# Mediterranean Europe

David Atkinson
Yvonne Byron
Duncan Garwood
Susie Grimshaw
Paul Hellander
Patrick Horton

Alex Landragin
Alex Leviton
Craig MacKenzie
Lisa Mitchell
Sally O'Brien
Jeanne Oliver
Tom Parkinson

Josephine Quintero
Rachel Suddart
Dani Valent
Vivek Wagle
David Willett
Pat Yale

LONELY PLANET PUBLICATIONS
Melbourne • Oakland • London • Paris

DENMARK
Odense

IRELAND
Dublin
Cork

Irish Sea
Liverpool
Manchester
Wales
Swansea
Cardiff
Bristol
England
Birmingham
BRITAIN

St George's Channel

NORTH
SEA

Hamburg
Bremen
GERMANY
Hanover
Leipzig

Elbe

London
Portsmouth
Plymouth

English Channel

Channel
Islands
Le Havre
Rouen
Lille
Rheims
Antwerp
Brussels
BELGIUM

NETHERLANDS
The Hague
Amsterdam
Düsseldorf
Cologne
Bonn

Frankfurt/
Main
Nuremberg

ATLANTIC

OCEAN

Brest
Quimper
St Malo
Caen
Rennes
Paris
LUXEMBOURG
Luxembourg

Seine

Nancy
Strasbourg
Freiberg

Heidelberg
Stuttgart
Munich

Rhine

Danube

La Coruña
Santiago de
Compostela
Vigo

Bay of
Biscay

Nantes
Tours
Blois
Dijon

Loire

Limoges
Clermont-
Ferrand
Lyon
St Étienne
Grenoble

Geneva
Bern
SWITZERLAND
Zürich
Basel

LIECHTENSTEIN
Innsbruck
AU
Lienz

Udine

Gijón
Santander
León
Bilbao
Valladolid
Burgos
San Sebastián
Bayonne
PYRENEES
Pamplona

Bordeaux

FRANCE

La Rochelle

Garonne

Toulouse

Nîmes
Avignon
Marseille
Cannes

Rhône

Turin
Milan
Verona

Genoa
La Spezia
MONACO
Nice

Venice
Po
Bologna

ALPS

Ligurian
Sea

SAN
MARINO
Ancona

APPENINES

Porto
Coimbra
PORTUGAL
Lisbon
Évora
Badajoz
Salamanca

Tagus

Douro

Zaragoza
Madrid

Ebro

Toledo

Guadiana

SPAIN

ANDORRA
Andorra
la Vella

Barcelona
Tarragona

Golfe de

Majorca
Menorca
Valencia
Ibiza
Palma
Balearic Islands

Florence
Pisa
Perugia

Corsica
Ajaccio
Elba

Rome

Sassan

Faro
Seville
Córdoba
Granada
Murcia
Alicante

Guadalquivir

Cádiz
Algeciras
Málaga
Almería
Gibraltar
UK
Sp
Cartagena

MEDITERRANEAN SEA

Sardinia
Cagliari

Tyrrhenian Sea

Strait of
Gibraltar
Tangier
Ceuta
Sp
Tetouan
Chefchaouen
Rabat
Fès
Meknès

Melilla
Sp
Oran
Oujda
Tlemcen

Algiers

Annaba
Constantine

Bizerte
Tunis
Sousse
Kairouan

Palermo
Sicily

Italy
Pantelleria

Valletta
MALTA

Isole
Pelagie

MOROCCO

ATLAS

ALGERIA

TUNISIA

Sfax
Tozeur
Gabès
Jerba

Gulf of
Gabès

Tripoli

SAHARA

LIBYA

0        250       500km
0     150     300mi

# Contents – Maps

## SLOVENIA

## SPAIN

## TURKEY

## YUGOSLAVIA

## MAP LEGEND                                                          back page

## METRIC CONVERSION                                    inside back cover

## MALTA 427

## MOROCCO 447

## PORTUGAL 495

## SLOVENIA 523

# 4  Contents – Text

## SPAIN 555

## TURKEY 635

## YUGOSLAVIA 685

## APPENDIX – TELEPHONES 710

## LANGUAGE 712

## THANKS 733

## INDEX 745

# The Authors

### David Atkinson
David worked on the France chapter. He is a London-based free-lance writer, specialising in travel, and has previously both lived and worked in Vietnam and Japan. During this time, he was mistaken for a gun-runner, ate freshly killed snake and learned to do a mean karaoke Elvis medley. His stories have been published in *The Guardian*, *The Weekend FT*, the *South China Morning Post* and *Time Magazine Asia*. He is a member of the British Guild of Travel Writers. Check out the website **W** www.travelwriters.com/davidatkinson for more information.

### Yvonne Byron
Yvonne updated the Getting There & Away chapter. After a quiet upbringing in rural Australia, Yvonne has travelled widely and lived in places as diverse as Dhaka, Oxford, Vancouver and Jakarta. After starting work as a defence analyst she has since been a pre-school teacher, university researcher and is now an editor with Lonely Planet. She has also co-authored or co-edited a number books on the relationship between people and forests. At Lonely Planet, Yvonne has been involved in the production of many guides, including 1st editions of the *Trans-Siberian Railway* and *Cyprus*. She now spends most weekends bushwalking in Victoria.

### Duncan Garwood
Duncan updated the Italy chapter. His writing career has so far taken him from the vaporous depths of London's largest sewage farm to the more traditional attractions of northern and central Italy. His first taste of travelling came with a four-month trip to India prior to a history degree at York University and a spell in corporate journalism. In 1997, however, he gave up leafy Berkshire for life in the Italian sun. Duncan currently lives in the wine-rich hills overlooking Rome, dividing his time between writing, dreaming and teaching English to, among others, Italian Miss World contenders.

### Susie Grimshaw
Susie worked on the Portugal chapter. Born in Cheshire, she was itching to travel from an early age and read American Studies at University in the hopes of securing an exchange placement on the other side of the pond. The economic climate at the time did not permit such frivolous behaviour, so she went off her own bat and has never looked back, chalking up the miles in the USA, Asia and Europe. Susie was delighted to return to Portugal so she could resume her comparative study of custard tarts. Previously, she nobly volunteered to review restaurants for *Out to Eat London*.

## Paul Hellander

Paul worked on the Albania and Cyprus chapters. He has never really stopped travelling since he first looked at a map in his native England. He graduated with a degree in Greek before heading for Australia where he trained interpreters and translators in Modern Greek before donning the hat of a travel writer. Paul has contributed to many LP titles including the following guides: *Greece*, *France*, *Cyprus*, *Israel & the Palestinian Territories*, *Singapore*, *Central America* and *South America*. His photos have also appeared in many LP guides. When not travelling, he lives in Adelaide, South Australia. He was last spotted heading once more to cover the prickly politics of Cyprus.

## Patrick Horton

Patrick Horton explored Serbia and Montenegro for the Yugoslavia chapter and if that wasn't enough then went straight on to research an 'interesting' part of Russia for a different title. Patrick, writer and photographer, was born with restless feet. He travelled extensively in his native Britain before hitting the around-the-world trail in 1985. He prefers the more arcane areas of the world, such as North Korea, Eritrea, East Timor or Tonga, or riding a motorcycle over the Himalaya. He lives in Melbourne with his long-suffering partner Christine, another ardent traveller whom he met in Paris. Patrick has had photographs published in many Lonely Planet guides and has worked on guides to *Australia*, *Eastern Europe*, *Ireland* and *Delhi*.

## Alex Landragin

Alex was born in France's Champagne region before his father landed an antipodean winemaking job and the family moved to Australia. After university studies in English and a couple of unremarkable careers, he worked as a staff writer and Web editor at Lonely Planet's Melbourne HQ before opting for a life on the road. During the sunny, tumultuous weeks of a presidential election campaign, Alex and his father drove the back roads of western France and Andorra at breakneck speed, racing from one restaurant to the next with bottomless appetites, with updating work slotted in between meals. Alex has also updated sections of the *Australia* and *Victoria* guides and between assignments writes fiction in wine country near Melbourne.

## Alex 'Pooky' Leviton

Alex updated the Slovenia chapter. Possibly Lonely Planet's shortest author ever at 4'9", Alex felt right at home in tiny Slovenia. She was raised in Los Angeles, but quickly escaped to the far reaches of Humboldt County. After college, she got a job at an alternative science/conspiracy theory magazine. This experience led her to leave the country, repeatedly. Alex has visited 46 countries on six continents. She worked on *Slovenia* while in her last semester at UC Berkeley's Graduate School of Journalism, and is currently a freelance writer and editor based in San Francisco.

**Mediterranean Europe**
**6th edition** – January 2003
**First published** – January 1993

**Published by**
**Lonely Planet Publications Pty Ltd**  ABN 36 005 607 983
90 Maribyrnong St, Footscray, Victoria 3011, Australia

**Lonely Planet Offices**
**Australia** Locked Bag 1, Footscray, Victoria 3011
**USA** 150 Linden St, Oakland, CA 94607
**UK** 10a Spring Place, London NW5 3BH
**France** 1 rue du Dahomey, 75011 Paris

**Photographs**
Many of the images in this guide are available for licensing from
Lonely Planet Images.
W www.lonelyplanetimages.com

**Front cover photograph**
Beach umbrellas, Ayvalık, Turkey
(Chris Sanders, Getty Images)

ISBN 1 74059 302 2

GR and PR are trademarks of the FRRP (Fédération Française de la
Randonée Pédestre).

Printed by SNP SPrint (M) Sdn Bhd
Printed in Malaysia

**Although the authors
and Lonely Planet try
to make the informa-
tion as accurate as
possible, we accept
no responsibility for
any loss, injury or
inconvenience sus-
tained by anyone
using this book.**

# Contents – Text

### Craig MacKenzie

Craig updated the Introduction and Facts for the Visitor chapters. Born in Kinlochleven in the Scottish West Highlands, his parents told him he was on a two-week holiday back in 1963 when he arrived in Melbourne, Australia, as an unwitting migrant. He's still in Melbourne having spent over 15 years with the Fairfax media group as a sports journalist and subeditor with freelance stints on SBS radio and TV. Seeking a haven for industrial misfits he joined Lonely Planet as a book editor in June, 1996. He's balding, overweight, smokes long panatellas and drinks pints of Guinness.

### Lisa Mitchell

Lisa updated the Greece chapter. She discovered the world was big on a spree across Europe, the UK, SE Asia and Australia in the '80s. She returned to earn her byline deciphering 'techno goss' in the computer press, spat the CPU, and became a writer and editor of lifestyle sections on a city newspaper. She sashayed momentarily into TV drama, later joining a women's magazine in dot com land. As deadlines and pocket money allow, Lisa pants up small mountains in high places. Her playgrounds include Alaska, Colorado, British Columbia, Patagonia, and New Zealand. She works as a freelance writer in Melbourne.

### Sally O'Brien

Sally updated the Italy chapter. Born in Melbourne, and raised in Seoul and Sydney, Sally edited various Lonely Planet titles before deciding to try her luck as an author. She's written for *Sydney*, *Australia* and *Sicily*, and covered Rome and Southern Italy for this book, where she amused one and all with her imaginative Italian and her version of driving on the right-hand side of the road. She's happy to keep getting sent there, despite predictably strange occurrences at train, bus and ferry stations and the aforementioned driving fiascos. When not authoring, she likes tea-drinking and procrastinating.

### Jeanne Oliver

Jeanne updated the Croatia chapter. Born in New Jersey, she spent her childhood mulling over the *New York Times'* travel section and plotting her future voyages. After a BA in English and a stint at the *Village Voice* newspaper, Jeanne got a law degree. Her legal practice was interrupted by ever-more-frequent trips to far-flung destinations and eventually she set off on around-the-world trip that landed her in Paris. A job in the tourist business led to freelance writing assignments for magazines and guidebooks. She joined Lonely Planet in 1996 and has written first editions of Lonely Planet's *Croatia*, *Normandy*, *Crete* and *Crete Condensed* as well as updating chapters in *Greece*, *Mediterranean Europe* and *France*.

## Tom Parkinson

Tom updated the Morocco chapter. A modern languages graduate, Tom's other travel experiences have taken him round Europe from Amsterdam to Zagreb, including a year in Berlin, as well as luring him further afield to Tanzania and Bali. After five years editing dictionaries in vacations, he was well aware of how annoying freelance authors can be, so jumped at the chance to become one, contributing to the Music section of LP *Britain* and visiting Morocco as his first full assignment. Currently straddling the difficult transition from feckless youth to irresponsible adult, Tom hopes to continue writing until he is utterly unemployable.

## Josephine Quintero

Josephine updated the Spain chapter. Born in England she started travelling with a backpack and guitar in the late '60s (didn't everyone?), stopping off in Israel on a kibbutz for a year. This led her, in a roundabout romantic sort of way, to move to California. After graduating from UC Berkeley, Josephine worked as a journalist for local newspapers and glossy magazines. Further travels took her to Kuwait where she edited the *Kuwaiti Digest*, and made several side trips, including to Yemen and India. She was briefly held hostage during the Iraqi invasion of Kuwait, and moved to the more relaxed shores of Andalucía shortly thereafter. She has worked as a ghostwriter on several books, including a spy thriller and several biographies. She has also contributed to more than 15 travel guidebooks, with an emphasis on the Iberian peninsula, and writes regularly for in-flight magazines, including *Highlife* (British Airways) and *Red Hot* (Virgin Airways).

## Rachel Suddart

Rachel updated the Getting Around and Malta chapters. Originally from the Lake District (UK) and a graduate of Manchester University she spent several years trying to work out how to combine her love for writing with her incurable wanderlust. In 2000 she had her first taste of authorship when she took part in a BBC documentary. After getting her foot stuck firmly in the door she took on a full-time role in Lonely Planet's London office. She has contributed to several LP titles.

## Dani Valent

Dani updated the France chapter. In eight years of travel writing for Lonely Planet, she has worked on over a dozen guides to destinations on four continents. She still loves coming home to Melbourne, Australia, where she dreams about making the perfect *crème brûlée* and playing Aussie Rules football for Carlton.

### Vivek Wagle

Vivek updated the Spain chapter. Dragging him kicking and screaming from his native land of India was probably the best way to introduce him to a life of itinerancy. After years of bouncing around the globe from Jakarta, Indonesia, to Washington, DC, with family and friends, he settled down long enough to earn an unbelievably practical degree in philosophy at Harvard University. But the experiential world soon won out over noumenal quandaries, propelling Vivek to enter the travel-writing business. After a stint as an editor in Lonely Planet's Oakland office, he hit the road once again as an author. To this day, he's not quite sure what time zone he's in at any given moment.

### David Willett

David updated the Greece chapter. He is a freelance journalist based near Bellingen on the mid-north coast of New South Wales, Australia. He grew up in Hampshire, England, and wound up in Australia in 1980 after stints working on newspapers in Iran (1975–8) and Bahrain. He spent two years working as a sub editor on the Melbourne *Sun* before trading a steady job for a warmer climate. Between jobs, David has travelled extensively in Europe, the Middle East and Asia. He is a regular visitor to Athens as coordinator of Lonely Planet's guide to *Greece* and co-author of the *Athens* city guide. He is also the author of Lonely Planet's guide to *Tunisia*, and has contributed to various other guides, including *Africa*, *Australia*, *Indonesia*, *South-East Asia*, *Mediterranean Europe* and *Western Europe*.

### Pat Yale

Pat updated the Turkey chapter. She first visited Turkey in 1974 in an old van that didn't look as if it would make it past Dover. Since throwing up sensible careerdom (ie, teaching), she has co-authored several editions of Lonely Planet's *Turkey* as well as worked on other Lonely Planet titles. At the time of writing she was living in a restored cave house with all mod cons and many cats in Göreme, Cappadocia.

### FROM THE AUTHORS

**David Atkinson** Ann Noon at the Maison de la France in London, Charles Page at Rail Europe, Nicole Mitchell at Eurostar, Sarah Barnes on behalf on Buzz, Daniel Spendrup in Chamonix, Sylvie Bonnafond in Lyon and Lonely Planet readers Paul Pederson, Anne Underwood & Katherine B for their useful input.

**Yvonne Byron** I'd like to thank Leonie Mugavin at Lonely Planet in Melbourne and Rachel Suddart, formerly in the London office, for their assistance in navigating my way around the abundance of websites and other valuable sources providing information on how to actually get to Europe.

**Duncan Garwood** Thanks, in no particular order, to Viviana, Daniele, Anna, Marco, Elisa and Marco in Bologna; Sabrina and Alessandro for their cheerful company in Milan and Maria Ferrara for her tips on that city's nightlife; Antonello and Dora in Genoa; Richard McKenna and everybody at the British School in Cinecittà, Rome, for giving me the time off and covering my courses; Sally O'Brien for her support and help; my mum for push-starting me into having a go; and Lidia for putting up with my absences and, probably worse for her, my presence.

**Susie Grimshaw** Thanks to Teresa Ventura at the Portuguese tourist office in London, Fernanda Reis at Porto Turismo, Vanda Brito at Ask Me Lisboa (I did) and to Carla Rodrigues at Arco de Cego for endless patience and good humour. Thanks also to Luis Kuski, Elsa Denninhoff Stelling, Celina Piedade and Carla Cavaço for insider tips and to Jorge and Ole for help researching entertainment sections. Also to Julia and John for moral (and practical) support and Paul Piaia for mapping expertise. Finally, a big thank you to Mark for putting up with the absence and remembering to feed the cat.

**Paul Hellander** The Balkans can occasionally be a taxing yet fascinating place to travel and so I would like to thank the following people who made the trip just that bit easier: Mimi Apostolov (Ohrid); Dimitri Gligorov (Skopje); Alma & Josef Tedeschini (Durrës); Anton Bushati (Tirana). For sharing their homes with me as I put it all together my gratitude also goes out to my friends in Greece: Maria Haristou & Andonis Konstantinidis (Thessaloniki); Angeliki Kanelli (Athens); Giannis and Vasilis Kambouris (Ikaria); Helga & Dimitris Ioannidopoulos (Ikaria). Stella, Byron & Marcus – thanks again for being there when needed.

**Patrick Horton** I want to acknowledge the help given to me by Miroslav Maric in translating, transporting me around Serbia and Montenegro and providing much background information. Thanks also to Leanne Smith of the Australian embassy in Belgrade for providing background information.

**Alex Landragin** I owe a huge debt of gratitude to Dani Valent, Annabel Hart and especially to the infinitely kind and diligent Miles Roddis. My thanks also to the editors at Lonely Planet for their patience and for giving me the job in the first place, to my father for navigating and for showing me a side of France I never knew, to various relatives for putting me up (read: putting up with me), and to the hundreds of thousands of protesters I bumped into in France's streets – *no pasaran!*

**Alex Leviton** This chapter would not have been possible without unending support from several incredibly wonderful and generous people, including my host Tanja Pajevic, my travelling partner and translator Freddy Wyss, and the helpful Ljubljana tourist-board team of Tatjana Radovič and Petra Čuk. I'd also like to thank Tadeja Urbas, John Whaley, Jerry Wagner, Dave Barnes, Tim Steyskal, Sarah Isakson, Rok Krančnik, Brigita Mark, Miha Rott, Franci at the Ljubljana bus station, the tourist offices in Maribor, Ptuj, and Bled, and Lonely Planet Slovenian pioneer Steve Fallon, for paving the way.

**Craig MacKenzie** I'm particularly grateful to Emma Sangster who provided invaluable assistance during a difficult period for her. Thanks also to Chris Adlam (Automobile Association), David Burnett, Yvonne Byron, Emma Cafferty (YHA England & Wales), Brigitte Ellemor, Paul Guy (HI Northern Ireland), Bibiana Jaramillo, Hilary Rogers, and Joyce Turton (HI Canada).

**Lisa Mitchell** To Matt Waite, my partner, for his patience, invaluable editorial support and encouragement. Enduring thanks to big sis Kerry Jones, for her editorial backup. Warm thanks to Yiannis and Katerina in Athens for their hospitality and contacts, and Spiros Gianotis from *Hellenic Travelling* magazine and Theo Spordilis on Chios for their research assistance. To Mike Emm Akalestos on Paros, could there be a more generous host? To Nikos and Angela Perlakis on Naxos, thank you for showing me the local delights. Thank you to the kind souls who offered refreshments and the busy travel agents and tourist information staff who answered my flurry of questions.

**Sally O'Brien** Thanks to Tony Davidson for the work; Duncan Garwood for his help and his great work; Craig MacKenzie for editing and Adrian Persoglia for designing the chapter; Maria Grazia Montenucci at APT Roma for her assistance; Marie-Claire Muir for the bar/restaurant research laughs in Rome and Naples; Jenny Hoskins, Sam Adams and Glenn for their kindness and humour in Naples; Fabian Muir for rekindling my interest in running madly across Rome; and the many tourist office staff, locals and travellers who offered opinions. Once again, a big salute to Lara and Jody for looking after my stuff and my parents, Barbara and Peter.

**Jeanne Oliver** In Croatia, my thanks go first to Renata Janekovic and the National Tourist Board. The helpful staff of the local tourist associations deserve my eternal gratitude with a special nod to the indefatigable Stanka Kraljević in Korčula and Goran Franinović in Pula. Jagoda Bracanović in Hvar, as well as Ratco Ojdanić and Aljoša Milat in Korčula, made my work a pleasure.

**Tom Parkinson** Cheers to all the travellers who kept me company along the way: Bea, Sarina, Jess and Hoyt in Meknès; James, Pat and Tom in Fès; Alan and Adam in Ceuta; Lou, Patrick, Andy and Chris in Tangier/Asilah; and Jan Dodd for extra info. *Shukran* to all the Moroccans who helped me out: Aziz at the Hotel de Paris; Rachid in Fès; Mohammed and the old couple on the train to Tarourirt; Mohamed Ait el Mokhtar in Tarourirt/Nador; Shakim in Nador; 'Killa' Adil in Tangier; M. Ziane at the Delegation in Rabat; and especially Dr Souad Hanafi, my Moroccan mother!

**Josephine Quintero** Josephine wishes to thank the following people: Hannah Reineck, Jonathan Symon, David Forrest, Naomi and Glen Mitchell, Craig Jenkins, Suman Bolar, Rose Brannon, Vijay Panjeti and Neil Allies.

**Rachel Suddart** Thanks to the MTA staff (especially Adriana Cacciottolo in London), Mr Philip Fenech (President of the GRTU's Hospitality and Leisure Division), Luisa Bonello (Malta Film Commission), Jacqui Roberts, Neil Wilson for his help and advice, Paul Gowen from the RAC for 'behind-the-wheel' knowledge, Mark Waters from the CTC for all things bicycle related, the UK IT team for all their patience and expertise, and Tom Hall for never getting sick of hearing 'Can I just run something past you...'. Thanks to Megan Hitchin for her tireless enthusiasm (and for saving me from being a billy-no-mates in the bars and restaurants), my Mum and Dad for their love and support and Paul for sending that all-important email. Thanks also to all the travellers that I met out on the road and those that took the time to write to our offices. Cheers to one and all.

**Dani Valent** Thanks to Karl Quinn, Liam Alexander-Quinn, Stephanie Bremner, Sally Ross, Miranda Epstein, Jeanne Oliver, Steve Fallon (who should never grow up) and the Corsican pigs that died to create all those brilliant sausages.

**Vivek Wagle** *Muchísimas gracias* to my fellow authors and to the production staff in Melbourne for making Spain such a smooth ride. Special thanks to Tony Davidson and Mary Neighbour for overseeing the project and to Ryan Ver Berkmoes for presenting me with the opportunity. *Un montón de agradecimiento* to travelling companion Cara Forster, whose support and assistance were invaluable. Love, as always, to Mom, Dad, Nani and Ayesha. And *mucho cariño* to all my US LP and ex-LP friends. It's been a great ride.

**David Willett** I'd like to thank all the friends who have contributed so much to my understanding of Greece over the years, especially Maria Economou from the Greek National Tourism Office; the Kanakis family; Ana Kamais; Matt Barrett; Tolis Houtzoumis; Petros and Dimitris in Nafplio; Yiannis in Sparti; the irrepressible Voula in Gythio; the Dimitreas family from Kardamyli; and Andreas the magician from Patras. Special thanks to my partner, Rowan, and our son Tom, who formed my support team around the Peloponnese and northern Greece.

**Pat Yale** Where would I be without all the people who routinely help me on my way around Turkey? Inevitably there are too many to mention by name, but particular thanks are owed to Aydın Şengül in Bergama; Zafer Küstü in Bodrum; Uğuur Çelikkol in Bursa; Corinne Parry in Fethiye; the Kiğuılı family in İstanbul; Mike and Karen Belton in Kaş; Şahin and Sami Sağuıroğulu in Köceğuiz; Sezgin Sağulam in Kuşadası; Rifat Koray, Ertan and Hakan Senkron in Pamukkale; Alison, Derviş, Jimmy and Shannon in Selçuk; Penny and Ali Yeşilipek in Side; and Remzi Bozbay in Van. In Cappadocia I owe a special *teşekkür ederim* to great friends Ahmet Diler in Avanos; Dawn Köse, Ruth Lockwood, Mustafa Güney and Ali Yavuz in Göreme; and Suha Ersoz and Aydın Güney in Ürgüp. Finally, Lisa Raffonelli, Golnaz Assadi and Paul Stockley went way beyond the normal demands of friendship in helping me track down plane fares from afar.

# This Book

Many people have helped to create this 6th edition. The list of authors for the last edition were Janet Austin, Verity Campbell, Carolyn Bain, Neal Bedford, Fionn Davenport, Matt Fletcher, Susan Forsyth, Kate Galbraith, Jeremy Gray, Paul Hellander, Mark Honan, John King, Sarah Mathers, John Noble, Tim Nollen, Jeanne Oliver, Daniel Robinson, Miles Roddis, David Rowson, Andrea Schulte-Peevers, Rachel Suddart, Bryn Thomas, Julia Wilkinson, David Willett, Nicola Williams, Neil Wilson and Pat Yale.

*Mediterranean Europe* is part of Lonely Planet's Europe series, which includes *Central Europe, Eastern Europe, Scandinavian Europe, Western Europe* and *Europe on a shoestring*. Lonely Planet also publishes phrasebooks to these regions.

## FROM THE PUBLISHER

The coordinating editor was Gina Tsarouhas who stepped into the breach when Tony Davidson took off to look after his new baby; the coordinating cartographer/designer was Adrian Persoglia. They were assisted by Susie Ashworth, Gus Poo ý Balbontin, Yvonne Bischofberger, Sonya Brooke, Yvonne Byron, Csanad Csutoros, Hunor Csutoros, Pete Cruttenden, Piotr Czajkowski, Michael Day, James Ellis, Simone Egger, Susannah Farfor, Justin Flynn, Huw Fowles, Karen Fry, Cris Gibcus, Errol Hunt, Nancy Ianni, Evan Jones, Joelene Kowalski, Valentina Kremenchutskaya, Kusnander, Chris Lee Ack, Craig MacKenzie, Sally Morgan, Leonie Mugavin, Jarrad Needham, Jacqueline Nguyen, Darren O'Connell, Leanne Peake, Cherry Prior, Nina Rousseau, Anastasia Safioleas, Jacqui Saunders, John Shippick, Sarah Sloane, Nick Stebbing, Nick Tapp, Ray Thomson, Simon Tillema, Tamsin Wilson, Celia Wood and Helen Yeates. The senior production staff were David Burnett, Liz Filluel, Quentin Frayne, Mark Germanchis, Mark Griffiths, Kieran Grogan, Rachel Imeson, Emma Koch, Chris Lee Ack, Adriana Mammarella, Mary Neighbour, Andrew Tudor, Vivek Wagle and Chris Wyness. The Managing Editors were Kerryn Burgess, Bruce Evans and Jane Thompson. The Commissioning Editor was Heather Dickson and Robert Reid steered at the helm as Series Publishing Manager. Design kudos go to Pepi Bluck, Tamsin Wilson and Daniel New. Thanks also to Lonely Planet Images.

## ACKNOWLEDGMENTS

Grateful acknowledgment is made for reproduction permission: Mountain High Maps ® Copyright © 1993 Digital Wisdom, Inc. Penguin Books Ltd: Excerpt from *The Italians*, Luigi Barzini (1964)

## THANKS

Many thanks to the travellers who used the last edition and wrote to us with helpful hints, advice and interesting anecdotes. Your names appear in the back of this book.

15

# Foreword

## ABOUT LONELY PLANET GUIDEBOOKS

The story begins with a classic travel adventure: Tony and Maureen Wheeler's 1972 journey across Europe and Asia to Australia. There was no useful information about the overland trail then, so Tony and Maureen published the first Lonely Planet guidebook to meet a growing need.

From a kitchen table, Lonely Planet has grown to become the largest independent travel publisher in the world, with offices in Melbourne (Australia), Oakland (USA), London (UK) and Paris (France).

Today Lonely Planet guidebooks cover the globe. There is an ever-growing list of books and information in a variety of media. Some things haven't changed. The main aim is still to make it possible for adventurous travellers to get out there – to explore and better understand the world.

At Lonely Planet we believe travellers can make a positive contribution to the countries they visit – if they respect their host communities and spend their money wisely. Since 1986 a percentage of the income from each book has been donated to aid projects and human rights campaigns, and, more recently, to wildlife conservation.

Although inclusion in a guidebook usually implies a recommendation we cannot list every good place. Exclusion does not necessarily imply criticism. In fact there are a number of reasons why we might exclude a place – sometimes it is simply inappropriate to encourage an influx of travellers.

## UPDATES & READER FEEDBACK

Things change – prices go up, schedules change, good places go bad and bad places go bankrupt. Nothing stays the same. So, if you find things better or worse, recently opened or long-since closed, please tell us and help make the next edition even more accurate and useful.

Lonely Planet thoroughly updates each guidebook as often as possible – usually every two years, although for some destinations the gap can be longer. Between editions, up-to-date information is available in our free, quarterly *Planet Talk* newsletter and monthly email bulletin *Comet*. The *Scoop* section of our website covers news and current affairs relevant to travellers. Lastly, the *Thorn Tree* bulletin board and *Postcards* section carry unverified, but fascinating, reports from travellers.

**Tell us about it!** We genuinely value your feedback. A well-travelled team at Lonely Planet reads and acknowledges every email and letter we receive and ensures that every morsel of information finds its way to the relevant authors, editors and cartographers.

Everyone who writes to us will find their name listed in the next edition of the appropriate guidebook, and will receive the latest issue of *Comet* or *Planet Talk*. The very best contributions will be rewarded with a free guidebook.

We may edit, reproduce and incorporate your comments in Lonely Planet products such as guidebooks, websites and digital products, so let us know if you don't want your comments reproduced or your name acknowledged.

**How to contact Lonely Planet:**
Online: e talk2us@lonelyplanet.com.au, w www.lonelyplanet.com
**Australia:** Locked Bag 1, Footscray, Victoria 3011
**UK:** 10a Spring Place, London NW5 3BH
**USA:** 150 Linden St, Oakland, CA 94607

# Introduction

Mediterranean Europe evokes images of sun-drenched beaches, the azure glow of the Mediterranean Sea, breathtaking landscapes speckled with olive and citrus groves, a multitude of outdoor cafés, wonderful food, friendly local people, exuberant festivals and a relaxed way of life. It *is* all this – and more.

This book offers an insight into the many different countries of this fascinating region, their peoples and cultures, and provides practical information to help you get the most out of your time and money. It covers the area from Portugal and Morocco in the west to Cyprus and Turkey over in the east. While Morocco and most of Turkey are not part of Europe, these countries have been included because of their proximity and accessibility, as well as their historical ties to the region.

Given the exceptional diversity of the countries and cultures in Mediterranean Europe, travellers are confronted by a seemingly endless choice of things to see and do. Some of Europe's earliest and most powerful civilisations flourished around the Mediterranean, and traces of them remain in the many archaeological sites and in the monuments, architecture, art, writings and music they spawned. There are countless churches, galleries and museums with works of art ranging from the Renaissance masters to 20th-century innovators. This region features architectural masterpieces as diverse as the Parthenon in Athens, Notre Dame in Paris, the Aya Sofya in İstanbul, St Peter's Basilica in Rome, the Alhambra in Granada and also Gaudí's extraordinary creations in Barcelona.

When museums and churches begin to overwhelm you, turn to the many outdoor pursuits Mediterranean Europe has to offer. There is skiing or trekking in Slovenia's Julian Alps or the Sierra Nevada mountain range in southern Spain, island-hopping in Greece, or you can simply laze on a beach anywhere along the coast. The food of the Mediterranean region is one of its principal delights, as is much of its world-renowned wine. There are even places where you can escape from other travellers, as relatively few tourists have made their way to some parts of Andalucía or southern Italy.

*Mediterranean Europe* includes much practical information on how to get there and how to get around once you've arrived, whether it's by road, rail or ferry. There are extensive details on what to see, when to see it and how much it all costs. The thousands of recommendations about places to stay range from *domatia* (rooms to rent) in Greece and cheap hotels in the medinas (old towns) of Morocco to luxurious hotels in Paris or Rome. Restaurant recommendations include outdoor cafés in France, trattorias in Italy and *gostilne* in Slovenia. If shopping appeals, the Mediterranean area offers outlets ranging from chic boutiques in Paris and İstanbul's Grand Bazaar to flea markets. Indeed, this is a book for all budgets and tastes.

It's 3000km from the Strait of Gibraltar to the Turkish coast – a huge region with a great diversity of beckoning attractions. To experience them, all you have to do is go, so don't linger a second longer.

# Facts for the Visitor

## HIGHLIGHTS
### The Top 10
There is so much to see in Mediterranean Europe that compiling a Top 10 is next to impossible. Nevertheless, we've compiled this list. You may agree with some entries, while some omissions may raise your hackles – it's OK, we've got broad shoulders:

1. Paris
2. Rome
3. Florence & Tuscany
4. Greek Island-hopping
5. Epiros in northwestern Greece
6. İstanbul
7. Venice
8. Cappadocia
9. The Dalmatian Coast
10. Barcelona

Other possibilities include Umbria, Provence, Slovenia's Soča Valley in spring, Andalucía, Corsica, Seville, Lisbon, the splendid Roman ruins of Ephesus, and Durmitor National Park in Montenegro.

## PLANNING
A bit of prior knowledge and careful planning can make your travel budget stretch further. You'll also want to make sure that the things you plan to see and do will be possible when you'll be travelling.

Lonely Planet's *Read This First – Europe* is an excellent source of preliminary information.

### When to Go
Any time is a good time to visit Mediterranean Europe, depending on what you want to do. Summer lasts roughly from June to September in the northern half of Europe and offers the most pleasant climate for outdoor pursuits. Along the Mediterranean coast, on the Iberian Peninsula and in southern Italy and Greece, where the summers tend to be hotter and longer, you can extend that period by one or even two months either way, when temperatures may also be more agreeable. The best times to visit most of Morocco are in spring and autumn.

You won't be the only tourist during the summer months in the region – everyone in France, Spain and Italy, for instance, goes on holiday in August. Prices can be high, accommodation fully booked and the sights packed. You'll find much better deals – and far fewer crowds – in the shoulder seasons either side of summer; in April and May, for instance, flowers are in bloom and the weather can be surprisingly mild, and Indian summers are common in Mediterranean Europe in September and October.

On the other hand, if you're keen on winter sports, resorts in the Dolomites, for example, begin operating in November or early December and move into full swing after the New Year, closing down again when the snow begins to melt in March or April.

The Climate and When to Go sections in the individual country chapters explain what to expect and when to expect it, and the climate charts in country chapters will help you compare the weather in different destinations. The Mediterranean coast is hotter and drier than the Atlantic seaboard with most rainfall occurring during the mild winter.

When summer and winter are mentioned throughout this book we generally mean high and low tourist seasons, ie, for summer read roughly May to September and for winter read October to April.

### What Kind of Trip
**Travelling Companions** If you decide to travel with others, keep in mind that travel can put relationships to the test like few other experiences. Make sure you agree on itineraries and routines beforehand and try to remain flexible about everything, even in the heat of an August afternoon in Rome or Madrid. Travelling with someone else does have financial benefits as a single room is more expensive per person than a double in most countries.

If travel is a good way of testing established friendships, it's also a great way of making new ones. Hostels and camping grounds are good places to meet fellow travellers, so even if you're travelling alone, you need never be lonely.

The Getting Around chapter has details on organised tours.

### Maps
Good maps are easy to come by once you're in Europe, but you might want to buy a few beforehand to plan and track your route. The

maps in this book will help you get an idea of where you might want to go and will be a useful first reference when you arrive in a city. Proper road maps are essential if you're driving or cycling around.

For some European cities Lonely Planet has detailed maps. Michelin maps are also good and, because of their soft covers, they fold up easily so you can stick them in your pocket. Some people prefer the maps meticulously produced by Freytag & Berndt, Kümmerly + Frey and Hallwag. As a rule, maps published by European automobile associations (the AA in Britain, the ADAC and AvD in Germany etc) are excellent and sometimes free if membership of your local association gives you reciprocal rights. Tourist offices are often another good source for (usually free and fairly basic) maps.

## What to Bring

It's very easy to find almost anything you may need in Mediterranean Europe and, since you'll probably buy things as you go along, it's better to start with too little rather than too much.

A backpack is still the most popular method of carrying gear as it is convenient, especially for walking.

Travelpacks, a combination backpack/shoulder bag, are also very popular. The backpack straps zip away inside the pack when they are not needed, so you almost have the best of both worlds. Backpacks or travelpacks can be made reasonably theft-proof with small padlocks. Another alternative is a large, soft, zip bag with a wide shoulder strap so it can be carried with relative ease. Forget suitcases unless you're travelling in style, but if you do take one, make sure it has wheels to allow you to drag it along behind you.

As for clothing, the climate will have a bearing on what you take along. Remember that insulation works on the principle of trapped air, so several layers of thin clothing are warmer than a single thick one (and will be easier to dry). You'll also be much more flexible if the weather suddenly turns warm. Be prepared for rain at any time of year. Bearing in mind that you can buy virtually anything on the spot, a minimum packing list could include:

- underwear, socks and swimming gear
- a pair of jeans and maybe a pair of shorts or a skirt
- a few T-shirts and shirts
- a warm sweater

- a solid pair of walking shoes
- sandals or thongs (flip-flops) for showers
- a coat or jacket
- a raincoat, waterproof jacket or umbrella
- a medical kit and sewing kit
- a padlock
- a Swiss Army knife
- soap and a towel
- toothpaste, toothbrush and other toiletries

## RESPONSIBLE TOURISM

As a visitor, you have a responsibility to the local people and to the environment. For guidelines on how to avoid offending the people you meet, read the following Appearances & Conduct section. When it comes to the environment, the key rules are to preserve natural resources and to leave the countryside as you find it. Those alpine flowers look much better on the mountainside than squashed inside your pocket (many species are protected anyway).

Wherever you are, littering is irresponsible and offensive. Mountain areas have fragile ecosystems, so stick to prepared paths whenever possible, and always carry your rubbish away with you. Don't use detergents or toothpaste (even if they are biodegradable) in or near watercourses. If you just gotta go when you're out in the wilderness somewhere, bury human waste in holes at least 15cm deep and at least 100m from any watercourse.

Recycling is an important issue in many Mediterranean countries, and you will be encouraged to follow suit. Traffic congestion on the roads is a major problem, and visitors will do themselves and residents a favour if they forgo driving and use public transport.

## Appearances & Conduct

Most Mediterranean countries attach a great deal of importance to appearance, so your clothes may well have some bearing on how you're treated, especially in Spain, Portugal, Italy and Greece.

By all means dress casually, but keep your clothes clean and ensure sufficient body cover (trousers or a knee-length dress) if your sightseeing includes churches, monasteries, mosques or synagogues. Wearing shorts away from the beach is not very common among men in Mediterranean Europe. Also keep in mind that in most Muslim countries, such as Morocco, Western women *or* men in shorts or sleeveless shirts are virtually in their underwear in the eyes of the more traditional locals. Many nightclubs and fancy restaurants refuse entry to anyone wearing jeans, or a tracksuit and sneakers (trainers); men might consider packing a tie as well, just in case.

On the beach, nude bathing is generally limited to particular areas, but topless bathing is common in many parts of Mediterranean Europe. Nevertheless, women should be wary of sunbathing topless in more conservative countries or untouristed areas. If nobody else seems to be doing it, you shouldn't do it either.

You'll soon notice that Europeans shake hands and even kiss when they greet one another. Don't worry about the latter with those you don't know well, but get into the habit of shaking hands with virtually everyone you meet. In some parts of Mediterranean Europe, it's also customary to greet the proprietor when entering a shop, café or quiet bar, and to say goodbye when you leave.

## VISAS & DOCUMENTS
### Passport
Your most important travel document is your passport, which should remain valid until well after you return home. If it's just about to expire, renew it before you go. This may not be easy to do overseas, and some countries insist that your passport remains valid for a specified period (usually three months beyond the date of your departure from that country).

Applying for or renewing a passport can take anywhere from an hour to several months, so don't leave it till the last minute. Bureaucratic wheels usually turn faster if you do everything in person rather than relying on the post or agents, but check first what you need to take with you: photos of a certain size, birth certificate, population register extract, signed statements, exact payment in cash etc.

Australian citizens can apply at a post office or the passport office in their state capital; Britons can pick up application forms from major post offices, and the passport is issued by the regional passport office; Canadians can apply at regional passport offices; New Zealanders can apply at any district office of the Department of Internal Affairs; US citizens must apply in person (but may usually renew by mail) at a US Passport Agency office or at some courthouses and post offices.

Once you start travelling, carry your passport at all times and guard it carefully (see Copies later in this section for advice about carrying copies of your passport and other important documents). Camping grounds and hotels sometimes insist that you hand over your passport for the duration of your stay, which is very inconvenient, but a driving licence or Camping Card International (see that section later for more information) usually solves the problem.

Citizens of the European Union (EU) and those from certain other European countries (eg, Switzerland) don't need a valid passport to travel to another EU country or even some non-EU countries; a national identity card is sufficient. If you want to exercise this option, check with your travel agent or the embassies of the countries you plan to visit.

Note that Cyprus, Malta, Slovenia and Turkey are among a group of countries trying to become EU members within the next few years, but they probably won't be admitted before 2004 at the earliest.

### Visas
A visa is a stamp in your passport or on a separate piece of paper permitting you to enter the country in question and stay for a specified period of time. Often you can get the visa at the border or at the airport on arrival, but not always – check first with the embassies or consulates of the countries you plan to visit. It's seldom possible on trains.

There's a wide variety of visas, including tourist, transit and business ones. Transit visas are usually cheaper than tourist or business visas, but they only allow a very short stay (one or two days) and can be difficult to extend. With a valid passport you'll be able to visit most of the countries around the Mediterranean for up to three months (sometimes even six), provided you have some sort of onward or return ticket and/or 'sufficient means of support' (money).

In line with the Schengen Agreement there are no passport controls at the borders between Austria, Belgium, Denmark, Finland, France, Germany, Greece, Iceland, Italy, Luxembourg, Netherlands, Norway, Portugal, Spain and Sweden; an identity card should suffice, but it's always safest to carry your passport.

Border procedures between EU and non-EU countries can still be thorough, but citizens of Australia, Canada, Israel, Japan, New Zealand and the USA do not need visas for tourist visits to any Schengen country.

All non-EU citizens visiting a Schengen country and intending to stay for longer than three days or to visit another Schengen country from there are supposed to obtain an official entry stamp in their passport, either at the point of entry or from the local police, within 72 hours. But in general registering at a hotel will be sufficient.

For those who do require visas, it's important to remember that these will have a 'use-by' date, and you'll be refused entry after that period has elapsed. Your visa may not be checked when entering these countries overland, but major problems can arise if it is requested during your stay or on departure and you can't produce it.

Visa requirements change, and you should always check with the individual embassies or a reputable travel agent before travelling. It's generally easier to get your visas as you go along, rather than arranging them all beforehand. Carry spare passport photos (you may need from one to four every time you apply for a visa).

## Travel Insurance

A travel-insurance policy to cover theft, loss and medical problems is a good idea. The policies handled by STA Travel and other student-travel organisations are usually good value. Some policies offer lower and higher medical expense options; the higher ones are chiefly for travellers from countries such as the USA that have extremely high medical costs. There is a wide variety of policies available, so check the small print.

Some policies specifically exclude 'dangerous activities', which can include scuba diving, motorcycling and even trekking. Some even exclude entire countries, such as Yugoslavia. A locally acquired motorcycle licence is not valid under some policies.

You may prefer a policy that pays doctors or hospitals directly rather than you having to pay on the spot and claim later. If you have to claim later make sure you keep all documentation. Some policies ask you to call back (reverse charges) to a centre in your home country where an immediate assessment of your problem is made.

Check that the policy covers ambulances or an emergency flight home.

EU nationals can obtain free emergency treatment in EU countries on the presentation of an E111 form, validated in their home country. Note, however, that this form does not provide health cover in Croatia, Malta, Morocco or Slovenia.

## Driving Licence & Permits

Many non-European driving licences are valid in Europe, but it's still a good idea to take along an International Driving Permit (IDP), which can make life much simpler, especially when hiring cars and motorcycles. Basically a multilingual translation of the vehicle class and personal details noted on your local driving licence, an IDP is not valid unless accompanied by your original licence. An IDP can be obtained for a small fee from your local automobile association – bring along a passport photo and a valid licence.

## Camping Card International

The Camping Card International (CCI) is a camping ground ID that can be used instead of a passport when checking into a camp site and includes third-party insurance. As a result, many camping grounds offer a small discount (usually 5% to 10%) if you sign in with one. CCIs are issued by automobile associations, camping federations and, sometimes, on the spot at camping grounds. In the UK, the AA and RAC issue them to their members for UK£6.50.

## Hostel Cards

A hostelling card is useful – if not always mandatory – for those staying at hostels. Some hostels in Mediterranean Europe don't require that you be a hostelling-association member, but they often charge less if you are and have a card. Many hostels will issue one on the spot or after a few stays, although this might cost a bit more than getting one in your home country. See also Hostels under Accommodation later in this chapter.

## Student & Youth Cards

The most useful of these is the International Student Identity Card (ISIC), a plastic ID-style card with your photograph, which provides discounts on many forms of transport (including airlines and local public transport), cheap or free admission to museums and sights, and inexpensive meals in some student cafeterias and restaurants.

If you're aged under 26 but not a student, you can apply for an International Youth Travel Card (IYTC, formerly GO25) issued by the Federation of International Youth Travel Organisations (FIYTO) or the Euro<26 card. Both go under different names in various countries and give much the same discounts and benefits as an ISIC. All these cards are issued by hostelling organisations, student unions or youth-oriented travel agencies.

## Seniors Cards

Museums and other sights, public swimming pools and spas, and transport companies frequently offer discounts to retired people/old-age pensioners/those over 60 (slightly younger for women). Make sure you bring proof of age; that suave *signore* in Italy or that polite Parisian *mademoiselle* is not going to believe you're a day over 39.

European nationals aged 60 and over can get a Railplus Card. For more information see Cheap Tickets under Train in the Getting Around chapter.

## International Health Certificate

You'll need this yellow booklet only if you're arriving in Europe from certain parts of Asia, Africa and South America, where diseases such as yellow fever are prevalent. See Immunisations under Health later in this chapter for more information.

## Copies

All important documents (passport data page and visa page, credit cards, travel insurance policy, air/bus/train tickets, driving licence etc) should be photocopied before you leave home. Leave one copy with someone at home and keep another with you.

While you're on the road add the serial numbers of your travellers cheques (cross them off as you cash them) to the photocopies of your important documents and keep all this emergency material separate from your passport, cheques and cash. Add some emergency money (eg, US$50 to US$100 in cash) to this separate stash as well. If you do lose your passport, notify the police immediately to get a statement, and contact your nearest consulate.

It's also a good idea to store details of your vital travel documents in Lonely Planet's free online Travel Vault in case you lose the photocopies or can't be bothered with them. Your password-protected Travel Vault is accessible online anywhere in the world – create it at **W** www.ekno.lonelyplanet.com.

## EMBASSIES & CONSULATES

See the listings in the individual country chapters for information on specific embassies and consulates.

## Getting Help from Your Embassy

As a tourist, it's important to realise what your own embassy – the embassy of the country of which you are a citizen – can and cannot do.

Generally speaking, it won't be much help in emergencies if the trouble you're in is remotely your fault. Remember that you are bound by the laws of the country you are in. Your embassy will not be sympathetic if you end up in jail after committing a crime locally, even if such actions are legal in your own country.

In genuine emergencies you might get some assistance, but only if other channels have been exhausted. For example, if you need to get home urgently, a free ticket home is exceedingly unlikely as the embassy would expect you to have insurance. If you have all your money and documents stolen, it might assist with getting a new passport, but a loan for onward travel is almost always out of the question.

## MONEY
## Exchanging Money

Most EU countries now have a single currency called the euro (see the boxed text 'The Euro' later).

US dollars, pounds sterling and Swiss francs are easily exchanged in Europe. You lose out through commissions and customer exchange rates every time you change money, so if you only visit Spain, for example, you are better off buying euros straight away from your bank at home.

The importation and exportation of certain currencies (eg, Moroccan dirham and Cypriot pounds) is restricted or banned entirely so get rid of any local currency before you leave those countries. Try not to have too many leftover Maltese lire and definitely get rid of any Yugoslavian dinar as it is impossible to change them back into hard currency. More and more banks and *bureaux de change* will now exchange Croatian kuna and Slovenian tolar but usually just in the neighbouring countries.

Most airports, central train stations, some fancy hotels and many border posts have banking facilities outside working hours, sometimes open on a 24-hour basis. Post offices in Europe often perform banking tasks, tend to have longer opening hours, and outnumber banks in remote places. Be aware that while they always exchange cash, they might not be prepared to change travellers cheques unless they're denominated in the local currency.

The best exchange rates are usually at banks. *Bureaux de change* usually, but not always by any means, offer worse rates or charge higher commissions. Hotels are almost always the worst places to change money. American Express and Thomas Cook offices usually do not charge commissions for changing their own cheques, but they may offer a less favourable exchange rate than banks.

**Cash** Nothing beats cash for convenience, or risk. If you lose it, it's gone forever and very few travel insurers will come to your rescue. Those that will, limit the amount to somewhere around US$300. For tips on carrying your money safely, see Theft under Dangers & Annoyances later in this chapter.

It's still a good idea, though, to bring some local currency in cash, if only to tide you over until you get to an exchange facility or find an automated teller machine (ATM). The equivalent of, say, US$50 or US$100 should usually be enough. Some extra cash in an easily exchanged currency (eg, US dollars) is also a good idea.

**Travellers Cheques & Eurocheques**
The main idea of carrying travellers cheques rather than cash is the protection they offer from theft, though they are losing their popularity as more travellers – including those on tight budgets – deposit their money in their bank at home and withdraw it as they go along through ATMs.

American Express, Visa and Thomas Cook travellers cheques are widely accepted and have efficient replacement policies. If you're going to remote places, it's worth sticking to American Express since small local banks may not always accept other brands.

When you change cheques, don't look at just the exchange rate; ask about fees and commissions as well. There may be a service fee per cheque, a flat transaction fee or a percentage of the total amount irrespective of the number of cheques. Some banks charge fees (often exorbitant) to cash cheques and not cash; others do the reverse.

## The Euro

The much-anticipated roll-out of new euro coins and banknotes by the European Central Bank took place on 1 January 2002 in all 12 participating euro-zone countries – Austria, Belgium, Finland, France, Germany, Greece, Ireland, Italy, Luxembourg, the Netherlands, Portugal and Spain.

The euro has the same value in all EU member countries. There are seven euro notes (5, 10, 20, 50, 100, 200 and 500 euros) and eight euro coins (1 and 2 euros, then 1, 2, 5, 10, 20 and 50 cents). One side is standard for all euro coins and the other side bears a national emblem of participating countries.

So, if you stumble across some Deutschmarks or francs on your travels, you're staring at museum pieces, albeit that old currencies can still be exchanged at central banks.

Treat the euro as you would any major world currency. Just as you'd exchange, say, US dollars for euros in the euro zone, you'll find yourself exchanging euros for a local currency outside the euro zone. And think of its portability and usability throughout much of Europe.

Rates of exchange of the euro and foreign currencies against local currencies are given in the appropriate country chapters.

| country | unit | | euro |
|---|---|---|---|
| Australia | A$1 | = | €0.59 |
| Canada | C$1 | = | €0.72 |
| Japan | ¥100 | = | €0.86 |
| New Zealand | NZ$1 | = | €0.48 |
| South Africa | R1 | = | €0.10 |
| UK | UK£1 | = | €1.64 |
| USA | US$1 | = | €1.15 |

Guaranteed personal cheques are another way of carrying money or obtaining cash. Eurocheques, which are available if you have a European bank account, are guaranteed up to a certain limit. When you cash them (eg, at post offices), you will be asked to show your Eurocheque card bearing your signature and registration number, and perhaps a passport or ID card. Your Eurocheque card should be kept separately from the cheques. Many hotels and merchants refuse to accept Eurocheques because of the fairly large commissions applied.

**ATMs & Credit Cards** If you're not familiar with the options, ask your bank to explain the workings and relative merits of credit, credit/debit, debit, charge and cash cards.

A major advantage of credit cards is that they allow you to pay for expensive items (eg, airline tickets) without you having to carry great wads of cash. They also allow you to withdraw cash at selected banks or from the many ATMs that are linked up internationally. However, if an ATM in Europe swallows a card that was issued outside Europe, it can be a major headache. Also, some credit cards aren't hooked up to ATM networks unless you specifically ask your bank to do this.

Cash cards, which you use at home to withdraw money from your bank account or savings account, can be used throughout Europe at ATMs linked to international networks, such as Cirrus and Maestro.

Credit and credit/debit cards such as Visa and MasterCard are widely accepted. MasterCard is linked to Europe's extensive Eurocard system, and Visa (sometimes called Carte Bleue) is particularly strong in France and Spain. However, these cards often have a credit limit that is too low to cover major expenses such as long-term car rental or airline tickets and can be difficult to replace if lost abroad. Also, when you get a cash advance against your Visa or MasterCard credit card account, your issuer charges a transaction fee and/or finance charge. With some issuers, fees can reach as high as US$10 *plus* interest per transaction so it's best to check with your card issuer before leaving home and compare rates.

Charge cards like American Express and Diners Club have offices in the major cities of most countries that will replace a lost card within 24 hours. However, charge cards are not widely accepted off the beaten track.

Another option is Visa TravelMoney, a prepaid travel card that gives 24-hour access to your funds in local currency via Visa ATMs. The card is PIN-protected and its value is stored on the system, not on the card. So if you lose the card, your money's safe. Visa TravelMoney can be purchased in any amount from Citicorp and Thomas Cook/Interpayment.

If you want to rely heavily on bits of plastic, go for two different cards – an American Express or Diners Club, for instance, along with a Visa or MasterCard. Better still is a combination of credit or cash card and travellers cheques so you have something to fall back on if an ATM swallows your card or the banks in the area are closed.

A word of warning – fraudulent shopkeepers have been known to quickly make several charge slip imprints with your credit card when you're not looking, and then simply copy your signature from the one that you authorise. Try not to let your card out of sight, and always check your statements upon your return.

**International Transfers** Telegraphic transfers are not very expensive but, despite their name, can be quite slow. Be sure to specify the name of the bank and the name and address of the branch where you'd like to pick it up.

It's quicker and easier to have money wired via an American Express office (which costs around US$60 for US$1000). Western Union's Money Transfer system (available at post offices in some countries) and Thomas Cook's MoneyGram service are also popular.

## Costs
This book provides a range of prices to suit every budget. See the Facts for the Visitor sections in the individual country chapters for specific information on travelling expenses.

## Tipping & Bargaining
In many European countries it's common (and the law in France) for a service charge to be added to restaurant bills, in which case no tipping is necessary. In others, simply rounding up the bill is sufficient. See the individual country chapters for details.

Some bargaining goes on in markets, but the best you should hope for (apart from in Morocco) is a 20% reduction in the initial asking price.

## Taxes & Refunds
Value-added tax (VAT) is a kind of sales tax that applies to most goods and services throughout many European countries; it's 20% in Italy, 19.6% in France, 19% in Slovenia, 18% in Greece and 16% in Spain. In most countries, visitors can claim back the VAT on purchases that are being taken out of the country. Those actually *residing* in one EU country are not entitled to a refund on VAT paid on goods bought in another EU country. Thus an American citizen living in London is not entitled to a VAT rebate on items bought in Paris, while an EU passport holder residing in New York is entitled to this rebate.

The procedure for making the claim is fairly straightforward, though it may vary somewhat from country to country, and there are minimum-purchase amounts imposed. First of all make sure the shop offers duty-free sales (often identified with a sign reading 'Tax-Free for Tourists'). When making your purchase, ask the shop attendant for a VAT-refund voucher (sometimes called a Tax-Free Shopping Cheque) filled in with the correct amount and the date. This can either be refunded directly at international airports on departure or stamped at ferry ports or border crossings and mailed back for refund.

## CUSTOMS

Duty-free goods are no longer sold to those travelling from one EU country to another. For goods purchased at airports or on ferries *outside* the EU, the usual allowances apply for tobacco (200 cigarettes, 50 cigars or 250g of loose tobacco), alcohol (1L of spirits or 2L of liquor with less than 22% alcohol by volume; 2L of wine) and perfume (50g of perfume and 0.25L of *eau de toilette*).

Do not confuse these with *duty-paid* items (including alcohol and tobacco) bought at normal shops and supermarkets in another EU country, where certain goods might be more expensive. (Cigarettes in France, for example, are half the price they are in the UK.) Then the allowances are more than generous: 800 cigarettes, 200 cigars or 1kg of loose tobacco; 10L of spirits (more than 22% alcohol by volume), 20L of fortified wine or aperitif, 90L of wine or 110L of beer; and unlimited quantities of perfume.

## POST & COMMUNICATIONS
### Post

From major European centres, airmail typically takes about five days to North America and a week to Australasian destinations. Postage costs vary from country to country, as does post office efficiency – the Italian post office is notoriously unreliable.

You can collect mail from poste-restante sections at major post offices. Ask people writing to you to print your name clearly and to underline your surname. When collecting mail, your passport may be required for identification and you may have to pay a small fee. If an expected letter is not awaiting you, ask to check under your given name; letters commonly get misfiled. Post offices usually hold

mail for about a month, but sometimes less. Unless the sender specifies otherwise, mail will always be sent to the city's main post office.

You can also have mail (but not parcels) sent to you at American Express offices so long as you have an American Express card or are carrying American Express travellers cheques. When you buy the cheques, ask for a booklet listing all the American Express offices worldwide.

## Telephone

You can ring abroad from almost any phone box in Europe. Public phones accepting stored value phonecards (available from post offices, telephone centres, newsstands and retail outlets) are virtually the norm now; in some countries, France, for example, coin-operated phones are almost impossible to find.

There's a wide range of local and international phonecards. Lonely Planet's ekno global communication service provides low-cost international calls, a range of innovative messaging services, an online travel vault where you can securely store all your important documents, free email and travel information, all in one easy service. You can join online at w www.ekno.lonelyplanet.com, where you can also find the best local access numbers to connect to the 24-hour customer service centre to join or find out more. Once you have joined always check the ekno website for the latest access numbers for each country and updates on new features.

For local calls you're usually better off with a local phonecard. Without a phonecard, you can ring from a booth inside a post office or telephone centre and settle your bill at the counter. Reverse-charge (collect) calls are often possible, but not always. From many countries, however, the Country Direct system lets you phone home by billing the long-distance carrier you use at home. The numbers can often be dialled from public phones without even inserting a phonecard.

Area codes for individual cities are provided in the country chapters. For country codes, see Appendix – Telephones at the back of this book.

Toll-free numbers throughout Mediterranean Europe generally have an 0800 prefix. You'll find toll-free emergency numbers (eg, ambulance, fire brigade, police) in the boxed texts 'Emergency Services' in the Facts for the Visitor sections of the country chapters.

## Fax

You can send faxes and telexes from most main post offices.

## Email & Internet Access

Major Internet service providers (ISPs) such as **AOL** (W *www.aol.com)*, **AT&T** (W *www .att.com)* and **CompuServe** (W *www.com puserve.com)* have dial-in nodes throughout Europe; it's best to download a list of the dial-in numbers before you leave home. If you access your Internet email account at home through a smaller ISP or your office or school network, your best option is either to open an account with a global ISP, like those mentioned above, or to rely on Internet cafés and other public access points to collect your emails.

If you do intend to rely on Internet cafés, you'll need to carry three pieces of information so you can access your Internet email account: your incoming (POP or IMAP) mail server name, your account name, and your password. Your ISP or network supervisor will give you these. Armed with this information, you should be able to access your Internet email account from any Internet-connected machine in the world, provided it runs some kind of email software (remember that Netscape and Internet Explorer both have mail modules). Most ISPs also enable you to receive your emails through its website, which only requires you to remember your account name and password. It pays to become familiar with the process for doing this before you leave home.

You'll find Internet cafés throughout Europe – check the individual country chapters in this book, and see W www.netcafeguide .com for an up-to-date list. You may also find public Internet access in post offices, libraries, hostels, hotels, universities and so on.

## DIGITAL RESOURCES

The World Wide Web is a rich resource for travellers. You can research your trip, hunt down bargain air fares, book hotels, check on weather conditions or chat with locals and other travellers about the best places to visit (or avoid).

**Airline Information** What airlines fly where, when and for how much.
W www.travelocity.com
**Airline Tickets** Name the price you're willing to pay for an airline seat and if an airline has an empty seat for which it would rather get something than nothing, US-based Priceline lets you know.
W www.priceline.com
**Currency Conversions** Has the exchange rates of hundreds of currencies worldwide.
W www.xe.net/ucc
**Lonely Planet** There's no better place to start your Web explorations than the Lonely Planet website. Here you'll find succinct summaries on travelling to most places on earth, postcards from other travellers and the Thorn Tree bulletin board, where you can ask questions before you go or dispense advice when you get back. You can also find travel news, and the subWWWay section links you to the most useful travel resources elsewhere on the Web.
W www.lonelyplanet.com
**Tourist Offices** Lists the tourist offices for most countries around the world.
W www.towd.com
**Train Information** Train fares and schedules on the most popular routes in Europe, including information on rail and youth passes.
W www.raileurope.com
**World Heritage List** Unesco keeps a list of 'cultural and natural treasures of the world's heritage'.
W www.worldheritagesite.org

## NEWSPAPERS & MAGAZINES

In larger towns and cities you can buy the excellent *International Herald Tribune* on the day of publication, as well as the colourful but superficial *USA Today*. Among other English-language newspapers widely available are the *Guardian*, the *Financial Times* and the *Times*. Also readily available are *Newsweek, Time* and the *Economist*.

## RADIO & TV

You can pick up a mixture of the BBC World Service and BBC for Europe on medium wave at 648kHz AM and on short wave at 1296kHz, 6195kHz, 9410kHz, 12095kHz (a good daytime frequency), 15485kHz and 17640kHz, depending on the time of day. BBC Radio 4 broadcasts on long wave at 198kHz.

The Voice of America (VOA) can usually be found at various times of the day on 7170kHz, 9530kHz, 9690kHz, 9760kHz, 11825kHz, 15165kHz, 15205kHz, 15335kHz and 15580kHz. There are also numerous English-language broadcasts (or even BBC World Service and VOA rebroadcasts) on local AM and FM radio stations.

Cable and satellite TV have spread across Europe with much more gusto than radio. Sky TV and Eurosport can be found in many upmarket hotels throughout Mediterranean Europe, as can CNN, BBC Prime and other networks.

## VIDEO SYSTEMS

If you want to record or buy video tapes to play back home, you won't get a picture if the image registration systems are different. Europe generally uses PAL (Secam in France), which is incompatible with the North American and Japanese NTSC system. Australia also uses PAL.

## PHOTOGRAPHY & VIDEO

Mediterranean Europe is extremely photogenic, but the weather and where you'll be travelling will dictate what film to use. In places like northern France where the sky can often be overcast, photographers should bring high-speed film (200 or 400 ISO), but for most of the sunny Mediterranean, slower film is the answer.

Lonely Planet's *Travel Photography* by Richard I'Anson will help you capture the pictures you've always wanted.

Film and camera equipment are available everywhere in the region, but obviously shops in the larger towns and cities will have a wider selection. Avoid buying film at tourist sites in Europe (eg, at the kiosks below the Leaning Tower of Pisa or at the entrance to the Acropolis). It may have been stored badly or have reached its sell-by date. It will certainly be more expensive.

Properly used, a video camera can give a fascinating record of your holiday. Unlike still photography, video 'flows' so, for example, you can shoot scenes of countryside rolling past the train window. Make sure you keep the batteries charged and have the necessary charger, plugs and transformer for the country you are visiting. In most countries, it is possible to obtain video cartridges easily in large towns and cities, but make sure you buy the correct format. It is usually worth buying at least a few cartridges duty-free at the start of your trip.

## TIME

Most of the countries covered in this book are on Central European Time (GMT/UTC plus one hour), the same time used from Spain to Poland. Morocco is on GMT/UTC (all year) while Greece, Turkey and Cyprus are on East European Time (GMT/UTC plus two hours).

Clocks are advanced one hour for daylight-saving time in most countries on the last Sunday in March, and set back on the last Sunday in September. At that time Central European Time is GMT/UTC plus two hours and East European Time is GMT/UTC plus two hours.

## ELECTRICITY
### Voltages & Cycles

Most of Mediterranean Europe runs on 220V, 50Hz AC. The exceptions are Malta, which has 240V (such as the UK), and also Spain, which usually has 220V but sometimes still the old 110V or 125V depending on the network (some houses have both). Some old buildings and hotels in Italy, including Rome, might also have 125V. All EU countries were supposed to have been standardised at 230V by now, but like many things in the EU, this is taking longer than anticipated.

Check the voltage and cycle (usually 50Hz) used in your home country. Most appliances set up for 220V will handle 240V without modifications (and vice versa); the same goes for 110V and 125V combinations. It's always preferable to adjust your appliance to the exact voltage if you can (some modern battery chargers and radios will do this automatically). Just don't mix 110/125V with 220/240V without a transformer (which will be built into an adjustable appliance).

Several countries outside Europe (such as the USA and Canada) use 60Hz AC, which will affect the speed of electric motors even after the voltage has been adjusted to European values, so CD and tape players (where motor speed is all-important) will be useless. But things like electric razors, hair dryers, irons and radios will be fine.

### Plugs & Sockets

Cyprus and Malta use a design like the one in the UK and Ireland: three flat pins (two for current and one for earth). The rest of Mediterranean Europe uses the 'europlug' with two round pins. Many europlugs and some sockets don't have provision for earth, since most local home appliances are double-insulated. When provided, earth usually consists of two contact points along the edge, although Italy and Greece use a third round pin. In Greece the standard two-pin plug still fits the sockets, but this is not always so in Italy.

If your plugs are of a different design, you'll need an adaptor. Get one before you leave, since the adaptors available in Europe usually go the other way. If you find yourself without one, however, a specialist electrical-supply shop should be able to help.

## WEIGHTS & MEASURES

The metric system is in use throughout Mediterranean Europe, which shows decimals with commas and thousands with full stops (for numbers with four or more digits the French use full stops or spaces).

There's a metric conversion chart on the inside back cover of this book.

## HEALTH

Travel health depends on your predeparture preparations, your daily health care while travelling and how you handle any medical problem that may arise.

### Predeparture Planning

**Immunisations** Before you leave, find out from your doctor, a travel health centre or an organisation such as the US-based **Centers for Disease Control and Prevention** (ⓦ *www .cdc.gov*) what the current recommendations are for travel to your destination. Remember to leave enough time so that you can get any vaccinations you need – six weeks before travel is ideal. Discuss your requirements with your doctor, but generally it's a good idea to make sure your tetanus, diphtheria and polio vaccinations are up to date before travelling. Other vaccinations that may be recommended for travel to your destination include typhoid, hepatitis A, hepatitis B, rabies and tick-borne encephalitis.

Although there is no risk of yellow fever in Europe, if you are arriving from a yellow-fever infected area (most of sub-Saharan Africa and parts of South America) you'll need proof of yellow fever vaccination before you will be allowed to enter Greece, Portugal (if you're arriving in or bound for the Azores and Madeira) and Malta.

All vaccinations should be recorded on an International Health Certificate.

**Malaria Medication** Antimalarial drugs do not prevent you from being infected, but kill the malaria parasites during their development and significantly reduce the risk of becoming very ill or dying. Expert advice on medication should be sought, as there are many factors to consider, including the area to be visited, the risk of exposure to malaria-carrying mosquitoes, the side effects of medication, your medical history and whether the medication is for a child, an adult or a pregnant woman. Travellers to isolated areas in high-risk countries may like to carry a treatment dose of medication for use if symptoms occur. See Malaria under Less Common Diseases later in this chapter for further information.

**Health Insurance** Make sure that you have adequate health insurance. See Travel Insurance under Visas & Documents earlier in this chapter for details.

**Travel Health Guides** *Travel with Children* from Lonely Planet includes advice on travel health for younger children.

There are also a number of excellent travel health sites on the Internet. The World Health Organization at ⓦ www.who.int and the US Centers for Disease Control and Prevention at ⓦ www.cdc.gov have good sites, while the Lonely Planet website at ⓦ www.lonelyplanet .com/weblinks/wlheal.htm has a number of excellent links.

**Other Preparations** Make sure you're healthy before you start travelling. If you are going on a long trip make sure your teeth are OK. If you wear glasses take a spare pair and your prescription.

If you require a particular medication take an adequate supply, as it may not be available locally. Take part of the packaging showing the generic name, rather than the brand, which will make getting replacements easier. To avoid any problems, it's a good idea to have a legible prescription or letter from your doctor to show that you legally use the medication.

### Basic Rules

**Food** Salads and fruit should be safe throughout Europe. Ice cream is usually OK, but beware if it has melted and been refrozen. Take great care with fish or shellfish (cooked mussels that haven't opened properly can be dangerous, for instance), and avoid undercooked meat.

If a place looks clean and well run, and if the vendor also looks clean and healthy, then the food is probably safe. In general, places that are packed with travellers or locals will be fine. Be careful with food that has been cooked and left to go cold.

## Travellers Thrombosis

Sitting inactive for long periods of time on any form of transport (bus, train or plane), especially if in cramped conditions, can give you swollen feet and ankles, and may increase the possibility of deep vein thrombosis (DVT).

DVT is when a clot forms in the deep veins of your legs. DVT may be symptomless or you may get an uncomfortable ache and swelling of your calf. What makes DVT a concern is that in a minority of people, a small piece of the clot can break off and travel to the lungs to cause a pulmonary embolism, a very serious medical condition.

To help prevent DVT during long-haul travel, you should move around as much as possible and while you are sitting you should flex your calf muscles and wriggle your toes every half-hour. It's also a good idea to drink plenty of water or juices during the journey to prevent dehydration, and, for the same reason, avoid drinking lots of alcohol or caffeinated drinks. In addition, you may also consider wearing support stockings if you have had leg swelling in the past or you are aged over 40.

If you are prone to blood clotting or you are pregnant, you will need to discuss preventive measures with your doctor before you leave.

Dairy products are fine throughout Europe, but should be treated with suspicion in Morocco and Turkey because milk is often unpasteurised. Boiled milk is fine if it is kept hygienically, and yogurt is always good.

**Water**   Tap water is almost always safe to drink in Europe, but it's best to stick to bottled water in parts of southern Italy. Be wary of water taken directly from rivers or lakes unless you can be sure that there are no people or cattle upstream. Run-off from fertilised fields is also a concern. Tap water is usually *not* safe to drink in Morocco or Turkey (although probably OK in Istanbul and major Moroccan cities), so stick to bottled water and avoid ice cubes and even fruit juice, as water may have been added to it. In these areas, use purified water rather than tap water to brush your teeth.

If you're going to spend some time in Morocco or Turkey, or are planning extended hikes where you have to rely on water from rivers or streams, you'll need to know about water purification. The simplest way of purifying water is to boil it thoroughly. Vigorous boiling should be satisfactory, although at high altitude water boils at a lower temperature, so germs are less likely to be killed. Boil it for longer in this situation.

Consider purchasing a water filter for a long trip. Alternatively, iodine is effective in purifying water and is available in tablet form. Follow the directions carefully and remember that too much iodine can be harmful. Chlorine tablets will kill many pathogens, but not some parasites such as giardia and amoebic cysts.

## Medical Problems & Treatment

Local pharmacies or neighbourhood medical centres are good places to visit if you have a small medical problem and can explain what the problem is. Hospital casualty wards will help if it's more serious. Major hospitals and emergency numbers are mentioned in the various country chapters of this book and sometimes indicated on the maps. Tourist offices and hotels can put you on to a doctor or dentist, and your embassy or consulate will probably know one who speaks your language.

## Environmental Hazards

**Altitude Sickness**   This affliction can occur above 3000m, but few treks or ski runs reach heights of 3000m or more so altitude sickness is unlikely. Headache, vomiting, dizziness, extreme faintness, and difficulty in breathing and sleeping are all signs to heed. Treat mild symptoms with rest and simple painkillers. If mild symptoms persist or get worse, descend to a lower altitude and seek medical advice.

**Heat Exhaustion & Prickly Heat**   Dehydration and salt deficiency can cause heat exhaustion and can lead to severe heatstroke (see that section later in this chapter). Take time to acclimatise to high temperatures, drink sufficient liquids such as tea and drinks rich in mineral salts (eg, clear soups, and fruit and vegetable juices) and do not do anything too physically demanding.

Salt deficiency is characterised by fatigue, lethargy, headaches, giddiness and muscle cramps; salt tablets may help, but adding extra salt to your food is better.

Prickly heat is an itchy rash caused by excessive perspiration trapped under the skin. It usually strikes people who have just arrived in a hot climate. Keeping cool, showering often, drying the skin and using a mild talcum or prickly heat powder, wearing loose cotton clothing, or resorting to air-conditioning may help.

**Sunburn** In the tropics, the desert or at high altitude you can get sunburn surprisingly quickly, even through cloud. Use a sunscreen, a hat, and a barrier cream for your nose and lips. Calamine lotion or a commercial after-sun preparation are good for mild sunburn. Protect your eyes with good quality sunglasses, particularly if you will be near water, sand or snow.

**Heatstroke** This serious, occasionally fatal, condition can occur if the body's heat-regulating mechanism breaks down and the body temperature rises to dangerous levels. Long, continuous periods of exposure to high temperatures and insufficient fluids can leave you vulnerable to heatstroke.

The symptoms are feeling unwell, not sweating very much (or at all) and a high body temperature (39°C to 41°C or 102°F to 106°F). Where sweating has ceased, the skin becomes flushed and red. Severe, throbbing headaches and lack of coordination will also occur, and the sufferer may be confused or aggressive. If untreated, severe cases will eventually become delirious or convulse. Hospitalisation is essential, but in the interim get victims out of the sun, remove their clothing, cover them with a wet sheet or towel and then fan continually. Give fluids if they are conscious.

**Hypothermia** Too much cold can be just as dangerous as too much heat. Be prepared for cold, wet or windy conditions even if you're just out walking.

Hypothermia occurs when the body loses heat faster than it can produce it and the core temperature of the body falls. It is surprisingly easy to progress from very cold to dangerously cold due to a combination of wind, wet clothing, fatigue and hunger, even if the air temperature is above freezing. It is best to dress in layers; silk, wool and some of the new artificial fibres are all good insulating materials. A hat is important, as a lot of heat is lost through the head. A strong, waterproof outer layer and a 'space' blanket for emergencies are essential. Carry basic supplies, including food containing simple sugars to generate heat quickly and fluid to drink.

Symptoms of hypothermia are exhaustion, numb skin (particularly toes and fingers), shivering, slurred speech, irrational or violent behaviour, lethargy, stumbling, dizzy spells, muscle cramps and violent bursts of energy. Irrationality may take the form of sufferers claiming they are warm and trying to take off their clothes.

To treat mild hypothermia, first get the person out of the wind and/or rain, remove their clothing if it's wet and replace it with dry, warm clothing. Give them hot liquids – but not alcohol – and some high-kilojoule, easily digestible food. Do not rub victims; instead, allow them to slowly warm themselves. This should be enough to treat the early stages of hypothermia. The early recognition and treatment of mild hypothermia is the only way to prevent severe hypothermia, which is a critical condition.

## Infectious Diseases

**Diarrhoea** Simple things like a change of water, food or climate can all cause a mild bout of diarrhoea, but a few rushed toilet trips with no other symptoms is not indicative of a major problem.

Dehydration is the main danger with any diarrhoea, particularly in children or the elderly as dehydration can occur quite quickly. Under all circumstances, fluid replacement is the most important thing to remember. Weak black tea with a little sugar, soda water, or soft drinks allowed to go flat and diluted 50% with clean water are all good. With severe diarrhoea a rehydrating solution is preferable, to replace minerals and salts lost. Commercially available oral rehydration salts (ORS) are very useful; add them to boiled or bottled water. In an emergency you can make up a solution of six teaspoons of sugar and half a teaspoon of salt to a litre of boiled or bottled water. Keep drinking small amounts often. Stick to a bland diet as you recover.

Over-the-counter diarrhoea remedies, such as loperamide or diphenoxylate (sold under many different brand names), can be used to bring relief from the symptoms, although they do not actually cure the problem. Only use these drugs if you do not have access to toilets, eg, if you *must* travel. Note that these drugs are not recommended for children under 12 years.

In some situations antibiotics may be needed: severe diarrhoea, diarrhoea with blood or mucus (dysentery), any diarrhoea accompanied by fever, profuse watery diarrhoea and persistent diarrhoea that does not improve after 48 hours. These suggest a more serious cause of diarrhoea and in these situations over-the-counter diarrhoea remedies should be avoided.

**Fungal Infections** These occur more commonly in hot weather and are usually found on the scalp, between the toes (athlete's foot) or fingers, in the groin and on the body (ringworm). You get ringworm (which is a fungal infection, not a worm) from infected animals or other people. Moisture encourages these infections.

To prevent fungal infections wear loose, comfortable clothes, avoid artificial fibres, wash frequently and dry yourself carefully. If you do get an infection, wash the infected area at least daily with a disinfectant or medicated soap and water, and rinse and dry well. Apply an antifungal cream or powder. Try to expose the infected area to air or sunlight as much as possible and wash all towels and underwear in hot water – change them often and let them dry in the sun.

**Hepatitis** A general term for inflammation of the liver, hepatitis is a common disease worldwide. The symptoms include fever, chills, headache, fatigue, feelings of weakness, and aches and pains, followed by loss of appetite, nausea, vomiting, abdominal pain, dark urine, light-coloured faeces, jaundiced (yellow) skin and yellowing of the whites of the eyes. People who have had hepatitis should avoid alcohol for some time after the illness, as the liver needs time to recover.

Hepatitis A is transmitted by contaminated food and drinking water. You should seek medical advice, but there is not much you can do apart from resting, drinking lots of fluids, eating lightly and avoiding fatty foods. Hepatitis E is transmitted in the same way as hepatitis A; it can be particularly serious in pregnant women.

Hepatitis B is spread through contact with infected blood, blood products or body fluids, for example through sexual contact, unsterilised needles and blood transfusions, or contact with blood via small breaks in the skin. Other risk situations include having a shave, and getting a tattoo or body piercing with contaminated equipment. The symptoms of type B may be more severe and may lead to long-term problems such as chronic liver damage. Hepatitis C and D are spread in the same way as hepatitis B and can also lead to long-term complications.

**HIV & AIDS** Infection with the human immunodeficiency virus (HIV) may lead to acquired immune deficiency syndrome (AIDS), which is a fatal disease. Any exposure to blood, blood products or body fluids may put the individual at risk. The disease is often transmitted through sexual contact or dirty needles – vaccinations, acupuncture, tattooing and body piercing can be as dangerous as intravenous drug use. HIV/AIDS can be spread through infected blood transfusions; but blood used for transfusions in European hospitals is screened for HIV and should be safe.

Anyone seeking residence, work and student permits in Spain must submit to a medical, which may include an AIDS test.

**Sexually Transmitted Infections** HIV/AIDS and hepatitis B can be transmitted through sexual contact – see the relevant sections earlier for more details. Other STIs include gonorrhoea, herpes and syphilis; sores, blisters or a rash around the genitals and discharges or pain when urinating are common symptoms. In some STIs, such as wart virus or chlamydia, symptoms may be less marked or not observed at all, especially in women. Chlamydia infection can cause infertility in men and women before any symptoms have been noticed. Syphilis symptoms eventually disappear completely but the disease continues and can cause severe problems in later years. While abstinence from sexual contact is the only 100% effective prevention, using condoms is also effective.

## Cuts, Bites & Stings

**Bedbugs & Lice** Bedbugs live in various places, but particularly in dirty mattresses and bedding, evidenced by spots of blood on bedclothes or on the wall. Bedbugs leave itchy bites in neat rows. Calamine lotion or a sting relief spray may help.

All lice cause itching and discomfort. They make themselves at home in your hair (head lice), your clothing (body lice) or in your pubic hair (crabs). You catch lice through direct contact with infected people or by sharing combs, clothing and the like. Powder or shampoo treatment will kill the lice and infected clothing should then be washed in very hot, soapy water and left in the sun to dry.

**Insect Bites & Stings** Mosquitoes can be a nuisance in southern Europe, but can almost drive you insane during the summer months in northern Europe, particularly around lakes and rivers. They also cause sleepless nights in swampy areas like the Camargue delta in southern France. Most people get used to mosquito bites after a few days as their bodies adjust, and the itching and swelling will become less severe. An antihistamine cream may help alleviate the symptoms. For some people, a daily dose of vitamin B will keep mosquitoes at bay. See also Malaria under Less Common Diseases.

**Ticks** You should always check all over your body if you have been walking through a potentially tick-infested area as ticks can cause skin infections and other potentially more serious diseases. If a tick is found attached, press down around the tick's head with tweezers, grab the head and gently pull upwards. Avoid pulling the rear of the body as this may squeeze the tick's gut contents through the attached mouth parts into the skin, increasing the risk of infection and disease. Smearing chemicals on the tick will not make it let go and is not recommended.

**Snakes** To minimise your chances of being bitten always wear boots, socks and long trousers when walking through undergrowth where snakes may be present. Don't put your hands into holes and crevices, and be careful when collecting firewood.

Snake bites do not cause instantaneous death, and antivenins are usually available. Immediately wrap the bitten limb tightly, as you would for a sprained ankle, and then attach a splint to immobilise it. Keep the victim still and seek medical help, if possible with the dead snake for identification. Don't attempt to catch the snake if there is a possibility of being bitten again. Tourniquets and sucking out the poison are comprehensively discredited.

## Women's Health

Antibiotic use, synthetic underwear, sweating and contraceptive pills can lead to fungal vaginal infections, especially when travelling in hot climates. Fungal infections are characterised by a rash, itch and discharge and can be treated with a highly diluted vinegar or lemon-juice douche, or with yogurt. Antifungal pessaries or vaginal cream are the usual treatment. Maintaining good personal hygiene and wearing loose-fitting clothes and cotton underwear may help prevent these infections.

Sexually transmitted infections are a major cause of vaginal problems. Symptoms include a smelly discharge, painful intercourse and sometimes a burning sensation when urinating. Medical attention should be sought and sexual partners must also be treated. For more details see the section on Sexually Transmitted Infections earlier. Besides abstinence, the best thing is to practise safer sex by using condoms.

## Less Common Diseases

The following diseases pose a small risk to travellers, and so are only mentioned in passing. Seek medical advice if you think you may have any of these diseases.

**Rabies** The only Mediterranean European countries that are rabies-free are Greece, Italy, Malta and Portugal. Many animals can be infected (such as dogs, cats, bats and monkeys) and it is their saliva which is infectious. Any bite, scratch or even lick from an animal should be cleaned immediately and thoroughly. Scrub with soap and running water, and then apply alcohol or iodine solution. Local medical advice should be sought immediately as to the possibility of rabies in the region. A course of injections may then be required in order to prevent the onset of symptoms and possible death.

**Leishmaniasis** This is a group of parasitic diseases transmitted by infected sandflies. Cutaneous leishmaniasis affects the skin tissue causing ulceration and disfigurement, and visceral leishmaniasis affects the internal organs. Seek medical advice, as laboratory testing is required for diagnosis and correct treatment. Avoiding sandfly bites is the best precaution. Bites are usually painless, itchy and yet another reason to cover up and apply repellent.

**Lyme Disease** This is a tick-transmitted infection that may be acquired in Europe. The illness usually begins with a spreading rash at the site of the tick bite and is accompanied by fever, headache, extreme fatigue, aching joints and muscles and mild neck stiffness. If untreated, these symptoms usually resolve over several weeks but over subsequent weeks or months disorders of the nervous system, heart and joints may develop. Treatment works best early in the illness. Medical help should be sought.

**Tick-borne Encephalitis** Ticks can carry encephalitis, a virus-borne cerebral inflammation. Tick-borne encephalitis can occur in most forest and rural areas of Europe. Symptoms include blotches around the bite, which is sometimes pale in the middle. Headache, stiffness and other flu-like symptoms, as well as extreme tiredness, appearing a week or two after the bite, can progress to serious problems. Medical help must be sought.

**Typhoid** This fever is a dangerous gut infection caused by contaminated water and food. Medical help must be sought. In its early stages sufferers may feel they have a bad cold or flu on the way, as early symptoms are a headache, body aches and a fever that rises a little each day until it is around 40°C (104°F) or more. The victim's pulse is often slow relative to the degree of fever present unlike a normal fever where the pulse increases. There may also be vomiting, abdominal pain, diarrhoea or constipation. In the second week the high fever and slow pulse continue and a few pink spots may appear on the body; trembling, delirium, weakness, weight loss and dehydration may occur. Complications such as pneumonia, perforated bowel or meningitis may also occur.

**Malaria** This serious and potentially fatal disease is spread by mosquito bites. If you are travelling in endemic areas it is extremely important to avoid mosquito bites and to take tablets to prevent this disease. Fortunately, mosquito-borne diseases such as malaria are for the most part unknown in Europe. Malaria is present in both Morocco and Turkey (not in the main tourist areas in Turkey's west and southwest). Symptoms range from fever, chills and sweating, headache, diarrhoea and abdominal pains to a vague feeling of ill-health. Seek medical help immediately if malaria is suspected. Without getting treatment malaria can rapidly become more serious and can be fatal.

There is a variety of medications, such as mefloquine, Fansidar and Malarone. You should seek medical advice, before you travel, on the right medication and dosage for you. If medical care is not available, malaria tablets can be used for treatment. You need to use a malaria tablet that is different from the one you were taking when you contracted malaria. See Malaria Medication earlier.

## WOMEN TRAVELLERS

Frustrating though it may be, women travellers continue to face more challenging situations when travelling than men do. If you are a woman traveller, especially a solo woman, you may find it helpful to understand the status of local women to better understand the responses you illicit from locals. Hopes of travelling inconspicuously, spending time alone and absorbing the surroundings are often thwarted by men who assume a lone woman desires company, or who seemingly find it impossible to avert their penetrating gaze. Bear in mind that most of this behaviour, which can come across as threatening, is more often than not harmless. Don't let it deter you! The more women that travel, alone or in pairs or groups, the less attention women will attract and, in time, the more freedom women will feel to gallivant across the globe, *sans* beau in tow.

Despite feminism's grip on many European countries, women remain underrepresented in positions of power, in both governmental and corporate spheres. Despite the exciting progress to elevate the status of women in recent years, women's leadership at the upper echelons of institutions still leaves a lot to be desired, and in many areas, you may notice the glut of women in low-paid, menial jobs. As is the case worldwide, women remain overrepresented among the illiterate and unemployed.

In Muslim countries, where conservative conceptions of the largely house-bound role of women still tend to prevail, women travelling alone or with other women will certainly be of interest or curiosity to both men and women. Unmarried men rarely have contact with women outside their family unit, which is why men in, for example, Morocco and

Turkey, will afford travelling women so much attention. In such areas, women travelling with a male companion will often experience the exact opposite, and may need to pinch themselves as a reminder that yes, they actually exist.

## GAY & LESBIAN TRAVELLERS

This book lists contact addresses and gay and lesbian venues in the individual country chapters; look in the Facts for the Visitor and Entertainment sections.

The *Spartacus International Gay Guide* (Bruno Gmünder, US$39.95) is a good male-only international directory of gay entertainment venues in Europe and elsewhere. It's best when used in conjunction with listings in local gay papers, usually distributed for free at gay bars and clubs. For lesbians, *Women's Travel in Your Pocket* (Ferrari Publications, US$15.95) is a good international guide.

## DISABLED TRAVELLERS

If you have a physical disability, get in touch with your national support organisation (preferably the 'travel officer' if there is one) and ask about the countries you plan to visit. They often have complete libraries devoted to travel, and they can put you in touch with travel agents who specialise in tours for the disabled.

The British-based **Royal Association for Disability & Rehabilitation** (*Radar; ☎ 020-7250 3222, fax 7250 0212;* **w** *www.radar .org.uk; 12 City Forum, 250 City Rd, London EC1V 8AF*) publishes a useful guide entitled *A Guide to Long Distance Travel for Disabled People* (UK£5), which gives a good overview of facilities available to disabled travellers in Europe.

## SENIOR TRAVELLERS

Senior citizens are entitled to many discounts in Europe on things like public transport and museum admission fees, provided proof of age can be shown. In some cases a special pass may be required. The minimum qualifying age is generally 60 or 65 for men and slightly younger for women.

In your home country, a lower age may already entitle you to all sorts of interesting travel packages and discounts (eg, on car hire) through organisations and travel agents that cater for senior travellers. Start hunting at your local senior citizens advice bureau.

European nationals aged 60 and over can get a Railplus Card, which entitles the holder to reduced fares. For more information see Cheap Tickets under Train in the Getting Around chapter.

## TRAVEL WITH CHILDREN

Successful travel with young children requires planning and effort. Don't try to overdo things; even for adults, packing too much into the time available can cause problems. And make sure the activities include the kids as well – balance that day at the Louvre with a day at Disneyland Paris. Include children in the trip planning; if they've helped to work out where you will be going, they will be much more interested when they get there. Europe is the home of Little Red Riding Hood, Cinderella, King Arthur and Tintin and is a great place to travel with kids. Lonely Planet's *Travel with Children* by Cathy Lanigan (with a foreword by Maureen Wheeler) is an excellent source of information.

Most car-rental firms in Europe have children's safety seats for hire at a nominal cost, but it's essential that you book them in advance. The same goes for highchairs and cots (cribs); they're standard in most restaurants and hotels, but numbers are limited. The choice of baby food, formulas, soy and cow's milk, disposable nappies (diapers) and the like is as great in the supermarkets of most European countries as it is at home, but the opening hours might be different. Run out of nappies on Saturday afternoon and you may be in for a messy weekend.

## DANGERS & ANNOYANCES

Overall, you should experience few problems travelling in Mediterranean Europe – even alone – as the region is well developed and relatively safe. But exercise common sense. The Basque separatist movement remains active as does soccer hooliganism.

Whatever you do, don't leave friends and relatives back home worrying about how to get in touch with you in case of emergency. Work out a list of places where they can contact you. Better still, phone home now and then or email.

### Theft

This is definitely a problem in Mediterranean Europe, and nowadays you also have to be wary of other travellers. The most important things to guard are your passport, papers, tickets and money – in that order. It's always best to carry these next to your skin or in a sturdy leather pouch on your belt. Train station lockers or luggage storage counters are useful places to store your bags (but *never* valuables) while you get your bearings in a new town. Be very suspicious of people who offer to help you operate your locker. Carry your own padlock for hostel lockers.

You can lessen the risks further by being careful of snatch thieves. Cameras or shoulder bags are an open invitation for these people, who sometimes operate from motorcycles or scooters and expertly slash the strap before you have a chance to react. A small daypack is better, but watch your rear. Be very careful at cafés and bars; loop the strap around your leg while seated.

Pickpockets are most active in dense crowds, especially in busy train stations and on public transport during peak hours. A common ploy is for one person to distract you while another whips through your pockets. Beware of gangs of kids – both dishevelled-looking *and* well dressed – waving newspapers and demanding attention. In the blink of an eye, a wallet or camera can go missing.

Be careful even in hotels; don't leave any valuables lying around in your room.

Parked cars containing luggage or other bags are prime targets for petty criminals in most cities, and in particular cars with foreign number plates and/or rental-agency stickers. While driving in cities, beware of snatch thieves when you pull up at the lights – keep doors locked and windows rolled up high.

In case of theft or loss, always report the incident to the police and ask for a statement. Otherwise your travel-insurance company won't pay up.

## Drugs

Always treat drugs with a great deal of caution. There are a lot of drugs available in Mediterranean Europe, but that doesn't mean they are legal. Even a little harmless hashish can cause a great deal of trouble in some places.

Don't even think about bringing drugs home with you either. With what may be considered 'suspect' stamps in your passport (eg, Morocco), energetic customs officials could well decide to take a closer look.

## ACTIVITIES

Mediterranean Europe offers countless opportunities to indulge in more active pursuits than sightseeing.

See the individual country chapters for more local information.

## Windsurfing

After swimming and fishing, windsurfing could well be the most popular of the many water sports on offer in Europe. It's easy to rent sailboards in many tourist centres, and courses are usually available for beginners.

## Boating

The Mediterranean itself is not the only body of water with opportunities for boating. The region's many lakes, rivers and other coastlines offer a variety of boating options unmatched anywhere in the world. You can kayak down rapids in Slovenia, charter a yacht in the Aegean, row on a peaceful Alpine lake, rent a sailing boat on the Côte d'Azur and cruise the canals of France – the possibilities are endless.

## Hiking

Keen hikers can spend a lifetime exploring Europe's many exciting trails. The spectacular Italian Dolomites are crisscrossed with well marked trails, and food and accommodation are available along the way in season. Hiking areas that are less well known but nothing short of stunning can be found in Corsica, Sardinia, Crete and Croatia.

## Cycling

Along with hiking, cycling is the best way to really get close to the scenery and the people, while keeping yourself fit in the process. It's also a good way to get around many cities and towns.

Much of Europe is ideally suited to cycling. In the northwest, the flat terrain ensures that bicycles are a popular form of everyday transport, though strong headwinds often spoil the fun. In the rest of the continent, hills and mountains can make for heavy going, but this is offset by the dense concentration of things to see. Cycling is a great way to explore many of the Mediterranean islands, though the heat can get to you after a while (make sure you drink enough fluids).

Popular cycling areas include the coastal areas of Sardinia (around Alghero) and Apulia, and the hills of Tuscany and Umbria in Italy, and the south of France.

If you are arriving from outside Europe, you can often bring your own bicycle along on the plane. Alternatively, this book lists many places where you can hire one.

See Bicycle in the introductory Getting Around chapter for more information on bicycle touring, and the Getting Around sections in the individual country chapters for rental agencies and tips on places to visit.

## Skiing
Skiing is quite expensive due to the costs of ski lifts, accommodation and the inevitable aprés-ski drinking sessions. Equipment hire (or even purchase), on the other hand, can be relatively cheap if you follow the tips in this book, and the hassle of bringing your own skis may not be worth it. As a rule, a skiing holiday in Europe will work out twice as expensive as a summer holiday of the same length. Cross-country skiing costs less than downhill since you don't rely as much on ski lifts.

The skiing season generally lasts from early December to late March, though at higher altitudes it may extend an extra month either way. Snow conditions can vary greatly from one year to the next and from region to region, but January and February tend to be the best (and busiest) months.

The Julian Alps in Slovenia offer great value and are luring skiers away from the flashier resorts just across the border in both Austria and Italy.

Some of the cheapest skiing in Europe can be found in the Sierra Nevada mountain range in the south of Spain. Greece also boasts a growing ski industry, and skiing there is good value.

## COURSES
If your interests are more cerebral, you can enrol in courses on anything from language to alternative medicine. Language courses are available to foreigners through universities or private schools, and are justifiably popular since the best way to learn a language is in the country where it's spoken. But you can also take courses in art, literature, architecture, drama, music, cooking, alternative energy, photography and organic farming, among other subjects.

The individual country chapters in this book give pointers on where to start looking.

In general, the best sources of information are the cultural institutes maintained by many European countries around the world; failing that, try their national tourist offices or embassies. Student-exchange organisations, student-travel agencies, and organisations such as the YMCA/YWCA and Hostelling International (HI) can also help to put you on the right track. Ask about special holiday packages that include a course.

## WORK
European countries aren't keen on handing out jobs to foreigners when unemployment rates are what they are in some areas. Officially, an EU citizen is allowed to work in any other EU country, but the paperwork isn't always straightforward for long-term employment and after three months they will probably need to apply for a residency permit. Other country/nationality combinations require special work permits that can be almost impossible to arrange, especially for temporary work. That doesn't prevent enterprising travellers from topping up their funds occasionally by working in the hotel or restaurant trades at beach or ski resorts or teaching a little English, and they don't always have to do this illegally either.

In France you can get a visa for work as an au pair if you are going to follow a recognised course of study (eg, a French-language course) and complete all the paperwork before leaving your country. Your national student-exchange organisation may be able to arrange temporary work permits to several countries through special programmes. For more details on working as a foreigner, see Work in the Facts for the Visitor sections of the individual country chapters.

If one of your parents or a grandparent was born in an EU country, you may have certain rights you never knew about. Get in touch with that country's embassy and ask about dual citizenship and work permits – if you go for citizenship, also ask about any obligations, such as military service and residency. Be aware that your home country may not recognise dual citizenship.

If you do find a temporary job, the pay may be less than that offered to local people. The one big exception is teaching English, but these jobs are hard to come by, at least officially. Other typical tourist jobs (picking grapes in France, washing dishes in Alpine resorts) often come with board and lodging, and the pay is little more than pocket money, but you'll have a good time partying with other travellers.

If you play an instrument or have other artistic talents, you could try working the streets. As every Peruvian pipe player (and his fifth cousin) knows, busking is fairly common in major cities of Mediterranean Europe, especially in France, Spain and Italy. Beware though: Many countries require municipal permits that can be hard to obtain. Talk to other buskers first.

Selling goods on the street, apart from at flea markets, is generally frowned upon and can be tantamount to vagrancy. It's also a hard way to make money if you're not selling something special. Most countries require permits for this sort of thing. In Spain it's fairly common, although officially illegal.

There are several references and websites that publicise specific positions in Mediterranean Europe. **Transitions Abroad** (W www.transabroad.com) publishes *Work Abroad: The Complete Guide to Finding a Job Overseas* and the *Alternative Travel Directory: The Complete Guide to Work, Study and Travel Overseas* as well as a colour magazine, *Transitions Abroad*. Its website lists paid positions and volunteer and service programmes. **Action Without Borders** (W www.idealist.org) and **GoAbroad.com** (W www.goabroad.com) list hundreds of jobs and volunteer opportunities.

*Work Your Way Around the World* by Susan Griffith gives good, practical advice on a wide range of issues. Its publisher, **Vacation Work** (W www.vacationwork.co.uk), has many other useful titles, including *Summer Jobs Abroad*, edited by David Woodworth. *Working Holidays*, published by the Central Bureau for Educational Visits & Exchanges in London, is another good source.

## Volunteer Work

Organising a volunteer work placement is a great way to gain a deeper insight into local culture. If you're staying with a family, or working alongside local colleagues, you'll probably learn much more about life here than you would if you were travelling through the country.

In some instances volunteers are paid a living allowance, sometimes they work for their keep, and other programmes require the volunteer to pay.

There are several Internet sites that can help you search for volunteer work opportunities in Mediterranean Europe. As well as websites mentioned earlier, **WorkingAbroad** (W www.workingabroad.com) has a good website for researching possibilities and applying for positions.

The **International Willing Workers On Organic Farms Association** (WWOOF; W www.wwoof.org) has some organisations in Mediterranean Europe. If you choose to join a WWOOF organisation, you can arrange to live and work on a host's organic farm.

## ACCOMMODATION

As with the rest of Europe, the cheapest places to stay in Mediterranean Europe are camping grounds, followed by hostels and accommodation in student dormitories; and guesthouses, *pensiones* and private rooms often offer good value. Self-catering flats and cottages are worth considering with a group, especially if you plan to stay somewhere for a while.

See the Facts for the Visitor sections in the individual country chapters for an overview of local accommodation options. During peak holiday periods, accommodation can be hard to find, and unless you're camping, it's advisable to book ahead. Even camping grounds can fill up, especially in or around big cities.

### Reservations

Cheap hotels in popular destinations (eg, Paris, Rome and Madrid), especially the well-run ones in desirable or central neighbourhoods, fill up quickly. It's a good idea to make reservations as many weeks ahead as possible – at least for the first night or two. A three-minute international phone call to reserve a room (followed, if necessary, by written confirmation and/or a deposit) is a lot cheaper than wasting your first day in a city looking for a place to stay.

If you arrive in a country by air and without a reservation, there is often an airport accommodation-booking desk, although it rarely covers the lower strata of hotels. Tourist offices often have extensive accommodation lists, and the more helpful ones will go out of their way to find you something suitable. In most countries the fee for this service is very low and if accommodation is tight it can save you a lot of running around. This is also an easy way to get around any language problems. Agencies offering private rooms can be good value. Staying with a local family doesn't always mean that you'll lack privacy, but you'll probably have less freedom than in a hotel.

Sometimes people will approach you on the street offering a private room or a hostel bed. This can be good or bad, there's no hard-and-fast rule – just make sure it's not way out in a dingy suburb somewhere and that you negotiate a clear price. As always, be careful when someone offers to carry your luggage; they might carry it off altogether.

## Camping

Camping is immensely popular in Mediterranean Europe (especially among German and Dutch tourists) and provides the cheapest accommodation. There's usually a charge per tent or site, per person and per vehicle. National tourist offices should have booklets or brochures listing camping grounds for their country. See Visas & Documents earlier in this chapter for information on the Camping Card International (CCI).

In large cities, most camping grounds will be some distance from the centre. For this reason, camping is most popular with people who have their own transport. If you're on foot, the money you save by camping can quickly be eaten up by the bus or train fares spent on commuting to and from a town centre. You may also need a tent, sleeping bag and cooking equipment, though not always. Many camping grounds hire bungalows or cottages accommodating from two to eight people.

Camping other than on designated camping grounds is difficult because the population density of Europe makes it hard to find a suitable spot to pitch a tent away from prying eyes. It is also illegal without permission from the local authorities (the police or local council office) or from the owner of the land (don't be shy about asking – you may be pleasantly surprised by the response).

In some countries (eg, France), free camping is illegal on all but private land, and in Greece it's illegal altogether. This doesn't prevent hikers from occasionally pitching their tent for the night, and they'll usually get away with it if they have only a small tent, are discreet, stay only one or two nights, take the tent down during the day and do not light a campfire or leave rubbish. At worst, they'll be woken up by the police and asked to move on.

## Hostels

Hostels offer the cheapest (secure) roof over your head in Mediterranean Europe, and you don't have to be a youngster to use them. Most hostels are part of the national youth hostel association (YHA), which is affiliated with what was formerly called the IYHF (International Youth Hostel Federation) and has been renamed Hostelling International (HI) in order to attract a wider clientele and move away from the emphasis on youth. The situation remains slightly confused, however. Some countries, such as canada and the USA, immediately adopted the new name, but many European countries will take a few years to change their logos. In practice it makes no difference – IYHF and HI are the same thing and the domestic YHA almost always belongs to the parent group.

Technically, you're supposed to be a YHA or HI member to use affiliated hostels, but you can often stay by paying an extra charge and this will usually be set against future membership. Stay enough nights as a non-member and you're automatically a member.

To join the HI, ask at any hostel or contact your local or national hostelling office. There's a useful website at Ⓦ www.iyhf.org with links to most HI sites. The offices for English-speaking countries appear below. Otherwise, check the individual country chapters for addresses.

**Australia** Australian Youth Hostels Association (☎ 02-9261 1111, fax 9261 1969, Ⓔ yha@yhansw.org.au), 422 Kent St, Sydney, NSW 2000

**Canada** Hostelling International Canada (☎ 613-237 7884, fax 237 7868, Ⓔ info@hihostels.ca), 205 Catherine St, Suite 400, Ottawa, Ont K2P 1C3

**England & Wales** Youth Hostels Association (☎ 01629-592600, fax 592702, Ⓔ customerservices@yha.org.uk), Trevelyan House, Dimple Rd, Matlock, Derbyshire DE4 3YH

**Ireland** An Óige (Irish Youth Hostel Association; ☎ 01-830 4555, fax 830 5808, Ⓔ mailbox@anoige.ie), 61 Mountjoy St, Dublin 7

**New Zealand** Youth Hostels Association of New Zealand (☎ 03-379 9970, fax 365 4476, Ⓔ info@yha.org.nz), PO Box 436, Level 3, 193 Cashel St, Christchurch

**Northern Ireland** Hostelling International Northern Ireland (☎ 028-9031 5435, fax 9043 9699, Ⓔ info@hini.org.uk), 22–32 Donegall Rd, Belfast BT12 5JN

**Scotland** Scottish Youth Hostels Association
(☎ 01786-891400, fax 891333,
e info@syha.org.uk), 7 Glebe Crescent,
Stirling FK8 2JA
**South Africa** Hostelling International South Africa
(☎ 021-424 2511, fax 424 4119,
e info@hisa.org.za), PO Box 4402,
St George's House, 73 St George's Mall,
Cape Town 8001
**USA** Hostelling International/American Youth
Hostels (☎ 202-783 6161, fax 783 6171,
e hiayhserv@hiayh.org), 733 15th St NW,
Suite 840, Washington DC 20005

At a hostel, you get a bed for the night, plus use of communal facilities, which often include a kitchen where you can prepare your own meals. You are usually required to have a sleeping sheet – simply using your sleeping bag is not permitted. If you don't have your own approved sleeping sheet, you can usually hire or buy one. Hostels vary widely in character, but the growing number of travellers and the increased competition from other forms of accommodation, particularly private 'backpacker hostels', have prompted many hostels to improve their facilities and cut back on rules and regulations. Increasingly, hostels are open all day, curfews are disappearing and the 'warden' with a sergeant-major mentality is an endangered species. In some places you'll even find hostels with single and double rooms.

There are many hostel guides with listings available, including the *HI Europe* (UK£8.50). Many hostels accept reservations by phone or fax, but usually not during peak periods, and they'll often book the next hostel you're heading to for a small fee. You can also book hostels through national hostel offices. Popular hostels can be heavily booked in summer and a limit may even be placed on how many nights you can stay.

## University Accommodation

Some university towns rent out student accommodation during holiday periods. This is very popular in France (see the France chapter for details). Accommodation will sometimes be in single rooms (more commonly in doubles or triples) and may have cooking facilities. Inquire at the college or university, at student information services or at local tourist offices.

## Guesthouses & Hotels

There's a huge range of accommodation above the hostel level. In some countries private accommodation may go under the name of *pensione*, guesthouse, *chambre d'hôte*, *domatia* and so on. Although the majority of guesthouses are simple affairs, there are more expensive ones where you will find attached bathrooms and other luxuries.

Above this level are hotels which, at the bottom of the bracket, may be no more expensive than guesthouses, but at the other extreme extend to luxury five-star properties with price tags to match. Although categorisation depends on the country, the hotels recommended in this book will generally range from no stars to one or two stars. You'll often find inexpensive hotels clustered around the bus and train station areas – always good places to start hunting.

Check your hotel room and the bathroom before you agree to take it, and make sure you know what it's going to cost; discounts are often available for groups or for longer stays. Ask about breakfast; sometimes it's included but at other times it may be obligatory and you'll have to pay extra for it. If the sheets don't look clean, ask to have them changed right away. Check where the fire exits are.

If you think a hotel room is too expensive, ask if there's anything cheaper. (Often hotel owners may have tried to steer you into more expensive rooms.) In southern Europe in particular, hotel owners may be open to a little bargaining if times are slack. In France it is now common practice for business hotels (usually rated higher than two stars) to slash their rates by up to 40% on Friday and Saturday nights when business is slow. Save your big hotel splurge for the weekend here.

## FOOD

Few regions in the world offer such a variety of cuisines in such a small area as Mediterranean Europe. Dishes are completely different from one country (and even region) to the next, and sampling the local food can be one of the most enjoyable aspects of travel. The Facts for the Visitor sections in the individual country chapters contain details of local cuisines, and the Places to Eat sections list many suggestions.

Restaurant prices vary enormously. The cheapest places for a decent meal are often the self-service restaurants in department stores. University restaurants are dirt cheap, but the food tends to be bland and you may not be allowed in if you're not a local student.

Kiosks often sell cheap snacks that can be as much a part of the national cuisine as the fancy dishes.

Self-catering – buying your ingredients at a shop or market and preparing them yourself – can be a cheap and wholesome way of eating. Even if you don't cook, lunch on a park bench with half a loaf of fresh bread, some local cheese and salami and a tomato or two, washed down with a bottle of local wine makes a nice change from restaurant food.

If you have dietary restrictions, you're a vegetarian or you keep kosher, for example, tourist organisations may be able to advise you or provide lists of suitable restaurants. In this book we list some vegetarian and kosher restaurants.

In general, vegetarians have no need to worry about going hungry in Mediterranean Europe; many restaurants have one or two vegetarian dishes, and southern European menus in particular tend to contain many vegetable dishes and salads.

## DRINKS

So much to drink, so little time. Mediterranean Europe is an alcohol connoisseur's haven. What else would you expect of the home of Chianti, ouzo, port and Estrella de Galicia (our favourite Spanish beer), not to mention the most famous wines in the history of viniculture? Can you feel the champagne bubbles tickling your nostrils?

Although Islam forbids the drinking of alcoholic beverages, they nevertheless are widely available in Morocco and Turkey.

Afterthought – nonalcoholic options such as coffee, tea (Morocco's national beverage is freshly brewed mint tea) and *aqua minerale* are readily available. See Drinks in the Facts for the Visitor sections of the country chapters for specific information.

# Getting There & Away

In these days of strong competition among airlines, there are many opportunities to find cheap tickets to a variety of European gateway cities for your Mediterranean Europe travel.

Forget shipping unless you are thinking about ferries across the Mediterranean. Only a handful of ships still carry passengers across the Atlantic; they don't sail often and are very expensive, even compared with full-fare air tickets. Some travellers still arrive or leave overland – the options being Africa, the Middle East and Asia via Russia on the Trans-Siberian Railway from China.

You can find useful websites with information on travel planning and ticket prices in the Digital Resources section of the Facts for the Visitor chapter of this book.

## AIR
### Buying Tickets

With a bit of research – ringing around travel agencies, checking Internet sites, perusing the travel ads in newspapers – you can often get yourself a good travel deal. Start early as some of the cheapest tickets need to be bought well in advance and popular flights can sell out.

Generally, there is nothing to be gained by buying a ticket direct from the airline. Discounted tickets are released to selected travel agencies and specialist discount agencies, and these are more than usually the cheapest deals going. One exception to this rule is the expanding number of 'no-frills' carriers, which mostly sell only direct to travellers. Unlike the 'full-service' airlines, no-frills carriers often make one-way tickets available at around half the return fare, meaning that it is easy to put together an open-jaw ticket when you fly to one place but leave from another.

The other exception is booking on the Internet. Many airlines, full-service and no-frills, offer some excellent fares to Web surfers. They may sell seats by auction or simply cut prices to reflect the reduced cost of electronic selling. Many travel agencies around the world have websites, which can make the Internet a quick and easy way to compare prices. There are also online agencies that operate only on the Internet. Online ticket sales work well if you are doing a simple one-way or return trip on specified dates. However, online superfast fare generators are no substitute for a travel

agent who knows all about special deals, has strategies for avoiding layovers and can offer advice on everything from which airline has the best vegetarian food to the best travel insurance to bundle with your ticket.

You may find the cheapest flights are advertised by obscure agencies. Most such firms are honest and solvent, but there are some rogue fly-by-night outfits around. Paying by credit card generally offers protection, as most card issuers provide refunds if you can prove you didn't get what you paid for. Similar protection can be obtained by buying a ticket from a bonded agency, such as one covered by the Air Travel Organisers' Licensing (ATOL) scheme in the UK. Agencies who accept only cash should hand over tickets straight away and not tell you to 'come back tomorrow'. After you've made a booking or paid your deposit, call the airline and confirm that the booking was made. It's not advisable to send money (even cheques) through the post unless the agency is very well established – some travellers have reported being ripped off by fly-by-night mail-order agencies.

If you purchase a ticket and later want to make changes to your route or get a refund, you need to contact the original travel agency. Airlines issue refunds only to the purchaser of a ticket – usually the travel agency who bought the ticket on your behalf. Many travellers change their routes halfway through their trips, so think carefully before you buy a ticket that is not easily refunded. Don't bother buying half-used tickets from other travellers; you won't be able to board the flight unless the name on the ticket matches that on your passport. You may decide to pay more than the rock-bottom fare by opting for the safety of a better-known travel agency. Firms such as STA Travel, with offices worldwide, are longstanding companies that offer good prices to most destinations.

Round-the-World (RTW) tickets are a useful option for long-haul travellers. Usually the tickets are valid for between 90 days and a year. Make sure you understand what restrictions may apply – there'll be a limit to how many stops (or kilometres/miles) you are permitted, and you won't be able to backtrack. Prices start at about UK£720, A$2250 or US$1450, depending on the number of stops, the route and the season. For short-term travel, cheaper fares are available by travelling mid-week, staying away at least one Saturday night or taking advantage of short-lived promotional fares.

## Student & Youth Fares

Full-time students and people aged under 26 years (under 30 in some countries) have access to better deals than other travellers. The better deals may not always be cheaper fares but can include more flexibility to change flights and/or routes. You have to show a document proving your date of birth or a valid International Student Identity Card (ISIC) or an International Youth Travel Card (IYTC) when buying your ticket and boarding the plane. See the website w www.istc .org for more information.

## Courier Flights

Another option is a courier flight, where an air-freight company uses your checked luggage allowance to send its parcels. The drawbacks are that your stay in Europe may be limited to one or two weeks, your luggage is usually restricted to hand luggage, and there is unlikely to be more than one courier ticket available for any given flight. Courier flights are occasionally advertised in newspapers, or

check the telephone book for air-freight companies. You may even have to go to the air-freight company to get an answer – the companies aren't always keen to give out information over the phone.

You can find out more about courier flights from the **International Association of Air Travel Couriers** (USA w www.courier.org; UK w www.aircourier.co.uk). Joining the association costs US$45 or UK£32, but this does not guarantee a flight. *Travel Unlimited* (PO Box 1058, Allston, MA 02134, USA) is a US-based monthly travel newsletter that publishes many courier flight deals from destinations around the world.

## Travellers with Special Needs

If they're warned early enough, airlines can often make special arrangements for travellers, such as wheelchair assistance at airports or vegetarian meals on the flight. Children under two years fly for 10% of the standard fare (or free on some airlines) as long as they don't occupy a seat. They don't get a baggage allowance. 'Skycots', baby food and nappies (diapers) should be provided by the airline if requested in advance. Children aged between two and 12 can usually occupy a seat for around two-thirds of the full fare, and they do get a baggage allowance.

The disability-friendly website w www .everybody.co.uk has an airline directory that provides information on the facilities offered by various airlines.

## The USA

Discount travel agencies in the USA are known as consolidators. San Francisco is the ticket consolidator capital of America, although some good deals can be found in Los Angeles, New York and other big cities. Consolidators can be found through the Yellow Pages or the major daily newspapers. **Priceline** (w www.priceline.com) is an online 'name-your-price' auction service.

**STA Travel** (☎ 800 781 4040; w www .statravel.com) is in all major American cities. The *New York Times, LA Times, Chicago Tribune* and *San Francisco Chronicle* all have weekly travel sections in which you'll find any number of travel agencies' ads.

Flight options across the North Atlantic, the world's busiest long-haul air corridor, are plentiful. You should be able to fly from New York to London or Paris and back for about

US$450 in the low season (September to May) and US$750 in the high season; even lower promotional or restricted validity flights are sometimes on offer. Equivalent fares from the west coast are US$100 to US$300 higher. Flights from the east coast to Lisbon start at around US$550 return and to/from Madrid cost from about US$850.

On a stand-by basis, one-way fares can work out to be cheap. New York–based **Airhitch** (☎ 212-864 2000; W www.airhitch .org) can get you to/from Europe for US$165/199/ 233 each way from the east coast/Midwest/ west coast, plus taxes and a processing fee.

Another option is a courier flight. A New York–London return ticket can cost as little as US$300 in the low season. See the Courier Flights section earlier.

## Canada

Canadian discount air ticket sellers are also known as consolidators and their air fares tend to be about 10% higher than those sold in the USA. The *Globe & Mail*, the *Toronto Star*, the *Montreal Gazette* and the *Vancouver Sun* carry travel agencies' ads and are a good place to look for cheap fares. **Travel CUTS** (☎ 800 667 2887; W www.travelcuts.com) is Canada's national student travel agency and has offices in all major cities.

Airhitch (see the USA section earlier) has stand-by fares to/from Toronto, Montreal and Vancouver.

## The UK

Discount air travel is big business in London. Advertisements for many travel agencies appear in the travel pages of the weekend broadsheets, such as the *Independent on Saturday* and the *Sunday Times*. Look out for the free magazines, such as *TNT*, which are widely available in London – often outside the main train and underground stations.

No-frills airlines, **Ryanair** (W www.ryan air.co.uk), **easyJet** (W www.easyjet .com) or **Go** (W www.go-fly.com), have cheap flights to Mediterranean countries. Some airlines give discounts for tickets purchased via the Internet. Fares from the UK to Barcelona, Madrid or Nice are highly competitive so you should be able to get a one-way flight for around UK£55. London is also a good centre for picking up cheap, restricted-validity tickets.

For those students and travellers aged under 26, a popular travel agency is STA

**Travel** (☎ 020-7361 6161; W www.sta travel.co.uk) with branches in London and across the country. STA sells tickets to all travellers but caters especially to young people and students. Other recommended travel agencies are **Trailfinders** (☎ 020-7938 1234; W www .trailfinders.co.uk; 215 Kensington High St, London W8), which also has branches in Manchester, Glasgow and other British cities; **Bridge the World** (☎ 020-7734 7447; W www.b-t-w.co.uk; 4 Regent Place, London W1); and **Flightbookers** (☎ 020-7757 2000; W www .ebookers.com; 34-42 Woburn Place, London WC1).

Charter flights can work out as a cheaper alternative to scheduled flights, especially if you do not qualify for the under-26 and student discounts. See your travel agency for possibilities.

## The Rest of Europe

Though London is the travel discount capital of Europe, there are several other cities in the region where you'll find a wide range of good deals. STA Travel has offices throughout Europe, where cheap tickets can be purchased and STA-issued tickets can be altered (usually for a fee). Check its website for locations and for its contact details. **Nouvelles Frontières** (W www.nouvelles-frontieres.com) is an organisation with branches around the world.

France has a network of student travel agencies that can supply discount tickets to travellers of all ages. **OTU Voyages** (☎ 0820 817 817; W www.otu.fr) and another, **Voyageurs du Monde** (☎ 01 42 86 16 00; W www.vdm .com), with branches throughout the country, offer some of the best services and deals.

Belgium, Switzerland and the Netherlands are also good places for buying discount air tickets. In Belgium, **Acotra Student Travel Agency** (☎ 02-512 86 07; W www.acotra .com; rue de la Madeline, Brussels) and **WATS Reizen** (☎ 03-233 70 20; de Keyserlei 44, Antwerp) are both well-known agencies. In Switzerland, **SSR Voyages** (☎ 01-297 11 11; W www.ssr.ch) specialises in student, youth and budget fares. There are branches in most major Swiss cities.

In the Netherlands, **NBBS Reizen** (☎ 020-624 09 89; Rokin 66, Amsterdam) is the official student travel agency. Another travel agency in Amsterdam that readers have recommended is **Malibu Travel** (☎ 020-626 32 30; Prinsengracht 230).

## Australia

Cheap flights from Australia to Europe generally travel via Southeast Asian capital cities, involving stopovers at Kuala Lumpur, Singapore or Bangkok. If a long stopover between connections is necessary, transit accommodation is sometimes included in the price of the ticket. If it's at your own expense, it may be worth considering a more expensive ticket.

Quite a few travel offices specialise in discount air tickets. Some travel agencies, particularly smaller ones, advertise cheap air fares in the travel sections of weekend newspapers, such as the *Age* in Melbourne and the *Sydney Morning Herald*.

**STA** (☎ *131 776;* ⓦ *www.statravel.com .au*) and **Flight Centre** (☎ *131 600;* ⓦ *www .flightcentre.com.au*) are major dealers in cheap air fares. **Student Uni Travel** (☎ *02-9232 7300;* ⓦ *sut.com.au*) specialises in the youth/backpacker market. Saturday's travel sections in the *Sydney Morning Herald* and Melbourne's *Age* have many ads offering cheap fares to Europe. With Australia's large and well-organised ethnic populations, it pays to check special deals in the ethnic press.

Thai, Malaysian, Qantas and Singapore Airlines to Europe start from about A$1500 (low season) up to A$2500. All have frequent promotional fares so it pays to check daily newspapers. Flights from Perth are a couple of hundred dollars cheaper than from east-coast cities.

Another option for travellers to get to Britain between November and February is to hook up with a returning charter flight. These low-season, one-way fares do have restrictions, but may work out to be considerably cheaper. Ask your travel agency for details.

## New Zealand

As in Australia, STA and Flight Centre are both popular travel agencies in New Zealand. **Student Uni Travel** (☎ *09-379 4224;* ⓦ *www .sut.co.nz*) has offices in the cities of Auckland, Christchurch and Hamilton. Also check the *New Zealand Herald* for ads. The cheapest fares to Europe are routed through Asia; a discounted return ticket to Europe from Auckland starts at around NZ$2100. A RTW ticket is about NZ$2850.

## Africa

Nairobi and Johannesburg are probably the best places in East and South Africa to buy tickets to Europe. One of the best agencies in Nairobi is **Flight Centre** (☎ *02-210024; 2nd floor, Lakhamshi House, Biashara St).* A return Nairobi–Zürich flight on Emirates Airlines starts as low as US$600, though with a limited period of validity. In Johannesburg **STA Travel** (☎ *011-447 5414;* ⓔ *rosebank@ statravel.co.za; Mutual Square, Rosebank)* and **Rennies Travel** (☎ *011-833 1441;* ⓦ *www .renniestravel.co.za, Unitas Bldg, 42 Marshall St)* are recommended.

If going to Morocco, you're better off getting a cheap return ticket to Paris, London, Madrid or Amsterdam and getting a cheap flight from there. Some West African countries, such as Burkina Faso, Gambia and Morocco, offer cheap charter flights to France.

## Asia

Hong Kong, Singapore and Bangkok are the discount air-fare capitals of Asia, but ask the advice of other travellers before handing over any money for tickets in these cities. In Singapore **STA** (☎ *737 7188;* ⓦ *www.sta travel.com.sg; 35a Cuppage Rd, Cuppage Terrace)* offers competitive fares. In Hong Kong try **Phoenix Services** (☎ *2722 7378; Rm B, 6th floor, Milton mansion, 96 Nathan Rd, Tsimshatsui).*

In India, cheap tickets can be bought from the bucket shops around Connaught Place in Delhi. Check with other travellers about the most trustworthy ones.

## LAND
### Bus

Europe's largest network of buses is run by **Eurolines** (ⓦ *www.eurolines.co.uk*), with six circular explorer routes, always starting and ending in London. Those taking in Paris start at UK£55. For details of bus passes that take in most of Mediterranean Europe, see Bus in the Getting Around chapter.

### Train

**UK** The Channel Tunnel allows for a land link between Britain and France. Eurostar is the passenger train service that travels between London and Paris and London and Brussels; cars travel on the Eurotunnel vehicle service.

***Eurostar*** The Eurostar service takes three hours to get from London's Waterloo station to the Gare du Nord in Paris. Passport and customs checks take place on board or very cursorily on arrival. There's quite a wide range of tickets; the cheapest are nonrefundable and have restrictions on departure times and length of stay, but you can get to Paris for as low as UK£79. There are often special deals on offer, so phone **Eurostar** *(UK ☎ 020-7928 5163; France ☎ 08 36 35 35 39;* ⓦ *www .eurostar.com)*. Tickets are available direct from Eurostar, from some travel agencies, at Waterloo station, at many of the UK's mainline train stations, and from **Rail Europe** *(☎ 0990 300 003;* ⓦ *www.raileurope.com)*, which also sells other European rail tickets. You can take a bicycle on Eurostar as part of your luggage only if it is in a bike bag.

***Eurotunnel*** The Eurotunnel vehicle service *(☎ 08705-353 535 in the UK, 03 21 00 61 00 in France;* ⓦ *www.eurotunnel.com)* travels between terminals in Folkestone and Calais. You can just drive into the terminal, buy your ticket and get on the next train but you'll almost always make a saving by buying your ticket in advance. Fares vary with the time of year and day. Bicycles can be taken on only two trains per day and they must be booked 24 hours in advance (use the phone number given). Trains run 24 hours a day, every day of the year, with up to four departures an hour. It takes about an hour from loading to unloading.

***Train-Boat-Train*** There are train boat train combos in association with **Hoverspeed** *(☎ 08705-240 241;* ⓦ *www.hoverspeed.co .uk)* and others from London's Charing Cross station to Paris' Gare du Nord that take between seven and eight hours and cost UK£39/58 one way/return or UK£49 for a five-day return. It's cheaper than Eurotunnel but takes a lot longer, and you've got to mess around transferring by bus between the train station and the ferry terminal on both sides.

***Africa & Asia*** Morocco and most of Turkey lie outside Europe, but the rail systems of both countries are still covered by Inter-Rail (Zone F & Zone G, respectively). The price of a cheap return train ticket from Paris to Morocco compares favourably with the equivalent bus fares. See the Getting Around chapter for details of rail passes.

It *is* possible to get to Mediterranean Europe by rail from central and eastern Asia, although count on spending at least eight days

doing it. There are four different routes to Moscow: the Trans-Siberian (from Vladivostok); the Trans-Mongolian (from Beijing); and the Trans-Manchurian (from Beijing via Harbin), which all use the same tracks across Siberia but have different routes east of Lake Baikal. There's also the Trans-Kazakhstan, which runs between Moscow and Urumqi in northwestern China. Prices vary enormously, depending on where you buy the ticket and what is included. Information is also available from the **Russian National Tourist Office** *(*ⓦ *www.interknowledge.com/Russia)*. *The Big Red Train Ride* by Eric Newby is good reading material to take along for the ride. Lonely Planet's *Trans-Siberian Railway* is a comprehensive guide to the route with details of costs, travel agencies who specialise in the trip and highlights.

## Overland Trails

The overland trail to/from Asia through Iran is still possible but, at the time of writing, unsettled conditions in Afghanistan, southern Pakistan and northwestern India make this route inadvisable without careful assessment of the situation. Check with your own foreign office before making a decision.

Discounting the complicated Middle East route, going to/from Africa involves a Mediterranean ferry crossing (see the following Sea section). Due to unrest in Africa, the most feasible overland routes through the continent have all but closed down.

Travelling by private transport beyond Mediterranean Europe requires plenty of paperwork and other preparations. A detailed description of what's required is beyond the scope of this book, but the following Getting Around chapter tells you what's required within the region. You could also check with your local automobile association.

## SEA
## Channel Ferries

Several different ferry companies compete for business on all the main Channel ferry routes. The resulting service is comprehensive but very complicated. The same ferry company can have a host of different prices for the same route depending upon the time of day or year, the validity of the ticket or, if you're driving, the length of your vehicle. Vehicle tickets include the driver and often up to five passengers free of charge. It is worth planning (and booking) ahead where possible as there may be special reductions on off-peak crossings and advance-purchase tickets. On Channel routes, apart from one-day or short-term excursion returns, there is little price advantage in buying a return ticket as against two singles.

The shortest cross-Channel routes between England and France (Dover to Calais or Folkestone to Boulogne) are also the busiest, though there is now competition from the Channel Tunnel. **P&O Stena Line** (Ⓦ *www.posl.com*) handles the short-hop Dover–Calais routes. **P&O Portsmouth** (Ⓦ *www.poportsmouth.com*) and **Brittany Ferries** (Ⓦ *www.brittany-ferries.com*) also sail direct between England and northern Spain, taking 24 to 35 hours, and between France and Ireland. The French line **Seafrance** (Ⓦ *www.seafrance.com*) also operates across the Channel. You can book ferry tickets online (often at a discount).

Rail-pass holders are entitled to discounts or free travel on some lines (see the earlier Train section), and most ferry companies give discounts to disabled drivers.

## Mediterranean Ferries

There are many ferries across the Mediterranean between Africa and Europe. The ferry you take will depend on your travels in Africa, but options include: Spain–Morocco, Italy–Tunisia, France–Morocco and France–Tunisia. There are also ferries between Greece and Israel via Cyprus. Ferries are often filled to capacity in summer, especially to/from Tunisia, so book well in advance if you're taking a vehicle across. Ferry companies operating on these routes include **Ferri-maroc** (Ⓦ *www.ferrimaroc.com*) and **SNCM** (Ⓦ *www.sncm.fr*).

## Passenger Ships & Freighters

Regular, long-distance passenger ships disappeared with the advent of cheap air travel, leaving a small number of luxury cruise ships. **Cunard** (Ⓦ *www.cunard.com*) has the *Queen Elizabeth 2*, which sails between New York and Southampton about 20 times a year; the trip takes six nights. Special deals are as low as US$999 for the crossing, including a one-way economy air fare.

A more adventurous alternative is as a paying passenger on a freighter. Freighters are far more numerous than cruise ships and there are many more routes from which to choose. With a bit of homework, you'll be able to sail between Europe and just about anywhere else in the world, with stopovers at exotic ports.

Passenger freighters typically carry five to 12 passengers (more than 12 would require a doctor on board) and, though these are less luxurious than dedicated cruise ships, you'll get a real taste of life at sea. Schedules tend to be flexible and costs are about $150 a day; vehicles can often be included for an additional fee. You can always get an idea of what's available from the website Ⓦ www.freighter-travel.com.

## DEPARTURE TAX

Some countries charge you a fee for the privilege of leaving from their airports. Some also charge port fees when departing by ship. Such fees are *usually* included in the price of your ticket, but it pays to check this when purchasing it. If not, you'll have to have the fee ready when leaving. Details of departure taxes are given at the end of the Getting There & Away sections of the individual country chapters.

# Getting Around

Travel within the European Union (EU) countries of the Mediterranean region, whether by air, rail or car, has been made easier following the Schengen Agreement, which abolished border controls between signed-up states. You shouldn't have too many problems getting around the non-EU countries either, thanks to a comprehensive transport network and good relations between neighbouring countries. The main exception to this is travelling between the Republic of Cyprus and the Turkish Republic of Northern Cyprus where there is a strict border control policy. See the Cyprus chapter for details.

Ensure that you have a valid passport and check any visa requirements before travelling (see also Visas & Documents in the Facts for the Visitor chapter earlier).

## AIR

Air travel is best viewed as a means to get you to the starting point of your itinerary rather than as your main means of travel. It lacks the flexibility of ground transport and tends to be expensive for short trips. Occasionally you will find low fares and special deals. In order to secure the best price, shop around and be prepared to travel on alternative dates.

Athens is a good place to purchase budget tickets in Mediterranean Europe. From here, you can also get good deals to elsewhere in the region. Depending on the season, there are cheap charter flights from Paris and Madrid to Morocco. For more information, see the Getting There & Away sections in the individual country chapters.

If you are travelling alone, courier flights are a possibility. You get cheap passage in return for accompanying a package or documents through customs and delivering it to a representative at the destination airport. There's a decreasing need for couriers, but you might find something.

Getting between airports and city centres is generally not a problem in Mediterranean Europe. If the public-transport network is poor then you may have to rely on taxis.

## BUS
### International Buses

International bus travel tends to take second place to train travel. The bus has the edge in terms of cost, sometimes quite substantially, but it generally slower and less comfortable. Europe's biggest network of international buses is provided by a group of companies operating under the name **Eurolines** (W *www .eurolines.com*).

Eurolines representatives include:

**Eurolines France** (☎ 08 36 69 52 52), Gare Routière Internationale, 28 Ave du Général de Gaulle, 75020 Paris
**Eurolines Italy** (☎ 064 40 40 09), Ciconvallazione Nonentana 574, Lato Stazione Tiburtina, Rome
**Eurolines Peninsular** (☎ 93 490 4000), Estació d'Autobuses de Sants, Calle Viriato, Barcelona

These companies may also be able to advise you on other bus companies and deals. See Bus in the Land section in the introductory Getting There & Away chapter for information on services between London and Mediterranean Europe. Eurolines return tickets are valid for six months, and youths under 26 and seniors over 60 pay less.

Eurolines also offers passes, which are cheaper but not as extensive or as flexible as rail passes. They cover 46 European cities with France, Spain and Italy well served in the Mediterranean region. Most of the trips must be international; a few internal journeys are possible between major cities. The cost is UK£229 for 30 days (UK£186 for youths/ senior citizens) or UK£267 for 60 days (UK£205). The passes are cheaper off-season.

**Busabout** (☎ 020-7950 1661; W *www .busabout.com; 258 Vauxhall Bridge Rd, Victoria, London SW1, England)*, operates buses that complete set circuits round Europe, stopping at major cities. You can start at any city, get unlimited travel per sector, and can 'hop-on, hop-off' at any scheduled stop, then resume with a later bus. Buses are often oversubscribed, so prebook each sector to avoid being stranded. Departures are every two days from April to October, or May to September for Spain and Portugal. The circuits cover the western countries of Mediterranean Europe, and you can pay to 'add-on' Greece, Morocco and Croatia. See its website for further information. There is also an office in Athens at Busabout Athens, Siva Travel, 65 Vassilis Sophias Ave, 11521 Athens.

Busabout's Consecutive Pass allows unlimited travel within the given time period. For a one month pass the cost is UK£329 for adults or UK£289 for students and those under 26. Passes are also available for 14/21 days, two or three months, or for the whole season. The Flexipass allows you to select travel days within the given time period. Six days in one month costs UK£169/149 for an adult/youth while 25 days in four months will set you back UK£549/499.

In conjunction with Eurolines, the Moroccan national bus line, CTM (Compagnie des Transports Marocains), operates buses from Spain, France and northern Italy to most of the large Moroccan towns.

See the individual country chapters for more information about long-distance buses.

## National Buses

Domestic buses provide a viable alternative to the rail network in most countries. Compared to trains they are slightly cheaper and, with the exception of Spain, Portugal and Greece, somewhat slower. Buses tend to be best for shorter hops such as getting around cities and reaching remote villages. They are often the only option in mountainous regions where railway tracks don't exist. Advance reservations are rarely necessary. On many city buses you usually buy your ticket in advance from a kiosk or machine and validate it upon boarding.

See the individual country chapters and city sections for more details on local buses.

## TRAIN

Trains are a popular way of getting around: they are comfortable, frequent and generally on time. In some countries, such as Spain, Portugal and (to some extent) Italy, fares are reasonably low; in others, European rail passes make travel more affordable. Supplements and reservation costs are not covered by passes, and pass-holders must always carry their passport for identification purposes.

If you plan to travel extensively by train, it might be worth getting hold of the *Thomas Cook European Timetable*, which gives a complete listing of train schedules and indicates where supplements apply or where reservations are necessary. It is updated monthly and is available from **Thomas Cook** (W *www.thomascook.com)* outlets in the UK, and in the USA from **Forsyth Travel Library**

(☎ *800-367 7984;* W *www.forsyth.com).* Check the websites. In Australia, look for it in the bigger bookstores, which can order in copies if they don't have any in stock.

If you are planning to do a lot of train travel in one or a handful of countries – Spain and Portugal, say – it might be worthwhile getting the national timetables published by the state railways. The *European Planning & Rail Guide* is an informative annual magazine, primarily geared towards North American travellers. To get a copy, call the toll-free US number ☎ 877-441 2387, or visit the website at W www.budgeteuropetravel.com. It's free within the USA; send US$3 if you want it posted to anywhere else.

Both Paris and Milan are important hubs for international rail connections in Mediterranean Europe; see the relevant city sections for details and budget ticket agents.

Note that European trains sometimes split en route in order to service two destinations, so even if you're on the right train, make sure you're also in the correct carriage.

## Express Trains

Fast trains or those that make few stops are identified by the symbols EC (Eurocity) or IC (InterCity). The French TGV and Spanish AVE are even faster. Supplements can apply on fast trains, and it is a good idea (sometimes obligatory) to make seat reservations at peak times and on certain lines.

## Overnight Trains

Overnight trains will usually offer a choice of couchette or sleeper if you don't fancy sleeping in your seat with somebody else's elbow in your ear. Again, reservations are advisable as sleeping options are allocated on a first-come, first-served basis.

Couchette bunks are comfortable enough, if lacking a bit in privacy. There are four per compartment in 1st class or six in 2nd class. A bunk costs from around UK£10 for most international trains, irrespective of the length of the journey.

Sleepers are the most comfortable option, offering beds for one or two passengers in 1st class, and two or three passengers in 2nd class. Charges vary depending upon the journey, but they are a lot more expensive than couchettes. Most long-distance trains have a dining (buffet) car or an attendant who wheels a snack trolley through the carriages.

If possible buy your food before travelling as onboard prices tend to be high.

## Security
You should be quite safe travelling on most trains in Mediterranean Europe but it pays to be security conscious nonetheless. Keep an eye on your luggage at all times (especially when stopping at stations) and lock the compartment doors at night.

## Rail Passes
Shop around, as pass prices can vary between different outlets. Once purchased, take care of your pass, as it cannot be replaced or refunded if lost or stolen. European passes can be used to get reductions on certain ferries. In the USA, **Rail Europe** (☎ 800-438 7245; W www .raileurope.com) sells all sorts of rail passes. See its website for more information. Its UK office (☎ 0870 584 8848; W www.raileurope .co.uk; 179 Piccadilly, London) has similar services.

**Eurail** These passes can only be bought by residents of non-European countries, and are supposed to be purchased before arriving in Europe. However, Eurail passes *can* be purchased within Europe, so long as your passport proves you've been there for less than six months, but the outlets where you can do this are limited, and the passes will be more expensive than getting them outside Europe. If you've lived in Europe for more than six months, you are eligible for an Inter-Rail pass, which is a better buy.

Eurail passes are valid for unlimited travel on national railways and some private lines in the Mediterranean countries of France (including Monaco), Greece, Italy, Portugal and Spain.

Eurail is also valid on some ferries between Italy and Greece. Reductions are given on some other ferry routes and on river/lake steamer services in various countries.

Eurail passes offer reasonable value to those aged under 26. A Youthpass gives unlimited 2nd-class travel within a choice of five validity periods: 15/21 days (UK£325/ 415) or one/two/three months (UK£525/740/ 925). The Youth Flexipass, also for 2nd class, is valid for freely chosen days within a two-month period: 10/15 days for UK£390/510. Overnight journeys commencing after 7pm count as the following day's travel. The traveller must fill out in ink the relevant box in the calendar before starting a day's travel.

For those aged over 26, the equivalent passes provide 1st-class travel. The standard Eurail pass costs UK£470/605 for 15/21 days or UK£750/1065/1320 for one/two/three months. The Flexipass costs UK£545/730 for 10/15 days within two months. Two to five people travelling together can get a 'saver' version of either pass, saving about 15%. Eurail passes for children are also available.

If you are travelling only within Mediterranean Europe the Europass seems to be a much better deal. See the following section.

**Europass** Also for non-Europeans, the Europass gives unlimited travel on freely chosen days within a two-month period. Youth (aged under 26) and adult (solo, or two sharing) versions are available, and purchasing requirements and sales outlets are as for Eurail passes. They are cheaper than Eurail passes as they cover fewer countries, including France, Italy and Spain. The youth/adult price is UK£190/295 for a minimum five travel days, or UK£430/615 for a maximum 15 days. 'Associate countries' can be added on to the basic pass. The prices vary. The associate Mediterranean countries are Greece (including ferries from Italy) and Portugal.

**Inter-Rail** Inter-Rail passes are available to European residents of at least six months standing (passport identification is required). Terms and conditions vary slightly from country to country, but in the country of origin there is a discount of around 50% on normal fares. The Inter-Rail pass is split into zones, covering most of the Mediterranean countries: Zone D includes Croatia; E includes France; F is Spain, Portugal and Morocco; G is Italy, Greece, Turkey, Slovenia and Italy–Greece ferries; and H includes Yugoslavia.

The normal Inter-Rail pass is for people under 26, although travellers over 26 can get the Inter-Rail 26+ version. The price for any one zone is UK£139 (UK£209 for 26+) for 22 days. Multizone passes are valid for one month: two zones cost UK£189 (UK£265), three zones UK£209 (UK£299) and the all-zone global pass is UK£249 (UK£355).

**Euro Domino** There is a Euro Domino pass for each of the countries covered in the

Inter-Rail pass, and they're worth considering if you're homing in on a particular region. They're sold in Europe to European residents. Adults (travelling 1st or 2nd class) and youths under 26 can opt for three to eight days valid travel within one month. Examples of adult/youth prices for eight days in 2nd class are UK£73/55 for Greece and UK£159/122 for Spain.

**National Rail Passes** If you intend to travel extensively within one country, check which national rail passes are available. These can sometimes save you a lot of money; details can be found in the Getting Around sections in the individual country chapters. You need to plan ahead if you intend to take this option, as some passes can only be purchased prior to arrival in the country concerned. Some national flexi passes, near-equivalents to the Domino passes mentioned previously, are only available to non-Europeans.

### Cheap Tickets

European rail passes are only worth buying if you plan to do a reasonable amount of inter-country travelling within a short space of time. Plan your itinerary carefully. Don't overdo the overnight travelling. Although it can work out to be a great way of saving time and money you don't want to be too tired to enjoy the next day of sightseeing.

When weighing up options, consider the cost of other cheap ticket deals, including advance purchase deals, one-off promotions or special circular-route tickets. Normal international tickets are valid for two months, and you can make as many stops as you like en route; make your intentions known when purchasing, and inform the train conductor how far you're going before they punch your ticket.

For a small fee, European residents can buy a Railplus Card, entitling the holder to a 25% discount on international train journeys. In most countries (eg, in the UK) it is sold only to people over 60 who hold a valid British Senior Card. The Railplus Card costs UK£12 and lasts for one year. However, some national rail networks may make the Railplus Card available also to young people or other travellers.

### CAR & MOTORCYCLE

Travelling with your own vehicle allows increased flexibility and the option to get off the beaten track. Unfortunately, cars can be inconvenient in city centres when you have to negotiate strange one-way systems or find somewhere to park amid a confusing or complex concrete jungle.

### Paperwork & Preparations

Proof of ownership of a private vehicle should always be carried (Vehicle Registration Document for British-registered cars) when touring Europe. An EU driving licence is acceptable for driving throughout Europe. However, old-style green UK licences are no good for Spain or Italy. If you have any other type of licence it is advisable or necessary to obtain an International Driving Permit (IDP) from your motoring organisation (see Driving Licence & Permits in the Visas & Documents section in the earlier Facts for the Visitor chapter). An IDP is recommended for Turkey even if you have aEuropean licence. Always check what type of licence is required in your chosen destination prior to departure.

Third-party motor insurance is compulsory in Europe. Most UK motor insurance policies automatically provide this for EU countries. Get your insurer to issue a Green Card (which may cost extra), an internationally recognised proof of insurance, and check that it lists all the countries you intend to visit. You'll need this in the event of an accident outside the country where the vehicle is insured. Also ask your insurer for a European Accident Statement form, which can simplify things if the worst happens. The European Accident Statement, also known in France as the 'Constat Amiable', is available from your insurance company and is carboned so that each party at an accident can record identical information for insurance purposes. The Association of British Insurers can give more information (see later for details). Never sign statements you can't read or understand – insist on a translation and sign that only if it's acceptable. For non-EU countries make sure you check the requirements with your insurer. For further advice and information contact the **Association of British Insurers** (☎ 020-7600 3333; ⓦ www.abi.org.uk) or check its website.

Taking out a European motoring assistance policy is a good investment, such as the AA Five Star Service or the RAC European Motoring Assistance. Expect to pay about UK£50 for 14 days cover with a 10% discount for association members. Non-Europeans might find it cheaper to arrange international coverage with their national motoring organisation before leaving home. Ask your motoring organisation for details about free services offered by affiliated organisations around Mediterranean Europe.

Vehicles crossing an international border should display a sticker showing its country of registration. A warning triangle, to be used in the event of breakdown, is compulsory almost everywhere. Recommended accessories are a first-aid kit (compulsory in Greece and several other Mediterranean European countries), a spare bulb kit (compulsory in Croatia and Spain) and a fire extinguisher (compulsory in Greece and Turkey). Bail bonds are no longer required for Spain. In the UK, contact the **RAC** (☎ 0800 550 005; W www.rac.co.uk) or the **AA** (☎ 0870 550 0600) for more information.

## Road Rules

Motoring organisations can supply members with country-by-country information on the motoring regulations, or they may produce motoring guidebooks for general sale. The RAC can provide you with comprehensive destination-specific notes. Contact the RAC by telephone or check the website (see earlier for details).

With the exception of Malta and Cyprus, driving in Mediterranean Europe is on the right-hand side. Vehicles brought over from the UK or Ireland, where driving is on the left, should have their headlights adjusted to avoid blinding oncoming traffic at night (a simple solution on older headlight lenses is to cover up a triangular section of the lens with tape). Priority is usually given to traffic approaching from the right in countries that drive on the right-hand side.

Take care with speed limits, as they vary from country to country. You may be surprised at the apparent disregard for traffic regulations in some places (particularly in Italy and Greece), but as a visitor it is always best to be cautious. Many driving infringements are subject to an on-the-spot fine in most countries. Always ask for a receipt.

Drink-driving laws are particularly strict. The blood-alcohol concentration (BAC) limit when driving is generally between 0.05% and 0.08%. See the introductory Getting Around sections in the individual country chapters for more details on traffic laws.

## Roads

Conditions and types of roads vary across Europe, but it is possible to make some generalisations. The fastest routes are four- or six-lane dual carriageways/highways (ie, two or three lanes either side) – called *autoroutes*, *autostrade* etc. These roads are great in terms of speed and comfort but driving can be quite dull with little or no interesting scenery. Some of these roads incur tolls, which are often quite hefty (eg, in Italy, France and Spain), but there's usually an alternative route you can take. Motorways and other primary routes are generally in good condition.

Road surfaces on minor routes are not so reliable in some countries (eg, Morocco, Malta and Greece) although normally they will be more than adequate. These roads are narrower and progress is generally much slower. However, you can expect much better scenery and plenty of interesting villages along the way.

## Rental

The big international firms will give you reliable service and a good standard of vehicle. Usually you will have the option of returning the car to a different outlet at the end of the rental period. Prebook for the lowest rates – if you walk into an office and ask for a car on the spot, you will pay over the odds, even allowing for special weekend deals. Fly-drive combinations and other programmes are worth looking into. You should be able to make advance reservations online. Check the websites for:

**Avis** W www.avis.com
**Budget** W www.budget.com
**Europcar** W www.europcar.com
**Hertz** W www.hertz.com

Brokers can cut hire costs. **Holiday Autos** (UK ☎ 0870 400 4477; W www.holidayautos .com) has low rates and offices or representatives in over 20 countries. In the USA call **Kemwel Holiday Autos** (☎ 877 820 0668). In the UK, a competitor with even lower prices is **Autos Abroad** (☎ 020-7287 6000; W www.autosabroad.co.uk).

If you want to rent a car and haven't prebooked, look for national or local firms, which can often undercut the big companies. Nevertheless, you need to be wary of dodgy deals where they take your money and point you towards some clapped-out wreck.

No matter where you rent, it is imperative to understand exactly what is included in your rental agreement (collision waiver, unlimited mileage etc). Make sure you are covered with an adequate insurance policy. Ask in advance if you can drive a rented car across borders from a country where hire prices are low into another where they're high.

The minimum rental age is usually 21 or even 23 (25 in Malta), and you'll probably need a credit card. Note that prices at airport rental offices are usually higher than at branches in the city centre.

Motorcycle and moped rental is common in some countries, such as Italy, Spain, Greece and the south of France. Sadly, it's also common to see inexperienced riders leap on rented bikes and very quickly fall off them again, leaving a layer or two of skin on the road in the process.

## Purchase

Britain is probably the best place to buy; second-hand prices are good and, whether buying privately or from a dealer, the absence of language difficulties will help you establish exactly what you are getting and what guarantees you can expect in the event of a breakdown. Bear in mind that you will be getting a car with the steering wheel on the right in Britain. If you want left-hand drive and can afford to buy new, prices are usually reasonable in Greece and France. Paperwork can be tricky wherever you buy, and many countries have compulsory roadworthiness checks on older vehicles.

## Leasing

Opting to lease a vehicle takes away the hassles of purchasing and can work out considerably cheaper than hiring over longer periods. The Renault Eurodrive scheme provides new cars for non-EU residents for a period of between 17 and 170 days. Under this arrangement, a Renault Clio 1.2 for 24 days, for example, would cost UK£340 (if picked up/dropped off in France), including insurance and roadside assistance. Check out the options before leaving home. In the US, Kemwel Holiday Autos (see under Rental earlier) arranges European leasing deals.

## Camper Van

A popular way to tour Europe is for three or four people to band together to buy or rent a camper van. London is the usual embarkation point. Look at the advertisements in London's free *TNT* magazine if you wish to form or join a group. *TNT* is also a good source for purchasing a van, as is the *Loot* newspaper. Some second-hand dealers offer a 'buy-back' scheme for when you return from the Continent, but we've received warnings that some dealers don't fully honour their refund commitments. Buying and re-selling privately should be more advantageous if you have the time. A reader recommended **Down Under Insurance** (☎ 020-7402 9211; W *www.down underinsurance.co.uk*) for European cover.

Camper vans usually feature a fixed high-top or elevating roof and two to five bunk beds. Apart from the essential camping gas cooker, professional conversions may include a sink, fridge and built-in cupboards. Prices and facilities vary considerably and it is certainly worth getting advice from a mechanic to see if you are being offered a fair price. Getting a mechanical check (from UK£35) is also a good idea. Once on the road you should be able to keep budgets lower than backpackers using trains, but don't forget to set some money aside for emergency repairs.

The main advantage of going by camper van is flexibility. Transport, accommodation and storage are all taken care of in one small unit. Unfortunately the self-contained factor can also prove to be one of the downsides. Conditions can get very cramped, tempers can become easily frayed and your romantic hippy-style trail may dissolve into the camper van trip from hell. Other disadvantages include having to leave your gear inside when you are exploring. You should invest in good locks and try to keep the inside tidy with your belongings stored away at all times.

## Motorcycle Touring

Most of Mediterranean Europe is made for motorcycle touring, with good-quality winding roads and an active motorcycling scene. In places where the roads aren't so good, the stunning scenery more than makes up for substandard surfaces. You'll need to kill the speed but if you pay the roads adequate attention you shouldn't incur any damages to you or your bike. Bear in mind that the weather is not always reliable. Make sure your wet weather gear is up to scratch. The wearing of crash helmets for rider and passenger is compulsory everywhere in Mediterranean Europe. It's recommended that motorcyclists use their headlights during the day.

On ferries, motorcyclists can sometimes be squeezed in without a reservation although booking ahead is advised in peak travelling periods. Take note of local custom about parking motorcycles on pavements (sidewalks). Though this is illegal in some countries, the police usually turn a blind eye so long as the vehicle doesn't obstruct pedestrians.

If you are thinking of touring Europe on a motorcycle try contacting the **British Motorcyclists Federation** (☎ *0116-254 8818)* for help and advice. An excellent source of information can be found at Ⓦ www.horizonsun limited.com for those who are interested in more adventurous biking activities.

## Fuel

Fuel prices can vary enormously from one country to the next, and may bear little relation to the general cost of living. You can make significant savings by filling up in the cheapest country. Motoring organisations such as the RAC can supply more details; in the UK call ☎ 0906 470 1740.

Unleaded petrol is now widely available throughout Europe (except in Morocco) and is usually cheaper than super (premium grade, the only 'leaded' choice in some countries). Diesel is usually significantly cheaper.

## TAXI

Taxis in Europe are metered and rates are usually high. There might also be supplements (depending on the country) for things such as luggage, time of day, the location from which you boarded and for extra passengers. Good bus, rail and underground (metro) railway networks make the taking of taxis all but unnecessary, but if you need one in a hurry they can usually be found idling near train stations or outside big hotels. Lower fares make taxis more viable in some countries, such as Spain, Greece and Portugal. Don't underestimate the local knowledge that can be gleaned from taxi drivers. They can often tell you about the liveliest places in town and know all about events happening during your stay.

## BICYCLE

A tour of Mediterranean Europe by bicycle may seem like a daunting prospect but help is at hand. The **Cyclists' Touring Club** (*CTC;*

☎ *0870 873 0060;* ⓔ *cycling@ctc.org.uk;* Ⓦ *www.ctc.org.uk; Cotterell House, 69 Meadrow, Godalming, Surrey GU7 3HS)* is based in the UK and offers its members an information service on all matters associated with cycling (including cycling conditions, detailed routes, itineraries and maps). If they are not able to answer your questions the chances are they will know someone who can. Membership costs UK£27 for adults, UK£10 for those aged under 25 and UK£16.50 for those over 65.

The key to a successful trip is to travel light. What you carry should be largely determined by your destination and type of trip. Even for the shortest and most basic trip it's worth carrying the tools necessary for repairing a puncture. Other things you might want to consider packing are spare brake and gear cables, spanners, Allen keys, spare spokes of the correct length and strong adhesive tape. Before you set off ensure that you are competent at carrying out basic repairs. There's no point in weighing yourself down with equipment that you haven't got a clue how to use. Always check over your bike thoroughly each morning and again at night when the day's touring is over. Take a good lock and always use it when you leave your bike unattended.

The wearing of helmets is not compulsory but is certainly advised. A seasoned cyclist can average about 80km a day but this depends on the terrain and how much weight you are carrying. Don't over do it – there's no point in burning yourself out during the initial stages.

For more information on cycling, see Activities in the earlier Facts for the Visitor chapter and in the individual country chapters.

## Rental

It is not as easy to hire bikes in some parts of Mediterranean Europe as it is elsewhere on the Continent, but where available they are hired out on an hourly, half-day, daily or weekly basis. Local tourist offices will carry information on rental outlets. Occasionally you can drop the bicycle off at a different location so you don't have to double back on yourself. See the individual country chapters for more details.

## Purchase

For major cycling tours, it's best to have a bike you are familiar with, so consider bringing your own (see Transporting a Bicycle section following) rather than buying one on arrival. If you can't be bothered with the hassle of taking one over then there are plenty of places to buy in Mediterranean Europe (shops sell new and second-hand bicycles or you can check local papers for private vendors) but you'll need a specialist bicycle shop for a machine capable of withstanding touring. CTC can provide members with a leaflet on purchasing. European prices are quite high (certainly higher than in North America), but non-Europeans should be able to claim back VAT on the purchase.

## Transporting a Bicycle

If you want to bring your own bicycle to Mediterranean Europe, you should be able to take it along with you on the plane relatively easily. You can either take it apart and pack everything in a bike bag or box, or simply wheel it to the check-in desk, where it should be treated as a piece of luggage. You may have to remove the pedals and turn the handlebars sideways so that it takes up less space in the aircraft's hold; check all this with the airline well in advance, preferably before you pay for your ticket. If your bicycle and other luggage exceed your weight allowance, ask about alternatives or you may suddenly find yourself being charged a fortune for excess baggage.

Within Mediterranean Europe, bicycles are usually transported as luggage on slower trains, subject to a small supplementary fee. Fast trains can rarely accommodate bikes: they might need to be sent as registered luggage and may end up on a different train from the one you take. This is often the case in France and Spain.

The European **Bike Express** (UK ☎ 01642-251 440; **w** www.bike-express.co.uk) is a coach service where cyclists can travel with their bicycles. It runs in the summer from northeast England to France, Italy and Spain, with pick-up/drop-off points en route. The maximum return fare is UK£179 (£10 off for CTC members); phone for details or visit its website.

## HITCHING

Hitching is never entirely safe in any country, and we don't recommend it. Travellers who decide to hitch should understand that they are taking a small but potentially serious risk. People who do choose to hitch will be safer if they travel in pairs and let someone know where they plan to go.

Hitching can be the most rewarding and frustrating way of getting around. Rewarding, because you get to meet and interact with local people and are forced into unplanned detours that may yield unexpected highlights off the beaten track. Frustrating, because you may get stuck on the side of the road to nowhere with nowhere (or nowhere cheap) to stay. Then it begins to rain…

That said, hitchers can end up making good time, but obviously your plans need to be flexible in case a trick of the light makes you appear invisible to passing motorists. A man and woman travelling together is probably the best combination. Two or more men must expect some delays; two women together will make good time and should be relatively safe. A woman hitching on her own is taking a big risk, particularly in places such as parts of southern Europe, Turkey and North Africa.

Don't try to hitch from city centres: take public transport to suburban exit routes. Hitching is usually illegal on motorways (freeways) – stand on the slip roads, or approach drivers at petrol stations and truck stops. Look presentable and cheerful and make a cardboard sign indicating your intended destination in the local language. Never hitch where drivers can't stop in good time or without causing an obstruction. At dusk, give up and think about finding somewhere to stay. If your itinerary includes a ferry crossing (from mainland France to Corsica, for instance), it's worth trying to score a ride before the ferry rather than after, since vehicle tickets sometimes include all passengers free of charge. This also applies to Eurotunnel, the vehicle-carrying train through the Channel Tunnel.

It is sometimes possible to arrange a lift in advance: scan student notice boards in colleges, or contact car-sharing agencies. Such agencies are particularly popular in France (eg, Allostop Provoya, Auto-Partage).

Travellers considering hitching as a way of getting around Mediterranean Europe may find the following two websites useful. For general facts, destination-based information and rideshare options visit **w** www.bug europe.com. The useful website **w** www .hitchhikers.org connects hitchhikers and drivers worldwide.

## BOAT
### Mediterranean Ferries

There are many ferries across the Mediterranean between southern Europe and North Africa, including routes between France and Spain and Morocco. There are also ferries between Italy and Greece (eg, Brindisi or Bari to Corfu, Igoumenitsa or Patras), and between Greece and Israel. Ferries are often filled to capacity in summer, so book well in advance if you're taking a vehicle across.

The Greek islands are connected to the mainland and each other by a spider's web of routings; Lonely Planet's *Greek Islands* gives details. Ferries also link other islands in the Mediterranean with mainland ports: Corsica with Nice, Marseille and Toulon in France and with Genoa, La Spezia, Piombino and Livorno in Italy; Sicily and Sardinia with Genoa and Naples (among other Italian ports) and Malta with Sicily and Naples. See the relevant country chapters in this book for more details.

## ORGANISED TOURS

Tailor-made tours abound; see your travel agent or look in the small ads in newspaper travel pages. Specialists include **Ramblers Holidays** (☎ 01707-331 133; **W** *www.ram blersholidays.co.uk*) in Britain for hiking trips

and **CBT Tours** (☎ 800-736-2453; **W** *www .cbttours.com*) in the USA for bicycle trips.

Young revellers can party on Europewide bus tours. Contiki and Top Deck offer camping or hotel-based bus tours for the 18 to 35 age group. The duration of Contiki's tours are five to 46 days. **Contiki** (☎ 020-8290 6777; **W** *www.contiki.com*) and **Top Deck** (☎ 020-7370 4555; **W** *www.topdecktravel.co.uk*) have London offices, as well as offices or representatives in Europe, North America, Australasia and South Africa. Check the websites.

For people aged over 50, **Saga Holidays** (**W** *www.sagaholidays.com*) offers holidays ranging from cheap coach tours to luxury cruises and it has cheap travel insurance. There's a **UK office** (☎ 0800 300 500; *Saga Building, Middelburg Square, Folkestone, Kent CT20 1AZ, England*) and a **US office** (☎ 617-262 2262; *222 Berkeley St, Boston, MA 02116*).

National tourist offices in most countries offer organised trips to points of interest. These may range from one-hour city tours to several-day circular excursions. They often work out more expensive than going it alone, but are sometimes worth it if you are pressed for time. A short city tour will give you a quick overview of the place and can be a good way to begin your visit.

# Albania

Albania was a closed communist country until 1990, but caught world attention in November of that year as the last domino to tumble in Eastern Europe's sudden series of democratic revolutions. Long considered fair prey by imperialist powers, Albania chose a curious form of isolation, with everything centred on the Stalinist rule and personality cult of Enver Hoxha, Albania's iron-fisted dictator from 1944 to his death in 1985. Hoxha did save the country from annexation by Yugoslavia after WWII, but few Albanians have positive feelings about him.

Albanians call their country the Republika e Shqipërisë, or 'Land of the Eagle'. Albania is Europe's last unknown, with some enchanting classical ruins at Apollonia, Butrint and Durrës, the charming 'museum towns' of Gjirokastra and Berat, vibrant towns like Tirana, Shkodra, Korça and Durrës, colourful folklore and majestic landscapes of mountains, forests, lakes and sea.

Albania's first years of attempted democracy were troubled. The country spiralled into violence and anarchy following the collapse of fraudulent pyramid schemes in late 1996. Since that difficult beginning the economic situation has improved enormously and the country is open to travellers once more. Those who do decide to visit Albania should mingle curiosity with a healthy caution, but visiting this country, as it slowly opens up to the world, is a rare experience.

## At a Glance

- **Tirana** – old bazaar town turned bustling metropolis
- **Ionian Coast** – towering mountains and dramatic ocean views
- **Gjirokastra** – picturesque fortress; the Drino Valley; tower houses
- **Butrint** – stunning well-preserved Roman ruins; an ancient Greek theatre; colourful mosaics

| | |
|---|---|
| **Capital** | Tirana |
| **Population** | 3.5 million |
| **Official Language** | Albanian (Tosk) |
| **Currency** | 1 lekë (L) = 100 quintars |
| **Time** | GMT/UTC+0100 |
| **Country Phone Code** | ☎ 355 |

# Facts about Albania

## HISTORY

During the 2nd millennium BC, the Illyrians, who were ancestors of today's Albanians, occupied the western Balkans. The Greeks arrived in the 7th century BC to establish self-governing colonies at Epidamnos (now Durrës), Apollonia and Butrint. They traded peacefully with the Illyrians, who formed tribal states in the 4th century BC. The south became part of Greek Epirus.

In the second half of the 3rd century BC, an expanding Illyrian kingdom based at Shkodra came into conflict with Rome, which sent a fleet of 200 vessels against Queen Teuta (who ruled over the Illyrian Ardian kingdom) in

228 BC. A long war resulted in the extension of Roman control over the entire Balkan area by 167 BC.

Like the Greeks, the Illyrians preserved their own language and traditions despite centuries of Roman rule. Under the Romans, Illyria enjoyed peace and prosperity, though the large agricultural estates were worked by slave labour. The main trade route between Rome and Constantinople, the Via Egnatia, ran from Durrës to Thessaloniki.

When the Roman Empire was divided in AD 395, Illyria fell within the Eastern Roman

ALBANIA

Empire, later known as Byzantium. Invasions by migrating peoples – Visigoths, Huns, Ostrogoths and Slavs – continued through the 5th and 6th centuries and only in the south did the ethnic Illyrians survive.

In 1344 Albania was annexed by Serbia, but after the defeat of Serbia by the Turks in 1389 the whole region was open to Ottoman attack. The Venetians occupied some coastal towns, and from 1443 to 1468 the national hero Skënderbeg (George Kastrioti) led Albanian resistance to the Turks from his castle at Kruja. Skënderbeg won all 25 battles he fought against the Turks, and even Sultan Mehmet-Fatih, conqueror of Constantinople, could not take Kruja.

From 1479 to 1912 Albania, the most backward corner of Europe, was under Ottoman rule. In the 15th and 16th centuries thousands of Albanians fled to southern Italy to escape Turkish rule and over half of those who remained converted to Islam.

In 1878 the Albanian League at Prizren, which is in present-day Kosova (Kosovo), began a struggle for autonomy that was put down by the Turkish army in 1881. Further Uprisings between 1910 and 1912 culminated in a proclamation of independence and the formation of a provisional government led by Ismail Qemali at Vlora in 1912. These achievements were severely compromised when Kosova, nearly half of Albania, was given to Serbia in 1913. With the outbreak of WWI, Albania was occupied by the armies of Greece, Serbia, France, Italy and Austria-Hungary in succession.

In 1920 the capital city was moved from Durrës to less-vulnerable Tirana. Thousands of Albanian volunteers converged on Vlora, forcing the occupying Italians to withdraw. Ahmet Zogu became the ruler of Albania and declared himself King Zogu I in 1928, but his close collaboration with Italy backfired in April 1939 when Mussolini ordered an invasion of Albania. Zogu fled to Britain and used gold looted from the Albanian treasury to rent a floor at London's Ritz Hotel.

On 8 November 1941 the Albanian Communist Party was founded with Enver Hoxha (pronounced Hodja) as first secretary, a position he held until his death in April 1985. The communists led the resistance against the Italians and, after 1943, against the Germans, ultimately tying down 15 combined German-Italian divisions.

## The Rise of Communism

After the fighting had died down, the communists consolidated power. In January 1946 the People's Republic of Albania was proclaimed, with Enver Hoxha as president.

In September 1948 Albania broke off relations with Yugoslavia, which had hoped to incorporate the country into the Yugoslav Federation. Instead, Albania allied itself with Stalin's USSR and put into effect a series of Soviet-style economic plans.

Albania collaborated closely with the USSR until 1960, when a heavy-handed Khrushchev demanded that a submarine base be set up at Vlora. Albania broke off diplomatic relations with the USSR in 1961 and reoriented itself towards the People's Republic of China.

From 1966 to 1967 Albania experienced a Chinese-style cultural revolution. Administrative workers were suddenly transferred to remote areas and younger cadres were placed in leading positions. The collectivisation of agriculture was completed and organised religion banned.

Following the Soviet invasion of Czechoslovakia in 1968, Albania left the Warsaw Pact and embarked on a self-reliant defence policy. Some 750,000 igloo-shaped concrete bunkers and pillboxes with narrow gun slits, built by Hoxha, serve as a reminder of this policy.

With the death of Mao Zedong in 1976 and the changes that followed in China after 1978, Albania's unique relationship with China came to an end.

## Post-Hoxha

Hoxha died in April 1985 and his long-time associate Ramiz Alia took over the leadership. Keenly aware of the economic decay caused by Albania's isolationist path, Alia began a liberalisation programme in 1986 and also broadened Albania's ties with foreign countries. Travellers arriving in Albania at this time no longer had their guidebooks confiscated and their beards and long hair clipped by border barbers, and short skirts were allowed.

In June 1990, inspired by the changes that were occurring elsewhere in Eastern Europe, some 4500 Albanians took refuge in Western embassies in Tirana. After a brief confrontation with the police and the Sigurimi (secret police) these people were allowed to board ships for Brindisi in Italy, where they were granted political asylum.

After student demonstrations in December 1990, the government agreed to allow opposition parties. The Democratic Party, led by heart surgeon Sali Berisha, was formed. Further demonstrations won new concessions, including the promise of free elections and independent trade unions. The government announced a reform programme and party hardliners were purged.

In early March 1991, as the election date approached, some 20,000 Albanians fled to Brindisi by ship, creating a crisis for the Italian government, which had begun to view them as economic refugees. Most were eventually allowed to stay.

The March 1992 elections ended 47 years of communist rule. After the resignation of Ramiz Alia, parliament elected Sali Berisha president in April. In September 1992 former president Ramiz Alia was placed under house arrest after he wrote articles critical of the Democratic government. In August 1993 the leader of the Socialist Party, Fatos Nano, was also arrested on corruption charges.

A severe crisis developed in late 1996, when private pyramid investment schemes – widely thought to have been supported by the government – collapsed spectacularly. Around 70% of Albanians lost their savings – in total over US$1 billion – and nationwide disturbances and violence resulted. New elections were called, and the victorious Socialist Party under Fatos Nano – who had been freed from prison by the rampaging mob – was able to restore some degree of security and investor confidence.

Albania shuddered again during November 1998 when Azem Hajdari, a very popular Democratic Party deputy, was assassinated, but the riots following his death were eventually contained.

In spring 1999 Albania faced a crisis of a different sort. This time, it was the influx of 465,000 refugees from neighbouring Kosova during the NATO bombing and the Serbian ethnic-cleansing campaign in Kosova. While this put a tremendous strain on resources, the net effect has in fact been positive. Substantial amounts of international aid money have poured in, the service sector has grown and inflation has declined to single digits.

By 2002 the country found itself in a kind of miniboom with much money being poured into construction projects and infrastructure renewal.

## GEOGRAPHY

More than three-quarters of this 28,748-sq-km country (a bit smaller than Belgium) consists of mountains and hills. There are three zones: a coastal plain, a mountainous region and an interior plain. The coastal plain extends approximately 200km from north to south and up to 50km inland. The 2000m-high forested mountain spine, which stretches for the entire length of Albania, culminates at Mt Jezerce (2694m) in the north, near the Yugoslav border. The country's highest peak is Mt Korab (2751m), which is located on the border with Macedonia to the east. Albania has been subject to some destructive earthquakes, such as the one that struck in 1979 leaving at least 100,000 people homeless.

The longest river in Albania is the Drin (285km), which drains Lake Ohrid. In the north the Drin flows into the Buna, Albania's only navigable river, which connects shallow Lake Shkodra to the sea. The Ionian littoral, especially the 'Riviera of Flowers' stretching from Vlora to Saranda, offers magnificent scenery. Forests cover 40% of the land, and the many olive trees, citrus plantations and vineyards give Albania a Mediterranean air.

## CLIMATE

Albania has a warm Mediterranean climate. The summers are hot, clear and dry, and the winters, when 40% of the rain falls, are cool, cloudy and moist. In winter the high interior plateau can be very cold as continental air masses move in. Along the coast the climate is moderated by sea winds. Gjirokastra and Shkodra receive twice as much rain as Korça, with November, December and April being the wettest months. The sun shines longest from May to September and July is the warmest month, but even April and October are quite pleasant.

The average maximum temperature in Tirana is 23.5°C in summer and 9°C in winter.

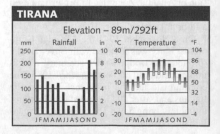

**TIRANA**

Elevation – 89m/292ft

## ECOLOGY & ENVIRONMENT

Large parts of the country were subjected to ecological vandalism during the communist years, particularly near the Fier oilfields in central Albania where unregulated extraction caused massive surface damage from waste products. The huge petrochemical factory at Elbasan belched enormous amounts of toxic fumes over the valley for years.

Albanians are now turning their attention to cleaning up their act and foreign interests are taking an active role in monitoring industrial operations. However, issues such as improving roads still take precedence.

## GOVERNMENT & POLITICS

Albania's political system is a presidential parliamentary democracy with Alfred Moisiu as president and head of state and Ilir Meta of the Socialist Party as prime minister. The main opposition, the Democratic Party, is chaired by Sali Berisha, the former president and rival to Socialist Party leader (and former prime minister) Fatos Nano.

## ECONOMY

Albania is a country rich in natural resources such as crude oil, natural gas, coal, copper, iron, nickel and timber and is the world's third-largest producer of chrome, accounting for about 10% of the world's supply. The Central Mountains yield minerals such as copper (in the northeast around Kukës), chromium (farther south near the Drin River) and iron nickel (closer to Lake Ohrid). The government is now making preparations for Albania's mining industry to be privatised through sales to foreign interests.

There are textile industries at Berat, Korça and Tirana. Oil was discovered in Albania in 1917 and the country at one point supplied all its own petroleum requirements. Oil and gas from Fier also enabled the production of chemical fertilisers.

There are several huge hydroelectric dams on the Drin River in the north. Albania obtains 80% of its electricity from such dams and by 1970 electricity had reached every village in the country.

Following a period of neglect in the agricultural sector, Albanian farmers have begun the long task of rebuilding rural infrastructure, and agriculture currently accounts for 55% of the country's GDP, estimated in 2002 at US$10.5 billion.

Albania continues to be heavily dependent on remittances coming from the Albanian communities abroad, particularly in Greece and Italy. Albania is also angling for more international aid money, particularly in light of its generous intake of Kosovar Albanian refugees in 1998. Priority projects for aid money involve infrastructure improvement.

Despite many challenges, Albania's economy was projected to grow at 7% to 8% for the third straight year in 2002, making it one of the fastest-growing economies in Europe.

## POPULATION & PEOPLE

Albanians are a hardy Mediterranean people, physically different from the more Nordic Slavs. Although the Slavs and Greeks look down on the Albanians, the Albanians themselves have a sense of racial superiority based on their descent from the ancient Illyrians, who inhabited the region before the Romans. The country's romanised name comes from the Albanoi, an ancient Illyrian tribe.

Approximately 95% of the country's population is Albanians. Over the years, the harsh economic conditions existing in Albania have unleashed waves of emigration: to Serbia in the 15th century, to Greece and Italy in the 16th century, to the USA in the 19th and 20th centuries and to Greece, Italy and Switzerland today. The Arbëreshi, long-time Albanian residents of 50 scattered villages in southern Italy, fled west in the 16th century to escape the Turks. As many as two million ethnic Albanians live in Turkey today, emigrants from Serb-dominated Yugoslavia between 1912 and 1966. Since 1990 hundreds of thousands of Albanians have migrated to Western Europe (especially Greece and Italy) to escape the economic hardships at home. Minorities in Albania include the Greeks (3% of the population) and Vlachs, Macedonians and Roma (comprising a further 2% of the population).

The Shkumbin River forms a boundary between the Gheg cultural region of the north and the Tosk region in the south. The people in these regions still vary in dialect, musical culture and traditional dress.

## ARTS
### Music

Polyphony, the blending of several independent vocal or instrumental parts, is a southern Albanian tradition dating from ancient Illyrian times. Peasant choirs perform in a variety of styles, and the songs, usually with an epic-lyrical or historical theme, may be dramatic to the point of yodelling or slow and sober, with alternate male and female voices combining in harmonies. Instrumental polyphonic *kabas* are played by small Roma ensembles usually led by a clarinet. Improvisation gives way to dancing at colourful village weddings. One well-known group, which often tours outside Albania, is the Lela Family of Përmet.

An outstanding recording of traditional Albanian music is the CD *Albania, Vocal and Instrumental Polyphony* (LDX 274 897) in the series 'Le Chant du Monde' (Musée de l'Homme, Paris).

## Literature

Prior to the adoption of a standardised orthography in 1909, very little literature was produced in Albania, though Albanians resident elsewhere in the Ottoman Empire and in Italy did write. Among these was the noted poet Naim Frashëri (1846–1900), who lived in İstanbul and wrote in Greek. Around the time of independence (1912), a group of romantic patriotic writers at Shkodra wrote epics and historical novels.

Perhaps the most interesting writer of the interwar period was Fan Noli (1880–1965). Educated as a priest in the USA, Fan Noli returned there to head the Albanian Orthodox Church in America after the Democratic government of Albania, in which he served as premier, was overthrown in 1924. Although many of his books are based on religion, the introductions he wrote to his own translations of Cervantes, Ibsen, Omar Khayyám and Shakespeare established him as Albania's foremost literary critic.

The poet Migjeni (1911–38) focused on social issues until his early death from tuberculosis. In his 1936 poem, *Vargjet e lira* (Free Verse), Migjeni seeks to dispel the magic of old myths and awaken the reader to present injustices.

Albania's best-known contemporary writer is Ismail Kadare, born in 1935, whose many novels have been translated into 20 languages. *Chronicle in Stone* (1971) relates wartime experiences in Kadare's birthplace, Gjirokastra, as seen through the eyes of a boy. *Broken April* (1990) deals with the blood vendettas of the northern highlands before the 1939 Italian invasion. Although Kadare lived in Tirana throughout the Hoxha years and even wrote a book, *The Great Winter* (1972), extolling Hoxha's defiance of Moscow, he sought political asylum in Paris in 1990. A more recent classic is *The Two-Arched Bridge* (1997), an ominous and beautiful 14th-century tale, told by a monk, of the troubled construction of a bridge during turbulent political times.

## Cinema

A film worth seeing is *Lamerica*, a brilliant and stark look at Albanian post-communist culture. Despite its title, it is about Albanians seeking to escape to Bari, Italy, in the immediate postcommunist era. The title is a symbol for ordinary Albanians seeking a better and more materially fulfilling life in the West. Woven loosely around a plot about a couple of Italian scam artists, the essence of the film is the unquenchable dignity of the ordinary Albanian in the face of adversity.

## SOCIETY & CONDUCT

Traditional dress is still common in rural areas, especially on Sunday and holidays. Men wear embroidered white shirts and knee trousers, the Ghegs with a white felt skullcap and the Tosks with a flat-topped white fez. Women's clothing is brighter than that of the men. Along with the standard white blouses with wide sleeves, women from Christian areas wear red vests, while Muslim women wear baggy pants tied at the ankles and coloured headscarves. Older Muslim women wear white scarves around the neck; white scarves may also be a sign of mourning.

The *Kanun* is an ancient social law, which outlines most aspects of social behaviour, including the treatment of guests. This has meant that Albanians can be hospitable in the extreme and will often offer travellers lodging and food free of charge. Travellers must be wary of exploiting this tradition and, while payment may well be acceptable in some cases, a small gift of a book or a memento from home will often suffice.

Be respectful when visiting the country's mosques – remove your shoes and try to avoid visits during prayer times.

## RELIGION

From 1967 to 1990 Albania was the only officially atheist state in Europe. Public religious services were banned and many churches were converted into theatres or cinemas. In mid-1990 this situation ended and in December of that year Nobel Prize-winner Mother Teresa of Calcutta, an ethnic Albanian from Macedonia, visited Albania and met with President Alia. Traditionally, Albania has been 70% Sunni Muslim, 20% Albanian Orthodox (mostly in the south) and 10% Roman Catholic (mostly in the north). It's the only country in Europe with an Islamic majority though the form of Islam is quite secular, similar to the situation in Turkey.

## LANGUAGE

Albanian (Shqipja) is an Indo-European dialect of ancient Illyrian, with a number of Latin, Slavonic and (modern) Greek words. The two main dialects of Albanian have diverged over the past 1000 years. In 1909 a standardised form of the Gheg dialect of Elbasan was adopted as the official language, but since WWII a modified version of the Tosk dialect of southern Albania has been used.

Outside the country, Albanians resident in former Yugoslavia speak Gheg, those in Greece speak Tosk, whereas in Italy they speak another dialect called Arberesh. With practice you can sometimes differentiate between the dialects by listening closely for the nasalised vowels of Gheg. In 1972 the Congress of Orthography at Tirana established a unified written language based on the two dialects, which is now universally accepted.

You'll find that Italian is the most useful foreign language to know in Albania, and English is a strong second. Greek is also useful in the south.

Many Albanian place names have two forms because the definite article is a suffix. In this book we use the form most commonly used in English, but Tirana actually means *the* Tiranë. Albanians, like Bulgarians, shake their heads to say yes and usually nod to say no.

See the Language chapter at the back of the book for pronunciation guidelines and useful words and phrases.

# Facts for the Visitor

## HIGHLIGHTS

The beauty and mystique of Albania's mountains and coastal region makes the country a highlight in itself. The fortress town of Gjirokastra in the south is worth a visit, as are the stunning and well-preserved Roman ruins at Butrint, also in the far south.

## PLANNING
### Maps

The best map of the country is the 1:300,000 *Albania* map published by Euro Map. It also includes several city and town plans. The 1:450,000 *Albania World Travel Map* published by Bartholomew is also very detailed. Buy them before you arrive in Albania as they may be hard to find in the country.

## TOURIST OFFICES

There are no tourist information offices in Albania, but hotel receptionists or travel agencies will sometimes help you with directions. You can buy city maps of Tirana in bookshops and larger kiosks in the capital, but in most of the other towns they're unobtainable. In addition, many streets lack signs and the buildings have no numbers marked on them! Some streets don't seem to have any name at all. However, you will find that most of the towns are small enough for you to get around without them.

## VISAS & DOCUMENTS

No visa is required by citizens of EU countries or nationals of Australia, New Zealand and the USA. Travellers from other countries should check with an Albanian embassy for appropriate visa requirements. Citizens of most countries – even those entering visa-free – will be required to pay an 'entry tax' at the border. The entry tax for almost all visitors is US$10. Israeli citizens pay US$30.

Upon arrival you will fill in an arrival and departure card. Keep the departure card, which will be stamped, with your passport and present it when you leave.

## EMBASSIES & CONSULATES
### Albanian Embassies & Consulates

Listed below are some of the main addresses for Albanian embassies.

**France** (☎ 01-45 53 51 32) 13 rue de la Pompe, Paris 75016
**Germany** (☎ 0302-593 0550, fax 593 0599) Friedrichstrasse 231, D-10969 Berlin
**Greece** (☎ 21 0723 4412, fax 21 0723 1972) Karahristou 1, GR-114 21 Athens
**UK** (☎ 020-7730 5709, fax 7828 8869) 24 Buckingham Gate, 2nd Floor, London SW1 E6LB
**USA** (☎ 202-223 4942, fax 628 7342) 2100 S St NW, Washington DC 20008

## Embassies & Consulates in Albania

The following embassies are in Tirana (area code ☎ 042):

**Bulgaria** (☎ 233 155, fax 232 272) Rruga Skënderbeg 12
**Germany** (☎ 232 048, fax 233 497) Rruga Skënderbeg 8
**Greece** (☎ 223 959, fax 234 443) Rruga Frederik Shiroka 3
**Macedonia** (☎ 233 036, fax 232 514) Rruga Lekë Dukagjini 2
**Turkey** (☎ 233 399, fax 232 719) Rruga E Kavajës 31
**UK** (☎ 234 973, fax 247 697) Rruga Skënderbeg 12
**USA** (☎ 247 285, fax 232 222) Rruga Elbasanit 103
**Yugoslavia** (☎ 232 089, fax 223 042) Rruga e Durrësit 192/196

## MONEY
### Currency

Albanian banknotes come in denominations of 100, 200, 500 and 1000 lekë. There are five, 10, 20 and 50 lekë coins. Notes that were issued after 1997 are smaller and contain a sophisticated watermark to prevent forgery. In 1964 the currency was revalued 10 times; prices on occasion may still be quoted at the old rate.

Everything in Albania can be paid for with lekë; however, bear in mind that most of the hotel and transport prices given in this chapter are quoted in US dollars or euros, both of which are readily accepted as alternative currencies for the lekë.

### Exchange Rates

Conversion rates for major currencies at the time of publication are listed below:

| country | unit | | lekë |
| --- | --- | --- | --- |
| Australia | A$1 | = | 73.18 lekë |
| Canada | C$1 | = | 88.57 lekë |
| euro zone | €1 | = | 118 lekë |
| Japan | ¥100 | = | 107.2 lekë |
| NZ | NZ$1 | = | 60 lekë |
| UK | UK£1 | = | 199.24 lekë |
| US | US$1 | = | 140 lekë |

To find the most up-to-date exchange rates for the Albanian lekë, point your Web browser at
Ⓦ www.xe.com/ucc/full.shtml.

### Exchanging Money

Some banks will change US-dollar travellers cheques into US dollars cash without any commission. Travellers cheques in small denominations may be used when paying bills at major hotels but cash is preferred everywhere. You'll find that credit cards are only accepted in the larger hotels and travel agencies, and a few places in Tirana and Durrës will offer credit-card advances (usually for MasterCard). At the time of research, one ATM had just opened in Tirana.

Every town has its free currency market, which usually operates on the street in front of the main post office or state bank. Look out for the men standing around with wads of money or pocket calculators in their hand. Such transactions are not dangerous and it all takes place quite openly, but be careful and make sure you count their money twice before tendering yours.

The advantages with changing money on the street are that you get a good rate and avoid the 1% commission some banks may charge. You also save time and don't have to worry about banking hours. Unlike the banks, private moneychangers never run out of currency notes.

In Albania, US dollars are the favourite foreign currency, though euros are also acceptable to all moneychangers. You will not be able to exchange Albanian currency outside of the country. Spend it or reconvert it before you leave.

### Tipping

Albania is a moderately tip-conscious society. You should round up the bill in restaurants. However, with taxi drivers you will normally agree on a fare beforehand so an extra tip will not be considered necessary.

## POST & COMMUNICATIONS
### Post

There are few public mail boxes in Albania outside of main towns, but there is an increasing number of modern post offices springing up around the country where you can hand in your mail directly.

Letters to the USA and Canada cost 90 lekë and postcards 50 lekë. Letters to Australia, Africa and Asia cost 60 lekë and postcards 40 lekë. Within Europe letters cost 50 lekë to send and postcards 30 lekë, while to neighbouring countries the rates are 30 lekë and 20 lekë respectively. Within Albania the rates are 20 lekë and 15 lekë.

## Telephone

Long-distance telephone calls made from main post offices are cheap, costing about 90 lekë a minute to Italy. Calls to the USA cost 230 lekë per minute. Phonecards are available from the post office in versions of 50 units (560 lekë), 100 units (980 lekë) and 200 units (1800 lekë). It's best not to buy the phonecards from the hawkers outside the post office.

Albania's country phone code is ☎ 355. Albania has two mobile/cellphone providers, and most areas of the country are now adequately covered. Roaming agreements with your home service provider may or may not exist. Owners of Greek mobile phones can roam in Albania. Local mobile numbers begin with 038 or 069.

To phone overseas from Albania, the international access code is ☎ 00. Dial ☎ 14 if you want domestic directory assistance and ☎ 12 for international directory assistance.

## Fax

Faxing can be done from the main post office in Tirana, or from major hotels, though they will charge more.

## Email & Internet Access

Places to access the Internet now abound in Tirana and most larger towns will have at least one place where you can access the Net. Rates are generally low – 300 lekë to 400 lekë an hour or part thereof. Some Internet centres also offer cheap international phone connections.

## DIGITAL RESOURCES

Websites that you might find useful include ⓦ www.albanian.com and ⓦ www.albania.co .uk (a good info source on current events).

## BOOKS

*The Albanians – A Modern History* (1999), by Miranda Vickers, is a comprehensive and very readable history of Albania from the time of Ottoman rule to the restoration of democracy after 1990.

*Biografi* (1993), by New Zealander Lloyd Jones, is a rather arresting story set in post-1990 Albania and is a mixture of both fact and fiction as the writer sets out to discover the alleged double of former communist dictator Enver Hoxha.

*The Accursed Mountains: Journeys in Albania* (1999), by Robert Carver, is a lively and colourful narrative about one journalist's entertaining, but occasionally credibility-stretching, journey through Albania in 1996.

*The Best of Albanian Cooking* (1999), by Klementina Hysa and R John Hysa, is one of scant few books on the subject of Albanian cuisine and contains a wide range of family recipes.

For a helpful list of Albanian words and phrases check out the *Mediterranean Europe phrasebook* from Lonely Planet, while *Colloquial Albanian* (1994), by Isa Zymberi, is a self-teach language course, accompanied by a cassette tape. It is part of the excellent Routledge teach-yourself language series.

An excellent source of rare and out-of-print books on Albania is **Harfield Books of London** (☎/fax 020-8871 0880; ⓦ www .harfieldbooks.com; 81 Replingham Rd, Southfields, London SW18 5LU). Also try **Oxus Books** (☎/fax 020-8870 3854; 121 Astonville St, London SW18 5AQ), which has a catalogue you can request.

## NEWSPAPERS & MAGAZINES

A wide variety of newspapers are published in Tirana. The independent daily *Koha Jonë* is the paper with the widest readership.

The *Albanian Daily News* is a fairly dry, English-language publication that has useful information on happenings around Albania. It's generally available from major hotels for 300 lekë, or you can read it online at ⓦ www .AlbanianNews.com.

## RADIO & TV

There are many TV channels available in Albania including the state TV service TVSH, the private station TVA and, among others, Eurosport, several Italian channels and even a couple of French ones.

The BBC World Service can be picked up in and around Tirana on 103.9FM, while the Voice of America's mainly music programme is on 107.4FM.

## TIME

Albania is one hour ahead of GMT/UTC, the same as Yugoslavia, Macedonia and Italy, but one hour behind Greece. Albania goes on summer time at the end of March, when clocks are turned forward an hour. At the end of September, they're turned back an hour.

## TOILETS

Public toilets should be used in dire circumstances only! There are only a handful in the whole of Tirana. Use hotel or restaurant toilets whenever you can. The ones in the main hotels in Tirana are very clean and modern. Plan your 'rest' stops carefully when travelling in the country.

## HEALTH

Health services are available to tourists for a small fee at state-run hospitals, but service and standards are not crash hot. Make sure your travel or health insurance covers treatment in Albania includes evacuation. Use the private clinics where available; the ABS Health Foundation in Tirana is a good one (see Information in the Tirana section later in this chapter).

## WOMEN TRAVELLERS

While women are not likely to encounter any predictable dangers, it is recommended that you travel in pairs or with male companions in order to avoid unwanted attention – particularly outside Tirana. Don't forget that Albania is a predominantly secular Muslim country. Dress should be conservative.

## GAY & LESBIAN TRAVELLERS

Homosexuality became legal in Albania early in 1995, however attitudes are still highly conservative.

## DISABLED TRAVELLERS

There are few special facilities for travellers in wheelchairs. However, there are toilets that cater for disabled people in the Tirana International and the Europapark Tirana hotels.

## DANGERS & ANNOYANCES

The security level in the country is now generally stable. You are advised however to avoid independent travel in the far north of the country around Bajram Curri and along the road corridor from Shkodra to Kukës, as banditry may still occur. Be warned that there

### Emergency Services

In the event of emergencies telephone ☎ 19 for the police, ☎ 17 for ambulance and ☎ 18 for the fire department. These numbers are valid nationwide.

may still be land mines near the northern border with Kosova around Bajram Curri.

Beware of pickpockets on crowded city buses and don't flash money around! Walking around larger towns is generally safe in the day, but at night beware of falling into deep potholes in the unlit streets, and occasional gangs of youths. Be aware of theft generally, but don't believe the horror stories you hear about Albania in Greece and elsewhere.

Take special care if accosted by Roma women and children begging; avoid eye contact and head to the nearest hotel.

As Albania was closed for so long, black travellers may encounter some curious stares. At worst, proprietors of small hotels may try to refuse service.

Corrupt police may attempt to extort money from you by claiming that something is wrong with your documentation, or they might try another pretext. Strongly resist paying them anything without an official receipt. If stopped, stay calm and smile. Allow the police to shoulder the onus of communication. They will probably give up if they can't make you understand. Always keep at least a copy of your passport with you.

You should also be aware of abysmal roads and chaotic driving conditions. Drive defensively and never at night.

Do not drink the tap water; plenty of bottled water is available.

## BUSINESS HOURS

Most businesses open at 8.30am, and some close for a siesta from noon to 4pm, opening again from 4pm to 7pm. Banking hours are shorter (generally 8.30am to 2pm).

## PUBLIC HOLIDAYS & SPECIAL EVENTS

Public holidays celebrated in Albania include New Year's Day (1 January), Easter Monday (March/April), Labour Day (1 May), Independence Day (28 November), Liberation Day (29 November) and Christmas Day (25 December).

Ramadan and Bajram, variable Muslim holidays, are also celebrated.

## COURSES

The **University of Tirana** (fax 042-241 09) runs a summer-school programme in Albanian language and culture from mid-August to mid-September. The registration fee is US$100.

## ACCOMMODATION

Accommodation has undergone a rapid transformation in Albania, with the opening of new, custom-built, private hotels to replace the dismal state hotels. Priced at about US$35 to US$50 and upwards per person per night (usually including breakfast), these are modern, well-appointed establishments.

Another positive development for visitors is the conversion of homes or villas into so-called private hotels. For budget travellers, these are without doubt the best way to go.

You can often find unofficial accommodation in private homes by asking around. However, for security reasons camping is not advisable.

## FOOD

Lunch is the main meal of the day, although eating out in the evening is very common in Tirana. The quality of restaurants in the capital has improved greatly. In the country and other towns more places to eat are opening up, so you should have no problem getting a decent meal.

Albanian cuisine, like that of Serbia, has been strongly influenced by Turkey. Grilled meats like *shishqebap* (shish kebab), *romstek* (minced meat patties) and *qofte* (meat balls) are served across all the Balkan countries. Some local dishes include *çomlek* (meat and onion stew), *fërges* (a rich beef stew), *rosto me salcë kosi* (roast beef with sour cream) and *tavë kosi* (mutton with yogurt). Lake Shkodra carp and Lake Ohrid trout are the most common fish dishes. For dessert, try the *akullore* (ice cream), which is very popular everywhere.

## DRINKS

Albanians take their coffee both as *kafe turke* (Turkish coffee) and *kafe ekspres* (espresso). If you ask for *kafe surogato* you will get what is the closest to filter coffee. Avoid unbottled drinks as they may contain tap water.

Albanian white wine is better than the vinegary red. However, the red *Shesi e Zi* from Librazhd or Berat is an excellent drop. Most of the beer consumed in Albania is imported from Macedonia or Greece, but look out for the locally produced and palatable Premium Tirana Pils. *Raki* (a clear brandy distilled from grapes) is taken as an aperitif – always ask for home-made if possible *(raki ë bërë në shtëpi)*. There's also *konjak* (cognac – the Skenderbey

cognac makes a good gift on your trip home), *uzo* (a colourless aniseed-flavoured liqueur like Greek ouzo) and various fruit liqueurs. *Fërnet* is a medicinal aperitif containing some herbal essences, made at Korça.

A good word to know is the favourite Albanian drinking toast – *gëzuar!*

## ENTERTAINMENT

Check with the local theatre for performances. These are generally advertised on painted boards either in front of the theatre or on main streets, but performances are invariably only in Albanian.

There's usually a disco or two to complement the zillions of cafés in a given town; ask around for what's hot.

## SPECTATOR SPORTS

Football (soccer) is played at local stadiums on weekend afternoons. As a foreigner, you may need someone to help you obtain tickets.

## SHOPPING

Most hotels have tourist shops where you can buy Albanian handicrafts such as carpets, silk, ornaments (made from silver, copper and wood), embroidery, handmade shoes, shoulder bags, picture books, musical instruments, and CDs and cassettes of folk music.

# Getting There & Away

## AIR

Rinas airport is 26km northwest of Tirana. Taxis ply the route to Tirana.

Ada Air arrives in Rinas from Athens, Bari, Prishtina, Skopje and Ioannina; Adria Airways from Ljubljana; Albanian Airlines from Bologna, Frankfurt, İstanbul, Prishtina, Rome and Zürich; Austrian Airlines from Vienna; Hemus Air from Sofia; Lufthansa Airlines from Frankfurt and Munich; Malév-Hungarian Airlines from Budapest; Olympic Airways from Athens via Ioannina or Thessaloniki; Swiss Internationl Air lines from Zürich; and Turkish Airlines from İstanbul.

Some examples of return fares are US$308 from Rome flying with Albanian Airlines; US$220 from Athens with Olympic and Ada; US$322 from Budapest with Malév; US$155 from Prishtina with Ada Air (US$171 with

Albanian Airlines); and US$250 from İstanbul with Turkish Airlines.

Before investing in any of the above fares, compare them with the price of a cheap flight to Athens or Thessaloniki, from where Albania is easily accessible by local bus with a change of bus at the border. Another option is a charter flight to Corfu, from where you can take a ferry to Saranda in southern Albania.

See Getting There & Away in the Tirana section for the phone numbers of the main airlines.

## LAND
### Bus
Buses to Thessaloniki (€35, 10 hours) leave at 6am each morning from in front of **Albanian Interlines** (☎ 222 272; Bulevardi Zogu I). Buses to Athens (€50, 24 hours) also leave from here three times a week.

Buses to Prishtina, the capital of Kosova, leave daily from beside the Tirana International Hotel at 6pm (€30, 12 hours). If you're bound for Macedonia, you will need to take the daily bus to Tetovo (also from here) and from Tetovo you can take a frequent local bus to Skopje.

Buses for İstanbul and Sofia leave from **Albtransport** (☎ 223 026; Rruga Mine Peza, Tirana; open 8am-4pm Mon-Fri). The Sofia bus (€35, 15 hours) leaves at 10am on Wednesday. Two buses depart for İstanbul (€55, 24 hours) at 10am and 1pm on Monday, and go via Sofia.

### Car & Motorcycle
Bringing a car or motorcycle to Albania is still a risky business as theft and the generally bad roads can be a problem. Additionally, your insurance Green Card may not cover Albania. But it is feasible to transit the country from, say, Yugoslavia to Macedonia or Greece in two days, if you are determined. You'll need to park the car in a secure park overnight in Tirana and continue the next day.

Roads are slowly being improved and there are quite decent sections between Tirana and Durrës and on the approaches to the main land borders. Drivers and riders will need to be extra careful of the poor driving techniques and be aware that traffic police regularly stop cars in an effort to extract fines for so-called infringements.

See also the Getting Around section later in this chapter for further information on local driving conditions.

The following highway border crossings are open to motorists, cyclists and pedestrians.

**Yugoslavia** The only border crossing is at Han i Hotit (between Shkodra and Podgorica), though a new crossing has been planned for some time at Muriqan/Sukobin, which would link Ulcinj, in Yugoslavia, and Shkodra much more conveniently.

**Kosova/Kosovo** The only really viable crossing for travellers is at Morinë/Vrbnica between Kukës and Prizren. However bear in mind that this whole area is not a good place to travel solo or independently as the corridor between Shkodra and the border can still be subject to random banditry and/or traveller harassment. Travellers on the through-buses should have no problems.

**Macedonia** The best two crossings are those on Lake Ohrid. The southern crossing is at Tushemisht (near Sveti Naum, 29km south of Ohrid), and the northern crossing is at Qafa e Thanës (between Struga and Pogradec). There is a third crossing at Maqellarë (between Debar and Peshkopi), but it is not recommended for travellers as Albanian-Macedonia tensions may flare up occasionally and delays or questioning of travellers may ensue.

**Greece** Border crossings are at Kapshtica/Krystallopigi (between Korça and Florina) and Kakavija/Kakavia (between Ioannina and Gjirokastra). A new border crossing north of the Greek port of Igoumenitsa at Konispoli/Sagiada is open, though facilities for vehicle crossings had not been completed at the time of research.

## SEA
The Italian company of **Adriatica di Navigazione** operates ferry services to Durrës from Bari (US$60, 8½ hours) daily and from Ancona (US$85, 19 hours) four times a week. Cars cost US$90/100 respectively. Bicycles are carried free.

In Bari you are able to buy ferry tickets from **Agestea** (☎ 080-553 1555; e agestea .bari02@interbusiness.it; Via Liside 4); and in Ancona it's **Maritime Agency Srl** (☎ 071-204 915; e tickets.adn@maritime.it; Via XXIX Settembre 10). In Albania tickets are sold by any number of the travel agencies in Durrës or Tirana.

The car ferry C/F *Grecia* runs each Tuesday and Saturday at 1pm to Durrës from Trieste (and returns on Wednesday and Sunday at 7pm). The trip on deck costs US$40/50 in low/high season. In Durrës contact **KAD Shipping** (☎ 052-25 154, fax 20 341) or any travel agency. In Trieste contact **Agemar** (☎ 39-40-363 222, fax 363 737; ℮ info@agemar.it) or any travel agency selling ferry tickets.

The fastest ferry connection between Bari and Durrës is via the passenger catamarans operated by **Quality Lines** (€60, 3½ hours). These high-speed vessels leave Durrës daily at 10am and 4.30pm. The Durrës agent can be contacted on ☎ 052-24 571.

See the Saranda Getting There & Away section for information on travel between Corfu and the small southern Albanian port of Saranda.

## ORGANISED TOURS
Package tours to Albania, which dwindled after the 1997 civil disturbances, currently are unavailable.

## DEPARTURE TAX
Airport departure tax is US$10, payable in dollars or lekë. A US$4 tariff is imposed on people leaving Albania by ferry, and there's a US$1 daily tariff on vehicles, payable upon crossing the border out of the country.

# Getting Around

## BUS
Most Albanians travel around their country in private minibuses or larger buses. These run fairly frequently throughout the day between Tirana and Durrës (38km) and other towns north and south. Buses to Tirana depart from towns all around Albania at the crack of dawn. Pay the conductor on board; the fares are low (eg, Tirana-Durrës is 100 lekë). Tickets are rarely issued.

City buses operate in Tirana, Durrës and Shkodra (pay the conductor). Watch your possessions on crowded city buses.

## TRAIN
Before 1948, Albania had no railways, but the communists built up a limited north-south rail network based at the port of Durrës. Today, however, nobody who can afford other types of transport takes the train, even though train fares are about a third cheaper than bus fares.

The reason will be obvious once you board – the decrepit carriages typically have broken windows and no toilets.

Daily passenger trains leave Tirana for Shkodra (3½ hours, 98km), Fier (4¼ hours), Ballsh (five hours), Vlora (5½ hours) and Pogradec (seven hours). Seven trains a day also make the 1½-hour trip between Tirana and Durrës.

## CAR & MOTORCYCLE
Albania has only acquired an official road traffic code in recent years and most motorists have only learned to drive in the last five years. The road infrastructure is poor and the roads badly maintained, but the number of cars on the road is growing daily. There are plenty of petrol stations in the cities and increasing numbers in the country.

Hazards include: pedestrians who tend to use the roads as an extension of the footpaths; animals being herded along country roads; gaping potholes; a lack of road warnings and signs; and occasionally reckless drivers. Security is also an issue. Park your vehicle in a secure location, such as hotel grounds, or in a guarded parking lot. An immobiliser alarm is also a very good idea.

Banditry is still an occasional threat in the northern part of the country between Shkodra and Kukës, though the Tirana-Montenegro corridor is generally safe. Never drive at night in any part of Albania.

Unleaded fuel is generally widely available along all major highways, but fill up when you can. A litre of unleaded petrol costs 100 lekë, while diesel costs close to 70 lekë.

**Avis** (☎ 04-235 011, fax 235 042; ℮ gazi@albaniaonline.net), based in the Europapark Tirana, is the only car-rental company in the country.

## HITCHING
With buses so cheap, hitching will probably only be an emergency means of transport. You can afford to be selective about the rides you accept as everyone will take you if they possibly can.

You can get an indication of where a car might be going from the letters on the licence plate: Berat (BR), Durrës (DR), Elbasan (EL), Fier (FR), Gjirokastra (GJ), Korça (KO), Kruja (KR), Lezha (LE), Pogradec (PG), Saranda (SR), Shkodra (SH), Tirana (TR) and Vlora (VL).

Lonely Planet does not recommend hitching as a form of transport.

## LOCAL TRANSPORT

Shared *furgon* (minibuses) run between cities when they are full or almost full. They usually cost about twice the bus fare, but for foreigners they're still cheap. Pay the driver or the driver's assistant once you leave the minibus.

# Tirana

☎ 042 • pop 440,000

It wasn't too long ago that the capital city of Albania was just a dusty, languid town virtually unknown to the outside world. Few cars ran along its wide boulevards and there was no building more than four storeys tall. Today it is a bustling, busy metropolis, with more cars than its streets can cope with; restaurants and cafés have mushroomed like bunkers and tall buildings now creep skywards where once only the minaret of a mosque had been the city's most distinguishing feature. Tirana (Tiranë) today is a fascinating city in the way that it is emerging from anonymity to a new maturity.

Tirana lies close to midway between Rome and İstanbul. Mt Dajti (1612m) rises to the east. Founded by a Turkish *pasha* (military governor) in 1614, Tirana developed into a craft centre with a lively bazaar. In 1920 the city was made the capital of Albania and in the 1930s the bulky Italianate government buildings went up. In the communist era, larger-than-life 'palaces of the people' blossomed in and around Skënderbeg Square and along Bulevardi Dëshmorët e Kombit (Martyrs of the Nation Boulevard). You'll also see Italian parks and a Turkish mosque, but the market area on the eastern side of Tirana is also worth exploring. The city is compact and can be explored on foot.

## Orientation

Orientation is easy in Tirana, as the whole city revolves around central Skënderbeg Square (Sheshi Skënderbeg). Running south from the square is Bulevardi Dëshmorët e Kombit, which leads to the three-arched university building. Running north Bulevardi Zogu I leads to the train station. Coming from the airport (26km) you will enter the city along Rruga Durrësit. Buses from the neighbouring countries will drop you off close to Skënderbeg Square. Most of the major services and hotels are within just a few minutes' walk of Skënderbeg Square.

## Information

**Tourist Offices** Tirana does not have any official tourist office, but there are travel agencies (for details see Travel Agencies later in this Information section). One helpful publication is *Tirana In Your Pocket*, available at bookshops and some of the larger kiosks for 300 lekë.

Another useful reference is *Tirana 2003: The Practical Guide of Tirana*. This gives telephone numbers and addresses for everything from hospitals to banks to embassies, though many of the entries are only in Albanian. This is also available at the main hotels and bookshops for around 300 lekë.

**Money** While there are plenty of banks in Tirana, a free currency market operates directly in front of the main post office. At the time of research just one ATM at the Greek-owned **Alpha Bank** *(Bulevardi Zogu I)* was in operation.

If you would prefer to avoid the swarms of independent currency exchangers, the Hotel Europapark Tirana has a **currency exchange booth** *(open 10.30am-5pm Mon-Fri)*, near the Swiss airline offices, which offers Master Card advances, cashes travellers cheques for 1% commission and exchanges cash. **American Bank of Albania** *(Rruga Ismail Qemali 27; open 9.30am-3.30pm Mon-Fri)* is also a reliable, secure place to cash your travellers cheques (2% commission). The American Express representative **World Travel** *(☎ 227 998; Mine Peza 2)* cashes travellers cheques for 2% commission.

The **Unioni Financiar Tiranë Exchange**, *(☎ 234 979; Rruga Dëshmorët e 4 Shkurtit)*, just south of the main post office, offers Western Union wire transfer services.

**Post & Communications** The **main post office** *(☎ 228 262; Sheshi Çameria; open 8am-8pm Mon-Fri)* and telephone centre are adjacent on a street jutting west from Skënderbeg Square. Another telephone centre is on Bulevardi Zogu I, about 400m past Skënderbeg Square on the right-hand side. There are additional sub-branch post offices on Bulevardi Zogu I and on Rruga Mohamet Gjollesha.

International courier service **DHL** (☎ 232 816, fax 257 294; **e** DHLAlbania@tia-co .al.dhl.com; Rruga Dëshmorët e 4 Shkurtit 7/1 • ☎ 227 667, fax 233 934; Rruga Ded Gjo Luli 6) has two offices in Tirana.

**Email & Internet Access** There are several places to access the Internet in Tirana. The best is **Net 1** (☎ 257 433; Rruga Nikolla Tupe 1/b; open 9am-11pm), with banks of gleaming machines. Another good choice is **F@stech** (☎/fax 251 947; Rruga Brigada e VIII; open 8.30am-11pm) four blocks north. Two blocks south is **Interalb Internet** (☎ 251 747; Rruga Dëshmorët 4 Shkurtit. Pall. 25/1; open 8am-10pm). All charge around 300 lekë per hour or part thereof.

**Travel Agencies** A good place to arrange ferry tickets from Durrës (see under Sea in the Getting There & Away section earlier in this chapter), or to book private rooms, is **Albania Travel & Tours** (☎ 329 83, fax 339 81; Rruga Durrësit 102; open 8am-8pm Mon-Fri, 8am-2pm Sat & Sun).

Other travel agencies abound, but not all operators speak English.

**Newspapers & Magazines** Foreign newspapers and magazines, including the *Times*, the *International Herald Tribune* and the *Economist*, are sold at most major hotels and at some central street kiosks, though they tend to be a few days old.

The **International Bookshop** (open 9am-9pm daily), in the Palace of Culture on the right-hand side, is another option. It has a selection of Penguin literary classics, maps of Tirana and Albania, and an excellent selection of books about Albania.

The **Qëndra Stefan** (see Places to Eat) has an attached bookshop with a selection of foreign publications.

**Medical & Emergency Services** Most of Tirana's foreigners use **ABS Health Foundation** (☎ 234 105; 360 Rruga Qemali Stafa; open Mon-Fri); it's across the street from the 'New School', but watch carefully for the small sign. Staffed by doctors trained in the West, it offers a range of services including regular (US$60) and emergency (US$90) consultations. The fee goes down if you pay a 12-month registration of US$120. Patients are seen by appointment 8am to 4pm weekdays.

## Things to See & Do

Most visits to Tirana begin at **Skënderbeg Square**, a great, open space in the heart of the city. Beside the 15-storey Tirana International Hotel, on the northern side of the square, is the **National Museum of History** (admission 300 lekë; open 8am-1pm Mon-Sat), the largest and finest museum in Albania. A huge, Stalinist-realism mosaic mural entitled *Albania* covers the facade of the museum building. Temporary exhibits are shown in the **gallery** (admission free) on the side of the building facing the Tirana International Hotel.

To the east is another massive building, the **Palace of Culture**, which has a theatre, shops and art galleries. Construction of the palace began as a gift from the Soviet people in 1960 and was completed in 1966, after the 1961 Soviet-Albanian split. The entrance to the **National Library** is on the south side of the building. Opposite this is the cupola and minaret of the **Et'hem Bey mosque** (1789–1823), one of the most distinctive buildings in the city. Inside the dome is beautifully painted. Built in 1830, Tirana's **clock tower** (☎ 243 292; open 9am-1pm & 4-6pm Mon, Wed & Sat) stands beside the mosque.

On the southern side of the square is the **Skënderbeg equestrian statue** (1968) looking straight up Bulevardi Zogu I north to the train station. Behind Skënderbeg's statue, the boulevard leads directly south to the three arches of **Tirana University** (1957). As you stroll down this tree-lined boulevard you'll see Tirana's **art gallery** (open Tues-Sun), a one-time stronghold of socialist realism, with a significant permanent collection that has been exhibited here since 1976.

**Stalinist Tirana** The wide and once vehicle-free Bulevardi Dëshmorët e Kombit was at one time the stomping ground of Albania's Stalinist *Nomenklatura* (political elite). It is along here and to the west of the boulevard that you can still see the sights of Tirana's not-too-distant Stalinist past.

Start your walk down Bulevardi Dëshmorët e Kombit, at the now brightly painted **government buildings**, housing various ministries. Just behind the last building on the left-hand side were the headquarters of the once much-feared **Sigurimi**, communist Albania's dreaded secret police.

Continue along Bulevardi Dëshmorët e Kombit to the bridge over the Lana River. On

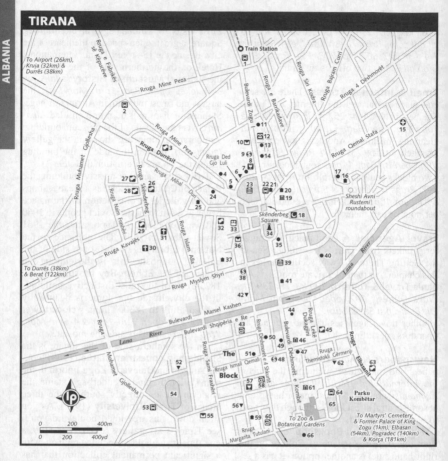

TIRANA

the left just over the river you'll see the sloping, white-marble walls of the **former Enver Hoxha Museum** (1988) – an expensive white elephant later used as a disco and conference centre. Just beyond and on the right, is the dour, four-storey, former **Central Committee building** (1955) of the Party of Labour, which also houses various ministries.

Opposite the Central Committee building is the **Prime Minister's Residence** now permanently guarded by strutting soldiers. On the balcony on the 2nd floor Enver Hoxha and cronies, such as Gog Nushi, Qemal Stafa and Hysni Kapo, would stand and review military parades.

Follow Rruga Ismail Qemali, the street on the southern side of the Central Committee building, and enter the once totally forbidden

**Block** – the former exclusive and strictly off-limits residential district of the Communist-party faithful. When the area was first opened to the general public in 1991, great crowds of Albanians flocked to see the style in which their 'proletarian' leaders lived. The three-storey pastel-coloured house on the corner of Rruga Dëshmorët e 4 Shkurtit and Rruga Ismail Qemali is the **former residence of Enver Hoxha**. The house is now guarded by a couple of bored-looking soldiers and doesn't seem to have any active function.

**Other Sights**  Beyond the university at the end of Bulevardi Dëshmorët e Kombit is **Parku Kombëtar** (National Park), with an open-air theatre (Teatri Veror) and an artificial lake. There's a superb view across the lake to

## TIRANA

| | | | | | |
|---|---|---|---|---|---|
| **PLACES TO STAY** | | 12 | Telephone Centre | 39 | Art Gallery |
| 16 | Qëndra Stefan | 13 | Albania Interlines | 40 | Parliament |
| 20 | Hotel Miniri | 14 | Olympic Airways | 43 | F@stech |
| 21 | Tirana International Hotel; | 15 | ABS Health Foundation | 44 | Former Enver Hoxha |
| | Turkish Airlines | 17 | Public Market | | Museum |
| 25 | Hotel California | 18 | Et'hem Bey Mosque; Clock | 45 | Macedonian Embassy |
| 37 | Europa International | | Tower | 46 | Prime Minister's |
| | Hotel | 19 | Palace of Culture; | | Residence |
| 41 | Hotel Dajti | | International Bookshop | 47 | Avis Car Rentals, Hotel |
| 59 | Hotel Endri | 22 | Bus Departure Point for | | Europapark Tirana; Swiss; |
| | | | Prishtina | | Austrian Airlines |
| **PLACES TO EAT** | | 23 | National Museum of | 48 | American Bank of Albania |
| 6 | Piazza Restaurant | | History; Alitalia | 49 | Former Central Committee |
| 42 | La Voglia | 24 | World Travel | | Building |
| 52 | Ujevara | 26 | Bulgarian Embassy | 50 | DHL |
| 56 | Il Passatore | 27 | German Embassy | 51 | Former Residence of Enver |
| 62 | Villa Ambassador | 28 | UK Embassy | | Hoxha |
| | | 29 | Greek Embassy | 53 | Southern Bus Station |
| **OTHER** | | 30 | Orthodox Church of | 54 | Selman Stërmasi (Dinamo) |
| 1 | Bus & Minibus Station to | | Holy Evangelist | | Stadium |
| | Durrës & North | 31 | Catholic Church of St | 55 | Post Office Sub Branch |
| 2 | Kruja Minibus Stop | | Anthony | 57 | Murphy's |
| 3 | Yugoslavia Embassy | 32 | Turkish Embassy | 58 | Net 1 |
| 4 | Albtransport | 33 | Kinema Millennium | 60 | Interalb Internet |
| 5 | Albania Travel & Tours | 34 | Skënderbeg Equestrian Statue | 61 | Palace of Congresses |
| 7 | DHL | 35 | Government Buildings; | 63 | US Embassy |
| 8 | London Bar | | Former Sigurimi HQ | 64 | Minibuses to Elbasan, |
| 9 | Alpha Bank ATM | 36 | Main Post Office | | Pogradec & Korça |
| 10 | Post Office Sub Branch | 38 | Unioni Financiar Tiranë | 65 | Qemal Stafa Stadium |
| 11 | Souvenir Stela | | Exchange | 66 | Tirana University |

the olive-coloured hills. Cross the dam retaining the lake to the rather moribund **Tirana Zoo**. Ask directions to the **botanical gardens**, just west of the zoo. If you're keen, you can hire a rowing boat and paddle on the lake.

About 1km southeast on Rruga Elbasanit is the **Martyrs' Cemetery** (Varrezat e Dëshmorëve), where some 900 partisans who died in WWII are buried. Large crowds once gathered here every 16 October, Enver Hoxha's birthday, since this is where he and other top Communist Party members were interred. (In May 1992 Hoxha's coffin was dug up and reburied in a common grave in a public cemetery on the other side of town.) The hill-top setting, with a great view over the city and mountains, is subdued, and a white figure of Mother Albania (1972) stands watch. Nearby, on the other side of the highway, is the **former palace of King Zogu**, now a government guesthouse.

## Places to Stay
**Private Rooms** Staying in private, rented apartments or with local families is the best budget accommodation in Tirana, but they can be hard to find. Owners expect you to call them and arrange a pick-up. Newer private hotels are pleasant but high priced.

**Albania Travel & Tours** (see Travel Agencies earlier in this section) has private rooms for around 2600 lekë per person. Other travel agencies may also find you a private room.

Tiny **Hotel Endri** (☎ 244 168, 229 334; Pall 27, Sh. 3 Ap. 30, Rruga Vaso Pasha 27; rooms US$20) is a decent deal. The 'hotel', essentially just two rooms next to manager Petrit Alikaj's apartment, is sparkling clean and new, with nice bathrooms and excellent showers. Handily, Petrit is also a taxi driver.

**Qëndra Stefan** (Stephen Center; ☎/fax 253 924; e stephenc@icc.al.eu.org; Rruga Hoxha Tasim 1; singles/doubles including breakfast $30/50) is a better option and much easier to find. Rooms are modern, bright and breezy and for nonsmokers and nondrinkers only. (See also Places to Eat later in this section.)

**Hotels** Just off Rruga Durrësit is the nifty **Hotel California** (☎/fax 232 228; Rruga Mihal Duri 21; singles/doubles US$50/70 including breakfast), which has clean rooms with minibar and TV.

A quite pleasant private hotel is **Europa International Hotel** (☎/fax 227 403; *Rruga Myslym Shyri 44/2; singles/doubles including breakfast US$60/70*), with modern rooms and parking out front. It can be hard to find this place as it is actually off Rruga Myslym Shyri in a back street. Ask for directions.

For a taste of Stalinist decor step into the somewhat dour and ageing **Hotel Dajti** (☎ 251 031, fax 251 036; *Bulevardi Dëshmorët e Kombit 6; singles US$50-60, doubles US$80*). The Dajti was erected in the 1930s by the Italians and has changed very little since then.

Just off Skënderbeg Square is the small **Hotel Miniri** (☎ 230 930, fax 233 096; *Rruga e Dibres 3; singles/doubles including breakfast US$60/96*), with adequate but unexciting rooms with phone and TV. Its main advantage is its central location.

The **Tirana International Hotel** (☎ 234 185, fax 234 188; W www.hoteltirana.albnet .net; *Skënderbeg Square; singles/doubles including breakfast US$140/190*) has well-appointed rooms. The hotel accepts MasterCard, American Express and Diner's Club.

## Places to Eat

There is no shortage of small restaurants, cafés and snack bars on and around Skënderbeg Square and Bulevardi Dëshmorët e Kombit.

Fancy breakfast, a cuppa or sandwich – perhaps a Chinese lunch, pizza, nachos or even fajitas? Call into **Qëndra Stefan** (☎ 253 924; *Rruga Hoxha Tasim 1; open 8am-10pm; open Mon-Sat*), a friendly, nonsmoking place run by Americans. Lunch specials are posted on a blackboard outside. It's near the fruit and vegetable market

Among Tirana's innumerable pizza places, the two-floor **La Voglia** (☎ 228 678; *Rruga Dëshmorët e 4 Shkurtit; pizza 350-400 lekë; open 8am-11pm*), close to the river, serves a very good pizza and has menus in English.

One of Tirana's more popular restaurants is **Il Passatore** (*Antonella's;* ☎ 233 420; *Rruga Vaso Pasha 22/1; mains per person 1200 lekë; open noon-4pm & 7pm-11pm Mon-Sat*). Convenient to Murphy's pub for the after-dinner wind-up, food and service here are excellent, with delicious specials of fish or pasta and a diverse salad bar.

**Piazza Restaurant** (☎ 230 706; *Rruga Ded Gjo Luli; mains per person 1400 lekë; open noon-4pm & 7pm-11pm*) is a tastefully designed and well-appointed establishment just

north of Skënderbeg Square. The food and service are excellent and prices, for what you get, are reasonable.

The **Villa Ambassador** (☎ 038-202 4293; *Rruga Themistokli Gërmenji; mains per person 1500 lekë; open noon-11.30pm*), tucked away on a small street near the US embassy, is among Tirana's best for atmosphere. Try to sample a plateful of Albanian specialities like rice wrapped in grape leaves, *burek* (cheese or meat pie) and more.

A little out of the way is the **Ujevara** (☎ 243 702; *Rruga Gjin Bue Shpata; open 12-11pm; pasta dishes 600-700 lekë*). Italian pasta and fresh salads are the key ingredients at this pleasant eatery near the southern bus station.

## Entertainment

For the low-down on events and exhibitions check out the leaflet *ARTirana*, which contains English, French, Italian and Albanian summaries of the cultural events currently showing in town.

Also check the posters outside the **Palace of Culture** (*Skënderbeg Square; performances from 7pm, winter from 6pm*) for ballet or opera. You can usually buy tickets half an hour before the show.

Tirana has an Irish pub: **Murphy's** (☎ 038-203 7854; *Rruga Abdyl Frashëri; open 2pm until late*) serves up Guinness on tap, Murphy's and a host of other brews, making it the before-and-after-dinner darling of the expat community.

**London Bar** (☎ 228 851; *Bulevardi Zogu I 51*), near the Tirana International Hotel, is also a popular hang-out with a restaurant.

Pop concerts and other musical events often take place in the **Qemal Stafa Stadium** next to the university. Look out for street banners bearing details of upcoming events. At the stadium there are also football matches held every Saturday and Sunday afternoon, except during July and August.

The biggest cinema in Tirana is the **Kinema Millennium** (☎ 248 647; *Rruga e Kavajës; admission 200-400 lekë*), near Skënderbeg Square, which shows recent box-office hits (earlier shows are cheaper).

## Shopping

Tirana's **public market**, north of the Sheshi Avni Rustemi roundabout several blocks east of the clock tower, is largest on Thursday and Sunday. A few shops sell folkloric objects such as carved wooden trays, small boxes, wall hangings and bone necklaces.

A good souvenir shop is **Souvenir Stela** *(Bulevardi Zogu I)*, where the offerings include brass plates with the Albanian insignia and ashtrays that are very cleverly modelled on Hoxha's bunkers.

## Getting There & Away

**Air** For information about routes and fares of flights to/from Rinas airport see the Getting There & Away section earlier in this chapter.

Many of the airline offices are on Rruga Durrësit, just off Skënderbeg Square. **Alitalia** *(☎ 230 023; Skënderbeg Square)* has an office behind the National Museum of History, and **Swiss International Air Lines** *(☎/fax 232 011)* and **Austrian Airlines** *(☎/fax 374 355)* are at Hotel Europapark Tirana. **Olympic Airways** *(☎ 228 960; Ve-Ve Business Centre, Bulevardi Zogu I)* is north of the Tirana International Hotel, and **Turkish Airlines** *(☎ 234 185)* is in the Tirana International Hotel.

**Bus** Buses and minibuses between Tirana and other towns are private. There are two main bus/minibus departure points: the Selman Stërmasi (Dinamo) Stadium for buses to the south, and the lot in front of the train station for buses to Durrës and the north. Minibuses to Elbasan, Pogradec and Korça leave from the north side of the Qemal Stafa Stadium, while minibuses to Kruja leave from a rather loosely defined area on Rruga Mine Peza.

The following table will give you an idea of distances and average costs of one-way bus trips from Tirana. Minibuses are usually 40% to 50% more expensive than buses, but buses do not cover all destinations.

| Destination | Distance | Duration | Cost (lekë) |
| --- | --- | --- | --- |
| Berat | 122km | 3½ hours | 250 |
| Durrës | 38km | 1 hour | 100 |
| Elbasan | 54km | 1½ hours | 300 |
| Fier | 113km | 3 hours | 260 |
| Gjirokastra | 232km | 7 hours | 700 |
| Korça | 181km | 4 hours | 700 |
| Kruja | 32km | 45 minutes | 150 |
| Kukës | 208km | 8 hours | 1000 |
| Pogradec | 150km | 3½ hours | 600 |
| Saranda | 284km | 8 hours | 800 |
| Shkodra | 116km | 2½ hours | 300 |
| Vlora | 147km | 4 hours | 300 |

Note that both buses and minibuses normally leave when full. Departures tend to commence early (5am to 8am) and sometimes cease operation by mid-afternoon. Pay the driver or conductor on the bus.

**Train** The train station is at the northern end of Bulevardi Zogu I. Eight trains daily go to Durrës (55 lekë, one hour, 36km). Trains also depart for Elbasan (160 lekë, four hours, three daily), for Pogradec (245 lekë, seven hours, twice daily), for Shkodra (150 lekë, 3½ hours, twice daily) and for Vlora (210 lekë, 5½ hours, twice daily).

## Getting Around

**To/From the Airport** A taxi to/from the airport should cost about €30 or US$20, depending on what currency you have in your pocket.

**Car & Motorcycle** Some of the major hotels offer guarded parking; others have parking available out the front. **Avis** *(☎ 235 011, fax 235 024; e gazi@albaniaonline.net)* in the Hotel Europapark Tirana is the only car-rental agency currently operating. Contact the office for rates.

**Taxi** Taxi stands dot the city and charge 400 lekë for a ride inside Tirana (600 lekë at night). Work out the price before getting in and reach an agreement with the driver *before* setting off. **Radio Taxi** *(☎ 377 777)*, with 24-hour service, is particularly reliable. These local taxis are much cheaper than the Mercedes taxis parked at the large hotels.

The older, private taxis are usually found around the market or at bus and train stations, and the shiny, Mercedes, tourist taxis park outside the Hotel Europapark Tirana and Tirana International Hotel (which quote fares in US dollars but also take lekë).

# Around Tirana

## DURRËS
☎ 052 • pop 85,000
If the bustle, dust and confusion of Tirana are too much for you, consider basing yourself in Durrës. Once the grim, workaday main port of Albania, Durrës is now a relaxed, more laid-back alternative to the capital, with some good places to eat and sleep. Moreover, Durrës still

retains the time-honoured tradition of the *xhiro* – the evening street promenade, when the main drag is closed and all the town comes out to walk and talk, to see and to be seen.

Unlike Tirana, Durrës is an ancient city. In 627 BC the Greeks founded Epidamnos (Durrës), whose name the Romans changed to Dyrrachium. It was the largest port on the eastern Adriatic and the start of the Via Egnatia (an extension of the Via Appia to Constantinople). The famous Via Appia (Appian Way) to Rome began 150km southwest of Durrës at the town of Brindisi, Italy.

Durrës changed hands frequently before being taken by the Turks in 1501, under whom the port dwindled into insignificance. A slow revival began in the 17th century and from 1914 to 1920 Durrës was the capital of Albania. Landings here by Mussolini's troops on 7 April 1939 met fierce though brief resistance, and those who fell are regarded as the first martyrs in the War of National Liberation.

Today, Roman ruins and Byzantine fortifications embellish the town, which lies 38km west of Tirana. On a bay southeast of the city there are long, sandy beaches where a collection of tourist hotels and restaurants have sprung up like Hoxha's bunkers during the bad old days of communism.

## Information

The **Savings Bank of Albania** *(open 8am-2pm Mon-Fri)*, across the bus parking lot from the train station, changes travellers cheques and offers MasterCard advances for a 1% commission.

The **post office** and **telephone centre** are located one block west of the train and bus stations. Several Internet cafés operate in the town. Among them are the **Interalb Internet** *(Rruga N Frashëri)*, the **Galaxy Internet Cafe** *(☎ 038-213 5637, Rruga Taulantia)* and **Patrik Internet** *(Rruga Aleksandër Goga)*. All charge around 240 lekë per hour.

## Things to See

The **Archaeological Museum**, on the waterfront promenade near the port, is worth a visit. Look out for the Belle of Durrës mosaic, which gives a view of ancient Dyrrachium and is one of its more notable exhibits.

Beyond the museum are the 6th-century **Byzantine city walls**, built after the Visigoth invasion of AD 481 and supplemented by round Venetian towers in the 14th century.

The impressive but unrestored **Roman amphitheatre**, built between the 1st and 2nd centuries AD, is on the hillside just inside the walls of the city. Much of the amphitheatre has now been excavated and you are able to see a small, built-in, 10th-century Byzantine church decorated with wall mosaics. Farther up the hill you will come to the **citadel**, which is the highest point of what must have once been an impressive fortification used for protection of the city.

The former **palace of King Ahmet Zogu** is on the hill top west of the amphitheatre. However it is a military area and you cannot get into the palace grounds. The 20-minute walk up the hills and the views are worth it though. The next hill beyond the enclosure bears a **lighthouse** that would afford a splendid view of Albanian coastal defences, Durrës and the entire coast, if you could get past the fence surrounding it.

As you're exploring the centre of the city, stop to see the **Roman baths** directly behind Aleksandër Moisiu Theatre, on the central square. The large **Xhamia e Madhe Durrës** mosque on the square was erected with Egyptian aid in 1993, to replace one destroyed in the 1979 earthquake.

## Places to Stay

Durrës has a handful of pleasant, mid-priced hotels in the centre and a string of new, resort-style hotels on the long, sandy beaches 8km south towards the settlement of Golem.

**Albania Travel & Tours** *(☎ 24 276, ☎/fax 254 50; Rruga Durrah; open 8am-8pm daily)*, near the port, may be able to help arrange a private room with advance notice.

The best budget choice is the **B&B Tedeschini** *(☎ 24 343, 038-224 6303; ⓔ ipmcrsp@ icc.al.eu.org; Dom Nikoll Kaçorri 5; B&B US$15)* in the gracious, 19th-century house of a personable Italian-Albanian couple. If you want lunch and dinner it's just US$10 more. The place is a bit hard to find; from the square fronting the mosque, walk towards the restaurant Il Castello. Take the first right, then a quick left, then a quick right. The house is 50m on the right down this street and has an unmarked red iron gate.

About 3km from Durrës and 400m back from the beach is the slightly more expensive **Green Villa** *(☎ 60 345; ⓔ bendushi_2001@ yahoo.com; singles/doubles from US$20/40)*. There are 16 rooms, all with private facilities.

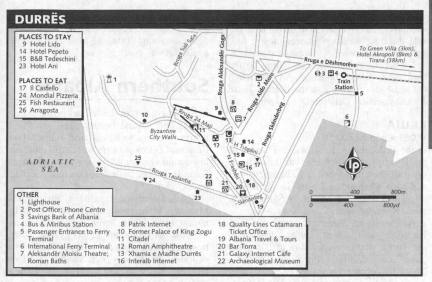

**DURRËS**

PLACES TO STAY
9   Hotel Lido
14  Hotel Pepeto
15  B&B Tedeschini
23  Hotel Ani

PLACES TO EAT
17  Il Castello
24  Mondial Pizzeria
25  Fish Restaurant
26  Arragosta

To Green Villa (3km),
Hotel Akropoli (8km) &
Tirana (38km)

Rruga e Dëshmorëve

Train
Station

Rruga Sali Saliu

Rruga Aleksandër Goga

Rruga Aldo Moro

Rruga 24 Maji

Byzantine
City Walls

Rruga Skenderbeg

ADRIATIC
SEA

Rruga Taulantia

H. Troplini

N. Frashëri

Skenderbeg

OTHER
1   Lighthouse
2   Post Office; Phone Centre
3   Savings Bank of Albania
4   Bus & Minibus Station
5   Passenger Entrance to Ferry
    Terminal
6   International Ferry Terminal
7   Aleksandër Moisiu Theatre;
    Roman Baths

8   Patrik Internet
10  Former Palace of King Zogu
11  Citadel
12  Roman Amphitheatre
13  Xhamia e Madhe Durrës
16  Interalb Internet

18  Quality Lines Catamaran
    Ticket Office
19  Albania Travel & Tours
20  Bar Torra
21  Galaxy Internet Cafe
22  Archaeological Museum

0        400        800m
0        400        800yd

Another 5km south you will find the **Hotel Akropoli** (☎ 0579-22 142, 038-214 0070; Golem; singles/doubles US$30/40). This is a modern and pleasant resort-style hotel with an in-house restaurant. Ring beforehand for a complimentary chauffeur service.

The 13-room **Hotel Lido** (☎/fax 27 941; Rruga Aleksandër Goga; singles/doubles US$35/46), in the centre of town, has clean, pleasant rooms with TV, phone, fridge, heating and air-conditioning. The cheery **Hotel Pepeto** (☎ 24 190, ☎/fax 26 346; singles/doubles US$40/60), just east of the square fronting the mosque, is another good choice, with rates that include breakfast and laundry. The owner speaks English.

At the waterfront is the more upmarket **Hotel Ani** (☎ 24 288, fax 30 478; Lagja 1, Rruga Taulantia; singles/doubles US$60/90), where the comfy rooms all have air-con, TV, telephone and minibar.

### Places to Eat

By far the best place to eat in town is the restaurant **Il Castello** (☎ 268 87; Rruga H Troplini 3), which has outstanding pastas (try the seafood pasta at 450 lekë) and a good selection of fish.

For a meal of fresh shrimp or fish on a patio overlooking the water, try the **Arragosta** (☎ 26 477, Rruga Taulantia), on the point about an 800m walk west of the town centre.

**Mondial Pizzeria** (☎ 27 946; Rruga Taulantia), which is on the waterfront on the way to Arragosta, is a busy little pizzeria serving good-sized pizzas and pasta dishes. Another option is the **Fish Restaurant** (Rruga Taulantia), which is universally recommended by the locals for its fresh fish. The Hotel Lido (see Places to Stay) also has its own restaurant for guests and outsiders alike.

Otherwise, if you happen to be along the beach strip south of Durrës, numerous restaurants offer seaside dining.

### Entertainment

The niftiest place for a coffee or beer is **Bar Torra** in the tower beside the port entrance. You can sip your beverage of choice while inside or atop the tower. Alternatively, you could pay a visit to the **Aleksandër Moisiu Theatre** in the centre of Durrës. Its frequent theatrical productions are performed only in Albanian however.

### Getting There & Away

Albania's 720km railway network centres on Durrës. There are eight trains a day to Tirana (55 lekë, one hour), two to Shkodra (150 lekë, 3½ hours) via Lezha, three to Pogradec (245 lekë, 6¾ hours) via Elbasan, and two to Vlora (210 lekë, five hours) via Fier. The train station is beside the Tirana highway, conveniently close to central Durrës.

Minibuses to Tirana (150 lekë, one hour) and buses (100 lekë, one hour) leave from beside the train station whenever they're full, and service elsewhere is frequent as well.

Numerous travel agencies along Rruga Durrah handle ferry bookings. All offer much the same service (see also the Getting There & Away section earlier in this chapter).

## KRUJA
☎ 053 • pop 17,400

In the 12th century, Kruja was the capital of the Principality of Arberit, but this hill-top town attained its greatest fame between 1443 and 1468 when national hero George Kastrioti (1405–68), also known as Skënderbeg, made Kruja his seat.

At a young age, Kastrioti, son of an Albanian prince, was handed over as a hostage to the Turks, who converted him to Islam and gave him a military education at Edirne. There he became known as Iskënder (after Alexander the Great) and Sultan Murat II promoted him to the rank of *bey* (governor), thus the name Skënderbeg.

In 1443 the Turks suffered a defeat at the hands of the Hungarians at Niš, which gave the nationally minded Skënderbeg the opportunity he had been waiting for to abandon the Ottoman army and Islam and rally his fellow Albanians against the Turks. Among the 13 Turkish invasions he subsequently repulsed was that led by Murat II himself in 1450. Pope Calixtus III named Skënderbeg the 'captain general of the Holy See' and Venice formed an alliance with him. The Turks besieged Kruja four times. Though beaten back in 1450, 1466 and 1467, they took control of Kruja in 1478 (after Skënderbeg's death) and Albanian resistance was suppressed.

The main sight in Kruja is the impressive **castle** and its rather retro-modernistic **Skënderbeg Museum** *(admission 300 lekë; open 8am-1pm & 3pm-8pm daily)*. The displays are mainly replicas of paintings and armour depicting Skënderbeg's struggle against the Ottomans.

The **Ethnographic Museum** *(☎ 22 225; admission 300 lekë; open 8am-1pm & 3pm-8pm daily)* is also worth a look for its reconstruction of a 19th-century Albanian house as well as folk dress, pottery and copper goods.

Kruja is 6.5km off the main road to Tirana and is visited as much for its crucial historical importance and striking hill-side location as

for its wide range of good-quality souvenirs, such as rugs and copperware. A cab to Kruja will cost around 3000 lekë from Tirana while a minibus will cost 150 lekë.

# Southern Albania

The southern part of the country is rich in historical and natural beauty. Apollonia and Butrint are renowned classical ruins, while Berat and Gjirokastra are wonderful museum towns and strongholds of the Tosk tradition. Saranda, on the Ionian Sea, is a developing resort town.

Southeast of the expansive, agricultural Myzaqeja Plain, the land becomes extremely mountainous, with lovely valleys such as those of the Osum and Drino Rivers, where Berat and Gjirokastra are situated. The 124km of Ionian coast north from Saranda to Vlora are stunning, with 2000m mountains falling directly to the sea.

## GJIROKASTRA
☎ 0762 • pop 24,500

Travellers from Greece may well find that this strikingly picturesque town, midway between Fier and Ioannina, is an ideal spot for the first night's stay in Albania. Gjirokastra (Gjirokastër) is reminiscent of an Albanian eagle perched on the mountainside with a mighty citadel for its head. The fortress surveys the Drino Valley above three- and four-storey tower houses clinging to the slopes. The town's Greek name of 'Argyrokastro' means 'silver castle'.

Gjirokastra was well established by the 13th century, but the arrival of the Turks during 1417 brought about a decline. By the 17th century Gjirokastra was thriving once again, with a flourishing bazaar where embroidery, felt, silk and the still-famous white cheese were traded. Ali Pasha Tepelena seized the town in the early 19th century and then he strengthened the citadel.

Gjirokastra was the birthplace of former dictator Enver Hoxha and for that reason special care was taken to retain its traditional architecture and both buildings and streets are made of the same white-and-black stone.

The old town, with its narrow, cobbled streets, sits high up on the hill side while the new town spills down to the main Kakavija-Tirana highway.

## Things to See

Gjirokastra's **castle** (500 lekë, open 8am-8pm daily) is its main feature, although in fairness its main drawcard is the walk up and the views it affords. The grounds are rather overgrown and the desultory collection of WWII armaments in its interior colonnades are rather uninspiring. The bizarre sight of a long-downed and disintegrating US military jet on the ramparts adds a rather unreal air to the scene. The castle courtyards were used as a political prison during the Hoxha years. The tiny cells are particularly grim.

## Places to Stay & Eat

The best place to stay is **Guest House Haxhi Kotoni** (☎ 35 26; Lagja Palorto 8, Rruga Bashkim Kokona; singles/doubles 1500/2000 lekë). This neat but tiny B&B offers clean and comfy double rooms with bathroom, TV and heating in a traditional old house. Look for the B&B sign 220m northeast of the mosque in the old town.

Eating options in the old town are pretty thin on the ground. **Bar Fantazia** (☎ 69 91), commanding the best view in the old town, is a café-bar and sometimes restaurant. Walk downhill into the new town to seek out a wider variety of choices. **First Pizza** is a Western-style fast-food place. It does excellent pizzas for around 280 lekë. Look for it on the north side of the long street leading from the old town to the main highway.

## Getting There & Away

Buses to and from Gjirokastra depart from or stop on the main highway, 1½km from the old town. Taxis can take you into town for about 200 lekë. Buses to Tirana (1000 lekë, five hours) are fairly frequent while there are four a day to Saranda (200 lekë, one hour). You'll need to take a taxi to get to the Greek border at Kakavija (1500 lekë, 30 minutes).

## SARANDA

☎ 0732 • pop 12,000

Saranda (Sarandë) is a small town on the Gulf of Saranda, between the mountains and the Ionian Sea, 61km southwest of Gjirokastra. An early Christian monastery dedicated to 40 saints (Santi Quaranta) gave Saranda its name. This southernmost harbour of Albania was once the ancient port of Onchesmos. It is now considered by most Albanians as their most 'exotic' holiday destination and in fact

it attracts a fair percentage of the domestic travel market. For foreigners Saranda's main attraction is that it is a useful entry point to and from Corfu in Greece. The sunny climate, a choice of good hotels and restaurants and the nearby ruins of Butrint also add to its traveller interest. The town's beaches are slowly being re-landscaped and the long promenade makes for some relaxed evening strolls.

## Information

Change money at **Exchange Mario** (☎ 23 61; Rruga Vangeli Gramoza) or with the crowds of moneychangers that hang out near the central square. Receive money at the **Western Union** office in the modern **post office** (☎ 23 45) nearby. Cardphones abound while mobile-phone users can pick up Greek transmitters as well as Albanian ones. Check email at **Ecom Internet** (☎ 39 95; Rruga Adem Shema), close to the centre.

## Things to See

The ancient ruins of **Butrint** (☎ 0732-46 00; 700 lekë; open 8am-7.30pm), 18km south of Saranda, are surprisingly extensive and interesting and are part of a 29-sq-km national park. The poet Virgil (70–19 BC) claimed that the Trojans founded Buthroton (Butrint), but no evidence of this has been found. Although the site had been inhabited long before, Greeks from Corfu settled on the hill in Butrint in the 6th century BC. Within a century Butrint had become a fortified trading city with an acropolis. The lower town began to develop in the 3rd century BC and many large stone buildings existed when the Romans took over in 167 BC. The site lies by a channel connecting salty Lake Butrint to the sea. A triangular **fortress**, erected by warlord Ali Pasha Tepelena in the early 19th century, watches over the ramshackle vehicular ferry that crosses the narrow channel.

Secluded in the forest below the acropolis is Butrint's 3rd-century BC **Greek theatre**, which was also in use during the Roman period. Close by are the small **public baths**, which have geometric mosaics. Deeper in the forest is a wall covered with crisp Greek inscriptions, and a 6th-century palaeo-Christian **baptistry** decorated with colourful mosaics of animals and birds. The mosaics are covered by protective sand. Beyond a 6th-century basilica stands a massive **Cyclopean wall** dating back to the 4th century BC. Over one gate is a splendid relief of a lion killing a bull, symbolic of a protective force vanquishing assailants.

In a crenellated brick building on top of the acropolis is a **museum** (if it is open) full of statuary from the site. There are good views from the terrace.

Butrint's prosperity continued throughout the Roman period and the Byzantines made it an ecclesiastical centre. Then the city declined; it was almost abandoned when Italian archaeologists arrived in 1927 and began carting off any relics of value to Italy until WWII interrupted their work. Some of these have been returned to Tirana's National Museum of History. A cab to Butrint will cost around 2000 lekë. There are no buses.

The **Blue Eye spring**, 15km east of Saranda, signposted *Syri i Kalter* to the left off the Gjirokastra road and before the ascent over the pass to the Drino Valley, is definitely worth seeing. Its iridescent blue water gushes from the depths of the earth and feeds into the Bistrica River. French divers have descended as far as 70m, but the spring's actual depth is still unknown.

### Places to Stay & Eat
An excellent budget choice is **Hotel Lili** (☎ *37 64; Lagja No. 3; singles/doubles 3000/5000 lekë*). All rooms have fridges, fans, TV and the use of a washing machine. There is a **restaurant** downstairs.

Excellent wood-oven pizzas are served up at **Pizzeri Evangjelos** (☎ *54 29; ne Shetitore; pizzas 350-600 lekë*), at the southern end of the promenade, while farther south and right on the waterside is the small and friendly **Restaurant Emmanueli** (*ne Shetitore; meals 700-800 lekë*).

### Getting There & Away
A daily ferry and hydrofoil service plies between Saranda and Corfu (€14 one way). Call **Finikas Lines** (☎ *30-9-4485 3228*) in Corfu for schedules from Corfu. The hydrofoil normally leaves Saranda at 10am.

Buses to Tirana (1000 lekë, eight hours) and Gjirokastra (300 lekë, 1½ hours) leave from Saranda's bus station four times daily, while there are two to three services a week to Korça (1000 lekë, eight hours).

A taxi to the Greek border at Kakavija will cost 3500 lekë while a cab to the border near Konispoli will cost around 3000 lekë.

## KORÇA
☎ 082 • pop 62,200
If you are heading to or from Greece via Florina or Kastoria then the small, breezy town of Korça may be the best stopover. Situated at the edge of a vast agricultural plain that stretches almost all the way to Lake Ohrid, this cultured, historical town is worth staying in for at least one day. Transport to and from the town is generally good and, while there's no specific drawcard, Korça's broad, tree-lined boulevards are a welcome respite from the often dreary, mud-stained streets of other rural Albanian towns.

### Places to Stay & Eat
The best budget option is the signposted **Hotel Gold** (☎ *46 894; Rruga Kiço Golniku 5; singles/doubles 1888/2830 lekë*). The clean rooms have TV and heating as well as private bathrooms. Follow the signs for 800m from the avenue leading from the bus stop to the main square.

In the centre of town you can't miss the modern **Hotel Grand** (☎ *43 168, fax 42 677; Central Square; singles/doubles including breakfast 2950/4720 lekë*). Once a grim, Stalinist-era guesthouse, this renovated hotel is now quite pleasant and comfortable. The rooms all have bathroom and TV.

Both the above hotels have their own restaurants. **Restaurant Alfa** (☎ *44 385; meals 700-800 lekë*) is just off the main square and is a pretty decent eating option. Fairly substantial Greek-style cuisine is on offer. Up a notch is the **Dolce Vita** (☎ *42 480; pizzas 380 lekë*), 200m to the left of the large Orthodox church and just south of the main square. This is the poshest restaurant-pizzeria in town.

### Getting There & Away
Buses and minibuses all congregate at the official – and thankfully mud-less – bus-parking area 200m, which is north of the main square. Arriving minibuses will normally drop their passengers off on the main square also. Minibuses to Tirana (700 lekë, four hours) depart when full.

For Greece there are three buses daily to Thessaloniki (€19, seven hours) and four a week to Athens (€30, 16 hours) at noon on Sunday, Monday, Thursday and Friday. Go to the **ticket office** in the street office behind the Grand Hotel to book your seat.

Note: you can take a minibus to the border for around 300 to 400 lekë, but a Greek taxi from the Albanian-Greek border to Florina or Kastoria alone will cost you a minimum of €30. There are only two to three inconveniently timed local buses daily linking the Greek border village of Krystallopigi with Florina, and none to Kastoria. The direct international bus from Korça is by far the best option.

## FIER & APOLLONIA
☎ 0623 • pop 48,500
Fier is a large town by the Gjanica River at a junction of road and rail routes, 89km south of Durrës. Albania's oil industry is centred on Fier, with a fertiliser plant, an oil refinery and a thermal power plant fuelled by natural gas. Fier has a pleasant **riverside promenade**, the imposing 13th-century **Orthodox Monastery of St Mary**, with wonderful icons inside, and the rich **Museum of Apollonia**.

By far the most interesting sight in the vicinity is the ruins of ancient Apollonia (Pojan), 12km west of Fier, set on a hill top surrounded by impressive bunkers. Apollonia was founded by Corinthian Greeks in 588 BC and quickly grew into an important city-state, minting its own currency. Under the Romans the city became a great cultural centre with a famous school of philosophy.

Julius Caesar rewarded Apollonia with the title 'free city' for supporting him against Pompey the Great during a civil war in the 1st century BC, and sent his nephew Octavius, the future Emperor Augustus, to complete his studies there. After a series of military disasters, the population moved southward into present-day Vlora (the ancient Avlon), and by the 5th century only a small village with its own bishop remained at Apollonia.

Only a small part of ancient Apollonia has so far been excavated, but look out for the very picturesque 3rd-century BC **House of Mosaics**, one of the site's highlights.

Fier and Apollonia are best visited on day trips from Tirana or Durrës.

## BERAT
☎ 062 • pop 47,700
Berat, Albania's second-most-important museum town, is sometimes called the 'city of a thousand windows' for the many openings in the white-plastered, red-roofed houses on terraces overlooking the Osum River. Along a ridge high above the gorge is a 14th-century **citadel** that shelters small Orthodox churches. On the slope below this, all the way down to the river, is **Mangalem**, the old Muslim quarter. A seven-arched stone bridge (1780) leads to **Gorica**, the Christian quarter.

In the 3rd century BC an Illyrian fortress called Antipatria was built here on the site of an earlier settlement. The Byzantines strengthened the hill-top fortifications in the 5th and 6th centuries, as did the Bulgarians 400 years later. The Serbs, who occupied the citadel in 1345, renamed it Beligrad, or 'White City', which has become today's Berat. In 1450 the Ottoman Turks took Berat. The town revived in the 18th and 19th centuries as a Turkish crafts centre specialising in woodcarving. For a brief time in 1944, Berat was the capital of liberated Albania.

While there is accommodation in the town, Berat is best visited on a day trip from Durrës or Tirana as the town does not really afford a convenient stopover for through travellers. You will need to retrace your steps as onwards travel is patchy and difficult at best.

# Northern Albania

Visits to northern Albania still involve some element of risk due to continuing instability of security. The main road corridor from Tirana to the Yugoslav border is generally fine, but travellers are advised to avoid independent travel west of Shkodra, between that town and Kukës, and farther north around Bajram Curri.

Shkodra, the old Gheg capital near the lake of the same name, is a pleasant introduction to Albania for those who are arriving from Yugoslavia. South of here is Lezha and Skënderbeg's tomb.

## SHKODRA
☎ 0224 • pop 91,300
Shkodra (also Shkodër and, in Italian, Scutari), the traditional centre of the Gheg cultural region, is one of the oldest cities in Europe. In 500 BC an Illyrian fortress already guarded the strategic crossing just west of the city where the Buna and Drin Rivers meet, and all traffic moving up the coast from Greece to Montenegro must pass. These rivers drain two of the Balkans' largest lakes: Shkodra, just northwest of the city, and Ohrid, far up the Drin River beyond massive hydroelectric dams. The route inland to Kosova also

begins in Shkodra. North of Shkodra, line after line of cement bunkers point the way to the Han i Hotit border crossing into Yugoslavia (33km). Tirana is 116km south.

Queen Teuta's Illyrian kingdom was based here in the 3rd century BC. Despite wars with Rome in 228 and 219 BC, Shkodra was not taken by the Romans until 168 BC. Later the region passed to Byzantium before becoming the capital of the feudal realm of the Balshas in 1350. In 1396 the Venetians occupied Shkodra's Rozafa Fortress, which they held against Suleiman Pasha in 1473 but lost to Mehmet Pasha in 1479. The Turks lost 14,000 men in the first siege and 30,000 in the second.

As the Ottoman Empire declined in the late 18th century, Shkodra became the centre of a semi-independent pashalik, which led to a blossoming of commerce and crafts. In 1913 Montenegro attempted to annex Shkodra (it succeeded in taking Ulcinj), but this was not recognised by the international community and the town changed hands often during WWI. Badly damaged by the 1979 earthquake, Shkodra was subsequently repaired and now is Albania's fourth-largest town.

Quality private accommodation has been slow to emerge in Shkodra. Travellers are advised to head for Durrës or Tirana.

## Rozafa Fortress

Two kilometres southwest of Shkodra, near the southern end of Lake Shkodra, is Rozafa Fortress, founded by the Illyrians in antiquity and rebuilt much later by the Venetians and Turks. From the highest point there's a marvellous view on all sides.

The fortress derived its name from a woman named Rozafa, who was allegedly walled into the ramparts as an offering to the gods so that the construction would stand. The story goes that Rozafa asked that two holes be left in the stonework so that she could continue to suckle her baby. Nursing women still come to the fortress to smear their breasts with milky water taken from a spring here.

# Andorra

The principality of Andorra, nestled in the Pyrenees mountains between France and Spain, covers an area of just 464 sq km. Although tiny, this political anomaly is at the heart of some of Europe's most dramatic scenery. It's also a budget skiing venue and duty-free shopping haven. These activities, together with great summer walking, attract over eight million visitors a year and bring not only wealth but some unsightly development around the capital of Andorra la Vella.

From the Middle Ages until as recently as 1993, Andorra's sovereignty was invested in two 'princes': the Catholic bishop of the Spanish town of La Seu d'Urgell and the French president (who inherited the job from France's pre-Revolutionary kings). Nowadays, democratic Andorra is a 'parliamentary co-princedom', the bishop and president remaining joint but largely nominal heads of state. Andorra is a member of the United Nations and the Council of Europe, but not a full member of the EU.

Andorrans form only about a quarter of the total population of 66,000, and are outnumbered by Spaniards. The official language is Catalan, which is related to both Spanish and French. Most people speak a couple of these languages and sometimes all three, while younger people, especially in the capital and ski resorts, manage more than a smattering of English also.

# Facts for the Visitor

## VISAS & DOCUMENTS
Visas aren't necessary; the authorities figure that if Spain or France let you in, that's good enough for them – but bring your passport or national ID card with you.

## EMBASSIES & CONSULATES
Andorra has embassies in France and Spain, both of whom have reciprocal diplomatic missions in Andorra.

## MONEY
Although it's not a full member of the EU, Andorra (which previously used the Spanish

## At a Glance

- **Andorra la Vella** – quaint Casa de la Vall, parliament of one of the world's smallest nations
- **La Massana** – gateway to the ski centres of Arinsal and Pal

| | |
|---|---|
| Capital | Andorra la Vella |
| Population | 66,000 |
| Official Language | Catalan |
| Currency | euro |
| Time | GMT/UTC+0100 |
| Country Phone Code | ☎ 376 |

peseta) has chosen to make life simpler for itself by opting for the euro. There are many ATMs and banks throughout the country, especially in Andorra la Vella.

## POST & COMMUNICATIONS
### Post
Andorra has no postal system of its own; France and Spain each operate separate systems with their own Andorran stamps, which are needed only for international mail (letters within the country are delivered free). Regular French and Spanish stamps cannot be used in Andorra.

It's usually swifter to route international mail (except letters to Spain) through the French postal system.

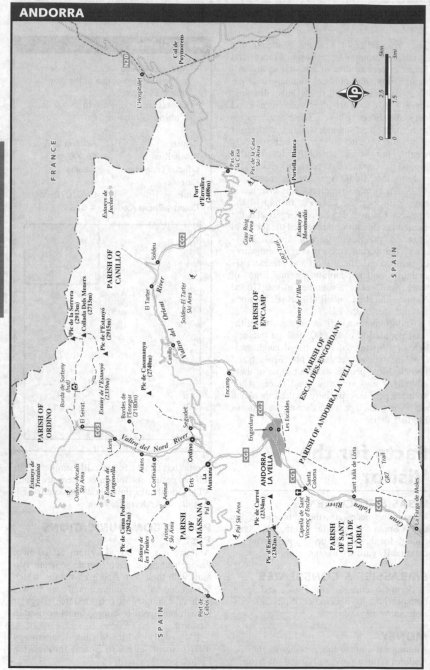

ANDORRA

## Telephone

Andorra's country code is ☎ 376. The cheapest way to make an international call is to buy a *teletarja* (phonecard, sold for €3 at tourist offices and kiosks) and ring off-peak (9pm to 7am plus all day Sunday). At these times a three-minute call to Europe or the US costs €1.62 (€2.31 to Australia). You can't make a reverse-charge (collect) call from Andorra.

## Email & Internet Access

There are a couple of Internet café options in Andorra la Vella (see Information under Andorra la Vella later in this chapter) and Hostal Poblado in Arinsal, 10km northwest of Andorra la Vella (see Places to Stay under Arinsal later in this chapter).

## TIME

Andorra is one hour ahead of GMT/UTC in winter (two hours ahead from the last Sunday in March to the last Sunday in September).

## BUSINESS HOURS

Shops in Andorra la Vella are generally open 9.30am to 1pm and 3.30pm to 8pm daily, except (usually) Sunday afternoon.

## ACTIVITIES

Above the main valleys, you'll find attractive lake-dotted mountain country, good for skiing in winter and walking in summer. The largest and best ski resorts are Soldeu-El Tarter and Pas de la Casa/Grau Roig. Others – Ordino-Arcalís, Arinsal and Pal – are a bit cheaper but often colder and windier. Ski passes cost €19 to €30 a day, depending on location and season; downhill ski-gear is €8 to €10 a day, and snowboards are €15 to €18 a day.

Tourist offices provide a useful English-language booklet, *Sport Activities*, describing numerous hiking and mountain-bike routes. In summer, mountain bikes can be rented in some resorts for around €18 a day.

## ACCOMMODATION

Tourist offices stock a comprehensive free brochure, *Hotels, Restaurants, Apartaments i Cámpings*. Be warned, however, that prices it quotes are merely indicative.

There are no youth hostels and, outside Andorra la Vella, few budget options for independent travellers. In compensation, there are plenty of camping grounds, many beautifully situated. In high season (December to March

### Emergency Services

The Europe-wide telephone number ☎ 112 can be used for the police, fire brigade and ambulance.

and July/August), some hotels put prices up substantially and others don't take in independent travellers.

For walkers, Andorra has 26 off-the-beaten-track *refugis* (mountain refuges); all except one are unstaffed and free. If you're trekking, ask at tourist offices for the free *Mapa de Refugis i Grans Recorreguts*, which pinpoints and describes them all.

# Getting There & Away

The only way to reach Andorra, unless you trek across the mountains, is by road.

## FRANCE

**Autocars Nadal** (☎ 821 138) operates two buses a day (€20, four hours) on Monday, Wednesday, Friday and Sunday, linking Toulouse's Gare Routière (bus station) and Andorra la Vella.

By rail, take a train from Toulouse to either L'Hospitalet (2¼ to 2¾ hours, four daily) or Latour-de-Carol (2½ to 3¼ hours). Two daily connecting buses link Andorra la Vella with both L'Hospitalet (€6.80) and Latour-de-Carol (€8.20). On Saturday, up to five buses run from L'Hospitalet to Pas de la Casa, just inside Andorra.

## SPAIN

**Alsina Graells** (☎ 827 379) runs up to seven buses daily between Barcelona's Estació del Nord and Andorra la Vella's bus station (€18, four hours).

**Eurolines** (☎ 860 010) has four services daily (€17.88) between Andorra (departing from the car park of Hotel Diplomàtic) and Barcelona's Sants bus station.

**Samar/Andor-Inter** (☎ 826 289) operates three times weekly between Andorra and Madrid (€27, nine hours) via Zaragoza (€13).

**La Hispano Andorrana** (☎ 821 372) operates five to eight buses daily between La Seu d'Urgell, just across the border, and Carrer

Doctor Nequi in Andorra la Vella (€2.05, hourly until 9pm).

# Getting Around

## BUS

Ask at a tourist office for a timetable of the eight bus routes, run by **Cooperativa Interurbana** (☎ 820 412), which follow Andorra's three main highways.

Destinations from the Avinguda Príncep Benlloch stop in Andorra la Vella include Ordino (€0.84, every half-hour), Arinsal (€1.38, four daily), Soldeu (€2.16, hourly) and Pas de la Casa (€4.36, up to four daily).

## CAR & MOTORCYCLE

The speed limit is 40km/h in populated areas and 90km/h elsewhere. Two problems are the recklessness of local drivers on the tight, winding roads and Andorra la Vella's horrendous traffic jams. Bypass the worst of the latter by taking the ring road around the south side of town.

Petrol in Andorra is about 25% cheaper than in Spain or France.

# Andorra la Vella

**pop 23,300**

The town of Andorra la Vella (elevation 1029m) is squeezed into the Riu Gran Valira Valley and is mainly engaged in retailing electronic and luxury goods. With the constant din of jackhammers and shopping-mall architecture, you might be in Hong Kong – but for the snowcapped peaks and an absence of noodle shops!

## Orientation

Andorra la Vella is strung out along the main drag, whose name changes from Avinguda del Príncep Benlloch to Avinguda de Meritxell to Avinguda de Carlemany. The tiny historic quarter is split by this heavily trafficked artery. The town merges with the once-separate villages of Escaldes and Engordany to the east and Santa Coloma to the southwest.

## Information

**Tourist Offices** The helpful **municipal tourist office** (☎ 827 117; Plaça de la Rotonda; open 9am-1pm & 4pm-8pm Mon-Sat,

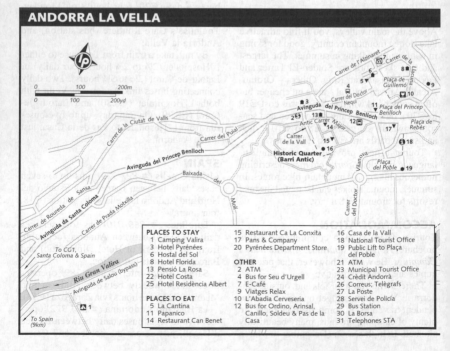

### ANDORRA LA VELLA

| PLACES TO STAY | 15 Restaurant Ca La Conxita | 16 Casa de la Vall |
|---|---|---|
| 1 Camping Valira | 17 Pans & Company | 18 National Tourist Office |
| 3 Hotel Pyrénées | 20 Pyrénées Department Store | 19 Public Lift to Plaça |
| 6 Hostal del Sol | | del Poble |
| 8 Hotel Florida | **OTHER** | 21 ATM |
| 13 Pensió La Rosa | 2 ATM | 23 Municipal Tourist Office |
| 22 Hotel Costa | 4 Bus for Seu d'Urgell | 24 Crèdit Andorrà |
| 25 Hotel Residència Albert | 7 E-Café | 26 Correus; Telègrafs |
| | 9 Viatges Relax | 27 La Poste |
| **PLACES TO EAT** | 10 L'Abadia Cerveseria | 28 Servei de Policia |
| 5 La Cantina | 12 Bus for Ordino, Arinsal, | 29 Bus Station |
| 11 Papanico | Canillo, Soldeu & Pas de la | 30 La Borsa |
| 14 Restaurant Can Benet | Casa | 31 Telephones STA |

9am-7pm Sun, 9am-9pm daily July & Aug) sells stamps and telephone cards.

The **national tourist office** (☎ 820 214; open 10am-1.30pm Mon-Sun, 3pm-7pm Mon-Sat Oct-June, 9am-1pm Mon-Sun, 3pm-7pm Mon-Sat July-Sept) is just off Plaça de Rebés.

**Money** There are ATMs sprinkled liberally throughout this mercantile city. **Crèdit Andorrà** (Avinguda de Meritxell 80) has a 24-hour banknote exchange machine that accepts 15 currencies. Banks abound, and are open 9am to 1pm and 3pm to 5pm weekdays and to noon Saturday.

American Express is represented by **Viatges Relax** (☎ 822 044; Carrer de Mossén Tremosa 2).

**Post & Communications** The French post office is **La Poste** (Carrer de Pere d'Urg 1) while **Correus i Telègrafs** (Carrer de Joan Maragall 10) is the Spanish one. Both are open 8.30am to 2.30pm weekdays and 9am to noon Saturday.

You can make international calls from pay phones or from the **Servei de Telecomunica-**

**cions d'Andorra** (STA; Avinguda de Meritxell 112; open 9am-9pm daily), which also has a fax service.

**E-Café** (☎ 865 677; Alzinaret 5; open 10am-9pm Mon-Fri & 4pm-8pm Sat Aug & Sep), just off Plaça de Guillemó, charges €3.60 an hour for Net access and is a cheerful place to log on. **Future@point** (☎ 828 202; Carrer de la Sardana 6; open 10am-11pm daily) charges €3.05 per hour.

### Things to See & Do

The small **Barri Antic** (Historic Quarter) was the heart of Andorra la Vella when the principality's capital was little more than a village. The narrow cobblestone streets around the **Casa de la Vall** are flanked by attractive stone houses.

Built in 1580 as a private home, the Casa de la Vall has served as Andorra's parliament building since 1702. Downstairs is **El Tribunal de Corts** (☎ 829 129), the country's only courtroom. Free guided tours (available in English) are given 9.30am to 1pm and 3pm to 7pm Monday to Saturday (daily in August, at other times 10am to 2pm Sunday). In summer, book at least a week ahead to ensure a

ANDORRA

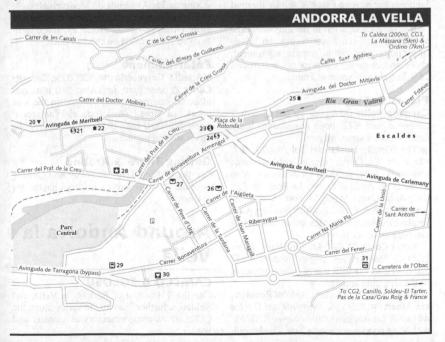

**ANDORRA LA VELLA**

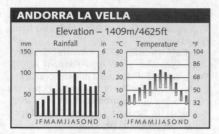

**ANDORRA LA VELLA**
Elevation – 1409m/4625ft

place – though individuals can often be squeezed in at the last minute.

The **Plaça del Poble**, a large public square just south of Plaça de Rebés, occupies the roof of a modern government office building. Giving excellent views, it's a very popular local gathering place, especially during the evening.

The free public lift in the southeast corner will whisk you away to the car park below.

Pamper yourself at **Caldea** (☎ 800 995; 3hr tickets €22.80; open 10am-11pm daily) in Escaldes, a 10-minute walk upstream from Plaça de la Rotonda.

Enclosed in what looks like a futuristic cathedral is Europe's largest spa complex of lagoons, hot tubs and saunas, fed by thermal springs.

If you've enough left in the kitty for some **shopping**, you can make savings on things like sports gear, photographic equipment, shoes and clothing, where prices are around 25% less than in Spain or France.

### Places to Stay
**Camping Valira** (Avinguda de Salou; sites 2 people & tent €12; open year-round) has a small indoor swimming pool.

The friendly **Hostal del Sol** (☎ 823 701; Plaça de Guillemó; singles/doubles with shower €12/24) provides spruce rooms. Also in the Barri Antic is **Pensió La Rosa** (☎ 821 810; Antic Carrer Major 18; dorm beds €13, singles/doubles €19/22) which provides plain singles/doubles, plus triples, quads and a room sleeping up to six people.

**Hotel Costa** (☎ 821 439; 3rd floor, Avinguda de Meritxell 44; singles/doubles €11/20) has clean, no-frills rooms – the entrance is in the shopping arcade.

Also very basic but clean is **Hotel Residència Albert** (☎ 820 156; Avinguda del Doctor Mitjavila 16; singles/doubles/triples €20/35/42). Most good-value rooms have a bathroom.

More upmarket, the delightful **Hotel Florida** (☎ 820 105, fax 861 925; e hotelflorida@andorra.ad; Carrer La Lacuna 15; singles/doubles low season €28/36, high season €40/67.30), one block from Plaça de Guillemó, provides well-equipped rooms (rates include breakfast).

Although the rooms are good value at **Hotel Pyrénées** (☎ 860 006, fax 820 265; e ph@mypic.ad; singles/doubles €33/52.30), you must take half-board in peak periods.

### Places to Eat
**Pans & Company** (Plaça de Rebés 2) is good for baguettes with a range of fillings (€2.50-3.30). **La Cantina** (Plaça de Guillemó; salads €4.50-6.60, 3-course set menu €7.20) is a friendly family-run place offering good salads and pizzas.

In the Barri Antic, **Papanico** (Avinguda del Príncep Benlloch; tapas €1.75-5) is fun for morning coffee to late-night snacks. **Restaurant Ca La Conxita** (Placeta de Monjó 3; meal €16-20) is a bustling family place. Around the corner there is the **Restaurant Can Benet** (Antic Carrer Major 9; mains €8.50-15), which is equally delightful.

There are fast-food outlets opposite the bus station and at Avinguda de Meritxell 105.

For self-caterers, the **Pyrénées department store** (Avinguda de Meritxell 21) has a well-stocked supermarket on the 2nd floor.

### Entertainment
**L'Abadia Cerveseria** (☎ 820 825; Cap del Carrer 2; open 6pm-3am Mon-Sat) is a great place to sample an amber liquid in the wee hours. **La Borsa** (Avinguda de Tarragona; open Thur-Sat) is an old favourite among the city's several nightclubs.

### Getting There & Around
See the Getting There & Away and Getting Around sections earlier in this chapter for options.

## Around Andorra la Vella

### CANILLO & SOLDEU
Canillo, 11km east of Andorra la Vella, and Soldeu, a further 7km up the valley along the CG2, are as complementary as summer and winter.

In summer, Canillo offers canyon clambering, a *vía ferrata* climbing gully and climbing wall, the year-round Palau de Gel with ice rink and swimming pool, guided walks and endless possibilities for hiking (including an easy, signposted nature walk which follows the valley downstream from Soldeu). The helpful **tourist office** (☎ 851 002) is on the main road at the east end of the village.

In winter, Soldeu and its smaller neighbour **El Tarter** come into their own as 23 lifts (including a cabin lift up from Canillo) connect 86km of runs with a vertical drop of 850m. The slopes, wooded in their lower reaches, are often warmer than Andorra's other more exposed ski areas and offer the Pyrenees' finest skiing and snowboarding. Lift passes for one/three days cost €24.50/63 (low season) and €27.50/70.50 (high season).

### Places to Stay

Year-round, accommodation in Canillo is markedly less expensive than in Andorra La Vella. Of its five camping grounds, **Camping Santa Creu** (☎ 851 462; person/tent/car €2.85/2.85/2.85) is the greenest and quietest. **Hostal Aina** (☎ 851 434, fax 851 747; beds €10.22, with breakfast €12.63) offers dormitory accommodation – ring ahead in winter as it is often full.

**Hotel Canigó** (☎ 851 024, fax 851 824, rooms €18.25 per person, with breakfast €21.85) provides comfortable and value-for-money lodging.

### Places to Eat

On Soldeu's main drag, the cheerful restaurant situated at the **Hotel Bruxelles** (sandwiches €2.70-3.50, menu €8) does well-filled sandwiches, whopping burgers and a tasty *menu*.

### Entertainment

The music pounds on winter nights in Soldeu. **Pussy Cat** and its neighbour, **Fat Albert**, both one block from the main drag, rock until far too late for impressive skiing next day.

### Getting There & Around

Buses run from Andorra la Vella to El Tarter and Soldeu (€2.16, 40 minutes, hourly) between 9am to 8pm. In winter there are free shuttle buses (just flash your ski pass) between Canillo and the two upper villages. These run approximately hourly (with a break from noon to 3pm) until 11pm.

All three villages are also on the bus route between Andorra la Vella and the French railheads of Latour-de-Carol and L'Hospitalet (see the main Getting There & Away section earlier in this chapter).

## ORDINO & AROUND

Despite recent development, Ordino (population 1000), on highway CG3 8km north of Andorra la Vella, retains its Andorran character, with most buildings still in local stone. At 1000m it's a good starting point for summer activity holidays. The **tourist office** (☎ 737 080; open 9am-1pm Mon-Sun, 3pm-7pm Mon-Sat) is beside the CG3.

### Things to See & Do

**Museu d'Areny i Plandolit** (☎ 836 908) is a 17th-century manor house with a richly furnished interior.

Within the same grounds is the far from nerdy **Museo Postal de Andorra**. It has an interesting 15-minute audiovisual program (available in English) and stamps by the thousand, issued by France and Spain specifically for Andorra (see Post & Communications earlier in this chapter). Admission to each museum costs €2.40. Both are open 9.30am to 1.30pm and 3pm to 6.30pm Tuesday to Saturday, plus Sunday morning.

There are some excellent walking trails around Ordino.

From the hamlet of **Segudet**, 500m east of Ordino, a path goes up through fir woods to the **Coll d'Ordino** (1980m), reached in about 1½ hours. **Pic de Casamanya** (2740m), with knock-me-down views, is some two hours north of the col.

Other trails lead off from the tiny settlements beside the CG3 north of Ordino. A track (three hours one way) heads west from **Llorts** (1413m) up the Riu de l'Angonella Valley to a group of lakes, the **Estanys de l'Angonella**, at about 2300m.

Just north of **El Serrat** (1600m), a secondary road leads 4km east to the **Borda de Sorteny** mountain refuge (1969m), from where trails lead into the high mountain area.

From **Arans** (1385m), a trail goes northeastwards to **Bordes de l'Ensegur** (2180m), where there's an old shepherd's hut.

### Places to Stay & Eat

The cheapest option you'll find in Ordino is the cavernous **Hotel Casamanya** (☎ 835 011;

ANDORRA

singles/doubles €28/32). **Bar Restaurant Quim** (Plaça Major; menu €8.50) has a basic menu. Next door, the **Restaurant Armengol** (menu €10) has a good range of meat dishes. Up the valley and some 200m north of Llorts is **Camping Mitxéu** (☎ 850 022; 2 people & tent €7.20; open mid-June–mid-Sept), one of Andorra's most beautiful camp sites. Bring your own provisions. **Hotel Vilaró** (☎ 850 225; singles/doubles €15/27.65) is 200m south of Ordino.

## Getting There & Away

Buses between Andorra la Vella and Ordino (€0.84) run about every half-hour from 7am to 9pm daily. Buses to El Serrat (€1.45) – via Ordino – leave Andorra la Vella at both 1pm and 8.30pm. The valley is also served by four buses daily (10 in the ski season) linking Ordino and Arcalís.

## ARINSAL

During winter, Arinsal, 10km northwest of Andorra la Vella, has good skiing and snowboarding and a lively après-ski scene. There are 13 lifts (including a smart cabin lift to hurtle you up from the village), 28km of pistes and a vertical drop of 1010m. In summer, Arinsal is a good departure point for medium mountain walks. From Aparthotel Crest at Arinsal's northern extremity, a trail leads northwest, then west to **Estany de les Truites** (2260m), a natural lake. The steepish walk up takes around 1½ hours. From here, it's another 1½ to two hours to bag **Pic de la Coma Pedrosa** (2964m), Andorra's highest point.

## Places to Stay

Just above Estany de les Truites is **Refugi de Coma Pedrosa** (☎ 327 955; €7; open June-late Sept). It does snacks and meals (dinner

€11). The large, well-equipped **Camping Xixerella** (☎ 836 613; sites per adult/tent/car €4.50/4.50/4.50; open year-round), between Arinsal and Pal, has an outdoor swimming pool. In Arinsal, **Hostal Poblado** (☎ 835 122, fax 836 879; e hospoblado@andornet.ad; basic singles/doubles €15/29, with shower €20/39, with bathroom €27.50/42; open July–mid-June), beside the cabin lift, is friendliness itself. It has a lively bar (which offers Internet access on the side), and breakfast is an extra €3.

## Places to Eat

As a change from the plentiful snack and sandwich joints, try **Refugi de la Fondue**, which does cheese or meat fondue dishes. **Restaurant el Moli** (pasta & pizza €5.50-7.50) bills itself as Italian – and indeed offers the usual staple pastas and pizzas – but also has more exotic fare. **Rocky Mountain** has a gringo menu with dishes such as T-bone steak and 'New York style cheesecake'. All three options are situated on the main road.

## Entertainment

In winter, Arinsal fairly throbs after sunset. In summer, it can be almost mournful. When the snow's around, call by **Surf** (meat dishes €7.50-13.50) near the base of the cabin lift. A pub, dance venue and restaurant, it specialises in juicy Argentinian meat dishes. **Quo Vadis** occasionally has live music.

## Getting There & Away

Buses leave Andorra la Vella for Arinsal (€1.38) via La Massana at 9.30am, 1pm and 6.15pm. There are also more than 10 buses daily between La Massana and Arinsal. In winter, Skibus (€2) runs five times daily between La Massana and Arinsal.

# Croatia

Crystal-clear seas, lush islands, unspoilt fishing villages, beaches, vineyards, Roman ruins and medieval walled cities are some of the many treasures that make Croatia (Hrvatska) a traveller's paradise. When Yugoslavia split apart in 1991, no less than 80% of the country's tourist resorts ended up in Croatia, mostly along the Adriatic coast. There is almost 6000km of coastline that winds around innumerable bays and inlets, rising to steep mountainous backdrops or flattening out to shingle beaches. An abundance of natural harbours lures yachties, and naturists have a wide choice of secluded coves.

Croatia extends in an arc from the Danube River in the east to Istria in the west and south along the Adriatic coast to Dubrovnik. Roman Catholic since the 9th century, the Croatian interior fell under Austro-Hungarian influence while the Istrian and Dalmatian coast was marked by Venetian and Italian rule. Croatia only united with Orthodox Serbia in 1918 and split from Yugoslavia in a painful struggle that lasted from 1991 to 1995. The war disrupted the tourist industry, which had always been the main source of hard currency, but the country is beginning to pull out of the slump. Italian and Central European visitors fill the coastal resorts for most of July and August but at any other time of year the pace slows considerably.

## Facts about Croatia

### HISTORY

In 229 BC the Romans began their conquest of the indigenous Illyrians by establishing a colony at Solin (Salona), close to Split in Dalmatia. Emperor Augustus then extended the empire and created the provinces of Illyricum (Dalmatia and Bosnia) and Pannonia (Croatia). In AD 285, Emperor Diocletian decided to retire to his palace fortress in Split, today the greatest Roman ruin in Eastern Europe. When the empire was divided in 395, what is now known as Slovenia, Croatia and Bosnia-Hercegovina stayed with the Western Roman Empire, while present Serbia, Kosovo and Macedonia went to the Eastern Roman Empire, later known as the Byzantine Empire.

Around 625, Slavic tribes migrated from present-day Poland. The Serbian tribe settled

| At a Glance | |
|---|---|

- **Zagreb** – charming avenues; bohemian cafés; fascinating galleries
- **Rovinj** – wooded hills; picturesque offshore islands; charming cobbled streets
- **Hvar Island** – lively seaside promenade; Gothic palaces; pine-covered slopes
- **Dubrovnik** – exquisite white-stone town and a mesmerising coastline

| | |
|---|---|
| **Capital** | Zagreb |
| **Population** | 4.4 million |
| **Official Language** | Croatian (Serbo-Croatian) |
| **Currency** | 1 Croatian kuna (KN) = 100 lipas |
| **Time** | GMT/UTC+0100 |
| **Country Phone Code** | ☎ 385 |

in the region that is now southwestern Serbia and extended their influence south and west. The Croatian tribe moved into what is now Croatia and occupied two former Roman provinces: Dalmatian Croatia along the Adriatic and Pannonian Croatia to the north.

By the early part of the 9th century, both settlements had accepted Christianity but the northern Croats fell under Frankish domination while Dalmatian Croats came under the nominal control of the Byzantine Empire. The Dalmatian duke Tomislav united the two groups in 925 in a single kingdom that prospered for nearly 200 years.

Late in the 11th century, the throne fell vacant and a series of power struggles weakened central authority and split the kingdom. The northern Croats, unable to agree upon a ruler, united with Hungary in 1102 for protection against the Orthodox Byzantine Empire.

In 1242 a Tatar invasion devastated Hungary and Croatia. In the 14th century the Turks began pushing into the Balkans, defeating the Serbs in 1389 and the Hungarians in 1526. Northern Croatia turned to the Habsburgs of Austria for protection against the Turks in 1527 and remained part of their empire until 1918. To form a buffer against the Turks, in the 16th century the Austrians invited Serbs to settle the Vojna Krajina (military frontier) along the Bosnian border. The Serbs in the borderlands had an autonomous administration under Austrian control; these areas were reincorporated into Croatia in 1881.

The Adriatic coast fell under Venetian influence as early as the 12th century, although Hungary continued to struggle for control of the region. Some Dalmatian cities changed hands repeatedly until Venice imposed its rule on the Adriatic coast in the early 15th century and occupied it for nearly four centuries. Only the Republic of Ragusa (Dubrovnik) maintained its independence. The Adriatic coast was threatened but never conquered by the Turks and, after the naval Battle of Lepanto in 1571 when Spanish and Venetian forces wiped out the Turkish fleet, this threat receded.

After Venice was shattered by Napoleonic France in 1797, the French occupied southern Croatia, abolishing the Republic of Ragusa (Dubrovnik) in 1808. Napoleon's merger of Dalmatia, Istria and Slovenia into the 'Illyrian provinces' in 1809 stimulated the concept of South Slav (Yugoslav) unity. Following the defeat of Napoleon at Waterloo in 1815, Austria-Hungary moved in to pick up the pieces along the coast.

A revival of Croatian cultural and political life began in 1835. In 1848 a liberal democratic revolution, which was led by Josip Jelačić, was suppressed, but serfdom was abolished. An 1868 reform transferred northern Croatia from Austria to Hungary, united the territory with Hungarian Slavonia and granted a degree of internal autonomy. Dalmatia remained under Austria. In the decade before WWI, some 50,000 Croats emigrated to the USA.

With the defeat of the Austro-Hungarian empire in WWI, Croatia became part of the Kingdom of Serbs, Croats & Slovenes (called Yugoslavia after 1929), with a centralised government in Belgrade. This was strongly resisted by Croatian nationalists, who organised the Marseilles assassination of the royal dictator King Alexander I in 1934. Italy had been promised control of the Adriatic coast as an incentive to join the war against Austria-Hungary in 1915 and it held much of northern Dalmatia from 1918 to 1943.

After the German invasion of Yugoslavia in March 1941, a puppet government dominated by the fascist Ustaša movement was set up in Croatia and Bosnia-Hercegovina under Ante Pavelić (who fled to Argentina after WWII). At first the Ustaša tried to expel all Serbs from Croatia to Serbia. But when the Germans stopped this because of the problems it was causing, the Ustaša launched an extermination campaign that rivalled the Nazis in its brutality. Although the number of victims is controversial, estimates indicate that from 60,000 to 600,000 ethnic Serbs, Jews and Roma (gypsies) were murdered. The Ustaša programme called for 'one-third of Serbs killed, one-third expelled and one-third converted to Catholicism'.

Not all Croats supported these policies, however. Josip Broz, known as Maršal Tito, was himself of Croat-Slovene parentage and tens of thousands of Croats fought bravely with his partisans. Massacres of Croats conducted by Serbian Četniks in southern Croatia and Bosnia forced almost all antifascist Croats into the communist ranks, where they joined the numerous Serbs trying to defend themselves from the Ustaša. In all, about a million people died violently in a war that was fought mostly in Croatia and Bosnia-Hercegovina.

## Recent History

After the war, Maršal Tito became the prime minister of the new Yugoslav Federation and divided it into five republics – Croatia, Serbia, Slovenia, Bosnia-Hercegovina and Macedonia. Even with a Stalin-style system of state planning, Croatia and Slovenia moved far ahead of the southern republics economically, leading to demands by reformers, intellectuals and students for greater autonomy. The 'Croatian Spring' of 1971 caused a backlash and purge of the reformers, who were jailed or expelled from the Communist Party.

CROATIA

Tito's habit of borrowing from abroad to flood the country with cheap consumer goods produced an economic crisis after his death in 1980. The sinking economy provoked greater tension among Yugoslavia's ethnic groups, which came to a head when Serbian politician Slobodan Milošević whipped Serbs into a nationalistic frenzy over the aspirations of the Albanian majority in the province of Kosovo.

Fearing a renewal of Serbian hegemony, many Croats felt the time had come to end more than four decades of communist rule and attain complete autonomy into the bargain. In the free elections of April 1990 Franjo Tudjman's Croatian Democratic Union (Hrvatska Demokratska Zajednica) easily defeated the old Communist Party. On 22 December 1990 a new Croatian constitution was promulgated, changing the status of Serbs in Croatia to a national minority.

The constitution's failure to guarantee minority rights, and mass dismissals of Serbs from the public service, led the 600,000-strong ethnic Serb community to demand autonomy. When Croatia declared independence on 25 June 1991, the Serbian enclave of Krajina proclaimed its independence from Croatia.

Heavy fighting broke out in Krajina (the area around Knin, north of Split), Baranja (the area north of the Drava River opposite Osijek) and Slavonia (the region west of the Danube). The 180,000-member, 2000-tank Yugoslav People's Army, dominated by Serbian communists, began to intervene on its own authority in support of Serbian irregulars under the pretext of halting ethnic violence.

In the three months following 25 June, a quarter of Croatia fell to Serbian militias and the federal army. In September the Croatian government ordered a blockade of 32 federal military installations in the republic, lifting morale and gaining much-needed military equipment. In response, the Yugoslav navy blockaded the Adriatic coast and laid siege to the strategic town of Vukovar on the Danube.

In early October 1991 the federal army and Montenegrin militia moved against Dubrovnik to protest against the ongoing blockade of their garrisons in Croatia. On 7 October the presidential palace in Zagreb was hit by rockets fired from Yugoslav air-force jets in an unsuccessful assassination attempt against President Tudjman. Heroic Vukovar finally fell on 19 November when the Yugoslav army ended a bloody three-month siege by concentrating 600 tanks and 30,000 soldiers there. During the six months of fighting in Croatia 10,000 people died, hundreds of thousands fled and tens of thousands of homes were deliberately destroyed.

## Independence

After the Croatian parliament amended its constitution to protect minority and human rights the European Community (EC), succumbing to strong pressure from Germany, recognised Croatia in January 1992. This was followed three months later by US recognition and in May 1992 Croatia was admitted to the United Nations.

In January 1993 the Croatian army suddenly launched an offensive in southern Krajina, pushing the Serbs back as much as 24km in some areas and recapturing strategic points. The Krajina Serbs vowed never to accept rule from Zagreb and in June 1993 they voted overwhelmingly to join the Bosnian Serbs (and eventually Greater Serbia).

The self-proclaimed 'Republic of Serbian Krajina' held elections in December 1993, which no international body recognised as legitimate or fair. Continued 'ethnic cleansing' left only about 900 Croats in Krajina out of an original population of 44,000.

While the world's attention turned to the grim events unfolding in Bosnia-Hercegovina, the Croatian government quietly began procuring arms from abroad. On 1 May 1995, the Croatian army and police entered and occupied western Slavonia, east of Zagreb, and seized control of the region. As the Croatian military consolidated its hold in the west of Slavonia, some 15,000 Serbs fled the region despite assurances from the Croatian government that they were safe from retribution.

Belgrade's silence througout this campaign made it clear that the Krajina Serbs had lost support of their Yugoslav sponsors, encouraging the Croats to forge on. At dawn on 4 August 1995 the military launched a massive assault on the rebel Serb capital of Knin. Outnumbered by two to one, the Serb army fled to northern Bosnia, along with about 150,000 civilians whose roots in the Krajina stretched back centuries. The military operation lasted days, but was followed by months of terror. Widespread looting and burning of Serb villages, as well as attacks on the few remaining elderly Serbs, seemed designed to ensure the permanence of this massive population shift.

The Dayton Agreement signed in Paris in December 1995 recognised Croatia's traditional borders and provided for the return of eastern Slavonia, a transition that was finally completed in January 1998.

Although stability has returned to the country, a key provision of the agreement was the promise by the Croatian government to allow the return of Serbian refugees. Housing, local industry and agriculture in Slavonia and Krajina were devastated by the war, which has made resettlement both complicated and costly. Although Serbian refugees face a real tangle of bureaucratic obstacles, Croatia's new government is finally acceding to the international community's demands and refugees are slowly trickling back.

## GEOGRAPHY

Croatia is half the size of present-day Yugoslavia in area (56,538 sq km) and population. The republic swings around like a boomerang from the Pannonian plains of Slavonia between the Sava, Drava and Danube Rivers, across hilly central Croatia to the Istrian Peninsula, then south through Dalmatia along the rugged Adriatic coast.

The narrow Croatian coastal belt at the foot of the Dinaric Alps is only about 600km long as the crow flies, but it's so indented that the actual length is 1778km. If the 4012km of coastline around the offshore islands is added to the total, the length becomes 5790km. Most of the 'beaches' along this jagged coast consist of slabs of rock sprinkled with naturists. Don't come expecting to find sand, but the waters are sparkling clean, even around large towns.

Croatia's offshore islands are every bit as beautiful as those off the coast of Greece. There are 1185 islands and islets along the tectonically submerged Adriatic coastline, 66 inhabited. The largest are Cres, Krk, Mali Lošinj, Pag and Rab in the north; Dugi Otok in the middle; and Brač, Hvar, Korčula, Mljet and Vis in the south. Most are barren and elongated from northwest to southeast, with high mountains that drop right into the sea.

## CLIMATE

The climate varies from Mediterranean along the Adriatic coast to continental inland. The high coastal mountains help to shield the coast from cold northerly winds, making for an early spring and late autumn. In spring and early summer a sea breeze called the *maestral* keeps the temperature down along the coast. Winter winds include the cold *bura* from the north and the humid *široko* from the south.

The sunny coastal areas experience hot, dry summers and mild, rainy winters, while the interior regions are cold in winter and warm in summer. Because of a warm current flowing northward along the Adriatic coast, the sea temperatures never fall below 10°C in winter and can be as high as 26°C in August. You can swim in the sea from mid-June until late September. The resorts south of Split are the warmest.

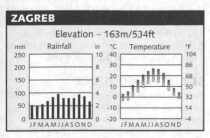

## ECOLOGY & ENVIRONMENT

The lack of heavy industry in Croatia has left the country largely free of industrial pollution, but its forests are under threat from acid rain from neighbouring countries. The dry summers and brisk *maestral* winds pose substantial fire hazards along the coast. The sea along the Adriatic coast is among the world's cleanest but scavenging for coral has nearly eliminated coral reefs. Purchasing the coral

jewellery and decorative objects on sale in many resorts only exacerbates the problem.

## NATIONAL PARKS

When the Yugoslav Federation collapsed, seven of its finest national parks ended up in Croatia. Brijuni near Pula is the most carefully cultivated park, with well-preserved Mediterranean holm oak forests. The mountainous Risnjak National Park near Delnice, east of Rijeka, is named after one of its inhabitants – the *ris*, or lynx.

Dense forests of beech trees and black pine in the Paklenica National Park near Zadar are home to a number of endemic insects, reptiles and birds, as well as the endangered griffon vulture. The abundant plant and animal life, including bears, wolves and deer, in the Plitvice Lakes National Park between Zagreb and Zadar has warranted its inclusion on Unesco's list of World Natural Heritage Sites. Both Plitvice Lakes and Krka National Parks (near Šibenik) feature a dramatic series of cascades and incredible turquoise lakes.

The 101 stark and rocky islands of the Kornati Archipelago and National Park make it the largest in the Mediterranean. The island of Mljet near Korčula also contains a forested national park.

## GOVERNMENT & POLITICS

Croatia is a parliamentary democracy with a powerful presidency. Croatia's first president was Franjo Tudjman, who died in December 1999. Beleaguered by allegations of corruption and cronyism, his party, the Croatian Democratic Union or HDZ, was resoundingly defeated in parliamentary elections that took place in January 2000.

The election of Ivica Račan as the prime minister and Stipe Mesic as president was a rejection of the strongly nationalistic policies of the HDZ and has ushered in a rapprochement with the West. The new government has moved to end Croatia's international isolation by cooperating with the War Crimes Tribunal being conducted at The Hague, speeding the return of Serbian refugees and enacting legislation expanding minority rights. During May 2000, Croatia was admitted into NATO's Partnership for Peace and in October 2001 Prime Minister Račan signed a Stabilization and Association Agreement (SAA) with the EU bringing Croatia closer to its goal of membership in the EU.

## ECONOMY

In addition to dealing with the residue of the banking crisis that occurred in the late 1990s, the current government is pushing ahead with a comprehensive privatisation of state assets. However, exports remain weak as the demand for Croatian products in Germany, Austria, Italy and Russia has slowed. Keeping inflation in check (2.6% in 2001) by limiting any wage increases in the public sector and maintaining a tight fiscal policy is now attracting international investment. There was a respectable 4.6% growth rate in the first quarter of 2002 but unemployment is high (22.3% in 2001) and the average wage is only about 3400KN (US$410) per month. Average Croatians have seen a steep decline in standard of living since the country's independence.

Tourism is expected to spearhead the new economy in Croatia. In the past, one-third of Croatia's national income came from tourism, but between 1991 and 1995 tourist numbers fell dramatically. Just as tourism was beginning to rebound, the 1999 war in Kosovo again labelled the region as a war zone and tourists stayed away in droves. Heavy investment in infrastructure and marketing is paying off; in 2002 tourism was expected to bring in US$4 billion, around 15% of the country's GDP.

## POPULATION & PEOPLE

Before the war, Croatia had a population of nearly five million, of which 78% were Croats and 12% were Serbs. Today's population includes just 201,000 Serbs, slightly less than 5%. Most live in eastern Croatia (Slavonia). The next largest ethnic group is Bosnians, followed by Italians, Hungarians and Slovenes. Small communities of Czechs, Roma and Albanians complete the mosaic. The largest cities in Croatia are Zagreb (780,000), Split (188,700), Rijeka (144,000), Osijek (114,600) and Zadar (72,700).

## ARTS

The Exhibition Pavilion in Zagreb is a good place to keep up with the latest developments in Croatian art.

### Painting

Vlaho Bukovac (1855–1922) was the most notable Croatian painter in the late 19th century. Important early-20th-century painters include Miroslav Kraljević (1885–1913) and Josip Račić (1885–1908). Post-WWII artists

experimented with abstract expressionism but this period is best remembered for the naive art that was typified by Ivan Generalić (1914–1992). Recent trends have included minimalism, conceptual art and pop art.

### Sculpture

The work of sculptor Ivan Meštrović (1883–1962) is seen in town squares throughout Croatia. Besides creating public monuments, Meštrović designed imposing buildngs, such as the circular Croatian History Museum in Zagreb. Both his sculptures and architecture display the powerful classical restraint he learnt from Auguste Rodin. Meštrović's studio in Zagreb and his retirement home at Split have been made into galleries of his work (for details see Gradec in the Zagreb section and Museums & Galleries in the Split section later in this chapter).

### Music & Dance

Croatian folk music has many influences. The *kolo,* a lively Slavic round dance where men and women alternate in the circle, is accompanied by Roma-style violinists or players of the *tambura,* a three- or five-string mandolin popular throughout the country. The measured guitar-playing and rhythmic accordions of Dalmatia have a gentle Italian air.

A recommended recording available locally on CD is *Narodne Pjesme i Plesovi Sjeverne Hrvatske* (Northern Croatian Folk Songs and Dances) by the Croatian folkloric ensemble Lado. The 22 tracks on this album represent nine regions, with everything from haunting Balkan voices reminiscent of Bulgaria to lively Mediterranean dance rhythms.

### SOCIETY & CONDUCT

As the Yugoslav years and the bitter struggle for independence recede into the past, the country's real personality is beginning to emerge. The long coastline that spent centuries under Italian domination is infused with a Mediterranean insouciance while the interior has a Central European sense of orderliness and propriety. The contrasting attitudes create a society that operates efficiently even though there seem to be few rules and the prevailing spirit is *'nema problema'* (no problem).

Croats take pride in keeping up appearances. Despite a fragile economy, money can usually be found in order to brighten up the town centre with a fresh coat of paint or to repair a historic building. Even as their bank accounts diminish, most people will cut out restaurants and movies to afford a shopping trip to Italy for some new clothes. The tidy streets and stylish clothes are rooted in the Croats' image of themselves as Western Europeans, not Yugoslavs, a word that makes Croats wince. Dressing neatly will go a long way towards gaining a traveller acceptance.

## RELIGION

Croats are overwhelmingly Roman Catholic, while virtually all Serbs belong to the Eastern Orthodox Church. In addition to doctrinal differences, Orthodox Christians venerate icons, allow priests to marry and do not accept the authority of the Roman Catholic pope. Long suppressed under communism, Catholicism is undergoing a strong resurgence in Croatia and churches have good attendances on Sunday. Muslims make up 1.2% of the population and Protestants 0.4%, with a tiny Jewish population in Zagreb.

## LANGUAGE

Croatian is a South Slavic language, as are Serbian, Slovene, Macedonian and Bulgarian. Prior to 1991 both Croatian and Serbian were considered dialects of a single language known as Serbo-Croatian.

As a result of history, tourism and the number of 'guest workers' who have returned from Germany, German is the most commonly spoken second language in Croatia. Most Istrians speak Italian and English is popular among young people.

The Lonely Planet *Mediterranean Europe phrasebook* includes a chapter on the Serbian and Croatian languages, with translations of key words and phrases from each appearing side by side, providing a clear comparison of the languages. For a basic rundown on words and phrases for the traveller, refer to the Language chapter at the end of this book.

# Facts for the Visitor

## HIGHLIGHTS
### Museums & Galleries

Art museums and galleries are easier for a foreign visitor to enjoy than historical museums, which are usually captioned in Croatian only. In Zagreb, the Museum Mimara contains an outstanding collection of Spanish, Italian and Dutch paintings, as well as an archaeological collection, exhibits of ancient art from Asia and collections of glass, textiles, sculpture and furniture. The Strossmayer Gallery of Old Masters, also in Zagreb, is worthwhile for its exhibitions of Italian, Flemish, French and Croatian paintings.

The Meštrović Gallery in Split is worth a detour and in Zagreb the Meštrović Studio gives a fascinating insight into the life and work of this remarkable sculptor.

### Beaches

Whether rocky, pebbly, gravelly or (rarely) sandy, Croatian beaches are often on the edge of a pine grove and slope into crystalline water that always seems to be the right temperature. The coastline is indented with wide bays and cosy coves where you just might be tempted to cast off your bathing suit along with the many naturists who flock to Croatian shores each summer.

### Historic Towns

All along the Adriatic coast are white-stone towns with narrow, winding streets enclosed by defensive walls. Each has its own flavour: Hilly Rovinj looks over the sea; the peninsula of Korčula town burrows into it. While Zadar retains echoes of its original Roman street plan, Hvar and Trogir are traditional medieval towns. None can match the exquisite harmony of Dubrovnik, with its blend of elements of Renaissance and baroque architecture.

### SUGGESTED ITINERARIES

Depending on how long you have in Croatia, you may like to visit the following places.

**Two days**
    Visit Dubrovnik
**One week**
    Visit Hvar or Korčula, Split and Dubrovnik
**Two weeks**
    Visit Zagreb, Istria and southern Dalmatia.

## PLANNING
### When to Go

May is a nice month to travel along the Adriatic coast, with good weather and few tourists. June is also good, but in the popular months of July and August all of Europe arrives and prices soar. September is perhaps the best month since it's not as hot as summer, though the sea remains warm, the crowds will have thinned out as children return to school, low-season accommodation rates apply and fruit, such as figs and grapes, will be abundant. In April and October it may be too cool for camping, but the weather should still be fine along the coast and private rooms will be plentiful and inexpensive.

## Maps

Kúmmerley + Frey's map *Croatia & Slovenia* (1:500,000) is detailed and shows the country's latest borders. Most tourist offices in the country have local maps, but make sure the street names are up to date.

## TOURIST OFFICES
### Local Tourist Offices

The **Croatian National Tourist Board** (☎ 46 99 333, fax 45 57 827; W *www.htz.hr; Iberov trg 10, Importanne Gallerija, 10000 Zagreb*) is a good source of information. Regional tourist offices supervise tourist development and municipal tourist offices that have free brochures and information on local events. Some arrange private accommodation.

Tourist information is also dispensed by the commercial travel agencies, such as **Atlas** (W *atlas-croatia.com*), Croatia Express, Generalturist and Kompas, which also arranges private rooms and sightseeing excursions. The agencies often sell local guidebooks, which are excellent value if you'll be staying for a while. Ask for the schedule for coastal ferries.

## Tourist Offices Abroad

Croatian tourist offices abroad include:

**UK** (☎ 020-8563 7979) Croatian National Tourist Office, 2 Lanchesters, 162-64 Fulham Palace Rd, London W6 9ER
**USA** (☎ 212-279 8672) Croatian National Tourist Office, Suite 4003, 350 Fifth Ave, New York, NY 10118

## VISAS & DOCUMENTS

Visitors from Australia, Canada, New Zealand, the EU and the USA do not require a visa for stays of less than 90 days. For other nationalities, visas are issued free of charge at Croatian consulates. Croatian authorities require all foreigners to register with the local police when they first arrive in a new area of the country, but this is a routine matter that is normally handled by the hotel, hostel, camping ground or agency that organises your private accommodation.

## EMBASSIES & CONSULATES
### Croatian Embassies & Consulates

Diplomatic representation abroad includes:

**Australia** (☎ 02-6286 6988) 14 Jindalee Crescent, O'Malley, ACT 2601, Canberra
**Canada** (☎ 613-562 7820) 229 Chapel St, Ottawa, Ontario K1N 7Y6
**Germany** (☎ 030-219 15 514) Ahornstrasse 4, Berlin 10787
**New Zealand** (☎ 09-836 5581) 131 Lincoln Rd, Henderson, Box 83200, Edmonton, Auckland
**South Africa** (☎ 012-342 1206) 1160 Church St, 0083 Colbyn, Pretoria
**UK** (☎ 020-738 72 022) 21 Conway St, London W1P 5HL
**USA** (☎ 202-588 5899) 2343 Massachusetts Ave NW, Washington, DC 20008

### Embassies & Consulates in Croatia

The following addresses are in Zagreb (area code ☎ 01), unless otherwise noted:

**Albania** (☎ 48 10 679) Jurišićeva 2a
**Australia** (☎ 48 36 600) Kršnjavoga 1
**Bosnia-Hercegovina** (☎ 46 83 761) Torbarova 9
**Bulgaria** (☎ 48 23 336) Novi Goljak 25
**Canada** (☎ 48 81 200) Prilaz Gjure Deželića 4
**Czech Republic** (☎ 61 77 246) Savska 41
**Germany** (☎ 61 58 105) avenija grada Vukovara 64
**Hungary** (☎ 48 34 990) Krležin Gvozd 11a
**New Zealand** (☎ 65 20 888) avenija Dubrovnik 15
**Poland** (☎ 48 34 579) Krležin Gvozd 3
**Romania** (☎ 24 30 137) Srebrnjak 150a
**Slovakia** (☎ 48 48 941) Prilaz Gjure Deželića 10
**Slovenia** (☎ 63 11 014) Savska 41
**UK** (☎ 45 55 310) Vlaška 121
    *Consulate:* (☎ 021-341 464) Obala hrvatskog narodnog preporoda 10, Split 21000
    *Consulate:* (☎ 020-412 916) Petilovrijenci 2, Dubrovnik 20000
**USA** (☎ 45 55 500) Andrije Hebranga 2
**Yugoslavia** (☎ 46 80 552) Mesićeva 19

## CUSTOMS

Travellers can bring their personal effects into the country, along with 1L of liquor, 1L of wine, 500g of coffee, 200 cigarettes and 50mL of perfume.

## MONEY
### Currency

In May 1994 the Croatian dinar was replaced by the kuna. Visitors are allowed to import or export Croatian banknotes up to a value of around 2000KN but there's no reason to do either. Like other Continental Europeans, Croats indicate decimals with commas and thousands with points.

## Exchange Rates

| country | unit | | kuna |
| --- | --- | --- | --- |
| Australia | A$1 | = | 4.25KN |
| Canada | C$1 | = | 4.94KN |
| Euro Zone | €1 | = | 7.65KN |
| Japan | ¥100 | = | 6.53KN |
| NZ | NZ$1 | = | 3.65KN |
| UK | UK£1 | = | 12.25KN |
| USA | US$1 | = | 7.83KN |

## Exchanging Money

There are numerous places to change money, all offering similar rates; ask at any travel agency for the location of the nearest exchange. Banks and exchange offices keep long hours. Exchange offices may deduct a commission of 1% to change cash or travellers cheques but some banks do not. Kuna can be converted into hard currency only at a bank and if you submit a receipt of a previous transaction. Hungarian currency is difficult to change in Croatia.

**Credit Cards** American Express (AmEx), MasterCard, Visa and Diners Club cards are widely accepted in large hotels, stores and many restaurants but don't count on cards to pay for private accommodation or meals in small restaurants. ATMs accepting Master-Card, Maestro, Cirrus, Plus and Visa are available in most bus and train stations, airports, all major cities and most small towns. Many branches of Privredna Banka have ATMs that allow cash withdrawals on an AmEx card. Make sure you have a four-digit personal identification number (PIN).

## Costs

Hotel prices, private accommodation and ferry fares are set in euros, though payment is in kuna calculated at the official daily rate. Accommodation is more expensive than it should be for a country trying to lure tourists, and real budget accommodation is in short supply. Transport, concert and theatre tickets, and meals are reasonably priced for Europe.

Accommodation costs vary widely depending on the season. If you travel in March you'll have no trouble finding a private room

for 90KN per person but prices climb to double that amount in July and August. Count on 25KN for a meal at a self-service restaurant and 35KN to 50KN for an average intercity bus fare. It's not that hard to survive on 250KN daily if you stay in hostels, private rooms or camping grounds. Unless you can survive on sandwiches, self-catering saves only a small amount of money since food is expensive in Croatia.

## Tipping

If you're served fairly and well at a restaurant, you should round up the bill as you're paying, but a service charge is always included. (Don't leave money on the table.) Bar bills and taxi fares can also be rounded up. Tour guides on day excursions expect to be tipped.

## Taxes & Refunds

A 22% Value Added Tax (VAT) is imposed upon most purchases and services and is included in the price. If your purchases exceed 500KN in one store you can claim a refund upon leaving the country. Ask the merchants for the paperwork but don't be surprised if they don't have it. You could try to bargain down the price if this happens.

## POST & COMMUNICATIONS

## Post

Mail sent to Poste Restante, 10000 Zagreb, Croatia, is held at the post office (open 24 hours) next to the Zagreb train station. A good coastal address to use is c/o Poste Restante, Main Post Office, 21000 Split, Croatia.

If you have an AmEx card, most Atlas travel agencies will hold your mail. Consult AmEx for a list of the cooperating agencies.

## Telephone

To call Croatia from abroad, dial your international access code, ☎ 385 (the country phone code for Croatia), the area code (without the initial zero) and the local number. When calling from one region to another within Croatia, use the initial zero but do not use the area code if calling within the region.

To make a phone call from Croatia, go to the main post office – phone calls placed from hotel rooms are much more expensive. You'll need a phonecard to use public telephones.

Phonecards are sold according to units (*impulsa*) and you can buy cards of 25/50/100/ 200 units for 15/25/40/70KN. These can be purchased at any post office and most to-bacco shops and newspaper kiosks. Many new phone boxes have a button on the upper left with a flag symbol. Press the button and you get instructions in English. Using a 100-unit phonecard, a three-minute call from Croatia will cost around 17KN to the UK and the USA, 25KN to Australia and 13KN to other European countries. The international access code is ☎ 00. For emergency and other useful service numbers see the boxed text 'Emergency Services' later.

## Email & Internet Access

Internet cafés are becoming increasingly plentiful in Croatia; their locations are noted in each city entry. The going rate is about 30KN per hour and the connections are usually good. America Online (AOL) has access numbers in Zagreb, Split, Rijeka and Dubrovnik.

## DIGITAL RESOURCES

All regions and many municipalities now have websites that range from collections of pretty pictures to detailed information on accommodation and activities. More hotels now have email addresses, which makes reservations easier. You can contact the Zagreb bus station at W www.akz.hr for information on schedules and fares. For train information check the Croatian Railways site on W www.hznet.hr and Croatian Telecom has an online phone directory in English at W imenik.hinet.hr. The useful website W www.visit-croatia.co.uk is a good stop for updated practical information.

## BOOKS

For a comprehensive account of the personalities and events surrounding the collapse of the former Yugoslavia it would be hard to go past *Yugoslavia: Death of a Nation* by Laura Silber & Allan Little, based on the 1995 BBC television series of the same name. Richard Holbrooke's *To End a War* is a riveting look at the people and events surrounding the Dayton peace agreement. *Café Europa* is a series of essays by a Croatian journalist, Slavenka Drakulić, which provides an inside look at life in the country since independence. Rebecca West's 1937 travel classic, *Black Lamb & Grey Falcon*, contains a long section on Croatia as part of her trip through Yugoslavia. Robert Kaplan's *Balkan Ghosts* touches on Croatia's part in the tangled web of Balkan history. Marcus Tanner's *Croatia: A Nation*

*Forged in War* provides an excellent overview of Croatia's history.

For a more comprehensive guide to Croatia, pick up Lonely Planet's *Croatia*. There's also Zoë Brân's *After Yugoslavia*, part of the Lonely Planet Journeys series, which recounts the author's recent trip through the country.

## NEWSPAPERS & MAGAZINES

The most respected daily in Croatia is *Vjesnik*, but the most daring is the satirical news weekly *Feral Tribune*. Its investigative articles and sly graphics keep Croatian politicians and businesspeople edgy. The English-language *Croatia Times* covers social, political and cultural developments and can be counted on for a rosy view of Croatian life. American, British and French newspapers and magazines can be hard to find outside large cities.

## RADIO & TV

The three national television stations fill a lot of their air time with foreign programming, generally American and always in the original language. For local news, residents of Zadar, Split, Vinkovci and Osijek turn to their regional stations. Croatian Radio broadcasts news in English four times daily (8am, 10am, 2pm and 11pm) on FM frequencies 88.9, 91.3 and 99.3.

## TIME

Croatia is on Central European Time (GMT/UTC plus one hour). Daylight saving comes into effect at the end of March, when clocks are turned forward an hour. At the end of September they're turned back an hour.

## LAUNDRY

Self-service laundrettes are virtually unknown outside of Zagreb. Most camping grounds have laundry facilities, hotels will wash clothes for a (hefty) fee or you could make arrangements with the proprietor if you're staying in private accommodation.

## TOILETS

Toilets in train or bus stations sometimes charge 2KN but it's usually not a problem to use the free toilets in a bar, café or restaurant.

## HEALTH

Everyone must pay to see a doctor at a public hospital (*bolnica*) or medical centre (*dom zdravcja*) but charges are reasonable. Travel insurance is important, especially if you have a serious accident and have to be hospitalised. Medical centres often have dentists on the staff, otherwise you can go to a private dental clinic *(zubna ordinacija)*.

## WOMEN TRAVELLERS

Women face no special danger in Croatia although women on their own may be harassed and followed in the larger coastal cities. Some local bars and cafés seem like private men's clubs; a woman alone is likely to be greeted with sudden silence and cold stares. There are few rules about appropriate dress and topless sunbathing is considered acceptable.

## GAY & LESBIAN TRAVELLERS

Homosexuality has been legal in Croatia since 1977 and is generally tolerated as long as it remains discreet. Public displays of affection between members of the same sex may meet with hostility, however, especially outside major cities. A small lesbian and gay community is developing in Zagreb but not to the extent of many Western European cities.

## DISABLED TRAVELLERS

Because of the number of wounded war veterans, more attention is being paid to the needs of disabled travellers. Public toilets at bus stations, train stations, airports and large public venues are usually wheelchair accessible. Large hotels are wheelchair accessible but very little private accommodation is. Bus and train stations in Zagreb, Zadar, Rijeka, Split and Dubrovnik are wheelchair accessible but the local Jadrolinija ferries are not. For further information, get in touch with **Savez Organizacija Invalida Hrvatske** *(☎/fax 01-48 29 394; Savska cesta 3, 10000 Zagreb)*.

## SENIOR TRAVELLERS

Although there are no transportation discounts available to seniors, most museums and attractions offer the same discounts to people over 60 as to students. Your passport usually suffices as proof of age.

## DANGERS & ANNOYANCES

Land mines left over from the war in Croatia pose no threat to the average visitor but it's most important to be aware that the former confrontation line between Croat and federal forces is still undergoing de-mining operations. Eastern Slavonia was heavily mined and, out of

### Emergency Services

In the event of an emergency call ☎ 92 for police, ☎ 93 for fire, ☎ 94 for emergency medical assistance and ☎ 901 for an operator-assisted call. Motorists can contact Hrvatski Autoclub (HAK; Croatian Auto Club) for help or advice – call ☎ 987 HAK *(vučna služba)* for road assistance.

These numbers can be dialled nationwide.

the main city of Osijek, de-mining is not yet complete. Main roads from Zagreb to the coast that pass through Karlovac and Knin are completely safe but it would be unwise to stray into fields or abandoned villages.

Personal security and theft are not problems in Croatia. The police and military are well disciplined and it's highly unlikely you'll have any problems with them in any of the places covered in this chapter.

See the boxed text 'Emergency Services' for emergency telephone numbers.

## BUSINESS HOURS

Banking hours are 7.30am to 7pm on weekdays and 8am to noon on Saturday. Many shops are open 8am to 7pm on weekdays and until 2pm on Saturday. Along the coast, life is more relaxed; shops and offices frequently close around 1pm for an afternoon break. Croats are early risers and by 7am there will be lots of people on the street and many places will already be open.

## PUBLIC HOLIDAYS & SPECIAL EVENTS

Public holidays are New Year's Day (1 January), Easter Monday (March/April), Labour Day (1 May), Bleiburg and Way of the Cross Victims Day (15 May), Statehood Day (30 May), Day of Antifascist Struggle (22 June), Homeland Thanksgiving Day (5 August), Feast of the Assumption (15 August), All Saints' Day (1 November) and Christmas and Feast of St Stephen (25 and 26 December). Statehood Day marks the anniversary of the declaration of independence in 1991, while Day of Antifascist Struggle commemorates the outbreak of resistance in 1941.

In July and August there are summer festivals in Dubrovnik, Opatija, Split and Zagreb. Mardi Gras celebrations marking the start of Lent have recently been revived in numerous towns with the attendant parades and festivities. The many traditional annual events held around Croatia are included under Special Events in the individual destination sections.

## ACTIVITIES
### Kayaking
There are countless possibilities for anyone with a folding sea kayak, especially in the Elafiti and Kornati Islands. Lopud is a good launching point to explore the Elafiti Islands and there's a daily ferry from Dubrovnik. Sali on Dugi Otok is close to the Kornati Islands and is connected by daily ferry to Zadar.

### Hiking
Risnjak National Park at Crni Lug, 12km west of Delnice between Zagreb and Rijeka, is a good hiking area in summer. Because of the likelihood of heavy snowfalls, hiking is only advisable from late spring to early autumn. It's a 9km, 2½-hour climb from the entrance of the park at Bijela Vodica to Veliki Risnjak (1528m). The steep gorges and beech forests of Paklenica National Park, 40km northeast of Zadar, also offer excellent hiking.

### Scuba Diving
The clear waters and varied underwater life of the Adriatic have led to a flourishing dive industry along the coast. Cave diving is the real speciality in Croatia; night diving and wreck diving are also offered and there are coral reefs in some places but in rather deep water.

You must get a permit for a boat dive but this is easy; go to the harbour captain in any port with your passport, certification card and 100KN. Permission is valid for a year in any dive spot in the country. If you dive with a dive centre it will take care of the paperwork.

Most of the coastal resorts mentioned in this chapter have dive shops. See the website for **Diving Croatia** (W *www.diving.hr*) for contact information.

## ACCOMMODATION
Along the Croatian coast, accommodation is priced according to three seasons, which tend to vary from place to place. Generally October to May are the cheapest months, June and September are mid-priced, but count on paying top price for the peak season, which runs for a six-week period in July and August. Prices quoted in this chapter are for the peak period and do not include 'residence tax', which runs

from about 4KN to 7.50KN depending on the location and season. Deduct about 25% if you come in June, the beginning of July and September, about 35% for May and October and about 50% for all other times. Note that prices for rooms in Zagreb are pretty much constant all year and that many hotels on the coast close in winter. Some places offer half-board which is bed and two meals a day, usually breakfast and one other meal.

### Camping
Nearly 100 camping grounds are scattered along the Croatian coast. Most operate only from mid-May to September, although a few are open in April and October. In May and late September, call ahead to make sure the camping ground is open before beginning the long trek out.

Many camping grounds, especially in Istria, are gigantic 'autocamps' with restaurants, shops and row upon row of caravans. Expect to pay up to 100KN for the site at some of the larger establishments but half that at most other camping grounds, in addition to 38KN to 48KN per person.

Nudist camping grounds (marked FKK) are among the best because their secluded locations ensure peace and quiet. However, bear in mind that freelance camping is officially prohibited.

### Hostels
The **Croatian YHA** (☎ *01-48 47 472, fax 48 47 474*; W *www.nncomp.com/hfhs/; Dežmanova 9, Zagreb*) operates youth hostels in Dubrovnik, Zadar, Zagreb and Pula. Nonmembers pay an additional 10KN per person daily for a stamp on a welcome card; six stamps entitles you to a membership. Prices in this chapter are for high season during July and August; prices fall the rest of the year. The Croatian YHA can also provide information about private youth hostels in Krk and Zagreb.

### Private Rooms
Private rooms in local homes are the best accommodation in Croatia. Although you may be greeted by offers of *sobe* (rooms) as you step off your bus and boat, rooms are most often arranged by travel agencies. The most expensive rooms are three-star and have private facilities in a place resembling a small guesthouse. Some of the better ones are listed in this chapter. It's best to call in advance as

the owners often will meet you at the bus station or ferry dock. In a two-star room, the bathroom is shared with one other room; in a one-star room, the bathroom is shared with two other rooms or with the owner who is usually an elderly widow. Breakfast is usually not included but sometimes can be arranged for an additional 25KN. Be sure to clarify whether the price agreed upon is per person or per room. If you're travelling in a small group, it may be worthwhile to get a small apartment with cooking facilities, which are widely available along the coast.

It makes little sense to price-shop from agency to agency since prices are fixed by the local tourist association. Whether you deal with the owner directly or book through an agency, you'll pay a 30% surcharge for stays of less than four nights and sometimes 50% or even 100% more for a one-night stay, although you may be able to get them to waive the surcharge if you arrive in the low season. Prices for private rooms in this chapter are for a four-night stay.

## Hotels

Hotels are ranked from one to five stars with the most in the two- and three-star range. Features, such as satellite TV, direct-dial phones, hi-tech bathrooms, minibars and air-con, are standard in four- and five-star hotels and one star hotels have at least a telephone in the room. Many two- and three-star hotels offer satellite TV but you'll find better decor in the higher categories. Unfortunately the country is saddled with too many 1970s, concrete-block hotels, built to warehouse package tourists, but some entrepreneurs are starting up smaller, more personal establishments that can be good value. Prices for hotels in this chapter are for the pricey six-week period that begins in mid-July and lasts until the end of August. During this period, some hotels may demand a surcharge for stays of less than four nights but this surcharge is usually waived the rest of the year and prices drop steeply.

## FOOD

A restaurant (*restauracija*) or pub may also be called a *gostionica* and a café is known as a *kavana*. Self-service cafeterias are quick, easy and inexpensive, though the quality of the food tends to vary quite a lot. Better restaurants aren't that much more expensive if you choose carefully. The cheapest dishes

are pasta and risotto, which can be a filling meal. Fish dishes are often charged by weight (from 220KN to 280KN a kilo), which makes it difficult to know how much a certain dish will cost but an average portion is about 250g. Some restaurants tack on a 10% cover charge, which is *supposed* to be mentioned on the menu.

Breakfast is included in the price of the hotels mentioned in this chapter and usually includes a juice drink, bread, cheese, yogurt, cereal and cold cuts, as well as coffee and tea. No restaurants serve breakfast. Throughout the former Yugoslavia the breakfast of the people is *burek* (a greasy layered pie made with meat) or *sira* (cheese), which is cut on a huge metal tray.

A load of fruit and vegetables from the local market can make a healthy, cheap picnic lunch. There are plenty of supermarkets in Croatia – cheese, bread, wine and milk are readily available and fairly cheap. The person behind the meat counter at supermarkets will make a big cheese or bologna sandwich for you upon request and you only pay the price of the ingredients.

## Regional Dishes

The Adriatic coast excels in seafood, including scampi, *prstaci* (shellfish) and Dalmatian *brodet* (mixed fish stewed with rice), all cooked in olive oil and served with boiled vegetables or *tartufe* (mushrooms) in Istria. In the Croatian interior, watch for *manistra od bobića* (beans and fresh maize soup) or *štrukle* (cottage cheese rolls). A Zagreb speciality is *štrukli* (boiled cheesecake).

Italian pizza and pasta are good options in Istria and Dalmatia, costing about half of what you'd pay in Western Europe.

## DRINKS

It's customary to have a small glass of brandy before a meal and to accompany the food with one of Croatia's fine wines. Ask for the local regional wine. Croatia is also famous for its *šljivovica* (plum brandies), *travarica* (herbal brandies), *vinjak* (cognacs) and liqueurs, such as maraschino, a cherry liqueur made in Zadar, or herbal *pelinkovac*. Italian-style espresso is popular in Croatia.

Zagreb's Ožujsko *pivo* (beer) is very good but Karlovačko beer from Karlovac is even better. You'll probably want to practise saying *živjeli!* (cheers!).

CROATIA

## ENTERTAINMENT

Culture was heavily subsidised by the communists and admission to operas, operettas and concerts is still reasonable. The main theatres offering musical programmes are listed in this chapter, so note the location and drop by some time during the day to see what's on and to purchase tickets. In the interior cities, winter is the best time to enjoy the theatres and concert halls. The main season at the opera houses of Rijeka, Split and Zagreb runs from October to May. These close for holidays in summer and the cultural scene shifts to the many summer festivals. Ask at municipal tourist offices about cultural events in their area.

Discos operate in summer in the coastal resorts and all year in the interior cities, but the best way to mix with the local population is to enjoy a leisurely coffee or ice cream in a café. With the first hint of mild weather, Croatians head for an outdoor terrace to drink, smoke and watch the passing parade. In the summer season, many resort hotels sponsor free dances on their terraces.

## SHOPPING

Tablecloths, pillowcases and blouses embroidered Croatian style in red geometric patterns make an easy souvenir to pack. Lavender and other fragrant herbs made into scented sachets or oils are found on most Dalmatian islands, especially Hvar, which is known for its lavender fields. Many of the jewellery stores are run by immigrants from Kosovo who have a centuries-old tradition in silver working. The workmanship on silver filigree earrings, bracelets and decorative objects is often of astonishingly high quality.

# Getting There & Away

## AIR

Croatia's main airline **Croatia Airlines** (☎ 01-48 19 633; **W** www.croatiaairlines.hr; Zrinjevac 17, Zagreb) has direct flights from Zagreb to Amsterdam, Berlin, Brussels, Frankfurt, İstanbul, London, Mostar, Munich, Paris, Prague, Sarajevo, Skopje, Tel Aviv, Vienna, Warsaw and Zürich. In summer there are also direct flights from London, Manchester and Rome to Dubrovnik and London and Manchester to Pula. There's a **Croatia Airlines**

minibus (reservations ☎ 051-330 207) that connects Zagreb airport with Rijeka daily (100KN). (Note that all batteries must be removed from checked luggage for all Croatia Airlines flights.)

## LAND
### Austria

**Bus** Eurolines Vienna runs a weekly bus from Vienna to Rijeka (€36, 8¼ hours), Split (€51, 15 hours) and Zadar (€43, 13 hours) and a twice daily bus (except Sunday) to Zagreb (€26, 4¾ hours).

**Train** The Ljubljana express travels daily from Vienna to Rijeka (€68.50, eight hours), via Ljubljana, and the EuroCity Croatia from Vienna to Zagreb (€62.30, 6½ hours); both services travel via Maribor, Slovenia.

### Benelux

Budget Bus/Eurolines offers a weekly bus year-round from Amsterdam to Zagreb (€106, 26 hours) and another bus to Rijeka and Split with an extra weekly bus to both destinations during summer. Eurolines operates a twice-weekly service all year from Brussels to Zagreb, and another weekly bus to Rijeka and the Dalmatian coast.

### Bosnia-Hercegovina

There are bus connections departing from Sarajevo (€21.50, six hours, daily) and Mostar (€10.50, three hours) for Dubrovnik; from Međugorje, Mostar and Sarajevo to Split (€16.50, seven hours), and also from Sarajevo to Zagreb (€26.50, eight hours) and Rijeka (€32).

### Germany

**Bus** Deutsche Touring GmbH runs many buses between German cities and Croatia, largely to service Croatian 'guest workers' in Germany. The prices and durations given below are for the entire journey from the German city where the bus originates to the final destination in Croatia.

There is a weekly bus leaving Frankfurt via Stuttgart, Ulm and Munich for Rijeka, Poreč, Rovinj and Pula (€85, 18½ hours); a daily bus from Bochum through Bonn, Düsseldorf, Frankfurt, Hamburg (twice weekly), Cologne, Stuttgart and Ulm to Rijeka, Zadar and Split (€115, 27½ hours); a twice-weekly bus from Berlin to Rijeka, Zadar and Split (€110, 24 hours); a weekly bus from Dortmund, Düsseldorf, Cologne, Bonn, Frankfurt, Stuttgart, Ulm and Munich to Dubrovnik (€125, 35 hours); a daily bus from Bochum that via Bonn, Hamburg (twice weekly) and Pforzheim to Zagreb (€105, 26 hours); and a direct bus from Berlin to Zagreb (€95, 17 hours, four times weekly). Information is available at bus stations in the cities mentioned. Baggage is €3 per piece.

**Train** There are three daily trains running from Munich to Zagreb (€75, nine hours) via Salzburg and Ljubljana and a daily train from Berlin to Zagreb (€162, 16 hours).

## Hungary

The four daily trains from Zagreb to Budapest (€21, 6½ hours) stop in Nagykanizsa, the first main junction inside Hungary (€9). The price of the fare is the same for one way and return.

## Italy

**Bus** Trieste is well connected with the Istrian coast. There are around six buses a day to Rijeka (€7.10, two to three hours), plus buses to Rovinj (€10.10, 3½ hours, three daily) Poreč (€8.05, 2¼ hours, three daily) and Pula (€13.75, 3¾ hours, four daily). There are fewer buses on Sunday. To Dalmatia there's a daily bus that leaves at 5.30pm and stops at Rijeka, Zadar (€23, 7½ hours), Split (€35.60, 10½ hours) and Dubrovnik (€53.20, 27 hours). There's also a bus from Venice leaving at 1.45pm Monday to Saturday that stops in Poreč (2½ hours), Rovinj (three hours) and Pula (€20, 3¼ hours). There's also a Friday night bus from Milan to Poreč, Rovinj and Pula (€49, 8½ hours).

For more information about bus travel, see W www.croazia travel.it.

**Train** Between Venice and Zagreb (€40, seven hours) there's an overnight direct train and a daily train via Trieste and Ljubljana.

## Slovenia

**Bus** Slovenia is also well connected with the Istrian coast. There are two buses a day between Pula and Portorož (€11, 1½ hours) and Koper (€12, four hours), as well as one weekday bus between Rovinj and Koper (€10.75, three hours) and Poreč and Portorož (€5, 1½ hours), as well as a daily bus in summer from Rovinj to Ljubljana (128KN, 2½ hours).

**Train** There are seven trains daily between Ljubljana and Zagreb (3853 SIT, three hours) and seven between Ljubljana and Rijeka (2466 SIT, three hours).

## Yugoslavia

**Bus** There's one bus each morning from Zagreb to Belgrade (€25, six hours). At Bajakovo on the border, a Yugoslav bus takes you on to Belgrade. The border between Montenegro and Croatia is open to visitors, allowing Americans, Australians, Canadians and Brits to enter visa-free. For further information regarding getting to/from Montenegro see the Dubrovnik Getting There & Away section of this chapter.

**Train** Five trains daily connect Zagreb with Belgrade (€16.50, six hours).

## Car & Motorcycle

The main highway entry/exit points between Croatia and Hungary are Goričan (between Nagykanizsa and Varaždin), Gola (23km east of Koprivnica), Terezino Polje (opposite Barcs) and Donji Miholjac (7km south of Harkány). There are 29 crossing points to/from Slovenia, too many to list here. There are 23 border crossings into Bosnia-Hercegovina and 10 into Yugoslavia, including the main Zagreb to Belgrade highway. Major destinations in Bosnia-Hercegovina, like Sarajevo, Mostar and Međugorje, are accessible from Zagreb, Split and Dubrovnik.

## SEA

Regular boats operated by several companies connect Croatia with Italy. All of the boat-company offices in Split are located inside the ferry terminal.

**Jadrolinija** (☎ 51-211 444, fax 211 485, W www.jadrolinija.hr; Riva 16, Rijeka; in Ancona ☎ 071-20 71 465, in Bari ☎ 080-52 75 439), Croatia's national boat line, runs three to six car ferries a week between Ancona and Split (€36.50, 10 hours). From June to September these ferries stop twice a week at Stari Grad on Hvar and at Korčula. There's also a line from Ancona to Zadar (€34, seven hours) two or three times weekly and one line from Bari to Dubrovnik up to four times each week (€36.50, 6½ hours). Prices are for deck passage in the low season and does not include the embarkation fee of €3 in Italian ports. Prices increase by about 25% in July and August.

SEM (☎ 21-338 292, fax 338 291; W www .sem-marina.hr; Gat Sv Duje, Split; in Ancona ☎ 071-20 40 90) connects Ancona with Split four times a week in winter and daily in summer and Ancona with Stari Grad on Hvar (8½ hours) in July and August.

SNAV (in Ancona ☎ 021-20 76 116, in Naples ☎ 081-76 12 348, in Split ☎ 21-322 252; W www.snavali.com) This company has a fast car-ferry that links Ancona and Split in only four hours (€62.50, daily) and a passenger boat that connects Split, Vela Luka on Korčula and Stari Grad with the Italian cities of Pescara, Vasto and Giulianova daily in summer. One-way/return fares are €98.50/ 150 in the low season and €114/181 in the high season.

From May to mid-September La Rivera (in Rome ☎ 06-509 16 061, in Naples ☎ 081-76 45 808; W www.lariverabus.it), an Italian company, offers a combination bus and boat trip two or three times a week from Rome and Naples to Korčula (both €117, 9¼ hours) and Dubrovnik (€139, 12½ hours). In Croatia, contact Marko Polo Tours (☎ 020-715 400, fax 715 800; e marko-polo-tours@du.tel.hr) in Korčula and Jadroagent in Dubrovnik.

In addition to connecting Ancona and Split two to four times a week for the same price as Jadrolinija, Adriatica Navigazione (in Venice ☎ 041-781 611, in Ancona 071-20 74 334; W www.adriatica.it) runs the Marconi between Trieste and Rovinj (€15.49, 3½ hours) from May to September stopping at the Brijuni Islands six times a week and stopping three times a week in July and August at Poreč (from Trieste €13.94, 2¾ hours). Book through Aurora Viaggi (☎ 040-631 300, Via Milano 20, Trieste) and any Jadroagent office in Croatia.

Until 2002 there was a regular ferry connecting Venice with Pula and Zadar. To see if the service has re-commenced, check with Agenzia Favret (☎ 041-25 73 511, via Appia 20) in Venice.

From mid-May to mid-September Ustica Lines (in Venice ☎ 041-27 12 646, in Trieste ☎ 040-67 02 711; W www.usticalines.it) runs five passenger boats a week from Trieste to Pula (€22, two hours) that stop twice a week in Poreč (€20, one hour). There are also up to six passenger boats a week mid-May to mid-October between Venice and Rovinj (€40, 2½ hours) that stop three times a week in Poreč (€40, one hour). In Croatia, Jadroagent

in Pula and Istra Line (☎ 52-451 067, Partizansko 2) in Poreč sell tickets.

## DEPARTURE TAX

Airport departure tax is US$11, which is included in the cost of the ticket. There is no port tax if you leave Croatia by boat but there is an embarkation tax of €3 from Italian ports.

# Getting Around

## AIR

Croatia Airlines has daily flights between Zagreb and Dubrovnik (906KN, one hour), Pula (483KN, 45 minutes), Split (627KN, 45 minutes) and Zadar (575KN, 40 minutes). Prices are somewhat lower in the low season and there are discounts for seniors and people aged under 26.

## BUS

Bus services in Croatia are excellent. Prices can vary substantially between companies and depend on the route taken, but the prices in this book should give you an idea of costs (and unless otherwise noted, all bus prices are for one-way fares). Luggage stowed in the baggage compartment under the bus costs extra (6KN a piece, including insurance).

At large stations, bus tickets must be bought at the office, not from drivers; try to book ahead to be sure of a seat. Tickets for buses that arrive from somewhere else are usually purchased from the conductor. Since there are several companies serving each route, buy only a one-way ticket or you'll be locked into one company's schedule for the return. On Croatian bus schedules, vozi svaki dan means 'every day', and ne vozi nedjeljom ni praznikom means 'not Sunday and public holidays'.

## TRAIN

Train travel is about 15% cheaper than bus travel and often more comfortable, though slower. Local trains usually have only unreserved, 2nd-class seats but they're rarely crowded. Reservations may be required on express trains. 'Executive' trains have only 1st-class seats and are 40% more expensive than local trains. Most train stations have left-luggage offices charging about 10KN apiece (passport required).

On timetables in Croatia the word for arrivals is dolazak and for departures odlazak or *polazak*. Other terms you may find include *poslovni* (express train), *brzi* or *ubrazni* (fast train), *putnički* (local train), *rezerviranje mjesta obvezatno* (compulsory seat reservation), *presjedanje* (change of trains), *ne vozi nedjeljom i blagdanom* (no service Sunday and holidays) and *svakodnevno* (daily).

## CAR & MOTORCYCLE

Motorists require vehicle registration papers and the green insurance card (see the introductory Getting Around chapter for details) to enter Croatia. Petrol is either leaded super, unleaded *(bezolovni)* or diesel. You have to pay tolls on the motorways around Zagreb, to use the Učka tunnel between Rijeka and Istria, the bridge to Krk Island, as well as the road from Rijeka to Delnice.

See the boxed text 'Emergency Services' earlier for emergency road assistance details.

Unless otherwise posted, the speed limits for cars and motorcycles are 50km/h in the built-up areas, 80km/h on main highways and 130km/h on motorways. On any of Croatia's winding two-lane highways, it's illegal to pass long military convoys or a line of cars caught behind a slow-moving truck. Drive defensively, as some local drivers lack discipline.

### Rental

The large car-rental chains represented in Croatia are Avis, Budget, Europcar and Hertz. Throughout Croatia, Avis is allied with the Autotehna company, while Hertz is often represented by Kompas.

Independent local companies are often much cheaper than the international chains, but Avis, Budget, Europcar and Hertz have the big advantage of offering one-way rentals that allow you to drop the car off at any one of their many stations in Croatia free of charge.

Prices at local companies begin at around 260KN a day with unlimited kilometres. Shop around as deals vary widely and 'special' discounts and weekend rates are often available. Third-party public liability insurance is included by law, but make sure your quoted price includes full collision insurance, called collision damage waiver (CDW). Otherwise your responsibility for damage done to the vehicle is usually determined as a percentage of the car's value. Full CDW begins at 40KN a day extra (compulsory for those aged under 25), theft insurance is 15KN a day and personal accident insurance another 40KN a day.

Sometimes you can get a lower car-rental rate by booking the car from abroad. Tour companies in Western Europe often have fly-drive packages that include a flight to Croatia and a car (two-person minimum).

## BOAT
### Jadrolinija Ferries

Year-round Jadrolinija car ferries operate along the Bari–Rijeka–Dubrovnik coastal route, stopping at Zadar, Split, and the islands of Hvar, Korčula and Mljet, with less frequent services in winter. The most scenic section is Split to Dubrovnik, which all Jadrolinija ferries cover during the day.

Ferries are a lot more comfortable than buses, though considerably more expensive. From Rijeka to Dubrovnik the deck fare is 226KN, but it's at least 10% cheaper from October to May and there's a 20% reduction on the return portion of a return ticket. With a through ticket, deck passengers can stop at any port for up to a week, provided they notify the purser beforehand and have their ticket validated. This is much cheaper than buying individual sector tickets but is only good for one stopover. Cabins should be booked a week ahead, but deck space is usually available on all sailings.

Deck passage on Jadrolinija is just that: reclining seats *(poltrone)* are about 36KN extra and four-berth cabins (if available) begin at 355KN (Rijeka to Dubrovnik). Cabins can be arranged at the reservation counter aboard ship, but advance bookings are recommended if you want to be sure of a place. You must buy tickets in advance at an agency or Jadrolinija office since they are not sold on board.

### Other Ferries

Local ferries connect the bigger offshore islands with each other and with the mainland. Some of the ferries operate only a couple of times a day and, once the vehicular capacity is reached, the remaining motorists must wait for the next available service. During summer the lines of waiting cars can be long, so it's important to arrive early.

Foot passengers and cyclists should have no problem getting on but you must buy your tickets at an agency before boarding since they are not sold on board. You should bear in mind that taking a bicycle on these services will incur an extra charge, which depends on the distance.

## HITCHING

Hitching is never entirely safe in any country in the world, and we don't recommend it. Those travellers who decide to hitch should understand that they are taking a small but potentially serious risk. If you do choose to hitch you'll be safer travelling in pairs and let someone know where you are planning to go.

Hitching in Croatia is undependable. You will have better luck on the islands but in the interior cars are small and usually full. Tourists never stop. Unfortunately, the image many Croats have of this activity is based on violent movies like *The Hitcher*.

## LOCAL TRANSPORT

Zagreb has a well-developed tram system as well as local buses but in the rest of the country you'll only find buses. In major cities, such as Rijeka, Split, Zadar and Dubrovnik buses run about every 20 minutes, and less often on Sunday. Small medieval towns along the coast are generally closed to traffic and have infrequent links to outlying suburbs.

### Taxi

Taxis are available in all cities and towns but must be called or boarded at a taxi stand; note that it's usually not possible to hail them in the street. Prices are high (flag fall is 25KN) and are generally the same throughout the country.

## ORGANISED TOURS

An interesting option for sailing enthusiasts is **Katarina Line** (☎ 051-272 110; W *www*.katarina-line.hr; *Tita 75, Opatija*), which offers week-long cruises from Opatija to Krk, Rab, Pag, Mali Lošinj and Cres or cruises from Split to Zadar that pass the Kornati Islands. Prices start at €250 a week per person and include half-board.

For specific tours in individual regions, see Organised Tours in the destination sections.

# Zagreb

☎ 01 • pop 780,000

Zagreb is not a city that dazzles you with its charms at first glance – it requires time to appreciate its value. Spreading up from the Sava River, Zagreb sits on the southern slopes of Mt Medvednica and throbs with the energy you would expect from a capital city.

The nightlife is good, a wealth of outdoor cafés are packed from the first hint of mild weather and there's a decent assortment of museums and galleries to explore. Medieval Zagreb developed from the 11th to the 13th centuries in the twin villages of Kaptol and Gradec, which make up the city's hilly old town. Kaptol grew around St Stephen's Cathedral (now renamed the Cathedral of the Assumption of the Blessed Virgin Mary) and Gradec centred on St Mark's Church.

The lower town is all business with stately Austro-Hungarian buildings housing stores, restaurants and businesses. Parks, fountains and several imposing monuments lighten the sober architecture of the town centre before the scene deteriorates into glum apartment blocks in the suburbs. Since the town centre is the liveliest and most attractive part of the city, it's worthwhile to find central accommodation if at all possible.

## Orientation

As you come out of the train station, you'll see a series of parks and pavilions directly in front of you and the twin neo-Gothic towers of the cathedral in the distance. Trg Jelačića, beyond the northern end of the parks, is the main city square. The bus station is 1km east of the train station. Tram Nos 2 and 6 run from the bus station to the nearby train station, with No 6 continuing to Trg Jelačića.

## Information

**Tourist Offices** The Zagreb **main tourist office** (☎ 48 14 051, fax 48 14 056; e *info@zagreb-touristinfo.hr*; *Trg Jelačića 11; open 8.30am-8pm Mon-Fri, 9am-7pm Sat, 10am-2pm Sun*) has city maps and the free leaflets, *Zagreb Info A-Z*, *Zagreb Events & Performances* and *City Walks*. There's a smaller **tourist office** (☎ 49 21 645; *Zrinjskog 14*) that has shorter opening hours. The tourist office also sells the Zagreb Card, which costs 60KN and includes 72 hours of free transport, a 50% discount on museums and sightseeing tours, and lists various discounts on car rentals, restaurants and parking.

The Croatian Auto Club (HAK) has an **information centre** (☎ 46 40 800; *Derenčinova 20*) in the city.

Plitvice Lakes National Park maintains an **information office** (☎ 46 13 586; *Trg Tomislava 19*). It also has information about other national parks around Croatia.

**Jadrolinija** (☎ 48 73 307; Zrinjevac 20) has information on coastal ferries.

**Money** There are ATMs at the bus and train stations and the airport as well as numerous locations around town. Exchange offices at the bus and train stations change money at the bank rate with 1.5% commission. Both the banks in the train station (open 7am to 9pm) and the bus station (open 6am to 8pm) accept travellers cheques.

The AmEx representative in Zagreb is **Atlas travel agency** (☎ 48 13 933; Zrinjevac 17).

**Post & Communications** Poste-restante mail is held (for one month) in the post office on the eastern side of the train station, which is open 24 hours Monday to Saturday and 1pm to midnight Sunday. Have your correspondence addressed to Poste Restante, 10000 Zagreb, Croatia.

This post office is also the best place for making long-distance telephone calls.

**Email & Internet Access** Zagreb's flashiest Internet café is **Art Net Club** (☎ 45 58 471; Preradovićeva 25; open 9am-11pm daily), which hosts frequent concerts and performances. There's also **Sublink** (☎ 48 11 329; Teslina 12; open 9am-10pm Mon-Sat, 3pm-10pm Sun), which charges 0.25KN a minute and offers a 10% discount to students. There are a number of smaller Internet cafés along Preradovićeva.

**Travel Agencies** Dali Travel (☎ 48 47 472, fax 48 47 474; e hfhs-cms@zg.hinet.hr; Dežmanova 9; open 9am-5pm Mon-Fri), the travel branch of the Croatian YHA, can provide information on HI hostels throughout Croatia and make advance bookings.

It also sells ISIC student cards (40KN) to those who have proof of attendance at an educational institution as well as Euro<26 cards for 30KN, which offer a variety of discounts in participating shops.

**Bookshops** The Algoritam bookshop in the Hotel Dubrovnik off Trg Jelačića has a wide selection of English-language books and magazines to choose from.

**Laundry** Predom (Draškovićeva 31; open 7am-7pm Mon-Fri) is one place to have your clothes cleaned. **Petecin** (Kaptol 11; open

---

### Street Names

In Zagreb, you may notice a discrepancy between the names used in this book and the names you'll actually see on the street. In Croatian, a street name can be rendered either in the nominative or genitive case. The difference is apparent in the name's ending. Thus, Ulica Ljedevita Gaja (street of Ljudevita Gaja) becomes Gajeva ulica (Gaja's street). The latter version is the one most commonly seen on the street sign and used in everyday conversation. The same principle applies to a square (trg) which can be rendered as Trg Petra Preradovića or Preradovićev trg. Some of the more common names are: Trg svetog Marka (Markov trg), Trg Josipa Jurja Strossmayera (Strossmayerov trg), Ulica Andrije Hebranga (Hebrangova), Ulica Pavla Radića (Radićeva), Ulica Augusta Šenoe (Šenoina), Ulica Ivana Tkalčića (Tkalčićeva) and Ulica Nikole Tesle (Teslina). Be aware also that Trg Nikole Sća Zrinskog is almost always called Zrinjevac.

---

8am-8pm Mon-Fri) is another option and it is generally quicker than Predom. Expect to pay about 3KN for underwear, 4KN for a shirt and 10KN for a skirt.

**Left Luggage** There are **left-luggage offices** (open 24hr) in the train station, and a **left luggage office** (open 5am-10pm Mon-Sat, 6am-10pm Sun) in the bus station. The price posted at the left-luggage office in the bus station is 1.20KN per hour, so be careful. At the train station you pay a fixed price of 10KN per day.

**Medical & Emergency Services** If you need to see a doctor, the closest health centre is **KBC Rebro** (☎ 23 88 888; Kišpatićeva 12; open 24hr year-round). It charges 200KN for an examination. The **police station** (☎ 45 63 311; Petrinjska 30) can assist foreigners with visa concerns.

### Things to See

**Kaptol** Zagreb's colourful **Dolac vegetable market** (open daily) is just up the steps from Trg Jelačića and continues north along Opatovina. The twin neo-Gothic spires of the 1899 **Cathedral of the Assumption of the Blessed Virgin Mary** (formerly known as St Stephen's Cathedral) are nearby. Elements of

# ZAGREB

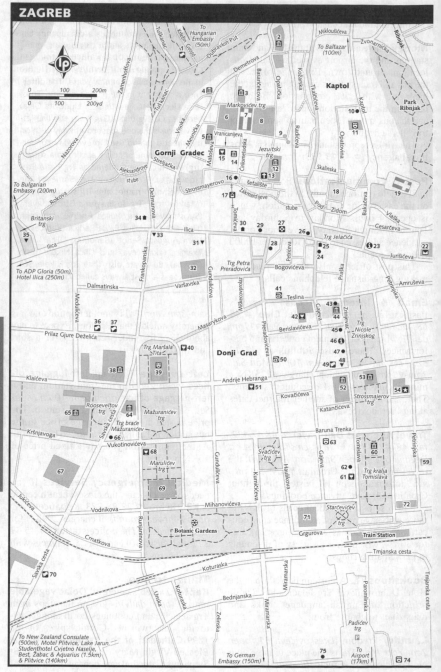

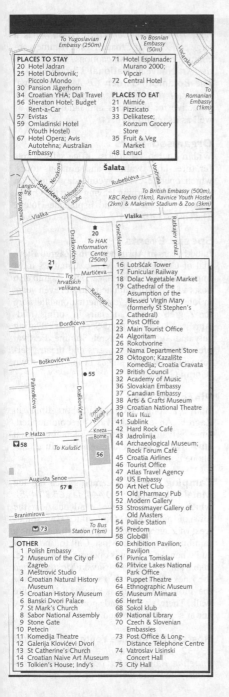

**PLACES TO STAY**
20 Hotel Jadran
25 Hotel Dubrovnik;
   Piccolo Mondo
30 Pansion Jägerhorn
34 Croatian YHA; Dali Travel
56 Sheraton Hotel; Budget
   Rent-a-Car
57 Evistas
59 Omladinski Hotel
   (Youth Hostel)
67 Hotel Opera; Avis
   Autotehna; Australian
   Embassy
71 Hotel Esplanade;
   Murano 2000;
   Vipcar
72 Central Hotel

**PLACES TO EAT**
21 Mimice
31 Pizzicato
33 Delikatese;
   Konzum Grocery
   Store
35 Fruit & Veg
   Market
48 Lenuci

**OTHER**
1 Polish Embassy
2 Museum of the City of
   Zagreb
3 Meštrović Studio
4 Croatian Natural History
   Museum
5 Croatian History Museum
6 Banski Dvori Palace
7 St Mark's Church
8 Sabor National Assembly
9 Stone Gate
10 Petecin
11 Komedija Theatre
12 Galerija Klovićevi Dvori
13 St Catherine's Church
14 Croatian Naive Art Museum
15 Tolkien's House; Indy's
16 Lotršćak Tower
17 Funicular Railway
18 Dolac Vegetable Market
19 Cathedral of the
   Assumption of the
   Blessed Virgin Mary
   (formerly St Stephen's
   Cathedral)
22 Post Office
23 Main Tourist Office
24 Algoritam
26 Rokotvorine
27 Nama Department Store
28 Oktogon; Kazalište
   Komedija; Croatia Cravata
29 British Council
32 Academy of Music
36 Slovakian Embassy
37 Canadian Embassy
38 Arts & Crafts Museum
39 Croatian National Theatre
40 Kav Kav
41 Sublink
42 Hard Rock Café
43 Jadrolinija
44 Archaeological Museum;
   Rock Forum Café
45 Croatia Airlines
46 Tourist Office
47 Atlas Travel Agency
49 US Embassy
50 Art Net Club
51 Old Pharmacy Pub
52 Modern Gallery
53 Strossmayer Gallery of
   Old Masters
54 Police Station
55 Predom
58 Glob@l
60 Exhibition Pavilion;
   Pavilijon
61 Pivnica Tomislav
62 Plitvice Lakes National
   Park Office
63 Puppet Theatre
64 Ethnographic Museum
65 Museum Mimara
66 Hertz
68 Sokol klub
69 National Library
70 Czech & Slovenian
   Embassies
73 Post Office & Long-
   Distance Telephone Centre
74 Vatroslav Lisinski
   Concert Hall
75 City Hall

the medieval cathedral on this site, destroyed by an earthquake in 1880, can be seen inside, including 13th-century frescoes, Renaissance pews, marble altars and a baroque pulpit. The baroque **Archiepiscopal Palace** surrounds the cathedral, as do 16th-century fortifications constructed when Zagreb was threatened by the Turks.

**Gradec** From ul Radićeva 5, off Trg Jelačića, a pedestrian walkway called stube Ivana Zakmardija leads to the **Lotršćak Tower** *(open Mon-Sat)* and a funicular railway (1888), which connects the lower and upper towns (2KN one way). The tower has a sweeping 360-degree view of the city. To the right is the baroque **St Catherine's Church**, with Jezuitski trg beyond. The **Galerija Klovićevi Dvori** *(Jezuitski trg 4; open Tues-Sun)* is Zagreb's premier exhibition hall where superb art shows are staged. Further north and to the right is the 13th-century **Stone Gate**, with a painting of the Virgin, which escaped the devastating fire of 1731.

The colourful painted-tile roof of the Gothic **St Mark's Church** *(☎ 48 51 611; Markovićev trg; open 11am-4pm & 5.30pm-7pm daily)* marks the centre of Gradec. Inside are works by Ivan Meštrović, Croatia's most famous modern sculptor. On the eastern side of St Mark's is the **Sabor** (1908), Croatia's National Assembly.

West of the church is the 18th-century **Banski Dvori Palace**, the presidential palace with guards at the door in red ceremonial uniform. Between April and September there is a changing of the guard ceremony at noon on the weekend.

Not far from the palace is the former **Meštrović Studio** *(☎ 48 51 123; Mletačka 8; adult/concession 20/10KN; open 9am-2pm Tues-Fri, 10am-6pm Sat)*, now housing an excellent collection of some 100 sculptures, drawings, lithographs and furniture created by the artist. Other museums nearby include the **Croatian History Museum** *(☎ 48 51 900; Matoševa 9; temporary exhibitions adult/concession 10/5KN; open 10am-5pm Mon-Fri, 10am-1pm Sat & Sun)*; the **Croatian Naive Art Museum** *(☎ 48 51 911; Ćirilometodska 3; adult/concession 10/5KN; open 10am-6pm Tues-Fri & 10am-1pm Sat & Sun)*; and also the **Croatian Natural History Museum** *(☎ 48 51 700; Demetrova 1; adult/concession 15/7KN; open 10am-5pm*

CROATIA

*Tues-Fri, 10am-1pm Sat & Sun).* The best is the **Museum of the City of Zagreb** *(☎ 48 51 364; Opatička 20; adult/concession 20/10KN; open 10am-6pm Tues-Fri, 10am-1pm Sat & Sun),* with a scale model of old Gradec. Summaries in English and German are in each room of the museum, which is in the former Convent of St Claire (1650).

**Lower Town** Zagreb really is a city of museums. There are four in the parks between the train station and Trg Jelačića. The yellow **exhibition pavilion** (1897) across the park from the station presents changing contemporary art exhibitions. The second building north, also in the park, houses the **Strossmayer Gallery of Old Masters** *(☎ 48 95 115; adult/student 20/15KN open 10am-1pm & 5pm-7pm Tues, 10am-1pm Wed-Sun),* paintings by old masters. It's closed on Monday, but you can enter the interior courtyard to see the Baška Slab (1102) from the island of Krk, one of the oldest inscriptions in the Croatian language.

The fascinating **Archaeological Museum** *(☎ 48 73 101; Trg Nikole Zrinjskog 19; adult/concession 20/10KN; open 10am-5pm Tues-Fri, 10am-1pm Sat & Sun)* has a wide-ranging display of artefacts from prehistoric times through to the medieval period. Behind the museum is a garden of Roman sculpture that is turned into a pleasant open-air café in the summer.

**West of the Centre** The **Museum Mimara** *(☎ 48 28 100; Rooseveltov trg 5; adult/concession 20/15KN; open 10am-5pm Tues, Wed, Fri & Sat, 10am-7pm Thur, 10am-2pm Sun)* houses a diverse collection amassed by Ante Topić Mimara and donated to Croatia. Housed in a neo-Renaissance palace, the collection includes icons, glassware, sculpture, Oriental art and works by renowned painters, such as Rembrandt, Velasquez, Raphael and Degas. The **Modern Gallery** *(☎ 49 22 368; Andrije Hebrangova 1; admission free; open 10am-6pm Tues-Sat & 10am-1pm Sun)* has an excellent collection of paintings by Croatian masters created from 1850 to 1950 when Croatian art was at its zenith and also presents temporary exhibitions.

The neo-baroque **Croatian National Theatre** *(Trg Maršala Tita 15),* dates from 1895, and has Ivan Meštrović's sculpture *Fountain of Life* (1905) in front. The **Ethnographic Museum** *(☎ 48 26 to 20; Trg Mažuranićev*

*14; adult/concession 15/10KN; open 10am-6pm Tues-Thur, 10am-1pm Fri-Sun)* has a large collection of Croatian folk costumes, accompanied by English captions. To the south the Art-Nouveau **National Library** (1907). The **Botanical Garden** *(ul Mihanovićeva; admission free; open 9am-7pm Tues-Sun)* is attractive for its plants and landscaping, as well as its restful corners.

## Organised Tours
Within Zagreb, the tourist office sells tickets for three-hour walking and minibus tours, which operate every Wednesday afternoon and Saturday morning leaving from the Opera, Sheraton, Dubrovnik and Esplanade Hotels. The cost is 120KN.

## Special Events
In odd years in April there's the Zagreb Biennial of Contemporary Music, Croatia's most important music event since 1961. Zagreb also hosts a festival of animated films in even years in June. Croatia's largest international fairs are the Zagreb grand trade fairs in spring (mid-April) and autumn (mid-September). During July and August the Zagreb Summer Festival presents a cycle of concerts and theatre performances on open stages in the upper town (Gornji Gradec).

## Places to Stay
Budget accommodation is in short supply in Zagreb. An early arrival is recommended, since private room-finding agencies are an attractive alternative and usually refuse telephone bookings.

**Camping** There's a camping area outside **Motel Plitvice** *(☎ 65 30 444, fax 65 30 445),* which is not in Plitvice at all but near the town of Lučko on the Obilazinica Hwy southwest of Zagreb. The motel sometimes runs a minibus from Savski Most. Call to find out if and when the service is operating. Otherwise, take tram No 7 or 14 to Savski Most and then the Lučko bus to Lučko village, from where the motel/camp site is about a 10-minute walk. There's a lake and sports centre nearby and it's open year-round.

**Hostels** The **Ravnice Youth Hostel** *(☎/fax 23 32 325;* e *ravnice-youth-hostel@zg .hinet.hr; Ravnice 38d; dorm beds 99KN)* is a fairly new and well-run private hostel that offers good value in its doubles, quads and one 10-bed dorm. Take either tram No 11 or 12 from Trg Jelačića.

Noisy **Omladinski Hotel** (☎ 48 41 261, fax 48 41 269; Petrinjska 77; dorm beds 65KN, singles/doubles 149/197KN, with private bathroom 202/267KN; open year-round) is actually a large youth hostel near the train station. Check-out is 9am.

**Studenthotel Cvjetno Naselje** (☎ 45 93 587; singles/doubles 240/360KN, students 165/230KN) is off Slavonska avenija in the southern part of the city. Breakfast is included. The rooms are good, each with private bathroom, although it's a long tram ride. To get there take tram No 4, 5, 14, 16 or 17 heading southwest on Savska cesta to 'Vjesnik'. Cvjetno Naselje is available to visitors only from mid-July to the end of September – for the rest of the year it's a student dormitory.

**Private Rooms** Convenient to the train station is **Evistas** (☎ 48 39 554, fax 48 39 543; e evistas@zg.tel.hr; Šenoina 28; rooms with shared bathroom 254KN, studios 365KN; office open 9am-8pm Mon-Fri, 9.30am-5pm Sat). Prices are based on a two-night stay; there's a 10% surcharge for staying only one night. You could also try **ADP Gloria** (☎ 48 23 567, fax 48 23 571; e gordana.gordic@zg.tel.hr; Britanski trg 5; doubles with private bathroom 257KN, apartments from 365KN; open 9am-8pm Mon-Fri, 9am-2pm Sat) It's wise to reserve in advance as accommodation in the town centre tends to fill rapidly.

**Hotels** For small hotels, you can't do better than the stylish **Hotel Ilica** (☎ 37 77 522, fax 37 77 622; e info@hotel-ilica.hr; Ilica 102; singles/doubles 349/449KN, twins 549KN, apartments 749KN), two tram stops heading west from Trg Jelačića, which offers 12 quiet, pleasant rooms and two apartments – all with air-con, TV and telephone.

The 110-room **Central Hotel** (☎ 48 41 122, fax 48 41 304; e hotel-central@zg .hinet.hr; Branimirova 3; singles/doubles 380/550KN), opposite the train station, is blandly modern. There are more expensive rooms available that have air-con.

The six-storey **Hotel Jadran** (☎ 45 53 777, fax 46 12 151; e jadran@hup-zagreb.hr; Vlaška 50; singles/doubles 390/520KN), near the city centre, has rooms with TV, telephone and the price includes breakfast. For a little

more money, **Pansion Jägerhorn** (☎ 48 33 877, fax 48 33 573; Ilica 14; singles/doubles 550/750KN, apartments 900KN) offers comfortable, modern rooms with TV, telephone and air-con, and a three- or four-person, two-room apartment.

**Hotel Dubrovnik** (☎ 48 73 555, fax 48 18 447; e hotel-dubrovnik@hotel-dubrovnik .tel.hr; Gajeva 1; singles/doubles from 585/890KN) is a business-like hotel well-located in the centre of town.

For a memorable stay, try the five-star **Hotel Esplanade** (☎ 45 66 666, fax 45 77 907; e esplanade@esplanade.hr; Mihanovićeva 1; singles/doubles 954/1521KN), next to the train station. This six-storey, 215-room hotel, built in 1924, is a *belle époque* masterpiece where the stately rooms make very few concessions to the 21st century. A continental/buffet breakfast will cost 90/135KN extra.

## Places to Eat
**Murano 2000** (Hotel Esplanade; mains from 90KN) offers the tastiest, most creative dishes in town. The vegetarian dishes that start at 60KN are truly wondrous and the restaurant specialises in *štrukli*, which could be a starter, main course or dessert.

**Paviljon** (mains from 60KN) is another elegant eatery with an Italian flavour – it's in the yellow exhibition pavilion across the park from the train station.

**Piccolo Mondo** (Hotel Dubrovnik; mains from 35KN) has an excellent location facing Trg Jelačića and the pastas and salads are surprisingly good. Pizza places are everywhere, but it would be hard to do better than the delicious, freshly made pizzas at **Pizzicato** (Gundulićeva 4; pizzas from 18KN) near the Academy of Music. The menu is translated into English.

For a change of pace, there's **Lenuci** (Zrinjevac 16 19), which turns out decent fajitas for 59KN.

The best restaurant for a meaty Croatian speciality, prepared the Croatian way is **Baltazar** (Nova Ves 4; mains from 60KN); to find it head north along Kaptol. **Mimiće** (Jurišićeva 21) has been a local favourite for decades, turning out plates of fried fish that cost from 11KN for 10 sardines and a hunk of bread.

**Delikatese** (Ilica 39) is a good place to pick up cheese, fruit, bread, yogurt and cold meat for a picnic. Next door is a **Konzum grocery**

CRCATIA

store that sells whole roasted chickens, an assortment of prepared salads and Pag cheese. Farther along Ilica at Britanski trg, there's a **fruit and vegetable market** *(open to 3pm daily)* that sells farm-fresh produce. Don't hesitate to bargain.

## Entertainment

Zagreb is a happening city. Its theatres and concert halls present a great variety of programmes throughout the year. Many (but not all) are listed in the monthly brochure *Zagreb Events & Performances*, which is available from the tourist office.

**Cafés & Bars** The liveliest scene in Zagreb is along bar-lined Bogovićeva, which turns into prime meet-and-greet territory each evening. Tkalčićeva, north of Trg Jelačića, attracts a slightly funkier crowd.

**Pivnica Tomislav** *(Trg Tomislava 18)*, facing the park in front of the train station, is a good local bar with inexpensive draught beer.

**Rock Forum Café** *(Gajeva 13; open summer)* occupies the rear sculpture garden of the Archaeological Museum, and across the street is **Hard Rock Café**, full of 1950s and '60s memorabilia. A couple of other cafés and music shops share this lively complex on the corner of Teslina and Gajeva Sts. Check out **BP Club** in the complex basement for jazz, blues and rock bands.

One of Zagreb's most pretentious cafés is Kazališna Kavana, known as **Kav Kaz** *(Trg Maršala Tita)*, opposite the Croatian National Theatre. **Old Pharmacy Pub** *(Andrije Hebranga 11a)* was once a pharmacy but now dispenses healthy doses of beer and spirits in a congenial environment. For a more offbeat experience, try **Tolkien's House** *(Vranicanijeva 8)*, which is decorated in the style of JRR Tolkien's books. **Indy's** *(Vranicanijeva 4)*, next door, presents a dazzling assortment of cocktails on an outdoor terrace.

**Discos & Clubs** Near the Hotel Sheraton, **Kulušić** *(Hrvojeva 6; open 8am-11pm Mon-Wed, 10pm-4am Thur-Sun)* is a casual, funky rock club that offers occasional live bands, fashion shows and record promos as well as standard disco fare.

A lot of the night action happens around Lake Jarun in the southwestern corner of the city. Take tram No 17 to the Jarun stop. Try **Best** *(☎ 36 91 601; Horvaćanski zavoj bb;* open 10pm-4am Fri & Sat)*, **Žabac** *(Jarunska ulica bb)* or **Aquarius** *(☎ 36 40 231; open 10pm-4am Wed-Sun)* on Lake Jarun. In town, **Sokol klub** *(☎ 48 28 510; Trg Maršala Tita 6; admission free for before midnight; open 10pm-4am Wed-Sun)*, across the street from the Ethnographic Museum, is a more polished place to dance till dawn.

**Gay & Lesbian Venues** At present there are no exclusively gay and lesbian venues in Zagreb but **Glob@l** *(☎ 48 76 146; P Hatza 14; open noon-4am Mon-Fri, 4pm-4am Sat & Sun)* is a friendly, relaxed spot that welcomes gays and straights.

**Theatre** It's worth making the rounds of the theatres in person to check their programmes. Tickets are usually available for performances, even for the best shows. A small office marked 'Kazalište Komedija' (look out for the posters) also sells theatre tickets; it's in the Oktogon, a passage connecting Trg Petra Preradovićeva to Ilica 3.

The neobaroque **Croatian National Theatre** *(☎ 48 28 532; Trg Maršala Tita 15; box office open 10am-1pm & 5pm-7.30pm Mon-Fri, 10am-1pm Sat, ½hr before performances Sun)* was established in 1895. It stages opera and ballet performances. **Komedija Theatre** *(☎ 48 14 566; Kaptol 9)*, near the cathedral, stages operettas and musicals.

The **Vatroslav Lisinski Concert Hall** *(ticket office ☎ 61 21 166; Trg Stjepana Radica 4; open 9am-8pm Mon-Fri, 9am-2pm Sat)*, just south of the train station, is a prestigious venue where symphony concerts are held regularly.

Concerts also take place at the **Academy of Music** *(☎ 48 30 822; Gundulićeva 6a)* off Ilica. Another entertainment option is the **Puppet Theatre** *(ul Baruna Trenka 3; performances 5pm Sat, noon Sun)*.

## Spectator Sports

Basketball is popular in Zagreb, and from October to April games take place in a variety of venues around town, usually on the weekend. The tourist office has the schedule.

Football (soccer) games are held every Sunday afternoon at the **Maksimir Stadium** *(Maksimirska 128; tram No 4, 7, 11 or 12 to Bukovačka)*, on the eastern side of Zagreb. If you arrive too early for the game, Zagreb's zoo is just across the street.

## Shopping

Ilica is Zagreb's main shopping street. You can get in touch with true Croatian consumerism at the **Nama department store**, near the square Trg Jelačića.

Croatia is the birthplace of the necktie (cravat); **Kroata Cravata** *(Oktogon)* has locally made silk neckties at prices that run from 165KN to 360KN. **Rokotvorine** *(Trg Jelačića 7)* sells traditional Croatian handicrafts, such as red-and-white embroidered tablecloths, dolls and pottery.

## Getting There & Away

**Air** For information about the flights to and from Zagreb, see the Getting There & Away and Getting Around sections at the start of this chapter.

**Bus** Zagreb's big, modern bus station has a large, enclosed waiting room and a number of shops, including grocery stores to stock up. You can buy most international tickets at window Nos 17 to 20.

Buses depart from Zagreb for most parts of Croatia, Slovenia and places beyond. Buy an advance ticket at the station if you're planning to travel far.

The following domestic buses depart from Zagreb:

| destination | cost (KN) | duration (hrs) | frequency (daily) |
| --- | --- | --- | --- |
| Dubrovnik | 195 | 11 | 7 |
| Korčula | 209 | 12 | 1 |
| Krk | 126 | 5 | 3 |
| Ljubljana | 150 | 2½ | 5 |
| Osijek | 95 | 4 | 6 |
| Plitvice | 72 | 2½ | 19 |
| Poreč | 120–155 | 5 | 6 |
| Pula | 122–147 | 7 | 13 |
| Rab | 138 | 6 | 2 |
| Rijeka | 100 | 4 | 21 |
| Rovinj | 133–146 | 5–8 | 8 |
| Split | 120–132 | 7–9 | 27 |
| Varaždin | 50 | 1¾ | 20 |
| Zadar | 94–110 | 5 | 20 |

For international bus connections see the Getting There & Away section at the beginning of this chapter.

**Train** The following domestic trains depart from Zagreb:

| destination | cost (KN) | duration (hrs) | frequency (daily) |
| --- | --- | --- | --- |
| Osijek | 88 | 4½ | 4 |
| Pula | 114 | 5½ | 2 |
| Rijeka | 77 | 5 | 5 |
| Split | 131 | 9 | 3–4 |
| Varaždin | 45 | 3 | 13 |
| Zadar | 131 | 11 | 2 |

Both daily trains to Zadar stop at Knin. Reservations are required on fast InterCity (IC) trains and there's a supplement that costs 5KN to 15KN for fast or express trains.

For international train connections see the Getting There & Away section at the beginning of this chapter.

## Getting Around

Public transport is based on an efficient but overcrowded network of trams, though the city centre is compact enough to make them unnecessary. Tram Nos 3 and 8 don't run on weekends. Buy tickets at newspaper kiosks for 6KN or from the driver for 7KN. You can use your ticket for transfers within 90 minutes but only in one direction.

A *dnevna karta* (day ticket), valid on all public transport until 4am the next morning, is 16KN at most Vjesnik or Tisak news outlets. (See Tourist Offices under Information earlier for details on the Zagreb Card.)

**To/From the Airport** The Croatia Airlines bus to Zagreb airport, 17km southeast of the city, leaves from the bus station every half-hour or hour from about 5.30am to 7.30pm, depending on flights, and returns from the airport on about the same schedule (30KN). A taxi would cost about 250KN.

**Car** Of the major car-rental companies, you could try **Budget Rent-a-Car** *(☎ 45 54 936)* in the Hotel Sheraton, **Avis Autotehna** *(☎ 48 36 006)* at the Hotel Opera and **Hertz** *(☎ 48 46 777; Vukotinovićeva 1)*. Bear in mind that local companies usually have lower rates. Try **Vipcar** *(☎ 45 72 148; Mihanovićeva 1)* at the Hotel Esplanade.

**Taxi** Zagreb's taxis ring up 7KN per kilometre after a flag fall of a whopping 25KN. On Sunday and at night from 10pm to 5am there's a 20% surcharge. Waiting time is 40KN an hour. The baggage surcharge is 5KN for every suitcase that the driver handles.

CROATIA

# Istria

Istria (Istra to Croatians), which is the heart-shaped 3600-sq-km peninsula just south of Trieste, Italy, is graced with a 430km-long indented shoreline and an interior of green rolling hills, drowned valleys and fertile plains. The northern part of the peninsula belongs to Slovenia, while the Dinaric Range in the northeastern corner separates Istria from the continental mainland.

Istria has been a political basketball. Italy took Istria from Austria-Hungary in 1919, then had to give it to Yugoslavia in 1947. A large Italian community lives in Istria and Italian is widely spoken. Tito wanted Trieste (Trst) as part of Yugoslavia, too, but in 1954 the Anglo-American occupiers returned the city to Italy so that it wouldn't fall into the hands of the 'communists'. Today the Koper-Piran strip belongs to Slovenia while the rest is held by Croatia. Visit Piran quickly, then move south to Rovinj, a perfect base from which to explore Poreč and Pula.

If you'll be visiting a number of museums in Istria, it may pay to buy the Istra Card for 60KN, which allows free or discounted admission to most of the region's museums. It's available in most tourist offices and many travel agencies.

## POREČ

☎ 052 • pop 17,460

Poreč (Parenzo in Italian), the Roman Parentium, sits on a low, narrow peninsula halfway down the western coast of Istria. The ancient Dekumanus with its polished stones is still the main street. Even after the fall of Rome, Poreč remained important as a centre of early Christianity, with a bishop and the famous Euphrasian Basilica, now a World Heritage Site. The town is the centre of a region packed with tourist resorts, but vestiges of earlier times and a quiet, small-town atmosphere (at least in the low season) make it well worth a stop. There are many places to swim in the clear water off the rocks north of the old town.

### Orientation & Information

The bus station, with a **left-luggage office** (open 5am-9pm Mon-Sat, 7.30am-1pm & 2.30pm-9pm Sun), is directly opposite the small-boat harbour just outside the old town. Follow Obala Maršala Tita into the old town.

For visitor information, head to the **tourist office** (☎ 451 293, fax 451 665; Ⓦ www .istra.com/porec; Zagrebačka 11; open 8am-10pm Mon-Sat Sept-June, 9am-1pm & 6pm-10pm Sun July & Aug). The **Atlas travel agency** (☎ 434 983; Eufrazijeva 63) represents AmEx. The **Sunny Way agency** (☎ 452 021; Alda Negrija 1) has information about boat connections to Italy.

The **telephone centre** (open 8am-3pm Mon-Fri, 8am-1pm Sat) is in the **main post office** (Trg Slobode 14). You can change money at any travel agency in town and there's an ATM at **Istarska Banka** (A Negrija 6). **Internet Center** (☎ 427 075; Grahaliĉa 1) offers Internet access.

### Things to See

The numerous historic sites in the old town include the ruins of two **Roman temples**, between Trg Marafor and the western end of the peninsula. Archaeology and history are featured in the **Regional Museum** (Dekumanus 9; adult/student 10/5KN; open 10am-1pm & 5pm-9pm daily July-Aug, 10am-1pm daily rest of year) in an old baroque palace. The captions are in German and Italian but there's an explanatory leaflet in English.

The main reason to visit Poreč, however, is to visit the 6th-century **Euphrasian Basilica** (☎ 431 635; admission free; open 7.30am-8pm daily, to 7pm Oct-Mar), which features some wonderfully preserved Byzantine gold mosaics. The sculpture and architecture of the basilica are survivors of that distant period. For a small fee you may visit the 4th-century mosaic floor of the adjacent Early Christian basilica or visit the baptistry and climb the bell tower.

From May to mid-October there are passenger boats (15KN return) every half-hour to **Sveti Nikola**, the small island opposite Poreč Harbour, departing from the wharf on Obala Maršala Tita.

### Special Events

Annual events in Poreč include the day-long Folk Festival (June) and the Musical Summer (May to September). Ask about these at the tourist office.

### Places to Stay

Accommodation in Poreč is tight in the summer but private-room prices are reasonable. Reserve in advance during July and August.

**Camping** There are two camping grounds at Zelena Laguna, 6km south of Poreč. Both **Autocamp Zelena Laguna** (☎ *410 541; camp sites 74KN plus per person 38KN*) and **Autocamp Bijela Uvala** (☎ *410 5511; camp sites 74KN plus per person 38KN*) are open from April to mid-October. Take the 'Zelena Laguna' resort tourist train (15KN) that runs half-hourly or hourly from the town centre between April and October.

**Private Rooms** In Poreč town centre **Di Tours** (☎ *432 100 or 452 018, fax 431 300; e di-tours@pu.tel.hr; Prvomajska 2*) arranges private accommodation. Near the vegetable market at Partizanska there's also **Istra-Line** (☎ *451 067, fax 432 116*) in a pink building. If you follow Nikole Tesle until it becomes Kalčića you'll come to Mate Vašića where you'll find **Fiore tours** (☎/fax 431 397; Mate Vašića 6), which also handles private accommodation. Expect to pay about 130/160KN for a single/double room with shared facilities in the high season plus a 30% surcharge for stays less than three nights.

**Hotels** Try the modern, five-storey **Hotel Poreč** (☎ *451 811, fax 451 730; e info@hotelporec.com; singles/doubles 310/465KN*) near the bus station, which has reasonably fresh rooms with TV. The front rooms are over a bar with a predictably noisy output during the summer. **Hotel Neptun** (☎ *400 800, fax 431 531; Obala Maršala Tita 15; singles/doubles 375/675KN with half-board*) overlooks the harbour and has more expensive rooms with harbour views. **Jadran** (☎ *431 236; Obala Maršala Tita; singles/doubles 325/600KN with half-board*) has simpler rooms with no TV.

## Places to Eat
The **Peškera Self-Service Restaurant** (*open 10am-8pm year-round*), just outside the northwestern corner of the old city wall, is good value and **Pizzeria Nono** (*Zagrebačka 4; mains from 40KN*) is a local favourite for its scrumptious pizzas.

There is a large **supermarket** and **department store** next to Hotel Poreč, near the bus station.

## Getting There & Away
There are buses to Rovinj (22KN, one hour, seven daily), Zagreb (144KN, five hours, eight

daily) and Rijeka (53KN, 5½ hours, eight daily), and Pula (31KN, 1¼ hours, 12 daily). Between Poreč and Rovinj the bus runs along the Lim Channel, a drowned valley. To see it clearly, sit on the right-hand side if you're southbound, or the left if you're northbound.

The nearest train station is at Pazin, 30km east (five buses daily from Poreč).

For information about bus and boat connections to Italy and Slovenia see the Getting There & Away section at the start of this chapter. The cheapest price for car rental is at **Follis** (☎ *427 103; Istarskog razvoda 11*).

## ROVINJ
☎ 052 • pop 14,200
Relaxed Rovinj (Rovigno in Italian), with its high peninsula topped by the 60m tower of the massive Cathedral of St Euphemia, is perhaps the best place to visit in Istria. Wooded hills punctuated by low-rise luxury hotels surround the town, while the 13 green, offshore islands of the Rovinj archipelago make for pleasant, varied views. The cobbled, inclined streets in the old town are charmingly picturesque. Rovinj is still an active fishing port, so you see local people going about their day-to-day business, and you can swim from the rocks in the sparkling water below Hotel Rovinj.

## Orientation & Information
The bus station is in the southeastern corner of the old town and there's an ATM next to the entrance, as well as Autotrans Travel Agency, which will change money. The Rovinj **tourist office** (☎ *811 566, fax 816 007; w www.tzgrovinj.hr; Obala Pina Budicina 12; open 8am-9pm Mon-Sat, 9am-1pm Sun*) is just off Trg Maršala Tita. **Planet Tourist Agency** (☎ *840 494, Sv Križ 1*) has a few computers to access the Internet and is in the centre of town. Otherwise, walk up Carducci about 500m to **Caffe-Bar Aurora** (☎ *830 333; Prolaz M Maretić 8*). The AmEx representative is **Atlas travel agency** (☎ *813 463*) next to Hotel Park at V Nazora BB.

Phone calls can be made from the post office that is across from the bus station. The bus station has a **left-luggage office** (*open 6am-9pm daily*) – ask at the ticket window.

## Things to See
The **Cathedral of St Euphemia** (*open 10am-6pm daily mid-June–mid-Sept, 10am-6pm Sun rest of year*), which completely dominates

the town from its hill-top location and built in 1736, is the largest baroque building in Istria. It reflects the period during the 18th century when Rovinj was the most populous town in Istria, an important fishing centre and the bulwark of the Venetian fleet.

Inside the cathedral, don't miss the tomb of St Euphemia (martyred in AD 304) behind the right-hand altar. The saint's remains were brought from Constantinople in 800. On the anniversary of her martyrdom (16 September) devotees congregate here. A copper statue of her tops the cathedral's mighty tower.

Take a wander along the winding narrow backstreets below the cathedral, such as **ul Grisia**, where local artists sell their work. Each year in mid-August Rovinj's painters stage a big open-air art show in town.

The Rovinj **Regional Museum** (*Trg Maršala Tita; adult/student 10/8KN; open 9.30am-12.30pm & 6pm-9.30pm Mon-Sat mid-June–mid-Sept, 10am-1pm Tues-Sat rest of year*) contains an unexciting collection of paintings and a few Etruscan artefacts that have been found in Istria. Captions are only in Croatian and Italian.

Somewhat interesting is the **Rovinj Aquarium** (*Obala Giordano Paliaga 5; admission 10KN; open 10am-6pm Mon-Sat mid-Apr–June & Sept–mid-Oct, 9am-9pm daily July & Aug*), dating from 1891. It exhibits a collection of local marine life, from poisonous scorpion fish to colourful anemones.

When you've seen enough of the town, follow the waterfront south past the Park Hotel to **Punta Corrente Forest Park**, which was established in 1890 by Baron Hütterodt, an Austrian admiral who kept a villa on Crveni otok (Red Island). Here you can swim off the rocks, climb a cliff or just sit and admire the offshore islands.

## Organised Tours
**Delfin Agency** (☎ 813 266), near the ferry dock for Crveni otok, runs half-day scenic cruises to the Lim Channel for 110KN per person, or you can go with one of the independent operators at the end of Alzo Rismondo that run half-day and full-day boat trips around the region. There's an hourly ferry to Crveni otok (20KN return) and a frequent ferry to nearby Katarina Island (15KN return) from the same landing. Get tickets on the boat or at the nearby kiosk. These boats operate only from May to mid-October.

## Special Events
The city's annual events include the Rovinj-Pesaro Regatta (early May), 'Rovinj Summer' concert series (July and August) and Rovinj Fair (August).

## Places to Stay
**Camping** The camping ground that is closest to Rovinj is **Porton Biondi** (☎ 813 557; per person/tent/car 30/16/16KN), less than a 1km from the town (on the Monsena bus route). Five kilometres southeast of Rovinj is **Polari Camping** (☎ 800 376; Villa Rubin bus; open May–mid-Oct).

**Private Rooms** The surcharge for a stay of less than three nights is 50% and guests who stay only one night are punished with a 100% surcharge, but you should be able to bargain the surcharge away outside of July and August. If not, it may be cheaper to stay in a hotel. **Natale-Lokva** (☎ 813 365, fax 830 239; e natale@pu.tel.hr; Via Carducci 4; singles/doubles with shared bathroom 185/315KN) is opposite the bus station.

You could also try **Futura Travel** (☎ 817 281; M Benussi 2) or **Marco Polo** (☎ 816 616, w www.marcopolo.hr; Trg Lokva 3), which have rooms at the same price. The prices are fixed by the local tourist association. Breakfast is an additional 30KN.

**Hotels** The **Hotel Rovinj** (☎ 811 288, fax 840 757; e hotel-rovinj@pu.hinet.hr; Svetoga Križa; singles/doubles from 352/487KN) has a splendid location overlooking the sea. Renovated rooms with air-con and/or sea view are more expensive. The cheapest hotel is the 192-room **Hotel Monte Mulin** (☎ 811 512, fax 815 882; singles/doubles with half-board 241/367KN), on the wooded hillside overlooking the bay just beyond Hotel Park. It's about a 15-minute walk heading south of the bus station. A new luxury hotel in a renovated Venetian building, **Hotel Villa Angelo D'Oro** (☎ 840 502, fax 840 112; e hotel.angelo@vip.hr; Via Svalba 38-42; singles/doubles 670/1160KN) offers plush, lavishly decorated rooms with air-con, satellite TV, minibar and a free sauna and Jacuzzi room.

## Places to Eat
Most of the fish and spaghetti places along the harbour cater to the more upmarket crowd, while **Cantinon** (obala Alzo Rismondo 18)

sells fresh grilled fish from 25KN to a local crowd. **Veli Jože** (*Svetoga Križa 1*) is somewhat more expensive, but is a good place to try Istrian dishes in an interior crammed with knick-knacks, or at tables outside.

Picnickers can buy supplies at the **supermarket** only about 25m downhill from the bus station or in one of the kiosks selling *burek* near the vegetable market.

### Getting There & Away

There's a bus from Rovinj to Pula (22KN, 40 minutes to 1¼ hours) every hour or so. There are up to eight daily to Poreč (22KN to 39KN, one hour), eight daily to Rijeka (73KN, 3½ hours), nine daily to Zagreb (140KN, five to eight hours), one daily to Koper (69KN, 1½ hours) and Split (263KN, 11¼ hours), and one daily to Dubrovnik (373KN, 17½ hours) and Ljubljana (128KN, 2½ hours, July to August). Prices and durations vary between different companies and routes.

The closest train station is Kanfanar, 19km away on the Pula-Divača line.

**Eurostar Travel** (☎ 813 144; *Obala Pina Budicina 1*) is the agent for Adriatica Navigazione and has schedules and tickets for boats to Italy.

## PULA
☎ 052 • pop 58,600

Pula (the ancient Polensium) is a large regional centre with some industry, a big naval base and a busy commercial harbour. An important base for the Romans, the city contains a wealth of Roman ruins topped by a remarkably well-preserved amphitheatre, which is now the centre of Pula's lively cultural scene. Nearby are some rocky wooded peninsulas overlooking the clear Adriatic waters, which explains the many resort hotels and camping grounds circling the city.

### Orientation

The **bus station** (*ul Carrarina*) is in the centre of town. One block south is Giardini, the central hub, while the harbour is just north of the bus station. The train station is near the water about 1km north of town.

### Information

**Tourist Offices** The helpful Pula **Tourist Information Centre** (☎ 219 197, fax 211 955; ⓦ *www.istra.com/pula; Forum 2; open 9am-8pm Mon-Sat, 10am-6pm Sun*) provides maps, brochures and schedules of upcoming events in Pula and around Istria.

**Money** You can exchange money in travel agencies and or the **post office** (*Istarska 5*) next to the bus station, where there is an ATM.

**Post & Communications** Long-distance telephone calls may be placed at the **main post office** (*Danteov trg 4; open to 8pm daily*). You can check your emails at **Enigma** (☎ 381 615; *Kandlerova 19*).

**Travel Agencies** The **Atlas travel agency** (☎ 214 172, fax 214 090; ⓔ *atl.pula@atlas .tel.hr; ul Starih Statuta 1*) organises tours to the Brijuni Islands (210KN), while **Jadroagent** (☎ 210 431; ⓔ *jadroagent-pula@pu .hinet.hr; Riva 14*) has schedules and tickets for boats connecting Istria with Italy and the islands.

**Left Luggage** The bus station has a **left-luggage office** (*open 4.30am-11.30pm daily with 2 half-hour breaks*). The train station also has a **left-luggage service** (*open 9am-4pm Mon-Sat*).

### Things to See

Pula's most imposing sight is the 1st-century **Roman amphitheatre** (*Flavijevska ul; adult/concession 16/8KN; open 7.30am-9pm daily Jun-Sept, 8am-4.30pm rest of year*) overlooking the harbour and northeast of the old town. Built entirely from local limestone, the amphitheatre was designed to host gladiatorial contests and could accommodate up to 20,000 spectators. The 30m-high outer wall is almost intact and contains two rows of 72 arches. Around the end of July a Croatian film festival is held in the amphitheatre, and there are pop, jazz and classical events, often with major international stars, throughout summer.

The **Archaeological Museum** (*Ulica Cararina 3; adult/concession 12/6KN; open 9am-8pm Mon-Sat, 10am-3pm Sun June-Sept, 9am-3pm Mon-Fri rest of year*) is on the hill opposite the bus station.

Even if you don't get into the museum be sure to visit the large sculpture garden around it, and the **Roman theatre** behind the museum. The garden is entered through 2nd-century twin gates.

Along the street facing the bus station are **Roman walls** that mark the eastern boundary

# PULA

**PLACES TO STAY**
2 Hotel Riviera; Arena Turist
4 Scaletta
20 Hotel Omir

**PLACES TO EAT**
14 Jupiter
17 Varaždin
21 Vesna
27 Splendid Self-Service

**OTHER**
1 Buses to Medulin, Premantura & Fažana
3 Atlas Travel Agency
5 Brijuni Excursion Boats
6 Roman Amphitheatre
7 Jadroagent
8 Cathedral
9 Enigma
10 Temple of Augustus; Old Town Hall
11 Cvajner
12 Tourist Information Centre
13 Venetian Citadel; Museum of History
15 Archaeological Museum; Roman Theatre
16 Post Office
18 Bus Station
19 Globtour
22 Triumphal Arch of Sergius
23 Main Post Office
24 Bounty
25 Hospital
26 Vegetable Market

of old Pula. Follow these walls south and continue down Giardini to the **Triumphal Arch of Sergius** (27 BC). The street beyond the arch winds right around old Pula, changing names several times. Follow it to the ancient **Temple of Augustus** and the **old town hall** (1296).

The 17th-century **Venetian Citadel**, on a high hill in the centre of the old town, is worth the climb for the view if not for the meagre exhibits in the tiny **Museum of History** (*Kaštel; admission 7KN; open 8am-7pm daily June-Sept, 9am-5pm Mon-Fri rest of year*) inside.

## Places to Stay

**Camping** The closest camping ground to the city centre is three kilometres southwest. **Autocamp Stoja** (*☎ 387 144, fax 387 748; bus No 1 to Stoja terminus; per person/tent*

*& car 50/100KN; open mid-Apr–mid-Oct*) has lots of space along the shady promontory, with swimming possible off the rocks. There are more camping grounds at Medulin and Premantura, which are coastal resorts southeast of Pula (take the buses heading southeast from town).

**Hostels** In a great location overlooking a clean, pebble beach **Ljetovalište Ferijalnog Saveza Youth Hostel** (*☎ 391 133, fax 391 106; e pula@hfhs.hr; tent sites 40KN, tent rental 10KN, B&B/half-board 90/155KN*) is 3km south of central Pula. Take the No 2 or 7 Verudela bus to the 'Piramida' stop, walk back to the first street, then turn left and look for the sign. The rate for camping includes breakfast. The hostel is heated.

**Private Rooms** In the Hotel Riviera **Arena Turist** (☎ 529 400, fax 529 401, W www .arenaturist.hr; Splitska 1a), **Globtour** (☎ 211 255; Giardini 10) and Atlas travel agency have private rooms for 148/184KN per single/ double with private bathroom, plus a selection of apartments to rent.

**Hotels** Most accommodation is outside town in the sprawling resorts on the Verudela Peninsula. The cheapest hotel in town is **Hotel Omlr** (☎ 210 614, fax 213 944; Dobricheva 6; singles/doubles 324/450KN), which has 14 small but adequate rooms. Prices stay the same year-round. For faded old-world elegance try **Hotel Riviera** (☎ 211 166, fax 211 166; Splitska ul 1; singles/doubles 465/ 705KN), overlooking the harbour. Neither the service nor the comfort justifies the price (which eases in the low season) in this one-star hotel, but the large front rooms have a view of the water and the wide shady hotel terrace is a relaxing place for a drink.

The most comfortable hotel in town is **Scaletta** (☎ 541 599, fax 541 025, W www .hotel-scaletta.com; Flavijeska 26; singles/ doubles 480/680KN), which offers beautifully decorated rooms with TV and telephone, including breakfast. The hotel restaurant is also excellent.

## Places to Eat
**Jupiter** (Castropola 38) serves up the best pizza in town and the pasta is good too. **Varaždin** (Istarska 32; mains from 40KN) offers carefully prepared soups, pastas, risottos and salads, as well as an assortment of fish and meat dishes.

**Splendid Self-Service** (Trg I Svibnja 5; open 9.30am-8.45pm daily), opposite the vegetable market, is easy since you see what you're getting and you pay at the end of the line. The people at the cheese counter in **Vesna** (Giardini; open 6.30am-8pm Mon-Fri, 6.30am-1.30pm Sat) prepare healthy sandwiches while you wait.

## Entertainment
Posters around Pula advertise live performances at the amphitheatre or the details of rave parties at two venues in Verudela: **Oasis** and **Fort Bourguignon**. The streets of Flanatička, Kandlerova and Sergijevaca, are lively people-watching spots and the Forum has several outdoor cafés that fill up in the early evening; the trendiest is café/gallery **Cvajner** with a stunning, art-filled interior.

**Bounty** (Veronska 8) is the place to go if Irish beer and cheer is your thing.

## Getting There & Away
**Bus** The buses that travel to Rijeka (58KN, 2½ hours, 20 daily) are sometimes crowded, especially the eight that continue to Zagreb, so be sure to reserve a seat in advance. Going from Pula to Rijeka, be sure to sit on the right-hand side of the bus for a stunning view of the Gulf of Kvarner.

Other destinations for buses from Pula include: Rovinj (22KN, 40 minutes, 18 daily); Poreč (31KN, one hour, 12 daily); Zagreb (135KN, five hours, 11 daily); Zadar (161KN, seven hours, four daily), Split (248KN, 10 hours, four daily) and to Dubrovnik (354KN, 15 hours, one daily).

**Train** There are two daily trains to Ljubljana (110KN, four hours) and two to Zagreb (110KN, 6½ hours) but you must board a bus for part of the trip.

**Boat** Until 2002 there was a regular ferry connecting Pula and Venice. To see if the service has recommenced, check with Jadroagent on the harbour (see Travel Agencies earlier in this section).

## Getting Around
The only city buses of use to visitors are bus No 1, which runs to the camping ground at Stoja, and bus Nos 2 and 7 to Verudela, which pass the youth hostel. Frequency varies from every 15 minutes to every 30 minutes, with service from 5am to 11.30pm daily. Tickets are sold at newsstands for 8KN and are good for two trips.

## AROUND PULA
### Brijuni Islands
The Brijuni (Brioni in Italian) island group consists of two main pine-covered islands and 12 islets off the coast of Istria and just northwest of Pula. Each year from 1949 until his death in 1980, Maršal Tito spent six months at his summer residences on Brijuni in a style any Western capitalist would have admired. In 1984 Brijuni was proclaimed a national park. Some 680 species of plants grow on the islands, including many exotic subtropical species, which were planted at Tito's request.

CROATIA

You may only visit Brijuni National Park with a group. Instead of booking an excursion with one of the travel agencies in Pula, Rovinj or Poreč, which costs 210KN, take a public bus from Pula to Fažana (8km), then sign up for a tour (170KN) at the **Brijuni Tourist Service** (☎ 525 883) office near the wharf. It's best to book in advance, especially in summer.

Also check along the Pula waterfront for excursion boats to Brijuni. The five-hour boat trips from Pula to Brijuni (60KN) may not actually visit the islands but only sail around them. Still, it makes a nice day out.

# Gulf of Kvarner

The Gulf of Kvarner (Quarnero in Italian) stretches 100km south from Rijeka, between the Istrian Peninsula to the west and the Croatian littoral to the east. The elongated islands are the peaks of a submerged branch of the Dinaric Alps, the range that follows the coast south all the way to Albania. Rijeka is a busy commercial port and transport hub at the northern end of the gulf while Krk, Cres and Pag are among the largest islands in Croatia.

## RIJEKA
☎ 051 • pop 144,000
Rijeka (Fiume in Italian), 126km south of Ljubljana, is such a transportation hub that it's almost impossible to avoid. The network of buses, trains and ferries that connect Istria and Dalmatia with Zagreb and points beyond all seem to pass through Rijeka. As Croatia's largest port, the city is full of boats, cargo, fumes, cranes and the bustling sense of purpose that characterises most port cities.

Although Rijeka is hardly one of the 'must see' destinations, the city does have a few saving graces, such as the pedestrian mall, Korzo, stately 19th-century buildings and a tree-lined promenade along the harbour.

### Orientation
The **bus station** (*Trg Žabica*) is south of the Capuchin Church in the centre of town. The **train station** (*ul Krešimirova*) is a seven-minute walk west of the bus station.

The Jadrolinija ferry wharf (there's no left-luggage section) is just a few minutes east of the bus station. Korzo runs in an easterly direction through the city centre towards the fast-moving Rječina River.

### Information
**Tourist Offices** The new and highly efficient **Turistička Zajednica** (☎ 335 882, fax 214 706, Ⓦ *www.multilink.hr/tz-rijeka; Korzo 33*) distributes *Rijeka Tourist Route*, a walking-tour guide that is so well produced it makes you actually want to stop and look around. For boat information, there's **Jadroagent** (☎ 211 276, fax 335 172; Trg Ivana Koblera 2) and the head office of **Jadrolinija** (☎ 211 444; Ⓦ *www.jadrolinija.hr; Riva 16*), the last word on its ever-changing schedule. **Hostelling International** (☎ 264 176; Korzo 22) sells HI cards and is a good source of information about Croatian hostels.

**Money** There's no ATM at the train station but the exchange offices adjacent to the train and bus stations keep long hours. There are a number of ATMs along Korzo and an exchange counter in the main post office.

**Post & Communications** The **telephone centre** (*open 7am-9pm Mon-Fri, 7am-2pm Sat & Sun*) is in the **main post office** (*Korzo*), opposite the old city tower. You can check your emails at **Ecomclub** (*24a Ivana Zajca; open 7am-10.30pm daily*) while enjoying a brew in a relaxed pub.

**Left Luggage** If the **left-luggage office** (*open 5.30am-10.30pm daily*) in the bus station is full, there's a **left-luggage office** (*open 24hr*) in the train station.

**Laundry** You'll find **Blitz** (*Krešimirova 3a; open 7am-8pm Mon-Fri, 7am-1pm Sat*) between the bus and train stations; it will do a small load of laundry for 60KN.

### Things to See
Rijeka's main orientation point is the **City Tower** (*Korzo*), which was originally one of the main gates to the city and one of the few monuments to have survived the earthquake in 1750.

The **Modern Art Gallery** (*Dolac 1; adult/concession 10/5KN; open 10am-1pm & 5pm-9pm Tues-Sun*) is in the upstairs scientific library opposite Hotel Bonavia. The **Naval and Historical Museum** (*Muzejski trg 1; adult/student 10KN/free; open 10am-1pm Tues-Sat*) traces the development of sailing, with models and paintings of ships and portraits of the captains. The **Natural History**

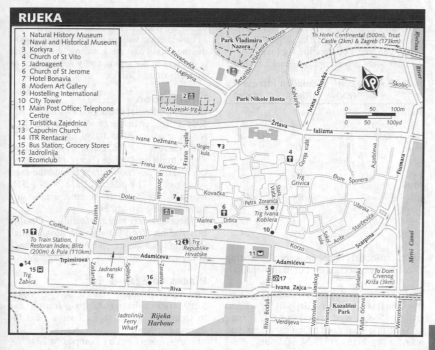

## RIJEKA

1. Natural History Museum
2. Naval and Historical Museum
3. Korkyra
4. Church of St Vito
5. Jadroagent
6. Church of St Jerome
7. Hotel Bonavia
8. Modern Art Gallery
9. Hostelling International
10. City Tower
11. Main Post Office; Telephone Centre
12. Turistička Zajednica
13. Capuchin Church
14. ITR Rentacar
15. Bus Station; Grocery Stores
16. Jadrolinija
17. Ecomclub

**Museum** (*Lorenzov prolaz 1; adult/student 10/5KN; open 9am-7pm Mon-Fri, 9am-2pm Sat*) is devoted to regional geology and botany.

Worth a visit is the 13th-century **Trsat Castle** (*admission free; open daily*), which is on a high ridge overlooking Rijeka, and the canyon of the Rječina River. If you have some more time to kill, stroll into some of Rijeka's churches, such as **Church of St Vito** (*Trg Grivica 11*), **Church of St Jerome** (*Trg Riječke Rezolucije*) or the ornate **Capuchin Church** (*Trg Žabica*).

### Places to Stay

The tourist office can direct you to the few options for private accommodation, most of which are a few kilometres out of town on the road to Opatija. It's just as easy to get to Opatija where there are more and better choices for hotels and private accommodation (for details on getting to/from Opatija see Getting There & Away in that section later).

The cheapest place to stay is **Dom Crvenog Križa** (*☎ 217 599, fax 335 380; Janka Polić Kamova 32; dorm beds 60KN*), a dorm run by the Red Cross, 3km east of town in Pećine. The only hotel in the centre is the four-star

**Hotel Bonavia** (*☎ 333 744, fax 335 969; Dolac 4; singles/doubles 967/1200KN*), which has all of the niceties that businesspeople on generous expense accounts find indispensable. **Hotel Continental** (*☎ 372 008; singles/doubles 315/390KN; Andrije Kašića Miočica*), northeast of the town centre, offers bland rooms in an unrenovated building.

### Places to Eat

**Restoran Index** (*ul Krešimirova 18*), between the bus and train stations, has a good self-serve section. **Korkyra** (*Slogin kula 5; mains from 35KN*) is a local favourite for specialities, such as *brodetto* (fish stew), *bakalar* (codfish stew) and various pastas. There are several 24-hour **grocery stores** in and around the bus station.

### Getting There & Away

**Air** The Croatia Airlines minibus (100KN) connects Zagreb with Rijeka. The bus goes to the central bus station in Rijeka and takes four hours.

**Bus** There are 13 buses daily between Rijeka and Krk (31KN, 1½ hours), via the huge Krk

Bridge. Buses to Krk are overcrowded and a reservation in no way guarantees a seat. Don't worry – the bus from Rijeka to Krk empties fast so you won't be standing for long.

Other buses departing from Rijeka include:

| destination | cost (KN) | duration (hrs) | frequency (daily) |
| --- | --- | --- | --- |
| Baška (Krk Island) | 41 | 2 | 1 |
| Dubrovnik | 306 | 13 | 2 |
| Poreč | 53 | 4½ | 5 |
| Pula | 58 | 2½ | 17 |
| Rab | 87 | 3½ | 2 |
| Rovinj | 70 | 3½ | 10 |
| Split | 196 | 8½ | 11 |
| Trieste | 58 | 2-3 | 3 |
| Zadar | 115 | 5 | 12 |
| Zagreb | 98 | 3½ | 24 |

For international connections see the Getting There & Away section earlier in this chapter.

**Train** Four trains daily run to Zagreb (77KN, five hours). There's also a daily direct train to Osijek (156KN, eight hours) and a daily train to Split that changes at Ogulin where you wait for two hours (135KN, 10 hours). Several of the seven daily services to Ljubljana (80KN, three hours) require a change of trains at the Slovenian border and again at Bifka or Bistrica in Slovenia but there are also two direct trains. Reservations are compulsory on some *poslovni* (express) trains.

**Car** Close to the bus station **ITR Rent a Car** (☎ 337 544; Riva 20) has rental cars from about 300/1820KN per day/week with unlimited kilometres, including tax.

**Boat** Croatia's national boat line, Jadrolinija, has tickets for the large coastal ferries that run all year between Rijeka and Dubrovnik, as well as the weekly passenger boat that runs from Zadar to Rijeka (230KN, 5¼ hours) in the summer, but not the other way. The return trip from Rijeka does not stop in Zadar. For fares, see the Getting Around section at the beginning of this chapter.

## OPATIJA
☎ 051 • pop 12,719

Opatija, just a few kilometres due west of Rijeka, was *the* fashionable seaside resort of the Austro-Hungarian empire until WWI. Many grand, old hotels remain from this time and the shady waterfront promenade stretches for 12km along the Gulf of Kvarner. The views of the indented coast are stunning, the nightlife is the best in the region and you're within an easy bus ride of Rijeka.

### Information
Head to the **tourist office** (☎ 271 310, fax 271 699; e tzgr.op@ri.tel.hr; Maršala Tita 101) for information. **Atlas travel agency** (☎ 271 032; Maršala Tita 116) can also assist visitors.

The **main post office** (Eugena Kumičića 2; open 8am-7pm Mon-Sat) is behind the market (tržnica). **The Internet Cafe** (☎ 271 511; Maršala Tita 85) offers Internet access in a comfortable environment.

There's no left-luggage facility at **Opatija bus station** (Trg Vladimira Gortana), which is in the town centre, but Autotrans Agency at the station will usually watch luggage.

### Places to Stay & Eat
**Preluk Autokamp** (☎ 621 913; open May-Sept) is beside the busy highway from Rijeka to Opatija. City bus No 32 stops near the camping ground.

For private rooms, try **Kompas** (☎ 271 912; Maršala Tita 110) or **GIT travel agency** (☎/fax 271 967; e gi-trade@ri.tel.hr; Maršala Tita 65). Both have rooms starting at 72/80KN per person for one-star accommodation inside/outside the town centre plus a 50% surcharge for single-room occupancy.

The hotel scene is competitive and offers good value for money especially outside of July and August. The two cheapest places to stay in town are **Hotel Paris** (☎ 271 911, fax 711 823; e lrh@lrh.tel.hr; Maršala Tita 198; singles/doubles from 262/405KN), and **Hotel Residenz** (☎ 271 399, fax 271 225; Maršala Tita 133; singles/doubles from 300/480KN). The **Hotel Kvarner** (☎ 271 233, fax 271 202; e hotel-kvarner@lrh.tel.hr; singles/doubles from 510/795KN) is a genteel 19th-century establishment with a swimming pool and easy access to the sea.

Maršala Tita is lined with a number of decent restaurants offering pizza, grilled meat and fish. There's the **supermarket/deli** (Maršala Tita 80) for self-caterers as well as the **Madonnina Pizzeria** (Pava Tomašića 3; mains from 35KN), not far from the Hotel Kvarner, which has a wide range of pizzas and pastas to choose from.

## Entertainment

An **open air cinema** *(Park Angiolina)* screens films and presents occasional concerts nightly at 9.30pm from May to September. There's a boisterous bar scene centred around the harbour and the ever-popular **Caffé Harbour** or **Hemingways**.

## Getting There & Away

Bus No 32 stops in front of the train station in Rijeka (11KN, ½ hour) and runs right along the Opatija Riviera, west of Rijeka, every 20 minutes until late in the evening. If you're looking for accommodation, it's easiest to get off at the first stop, opposite the GIT travel agency and walk downhill, passing hotels and other agencies on the way to the bus station.

## KRK ISLAND

☎ 051 • pop 18,000

Croatia's largest island, the 409-sq-km Krk (Veglia in Italian), is very barren and rocky. In 1980 Krk was joined to the mainland by the enormous Krk Bridge, the largest concrete arch bridge in the world, with a span of some 390m. Since then, Krk has suffered from too-rapid development, from Rijeka airport and some tourist hotels at the northern end of Krk to big tourist hotels in the middle and far south. Still, the main town (also called Krk) is rather picturesque and the popular resort of Baška at the island's southern end has a 2km pebbly beach set below a high ridge.

## Krk Town

Tiny Krk town has a compact medieval centre that opens onto a scenic port. From the 12th to 15th centuries, Krk town and the surrounding region remained semi-independent under the Frankopan Dukes of Krk, an indigenous Croatian dynasty, at a time when much of the Adriatic was controlled by Venice. This history explains the various medieval sights in Krk town, the ducal seat.

The bus from Baška and Rijeka stops by the harbour, a few minutes' walk from the old town of Krk. There's no left-luggage facility at Krk bus station. The **Turistička Zajednica** *(☎/fax 221 414; Velika Placa 1)* is in the city wall's Guard Tower. You can change money at any travel agency and there's an ATM accepting MasterCard and Cirrus in the shopping centre near the bus station.

The lovely 14th-century **Frankopan Castle** and 12th-century Romanesque **cathedral** are in the lower town near the harbour. In the upper part of Krk town are three old **monastic churches**. The narrow streets of Krk are worth exploring.

**Places to Stay & Eat** There is a range of accommodation in and around Krk, but many places only open during summertime. The closest camping ground is **Autocamp Ježevac** *(☎ 221 081; per person/tent/car 28/19/ 18KN)* on the coast, a 10-minute walk south-west of Krk town.

Private rooms can be organised through **Autotrans** *(☎ 221 172)* at the bus station. You can expect to pay from about 140/160KN for a single/double.

The new hostel **Veli Jože** *(☎/fax 220 212; Vitezića 32; dorm beds 132KN)* is located in a spruced-up older building and is open year-round. Rates go down considerably during the low season.

There are a number of restaurants around the harbour, but for something different, try **Konobo Nono** *(Krčkih iseljenika 8; mains around 50KN)* which offers *šurlice*, homemade noodles topped with goulash, as well as grilled fish and meat dishes.

## Baška

At the southern end of Krk Island, Baška is popular for its 2km-long pebbly beach set below a dramatic, barren range of mountains. Although crowded in summer, the old town and harbour make a pleasant stroll and there's always that splendid beach. The bus from Krk stops at the top of a hill on the edge of the old town, between the beach and the harbour.

The main street of Baška is Zvonimirova, overlooking the harbour, and the beach begins at the western end of the harbour, continuing southwards past a big sprawling hotel complex. The town's **tourist office** *(☎ 856 817; e tz-baska@ri.tel.hr; Zvonimirova 114; open 8am-8pm daily mid-June–Sept, 8am-3pm Mon-Fri rest of year)* is just down the street from the bus stop.

## Getting There & Away

About 14 buses a day travel between Rijeka and Krk town (31KN, 1½ hours), of which six continue on to Baška (up to one hour). One of the Rijeka buses is to/from Zagreb (four hours). To go from Krk to Zadar, take one of the many buses to Kraljevica and then change to a southbound bus.

# Dalmatia

Dalmatia (Dalmacija) occupies the central 375km of Croatia's Adriatic coast, from the Gulf of Kvarner in the north to the Bay of Kotor in the south. With its Roman ruins, spectacular beaches, old fishing ports, medieval architecture and unspoilt offshore islands, Dalmatia offers an unbeatable combination of hedonism and historical discovery.

The dramatic coastal scenery is due to the rugged Dinaric Range, which forms a 1500m-long barrier that separates Dalmatia from Bosnia-Hercegovina. After the last Ice Age, part of the coastal mountains were flooded, creating the sort of long, high islands seen in the Gulf of Kvarner. The deep, protected passages between these islands are a paradise for sailors and cruisers.

Split is the largest city in the region and a hub for bus and boat connections along the Adriatic, as well as home to the late Roman Diocletian's Palace. Zadar has more Roman ruins and a wealth of churches. The architecture of Hvar and Korčula recalls the days when these places were outposts of the Venetian empire. None can rival majestic Dubrovnik, a cultural and aesthetic jewel. The ferry trip from Split to Dubrovnik is the Mediterranean at its best and one of the classic journeys of Eastern Europe.

## ZADAR

☎ 023 • pop 72,700

Zadar (ancient Zara), the main city of northern Dalmatia, occupies a long peninsula separating the harbour on the east from the Zadarski Channel on the west. Its strategic position on the Adriatic coast made Zadar a target for the Romans, the Byzantine, Venetian, Austro-Hungarian empires and Italy. Although it was damaged by Allied bombing raids in 1943–44 and Yugoslav rockets in 1991, the resilient city has been rebuilt and restored, retaining much of its old flavour. The marble, traffic-free streets of the old town are replete with Roman ruins, medieval churches and several fascinating museums. Massive 16th-century fortifications still shield the city on the landward side, with high walls running along the harbour. The tree-lined promenade along Obala kralja Petra Krešimira IV is perfect for a lazy stroll or a picnic and there are several small beaches east of the old town. More

beaches lie to the west at Borik as well as on the islands of Ugljan and Dugi Otok, within easy reach of the town. Don't forget to sample Zadar's famous maraschino cherry liqueur.

### Orientation

The train and bus stations are adjacent and are a 15-minute walk southeast of the harbour and old town. From the stations, Zrinsko-Frankopanska ul leads northwest past the main post office to the harbour. Buses marked 'Poluotok' run from the bus station to the harbour. Narodni trg is the heart of Zadar.

### Information

The main tourist office is **Turistička Zajednica** *(☎ 212 222; e tzg-zadar@zd.tel.hr; Smiljanića 4; open 8am-8pm Mon-Sat, 8am-1pm Sun June-Sept, 8am-6pm Mon-Sat Oct-May).*

The AmEx representative is **Atlas travel agency** *(☎ 235 850; Branimirova Obala 12),* across the footbridge over the harbour, and just northeast of Narodni trg. **Croatia Express** *(☎ 250 502; Široka ul)* is next to an ATM. **Croatia Airlines** *(☎ 250 101; Poljana Natka Nodila 7)* has flight information. You can exchange money at any travel agency, at the Jadrolinija office or in the main post office. There is also an exchange office and an ATM at the bus station.

Telephone calls can be made from the **post office** *(Pojana Pape Aleksandra III)*. Computers and an Internet connection are available at **Cybercafe** *(☎ 313 995; Špire Brusine 8; open 8am-10pm Mon-Sat).*

There are **left-luggage** *(open 24hr)* facilities at the train station, a **left-luggage office** *(open 7am-9pm Mon-Fri)* at the bus station and yet another near the Jadrolinija dock *(open 7am-8pm Mon-Fri, 7am-3pm Sat).*

### Things to See & Do

Most attractions are near **St Donatus Church** *(Šimuna Kožičića Benje; admission 5KN; open 9.30am-2pm & 5pm-8pm daily Mar-Oct),* a circular 9th-century Byzantine structure built over the Roman forum. Slabs for the ancient forum are visible in the church and there is a pillar from the Roman era on the northwestern side. In summer, ask about the musical evenings here (Renaissance and early baroque music). The outstanding **Museum of Church Art** *(Poljana Opatice Čike bb; adult/student 20/10KN; open 10am-1pm daily, 6pm-8pm Mon-Sat),* in the Benedictine

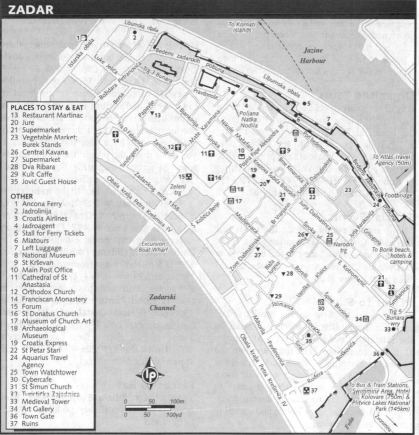

## ZADAR

**PLACES TO STAY & EAT**
13 Restaurant Martinac
20 Jure
21 Supermarket
23 Vegetable Market;
   Burek Stands
26 Central Kavana
27 Supermarket
28 Dva Ribara
29 Kult Caffe
35 Jović Guest House

**OTHER**
1 Ancona Ferry
2 Jadrolinija
3 Croatia Airlines
4 Jadroagent
5 Stall for Ferry Tickets
6 Miatours
7 Left Luggage
8 National Museum
9 St Krševan
10 Main Post Office
11 Cathedral of St
   Anastasia
12 Orthodox Church
14 Franciscan Monastery
15 Forum
16 St Donatus Church
17 Museum of Church Art
18 Archaeological
   Museum
19 Croatia Express
22 St Petar Stari
24 Aquarius Travel
   Agency
25 Town Watchtower
30 Cybercafe
31 St Šimun Church
32 Turistička Zajednica
33 Medieval Tower
34 Art Gallery
36 Town Gate
37 Ruins

monastery opposite St Donatus, offers three floors of elaborate gold and silver reliquaries, religious paintings, icons and local lacework. The 13th-century Romanesque **Cathedral of St Anastasia** *(Trg Svete Stoš; open only for Mass )* has some fine Venetian carvings in the 15th-century choir stalls. The **Franciscan Monastery** *(Zadarscog mira 1358; admission free; open 7.30am-noon & 4.30pm-6pm daily)* is the oldest Gothic church in Dalmatia (consecrated in 1280), with lovely interior Renaissance features and a large Romanesque cross in the treasury, behind the sacristy.

The most interesting museum is the **Archaeological Museum** *(Trg Opatice Čike 1; adult/student 10/5KN; open 9am-1pm & 6pm-8.30pm Mon-Fri, 9am-1pm Sat)*, across from St Donatus, with an extensive collection

of artefacts from the Neolithic period through the Roman occupation to the development of Croatian culture under the Byzantines. Some captions are in English and you are handed a leaflet in English when you buy your ticket.

Less interesting is the **National Museum** *(Poljana Pape Aleksandra III; admission 5KN; open 9am-2pm Mon-Fri)*, just inside the sea gate, featuring photos of Zadar from different periods, and old paintings and engravings of many coastal cities. The same admission ticket will get you into the **art gallery** *(Smiljanića; open 9am-noon & 5pm-8pm Mon-Fri, 9am-1pm Sat)*. Notable churches include **St Šimun Church** *(Trg Šime Budinica; open 8am-noon & 6pm-8pm daily June-Sept)*, with a 14th-century gold chest, and **St Petar Stari** with Roman-Byzantine frescoes.

There's a swimming area with diving boards, a small park and a café on the coastal promenade off Zvonimira. Bordered by pine trees and parks, the promenade takes you to a beach in front of Hotel Kolovare and then winds on for about a kilometre up the coast.

## Organised Tours

Any of the many travel agencies around town can supply information on tourist cruises to the beautiful Kornati Islands, river-rafting and half-day excursions to the Krka waterfalls. Check with **Miatours** (*☎/fax 212 788; e miatrade@zd.tel.hr; Vrata Sveti Krševana*) or **Aquarius Travel Agency** (*☎/fax 212 919; e juresko@zd.tel.hr; Nova Vrata bb*).

## Special Events

Major annual events include the town fair (July and August), the Dalmatian Song Festival (July and August), the musical evenings in St Donatus Church (August) and the Choral Festival (October).

## Places to Stay

Most visitors head out to the 'tourist settlement' at Borik, 3km northwest of Zadar, on the Puntamika bus (6KN, every 20 minutes from the bus station). Here there are hotels, a hostel, a camping ground and numerous 'sobe' signs; you can arrange a private room through an agency in town. If you arrive in the low season, try to arrange accommodation in advance, as some hotels and camping grounds will be closed.

**Camping** The huge autocamp **Zaton** (*☎ 280 280; camp sites per person/tent & car 68/60KN; open May-Sept*) is 16km northwest of Zadar on a sandy beach. There are 12 buses marked Zaton that leave daily from the bus station. Nearer to Zadar is **Autocamp Borik** (*☎ 332 074; camp sites per person/tent/car 30/18/26KN*), which is only steps away from Borik beach.

**Hostels** The **Borik Youth Hostel** (*☎ 331 145, fax 331 190; Obala Kneza Trpimira 76; B&B/half-board 90/155KN*) is near the beach at Borik.

**Private Rooms** Agencies that arrange private accommodation include Miatours and Aquarius Travel Agency (see under Organised Tours earlier in this section). Expect to pay

about 140KN per person for accommodation in the town centre with private bathroom.

**Hotels** If you want to stay in the town, there is only one choice but it's a good one. **Jović Guest House** (*☎ 214 098, ☎ 098 330 958; Šime Ljubića 4a; rooms 150KN per person*) is a new 12-room guesthouse in the heart of town with smallish but cool and attractive rooms with private bathroom. The price does not include breakfast but there are plenty of cafés around to have your morning meal. If you can't reach the owner, the rooms can be reserved through Aquarius Travel Agency (see Organised Tours, earlier).

Located right next door to the train station is **Hotel Kolovare** (*☎ 203 200, fax 203 300; e hotel-kolovare-zadar@zd.tel.hr; Bože Peričića 14; singles/doubles 487/735KN*), a more elaborate, but impersonal establishment. On Borik, **Hotel Mediteran** (*☎ 337 500, fax 337 528; e info@hotelmediteran-zd.hr; M Gupca 19; singles/doubles 320/416KN*) has comfortable rooms; dearer ones have air-con. You can also try **Hotel Puntamika** (*singles/doubles 350/460KN*), **Hotel Donat** or **Hotel Barbara** (*singles/doubles 285/375KN*), all in the Borik tourist complex. Each of these can be reserved at the **Hoteli Borik** (*☎ 206 400, fax 332 065; e prodaja@hoteliborik.hr*).

## Places to Eat

The eatery **Dva Ribara** (*Blaža Jurjeva 1; mains from 35KN*) is justifiably popular with the local crowd.

**Restaurant Martinac** (*Papavije 7; mains from 45KN*) has a secluded backyard terrace behind the restaurant that provides a relaxed ambience to sample delicious risotto and fish.

**Jure** (*Knezova Šubića Bribirskih 11; mains from 25KN*) is a self-service restaurant.

There's a **supermarket** (*cnr Široka & Sabora*) that keeps long hours and you'll find a number of **burek stands** around the vegetable market.

## Entertainment

**Central Kavana** (*Široka ul*) is a spacious café and hang-out with live music on the weekend. **Kult Caffe** (*Stomarica*) draws a young crowd; listen to rap music indoors or relax on the large shady terrace outside. In summer the many cafés along Varoška and Klaića place their tables on the street; it's great for people-watching.

## Getting There & Away

**Air** Zadar's airport, 12km east of the city, receives charter flights and Croatia Airlines flights from Zagreb (575KN) daily. A Croatia Airlines bus meets all flights and costs 25KN. A taxi into town costs around 150KN.

**Bus & Train** Zadar is on the coastal route that goes from Rijeka down to Split and Dubrovnik. There are four daily trains to Zagreb (131KN, 11 hours) that change at Knin, but the bus to Zagreb is quicker and passes by Plitvice Lakes National Park (three hours).

Croatia Express (see Information earlier) sells bus tickets to many German cities. See the introductory Getting There & Away section earlier in this chapter for more information.

**Boat** The Jadrolinija coastal ferry from Rijeka to Dubrovnik calls at Zadar twice weekly (138/168KN low/high season, six hours). It arrives around midnight.

For information on the boat connections to Italy see the Getting There & Away section at the beginning of this chapter and contact **Jadroagent** (☎ 211 447; ul Natka Nodila), just inside the city walls. **Jadrolinija** (☎ 254 800; Liburnska obala 7), on the harbour, has tickets for all local ferries, or you can buy ferry tickets from the Jadrolinija stall on Liburnska obala.

## AROUND ZADAR
## Plitvice Lakes
☎ 053

**Plitvice Lakes National Park** (admission Oct-May/June-Sept 70/90KN, students 40/55KN) lies midway between Zagreb and Zadar. The 19.5 hectares of wooded hills enclose 16 turquoise lakes, which are connected by a series of waterfalls and cascades. The mineral-rich waters carve new paths through the rock, depositing tufa in continually changing formations. Wooden footbridges follow the lakes and streams over, under and across the rumbling water for an exhilaratingly damp 18km. Swimming is not allowed. Your park admission is valid for the entire stay and also includes the boats and buses you need to use to see the lakes. There is accommodation on the site, as well as private accommodation nearby. Check options with the Plitvice Lakes National Park information office in Zagreb (see Information in the Zagreb section earlier in this chapter).

**Getting There & Away** All buses from Zadar to Zagreb stop at Plitvice (three hours). It is possible to visit Plitvice for the day on the way to or from the coast but be aware that buses will not pick up passengers at Plitvice if they are full. Luggage can be left at the **tourist information centre** (☎ 751 015; open 7am-8pm daily) at the first entrance to the park.

## SPLIT
☎ 021 • pop 188,700

Split (Spalato in Italian), the largest Croatian city on the Adriatic coast, is the heart of Dalmatia and lies on the southern side of a high peninsula sheltered from the open sea by many islands. Ferries to these islands are constantly coming and going. Within the ancient walls of Diocletian's Palace in the centre of town rises the majestic cathedral surrounded by a tangle of marble streets containing shops and businesses.

The entire western end of the peninsula is a vast, wooded mountain park, while industry, shipyards, limestone quarries and the ugly commercial-military port are mercifully far enough away on the northern side of the peninsula. High coastal mountains set against the blue Adriatic provide a striking frame to the scene.

Split achieved fame when Roman emperor Diocletian (AD 245–313), who was noted for his persecution of the early Christians, had his retirement palace built here from 295 to 305. After his death the great stone palace continued to be used as a retreat by Roman rulers. When the neighbouring colony of Salona was abandoned in the 7th century, many of the Romanised inhabitants fled to Split and barricaded themselves behind the high palace walls, where their descendants continue to live to this day.

Since 1945, Split has grown into a major industrial city ringed with apartment-block housing of stupefying ugliness, but the remarkable Diocletian's Palace (which is a now World Heritage Site) makes a visit to the city worthwhile. Split would make a great base for day trips to the surrounding islands, but finding some reasonable accommodation is a major problem.

## Orientation

The bus, train and ferry terminals are adjacent on the eastern side of the harbour, a short walk from the old town. Obala hrvatskog narodnog

## SPLIT

Franciscan Monastery

Park Skojevaca

To Solin (5km), Trogir (20km) & Ribnjak (20km)

Sports Stadium

Poljud Harbour

Hrvatske mornarice

Archaeological Museum

Lučićeva

Lovretska

Radničko Šetalište

Bus to Trogir & Airport

Šetalište M Tartaglie

Matoševa

Kaštelanska

Zrinsko-Frankopanska

Domovinska

Marjan Hill

Prilaz Vladimira Nazora

Plinarska

Ujevićeva Poljana

Sinjskih

Šubićeva

Slavićeva

Istarska

Zagrebačka

Vukovarska

To Lisičina

Milićeva

Križeva

Kralja Tomislava

Kneza Držislava

Slobode

Senjska

Jewish Cemetery

Stairway to Marjan Hill

Obala hrvatskog narodnog preporoda

Hrvojeva

Vrzov dolac

Matice hrvatske

Marasovica

Hotel Marjan

Kralja Zvonimira

Ratvice

Put Meja ul

Obala kneza Branimira

See Central Split Map

Obala kneza Domagoja

Train Station

Blankinijeva

Šetalište

Matije Gupca

To Meštrović Gallery (200m)

Šetalište Ivana Meštrovića

Hotel Jadran Koteks

Split Harbour

Yacht Harbour

Ferry Terminal

Bačvice

Beach

Put Firula

Vilka

**ADRIATIC SEA**

preporoda, the waterfront promenade, is your best central reference point in Split.

## Information

**Tourist Offices** The **Turistička Zajednica** (☎/fax 342 606; ⓦ www.visitsplit.com; open 9am-8pm Mon-Fri, 9am-1pm Sat) on Peristyle has several brochures about Split but very little more. The **Turistička Biro** (☎/fax 342 142; Obala hrvatskog narodnog preporoda 12; ⓔ turist-biro-split@st.hinet.hr) arranges private accommodation and also sells guidebooks.

**Money** There are several ATMs around the bus and train station. The AmEx representative is **Atlas travel agency** (☎ 343 055; Nepotova 4). You can change money here or

at any travel agency. There's also an ATM next to the **Croatia Airlines office** (Obala hrvatskog narodnog preporoda 9).

**Post & Communications** Poste-restante mail can be collected from window No 7 at the **main post office** (Kralja Tomislava 9; open 7am-8pm Mon-Fri, 7am-3pm Sat). There's also a **telephone centre** (open 7am-9pm Mon-Sat) here. **Internet Games** (☎ 338 548; Obala Kneza Domagoja 3) caters to backpackers and offers an Internet connection.

**Bookshop** The **Algoritam** (Bajamontijeva 2) is a good English-language bookshop.

**Left Luggage** There's a **garderoba kiosk** (open 6am-10pm daily) at the bus station. The train station's **left-luggage office** *(Domagoja 6; open 7am-9pm daily)* is about 50m north of the station.

## Things to See

The old town is a vast open-air museum and the new information signs at the important sights explain a great deal of Split's history. **Diocletian's Palace** *(entrance: Obala hrvatskog narodnog preporoda 22)*, facing the harbour, is one of the most imposing Roman ruins in existence. It was built as a strong rectangular fortress, with walls measuring 215m from east to west and 181 m wide at the southernmost point and reinforced by square corner towers. The imperial residence, mausoleum and temples were south of the main street, connecting the east and west gates.

Enter through the central ground floor of the palace. On the left are the excavated **basement halls** *(adult/concession 6/3KN; open 10am-6pm daily)*, which are empty but still impressive. Go through the passage to the **Peristyle**, a picturesque colonnaded square, with a neo-Romanesque cathedral tower rising above. The **vestibule**, an open dome above the ground-floor passageway at the southern end of the Peristyle, is overpowering. A lane off the Peristyle opposite the cathedral leads to **Temple of Jupiter**, which is now a baptistry.

On the eastern side of the Peristyle is the **cathedral**, originally Diocletian's mausoleum. The only reminder of Diocletian in the cathedral is a sculpture of his head in a circular stone wreath below the dome directly above the baroque white-marble altar. The Romanesque wooden doors (1214) and stone pulpit are notable. Climb the tower for a small fee.

The west palace gate opens onto medieval Narodni trg, dominated by the 15th-century Venetian Gothic **old town hall**. Trg Braće Radića, between Narodni trg and the harbour, contains the surviving north tower of the 15th-century Venetian garrison castle, which once extended to the water's edge. The east palace gate leads into the market area.

In the Middle Ages the nobility and rich merchants built their residences within the old palace walls; the **Papalic Palace** *(Papalićeva – also known as Žarkova – ul 5)* is now the town museum. Go through the north palace gate to see the powerful **statue** (1929) by Ivan Meštrović of 10th-century Slavic religious leader Gregorius of Nin, who fought for the right to perform Mass in Croatian. Notice that

his big toe has been polished to a shine; it's said that touching it brings good luck.

**Museums & Galleries** Many of Split's museums have been closed for the last 10 years awaiting money for renovation.

The **town museum** *(Papalićeva ul 5; adult/concession 10/5KN; open 9am-noon & 6pm-9pm Tues-Fri, 10am-noon Sat & Sun)*, east of Narodni trg, has a tidy collection of artefacts, paintings, furniture and clothes from Split; captions are in Croatian. The **Ethnographic Museum** *(Narodni trg; adult/student 10/5KN; open 9am-noon & 6pm-9pm Tues-Fri, 9am-noon Sat-Mon)* has a mildly interesting collection of photos of Old Split, traditional costumes and memorabilia of important citizens, but captions are in Croatian.

The **archaeological museum** *(Zrinjsko-Frankopanska 25; adult/student 10/5KN; open 9am-noon & 5pm-8pm Tues-Fri, 9am-noon Sat & Sun)*, north of the town, is worth the walk for its exhibits devoted to burial sculpture and excavations at Salona.

The best art museum in Split is **Meštrović Gallery** *(Šetalište Ivana Meštrovića 46; adult/student 15/10KN; open 10am-6pm Mon-Sat, 10am-2pm Sun)*. You'll see a comprehensive, well-arranged collection of works by Ivan Meštrović, Croatia's premier modern sculptor, who built the gallery as his home in 1931–39. Although Meštrović intended to retire here, he emigrated to the USA soon after WWII. Bus No 12 runs to the gallery from Trg Republike every 40 minutes.

From the Meštrović Gallery it's possible to hike straight up **Marjan Hill**. Go up ul Tonća Petrasova Marovića on the western side of the gallery and continue straight up the stairway to Put Meja ul. Turn left and walk west to Put Meja 76. The trail begins on the western side of this building. Marjan Hill offers trails through the forest, lookouts and old chapels.

## Organised Tours

Atlas travel agency (see Information earlier) runs excursions to Krka waterfalls (225KN) and Zlatni Rat beach on the island of Brač (140KN), as well as other excursions.

## Special Events

The Split Summer Festival (mid-July to mid-August) features open-air opera, ballet, drama and musical concerts. There's also the Feast of St Dujo (7 May), a flower show (May) and

CROATIA

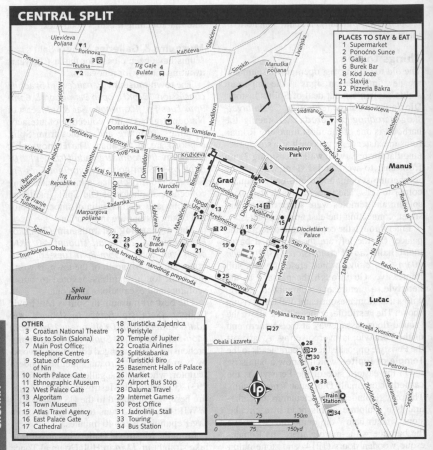

## CENTRAL SPLIT

**PLACES TO STAY & EAT**
1   Supermarket
2   Ponoćno Sunce
5   Galija
6   Burek Bar
8   Kod Joze
21   Slavija
32   Pizzeria Bakra

**OTHER**
3   Croatian National Theatre
4   Bus to Solin (Salona)
7   Main Post Office;
      Telephone Centre
9   Statue of Gregorius
      of Nin
10   North Palace Gate
11   Ethnographic Museum
12   West Palace Gate
13   Algoritam
14   Town Museum
15   Atlas Travel Agency
16   East Palace Gate
17   Cathedral
18   Turistička Zajednica
19   Peristyle
20   Temple of Jupiter
22   Croatia Airlines
23   Splitskabanka
24   Turistički Biro
25   Basement Halls of Palace
26   Market
27   Airport Bus Stop
28   Daluma Travel
29   Internet Games
30   Post Office
31   Jadrolinija Stall
33   Touring
34   Bus Station

the Festival of Popular Music (end of June). The traditional February Carnival is from June to September and a variety of evening entertainment is presented in the old town.

### Places to Stay

Budget travellers are out of luck in Split. There's only one one-star hotel in the town centre and the two-star hotels are a long bus or expensive taxi ride away. The closest camping ground is **Ribnjak** (☎ 864 430), 20km southeast of Split, near Omiš.

Turistička Biro (see Information) and **Daluma Travel** (☎/fax 338 439; e daluma-st@ st.tel.hr; Obala Kneza Domagoja 1) have two-star singles/doubles for 145/265KN. **Slavija** (☎ 347 053, fax 591 558; Buvinova 3; singles/ doubles 190/230KN, with private bathroom

230/280KN) has the cheapest rooms in town but they're still over-priced for the meagre amenities. Three-star **Hotel Marjan** (☎ 302 111, fax 302 930; Obala Kneza Branimira 8; singles/doubles 500/630KN) and the two-star **Hotel Jadran Koteks** (☎ 398 622, fax 398 586; e koteks-zvoncac@st.hinet.hr; Sustje-panski; singles/doubles 400/520KN), east of the town, offer rooms with TV and air-con but the Jadran Koteks has a swimming pool and is on the beach.

### Places to Eat

The best pizza in town is at **Galija** (Tončićeva; pizzas from 26KN; open to 11pm daily), but **Pizzeria Bakra** (Radovanova 2; pizzas from 32KN), off ul Sv Petra Starog and just down from the vegetable market, is not bad either.

The vegetarian salad bar at **Ponoćno Sunce** (*Teutina 15*) is good value at 40KN. It also serves pasta and grilled meat. For some excellent Dalmatian specialities at a reasonable price, try **Kod Joze** (*Sredmanuška 4; mains from 40KN*).

There's a spiffy **Burek Bar** (*Domaldova 13*), near the main post office, and the vast **supermarket/delicatessen** (*Svačićeva 1*) has a wide selection of meat and cheese for sandwiches. The **vegetable market** has a wide array of fresh local produce.

## Entertainment

In summer everyone starts the evening at one of the cafés along Obala hrvatskog narodnog preporoda and then heads towards the **Bačvice** complex on the beach. These former public baths offer restaurants, cafés, discos and venues for live rock and salsa. During winter, opera and ballet are presented at the **Croatian National Theatre** (*Trg Gaje Bulata; best seats about 60KN*); tickets for the same night are usually available. Erected in 1891, the theatre was fully restored in 1979 in the original style; it's worth attending a performance for the architecture alone.

## Getting There & Away

**Air** The country's national air carrier, **Croatia Airlines** (☎ 362 997), operates flights between Zagreb and Split up to four times every day (627KN, one hour).

**Bus** Advance bus tickets with seat reservations are recommended. There are buses from the main bus station beside the harbour to:

| destination | cost (KN) | duration (hrs) | frequency (daily) |
|---|---|---|---|
| Dubrovnik | 100 | 4½ | 12 |
| Ljubljana | 234 | 10 | 1 |
| Međugorje | 70 | 3 | 4 |
| Mostar | 74 | 4 | 4 |
| Osijek | 204 | 10½ | 1 |
| Pula | 250 | 10 | 3 |
| Rijeka | 104 | 8 | 14 |
| Sarajevo | 121 | 7 | 11 |
| Zadar | 78–88 | 3 | 26 |
| Zagreb | 130 | 8s | 26 |

Bus No 37 to Solin, Split airport and Trogir leaves from a local bus station on Domovinskog, 1km northeast of the city centre (see the Split map).

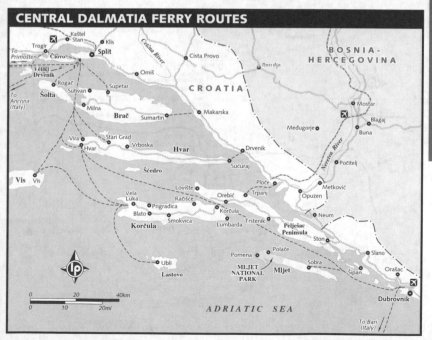

**CENTRAL DALMATIA FERRY ROUTES**

**Touring** (☎ *338 503; Obala Domagojeva 10*), near the bus station, represents Deutsche Touring and sells tickets to German cities.

**Train** There are four trains daily that run between Split and Zagreb (90KN to 131KN, eight to nine hours depending on the service and the time of day), and Split and Šibenik (31KN, 90 minutes).

**Boat** In the large ferry terminal opposite the bus station, **Jadrolinija** (☎ *338 333*) handles all car ferry services that depart from the docks around the ferry terminal. For passenger ferries, buy tickets at the Jadrolinija stall on Obala Kneza Domagoja near the train station and the departure point for passenger ferries. **Jadroagent** (☎ *338 335*), in the ferry terminal, represents Adriatica Navigazione for its connections between Split and Ancona (see Sea in the Getting There & Away section at the beginning of this chapter). There's also an **SMC agency** (☎ *338 292*) in the terminal for tickets between Ancona and Split, Hvar and Vis, as well as **SNAV** (☎ *322 252*) for a four-hour connection to Ancona, and other connections to Pescara, Giulianova and Vasto. For details on connections to/from Italy see the Getting There & Away section at the beginning of this chapter

## Getting Around
The bus to Split airport (30KN) leaves from Obala Lazareta 3, about 90 minutes before flight times or you can take bus No 37 from the bus station on Domovinskog (9.50KN for a two-zone ticket).

A one-zone ticket costs 7KN for one trip in Central Split if you buy it from the driver but 11KN for two trips and 55KN for 10 trips if you buy it from a kiosk. There's a kiosk that also distributes bus maps at the city bus stop.

## SOLIN (SALONA)
The ruins of the ancient city of Solin (known as Salona by the Romans), among the vineyards at the foot of mountains 5km northeast of Split, are the most interesting archaeological site in Croatia. Today surrounded by noisy highways and industry, Salona was the capital of the Roman province of Dalmatia from the time Julius Caesar elevated it to the status of colony. Salona held out against the barbarians and was only evacuated in AD 614 when the

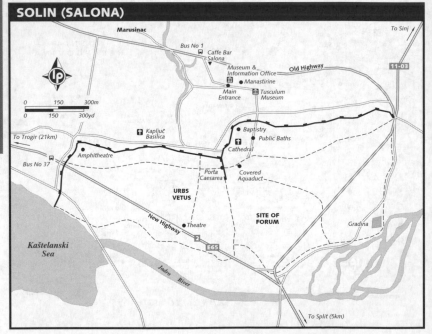

inhabitants fled to Split and neighbouring islands in the face of Avar and Slav attacks.

## Things to See

A good place to begin your visit is at the main entrance near Caffe Bar Salona. There's a small **museum** *(admission 10KN; open 8am-3pm Mon-Fri)* at the entrance, which also provides a helpful map and some literature about the complex.

**Manastirine**, the fenced area behind the car park, was a burial place for early Christian martyrs before the legalisation of Christianity. Excavated remains of the cemetery and the 5th-century basilica are highlights, although this area was outside the ancient city itself. Overlooking Manastirine is **Tusculum** with interesting sculptures embedded in the walls and in the garden.

The Manastirine-Tusculum complex is a part of an **archaeological reserve** *(admission 10KN; open 7am-8pm daily)*. A path bordered by cypress trees runs south towards the northern **city wall** of Salona. Note the covered aqueduct along the inside base of the wall. The ruins in front of you as you stand on the wall were the Early Christian cult centre, which include the three-aisled, 5th-century **cathedral** and a small **baptistry** with inner columns. **Public baths** adjoin the cathedral on the east.

Southwest of the cathedral is the 1st-century east city gate, **Porta Caesarea**, later engulfed by the growth of Salona in all directions. Grooves in the stone road left by ancient chariots can still be seen at this gate.

Walk west along the city wall for about 500m to **Kapljuč Basilica** on the right, another martyrs' burial place. At the western end of Salona is the huge 2nd-century **amphitheatre**, destroyed in the 17th century by the Venetians to prevent it from being used as a refuge by Turkish raiders.

## Getting There & Away

The ruins are easily accessible on Split city bus No 1 direct to Solin every half-hour from the city bus stop at Trg Gaje Bulata.

From the amphitheatre at Solin it's easy to continue to Trogir by catching a westbound bus No 37 from the nearby stop on the adjacent new highway. If, on the other hand, you want to return to Split, use the underpass to cross the highway and catch an eastbound bus No 37 (buy a four-zone ticket in Split if you plan to do this).

## TROGIR
☎ 021 • pop 600

Trogir (formerly Trau), a lovely medieval town on the coast just 20km west of Split's city limits, is well worth a stop if you're coming south from Zadar. A day trip to Trogir from Split can easily be combined with a visit to the Roman ruins of Solin.

The old town of Trogir occupies a tiny island in the narrow channel lying between Čiovo Island and the mainland, and is just off the coastal highway. There are many sights on the 15-minute walk around this island.

## Orientation & Information

The heart of the old town is a few minutes' walk from the bus station. After crossing the small bridge near the station, go through the north gate. Trogir's finest sights are around Narodni trg to the southeast.

A private tourist office, **Cipiko Tourist Office** *(☎ 881 554; open 9am-12.30pm & 2.30pm-5pm Mon-Fri Sept-June, 9am-8pm Mon-Sat July & Aug)* opposite the cathedral, sells a map of the area and arranges private accommodation. There's no left-luggage office in Trogir bus station, so you may end up toting your bags around town.

## Things to See

The glory of the three-nave Venetian **Cathedral of St Lovro** *(Trg Ivana Pavla II; open 8am-noon year-round & 4pm-7pm daily during summer)* is the Romanesque portal of *Adam and Eve* (1240) by Master Radovan, the earliest example of the nude in Dalmatian sculpture. Enter the building via an obscure back door to see the perfect Renaissance Chapel of St Ivan and the choir stalls, pulpit, ciborium and treasury. You can even climb the cathedral tower, if it's open, for a great view. Also located on the square is the renovated **Church of St John the Baptist** with a magnificent carved portal and an interior showcasing a *Pietá* by Nicola Firentinac.

## Getting There & Away

In Split, bus No 37 leaves from the local bus station. If you're making a day trip to Trogir also buy your return ticket back to Split, as the ticket window at Trogir bus station is often closed. Drivers will also sell tickets if you're stuck. The city bus No 37 runs between Trogir and Split every 20 minutes throughout the day, with a short stop at Split airport en route.

CROATIA

There's also a ferry once a week between Trogir and Split.

Southbound buses from Zadar (130km) will drop you off in Trogir. Getting buses north can be more difficult, as they often arrive full from Split.

## HVAR ISLAND
☎ 021 • pop 12,600

Called the 'Croatian Madeira', Hvar is said to receive more sunshine than anywhere else in the country – 2724 hours each year. Yet the island is luxuriantly green, with brilliant patches of lavender, rosemary and heather. The fine weather is so reliable that hotels give a discount on cloudy days and a free stay if you ever see snow.

### Hvar Town

Medieval Hvar lies between protective pine-covered slopes and the azure Adriatic, its Gothic palaces hidden among narrow backstreets below the 13th-century city walls. A long seaside promenade dotted with small, rocky beaches stretches from either end of Hvar's welcoming harbour. The traffic-free marble streets of Hvar have an air of Venice, and it was under Venetian rule that Hvar's citizens developed the fine stone-carving skills evident in a profusion of beautifully ornamented buildings.

**Orientation & Information** The town centre is Trg Sv Stjepana, 100m west of the bus station. Passenger ferries tie up on Riva, the eastern quay running south of Trg Sv Stjepana. Travel agencies, shops and banks are spread along the harbour and there is no lack of ATMs on the island.

The **tourist office** (☎/fax 742 977, 741 059; e tzg-hvar@st.tel.hr; w www.hvar.hr; open 8am-noon & 4pm-10pm daily, mornings only Oct-May) is located in the arsenal building on the corner of Trg Sv Stjepana. The travel agencies **Mengola Travel** (☎/fax 742 099; e mengola-hvar@st.tel.hr), on the western side of the harbour, and **Pelegrini** (☎/fax 742 250), on Riva, are generally more informative. There's a **left-luggage office** (open 7am-midnight daily) in the bathroom next to the bus station and Internet access at the hotel Slavija for 15KN an hour (for details see Places to Stay later in this section).

**Atlas travel agency** (☎ 741 670) is on the western side of the harbour. Public telephones

are in the **post office** (open 7am-8pm Mon-Fri, 7am-3pm Sat) on Riva.

**Things to See & Do** The full flavour of medieval Hvar is best savoured on the backstreets of the old town. At each end of Hvar is a monastery with a prominent tower. The Domininican **Church of St Marko** at the head of the bay was largely destroyed by Turks in the 16th century but you can visit the local **archaeological museum** (admission 10KN; open 10am-noon daily) in the ruins. If it is closed you'll still get a good view of the ruins from the road just above, which leads up to a stone cross on a hill top offering a picture-postcard view of Hvar.

At the southeastern end of Hvar you'll find the 15th-century Renaissance **Franciscan monastery** (open 10am-noon & 5pm-7pm daily July & Aug, plus Christmas week & Holy Week), with a wonderful collection of Venetian paintings in the church and adjacent **museum** (admission 10KN; open 10am-noon & 5pm-7pm Mon-Sat), including The Last Supper by Matteo Ingoli.

Smack in the middle of Hvar is the imposing Gothic **arsenal**, its great arch visible from afar. The local commune's war galley was once kept here. Upstairs off the arsenal terrace is Hvar's prize, the first **municipal theatre** (admission 10KN; open 10am-noon & 5pm-7pm daily) in Europe (1612), rebuilt in the 19th century. Hours can vary and you enter through the adjoining **Gallery of Contemporary Croatian Art** (Arsenal; admission 10KN; open 10am-noon & 7pm-11pm July & Aug, plus Christmas week & Holy Week, 10am-noon low season).

On the hill high above Hvar town is a **Venetian fortress** (1551) and it's worth the climb for the sweeping panoramic views. The fort was built to defend Hvar from the Turks, who sacked the town in 1539 and 1571.

There is a small town beach next to the Franciscan Monastery but the best beach is in front of the Hotel Amphora, around the western corner of the cove. Most people take a launch to the offshore islands that include the naturist islands of Jerolim and Stipanska and lovely Palmižana; the cost is 20KN to 30KN.

In front of the Hotel Amphora, **Diving Centar Jurgovan** (☎ 742 490; w www.jurgovan.com) is a large operation that offers a certification course, dives (€34.15 with equipment) and all sorts of water sports (banana boating, snorkelling, water-skiing), as well as hotel packages. **Dinko Petrić** (☎ 741 792), in front of Hotel Bodul, is a smaller operator that offers day-long dive trips including lunch for about 220KN.

**Places to Stay** Accommodation in Hvar is extremely tight in July and August. A reservation is highly recommended.

The closest camping ground is **Mala Milna** (☎ 745 027), 2km southeast of town. For private accommodation, try Mengola Travel or Pelegrini. Expect to pay from 160/262KN per single/double with private bathroom in the town centre.

**Jagoda & Ante Bracanović Guesthouse** (☎ 741 416, 091 520 3796; e virgilye@ yahoo.com; Poviše Škole; singles/doubles 100/190KN) is a friendly place that offers six spacious rooms – each with a private bathroom, balcony and kitchen access – it's close to the town centre and is open all year.

About 1km southwest of the town centre is the two-star **Hotel Croatia** (☎ 742 707, fax 742 400; e croatia-hvar@st.tel.hr; singles/ doubles 290/510KN) that has 36 attractive and newly renovated rooms with telephones; the slightly more expensive rooms have balconies. The hotel is surrounded by a pine grove and has easy access to a small cove. Half-board is also available.

In town, there's the **Slavija** (☎ 741 820, fax 741 147; Riva; singles/doubles 444/664KN) right on the harbour and the century-old **Hotel Palace** (☎ 741 966, fax 742 420; singles/ doubles 544/878KN). One hotel or the other is open all year and the prices drop 50% during the low season. Reservations for both are handled by **Sunčani Hvar** (☎ 741 026, fax 742 014; w www.suncanihvar.hr), which also handles other hotels in town. The tourist office can also make hotel reservations.

**Places to Eat** Pizzerias along the harbour offer the most predictable but least expensive eating. **Bounty** (☎ 742 565; mains from 60KN), next to Mengola Travel Agency, is the cheapest of the options, but it's worthwhile to head up the stairs from the northern side of Trg Sv Stjepana to **Macondo** (☎ 741 851; mains from 50KN) or farther east to the **Paradise Garden** (☎ 741 310; mains from 60KN) up the stairs on the northern side of the cathedral, where dining is outdoors on an enclosed patio.

The **grocery store** (Trg Sv Stjepana) is a viable restaurant alternative and there's a morning **market** next to the bus station.

**Getting There & Away** The Jadrolinija ferries between Rijeka and Dubrovnik stop in Stari Grad before continuing to Korčula. The **Jadrolinija agency** (☎ 741 132) beside the landing sells tickets.

Car ferries from Split call at Stari Grad (32KN, one hour) three times daily (five daily in July and August) and there's an afternoon passenger boat from Split to Hvar town (23KN) that goes on to Vela Luka on Korčula Island (22KN, one hour). See the introductory Getting There & Away section of this chapter for information on international connections. Buses meet all ferries that dock at Stari Grad in July and August, but if you come in winter it's best to check first with one of the travel agencies to make sure the bus is running.

It's possible to visit Hvar on a (hectic) day trip from Split by catching the morning Jadrolinija ferry to Stari Grad, a bus to Hvar town, then the last ferry from Stari Grad directly back to Split.

## KORČULA ISLAND
☎ 020 • pop 16,200

Korčula is the largest island in an archipelago of 48 islets. Rich in vineyards and olive trees, the island was named Korkyra Melaina (Black Korčula) by the original Greek settlers because of its dense woods and plant life. The southern coast is dotted with quiet coves and small beaches linked to the interior by winding, scenic roads.

### Korčula Town

The town of Korčula (Curzola in Italian), at the northeastern tip of the island, hugs a small, hilly peninsula jutting into the Adriatic Sea. With its round, defensive towers and compact cluster of red-roofed houses, Korčula is a typical medieval Dalmatian town. Korčula Island was controlled by Venice from the 14th to the 18th centuries, as is evident from the Venetian coats of arms adorning the official buildings. The gated, walled old town is criss-crossed by narrow stone streets designed to protect its inhabitants from the winds swirling around the peninsula. If you didn't plan a stop in Korčula, one look at this unique town from the Jadrolinija ferry will make you regret it.

CROATIA

**Orientation** The big Jadrolinija car ferry drops you off either in the west harbour next to the Hotel Korčula or the east harbour next to Marko Polo Tours. The old town lies between the two harbours. The large hotels and main beach lie south of the east harbour and the residential neighbourhood Sveti Nikola (with a smaller beach) is southwest of the west harbour.

**Information** Korčula **Turistička Agencija** (☎ 711 067, fax 715 067; W www.korcula .net) is a good source of information on the west harbour as you enter the old town and the website gives a good range of accommodation options. **Atlas travel agency** (☎ 711 231) is the local AmEx representative and there's a **Jadrolinija office** (☎ 715 410) about 25m up from the west harbour.

The **post office** (with public telephones) is rather hidden next to the stairway up to the old town. There's Internet access at **Tino's Internet** (Ul Tri Sulara) or Tino's other outlet at the **ACI Marina**, both of which are open long hours.

There are ATMs in town at Splitska Banka and Dubrovačka Banka. You can change money there, at the post office or any of the travel agencies. There's no left-luggage office at the bus station.

**Things to See** Other than following the circuit of the former city walls or walking along the shore, sightseeing in Korčula centres on Cathedral Square. The Gothic **Cathedral of St Mark** features two paintings by Tintoretto (*Three Saints* on the altar and *Annunciation* to one side).

The **treasury** (☎ 711 049; Trg Sv Marka Statuta; admission 10KN; open 9am-7pm daily June-Aug) in the 14th-century Abbey Palace next to the cathedral is worth a look; even better is the **Town Museum** (☎ 711 420; Trg Sv Marka Statuta; admission 10KN) in the 15th-century Gabriellis Palace opposite. The exhibits of Greek pottery, Roman ceramics and home furnishings have English captions. It's said that Marco Polo was born in Korčula in 1254; you can climb the **tower** (admission 5KN) of what is believed to have been his house.

There's also an **Icon Museum** (Trg Svih Svetih; admission 8KN; open 10am-1pm Mon-Sat year-round) in the old town. It isn't much of a museum, but visitors are let into the

beautiful old **Church of All Saints**. Museums keep longer hours in the summer.

In the high summer season, water taxis at the east harbour collect passengers to visit various points on the island, as well as **Badija Island**, which features a 15th-century Franciscan monastery (now a dormitory), as well as Orebić and the nearby village of Lumbarda, which both have sandy beaches.

**Organised Tours** Both Atlas travel agency (for contact details see Information earlier) and **Marko Polo Tours** (☎ 715 400, fax 715 800; e marko-polo-tours@du.tel.hr) offer an Island Tour by boat (185KN), a tour to Mljet Island (170KN) or a half-day boat trip around the surrounding islands (100KN).

**Places to Stay** Korčula offers a range of accommodation, although prices are high in July and August. **Autocamp Kalac** (☎ 711 182, fax 711 146) is behind Hotel Bon Repos in a dense pine grove near the beach. Turistička Agencija and Marko Polo Tours arrange private rooms, charging 155/295KN per single/double with private bathroom and apartments starting at 335KN.

You may get a better deal from guesthouses, which are less likely to insist on a 30% surcharge for short stays. Try **Tarle** (☎ 711 712, fax 711 243; e croatia-osiguranje1@ du.tel.hr; Stalište Frana Kršinića; doubles with/without kitchen 200/170KN, apartments 440KN) next to Hotel Marko Polo about 500m southeast of the bus station, which has a pretty enclosed garden and rooms with balconies. Air-con is planned.

Closer to the old town is the residential neighbourhood of Sveti Nikola, about 100m west of the bus station. Here you'll find the **Depolo** (☎/fax 711 621; e tereza.depolo@ du.hinet.hr; doubles with/without sea view 200/160KN), which has spiffy rooms, some with air-con. Other guesthouses nearby for about the same price include **Peručić** (☎/fax 711 458; e tonci.perucic@du.hinet.hr) with great balconies and the homy **Ojdanić** (☎/fax 711 708; e roko-taxi@du.hinet.hr). Ratko Ojdanić also has a water taxi and much experience in fishing trips around the island.

The hotel scene is far from inspiring. The large **Hotel Park** (☎ 726 004, fax 711 746; e htp-korcula@du.tel.hr; singles/doubles 425/525KN) is the cheapest and can put you in touch with the four other large hotels.

CROATIA

**Places to Eat** Just around the corner from Marco Polo's house **Adio Mare** *(mains about 80KN)* is a reliable choice for fresh fish and has a charming maritime decor. **Marco Polo** *(mains from 35KN)* does a good job with its Italian-style dishes and is open year-round. **Gradski Podrum** *(mains from 65KN)* serves up local specialities, such as fish Korčula style – boiled with potatoes and topped with tomato sauce. There's a **supermarket** next to Marko Polo Tours.

**Entertainment** Between May and September there's **moreška sword dancing** *(tickets 50KN; 9pm Thur)* by the old town gate, more often during July and August. The clash of swords and the graceful movements of the dancers/fighters make an exciting show. Atlas, the Turistička Agencija or Marko Polo Tours sell tickets.

**Getting There & Away** Transport connections to Korčula are good. There's one bus every day to Dubrovnik and Zagreb (209KN, 12 hours) and one a week to Sarajevo (145KN, eight hours).

*Boat* There's a regular afternoon car ferry between Split and Vela Luka (35KN, three hours) on the island's western end that stops at Hvar most days. Six daily buses link Korčula town to Vela Luka (24KN, one hour) but services from Vela Luka are reduced on the weekend.

From Orebić, look for the passenger launch (10KN, 15 minutes, at least four times daily year-round), which will drop you off near Hotel Korčula right below the old town's towers. There's also a car ferry to Dominče (7KN, 15 minutes) which stops near the hotel Bon Repos where you can pick up the bus from Lumbarda or take a water taxi to town (6KN). For international connections see the Getting There & Away section at the beginning of this chapter.

## OREBIĆ
Orebić, on the southern coast of the Pelješac Peninsula between Korčula and Ploče, offers better beaches than those found at Korčula, 2.5km across the water. The easy access by ferry from Korčula makes it the perfect place to go for the day. The best beach in Orebić is Trstenica cove, a 15-minute walk east along the shore from the port.

## Getting There & Away
In Orebić the ferry terminal and the bus station are adjacent to each other. Korčula buses to Dubrovnik, Zagreb and Sarajevo stop at Orebić. See the Korčula section for additional bus and ferry information.

## MLJET ISLAND
☎ 020 • pop 1111
Created in 1960, **Mljet National Park** occupies the western third of the green island of Mljet (Meleda in Italian), between Korčula and Dubrovnik. The park is centred around two saltwater lakes surrounded by pine-clad slopes. Most people visit the island on day trips from Korčula or Dubrovnik but it is possible to get here by the regular ferry from Dubrovnik, stay a few days and go hiking, cycling and boating.

## Orientation
Tour boats and the Atlant passenger boats arrive at Pomena wharf at Mljet's western end, where a good map of the island is posted. Jadrolinija ferries arrive at Sobra on the eastern end and they are met by a local bus for the 1½-hour ride to Pomena. The admission price for the national park is 55/35KN per adult/concession during July and August, 38.50/24.50KN from September to June but there is no park admission price if you stay overnight on the island.

## Things to See & Do
From Pomena it's a 15-minute walk to a jetty on **Veliko jezero**, the larger of the two lakes. Here you can board a boat (the price is included in the park admission fee) to a small lake islet and have lunch at a 12th-century **Benedictine monastery**, which is now a restaurant.

Those who don't want to spend the rest of the afternoon swimming and sunbathing on the monastery island can catch an early boat back to the main island and spend a couple of hours walking along the lakeshore before taking the late-afternoon excursion boat back to Korčula or Dubrovnik. There's a small landing opposite the monastery where the boat operator drops off passengers upon request. It's not possible to walk right around the larger lake because there's no bridge over the channel that connects the lakes to the sea.

Mljet is good for cycling; the Odisej hotel rents bicycles (70KN per half-day).

CROATIA

## Organised Tours

See Organised Tours in the Korčula and Dubrovnik sections for agencies offering excursions to Mljet. The tour lasts from 8.30am to 6pm and includes the park entry fee. The boat trip from Korčula to Pomena takes at least two hours, less by hydrofoil. From Dubrovnik takes longer. Lunch isn't included in the tour price.

## Places to Stay

There's no camping permitted inside the national park but **Marina** (☎ 745 071; open June-Sept) is a small camping ground in Ropa, about 1km from the park. The Polače **tourist office** (☎ 744 086; e np-mljet@np-mljet.hr) arranges private accommodation at 200KN per double room in peak season but it is essential to make arrangements before arrival. Don't count on 'sobe' signs and in high season you'll have trouble renting for less than four nights.

The only hotel option available on the island is the upmarket **Odisej** (☎ 744 022, fax 744 042; e odisej@plavalaguna.hr; 294KN per person) in Pomena. There's a 50% reduction on the rates in the low season.

## Getting There & Away

It's possible to make a quick visit to Mljet by a regular morning ferry (32KN, two hours) from Dubrovnik in July and August. The rest of the year, the ferry leaves Dubrovnik in mid-afternoon Monday to Saturday or Sunday evening. The ferry docks in Sobra where it is met by a bus. The big Jadrolinija coastal ferries also stop at Mljet twice a week in summer and once a week during the rest of the year.

**Atlant Shipping & Travel Agency** (☎ 419 044; Radića 26) in Dubrovnik runs a fast boat, the *Nona Anna*, daily from June to September (30KN, one hour 40 minutes) to Pomena and Polače. It leaves from Gruž harbour, Dubrovnik, at 8am and returns at 7pm, allowing Mljet to be visited on a day trip. Tickets can be bought at the agency or on board the boat.

## DUBROVNIK

☎ 020 • pop 43,770

Lord Byron called it 'the pearl of the Adriatic'; Agatha Christie spent her second honeymoon there; George Bernard Shaw said it was 'paradise on earth'. Behind the stone curtain of Dubrovnik's walls lay marble-paved squares, steps and streets ornamented with numerous

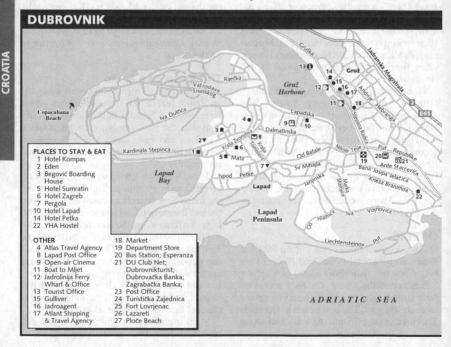

# DUBROVNIK

**PLACES TO STAY & EAT**
1 Hotel Kompas
2 Eden
3 Begović Boarding House
5 Hotel Sumratin
6 Hotel Zagreb
7 Pergola
10 Hotel Lapad
14 Hotel Petka
22 YHA Hostel

**OTHER**
4 Atlas Travel Agency
8 Lapad Post Office
9 Open-air Cinema
11 Boat to Mljet
12 Jadrolinija Ferry Wharf & Office
13 Tourist Office
15 Gulliver
16 Jadroagent
17 Atlant Shipping & Travel Agency
18 Market
19 Department Store
20 Bus Station; Esperanza
21 DU Club Net; Dubrovniknturist; Dubrovačka Banka; Zagrabačka Banka; 
23 Post Office
24 Turistička Zajednica
25 Fort Lovrjenac
26 Lazareti
27 Ploče Beach

finely carved fountains and palaces. Churches, monasteries and museums recall an eventful history and a vibrant artistic tradition that is still flourishing. Beyond the walls stretch the crystal-blue waters of the southern Adriatic, sprinkled with tiny islands for the hedonistic.

Founded 1300 years ago by refugees from Epidaurus in Greece, medieval Dubrovnik (Ragusa until 1918) shook off Venetian control in the 14th century and became one of Venice's more important maritime rivals, trading with Egypt, Syria, Sicily, Spain, France and later Turkey. The double blow of an earthquake in 1667 and the opening of new trade routes to the east sent Ragusa into a slow decline, ending with Napoleon's conquest of the town in 1806.

The deliberate and militarily pointless shelling of Dubrovnik by the Yugoslav army in 1991 sent shockwaves through the international community but, when the smoke cleared in 1992, traumatised residents cleared the rubble and set about repairing the damage. With a substantial amount of international aid, the famous monuments were rebuilt and re-sculpted, the streets sealed and the clay roofs retiled. The reconstruction has been skilful but you will notice different shades of rose-tiled roofs as you walk around the city walls.

After a steep postwar decline, visitors are once again discovering Dubrovnik's magic. Tourism is the town's main (if not only) money-earner and its comeback has been striking, particularly in the warm summer months. Whatever the time of year the interlay of light and stone is enchanting. Don't miss it.

## Orientation

The Jadrolinija ferry terminal and the bus station are a few hundred metres apart at Gruž, several kilometres northwest of the old town, which is closed to cars. The main street in the old town is Placa (also called Stradun). Most accommodation is on the leafy Lapad Peninsula, west of the bus station.

## Information

**Tourist Offices** The main **Turistička Zajednica** (☎ 427 591, fax 426 253; e ured.pile@ tzdubrovnik.hr; Starčevića 7; open 8am-8pm daily) is outside Pile Gate and there's another **tourist office** (☎ 417 983; Gruž) near the Jadrolinija dock. There's also a private **Tourist Information Centar** (☎ 323 350, fax 323 351; Placa 1) opposite the Franciscan monastery. Look for the booklet *Dubrovnik Riviera Guide* with useful information. **Jadrolinija** (☎ 418 000) sells ferry tickets.

**Money** You can change money at any travel agency or, if you arrive by a bus, at the post office in the department store near the bus station. There are ATMs southeast of the bus station at **Dubrovačka Banka** (Put Republike 9), for Visa and Plus, and at **Zagrabačka Banka** (Put Republike 5) for other cards. The same two banks also have ATMs on Gruž harbour near the Jadrolinija dock. There are also several ATMs on Placa.

**Post & Communications** The main post office (cnr Široka & Od Puća; open 8am-7pm Mon-Fri, 8am-2pm Sat) is in town and there's a branch at Ante Starčevića 2, a block from Pile Gate. There's another post office on the way to the Hotel Kompas, as well as one in Lapad. **DU Club Net** (☎ 356 894; Put Republike 7; open 8am-midnight daily) has Internet access and in town at the **Library** (cnr Od Puća & Miha Pracata; open 8am-8.30pm Mon-Fri, 8am-1pm Sat), which has cheaper access at 10/20KN per 30 minutes/one hour.

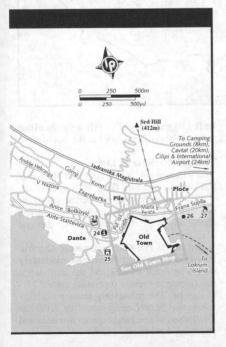

CRCATIA

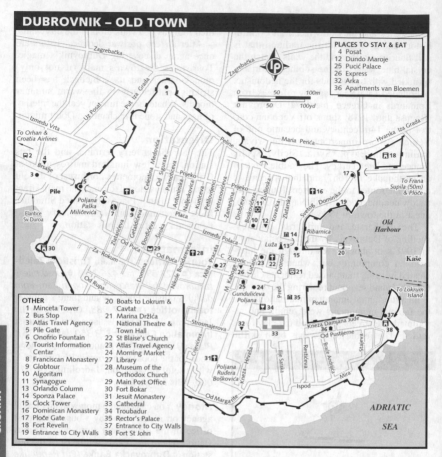

## DUBROVNIK – OLD TOWN

**PLACES TO STAY & EAT**
4 Posat
12 Dundo Maroje
25 Pucić Palace
26 Express
32 Arka
36 Apartments van Bloemen

**OTHER**
1 Minceta Tower
2 Bus Stop
3 Atlas Travel Agency
5 Pile Gate
6 Onofrio Fountain
7 Tourist Information Centar
8 Franciscan Monastery
9 Globtour
10 Algoritam
11 Synagogue
13 Orlando Column
14 Sponza Palace
15 Clock Tower
16 Dominican Monastery
17 Ploče Gate
18 Fort Revelin
19 Entrance to City Walls
20 Boats to Lokrum & Cavtat
21 Marina Držlća National Theatre & Town Hall
22 St Blaise's Church
23 Atlas Travel Agency
24 Morning Market
27 Library
28 Museum of the Orthodox Church
29 Main Post Office
30 Fort Bokar
31 Jesuit Monastery
33 Cathedral
34 Troubadur
35 Rector's Palace
37 Entrance to City Walls
38 Fort St John

**Travel Agencies** The AmEx representative is **Atlas travel agency** (☎ 442 574; Sv Đurđa 1), outside Pile Gate next to the old town; it also holds mail. There are also other **Atlas offices** (☎ 418 001; Gruž harbour • ☎ 442 528; Lučarica 1). The travel agency closest to the bus station is **Dubrovnikturist** (☎ 356 959, fax 356 885; e dubrovnikturist@net.hr; Put Republike 7). **Globtour** (☎ 323 991; Placa) is in town and **Gulliver** is near Jadrolinija dock (☎ 313 300, fax 419 119; Radića 32).

**Jadroagent** (☎ 419 009, fax 419 029; Radića 32) handles tickets for most international boats from Croatia.

**Bookshops** You'll find a good selection of English-language books at **Algoritam** (Placa), including guidebooks.

**Left Luggage** There's a **left-luggage office** (open 5.30am-9pm daily) at the bus station.

### Things to See & Do
You will probably begin your visit at the city bus stop outside **Pile Gate**. As you enter the city Dubrovnik's wonderful pedestrian promenade, Placa or Stradun, extends before you all the way to the clock tower at the other end of town.

Just inside Pile Gate is the huge **Onofrio Fountain** (1438) and **Franciscan monastery** with a splendid cloister and the third-oldest functioning pharmacy (operating since 1391) in Europe. The **monastery museum** (adult/concession 5/3KN; open 9am-4pm daily) has a collection of liturgical objects, paintings and pharmacy equipment.

In front of the clock tower at the eastern end of Placa, is the **Orlando Column** (1419) – a favourite meeting place. On opposite sides of Orlando are the 16th-century **Sponza Palace** (which was originally a Customs House then later a bank), which now houses the **State Archives** (☎ 321 032; admission free; open 8am-4pm Mon-Fri), and **St Blaise's Church**, a lovely Italian baroque building built in 1715 to replace an earlier church destroyed in the 1667 earthquake.

At the end of Pred Dvorom, the wide street beside St Blaise, is the baroque **Cathedral of the Assumption of the Virgin**. Between the two churches, the 1441 Gothic **Rector's Palace** (adult/concession 15/10KN; open 9am-2pm Mon-Sat) houses a museum with furnished rooms, baroque paintings and historical exhibits. The elected rector was not permitted to leave the building during his one-month term without permission of the senate. The narrow street opposite opens onto Gundulićeva Poljana, a bustling morning market. Up the stairs at the southern end of the square is the **Jesuit monastery** (1725).

As you proceed up Placa, make a detour to the **Museum of the Orthodox Church** (adult/concession 10/5KN; open 9am-1pm Mon-Sat) for a look at a fascination collection of 15th- to 19th-century icons.

By this time you'll be ready for a leisurely walk around the **city walls** (adult/concession 15/5KN; open 9am-7pm daily), which has entrances just inside Pile Gate, across from the Dominican monastery and near Fort St John. Built between the 13th and 16th centuries and still intact, these powerful walls are the finest in the world and Dubrovnik's main claim to fame. They enclose the entire city in a protective veil over 2km long and up to 25m high, with two round towers, 14 square towers, two corner fortifications and a large fortress. The views over the town and sea are great – this walk could be the high point of your visit.

Whichever way you go, you'll notice the 14th-century **Dominican monastery** (adult/concession 10/5KN; open 9am-6pm daily) in the northeastern corner of the city, whose forbidding fortress-like exterior shelters a rich trove of paintings from Dubrovnik's finest 15th- and 16th-century artists.

Dubrovnik has many other sights, such as the unmarked **synagogue** (ul Žudioska 5; admission free; open 10am-1pm Mon-Fri), near the clock tower, which is the second oldest synagogue in Europe. The uppermost streets of the old town below the north and south walls are pleasant to wander along.

**Beaches** Ploče, the closest beach to the old city, is just beyond the 17th-century **Lazareti** (former quarantine station) outside Ploče Gate. There are also hotel beaches along the **Lapad Peninsula**, which you are able to use without a problem. The largest is outside the Hotel Kompas.

An even better option is to take the ferry that shuttles half-hourly in summer to lush **Lokrum Island** (25KN return), a national park with a rocky nudist beach (marked FKK), a botanical garden and the ruins of a medieval Benedictine monastery.

### Organised Tours

Atlas offers full day tours to Mostar (240KN), Međugorje (220KN), the Elaphite Islands (210KN) and Mljet (320KN), among other destinations. Its tour to Montenegro (220KN) is a good alternative to taking the morning bus to Montenegro since the bus schedules make a day trip there impractical.

### Special Events

The Dubrovnik Summer Festival from mid-July to mid-August is a major cultural event with over 100 performances at a number of different venues in the old city. The Feast of St Blaise (3 February) and carnival (February) are also celebrated.

### Places to Stay

**Camping** The camping grounds that are closet to Dubrovnik are **Porto** (☎ 487 078; camp sites per person/tent/car 28/38/36KN) and **Matkovica** (☎ 486 096; camp sites per person/tent/car 28/38/36KN), both 8km south of Dubrovnik near a quiet cove. Bus No 10 to Srebeno leaves you close to both.

**Hostels** The YHA hostel (☎ 423 241, fax 412 592; B&B/half-board 90/120KN), up Vinka Sagrestana from Bana Josipa Jelačića 17, is a party place. Full board can be arranged but the hostel is on one of the liveliest streets in Lapad, full of bars, cafés and pizzerias.

**Private Rooms** Agencies that organise private accommodation include Atlas, Globtour, Dubrovnikturist and Gulliver. Turistička Zajednica will put you in touch with proprietors but does not make reservations. In the high season, prices are about 93/76KN per person for rooms with private/shared shower with a 30% surcharge for single occupancy.

**Hotels** Staying in the old town is clearly desirable and there are a number of interesting options. The most personal and original accommodation to be found in Dubrovnik is **Apartments van Bloemen** (☎ 323 433, 91 33 24 106; ⓔ marc.van-bloemen@du.hinet.hr; Bandureva 1; apartments 680KN) with four beautifully decorated, air-conditioned apartments that sleep three. The **Pucić Palace** (☎/fax 324 111; ⓔ info@thepucicpalace .com; Od Puča 1; rooms from 1460KN) was about to open at the time of research and is clearly aiming to mine very deep pockets by offering the most deluxe digs in Croatia, which include the use of a private yacht.

Most hotels are in Lapad. Bus No 6 runs from the old town and the bus station to Lapad. From Jadrolinija wharf take bus No 7b. **Begović Boarding House** (☎ 435 191; Primorska 17; rooms per person 100KN, apartments per person 135KN), is a friendly place with three rooms with shared bathroom and three small apartments. There's a terrace out the back with a good view.

**Hotel Sumratin** (☎ 436 333, fax 436 006; singles/doubles 278/452KN), with a lift and parking, and **Hotel Zagreb** (☎ 436 146, fax 436 006; singles/doubles 307/510KN) are near each other in a tranquil part of Lapad, but Hotel Zagreb has a more traditional European flavour and its rooms also have TVs.

Renovated **Hotel Petka** (☎ 418 008, fax 418 058; Obala Stjepana Radića 38; singles/ doubles from 320/470KN), opposite the Jadrolinija ferry landing, has 104 nondescript rooms with air-con. **Hotel Lapad** (☎ 432 922, fax 424 782; ⓔ hotel-lapad@du.tel.hr; Lapadska Obala 37; singles/doubles 474/ 627KN) is a better bet with 200 rooms; the more expensive ones have air-con and satellite TV. The hotel is a solid, old limestone structure with simple but cheerful rooms and an outdoor swimming pool.

## Places to Eat

The dining scene in the old town is not stupendous. Most places serve more or less the same thing at the same price.

The best dining in Lapad is at **Eden** (Kardinala Stepinca 54; mains 50-80KN). The leafy terrace upstairs is an agreeable spot to enjoy meat, pasta or fish dishes. **Pergola** (Tomislava 1; mains from 50KN) is another consistently satisfying place with an outdoor terrace and good seafood.

The spaghetti with shrimp and squid risotto at **Dundo Maroje** (Kovačka; mains from 45KN) are a cut above average. Vegetarians will like **Arka** (Uz Jezuite bb; mains from 40KN), which is Italian influenced but also has soybean-based dishes. **Express** (Kaboge 1; mains from 16KN) is a self-service restaurant that serves up freshly prepared food at unbeatable prices. **Posat** (Uz Posat 1; mains from 50KN) is the place to go for a romantic dinner on its outdoor terrace.

The cheapest way to fill up in Dubrovnik is to buy the makings of a picnic at a local supermarket, such as the one in the department store near the bus station.

## Entertainment

**Esperanza** (☎ 357 144; Put Republike 30; open 10pm-4am daily), next to the bus station, is a popular disco and Jelačića, dubbed 'Bourbon' street, has a cluster of clubs on both sides of the youth hostel. The **open-air cinema** (Kumičića) in Lapad allows you to watch movies by starlight. **Troubadur** (☎ 412 154; Gundulićeva) is a local favourite for live music, which occasionally includes jazz.

Ask at the tourist office about concerts and folk dancing.

## Getting There & Away

**Air** Daily flights to/from Zagreb are operated by Croatia Airlines. It's about 906KN one way in summer but less during the off-peak season.

There are also nonstop flights to Rome, and flights to Tel Aviv, London and Manchester from April to October.

**Bus** Buses from Dubrovnik include:

| destination | cost (KN) | duration (hrs) | frequency (daily) |
| --- | --- | --- | --- |
| Korčula | 69 | 3 | 1 |
| Mostar | 77 | 3 | 2 |
| Orebić | 42 | 2½ | 1 |
| Rijeka | 295–309 | 12 | 4 |
| Sarajevo | 157 | 5 | 1 |
| Split | 72–111 | 4½ | 14 |
| Zadar | 131–185 | 8 | 7 |
| Zagreb | 165–199 | 11 | 8 |

There's a daily 11am bus to the Montenegrin border from where a Montenegrin bus takes you to Herceg-Novi (57KN, two hours) and on to Kotor (72KN, 2½ hours) and Bar (120KN, three hours). In the busy summer season and on the weekend, buses out of Dubrovnik can be crowded, so book a ticket well before the scheduled departure time.

**Boat** In addition to the Jadrolinija coastal ferry north to Hvar, Split, Zadar and Rijeka, there's a local ferry that leaves Dubrovnik for Sobra on Mljet Island (26KN to 32KN, 2½ hours, 2pm Monday to Saturday, 8.30pm Sunday) throughout the year. In summer there are two ferries a day. There are several ferries a day year-round to the outlying islands of Šipanska, Sugjuraj, Lopud and Koločep. Information on domestic ferries is available from **Jadrolinija** (☎ 418 000; Obala S Radića 40). See also the Central Dalmatia Ferry Routes map in the Split Getting There & Away section earlier in this chapter.

For information on international connections see the Getting There & Away section at the beginning of this chapter.

## Getting Around

Čilipi international airport is 24km southeast of Dubrovnik. The Croatia Airlines airport buses (25KN) leave from the main bus station 1½ hours before flight times. A taxi costs around 200KN.

Dubrovnik's buses run frequently and generally on time. The fare is 10KN if you buy from the driver but only 7KN if you buy a ticket at a kiosk.

## AROUND DUBROVNIK

**Cavtat** is a small town that curves around an attractive harbour bordered by nice beaches. Although it does not have as many interesting sights as Dubrovnik, it does make a good alternative place to stay if Dubrovnik is fully booked out or the summer crowds become overwhelming. Don't miss the memorial chapel to the Račić family designed by Ivan Meštrović.

A day trip can be made from Dubrovnik to the resort town just to the southeast. Bus No 10 runs often to Cavtat from Dubrovnik's bus station and there are three daily boats during the summer (30KN).

# Cyprus (Κύπρος, Kıbrıs)

Cyprus, the Mediterranean's third-largest island, is deemed the legendary birthplace of Aphrodite. Close to Greece, Turkey, Jordan, Israel and Egypt, it is a useful stepping stone for those travelling between east and west.

Cyprus presents an infinite variety of natural and architectural delights. Two high mountain ranges tower above a fertile plain. Landscapes are dotted with ancient Greek and Roman ruins, Orthodox monasteries and crusader castles.

There's an easy-going lifestyle on the island, the crime rate is low and the sun shines a lot. All of this makes Cyprus sound like a paradise, and perhaps it would be, were it not for the Turkish invasion of 1974 and subsequent partition of the island. Despite this, its people are friendly, relaxed and hospitable.

# Facts about Cyprus

## HISTORY
Cyprus' position in the eastern Mediterranean has meant that since ancient times it has been an important trading post, and consequently, has a rich history fraught with battles and conquest.

Inhabited since Neolithic times, Cyprus has been colonised by Myceneans, Phoenicians, Egyptians, Assyrians and the Persians. In 295 BC, Ptolemy I, one of Alexander's generals who became king of Egypt, won control of the island. His dynasty ruled Cyprus until it was annexed by Rome in 58 BC.

As part of the Roman Empire, Cyprus enjoyed relative peace and prosperity. Later it came to be torn between the warring Byzantine and Islamic empires, and from the 7th to the 11th century it changed hands at least 11 times.

Richard the Lionheart conquered the island in 1191 during the Third Crusade, but when the Cypriots rebelled, he sold the island to the Knights Templar. They in turn sold it to Guy de Lusignan, the deposed king of Jerusalem, whose French dynasty ruled Cyprus for the next three centuries. This was a period of prosperity but also oppression of Cypriot culture and Greek Orthodoxy.

By the late 14th century the Lusignans were in decline and the Venetians took control in 1489. They strengthened the island's

## At a Glance

- **Troödos Massif** – Omodos and other wine-making villages, walks through enchanting pine forests
- **Akamas Peninsula** – baths of Aphrodite, the wide, sandy beach of Polis'
- **Kyrenia** – pretty horseshoe-shaped harbour, lofty castles

| | |
|---|---|
| **Capital** | Lefkosia (formerly Nicosia, Lefkoşa in Turkish) |
| **Population** | 762,900 |
| **Official Language** | Greek (Republic) Turkish (Northern Cyprus) |
| **Currency** | 1 Cypriot pound (CY£) = 100 cents (Republic) 1 Turkish lira (TL) = 100 kurus (Northern Cyprus) |
| **Time** | GMT/UTC+0200 |
| **Country Phone Code** | ☎ 357 (Republic) ☎ 90 392 (Northern Cyprus) |

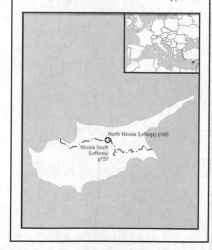

North Nicosia (Lefkoşa) p165
Nicosia South (Lefkosia) p157

CYPRUS

fortifications, but in 1570 the Turks attacked, killing some 2000 people; this began 300 years of Ottoman rule.

147

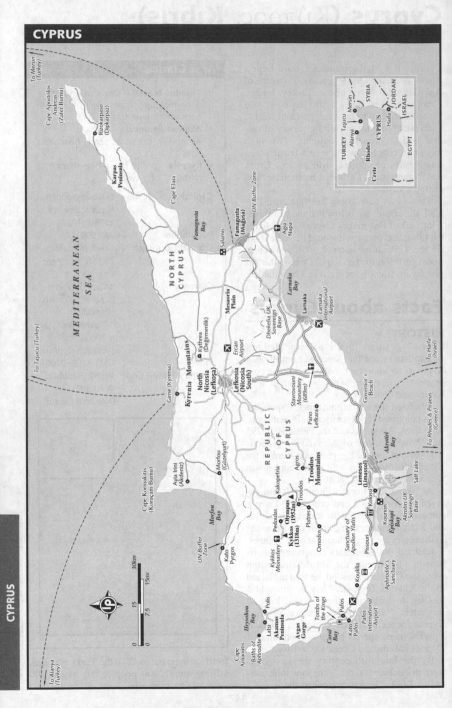

CYPRUS

In 1878 the administration of Cyprus was ceded to Britain. This was done out of fear of Russia's expansionist policy, with Britain promising in return to aid Turkey in the event of a Russian attack.

In 1925 Cyprus became a UK crown colony. By now, Cypriots were deeply frustrated by their lack of self-determination, and the first stirring of the *enosis* movement (which wanted union with Greece) were felt. This led to intercommunal riots between Greeks and Turks. The latter (18% of the population) opposed *enosis*, believing that it would lead to even greater oppression. By the late 1940s, the Cypriot Orthodox Church openly supported *enosis*, and a 1951 plebiscite showed that 96% of Greek Cypriots were also in favour.

In 1954 Britain prepared a new constitution for Cyprus that was accepted by the Turkish population, but not the extremist National Organisation of Cypriot Freedom Fighters (EOKA), which wanted *enosis*. EOKA began guerrilla activities against the British administration, causing many deaths and much suffering.

In August 1960 the UK granted independence to Cyprus. Archbishop Makarios became president, with a Turk, Faisal Kükük, as vice president. In December 1963 Makarios proposed constitutional amendments that would have given the Greeks greater control. The Turkish government rejected these and threatened military intervention, but was restrained by international pressure. Intercommunal violence increased significantly and in 1964 the United Nations (UN) sent in a peacekeeping force.

In 1967 a military junta seized power in Greece and the demands for *enosis* ceased – nobody wanted union with such a repressive regime. However, on 15 July 1974, Greece overthrew Makarios in a coup d'etat. When he escaped assassination and fled the country, Greece put ex-guerrilla leader Nikos Sampson in power. The Turks responded by invading Cyprus, and the Greek junta realised the magnitude of the mistake. Sampson was removed and the Greek offensive collapsed. The Turkish troops continued to advance until they occupied the northern third of the island, forcing some 180,000 Greek Cypriots to flee their homes for the safety of southern Cyprus. Neither the UK nor the USA chose to intervene.

Cyprus remains a divided island. From time to time violence between the two sides erupts, like that which occurred in August 1996. Unsuccessful peace talks, mostly under the auspices of the UN, have been held sporadically, the most recent ones being extended negotiations between the presidents of both communities during 2002. These negotiations sought to find an acceptable solution for Cyprus' accession to the EU. At the time of research, no proposal had been agreed to.

## GEOGRAPHY & CLIMATE

There are two mountain ranges: the Kyrenia Mountains in Northern Cyprus and the Troödos Massif in the centre of the Republic in the south. Between them is the Mesaoria Plain.

Cyprus enjoys an intense Mediterranean climate with a typically strongly marked seasonal rhythm. Summers are hot and dry and last from June until September. Winters are changeable, with cold and warmer weather alternating and conditions also varying with the elevation.

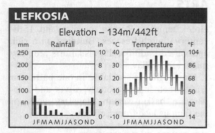

## ECOLOGY & ENVIRONMENT

Much of southern Cyprus' coastline has been spoilt by tourism, so most of the island's impressive range of flora and fauna is restricted to the well-managed areas of the Troödos Mountains and the Akamas Peninsula.

In the North, where authorities have not yet experienced mass tourism, they have had the chance to monitor encroachment more carefully. In some large areas – notably the Karpas Peninsula – large-scale development is now banned.

## GOVERNMENT & POLITICS

In 1960 Cyprus was declared an independent sovereign republic with a presidential system of government. It is currently ruled by the Democratic Rally Party (DISY) led by Glafkos Kliridis.

CYPRUS

In November 1983, Rauf Denktaş declared northern Cyprus the independent Turkish Republic of Northern Cyprus, with himself as president. Only Turkey recognises this self-styled nation.

## ECONOMY

Partition had a devastating effect on the Cypriot economy. The Republic (southern Cyprus) has made a steady recovery and tourism is now its biggest source of income.

The North uses the Turkish lira, tying the area's economy to Turkey's high inflation; agriculture and a developing tourist industry provide most of the income.

## POPULATION & PEOPLE

Since partition, the vast majority of Greek Cypriots live in the Republic, while Turkish Cypriots and Turkish mainland colonists live in the North. The total population of Cyprus' is 762,900 with approximately 143,500 living in the North.

## ARTS

Reminders of Cyprus' history include ancient Greek temples, Roman mosaics and 15th-century church frescoes. Building on a rich and varied tradition, the visual arts are very much alive today.

Many villages specialise in one particular craft, whether it be pottery, silver and copperware, basket-weaving, tapestry work, or the famous lace from Lefkara.

## SOCIETY & CONDUCT

Since the island's split, Greek Cypriots have become more culturally defined. For example, the Republic decided to Hellenise some of its hitherto anglicised place names. In the North, the Turks have succeeded in imbuing the region with an all-pervasive Turkishness. They have changed Greek place names to Turkish ones and embraced the Turkish culture.

On both sides of the Green Line, people are friendly, honest and law-abiding (there is hardly any crime or vandalism anywhere). Family life, marriage and children still play a central role in society, as does religion. Greek and Turkish Cypriots are fiercely patriotic.

## RELIGION

Most Greek Cypriots belong to the Greek Orthodox Church and most Turkish Cypriots are Sunni Muslims.

## LANGUAGE

A large number of Cypriots in the Republic speak English and many road signs are in Greek and English. In Northern Cyprus this is not the case outside the touristy areas and you'll have to brush up on your Turkish.

Since 1995 the Republic has changed some of the place names to their official Greek version. As a result, Nicosia has become Lefkosia, and Limassol is now Lemesos. Throughout this chapter the places names are given in their anglicised, Greek and Turkish versions.

See the Turkish and Greek language sections at the back of the book for guidelines for pronunciation, and useful words and phrases.

# Facts for the Visitor

## HIGHLIGHTS
### Republic of Cyprus

Nine of the frescoed Byzantine churches in the Troödos Massif are on Unesco's World Heritage List and they really are special. The Tombs of the Kings, dating back to the 3rd century BC, are a lot more fun than the more famous Pafos Mosaics, and only get half the crowds.

### Northern Cyprus

With the castle at one end, Kyrenia's waterfront must be one of the most beautiful in the Mediterranean. A trio of romantic, lofty castles studding the Kyrenia mountain range are a must for romantics, history buffs and walkers.

## SUGGESTED ITINERARIES

Depending on the length of your stay, you might want to see and do the following things:

### Republic of Cyprus

**One week** Allow two days for Lefkosia, two days for Pafos, one day for exploring the ancient coastal sites between Pafos and Lemesos, and the rest in the Troödos Massif.

**Two weeks** As above but make two trips into Northern Cyprus, add Polis and the Akamas Peninsula (beaches and walks) and have yourself a steam and/or massage at the excellent hammam in Lemesos.

### Northern Cyprus

**One week** Allow one day for North Nicosia (Lefkoşa), one day for Famagusta, half a day for Salamis, and spend the rest staying in Kyrenia and visiting the castles in the Kyrenia Mountains.

**Two weeks** As above but have a Turkish bath in North Nicosia and spend some time exploring the Kantara Castle and the near-deserted Karpas Peninsula.

## PLANNING

Cyprus has a typical Mediterranean climate. April to May and September to October are the most pleasant times to visit.

Most tourist offices have free tourist maps that are adequate for most purposes. The 1:200,000 *Cyprus Travel Map* by Insight is the best map for both sides of the island and lists both Turkish and Greek place names for Northern Cyprus.

## TOURIST OFFICES
### Local Tourist Offices

The Cyprus Tourism Organisation (CTO) has offices in major towns in the Republic. Its leaflets and maps are excellent.

In Northern Cyprus there are tourist offices in North Nicosia (Lefkoşa), Famagusta (Mağusa) and Kyrenia (Girne), which have free country and town maps plus many comprehensive brochures.

### Tourist Offices Abroad

The CTO has branches in most European countries, the USA, Russia, Israel and Japan.

Northern Cyprus tourist offices can be found in the UK, Belgium, the USA, Pakistan and Turkey; otherwise inquiries are handled by Turkish tourist offices.

## VISAS & DOCUMENTS

In both the Republic and Northern Cyprus, nationals of the USA, Australia, Canada, Japan, New Zealand, Singapore and EU countries can enter and stay for up to three months without a visa.

If you have a Northern Cyprus stamp in your passport you can still visit Greece, but the Republic authorities may take a dim view and refuse you entry to the South. It is thus advisable to get immigration to stamp a separate piece of paper instead of your passport when entering Northern Cyprus.

## EMBASSIES & CONSULATES
### Cypriot Embassies & Consulates

The Republic of Cyprus has diplomatic representation in 27 countries, including:

**Australia** (☎ 02-6281 0832) 30 Beale Crescent, Deakin, ACT 2600
**Germany** (☎ 030-308 6830) Wallstrasse, D-10179 Berlin
**Greece** (☎ 21 0723 2727) Irodotou 16, GR-10675, Athens
**Israel** (☎ 03-525 0212) 50 Dizengoff St, 14th floor, Top Tower, Dizengoff Centre, 64322 Tel Aviv
**UK & Ireland** (☎ 020-7499 8272) 93 Park St, London W1Y 4ET
**USA** (☎ 202-462 5772) 2211 R St North West, Washington, DC, 20008

The Northern Cyprus Administration has offices in:

**Canada** (☎ 905-731 4000) 328 Highway 7 East, Suite 308, Richmond Hill, Ontario L4B 3P7
**Germany** (☎ 02683-32748) Auf Dem Platz 3, D-53577 Neustadt Wied-Neschen
**Japan** (☎ 03-203 1313) 4th Floor, 6th Arai Blog-1-4, Kabohi-Cho, Shinytku-Ku, Tokyo 160
**Turkey** (☎ 0312-437 6031) Rabat Sokak No 20, Gaziosmanpaşa 06700, Ankara
**UK** (☎ 020-7631 1920) 29 Bedford Square, London WC1B 3EG
**USA** (☎ 212-687 2350) 821 United Nations Plaza, 6th floor, New York, NY 10017

## Embassies & Consulates in Cyprus

Countries with diplomatic representation in the Republic of Cyprus include:

**Australia** (☎ 2275 3001) Gonia Leoforos Stasinou 4 & Annis Komninis, 2nd floor, 1060 Lefkosia
**Canada** (☎ 2245 1630) Office 403, Themistokli Dervi 15, Lefkosia
**Germany** (☎ 2245 1145) Nikitara 10, 1080 Lefkosia
**Greece** (☎ 2268 0645) Leoforos Vyronos 8–10, 1513 Lefkosia
**Israel** (☎ 2266 4195) I Grypari 4, 1500 Lefkosia
**UK** (☎ 2286 1100) Alexandrou Palli, 1587 Lefkosia
**USA** (☎ 2277 6400) Gonia Metochiou & Ploutarchou, 2406 Egkomi, Lefkosia

Countries with diplomatic representation in Northern Cyprus include:

**Australia** (☎ 227 7332) Güner Türkmen Sokak 20, North Nicosia
**Germany** (☎ 227 5161) Kasım Sokak 15, North Nicosia
**Turkey** (☎ 227 2314) Bedrettin Demirel Caddesi, North Nicosia

UK (☎ 228 3861) Mehmet Akif Sokak 29, North Nicosia

USA (☎ 227 3930) Şerif Arzık Sokak, Keşluçiftlık, North Nicosia

## CUSTOMS

Items that can be imported duty-free into the Republic are 250g of tobacco or the equivalent in cigarettes, 2L of wine or 1L of spirits, and one bottle of perfume not exceeding 600ml. In Northern Cyprus it is 500g of tobacco or 400 cigarettes, and 1L of spirits or 1L of wine.

## MONEY
### Currency

The Republic's unit of currency is the Cyprus pound (CY£), divided into 100 cents. There is no limit on the amount of Cyprus pounds you can bring into the country, but foreign currency equivalent to US$1000 or above must be declared. You can leave Cyprus with up to CY£500, or the initial amount with which you entered. The unit of currency in Northern Cyprus is the Turkish lira (TL), and there are no restrictions.

Banks throughout Cyprus will exchange all major currencies in either cash or travellers cheques. Most shops, hotels etc in Northern Cyprus readily accept UK£, euros and CY£.

In the Republic you can get a cash advance on Visa, MasterCard, Diners Club, Eurocard and American Express at one or more banks, and there are plenty of ATMs. In Northern Cyprus cash advances are given on Visa cards at the Vakıflar and Türk banks in North Nicosia (Lefkoşa) and Kyrenia; major banks in large towns have ATMs.

### Exchange Rates

Following are current exchange rates at the time of publication.

| country | unit | | pound |
|---|---|---|---|
| Australia | A$1 | = | CY£0.35 |
| Canada | C$1 | = | CY£0.40 |
| euro zone | €1 | = | CY£0.58 |
| Israel | NS1 | = | CY£0.12 |
| Japan | ¥100 | = | CY£0.50 |
| New Zealand | NZ$1 | = | CY£0.30 |
| Turkey | TL1,000,000 | = | CY£0.43 |
| UK | £1 | = | CY£0.90 |
| USA | US$1 | = | CY£0.62 |

Note that exchange rates for the Turkish lira are particularly volatile because of the high inflation rate. Check out the Oanda website (Ⓦ www.oanda.com/convert/classic) for the latest exchange rates.

Accommodation prices quoted in the Northern Cyprus section are in UK pounds, while food and transport prices are given in Turkish lira.

### Costs

Cyprus is a cheaper place to visit than most Western European countries, and in Northern Cyprus costs are slightly lower still. Living frugally, you could just get by on CY£20 a day, or live quite adequately on CY£40. Accommodation costs tend to go up between April and November, peaking during July and August.

If not free, admission costs to all museums and sites are between CY£0.50 and CY£2, and so are not detailed in the text. Admissions to museums in Northern Cyprus range from one to seven million Turkish lira.

### Tipping & Bargaining

In all parts of the island a 10% service charge is sometimes added to a restaurant bill, otherwise a tip of similar percentage is expected. Taxi drivers and hotel porters always appreciate a small tip. It is not normal to bargain for goods in markets.

## POST & COMMUNICATIONS
### Post

In the Republic, postal rates for cards and letters are between 26 cents and 41 cents. There are poste restante services in Lefkosia, Pafos, Larnaka and Lemesos.

In Northern Cyprus, rates are between UK£0.40 and UK£0.46. There are poste restante services in North Nicosia, Kyrenia and Famagusta. All mail must be addressed to Mersin 10, Turkey, *not* Northern Cyprus.

### Telephone & Fax

In the Republic, you can make overseas calls from all telephone boxes, but they only take phonecards which are available from newsagencies, some banks or the Republic's telephone company (CYTA). At peak times, a three-minute call to the USA will cost CY£1.83, and CY£1.53 during off-peak time (10pm to 8am, and Sunday). The Republic's country code is ☎ 357.

In Northern Cyprus most public telephone boxes only take phonecards bought at Turkish Telecom administration offices or shops. A peak three-minute call to the USA will set you back UK£1.35 and off-peak UK£0.90. To call Northern Cyprus from abroad dial ☎ 90 (Turkey), the regional code ☎ 392, and then the actual number.

To call the North from the South dial ☎ 0139 followed by the local number. To call the South from the North call ☎ 0132 followed by the local number.

In both regions most people now use mobile phones and your own phone will probably pick up both Turkish and Greek Cypriot networks as long as it is rigged up for global roaming.

In the South you can send faxes from the post office, in the North from the Turkish Telecom administration offices, or from shops in both regions.

## Email & Internet Access

There are Internet cafés in all main towns in southern Cyprus and several in the North. The majority open late, close in the early hours of the morning and have become real social centres. They all charge in the region of CY£2.50/TL1,000,000 for the first hour and CY£1/TL750,000 for subsequent hours.

## DIGITAL RESOURCES

The Internet has lots of interesting information on Cyprus, but the most comprehensive site on Northern Cyprus is at W www.cypnet.com/cyradise/cyradise.html. The best site for the South can be found at W www.cyprustourism.org.

## BOOKS

Lonely Planet's *Cyprus* by Paul Hellander provides a full and comprehensive guide to the whole island. *Bitter Lemons* by Lawrence Durrell is an excellent read, while Colin Thubron's *Journey Into Cyprus* was the last significant travelogue written of the once-undivided Cyprus.

## NEWSPAPERS & MAGAZINES

The Republic's English-language papers are the *Cyprus Mail* and the *Cyprus Weekly*. Northern Cyprus publications are the *Turkish Daily News* and *Cyprus Today*, while the *New Colonial* is a bilingual, newsy and informative free magazine on the North.

## RADIO & TV

CyBC (Cyprus Broadcasting Corporation) has programmes and news bulletins in English on RIK-2 (FM 91.1, 92.4, 94.2 and 96.5) at 10am, 2pm and 8pm. There are a couple of commercial English/Greek stations in southern Cyprus that are worth noting – Kiss FM (FM 89.0) in Lefkosia and Sky FM (FM 88.7) in Lemesos. In Northern Cyprus, Bayrak International (FM 87.8 and 105) is a mainly English-language station broadcasting out of North Nicosia. BFBS (British Forces Broadcasting Services) broadcasts 24 hours a day in English on different frequencies within the country: BFBS-1 can be heard on FM 89.7 in Lefkosia, FM 92.1 in Lemesos and FM 99.6 in Larnaka; BFBS-2 has a frequency of FM 89.9 in Lefkosia, FM 91.7 in Lemesos and FM 95.3 in Larnaka. The BBC World Service can be heard on AM 1323.

CyBC TV has news in English at 8pm on Channel 2. Satellite dishes are very common, so many hotels have CNN, BBC, SKY or NBC.

## TIME

Cyprus is two hours ahead of GMT/UTC. Clocks go forward one hour on the last weekend in March and back one hour on the last weekend in October.

## LAUNDRY

There are plenty of dry cleaners and laundrettes can be found in all main towns, but they are not common. Most hotels have a laundry service.

## TOILETS

There are public toilets in the main towns and at tourist sites. They are invariably clean and Western-style, although in Northern Cyprus you occasionally come across dirtier ones or those of the squat variety.

## WOMEN TRAVELLERS

Women travelling alone will receive a lot of attention, especially when exploring the less touristy areas. A firm 'no thank you' should be enough to deter any unwanted interest.

## GAY & LESBIAN TRAVELLERS

Homosexuality is legal in the Republic but still illegal in Northern Cyprus where the secular Muslim population is intolerant of the practice. In the South, open gay attitudes only find room to breathe in Lemesos and also in Pafos, where there are a sprinkling of gay clubs. In general, Greek Cypriots are pretty conservative about homosexuality, too.

## DISABLED TRAVELLERS

Any CTO can send you the *What the Disabled Visitor Needs to Know about Cyprus* fact sheet, which lists some useful organisations. The Republic's airports have truck-lifts for arriving or departing disabled travellers. Some hotels have facilities for the disabled, but there's little help at sites or museums.

In Northern Cyprus there are few facilities for the disabled visitor.

## SENIOR TRAVELLERS

Cyprus is a popular holiday destination with older visitors and they will find travelling around both the Republic and Northern Cyprus fairly easy. In general, no concessions exist for seniors.

### Emergency Services

In an emergency you can ring either ☎ 112 or ☎ 199 for an ambulance, the police or for the fire service.

## BUSINESS HOURS

Opening hours vary according to whether it is winter, spring or summer.

During summer, banks in the Republic are open 8.15am to 12.30pm Monday to Friday, and 3.15pm to 4.45pm on Monday; some large banks offer a tourist service on other afternoons. In Northern Cyprus, banks are open 8am to noon and in winter from 2pm to 4pm as well.

In summer (15 June to 1 August), shops are open 8am to 2pm and 5pm to 8.30pm Monday to Saturday, closing at 2pm on Wednesday and Saturday. In Northern Cyprus they are open 4pm to 7pm Monday to Saturday.

## PUBLIC HOLIDAYS & SPECIAL EVENTS

Holidays in the Republic are the same as in Greece, with the addition of Greek Cypriot Day (1 April) and Cyprus Independence Day (1 October). Easter is the most important religious festival and just about everything stops. Fifty days before this is carnival time.

A useful publication is the *Diary of Events* available from any CTO. The Kataklysmos (Deluge) Festival is observed in most coastal cities 50 days after Easter.

Northern Cyprus observes Muslim holidays, including the month of Ramazan, which means the North can sometimes shut down for periods of up to a week. It also has National Children's Day (23 April), Victory Day (30 August), Turkish Republic Day (20 October) and the Proclamation of the Turkish Republic of Northern Cyprus Day (15 November).

## ACTIVITIES

Cyprus has a wide range of activities catering to different interests. The coast has beautiful beaches for those wanting to relax, as well as water sports, such as parasailing, for the more adventurous. Travel agencies and tour operators have many day trips and cruises that cater for all ages and interests. Those with a taste for history and archaeology are spoilt for choice. There are many sites dotted all over the island but take a guidebook – information is not always comprehensive and it is sometimes difficult to know what you are looking at. The inland area around the Troödos Massif is home to a vast variety of flora and fauna. The graded walking and hiking trails are well marked.

## WORK

In the Republic, work permits can only be obtained through a prospective employer applying on your behalf. The best place to look for jobs is in the *Cyprus Weekly*. During the tourist season you can sometimes pick up bar or café work in return for bed and board (payment is rare if you don't have a permit).

To work in Northern Cyprus, a permit must also be obtained through a prospective employer applying on your behalf. The application is examined by the Department of Labour and granted where the qualifications sought are not locally available.

## ACCOMMODATION
### Camping

There are seven licensed camping grounds in the Republic, mostly with limited opening times. They are all equipped with hot showers, a minimarket and a snack bar, and charge around CY£1.50 a day for a tent space, plus CY£1 per person per day. In the North there are four camping grounds.

## Hostels

There are four Hostelling International (HI) hostels in the Republic; these are slightly cheaper if you are a member. Contact the **Cyprus Youth Hostel Association** (☎ *2267 0027; PO Box 1328, 1506 Lefkosia*). There are no HI hostels in Northern Cyprus.

## Hotels

Prices for a double room in a hotel range from CY£17 to CY£210. A room in a guesthouse costs between CY£10 and CY£32. Prices are negotiable in winter. In Northern Cyprus these prices are slightly lower.

## Other Accommodation

In southern Cyprus you can sometimes stay overnight in monasteries, ostensibly for free, but a donation is expected.

## FOOD

Cypriot food is a combination of Greek and Turkish cuisine, based primarily on meat, salad and fruit. The local cheese is *halloumi*. Barbecues are a very popular way of cooking meat and fish, and a *meze* is a traditional meal consisting of about 20 different small dishes.

## DRINKS

Cypriot wine, made in the villages of the Troödos, is excellent. Greek and Turkish coffee and instant coffee (called Nescafe) is popular. *Zivania* – a strong spirit distilled from grape pressings – is widely available in both the Republic and in Northern Cyprus.

## ENTERTAINMENT

Restaurants sometimes have live music and there are cinemas, clubs and Internet cafés open until 2am or later in most major towns.

## SHOPPING

Good buys include local wine and spirits, most leather items and crafts, such as pottery, silver and copperware, basket-weaving, tapestry and lace work.

# Getting There & Away

## AIR

The Republic's airports are at Larnaka and Pafos. There are scheduled and charter flights from most European cities and the Middle East (around UK£230 return from London, including tax), with discounts for students, but they are heavily booked in the high season. From Cyprus there are daily flights to Greece (CY£87), and frequent services to Israel (CY£79), Egypt (CY£87), Lebanon (CY£68), Jordan (CY£70) and also Syria (CY£58); prices include taxes.

Ercan airport in Northern Cyprus is not recognised by the international airline authorities, so you can't fly there direct. Turkish airlines touch down in Turkey and then continue onto Ercan in Northern Cyprus (except on the few occasions during the year when flights get sent to Gecitkale airport) for around UK£315 from London, including tax; and other airlines can fly you to Turkey, where you change planes.

## SEA

The Republic's passenger ferry port is in Lemesos. In 2002 passenger ferry services to and from Greece and Israel had been suspended, but two- to three-day cruises still operated out of Lemesos. Check with travel agencies if passenger services with Salamis Tours or Poseidon Lines have been restored by the time you read this.

From Northern Cyprus there are two routes to mainland Turkey: Famagusta to Mersin (TL50,000,000; students TL37,500,000) and Kyrenia to Taşucu (from TL33,500,000 to TL41,500,000).

## DEPARTURE TAX

In the Republic, departure tax is CY£7 when leaving by air and CY£11 when leaving by sea. In Northern Cyprus, it is UK£6 for both air and sea departures. At the time of purchase make sure that the taxes are included in your ticket price.

# Getting Around

You can make a day trip into Northern Cyprus from the Republic (see the Lefkosia section). It is *illegal* to travel in the opposite direction.

You should not attempt to cross from the North to the South if you entered Cyprus initially via the North. You will be questioned, your details taken down and sent back to the North by the South's authorities. You will probably be refused subsequent entry to the South even if you enter via one of the South's official ports of entry.

### BUS

Urban and long-distance buses run Monday to Saturday and are operated by a host of private companies. There are few services on Sunday. Buses between major towns are frequent and efficient, charging CY£0.50 to CY£5 for most journeys.

### SERVICE TAXI

Service taxis, which take up to eight people, are run by a central company called **Travel & Express** *(head office: ☎ 077 7474)*. Each region has its own contact number but call head office for bookings anywhere. The fixed fares are still competitive with bus travel. For details of departure and arrivals call the above number. Northern Cyprus has service taxis between Kyrenia, Famagusta and North Nicosia. There are also more-expensive private taxis everywhere.

### CAR & MOTORCYCLE

Cars and 4WD vehicles are widely available for hire and cost between CY£12 and CY£50 a day. You can also rent motorcycles (from CY£12) or mopeds (CY£8) in some towns. Driving is on the left and international road signs are used.

In the Republic, children aged under five must not sit in the front seat and you are advised against travelling due west in the late afternoon because of the sun's severe glare. The blood alcohol limit is 0.09%. Any car or motorcycle licence is valid in the Republic, but you must be over 21 years of age to drive a car. If you're over 18 you can ride a motorcycle of 50cc and above, and 17-year-olds can ride a motorcycle of 49cc or less. In Northern Cyprus you can drive from the age of 18. Officially, you need either a British or an international driving licence to drive there. Both of these laws also apply to riders of motorcycles.

Parking in the South is quite cheap. In the North parking is generally free. At the time of research unleaded petrol cost CY£0.45 per litre in the South and TL1,220,000 per litre in the North.

For more information you can contact the **Cyprus Automobile Association** *(☎ 2231 3131; Hristou Mylona 12, Lefkosia)*.

### BICYCLE

Bicycles can be hired in most areas but particularly in coastal resorts. Rates start from around CY£4 a day.

# The Republic of Cyprus

In the Republic, which comprises 63% of the island, you'll find a real mix of Greek, Eastern and Western cultures. The British legacy lives on in the island's two UK military bases – at Akrotiri and Dekelia.

## NICOSIA SOUTH (LEFKOSIA)

(ΛΕΥΚΩΣΙΑ, LEFKOŞA)

**pop 197,800**

Nicosia South (known officially in Greek as Lefkosia) is the capital, bisected by the Green Line separating the Republic from Northern Cyprus. According to the sign at the UN-patrolled barrier at Lidras St, this is 'the last divided capital', and a visit is essential to appreciate the island's plight. Being inland, it attracts far fewer visitors, and so is much more genuinely Cypriot than the coastal towns.

### Orientation

The old town is inside the 16th-century Venetian wall and is the most interesting area to visit; the new town sprawls around it. Reduced in height and dissected by thoroughfares, the wall is hardly visible in places.

The city centre is Plateia Eleftherias on the southwestern edge of the wall. The UN crossover point (Ledra Palace Hotel checkpoint) is at the far west and Famagusta Gate is to the east. At the base of the wall there are car parks and municipal gardens.

### Information

**Tourist Offices** The **CTO** *(☎ 2267 4264; open 8.30am-4pm Mon-Fri, 8.30am-2pm Sat)* in the old town is in Laïki Yitonia, a fairly touristy, restored area. The staff are very helpful and they hand a out a wide range of free material.

**Money** The **Hellenic Bank** *(Leoforos Konstantinou Paleologou 5; open 8.15am-12.30pm Mon-Fri)* is near the CTO. There are plenty of central ATMs, but hardly any private exchange bureaus.

# NICOSIA SOUTH (LEFKOSIA)

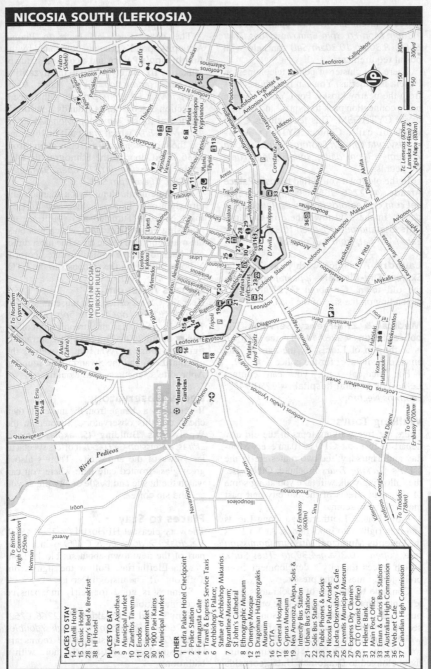

**PLACES TO STAY**
14 Castelli Hotel
15 Classic Hotel
28 Tony's Bed & Breakfast
38 HI Hostel

**PLACES TO EAT**
3 Taverna Axiothea
9 Municipal Market
10 Zanettos Taverna
11 Erodos
20 Supermarket
30 1900 Paei Kairos
35 Municipal Market

**OTHER**
1 Ledra Palace Hotel Checkpoint
2 Police Station
4 Famagusta Gate
5 Travel & Express Service Taxis
6 Archbishop's Palace;
   Statue of Archbishop Makarios
7 Byzantine Museum;
   St John's Cathedral
8 Ethnographic Museum
12 Omeriye Mosque
13 Dragoman Hatzigeorgakis
   Museum
16 CYTA
17 General Hospital
18 Cyprus Museum
19 Nea Amoroza, Alepa, Solis &
   Intercity Bus Station
21 Urban Bus Station
22 Solis Bus Station
23 Public Phones & Kiosks
24 Nicosia Palace Arcade
25 Ledra Observatory & Cafe
26 Leventis Municipal Museum
27 Express Dry Cleaners
29 CTO (Tourist Office)
31 Hellenic Bank
32 Main Post Office
33 Eman & Clarios Bus Stations
34 Australian High Commission
36 Web.net Cafe
37 Canadian High Commission

**Post & Communications** The **main post office** *(Plateia Eleftherias; open 7.30am-1.30pm Mon-Fri, 3pm-6pm Mon, Tues, Thur & Fri, 8.30am-10.30am Sat)* can help with postal requirements.

There is a cluster of public telephones on Plateia Eleftherias. You can buy phonecards from the nearby kiosks. For CY£29 you can buy a connection pack to Cyprus' mobile network, CYTAGSM. This fee includes CY£5 worth of calls. Contact **CYTA** (W *www .soeasy.cyta.com.cy; Leoforos Egyptou; open 7.30am-1.30pm daily, 3pm-5.30pm Tues)* for details.

In the old town you'll find **Nicosia Palace Arcade** (☎ 2266 3653; e *n.palace@cyta net.com.cy; Leoforos Kostaki Pantelidi; open daily).* In the new town there is **Web.net Café** *(Stasandrou 10C; open 10.30am–about 2am Mon-Sat, from 5.30pm Sun).*

**Laundry** A service wash is available at **Express Dry-Cleaners** *(Ippokratous 49)*, in the old town, for about CY£1 to CY£2 depending on the size of the load.

**Medical & Emergency Services** The **police station** *(☎ 2267 1434)* in the old town is at the top of Lidras, by the barrier. The emergency number for the police is ☎ 199.

For medical care, you can contact Lefkosia's **general hospital** *(☎ 2280 1400; Leoforos Nechrou).*

## Walking Tours
There are free walking tours of the old city departing from the CTO at 10am every Monday and Thursday; the two routes are in the CTO's *Walking Tours* brochure. Otherwise, the following walk will take you along some of the main streets of the old city and past many of its museums.

From Plateia Eleftherias go along Lidras and turn right onto Ippokratous. At No 17 is the **Leventis Municipal Museum** *(admission free; open 10.30am-4.30pm Tues-Sun)*, which traces the city's development from prehistoric times to the present.

Continue to the end of Ippokratous, turn left onto Thrakis, take the dogleg onto Trikoupi and continue northwards. Soon you'll see the Omeriye Mosque on your right, after which you turn right onto Patriarhou Grigoriou. On the right is the 18th-century house that belonged to **Dragoman Hatzigeorgakis**

*(admission CY£0.75; open 8am-2pm Mon-Fri, 9am-1pm Sat)*, which is now a museum.

The next street left leads to Plateia Arhiepiskopou Kyprianou, dominated by the **Archbishop's Palace** and a colossal statue of Makarios III. Here you'll find the **Byzantine Museum** *(admission CY£1; open 9am-4.30pm Mon-Fri, 9am-1pm Sat)*, with a superb collection of icons. In its grounds is **St John's Cathedral** *(open 9am-noon Mon-Sat, 2pm-4pm Mon-Fri)*, which was built in 1662 and has the most wonderful frescoes dating from 1736. Next door is the **Ethnographic Museum** *(admission CY£1; open 9am-4pm Mon-Fri, 10am-1pm Sat).*

Continue north along Agiou Ioannou and turn right onto Thiseos, which leads to Leoforos N Foka. Turn left and you'll see the imposing **Famagusta Gate**, which was once the main entrance to the city. The most direct way back to Laïki Yitonia is to take Leoforos N Foka, following the signposts to the CTO.

## Cyprus Museum
Near the CYTA office, this museum *(admission CY£1.50; open 9am-5pm Mon-Sat, 10am-1pm Sun)* has an extraordinary collection of about 2000 7th-century BC terracotta figurines found at Ayia Irini, as well as the original Leda and the Swan mosaic found at Aphrodite's sanctuary near Kouklia.

## Ledra Observatory
If you fancy a change from the museums then check out this observatory. Situated in the Woolworths Building *(Shiakolas Tower; Lidras; admission CY£0.50)* it offers spectacular views of the entire city. There's also a great glass-fronted café here where you can watch the hustle and bustle of city life as you eat and sip coffee.

## Places to Stay
The very pleasant HI **Hostel** *(☎ 2267 4808; Hatzidaki 5; dorm beds CY£5)* is in a quiet part of the new town about six blocks from Plateia Eleftherias. Follow the signs from Tefkrou, off Themistokli Dervi.

Solonos is good for fairly inexpensive accommodation.

**Tony's Bed & Breakfast** *(☎ 2266 6752; fax 2266 2225; Solonos 13; singles/doubles CY£18/28)* is the best, but the rooms are rather small and cost slightly more with a bathroom.

Most of the more-expensive hotels are found in the new town, but inside the walls is the three star **Classic Hotel** (☎ 2266 4006, fax 2267 0072; Rigenis 90; singles/doubles CY£38/48), where rates include breakfast.

**Castelli Hotel** (☎ 2271 2812; fax 2268 1076; e hinnicres@cytanet.com.cy; Ouzounian 38; doubles/single CY£72/99), close to the Classic Hotel, is a business hotel with somewhat stuffy staff but, otherwise, it has excellent rooms.

## Places to Eat
For a drink or snack during the day or night there are plenty of cafés lining the streets of the old city. For a filling *mezes* meal, head for **Zanettos Taverna** (☎ 2276 5501; Trikoupi 65; mains CY£2.50-3).

Also worth checking out is **1900 Paei Kairos** (☎ 2266 7668; Pasikratous 11-15; mezes CY£2.20-4.50) is a Greek-style *mezes* restaurant where you only order the *mezes* you want.

**Erodos** (☎ 2275 2250; Patriarhou Grigoriou 1; mains CY£3.50-5), near the Omeriye Mosque, is a relaxing place where you can have snacks or a full meal. Although the business card for this place states the above address, it is actually on Plateia Tyllirias.

**Taverna Axiothea** (☎ 2243 0787; Axiotheas 9; mezes CY£5), hard up against the Green Line in the yuppie enclave of the Famagusta Gate area, is this unassuming taverna, which is good for cheap and tasty *mezes*.

Also in the old town is the **municipal market** (Diogenous), and in the new town there's a market on the corner of Leoforos Evgenias & Antoniou Theodotou and Digeni Akrita. There's a decent **supermarket** on Plateia Solomou.

## Getting There & Away
Lefkosia's international airport is in the UN buffer zone and no longer deals with tourists.

There are lots of private bus companies operating out of Lefkosia. **Intercity** (☎ 2266 5814; Plateia Solomou), has seven buses a day to Lemesos (CY£1.50; two on Saturday) and six buses a day to Larnaka (CY£1.50). **Nea Amoroza** (☎ 2693 6822) and **Alepa** (☎ 2266 4636) both operate at least one daily bus to Pafos (CY£3), while **Klarios** (☎ 2275 3234; Constanza Bastion) runs at least one bus daily to Troödos (CY£1.50) and 12 buses to Kakopetria (CY£1.20). **EMAN** goes to

Agia Napa (CY£2) Monday to Saturday at 3pm. Eman and Klarios depart from depots at Constanza Bastion; Alepa, Nea Amoroza and Intercity depart from Plateia Solomou.

There is one bus at noon run by **Solis** (☎ 2266 6388; Tripolis Bastion; Mon-Sat) directly to Polis (CY£5).

**Travel & Express** (☎ 077 7474; Podocataro Bastion) has service taxis that operate to Larnaka (CY£2.50) and Lemesos (CY£3.50).

At Plateia Solomou is **A Petsas & Sons** (☎ 2266 2650), where you can hire cars.

**Northern Cyprus** Depending on the prevailing diplomatic relations, you're usually allowed into Northern Cyprus for one day, but check at the CTO first. The border crossing at the Ledra Palace Hotel is open 8am to 1pm, returning at 5pm. You simply walk to the Turkish checkpoint with your passport and request an entry permit. Private cars can be taken over the border, but not hired ones. There is no limit to the number of times you can do this.

## Getting Around
The **city bus station** (Plateia Solomou) serves local buses; Lefkosia Buses operates many routes between the city and suburbs.

There are no bicycles for rent in or around the old city.

## LARNAKA (ΛΑΡΝΑΚΑ)
### pop 69,700
Larnaka is a coastal resort built over the ancient city of Kition. It has a city beach, a long waterfront promenade, an old Turkish area and a fort. North of the fort, touristy cafés line the seafront, but the other side is more easy going and less spoilt.

The **CTO** (☎ 2465 4322; Plateia Vasileos Pavlou; open 8.15am-2.30pm Mon-Fri; 3pm-6.15pm Mon, Tues, Thur & Fri; 8am-1.30pm Sat) is at the north end of town. There is also a CTO at the airport.

There are not too many Internet cafés in town these days. **Alto Internet Cafe** (☎ 2465 9625; Grigoriou Afxentiou) is the easiest to find. It is open from 10am to 2am and access charges are CY£2 per hour.

## Things to See & Do
Larnaka's promenade beach is not Waikiki, but the water is clean and fairly shallow. Head about 2km south to **Makenzy (McKenzie)**

CYPRUS

Beach for a better deal or 3km north along the bay for less-crowded swimming.

Larnaka's **Fort** (*☎ 2463 0576; admission CY£0.75; open 9am-7pm Mon-Fri*) is worth ducking into for a glimpse of the city's past. The open area inside the fort is occasionally used for concerts and other cultural events.

The ornate Byzantine church of **St Lazaros** and the church's **museum** (*☎ 2465 2498; Agiou Lazarou; admission CY£0.50*) are worth a visit; it's here that St Lazaros (the one who rose from the dead) was laid to rest.

### Places to Stay & Eat

The nearest camping ground is **Forest Beach Camping** (*☎ 2464 4514; 1 person & tent CY£2.50*), 8km along the beach road towards Agia Napa, but it can get pretty run down. To get there take the tourist bus from the north side of Sun Hall Hotel.

The HI **Hostel** (*☎ 2462 1188; N Rossou 27; dorm beds/family room CY£4/5*) is just east of St Lazaros church. It's fairly basic but the rooms are clean enough.

**Onisillos Hotel** (*☎ 2465 1100, fax 2465 4468; e onisillos@cytanet.com.cy; Onisillos 17; singles/doubles with bathroom CY£25/33*), in a very quiet part of town, 500m west of the fort, is a friendly two-star. Rooms all have phone, TV and air-con, and prices include breakfast.

**Prasino Amaxoudi** (*☎ 2462 2939; kebabs CY£2*), south, beside the mosque, is where you'll get good-value, fresh souvlaki, doner kebab or *haloumi* pitta-bread sandwiches.

**Militzis Restaurant** (*☎ 2465 5867; Piyale Pasha 28; mains CY£4*), south of the fort on the waterfront, is where all the locals eat.

**1900 Art Café** (*☎ 2462 3730; Stasinou 6; snacks CY£1-2*) is at the other end of town, near the CTO. It's an art gallery, a bookshop and also a restaurant with an ever-changing menu of home-cooked Cypriot dishes.

The **municipal market** is at the northern end of N Rossou.

### Getting There & Away

The bus stop for Lefkosia (CY£1.50), Lemesos (CY£1.70) and Agia Napa (CY£1) is almost opposite the Dolphin Café Restaurant on the waterfront. On Sunday the only service is to Agia Napa.

**Travel & Express** (*☎ 077 7474*) operates service taxis to Lemesos (CY£3) as well as Lefkosia (CY£2.50).

### Getting Around

**To/From the Airport** Bus Nos 22 and 24 from Ermou St go to the airport (6km away) on request. The first bus is at 6.30am and the last at 7pm in summer and 5.30pm in winter. A private taxi costs from CY£3 to CY£5.

**Bus** Every 30 minutes from 7.30am to 6pm Bus No 18 runs from the Larnaka Tourist Information Office to the tourist hotel area, 8km along the coast towards Agia Napa (CY£0.50).

**Car & Motorcycle** Next door to A Makris, **Thames** (*☎ 2465 6333*) rents cars and there are also car-rental booths at the airport. You can hire motorcycles or mopeds from **Anemayia** (*☎ 2465 8333*) on the Larnaka to Dhekelia road; ring for free delivery.

**Bicycle** You can hire bicycles at **Anemayia** (*☎ 2465 8333*).

### AGIA NAPA (ΑΓΙΑ ΝΑΠΑ)

On the coast, 35km east of Larnaca, is Agia Napa. Once a small fishing village with a coastline of beautiful beaches, it is now Cyprus' main package-tourist resort and accommodation is scarce if not booked through a tour operator. Bars, clubs and pubs line the streets and if you're after 24-hour nightlife then Agia Napa is the place to be. See Larnaka and Lefkosia for transport details.

**Leros Hotel** (*☎ 2372 1126; Arhiepiskopou III; singles/doubles CY£17.50/28*) is a cheap place to stay. It's small and homey and has a bar. Grab a bite of Cypriot fare at the **Limelight Taverna** (*☎ 2372 1650; Dionysiou Solomou 10*). Try the suckling pig.

The funkiest club in town has to be the **Castle Club** (*☎ 9962 3126; Grigoriou Afxentiou*). Chill out at **Insomnia** (*☎ 2372 4868; Nisiou 4*).

### LIMASSOL (ΛΕΜΕΣΟΣ, LİMASOL)
pop 157,600

Limassol (which is referred to more popularly as Lemesos) is Cyprus' second-largest city and the main passenger and cargo port. Bland apartments and public gardens line the waterfront; behind these to the west is the more attractive old town with crumbling houses, a mosque, old-fashioned artisans' shops and a castle. Behind the old section sprawls the new town.

Dramatic and alluring – the Andorran Pyrenees are popular for skiing and snowboarding

The picturesque Albanian town of Gjirokastra nestles on the side of a mountain

Dubrovnik, the 'pearl of the Adriatic', is a spectacular feature of the southern Dalmation coast

GUY MCBERLY

Busking on the streets of Zagreb, Croatia

JON DAVISON

Fun by the water in Cavtat, Croatia

MARTIN MOOS

Fine art: Zagreb's Museum Mimara contains a wealth of European paintings

PAUL DAVID HELLANDER

Love is in the air: Aphrodite's Rock, Cyprus

JON DAVISON

Kykkos Monastery, Troödos Massif, Cyprus

The **CTO** (☎ 2536 2756; Spyros Araouzou 115a; open 8.15am-2.30pm Mon-Sat, 3pm-6pm Mon, Tues, Thur & Fri) is on the waterfront near the old harbour.

There are a number of Internet cafés in Lemesos. The most convenient is **CyberNet** (Eleftherias 79; open 3pm-2am daily), a couple of blocks behind the CTO. Access costs CY£2 per hour.

## Things to See

The main attraction is the well-restored **Medieval Castle & Museum** (☎ 2533 0419; admission CY£1; open 9am-5pm Mon-Sat, 10am-1pm Sun) where Richard the Lionheart married Berengaria of Navarre in 1191.

For a hi-tech review of Lemesos' and Cyprus' history visit the **Time Elevator** (☎ 2576 2828; e elevator@nplanitis.com; Vasilissis 1; admission CY£7) housed in Lemesos' restored Carob Mill behind the Mediaeval Castle. Covering the period from 8500 BC to 1974 and beyond this virtual ride is an exciting way to learn about Cyprus' history.

Of more tangible interest are the historical sites to the west. Fourteen kilometres along the road to Pafos is **Kolossi Castle**, and a further 5km away are the extensive remains of **Kourion** and the nearby **Sanctuary of Apollon Ylatis**. It's probably the most-visited site in Cyprus.

## Places to Stay & Eat

The nearest camping ground is **Governor's Beach Camping** (☎/fax 2563 2878; 1 person & tent CY£2.50), 20km east of town.

The cheapest hotels are clustered in the old town, to the east of the castle. A good one with large, clean rooms is the **Luxor Guest House** (☎ 2536 2265; Agiou Andreou 101; singles/doubles CY£6/12). Breakfast is extra.

**Continental Hotel** (☎ 2536 2530, fax 2537 3030; Spyrou Araouzou 137; singles/doubles CY£16/28), a two-star on the waterfront, has reasonable rooms with bathroom and prices quoted include breakfast.

**Richard & Berengaria** (☎ 2536 3863; Irinis 23; lunch CY£5.50), a small café, just by the castle, is a simple, good place to lunch or grab a snack.

**Rizitiko Tavern** (☎ 2534 8769; Tzamiou 4-8; mains CY£4-5), tucked away down a side street, is a good place to try for an evening meal. The friendly atmosphere is only beaten by the delicious traditional food that it serves.

The **municipal market** is at the northern end of Saripolou.

## Getting There & Away

**Intercity** (Lefkosia: ☎ 2266 5814 • Larnaka: ☎ 2464 3492) has frequent daily services to Lefkosia (CY£1.50) and also goes to Larnaka (CY£1.70). **Nea Amoroza** (2693 6822) has services to Pafos (CY£2). All of these buses depart from the Old Port. From here there is also a weekday bus at noon to Agros (CY£1) in the Troödos Mountains.

**Travel Express** (☎ 077 7474) has service taxis operating to Lefkosia (CY£3.50), Larnaka (CY£3) and Pafos (CY£2.75). Sunday fares are 10% higher.

There are currently no passenger ferries from Lemesos to either Israel or Greece. Check with **Salamis Tours Ltd** (☎ 2535 5555) or **Poseidon Lines** (☎ 2574 5666) in case they have been reinstated. The port is 5km southwest of town.

## Getting Around

The **city bus station** (A Themistokleous) is close to the municipal market. Bus No 1 goes towards the port, buses Nos 16 and 17 go to Kolossi and No 30 goes northeast along the seafront. Frequent buses also run from the castle to Kourion and its beach. Fares are between CY£0.45 and CY£0.80. From April to November there's a daily Governor's Beach bus that leaves from the CTO at 9.50am, returning at 4.30pm (CY£0.80).

**Lipsos Rent-a-Car** (☎ 2536 5295; Richard & Berengaria 6) is opposite the castle. The **Oceanic Supermarket** (28 Oktovriou 232) rents mopeds and bicycles.

## TROÖDOS MASSIF (ΤΡΟΟΔΟΣ)

The mountains of the Troödos region are beautiful with their secluded Byzantine monasteries, 15th-century frescoed churches, small wine-making villages, pine forests and numerous walking trails. In summer the area offers some respite from the heat, and in winter there's enough snow to ski. The tallest peak is Mt Olympus at 1952m.

The **CTO** (☎ 2542 1316; e platresinfo@cto.org.cy; open 9am-3.30pm Mon-Fri, 9am-2.30pm Sat) is in the square at Platres. There's enough in this area to keep you busy for at least a week. Check at the CTO for suggested walking trails and information on the flora and fauna you may encounter.

## Things to See & Do

The **Kykkos Monastery**, 20km west of Pedoulas, is the best known but also the most touristy of the monasteries. Although it dates from the 12th century, it has been completely renovated and all the mosaics, frescoes and stonework are new. It also has a museum containing priceless religious icons and relics.

In Pedoulas is the small, World Heritage–listed **Church of Arhangelos**, with frescoes dating from 1474. The key to the church is at a nearby house (signposted). Another fine World Heritage–listed church is **St Nikolaos of the Roof** *(open 9am-4pm Tues-Sat, 11am-4pm Sun)*, near Kakopetria. Entry is free but donations are welcomed.

**Omodos**, almost directly south of Pedoulas, is a village in the wine-growing region where local wine is available for sale and tastings. You can also visit **Socrates' Traditional House**, a 500-year-old house with a wine cellar and period distillery. Also in Omodos is the **Stavros Monastery**, which is more intimate than the larger and more-renowned monasteries.

## Places to Stay & Eat

Even though there are hotels or rooms in almost all the villages, there aren't enough so in July and August you should book. Outside these months, you can negotiate on prices.

**Troödos** (Τρόοδος) About 1km downhill from Troödos, which has a population of only 200, on the Lefkosia road, in a pine forest, there is a **camping ground** *(☎ 2542 0124; open May-Oct; 1 person & tent CY£2.50)*.

**Troödos HI Hostel** *(☎ 2542 0200; dorm beds 1st/subsequent nights CY£5/4; usually open May-Oct)* with its 10 bunk beds is the cheapest option. It's airy and clean and there's a big common area with kitchen. If no-one's around find a bed and unpack.

**Jubilee Hotel** *(☎ 2542 0107, fax 2267 3951;* e *jubilee@cytanet.com.cy; Troödos; singles/doubles CY£27/38)*, where rates include breakfast, is a rather more luxurious two-star. It's about 1km west of the hostel.

Eat anglicised food at **Fereos Restaurant** *(☎ 2542 0114; kebab CY£5)* on the main drag. The food is filling if not flash.

**Platres** (Πλάτρες) With a population of 1000 accommodation options here are much more favourable than uphill in Troödos.

**Lantern Hotel** *(☎ 9945 2307; Makariou 6; singles/doubles CY£12/18)* is an excellent, central, budget choice. It's unpretentious and clean, and most rooms have a bathroom.

Situated on the top road, a five-minute walk from the centre of Platres is **Minerva Hotel** *(☎ 2542 1731, fax 2542 1075;* e *minerva@globalsoftmail.com; singles/doubles CY£18/28)*. It's a cosy place, and the prices quoted include breakfast.

**Petit Palais** *(☎ 2542 1723, fax 2542 1065;* e *petitpalais@spidernet.com.cy; singles/doubles CY£32/36)* is a Swiss-style place with smallish but tidy rooms that is also very central; prices quoted include breakfast.

**Pigasos** *(☎ 2542 1744; Faneromenis 1, Platres; sandwiches CY£2; open lunch only)* right in the centre, is good for a quick snack and a cold beer. It's also great for *haloumi* and *lountza* (smoked, marinated loin of pork) sandwich concoctions, or *lahmajoun* – pitta bread stuffed with spicy mince.

**Village Tavern** *(☎ 2542 2777; Leoforos Makariou; mains CY£4-5)* is an excellent place for an evening meal – the *stifado* (rich meat stew) and *kleftiko* (oven-baked lamb with herbs) are just mouth-watering.

**Skylight Restaurant** *(☎ 2542 2244; mezes CY£6.75)* is also good and it has a pool. Enjoy a swim before a filling jacket-potato lunch (CY£2.75 to CY£3.50).

## Getting There & Away

Only expensive taxis currently link Platres with Lemesos (CY£17).

There is a **bus service** *(☎ 9961 8865)* from Lefkosia to Platres (via Pedoulas) at 12.15pm (CY£2, Monday to Friday). From Platres to Lefkosia the bus departs at 6am.

There is an additional service from Lefkosia to Troödos at 11.30am (CY£1.50, Monday to Friday) with a further 10 services (12 in summer) from Lefkosia to Kakopetria (CY£1.20, Monday to Friday). Call ☎ 2275 3234 for more information.

For the Kykkos Monastery there is one bus from Lefkosia that leaves at noon (CY£1.90, Monday to Saturday) and returns the next day at 6am.

## PAFOS (ΠΑΦΟΣ, BAF)

**pop 40,000**

Once the capital of Cyprus, Pafos has always been historically and mythologically important. Today it consists of Kato (lower) Pafos on the coast, where you'll find most of the places of interest, and Pafos, which is 1km inland. Kato Pafos is full of huge hotels and expensive bars and eateries which spoil the old harbour and port area. Pafos itself is much more pleasant, with an authentic life of its own.

The **tourist office** (☎ 2693 2841; Gladstonos 3; open 8.15am-2.30pm Mon-Sat, 3pm-6pm Mon, Tues, Thur & Fri Sept-June, often closes 3.45pm July & Aug) is just down from Pafos' main square. There's another tourist office at the airport.

For those who need to hop online, the easiest Internet café to find is **Maroushia Internet** (☎ 2694 7240; Akti Posidonos; open 10am-11pm Mon-Sat, 3pm-10pm Sun), just back from the seafront in Kato Pafos.

## Things to See

There is lots to see in Pafos but most renowned are the **Pafos Mosaics** (☎ 2694 0217; admission CY£1.50; open 8am-7.30pm daily), with its well-preserved (if dusty) floors from the villas of 3rd-century-AD Roman nobles. They mostly depict mythological themes, emphasising the exploits of Dionysos, the uninhibited god of wine. On the way to the mosaics you pass the remains of a **Byzantine castle** and an **odeion** (an ancient music and dance school).

About 2km north of Kato Pafos, on the coastal road to Polis, are the **Tombs of the Kings** (☎ 2694 0295; admission CY£0.75; open 8.30am-7.30pm daily), which date from the 3rd century BC. These underground tombs are quite fascinating.

## Places to Stay & Eat

The HI **Hostel** (☎ 2693 2588; Eleftheriou Venizelou 37; dorm beds 1st/subsequent nights CY£5/4) is quite a way north of Ano Pafos centre. To get there, walk up Leoforos Evagora Pallikaridi and it is off on the right.

**Trianon Hotel** (☎ 2693 2193; Arhiepiskopou Makariou III 99; singles/doubles CY£5/12) has bright and airy rooms, but the bathroom and kitchen facilities are shared.

**Axiothea Hotel** (☎ 2693 2866, fax 2694 5790; Ivis Malioti 2; singles/doubles with bathroom CY£24/32) is a friendly two-star which includes breakfast in its rates. On the high ground to the south of the CTO, it has a glass-fronted bar and reception with wonderful views of the sea – perfect for watching the sunset.

**Nikos Tyrimos Fish Tavern** (☎ 2694 2846; Agapinoros 71; fish dishes CY£3.75-8), in Kato Pafos, is the place to head if you plan to eat fish in Pafos. It *smells* of fresh fish as soon as you walk in. There is no other place like this; fish are caught from the owner's boat and served up the same day to discerning seafood-lovers.

**Argo** (☎ 2629 3327; Pafias Afroditis 21; set dinner CY£6), also in Kato Pafos, situated 100m west of the main entertainment area, is popular. The moussaka in a clay pot and the *kleftiko* are the two best dishes.

The **municipal market** (Ano Pafos) is near the covered bazaar area, not far from the Trianon Hotel.

## Getting There & Away

**Nea Amaroza Co** (☎ 2693 6822; Evagora Palikaridi 79) operates to Polis, Lemesos and Pomos. Its office is north of Pafos' main square. There are around 10 buses a day to Polis (CY£1) and one daily to Lemesos (CY£1.50) at 2.30pm.

**Alepa Bus Co** (☎ 2693 4410) runs one morning bus daily to Lefkosia (CY£3) and every 10 to 15 minutes to Kato Pafos (CY£0.50). All buses depart from the Central (Karavella) Bus Station.

**Travel & Express** (☎ 077 7474) has service taxis operating to Lemesos (CY£2.75).

## Getting Around

There are no buses or service taxis to/from the airport; a normal taxi costs about CY£5 to CY£7.

The urban bus station is at Karavella Parking, behind the Amaroza bus company office. Bus No 1 goes to Geroskipou Tourist Beach, 9km north of Pafos; bus No 11 goes to Kato Pafos; and bus No 10 goes to Coral Bay. They all stop at the municipal market.

**D Antoniades Ltd** (☎ 2623 3301; Evagora Pallikaridi 111-113) rents mountain bikes, motorcycles and mopeds.

## POLIS (ΠΟΛΙΣ)
### pop 4500

In the heart of Hrysohou Bay, near the wild, remote hiking region of the Akamas Peninsula is the large village of Polis. At present it isn't as spoilt by tourism as Cyprus' other coastal towns and this small town is ideally situated for holidays that actually leave you time to relax.

The **CTO** (☎ 2632 2468; Vasileos Stasioikou 2; open 9am-1pm Mon, Tues, Thur & Fri, 2.30pm-5.45pm Mon-Sat) is very central. There are a number of mountain bike, motorcycle and car-rental companies.

### Things to See & Do
The **Akamas Peninsula** is a rugged patchwork of barren rock and lush vegetation, with a wide variety of flora and fauna, including some rare species. A network of paths crisscrosses the peninsula, making it ideal for walkers.

At the start of these trails are the famous and much-visited **Baths of Aphrodite**, 10km west of Polis. According to one legend, the goddess bathed there to restore her virginity after encounters with her many lovers.

In the village, Byzantine frescoes have recently been uncovered in the church of **Agios Andronikos**. The key to the church is held at the **Archaeological Museum**.

**Polis' beach** near the camping ground (2km) is wide and sandy with lots of shade, lifesavers and a beachside tavern for lunch.

### Places to Stay & Eat
About 1km north of Polis towards the sea is the CTO **camping ground** (☎ 2632 1526; 1 person & tent CY£2.50) surrounded by eucalyptus trees; it is signposted from the town centre. Many houses have rooms to rent from CY£11, and there are plenty of apartments for hire.

**Odysseas & Eleni** (☎ 2632 1172; fax 2632 2279; Vasileos Filippou; singles/doubles CY£12/24) is one decent option that's close to the centre.

**Nikos & Olympia** (☎ 2632 1274; Arsinois 1-2; singles/doubles CY£13/26), with airconditioned apartments and swimming pool, also nearby, is another good choice.

**Bougainvillea Hotel Apartments** (☎ 2632 2201, fax 2632 2203; Verginas 13; 2-person studios CY£30-32) is a lovely flower-covered complex with pleasant and airy two-person studios; breakfast is included for CY£2. Prices drop by up to 50% in low season.

There are now lots of reasonably priced cafés and restaurants, but the best budget option by far with perhaps the best food in Polis is **Alekos Restaurant** (☎ 2632 3381; Leoforos Makariou; mains CY£3-4). Look for the nutritious home-cooked Cypriot specials such as black-eyed, or garden beans with or without meat. There's a free litre of wine for two diners.

### Getting There & Away
**Nea Amaroza Co** (☎ 2632 1114; Kyproleontos) has an office beside the Old Town Restaurant. It runs 10 buses a day to Pafos (CY£1) and in summer it also has three services to Latsi (CY£0.50) and the Baths of Aphrodite (CY£0.50).

There are daily buses to Lefkosia at 5am or 5.30am, depending on the company, that cost CY£5. Seats must be reserved one day in advance by ringing Nea Amaroza Co, or by calling into their office on Kyproleontos.

# Northern Cyprus

The Turkish Republic of Northern Cyprus (TRNC) occupies 37% of the island. Almost completely unspoilt by tourism, it has some of the island's best beaches, as well as awe-inspiring monasteries, archaeological sites and castles.

In this section, Turkish place names are used with their Greek names in brackets.

## NORTH NICOSIA (LEFKOŞA, ΛΕΥΚΩΣΙΑ)
**pop 40,000**
North Nicosia (Lefkoşa to the Turks), the capital of Northern Cyprus, is a quiet city with some good examples of Gothic and Ottoman architecture. If you wander the backstreets of the old town you'll find lots of locals toiling away in small workshops, making or mending a whole variety of everyday articles. It's a great place for a day excursion but budget accommodation options are not so hot.

### Orientation
The city centre is Atatürk Meydanı in the old city. Girne Caddesi is the main thoroughfare which runs north from Atatürk Meydanı to the well-preserved Kyrenia Gate (Girne Kapısı). To the east of the square is the Selimiye quarter, where you'll find most of the interesting places.

### Information
Inside Kyrenia Gate there's an excellent tourist office with all the relevant maps and brochures for Northern Cyprus. There's also a tourist office at the **Ministry of Tourism**

(☎ 227 9112, fax 228 5625; Bedrettin Demirel Caddesi), about 2km north in the new town. Both are closed on Sunday, but the one at Ledra checkpoint is open.

The **main post office** (Sarayönü Sokak) is just west of Atatürk Meydanı. The **telecommunications office** (Kizilay Sokak; open 8am-midnight daily) is in the new town.

The easiest Internet outlet to find is the central **Deep Net City** (☎ 227 9669; e deep netcity@kktc.net; Girne Caddesi 73). This busy place is open 24 hours a day and access costs TL1,000,000 per hour.

## Things to See & Do

The **Turkish Museum** (Mevlevi Tekke Müzesi; admission TL2,500,000; open 7.30am-2pm Mon-Fri) is at the northern end of Girne Caddesi in a 17th-century Islamic monastery that was used by 19-century Whirling Dervishes (Muslim ascetics), and now displays dervish artefacts. Extending from the museum is a long, thin mausoleum containing the tombs of 16 sheikhs.

The old quarter, east of Atatürk Meydanı, is dominated by the **Selimiye Mosque**, (Agios Nikolaos Cathedral), which was originally a cathedral built between 1209 and 1326. Next door is the **Bedesten**, a building comprising two churches, which became an Ottoman bazaar.

A few blocks west of the Bedesten is the **Büyük Hamam**, a popular Turkish bath frequented by locals and tourists of both genders (male masseurs only). A steam bath and a massage costs UK£10.

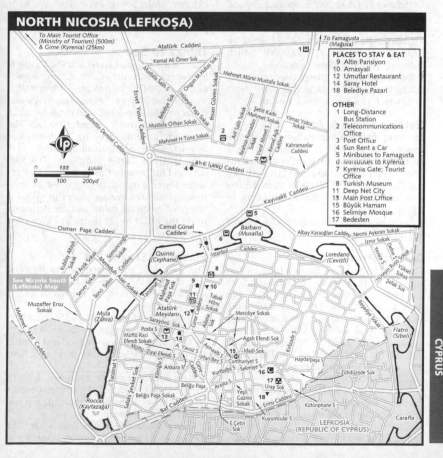

NORTH NICOSIA (LEFKOŞA)

PLACES TO STAY & EAT
9    Altin Pansiyon
10   Amasyali
12   Umutlar Restaurant
14   Saray Hotel
18   Belediye Pazari

OTHER
1    Long-Distance Bus Station
2    Telecommunications Office
3    Post Office
4    Sun Rent a Car
5    Minibuses to Famagusta
6    Minibuses to Kyrenia
7    Kyrenia Gate; Tourist Office
8    Turkish Museum
11   Deep Net City
13   Main Post Office
15   Büyük Hamam
16   Selimiye Mosque
17   Bedesten

CYPRUS

## Places to Stay & Eat

Most of the budget accommodation is intended for the local workforce and is not recommended for tourists (particularly lone female travellers).

**Altin Pansiyon** (☎ 228 5049; Girne Caddesi 63; singles/doubles UK£6/8) is only just passable for budget travellers and it doesn't include breakfast in its rates.

**Saray** (☎ 228 3115, fax 228 4808; e saray@northcyprus.net; Atatürk Meydanı; singles/doubles UK£27/41) is the best three-star hotel in the Old Town, and breakfast is included.

Along Girne Caddesi you'll find there are two very friendly low-key kebab restaurants fairly close to each other.

**Amasyali** (☎ 228 3294; Girne Caddesi 186; doner TL1,500,000) is open all day and serves up staples such as doner kebabs to eat in or take away.

**Umutlar Restaurant** (☎ 227 3236; Girne Caddesi 51; kebabs TL1,500,000), which dishes up a similar menu, is close by.

**Belediye Pazarı** is a large covered market selling fresh produce, as well as many items from which you can organise a picnic.

## Getting There & Away

The **long-distance bus station** (cnr Atatürk Caddesi & Kemal Aşik Caddesi) is in the new town. However, it is much easier to catch the frequent minibuses to Kyrenia (TL1,000,000) and Famagusta (TL1,500,000) from the bus stop and İtimat bus station just east of Kyrenia Gate.

Local minibuses leave from just west of Kyrenia Gate.

## Getting Around

There are no buses to Ercan airport. A taxi will cost TL16,000,000. There are plenty of taxi ranks, and cars can be hired from **Sun Rent a Car** (☎ 227 2303, fax 228 3700; e info@sunrentacar.com, w www.sunrentacar.com; Abdi İpekçi Caddesi 10) a five-minutes' walk north of Kyrenia Gate. A Renault Clio costs from UK£21 to UK£26 per day, while a Suzuki Vitara jeep costs from UK£24 to UK£29.

When you cross into Northern Cyprus from the South there are usually a number of taxi drivers waiting to show you all the sights in one day for around UK£35. This is a reasonable deal for two to three persons, especially if you have limited time and want to see a lot. The taxis are modern air-conditioned Mercedes and are very comfortable.

## KYRENIA (GİRNE, KEPYNEIA)
**pop 12,600**

Kyrenia is a very attractive town built around a horseshoe-shaped harbour dominated on one side by an impressive Byzantine castle. Behind the harbour is Hürriyet Caddesi, which runs from the town hall roundabout westward; at the western end of the harbour you'll find the **tourist office** (☎ 815 2145). The waterfront is lined with shaded outdoor cafés and restaurants where it is relaxing to sit and watch the boats.

Just down from the roundabout you will find **Café Net** (☎ 815 9259; e cafenet@kktc.net, Efeler Sokak; open 10am-midnight daily) where Internet access is TL1,500,000 per hour.

## Things to See

The star attraction of Kyrenia is the **Castle & Shipwreck Museum** (Girne Kalesi; admission TL7,000,000; open 9am-6.45pm daily), which houses Cyprus' oldest shipwreck and its cargo. The ship is believed to have sunk in a storm near Kyrenia around 3000 BC. The imposing castle was built by the Byzantines as a defence against marauding Arabs.

**St Hilarion Castle** (admission TL4,500,000) and **Buffavento Castle** (admission free) in the Kyrenia mountain ranges not far from Kyrenia, are fascinating places to visit for lovers of medieval ruins, and are definitely worth the effort to get there. The views are stupendous.

## Places to Stay & Eat

There's lots of accommodation in Kyrenia, with many of the cheaper options along Ecevit Caddesi and between Hürriyet Caddesi and the harbour.

**Bingöl Guest House** (☎ 815 2749; Efeler Sokak, Kyrenia; singles/doubles UK£4/10) on the main roundabout is good and central. Breakfast is included and they also have triples and quads.

**New Bristol Hotel** (☎ 815 6570, fax 815 7365; Hürriyet Caddesi 114; singles/doubles UK£15/19) is a bit old-fashioned, but has decent-enough rooms.

**Girne Harbour Lodge Motel** (☎ 815 7392, fax 815 3744; Cambulat Sokak 46;

*singles/doubles UK£16/32)* at the west end of the harbour is the place to try if you want a sea view and old-fashioned charm. The prices includes breakfast.

**Ergenekon Hotel** *(☎ 815 4677, fax 815 6010; e ergenekon@iecnc.org; Girne Limanı; singles/doubles UK£20/30)* is an excellent mid-range choice which overlooks the western harbour. It has very airy and comfortable rooms and the room price includes breakfast.

**Little Arif's Restaurant** *(☎ 852 0281; Hürriyet Caddesi; kebabs TL5,000,000)* is a bit of an institution and is also excellent value. Pitched almost exclusively at a local clientele, the no-frills Little Arif's is both unpretentious and cheap.

**Kyrenia Restaurant** *(Paşabahçe Restaurant; ☎ 815 1799; Türkmen Caddesi 2; mains TL8,000,000-10,000,000)* is run by a distinguished elderly couple. This neat eatery oozes simplicity laced with culinary rusticity.

### Getting There & Away

The long-distance bus station is on Ecevit Caddesi in the south of the New Town. Minibuses to Famagusta (TL2,000,000) and North Nicosia (TL1,000,000), as well as shared taxis to North Nicosia (TL1,000,000), all depart from Belediye Meydanı.

There are express boats to Taşucu in Turkey at 9.30am daily, taking three hours. There's also a slower daily ferry that takes about seven hours. One-way tickets cost TL41,500,000 and TL33,500,000 respectively and can be bought from the passenger lounge at the port or from **Fergün Denizcilik Şirketi Ltd** *(☎ 815 2344; Mustafa Çağatay Caddesi 6/2C)*. During peak season there is also a twice-weekly express ferry to Alanya in Turkey (US$30, four to five hours).

### FAMAGUSTA (MAĞUSA, ΑΜΜΟΧΩΣΤΟΣ)

**pop 28,000**

The old part of Famagusta (also known as Gazimağusa) is enclosed by an impressive, well-preserved Venetian wall. The **tourist office** *(☎ 366 2864; Fevzi Cakmak Caddesi)* is outside the wall, about 300m east of the **Victory Monument** (a huge black statue of Kemal Atatürk and his soldiers in battle).

### Things to See

Famagusta's **St Nicholas Cathedral**, now the Mustafa Paşa Mosque, is the finest example

of Lusignan Gothic architecture in Cyprus and was modelled on the Cathedral of Rheims in France. The Cathedral of St Nicholas was the centrepiece of Famagusta's Lusignan heyday and the last Lusignan king, Jacques II. It is now a working mosque.

**Othello's Tower** *(Othello Kalesi; admission TL4,500,000; open 9am-4.45pm daily)* part of the city walls and battlements, was built by the Lusignans in the 13th century. According to legend, it was here that Cristoforo Moro (Venetian governor of Cyprus from 1506 to 1508) killed his wife, Desdemona, in a fit of jealous rage. It is said that Shakespeare, confusing Moro's surname with his race, based his tragedy on this tale. There are good views from the ramparts.

### Places to Stay & Eat

Inside the city walls is pleasant **Altun Tabya Hotel** *(☎ 366 5363; Altun Tabya Sokak; singles/doubles US$20/25)*. Follow the signs from the gate east of the Victory Monument. The prices quoted include breakfast.

**Panorama Hotel** *(☎ 366 5880, fax 366 5990; İlker S Körler Caddesi; singles/doubles UK£8/12)*, in a run-down section of the new town (not far from the tourist office), has cosy rooms. It also offers reduced rates for weekly stays.

**Viyana Restaurant** *(☎ 366 6037; Liman Yolu Sokak 19; meals TL10,000,000)*, in the old town opposite St Nicholas Cathedral, is where good food is served in a shaded outside eating area.

**Petek Confectioner** *(☎ 366 7104; Yeşil Deviz Sokak 1)*, also on the same street, is the where you can drink tea and eat cake and Turkish delight.

On the north side of the square in front of Lala Mustafa Paşa Cami, **La Veranda** *(☎ 367 0153; Namık Kemal Meydanı; hamburger, chips & beer TL5,500,000)* is good for a cool beer and a quick snack.

### Getting There & Away

Minibuses to North Nicosia (TL1,000,000) depart frequently from the İtimat bus station on the Victory Monument roundabout and from the small bus terminus on Lefkoşa Yolu, west of the Monument. Also from here minibuses for Kyrenia leave every half hour or so (TL1,500,000).

Ferries to Mersin in Turkey leave at 10pm on Tuesday, Thursday and Sunday from the port behind Canbulat Yolu. They take 12 hours and the trip costs about TL50,000,000 (students TL37,500,000) one way. The ticket agents are **Turkish Maritime Lines** (☎ *366 5786, fax 366 7840; ℮ cypship@superon line.com; Bulent Ecevit Bulvarı).*

## ANCIENT SALAMIS
Nine kilometres north of Famagusta is the huge site of Cyprus' most important classical city, Salamis *(Salamis Harabeleri; admission TL4,500,000; open 8am-6pm daily summer).* Among other remains, there's a fully restored Roman amphitheatre, a gymnasium still surrounded by the majority of its marble columns with adjacent baths and some mosaics. There's a bar/restaurant in the car park.

Allow at least half a day here at this place as there is also a long sandy beach next to the site and a camping ground. There are no buses to Salamis and a return taxi will cost you around TL16,000,000.

## KANTARA CASTLE
This lofty mountain-top castle *(Kantara Kalesi; admission TL3,500,000)* is a definite daytrip highlight from Famagusta. Perched on a craggy peak an hour's drive north of Famagusta it is the third and perhaps most romantic of the trio of Cyprus' castles. You can see the sea on both sides of the **Karpas Peninsula** and on a good, clear day the coast of Turkey or even Syria. You'll need your own transport to get there.

# France

France has its share of coiffed, caffeinated croissant-munchers with arrogant sneers at the ready. It also has its share of warm-hearted souls who accept that decent human beings may not always speak fluent French. Endearing, delicious, beautiful, diverse and occasionally maddening, France is the 'quoi' in 'je ne sais quoi'.

The largest country in Western Europe, France stretches from the rolling hills of the north to the seemingly endless beaches of the south.

Over the centuries, France has received more immigrants than any other country in Europe. From the ancient Celtic Gauls and Romans to the more recent arrivals from France's former colonies in Indochina and Africa, these peoples have introduced their own culture, cuisine and art.

Once on the western edge of Europe, today's France stands firmly at the cross-roads: between England and Italy, Belgium and Spain, North Africa and Scandinavia. Of course, this is exactly how the French have always regarded their country – at the very centre of things.

## At a Glance

- **Paris** – art treasures of the Louvre, walks along the romantic River Seine
- **Provence** – Van Gogh's old haunts in Arles, Avignon's immense Palais des Papes
- **Côte d'Azur** – glamorous St Tropez, star-spotting in Cannes, sunning with the rich and famous in Monaco
- **Corsica** – Bonifacio's huge limestone cliffs, Les Calanques mountain trails

| | |
|---|---|
| **Capital** | Paris |
| **Population** | 58.5 million |
| **Official Language** | French |
| **Currency** | euro |
| **Time** | GMT/UTC+0100 |
| **Country Phone Code** | ☎ 33 |

Paris Maps
Paris pp188-9
Central Paris p192
The Latin Quarter & Île de la Cité p198
Montmartre p201
Marais & Île Saint Louis p204

BRITAIN
BELGIUM
✪ Paris
LUXEMBOURG
GERMANY
AUSTRIA
SWITZERLAND
ITALY
Avignon p218
ANDORRA
Marseilles p214
Monaco p230
Nice p222-3
Cannes p226
SPAIN
Ajaccio p233

# Facts about France

## HISTORY
### Prehistory to Medieval
Human presence in France dates from the middle Palaeolithic period, about 90,000 to 40,000 years ago. Around 25,000 BC the Stone Age Cro-Magnon people appeared and left their mark in the form of cave paintings and engravings.

The Celtic Gauls moved into what is now France between 1500 and 500 BC. Julius Caesar's Roman legions took control of the territory around 52 BC, and France remained under Roman rule until the 5th century, when the country was overrun by Franks (thus 'France') and other Germanic groups.

Two Frankish dynasties, the Merovingians and the Carolingians, ruled from the 5th to the 10th centuries. In AD 732, Charles Martel defeated the Moors at Poitiers, ensuring that France would not follow Spain and come under Muslim rule. Charles Martel's grandson, Charlemagne, extended the boundaries of

the kingdom and was crowned Holy Roman Emperor in AD 800. During the 9th century, Scandinavian Vikings (the Normans) began raiding France's western coast and eventually founded the Duchy of Normandy.

Under William the Conqueror (the Duke of Normandy), Norman forces occupied England in 1066, making Normandy – and later, Plantagenet-ruled England – a formidable rival of the kingdom of France. A further one-third of France came under the control of the English Crown in 1154, when Eleanor of

FRANCE

Aquitaine married Henry of Anjou (later King Henry II of England).

In 1415, French forces were defeated at Agincourt; in 1420, the English took control of Paris, and two years later King Henry IV of England became king of France. But a 17-year-old peasant girl known to history as Jeanne d'Arc (Joan of Arc) surfaced in 1429 and rallied the French troops at Orléans. She was captured, convicted of heresy and burned at the stake two years later, but her efforts helped to turn the war in favour of the French.

## Renaissance & Reformation

The ideals and aesthetics of the Italian Renaissance were introduced in the 15th century, partly by the French aristocracy returning from military campaigns in Italy. The influence was most evident during the reign of François I, and the chateaux of Fontainebleau, near Paris, is a good example of Renaissance architectural style.

By the 1530s the Protestant Reformation had been strengthened in France by the ideas of the Frenchman John Calvin, an exile in Geneva. The Wars of Religion (1562–98) involved three groups: the Huguenots (French Protestants); the Catholic League, led by the House of Guise; and the Catholic monarchy. The fighting brought the French state close to disintegration. Henry of Navarra, a Huguenot who embraced Catholicism, eventually became King Henry IV. In 1598, he promulgated the Edict of Nantes, which guaranteed the Huguenots many civil and political rights.

## Louis XIV & the Ancien Régime

Louis XIV – also known as Le Roi Soleil (the Sun King) – ascended the throne in 1643 at the age of five and ruled until 1715. Throughout his long reign, he sought to extend the power of the French monarchy. He also involved France in a long series of costly wars and poured huge sums of money into his extravagant palace at Versailles.

His successor, Louis XV (r. 1715–74), was followed by the incompetent – and later universally despised – Louis XVI. As the 18th century progressed, new economic and social circumstances rendered the *ancien régime* (old order) dangerously at odds with the needs of the country.

The Seven Years' War (1756–63), fought by France and Austria against Britain and Prussia, was one of a series of ruinous wars pursued by Louis XV, culminating in the loss of France's flourishing colonies in Canada, the West Indies and India to the British.

## The French Revolution

By the late 1780s, Louis XVI and his queen, Marie-Antoinette, had managed to alienate virtually every segment of society. When the king tried to neutralise the power of reform-minded delegates at a meeting of the Estates General in 1789, the urban masses took to the streets and, on 14 July, a Parisian mob stormed the Bastille prison.

The Revolution began in the hands of the moderate, republican Girondists (Girondins in French), but they soon lost power to the radical Jacobins, led by Robespierre, Danton and Marat, who established the First Republic in 1792. In January 1793, Louis was guillotined in what is now place de la Concorde in Paris. Two months later the Jacobins set up the notorious Committee of Public Safety, which had near-dictatorial control during the Reign of Terror (September 1793 to July 1794).

In the resulting chaos, a dashing young general by the name of Napoleon Bonaparte chalked up a string of victories in the Italian campaign of the war against Austria, and his success soon turned him into an independent political force.

## Napoleon

In 1799, when it appeared that the Jacobins were again on the ascendancy, Napoleon assumed power himself. Five years later he had himself crowned Emperor of the French by Pope Pius VII, and the scope and nature of Napoleon's ambitions became obvious to all.

In 1812, in an attempt to do away with his last major rival on the continent, Tsar Alexander I, Napoleon invaded Russia. Although his Grande Armée (Grand Army) captured Moscow, it was wiped out shortly thereafter by the brutal Russian winter. Prussia and Napoleon's other enemies quickly recovered from earlier defeats, and less than two years later the Allied armies entered Paris. Napoleon abdicated and was exiled to Elba, his tiny Mediterranean island-kingdom.

At the Congress of Vienna (1814–15), the Allies restored the House of Bourbon to the French throne. But in March 1815, Napoleon escaped from Elba, landed in southern France and gathered a large army as he marched towards Paris. His 'Hundred Days' back in power ended when his forces were defeated by the English at Waterloo in Belgium. Napoleon was banished to the remote South Atlantic island of St Helena where he died in 1821.

## 19th Century

The 19th century was a chaotic one for France. Louis XVIII's reign (1815–24) saw a struggle between extreme monarchists and those who saw the changes wrought by the Revolution as irreversible. Charles X (r. 1824–30) handled the struggle between reactionaries and liberals with great ineptitude and was overthrown in the July Revolution of 1830. Louis-Philippe (r. 1830–48), an ostensibly constitutional monarch of upper bourgeois sympathies and tastes, was then chosen by parliament to head what became known as the July Monarchy.

Louis-Philippe was in turn ousted in the February Revolution of 1848, in whose wake the Second Republic was established. In the presidential elections, Napoleon's undistinguished nephew Louis-Napoleon Bonaparte was overwhelmingly elected. A legislative deadlock led Louis-Napoleon to lead a coup d'etat in 1851, after which he was proclaimed Napoleon III, Emperor of the French.

The second empire lasted from 1852 until 1870, when the Prussian prime minister, Bismarck, goaded Napoleon III into declaring war on Prussia. Within months the unprepared French army had been defeated and the emperor taken prisoner. When news of the debacle reached the French capital, the Parisian masses took to the streets and demanded that a republic be declared – the Third Republic.

## WWI

Central to France's entry into WWI was the desire to regain Alsace and Lorraine, lost to Germany in 1871. This was achieved but at immense human cost: of the eight million French men who were called to arms, 1.3 million were killed and almost one million crippled. The war was officially ended by the Treaty of Versailles in 1919, which laid down severe terms (Germany was to pay US$33 billion in reparations).

## WWII

During the 1930s the French, like the British, did their best to appease Hitler, but two days after the 1939 German invasion of Poland, the two countries reluctantly declared war on Germany. By June of the following year, France had capitulated. The British forces sent to help the French barely managed to avoid capture by retreating to Dunkirk and crossing the English Channel in small boats.

The Germans divided France into zones of direct occupation (in the north and along the west coast) and a puppet state based in the spa town of Vichy. Both the collaborationist government and French police forces in the German-occupied areas were very helpful to the Nazis in rounding up French Jews and other targeted groups for deportation to concentration camps.

General Charles de Gaulle, France's under-secretary of war, fled to London and set up a French government-in-exile. He also established the Forces Françaises Libres (Free French Forces), dedicated to continuing the fight against Germany. The liberation of France began with the USA, British and Canadian landings in Normandy on D-Day (6 June 1944). Paris was liberated on 25 August.

## The Fourth Republic

De Gaulle soon returned to Paris and set up a provisional government, but in January 1946 he resigned as its president, miscalculating that this move would create a popular outcry for his return. A few months later, a new constitution was approved by referendum. The Fourth Republic was a period of unstable coalition cabinets, characterised by slow economic recovery fuelled by massive US aid, an unsuccessful war to reassert French colonial control of Indochina and an uprising by Arab nationalists in Algeria, whose population included more than a million French settlers.

## The Fifth Republic

The Fourth Republic came to an end in 1958; de Gaulle was brought back to power to prevent a military coup and even civil war. He soon drafted a new constitution that gave considerable powers to the president at the expense of the national assembly.

In 1969, de Gaulle was succeeded as president by Gaullist leader Georges Pompidou, who in turn was followed by Valéry Giscard d'Estaing in 1974. François Mitterrand, a Socialist, was elected president in 1981 and re-elected seven years later. Smooth, irksome Jacque Chirac was elected president in 1995 and re-elected in 2002. In 2002, he won with an overwhelming majority (82% of the vote) after French voters boxed themselves into a corner by setting up a presidential contest with National Front right-winger Jean Marie Le Pen as the only alternative. Le Pen's strongest support is along the Mediterranean coast, in southern Corsica and in pockets of France's northeast.

## GEOGRAPHY

France (551,000 sq km) is the third-largest country in Europe, after Russia and Ukraine. It's shaped like a hexagon bordered by either mountains or water, except for the relatively flat, northeast frontier that abuts Germany, Luxembourg and Belgium.

## CLIMATE

France has a temperate climate with mild winters. A pleasant Mediterranean climate extends from the southern coast as far inland as the southern Alps, the Massif Central and the eastern Pyrenees.

The Paris basin records France's lowest rainfall overall (about 575mm a year) but enough erratic showers to keep you on your toes. Paris' average yearly temperature is 12°C, with extremes ranging from below zero in January and days in the mid-30s in August.

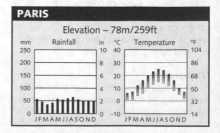

## ECOLOGY & ENVIRONMENT

France has a rich variety of flora and fauna, including some 113 species of mammals (more than any other country in Europe).

About three-quarters of France's electricity is produced by nuclear power plants. France maintains an independent arsenal of nuclear weapons; in 1992, the government finally agreed to suspend nuclear testing on the Polynesian island of Moruroa and a nearby atoll. However, one last round of tests was concluded in January 1996 before France signed a nuclear test-ban treaty in April 1998.

## GOVERNMENT & POLITICS

Despite a long tradition of highly centralised government, the country remains linguistically and culturally heterogeneous. There are even small groups in the Basque Country, Brittany and Corsica who still demand complete independence from France.

France has had 11 constitutions since 1789. The present one, instituted by de Gaulle in 1958, established what is known as the Fifth Republic (see History earlier). It gives considerable power to the president of the republic.

The 577 members of the national assembly are directly elected in single-member constituencies for five-year terms. The 321 members of the rather powerless Sénat, most of whom serve for nine years, are indirectly elected. The president of France is elected directly for a five-year term (recently reduced from a seven-year term).

Executive power is shared by the president and the council of ministers, whose members, including the prime minister, are appointed by the president but are responsible to parliament. The president, who resides in the Palais de l'Élysée in Paris, makes all major policy decisions.

France is a member of the European Union and one of the five permanent members of the UN Security Council. It withdrew from NATO's joint military command in 1966.

### Local Administration

Regional names still exist, but for administrative purposes the country has been divided into units called *départements*, of which there are 96 in metropolitan France and another six abroad. The government in Paris is represented in each department by a *préfet* (prefect). A department's main town, where the departmental government and the prefect are based, is known as a *préfecture*.

## ECONOMY

After sluggish growth through much of the 1990s, the French economy has finally started to hum again. Economists are predicting that GDP growth will rebound to 2.6% in 2003 and a couple of years at around 1.5% as money filters through from a trade surplus. Unemployment – which was stuck around 12% in the late 1990s – has dropped to around 9%.

The government has long played a significant interventionist *(dirigiste)* role in the French economy. About 24% of GDP is spent by the state, despite a series of heavyweight privatisations during the 1990s.

Being ignored by waiters may make you doubt it but France is one of the world's most service-oriented countries; the services sector accounts for around 72% of GDP. France is also the largest agricultural producer and exporter in the EU. Nearly one in 10 workers is engaged in agricultural production, which helps to account for the attention given by the government to protests by French farmers.

## POPULATION & PEOPLE

France has a population of 58.5 million, more than 20% of whom live in the Paris metropolitan area. During the last 150 years France has received more immigrants than any other European country (4.3 million between 1850 and WWI), including significant numbers of political refugees. In the late 1950s and early 1960s, as the French colonial empire collapsed, over a million French settlers returned to France from North Africa and Indochina.

Today, France has about five million foreign-born residents. In recent years, there has been a racist backlash against France's nonwhite immigrant communities, led by the extreme-right Front National (FN) party. Assaults on Jewish property and people, perpetrated by white and Muslim racists, are also on the rise.

## ARTS
### Architecture

A religious revival in the 11th century led to the construction of a large number of Romanesque churches, so called because their architects adopted elements from austere Gallo-Roman buildings, such as round arches and heavy walls.

The Gothic style originated in the mid-12th century in northern France. Gothic structures are characterised by ribbed vaults, pointed arches and stained-glass windows, with the emphasis on space, verticality and light. The invention of the flying buttress meant that greater height and width were now possible. By the 15th century, decorative extravagance led to the Flamboyant Gothic style with its characteristic wavy stone carving.

## Painting

An extraordinary flowering of artistic talent occurred in France during the late 19th and early 20th centuries. The impressionists, who endeavoured to capture the ever-changing aspects of reflected light, included Édouard Manet, Claude Monet, Edgar Degas, Camille Pissarro and Pierre-Auguste Renoir. They were followed by the postimpressionists, among whose ranks were Paul Cézanne, Paul Gauguin and Georges Seurat. A little later, the Fauves (literally, 'wild beasts'), the most famous of whom was Henri Matisse, became known for their radical use of vibrant colour. In the years before WWI Pablo Picasso, who was living in Paris, and Georges Braque, pioneered cubism, a school of art which concentrated on the analysis of form through abstract and geometric representation.

## Music

When French music comes to mind, most people hear accordions and *chansonniers* (cabaret singers) like Édith Piaf. But at many points in history, France has been at the centre of musical culture in Europe.

France's two greatest classical composers of the 19th century were the Romantic Hector Berlioz, the founder of modern orchestration, and César Franck, who specialised in organ compositions. Their output sparked a musical renaissance that would produce such greats as Gabriel Fauré and the impressionists Claude Debussy and Maurice Ravel.

Jazz hit Paris in the 1920s and has remained popular ever since. Violinists Stéfane Grappelli and Jean-Luc Ponty, and pianist Michel Petrucciani have all left their mark on the world jazz scene.

Popular music has come a long way since the *yéyé* (imitative rock) of the 1960s sung by Johnny Halliday. Evergreen balladeers/folk singers include Francis Cabrel and Julien Clerc. Watch out for rap group IAM and

modern troubadours Massilia Sound System from Marseille. New and groovy are the ethereal François Breut and the jazzy Paris Combo. *Sono mondial* (world music) coming out of France includes Senegalese *mbalax*, Algerian *raï* and West Indian *zouk*.

## Literature

To get a feel for France and its literature of the 19th century, you might pick up novels by Victor Hugo (*Les Misérables* or *The Hunchback of Notre Dame*), Stendahl (*The Red and the Black*), Honoré de Balzac (*Old Goriot*), Émile Zola (*Germinal*) or Gustave Flaubert (*A Sentimental Education* or *Madame Bovary*).

After WWII, existentialism emerged – a significant literary movement based upon the philosophy that people are self-creating beings. Its most prominent figures were Jean-Paul Sartre (*Being and Nothingness*), Simone de Beauvoir, and Albert Camus (*The Plague*). De Beauvoir also wrote *The Second Sex*, which has had a profound influence on feminist thinking.

Contemporary authors who enjoy a wide following include Françoise Sagan, Emmanuel Carrère, Michel Houellebecq and Algerian-born Anouar Benmalek.

## Cinema

Film is taken very seriously as an art form in France. Some of the most innovative and influential filmmakers of the 1920s and 1930s were Jean Vigo, Marcel Pagnol and Jean Renoir.

After WWII, a *nouvelle vague* (new wave) of directors burst onto the scene, including Jean-Luc Godard, François Truffaut, and Claude Chabrol.

Contemporary directors of note include Luc Besson (*The Fifth Element, Nikita*), Claire Denis (*Chocolat, Beau Travail*) and Jean-Pierre Jeunet (*Delicatessen, Amelie*). The French film industry's main annual event is the Cannes Film Festival held in May.

## SOCIETY & CONDUCT

Some visitors to France conclude that it would be a lovely country if it weren't for the French. The following tips might prove useful: never address a waiter or bartender as *garçon* (boy) – *s'il vous plaît* is the way it's done nowadays; avoid discussing money; keep off the manicured French lawns; resist handling produce in markets; and always address people as *Monsieur* (Mr/sir), *Madame* (Mrs) and *Mademoiselle* (Miss) – when in doubt use 'Madame'.

Finally, when you go out for the evening, it's a good idea to follow the local custom of dressing relatively well, particularly in a restaurant.

## RELIGION

Some 80% of French people say they are Catholic, but although most have been baptised very few attend church. Protestants, who were severely persecuted during much of the 16th and 17th centuries, now number about one million.

France now has more than five million Muslims, making Islam the second-largest religion in the country. The majority are immigrants (or their offspring) who came from North Africa during the 1950s and 1960s.

There has been a Jewish community in France almost continuously since Roman times. About 75,000 French Jews were killed during the Holocaust. The country's Jewish community now numbers around 700,000.

## LANGUAGE

Around 77 million people worldwide speak French as their first language, and various forms of Creole are used in Haiti, French Guiana and southern Louisiana. French was the international language of culture and diplomacy until WWI – in France it tends to be assumed that all decent human beings speak French.

Your best bet is always to approach people politely in French, even if the only words you know are *'Pardon, Monsieur/Madame/ Mademoiselle, parlez-vous Anglais?'* ('Excuse me sir/madam/miss, do you speak English?').

See the Language chapter at the back of this book for pronunciation guidelines and useful words and phrases.

# Facts for the Visitor

## HIGHLIGHTS
### Museums

Many of the country's most exceptional museums are in Paris. Besides the rather overwhelming Louvre, Parisian museums not to be missed include the Musée d'Orsay (late-19th and early-20th-century art), the Pompidou Centre (modern and contemporary art), the Musée Rodin, and the Musée National du Moyen Age (Museum of the Middle Ages) at Hôtel de Cluny. Nice is also well known for its museums.

### Beaches

The Côte d'Azur – the French Riviera – has some of the best-known beaches in the world, but you'll also find lovely beaches further west on the Mediterranean.

## SUGGESTED ITINERARIES
**Two days**
   See Paris – the most beautiful city in the world
**One week**
   Spend more time in Paris and visit Arles and the Côte d'Azur
**Two weeks**
   As above plus Avignon and Carcassonne
**One month**
   As above, but spending more time in each place and also visit Corsica

## PLANNING
### When to Go

France is at its best in spring, although wintry relapses aren't uncommon in April and the beach resorts only begin to pick up in mid-May. Autumn is pleasant, too, but by late October it's a bit cool for sunbathing. Winter is great for snow sports in the Pyrenees, but Christmas, New Year and the February/March school holidays create surges in tourism. Paris always has all sorts of cultural activities during its rather wet winter.

In summer, the weather is warm and even hot, especially in the south, and the beaches, resorts and camping grounds get packed to the gills. Also, millions of French people take their annual month-long *congé* (holiday) in August. Resort hotel rooms and camp sites are in extremely short supply, while in the half-deserted cities many shops, restaurants, cinemas, cultural institutions and even hotels simply shut down. Avoid travelling in France during August.

### Maps

For driving, the best road map is Michelin's *Motoring Atlas France* (1:200,000), which covers the entire country. Éditions Didier Richard's 1:50,000 trail maps are adequate for most hiking and cycling excursions.

The Institut Géographique National (IGN) publishes maps of France in both 1:50,000 and 1:25,000 scale. Topoguides are booklets for hikers that include trail maps and information (in French) on trail conditions, flora, fauna, villages en route and more.

## TOURIST OFFICES
### Local Tourist Offices
Every city, town, village and hamlet seems to have either an *office de tourisme* (a tourist office run by some unit of local government) or a *syndicat d'initiative* (a tourist office run by an organisation of local merchants). Both are excellent resources and can almost always provide a local map at the very least. Many tourist offices will make local hotel reservations, usually for a small fee.

Details on local tourist offices appear under Information at the beginning of each city, town or area listing.

### Tourist Offices Abroad
The French Government Tourist Offices in the following countries can provide brochures and tourist information.

**Australia** (☎ 02-9231 5244, fax 9221 8682, e france@bigpond.net.au) 25 Bligh St, 22nd floor, Sydney, NSW 2000
**Canada** (☎ 514-876 9881, fax 845 4868; e mfrance@attcanada.net) 1981 McGill College Ave, Suite 490, Montreal, Que H3A 2W9
**UK** (☎ 090-6824 4123, fax 020-7493 6594, e info@mdlf.co.uk) 178 Piccadilly, London W1J 9AL
**USA** (☎ 212-838 7800, fax 838 7855, e info@francetourism.com) 444 Madison Ave, New York, NY 10020

## VISAS & DOCUMENTS
Citizens of the USA, Canada, Australia and New Zealand, and most European countries can enter France for up to three months without a visa. South Africans, however, must have a visa to visit France (to avoid delays, apply before leaving home).

If you're staying in France for more than three months to study or work, apply to the French consulate nearest where you live for a long-stay visa. If you're not an EU citizen, it's extremely difficult to get a work visa; one of the few exceptions allows holders of student visas to work part-time. Begin the paperwork several months before you leave home.

By law, everyone in France, including tourists, must carry identification with them.

For visitors, this means a passport. A national identity card is sufficient for EU citizens.

### Visa Extensions
Tourist visas *cannot* be extended. However, if you qualify for an automatic three-month stay upon arrival, you'll get another three months if you exit and then re-enter France. At many French borders, though, it's hard to get exit and entry stamps in your passport (even if you want them) so you can more or less stay as long as you like.

## EMBASSIES & CONSULATES
### French Embassies & Consulates
French embassies abroad include:

**Australia** (☎ 02-6216 0100, fax 6216 0127, e embassy@ambafrance-au.org) 6 Perth Ave, Yarralumla, ACT 2600
**Canada** (☎ 613-789 1795, fax 562 3704, e consulat@amba-ottowa.fr) 42 Sussex Dr, Ottawa, Ont K1M 2C9
**Germany** (☎ 030-206 39000, fax 206 39010, e consulat.berlin@diplomatie.gouv.fr) Pariser Platz 5, 10117 Berlin
**Italy** (☎ 06-686 011, fax 860 1360, e france-italia@france-italia.it) Piazza Farnese 67, 00186 Rome
**New Zealand** (☎ 04-384 2555, fax 384 2577, e consulfrance@actrix.gen.nz) Rural Bank Bldg, 34-42 Manners St, Wellington
**Spain** (☎ 91-423 8900, fax 423 8901) Calle de Salustiano Olozaga 9, 28001 Madrid
**UK** (☎ 020-7073 1000, fax 7073 1004, e info-londres@diplomatie.gouv.fr) 58 Knightsbridge, London SW1X 7JT. Visa inquiries: ☎ 0891-887733
**USA** (☎ 202-944 6060, fax 944 6040, e info-washington@diplomatie.gouv.fr) 4101 Reservoir Rd, NW Washington, DC, 20007

### Embassies & Consulates in France
Countries with embassies in Paris include:

**Australia** (☎ 01 40 59 33 00, fax 01 40 59 33 10, e information.paris@dfat.gov.au) 4 rue Jean Rey, 15e (metro Bir Hakeim)
**Canada** (☎ 01 44 43 29 00, 01 44 43 29 99) 35 ave Montaigne, 8e (metro Franklin D Roosevelt)
**New Zealand** (☎ 01 45 01 43 43, fax 01 45 01 43 44, e nzembassy.paris@wanadoo.fr) 7ter rue Léonard de Vinci, 16e (metro Victor Hugo)
**Spain** (☎ 01 44 43 18 00, fax 01 47 23 59 55, e emba.espa@wanadoo.fr) 22 ave Marceau, 8e (metro Alma Marceau)

Grande Arche in La Defense, Paris

Contemporary sculpture in La Defense, Paris

Parisian silhouette: the iconic Eiffel Tower

Snorkelling at Ile Lavezzi, Corsica, France

Set sail from Marseille, France

RICHARD I'ANSON

Reflect on Paris' artistic treasures: The Louvre and eye-catching glass pyramid

GEORGE TSAFOS

Olymbos, Karpathos Island

PAUL DAVID HELLANDER

Take a dip at Ammoöpi, Karpathos' premier holiday resort

JOHN ELK III

The Acropolis, crowned by the Parthenon, is a powerful reminder of ancient Greece's prowess

UK (☎ 01 44 51 31 00, fax 01 44 51 31 27,
  e ambassade@amb-grandebretagne.fr) 35
  rue du Faubourg St Honoré, 8e (metro
  Concorde)
USA (☎ 01 43 12 22 22, fax 01 42 66 97 83,
  e citizeninfo@state.gov) 2 rue St Florentin,
  1er (metro Concorde)

# MONEY
## Currency
The official currency of France is the euro.

**Cash & Travellers Cheques** Generally
you'll get a better exchange rate for travellers
cheques than for cash. The most widely accepted ones are issued by American Express
(AmEx) in US dollars or euros.

Visa (Carte Bleue in France) is more
widely accepted than MasterCard (Eurocard).
Visa card-holders with a PIN can get cash advances from banks and ATMs nationwide.
AmEx cards aren't very useful, except to get
cash at AmEx offices in big cities or to pay
in upmarket shops and restaurants.

Many post offices make exchange transactions at a very good rate and accept AmEx
travellers cheques; there's 2.5% commission
on cash and 1.5% commission on US dollar
travellers cheques.

Banque de France no longer offers currency exchange. Commercial banks usually
charge a stiff €3 to €5 per foreign currency
transaction. In larger cities, exchange bureaus
are faster, easier, open longer hours and often
give better rates than the banks.

If your AmEx travellers cheques are lost or
stolen, call ☎ 0800 90 86 00, a 24-hour toll-
free number. For lost or stolen Visa cards,
call ☎ 0800 90 11 79.

## Costs
If you stay in hostels, buy provisions from
grocery stores and don't travel much, it's
possible to survive in France for US$30 a
day (US$35 in Paris). A frugal – but less mis-
erable – budget is more like US$55 a day.
Eating out, travelling a lot or treating yourself
to France's many little luxuries can increase
this figure dramatically.

**Discounts** Museums, cinemas, the SNCF,
ferry companies and other institutions offer
price breaks to people under the age of either
25 or 26, students with ISIC cards (age limits may apply), and seniors (people over 60
or, in some cases, 65.) Look for the words

demi-tarif or tarif réduit (half-price tariff or
reduced rate) on rate charts.

## Tipping & Bargaining
It's not necessary to leave a pourboire (tip) in
restaurants or hotels; under French law, the bill
must already include a 15% service charge.
However, it's usual to leave €0.50 or €1 for
a casual meal, about €1 per person for a more
formal meal and about 10% of the bill in a
truly posh restaurant. For a taxi ride, the usual
tip is about €1 no matter what the fare (10%
in Paris). You'll rarely have an opportunity to
bargain in France.

## Taxes & Refunds
France's VAT (value-added tax, ie, sales tax)
is known in French as TVA (taxe sur la valeur
ajoutée). The TVA is 19.6% on the purchase
price of most goods (and for noncommercial
vehicle rental). Prices that include TVA are
often marked TTC (toutes taxes comprises),
which means 'all taxes included'.

It's possible (though rather complicated) to
get a reimbursement for TVA if you meet several conditions: you are not an EU national
and are over 15 years of age; you have stayed
in France less than six months; you are buying more than €175 worth of goods (not more
than 10 of the same item); and the shop offers
vente en détaxe (duty-free sales).

To claim a TVA, you fill out an bordereau
de vente (export sales invoice) when you make
your purchase, and this is stamped at your port
of exit. The shop then reimburses you – by
mail or bank transfer within 30 days – for the
TVA you've paid. Note that there's no duty-
free shopping within the EU.

# POST & COMMUNICATIONS
## Postal Rates
La Poste, the French postal service, is fast,
reliable and expensive. Postcards and letters
up to 20g cost €0.46 within the EU, €0.67 to
the USA, Canada and the Middle East, and
€0.79 to Australasia. Aerograms cost €0.69
to all destinations. Overseas packages are
sent by air only, which is expensive.

**Receiving Mail** Mail to France *must* include the area's five-digit postcode, which
begins with the two-digit number of the
department. In Paris, all postcodes begin with
750 and end with the arrondissement number,
eg, 75004 for the 4th arrondissement.

FRANCE

Poste restante mail is held alphabetically by family name, so make sure your last name is written in capital letters. If not addressed to a particular branch, poste restante mail ends up at the town's *recette principale* (main post office). In Paris, this means the **central post office** (☎ *01 40 28 20 00; 52 rue du Louvre, 1er; metro Sentier or Les Halles*). There's a €0.46 charge for every poste-restante item claimed.

You can also receive mail at AmEx offices, although if you don't have an AmEx card or travellers cheques there's a €0.76 charge each time you check to see if you have received any mail.

## Telephone

**Public Telephones** Almost all public phones now require *télécartes* (phonecards), which are sold at post offices, *tabacs* (tobacco shops), Paris metro ticket counters and supermarket check-out counters. Cards worth 50/120 units cost €7.50/15. Each unit is good for one three-minute local call. To make a call with a phonecard, pick up the receiver, insert the card and dial when the LCD screen reads '*Numérotez*'. All telephone cabins can take incoming calls; give the caller the 10-digit number written after the words '*ici le*' on the information sheet next to the phone.

**Domestic Dialling** France has five telephone zones and all phone numbers comprise 10 digits. Paris and Île de France numbers begin with 01. The other codes are: ☎ 02 for the northwest; ☎ 03 for the northeast; ☎ 04 for the southeast (including Corsica); and ☎ 05 for the southwest.

Numbers beginning with 0800 are free, but others in the series (eg, 0826) generally cost €0.15 per minute. For directory assistance, dial ☎ 12.

**International Dialling** France's international country code is ☎ 33. When dialling from abroad, omit the initial '0' that's at the beginning of 10-digit phone numbers.

To place a direct call, dial ☎ 00 and then the country code, area code and local number. Peak rates are about €0.25 per minute to North America and €0.65 per minute to Asia.

To make a reverse-charge (collect) call *(en PCV)* or person-to-person *(avec préavis)* from France to other countries, call ☎ 3123 or

☎ 0800 990 011 (for the USA and Canada) and ☎ 0800 990 061 for Australia. It's about US$10 for a three-minute call.

For directory inquiries outside France, dial ☎ 3212. It costs about €2.25. For information on home-country direct calls, see Appendix – Telephones at the back of this book.

**Telephone Cards** Lonely Planet's ekno Communication Card is aimed specifically at independent travellers and provides budget international calls, a range of messaging services, free email and travel information – for local calls, you're usually better off with a télécarte (see Public Telephones earlier). You can join online at **w** www.ekno.lonely planet.com, or by phone from France by dialling ☎ 08 00 90 08 50. To use ekno in France, dial ☎ 08 00 90 91 18.

**Minitel** This is a computerised information service peculiar to France. Though useful, it can be expensive to use and the Internet has more or less overtaken it. Minitel numbers consist of four digits (eg, 3611, 3614, 3615) and a string of letters. Most of the terminals in post offices are free for directory inquiries.

## Fax

Virtually all French post offices can send and receive domestic and international faxes *(télécopies* or *téléfaxes)*. It costs around €1.20/4.60 to send a one-page fax within France/to the USA.

## Email & Internet Access

Email can be sent and received at Internet cafés throughout France. La Poste has Internet centres at many post offices around France; a €7 Cybercarte gives you an hour's access, and each €4.50 'recharge' is good for another hour. Commercial Internet cafés charge about €3 for 30 minutes of surfing.

## DIGITAL RESOURCES

Useful websites in English include the **Paris Tourist Office** (**w** *www.paris-touristoffice .com*), the USA's **French Government Tourist Office** (**w** *www.francetourism.com*) and **GuideWeb** (**w** *www.guideweb.com*), which has information about selected regions in France. Many towns have their own websites. Gay and lesbian travellers should check the **Queer Resources Directory** (**w** *www .france.qrd.org*).

# BOOKS
## Lonely Planet
Lonely Planet's *France* guide has comprehensive coverage of France and includes chapters on Andorra and Monaco. *Paris Condensed* is a pocket companion with short visits in mind. Regional guides include *Provence & the Côte D'Azur, Normandy, Brittany, The Loire, Southwest France* and *Corsica*. The *French phrasebook* is a complete guide to *la langue française*.

## Guidebooks
Michelin's hardcover *Guide Rouge* (red guide) lists mid-range and top-end hotels and rates France's greatest restaurants with the famous stars. Michelin's *guides verts* (green guides) cover all of France in 24 regional volumes (12 in English).

The best general French-language guides are by *Guide Bleu*. Its blue-jacketed all-France and regional guides provide accurate, balanced information on history, culture and architecture.

## Travel
Paul Rambali's *French Blues* is a series of uncompromising yet sympathetic snapshots of modern France. *A Year in Provence* by Peter Mayle is an irresistible account of country life in southern France. *A Moveable Feast* by Ernest Hemingway portrays Bohemian life in 1920s Paris. Henry Miller also wrote some pretty dramatic stuff set in the French capital of the 1930s, including *Tropic of Cancer*. Gertrude Stein's *The Autobiography of Alice B Toklas* is an entertaining account of Paris' literary and artistic circles from WWI to the mid-1930s.

## History & Politics
There are many excellent histories of France in English. Among the best is Fernand Braudel's two-volume *The Identity of France*. *France Today* by John Ardagh provides excellent insights into the way French society has evolved since WWII. Both are out of print but available in second-hand stores. *The Days of the French Revolution* by Christopher Hibbert is a highly readable account.

## NEWSPAPERS & MAGAZINES
The *International Herald Tribune* is sold at many news kiosks throughout France for €1.85. Other English-language papers you can find include the *Guardian* and *USA Today*. *Newsweek* and *Time* are also widely available.

## RADIO & TV
The BBC World Service can be picked up on 195kHz AM and 6195kHz, 9410kHz, 9760kHz and 12095kHz short wave. In northern France, BBC for Europe is on 648kHz AM. Top-end hotels often offer cable TV access to CNN, BBC Prime, Sky and other networks. Canal+ (pronounced ka-**nahl**-pluce), a French subscription TV station available in many mid-range hotels, sometimes shows undubbed English movies.

## PHOTOGRAPHY & VIDEO
Be prepared to have your camera and film forced through the ostensibly film-safe x-ray machines at airports and when entering sensitive public buildings. Ask to have your film hand-checked, if not your entire camera. Film is widely available, and costs about €5.50/7 for a 36-exposure roll of 100ASA print/slide film, excluding processing.

French videotapes use the Secam system and cannot be played on many American, British or Australian video cassette recorders.

## TIME
France is GMT/UTC plus one hour. Clocks are turned one hour ahead on the last Sunday in March and then back again on the last Sunday in September.

## LAUNDRY
Self-service *laveries libre service* (laundrettes) generally charge €3.35 to €5 a load and around €0.30 for five minutes of drying. Bring lots of coins; few laundrettes have change machines.

## TOILETS
Public toilets are scarce, though small towns often have one near the *mairie* (town hall). In Paris, you're more likely to come upon one of the tan, self-disinfecting toilet pods. Many public toilets cost €0.30 or even €0.50. Except in the most tourist-filled areas, café owners usually allow you to use their toilets provided you ask politely.

## WOMEN TRAVELLERS
In general, women need not walk around in fear, although the French seem to have given little thought to sexual harassment – many

men tend to stare hard at passing women, for instance. If you're subject to catcalls or hassled on the street, the best strategy is usually to walk on and ignore the comment. Making a cutting retort is ineffective in English and risky in French if your slang isn't proficient.

France's national rape crisis hotline, run by women's organisation **Viols Femmes Informations** *(☎ 0800 05 95 95; staffed 10am-7pm Mon-Fri)*, can be reached toll free.

## GAY & LESBIAN TRAVELLERS

**Centre Gai et Lesbien** *(CGL; ☎ 01 43 57 21 47; 3 rue Keller, 11e; metro Ledru Rollin; open 4pm-8pm daily)*, 500m east of place de la Bastille, is headquarters for numerous organisations. It has a bar, and library among its facilities. Paris' Gay Pride parade is held on the last weekend in June. Gay publications include the monthlies *3 Keller*, *Action* and the newsstand magazine *Têtu*. The monthly *Lesbia* gives a rundown of what's happening around the country.

## DISABLED TRAVELLERS

France isn't well-equipped for *handicapés* – kerb ramps are few and far between, older public facilities and budget hotels often lack lifts, and the Paris metro is hopeless. Details of train travel for wheelchair users are available in SNCF's booklet *Guide du Voyageur à Mobilité Réduite*. You can also contact the French rail company **SNCF Accessibilité** *(☎ 0800 15 47 53)*.

Hostels in Paris that cater to disabled travellers include Foyer International d'Accueil de Paris Jean Monnet and Centre International de Séjour de Paris Kellermann (see Hostels in the Paris Places to Stay section later).

## SENIOR TRAVELLERS

Senior travellers are generally treated with a great deal of respect in France and are entitled to discounts on public transport, museum admission fees and so on, provided they show proof of age. If you're doing a lot of travel, the SNCF's Carte Senior, entitling the holder to further reductions on train travel, may be a good deal.

## DANGERS & ANNOYANCES

The biggest crime problem for tourists in France is theft – especially of and from cars. Pickpockets are a problem, and women are a common target because of their handbags.

## Emergency Services

Nationwide emergency numbers are police ☎ 17, ambulance ☎ 15 and fire ☎ 18.

You should be especially careful at airports and on crowded public transport in cities.

France's laws regarding even small quantities of drugs are very strict, and the police have the right to search anyone at any time.

The rise in support for the extreme right-wing Front National in recent years reflects growing racial intolerance in France. Especially in the south, entertainment places such as bars and discos are, for all intents and purposes, segregated.

## BUSINESS HOURS

Most museums are closed on either Monday or Tuesday and on public holidays, though in summer some open daily. Most small businesses open 9am or 10am to 6.30pm or 7pm daily except Sunday and perhaps Monday, with a break between noon and 2pm or between 1pm and 3pm. In the south, middle-of-the-day closures are more like siestas and may continue until 3.30pm or 4pm.

Many food shops open daily except Sunday afternoon and Monday. Most restaurants open only for lunch (noon to 2pm or 3pm) and dinner (6.30pm to about 10pm or 11pm); outside Paris, very few serve meals throughout the day. In August, lots of establishments simply close down for the annual month-long holiday.

Banks open Monday to Friday but may only change money and travellers cheques in the morning (usually 8.45am to 12.15pm).

## PUBLIC HOLIDAYS & SPECIAL EVENTS

National *jours fériés* (public holidays) in France include New Year's Day, Easter Sunday and Monday, 1 May (May Day), 8 May (1945 Victory Day), Ascension Thursday, Pentecost/Whit Sunday and Whit Monday, 14 July (Bastille Day), 15 August (Assumption Day), 1 November (All Saints' Day), 11 November (1918 Armistice Day) and also Christmas Day.

Some of the biggest and best events in France include: the Festival d'Avignon (early July to early August), with some 300 daily music, dance and drama events; Bastille Day celebrations, on 13 and 14 July; the Carnaval de Nice, held in Nice every spring around Mardi Gras (Shrove Tuesday); and the Nice Jazz Festival in July.

## ACTIVITIES

There are low-altitude ski stations in the Pyrenees for those who love **skiing** in Europe; w www.skifrance.fr provides information in English about ski resorts, services, conditions and more.

France has thousands of kilometres of **hiking** trails in every region of the country. These include *sentiers de grande randonnée*, long-distance hiking paths with alphanumeric names that begin with the letters GR and are sometimes hundreds of kilometres long (as in Corsica). These paths are run by an organisation called **Fédération Française de Randonnée Pédestre** (FFRP; ☎ 01 44 89 93 93, fax 01 40 35 85 67; e info@ffrp .asso.fr), which also publishes guides to these routes.

The **Fédération Française de Canoë-Kayak** (☎ 01 45 11 08 50; e ffck@ffcanoe .asso.fr; 87 quai de la Marne, 94344 Joinville-le-Pont) can supply information on **canoeing** and **kayaking** clubs around the country.

The French take their **cycling** very seriously, and parts of the country almost grind to a halt during the annual Tour de France. Lonely Planet's *Cycling in France* is an essential resource when touring. *France by Bike: 14 Tours Geared for Discovery* by Karen and Terry Whitehall is a worthy rival. Details on places that rent bikes appear at the end of individual city or town listings under Getting Around.

## COURSES

For details see Language Courses in the Paris section later. Information on studying in France is available from French consulates and French Government Tourist Offices abroad. In Paris, you might also get in touch with the Ministry of Tourism-sponsored **International Cultural Organisation** (ICO; ☎ 01 42 36 47 18, fax 01 40 26 34 45; 55 rue de Rivoli, 1er, BP 2701, 75027 Paris CEDEX; metro Châtelet).

## WORK

All EU citizens are allowed to work in France. For anyone else it's almost impossible, although the government tolerates undocumented workers helping out with basic agricultural work.

Working as an au pair is very common in France, especially in Paris. Single young people – particularly women – receive board, lodging and a bit of money in exchange for taking care of the kids. Knowing some French may be a prerequisite. For au pair placements contact a French consulate or private agencies such as **Agence Nurse Au Pair Placement** (NAPP; ☎ 01 45 00 33 88, fax 01 45 00 33 99; w www.napp.fr; 16 rue Le Sueur, Paris 75016).

## ACCOMMODATION
### Camping

France has thousands of seasonal and year-round camping grounds. Facilities and amenities, reflected in the number of stars the site has been awarded, determine the price. At the less fancy places, two people with a small tent pay €10 to €15 a night. Campers without a vehicle can usually get a spot, even late in the day, but not in July and August, when most are packed with families.

### Refuges & Gîtes d'Étape

*Refuges* (huts or shelters) are basic dorms operated by national park authorities, the Club Alpin Français and other private organisations. They are marked on hiking and climbing maps. Some open year-round.

In general, *refuges* have mattresses and blankets but not sheets. Charges average €10 to €16 per night (more in popular areas), and meals are sometimes available. It's a good idea to call ahead and make a reservation.

*Gîtes d'étape*, which are usually better equipped and more comfortable than *refuges*, are found in less-remote areas, often villages. They cost around €9 to €11 per person.

### Chambre d'Hôtes

A chambre d'hôte, basically a B&B, is a room in a private house rented to travellers by the night. Breakfast is included.

### Hostels

In the provinces, *Auberges de Jeunesse* (hostels) generally charge €9 to €12 for a bunk in a single-sex dorm. In Paris and the Côte d'Azur, expect to pay €15 to €20 a night, including breakfast. In the cities, especially Paris, you'll also find *foyers*, student dorms used by travellers in summer. Most of

France's hostels belong to one of three Paris-based organisations:

**Fédération Unie des Auberges de Jeunesse** (FUAJ; ☎ 01 44 89 87 27, fax 01 44 89 87 10, W www.fuaj.org) 27 rue Pajol, 18e, 75018 Paris (metro La Chapelle)

**Ligue Française pour les Auberges de la Jeunesse** (LFAJ; ☎ 01 44 16 78 78, fax 01 44 16 78 80) 67 rue Vergniaud, 75013 Paris (metro Glacière)

**Union des Centres de Rencontres Internationales de France** (UCRIF; ☎ 01 40 26 57 64, fax 01 40 26 58 20, W www.ucrif.asso.fr) 27 rue de Turbigo, 2e, 75002 Paris (metro Étienne Marcel)

Only FUAJ is affiliated with the Hostelling International (HI) organisation.

## Hotels

For two people sharing a room, budget hotels are often cheaper than hostels. Doubles tend to cost only marginally more than singles; most have only one bed *(un grand lit)*. Doubles with two beds usually cost a little more. A hall *douche* (shower) can be free or cost between €2 and €3. If you'll be arriving after noon (after 10am at peak times), it's wise to book ahead, though if you phone on the day of your arrival, many will hold a room for you until a set hour. Local tourist offices also make reservations, usually for a small fee. Check whether your hotel is part of the Bon Weekend en Ville scheme whereby one night's stay at the weekend gives you a second night free.

The prices listed in this chapter are high season prices (usually June to August, except in ski areas); discounts of 30% to 50% are possible at other times of year.

## FOOD

A fully-fledged traditional French dinner – usually begun about 8.30pm – has quite a few distinct courses: an apéritif or cocktail; an *entrée* (first course); the *plat principal* (main course); *salade* (salad); *fromage* (cheese); *dessert*; *fruit* (fruit; pronounced fwee); *café* (coffee); and a *digestif* liqueur.

Restaurants usually specialise in a particular cuisine while brasseries – which look very much like cafés – serve quicker meals of more standard fare (eg, steak and chips/ french fries or omelettes). Restaurants tend to open only for lunch (noon to 2pm or 3pm)

and dinner (about 6.30pm to about 10pm or 11pm); brasseries serve meals throughout the day.

Most restaurants offer at least one fixed-price multicourse meal known in French as a *menu*. In general, *menus* cost much less than ordering each dish *à la carte* (separately). Many restaurants close on Sunday (some on Monday too) and it can be genuinely hard to find a place to eat on a Sunday in a provincial French town.

Sitting in a café to read, write or talk with friends is an integral part of everyday life in France. A café located on a grand boulevard will charge considerably more than a place that fronts a side street. Once inside, progressively more expensive tariffs apply at the *comptoir* (counter), in the café itself *(salle)* and outside on the *terrasse*. The price of drinks goes up at night, usually after 8pm.

## DRINKS
## Nonalcoholic Drinks

Tap water in France is perfectly safe. Make sure you ask for *une carafe d'eau* (a jug of water) or *de l'eau du robinet* (tap water) or you may get costly *eau de source* (mineral water). A small cup of espresso is called *un café*, *un café noir* or *un express*; you can also ask for a *grand* (large) one. *Un café crème* is espresso with steamed cream. *Un café au lait* is espresso served in a large cup with lots of steamed milk. Decaffeinated coffee is *un café décaféiné* or simply *un déca*.

Other popular hot drinks include *thé* (tea) – if you want milk you ask for *'un peu de lait frais'*; *tisane* (herbal tea); and *chocolat chaud* (hot chocolate).

## Alcoholic Drinks

The French almost always take their meals with wine – *rouge* (red), *blanc* (white) or *rosé*. The least-expensive wines cost less per litre than soft drinks. The cheapest wines are known as *vins ordinaires* or *vins de table* (table wines).

Alcoholic drinks other than wine include apéritifs, such as *kir* (dry white wine sweetened with *cassis* – blackcurrant liqueur), *kir royale* (champagne with cassis), and *pastis* (anise-flavoured alcohol drunk with ice and water); and *digestifs* such as brandy or Calvados (apple brandy). A *demi* of beer (about 250ml) is cheaper *à la pression* (on draught) than from a bottle.

# Getting There & Away

## AIR

Air France and scores of other airlines link Paris with every part of the globe. Other French cities with international air links (mainly to places within Europe) include Marseille, Nice and Toulouse. For information on Paris' two international airports, Orly and Roissy-Charles de Gaulle, see Getting There & Away in the Paris section later in this chapter.

The Internet is the best place to find cheap seats on discount airlines – flights between London and Paris are sometimes available for as little as €25 return. Regular tickets with the larger companies for the same trip are more like €120. One-way discount fares to Paris start at €110 from Rome, €160 from Athens, €140 from Dublin, 220 million Turkish lira from İstanbul, and €110 from Madrid. Student travel agencies can supply more details.

In France, inexpensive flights offered by discount airlines and charter clearing houses can be booked through many regular travel agencies – look in agency windows and pamphlets advertising **Go Voyages** (☎ 01 53 40 44 29; ⓦ www.govoyages.com) or **Look Voyages** (☎ 01 55 49 49 60, 0825 82 38 23; ⓦ www.look-voyages.fr). Reliable travel agency chains include the French student travel company **OTU** (☎ 0820 81 78 17; ⓦ www.otu.fr) and **Nouvelles Frontières** (☎ 0825 00 08 25; ⓦ www.nouvelles -frontieres.fr).

## LAND
### Britain

The highly civilised **Eurostar** (UK: ☎ 08705-186 186 • France: ☎ 0892 35 35 39; ⓦ www .eurostar.com) links London's Waterloo Station with Paris' Gare du Nord via the Channel Tunnel, which passes through a layer of impermeable chalk marl 25m to 45m below the floor of the English Channel. The journey takes about three hours (including 20 minutes in the tunnel), not including the one-hour time change. Tickets for people aged 25 and under cost UK£40/69 one way/return; return fares booked 14/seven days ahead cost UK£79/95.

Discount return fares start at around UK£60. Student travel agencies often have youth fares that are not available direct from Eurostar.

**Eurotunnel shuttle trains** (UK: ☎ 08705 35 35 35; • France: ☎ 03 21 00 61 00; ⓦ www.eurotunnel.com) whisk buses and cars (and their passengers) from near Folkstone to Coquelles (just west of Calais) in 35 minutes. The regular one-way fare for a car and its passengers ranges from UK£147.50 (February and March) to UK£162.50 (July and August). For promotional fares you must book at least one day ahead.

### Elsewhere in Europe

**Bus** For details on Eurolines coach services (France: ☎ 0836 69 52 52; ⓦ www.euro lines.fr) linking France with other European countries, see Getting There & Away in the Paris section.

**Train** Paris, France's main rail hub, is linked with every part of Europe. Depending on where you're coming from, you sometimes have to change train stations in Paris to reach the provinces. For details on Paris' six train stations, see Getting There & Away in the Paris section later.

People aged 25 or under are eligible for at least 20% discounts on most international 2nd-class rail travel; on some routes discounts are limited to night trains. On the super-fast *Thalys* trains that link Paris with Brussels, Amsterdam and Cologne, seniors also get significant discounts.

## SEA

Ferry tickets are available from almost all travel agencies.

### Britain & the Channel Islands

**Hoverspeed** (UK: ☎ 0870 240 8070 • France: ☎ 0800 1211 1211; ⓦ www.hoverspeed.co .uk) runs giant catamarans (SeaCats) from Folkestone to Boulogne (55 minutes, 17 daily). Foot passengers are charged UK£24 one way (or return if you come back within five days). Depending on the season, a car with up to five passengers is charged UK£115 to UK£189 one way.

The Dover-Calais crossing is also handled by car ferries (one to 1½ hours, 15 daily) run by **SeaFrance** (UK: ☎ 0870-571 1711 • France: ☎ 0803 04 40 45; ⓦ www.seafrance

*.com)* and **P&O Stena** *(UK: ☎ 0870-600 0611 ● France: ☎ 0802 01 00 20; ☧ www .posl.com)*. Pedestrians pay UK£17/26 with SeaFrance/P&O Stena; cars are charged UK£130 to UK£170 one way.

If you're travelling to Normandy, the Newhaven-Dieppe route is handled by Hoverspeed's SeaCats (2¼ hours, one to three daily). Poole is linked to Cherbourg by **Brittany Ferries** *(UK: ☎ 0870-536 0360 ● France: ☎ 0825 82 88 28; ☧ www.brittany -ferries.com)*, which has one or two 4¼-hour crossings daily; the company also has ferries from Portsmouth to Caen (Ouistreham). On the Portsmouth-Cherbourg route, **P&O Portsmouth** *(UK: ☎ 0870-598 0555 ● France: ☎ 0803 01 30 13; ☧ www.poportsmouth .com)* has two car ferries daily and, from mid-March to mid-October (UK£117 with car), two faster catamarans daily; the company also links Portsmouth with Le Havre.

### Ireland
**Irish Ferries** *(Ireland: ☎ 1890 31 31 31 ● Cherbourg, France: ☎ 02 33 23 44 44; ☧ www .irishferries.com)* has overnight runs from Rosslare to either Cherbourg (19½ hours) or Roscoff (17 hours) between six and 13 times a month. Pedestrians pay €60 to €120 (€48 to €96 for students and seniors). Eurailpass holders are charged at 50% of the adult pedestrian fare.

### Italy
For information on ferry services between Corsica and Italy, see Getting There & Away in the Corsica section.

### North Africa
France's **SNCM** *(☎ 0836 67 21 00; ☧ www .sncm.fr)* and the **Compagnie Tunisienne de Navigation** *(CTN; Tunis: ☎ 01-341 777 ● Marseille: ☎ 04 91 91 55 71)* link Marseille with Tunis (about 24 hours, three or four a week). The standard adult fare is TD196/356 one way/return.

Sète, 29km southwest of Montpellier, is linked with the Moroccan port of Tangier (Tanger; 36 hours, five to seven a month) by the **Compagnie Marocaine de Navigation** *(Marseille: ☎ 04 91 56 40 88 ● Tangier: ☎ 09-94 40 57; ☧ www.comanav.co.ma)*. The cheapest one-way berth costs Dh1940. Discounts are available if you're aged under 26 or in a group of four or more.

# Getting Around

## AIR
France's long-protected domestic airline industry has been opened up to competition, though Air France still handles the majority of domestic flights.

Full-fare flying within France is extremely expensive, but very significant discounts are available to people aged 12 to 24, couples, families and seniors. Heavily discounted flights may be cheaper than long-distance rail travel. Details on France's complicated fare structures are available from travel agencies.

## BUS
Because the French train network is state-owned and the government prefers to operate a monopoly, the country has only a very limited intercity bus service. However, buses (some run by the SNCF, see Train following) are widely used for short-distance trips, especially in rural areas with relatively few train lines.

## TRAIN
Eurail and Inter-Rail passes are valid in France.

France's excellent rail network, operated by the **Société Nationale des Chemins de Fer Français** *(SNCF; ☧ www.sncf.com)* reaches almost every part of the country. The most important train lines fan out from Paris like the spokes of a wheel. The SNCF's nationwide telephone number for inquiries and reservations (☎ 0836 35 35 39 in English) costs €0.34 per minute.

The pride and joy of the SNCF is the high-speed TGV ('teh-zheh-veh') network. The TGV Sud-Est and TGV Midi-Mediterranée link Paris' Gare de Lyon with the southeast, including Avignon, Marseille, Nice and Montpellier; the TGV Atlantique Sud-Ouest and TGV Atlantique Ouest link Paris' Gare Montparnasse with western and southwestern France, including Toulouse; and the TGV Nord links Paris' Gare du Nord with Arras, Lille and Calais.

Reservation fees are optional unless you're travelling by TGV or want a couchette or special reclining seat. On popular trains (eg, on holiday weekends) you may have to reserve ahead to get a seat. Eurail-pass holders must pay all applicable reservation fees.

Before boarding the train, you must validate your ticket (and your reservation card, if it's separate) by time-stamping it in one of the *composteurs*, the bright orange posts that are located somewhere between the ticket windows and the tracks. Eurail and some other rail passes *must* be validated at a train station ticket window to initiate the period of validity.

## Discounts

### Passes for Nonresidents of Europe

The France Railpass allows unlimited rail travel within France for to 10 days during the course of a month. In 2nd class, the three-day version costs US$210 (US$171 each for two people travelling together); each additional day of travel costs US$30. The France Youthpass, available if you're 25 and under, costs US$148 for four days of travel in a month; additional days (up to a maximum of six) cost US$18. **Rail Europe** *(USA: ☎ 877-456-RAIL;* ⓦ *www.raileurope.com)* has details.

**Passes for Residents of Europe** The Euro Domino France flexipass gives European residents who don't live in France three to eight days of midnight-to-midnight travel over a period of one month. The youth version (for people 25 and under) costs €84 for three days plus about €15 each additional day; the adult version costs €115 for three days plus about €20 each additional day.

**Other Discounts** Discounts of 25% on one-way or return travel within France are available at all train station ticket windows to: people aged 12 to 25 (the Découverte 12/25 fare); one to four adults travelling with a child aged four to 11 (the Découverte Enfant Plus fare); people over 60 (the Découverte Senior fare); and – for return travel only – any two people who are travelling together (the Découverte À Deux fare).

No matter what age you are, the Découverte Séjour excursion fare gives you a 25% reduction for return travel within France if you meet two conditions: the total length of your trip is at least 200km; and you'll be spending a Saturday night at your destination.

The Découverte J30, which must be purchased 30 to 60 days before the date of travel, offers savings of 45% to 55%. The Découverte J8, which you must buy at least eight days ahead, gets you 20% to 30% off.

## CAR & MOTORCYCLE

Travelling by car or motorcycle is expensive; petrol is costly and tolls add up quickly if you're going cross-country in a hurry. Three or four people travelling together, however, may find that renting a car is cheaper than taking the train. In the centres of almost all French cities, parking is metered.

Unless otherwise posted, speed limits are 130km/h (110km/h in the rain) on *autoroutes* (dual carriageways/divided highways with names beginning with A); 110km/h (100km/h in the rain) on *routes nationales* (highways with names beginning with N) that have a divider down the middle; and 90km/h (80km/h if it's raining) on nondivided routes nationales and rural highways. When you pass a sign with a place name, you have entered the boundaries of a town or village; the speed limit automatically drops to 50km/h until you pass an identical sign with a red bar across it.

The maximum permissible blood-alcohol level in France is 0.05%.

Petrol *sans plomb* (unleaded) costs around €1.10 a litre, give or take 10%. *Gasoil* or *gazole* (diesel) is about €0.75 to €1 a litre. Fuel is most expensive at the autoroute rest stops, and tends to be cheapest at the big supermarkets on the outskirts of towns.

If you don't live in the EU and need a car in France (or Europe) for 17 days (or a bit more) to six months, it's much cheaper to 'purchase' one from the manufacturer and then 'sell' it back than it is to rent one. The *achat-rachat* (purchase-repurchase) paperwork is not your responsibility. Both Renault's **Eurodrive** *(USA: ☎ 800-221 1052;* ⓦ *www.eurodrive.renault.com)* and Peugeot's **Vacation Plan/Sodexa** *(USA: ☎ 212-581 3040;* ⓦ *www.sodexa.com)* offer great deals that – incredibly – include insurance with no deductible (excess).

## HITCHING

Hitching in France can be difficult, and getting out of big cities such as Paris and Marseille or travelling around the Côte d'Azur by thumb is well nigh impossible. Remote rural areas are your best bet, but few cars are likely to be going further than the next large town. Women should not hitch alone.

It's an excellent idea to hold up a sign with your destination followed by the letters *s.v.p.* (for *s'il vous plaît* – 'please'). Some people have reported good luck hitching with truck

FRANCE

drivers from truck stops. It's illegal to hitch on autoroutes, but you can stand near the entrance ramps.

FUAJ, the French youth hostel association, has a car-pooling registry that matches drivers and passengers for car journeys within Europe. Check it out at ⓦ www.fuaj.org

# Paris

**pop 2.2 million, metropolitan area 10.6 million**
Paris has almost exhausted the superlatives that can reasonably be applied to a city. Notre Dame and the Eiffel Tower – at sunrise, at sunset, at night – have been described ad nauseam, as have the Seine and the subtle (and not-so-subtle) differences between the Left and Right banks. But what writers rarely capture is the grandness and the magic of strolling along the city's broad, 19th-century avenues leading from impressive public buildings and exceptional museums to parks, gardens and esplanades. Paris is enchanting at any time, in every season.

## ORIENTATION
In central Paris (which the French call Intra-Muros – 'within the walls'), the Rive Droite (Right Bank) is north of the Seine, while the Rive Gauche (Left Bank) is south of the river. For administrative purposes, Paris is divided into 20 *arrondissements* (districts) that spiral out from the centre. Paris addresses always include the arrondissement number, listed here after the street address, using the usual French notation, ie, 1er stands for *premier* (1st), 19e for *dix-neuvième* (19th) etc. When an address includes the full five-digit postal code, the last two digits indicate the arrondissement, eg, 75014 for the 14e.

## Maps
Lonely Planet's *Paris City Map* includes central Paris, the Métro, Montmartre, a walking tour and an index of all streets and sights.

## INFORMATION
### Tourist Offices
Paris' **main tourist office** (☎ 0836 68 31 12, fax 01 49 52 53 00; ⓔ info@paris-tourist office.com; 127 ave des Champs-Élysées, 8e; metro Georges V; open 9am-8pm daily, 11am-7pm Sun winter • branches: Gare de Lyon; open 8am-8pm Mon-Sat • base of Eif-

*fel Tower; open 11am-6pm daily May-Sept)* is the best source of information on what's going on in the city. For a small fee (€3 for a one-star hotel), the office can find your accommodation in Paris for that night only.

## Money
All of Paris' six major train stations have exchange bureaus open seven days a week until at least 7pm. Exchange offices at both airports are open until 10.30pm.

**American Express** Paris' landmark AmEx office (☎ 01 47 77 77 75; metro Auber or Opéra) at 11 rue Scribe, 9e, faces the west side of Opéra Garnier. Exchange services are available 9.30am to 6.30pm (to 7pm June to September) Monday to Friday and 9am to 5.30pm Saturday and Sunday.

**Notre Dame (4e & 5e)** Société Française de Change (☎ 01 43 26 01 84, 21 rue Chanoinesse; metro Cité) has good rates and is open 8.30am to 7pm daily.

**Champs-Élysées (8e)** Thanks to fierce competition, the Champs-Élysées is an excellent place to change money. There's a bureau de change inside the tourist office at 127 ave des Champs-Élysées and a Thomas Cook branch next door.

**Grands Boulevards (9e)** FCO (☎ 01 47 70 02 59, 19 rue du Faubourg Montmartre; metro Grands Blvds) tends to have decent rates and is open 8.30am to 7pm daily.

## Post & Communications
Paris' **main post office** (☎ 01 40 28 76 00; 52 rue du Louvre, 1er; metro Sentier or Les Halles; open 24hr) has foreign exchange available during regular post office hours – 8am to 7pm Monday to Friday and to noon on Saturday.

## Email & Internet Access
The cheapest Internet cafés are **EasyInternet** (31-37 blvd de Sébastopol, 2e; metro Châtelet-Les Halles • 6 rue de la Harpe, 6e; metro St Michel • 15 rue de Rome, 8e; metro St-Lazare; all open 24hr daily) where you can get a 24-hour Internet access pass for €5. More pleasant, but more expensive is the cool **Web Bar** (☎ 01 42 72 66 55; 32 rue de Picardie, 3e; metro Temple or Républic; open 8.30am-2am daily), which charges €4 for one hour of Internet access.

Also try **Mike's Bike Tours** (24 rue Edgar Faure, 15e) with its English keyboards and a tourist-friendly atmosphere.

## Travel Agencies

**Nouvelles Frontières** *(☎ 0825 000 825; 66 blvd St Michel, 6e; metro Luxembourg; open 9am-7pm Mon-Sat)* has 15 outlets around the city. **Voyageurs du Monde** *(☎ 01 42 86 16 00; 55 rue Ste Anne, 2e; metro Pyramides or Quartre Septembre; open 9.30am-7pm Mon-Sat)* is a huge agency.

## Bookshops

The famous English language bookshop **Shakespeare & Company** *(☎ 01 43 26 96 50; 37 rue de la Bûcherie, 5e; metro St Michel)* is across the Seine from Notre Dame Cathedral.

**WH Smith** *(☎ 01 44 77 88 99; 248 rue de Rivoli; metro Concorde)* is the largest English-language bookshop in Paris. Mellow, Canadian-run **Abbey Bookshop** *(☎ 01 46 33 16 24; 29 rue de la Parcheminerie, 5e; metro Cluny-La Sorbonne)* has an eclectic selection of new and used fiction titles. **Les Mots à la Bouche** *(☎ 01 42 78 88 30; 6 rue Ste Croix de la Bretonnerie, 4e; metro Hôtel de Ville)* is Paris' premier gay bookshop.

## Cultural & Religious Centres

The **British Council** *(☎ 01 49 55 73 00; 9 rue de Constantine, 7e; metro Invalides)* has a library. The **American Church** *(☎ 01 40 62 05 00; 65 quai d'Orsay, 7e; metro Invalides)* is a place of worship and a community centre for English speakers; its announcement board is an excellent source of information regarding accommodation and employment.

## Laundry

The *laveries* (laundrettes) mentioned here open daily and are near many of the places to stay listed later. **Laverie Libre Service** *(7 rue Jean-Jacques Rousseau; metro Louvre Rivoli)* is near the BVJ hostel, or there's another **branch** *(25 rue des Rosiers; metro St Paul)* in the Marais. There's also another **branch** *(4 rue Burq, Montmartre; metro Blanche)*. There's another **laundrette** *(216 rue St Jacques; metro Luxembourg)* four blocks southwest of the Panthéon. **Lavomatique** *(63 rue Monge; metro Monge)* is another option. Near Gare de l'Est is the **Lav' Club** *(55 blvd de Magenta; metro Gare de l'Est)*.

## Lost Property

Paris' **Bureau des Objets Trouvés** *(Lost & Found Office; ☎ 01 55 76 20 20; 36 rue des Morillons, 15e; metro Convention; open 8.30am-5pm Mon, Wed & Fri, 8.30am-8pm Tues & Thur)* is the first place to contact. Since telephone inquiries are impossible, the only way to find out if a lost item has been located is to go there and fill in the forms. For items lost on the metro, call ☎ 01 40 30 52 00.

## Medical & Emergency Services

An easy *Assistance Publique* (public health service) to find is the **Hôtel Dieu hospital** *(☎ 01 42 34 82 34; 1 place du Parvis Notre Dame, 4e; metro Cité)* on the northern side of the square. A 24-hour *service des urgences* (emergency service) is provided.

## Dangers & Annoyances

For its size, Paris is a safe city but you should always use common sense; for instance, avoid the large Bois de Boulogne and Bois de Vincennes parks after nightfall. And some stations are best avoided late at night, especially if you are on your own. These include Châtelet and its seemingly endless tunnels, Château Rouge in Montmartre, Gare du Nord, Strasbourg–St Denis, Montparnasse-Bienvenüe and Réaumur-Sébastopol.

## THINGS TO SEE

The Carte Musées et Monuments museum pass gets you into some 60 museums and monuments without having to queue for a ticket. The card costs €15/30/45 for one/three/five consecutive days and is on sale at the museums and monuments, at some metro ticket windows, at the tourist office and FNAC outlets. Most museums offer discounts for 18 to 25 year olds, free admission to children and many are free on the first Sunday of each month.

### Left Bank

**Île de la Cité (1er & 4e)** Paris was founded sometime during the 3rd century BC when members of a tribe known as the Parisii set up a few huts on Île de la Cité. By the Middle Ages the city had grown to encompass both banks of the Seine, though Île de la Cité remained the centre of royal and ecclesiastical power.

**Notre Dame (4e)** Paris' cathedral *(☎ 01 42 34 56 10; metro Cité or St Michel; admission free; open 8am-6.45pm daily)* is one of the most magnificent achievements of Gothic architecture. Begun in 1163 and completed around 1345, features include the three

# PARIS

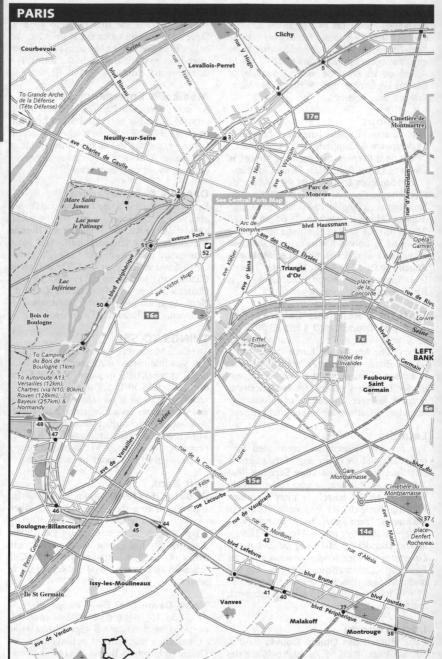

Courbevoie

Clichy

6

rue V Hugo

Levallois-Perret

rue A France

5

blvd Bineau

4

Seine

17e

Cimetière de
Montmartre

To Grande Arche
de la Défense
(Tête Défense)

Neuilly-sur-Seine

3

ave de Wagram

ave Niel

Parc de
Monceau

rue d'Amsterdam

ave Charles de Gaulle

2

See Central Paris Map

Mare Saint
James

1

Arc de
Triomphe

blvd Haussmann

Opéra-
Garnier

Lac pour
le Patinage

5

avenue Foch

ave des Champs Élysées

8e

52

ave Kléber

Triangle
d'Or

place
de la
Concorde

rue de Rivo

Lac
Inférieur

ave Victor Hugo

ave d'Iéna

ave d'léna

Louvre

16e

50

Seine

blvd Périphérique

Bois de
Boulogne

Eiffel
Tower

7e

blvd Saint

LEFT
BANK

49

Germain

To Camping
du Bois de
Boulogne (1km)

Hôtel des
Invalides

Faubourg
Saint
Germain

To Autoroute A13,
Versailles (12km),
Chartres (via N10, 80km),
Rouen (128km),
Bayeux (257km) &
Normandy

6e

48

Seine

47

ave de Versailles

rue de la Convention

Faure

15e

Gare
Montparnasse

blvd du

46

ave Félix

Cimetière du
Montparnasse

Boulogne-Billancourt

45

44

rue Lecourbe

rue de Vaugirard

14e

ave du Maine

37

place
Denfert
Rochereau

ave Pierre Grenier

rue des Morillons

42

Issy-les-Moulineaux

blvd Lefebvre

rue d'Alésia

Île St Germain

43

blvd Brune

blvd Jourdan

41  40

Vanves

39

blvd Périphérique

blvd

38

ave de Verdun

Malakoff

Montrouge

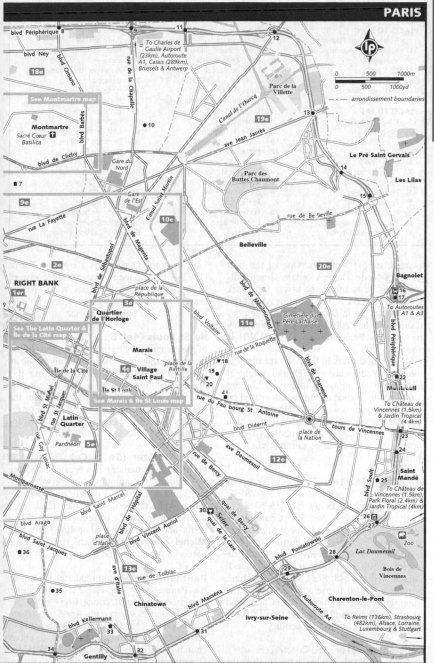

## PARIS

| PLACES TO STAY | | 10 | Fédération Unie des | | 31 | Porte d'Ivry |
|---|---|---|---|---|---|---|
| 7 | Hôtel des Trois Poussins | | Auberges de Jeunesse | | 32 | Porte d'Italie |
| 21 | Auberge Internationale des | 11 | Porte d'Aubervilliers | | 34 | Porte de Gentilly |
| | Jeunes | 12 | Porte de la Villette | | 35 | Ligue Française pour les |
| 25 | CISP Ravel | 13 | Porte de Pantin | | | Auberges de la Jeunesse |
| 33 | CISP Kellermann | 14 | Porte du Pré St Gervais | | 37 | Catacombes |
| 36 | FIAP Jean Monnet | 15 | Porte des Lilas | | 38 | Porte d'Orléans |
| | | 16 | Gare Routière Internationale | | 39 | Porte de Châtillon |
| PLACES TO EAT | | | (International Bus | | 40 | Porte de Vanves |
| 18 | Ethnic Restaurants | | Terminal) | | 41 | Porte Brancion |
| 20 | Havanita Café | 17 | Porte de Bagnolet | | 42 | Lost Property Office |
| | | 19 | Centre Gai et Lesbien | | 43 | Porte de la Plaine |
| OTHER | | 22 | Porte de Montreuil | | 44 | Porte de Sèvres |
| 1 | Paris Cycles | 23 | Porte de Vincennes | | 45 | Paris Heliport |
| 2 | Porte Maillot | 24 | Porte de St Mandé | | 46 | Porte de St Cloud |
| 3 | Porte de Champerret | 26 | Musée des Arts d'Afrique et | | 47 | Porte Molitor |
| 4 | Porte d'Asnières | | d'Océanie | | 48 | Porte d'Auteuil |
| 5 | Porte de Clichy | 27 | Porte Dorée | | 49 | Porte de Passy |
| 6 | Porte de Saint Ouen | 28 | Porte de Charenton | | 50 | Porte de la Muette |
| 8 | Porte de Clignancourt | 29 | Porte de Bercy | | 51 | Porte Dauphine |
| 9 | Porte de la Chapelle | 30 | Batofar | | 52 | New Zealand Embassy |

spectacular rose windows. One of the best views of Notre Dame's ornate flying buttresses can be had from the lovely little park behind the cathedral. The haunting **Mémorial des Martyrs de la Déportation**, in memory of the more than 200,000 people deported by the Nazis and French fascists during WWII, is close by.

Free **guided tours** in English take place at noon on Wednesday and Thursday and at 2.30pm on Saturday. Concerts held here don't keep to a schedule but are advertised on posters around town. The **North Tower** (adult/concession €5.50/3.50), from which you can view many of the cathedral's fierce-looking gargoyles, can be climbed via long, spiral steps.

**Ste Chapelle (1er)** The gem-like upper chapel of Ste Chapelle (☎ 01 53 73 78 50; metro Cité; adult/concession €5.50/3.50, combination ticket for Ste Chapelle & Conciergerie €8/5; open 9.30am-6pm daily), illuminated by a veritable curtain of 13th-century stained glass, is inside the **Palais de Justice** (Law Courts; 4 blvd du Palais, 1er). Consecrated in 1248, Ste Chapelle was built in three years to house a crown of thorns (supposedly worn by the crucified Christ) and other relics purchased by King Louis IX (later St Louis) earlier in the 13th century.

**Conciergerie (1er)** The Conciergerie was a luxurious royal palace when it was built in the

14th century. During the Reign of Terror (1793–94), it was used to incarcerate 'enemies' of the Revolution before they were brought before the tribunal, which met next door in what is now the Palais de Justice.

**Île St Louis (4e)** The 17th-century houses of grey stone and the small-town shops lining the streets and quays of Île St Louis create an almost provincial atmosphere, making it a great place for a quiet stroll. On foot, the shortest route between Notre Dame and the Marais passes through Île St Louis. For reputedly the best ice cream in Paris, head for **Berthillon** (31 rue St Louis en l'Île).

**Latin Quarter (5e & 6e)** This area is known as the Quartier Latin because, until the Revolution, all communication between students and their professors here took place in Latin. While the 5e has become increasingly touristy, there's still a large population of students and academics. Shop-lined **Blvd St Michel**, known as 'Boul Mich', runs along the border of the 5e and the 6e.

**Panthéon (5e)** A Latin Quarter landmark, the Panthéon (☎ 01 44 32 18 00; metro Luxembourg; adult/concession €7/4.50; open 9.30am-5.45pm daily Apr-Sept, 10am-5.15pm daily Oct-Mar), at the eastern end of rue Soufflot, was commissioned as an abbey church in the mid-18th century. In 1791, the Constituent Assembly converted it into a mausoleum for the 'great men of the era of French liberty'. Permanent residents include Victor Hugo, Voltaire and Jean-Jacques Rousseau.

**Sorbonne (5e)** Founded in 1253 as a college for 16 poor theology students, the Sorbonne was closed in 1792 by the Revolutionary government but reopened under Napoleon. **Place de la Sorbonne** links blvd St Michel with **Église de la Sorbonne**, the university's domed 17th-century church.

**Jardin du Luxembourg (6e)** The gardens' main entrance is opposite 65 blvd St Michel. The **Palais du Luxembourg**, fronting rue de Vaugirard at the northern end of the Jardin du Luxembourg, was built for Maria de' Medici, queen of France from 1600 to 1610. It now houses the Sénat, the upper house of the French parliament.

**Musée National du Moyen Age (5e)** The Museum of the Middle Ages (*☎ 01 53 73 78 16; metro Cluny-La Sorbonne; adult/ concession €5.50/4; open 9.15am-5.45pm Wed-Mon*), also known as the Musée de Cluny, houses one of France's finest collections of medieval art. Its prized possession is a series of six late-15th-century tapestries from the southern Netherlands known as *La Dame à la Licorne* (The Lady and the Unicorn).

**Mosquée de Paris (5e)** Paris' ornate central mosque (*☎ 01 45 35 97 33; place du Puits de l'Ermite; metro Monge; open 9am-noon & 2pm-6pm Sat-Thur*) was built between 1922 and 1926. The mosque complex includes a small souk (marketplace), a *salon de thé* (tearoom), an excellent couscous restaurant and a *hammam* (Turkish bath).

The mosque is opposite the **Jardin des Plantes** (Botanical Gardens), which includes a small **zoo** as well as the **Musée d'Histoire Naturelle** (*Museum of Natural History; ☎ 01 40 79 30 00; metro Monge; adult/concession €4.57/3.05; open 10am-5pm; Wed-Mon*).

**Catacombes (14e)** In 1785, the bones of millions of Parisians were exhumed from overflowing cemeteries and moved to three disused quarries. One such ossuary is the Catacombes (*☎ 01 43 22 47 63; metro Denfert Rochereau; adult/student or senior/child €5/ 3.30/2.59; open 11am-4pm Tues, 9am-4pm Wed-Sun*). During WWII, these tunnels were used by the Résistance as headquarters. The route through the Catacombes begins from the small green building at 1 place Denfert Rochereau. Take a flashlight (torch).

**Musée d'Orsay (7e)** This museum (*☎ 01 40 49 48 48; 1 rue de la Légion-d'Honneur; metro Musée d'Orsay; adult/concession €7/5, both €5 Sun; open 10am-6pm Tues-Wed & Fri-Sat, 10am-9.45pm Thur, 9am-6pm Sun, from 9am in summer*) exhibits works of art produced between 1848 and 1914, and is spectacularly housed in a 1900 train station. Tickets are valid all day.

**Musée Rodin (7e)** The Musée Rodin (*☎ 01 44 18 61 10; 77 rue Varenne; metro Varenne; adult/concession €5/3; open 9.30am-5.45pm daily Apr-Sept, 9.30am-4.45pm daily Oct-Mar*) is one of the most pleasant museums in Paris. Visiting just the garden (5pm close) costs €1.

**Invalides (7e)** The **Hôtel des Invalides** (*metro Invalides for Esplanade, metro Varenne or Latour Maubourg for main building*) was built in the 1670s by Louis XIV to provide housing for 4000 *invalides* (disabled veterans). It also served as the headquarters of the military governor of Paris, and was used as an armoury. On 14 July 1789 the Paris mob forced its way into the building and took all 28,000 firearms before heading for the Bastille prison.

The **Église du Dôme**, built between 1677 and 1735, is considered one of the finest religious edifices constructed under Louis XIV. In 1861 it received the remains of Napoleon, encased in six concentric coffins.

The buildings on either side of the **Cour d'Honneur** (Main Courtyard) house the **Musée de l'Armée** (*☎ 01 44 42 37 72; adult/concession €6/4.50; open 10am-5pm daily, 10am-6pm in summer*), a huge military museum that includes the light and airy **Tombeau de Napoléon 1er** (Napoleon's Tomb).

**Tour Eiffel (7e)** The Tour Eiffel (*☎ 01 44 11 23 23; metro Champ de Mars-Tour Eiffel; open 9.30am-11pm daily Sept–mid-June, 9am-midnight mid-June–Aug*) faced massive opposition from Paris' artistic and literary elite when it was built for the 1889 Exposition Universelle (World's Fair), which was

# CENTRAL PARIS

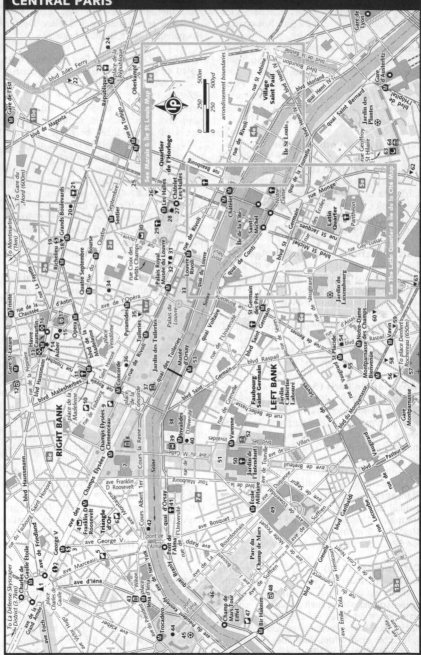

## CENTRAL PARIS

| PLACES TO STAY | 5 | Spanish Embassy | 36 | WH Smith Bookshop |
|---|---|---|---|---|
| 24 Auberge de Jeunesse Jules | 6 | Canadian Embassy | 37 | Musée de l'Orangerie |
| Ferry | 7 | Grand Palais | 38 | Palais Bourbon |
| 31 Centre International BVJ | 8 | Musée du Petit Palais | | (National Assembly Building) |
| Paris-Louvre & Laundrette | 9 | US Embassy | 39 | Aérogare des Invalides |
| | 10 | UK Embassy | | (Buses to Orly) |
| PLACES TO EAT | 11 | La Madeleine Church | 40 | British Council |
| 18 Chartier Restaurant | 12 | EasyInternet | 41 | American Church |
| 22 Chez Prune | 13 | Au Printemps | 42 | Bateaux Mouches |
| 26 Joe Allen | | (Department Store) | | (Boat Tours) |
| 32 Le Petit Mâchon | 14 | Eurostar & Ferry Offices | 43 | Musée Guimet |
| 35 Food Shops | 15 | American Express | 44 | Palais de Chaillot |
| 56 Le Flibustier | 16 | Galeries Lafayette | | (Musée de l'Homme) |
| 58 Mustang Café | | (Department Store) | 45 | Jardins du Trocadéro |
| 59 Le Caméléon Restaurant | 17 | Opéra Garnier | 46 | Eiffel Tower |
| 60 CROUS Restaurant | 19 | FCO Currency Exchange | 47 | Australian Embassy |
| Universitaire Assas | 20 | Accord Language School | 48 | Mike's Bike Tours Office |
| 61 CROUS Restaurant | 21 | De La Ville Café | 49 | École Militaire |
| Universitaire Bullier | 23 | Favela Chic | 50 | Église du Dôme |
| 62 Founti Agadir | 25 | Rue Saint Denis Sex District | 51 | Hôtel des Invalides |
| | 27 | Roue Libre | 52 | Musée Rodin |
| OTHER | 28 | Forum des Halles | 53 | Musée d'Orsay |
| 1 Arc de Triomphe | | (Shopping Mall & Park) | 54 | Alliance Française |
| 2 Main Tourist Office | 29 | Église Saint Eustache | 55 | FNAC Store & Ticket Outlet |
| 3 24hr Currency exchange | 30 | Main Post Office | 57 | Cimetière du Montparnasse |
| machine | 33 | Louvre Museum | 63 | Paris Mosque & Hammam |
| 4 Post Office | 34 | Voyageurs du Monde | 64 | Musée d'Histoire Naturelle |

held to commemorate the Revolution. It was almost torn down in 1909 but was spared for practical reasons – it proved an ideal platform for newfangled transmitting antennae. The Eiffel Tower is 320m high, including the television antenna at the very tip.

Three levels are open to the public. The lift (west and north pillars) costs €3.70 for the 1st platform (57m), €6.90 for the 2nd (115m) and €9.90 for the 3rd (276m). Children three to 12 pay €2.10/3.80/5.30 respectively; there are no other discounts. The escalator in the south pillar to the 1st and 2nd platforms costs €3.

### Champ de Mars (7e)
The Champ de Mars, a grassy park around the Eiffel Tower, was once a parade ground for the 18th-century **École Militaire** (France's military academy) at the southeastern end of the lawns.

## Right Bank
### Jardins du Trocadéro (16e)
The Trocadéro gardens *(metro Trocadéro)*, with its fountain and nearby sculpture park grandly illuminated at night, are across the pont d'Iéna from the Eiffel Tower. The colonnaded Palais de Chaillot, built in 1937, houses the anthropological and ethnographic **Musée de**

l'Homme *(Museum of Mankind; ☎ 01 44 05 72 72; adult/concession €4.57/3.05; open 9.45am-5.15pm Wed-Mon)*; and the **Musée de la Marine** *(Maritime Museum; ☎ 01 53 65 69 69; adult/concession €6.86/5.34; open 10am-5.50pm Wed-Mon)*, known for its beautiful model ships.

### Musée National des Art Asiatiques-Guimet (16e)
The Guimet Museum *(☎ 01 56 52 53 00; 6 place d'Iéna; metro Iéna; adult/concession €7/5; open 10am-6pm Wed-Mon)* displays antiquities and art from throughout Asia.

### Louvre (1er)
The Louvre Museum *(☎ 01 40 20 53 17, recorded message ☎ 01 40 20 51 51; metro Palais Royal-Musée du Louvre; permanent collection admission €7.50, after 3pm & Sun €5; open 9am-6pm Thur-Sun, 9am-9.45pm Mon & Wed)*, built around 1200 as a fortress and rebuilt in the mid-16th century as a royal palace, became a public museum in 1793. The collections have been assembled by French governments over the past five centuries and include works of art and artisanship from all over Europe as well as important collections of Assyrian, Egyptian, Etruscan, Greek, Coptic, Roman and Islamic

art. The Louvre's most famous work is undoubtedly Leonardo da Vinci's *Mona Lisa*.

Ticket sales end 45 minutes before closing time. Admission to temporary exhibits varies. Tickets are valid for the whole day, so you can leave and re-enter as you please. By advance purchasing your tickets at the *billeteries* (ticket office) at FNAC, or other department stores, for an extra €1.10, you can walk straight in without queuing.

For English-language guided tours (€6/ 4.50 per adult/concession; 11am, 2pm and 3.45pm most days) and audioguide tours (€5), go to the mezzanine level beneath the glass pyramid.

**Place Vendôme (1er)** The 44m-high column in the middle of place Vendôme consists of a stone core wrapped in bronze from 1250 cannons captured by Napoleon at the Battle of Austerlitz (1805). The shops around the square are among Paris' most fashionable and expensive.

**Musée de l'Orangerie (1er)** This museum (☎ 01 42 97 48 16; metro Concorde), usually home to important impressionist works including a series of Monet's spectacular *Nymphéas* (Water Lilies), is closed for renovations until the end of 2004.

**Place de la Concorde (8e)** This vast, cobbled square between the Jardin des Tuileries and the Champs-Élysées was laid out between 1755 and 1775. Louis XVI was guillotined here in 1793 – as were another 1343 people, including his wife Marie Antoinette, during the next two years. The 3300-year-old Egyptian **obelisk** in the middle of the square was given to France in 1829 by the ruler of Egypt, Mohammed Ali.

**La Madeleine (8e)** The church of St Mary Magdalene (metro Madeleine), built in the style of a Greek temple, was consecrated in 1842 after almost a century of design changes and construction delays.

**Champs-Élysées (8e)** The 2km-long ave des Champs-Élysées links the Arc de Triomphe with place de la Concorde. Once popular with the aristocracy as a stage on which to parade their wealth, it has, in recent decades, been partly taken over by fast-food restaurants and overpriced cafés. The nicest

bit is the park between place de la Concorde and Rond Point des Champs-Élysées.

**Musée du Petit Palais (8e)** The Petit Palais (☎ 01 42 65 12 73) is due to reopen in 2003 after refurbishment.

West of the Petit Palais, the **Grand Palais** (☎ 01 44 13 17 17; 3 ave du Général du Eisenhower; admission varies; open 10am-8pm Thur-Mon, 10am-8pm Wed), which was constructed for the 1900 World Fair, is now used for temporary exhibitions.

**Arc de Triomphe (8e)** Paris' second most famous landmark, the Arc de Triomphe (☎ 01 55 37 73 77; metro Charles de Gaulle-Étoile; viewing platform adult/concession €7/4.50; viewing platform open 10am-11pm daily Apr-Sept, 10am-10.30pm Oct-Mar) is 2.2km northwest of place de la Concorde in the middle of place Charles de Gaulle. Also called place de l'Étoile, this is the world's largest traffic roundabout and the meeting point of 12 avenues. Commissioned in 1806 by Napoleon to commemorate his imperial victories, it remained unfinished until the 1830s. An Unknown Soldier from WWI is buried under the arch, his fate and that of countless others like him commemorated by a memorial flame lit each evening at around 6.30pm.

The platform atop the arch is accessed by a lift going up, and by steps heading down. The only sane way to get to the arch's base is via the underground passageways.

The **Voie Triomphale** (Triumphal Way) stretches 4.5km from the Arc de Triomphe along ave de la Grande Armée to the skyscraper district of **La Défense**, known for its landmark, the **Grande Arche** (Grand Arch), a hollow cube (112m to a side).

**Centre Georges Pompidou (4e)** Thanks in part to its outstanding temporary exhibitions, Centre Pompidou (☎ 01 44 78 12 33; metro Rambuteau or Châtelet-Les Halles) – also known as Centre Beaubourg – is by far the most frequented sight in Paris. **Place Igor Stravinsky**, south of the centre, and the large square to the west attract all kinds of street artists.

The **Musée National d'Art Moderne** (National Museum of Modern Art; adult/ concession €5.50/3.50; open 11am-9pm Wed-Mon, 11am-11pm Thur) on the 4th floor displays France's brilliant collection of modern art, from 1905 to the present. The fee includes admission to Brancusi's studio, reconstructed at the north of the forecourt. The **Bibliothèque Publique d'Information**, a huge, nonlending library, is on the 2nd floor (enter from Rue du Renard).

**Les Halles (1er)** Paris' main wholesale food market, Les Halles, occupied this site from the 12th century until 1969, when it was moved out to the suburb of Rungis; a huge underground shopping mall (Forum des Halles) was built in its place. Just north of the grassy area on top of Les Halles is the mostly 16th-century **Église St Eustache**, noted for its wonderful pipe organ.

**Hôtel de Ville (4e)** Paris' magnificent city hall (☎ 01 42 76 50 49; place de l'Hôtel de Ville; metro Hôtel de Ville) was burned down during the Paris Commune of 1871 and rebuilt (1874–82) in the neo-Renaissance style.

**Marais Area (4e)** A *marais* (marsh) converted to agricultural use in the 13th century, this area was, during the 17th century – when the nobility erected luxurious but discreet mansions known as *hôtels particuliers* – the most fashionable part of the city. Eventually the marais was taken over by ordinary Parisians and by the time renovation began in the 1960s, it had become a poor but lively Jewish neighbourhood. In the 1980s the area underwent serious gentrification and today it is the centre of Paris' gay life.

**Place des Vosges (4e)** Built in 1605 and originally known as place Royal, place des Vosges (metro Chemin Vert) is a square ensemble of 36 symmetrical houses. Duels were once fought in the elegant park in the middle. Today, the arcades around place des Vosges are occupied by upmarket art galleries, antique shops and boutiques.

The nearby **Maison de Victor Hugo** (☎ 01 42 72 10 16; adult/concession €3.50/2.50; open Tues-Sun) is where the author lived from 1832 to 1848.

**Musée Picasso (3e)** The Picasso Museum (☎ 01 42 71 25 21; 5 rue de Thorigny; metro St Paul; adult/concession €5.50/4; open 9.30am-6pm, 9.30am-8pm Thur; closes 5.30pm Oct-Mar) is just northeast of the Marais. Paintings, sculptures, ceramics, engravings and drawings donated to the French government by the heirs of Pablo Picasso (1881–1973) to avoid huge inheritance taxes, are on display, as is Picasso's personal art collection (which includes Braque, Cézanne, Matisse, Rousseau etc).

**Bastille (4e, 11e & 12e)** The Bastille is the most famous nonexistent monument in Paris; the notorious prison was demolished shortly after the mob stormed it on 14 July 1789. The site is known as place de la Bastille. The 52m-high **Colonne de Juillet** in the centre was erected in 1830. There's also the new (and rather drab) **Opéra Bastille** (☎ 0836 69 78 68; place de la Bastille; metro Bastille).

**Opéra Garnier (9e)** Paris' renowned opera house (see Opera & Classical Music under Entertainment later) was designed in 1860 by Charles Garnier. The **ceiling** of the auditorium was painted by Marc Chagall in 1964. The building also houses the **Musée de l'Opéra** (adult/concession €6/4; open 10am-5pm daily).

**Montmartre (18e)** During the 19th century Montmartre was a vibrant centre of artistic and literary creativity. Today it's an area of mimes, buskers, tacky souvenir shops and commercial artists.

***Basilique du Sacré Cœur*** Sacré Cœur (☎ 01 53 41 89 00; metro Anvers; admission free; open 7am-11pm daily; admission to dome & crypt adult/student €4.50/2.50; dome & crypt open 10am-5.45pm daily) was built to fulfil a vow taken by Parisian Catholics after the disastrous Franco-Prussian War of 1870–71. The funicular up the hill's southern slope costs one metro/bus ticket each way.

***Place du Tertre*** Just west of **Église St Pierre**, place du Tertre is filled with cafés, restaurants, portrait artists and tourists – though the real attractions of the area are the quiet, twisting streets. Look for the **windmills** on rue Lepic and Paris' last **vineyard**, on the corner of rue des Saules and rue St Vincent.

**Pigalle (9e & 18e)** The area along blvd de Clichy between the Pigalle and Blanche metro stops is lined with sex shops, striptease parlours and bad nightclubs.

FRANCE

Musée de l'Érotisme (Museum of Eroticism; ☎ 01 42 58 28 73; 72 blvd de Clichy; metro Blanche; adult/student €7/5; open 10am-2am daily) tries to raise erotic art, both antique and modern, to a loftier plane – but we know why we visited. The **Moulin Rouge** (☎ 01 53 09 82 82; 82 blvd de Clichy; metro Blanche; tickets from €60), founded in 1889, is known for its thrice-nightly revues of near-naked women.

**Cimetière du Père Lachaise (20e)** Père Lachaise Cemetery (☎ 01 55 25 82 10; metro Père Lachaise; admission free; open to at least 5.30pm daily), final resting place of such notables as Chopin, Proust, Oscar Wilde and Édith Piaf, may be the most visited cemetery in the world. The best known tomb is that of 1960s rock star Jim Morrison, lead singer of The Doors, who died in 1971.

**Bois de Vincennes (12e)** Highlights of this 9.29-sq-km English-style park include the **Parc Floral** (Floral Garden; metro Château de Vincennes); the **Parc Zoologique de Paris** (Paris Zoo; ☎ 01 44 75 20 10; metro Porte Dorée); and the **Jardin Tropical** (Tropical Garden; RER stop Nugent-sur-Marne).

**Château de Vincennes (12e)** A bona fide royal chateau, the Château de Vincennes (☎ 01 48 08 31 20; metro Château de Vincennes; open 10am-noon & 1pm-5pm daily) is at the northern edge of the Bois de Vincennes. You can walk around the grounds for free, but to see the Gothic **Chapelle Royale** and the 14th-century **donjon** (keep), you must take a tour (in French, with an information booklet in English).

**Musée des Arts d'Afrique et d'Océanie (12e)** This museum (☎ 01 44 74 84 80; 293 ave Daumesnil; metro Porte Dorée; adult/concession €4.50/3; open 10am-5.30pm Wed-Mon) specialises in art from Africa and the South Pacific.

**Bois de Boulogne (16e)** This 8.65-sq-km park is endowed with meandering trails, forests, cycling paths and belle époque–style cafés. Rowing boats can be rented at the **Lac Inférieur** (metro Ave Henri Martin).

**Paris Cycles** (☎ 01 47 47 76 50; Rond-Point du Jardin d'Acclimation; metro Les Sablons) rents cycles for €5/12 one hour/day.

## LANGUAGE COURSES

**Alliance Française** (☎ 01 45 44 38 28; 101 blvd Raspail, 6e; metro St Placide) offers month-long French courses; it can also help you find a family to stay with. **Accord Language School** (☎ 01 42 36 24 95; 14 blvd Poissonière, 9e; metro Bonne Nouvelle) gets high marks from students.

## ORGANISED TOURS
### Bus

From April to late September, RATP's Balabus follows a 50-minute return route from Gare de Lyon to the Grande Arche in La Défense. Buses depart about every 20 minutes; the whole circuit costs three metro/bus tickets. **L'Open Tour** (☎ 01 43 46 52 06) runs open-deck buses along three circuits year-round, allowing you to jump on and off at more than 30 stops. Tickets cost €24/26 for one/two days (€20 if you're holding a Carte Orange, Paris Visite or Batobus pass).

### Bicycle

**Paris à Vélo C'est Sympa!** (☎ 01 48 87 60 01; e info@parisvelosympa.com; 37 blvd Bourdon, 4e; metro Bastille; €30/26 for over/under 26s) offers three-hour bicycle tours on Saturday and Sunday (and during the week depending on demand). **Mike's Bike Tours** (☎ 01 56 58 10 54; w www.MikesBikeToursParis.com, e info@MikesBikeToursParis.com) head off from the south leg of the Eiffel Tower daily at 11am and 3pm 15 May to August 31 and at 3pm only 1 March to 14 May and 1 September to 15 November (€22). Night tours (€26) leave at 7pm (daily 1 March to 15 November). Both include a guide, the bicycle and insurance.

### Boat

Every 25 minutes, from April to early November, the **Batobus river shuttle** (☎ 01 44 11 33 99) docks at eight places including Notre Dame and the Musée d'Orsay. A one-/two-day pass costs €10/12.50 (€5.50/6.50 for children aged under 12). Another company, **Bateaux Mouches** (☎ 01 42 25 96 10, English-language recording ☎ 01 40 76 99 99; metro Alma Marceau) makes a one-hour cruise for €7 (€4 for children four to 12) with commentary. **Vedettes du Pont Neuf** (☎ 01 46 33 98 38; metro Pont Neuf) operates one-hour boat circuits day and night for €9 (€4.50 for under 12s).

## PLACES TO STAY
## Accommodation Services

**OTU Voyages** (☎ 01 40 29 12 12; ⓦ www
.otu.fr; 119 rue St Martin, 4e; metro Rambuteau; open 9.30am-6.30pm Mon-Fri,
10am-5pm Sat), directly across the square
from the Centre Pompidou, can find you accommodation for the same or following day
for a €3 fee. The staff will give you a voucher
to take to the hotel.

The main tourist office (see Information
earlier) and its Gare de Lyon annexe can also
make same-day bookings.

## Camping

**Camping du Bois de Boulogne** (☎ 01 45 24
30 81, fax 01 42 24 42 95; ⓔ resa@mobil
home-paris.com; Allée du Bord de l'Eau, 16e;
2 people & tent without/with vehicle from
€11/17), at the far western edge of the Bois
de Boulogne, is Paris' only camping ground.
The Porte Maillot metro stop is linked to the
camping ground by RATP bus No 244 (6am
to 8.30pm) and, April to October, by privately
operated shuttle bus (€1.70).

## Hostels

Many hostels allow a three-night maximum
stay, especially in summer. Only official
auberges de jeunesse (youth hostels) require
guests to present Hostelling International
(HI) cards or equivalent. Curfew – if enforced – tends to be 1am or 2am. Few hostels
accept reservations by telephone.

**Louvre Area (1er)** There are bunks in the
single-sex rooms at **Centre International
BVJ Paris-Louvre** (☎ 01 53 00 90 90; 20 rue
Jean-Jacques Rousseau; metro Louvre-
Rivoli; dorm beds €26) and the rates include
breakfast.

**Marais (4e)** The **Maison Internationale de
la Jeunesse et des Étudiants** (MIJE; ☎ 01 42
74 23 45, fax 01 40 27 81 64; dorm
beds/singles from €23/38) runs three hostels
in attractively renovated 17th- and 18th-
century Marais residences. Rates include
breakfast. **MIJE Maubisson** (12 rue des Bar-
res; metro Hôtel de Ville) is, in our opinion,
the best. **MIJE Fourcy** (6 rue de Fourcy; metro
St Paul), the largest hostel, and **MIJE Fauconnier** (11 rue du Fauconnier; metro Pont
Marie), two blocks south of MIJE Fourcy, are
the other options.

**Panthéon Area (5e)** Friendly Y&H Hostel (☎ 01 45 35 09 53, fax 01 47 07 22 24;
ⓔ smile@youngandhappy.fr; 80 rue Mouffetard; metro Monge; dorm beds/doubles
€22/50) is popular with a younger crowd.

**11e Arrondissement** Breakfast is included
in the rates at **Auberge de Jeunesse Jules
Ferry** (☎ 01 43 57 55 60; ⓔ auberge@easynet
.fr; 8 blvd Jules Ferry; metro République;
dorm beds €18, €20.90 without HI card).

The clean and friendly **Auberge Internationale des Jeunes** (☎ 01 47 00 62 00, fax
01 47 00 33 16; ⓔ aij@aijparis.com; 10 rue
Trousseau, 11e; metro Ledru Rollin; dorm
beds Nov-Feb €13, Mar-Oct €14) attracts a
young crowd and gets full in summer. Rates
include breakfast.

**12e Arrondissement** Breakfast is included in the tariff at **Centre International de
Séjour de Paris (CISP) Ravel** (☎ 01 44 75 60
00, fax 01 43 44 45 30; ⓔ reservation@
cisp.asso.fr; 6 ave Maurice Ravel; metro Porte
de Vincennes; beds in 2- to 4-bed rooms
€19.20, singles/doubles €30/48).

**13e & 14e Arrondissements** The **Foyer
International d'Accueil de Paris (FIAP) Jean
Monnet** (☎ 01 43 13 17 00, fax 01 45 81 63
91; ⓔ fiapadmi@fiap.asso.fr; 30 rue Cabanis;
metro Glacière; dorm beds from €22, singles
€48.50) has modern rooms, and rates include
breakfast. Rooms specially outfitted for
handicapés (disabled people) are available.
Reservations are accepted.

The **Centre International de Séjour de
Paris (CISP) Kellermann** (☎ 01 44 16 37 38,
fax 01 44 16 37 39; 17 blvd Kellermann;
metro Porte d'Italie; dorm beds/singles
€15.40/22.40) includes sheets and breakfast
in its rates. There are facilities for disabled
people on the 1st floor. Reservations are
accepted up to 48 hours in advance.

## Hotels

**Marais (4e)** Friendly **Hôtel Rivoli** (☎ 01 42
72 08 41; 44 rue de Rivoli; metro Hôtel de
Ville; singles without bath from €26, doubles
with bath & toilet €48) is a good deal. **Hôtel
de Nice** (☎ 01 42 78 55 29, fax 01 42 78 36
07; 42bis rue de Rivoli; metro Hôtel de Ville;
singles/doubles/triples €60/95/115) is a
family-run place; some rooms have balconies.
**Grand Hôtel Malher** (☎ 01 42 72 60 92, fax

FRANCE

# THE LATIN QUARTER & ÎLE DE LA CITÉ

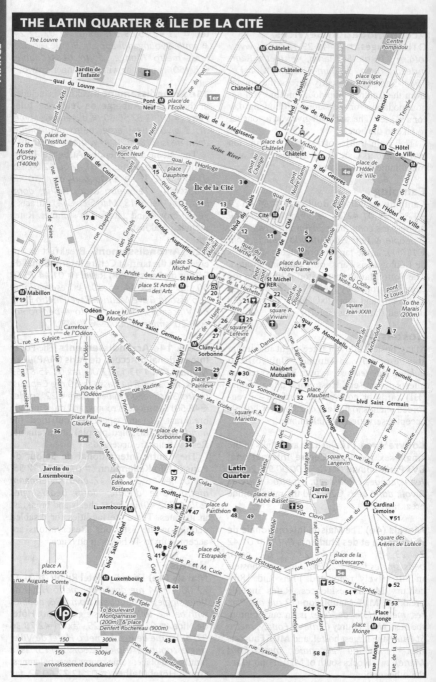

# THE LATIN QUARTER & ÎLE DE LA CITÉ

**PLACES TO STAY**
15  Hôtel Henri IV
17  Hôtel de Nesle
23  Hôtel Esmeralda
35  Hôtel de la Sorbonne
40  Hôtel de Médicis
43  Grand Hôtel du Progrès
44  Hôtel Gay Lussac
53  Hôtel St Christophe
58  Y & H Hostel

**PLACES TO EAT**
18  Food Shops
19  CROUS
24  Le Grenier de Notre-Dame
26  Restaurants ('Bacteria Alley')
31  Food Shops
32  Fromagerie (Cheese Shop)
39  Douce France Sandwich Bar
45  Food Shops
46  Tashi Delek Tibetan
    Restaurant
47  Perraudin
51  Le Petit Légume
54  Ed l'Épicier Supermarket

56  Le Petit Grec
57  Restaurants

**OTHER**
1   Samaritaine (Department
    Store)
2   Noctambus (All-Night Bus)
    Stops
3   Conciergerie Entrance
4   Flower Market
5   Hôtel Dieu (Hospital)
6   Société Française de Change
7   Mémorial des Martyrs de la
    Déportation
8   Notre Dame Cathedral
9   Notre Dame Tower Entrance
10  Hospital Entrance
11  Préfecture Entrance
12  Préfecture de Police
13  Sainte Chapelle
14  Palais de Justice &
    Conciergerie
16  Vedettes du Pont Neuf (Boat
    Tours)
20  EasyInternet

21  Caveau de la Huchette Jazz
    Club
22  Shakespeare & Co Bookshop
25  Abbey Bookshop
27  Église Saint Séverin
28  Musée du Moyen Age
    (Thermes de Cluny)
29  Musée du Moyen Age
    Entrance
30  Eurolines Bus Office
33  Sorbonne (University of
    Paris)
34  Église de la Sorbonne
36  Palais du Luxembourg
    (French Senate Building)
37  Post Office
38  Café Oz
41  Laundrette
42  Nouvelles Frontières
48  Panthéon Entrance
49  Panthéon
50  Église Saint Étienne
    du Mont
52  Laundrette
55  La Contrescarpe

01 42 72 25 37; e ghmalher@yahoo.fr; 5 rue Malher; metro St Paul; singles/doubles from €103/118) has nice rooms with satellite TV. Rates drop by €20 in the low season.

**Bastille (11e)** Above the bistro of the same name, **Hôtel Les Sans-Culottes** (☎ 01 49 23 85 80, fax 01 48 05 08 56; 27 rue de Lappe; metro Bastille; singles/doubles €53/61) has nine pleasant rooms with TV.

**Notre Dame Area (5e)** Scruffy but well-loved **Hôtel Esmeralda** (☎ 01 43 54 19 20, fax 01 40 51 00 68; 4 rue St Julien; metro St Michel; singles €30, doubles with shower & toilet from €60) is an institution. Its simple rooms are booked well in advance.

**Panthéon Area (5e)** Shabby **Hôtel de Médicis** (☎ 01 43 54 14 66; e hotelmedicis@aol.com; 214 rue St Jacques; metro Luxembourg; singles/doubles €16/31) has some good-sized basic rooms. Triples are available too. Much nicer is **Grand Hôtel du Progrès** (☎ 01 43 54 53 18, fax 01 56 24 87 80; 50 rue Gay Lussac; metro Luxembourg; singles/doubles from €27/42, with shower & toilet from €54/56 including breakfast) with good views from some rooms. There are some spacious rooms at older-style **Hôtel Gay Lussac** (☎ 01 43 54 23 96, fax 01 40 51 79 49; 29 rue Gay Lussac; metro Luxembourg; singles/doubles/quads from €55/49/95). **Hôtel St Christophe** (☎ 01 43 31 81 54, fax 01 43 31 12 54; e saintchristophe@wanadoo.fr; 17 rue Lacépède; metro place Monge; singles/doubles €111/123) is a classy small hotel with 31 well-equipped rooms. Wipe off about €10 in low season. **Hotel de la Sorbonne** (☎ 01 43 54 58 08, fax 01 40 51 05 18; e reservation@hotelsorbonne.com; 6 rue Victor Cousin; rooms with shower/bath €79/89) is a comfortable place near Boulevard St Michel. Breakfast is €5.

**St Germain des Prés (6e)** The whimsically decorated **Hôtel de Nesle** (☎ 01 43 54 62 41; e contact@hoteldenesle.com; 7 rue de Nesle; metro Odéon or Mabillon; singles/doubles from €35/69) is hospitable, with a tranquil garden. The well-positioned **Hôtel Henri IV** (☎ 01 43 54 44 53; 25 place Dauphine; metro Pont Neuf; singles/doubles from €22/25, no credit cards) at the western end of Île de la Cité, has adequate rooms (hall showers €2.50). Book well ahead.

**Montmartre (18e)** An attractive place is **Hôtel des Arts** (☎ 01 46 06 30 52, fax 01 46 06 10 83; e hotel.arts@wanadoo.fr; 5 rue Tholozé; metro Abbesses; singles/doubles from €64/78). **Hôtel de Rohan** (☎ 01 42 52

32 57, fax 01 55 79 79 63; 90 rue Myrha; metro Château Rouge; singles/doubles €19/ 23, with shower & toilet €28/31) has recently renovated most of its rooms (hall showers €3). Lovely **Hôtel des Trois Poussins** (☎ 01 53 32 81 81, fax 01 53 32 81 82; e h3p@les3poussins.com; 15 rue Clauzel; metro St Georges; singles/doubles from €120/135) is south of place Pigalle. Rooms with kitchen facilities cost an extra €15.

## PLACES TO EAT
### Restaurants
Except for those in the very touristy areas, most of the city's thousands of restaurants are pretty good value for money.

**Forum des Halles** There are Lyon-inspired specialities at **Le Petit Mâchon** (☎ 01 42 60 08 06; 158 rue St Honoré; metro Palais Royal; menu €15) bistro. American bar/restaurant **Joe Allen** (☎ 01 42 36 70 13; 30 rue Pierre Lescot; metro Étienne Marcel; burgers €12) promises the best burgers in Paris.

**Opéra Area (2e & 9e)** Although the food is so-so, **Chartier** (☎ 01 47 70 86 29; 7 rue du Faubourg Montmartre; metro Grands Boulevards; mains from €6.25, 3-course menu with wine €13.65) is worth it for the atmosphere and fabulous *belle époque* dining room.

**Marais (4e)** Rue des Rosiers (metro St Paul), heart of the old Jewish neighbourhood, has a few *kascher* (kosher) restaurants. Paris' best known Jewish (but not kosher) restaurant, founded in 1920, is **Restaurant Jo Goldenberg** (☎ 01 48 87 20 16; mains around €13) at No 7. **Minh Chau** (10 rue de la Verrerie; metro Hôtel de Ville; mains about €4.50) is a tiny but welcoming Vietnamese/Chinese place with tasty dishes. For vegetarian fare head to **Aquarius** (☎ 01 48 87 48 71; 54 rue Ste Croix de la Bretonnerie; metro Rambuteau; 2-course lunch €11, 3-course dinner €15.40; closed Sun), which has tasty dishes such as soy sausages and tofu omelette.

**Au Gamin de Paris** (☎ 01 42 78 97 24; 51 rue Vieille du Temple; metro St Paul) is a lively restaurant with great salads, steak and pasta. Count on spending at least €15 per person. **Le Colimacon** (☎ 01 48 87 12 01; 44 rue Vieille du Temple; metro St Paul; 2-/3-course menus €14.50/20.70) serves very delicious modern French food.

**République (10e)** On the Canal St Martin, **Chez Prune** (☎ 01 42 41 30 47; 36 rue Beaurepaire, 10e; metro République; lunch about €10) is a hip café that serves tasty French food.

**Bastille (4e, 11e & 12e)** The area around Bastille has many ethnic and traditional restaurants. Rue de Lappe, a happening strip since the 17th century, has heaps of eateries and bars. **Havanita Café** (☎ 01 43 55 96 42; mains €10-17), at No 11, is a loud, brassy lounge serving Cuban-inspired food and drinks. For good French food in a charming room try **Les Sans-Culottes** (☎ 01 48 05 42 92; menu €20) at No 27.

**Bofinger** (☎ 01 42 72 87 82; 5-7 rue de la Bastille; metro Bastille; lunch/dinner menus €20/30; open daily) is a brasserie with an Art Nouveau interior and seafood specialities.

**Latin Quarter (4e, 5e & 6e)** This area has plenty of good Greek, North African and Middle Eastern restaurants – but avoid rue de la Huchette (aka 'bacteria alley') and its nearby streets, unless you're after shwarma (€4), available at several places.

The Moroccan **Founti Agadir** (☎ 01 43 37 85 10; 117 rue Monge; metro Censier Daubenton; lunch menus €12 & €14) has some of the best couscous, grills and tajines on the Left Bank. Or, if you fancy classics such as *bœuf bourguignon* (€12.20), try **Perraudin** (☎ 01 46 33 15 75; 157 rue St Jacques; metro Luxembourg; open Mon-Fri), a reasonably priced traditional French place.

**Le Petit Légume** (☎ 01 40 46 06 85; 36 rue des Boulangers; metro Cardinal Lemoine; menus €8, €10.50 & €13) is a great choice for organic vegetarian fare.

Some of the best crepes in Paris are sold at **Le Petit Grec** (68 rue Mouffetard; crepes about €3), which has upgraded from the cart it used to operate across the street. **Tashi Delek** (☎ 01 43 26 55 55; 4 rue des Fossés St Jacques; metro Luxembourg; dinner menus €17.50, vegetarian dishes €6.40-8.40) offers good, cheap, Tibetan fare. **Douce France** (7 rue Royer Collard; metro Luxembourg) is a popular hole-in-the-wall selling great sandwiches for €2.20.

**Le Grenier de Notre-Dame** (☎ 01 43 29 98 29; 18 rue de la Bûcherie; menu €12) is a vegetarian restaurant with dishes such as lasagne and cassoulet.

FRANCE

# MONTMARTRE

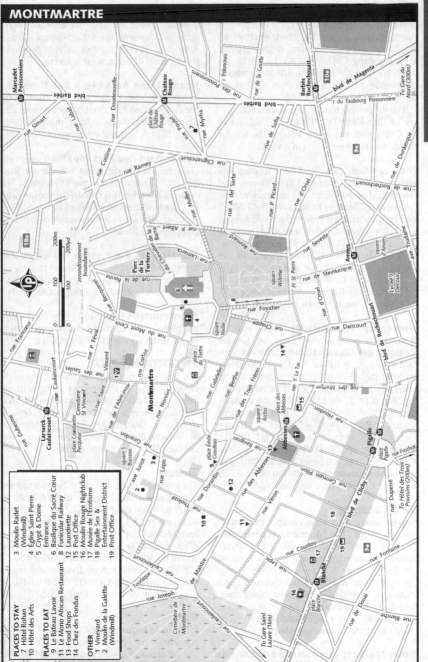

**PLACES TO STAY**
7   Hôtel Rohan
10  Hôtel des Arts

**PLACES TO EAT**
9   Le Bateau Lavoir
11  Le Mono African Restaurant
13  Food Shops
14  Chez des Fondus

**OTHER**
1   Vineyard
2   Moulin de la Galette
    (Windmill)
3   Moulin Radet
    (Windmill)
4   Eglise Saint Pierre
5   Crypt & Dome
    Entrance
6   Basilique du Sacré Cœur
8   Funicular Railway
12  Laundrette
15  Post Office
16  Moulin Rouge Nightclub
17  Musée de l'Erotisme
18  Pigalle Sex &
    Entertainment District
19  Post Office

**Montparnasse (6e & 14e)** One of many Breton-style creperies along rue d'Odessa and rue du Montparnasse is **Le Flibustier** (☎ 01 43 21 70 03; 20 rue d'Odessa; crepes around €6). **Mustang Café** (☎ 01 43 35 36 12; 84 blvd du Montparnasse; metro Montparnasse-Bienvenüe; platters & chilli from €10; open to 5am) serves passable Tex-Mex.

For innovative food in a traditional setting, try **Le Caméléon** (☎ 01 43 20 63 43; 6 rue de Chevreuse, 6e; metro Vavin); the lobster ravioli (€16) alone is worth a visit.

**Montmartre (9e & 18e)** Restaurants around place du Tertre tend to be touristy and overpriced – but there are alternatives. A favourite is **Chez des Fondus** (☎ 01 42 55 22 65; 17 rue des Trois Frères; metro Abbesses; open 7pm-2am daily) where €15 buys an apéritif, wine, and either cheese or meat fondue. **Le Mono** (☎ 01 46 06 99 20; 40 rue Véron; dishes €8-12) has West African fare.

Atmospheric **Le Bateau Lavoir** (☎ 01 42 54 23 92; 8 rue Garreau; entrees/mains €7/ 14) is a traditional French restaurant.

**University Restaurants** Paris has 17 *restaurants universitaires* run by **Centre Régional des Œuvres Universitaires et Scolaires** (Crous; ☎ 01 40 51 37 01). Students with ID pay €2.40. Opening times vary, so check the schedule outside any of the following: **Assas** (☎ 01 46 33 61 25; 92 rue d'Assas, 6e; metro Port Royal or Notre Dame des Champs); **Bullier** (☎ 01 43 54 93 38; 39 ave Georges Bernanos, 5e; metro Port Royal); **Châtelet** (☎ 01 43 31 51 66; 10 rue Jean Calvin, 5e; metro Censier Daubenton), just off rue Mouffetard; and **Mabillon** (☎ 01 43 25 66 23; 3 rue Mabillon, 6e; metro Mabillon).

## Self-Catering

Supermarkets are always cheaper than small grocery shops. The **Monoprix supermarket** (23 ave de l'Opéra) opposite metro Pyramides is convenient for the Louvre area, or try **Ed l'Épicier** (37 rue Lacépède; metro Monge) if you're in the Latin Quarter. For a different shopping experience altogether, head to **Fauchon** (☎ 01 47 42 91 10; 26 place de la Madeleine; metro Madeleine), Paris' most famous gourmet-food shop.

**Food Markets** Paris' marchés découverts (open-air markets; open 7am-2pm) pop up in various squares and streets two or three times a week. There are also **marchés couverts** (covered markets; open 8am–about 1pm & 4pm-7pm Tues-Sun). Ask at your hotel for the location of the nearest market.

**Notre Dame Area (4e & 5e)** There are a number of *fromageries* and **groceries** along rue St Louis en l'Île (metro Pont Marie) and place Maubert hosts a **food market** (open Tues, Thur & Sat) and other food shops.

**St Germain des Prés (6e)** Food shops are clustered on **rue de Seine** and **rue de Buci** (metro Mabillon) and at rue St Jacques. The covered **Marché St Germain** (rue Lobineau), just north of the eastern end of Église St Germain des Prés, has a huge array of produce and prepared foods.

**Marais (4e)** Flo Prestige (10 rue St Antoine; metro Bastille; open 8am-11pm daily) has fancy picnic supplies and, more importantly, delectable pastries and baked goods.

**Montmartre (18e)** Most of the food shops are along rue Lepic and rue des Abbesses, about 500m southwest of Sacré Cœur.

## ENTERTAINMENT

It's virtually impossible to sample the richness of Paris' entertainment scene without consulting *Pariscope* (€0.40; with an English-language insert from Time Out) or *L'Officiel des Spectacles* (€0.35), both published on Wednesday and available at newsstands. Look out for *LYLO*, a free listings zine.

## Tickets

Theatre and concert tickets can be reserved and bought at the ticket outlets in **FNAC stores** (☎ 01 43 42 04 04; 4 place Bastille, 12e; metro Bastille • ☎ 01 40 41 40 00; 3rd underground level, Forum des Halles shopping mall, 1 rue Pierre Lescot, 1er; metro Châtelet-Les Halles) and in the **Virgin Megastores** (☎ 01 49 53 50 00; 52 ave des Champs-Élysées, 8e; metro Franklin D Roosevelt • ☎ 01 44 50 03 10; 99 rue de Rivoli, 1er; metro Pont Neuf).

## Bars

**L'Etoile Manquante** (☎ 01 42 72 47 47; 34 rue Vieille du Temple, 4e; metro St Paul) is a gay/mixed bar with funky art. Meals are available. Anglophone and always crowded,

Stolly's (☎ 01 42 76 06 76; 16 rue de la Cloche Percée, 4e; metro Hôtel de Ville) is on a tiny street just off rue de Rivoli.

De La Ville Café (☎ 01 48 24 48 09; 36 blvd Bonne Nouvelle, 10e; metro Bonne Nouvelle) is a fashionable but welcoming bar. Café Oz (☎ 01 43 54 30 48; 18 rue St Jacques; metro Luxembourg) is a casual, friendly pub with Foster's on tap.

Relaxed La Contrescarpe (☎ 01 43 36 82 88; 57 rue Lacépède, 5e), on place Contrescarpe, is as nice for morning coffee or cocktail hour.

## Clubs & Dance Venues

The clubs and other dancing venues favoured by the Parisian 'in' crowd change frequently, and many are officially private, which means bouncers can deny entry to whomever they don't like the look of. For example, single men may not be admitted; women, on the other hand, get in free some nights.

Favela Chic (☎ 01 40 21 38 14; 18 rue du Faubourg du Temple, 9e; metro Republique; admission free; open 7.30pm-2am Tues-Sat) morphs from a Brazilian restaurant into a heaving dance spot.

Batofar (☎ 01 45 83 33 06; quai de la Gare, 13e; metro Bibliothèque Nationale) is the best known of a number of floating barges, all of which host parties and concerts.

Café de la Danse (☎ 01 47 00 57 59; 5 passage Louis Philippe; metro Bastille) is a good venue with a varied line-up. It's off 21 rue de Lappe. Pick up a programme at Web Bar (see Email & Internet Access earlier).

## Jazz

Caveau de la Huchette (☎ 01 43 26 65 05; 5 rue de la Huchette, 5e; metro St Michel; adult/student €10.50/9 Mon-Fri, all €13 Sat-Sun; open 9.30pm-2am, later Sat-Sun) is touristy but still a favourite for live jazz.

## Opera & Classical Music

Paris plays host to dozens of concerts each week. The Opéra National de Paris (☎ 0892 69 78 68; W www.opera-de-paris.fr) splits its performances between Opéra Garnier, its original home built in 1875, and the modern Opéra Bastille, which opened in 1989. Both opera houses also stage ballets and concerts. Opera tickets (September to July only) cost €7 to €109; ballets €8 to €67; and concerts €7 to €39. Unsold tickets are offered 15 min-

utes prior to showtime to students and under 25s for about €15 – ask for the tarif spécial.

## Cinemas

Going to the movies in Paris is expensive (about €8), although most cinemas give discounts on Wednesday (and sometimes Monday and mornings). Check Pariscope and L'Officiel des Spectacles for listings: 'vo' (version originale) indicates subtitled movies.

## SHOPPING
## Fashion

Some of Paris' fanciest shops are along ave Montaigne and rue du Faubourg St Honoré, 8e; rue St Honoré, 1er and 8e; and place Vendôme, 1er. Rue Bonaparte, 6e, offers a good choice of mid-range boutiques.

## Department Stores

Paris' three main department stores, open 9.30am to 7pm Monday to Saturday (10pm on Thursday), are: Au Printemps (☎ 01 42 82 50 00; 64 blvd Haussmann; metro Havre Caumartin); Galeries Lafayette (☎ 01 42 82 36 40; 40 blvd Haussmann; metro Auber or Chaussée) and Samaritaine (☎ 01 40 41 20 20; metro Pont Neuf), which provides an amazing view from the 10th-floor terrace of Magasin Principal at 19 rue de la Monnaie.

## GETTING THERE & AWAY
## Air

Paris has two major international airports. Aéroport d'Orly (flight & other information ☎ 01 49 75 15 15, 0836 25 05 05) is 14km south of central Paris. Aéroport Charles de Gaulle (☎ 01 48 62 22 80, 0836 25 05 05), also known as Roissy-Charles de Gaulle in the suburb of Roissy, is 23km northeast of central Paris.

Telephone numbers for information at Paris' airline offices are:

|  |  |
|---|---|
| Air France | ☎ 0836 68 10 48 |
| Air Liberté | ☎ 0825 80 58 05 |
| Air New Zealand | ☎ 01 40 53 82 23 |
| Air UK | ☎ 01 44 56 18 08 |
| American Airlines | ☎ 0810 87 28 72 |
| British Airways | ☎ 0825 82 54 00 |
| Continental | ☎ 01 42 99 09 09 |
| Lufthansa | ☎ 0802 02 00 30 |
| Northwest Airlines | ☎ 0810 55 65 56 |
| Qantas | ☎ 0820 82 05 00 |
| Singapore Airlines | ☎ 01 53 65 79 01 |
| Thai Airways International | ☎ 01 44 20 70 15 |
| United Airlines | ☎ 0801 72 72 72 |

FRANCE

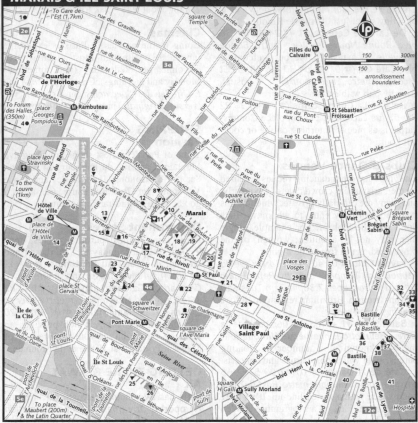

## MARAIS & ÎLE SAINT LOUIS

## Bus

The Eurolines terminal **Gare Routière Internationale** (☎ *0836 69 52 52; Porte de Bagnolet, 20e; metro Gallieni*) is on the eastern edge of Paris. There's a ticket office in town (☎ *01 43 54 11 99; 55 rue St Jacques, 5e; metro Cluny-La Sorbonne; open 9.30am-6.30pm Mon-Fri, 10am-1pm & 2pm-6pm Sat*). There is no domestic, intercity bus service to or from Paris.

## Train

Paris has six major train stations (*gares*), each handling traffic to different destinations. For information in English call ☎ 0836 35 35 35 from 7am to 10pm. The metro station attached to each train station bears the same name as the gare. Paris' major train stations are:

**Gare d'Austerlitz (13e)** Spain and Portugal and non-TGV trains to southwestern France

**Gare de l'Est (10e)** Parts of France east of Paris, Luxembourg, parts of Switzerland (Basel, Lucerne, Zürich), southern Germany (Munich, Frankfurt) and points further east

**Gare de Lyon (12e)** Regular and TGV Sud-Est trains to places southeast of Paris, including Provence, the Côte d'Azur, parts of Switzerland (Bern, Geneva, Lausanne), Italy and points beyond

**Gare Montparnasse (15e)** Destinations in southwestern France

**Gare du Nord (10e)** Northern suburbs of Paris, northern France, the UK, Belgium, northern Germany, Scandinavia, Moscow etc; terminus of the TGV Nord (Lille and Calais) and the Eurostar to London

**Gare St Lazare (8e)** Destinations in northwestern France

## MARAIS & ÎLE SAINT LOUIS

| PLACES TO STAY | | |
|---|---|---|
| 15 Hôtel Rivoli | 21 Food Shops | 7 Musée Picasso |
| 16 Hôtel de Nice | 25 Berthillon Ice Cream | 10 Laundrette |
| 20 Grand Hôtel Malher | 26 Food Shops | 11 L'Etoile Manquante |
| 22 MIJE Fourcy | 28 Monoprix Supermarket | 12 Les Mots à la Bouche Bookshop |
| 23 MIJE Maubisson | 30 Bofinger | 14 Hôtel de Ville (City Hall) |
| 27 MIJE Fauconnier | 31 Flo Prestige | 17 Stolly's |
| 35 Hôtel Les Sans-Culottes | 32 Restaurants | 24 Memorial to the Unknown |
| | 34 Havanita | Jewish Martyr |
| | | 29 Maison de Victor Hugo |
| PLACES TO EAT | OTHER | 33 Café de la Danse |
| 6 Aquarius Vegetarian | 1 Union des Centres de | 36 Colonne de Juillet |
| Restaurant | Rencontres Internationales de | 37 FNAC Store NEW; ticket office |
| 8 Au Gamin de Paris | France (UCRIF) | 38 Entrance to Opéra-Bastille |
| 9 Le Colimacon | 2 Web Bar | 39 Paris à Vélo C'est Sympa! |
| 13 Minh Chau | 3 EasyInternet | 40 Port de Plaisance de Paris |
| 18 Restaurants | 4 OTU Voyages | Arsenal |
| 19 Restaurant Jo Goldenberg | 5 Centre Pompidou | 41 Opéra-Bastille |

## GETTING AROUND

Paris' public transit system, most of which is operated by the **RATP** (*Régie Autonome des Transports Parisiens;* ☎ *0836 68 77 14; English information* ☎ *0892 68 41 14)* is cheap and efficient.

### To/From Orly Airport

Orly Rail is the quickest way to reach the Left Bank and the 16e. Take the free shuttle bus to the Pont de Rungis-Aéroport d'Orly RER station, which is on the C2 line, and get on a train heading into the city. Another fast way into town is the Orlyval shuttle train (€7, 35 to 40 minutes); it stops near Orly-Sud's Porte F and links Orly with the Antony RER station, which is on line B4. Orlybus (€5.50, 30 minutes) takes you to the Denfert-Rochereau metro station, 14e. Air France buses (€7.50) go to/from Gare Montparnasse, 15e (every 15 minutes) along Aérogare des Invalides in the 7e. RATP bus No 183 (one bus/metro ticket) goes to Porte de Choisy, 13e, but is very slow. Jetbus, the cheapest option, links both terminals with the Villejuif-Louis Aragon metro stop (€4.50, 15 minutes). All services between Orly and Paris run every 15 minutes or so (less frequently late at night) from 5.30am or 6.30am to 11pm or 11.30pm. A taxi to/from Orly costs about €45 to €55, plus €0.90 per piece of luggage weighing more than 5kg.

### To/From Charles de Gaulle Airport

Roissybus links the city with both of the airport's train stations (€8, 50 minutes). To get to the airport, take any line B train whose four letter destination code begins with E (eg, EIRE). Regular metro ticket windows can't always sell these tickets, so you may have to buy one at the RER station where you board. Trains run every 15 or 20 minutes from 6am to around 11pm.

Air France bus No 2 will take you to Porte Maillot and the corner of ave Carnot near the Arc de Triomphe for €10; bus No 4 to Gare Montparnasse costs €11.50.

RATP bus No 350 (€3.90 or three bus/metro tickets) links both aérogares with Porte de la Chapelle, 18e, and stops at Gare du Nord and Gare de l'Est, both in the 10e. RATP bus No 351 goes to ave du Trône, on the eastern side of place de la Nation in the 11e and runs every half-hour or so until 8.20pm (9.30pm from the airport to the city). The trip costs €3.90 or three bus/metro tickets.

A taxi to/from Charles de Gaulle costs about €40.

### Bus

Short trips cost one bus/metro/RER ticket (see Metro/RER/Bus Tickets later), while longer rides require two. Travellers without tickets can purchase them from the driver. Whatever kind of *coupon* (ticket) you have, you must cancel it in the little machine next to the driver. The fines are hefty if you're caught without a ticket or without a cancelled ticket. If you have a Carte Orange or Paris Visite pass (see the following Metro & RER section), just show it to the driver – do not cancel it in the machine.

After the metro shuts down at around 12.45am, the Noctambus network (its symbol is a black owl silhouetted against a yellow moon) links the Châtelet-Hôtel de Ville area with most parts of the city. Noctambuses begin their runs from ave Victoria, 4e, between the Hôtel de Ville and place du Châtelet between 1am and 5.30am seven days a week. A single ride costs €2.40 and allows one transfer onto another Noctambus.

## Metro & RER

Paris' underground rail network consists of two separate but linked systems: the Métropolitain, known as the metro, which now has 14 lines and more than 300 stations, and the suburban commuter rail network, the RER which, along with certain SNCF lines, is divided into eight concentric zones. The whole system has been designed so that no point in Paris is more than 500m from a metro stop.

**How it Works**  Each metro train is known by the name of its terminus; trains on the same line have different names depending on which direction they are travelling. On lines that split into several branches and thus have more than one end-of-the-line station, the final destination of each train is indicated on the front, sides and interior of the train cars. In the stations, white-on-blue *sortie* signs indicate exits and black-on-orange *correspondance* signs show how to get to connecting trains. The last metro train sets out at 12.30am. Plan ahead so as not to miss your connection. The metro starts up again at 5.30am.

## Metro/RER/Bus Tickets

The same tickets are valid on the metro, the bus and, for travel within the Paris city limits, the RER's 2nd-class carriages. They cost €1.30 if bought individually and €9.30 (half for children aged four to 11) for a *carnet* of 10. One ticket lets you travel between any two metro stations, including stations outside of the Paris city limits, no matter how many transfers are required. You can also use it on the RER system within zone 1.

For travel on the RER to destinations outside the city, purchase a special ticket *before* you board the train or you won't be able to get out of the station and could be fined. Always keep your ticket until you reach your destination and exit the station.

The cheapest and easiest way to travel the metro is with a Carte Orange, a bus/metro/RER pass that comes in weekly and monthly ver-

sions. You can get tickets for travel in up to eight urban and suburban zones; the basic ticket – valid for zones 1 and 2 – is probably sufficient.

The weekly ticket costs €13.25 for zones 1 and 2 and is valid Monday to Sunday. Even if you'll be in Paris for only three or four days, it may very well work out cheaper than purchasing a carnet – you'll break even at 15 rides – and it will certainly cost less than buying a daily Mobilis or Paris Visite pass. The monthly Carte Orange ticket (€44.35 for zones 1 and 2) begins on the first day of each calendar month. Both are on sale in metro and RER stations and at certain bus terminals.

To get a monthly Carte Orange, bring a passport-size photograph of yourself to the ticket counter (automatic photo booths are in most stations). You don't need a photo for a weekly carte.

Mobilis and Paris Visite passes, designed for tourists, are on sale in many metro and train stations and international airports. The Mobilis card (and its *coupon*) allows unlimited travel for one day in two to eight zones (€5 to €17.95). Paris Visite transport passes, providing discounts on entries to certain museums and activities as well as transport, are valid for one/two/three/five consecutive days of travel in either three, five or eight zones. The one- to three-zone version costs €8.35/13.70/18.25/26.65 for one/two/three/five days. Children aged four to 11 pay half-price. They can be purchased at larger metro and RER stations, at SNCF bureaus in Paris and at the airports.

## Taxi

The *prise en* charge (flag fall) is €2. Within the city limits, it costs €0.60 per kilometre for travel 7am to 7pm Monday to Saturday (tariff A). At night and on Sundays and holidays (tariff B), it's €1 per kilometre. An extra €2.45 is charged for taking a fourth passenger, but most drivers refuse to take more than three people because of insurance constraints. Luggage more than 5kg costs €0.90 extra and for pick-up from SNCF mainline stations there's a €0.70 supplement. The usual tip is 10% no matter what the fare.

There are 500 *tête de station* (taxi stands) in Paris. Radio-dispatched taxis include **Taxis Bleus** (☎ 01 49 36 10 10) and **G7 Taxis** (☎ 01 47 39 47 39). If you order a taxi by phone, the meter is switched on as soon as the driver gets your call.

## Car & Motorcycle

Driving in Paris is nerve-wracking but not impossible. The fastest way to get across Paris is usually via the Périphérique, the ring road that encircles the city.

Street parking can cost €2 per hour; large municipal parking garages charge about €2.50/5/18 for one/two/24 hours.

Renting a small car (Opel Corsa 1.2) for one day with insurance and 250km costs about €85, but cheaper deals are often available.

Rental agencies in Paris include:

**Avis** (☎ 0820 05 05 05, 01 43 48 29 26)
**Budget** (☎ 01 45 44 62 00)
**Europcar** (☎ 0825 35 23 52)
**Hertz** (☎ 01 39 38 38 38)
**National/Citer** (☎ 01 42 06 06 06)

## Bicycle

There are 130km of bicycle lanes running throughout Paris. Some of them aren't particularly attractive or safe, but cyclists may be fined about €40 for failing to use them. The tourist office distributes a free brochure-map called *Paris à Vélo*.

Paris à Vélo (see Bicycle under Organised Tours earlier) rents bikes for €12.20/30.50 for one/three days. Also try the RATP-sponsored Roue Libre (☎ 0810 44 15 34; 1 passage Mondétour).

# Around Paris

The region surrounding Paris is known as the Île de France (Island of France) because of its position between the rivers Aube, Marne, Oise and Seine.

## DISNEYLAND PARIS

It took US$4.4 billion to turn beet fields 32km east of Paris into the much heralded Disneyland Paris (adult/child 3-11 years €39/29 Apr–early Jan, €29/25 early Jan–Mar; open 9am-8pm daily, 9am-11pm July-Aug), now the most popular tourist attraction in Europe. Three-day passes are available.

## VERSAILLES

**pop 95,000**

Versailles served as the country's political capital and the seat of the royal court from 1682 until 1789. After the Franco-Prussian War of 1870–71, the victorious Prussians proclaimed the establishment of the German empire from the chateau's Galerie des Glaces (Hall of Mirrors), and in 1919 the Treaty of Versailles was signed in the same room, officially ending WWI.

The chateau can be jammed with tourists, especially on weekends, in summer and most especially on summer Sundays. Arrive early to avoid the queues or beat most of the queues by prebuying or buying a guided tour ticket when you arrive which includes general admission.

### Information

The **tourist office** (☎ 01 39 24 88 88; e tourisme@ot-versailles.fr; 2 bis ave de Paris; open 9am-7pm daily Apr-Oct, 9am-6pm Nov-Mar) is just north of the Versailles-Rive Gauche train station.

### Château de Versailles

The enormous Château de Versailles (☎ 01 30 83 78 00, 01 30 83 77 77) was built in the mid-17th century during the reign of Louis XIV (the Sun King). The chateau essentially consists of four parts: the main palace building; the impressive vast 17th-century gardens; the late-17th century Grand Trianon; and the mid-18th century Petit Trianon.

**Opening Hours & Tickets** The main building opens 9am to 5.30pm (6.30pm April to October) Tuesday to Sunday. Admission to the **Grands Appartements** (State Apartments), including the 73m-long **Galerie des Glaces** (Hall of Mirrors) and the **Appartement de la Reine** (Queen's Suite) costs €7.50 (€5.30 after 3.30pm, free for under 18s). Tickets are on sale at Entrée A (Entrance A) off to the right from the equestrian statue of Louis XIV as you approach the building. You won't be able to visit other parts of the main palace unless you take one of the guided tours (see Guided Tours later). Entrée H has facilities for the disabled, including a lift.

The **Grand Trianon** (admission €5, €3 reduced rate; admits to Petit Trianon too) opens noon to 6.30pm daily April to October; the rest of the year it closes at 5.30pm. The **Petit Trianon** is open the same days and hours.

The gardens (€3) are open 8am (9am in winter) to nightfall daily (except if it's snowing). On Saturday, July to September, and Sunday early April to early October, the baroque fountains 'perform' the **Grandes**

Eaux (☎ *01 30 83 78 78; admission €5.50; times vary).*

A 'passport' (€21.20) includes admission to the Chateau, an audio tour, the Grand Trianon, Petit Trianon and the garden; it's available from FNAC stores and some SNCF stations.

**Guided Tours** To make a reservation go to entrées C or D. A one-hour tour costs €4.20 in addition to the regular entry fee; 80-minute audioguide tours are available at entrée A for €3.50.

## Getting There & Away
Bus No 171 (€1.30 or one metro/bus ticket, 35 minutes) links Pont de Sèvres in Paris with the place d'Armes and Versailles but it's faster to go by train. Each of Versailles' three train stations is served by RER and/or SNCF trains coming from a different group of Paris stations.

RER line C4 takes you from Paris' Left Bank RER stations to Versailles-Rive Gauche station (€2.20). From Paris, catch any train with a four-letter code beginning with V. There are up to 70 trains daily (around 35 on Sunday), and the last train back to Paris leaves shortly before midnight.

RER line C5 links Paris' Left Bank with Versailles-Chantiers station (€2.20). From Paris, take any train whose code begins with 'S'. Versailles-Chantiers is also served by some three dozen SNCF trains daily (20 on Sunday) from Gare Montparnasse (€2.20, 15 minutes); all trains on this line continue on to Chartres.

From Paris' Gare St Lazare (€3) and La Défense (€2), the SNCF has about 70 trains daily to Versailles-Rive Droite, which is 1200m from the chateau. The last train to Paris leaves a bit past midnight.

## CHARTRES
**pop 42,059**
The impressive 13th-century cathedral of Chartres rises spectacularly from the fields 88km southwest of Paris. The amenable town is an easy place to spend a day or two.

## Orientation
The medieval sections of Chartres are situated along the Eure River and the hillside to the west. The cathedral is about 500m east of the train station.

## Information
The **tourist office** (☎ *02 37 18 26 26;* e *char tres.tourism@wanadoo.fr)* is across place de la Cathédrale from the cathedral's main entrance. The **post office** *(place des Épars)* handles money exchange.

## Cathédrale Notre Dame
There have been churches on this site since the 4th century. The current 13th-century cathedral (☎ *02 37 21 75 02; open 8am-8pm Easter-Oct, 8.30am-7.30pm Nov-Easter, except during services)* has a high degree of architectural unity, having been built in 30 years after a Romanesque cathedral on this site was destroyed by fire in 1194. Unlike so many of its contemporaries, this early Gothic masterpiece has not been significantly modified, apart from a 16th-century steeple.

Fascinating **tours** (☎ *02 37 28 15 58; adults/students €5.50/4)* are conducted by Englishman Malcolm Miller from Easter to November; audioguides (€2.50 to €5.65) are available from the cathedral bookshop. The 112m-high **Clocher Neuf** *(new bell tower; adult/concession 18-25 years €4/ 2.50)* is well worth the ticket price and the long, spiral climb.

Inside, the cathedral's most exceptional feature is its 172 **stained-glass windows**, most of which are 13th-century originals. The **trésor** (treasury) displays a piece of cloth said to have been worn by the Virgin Mary.

The early-11th century Romanesque **crypt**, the largest in France, can be visited by a half-hour guided tour in French (with a written English translation) for €2.30.

## Old City
Streets with buildings of interest include **rue de la Tannerie**, which runs along the Eure, and **rue des Écuyers**, midway between the cathedral and the river. **Église St Pierre** *(place St Pierre)* has a massive bell tower dating from around 1000 and some fine (often overlooked) medieval stained-glass windows.

## Places to Stay
**Camping** About 2.5km southeast of the train station there's **Les Bords de l'Eure** (☎ *02 37 28 79 43, fax 02 37 23 41 99; 9 rue de Launay; open May-early Sept).* Bus No 8 (direction Hôpital) from the train station goes to the Vignes stop.

**Hostel** The pleasant and calm **Auberge de Jeunesse** (☎ 02 37 34 27 64, fax 02 37 35 75 85; 23 ave Neigre; dorm beds €10.50; reception open 2pm-10pm daily) includes breakfast in its rates. From the train station, take bus No 5 (direction Mare aux Moines) to the Rouliers stop.

**Hotels** It's fair to say that **Hôtel de l'Ouest** (☎ 02 37 21 43 27, fax 02 37 21 47 80; 3 place Pierre Sémard; singles/doubles from €15/23) is pretty dingy. Better is **Hôtel Jehan de Beauce** (☎ 02 37 21 01 41, fax 02 37 21 59 10; e jehan_de_beauce@club-internet.fr; 19 ave Jehan de Beauce; singles/doubles from €37/45).

Le Boeuf Couronné (☎ 02 37 18 06 06, fax 02 37 21 72 13; 15 place Châtelet; singles/doubles from €26/29) is quiet but it's central with a decent restaurant.

## Places to Eat
Across from the south porch of the cathedral is **Café Serpente** (☎ 02 37 21 68 81; 2 rue du Cloître Notre Dame; mains €13-18). Nearby, **La Vieille Maison** (☎ 02 37 34 10 67; 5 rue au Lait; menus €28 & €45; open Tues-Sat lunch & dinner, Sun lunch only) is a much-lauded restaurant.

Le Vesuve (☎ 02 37 21 56 35; 30 place des Halles; pizzas €6.50-9.50) serves light meals. There's a **Monoprix supermarket** (21 rue Noël Ballay) northeast of place des Épars.

## Getting There & Around
**Train** There are three dozen trains daily (20 on Sunday) to/from Paris' Gare Montparnasse (€11.40, 55 to 70 minutes) also stopping at Versailles' Chantiers station (€9.70, 45 to 60 minutes). The last train back to Paris leaves Chartres a bit after 9pm (7.55pm on Saturday, after 10pm on Sunday and holidays).

# Languedoc-Roussillon

Languedoc-Roussillon stretches in an arc along the coast from Provence to the Pyrenees. The plains of Bas Languedoc (Lower Languedoc) extend to the coast, where beaches are generally broad and sandy. The wine – Languedoc is France's largest wine-producing area – is red, robust and cheap. Inland are the rugged, sparsely populated mountains of Haut Languedoc (Upper Languedoc), a region of bare limestone plateaus and deep canyons.

Transport is frequent between cities on the plain but buses in the interior are about as rare as camels. For train information in the region, ring ☎ 08 36 35 35 35.

## MONTPELLIER
**pop 229,000**
Montpellier is one of the nation's fastest-growing cities. It's also one of the youngest, with students making up nearly one-quarter of its population.

Montpellier hosts a popular theatre festival in June and a two-week international dance festival in June/July.

### Orientation & Information
The Centre Historique has at its heart place de la Comédie, an enormous pedestrianised square. Westward from it sprawls a network of lanes between rue de la Loge and rue Grand Jean Moulin.

Montpellier's **main tourist office** (☎ 04 67 60 60 60; open 9am-6.30pm Mon-Fri, reduced hours Sat & Sun, later closing in summer) is on esplanade Charles de Gaulle.

To snack and surf, visit the **Dimension 4 Cybercafé** (11 rue des Balances; open 10am-1am daily). It charges €4 per hour.

### Things to See
**Musée Fabre** (39 blvd Bonne Nouvelle) has one of France's richest collections of French, Italian, Flemish and Dutch works from the 16th century onwards. **Musée Languedocien** (7 rue Jacques Cœur) displays the region's archaeological finds. Both charge €5.50/3 per adult/concession.

**Beaches** The closest beach is at **Palavas-les-Flots**, 12km south of the city. Take bus No 17 or 28.

### Places to Stay
**Camping** Some 4km south of town is **L'Oasis Palavasienne** (☎ 04 67 15 11 61; Route de Palavas; bus No 17 to Oasis stop; 2 people & tent low/high season €16.40/24.05; open mid-Apr–Aug).

**Hostels** The **Auberge de Jeunesse** (☎ 04 67 60 32 22, fax 04 67 60 32 30; e montpellier@fuaj.org; 2 impasse de la Petite Corraterie;

FRANCE

dorm beds €8; open mid-Jan–mid-Dec) is just off rue des Écoles Laïques. Take the tram to the Louis Blanc stop.

**Hotels** Just off place de la Comédie is **Hôtel des Touristes** (☎ 04 67 58 42 37, fax 04 67 92 61 37; 10 rue Baudin; singles/doubles/triples with shower from €24.40/29.75/49.55) with spacious rooms. Friendly **Hôtel des Étuves** (☎/fax 04 67 60 78 19; 24 rue des Étuves; singles/doubles with bathroom from €27.45/33.55) is another option. Close by is **Hôtel Majestic** (☎ 04 67 66 26 85; 4 rue du Cheval Blanc; singles/doubles €18/23, doubles/triples/quads with bathroom €29/46/53).

### Places to Eat
Eating places abound in Montepellier's old quarter. **Tripti Kulai** (20 rue Jacques Cœur; menus €10.50 & €14.50) is vegetarian. **La Tomate** (6 rue Four des Flammes; menus from €8) does great regional dishes, salads the size of a kitchen, plus dessert.

### Entertainment
For a drink, try the bars flanking rue En-Gondeau, off rue Grand Jean Moulin. **Mash Disco Bar** (5 rue de Girone) is a popular student hang-out. For more entertainment options, look out for a free copy of Sortit à Montpellier in restaurants and shops.

### Getting There & Away
Montpellier's **bus station** (☎ 04 67 92 01 43) is immediately southwest of the train station, itself 500m south of place de la Comédie.

Rail destinations include Paris' Gare de Lyon (€63.10/77.10 weekdays/weekends, 4½ hours by TGV, about 10 daily), Carcassonne (€17.70, 1½ hours, at least 10 daily) and Nîmes (€7.20, 30 minutes, 15 or more daily).

## NÎMES
**pop 133,000**
Nîmes has some of Europe's best-preserved Roman buildings. **Les Arènes** (the amphitheatre; adult/child €4.50/3.20), constructed around AD 100 to seat 24,000 spectators, is used to this day for theatre performances, music concerts and bullfights.

The rectangular **Maison Carrée**, a well-preserved 1st-century Roman temple, has survived the centuries as a meeting hall, private residence, stable, church and archive.

Try to coincide with one of Nîmes' three wild férias (festivals) – Féria Primavera (Spring Festival) in February, Féria de Pentecôte (Whitsuntide Festival) in June, and the Féria des Vendanges coinciding with the grape harvest in September.

The **main tourist office** (☎ 04 66 58 38 00; 6 rue Auguste) can help with information.

To check your email, log on at **Netgames** (25 rue de l'Horloge), beside the Maison Carrée, which charges €3 an hour.

### Places to Stay
**Domaine de la Bastide** (☎/fax 04 66 38 09 21; tent sites for 2 people with car €11.30; open year-round) is 4km south of town on route de Générac (the D13). Take bus D and get off at La Bastide, the terminus.

**Hôtel de la Maison Carrée** (☎ 04 66 67 32 89, fax 04 66 76 22 57; 14 rue de la Maison Carrée; singles/doubles with washbasin €22/26, singles/doubles with bathroom €28-37/34-43, triples/quads €50/53) is a welcoming, highly recommended place.

### Places to Eat
**La Truye qui Filhe** (9 rue Fresque; menu €8.40; open noon-2pm Mon-Sat; closed Aug), beneath the vaults of a restored 14th-century inn, is a self-service format with a warm atmosphere and a superb-value menu that changes daily.

### Getting There & Away
**Bus** Nîmes' bus station is by the train station. Destinations include Pont du Gard (€5.40, 45 minutes, five to six daily), Avignon (€7.10, 30 minutes, 10 or more daily) and Arles (€5.25, 30 to 45 minutes, four to eight daily).

**Train** The train station is at the southeastern end of ave Feuchères. Destinations include Paris' Gare de Lyon (€62.50, four hours by TGV, seven daily), Avignon (€7.10, 30 minutes, 10 or more daily), Marseille (€15.30, 1¼ hours, 12 daily) and Montpellier (€7.20, 30 minutes, 15 or more daily).

## AROUND NÎMES
### Pont du Gard
The Roman general Agrippa slung the mighty Pont du Gard over the Gard River around 19 BC. You won't be alone; this three-tier aqueduct, 275m long and 49m high, receives more than two million visitors a year.

There's a tourist kiosk on each bank and a brand new information centre on the left bank, set back from the river.

Buses from Avignon (26km) and Nîmes (23km) stop 1km north of the bridge.

## CARCASSONNE
**pop 46,250**
From afar, the old walled city of Carcassonne looks like a fairy-tale medieval city. Once inside the fortified walls, however, the magic rubs off. Luring some 200,000 visitors in July and August alone, it can be a tourist hell in high summer. Purists may sniff at Carcassonne's 'medieval' Cité – whose impressive fortifications were extensively renovated and rebuilt in the 19th century – but what the heck; it *is* magic, one of France's greatest skylines.

The Ville Basse (lower town), a more modest stepsister to camp Cinderella up the hill, has cheaper eating places and accommodation and also merits a browse.

### Orientation & Information
The Aude River separates the Ville Basse from the Cité on its hillock. The **main tourist office** (☎ 04 68 10 24 30) is in the Ville Basse opposite square Gambetta.

**Alerte Rouge** (Red Alert; 73 rue Verdun; open 10am-11pm daily) is an Internet café charging €4.80 per hour.

### Things to See
The 1.7km-long double ramparts of **La Cité** (spectacularly floodlit at night) are spiked with 52 witches' hat towers. Within are narrow, medieval streets and the 12th-century **Château Comtal** (Count's Castle), visited by guided tour only (adult/concession €4.50/3.50). A 40-minute tour in English departs up to five times daily, according to season.

### Places to Stay
**Camping** About 2km south of square Gambetta is **Camping de la Cité** (☎ 04 68 25 11 77, fax 04 68 47 33 13; route de St-Hilaire; tent site 2 people & car €12.20-16.80 according to season; open mid-Mar–early Oct). From mid-June to mid-September, bus No 8 connects the camp site with La Cité and the train station.

**Hostels** In the heart of the Cité, the large, cheery **Auberge de Jeunesse** (☎ 04 68 25 23 16; rue Vicomte Trencavel; dorm beds €12.20 including breakfast) has a snack bar offering light meals and a great outside terrace. The B&B at the **Centre International de Séjour** (☎ 04 68 11 17 00; 91 rue Aimé Ramon; dorm beds €8) in the Ville Basse is another option.

**Hotels** Handy for the train station is the recommended **Hôtel Astoria** (☎ 04 68 25 31 38; 18 rue Tourtel; singles/doubles from €18/ 20, with bathroom from €27).

Pricing policy at welcoming **Relais du Square** (☎ 04 68 72 31 72; 51 rue du Pont Vieux; 1- to 3-person room €30) couldn't be simpler; all the large rooms, accommodating one to three people, cost the same, whatever their facilities. So in summer get there early if you want your own bathroom.

### Places to Eat
In the Ville Basse, **Le Gargantua** (Mon-Fri menu €10.55, other menus from €21) is the restaurant of Relais du Square. **L'Italia** (32 route Minervoise), near the station, is a pizza-plus joint that also does takeaways. Next door is the more stylish **Restaurant Gil** (menus from €14) with Catalan-influenced meals.

### Getting There & Away
The train station is at the northern end of pedestrianised rue Georges Clemenceau. Carcassonne is on the main line linking Toulouse (€11.70, 50 minutes, 10 or more daily) with Béziers (€11.10, 50 minutes, five daily) and Montpellier (€17.70, 1½ hours, 10 or more daily).

## TOULOUSE
**pop 690,000**
Toulouse, France's fourth-largest city, is renowned for its high-tech industries, especially aerospace; local factories have built the Caravelle, Concorde and Airbus passenger planes and also the Ariane rocket. Like Montpellier, it's a youthful place with more than 110,000 students – more than any other French provincial city.

Most older buildings in the city centre are in rose-red brick, earning the city its nickname *la ville rose* (the pink city).

### Orientation
The heart of Toulouse is bounded to the east by blvd de Strasbourg and its continuation, blvd Lazare Carnot and, to the west, by the Garonne

River. Its two main squares are place du Capitole and, 300m eastwards, place Wilson.

## Information

The busy **tourist office** (☎ 05 61 11 02 22; *open 9am-6pm Mon-Fri, 9am-12.30pm & 2pm-6pm Sat, 9am-12.30pm & 2pm-5pm Sun Oct-Apr, 9am-7pm Mon-Sat, 10am-1pm & 2pm-6.15pm Sun May-Aug)* is in the Donjon du Capitole, a 16th-century tower on Square Charles de Gaulle.

Online time at Internet café **Résomania** *(85 rue Pargaminières; open until midnight daily)* is €3 per hour before noon and €4 between noon and midnight.

Major annual events include Festival Garonne with riverside music, dance and theatre (July), Musique d'Été with music of all definitions around town (July and August) and Jazz sur Son 31, an international jazz festival (October).

## Things to See & Do

**Cité de l'Espace** Space City (☎ 05 62 71 48 71; *adult/concession €12/10)* is a truly mind-boggling interactive space museum and planetarium. To get there, take bus No 15 from Allées Jean Jaurès to the end of the line, from where it's a 600m walk.

The **Galerie Municipale du Château d'Eau** *(place Laganne; adult/concession €2.30/1.50; open 1pm-7pm Wed-Mon)* is a world-class photographic gallery inside a 19th-century water tower at the western end of pont Neuf, just across the Garonne River.

**Musée des Augustins** *(21 rue de Metz; adult/student €2.20/free)* has a superb collection of paintings and stone artefacts.

Within the magnificent Gothic **Église des Jacobins**, the remains of St Thomas Aquinas (1225–74), an early head of the Dominican order, are interred on the north side.

The **Basilique St Sernin** is France's largest and most complete Romanesque structure. It's topped by a magnificent eight-sided 13th-century **tower**.

The **Jardin des Plantes** *(allée Jules Guesde)* is open until dusk daily. As well as being the site of the **Natural History Museum**, it has a fine collection of modern sculpture.

## Places to Stay

**Camping** The oft-packed **Camping de Rupé** (☎ 05 61 70 07 35; *21 chemin du Pont de Rupé; 2 people, car & tent €11.50; open*

*year-round)* is 6km northwest of the train station. Take bus No 59 (last departure 7.25pm) from place Jeanne d'Arc to the Rupé stop.

**Hotels** Avoid the cheap hotels near the train station; most are fairly sordid.

The exceptionally friendly **Hôtel Beauséjour** (☎/fax 05 61 62 77 59; *4 rue Caffarelli; basic rooms from €20, doubles/triples with bath €25/33)*, off Allées Jean Jaurès, is great value. **Hôtel Splendid** (☎/fax 05 61 62 43 02; *basic rooms from €13.72, singles/doubles/triples with bath €21.40/24.40/33.55)* is at No 13.

## Places to Eat

Fill yourself at lunchtime when there are some amazing deals. Look around – many places have lunch *menus* for €8 to €10. Unmissable and an essential Toulouse experience are the small, spartan, lunchtime-only **restaurants** on the 1st floor of Les Halles Victor Hugo covered market (great in itself for atmosphere and fresh produce). These places serve up generous quantities of hearty fare for €9 to €20.

Place St Georges is almost entirely taken over by café tables. Both blvd de Strasbourg and place du Capitole are lined with cafés and restaurants.

**Restaurant Saveur Bio** *(22 rue Maurice Fonvieille; lunch mixed plate or buffet €8, menus €19.50)* serves vegetarian food including a great-value buffet, and three *menus*.

## Entertainment

For what's on where, pick up a copy of *Toulouse Hebdo* (€0.90) or *Intramuros* (free from selected restaurants and bars). For life after dark, ask at the tourist office for its free listing *Toulouse By Night*.

Cafés around place St-Pierre beside the Garonne pull in a mainly young crowd. Nearby, the **Why Not Café** *(5 rue Pargaminières)* has a beautiful terrace while **Café des Artistes** *(13 place de la Daurade)* is an art-student hang-out.

Two hot discos near the centre are **La Strada** *(4 rue Gabriel Péri)* and **L'Ubu** *(16 rue St-Rome)*.

## Getting There & Away

**Bus** Toulouse's **bus station** (☎ 05 61 61 67 67), just north of the train station, serves mainly regional destinations that include

Andorra (€20, four hours, one to two daily). For longer distance travel, both **Intercars** (☎ 05 61 58 14 53) and **Eurolines** (☎ 05 61 26 40 04) have offices in Toulouse.

**Train** The train station, Gare Matabiau, is on blvd Pierre Sémard, about 1km northeast of the city centre.

Destinations served by multiple daily direct trains include Bayonne (€31, 3¾ hours), Bordeaux (€26.10, 2½ hours) and also Carcassonne (€11.70, 50 minutes). The fare to Paris is €56 by Corail (6½ hours, Gare d'Austerlitz) and €70.40 to €80 by TGV (5½ hours, Gare Montparnasse via Bordeaux).

**SNCF** (5 rue Peyras) provides information and ticketing.

# Provence

Provence was settled by the Ligurians, the Celts and the Greeks, but it was after its conquest by Julius Caesar in the mid-1st century BC that the region really began to flourish.

Many well-preserved amphitheatres, aqueducts and other buildings from the Roman period can still be seen in Arles and Nîmes (see the Languedoc-Roussillon section later). During the 14th century, the Catholic Church, then led by a series of French-born popes, moved its headquarters from feud riven Rome to Avignon, thus beginning the most resplendent period in that city's history.

## MARSEILLE
**pop 797,491**

The cosmopolitan and much maligned port of Marseille, France's second-largest city and third-most populous urban area, isn't in the least bit prettified for the benefit of tourists. Its urban geography and atmosphere derive from the diversity of its inhabitants, the majority of whom are immigrants (or their descendants) from the Mediterranean basin, West Africa and Indochina. Although Marseille is notorious for organised crime and racial tensions, the city is a vibrant and interesting place to explore.

### Orientation

The city's main street, La Canebière, stretches eastward from the Vieux Port. The train and bus stations are north of La Canebière at the top of blvd d'Athènes. The city centre is

around rue Paradis, which becomes more fashionable as you move south.

### Information

The **tourist office** (☎ 04 91 13 89 00, fax 04 91 13 89 20; ⓔ accueil@marseille-tourisme .com; 4 La Canebière; open 9am-7pm Mon-Sat, 10am-6pm Sun Oct-June, 9am-7.30pm Mon-Sat, 10am-6pm Sun July-Sept) is next to the Vieux Port. There are **annexes** (open Mon-Fri Sept-June, Mon-Sat July & Aug) at the train station and place des Pistoles.

**Info-Café** (☎ 04 91 33 74 98; 1 quai de Rive-Neuve; open 9am-10pm Mon-Sat, 2pm-7pm Sun) charges €3.60 an hour for Internet access, has more than 50 computer terminals, fast connections, a bar and harbour views.

**Dangers & Annoyances** Despite its fearsome reputation, Marseille is probably no more dangerous than other French cities. At night it's best to avoid the Belsunce area – the neighbourhood southwest of the train station and streets bordering La Canebière.

### Things to See & Do

Marseille grew up around the **Vieux Port**, where Greeks from Asia Minor established a settlement around 600 BC. The quarter north of quai du Port (around the Hôtel de Ville) was blown up by the Germans in 1943 and rebuilt after the war. The lively **place Thiars** pedestrian zone, with its many late-night restaurants and cafés, is south of the quai de Rive Neuve.

For panoramic views and overwrought mid-19th-century architecture, take Bus No 60 1km south of the Vieux Port to the **Basilique Notre Dame de la Garde**, the city's highest point.

**Museums** Unless otherwise noted, the museums listed are open 10am to 5pm Tuesday to Sunday, with extended hours in summer; all charge €2 to €3 for admission and admit students for half-price. The **Carte Privilèges** (€15.25/22.87/30.49 for 1/2/3 days) includes admission to all museums, boat fare to Le Château d'If and all public transport. It's only a good deal if you're going to the islands.

The **Centre de la Vieille Charité** (☎ 04 91 14 58 80; 2 rue de la Charité) is home to Marseille's **Museum of Mediterranean Archaeology** and has superb permanent exhibits on ancient Egypt and Greece. It's in the mostly North African Panier quarter (north of the Vieux Port).

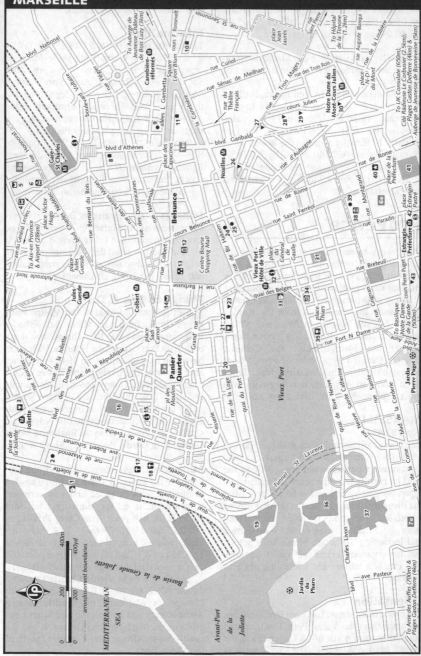

# MARSEILLE

## MARSEILLE

| PLACES TO STAY | | 2 | SNCM Ferries Office | 20 | Hôtel de Ville |
|---|---|---|---|---|---|
| 8 | Hôtel d'Athènes | 3 | Le Web Bar | 21 | La Caravelle |
| 10 | Hôtel Ozea; Hôtel Pied-à-Terre | 4 | Bus Station | 24 | Espaces Infos RTM |
| 11 | Hôtel Lutetia | 5 | Post Office | 25 | American Express |
| 22 | Hôtel Résidence du Vieux Port | 6 | Taxi Stand | 31 | Opéra |
| | | 7 | Tourist Information Annexe | 32 | Tourist Office |
| PLACES TO EAT | | 9 | Laverie des Allées | 33 | Boats to Château d'If & Îles |
| 23 | Restaurant Miramar | | Laundrette | | du Frioul |
| 26 | Marché des Capucins | 12 | Musée d'Histoire de | 34 | Info-Café |
| 27 | Restaurant Antillais | | Marseille | 35 | O'Malleys |
| 28 | Mosaic La Poudriere | 13 | Jardin des Vestiges | 36 | Bas Fort Saint Nicolas |
| 29 | Le Resto Provençal | 14 | Main Post Office | 37 | Fort d'Entrecasteaux & Fort |
| 30 | Le Chalet Berbere | 15 | Tourist Office Annexe | | Saint Nicolas |
| 43 | Fruit & Vegetable Market | 16 | Centre de la Vieille Charité | 38 | Musée Cantini |
| | | 17 | Nouvelle Cathédrale | 39 | SNCF Office |
| OTHER | | 18 | Ancienne Cathédrale de la | 40 | Préfecture de Police |
| 1 | Passenger Ferry Terminal | | Major | 41 | Préfecture |
| | (Gare Maritime) | 19 | Fort Saint Jean | 42 | Banque de France |

The **Musée Cantini** (☎ 04 91 54 77 75; 19 rue Grignan), off rue Paradis, hosts modern art exhibitions.

Roman history buffs will love the **Musée d'Histoire de Marseille** (☎ 04 91 90 42 22; ground floor, Centre Bourse shopping mall; open noon-7pm Mon-Sat), north of La Canebière. Its exhibits include the remains of a merchant ship dating to the 2nd century AD.

**Château d'If** Château d'If (☎ 04 91 59 02 30; admission €4; open 9am-7pm Tues-Sun Apr-Sept, 9am-7.30pm Tues-Sun Oct-Mar) is the 16th-century island fortress-turned-prison made infamous by Alexandre Dumas' The Count of Monte Cristo. Boats (€8 return; 20 minutes each way) depart from quai des Belges in the Vieux Port and continue to the nearby **Îles du Frioul** (€13 return for both islands).

**Cité Radieuse Le Corbusier** Finished in 1952, Le Corbusier's apartment building (☎ 04 91 77 14 07; 280 blvd Michelet, 8e; bus No 21 from La Canebière) has been much imitated but rarely with the famous architect's careful dimensions. Ask at the 3rd floor hotel (see Places to Stay) about **tours** (€5; minimum 3 people).

## Places to Stay

**Hostels** In the Montolivet neighbourhood, 4.5km east of the city centre, is **Auberge de Jeunesse Château de Bois Luzy** (☎/fax 04 91 49 06 18; Allées des Primevères, 12e; bus No 8 from La Canebière; dorm beds €7.62). HI cards are required.

The **Auberge de Jeunesse de Bonneveine** (☎ 04 91 17 63 30, fax 04 91 73 97 23; e ajemb@freesurf.fr; Impasse du Docteur Bonfils, 8e; dorm beds €11.90-16.40; closed Jan) is 4.5km south of the Vieux Port. Take bus No 44 from the Rond-Point du Prado metro stop to place Louis Bonnefon.

**Hotels – Train Station Area** Two-star **Hôtel d'Athènes** (☎ 04 91 90 12 93, fax 04 91 90 72 03; 37-39 blvd d'Athènes, 1er; rooms with bath/shower & toilet €34.30/38.15) is at the foot of the staircase leading from the train station into town. The well-kept rooms are comfortable but can be noisy.

**Hotels – Around La Canebière** New guests can arrive 24 hours a day at clean, simple **Hôtel Ozea** (☎/fax 04 91 47 91 84; 12 rue Barbaroux, 1er; doubles with/without shower €23/27; hall shower €3). At night just ring the bell to wake up the night clerk. There are well-kept rooms, but no hall showers, at **Hôtel Pied-à-Terre** (☎ 04 91 92 00 95; 18 rue Barbaroux, 1er; singles/doubles €26.50/20).

More expensive but worth the money is homey **Hôtel Lutetia** (☎ 04 91 50 81 78, fax 04 91 50 23 52; 38 Allées Léon Gambetta; singles/doubles €40/45, with bath €44/49) with smallish rooms with TV and phone.

**Hotels – Elsewhere** For water views, try three-star, seven-storey **Hôtel Résidence du Vieux Port** (☎ 04 91 91 91 22, fax 04 91 56 60 88; e hotel.residence@wanadoo.fr; 18 Quai du Port, 1er; singles/doubles €85/100, 5-person apartment €138).

**Hôtel Corbusier** (☎ *04 91 16 78 00, fax 04 91 16 78 28;* e *hotelcorbusier@wana doo.fr; 280 blvd Michelet, 8e; doubles €38)* has simple but stylish rooms in a famous apartment block.

## Places to Eat

Fresh fruit and vegies are sold at the **Marché des Capucins** *(place des Capucins; open Mon-Sat)*, one block south of La Canebière.

Restaurants along pedestrianised cours Julien, a few blocks south of La Canebière, offer an incredible variety of cuisines: Antillean, Pakistani, Thai, Lebanese, Tunisian and even French.

**Restaurant Antillais** *(10 cours Julien; mains from €6.50, menu with house wine €16)* features West Indian cuisine. **Mosaic La Poudriere** (☎ *04 91 47 48 32; 36-38 cours Julien; dinner menu €14; open 10am-midnight Tues-Sat, 2pm-midnight Mon)* is a bar, restaurant and illustrated book store. **Le Resto Provençal** *(62 cours Julien; menu €20; open Tues-Sat)* does regional French cuisine.

**Le Chalet Berbere** (☎ *04 96 12 08 47; 94 cours Julien; mains from €7; open Tues-Sun lunch, Mon-Sat dinner)* is a small but smart Algerian couscous place.

Restaurants line the streets around place Thiars on the south side of the Vieux Port. Though many offer bouillabaisse, the rich fish stew for which Marseille is famous, you must wander to the other side of the harbour to **Restaurant Miramar** (☎ *04 91 91 10 40; 12 quai du Port)* to find the real (and really expensive at €48) thing.

## Entertainment

Listings magazines such as *Vox Mag, Ventilo* and *Cesar* are distributed for free at the tourist office. *Sortir* comes out with the Friday edition of *La Provence* newspaper; look out for *PAF*, a monthly one-page gig guide.

**Le Web Bar** (☎ *04 96 11 65 11; 114 Rue République; open 10am-2am daily)* hosts all kinds of funky music events including brunch concerts.

Atmospheric **La Caravelle** (☎ *04 91 90 36 64; 34 quai du Port)* is a jazzy bar with views of the port. On the other side of the water is **O'Malleys Irish pub** *(9 quai de Rive Neuve)*.

## Getting There & Away

**Bus** The bus station (☎ *04 91 08 16 40; place Victor Hugo)*, 150m to the right as you

exit the train station, offers services to Aix-en-Provence, Avignon, Cannes, Nice, Nice airport and Orange, among others.

**Eurolines** (☎ *04 91 50 57 55)* has buses to Spain, Italy, Morocco, the UK and other countries. Its counter in the bus station is open from 9am to noon and 2pm to 5.30pm (closed Sunday).

**Train** Marseille's passenger train station, served by both metro lines, is called **Gare St Charles** (☎ *0836 35 35 35)*. Services along Voie (platform A) include a busy ticket office, sparkling **toilets** *(admission €0.40; open 6am-midnight daily)* and **left luggage** *(from €3 per piece for 72hr; open 7.15am-10pm)*. There's a **tourist information annexe** out the side door at the top of the platform.

From Marseille there are trains to more or less any place in France. Some sample destinations are Paris' Gare de Lyon (€77.10, 3¼ hours by TGV, 18 daily), Avignon via Arles (€17.10, one hour, 20 daily), Nice (€25, 1½ hours), Barcelona (€60.40, 8½ hours) and Geneva (€49.50, 6½ hours).

**Ferry** The **Société Nationale Maritime Corse-Méditerranée** *(SNCM;* ☎ *08 36 67 95 00, fax 04 91 56 35 86)* runs ferries from the *gare maritime* (passenger ferry terminal) at the foot of blvd des Dames. There's also an **SNCM office** *(61 blvd des Dames; open Mon-Sat)*. For ferries to Corsica, Italy and Sardinia call ☎ 0891 701 801 and for Algeria and Tunisia call ☎ 0891 702 802.

## Getting Around

**Bus & Metro** Marseille has a trolley bus line and an extensive bus network, operating from 5am to 9pm. Night buses and tram No 68 run from 9pm to 1am (12.30am Saturday and Sunday). Two easy-to-use metro lines run to about 9pm (to 12.30am Friday to Sunday). Tickets (single/carnet of six €1.40/6.50) are valid on all services for one hour. Time-stamp your ticket when you board the bus. For more information, visit the **Espace Infos RTM** (☎ *04 91 91 92 10; 6-8 rue des Fabres)*.

## AROUND MARSEILLE
### Aix-en-Provence
pop 134,324

One of the most appealing cities in Provence, Aix owes its atmosphere to the students who make up more than 20% of the population.

The city is renowned for its *calissons*, almond-paste confectionery, and also for being the birthplace of the postimpressionist painter Cézanne. Aix hosts the Festival International d'Art Lyrique each July.

The **tourist office** (☎ *04 42 16 11 61, fax 04 42 16 11 62;* e *infos@aixenprovence tourism.com; place Général de Gaulle)* has walking tour brochures. Aix is easy to see on a day trip from Marseille, and frequent trains (€4.10) make the 35-minute trip.

**Things to See** The mostly pedestrianised old city is a maze of tiny streets of ethnic restaurants and specialist food shops, along with elegant 17th- and 18th-century mansions.

Aix also has several interesting museums, the finest of which is the **Musée Granet** *(place St Jean de Malte; admission varies; open Wed-Mon).* The collection includes paintings from the 16th to 19th centuries, including some lesser known Cézanne works. Slow-moving renovations mean the museum may be only partially open.

**Places to Stay** About 2km southeast of town is **Camping Arc-en-Ciel** (☎ *04 42 26 14 28; route de Nice; camp sites €17.10; open Apr-Sept)* at Pont des Trois Sautets. Take bus No 3 to Les Trois Sautets stop. **Auberge de Jeunesse du Jas de Bouffan** (☎ *04 42 20 15 99, fax 04 42 59 36 12; 3 ave Marcel Pagnol; beds €14 including breakfast & sheets)* is 2km west of the centre. Rooms are locked between 9am and 5pm. Take bus No 4 from La Rotonde to the Vasarely stop. **Hôtel Cardinal** (☎ *04 42 38 32 30, fax 04 42 26 39 05; 24 rue Cardinale; singles/doubles €46/58, self-catering suites €73)* has large rooms with shower, toilet and a mix of modern and period furniture. The small self-catering suites are in its annexe at 12 rue Cardinale.

**Places to Eat** Pop your head into **Les Deux Garçons** *(53 cours Mirabeau),* the café where everyone from Cézanne to Sartre drank and chatted. **Restaurant Gu et Fils** *(3 rue Frédéric Mistral)* serves delicious regional meals.

## AVIGNON
**pop 85,937**
Avignon acquired its ramparts and its reputation as a city of art and culture during the 14th century, when Pope Clement V and his court, fleeing political turmoil in Rome, established themselves here. From 1309 to 1377 huge sums of money were invested in building and decorating the popes' palace. Even after the pontifical court returned to Rome amid bitter charges that Avignon had become a den of criminals and brothel-goers, the city remained an important cultural centre.

Today, Avignon maintains its tradition as a patron of the arts, most notably through its annual performing arts festival. The city also has interesting museums, including several across the Rhône in Villeneuve-lès-Avignon.

The world-famous Festival d'Avignon in July attracts hundreds of artists who put on some 300 performances of all sorts each day.

## Orientation
The main avenue in the walled city runs northward from the train station to place de l'Horloge; it's called cours Jean Jaurès south of the tourist office and rue de la République north of it. Rue des Teinturiers in the southeastern segment of the walled city is dotted with cool cafés, galleries and shops. The island that runs down the middle of the Rhône between Avignon and Villeneuve-lès-Avignon is known as Île de la Barthelasse.

## Information
The helpful **tourist office** (☎ *04 32 74 32 74, fax 04 90 82 95 03;* e *information@ot -avignon.fr; 41 cours Jean Jaurès; open 9am-6pm Mon-Sat, 10am-5pm Sun Apr-Oct, 9am-7pm Mon-Sat, 10am-5pm Sun July, 9am-6pm Mon-Fri, 9am-5pm Sat, 10am-noon Sun Nov-Mar)* is 300m north of the train station. There's an annexe at pont St Bénézet (open April to October).

The **main post office** *(cours Président Kennedy)* can be accessed via Porte de la République from the train station.

**Cyberdrome** (☎ *04 90 16 05 15;* e *cyber drome@wanadoo.fr; 68 rue Guillaume Puy; open 7am-1am)* is a decent Internet café charging €4.60 an hour.

## Things to See & Do
**Palais des Papes & Around** Avignon's leading tourist attraction is the fortified Palace of the Popes *(adult/concession €11/7.50 including admission to pont St Bénézet; open 9am-7pm daily Apr-June, 9am-8pm July-Sept, 9.30am-5.45pm Oct-Mar),* built during the 14th century. The seemingly endless halls, chapels, corridors and staircases were once

FRANCE

# AVIGNON

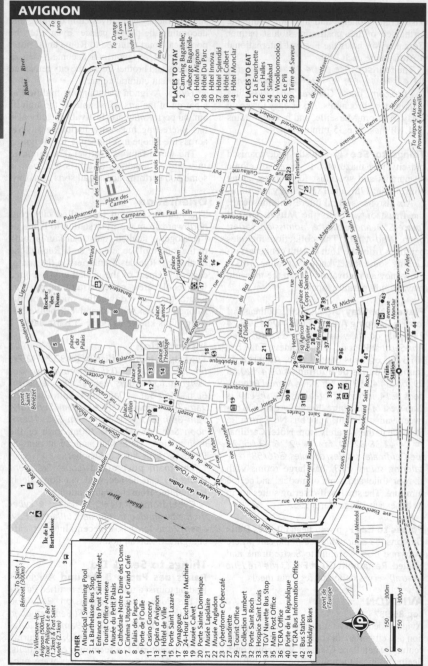

PLACES TO STAY
2  Camping Bagatelle;
   Auberge Bagatelle
10 Hôtel Mignon
28 Hôtel Du Parc
30 Hôtel Innova
37 Hôtel Splendid
38 Hôtel Colbert
44 Hôtel Monclar

PLACES TO EAT
12 La Fourchette
16 Les Halles
24 Sindabad
25 Woolloomooloo
26 Le Pili
39 Terre de Saveur

OTHER
1  Municipal Swimming Pool
3  La Barthelasse Bus Stop
4  Entrance to Pont Saint Bénézet;
   Tourist Office Annexe
5  Musée du Petit Palais
6  Cathédrale Notre Dame des Doms
7  Cinéma Utopia; Le Grand Café
8  Palais des Papes
9  Porte de l'Oulle
11 Casino Grocery
13 Opéra d'Avignon
14 Hôtel de Ville
15 Porte Saint Lazare
18 24-Hour Exchange Machine
19 Musée Calvet
20 Porte Sainte Dominique
21 Musée Lapidaire
22 Musée Angladon
23 Cyberdrome Cybercafé
27 Laundrette
29 Tourist Office
31 Collection Lambert
32 Porte Saint Roch
33 Hospice Saint Louis
34 TGV Navette Bus Stop
35 Main Post Office
36 TCRA Office
40 Porte de la République
41 TCRA Bus Information Office
42 Bus Station
43 Holiday Bikes

To Villeneuve-lès-
Avignon (500m), Bel
Tranquille & Rel
(1.2km) & Pont Saint
André (2.1km)

To Saint
Bénézet (300m)

sumptuously decorated, but these days they are nearly empty except for a few damaged frescoes.

At the far northern end of place du Palais, the **Musée du Petit Palais** *(adult/concession €4.50/2.50; open 9.30am-1pm & 2pm-5.30pm Wed-Mon Oct-May, 10am-1pm & 2pm-6pm Wed-Mon June-Sept)* houses an outstanding collection of 13th- to 16th-century Italian religious paintings. Just up the hill is **Rocher des Doms**, a park with great views of the Rhône, pont St Bénézet and Villeneuve-lès-Avignon.

**Pont St Bénézet** Originally built in the 12th century to link Avignon and Villeneuve-lès-Avignon, this is the **'pont d'Avignon'** *(same hours as Palais des Papes)* mentioned in the French nursery rhyme. Once 900m long, the bridge was repaired and rebuilt several times until all but four of its 22 spans were washed away in the 17th century.

**Museums** Housed in an 18th-century mansion, the **Musée Calvet** *(☎ 04 90 86 33 84; 65 rue Joseph Vernet; adult/concession €5/3; open Wed-Mon)* has a collection of ancient Egyptian, Greek and Roman artefacts as well as paintings from the 16th to 20th centuries. Its annexe, the **Musée Lapidaire** *(27 rue de la République; adult/concession €5/3; open Wed-Mon)* houses sculpture and statuary from the Gallo-Roman, Romanesque and Gothic periods.

The **Collection Lambert** *(☎ 04 90 16 56 20; 5 rue Violette; adult/concession €5/4; open Tues-Sun)* is a new contemporary art museum displaying the astonishing collection of art dealer Yvon Lambert.

The **Musée Angladon** *(☎ 04 90 82 29 03; 5 rue Laboureur; adult/concession €5/3; open 1pm-6pm Wed-Sun, also Tues mid-June–mid-Oct)* was once a private home; now it shows 19th- and 20th-century paintings to the public. It's the only place in the region you can see a Van Gogh painting.

**Villeneuve-lès-Avignon** Avignon's picturesque sister city can be reached by foot or bus No 10 from the main post office. A pass for the following attractions costs €6.86.

The **Chartreuse du Val de Bénédiction** *(☎ 04 90 15 24 24; 60 rue de la République; adult/concession €5.50/3.50)* was once the largest and most important Carthusian

monastery in France. The **Musée Pierre de Luxembourg** *(☎ 04 90 27 49 66; 3 rue de la République; adult/concession €3/1.90; open Tues-Sun, closed Feb)* has a fine collection of religious paintings. The **Tour Philippe le Bel** *(☎ 04 32 70 08 57; admission €1.60/0.90)*, a defensive tower built in the 14th century at what was then the northwestern end of pont St Bénézet, has great views of Avignon's walled city, the river and the surrounding countryside. Another Provençal panorama can be enjoyed from the 14th-century **Fort St André** *(☎ 04 90 25 45 35; adult/concession €4/2.50)*.

## Special Events
The **Festival d'Avignon** *(☎ 04 90 14 14 60, fax 04 90 27 66 83; ⓦ www.festival-avignon .com)* is held every year during the last three weeks of July. Tickets can be reserved from mid-June onwards.

## Places to Stay
**Camping** Three-star **Camping Bagatelle** *(☎ 04 90 86 30 39, fax 04 90 27 16 23; Île de la Barthelasse; bus No 10 from main post office to Barthelasse stop; sites per adult/tent €3.78/2.59; reception open 8am-9pm year-round)* is an attractive, shaded camping ground just north of pont Édouard Daladier, 850m from the walled city.

**Hostels** The 210-bed **Auberge Bagatelle** *(☎ 04 90 86 30 39, fax 04 90 27 16 23; Île de la Barthelasse; dorm beds €10.17)* is part of a large, park-like area that includes Camping Bagatelle. See Camping for bus directions.

**Hotels – Within the Walls** There are three hotels all close to each other on the same street. **Hôtel Du Parc** *(☎ 04 90 82 71 55, fax 04 90 85 64 86; ⓔ hotelsurparc@aol.com; 18 rue Agricol Perdiguier; singles/doubles without shower €29/34, with shower €36/42)* is an option.

**Hôtel Splendid** *(☎ 04 90 86 14 46, fax 04 90 85 38 55; ⓔ contacthotel@infonie.fr; 17 rue Agricol Perdiguier; singles/doubles with shower €34/43, with shower & toilet €36/46)* is a friendly place.

Two-star **Hôtel Colbert** *(☎ 04 90 86 20 20, fax 04 90 85 97 00; ⓔ colberthotel@wanadoo .fr; 7 rue Agricol Perdiguier; singles with shower €42, doubles/triples with shower & toilet €52/79)* is the third in the trio.

The always-busy **Hôtel Innova** (☎ 04 90 82 54 10, fax 04 90 82 52 39; e hotel.in nova@wanadoo.fr; 100 rue Joseph Vernet; rooms €23-41) has comfortable rooms that are soundproofed.

**Hôtel Mignon** (☎ 04 90 82 17 30, fax 04 90 85 78 46; e hotel.mignon@wanadoo.fr; 12 rue Joseph Vernet; singles/doubles with shower & toilet €37/43) has spotless rooms with English-language cable TV and decent breakfasts (€4).

**Hotels – Outside the Walls** The noisy, family-run **Hôtel Monclar** (☎ 04 90 86 20 14, fax 04 90 85 94 94; e hmonclar 84@aol.com; 13 ave Monclar; rooms for 1 or 2 people with shower & toilet from €45, triples/quads from €45/55) is just across the tracks from the train station. The hotel has its own car park (€4.50) and a pretty back garden.

## Places to Eat

For self-catering try **Les Halles food market** (place Pie; open 7am-1pm Tues-Sun).

**Le Grand Café** (☎ 04 90 86 86 77; la Manutention, 4 rue des Escaliers Ste Anne; mains around €15; open Tues-Sat) in the Cinèma Utopia complex is a sophisticated place for a Provençal lunch, dinner or drink.

**La Fourchette** (☎ 04 90 85 20 93; 17 rue Racine; menus €21-26; open Mon-Fri) is a homey Michelin-recommended place. Try the salmon with saffron and lentil salad.

On the other side of town, in a groovy little strip, **Woolloomooloo** (16 bis rue des Teinturiers; lunch menu €11; open Tues-Sat) draws a young crowd with its international menu.

**Terre de Saveur** (☎ 04 90 86 68 72; 1 rue St Michel; vegetarian lunch menu €13; open 11.30am-2.30pm Tues-Sat, 7pm-9.30pm Fri & Sat), just off place des Corps Saints, has vegetarian dishes like tortilla da quinoa.

Nearby, **Le Pili** (☎ 04 90 27 39 53; 34-36 place des Corps Saints; meals about €8) has good wood-fired pizza and steaks.

## Entertainment

**Cinèma Utopia** (☎ 04 90 82 65 36; 4 rue des Escaliers Ste Anne; tickets €3-5) is a student entertainment/cultural centre with a jazz club, café and four cinemas screening nondubbed films. There's an annexe at 5 Rue Figuiere. The tourist office has programmes.

## Getting There & Away

**Bus** The bus station (☎ 04 90 82 07 35; 5 ave Monclar) is down the ramp as you exit the train station. Destinations include Aix-en-Provence (€12, 1¼ hours), Arles (€7.80, one hour), Nice (€27), and Marseille (€15.20, 2½ hours). Tickets are sold on the buses.

**Train** The train station (Gare Avignon Centre; ☎ 0893 35 35 35) is across blvd St Roch from Porte de la République. There are frequent trains to Arles (€7, 20 minutes), Nice (€35.40, three hours), Nîmes (€7.10, 35 minutes) and Paris (€63.70, three hours via TGV). Most TGV services leave from **Gare Avignon TGV** (Quartier de Courtine), accessible by frequent shuttle bus from outside the main post office. The tourist office has timetables.

## Getting Around

TCRA municipal buses operate 7am to about 7.40pm. Tickets cost €1 or €7.80 for a carnet of 10 tickets; they're available from drivers, tabacs and the **TCRA office** (☎ 04 32 74 18 32; ave de Latre de Tassigny).

**Holiday Bikes** (☎ 04 90 27 92 61, fax 04 90 95 66 41; e motovelo@provencebike.com; 52 blvd St Roch; open 9am-6.30pm daily) rents road bikes (€14 per day) and scooters (from €30).

## ARLES
**pop 50,467**

Arles began its ascent to prosperity in 49 BC when Julius Caesar, to whom the city had given its support, sacked Marseille, which had backed the Roman general Pompey. It soon became a major trading centre and by the late 1st century AD, needed a 20,000-seat amphitheatre and a 12,000-seat theatre. Now known as the **Arènes** and the **Théâtre Antique** respectively, they are still used to stage bullfights and cultural events.

Arles is also known for its **Église St Trophime** and **Cloître St Trophime**. Significant parts of both date from the 12th century and are in the Romanesque style. But the city is probably best known as the place where Van Gogh painted some of his most famous works, including The Sunflowers. The **tourist office** (☎ 04 90 18 41 20; e ot-arles@visit provence.com; esplanade des Lices) can help with information.

There are bus services to Marseille (€14.60, 2½ hours), Aix-en-Provence (€11.40, 1¾ hours) and Avignon (€6, 1½ hours, including a shuttle that connects with the TGV to Lyon and Paris).

# Côte d'Azur

The Côte d'Azur, which includes the French Riviera, stretches along France's Mediterranean coast from Toulon to the Italian border. Many of the towns here – budget-busting St Tropez, Cannes, Antibes, Nice and Monaco – have become world-famous thanks to the recreational activities of the tanned and idle rich. The reality is rather less glamorous, but the Côte d'Azur still has a great deal to attract visitors: sunshine, 40km of beaches, all sorts of cultural activities and, sometimes, even a bit of glitter.

Unless you're camping or hostelling, your best bet is to stay in Nice, which has a generous supply of cheap hotels, and make day trips to other places. Note that theft from backpacks, pockets, cars and even laundrettes is a serious problem along the Côte d'Azur, especially at train and bus stations.

## NICE
### pop 343,123
Known as the capital of the Riviera, the fashionable yet relaxed city of Nice makes a great base from which to explore the entire Côte d'Azur. The city, which did not become part of France until 1860, has plenty of relatively cheap accommodation and is only a short train or bus ride from the rest of the Riviera. Nice's beach may be nothing to write home about, but the city has some fine museums.

### Orientation
Ave Jean Médecin runs from near the train station to place Masséna. Vieux Nice is the area delineated by the quai des États-Unis, blvd Jean Jaurès and the 92m hill known as Le Château. The neighbourhood of Cimiez, home to several very good museums, is north of the town centre.

### Information
The **main tourist office** (☎ 04 93 87 07 07, fax 04 93 16 85 16; e info@nicetourism.com; open 8am-7pm Mon-Sat, 9am-6pm Sun, 9am-8pm July-Sept) is at the train station. There's an **annexe** (☎ 04 92 14 48 00; 5 promenade des Anglais; open 9am-6pm Mon-Sat).

The **main post office** (23 ave Thiers) is one block from the train station.

Opposite the train station, **Le Change** (☎ 04 93 88 56 80; 17 ave Thiers; open 7.30am-9pm), to the right as you exit the terminal, offers decent rates. **American Express** (☎ 04 93 16 53 53; 11 promenade des Anglais; open Mon-Sat) also has currency exchange.

Access the Internet for €5 an hour at **Société Sencom** (☎ 04 97 03 23 10; cnr Paganini & Rue Belgique; open 10am-8pm daily). **Master Home** (☎ 04 93 80 33 82; 11 rue de la Préfecture), a pub in the old town, charges €6 an hour.

### Things to See
An excellent-value museum pass (€8/25 for one/seven days), available at tourist offices and participating museums, gives free admission to 60 Côte d'Azur museums. There's a cheaper one for Nice's museums. Unless otherwise noted, the following museums are open Wednesday to Monday from around 10am to 5pm or 6pm (sometimes with a break for lunch in the off season), and entry is around €4/2 per adult/concession.

The **Musée d'Art Moderne et d'Art Contemporain** (Museum of Modern and Contemporary Art; ave St Jean Baptiste; bus Nos 3, 5, 7, 16 & 17) has conceptual works by artists such as Arman and Yves Klein.

Vivid paintings of Old Testament scenes dominate the **Musée Marc Chagall** (☎ 04 93 53 87 20; 16 ave Docteur Ménard, opposite No 4; adult/concession €5.50/4). Ask at the ticket counter for a free bus ticket to Cimiez.

A 17th-century Genoese villa houses the **Musée Matisse** (☎ 04 93 81 08 08; 164 ave des Arènes de Cimiez) in Cimiez. Bus No 15 is convenient; get off at the Arènes stop.

The **Musée Archéologique** (Archaeology Museum; ☎ 04 93 81 59 57; 160 ave des Arènes de Cimiez) and nearby **Gallo-Roman ruins** (which include public baths and an amphitheatre) are next to the Musée Matisse.

Nice's **Russian Orthodox Cathedral of St Nicholas** (admission €2; open Mon-Sat, & Sun afternoon, closed noon-2.30pm), built between 1903 and 1912, is crowned by six onion-shaped domes. Shorts, short skirts and sleeveless shirts are forbidden.

### Activities
Nice's **beach** is covered with pebbles, not sand. Between mid-April and mid-October,

FRANCE

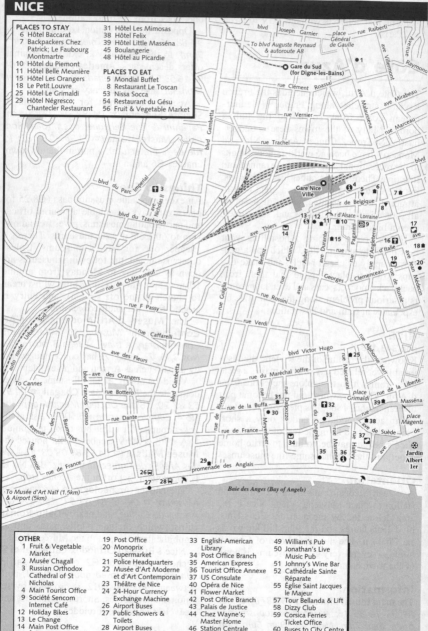

# NICE

**PLACES TO STAY**
6 Hôtel Baccarat
7 Backpackers Chez
Patrick; Le Faubourg
Montmartre
10 Hôtel du Piemont
11 Hôtel Belle Meunière
15 Hôtel Les Orangers
18 Le Petit Louvre
25 Hôtel Le Grimaldi
29 Hôtel Négresco;
Chantecler Restaurant

31 Hôtel Les Mimosas
38 Hôtel Felix
39 Hôtel Little Masséna
45 Boulangerie
48 Hôtel au Picardie

**PLACES TO EAT**
5 Mondial Buffet
8 Restaurant Le Toscan
53 Nissa Socca
54 Restaurant du Gésu
56 Fruit & Vegetable Market

**OTHER**
1 Fruit & Vegetable
Market
2 Musée Chagall
3 Russian Orthodox
Cathedral of St
Nicholas
4 Main Tourist Office
9 Société Sencom
Internet Café
12 Holiday Bikes
13 Le Change
14 Main Post Office
16 Église Notre Dame
17 UK Consulate

19 Post Office
20 Monoprix
Supermarket
21 Police Headquarters
22 Musée d'Art Moderne
et d'Art Contemporain
23 Théâtre de Nice
24 24-Hour Currency
Exchange Machine
26 Airport Buses
27 Public Showers &
Toilets
28 Airport Buses
30 Laundrette
32 Anglican Church

33 English-American
Library
34 Post Office Branch
35 American Express
36 Tourist Office Annexe
37 US Consulate
40 Opéra de Nice
41 Flower Market
42 Post Office Branch
43 Palais de Justice
44 Chez Wayne's;
Master Home
46 Station Centrale
Terminus
47 Intercity Bus Station

49 William's Pub
50 Jonathan's Live
Music Pub
51 Johnny's Wine Bar
52 Cathédrale Sainte
Réparate
55 Église Saint Jacques
le Majeur
57 Tour Bellanda & Lift
58 Dizzy Club
59 Corsica Ferries
Ticket Office
60 Buses to City Centre
61 Ferry Terminal;
SNCM Office

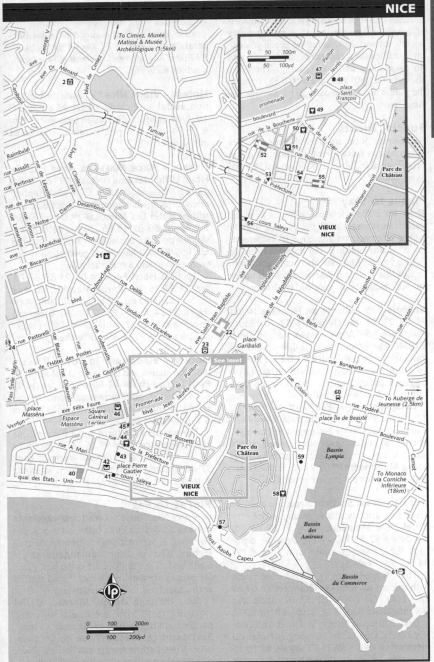

NICE

FRANCE

To Cimiez, Musée
Matisse & Musée
Archéologique (1.5km)

0    50    100m
0    50    100yd

ave George V
ave Dr Ménard
blvd de Cimiez
Cambou

2

47
du Paillon
Jean Jaurès
48 place
Saint
François

promenade
boulevard
rue de la Boucherie
49

pkwy de Cimiez
ave de Cimiez
Tunnel

50
rue de la Loge
51

Raimbaldi
rue Assalit
rue de la Répartie
rue Pertinax
rue de Paris
rue Lamartine
rue Miron
Notre
Dame Desambrois
Maréchal

52
rue Rossetti
53
rue de la Préfecture
54
55

Parc du
Château

allée Professeur Benoît

56    cours Saleya

VIEUX
NICE

ave Biscarra

Foch
21
blvd Carabacel
Dubouchage
rue Delille
rue Tonduti de l'Escarène

ave Saint Jean Baptiste
ave Gallieni
esplanade Kennedy
ave de la République

rue Augusta Gal
rue Arson

24
rue Pastorelli
rue Gioffredo
rue Barla

rue de l'Hôtel des Postes
rue Blacas
rue Charvain
Alberti

22
23
place
Garibaldi

rue Bonaparte

rue Cassini
60
rue Fodéré

To Auberge de
Jeunesse (2.5km)

Pass Émile Négrin
place
Masséna
Espace
Masséna
ave Félix Faure
Square
Général
Leclerc
46
45
44
43
Promenade
Jean Jaurès
blvd
du Paillon

rue Rossetti
rue de la Préfecture
place
Île de Beauté

Verdun
rue A. Mari
42    place Pierre
Gautier
41    cours Saleya
40
quai des États-Unis

VIEUX
NICE

Parc du
Château

59

58

Bassin
Lympia

Boulevard
Carnot

To Monaco
via Corniche
Inférieure
(18km)

57

Quai Rauba Capeu

Bassin
des
Amiraux

Bassin
du Commerce

61

See Inset

0    100    200m
0    100    200yd

free public beaches alternate with private beaches (€8 to €13 a day) that have all sorts of amenities (mattresses, showers, changing rooms, security etc). Along the beach you can hire paddle boats, sailboards and jet skis, and go parasailing and water-skiing. There are showers (€1.80) and toilets (€0.35) open to the public located opposite 50 promenade des Anglais.

## Special Events

Parties in Nice include the Festin des Cougourdons (gourd feast) in March, a jiving Jazz Festival in July and the Vineyard Festival in September.

## Places to Stay

There are quite a few cheap hotels near the train station and lots of places in a slightly higher price bracket along rue d'Angleterre, rue d'Alsace-Lorraine, rue de Suisse, rue de Russie and rue Durante, also near the station. In summer the inexpensive places fill up by late morning – book your bed by 10am.

**Hostels** The **Auberge de Jeunesse** (☎ 04 93 89 23 64, fax 04 92 04 03 10; Route Forestière de Mont Alban; dorm beds €13.40; curfew midnight) is 4km east of the train. It's often full – call ahead. Take bus No 14 from the Station Centrale terminus on Square Général Leclerc, linked to the train station by bus Nos 15 and 17.

**Backpackers Chez Patrick** (☎ 04 93 80 30 72; 32 rue Pertinax; e chezpatrick@viola.fr; dorm beds €18) is well-managed and friendly. There's no curfew or daytime closure. If it's full, ask downstairs at the restaurant **Le Faubourg Montmartre** (☎ 04 93 62 55 03; 32 rue Pertinax; rooms per person about €15).

**Hotels – Train Station Area** For a cruisy place that attracts lots of young people try **Hôtel Belle Meunière** (☎ 04 93 88 66 15, fax 04 93 82 51 76; 21 ave Durante; dorm beds €13, doubles/triples with bath €79/94.50; open Feb-Nov).

The welcome is patchy, but there are rooms with balcony at **Hôtel Les Orangers** (☎ 04 93 87 51 41, fax 04 93 82 57 82; 10bis ave Durante; dorm beds €14, doubles from €34).

Rue d'Alsace-Lorraine is dotted with two-star hotels. One of the cheapest is **Hôtel du Piemont** (☎ 04 93 88 25 15, fax 04 93 16 15 18; singles/doubles with washbasin & shower

from €24.50/28.50), at No 19. There are kitchenettes in the old-fashioned rooms.

Also in this neighbourhood is **Hôtel Baccarat** (☎ 04 93 88 35 73, fax 04 93 16 14 25; 39 Rue d'Angleterre; dorm beds €14, singles/doubles €29/36).

**Hotels – Vieux Nice** Opposite the bus station, **Hôtel au Picardie** (☎ 04 93 85 75 51; 10 blvd Jean Jaurès; singles/doubles from €19/24) also has pricier rooms with toilet and shower.

**Hotels – Place Masséna Area** Friendly **Hôtel Little Masséna** (☎/fax 04 93 87 72 34; 22 rue Masséna; doubles €26-42; reception open to 8pm) has rooms with hotplate and fridge. **Hôtel Les Mimosas** (☎ 04 93 88 05 59, fax 04 93 87 15 65; 26 rue de la Buffa; singles/doubles/triples with shared facilities €30.50/37/48) has clean, good-sized rooms with air-con and a cute sheep dog.

Spotless **Hôtel Felix** (☎ 04 93 88 67 73, fax 04 93 16 15 78; rue Masséna; doubles €75) is hard to beat. **Hôtel Le Grimaldi** (☎ 04 93 16 00 24, fax 04 93 87 00 24; e zedde@le-grimaldi.com; 15 Rue Grimaldi; singles/doubles €80/90) has stylish, cheery rooms.

**Hotels – Elsewhere in Town** Between the train station and the beach is colourful **Le Petit Louvre** (☎ 04 93 80 15 54, fax 04 93 62 45 08; e petitlouvre@aol.com; 10 rue Emma Tiranty; singles/doubles with shower & toilet €34/43).

The top rooms in town are at belle epoque **Hôtel Négresco** (☎ 04 93 16 64 00, fax 04 93 88 35 68; e direction@hotel-negresco.com; 37 promenade des Anglais; rooms without/with seaview from €213/297).

## Places to Eat

In Vieux Nice, there's a **fruit and vegetable market** (cours Saleya; open 6am-5.30pm Tues-Sat, & Sun morning) in front of the préfecture. The no-name **boulangerie** at the south end of rue du Marché is the best place for pizza slices and michettes (bread stuffed with cheese, olives, and anchovies).

Near the train station, **Mondial Buffet** (☎ 04 93 16 15 51; 7 ave Thiers) has cheap noodles and rice dishes. In the same vicinity, **Restaurant Le Toscan** (1 rue de Belgique; open Tues-Sat), a family-run Italian place, offers large portions of home-made ravioli.

Nearby, **Le Faubourg Montmartre** (☎ *04 93 62 55 03; 32 rue Pertinax; menu €11)*, beneath the Backpackers Hotel, is always crowded. The house speciality is *bouillabaisse* (€28 for two).

In the old city, **Nissa Socca** (*5 rue Ste Reparate; menu €13)* is a perennial favourite. Its Niçois specialities include *socca* (chickpea pancakes), *farcis* (stuffed vegetables) and ratatouille.

**Restaurant du Gésu** (*1 place du Jésus; pasta about €7; no credit cards)* is local, cheap and loud.

**Chantecler** (*lunch/dinner menus from €40/90)* is the much-fêted restaurant at Hôtel Négresco (see Places to Stay earlier).

## Entertainment

**William's Pub** (*4 rue Centrale; open Mon-Sat)* has live music starting at around 9pm. There's pool, darts and chess in the basement. **Jonathan's Live Music Pub** (*1 rue de la Loge)* has live music every night in summer. **Chez Wayne's** (☎ *04 93 13 46 99; 15 rue de la Préfecture)* is an expat pub with live bands on Friday and Saturday and karaoke on Sunday. Happy hour is 6pm to 9pm.

Local students and backpackers come for the live music and cheap pasta (€7.95) at **Johnny's Wine Bar** (*1 Rue Rossetti; open Mon-Sat)*, east of Cathédrale Ste Réparate.

At the port there's **Dizzy Club** (☎ *06 13 16 78 81; 26 quai Lunel; open from 11.30pm Wed-Sun)* with an eclectic roster of drum 'n' bass, breakbeat and pure house nights.

## Getting There & Away

**Air** Nice's **airport** (☎ *04 93 21 30 30)* is 6km west of the city centre. Bus No 98 runs along the beach between the airport and the city centre (€3.50).

**Bus** The intercity bus station, opposite 10 blvd Jean Jaurès, is served by around two dozen bus companies. There are slow but frequent services daily until about 7.30pm to Cannes (€5.70, 1½ hours), Antibes (€4.50, 1¼ hours), Menton (€4.90 return, 1¼ hours) and Monaco (€3.70 return, 45 minutes).

**Train** Nice's main train station, Gare Nice Ville, is 1.2km north of the beach on ave Thiers. There are fast, frequent services (up to 40 daily trains) to points all along the coast, including Monaco (€2.90, 20 min-

utes), Cannes (€5, 40 minutes) and Marseille (€25.10, 2¾ hours).

About six daily TGVs link Nice with Paris' Gare de Lyon (€80 to €90, six hours; discounts available). Trains go to Spain, too.

Trains for Digne-les-Bains (€17, 3¼ hours) make the scenic trip five times daily from Nice's **Gare du Sud** (☎ *04 93 82 10 17; 4 bis rue Alfred Binet)*.

## Getting Around

Local buses, run by Sunbus, cost €1.30/4 for a single ticket/daily pass (available on the bus). The **Sunbus information office** (☎ *04 93 16 52 10; ave Félix Faure)* is at the Station Centrale. From the train station to Vieux Nice and the bus station, take bus No 2, 5 or 17. Bus No 12 links the train station with the beach. Bus Nos 9 and 10 go to the port.

**Holiday Bikes** (☎ *04 93 16 01 62; 34 ave Auber)* rents bicycles (€12 per day) and motor scooters (from €30 per day).

## CANNES
### pop 67,406

The harbour, the bay, Le Suquet hill, the beachside promenade, and the sun-worshippers on the beach provide more than enough natural beauty to make Cannes worth at least a day trip. It's also fun watching the rich drop their money with such nonchalance.

Cannes is renowned for its many festivals and cultural activities, the most famous being the International Film Festival, which runs for two weeks in mid-May. People come to Cannes all year long, but the main tourist season runs from May to October.

## Orientation

From the train station, follow rue Jean Jaurès west and turn left onto rue Vénizélos, which runs west into the heart of the Vieux Port. Place Bernard Cornut Gentille (formerly place de l'Hôtel de Ville), where the bus station is located, is on the northwestern edge of the Vieux Port. Cannes' most famous promenade, the magnificent blvd de la Croisette, begins at the Palais des Festivals and continues eastward around the Baie de Cannes to Pointe de la Croisette.

## Information

The **main tourist office** (☎ *04 93 39 24 53, fax 04 92 99 84 23;* e *semoftou@palais festivals-cannes.fr; open 9am-7pm Mon-Fri,*

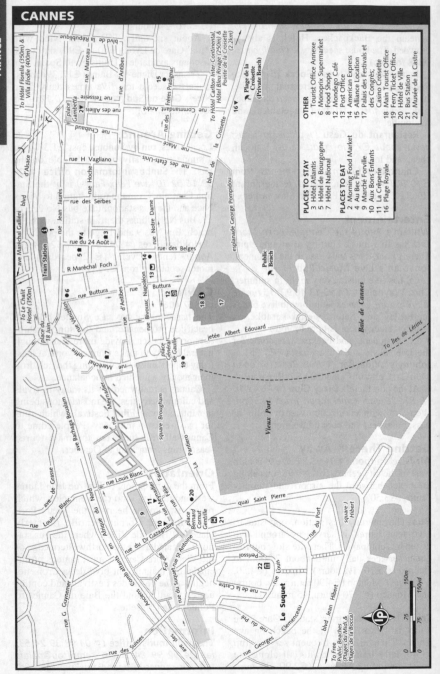

# CANNES

**PLACES TO STAY**
3 Hôtel Atlantis
5 Hôtel de Bourgogne
7 Hôtel National

**PLACES TO EAT**
2 Morning Food Market
9 Au Bec Fin
10 Aux Bons Enfants
11 La Crêperie
16 Plage Royale

**OTHER**
1 Tourist Office Annexe
6 Monopix Supermarket
8 Food Shops
12 Mondego Café
13 Post Office
14 American Express
15 Alliance Location
17 Palais des Festivals et
   des Congrès;
   Casino Croisette
18 Main Tourist Office
19 Ferry Ticket Office
20 Hôtel de Ville
21 Bus Station
22 Musée de la Castre

10am-6pm Sat & Sun Sept-June, 9am-8pm July & Aug) is on the ground floor of the **Palais des Festivals**. There's an **annexe** (☎ 04 93 99 19 77; open Mon-Fri) at the train station; turn left as you exit the station and walk up the stairs next to Buffet de la Gare.

The main **post office** (22 rue Bivouac Napoléon) is not far from the Palais des Festivals. There are Internet terminals for €4/7 for 30 minutes/one hour at **Mondego Café** (☎ 04 93 68 19 21; 15 square Merimée), opposite Palais des Festivals.

## Things to See & Do

**Vieux Port** Some of the largest yachts you'll ever see are likely to be sitting in the Vieux Port, a fishing port now given over to pleasure craft. The streets around the old port are particularly pleasant on a summer's evening, when the many restaurants and cafés light up the area.

The hill just west of the Vieux Port, **Le Suquet**, affords magnificent views of Cannes. The **Musée de la Castre** (☎ 04 93 38 55 26; Le Suquet; adult/student €3/free; open 10am-1pm & 2pm-5pm Tues-Sun Dec-Oct), housed in a chateau atop Le Suquet, has Mediterranean and Middle Eastern antiquities as well as objects of ethnographic interest from all over the world.

**Beaches** Each of the fancy hotels that line blvd de la Croisette has its own private section of the beach. You can pay to roast alongside the hotel guests; a sunlounge at the Hotel Carlton beach starts at €21. There's a small strip of public sand near the Palais des Festivals. Other free public beaches – the **Plages du Midi** and **Plages de la Bocca** – stretch several kilometres westward from the old port.

**Îles de Lérins** The eucalyptus and pine-covered **Île Ste Marguerite**, where the man in the iron mask (made famous in the novel by Alexandre Dumas) was held captive during the late 17th century, is a little more than 1km from the mainland. The island is criss-crossed by many trails and paths. The smaller **Île St Honorat** is home to Cistercian monks who welcome visitors to their monastery, the ruins of a cloister and the small chapels dotted around the island. Bring a picnic to eat on the rocky shores of this tiny island.

**Compagnie Maritime Cannoise** (CMC; ☎ 04 93 38 66 33) is one of many companies running ferries to Île Ste Marguerite (€8 return, 15 minutes). The ticket offices are at the Vieux Port near the Palais des Festivals. Ferries to St Honorat are less common but you'll find one at the same port. Many companies offer day trips to Monaco and St Tropez (about €27).

## Places to Stay

Tariffs can be up to 50% higher in July and August – when you'll be lucky to find a room at all – than in winter. Hotels are booked up to a year in advance for the film festival.

**Hostels** The pleasant **Le Chalit** (☎/fax 04 93 99 22 11; ⓔ le_chalit@libertysurf.fr; 27 ave du Maréchal Galliéni; dorm beds €20; open year-round no curfew, reception closed 10.30am-5pm) is a five-minute walk north-west of the station.

**Hotels** The very friendly **Hôtel Florella** (☎ 04 93 38 48 11, fax 04 93 99 22 15; ⓔ reservations@hotelflorella.com; 55 blvd de la République; singles/doubles/triples/quads with shower & toilet €30/35/45/60) is run by an Irish couple.

**Villa Elodie** (☎/fax 04 93 39 39 91; ⓔ villaelodie@wanadoo.fr; 35 ave de Vallauris; 2-person studio/8-person apartment €39/80) is about 400m northeast of the train station. There's a two night minimum and you need to call because there's no reception. To get there, follow blvd de la République for 300m and ave de Vallauris runs off to the right.

Large **Hôtel Atlantis** (☎ 04 93 39 18 72, fax 04 93 68 37 65; ⓔ hotel.atlantis@wanadoo.fr; 4 rue du 24 Août; singles/doubles with TV & shower €55/65) has access to a private beach. **Hôtel de Bourgogne** (☎ 04 93 38 36 73, fax 04 92 99 28 41; 11 rue du 24 Août; singles/doubles with washbasin €24/31, with bath & toilet €45) is another option, or try **Hôtel National** (☎ 04 93 39 91 92, fax 04 92 98 44 06; ⓔ hotelnationalcannes@wanadoo.fr; 8 rue Maréchal Joffre; singles/doubles with shower & TV from €40/55).

Next to the famous **Hôtel Carlton Inter-Continental** (☎ 04 93 06 40 06, fax 04 93 06 40 25; ⓔ cannes@interconti.com; 58 La Croisette; rooms/suites from €370/1310) is the much more affordable **Hôtel Bleu Rivage** (☎ 04 93 94 24 25, fax 04 93 43 74 92; ⓔ bleurivage@wanadoo.fr; 61 La Croisette; rooms from €175).

## Places to Eat

Morning **food markets** *(open Tues-Sun, daily in summer)* are held on place Gambetta, and at the **Marché Forville** north of place Bernard Cornut Gentille.

There are a few budget restaurants around the Marché Forville and many small (but not necessarily cheap) restaurants along rue St Antoine, which runs northwest from place Bernard Cornut Gentille.

Near the train station is **Au Bec Fin** *(☎ 04 93 38 35 86; 12 rue du 24 Août; menus €18 & 22; open Mon-Fri & Sat lunch)*. Try the lovely *soupe au pistou*.

Another good choice is the popular **Au Bons Enfants** *(80 rue Meynadier; open Mon-Sat; menu €15.50)* with regional dishes.

**La Crêperie** *(☎ 04 92 99 00 00; 66 rue Meynadier; menu €8.85; open Mon-Sat)* has dozens of buckwheat crepe options.

**Plage Royale** *(☎ 04 93 38 22 00; La Croisette; menu €22.50)* serves seafood-skewed lunches on the beach.

## Getting There & Away

Buses to Nice (€5.10, 1½ hours) and other destinations, most operated by Rapides Côte d'Azur, leave from place Bernard Cornut Gentille.

From the **train station** *(☎ 0836 35 35 39)* there are regular services to Nice (€5, 40 minutes), Marseille (€20.90, two hours) and St Raphaël (€5.30, 20 minutes), where you can pick up a bus to St Tropez.

## Getting Around

**Bus Azur** *(☎ 04 93 45 20 08; place Bernard Cornut Gentille)* has an office in the same building as Rapides Côte d'Azur. It serves Cannes and destinations up to 7km from town. Tickets cost €1.22.

**Alliance Location** *(☎ 04 93 38 62 62; 19 rue des Frères Pradignac)* rents mountain bikes/scooters for €15/26 a day.

## ST TROPEZ
**pop 19,858**

Since 1956 when the small fishing village of St Tropez found fame through the patronage of French actor Brigitte Bardot and her acolytes, things have never been the same. The once-isolated fishing village now draws in thousands of visitors a year. If you can, come by boat since the road traffic into and out of the town can be horrendous. If watch-ing the rich dining on yachts is not your flute of Moët then head for the backstreets where men still play pétanque and you might spy a famous face or two.

## Information

The **tourist office** *(☎ 04 94 97 45 21, fax 04 94 97 82 66; e tourisme@saint-tropez.st; quai Jean Jaurès; open 9.30am-8.30pm July & Aug, hours vary outside high season)* has information and guided tours.

## Things to See & Do

You might care to visit the **Musée de l'Annonciade** *(place Grammont)*, which is a dis-used chapel in the Old Port containing an impressive collection of modern art, including works by Matisse, Bonnard, Dufy, Derain and Rouault. The **Musée Naval** in the dungeon of the citadel at the end of Montée de la Citadelle has displays on the town's maritime history and the Allied landings in 1944.

For a decent beach you need to get 4km out of town to the excellent **Plage de Tahiti**.

## Places to Stay & Eat

Accommodation isn't cheap, even if you camp. St Tropez's cheapest hotel is dingy **Hôtel La Méditerranée** *(☎ 04 94 97 00 44, fax 04 94 97 47 83; 21 blvd Louis Blanc; sin-gles/doubles €63/99)*. **Hôtel Le Baron** *(☎ 04 94 97 06 57, fax 04 94 97 58 72; e contact@hotel-le-baron.com; 23 rue de l'Aïoli; singles/doubles with bath €69/100)* is more classy.

Extremely tasteful is **Café Sud** *(☎ 04 94 97 71 72; 12 rue Étienne Berny; mains about €22)*, tucked down a narrow street off places des Lices. Tables are outside in a star-topped courtyard. Close by, **Bistrot des Lices** *(☎ 04 94 55 82 82; 3 places des Lices; mains €18-30)* serves traditional Provençal cuisine, including wonderful ratatouille.

## Getting There & Away

The **bus station** *(ave Général de Gaulle)* is on the southwest edge of town on the main road. Frequent taxi boats run to Port Grimaud nearby and excursion boats run regularly to and from St Maxime and St Raphaël.

## MENTON
**pop 28,792**

Reputed to be the warmest spot on the Côte d'Azur, Menton is encircled by mountains. The town is renowned for lemons and holds a two-week Fête du Citron (Lemon Festival) between mid-February and early March. The helpful **tourist office** (☎ 04 92 41 76 76; 8 ave Boyer) is in the Palais de l'Europe.

It's pleasant to wander around the narrow, winding streets of the Vieille Ville (old town) and up to the cypress-shaded **Cimetière du Vieux Château**, with the graves of English, Irish, North Americans, New Zealanders and others who died here during the 19th century. The view alone is worth the climb.

### Église St Michel
The grandest baroque church in this part of France sits perched in the centre of the Vieille Ville. The **beach** along the promenade du Soleil is public and, like Nice's, carpeted with smooth pebbles. Better private beaches are found east of the old city in the port area, the main one being **Plage des Sablettes**.

### Places to Stay
**Camping St Michel** (☎ 04 93 35 81 23, fax 04 93 57 12 35; Plateau St Michel; adult/tent/car from €3.20/3.70/3.50; open Apr-Oct) is 1km northeast of the train station up steep steps. Terraced sites are interspersed with olive trees and the facilities are clean. The adjacent **Auberge de Jeunesse** (☎ 04 93 35 93 14, fax 04 93 35 93 07; e menton@fuaj.org; Plateau St Michel; dorm beds €11.34; open Feb-Oct) takes HI members only.

**Hôtel St Michel** (☎ 04 93 57 46 33, fax 04 93 57 71 19; 1684 promenade du Soleil; rooms from €65) has some rooms that overlook the water.

### Getting There & Away
The **bus station** (☎ 04 93 28 43 27) has services to Monaco (€2 return, 30 minutes) and Nice (€4.90 return, 1¼ hours). Take the train to get to Ventimiglia in Italy.

# Monaco (Principauté de Monaco)

**pop 30,000**
The Principality of Monaco, a sovereign state whose territory covers only 1.95 sq km, has been ruled by the Grimaldi family for most of the period since 1297. Prince Rainier III (born in 1923), whose sweeping constitutional powers make him far more than a figurehead, has

reigned since 1949. The citizens of Monaco (Monégasques), of whom there are only 5000 out of a total population of 30,000, pay no taxes. The official language is French, although efforts are being made to revive the principality's traditional dialect. There are no border formalities and Monaco makes a perfect day trip from Nice.

### Orientation
Monaco consists of four principal areas: Monaco Ville, also known as the old city or the Rocher de Monaco, perched atop a 60m-high crag overlooking the Port de Monaco; Monte Carlo, famed for its casino and its Grand Prix motor race, north of the harbour; La Condamine, the flat area surrounding the harbour; and Fontvieille, an industrial area southwest of Monaco Ville and the Port de Fontvieille.

### Information
**Tourist Offices** Monaco's **Direction du Tourisme et des Congrès de la Principauté de Monaco** (☎ 92 16 61 66, fax 92 16 60 00; e dtc@monaco-tourisme.com; 2a blvd des Moulins; open 9am-7pm Mon-Sat, 10am-noon Sun Oct–mid-June, 8am-8pm daily mid-June–Sept) is across the public gardens from the casino. There's a helpful counter at the train station open the same hours; in summer, several tourist office kiosks operate around the principality.

**Money** Unsurprisingly, there are lots of **banks** in the vicinity of the casino. **American Express** (☎ 93 25 74 45; 35 blvd Princesse Charlotte; open Mon-Fri) is near the main tourist office.

**Post & Communications** Monégasque stamps are valid only within Monaco, and postal rates are the same as in France. The **main post office** (1 ave Henri Dunant) is inside the Palais de la Scala.

Calls between Monaco and France are treated as international calls. Monaco's country code is ☎ 377. To call France from Monaco, dial ☎ 00 and France's country code (☎ 33). This applies even if you are only making a call from the east side of blvd de France (in Monaco) to its west side (in France)!

**Email & Internet Access** For Internet access, head to **Stars 'n' Bars** (☎ 97 97 95 95; 6 quai Antoine, 1er; open 11am-midnight

# MONACO

**PLACES TO STAY**
24 Centre de la Jeunesse
   Princesse Stéphanie

**PLACES TO EAT**
8 Le Louis XV
13 Stars 'n' Bars Restaurant;
   Internet Café
19 U Cavagnetu

**OTHER**
1 Plages de Larvotto
2 Public Lift Entrance
3 Public Lift Entrance
4 Public Lift
5 American Express
6 Tourist Office
7 Casino de Monte Carlo

9 Main Post Office
10 Public Lift Entrance
11 Public Lift Entrance
12 Casino Supermarket
14 Fort Antoine
15 Post Office
16 Public Lift to Parking
   Pêcheurs
17 Musée Océanographique
18 Cathédrale de Monaco
20 Musée des Souvenirs
   Napoléoniens
21 Palais du Prince
22 Rampe Major
23 Food Market
25 Musée d'Anthropologie
   Préhistorique
26 Public Lift

*Tues-Sun)*, an American-style bar/restaurant, charging €6 for 30 minutes of surfing.

## Things to See & Do

**Palais du Prince** The changing of the guard takes place outside the Prince's Palace *(adult/concession €6/3; open 9.30am-6.20pm daily June-Oct)* daily at 11.55am. About 15 state apartments are open to the public. Guided tours (35 minutes) in English leave every 15 or 20 minutes. Entry to the **Musée des Souvenirs Napoléoniens** – a display of Napoleon's personal effects in the palace's south wing – is €4/2.

**Musée Océanographique** If you're planning on visiting one aquarium on your whole trip, the world-famous Oceanographic Museum *(ave St Martin in Monaco Ville; adult/concession €11/6; open 9am-7pm daily, 9am-8pm July & Aug)*, with its 90 seawater tanks, should be it.

**Cathédrale de Monaco** The unspectacular 19th-century cathedral *(4 rue Colonel)* has one major attraction – the grave of Grace Kelly (1929–1982). The Hollywood star married Prince Rainier III in 1956, but was killed in a car crash in 1982. The remains of other members of the royal family, buried in the church crypt since 1885, rest behind Princess Grace's tomb.

**Jardin Exotique** The steep slopes of the wonderful Jardin Exotique *(bus No 2 from tourist office to end of line; adult/concession €6.40/3.60)* are home to some 7000 varieties of cacti and succulents from all over the world. The spectacular view is worth at least half the admission fee, which also gets you into the **Musée d'Anthropologie Préhistorique** and includes a half-hour guided visit to the **Grottes de l'Observatoire**, a system of caves 279 steps down the hillside.

## Places to Stay

Monaco's HI hostel, **Centre de la Jeunesse Princesse Stéphanie** *(☎ 93 50 83 20, fax 93 25 29 82; 🖃 info@youthhostel.asso.mc; 24 ave Prince Pierre; dorm beds €16)* is 120m uphill from the train station. You must be aged between 16 and 31 to stay here. Beds are given out each morning on a first-come, first-served basis, though you can book ahead with a deposit.

The two-star **Hôtel de France** *(☎ 93 30 24 64, fax 92 16 13 34; 🖃 hotel-france@ monte-carlo.mc; 6 rue de la Turbie; singles/ doubles €67/85)* has rooms with shower, toilet and TV.

## Places to Eat

There are a few cheap restaurants in La Condamine along rue de la Turbie. Lots of touristy restaurants can be found in the streets leading off from place du Palais. The flashy **Stars 'n' Bars** *(☎ 93 50 95 95; 6 Quai Antoine 1er; open Tues-Sun, food until midnight)* does Tex-Mex, burgers and salads.

One of the very few affordable restaurants that specialises in Monégasque dishes is **U Cavagnetu** *(☎ 93 30 35 80; 14 rue Comte Félix-Gastaldi; lunch/dinner menus from €13/18)*.

If you need to know the prices, you can't afford to eat at Alain Ducasse's landmark **Le Louis XV** *(☎ 92 16 30 31; place du Casino Monte Carlo)*.

## Getting There & Away

There is no single bus station in Monaco – intercity buses leave from various points around the city.

The flash **train station** *(☎ 0836 35 35 39; ave Prince Pierre)* is part of the French SNCF network. There are frequent trains to Menton (€2, 10 minutes), Nice (€?.90, 20 minutes) and Ventimiglia in Italy (€3, 25 minutes).

# Corsica (Corse)

Corsica, the most mountainous and geographically diverse of all the Mediterranean islands, has spent much of its history under foreign rule. From the 13th century it remained under Genoese control until the Corsicans, led by the extraordinary Pasquale Paoli, declared the island independent in 1755. But France took over in 1769 and has ruled Corsica since – except in 1794–96, when it was under English domination, and during the German and Italian occupation of 1940–43.

The island has 1000km of coastline, soaring granite mountains that stay snowcapped until July, a huge national park, flatland marshes, an uninhabited desert in the north-west and a 'continental divide' running down the middle of the island. It's a popular holiday destination for the French and increasingly for foreign travellers who come here for its exceptional hiking and diving opportunities.

**Dangers & Annoyances** In 2002, Corsica gained a smidgeon of administrative autonomy from France and the right to teach Corsican in local schools. That's not enough for the small core of committed activists, who continue to agitate for independence. As a traveller, there's no need to be nervous; defaced road signs are the only evidence you're likely to see of unrest in Corsica.

## AJACCIO (AIACCIU)
pop 52,850

The port city of Ajaccio, birthplace of Napoleon Bonaparte (1769–1821), is a great place to begin a visit to Corsica and a fine place for strolling. The many museums and statues dedicated to Bonaparte speak volumes – not about Napoleon himself, but about how the people of his native town prefer to think of him.

### Orientation

The main street is cours Napoléon, which stretches from place du Général de Gaulle northward to the train station and beyond. The old city is south of place Foch. The ferry port is central to both the old and new town.

### Information
**Tourist Offices** The tourist office (☎ 04 95 51 53 03, fax 04 95 51 53 01; e ajaccio .tourisme@wanadoo.fr; 1 place Foch; open 8am-7pm Mon-Sat, 9am-1pm Sun Apr-June & Sept-Oct, 8am-8.30pm Mon-Sat, 9am-1pm & 2pm-7pm Sun July-Aug, 8am-6pm Mon-Fri, 8am-noon & 2pm-5pm Sat & Sun Nov-Mar) is boosted by a **chamber of commerce counter** (☎ 04 95 23 56 56; open 6am-10.30pm daily) at the airport.

**Gare.Net** (☎ 04 95 50 72 79; 2 ave de Paris) charges €5 for an hour's Internet access.

**Money & Post** Money can be exchanged at the **main post office** (13 cours Napoléon).

**Hiking** The **Maison d'Information Randonnées** (☎ 04 95 51 79 00, fax 04 95 21 88 17; e infos@parc-naturel-corse.com; 2 rue du sergent Casalonga; open 8.30am-12.30pm & 2pm-6pm Mon-Thur, to 5pm Fri) provides information on the Parc Naturel Régional de la Corse and its hiking trails.

## Things to See & Do
**Museums** The house where Napoleon was born and raised, the **Maison Bonaparte** (☎ 04 95 21 43 89; rue St Charles; adult/concession €4/2.60; open 10am-noon & 2pm-4.45pm Oct-Mar, 9am-noon & 2pm-6pm Apr-Sept, closed Mon morning year-round), in the old city, was sacked by Corsican nationalists in 1793 but rebuilt later in the decade.

The sombre **Salon Napoléonien** (☎ 04 95 21 90 15; 1st floor, Hôtel de Ville, place Foch; admission €2.29; open 9am-11.45am & 2pm-4.45pm Mon-Fri mid-Sept–mid-June, 9am-11.45am & 2pm-5.45pm Mon-Sat mid-June–mid-Sept) exhibits a collection of the emperor's memorabilia.

The **Musée A Bandera** (☎ 04 95 51 07 34; 1 rue Général Lévie; adult/concession €3.85/2.30; open 9am-7pm Mon-Sat, 9am-noon Sat July–15 Sept, 9am-noon & 2pm-6pm Mon-Sat 16 Sept–June) deals with Corsican military history.

**Musée Fesch** (☎ 04 95 21 48 17; 50 rue du Cardinal Fesch; adult/concession €5.34/3.81; open 1.30pm-6pm Mon, 9am-6.30pm Tues-Thur, 9am-6.30pm & 9pm-midnight Fri, 10.30am-6pm Sat & Sun July-Aug, 1pm-5.15pm Mon, 9.15am-12.15pm & 2.15pm-5.15pm Tues-Sun Apr-June & Sept, 9.15am-12.15pm & 2.15pm-5.15pm Tues-Sat Oct-Mar) houses a truly awesome assembly of 14th- to 19th-century Italian paintings.

## Places to Stay
**Camping** About 3km north of the town centre, **Camping Les Mimosas** (☎ 04 95 20 99 85, fax 04 95 10 01 77; Route d'Alata; sites per adult/tent/car €4.80/2/2; open Apr-Oct) offers 10% discounts out of season. Take bus No 4 from cours Napoléon to the corner of route d'Alata and chemin des Roseaux, and walk up route d'Alata for 1km.

**Hotels** Efficient **Hôtel Kallisté** (☎ 04 95 51 34 45, fax 04 95 21 79 00; e hotelkalliste@ cyrnos.com; 51 cours Napoléon; singles/doubles with shower & toilet €56/69) has classy rooms with terracotta tiles. Prices drop by 33% during low season. Breakfast (€6.50) is served in your room.

Only 200m from the ferry terminal, **Hôtel Le Dauphin** (☎ 04 95 21 12 94, fax 04 95 21 88 69; 11 blvd Sampiero; singles/doubles with shower & toilet €49/60) includes breakfast in the price.

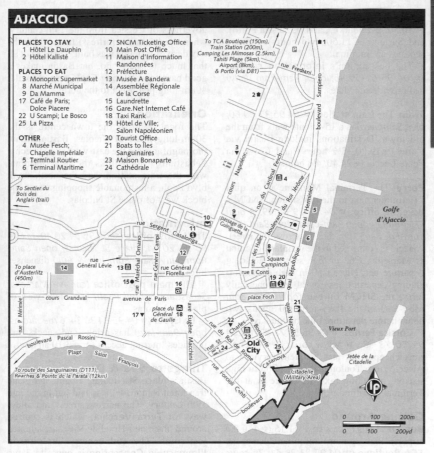

## AJACCIO

**PLACES TO STAY**
1  Hôtel Le Dauphin
2  Hôtel Kallisté

**PLACES TO EAT**
3  Monoprix Supermarket
8  Marché Municipal
9  Da Mamma
17  Café de Paris;
    Dolce Piacere
22  U Scampi; Le Bosco
25  La Pizza

**OTHER**
4  Musée Fesch;
    Chapelle Impériale
5  Terminal Routier
6  Terminal Maritime

7  SNCM Ticketing Office
10  Main Post Office
11  Maison d'Information
    Randonnées
12  Préfecture
13  Musée A Bandera
14  Assemblée Régionale
    de la Corse
15  Laundrette
16  Gare.Net Internet Café
18  Taxi Rank
19  Hôtel de Ville;
    Salon Napoléonien
20  Tourist Office
21  Boats to Îles
    Sanguinaires
23  Maison Bonaparte
24  Cathédrale

To TCA Boutique (150m),
Train Station (200m),
Camping Les Mimosas (2.5km),
Tahiti Plage (5km),
Airport (8km),
& Porto (via D81)

*Golfe d'Ajaccio*

To Sentier du
Bois des
Anglais (trail)

To place
d'Austerlitz
(450m)

To route des Sanguinaires (D111),
Beaches & Pointe de la Parata (12km)

*Vieux Port*

Citadelle
(Military Area)

Jetée de la
Citadelle

0    100    200m
0    100    200yd

## Places to Eat

Most of Ajaccio's restaurants are seasonal. Cafés can be found along blvd du Roi Jérôme, quai Napoléon and the north side of place de Gaulle. **Café de Paris** and the neighbouring **Dolce Piacere**, on the west side of place du Général de Gaulle, both have giant terraces with sea views.

The best pizza is served at **La Pizza** (*☎ 04 95 21 30 71; 2 rue des Anciens Fosées; pizza €8.50-10.50*). Try the tasty *quatre saisons*, drizzled with chilli-laced olive oil.

Popular **U Scampi** (*☎ 04 95 21 38 09; 11 rue Conventionnel Chiappe; menus from €13; open Mon-Thur, Fri lunch & Sat dinner year-round*) serves Corsican specialities that includes octopus stew, on a flower-filled terrace. **Le Bosco** (*☎ 04 95 21 25 06*) shares the

terrace with U Scampi and has the same sort of food, including a €31.25 shellfish platter.

**Da Mamma** (*☎ 04 95 21 39 44; Passage de la Guinguetta; menus from €10.50*), tucked away off cours Napoléon, does paella, pasta and Corsican specialities.

There's an open-air **Marché Municipal** (*square Campinchi; open 8am-noon Tues-Sun*) and a **Monoprix supermarket** (*33 cours Napoléon; open Mon-Sat*) for supplies.

## Getting There & Away

**Bus** The Terminal Maritime et Routier on Quai l'Herminier houses Ajaccio's bus station. **Eurocorse** (*☎ 04 95 21 06 30; open 8.30am-4pm Mon-Sat*) is responsible for most lines. Destinations include Bastia (€18, three hours), Bonifacio (€19.50, four hours),

Corte (€10.50, 1½ hours), Porto and Ota (€10.50, 2½ hours), Calvi (€22, via Porto), and Sartène (€11.50, two hours). Sunday services are minimal.

The bus station's **information counter** (☎ 04 95 51 55 45; open 7am-7pm daily) can provide schedules.

**Train** The **train station** (☎ 04 95 32 80 60; blvd Sampiero) is a 15-minute walk from the old town. Destinations include Bastia via Corte (€19.90, 3½ hours) and Calvi via Ponte Leccia (€24.40, 4½ hours).

**Ferry** The Terminal Maritime is on quai l'Herminier next to the bus station. SNCM's **ticketing office** (☎ 04 95 29 66 99; 3 quai l'Herminier; open 8am-6pm Mon, 8am-8pm Tues-Fri, 8am-1pm Sat) is across the street. Ajaccio is connected to the mainland (Toulon or Marseille, €62 in high season, including departure tax; Nice, €50 in high season including departure tax) by at least one daily ferry; the **SNCM bureau** (open 7am-8pm Mon-Sat) in the ferry terminal opens two hours before departure time on Sunday.

**Corsica Ferries** (☎ 04 95 50 78 82, fax 04 95 50 78 83; W www.corsicaferries.com) runs cheaper but less frequent services to Ajaccio from Toulon and Nice (€35 in high season, including tax). Its office is at the Terminal Maritime.

### Getting Around

**Bus** Local bus tickets cost €1.15 (€4 to the airport). Pick up maps and timetables at the **TCA Boutique** (☎ 04 95 23 29 41; 75 cours Napoleon; open 8am-noon & 2.30pm-6pm Mon-Sat).

**Taxi** There's a taxi rank on place du Général de Gaulle, or call **ABC Taxis Ajacciens** (☎ 06 62 55 71 38).

**Car** Driving is a good – if heartstopping – way to see Corsica. **Rent A Car** (☎ 04 95 51 61 81, fax 04 95 21 79 00; W www.rentacar.fr) has an office at Hôtel Kallisté (see Places to Stay earlier). Small cars start at €49/227 a day/week. Scooters are also available.

## BASTIA
pop 37,880

Pleasant, bustling Bastia, Corsica's most important commercial centre, has rather an Italian feel to it. It was the seat of the Genoese governors of Corsica from the 15th century, when the *bastiglia* (fortress) from which the city derives its name was built. There's not all that much to see or do, but Bastia makes a good base for exploring **Cap Corse**, the wild, 40km-long peninsula to the north.

### Orientation

The focal point of the town centre is the 300m-long place St Nicolas. Bastia's main thoroughfares are the east-west ave Maréchal Sébastiani, which links the ferry terminal with the train station, and the north-south blvd Paoli, a fashionable shopping street one block west of place St Nicolas.

### Information

The **tourist office** (☎ 04 95 54 20 40, fax 04 95 54 20 41; place St Nicolas; open 8am-6pm daily, 8am-8pm July & Aug) dispenses information.

The **main post office** (cnr ave Maréchal Sébastiani & blvd Paoli) is a block west of place St Nicolas.

**Le Cyber** (☎ 04 95 34 30 34; 6 rue Jardins; open 9am-late) has drinks and snacks and provides Internet access for €3.10 an hour.

### Things to See & Do

Bastia's **place St Nicolas**, a palm and plane tree-lined esplanade, was laid out in the late 19th century. The narrow streets and alleyways of **Terra Vecchia**, which is centred around place de l'Hôtel de Ville, are situated just south. The 16th-century **Oratoire de l'Immaculée Conception** is opposite 3 rue Napoléon and was decorated in rich baroque style in the early 18th century.

The picturesque, horseshoe-shaped **Vieux Port** is between Terra Vecchia and the **Citadelle** and is the most colourful part of Bastia with its crumbling buildings and lively restaurants.

### Places to Stay

**Camping** Small and sweet **Camping Les Orangers** (☎ 04 95 33 24 09; sites per tent/parking/adult €2/1.60/4; open Apr-mid-Oct) is about 4km north of Bastia in Miomo. Take the bus to Sisco from opposite the tourist office.

**Hotels** Book ahead because Bastia's hotels fill up with business travellers.

**Hôtel Le Riviera** *(☎ 04 95 31 07 16, fax 04 95 34 17 39; 1bis rue du Nouveau Port; doubles with shower & toilet €58)* is very close to the ferry. The family-run **Hôtel Central** *(☎ 04 95 31 71 12, fax 04 95 31 82 40; ℮ info@centralhotel.fr; 3 rue Miot; singles/ doubles with shower & toilet 40/50, with kitchenette €75/90)* has recently renovated its rooms.

Don't be discouraged by the dingy stairs – once you get inside, the rooms are fresh and comfortable at **Hôtel Le Forum** *(☎ 04 95 31 02 53, fax 04 95 31 65 60; ℮ hotel_leforum@ wanadoo.fr; 20 blvd Paoli; rooms with shower & toilet from €60)*. Prices drop about €10 outside July and August.

## Places to Eat
Cafés and brasseries line the western side of place St Nicolas. There are more restaurants at the Vieux Port, on quai des Martyrs de la Libération and on place de l'Hôtel de Ville in Terra Vecchia, where the **Café Pannini** sells great jumbo sandwiches.

**La Barcarolle** *(☎ 04 95 31 42 45; Corsican menu €19)* at the Vieux Port, serves pizzas and seafood dishes.

A delightful **food market** *(place de l'Hôtel de Ville; open 8am-1pm Tues-Sun)* takes place in Terra Vecchia, and there's a **Spar supermarket** *(cnr rue César Campinchi & rue Capanelle)*.

## Getting There & Away
**Air** France's fifth-busiest airport, **Aéroport de Bastia-Poretta** *(☎ 04 95 54 54 54)*, is 20km south of the town. Municipal buses to the airport (€8) depart from the roundabout opposite the train station about an hour before each flight (seven to 12 times daily). The tourist office has timetables.

**Bus** Buses to Porto-Vecchio (€16.30, three hours) are run by **Rapides Bleus** *(☎ 04 95 31 03 79; 1 ave Maréchal Sebastiani)*, which also handles tickets for Eurocorse buses to Corte and Ajaccio. The afternoon bus to Calvi run by **Les Beaux Voyages** *(☎ 04 95 65 02 10)* leaves from outside the train station.

**Train** The train station *(☎ 04 95 32 60 06)* is at the northern end of ave Maréchal Sébastiani. Destinations include Corte (€9.40, two hours), Ajaccio (€19.90, 3½ hours) and Calvi via Ponte Leccia (€15, 4½ hours).

**Ferry** Bastia is linked by ferry to France and Italy. The ferry terminal is at the eastern end of ave Pietri. **SNCM's office** *(☎ 04 95 54 66 81; open 7.15am-6.30pm Mon-Fri, 8am-11.45am Sat)* handles ferries to mainland France. The SNCM counter in the terminal opens two hours before each sailing.

**Corsica Ferries** *(☎ 04 95 32 95 95, fax 04 95 32 14 71; 15bis rue Chanoine Leschi; open 8.30am-noon & 2pm-6pm Mon-Sat)* runs to Toulon, Nice and Italy. For more Italian destinations, try **Mobylines** *(☎ 04 95 34 84 94, fax 04 95 32 17 94; 4 rue du Commandant Luce de Casabianca; open 8am-noon & 2pm-6pm Mon-Fri, 8am-noon Sat)*, 200m north of place St Nicolas. Mobylines and Corsica Ferries also have ticket windows in the ferry terminal with restricted hours.

Standard fares to/from mainland France are around €30/15 for passengers over/under 25 years of age, including departure tax.

## CALVI
**pop 6219**
Calvi, where Admiral Horatio Nelson lost his eye, serves as a military town and an upmarket holiday resort. The Citadelle, garrisoned by a crack regiment of the French Foreign Legion, sits atop a promontory at the western end of a beautiful half-moon-shaped bay.

## Orientation
The Citadelle – also known as the Haute Ville (upper town) – is northeast of the port. Blvd Wilson, the main thoroughfare in the Basse Ville (lower town), is up the hill from quai Landry and the marina.

## Information
The **tourist office** *(☎ 04 95 65 16 67, fax 04 95 65 14 09; open 9am-noon & 2pm-6pm Mon-Sat Oct-May, 8.30am-1pm & 2.30pm-7pm daily June-Sept)* is near the marina.

**Crédit Lyonnais** *(7 blvd Wilson; open 8.15am-noon & 2pm-5pm Mon-Fri)* is on the same street as the **main post office**, about 100m to the south.

**Café de L'Orient** *(☎ 04 95 65 00 16; quai Landry)* has Internet-connected computers for €1 plus €0.10 a minute.

## Things to See & Do
The **Citadelle**, set atop an 80m-high granite promontory and enclosed by massive Genoese ramparts, affords great views of the

surrounding area. The 13th-century **Église St Jean Baptiste** was rebuilt in 1570; inside is a miraculous ebony icon of Christ. West of the church, a marble plaque marks the site of the house where, according to local tradition, Christopher Columbus was born. The imposing 13th-century **Palais des Gouverneurs** (Governors' Palace) is above the entrance to the citadel. Now known as Caserne Sampiero, it serves as a barracks and mess hall for officers of the French Foreign Legion.

**Beaches** Calvi's 4km-long beach begins just south of the marina and stretches around the Golfe de Calvi. Other nice beaches, including one at **Algajola**, are west of town. The port and resort town of L'Île Rousse (Isula Rossa) east of Calvi is also endowed with a long, sandy beach with incredibly clean water.

### Places to Stay
**Camping & Bungalows** Just less than 1km southeast of town is **Camping La Clé des Champs** (*☎/fax 04 95 65 00 86;* e *cam agni@wanadoo.fr; route de Pietra Maggiore; sites per adult/tent/car €5.35/1.55/1.55; bungalows per week for 2 people from €185; open Apr-Oct*).

**Hostels** The 130-bed **Auberge de Jeunesse BVJ Corsotel** (*☎ 04 95 65 14 15, fax 04 95 65 33 72; ave de la République; dorm beds €20.60; open late Mar–Oct*) has beds in two- to eight-person rooms, and rates include a filling breakfast.

**Hotels** A cheap option is **Hôtel du Centre** (*☎ 04 95 65 02 01; 14 rue Alsace-Lorraine; rooms with showers €31-42; open 1 June-5 Oct*). A step up are the deluxe rooms at **Hôtel Balanea** (*☎ 04 95 65 94 94, fax 04 95 65 29 71;* e *info@hotel-balanea.com; rooms without/with sea view €81/185*). Prices drop about 40% out of season.

### Places to Eat
Calvi's attractive marina is lined with pricey restaurants, but there are several budget places on rue Clemenceau, which runs parallel to blvd Wilson. **Best Of**, at the south end of the street, sells good sandwiches (about €4.50).

Quai Landry's line-up of waterfront cafés and nice seafood restaurants includes **Callelu** (*☎ 04 95 65 22 18; fish dishes €18.30-20.60*).

It doesn't have sea views but **U Fornu** (*☎ 04 95 65 27 60; Impasse du blvd Wilson; mains €15-19*) has the best Corsican food in town. You'll find it up the stairs next to Banque Lyonnais on blvd Wilson.

The tiny **Marché Couvert** (*open 8am-noon daily*) is near Église Ste Marie Majeure. The **Super U supermarket** (*ave Christophe Colomb*) is south of the town centre.

### Getting There & Away
**Bus** Buses to Bastia are run by **Les Beaux Voyages** (*☎ 04 95 65 15 02; place de la Porteuse d'Eau*). From mid-May to mid-October **Autocars SAIB** (*☎ 04 95 26 13 70*) trundles to Porto (€16, 2½ hours) along Corsica's spectacular western coast.

**Train** Calvi's **train station** (*☎ 04 95 65 00 61*) is just off ave de la République. From mid-April to mid-October, *navettes* (one-car trains) make 19 stops between Calvi and L'Île Rousse (€6, 45 minutes).

**Ferry** SNCM ferries (*☎ 04 95 65 01 38*) sail to Calvi from Nice and Marseille, but during winter they can be very infrequent. **Corsica Ferries** (*☎ 04 95 65 43 21*) links Calvi with Nice and Savone, Italy about once a week (more in summer).

## PORTO (PORTU)
**pop 460**
The pleasant seaside town of Porto, nestled among huge outcrops of red granite and renowned for its sunsets, is an excellent base for exploring some of Corsica's natural wonders. **Les Calanques**, a spectacular mountain landscape of red and orange granite outcrops, towers above the azure waters of the Mediterranean slightly south of Porto along route D81. The **Gorges de Spelunca**, Corsica's most famous river gorge, stretches almost from the town of Ota, 5km east of Porto, to the town of Evisa, 22km away.

### Orientation & Information
The marina is located about 1.5km downhill from Porto's pharmacy – the local landmark – on the D81. The area, known as Vaïta, is spread out along the road linking the D81 to the marina. The Porto River just south of the marina is linked by an arched pedestrian bridge to a eucalyptus grove and a small pebble beach.

The **tourist office** (☎ 04 95 26 10 55, fax 04 95 26 14 25; open 9am-noon & 2pm-6pm Mon-Fri Sept-June, 9am-8pm daily July & Aug) is near the marina. The only ATM between Ajaccio and Calvi is here at Porto – it's outside the post office, halfway between the pharmacy and the marina.

### Things to See & Do

A short trail leads to the 16th-century **Genoese tower** (admission €2.50; open 10am-12.30pm & 3pm-7pm Apr-Oct) on the outcrop above the town.

From March to November, **Nave Va** (☎ 04 95 26 15 16) runs boat excursions (€25.50) to the fishing village of Girolata (passing by the Scandola Nature Reserve), and occasionally to Les Calanques in the evenings (€12).

### Places to Stay

**Camping** Friendly **Funtana al' Ora** (☎ 04 95 26 11 65, fax 04 95 26 10 83; ℮ info@porto -tourisme.com; sites per tent/person/car €2.15/5.20/2.15, bungalows per week from €183; open 15 April–Oct) is 2km east of Porto on the road to Évisa.

**Hostels** In the nearby village of Ota, **Gîte d'Étape Chez Félix** (☎/fax 04 95 26 12 92) and **Gîte d'Étape Chez Marie** (☎/fax 04 95 26 11 37) both open year-round and charge €11 for a dorm bed.

**Hotels** There's lots of hotels in Vaïta and at the marina but most close between November and March. One of the best deals is **Hôtel du Golfe** (☎/fax 04 95 26 13 33; doubles/triples with shower & toilet €40/49). **Hôtel Monte Rosso** (☎ 04 95 26 11 50, fax 04 95 26 12 30; doubles with shower & toilet €51) is nearby.

### Getting There & Away

**Autocars SAIB** (☎ 04 95 22 41 99) has two buses daily (Sunday service July to mid-September only) linking Porto and nearby Ota with Ajaccio (€10.50, 2½ hours). From mid-May to mid-October a bus also goes from Porto to Calvi (€16, 2½ hours).

## PIANA

### pop 428

A good base for walks to Les Calanques, this hillside village has stunning views and a cruisy atmosphere, even when it's overrun by summer hordes.

### Places to Stay & Eat

Just 100m south of the centre, **Hôtel Continental** (☎ 04 95 27 89 00, fax 04 95 27 84 71; annexe rooms €45; singles/doubles/triples/ quads €27/33/40/47; open Apr-Sept) has annexe rooms with groovy 1960s furniture and terrific views.

Wonderful **Les Roches Rouges** (☎ 04 95 27 81 81, fax 04 95 27 81 76; singles/ doubles/triples/quads €69/69/84/115; open Apr-Oct) opened in 1912 and has an Agatha Christie atmosphere. It's just north of Piana, below the D81.

**Le Casanova** (☎ 04 95 27 84 20; place de la Coletta) is one of a number of pleasant terrace restaurants in Piana's central plaza.

## CORTE (CORTI)

### pop 6335

When Pasquale Paoli led Corsica to independence in 1755, he made Corte, a fortified town at the centre of the island, the country's capital. To this day, the town remains a potent symbol of Corsican independence. In 1765, Paoli founded a national university there, but it was closed when his short-lived republic was taken over by France in 1769. The Università di Corsica Pasquale Paoli was reopened in 1981 and now has about 4000 students, making Corte the island's liveliest and least touristy town.

Ringed with mountains, snowcapped until as late as June, Corte is an excellent base for hiking; some of the island's highest peaks rise west of the town.

### Information

The **tourist office** (☎ 04 95 46 26 70, fax 04 95 46 34 05; ℮ corte.tourisme@wanadoo.fr; La Citadelle; open 9am-noon & 2pm-6pm Mon-Fri Oct-Apr, 9.30am-6pm Mon-Sat May-June, 9am-8pm Mon-Sat, 10am-11am & 2pm-7pm Sun July-Aug, 9am-1pm & 2pm-7pm Mon-Sat Sept) has helpful staff.

There are several **banks** with ATMs along cours Paoli. The **post office** (ave Baron Mariani) also has an ATM.

There's Internet access for €3.50 an hour at **Grand Café du Cours** (22 cours Paoli).

### Things to See & Do

The **Citadelle**, built in the early 15th century and largely reconstructed during the 18th and 19th centuries, is perched on top of a hill, with the steep and twisted alleyways and streets of the **Ville Haute** and the Tavignanu and Restonica river valleys below.

The **Château** – the highest part, also known as the Nid d'Aigle (Eagle's Nest) – was built in 1419 by a Corsican nobleman and expanded by the French.

The outstanding **Museu di a Corsica** (*Musée de la Corse;* ☎ *04 95 45 25 45; adult/concession €5.34/3.05; open 10am-6pm Tues-Sun, to 8pm July & Aug*) houses exhibitions on Corsican folk traditions, crafts, agriculture, economy and anthropology. It also hosts temporary art exhibitions.

The **Gorges de la Restonica**, a deep valley cut through the mountains by the Restonica River, is a favourite with hikers. The river passes Corte, but some of the choicer trails begin about 16km southwest of town at the Bergeries Grotelle sheepfolds.

### Places to Stay

**Camping** Just south of pont Restonica is **Camping Alivetu** (☎ *04 95 46 11 09, fax 04 95 46 12 34;* e *camping.alivetu@laposte.net; Faubourg de St Antoine; sites per tent/ adult/car €6/2.50/2.50; open 1 Apr–15 Oct*).

**Hostels** Very rural and pretty is **Gîte d'- Étape U Tavignanu** (☎ *04 95 46 16 85, fax 04 95 61 14 01; chemin de Baliri; dorm beds with breakfast/full pension €14/34.30, camping per tent/adult €1.90/3.80; open year-round*). From pont Tavignanu (the first bridge on Allée du Neuf Septembre), walk westward along chemin de Baliri and follow the signs and orange paint splodges (almost 1km). There's parking down below.

**Hotels** The 135-room **Hôtel HR** (☎ *04 95 45 11 11, fax 04 95 61 02 85;* e *hr2b@aol.com; 6 allée du 9 Septembre; singles/doubles from €21/25*) has clean, utilitarian rooms. **Hôtel de la Poste** (☎ *04 95 46 01 37; 2 place Padoue; rooms with shower/shower & toilet €29/41.50*) has spacious, simple rooms with shower.

The atmospheric **Hôtel du Nord et de L'Europe** (☎ *04 95 46 00 68, fax 04 95 46 03 40;* e *info@hoteldunord-corte.com; 22 cours Paoli; rooms with shower & toilet €55*) has recently been renovated.

### Places to Eat

Corte's best restaurant is **U Museu** (☎ *04 95 61 08 36; Rampe Ribanella; 2-/3-course*

menus €11.50/13.60). Tasty local fare includes *civet de sanglier aux myrtes sauvages* (wild boar stew with myrtle).

**Restaurant Le Bip's** (☎ *04 95 46 06 26; 14 cours Paoli; menus from €12; open Sun-Fri*) is a nice cellar restaurant at the bottom of the flight of stairs beside **Brasserie Le Bip's** (☎ *04 95 46 04 48*).

**Grand Café du Cours** (*22 cours Paoli; open 7am-2am daily*) is a cruisy student bar with Internet facilities. It serves light snacks.

There's a **Spar supermarket** (*7 ave Xavier Luciani*) and a **Casino supermarket** (*allée du 9 Septembre*).

### Getting There & Away

Corte is on Eurocorse's Bastia-Ajaccio route, served by two buses daily in each direction (no Sunday service). The stop is at 3 ave Xavier Luciani where a schedule is posted.

The **train station** (☎ *04 95 46 00 97; open 6.25am-8pm Mon-Sat, 8.50am-11.20am & 3.30pm-8.25pm Sun*) is at the eastern end of allée du 9 Septembre.

## BONIFACIO (BUNIFAZIU)
### pop 2661

The famed **Citadelle** of Bonifacio sits 70m above the translucent waters of the Mediterranean, atop a narrow and easily defensible promontory – 'Corsica's Gibraltar'. On all sides, limestone cliffs sculpted by the wind and the waves drop almost vertically to the sea; the north side looks out on 1.6km-long Bonifacio Sound, at the eastern end of which is the **marina**. The southern ramparts afford views of the coast of Sardinia, 12km away.

Bonifacio was long associated with the Republic of Genoa. The local dialect – unintelligible to other Corsicans – is Genoese and many local traditions (including cooking methods) are Genoa-based.

### Information

The **tourist office** (☎ *04 95 73 11 88, fax 04 95 73 14 97;* e *tourisme.bonifacio@wanadoo .fr; 2 rue Fred Scamaroni; open 9am-8pm daily May-Oct, 9am-noon & 2pm-6pm Mon-Fri, 9am-noon Sat Nov-Apr*) is in the Citadelle.

The **Société Générale** (*38 rue St Érasme; open Mon-Fri*), outside the Citadelle, has poor rates, charges €5.30 plus a percentage commission, and has the only ATM in town. In summer, there are exchange bureaus along the marina.

## Things to See & Do

Looking down the dramatic cliffs to the sea is a delight; the best views are to be had from **place du Marché** and from the walk west towards and around the cemetery. Don't miss **Porte de Gênes**, which is reached by a tiny 16th-century drawbridge, or the Romanesque **Église Ste Marie Majeure**, the oldest building in Bonifacio. **Rue des Deux Empereurs** (Street of the Two Emperors) is so-called because both Charles V and Napoleon slept there; look for the plaques at Nos 4 and 7. The **Foreign Legion Monument** east of the tourist office was brought back from Algeria in 1963 when that country won its independence.

## Places to Stay

The olive-shaded **Camping Araguina** (☎ 04 95 73 02 96, fax 04 95 73 01 92; ℮ camp ing.araguina@wanadoo.fr; ave Sylvère Bohn; sites per person/tent €6.25/1.90, bungalows €53.50; open mid-Mar–Oct) is 400m north of the marina.

In the Citadelle, **Hôtel Le Royal** (☎ 04 95 73 00 51, fax 04 95 73 04 68; rue Fred Scamaroni; rooms from €91.50 Aug, from €68.60 July & Sept, €38.20 Nov-Mar) is a friendly place with restaurant attached.

Near the cemetery at the end of the promontory is **Hôtel Santateresa** (☎ 04 95 73 11 32, fax 04 95 73 15 99; rooms €131); prices are halved in low season.

## Places to Eat

In the Citadelle, **Pizzeria-Grill de la Poste** (☎ 04 95 73 13 31; 5 rue Fred Scamaroni) has Corsican dishes, pizza (from €7) and pasta (€8 to €20). **Cantina Doria** (☎ 04 95 73 50 49; 27 rue Doria) is a rustic hole-in-the-wall popular with locals. The enormous *soupe Corse* (€6) is enough for two people.

**Super Marché Simoni** (93 quai Jérôme Comparetti) is at the marina.

## Getting There & Away

**Bus** For buses to Ajaccio via Sartène (€19.50, four hours, two or three daily with some Sunday services) and Porto-Vecchio (€6, 30 minutes, two buses daily, four in the summer months), there's **Eurocorse** (Bastia ☎ 04 95 31 73 76; 1 Rue du Nouveau Port). All buses leave from the car park next to the Eurocorse kiosk at the eastern end of the marina.

**Ferry** From Bonifacio's ferry port, both **Saremar** (☎ 04 95 73 00 96) and **Moby Lines** (☎ 04 95 73 00 29) offer car and passenger ferry service year-round that go to Santa Teresa (50 minutes, two to seven per day).

Saremar charges €6.71/8.52 for a one-way passenger fare in low/high season while Moby Lines charges €8.50/12. There's an additional €3.10 port tax.

# Greece

The first travel guide to Greece was written 1800 years ago by the Greek geographer and historian Pausanias, so the tourism industry isn't exactly in its infancy.

The country's enduring attraction is its wonderful archaeological sites; those who travel through Greece journey not only through the landscape but also through time, witnessing the legacy of Europe's greatest ages – the Mycenaean, Minoan, classical, Hellenistic and Byzantine.

You cannot wander far in Greece without stumbling across a broken column, a crumbling bastion or a tiny Byzantine church, each perhaps neglected and forgotten but still retaining an aura of its former glory.

Greece's culture is a unique blend of East and West, inherited from the long period of Ottoman rule, which is apparent in its food, music and traditions. The mountainous countryside is a walker's paradise crisscrossed by age-old donkey tracks leading to stunning vistas.

The magnetism of Greece is also due to less tangible attributes – the dazzling clarity of the light, the floral aromas that permeate the air, the spirit of places – for there is hardly a grove, mountain or stream which is not sacred to a deity, and the ghosts of the past still linger.

Then again, many visitors come to Greece simply to get away from it all and relax in one of Europe's friendliest and safest countries.

## Facts about Greece

### HISTORY

Greece's strategic position at the crossroads of Europe and Asia has resulted in a long and turbulent history.

During the Bronze Age, which lasted from 3000 to 1200 BC in Greece, the advanced Cycladic, Minoan and Mycenaean civilisations flourished. The Mycenaeans were eventually swept aside in the 12th century BC and replaced by the Dorians, who introduced Greece to the Iron Age. The next 400 years are often referred to as the Dark Ages, a period about which very little is known. Homer's *Odyssey* and *Iliad* were composed at this time.

## At a Glance

- **Athens** – lively tavernas, the most famous monument in the ancient world: the Acropolis
- **Delphi** – awe-inspiring ruins, home of the Delphic oracle
- **Naxos** – dramatic coastal landscape and a crumbling 13th-century castle
- **Crete** – Knossos' ancient Minoan sites, idyllic beaches, Hania's web of narrow streets
- **Rhodes** – fortress city built by the Knights of St John, largest inhabited medieval town in Europe

| | |
|---|---|
| **Capital** | Athens |
| **Population** | 10.9 million |
| **Official Language** | Greek |
| **Currency** | euro |
| **Time** | GMT/UTC+0200 |
| **Country Phone Code** | ☎ 30 |

By 800 BC, when Homer's works were first written down, Greece was undergoing a cultural and military revival with the evolution of the city-states, the most powerful of which were Athens and Sparta. Greater Greece – Magna Graecia – was created, with southern Italy as an important component. The unified Greeks repelled the Persians twice, at Marathon (490 BC) and Salamis (480 BC).

GREECE

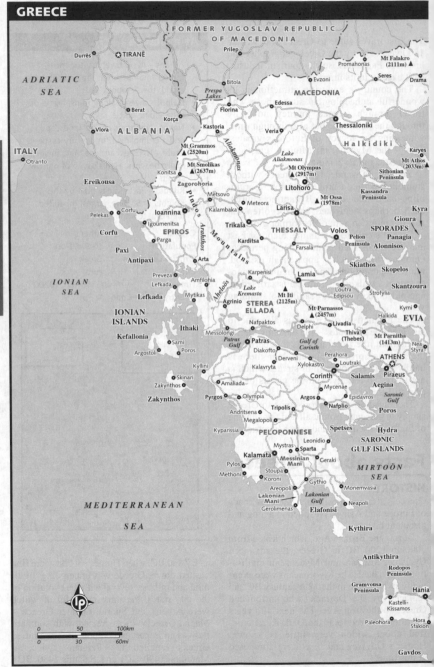

# GREECE

FORMER YUGOSLAV REPUBLIC OF MACEDONIA

Prilep

Durrës
TIRANË
Promahonas
Mt Falakro (2111m)
Seres
Drama

ADRIATIC SEA

Bitola

Prespa Lakes
MACEDONIA
Evzoni

Berat
Edessa
Florina
Korça
Veria
Thessaloniki

Vlora
ALBANIA
Kastoria
Halkidiki

ITALY
Karyes

Otranto
Mt Grammos ▲(2520m)
Lake Aliakmonas
Mt Athos (2033m)▲

Ereikousa
Mt Smolikas ▲(2637m)
Mt Olympus ▲(2917m)
Sithonian Peninsula

Konitsa
Litohoro
Kassandra Peninsula

Zagorohoria
Metsovo
Kyra

Pelekas
Corfu
Ioannina
Meteora
Mt Ossa ▲(1978m)
Gioura

Corfu
Igoumenitsa
Kalambaka
Larisa
SPORADES
Panagia

Paxi
EPIROS
Trikala
THESSALY
Volos
Pelion
Alonnisos

Antipaxi
Parga
Karditsa
Farsala
Peninsula

Arta
Skiathos

Preveza
Karpenisi
Lamia
Skopelos

IONIAN SEA
Amfilohia
Loutra Edipsou
Skantzoura

Lefkada
Lake Kremasta
Mt Iti (2125m)
Strofylia
Kymi

Lefkada
Mytikas
Agrinio
STEREA ELLADA
Mt Parnassos ▲(2457m)
Halkida
EVIA

IONIAN ISLANDS
Nafpaktos
Delphi
Livadia
Nea Styra

Kefallonia
Ithaki
Messolongi
Patras
Thiva (Thebes)
Mt Parnitha (1413m) ▲

Sami
Poros
Patras Gulf
Diakofto
Gulf of Corinth
Perahora
ATHENS

Argostoli
Kyllini
Derveni
Xylokastro
Loutraki
Piraeus

Skinari
Kalavryta
Corinth
Salamis
Aegina

Zakynthos
Amaliada
Mycenae
Saronic Gulf

Zakynthos
Pyrgos
Olympia
Argos
Epidavros
Poros

Andritsena
Tripolis
Nafplio

Megalopoli
Spetses
Hydra

Kyparissia
PELOPONNESE
Leonidio
SARONIC GULF ISLANDS

Mystras
Sparta

Kalamata
Messinian Mani
Geraki
MIRTOÖN SEA

Pylos
Koroni
Gythio

Methoni
Stoupa
Lakonian Gulf

Areopoli
Monemvasia

Lakonian Mani
Gerolimenas
Elafonisi
Neapoli

Kythira

MEDITERRANEAN SEA

Antikythira

Rodopos Peninsula

Gramvousa Peninsula
Hania

Kastelli-Kissamos

Paleohora
Hora Sfakion

0    50    100km
0    30    60mi

Gavdos

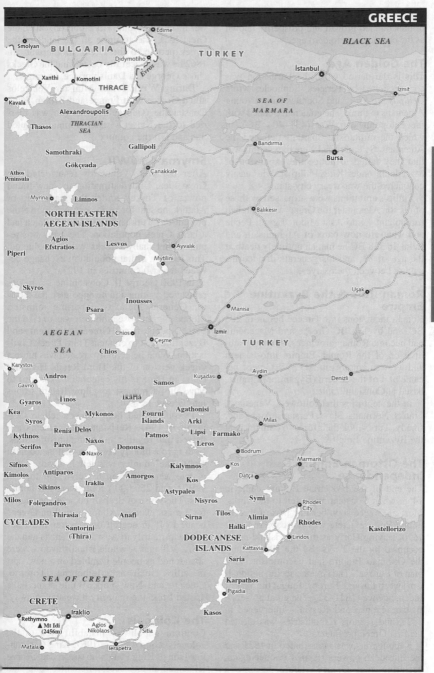

Victory over Persia was followed by a period of unparalleled growth and prosperity known as the classical (or golden) age.

## The Golden Age

This is the period when the Parthenon was commissioned by Pericles, Sophocles wrote *Oedipus the King*, and Socrates taught young Athenians to think. The golden age ended with the Peloponnesian War (431–404 BC), in which the militaristic Spartans defeated the Athenians. So embroiled were they in this war that they failed to notice the expansion of Macedonia under King Philip II, who easily conquered the war-weary city-states.

Philip's ambitions were surpassed by those of his son Alexander the Great, who marched triumphantly into Asia Minor, Egypt, Persia and what are now parts of Afghanistan and India. In 323 BC he met an untimely death at the age of 33, and his generals divided his empire between themselves.

## Roman Rule & the Byzantine Empire

Roman incursions into Greece began in 205 BC, and by 146 BC Greece and Macedonia had become Roman provinces. After the subdivision of the Roman Empire into eastern and western empires in AD 395, Greece became part of the eastern (Byzantine) Empire, based at Constantinople.

In the centuries that followed, Venetians, Franks, Normans, Slavs, Persians, Arabs and, finally, Turks took their turns to chip away at the Byzantine Empire.

## The Ottoman Empire & Independence

The end of the Byzantine Empire came in 1453, when Constantinople fell to the Turks. Most of Greece soon became part of the Ottoman Empire. Crete was not captured until 1670, leaving Corfu as the only island never occupied by the Turks. By the 19th century the Ottoman Empire had become the 'sick man of Europe'. The Greeks, seeing nationalism sweep through Europe, fought the War of Independence (1821–32). The great powers – Britain, France and Russia – intervened in 1827, and Ioannis Kapodistrias was elected the first Greek president.

Kapodistrias was assassinated in 1831 and the European powers stepped in once again, declaring that Greece should become a monarchy. In January 1833, Otho of Bavaria was installed as king. His ambition, called the Great Idea, was to unite all the lands of the Greek people to the Greek motherland. In 1862 he was peacefully ousted and the Greeks chose George I, a Danish prince, as king.

During WWI, Prime Minister Venizelos allied Greece with France and Britain. King Constantine (George's son), who was married to the Kaiser's sister Sophia, disputed this and left the country.

## Smyrna & WWII

After the war, Venizelos resurrected the Great Idea. Underestimating the new-found power of Turkey under the leadership of Atatürk, he sent forces to occupy Smyrna (the present-day Turkish port of İzmir), which had a large Greek population. The army was repulsed and many Greeks were slaughtered. This led to a brutal population exchange between the two countries in 1923.

In 1930 George II, Constantine's son, was reinstated as king and he appointed the dictator General Metaxas as prime minister. Metaxas' grandiose ambition was to take the best aspects from Greece's ancient and Byzantine past to create a Third Greek Civilisation. What he actually created was more a Greek version of the Third Reich. His chief claim to fame is his celebrated *okhi* (no) to Mussolini's request to allow Italian troops into Greece in 1940.

Despite Allied help, Greece fell to Germany in 1941. Resistance movements polarised into royalist and communist factions, leading to a bloody civil war that lasted until 1949. The country was left in chaos. More people were killed in the civil war than in WWII, and 250,000 people were left homeless. The sense of despair became the trigger for a mass exodus. Almost a million Greeks headed off in search of a better life elsewhere, primarily to Australia, Canada and the USA. Villages – whole islands even – were abandoned as people gambled on a new start in cities such as Melbourne, Toronto, Chicago and New York. While some have drifted back, the majority have stayed away.

## The Colonels

Continuing political instability led to the colonels' coup d'etat in 1967. King Constantine (son of King Paul, who succeeded George II) staged an unsuccessful counter-coup, and then fled the country. The colonels' junta distinguished itself by inflicting appalling brutality, repression and political incompetence upon the Greek people. In 1974 they attempted to assassinate Cyprus' leader, Archbishop Makarios. When Makarios escaped, the junta replaced him with the extremist Nikos Samson, prompting Turkey to occupy North Cyprus. The continued Turkish occupation of Cyprus remains one of the most contentious issues in Greek politics. The junta, now discredited, had little choice but to hand back power to civilians. In November 1974 a plebiscite voted against restoration of the monarchy, and Greece became a republic. An election brought the right-wing New Democracy (ND) party into power.

## The Socialist 1980s

In 1981 Greece entered the then EC (European Community, now the EU). Andreas Papandreou's Panhellenic Socialist Movement (Pasok) won the next election, giving Greece its first socialist government. Pasok promised the removal of US air bases and withdrawal from NATO, which Greece had joined in 1951. Instead Papandreou presided over seven years of rising unemployment and spiralling debt.

He was forced to step aside in 1989 while an unprecedented conservative and communist coalition took over to investigate a scandal involving the Bank of Crete. Papandreou and four ministers were ordered to stand trial, and the coalition ordered fresh elections in October 1990.

## The 1990s

The elections brought the ND party back to power with a majority of two. Tough economic reforms introduced by Prime Minister Konstantinos Mitsotakis soon made his government unpopular. By late 1992, allegations emerged about the same sort of corruption and dirty tricks that had brought Papandreou unstuck. Mitsotakis himself was accused of having a secret hoard of Minoan art, and he was forced to call an election in October 1993.

Greeks again turned to Pasok and the ailing Papandreou, who eventually had been cleared of all charges. He had little option but to continue with the austerity programme begun by Mitsotakis, quickly making his government equally unpopular.

Papandreou was forced to step down in January 1996 after a lengthy spell in hospital.

His departure produced a dramatic change of direction for Pasok, with the party abandoning its leftist policies and electing experienced economist and lawyer Costas Simitis as its new leader. Cashing in on his reputation as the Mr Clean of Greek politics, Simitis romped to a comfortable majority at a snap poll called in October 1996.

His government has since focused almost exclusively on the push for further integration with Europe. Simitis's prime goal of admission to the euro club was achieved in January 2001 when the EU agreed that Greece had met the economic requirements for monetary union. Greece duly adopted the euro as its currency in 2002.

Simitis was rewarded with a further four-year mandate in April 2000, but was suffering a serious mid-term popularity slump at the time of research. Newspaper polls in May 2002 showed Pasok trailing the opposition ND party by more than 7%. The next election is due before April 2004.

## Foreign Policy

Greece's foreign policy is dominated by its extremely sensitive relationship with Turkey, its giant Muslim neighbour to the east.

After decades of constant antagonism, these two uneasy NATO allies were jolted to their senses (literally) by the massive earthquake which devastated the İzmit area of western Turkey in August 1999. According to geologists, the quake moved Turkey 1.5m closer to Greece. It had the same effect on the Greek people, who urged their government to join the rescue effort. Greek teams were among the first on the scene, where they were greeted as heroes. The Turks were quick to return the favour after the Athens quake which followed on 7 September 1999. The relationship has continued to blossom, despite the occasional hiccup, and at the time of research the two countries were discussing a joint bid to stage the 2008 European soccer championships.

While Turkey remains the country's top priority, Greece has also had its hands full in recent years coping with events to the north precipitated by the break-up of former Yugoslavia and the collapse of the communist regimes in Albania and Romania.

## GEOGRAPHY

Greece consists of the southern tip of the Balkan Peninsula and about 2000 islands,

GREECE

only 166 of which are inhabited. The land mass is 131,900 sq km and Greek territorial waters cover a further 400,000 sq km.

Most of the country is mountainous. The Pindos Mountains in Epiros are the southern extension of the Dinaric Alps, which run the length of former Yugoslavia. The range continues down through central Greece and the Peloponnese, and re-emerges in the mountains of Crete. Less than a quarter of the country is suitable for agriculture.

## GEOLOGY

Greece lies in one of most seismically active regions in the world, recording over 20,000 earthquakes in the last 40 years. Fortunately, most of them are very minor – detectable only by sensitive seismic monitoring equipment. The reason for all this activity is that the eastern Mediterranean lies at the meeting point of three continental plates: the Eurasian, African and Arabian. The three grind away at each other constantly, generating countless earthquakes as the land surface reacts to the intense activity beneath the earth's crust.

The system has two main fault lines. The most active is the North Aegean Fault, which starts as a volcano-dotted rift between Greece and Turkey, snakes under Greece and then runs north up the Ionian and Adriatic coasts. Less active but more dramatic is the North Anatolian Fault that runs across Turkey, which is renowned for major tremors like the 7.4 monster that struck more than 40,000 dead in western Turkey in August 1999. Seismologists maintain that activity along the two fault lines is not related.

## CLIMATE

Greece's climate is typically Mediterranean with mild, wet winters followed by very hot, dry summers.

There are regional variations. The mountains of northern Greece have a climate similar to the Balkans, with freezing winters and very hot, humid summers, while the west coast and the Ionian Islands have the highest rainfall.

Mid-October is when the rains start in most areas, and the weather stays cold and wet until February – although there are also plenty of winter days with clear blue skies and sunshine. Crete stays warm the longest and you can swim off its southern coast from mid-April to November.

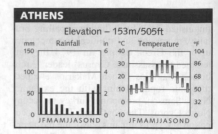

## ECOLOGY & ENVIRONMENT

Greece is belatedly becoming environmentally conscious; regrettably, it is often a case of closing the gate after the horse has bolted. Deforestation and soil erosion are problems that go back thousands of years. Olive cultivation and goats have been the main culprits, but firewood gathering, shipbuilding, housing and industry have all taken their toll.

Forest fires are also a major problem, with an estimated 25,000 hectares destroyed every year. The 2000 season was one of the worst on record, particularly in the Peloponnese and on the island of Samos. Epiros and Macedonia in northern Greece are the only places where extensive forests remain.

General environmental awareness remains at a depressingly low level, especially where litter is concerned. The problem is particularly bad in rural areas, where roadsides are strewn with soft drink cans and plastic packaging hurled from passing cars. Environmental education has begun in schools, but it will be some time before community attitudes change.

The news from the Aegean Sea is both good and bad. According to EU findings, it is Europe's least-polluted sea – apart from areas immediately surrounding major cities. Like the rest of the Mediterranean, the Aegean has been overfished.

## FLORA & FAUNA

The variety of flora in Greece is unrivalled in Europe. The wildflowers are spectacular. They continue to thrive because much of the land is too poor for agriculture and has escaped the ravages of modern fertilisers. The best places to see the dazzling array of wildflowers are the mountains of Crete and the southern Peloponnese.

You won't encounter many animals in the wild, mainly due to the macho Greek habit of blasting to bits anything that moves. Wild boar are still found in reasonable numbers in the north and are a favourite target for hunters. Squirrels, rabbits, hares, foxes and weasels are all fairly common on the mainland; less common is the cute European suslik – a small ground squirrel. Reptiles are well represented. Snakes include several viper species, which are poisonous.

Bird-watchers have more chance of coming across something unusual than animal-spotters. Lake Mikri Prespa in Macedonia has the richest colony of fish-eating birds in Europe, while the Dadia Forest Reserve in Thrace numbers such majestic birds as the golden eagle and the giant black vulture among its residents.

### Endangered Species

The brown bear, Europe's largest land mammal, still survives in very small numbers in the mountains of northern Greece, as does the grey wolf.

Europe's rarest mammal, the monk seal, was once very common in the Mediterranean Sea, but is now on the brink of extinction in Europe. There are about 400 left in Europe, half of which live in Greece. There are about 40 in the Ionian Sea and the rest are found in the Aegean.

The waters around Zakynthos are home to the last large sea turtle colony in Europe, that of the loggerhead turtle (*Careta careta*) The **Sea Turtle Protection Society of Greece** (☎/fax 21 0523 1342; e stps@compulink .gr; Solomou 57, Athens 104 32) runs monitoring programmes and is always looking for volunteers.

### National Parks

Visitors who expect Greek national parks to provide facilities on par with those in countries such as Australia and the USA will be very disappointed. Although they all have refuges and some have marked hiking trails, Greek national parks have little else in the way of facilities.

The most visited parks are Mt Parnitha, just north of Athens, and the Samaria Gorge on Crete. The others are Vikos-Aoös and Prespa national parks in Epiros; Mt Olympus on the border of Thessaly and Macedonia; and Parnassos and Iti national parks in central Greece.

If you want to see wildlife, the place to go is the Dadia Forest Reserve in eastern Thrace.

There is also a National Marine Park off the coast of Alonnisos, and another around the Bay of Laganas area off Zakynthos.

## GOVERNMENT & POLITICS

Since 1975, democratic Greece has been a parliamentary republic with a president as its head of state. The president and parliament, which has 300 deputies, have joint legislative power. Prime Minister Costas Simitis heads a 43-member cabinet.

## ECONOMY

Traditionally, Greece has been an agricultural country, but the importance of agriculture in the economy is declining. Tourism is by far the biggest industry; shipping comes next.

## POPULATION & PEOPLE

The 2001 census recorded a population of 10,964,080. Women outnumber men by more than 200,000. Greece is now a largely urban society, with 68% of people living in cities. By far the largest city is Athens, with more than 3.7 million people in the greater Athens area, which includes Piraeus (171,000). Other major cities are: Thessaloniki (750,000), Patras (153,300), Iraklio (127,600), Larisa (113,400) and Volos (110,000). Less than 15% of the population live on the islands. The most populous are Crete (537,000), Evia (209,100) and Corfu (107,592).

Contemporary Greeks are a mixture of all of the invaders who have occupied the country since ancient times. There are a number of distinct ethnic minorities: about 300,000 ethnic Turks in Thrace; about 100,000 Britons; about 5000 Jews; Vlach and Sarakatsani shepherds in Epiros; Roma (Gypsies); and, recently, a growing number of Albanians.

## ARTS

The arts have been integral to Greek life since ancient times. In summer, Greek dramas are staged in the ancient theatres where they were originally performed.

The visual arts follow the mainstream of modern European art, and traditional folk arts such as embroidery, weaving and tapestry continue.

The *bouzouki* (a stringed instrument similar to a mandolin) is the most popular musical instrument, but each region has its own special instruments and sounds. *Rembetika* music, with its themes of poverty and suffering, was

GREECE

banned by the junta, but is now enjoying a revival. Rembetika is the music of the working classes and has its roots in the sufferings of the refugees from Asia Minor in the 1920s. Songs are accompanied by bouzouki, guitar, violin and accordion.

The blind bard Homer composed the narrative poems *Odyssey* and *Iliad*. These tales of the Trojan War and the return to Greece of Odysseus, King of Ithaki, link together the legends sung by bards during the dark age.

Plato was the most devoted pupil of Socrates, writing down every dialogue he could recall between Socrates, other philosophers and the youth of Athens. His most widely read work is the *Republic*, where it argues that the perfect state could only be created with philosopher-rulers at the helm.

Nikos Kazantzakis, author of *Zorba the Greek* and numerous other novels, plays and poems, is the most famous of 20th-century Greek novelists. The Alexandrian, Constantine Cavafy (1863–1933), revolutionised Greek poetry by introducing a personal, conversational style. He is considered to be the TS Eliot of Greek literary verse. Poet George Seferis (1900–71) won the Nobel Prize for literature in 1963, and Odysseus Elytis (1911–96) won the same prize in 1979.

Theophilos (1866–1934) is famous for his primitive style of painting. The country's most famous painter was a young Cretan called Domenikos Theotokopoulos, who moved to Spain in 1577 and became known as the great El Greco.

## SOCIETY & CONDUCT

Greece is steeped in traditional customs. Name days (celebrated instead of birthdays), weddings and funerals all have great significance. On someone's name day there is an open house and refreshments are served to well-wishers who stop by with gifts. Weddings are highly festive with dancing, feasting and drinking sometimes continuing for days.

If you want to bare all, other than on a designated nude beach, remember that Greece is a conservative country, so take care not to offend the locals.

## MYTHOLOGY

The myths are accounts of the gods whom the Greeks worshipped and heroes idolised in ancient times. The main characters are the 12 principle deities, who lived on Mt Olympus –

which the Greeks thought to be at the exact centre of the world.

The supreme deity was Zeus, who was also god of the heavens. He was the possessor of an astonishing libido and mythology is littered with his offspring. Zeus was married to his sister, Hera, who was the protector of women and the family. She was able to renew her virginity each year by bathing in a spring. She was the mother of Ares, the god of war, and Hephaestus, god of the forge.

Demeter was the goddess of earth and fertility, while the goddess of love (and lust) was the beautiful Aphrodite. The powerful goddess of wisdom and guardian of Athens was Athena, who is said to have been born (complete with helmet, armour and spear) from Zeus' head.

Poseidon, the brother of Zeus, was god of the sea and preferred his sumptuous palace in the depths of the Aegean to Mt Olympus. Apollo, god of the sun, was also worshipped as the god of music and song. His twin sister, Artemis, was the goddess of childbirth and the protector of suckling animals.

Hermes, messenger of the gods, completes the first 11 – the gods whose position in the pantheon is agreed by everyone. The final berth is normally reserved for Hestia, goddess of the hearth. She was too virtuous for some, who promoted the fun-loving Dionysos, god of wine, in her place.

Other gods included Hades, the god of the underworld; Pan, god of the shepherds; Asclepius, the god of healing; and Eros, the god of love.

Heroes such as Heracles and Theseus were elevated almost to the ranks of the gods.

## RELIGION

About 97% of Greeks nominally belong to the Greek Orthodox Church. The rest of the population is split between the Roman Catholic, Protestant, Evangelist, Jewish and Muslim faiths. While older Greeks and those in rural areas tend to be deeply religious, most young people are decidedly more interested in the secular.

## LANGUAGE

Greeks are naturally delighted if you can speak a little of their language, but you don't need to be able to speak Greek to get around. English is almost a second language, especially among younger people. You'll also find many Greeks have lived abroad, usually in Australia or the USA, so even in remote villages there are invariably one or two people who can speak English.

See the Language chapter at the back of this book for pronunciation guidelines and useful Greek words and phrases.

## Transliteration

Travellers in Greece will frequently encounter confusing and seemingly illogical English transliterations of Greek words. Transliteration is a knotty problem – there are six ways of rendering the vowel sound 'ee' in Greek, and two ways of rendering the 'o' sound and the 'e' sound.

This guidebook has merely attempted to be consistent within itself, not to solve this long-standing difficulty.

As a general rule, the Greek letter gamma (g) appears as a 'g' rather than a 'y'; therefore it's *agios,* not ayios. The letter delta (d) appears as 'd' rather than 'dh', so it's *domatia,* not dhomatia. The letter phi (f) can be either 'f' or 'ph'. Here, we have used the general rule that classical names are spelt with a 'ph' and modern names with an 'f' – so it's Phaestos (not Festos), but Folegandros, not Pholegandros. Please bear with us if signs in Greek don't agree with our spelling. It's that sort of language.

# Facts for the Visitor

## HIGHLIGHTS
### Islands

Many islands are overrun with visitors in summer. For tranquillity, head for the lesser-known islands, such as Kassos, Sikinos and Kastellorizo. If you enjoy mountain walks, Crete, Lesvos, Naxos and Samos are ideal destinations.

## Museums & Archaeological Sites

Greece has more ancient sites than any other country in Europe. It's worth seeking out some of the lesser lights where you won't have to contend with the crowds that pour through famous sites, such as the Acropolis, Delphi, Knossos and Olympia.

The counrty's leading museum is the National Archaeological Museum in Athens, which houses Heinrich Schliemann's finds from Mycenae, and Minoan frescoes from Akrotiri on Santorini (Thira). The Thessaloniki Museum contains treasures from the graves of the Macedonian royal family, and the Iraklio Museum houses a vast collection from the Minoan sites of Crete.

Visiting the museums and sites is free for card-carrying students and teachers from EU countries. An International Student Identification Card (ISIC) gets non-EU students a 50% discount.

## Historic Towns

Two of Greece's most spectacular medieval cities are in the Peloponnese. The ghostly Byzantine city of Mystras, west of Sparta, clambers up the slopes of Mt Taygetos, its winding paths and stairways leading to deserted palaces and churches. In contrast, Byzantine Monemvasia is still inhabited, but is equally dramatic and full of atmosphere.

There are some stunning towns on the islands. Rhodes is the finest surviving example of a fortified medieval town in Europe, while Naxos' *hora* (main village or town) is a maze of narrow, stepped alleyways of whitewashed Venetian houses, their tiny gardens ablaze with flowers.

## SUGGESTED ITINERARIES

Depending on the length of your stay, you might want to see and do the following:

**Two days**
  Spend the time in Athens seeing its museums and ancient sites.
**One week**
  Spend one day in Athens, two days in the Peloponnese visiting Nafplio or Mycenae and Olympia, and four days in the Cyclades.
**Two weeks**
  Spend two days in Athens, two days in the Peloponnese, and two days in central Greece visiting Delphi and Meteora. Follow up with a week of island-hopping through the Cyclades.
**One month**
  Spend two days in Athens, two days in the Peloponnese and then catch an overnight ferry from Patras to Corfu for two days. Head to Ioannina and spend two days exploring the Zagorohoria villages of northern Epiros before spending three days travelling back to Athens via Meteora and Delphi. Take a ferry from Piraeus to Chios and spend two weeks island-hopping your way back through the north-eastern Aegean Islands, the Dodecanese and the Cyclades.

GREECE

## PLANNING
### When to Go
Spring and autumn are the best times to visit. Outside the major cities, winter is pretty much a dead loss – unless you're going to take advantage of the cheap skiing. The islands go into hibernation between late November and early April. Hotels and restaurants are closed, and buses and ferries operate on drastically reduced schedules.

The cobwebs are dusted off in time for Easter, and conditions are perfect until the end of June. Everything is open, public transport operates normally, but the crowds have yet to arrive. From July until mid-September, it's on for young and old as northern Europe heads for the Mediterranean en masse. If you want to party, this is the time to go. The flip side is that everywhere is packed out, and rooms can be hard to find.

The pace slows down again by about mid-September, and conditions are ideal once more until the end of October.

### Maps
Unless you are going to trek or drive, the free maps given out by the tourist offices will probably suffice. The best motoring maps are produced by local company Road Editions, which also produces a good trekking series.

### What to Bring
In summer, bring light cotton clothing, a sun hat and sunglasses; bring sunscreen, too, as it's expensive in Greece. In spring and autumn, you will need light jumpers (sweaters) and thicker ones for the evenings. In winter, thick jumpers and a raincoat are essential.

You will need to wear sturdy walking shoes for trekking in the country, and comfortable shoes are a better idea than sandals for walking around ancient sites. An alarm clock for catching early-morning ferries, a torch (flashlight) and a small day-pack will also be useful.

### TOURIST OFFICES
The Greek National Tourist Organisation (GNTO) is known as EOT in Greece. There is either an EOT office or a local tourist office in almost every town of consequence and on many of the islands. Most do no more than give out brochures and maps. Popular destinations have tourist police, who can often help in finding accommodation.

### Local Tourist Offices
The EOT main tourist office (☎ 21 0331 0561/0562, fax 21 0325 2895; ℮ info@ gnto.gr; ⓦ www.gnto.gr; Amerikis 2, Athens 105 64) helps with information. Other tourist offices are listed throughout this chapter.

### Tourist Offices Abroad
**Australia** (☎ 02-9241 1663) 51–57 Pitt St, Sydney, NSW 2000
**Canada** (☎ 416-968 2220) 91 Scollard St, Toronto, Ontario M5R 1G4
(☎ 514-871 1535) 1170 Place Du Frere Andre, Montreal, Quebec H3B 3C6
**France** (☎ 1-42 60 65 75) 3 Ave de l'Opéra, Paris 75001
**Germany** (☎ 069-236 561) Neue Mainzerstrasse 22, 60311 Frankfurt
(☎ 089-222 035) Pacellistrasse 5, 2W 80333 Munich
(☎ 040-454 498) Neurer Wall 18, 20254 Hamburg
(☎ 030-217 6262) Wittenbergplatz 3A, 10789 Berlin 30
**Italy** (☎ 06-474 4249) Via L Bissolati 78-80, Rome 00187
(☎ 02-860 470) Piazza Diaz 1, 20123 Milan
**Japan** (☎ 03-350 55 917) Fukuda Bldg West, 5th Floor 2-11-3 Akasaka, Minato-ku, Tokyo 107-0052
**UK** (☎ 020-7734 5997) 4 Conduit St, London W1R ODJ
**USA** (☎ 212-421 5777) Olympic Tower, 645 Fifth Ave, New York, NY 10022
(☎ 312-782 1084) Suite 160, 168 North Michigan Ave, Chicago, IL 60601
(☎ 213-626 6696) Suite 2198, 611 West 6th St, Los Angeles, CA 92668

### VISAS & DOCUMENTS
Nationals of Australia, Canada, EU countries, Israel, New Zealand and the USA are allowed to stay in Greece for up to three months without a visa. For longer stays, apply at a consulate abroad or at least 20 days in advance to the **Aliens Bureau** (☎ 21 0770 5711; Leoforos Alexandras 173, Athens) at Athens Central Police Station. Elsewhere in Greece, apply to the local police authority.

In the past, Greece has refused entry to those whose passport indicates that they have visited Turkish-occupied North Cyprus, although there are reports that this is less of a problem now. To be on the safe side, however, ask the North Cyprus immigration officials to stamp a piece of paper rather than your passport. If you enter North Cyprus from the Greek Republic of Cyprus, no exit stamp is put in your passport.

## Driving Licence & Permits

Greece recognises all national driving licences, provided the licence has been held for at least one year. It also recognises an International Driving Permit, which should be obtained before you leave home.

## Discount Cards

A Hostelling International (HI) card is of limited use in Greece. The only place you will be able to use it is at the Athens International Youth Hostel (see Places to Stay under Athens, later).

The most widely recognised (and thus the most useful) form of student ID is the International Student Identity Card (ISIC). Holders qualify for half-price admission to museums and ancient sites and for discounts at some budget hotels and hostels.

See Senior Travellers, later in this chapter, for more information.

## EMBASSIES & CONSULATES
## Greek Embassies Abroad

Greece has diplomatic representation in the following countries:

**Australia** (☎ 02-6273 3011) 9 Turrana St, Yarralumla, ACT 2600
**Canada** (☎ 613-238 6271) 76–80 Maclaren St, Ottawa, Ontario K2P 0K6
**France** (☎ 01-47 23 72 28) 17 Rue Auguste Vaquerie, 75116 Paris
**Germany** (☎ 0228-83010) An Der Marienkapelle 10, 53 179 Bonn
**Italy** (☎ 06-854 9630) Via S Mercadante 36, Rome 3906
**Japan** (☎ 03-340 0871/0872) 3-16-30 Nishi Azabu, Minato-ku, Tokyo 304-5853
**New Zealand** (☎ 04-473 7775) 5–7 Willeston St, Wellington
**South Africa** (☎ 12-437 351/352) 1003 Church St, Hatfield, Pretoria 0028
**Turkey** (☎ 312-436 8860) Ziya-ul-Rahman Caddesi 9–11, Gazi Osman Pasa 06700, Ankara
**UK** (☎ 020-7229 3850) 1A Holland Park, London W11 3TP
**USA** (☎ 202-939 5818) 2221 Massachusetts Ave NW, Washington, DC 20008

## Foreign Embassies in Greece

The following countries do have diplomatic representation in Greece:

**Australia** (☎ 21 0645 0404) Dimitriou Soutsou 37, Athens 115 21
**Canada** (☎ 21 0727 3400) Genadiou 4, Athens 115 21
**France** (☎ 21 0361 1663) Leoforos Vasilissis Sofias 7, Athens 106 71
**Germany** (☎ 21 0728 5111) Dimitriou 3 & Karaoli, Kolonaki 106 75
**Italy** (☎ 21 0361 7260) Sekeri 2, Athens 106 74
**Japan** (☎ 21 0775 8101) Athens Tower, Leoforos Messogion 2-4, Athens 115 27
**New Zealand** (☎ 21 0687 4701) Kifissias 268, Halandri 152 32; honorary consulate
**South Africa** (☎ 21 0680 6645) Kifissias 60, Maroussi, Athens 151 25
**Turkey** (☎ 21 0724 5915) Vasilissis Georgiou 8, Athens 106 74
**UK** (☎ 21 0723 6211) Ploutarhou 1, Athens 106 75
**USA** (☎ 21 0721 2951) Leoforos Vasilissis Sofias 91, Athens 115 21

## CUSTOMS

Duty-free allowances in Greece are the same as for other EU countries. Import regulations for medicines are strict; if you are taking medication, make sure you get a statement from your doctor before you leave home. It is illegal, for example, to take codeine into Greece. The export of antiques is prohibited. You can bring as much foreign currency as you like, but if you want to leave with more than US$1000 in foreign banknotes the money must be declared on entry.

## MONEY

Banks will exchange all major currencies, in either cash or travellers cheques and also Euro cheques. Post offices charge less commission than banks, but won't cash travellers cheques.

All major credit cards are accepted, but only in larger establishments. You'll find ATMs everywhere, particularly in tourist areas.

## Currency

Greece adopted the euro at the beginning of 2002, and the Greek drachma disappeared at the end of February after a two-month period of dual circulation. Most people appear to welcome the change, although older people have struggled to adapt.

The only place that will now convert outstanding drachma into euro is the Bank of Greece, and only at its central offices in major cities such as Athens, Patras and Thessaloniki. The Athens branch is at Panepistimiou 15, near Syntagma.

## Costs

Greece is still a cheap destination by northern European standards, but it is no longer

GREECE

dirt-cheap. A rock-bottom daily budget would be €25. This would mean hitching, staying in youth hostels or camping, staying away from bars, and only occasionally eating in restaurants or taking ferries. Allow at least €50 per day if you want your own room and plan to eat out regularly as well as seeing the sights. If you really want a holiday – comfortable rooms and restaurants all the way – you will need closer to €100 per day.

Your money will go a lot further if you travel in the quieter months. Accommodation, which eats up a large part of the daily budget, is generally about 25% cheaper outside the high season. There are fewer tourists around and more opportunities to negotiate even better deals.

## Tipping & Bargaining

In restaurants the service charge is included on the bill, but it is the custom to leave a small tip – just round off the bill. Accommodation is nearly always negotiable outside peak season, especially if you are staying more than one night. Souvenir shops are another place where substantial savings can be made. Prices in other shops are normally clearly marked and non-negotiable.

## Taxes & Refunds

Value-added tax (VAT) varies from 15% to 18%. A tax-rebate scheme applies at a restricted number of shops and stores; look for a Tax Free sign in the window. You must fill in a form at the shop and then present it with the receipt at the airport on departure. A cheque will (hopefully) be sent to your home address.

## POST & COMMUNICATIONS
### Post

The postal rate for postcards and airmail letters is €0.60 to all destinations. Post within Europe takes five to eight days and to the USA, Australia and New Zealand, nine to 11 days.

Post offices are usually open from 7.30am to 2pm. In major cities they stay open until 8pm and are also open 7.30am to 2pm on Saturday. Do not wrap up a parcel until it has been inspected at the post office. Some tourist shops also sell stamps, but with a 10% surcharge.

Mail can be sent poste restante to any main post office and is held for up to one month.

Your surname should be underlined and you will need to show your passport when you collect your mail. Parcels are not delivered in Greece – they must be collected from a post office.

## Telephone & Fax

The phone system is modern and efficient. All public phone boxes use phonecards, sold at Organismos Tilepikoinonion Ellados (OTE) offices and *periptera* (street kiosks). The cards cost €2.95 for 1000 units, €5.60 for 2000 units, €12.35 for 5000 units, and €24.10 for 10,000 units. The 1000-unit cards are widely available at *periptera*, corner shops and tourist shops; the others can be bought at OTE offices.

It's also possible to use these phones using a growing range of discount-card schemes, such as Kronokarta and Teledome, which involve dialling an access code and then punching in your card number. The cards come with instructions in Greek and English. They are easy to use and buy double the time.

It is no longer possible to use public phones to access other national card schemes, such as Telstra Australia's Telecard, for international calls. These calls can be made from private digital phones, but the time you spend on the phone is also charged at local call rates. It's better to use Kronokarta or Teledome.

If you're calling Greece from abroad, the country code is ☎ 30. If you need to make an international call from Greece, the international access code is ☎ 00.

Main city post offices have fax facilities.

## Email & Internet Access

Greece was slow to embrace the wonders of the Internet, but is now striving to make up for lost time. Internet cafés are springing up everywhere, and are listed under Information for cities and islands where available. Charges differ radically – from less than €3.50 per hour in big cities up to €15 per hour on Mykonos.

There has also been a huge increase in the number of hotels and businesses using email, and addresses have also been listed in this chapter where available.

## DIGITAL RESOURCES

There has also been a huge increase in the number of websites providing information about Greece.

A good place to start is the 500 Links to Greece listed at W www.viking1.com/corfu/link.htm. It has links to a huge range of sites covering everything from accommodation to Zeus. One site that it doesn't provide a link to, however, is W www.greektravel .com, the front door for an assortment of interesting sites by Matt Barrett.

The Greek Ministry of Culture has put together an excellent site ath at W www.culture .gr, which has loads of information about museums and ancient sites. Other websites include W www.gogreece.com/travel and W www.aegean.ch. You'll find more specialist websites listed through the chapter.

## BOOKS
### Lonely Planet
Lonely Planet's *Greece* contains more comprehensive information on the areas covered by this chapter, as well as coverage of less-visited areas, particularly in central and northern Greece. The *Greek Islands* guide is especially tailored for island-hoppers. If you want to concentrate on specific regions, pick up Lonely Planet's guides to *Athens*, *Corfu & the Ionians*, *Crete* and *Rhodes & the Dodecanese*. *Peloponnese* will be published in 2003.

### Travel
The ancient Greek traveller Pausanias is acclaimed as the world's first travel writer. His *Guide to Greece* was written in the 2nd century AD and even now makes fascinating reading.

### History
*A Traveller's History of Greece* by Timothy Boatswain & Colin Nicholson is probably the best choice for the layperson who wants a good general reference.

### General
There are numerous books to choose from if you want to get a feel for the country. *Zorba the Greek* by Nikos Kazantzakis may seem an obvious choice, but read it and you'll understand why it's the most popular of all Greek novels translated into English.

English writer Louis de Bernières has become almost a cult figure following the success of *Captain Corelli's Mandolin*, which tells the emotional story of a young Italian army officer sent to the island of Kefallonia during WWII.

Athenian writer Apostolos Doxiadis has charmed critics the world over with his latest novel, *Uncle Petros and Goldbach's Conjecture*, an unlikely blend of family drama and mathematical theory.

## NEWSPAPERS & MAGAZINES
The weekly *Athens News* (€1.50) appears on Friday with an assortment of news, local features and entertainment listings. The Athens edition of the *International Herald Tribune* (€1.60) carries an eight-page English translation of the popular Greek daily *Kathimerini*.

Foreign newspapers are widely available, although only between April and October in smaller resort areas.

## RADIO & TV
There are plenty of radio stations to choose from, especially in Athens, but not many broadcast in English. If you have a shortwave radio, the best frequencies for the World Service are 618, 941 and 1507MHz.

The nine TV channels generate nine times as much rubbish as one channel. You'll find the occasional American action drama in English (with Greek subtitles). Reality show junkies will find local versions of shows such as Big Brother and Survivor.

## PHOTOGRAPHY
Major brands of film are widely available, but quite expensive outside major towns and on the islands.

Never photograph military installations or anything else with a sign forbidding pictures.

## TIME
Greece is two hours ahead of GMT/UTC, and three hours ahead on daylight-saving time, which begins at 12.01am on the last Sunday in March when clocks are put forward one hour. Clocks are put back an hour at 12.01am on the last Sunday in September.

Out of daylight-saving time, at noon in Greece it is also noon in İstanbul, 10am in London, 2am in San Francisco, 5am in New York and Toronto, 8pm in Sydney and 10pm in Auckland. Note: These times do not make an allowance for daylight saving in other countries.

## LAUNDRY
Large towns and some islands have laundrettes. They charge from €8 to €10 to wash

and dry a load. Hotel managers and room owners will usually provide you with a wash-tub if requested.

## TOILETS

You'll find public toilets at all major bus and train stations, but they are seldom very pleasant. You will need to supply your own paper. In town, a café is the best bet, but the owner won't be impressed if you don't at least buy something.

Greek plumbing cannot handle toilet paper; always put it in the bin provided.

## WOMEN TRAVELLERS

Many foreign women travel alone in Greece. Hassles occur, but they tend to be a nuisance rather than threatening. Violent offences are very rare. Women travelling alone in rural areas are usually treated with respect. In rural areas it's sensible to dress conservatively; it's perfectly OK to wear shorts, short skirts etc in touristy places.

## GAY & LESBIAN TRAVELLERS

In a country where the church still plays a major role in shaping society's views on issues such as sexuality, it should come as no surprise that homosexuality is generally frowned upon. Although there is no legislation against homosexual activity, it is wise to be discreet and to avoid open displays of togetherness.

However, this has not prevented Greece from becoming a popular destination for gay travellers. Athens has a busy gay scene, but most people head for the islands – Mykonos and Lesvos in particular. Paros, Rhodes, Santorini (Thira) and Skiathos also have their share of gay hang-outs.

## DISABLED TRAVELLERS

If mobility is a problem, the hard fact is that most hotels, museums and ancient sites are not wheelchair accessible.

## SENIOR TRAVELLERS

Elderly people are shown great respect in Greece. There are some good deals available for EU nationals. For starters, those over 60 qualify for a 50% discount on train travel plus five free journeys per year. Take your ID card or passport to a Greek Railways (OSE) office and you will be given a Senior Card. Pensioners also get a discount at museums and ancient sites.

## DANGERS & ANNOYANCES

Greece has the lowest crime rate in Europe. Athens is developing a bad reputation for petty theft and scams, but elsewhere crimes are most likely to be committed by other travellers.

### Emergency Services

The emergency number for the police is ☎ 100, tourist police ☎ 171, fire brigade ☎ 199, and ambulance (Athens only) ☎ 166. The Europe-wide emergency telephone number ☎ 112 can also be used. See Car & Motorcycle in the introductory Getting Around section later in this chapter for information on assistance in the event of breakdown.

## LEGAL MATTERS

Greek drug laws are the strictest in Europe. There is no distinction between possession and pushing. Possession of a small amount of marijuana is likely to land you in jail.

## BUSINESS HOURS

Banks are open from 8.30am to 2.30pm Monday to Thursday, and 8.30am to 2pm Friday. Some city banks also open from 3.30pm to 6.30pm and on Saturday morning. Shops are open from 8am to 1.30pm and 5.30pm to 8.30pm on Tuesday, Thursday and Friday, and 8am to 2.30pm on Monday, Wednesday and Saturday, but these times are not always strictly adhered to. *Periptera* are open from early morning to midnight. All banks and shops, and most museums and archaeological sites, close during public holidays.

## PUBLIC HOLIDAYS & SPECIAL EVENTS

Public holidays are as follows:

**New Year's Day** 1 January
**Epiphany** 6 January
**First Sunday in Lent** February
**Greek Independence Day** 25 March
**Good Friday/Easter Sunday** March/April
**Spring Festival/Labour Day** 1 May
**Feast of the Assumption** 15 August
**Okhi Day** 28 October
**Christmas Day** 25 December
**St Stephen's Day** 26 December

Easter is Greece's most important festival, with candle-lit processions, feasting and firework displays. The Orthodox Easter is 50 days after the first Sunday in Lent.

There are a number of cultural festivals that are also held during the summer months. The most important is the Athens Festival, when plays, operas, ballet and classical music concerts are staged at the Theatre of Herodes Atticus. The festival also features performances of ancient Greek dramas at the Theatre of Epidavros in the Peloponnese.

## ACTIVITIES
### Windsurfing
Sailboards are widely available for hire, priced from €12. The top spots for windsurfing are Hrysi Akti on Paros, and Vasiliki on Lefkada, which is reputedly one of the best places in the world to learn.

### Sailing
Sailing facilities are harder to find, although the same locations recommended previously for windsurfing are all also ideal for sailing.

Hrysi Akti on Paros and Mylopotas Beach on Ios are two of the best locations. Hire charges for Hobie Cats (catamarans) range from €20 to €25.

### Skiing
Greece offers some of the cheapest skiing in Europe. There are 16 resorts dotted around the mainland, most of them in the north. They have all the basic facilities and are a pleasant alternative to the glitzy resorts of northern Europe.

The season depends on snow conditions but runs approximately from January to the end of April. You'll find information about the latest snow conditions on the Internet at ⓦ www.snowreport.gr.

### Hiking
The mountainous terrain of the Greek countryside is perfect for trekkers who want to get away from the crowds. The popular routes are well marked and well maintained, including the E4 and E6 trans-European treks, which both end in Greece.

A number of companies run organised treks. **Trekking Hellas** (☎ 21 0323 4548, fax 21 0325 1474; ⓔ trekking@compulink.gr; ⓦ www.trekking.gr; Filellinon 7, Athens 105 57) operates treks on the islands as well as on the mainland, while **Alpin Club** (☎ 21 0729 5486, fax 21 0721 2773; ⓔ alpinclub@inte net.gr; ⓦ www.alpinclub.gr; Mihalakopoulou

39, Athens 115 28) concentrates on the Peloponnese and central Greece.

## LANGUAGE COURSES
If you are serious about learning Greek, an intensive course at the start of your stay is a good way to go about it. Most of the courses are in Athens and are covered under Athens, later in this chapter. More information about courses is available from EOT offices and Greek embassies.

## WORK
Your best chance of finding work is to do the rounds of the tourist hotels and bars at the beginning of the season. The few jobs available are hotly contested, despite the menial nature of the work and dreadful pay. EU nationals don't need a work permit, but everyone else does.

## ACCOMMODATION
There is a range of accommodation in Greece to suit every taste and pocket. All places to stay are subject to strict price controls set by the tourist police. By law, a notice must be displayed in every room, which states the category of the room and the price for each season. If you think you've been ripped off, contact the tourist police. Prices quoted in this book are for the high season, unless otherwise stated. Prices are about 40% cheaper between October and May.

### Camping
Greece has almost 350 camping grounds, and a lot of them in great locations. Standard facilities include hot showers, kitchens, restaurants and minimarkets – and often a swimming pool. Prices vary according to facilities, but reckon on €4.50 per adult and €3 for a small tent.

### Refuges
Greece has 55 mountain refuges, which are listed in the booklet *Greece Mountain Refuges & Ski Centres*, available free of charge at EOT and EOS (Ellinikos Orivatikos Syndesmos, the Greek Alpine Club) offices.

### Hostels
You'll find youth hostels in most major towns and on half a dozen islands. The only place affiliated to Hostelling International (HI) is the excellent **Athens International**

Youth Hostel (☎ 21 0523 4170); see Places to Stay under Athens, later.

Most other youth hostels throughout Greece are run by the **Greek Youth Hostel Organisation** (☎ 21 0751 9530, fax 21 0751 0616; ⓔ y-hostels@otenet.gr; Damareos 75, Athens 116 33). There are affiliated hostels in Athens, Olympia, Patras and Thessaloniki on the mainland, and on the islands of Crete and Santorini (Thira). Most charge €7 to €8, and you don't have to be a member to stay in any of them.

## Domatia
*Domatia* are the Greek equivalent of the British bed and breakfast, minus the breakfast. Once upon a time, *domatia* consisted of little more than spare rooms that families would rent out in summer to supplement their income. Nowadays many of these *domatia* are purpose-built appendages to the family house. The rates start at about €18/25 for singles/doubles.

## Hotels
Hotels in Greece are classified as deluxe, A, B, C, D or E class. The ratings seldom seem to have much bearing on the price, but expect to pay €18/25 for singles/doubles in D and E class, and anything from €35/45 to €60/80 for singles/doubles in a decent C-class place with private bathroom.

Some places are classified as pensions and are rated differently. Both are allowed to levy a 10% surcharge for stays of less than three nights, but they seldom do. It normally works the other way – you can bargain a cheaper rate if you're staying more than one night.

## Apartments
Self-contained family apartments are available in some hotels and *domatia*, particularly on the islands.

## Houses & Flats
For long-term rental accommodation in Athens, you can check the advertisements in the English-language newspapers. In rural areas, ask around in tavernas.

## FOOD
If Greek food conjures up an uninspiring vision of lukewarm *mousakas* collapsing into a plate of olive oil, take heart – there's a lot more on offer.

## Snacks
Greece has a great range of fast-food options for the inveterate snacker. Foremost among them are the *gyros* and the *souvlaki*. The gyros is a giant skewer laden with seasoned meat that grills slowly as it rotates, the meat being steadily trimmed from the outside. Souvlaki are small, individual kebabs. Both are served wrapped in pitta bread with salad and lashings of *tzatziki* (a yogurt, cucumber and garlic dip). Other snacks are pretzel rings, *spanakopitta* (spinach and cheese pie) and *tyropitta* (cheese pie).

## Starters
Greece is famous for its appetisers, known as *mezedes* (literally, 'tastes'; *meze* for short). Standards include tzatziki, *melitzanosalata* (aubergine or eggplant dip), *taramasalata* (fish-roe dip), *dolmades* (stuffed vine leaves), *fasolia* (beans) and *oktapodi* (octopus). A selection of three or four starters represents a good meal and can be a very good option for vegetarians.

## Main Dishes
You'll find *mousakas* (layers of aubergine and mince, topped with bechamel sauce and baked) on every menu, alongside a number of other taverna staples. They include *moschari* (oven-baked veal and potatoes), *keftedes* (meatballs), *stifado* (meat stew), *pastitsio* (baked dish of macaroni with minced meat and bechamel sauce) and *yemista* (either tomatoes or green peppers stuffed with minced meat and rice). Most mains cost between €4 and €8.

The most popular fish are *barbouni* (red mullet) and *sifias* (swordfish), but they don't come cheap. Prices start at about €10 for a serve. *Kalamaria* (fried squid) is readily available and cheap at about €4.50.

Fortunately for vegetarians, salad is a mainstay of the Greek diet. The most popular is *horiatiki salata*, normally listed on English menus as Greek or country salad. It's a mixed salad comprising cucumbers, peppers, onions, olives, tomatoes and feta (sheep's- or goat's-milk white cheese).

## Desserts
Turkish in origin, most Greek desserts are variations on pastry soaked in honey. Popular ones include *baklava* (thin layers of pastry filled with honey and nuts) and *kadaïfi* (shredded wheat soaked in honey).

## Restaurants

There are several varieties of restaurants. An *estiatorio* is a straightforward place with a printed menu. A taverna is often cheaper and more typically Greek, and you'll probably be invited to peer into the pots. A *psistaria* specialises in charcoal-grilled dishes. *Ouzeria* (ouzo bars) often have such a range of *mezedes* that they can be regarded as eating places.

## Kafeneia

*Kafeneia* are the smoke-filled cafés where men gather to drink coffee, play backgammon and cards and engage in heated political discussion. They are a bastion of male chauvinism. Female tourists tend to avoid them, but those who venture in invariably find they are treated courteously.

## Self-Catering

Buying and preparing your own food is easy – every town of consequence has a supermarket, as well as fruit and vegetable shops.

## DRINKS
### Nonalcoholic Drinks

Bottled mineral water is cheap and available everywhere, as are soft drinks and packaged juices.

## Alcoholic Drinks

Greece is traditionally a wine-drinking society. If you're spending a bit of time in the country, it's worth acquiring a taste for retsina (resinated wine). The best (and worst) flows straight from the barrel in the main production areas of Attica and central Greece, but it's available by the bottle everywhere. Greece also produces a large range of regular wines from traditional grape varieties.

Mythos and Alpha are two Greek beers to look out for. Amstel is the most popular of several northern European beers produced locally under licence. You can expect to pay about €0.80 in a supermarket, or €1.50 in a restaurant for a beer. The most popular aperitif is the aniseed-flavoured ouzo.

## ENTERTAINMENT

The busy nightlife is a major attraction for many travellers. Nowhere is the pace more frenetic than on the islands in high season. Discos abound in all resort areas and Ios and Paros especially are famous for their raging discos and bars. If you enjoy theatre and classical music, Athens and Thessaloniki are the places to be.

Greeks are great film-goers. Cinemas show films in the original language (usually English) with Greek subtitles.

## SPECTATOR SPORTS

Greek men are sports mad. Basketball has almost overtaken soccer as the main attraction. If you happen to be eating in a taverna on a night when a big match is being televised, expect indifferent service.

## SHOPPING

Greece produces a vast array of handicrafts, including woollen rugs, ceramics, leather work, hand-woven woollen shoulder bags, embroidery, copperware and carved-wood products.

# Getting There & Away

## AIR

There are no less than 16 international airports in Greece, but most of them handle only summer charter flights to the islands. Eleftherios Venizelos International Airport in Athens handles the vast majority of international flights, including all intercontinental flights. Athens has regular scheduled flights to all the European capitals. Thessaloniki is also well served.

Most flights are with the national carrier, Olympic Airways, or the flag carrier of the country concerned.

## Departure Tax

The airport tax is €12 for passengers travelling to destinations within the EU, and €22 for other destinations. It applies to travellers aged over five, and is paid when you buy your ticket, not at the airport.

Travellers using Athens airport must fork out an additional €10.30 for the privilege of using the swish new terminal, as well as a security charge of €1.29. These charges apply to all passengers aged over two, and are paid when you buy your ticket.

## The USA & Canada

Olympic Airways has daily flights to Athens from New York and up to three a week from

Boston. Delta also has daily flights from New York. Apex fares range from US$960 to US$1550. It's worth shopping around for cheaper deals from major European airlines.

You should be able to get to Athens from Toronto and Montreal for about C$1150 or from Vancouver for C$1500. Olympic has up to five flights a week to Athens from Toronto via Montreal.

### Australia
Olympic flies to Athens twice a week from Sydney via Melbourne. Fares range from A$1695 to A$2400.

### Europe
Flying is the fastest, easiest and cheapest way of getting to Greece from northern Europe. What's more, scheduled flights are so competitively priced that it's hardly worth hunting around for charter cheapies.

Olympic Airways and British Airways both offer 30-day return tickets from London for about UK£240 (midweek departures) in high season, as well as returns to Thessaloniki for about UK£225.

At the time of writing, the cheapest fares were being offered by **EasyJet** (☎ 0870 600 0000), which had flights from London (Stansted) to Athens from UK£69 one way.

Charter flights from London to Athens are readily available for around UK£99/189 one way/return in high season, dropping to UK£79/129 in low season. Fares are about UK£109/209 to most island destinations in high season. Similar deals are available from charter operators throughout Europe.

Athens is a good place to buy cheap air tickets. Examples of one-way fares include London (€75), Madrid (€220), Paris (€165) and Rome (€125).

### LAND
### Northern Europe
Overland travel between northern Europe and Greece is virtually a thing of the past. Buses and trains can't compete with cheap air fares, and the turmoil in the former Yugoslavia has cut the shortest overland route. All bus and train services now go via Italy and take the ferries over to Greece.

Unless you have a Eurail pass, travelling to Greece by train is prohibitively expensive. Greece is part of the Eurail network, and passes are valid on the ferries operated by

Adriatica di Navigazione and Hellenic Mediterranean Lines from Brindisi to Corfu, Igoumenitsa and Patras.

### Neighbouring Countries
The Hellenic Railways Organisation (OSE) has buses from Athens to İstanbul (€67.50, 22 hours) at 7pm from Thursday to Tuesday, and to Tirana (€35.20, 21 hours) at 7pm daily.

There are daily trains between Athens and İstanbul for €58.70, leaving from Larisis station at 11.15pm. The trip takes 23 hours.

The crossing points into Turkey are at Kipi and Kastanies, the crossings into the Former Yugoslav Republic of Macedonia (FYROM) are at Evzoni and Niki, and the Bulgarian crossing is at Promahonas. All are open 24 hours a day. The crossing points to Albania are at Kakavia and Krystallopigi.

If you want to hitchhike to Turkey, look for a through-ride from Alexandroupolis because you cannot hitchhike across the border.

### SEA
### Departure Tax
Port taxes are €5.50 to Italy and €8.80 to Turkey, Cyprus and Israel.

### Italy
The most popular crossing is from Brindisi to Patras (18 hours), via Corfu (nine hours) and Igoumenitsa (10 hours). There are numerous services. Deck-class fares start at about €35 one way in low season and €45 one way in high season. Eurail pass-holders can travel free with Blue Star Ferries and Hellenic Mediterranean. You still need to make a reservation and pay port taxes.

There are also ferries to Patras from Ancona, Bari, Trieste and Venice, stopping at either Corfu or Igoumenitsa on the way. In summer you can get ferries from Bari and Brindisi to Kefallonia.

### Turkey
There are five regular ferry services between the Greek Islands and places in Turkey, these are between: Lesvos–Ayvalık, Chios–Çeşme, Samos–Kuşadası, Kos–Bodrum and Rhodes–Marmaris. All are daily services in summer, dropping to weekly in winter. Tickets must be bought a day in advance and you will be asked to hand over your passport. It will be returned on the boat.

### Cyprus & Israel

Salamis Lines and Poseidon Lines operate services from Piraeus to the Israeli port of Haifa, via Rhodes and Lemessos (formerly Limassol) on Cyprus. Deck-class fares from Piraeus are €70.50 to Lemessos and €106 to Haifa.

Students and travellers aged under 30 qualify for a 20% discount on these fares.

# Getting Around

## AIR

Most domestic flights are operated by **Olympic Airways** (W *www.olympic-airways .gr*) and its offshoot, Olympic Aviation. They offer a busy schedule in summer with flights from Athens to 25 islands and a range of mainland cities. Sample fares include Athens to Iraklio for €89, Athens to Rhodes for €96 and Athens to Santorini (Thira) for €84. There are also flights from Thessaloniki to the islands. It is advisable to book at least two weeks in advance, especially in summer. Services to the islands are fairly skeletal in winter. **Aegean Airlines** (W *www.aegeanair.com*) provides competition on a few major routes.

These fares include the €12 tax on domestic flights, paid when you buy your ticket.

## BUS

Buses are the most popular form of public transport. They are comfortable, they run on time and there are frequent services on all the major routes. Almost every town on the mainland (except in Thrace) has at least one bus a day to Athens. Local companies can get you to all but the remotest villages. Reckon on paying about €4 per hour of journey time. Sample fares from Athens include €28 to Thessaloniki (7½ hours) and €12.25 to Patras (three hours). Tickets should be bought at least an hour in advance to ensure a seat.

Major islands also have comprehensive local bus networks. In fact, every island with a road has a service of some sort, but they tend to operate at the whim of the driver.

## TRAIN

Trains are generally looked on as a poor alternative to bus travel. The main problem is that there are only two main lines: to Thessaloniki and Alexandroupolis in the north,

and to the Peloponnese. In addition there are a number of branch lines, such as the Pyrgos–Olympia line and the spectacular Diakofto–Kalavryta mountain railway.

If there are trains going in your direction, they are a good way to travel. Be aware that there are two distinct levels of service: the painfully slow, dilapidated trains that stop at all stations, and the faster, modern intercity trains.

The slow trains represent the cheapest form of transport. It may take five hours to crawl from Athens to Patras, but the 2nd-class fare is only €5.30. Intercity trains do the trip in 3½ hours for €10, which is still cheaper than the bus.

Inter-Rail and Eurail passes are valid in Greece, but you still need to make a reservation. In summer, make reservations at least two days in advance.

## CAR & MOTORCYCLE

Car is a great way to explore areas that are off the beaten track. Bear in mind that roads in remote regions are often poorly maintained. You'll need a good road map.

You can bring a vehicle into Greece for four months without a carnet – if you have a Green Card (international third-party insurance).

Average prices for fuel are €0.70 to €0.82 per litre for super, €0.68 to €0.80 for unleaded and €0.65 to €0.73 for diesel.

Most islands are served by car ferries. Sample fares for small cars from Piraeus include €65 to Crete and €78 to Rhodes.

The Greek automobile club, ELPA, offers reciprocal services to members of other national motoring associations. If your vehicle breaks down, dial ☎ 104.

### Road Rules

Greek motorists are famous for ignoring the road rules, which is probably why the country has one of the highest road-fatality rates in Europe. No casual observer would ever guess that it is compulsory to wear seat belts in the front seats of vehicles, nor that it is compulsory to wear a crash helmet on motorcycles of more than 50cc – always insist on a helmet when renting a motorcycle.

The speed limit for cars is 120km/h on toll roads, 90km/h outside built-up areas and 50km/h in built-up areas. For motorcycles, the speed limit outside built-up areas is 70km/h. Speeding fines start at €60.

Drink-driving laws are strict; a blood alcohol content of 0.05% incurs a penalty and over 0.08% is a criminal offence.

## Rental

Car hire is expensive, especially from the multinational hire companies. High-season weekly rates with unlimited mileage start at about €380 for the smallest models, dropping to €300 in winter – and that's without tax and extras.

You can generally do much better with local companies. Their advertised rates are about 25% lower and they're often willing to bargain.

Mopeds, however, are cheap and available everywhere. Most places charge about €15 per day.

**Warning** If you plan to hire a motorcycle or moped, check that your travel insurance does cover you for injury resulting from motorcycle accidents. Many policies don't.

Lonely Planet receives a lot of letters complaining about companies hiring out poorly maintained machines. Most insurance policies won't pay out for injuries caused by defective machines.

## BICYCLE

Cycling is becoming a popular way to visit Greece. Bicycles are an ideal way to explore some of the larger islands, and are carried free on ferries. The Peloponnese is another favourite destination, but you need strong leg muscles to tackle some of the mountainous terrain.

GREECE

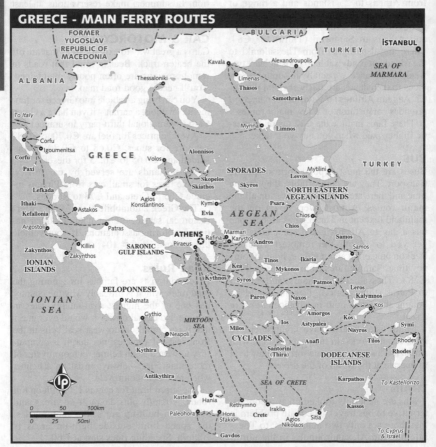

**GREECE - MAIN FERRY ROUTES**

You can hire bicycles, but they are not nearly as widely available as cars and motorcycles. Prices range from about €5 to €15, depending on the age and style of bike and the location.

## HITCHING

The further you are from a city, the easier hitching becomes. Getting out of major cities can be hard work, and Athens is notoriously difficult. In remote areas, people may stop to offer a lift even if you aren't hitching.

## BOAT
## Ferry

Every island has a ferry service of some sort. They come in all shapes and sizes, from the state-of-the-art 'superferries' that run on the major routes to the ageing open ferries that operate local services to outlying islands.

The hub of the vast ferry network is Piraeus, the main port of Athens. It has ferries to the Cyclades, Crete, the Dodecanese, the Saronic Gulf Islands and the northeastern Aegean Islands. Patras is the main port for ferries to the Ionian Islands, while Volos and Agios Konstantinos are the ports for the group of islands called Sporades.

Some of the smaller islands are virtually inaccessible during winter, when schedules are cut back to a minimum. Services start to pick up in April and are running at full steam from June to September.

Fares are fixed by the government. The small differences in price you may find between ticket agencies are the result of some agencies sacrificing part of their designated commission to qualify as a 'discount service'. The discount offered seldom amounts to much. Tickets can be bought at the last minute from quayside tables set up next to the boats. Prices are the same, contrary to what you will be told by agencies.

When buying your ticket, unless you specify otherwise, you will automatically be sold deck class, which is the cheapest fare. Sample fares from Piraeus include €17.30 to Mykonos and €21 to Santorini (Thira).

## Hydrofoil

Hydrofoils offer a faster alternative to ferries on some routes, particularly to islands close to the mainland. They take half the time, but cost twice as much. Most routes operate only during high season.

## Catamaran

High-speed catamarans have become an important part of the island travel scene. They are just as fast as hydrofoils, if not faster, and are much more comfortable. They are also much less prone to cancellation in rough weather.

## Yacht

It's hardly a budget option, but *the* way to see the islands is by yacht. There are many places to hire boats, both with and without a crew. If you want to go it alone, two crew members must have sailing certificates. Prices start at about US$1500 per week for a four-person boat. A skipper is an extra US$800 per week.

## LOCAL TRANSPORT

You'll find taxis almost everywhere. Flag fall is €0.75, followed by €0.23 per kilometre in towns and €0.46 per kilometre outside towns. The rate doubles from midnight to 5am. There's a surcharge of €0.90 from airports and €0.60 from ports, bus stations and train stations. Luggage is €0.30 per item over 10kg.

Taxis in Athens and Thessaloniki often pick up extra passengers along the way (yell out your destination as they cruise by; when you get out, pay what's on the meter, minus what it read when you got in, plus €0.75).

In rural areas taxis don't have meters, so make sure you agree on a price with the driver before you get in.

## ORGANISED TOURS

Greece has many companies which operate guided tours, predominantly on the mainland, but also on larger islands. The major operators include CHAT, Key Tours and GO Tours, which are all based in Athens. It is cheaper to travel independently – tours are only worthwhile if you have extremely limited time.

## STREET NAMES

*Odos* means street, *plateia* means square and *leoforos* means avenue. These words are often omitted on maps and other references, so we have done the same throughout this chapter, except when to do so would cause confusion.

# Athens Αθήνα

☎ 21 • pop 3.7 million

Ancient Athens ranks alongside Rome and Jerusalem for its glorious past and its influence

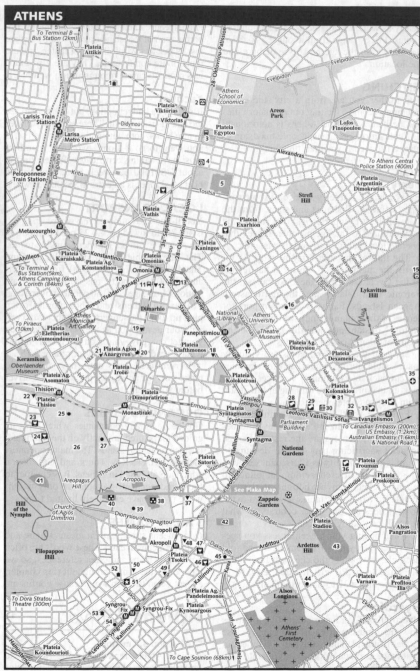

# ATHENS

To Terminal B
Bus Station (2km)

Plateia
Attikis

28-Oktovriou-Patission

Evelpidon

Evelpidon

Pringiponnison

Valtinon

Plateia
Viktorias

Viktorias

Athens
School of
Economics

Areos
Park

Lofos
Finopoulou

Larisis Train
Station

Didymou

Plateia
Egyptou

Larisa
Metro Station

Alexandras

To Athens Central
Police Station (400m)

Peloponnese
Train Station

Kritis

Tositsa

Strefi
Hill

Plateia
Argentinis
Dimokratias

Delgianni

Metaxourghio

Plateia
Vathis

Plateia
Exarhion

Koletti

Emmanuil Benaki

Ahilleos

31s-Septemvriou

28-Oktovriou-Patission

Plateia
Karaiskaki

Ag. Konstantinou

Plateia Ag.
Konstandinou

Plateia
Kaningos

Lofos

To Terminal A
Bus Station(5km),
Athens Camping (6km)
& Corinth (84km)

Plateia
Omonias

Omonia

Eolou

Panepistimiou

Plateia
Karaiskaki

Lykavittos
Hill

Pireos (Tsaldari-Panag)

Dimarhio

National
Library

Athens
University

Plateia Ag.
Dionysiou

To Piraeus
(10km)

Athens
Municipal
Art Gallery

Plateia
Eleftherias
(Koumoundourou)

Plateia Agion
Anargyron

Panepistimiou (El Venizelou)

Theatre
Museum

Plateia
Dexameni

Plateia
Iroön

Plateia
Klafthmonos

Keramikos
Oberlaender
Museum

Plateia Ag.
Asomaton

Plateia
Kolokotroni

Plateia
Kolonakiou

Thision

Plateia
Thisiou

Plateia
Dimopratiriou

Monastiraki

Ermou

Vassileos
Georgiou

Plateia
Syntagmatos
Syntagma

Leoforos Vasilissis Sofias

Evangelismos

Syntagma

To Canadian Embassy (200m),
US Embassy (1.2km),
Australian Embassy (1.6km)
& National Road 1

Parliament
Building

Nikis

Pratiniou

Plateia
Satoris

National
Gardens

Plateia
Trouman

Areopagus
Hill

Acropolis

Thespou

Kydathineon

Leoforos Amalias

See Plaka Map

Plateia
Proskopon

Hill
of the
Nymphs

Church
of Agios
Dimitrios

Dionysiou-Areopagitou

Zappeio
Gardens

Zappeio
Gardens

Plateia
Stadiou

Alsos
Pangratiou

Filopappos
Hill

Kallisperi

Akropoli

Leof. Vas.-Olgas

Plateia
Stadiou

Akropoli

Plateia
Tsokri

Diakou Ath

Ardittou

Ardettos
Hill

Plateia
Varnava

Plateia
Profitou
Ilia

To Dora Stratou
Theatre (300m)

Syngrou-
Fix

Syngrou-Fix

Plateia Ag.
Pandeleimonos

Plateia
Kynosargous

Alsos
Longinou

Athens'
First
Cemetery

Leof. Vas.-Konstantinou

Plateia
Koundourioti

Leoforos Syngrou

Kallirois

To Cape Sounion (68km)

Leof. Voullagmenis

1
2
3
4
5
6
7
8
9
10
11
12
13
14
15
16
17
18
19
20
21
22
23
24
25
26
27
28
29
30
31
32
33
34
35
36
37
38
39
40
41
42
43
44
45
46
47
48
49
50
51
52
53
54

## ATHENS

| PLACES TO STAY | | 3 | Mavromateon Bus Terminal | 29 | Italian Embassy |
|---|---|---|---|---|---|
| 1 | Hostel Aphrodite | 4 | Museum Internet Café | 30 | Benaki Museum |
| 8 | Athens International Youth | 5 | National Archaeological | 31 | British Council |
| | Hostel | | Museum | 32 | Goulandris Museum of |
| 20 | Hotel Cecil | 6 | AN Club | | Cycladic & Ancient Greek Art |
| 52 | Art Gallery Hotel | 7 | Rodon Club | 33 | German Embassy |
| 53 | Marble House Pension | 9 | OSE Office | 34 | British Embassy |
| | | 10 | Bus No 051 to Bus | 35 | Evangelismos Hospital |
| PLACES TO EAT | | | Terminal A | 36 | Turkish Embassy |
| 12 | Marinopoulos (Supermarket) | 11 | Bus No 049 to Piraeus | 38 | Theatre of Dionysos |
| 18 | Vasilopoulou (Supermarket) | 13 | Athens' Central Post Office | 39 | Stoa of Eumenes |
| 19 | Fruit & Vegetable Market | 14 | Bits and Bytes Internet Café | 40 | Theatre of Herodes Atticus |
| 21 | Embros | 15 | Lykavittos Theatre | 41 | Hill of the Pynx Theatre |
| 22 | To Steki tou Elia | 16 | Hellenic American Union | 42 | Temple of Olympian Zeus |
| 37 | Daphne Restaurant | 17 | OSE Office | 43 | Roman Stadium |
| 48 | Oinomageireion ton Theon | 23 | Stavlos | 44 | Athens Centre |
| 49 | To 24 Hours | 24 | To Lizard | 45 | Key Tours Office & Terminal |
| 50 | Veropoulos (Supermarket) | 25 | Temple of Hephaestus | 46 | Granazi Bar |
| | | 26 | Ancient Agora | 47 | Lamda Club |
| OTHER | | 27 | Church of the Holy Apostles | 51 | Tourist Police |
| 2 | OTE Main Office | 28 | French Embassy | 54 | Olympic Airways Head Office |

on Western civilisation, but the modern city is a place that few people fall in love with.

However inspiring the Acropolis might be, most visitors have trouble coming to terms with the surrounding urban sprawl, the appalling traffic congestion and the pollution. Most stop no longer than is required to take in the two main attractions: the Acropolis and the treasures of the National Archaeological Museum.

The city's well-publicised deficiencies are coming under the spotlight as never before as it struggles to prepare to host the 2004 Olympic Games. Progress has been exasperatingly slow, and some major public works projects have been scaled back before leaving the drawing board. The International Olympic Committee, however, remains publicly optimistic that preparations are almost on track.

Culturally, Athens is a fascinating blend of East and West. King Otho and the middle class that emerged after independence may have been intent on making Athens a European city, but the influence of Asia Minor is everywhere – the coffee, the kebabs, the raucous street vendors and the colourful markets.

## ORIENTATION

Although Athens is a huge, sprawling city, nearly everything of interest to travellers is located within a small area bounded by Omonia Square (Plateia Omonias) to the north, Monastiraki Square (Plateia Monastirakiou)

to the west, Syntagma Square (Plateia Syntagmatos) to the east and the Plaka district to the south. The city's two major landmarks, the Acropolis and Lykavittos Hill, can be seen from just about everywhere in this area.

Syntagma is the heart of modern Athens. Flanked by luxury hotels, banks and fast-food restaurants, the square is dominated by the old royal palace – home of the Greek parliament since 1935.

Omonia has developed a sorry reputation for sleaze in recent years, but this is set to change with the announcement of plan to transform Plateia Omonias from a traffic hub into an expanse of formal gardens. This is guaranteed to create traffic chaos, since all the major streets of central Athens meet here. Panepistimiou (El Venizelou) and Stadiou run parallel southeast to Syntagma, while Athinas leads south to the market district of Monastiraki. Monastiraki is in turn linked to Syntagma by Ermou – home to some of the city's smartest shops – and Mitropoleos.

Mitropoleos skirts the northern edge of Plaka, the delightful old quarter which was virtually all that existed when Athens was declared the capital of independent Greece. Its labyrinthine streets are nestled on the northeastern slope of the Acropolis, and most of the city's ancient sites are close by. It may be touristy, but it's the most attractive and interesting part of Athens and the majority of visitors make it their base.

Streets are clearly signposted in Greek and English. If you do get lost, it's very easy to find help. A glance at a map is often enough to draw an offer of assistance. Anyone you ask will be able to direct you to Syntagma (say **syn**-tag-ma).

## INFORMATION
### Tourist Offices
Athens' main **EOT tourist office** (☎ 21 0331 0561/0562, fax 21 0325 2895; e info@ gnto.gr; Amerikis 2; open 9am-4pm Mon-Fri) is close to Syntagma. It has a useful free map of Athens, as well as information about public transport in Athens, including ferry departures from Piraeus.

The airport also has an **EOT office** (☎ 21 0353 0445; open 9am-7pm daily).

The **tourist police** (☎ 21 0920 0724; Veikou 43, Koukaki; trolleybus No 1, 5 or 9 from Syntagma; open 24hrs) also has a 24-hour **information service** (☎ 171).

## Money
Most of the major banks have branches around Syntagma, which are open from 8am to 2pm Monday to Thursday and 8am to 1.30pm Friday. The **National Bank of Greece** (cnr Karageorgi Servias & Stadiou) is open extended hours for foreign-exchange dealings only: 3.30pm to 6.30pm Monday to Thursday; 3pm to 6.30pm on Friday; 9am to 3pm on Saturday; and 9am to 1pm on Sunday. It also has an ATM.

For money exchange try **American Express** (AmEx; ☎ 21 0324 4975; Ermou 2) or **Eurochange** (☎ 21 0322 0155; Karageorgi Servias 4), which has an office nearby. It changes Thomas Cook travellers cheques without commission.

**Acropole Foreign Exchange** (Kydathineon 23; open 9am-midnight daily) is in Plaka. The banks at the airport are open from 7am to 9pm. The airport also has several ATMs.

## Post & Communications
**Athens Central Post Office** (Eolou 100, Omonia) is where mail addressed to poste restante will be sent unless specified otherwise; its postcode is 102 00. If you're staying in Plaka, it's best to get mail sent to the Syntagma post office (postcode 103 00) on the corner of Plateia Syntagmatos and Mitropoleos. Both are open 7.30am to 8pm

Monday to Friday, 7.30am to 2pm Saturday, and 9am to 1.30pm Sunday. Parcels over 2kg going abroad must be posted from the **parcels office** (Stadiou 4) in the arcade. They should not be wrapped until they've first been inspected.

The city's main **OTE telephone office** (28 Oktovriou-Patission 85) is open 24 hours.

## Email & Internet Access
Internet cafés are popping up like mushrooms all over Athens. Most charge from €4 to €6 per hour of computer time, whether you log on or not. They include:

**Bits and Bytes Internet Café** Akadimias 78, Exarhia; open 24 hours
**Museum Internet Café** Oktovriou-Patission 46, Omonia (next to the National Archaeological Museum); open 9am to 3am daily
**Plaka Internet World** Pandrosou 29, Monastiraki; open 11am to 11pm daily
**Skynet Internet Centre** Cnr Voulis & Apollonos, Plaka; open 9am to 11pm Monday to Saturday
**Sofokleous.com Internet Café** Stadiou 5, Syntagma (behind Flocafé); open 10am to 10pm Monday to Saturday, 1pm to 9pm Sunday

## Travel Agencies
The bulk of the city's travel agencies are around Plateia Syntagmatos, particularly in the area just south of the square on Filellinon, Nikis and Voulis.

Reputable agencies include **STA Travel** (☎ 21 0321 1188, 21 0321 1194; e statrav el@robissa.gr; Voulis 43) and **USIT-Etos Travel** (☎ 21 0324 0483, fax 21 0322 8447; e usit@usitetos.gr; Filellinon 7). Both these places also issue ISIC cards.

## Bookshops
There are several good English-language bookshops around the city centre. The biggest, with two branches, is **Eleftheroudakis Books** (Panepistimiou 17 • Nikis 20). Others include **Pantelides Books** (Amerikis 11), and **Compendium Books** (Nikis 28). Compendium also has a second-hand books section.

## Cultural Centres
The **British Council** (☎ 21 0369 2314; Plateia Kolonakiou 17) and the **Hellenic American Union** (☎ 21 0362 9886; Massalias 22) hold frequent concerts, film shows, exhibitions and the like. Both also have libraries.

## Laundry

Plaka has a convenient **laundrette** *(Angelou Geronta 10)*, just off Kydathineon, near the outdoor restaurants.

## Medical & Emergency Services

For emergency medical treatment, ring the **tourist police** *(☎ 171)* and they'll tell you where the nearest hospital is. Hospitals give free emergency treatment to tourists. For hospitals with outpatient departments on duty, call ☎ 106. For first-aid advice, ring ☎ 166. You can get free dental treatment at the **Evangelismos Hospital** *(Ipsilandou 45)*.

## Dangers & Annoyances

Athens has its share of petty crime.

**Pickpockets** A major problem in Athens are pickpockets. Their favourite hunting grounds are the metro system and the crowded streets around Omonia, particularly Athinas. The Sunday market on Ermou is another place where it pays to take extra care of your valuables.

**Taxi Touts** Working in league with some overpriced C-class hotels around Omonia, some taxi drivers have become a problem. The scam involves taxi drivers picking up late-night arrivals, particularly at the airport and Bus Terminal A, and persuading them that the hotel they want to go to is full. The taxi driver will pretend to phone the hotel of choice, announce that it's full and suggest an alternative. You can ask to speak to your chosen hotel yourself, or insist on going where you want.

**Bar Scams** Lonely Planet receives a steady flow of letters warning about bar scams, particularly around Syntagma. The most popular version runs something like this: friendly Greek approaches solo male traveller and discovers that the traveller knows little about Athens; friendly Greek then reveals that he, too, is from out of town. Why don't they go to this great little bar that he's just discovered and have a beer? They order a drink, and the equally friendly owner then offers another drink. Women appear, more drinks are provided and the visitor relaxes as he realises that the women are not prostitutes, just friendly Greeks. The crunch comes at the end of the evening when the traveller is presented

with an exorbitant bill and the smiles disappear. The con men who cruise the streets playing the role of the friendly Greek can be very convincing – some people have been taken in more than once.

## ACROPOLIS

Most of the buildings now gracing the Acropolis *(combined site & museum admission €12; site open 8am-6.30pm daily, museum open 8am-6.30pm Tues-Sun, noon-6.30pm Apr-Oct; site & museum open 8am-2.30pm daily Nov-Mar)* were commissioned by Pericles during the golden age of Athens in the 5th century BC. The site had been cleared for him by the Persians, who destroyed an earlier temple complex on the eve of the Battle of Salamis.

The entrance to the Acropolis is through the **Beule Gate**, a Roman arch that was added in the 3rd century AD. Beyond this is the **Propylaia**, the monumental gate that was the entrance to the city in ancient times. It was damaged by Venetian bombing in the 17th century, but it has since been restored. To the south of the Propylaia is the small, graceful **Temple of Athena Nike**, which is not accessible to visitors.

Standing supreme over the Acropolis is the monument which more than any other epitomises the glory of ancient Greece – the **Parthenon**. Completed in 438 BC, this building is unsurpassed in grace and harmony. To achieve perfect form, its lines were ingeniously curved to counteract unharmonious optical illusions. The base curves upward slightly towards the ends, and the columns become slightly narrower towards the top, with the overall effect of making them both look straight.

Above the columns are the remains of a Doric frieze, which was partly destroyed by Venetian shelling in 1687. The best surviving pieces are the controversial Elgin Marbles,

### Admission

The €12 admission charge buys a collective ticket that also gives entry to all the other significant ancient sites: the Ancient Agora, the Roman Agora, the Keramikos, the Temple of Olympian Zeus and the Theatre of Dionysos. The ticket is valid for 48 hours, otherwise individual site fees apply.

GREECE

GREECE

carted off to Britain by Lord Elgin in 1801. The Parthenon, dedicated to Athena, contained an 11m-tall gold-and-ivory statue of the goddess completed in 438 BC by Phidias of Athens (only the statue's foundations exist today).

To the north is the **Erechtheion** and its much-photographed Caryatids, the six maidens who support its southern portico. These are plaster casts – the originals (except for the one taken by Lord Elgin) are in the site's **museum**.

## SOUTH OF THE ACROPOLIS

The importance of theatre in the life of the Athenian city-state can be gauged from the dimensions of the enormous **Theatre of Dionysos** *(entrance: Dionysiou Areopagitou; admission €2; open 8am-7pm Tues-Fri, 8.30am-3pm Sat-Sun Apr-Oct, 8.30am-3pm daily Nov-Mar)*, just south of the Acropolis. Built between 342 and 326 BC on the site of an earlier theatre, in its time it could hold 17,000 people spread over 64 tiers of seats, of which about 20 tiers survive.

The **Stoa of Eumenes**, built as a shelter and promenade for theatre audiences, runs west from the Theatre of Dionysos to the **Theatre of Herodes Atticus**, which was built in Roman times. It is used for performances during the Athens Festival, but is closed at other times.

## TEMPLE OF OLYMPIAN ZEUS

Begun in the 6th century BC, this massive temple *(admission €2; open 8.30am-3pm Tues-Sun)* took more than 700 years to complete. Emperor Hadrian eventually finished the job in AD 131. It was the largest temple in Greece, impressive for the sheer size of its 104 **Corinthian columns** (17m high with a base diameter of 1.7m). The site is just southeast of Plaka, and the 15 remaining columns are a useful landmark.

## ROMAN STADIUM

The stadium, east of the Temple of Olympian Zeus, hosted the first Olympic Games of modern times in 1896. It was originally built in the 4th century BC as a venue for the Panathenaic athletic contests. The seats were rebuilt in Pentelic marble by Herodes Atticus in the 2nd century AD, and faithfully restored in 1895.

## ANCIENT AGORA

The agora *(admission €4; open 8am-7pm daily Apr-Oct, 8.30am-3pm Tues-Sun Nov-Mar)* was the marketplace of ancient Athens

and the focal point of civic and social life. Socrates spent much time here expounding his philosophy. The main monuments are the well-preserved **Temple of Hephaestus**, the 11th-century **Church of the Holy Apostles** and the reconstructed **Stoa of Attalos**, which houses the site's museum.

## ROMAN AGORA

The Romans built their agora *(admission €2; open 8.30am-2.30pm Tues-Sun)* just west of its ancient counterpart. Its principle monument is the wonderful **Tower of the Winds**, built in the 1st century BC by a Syrian astronomer named Andronicus. Each side represents a point of the compass, and has a relief carving depicting the associated wind.

## MUSEUMS

Athens has no less than 28 museums, displaying everything from ancient treasures to old theatre props. You'll find a complete list at the tourist office. These are the highlights:

### National Archaeological Museum

This is the undoubted star of the show – the most important museum *(28 Oktovriou-Patission 44; admission €6; open 12.30pm-7pm Mon, 8am-7pm Tues-Sun Apr-Oct, 10.30am-5pm Mon, 8.30am-3pm Tues-Sun Nov-Mar)* in Greece, with finds from all the major sites. The crowd-pullers are the magnificent, exquisitely detailed gold artefacts from Mycenae and spectacular Minoan frescoes from Santorini (Thira), which are here until a suitable museum is built on the island.

### Benaki Museum

This museum *(cnr Vasilissis Sofias & Koumbari; admission €5.90; open 9am-5pm Mon, Wed, Fri & Sat, 9am-midnight Thur, 9am-3pm Sun)* houses the collection of Antoine Benaki, the son of an Alexandrian cotton magnate named Emmanual Benaki. The collection includes ancient sculpture, Persian, Byzantine and Coptic objects, Chinese ceramics, icons, two El Greco paintings and a superb collection of traditional costumes.

### Goulandris Museum of Cycladic & Ancient Greek Art

This private museum *(Neofytou Douka 4; admission €2.95; open 10am-4pm Mon &*

*Wed-Fri, 10am-3pm Sat)* was custom-built to display a fabulous collection of Cycladic art, with an emphasis on the early Bronze Age. Particularly impressive are the beautiful marble figurines. These simple, elegant forms, mostly of naked women with arms folded under their breasts, inspired 20th-century artists such as Brancusi, Epstein, Modigliani and Picasso.

## LYKAVITTOS HILL

Pine-covered Lykavittos is the highest of the eight hills dotted around Athens. From the summit there are all-embracing views of the city, the Attic basin and the islands of Salamis and Aegina – pollution permitting of course.

The open-air Lykavittos Theatre, northeast of the summit, is used for concerts in summer.

The southern side of the hill is occupied by the posh residential suburb of Kolonaki. The main path to the summit starts at the top of Loukianou, or you can take the funicular railway from the top of Ploutarhou (€2/4 single/return, 9.15am to 11.45pm daily).

## CHANGING OF THE GUARD

Every Sunday at 11am a platoon of traditionally costumed *evzones* (guards), accompanied by a band, marches down Vasilissis Sofias to the Tomb of the Unknown Soldier located in front of the parliament building on Syntagma.

## LANGUAGE COURSES

Try the **Athens Centre** (☎ 21 0701 2268, fax 21 0701 8603; e athenscr@compulink.gr; w www.athenscentre.gr; Arhimidous 48, Mets), or the **Hellenic American Union** (☎ 21 0362 9886, fax 21 0363 3174; e vioannou@hau.gr; w www.hau.gr; Massalias 22, Kolonaki) for language courses.

## ORGANISED TOURS

**Hop In Sightseeing** (☎ 21 0428 5500; Zanni 29, Piraeus), **Key Tours** (☎ 21 0923 3166; Kallirois 4); **CHAT Tours** (☎ 21 0322 3137; Stadiou 4); and **GO Tours** (☎ 21 0322 5951; Voulis 31-33) are the main organised-tour operators – you'll see their brochures everywhere, offering similar tours and prices. They include a half-day sightseeing tour of Athens (€29.35), which does nothing more than point out all the major sights, and Athens by Night (€40), which takes in a *son et lumière*

(sound-and-light show) before taking in a taverna dinner with folk dancing.

Every hotel mentioned later in the Places to Stay section handles bookings for at least one of the tour companies. Some offer substantial discounts for hotel clients. You will be told of your pick-up point when you book.

## HELLENIC FESTIVAL

The annual Hellenic Festival is the city's most important cultural event, running from mid-June to late September. It features a line-up of international music, dance and theatre at the Theatre of Herodes Atticus. The setting is superb, backed by the floodlit Acropolis. Information and tickets are available from the **Athens Festival Box Office** (Stadiou 4). You'll find details of events on the Internet at w www.greekfestival.gr.

## PLACES TO STAY
## Camping

The closest camping ground is **Athens Camping** (☎ 21 0581 4114, fax 21 0582 0353; Athinon 198), 7km west of the city centre on the road to Corinth. There are several camping grounds southeast of Athens on the coast road to Cape Sounion.

## Hostels

There are a few places around town making a pitch for the hostelling market by tagging 'youth hostel' onto their name. There are some dreadful dumps among them.

There is only one youth hostel worth knowing about, the excellent HI-affiliated **Athens International Youth Hostel** (☎ 523 4170, fax 523 4015; e info2002yh@ yahoo.com; Victor Hugo 16; dorm beds HI members €8.40). Location is the only drawback, otherwise the place is almost too good to be true. The spotless rooms, each with bathroom, sleep two to four people. You need to become a HI member to stay here; if you're not a member the joining fee is €12.35, or it's €2.05 for a daily stamp.

## Hotels

Athens is a noisy city and Athenians keep late hours, so an effort has been made to select hotels in quiet areas. Plaka is the most popular place to stay, and it has a good choice of accommodation right across the price spectrum. Rooms fill up quickly during July and August, so it's wise to make a reservation.

**Plaka** Most backpackers head to the **Student & Travellers' Inn** (☎ 21 0324 4808, fax 21 0321 0065; e students-inn@ath.forth net.gr; Kydathineon 16; dorm beds €18, singles/doubles with shared bathroom €32/42, singles/doubles with private bathroom €36/52). Facilities include a courtyard with big-screen TV, Internet access and a travel service.

**Festos Youth & Student Guest House** (☎ 21 0323 2455, fax 21 0321 0907; e con solas@hol.gr; Filellinon 18) is the main budget alternative.

Plaka also has some good mid-range accommodation.

**Acropolis House Pension** (☎ 21 0322 2344, fax 21 0322 6241; Kodrou 6-8; singles/doubles with bathroom from €49.50/66) occupies a beautifully preserved 19th-century house.

**Hotel Adonis** (☎ 21 0324 9737, fax 21 0323 1602; Kodrou 3; singles/doubles from €39/55.70), opposite the Acropolis House Pension, is a comfortable modern hotel with air-con rooms. It has good views of the Acropolis from the 4th-floor rooms and from the rooftop bar.

**Monastiraki** The friendly and family-run **Hotel Tempi** (☎ 21 0321 3175, fax 21 0325 4179; e tempihotel@travelling.gr; Eolou 29; singles with shared bathroom €28, doubles/triples with private bathroom €42/50) is a quiet place on the pedestrian precinct part of Eolou. Rooms at the front overlook a small square with a church and a flower market. It has a small communal kitchen where guests can prepare breakfast.

**Hotel Cecil** (☎ 21 0321 7909, fax 21 0321 8005; e cecil@netsmart.gr; Athinas 39; singles/doubles with bathroom €50/70.50) occupies a fine old classical building with beautiful high, moulded ceilings. It looks immaculate after a complete refit, and rates include breakfast.

**Koukaki** It isn't exactly backpacker territory, but **Marble House Pension** (☎ 21 0923 4058, fax 21 0922 6461; Zini 35A; singles/doubles without bathroom €27/35; singles/doubles with bathroom €32/41), on a quiet cul-de-sac off Zini, is one of Athens' better budget hotels. All rooms have a bar fridge, ceiling fans and safety boxes for valuables, and air-con is available.

**Art Gallery Hotel** (☎ 21 0923 8376, fax 21 0923 3025; e ecotec@otenet.gr; Erehthiou 5; singles/doubles/triples with bathroom €58.60/70.40/84.50) is a friendly place that's always brimming with fresh flowers.

**Omonia Area** There are dozens of hotels around Omonia, but most of them are either bordellos masquerading as cheap hotels or are uninspiring, overpriced C-class places.

**Hostel Aphrodite** (☎ 21 0881 0589, fax 21 0881 6574; e hostel-aphrodite@ath .forthnet.gr; Einardou 12; dorm beds €17, singles/doubles/triples with shared bathroom €30/40/54; singles/doubles with private bathroom €32/42) is a fair way north of Omonia, but it's only 10 minutes from the train stations. It offers Internet access and there's a bar.

## PLACES TO EAT
### Plaka
For most people, Plaka is the place to be. It's hard to beat the atmosphere of dining out beneath the floodlit Acropolis. You do, however, pay for the privilege – particularly at the many outdoor restaurants around the square on Kydathineon. The best of this bunch is **Byzantino** (☎ 21 0322 7368; Kydathineon 20; mains €3.50-12), which prices its menu more reasonably and is popular with Greek family groups.

**Eden Vegetarian Restaurant** (☎ 21 0324 8858; Lyssiou 12; mains €8-12; open Wed-Mon) is one of only two vegie restaurants, which are thin on the ground in Athens. The Eden has been around for years, substituting soya products for meat in tasty vegetarian versions of mousakas and some other Greek favourites.

**Daphne Restaurant** (☎ 21 0322 7971; Lysikratous 4; meals around €30; open from 7pm nightly) is the place to head for a real treat. It's an exquisitely restored 1830s neoclassical mansion decorated with frescoes from Greek mythology. The menu includes regional specialties, such as rabbit cooked in mavrodaphne wine.

### South of the Acropolis
**Oinomageireion ton Theon** (☎ 21 0924 3721; Makrigianni 23-27; mains €4-9) is a new place just five minutes' walk from Plaka. It's got a great selection of meze, priced from €2, as well as tasty versions of favourites such

## PLAKA

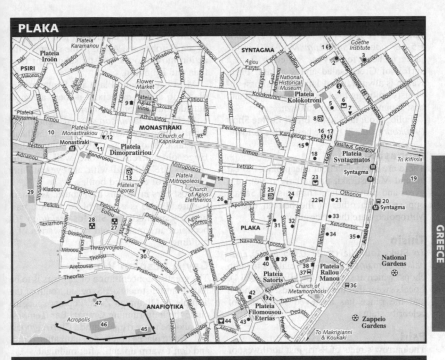

## PLAKA

### PLACES TO STAY
9 Hotel Tempi
38 Festos Youth & Student Guest House
39 Hotel Adonis
40 Acropolis House Pension
42 Student & Travellers' Inn

### PLACES TO EAT
7 Brazil Coffee Shop
11 Thanasis
12 Savas
24 Furin Kazan Japanese Fast-Food Restaurant
30 Eden Vegetarian Restaurant

### OTHER
1 Bank of Greece
2 Eleftheroudakis Books
3 Pantelides Books
4 EOT Main Tourist Office
5 Athens Festival Box Office
6 Parcels Office
8 Sofokleous.com Internet Café
10 Athens Flea Market
13 Plaka Internet World
14 Athens Cathedral
15 Eleftheroudakis Books
16 Eurochange
17 National Bank of Greece
18 American Express
19 Parliament Building
20 Bus E95 to Airport
21 USIT-Etos Travel
22 Bus No 040 to Piraeus
23 Syntagma Post Office
25 Skynet Internet Centre
26 National Welfare Organisation Shop
27 Tower of the Winds
28 Roman Agora
29 Stoa of Attalos
31 STA Travel
32 Compendium Books
33 Trekking Hellas
34 Olympic Airways Branch Office
35 CHAT Tours Terminal
36 Bus No 024 to Bus Terminal B
37 Trolley-bus Stop for Plaka
41 Acropole Foreign Exchange
43 Laundrette
44 Brettos
45 Acropolis Museum
46 Parthenon
47 Erechtheion

as beef *stifado* and *mousakas*. There are good views of the Acropolis from the window seats.

**To 24 Hours** *(☎ 21 0922 2749; Syngrou 44; mains €4-6.50)* is a great favourite with Athenian night owls. As the name suggests, it's open 24 hours. It calls itself a *patsadiko*, which means that it specialises in *patsas* (tripe

soup), but it always has a wide selection of taverna dishes.

### Syntagma
Fast food is the order of the day around busy Syntagma with an assortment of Greek and international offerings.

**Furin Kazan Japanese Fast-Food Restaurant** *(☎ 21 0322 9170; Apollonos 2; mains €5-16; open 11am-11pm Mon-Sat)* is the place to head for anyone suffering from a surfeit of Greek salad and souvlaki. Furin Kazan is always full of Japanese visitors, obviously enjoying the food at the cheapest and best Japanese restaurant in town.

Follow your nose to the **Brazil Coffee Shop** *(Voukourestiou 2)* for the best coffee in town.

## Monastiraki

There are some excellent cheap places to eat around Monastiraki, particularly if you're a gyros and souvlaki fan. **Thanasis** and **Savas**, opposite each other at the bottom end of Mitropoleos, are the places to go.

## Thisio

**To Steki tou Elia** *(☎ 21 0345 8052; Epahalkou 5; mains €4.50-6)* specialises in lamb chops, which are sold by the kilogram (€14). Locals swear that they are the best in Athens, and the place has achieved some sort of celebrity status.

## Psiri

The narrow streets of Psiri, just northwest of Monastiraki, are now dotted with numerous trendy ouzeris, tavernas and music bars, particularly the central area between Plateia Agion Anargyron and Plateia Iroön.

**Embros** *(☎ 21 0321 3285; Plateia Agion Anargyron 4; meze €3.50-12)* is a popular spot to try with seating in the square and a choice of about 20 *mezedes*.

## Self-Catering

The following are among the main **supermarkets** in central Athens:

**Marinopoulos** Athinas 60, Omonia • Kanari 9, Kolonaki
**Vasilopoulou** Stadiou 19, Syntagma
**Veropoulos** Parthenos 6, Koukaki

You'll find the best selection of fresh produce at the **fruit and vegetable market** on Athinas.

## ENTERTAINMENT

The weekly *Athens News* carries a 16-page entertainment guide listing weekly events, while the *Kathimerini* supplement that accompanies the *International Herald Tribune* has daily listings.

## Discos & Bars

Discos operate in central Athens only between October and April. In the summer, the action moves to the coastal suburbs of Glyfada and Ellinikon.

Most bars around Plaka and Syntagma are places to avoid, especially if there are guys outside touting for customers.

**Brettos** *(Kydathineon 41)*, a delightful, old family-run place, which is right in the heart of Plaka, is one bar that's recommended. Huge old barrels line one wall, and the shelves are stocked with an eye-catching collection of coloured bottles.

Most bars in Athens have music as a main feature. Thisio is a good place to look, particularly on Iraklidon. **Stavlos** *(Iraklidon 10)* occupies an amazing old rabbit warren of a building.

## Gay & Lesbian Venues

The greatest concentration of gay bars is to be found on the streets off Syngrou, south of the Temple of Olympian Zeus. Popular spots include the long-running **Granazi Bar** *(Lembesi 20)* and the more risque **Lamda Club** *(Lembesi 15)*. These places don't open until after 10pm, and don't warm up until after midnight.

**To Lizard** *(Apostolou Pavlou 31)*, in Thisio, is a party bar which operates Friday to Sunday nights from 11pm. The crowd is mostly lesbian, with a few gays and the occasional straight.

## Rock & Jazz

**Rodon Club** *(Marni 24)*, north of Omonia, hosts touring international rock bands, while local bands play at the **AN Club** *(Solomou 20, Exarhia)*.

## Folk Dancing

**Dora Stratou Dance Company** *(☎ 21 0921 6650; tickets €11.75)* performs at its theatre on Filopappos Hill at 10.15pm every night from mid-May to October, with additional performances at 8.15pm on Wednesday. Filopappos Hill is west of the Acropolis, off Dionysiou Areopagitou. Bus No 230 from Syntagma will get you there.

## Sound-&-Light Show

Athens' endeavour at this spectacle is not one of the world's best. There are shows in English every night at 9pm from April to October at the theatre on the **Hill of the Pnyx**

*(☎ 21 0322 1459; tickets €8.80)*. The Hill of the Pnyx is opposite Filopappos Hill, and the show is timed so that you can cross straight to the folk dancing.

## SPECTATOR SPORTS

Almost half of the 18 soccer teams in the Greek first division are based in Athens or Piraeus. The most popular are Panathinaikos (Athens) and Olympiakos (Piraeus).

## SHOPPING

The **National Welfare Organisation shop** *(cnr Apollonos & Ipatias, Plaka)* is a good place to go shopping for handicrafts. It has top-quality goods and the money goes to a good cause – the organisation was formed to preserve and promote traditional Greek crafts.

For some serious bargaining, check out the famous **Flea Market**, west of Monastiraki metro station.

## GETTING THERE & AWAY
### Air

Athens is served by Eleftherios Venizelos International Airport at Spata, 27km east of Athens.

Facilities at the new airport, named in honour of the country's leading 20th-century politician, are immeasurably better than at the city's former airport at Ellinikon. Where Ellinikon was shabby and outdated, the new airport gleams. Built by a German consortium, everything is absolutely state of the art. It also has good selection of cafés, and some very reasonably priced eating places.

For Olympic Airways flight information ring ☎ 21 0936 3363; for all other airlines ring ☎ 21 0969 4466/4467. The head office of **Olympic Airways** *(☎ 21 0926 7251/4)* is at Leoforos Syngrou Andrea 96. The most central **Olympic Airways branch office** *(☎ 21 0926 7444, international ☎ 21 0926 7489)* is at Filellinon 13, just off Plateia Syntagmatos.

### Bus

Athens has two main intercity bus stations. EOT gives out schedules for both stations detailing departure times, journey times and fares.

**Terminal A** *(Kifissou 100)*, northwest of Omonia, has departures to the Peloponnese, the Ionian Islands and western Greece. To get to Terminal A, take bus No 051 from the junction of Zinonos and Menandrou, near Plateia Omonia. Buses run every 15 minutes from 5am to midnight.

**Terminal B** *(off Liossion)* is north of Omonia and has departures to central and northern Greece, as well as to Evia. To get to Terminal B, take bus No 024 from outside the main gate of the National Gardens on Amalias. EOT misleadingly gives the terminal's address as Liossion 260, which turns out to be a small workshop. Liossion 260 is where you should get off the bus. Turn right onto Gousiou and you'll see the terminal at the end of the road.

Buses for Attica leave from the Mavromateon bus terminal at the junction of Alexandras and 28 Oktovriou-Patission.

### Train

Athens has two train stations, about 200m apart on Deligianni, approximately 1km northwest of Omonia. Trains to the Peloponnese leave from the Peloponnese station, while trains to the north leave from Larisis station – as do all international services.

Services to the Peloponnese include eight trains to Patras, four of which are intercity express (€10, 3½ hours), while services north include 10 trains a day to Thessaloniki, five of which are intercity express (€27.60, six hours). The 7am service from Athens is express right through to Alexandroupolis, arriving at 7pm. There are also trains to Volos and Halkida in Evia. The easiest way to get to the stations is on metro Line 2 to Larisa, outside Larisis station. The Peloponnese station is across the footbridge at the southern end of Larisis station. Tickets can be bought at the stations, or at **OSE offices** *(Sina 6 • Karolou 1)*.

### Car & Motorcycle

National Rd 1 is the main route north from Athens. It starts at Nea Kifissia. To get there from central Athens, take Vasilissis Sofias from Syntagma and follow the signs. National Rd 8, which begins beyond Dafni, is the road to the Peloponnese; take Agiou Konstantinou from Omonia.

The northern reaches of Syngrou, just south of the Temple of Olympian Zeus, are packed solid with car-rental firms.

### Hitching

Athens is the most difficult place in Greece to hitchhike from. Your best bet is to ask the truck drivers at the Piraeus cargo wharves. Otherwise, for the Peloponnese, take a bus from Panepistimiou to Dafni, where National Rd 8 begins. For northern Greece, take the metro to Kifissia, then a bus to Nea Kifissia and walk to National Rd 1.

### Ferry
See Piraeus, later in this chapter, for information on ferries travelling to and from the islands.

### GETTING AROUND
### To/From the Airport
There are two special express-bus services operating between the airport and the city, as well as a service between the airport and Piraeus.

Bus service E94 operates between the airport and the eastern terminus of Metro Line 3 at Ethniki Amyna. According to the official timetable there are departures every 16 minutes between 6am and midnight. The journey takes about 25 minutes.

Service E95 operates between the airport and Plateia Syntagmatos. This line operates 24 hours a day with services approximately every 30 minutes. The bus stop is outside the National Gardens on Amalias on the eastern side of Plateia Syntagmatos. The journey takes between an hour and 90 minutes, depending on traffic conditions.

Service E96 operates between the airport and Plateia Karaïskaki in Piraeus. This line also operates 24 hours, with services approximately every 40 minutes.

Tickets for all these services cost €2.95. The tickets are valid for 24 hours, and can be used on all forms of public transport in Athens – buses, trolleybuses and the metro.

Taxi fares vary according to the time of day and level of traffic, but you should expect to pay €15 to €20 from the airport to the city centre, and €20 to €25 from the airport to Piraeus, depending on traffic conditions. Neither trip should take longer than an hour.

### Bus & Trolleybus
Blue-and-white suburban buses operate from 5am to midnight. Route numbers and destinations, but not the actual routes, are listed on the free EOT map. The map does, however, mark the routes of the yellow trolleybuses, making them easy to use. They also run from 5am to midnight.

There are special buses that operate 24 hours a day to Piraeus. Bus No 040 leaves from the corner of Syntagma and Filellinon, and No 049 leaves from the Omonia end of Athinas. The buses run every 20 minutes from 6am to midnight, and then hourly until 6am.

Tickets for all these services cost €0.45, and must be purchased before you board – either from a ticket booth or from a *periptero*. The same tickets can be used on either buses or trolleybuses and must be validated as soon as you board. The penalty for travelling without a validated ticket is €17.60.

### Metro
The opening of the first phase of the long-awaited new metro system has transformed travel around central Athens. Coverage is still largely confined to the city centre, but that's good enough for most visitors. The following is a brief outline of the three lines that make up the network:

**Line 1** This line is the old Kifissia–Piraeus line. Until the opening of lines 2 and 3, this was the metro system. It is indicated in green on maps and signs. Useful stops include Piraeus (for the port), Monastiraki and Omonia (city centre), Plateia Viktorias (National Archaeological Museum) and Irini (Olympic Stadium). Omonia and Attiki are transfer stations with connections to Line 2; Monastiraki will eventually become a transfer station with connections to Line 3.

**Line 2** This line runs from Sepolia in the northwest to Dafni in the southeast. It is indicated in red on maps and signs. Useful stops include Larisa (for the train stations), Omonia, Panepistimiou and Syntagma (city centre) and Akropoli (Makrigianni). Attiki and Omonia are transfer stations for Line 1, while Syntagma is the transfer station for Line 3.

**Line 3** This line runs northeast from Syntagma to Ethniki Amyna. It is indicated in blue on maps and signs. Useful stops are Evangelismos (for the museums on Vasilissis Sofias) and Ethniki Amyna (buses to the airport). Syntagma is the transfer station for Line 2.

Travel on lines 2 and 3 costs €0.75, while Line 1 is split into three sections: Piraeus–Monastiraki, Monastiraki–Attiki and Attiki–Kifissia. Travel within one section costs €0.60, and a journey covering two or more sections costs €0.75. The same conditions apply everywhere though: tickets must be validated at the machines at platform entrances before travelling. The penalty for travelling without a validated ticket is €23.50.

The metro operates from 5am to midnight. Trains run every three minutes during peak periods, and every 10 minutes at other times.

## Taxi

Athenian taxis are yellow. The flag fall is €0.75, and there's an additional surcharge of €0.60 from ports and train and bus stations, as well as a €0.90 surcharge from the airport. After that, the day rate (tariff 1 on the meter) is €0.23/km. The rate doubles between midnight and 5am (tariff 2 on the meter). Baggage is charged at the rate of €0.30 per item over 10kg. The minimum fare is €1.50, which covers most journeys in central Athens.

# Around Athens

## PIRAEUS Πειραιάς
**☎ 21 • pop 171,000**

Piraeus has been the port of Athens since classical times. These days it's little more than an outer suburb of the space-hungry capital, linked by a mish-mash of factories, warehouses and apartment blocks. The streets are every bit as traffic-clogged as in Athens, and behind the veneer of banks and shipping offices most of Piraeus is pretty seedy. The only reason to come here is to catch a ferry or hydrofoil.

## Orientation & Information

Piraeus consists of a peninsula surrounded by harbours. The most important of them is the

**GREECE**

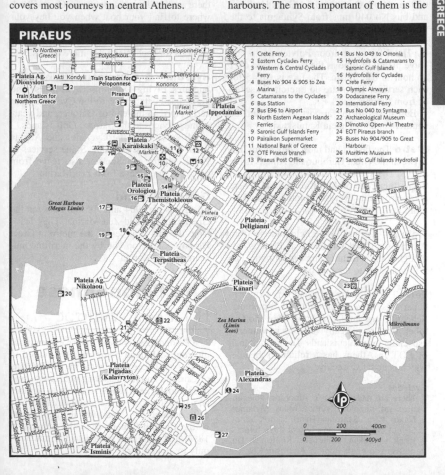

**PIRAEUS**

| | | |
|---|---|---|
| 1 | Crete Ferry | 14 Bus No 049 to Omonia |
| 2 | Eastern Cyclades Ferry | 15 Hydrofoils & Catamarans to |
| 3 | Western & Central Cyclades | Saronic Gulf Islands |
| | Ferry | 16 Hydrofoils for Cyclades |
| 4 | Buses No 904 & 905 to Zea | 17 Crete Ferry |
| | Marina | 18 Olympic Airways |
| 5 | Catamarans to the Cyclades | 19 Dodacanese Ferry |
| 6 | Bus Station | 20 International Ferry |
| 7 | Bus E96 to Airport | 21 Bus No 040 to Syntagma |
| 8 | North Eastern Aegean Islands | 22 Archaeological Museum |
| | Ferries | 23 Dimotiko Open-Air Theatre |
| 9 | Saronic Gulf Islands Ferry | 24 EOT Piraeus branch |
| 10 | Pairaikon Supermarket | 25 Buses No 904/905 to Great |
| 11 | National Bank of Greece | Harbour |
| 12 | OTE Piraeus branch | 26 Maritime Museum |
| 13 | Piraeus Post Office | 27 Saronic Gulf Islands Hydrofoil |

Great Harbour (Megas Limin). All ferries leave from here, as do hydrofoil and catamaran services to Aegina and the Cyclades. There are dozens of shipping agencies around the harbour, as well as banks and a post office.

Zea Marina (Limin Zeas), on the other side of the peninsula, is the main port for hydrofoils to all the Saronic Gulf Islands, except for Aegina. Northeast of here is the picturesque Mikrolimano (Small Harbour), which is lined with countless fish restaurants. There's an **EOT office** *(☎ 21 0452 2586)* at Zea Marina.

### Getting There & Away

**Bus** There are two 24-hour bus services between central Athens and Piraeus. Bus No 049 runs from Omonia to the Great Harbour, and bus No 040 runs from Syntagma to the tip of the Piraeus peninsula. No 040 is the service to catch for Zea Marina – get off at the Hotel Savoy on Iroön Polytehniou – and leave plenty of time as the trip can take over an hour in bad traffic. The fare is €0.45 for each service. There are no intercity buses to or from Piraeus.

E96 buses to the airport leave from the southern side of Plateia Karaïskaki.

**Metro** The fastest and most convenient link between the Great Harbour and Athens is the metro. The station is close to the ferries, at the northern end of Akti Kalimassioti. There are metro trains every 10 minutes from 5am to midnight.

**Train** All services to the Peloponnese from Athens start and terminate at Piraeus, although some schedules don't mention it. The station is next to the metro.

**Ferry** The following information is a guide to departures between June and mid-September. Schedules are similar in April, May and October, but are radically reduced in winter – especially to smaller islands. The main branch of EOT in Athens has a reliable schedule, which is updated weekly.

#### Cyclades
There are daily ferries to Amorgos, Folegandros, Ios, Kimolos, Kythnos, Milos, Mykonos, Naxos, Paros, Santorini (Thira), Serifos, Sifnos, Sikinos, Syros and Tinos; two or three ferries a week to Iraklia, Shinoussa, Koufonisi, Donoussa and Anafi; none to Andros or Kea.

#### Crete
There are two boats a day to Iraklio; daily services to Hania and Rethymno; and three a week to Agios Nikolaos and Sitia.

#### Dodecanese
There are daily ferries to Kalymnos, Kos, Leros, Patmos and Rhodes; three a week to Karpathos and Kassos; and weekly services to the other islands.

#### Northeastern Aegean Islands
There are daily ferries to Chios, Lesvos (Mytilini), Ikaria and Samos; and two a week to Limnos.

#### Saronic Gulf Islands
There are daily ferries to Aegina, Poros, Hydra and Spetses year-round.

The departure points for the ferry destinations are shown on the map of Piraeus. Note that there are two departure points for Crete. Check where to find your boat when you buy your ticket. See Boat under Getting Around, earlier in this chapter, and the Getting There & Away sections for each island, for more details.

**Hydrofoil & Catamaran** Minoan Lines operates Flying Dolphins (hydrofoils) and high-speed catamarans to the Cyclades from early April to the end of October, and year-round services to the Saronic Gulf Islands.

All services to the Cyclades and Aegina leave from Great Harbour. Some services to Poros, Hydra and Spetses also leave from here, but most leave from Zea Marina.

### Getting Around
Local bus Nos 904 and 905 run between the Great Harbour and Zea Marina. They leave from the bus stop beside the metro at Great Harbour, and drop you by the maritime museum at Zea Marina.

# The Peloponnese
## Η Πελοπόννησος

The Peloponnese is the southern extremity of the rugged Balkan peninsula. It's linked to the rest of Greece only by the narrow Isthmus of Corinth, and this has long prompted some people to declare the Peloponnese to be more an island than part of the mainland. It technically became an island after the completion of the Corinth Canal across the isthmus in 1893, and it is now linked to the mainland only by road and rail bridges.

The Peloponnese is an area rich in history. The principal site is Olympia, which is the birthplace of the Olympic Games, but there are many other sites which are worth seeking out. Epidavros, Corinth and Mycenae in the northeast are all within easy striking distance of the pretty Venetian town of Nafplio.

In the south are the magical old Byzantine towns of Monemvasia and Mystras. The rugged Mani Peninsula is famous for its spectacular wild flowers in spring, as well as for the bizarre tower settlements sprinkled across its landscape.

## PATRAS Πάτρα
☎ 261 • pop 153,300

Patras is Greece's third-largest city and the principal port for ferries to Italy and the Ionian Islands. It's not particularly exciting and most travellers hang around only long enough for transport connections.

## Orientation & Information

The city is easy to negotiate and is laid out on a grid stretching uphill from the port to the old *kastro* (castle). Most services of importance to travellers are to be found along the waterfront, which is known as Othonos Amalias, in the middle of town, and Iroön Politehniou to the north. The train station is right in the middle of town on Othonos Amalias, and the main bus station is close by.

The **EOT office** (☎ 261 062 0353) is inside the port fence, off Iroön Politehniou, and the **tourist police** (☎ 261 045 1833) are upstairs in the embarkation hall.

GREECE

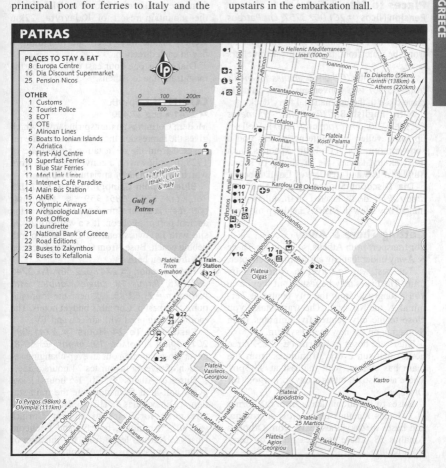

**PATRAS**

**PLACES TO STAY & EAT**
8 Europa Centre
16 Dia Discount Supermarket
25 Pension Nicos

**OTHER**
1 Customs
2 Tourist Police
3 EOT
4 OTE
5 Minoan Lines
6 Boats to Ionian Islands
7 Adriatica
9 First-Aid Centre
10 Superfast Ferries
11 Blue Star Ferries
12 Med Link Lines
13 Internet Café Paradise
14 Main Bus Station
15 ANEK
17 Olympic Airways
18 Archaeological Museum
19 Post Office
20 Laundrette
21 National Bank of Greece
22 Road Editions
23 Buses to Zakynthos
24 Buses to Kefallonia

The **National Bank of Greece** *(Plateia Trion Symahon)* has a 24-hour ATM.

You can send mail at the **post office** *(cnr Zaïmi & Mezonos)*. There's an **OTE telephone office** opposite the tourist office at the port. For Internet access, try **Internet Café Paradise** *(Zaïmi 7; open 5am-1am daily)*.

**Road Editions** *(Agiou Andreou 50)* stocks a large range of Lonely Planet guides as well as maps and travel literature.

### Things to See & Do

There are great views of Zakynthos and Kefallonia from the Byzantine **kastro**, which is reached by the steps at the top of Agiou Nikolaou.

### Places to Stay & Eat

**Pension Nicos** *(☎ 261 062 3757; cnr Patreos & Agiou Andreou 121; singles/doubles/ triples with bathroom €18/30/40)*, just up from the waterfront, is where most travellers head.

**Europa Centre** *(Othonos Amalias 10; meals from €3.50)* is a convenient cafeteria-style place close to the international ferry dock.

**Nitro English Bar** *(Pantanasis 9; mains €7.50-10.50; open 1pm until late)* is well set up for travellers with Internet access and a shower room. You'll find daily specials, such as steak-and-kidney pie or shepherd's pie, Sunday roasts and a choice of English beers.

**Dia Discount Supermarket** *(Agiou Andreou 29)* is ideally located for travellers planning to buy a few provisions and keep moving.

### Getting There & Away

For transport from Athens, see Getting There & Away under that city earlier in this chapter.

The best way to travel to Athens is by train. The buses may be faster, but they drop you a long way from the city centre at Terminal A on Kifissou. The trains take you close to the city centre, five minutes from Syntagma on the new metro system.

There are buses to Athens (€12.25, three hours) that run every 30 minutes from the main bus station, with the last at 9.45pm. There are also 10 buses a day to Pyrgos (for Olympia).

Buses to Kefallonia leave from the corner of Othonos Amalias and Gerokostopoulou, and buses to Zakynthos leave from Othonos Amalias 58. These services travel by ferry from Kyllini.

There are nine trains a day to Athens. Four are slow trains (€5.30, five hours) and five are intercity express trains (€10, 3½ hours). The last intercity train leaves at 6.30pm. Trains also run south to Pyrgos and to Kalamata.

There are daily ferries to Kefallonia (€10, 2½ hours), Ithaki (€10.90, 3¾ hours) and Corfu (€17.90, seven hours). Services to Italy are covered under Getting There & Away at the start of this chapter. Ticket agencies line the waterfront.

## DIAKOFTO–KALAVRYTA RAILWAY

This spectacular rack-and-pinion line climbs up the deep gorge of the Vouraikos River from the small coastal town of **Diakofto** to the mountain resort of **Kalavryta**, 22km away. It is a thrilling journey, with dramatic scenery all the way. There are four trains a day in each direction.

Diakofto is one hour east of Patras on the main train line to Athens.

## CORINTH Κόρινθος

☎ 2741 • pop 27,400

Modern Corinth is an uninspiring town which gives the impression that it has never quite recovered from the devastating earthquake of 1928. It is, however, a convenient base from which to visit nearby ancient Corinth.

**Blue Dolphin Campground** *(☎ 2741 025 766, fax 2741 085 959; ℮ skoupos@ otenet.gr)* is about 4km west of town near the ancient port of Lecheon. It's a well-organised site with its own stretch of Gulf of Corinth pebble beach. Buses from Corinth to Lecheon can drop you here.

**Hotel Apollon** *(☎ 2741 022 587, fax 2741 083 875; Pirinis 18; singles/doubles with bathroom €23.50/35.20)*, near the train station, is the best of Corinth's budget hotels. The rooms are equipped with air-con and TV.

**Restaurant To 24 Hours** *(☎ 2741 083 201; Agiou Nikolaou 19; mains €3.50-8)* never closes, turning out an ever-changing selection of taverna favourites 24 hours a day.

Buses to Athens (€5.70, 1½ hours) leave every half-hour from opposite the train station at Dimocratias 4. This is also the departure point for buses to ancient Corinth (€0.80, 20 minutes, hourly) and Lecheon. Buses to Nafplio leave from the junction of Ethnikis Antistaseos and Aratou.

There are 14 trains a day to Athens, five of which are intercity services. There are also trains to Kalamata, Nafplio and Patras.

## ANCIENT CORINTH & ACROCORINTH

The ruins of ancient Corinth (admission €4; open 8am-7pm May-Oct, 8am-5pm Nov-Mar) lie 7km southwest of the modern city. Corinth (Κόρινθος) was one of ancient Greece's wealthiest and most wanton cities. When Corinthians weren't clinching business deals, they were paying homage to Aphrodite in a temple dedicated to her, which meant they were frolicking with the temple's sacred prostitutes. The only ancient Greek monument remaining here is the imposing **Temple of Apollo**; the others are Roman. Towering over the site is Acrocorinth (admission free; open 8am-6pm daily), the ruins of an ancient citadel built on a massive outcrop of limestone.

## NAFPLIO Ναύπλιο
☎ 2752 • pop 11,900

Nafplio ranks as one of Greece's prettiest towns. The narrow streets of the old quarter are filled with elegant Venetian houses and neoclassical mansions.

The **municipal tourist office** (☎ 2752 024 444; 25 Martiou; open 9am-1.30pm & 4.30pm-9pm daily) is about as unhelpful as tourist offices get.

The bus station is on Syngrou, the street which separates the old town from the new. There are hourly buses to Athens (€8.50, 2½ hours) via Corinth, as well as services to Argos (for Peloponnese connections), Mycenae and Epidavros.

### Palamidi Fortress

There are terrific views of the old town and the surrounding coast from this magnificent hill-top fortress (admission €4; open 8am-6.45pm Apr-Oct, 8am-5pm Nov-Mar), built by the Venetians at the beginning of the 18th century. The climb is strenuous – there are almost 1000 steps – so start early and take water with you.

### Places to Stay

The cheapest rooms are in the new part of town along Argous, the road to Argos.

**Hotel Argolis** (☎/fax 2752 027 721; Argous 32; singles/doubles with bathroom

€18/25) is a good place to start. It normally discounts rooms to a bargain €8/16 for singles/doubles. If you're arriving by bus, ask to be let off at the Thanasenas stop, which is right opposite the hotel.

Most people prefer to stay in the old town, which is the most interesting place to be. Unfortunately, there is very little budget accommodation here.

**Dimitris Bekas** (☎ 2752 024 594; Efthimiopoulou 26; singles/doubles/triples with shared bathroom €15/21/24) offers top value for a great location above the church on the slopes of the Akronafplia. The rooftop terrace has great views over the old town.

**Pension Marianna** (☎ 2752 024 256, fax 2752 021 783; e petros4@otenet.gr; Potamianou 9; singles/doubles/triples with bathroom €40/50/60), nearby, also has great views. The rooms have air-con and TV, and prices include breakfast.

**Hotel Epidauros** (☎/fax 2752 027 541; Kokinou 2; doubles with bathroom €35.20) is a good fallback if the above are full. There is a selection of rooms here and at the co-owned **Hotel Tiryns** (☎ 2752 021 020) nearby.

### Places to Eat

**Mezedopoleio O Noulis** (☎ 2752 025 541; Moutzouridou 21; meze €1.50-7.35) serves a fabulous range of meze which can easily be combined into a meal. Check the saganaki flambé, ignited with Metaxa (brandy) as it reaches your table.

**Taverna O Vassilis** (☎ 2752 025 334; Staikopoulou 20-24; mains €4-8.50) is a popular family-run place at the heart of the restaurant strip on Staikopoulou. It has a large choice of starters, and a good selection of mains – including a very tasty rabbit stifado for €4.85.

## EPIDAVROS Επίδαυρος

The crowd-puller at this site is the huge and well-preserved **Theatre of Epidavros** (admission €6; open 8am-7pm daily Apr-Oct, 8am-5pm daily Nov-Mar), but don't miss the more peaceful **Sanctuary of Asclepius** nearby. Epidavros was regarded as the birthplace of Asclepius, the god of healing, and the sanctuary was once a flourishing spa and healing centre.

You can enjoy the theatre's astounding acoustics first-hand during the Epidavros Festival from mid-June to mid-August.

GREECE

There are two buses a day from Athens (€8.40, 2½ hours,), as well as four a day from Nafplio (€2, 40 minutes).

## MYCENAE Μυκήνες

Mycenae *(admission €6; open 8am-7pm daily Apr-Oct, 8am-5pm daily Nov-Mar)* was the most powerful influence in Greece for three centuries until about 1200 BC. The rise and fall of Mycenae is shrouded in myth, but the site was settled as early as the sixth millennium BC. Historians are divided as to whether the city's eventual destruction was wrought by invaders or internal conflict between the Mycenaean kingdoms. Described by Homer as 'rich in gold', Mycenae's entrance, the **Lion Gate**, is Europe's oldest monumental sculpture.

Excavations have uncovered the palace complex and a number of tombs. The so-called **Mask of Agamemnon**, discovered by Heinrich Schliemann in 1873, now holds pride of place at the National Archaeological Museum in Athens along with other finds from the site.

Most people visit on day trips from Nafplio, but there are several hotels in the modern village below the site. The **Belle Helene Hotel** *(☎ 2751 076 225, fax 2751 076 179; Christou Tsounta; singles/doubles €26.40/38.15)*, on the main street, is where Schliemann stayed during the excavations.

There are buses to Mycenae from Argos and Nafplio.

## SPARTA Σπάρτη
☎ 2731 • pop 14,100

The bellicose Spartans sacrificed all the finer things in life to military expertise and left no monuments of any consequence. Ancient Sparta's forlorn ruins lie amid olive groves at the northern end of town. Modern Sparta is a neat, unspectacular town, but it's a convenient base from which to visit Mystras.

Sparta is laid out on a grid system. The main streets are Palaeologou, which runs north-south through the town, and Lykourgou, which runs east-west. The **tourist office** *(☎ 2731 024 852; open 8am-2.30pm Mon-Fri)* is in the town hall on Plateia Kentriki.

**Camping Paleologou Mystras** *(☎ 2731 022 724; open year-round)*, 2km west of Sparta on the road to Mystras, is a well-organised site with good facilities, including a swimming pool. Buses to Mystras can drop you there.

**Hotel Cecil** *(☎ 2731 024 980, fax 2731 081 318; Palaeologou 125; singles/doubles with bathroom €30/40)* is a family-run place and one of the many good hotels back in town. Rooms here have TV.

**Restaurant Elysse** *(☎ 2731 029 896; Palaeologou 113; mains €4.50-8.80)* offers Lakonian specialties such as chicken *bardouniotiko*, which is chicken cooked with onions and feta cheese.

The bus station is at the eastern end of Lykourgou. There are 10 buses a day that go to Athens (€12.65, four hours), three that go to Monemvasia and two to Kalamata. There are also frequent buses to Mystras (€0.80, 30 minutes).

## MYSTRAS Μυστράς

Mystras *(admission €5; open 8am-6pm Apr-Oct, 8am-3.30pm Nov-Mar)*, 7km from Sparta, was once the shining light of the Byzantine world. Its ruins spill from a spur of Mt Taygetos, and are crowned by a mighty fortress built by the Franks in 1249. The streets of Mystras are lined with palaces, monasteries and churches, most of them dating from the period between 1271 and 1460, when the town was the effective capital of the Byzantine Empire.

## MONEMVASIA Μονεμβασία
☎ 2732

Monemvasia is no longer an undiscovered paradise, but mass tourism hasn't lessened the impact of one's first encounter with this extraordinary old town – nor the thrill of exploring it.

Monemvasia occupies a great outcrop of rock that rises dramatically from the sea opposite the village of Gefyra. It was separated from the mainland by an earthquake in AD 375 and access is by a causeway from Gefyra. From the causeway, a road curves around the base of the rock for about 1km until it comes to a narrow L-shaped tunnel in the massive fortifying wall. You emerge, blinking, into the **Byzantine town**, hitherto hidden from view.

The cobbled main street is flanked by stairways leading to a complex network of stone houses with tiny walled gardens and courtyards. Signposted steps lead to the ruins of the **fortress** built by the Venetians in the 16th century. The views are great, and there is the added bonus of being able to explore the

Byzantine **Church of Agia Sophia**, perched precariously on the edge of the cliff.

There is no budget accommodation in Monemvasia, but there are *domatia* in Gefyra, as well as cheap hotels.

**Hotel Monemvasia** (☎ *2732 061 381, fax 2732 061 707; singles/doubles with bathroom €25/38)* is a small modern hotel 500m north of Gefyra on the road to Molai. It has large balconies looking out to Monemvasia, and prices include breakfast.

If your budget permits, treat yourself to a night in one of the beautifully restored traditional settlements in Monemvasia. **Malvasia Guest Houses** (☎ *2732 061 113, fax 2732 061 722; singles/doubles from €35/40)* has a wide choice of rooms, and prices include breakfast.

**Taverna O Botsalo** is the place to go for a hearty meal in Gefyra, while **To Kanoni**, on the right of the main street in Monemvasia, has an imaginative menu.

There are four buses a day to Athens (€18.65, six hours), travelling via Sparta, Tripolis and Corinth.

In July and August, there are at least two hydrofoils a day to Piraeus via the Saronic Gulf Islands.

## GYTHIO Γύθειο
☎ 2733 • pop 4900

Gythio, once the port of ancient Sparta, is an attractive fishing town at the head of the Lakonian Gulf. It is the gateway to the rugged Mani Peninsula to the south.

The main attraction is the picturesque islet of **Marathonisi**, linked to the mainland by a causeway. According to mythology this islet is ancient Cranae, where Paris (a prince of Troy) and Helen (the wife of Menelaus of Sparta) consummated the love affair that sparked the Trojan War. An 18th-century tower on the islet has been turned into a **museum** of Mani history.

**Meltemi Camping** (☎ *2733 022 833)* is the pick of the sites along the coast south of town. Buses to Areopoli can drop you there. You'll find plenty of *domatia* signs around town. They include **Xenia Rooms to Rent** (☎ *2733 022 719; singles/doubles with bathroom €15/20)*, opposite the causeway to Marathonisi. **Saga Pension** (☎ *2733 023 220, fax 2733 024 370; singles/doubles €25/30)*, nearby, is another good choice and rooms have TV.

The waterfront is lined with countless fish tavernas with similar menus. For something completely different, head inland to the tiny **General Store & Wine Bar** (☎ *2733 024 113; Vasileos Georgiou 67)*. It has an unusually imaginative menu featuring such dishes as orange-and-pumpkin soup (€3.50) and fillet of pork with black pepper and ouzo (€11).

There are five buses a day to Athens (€15.10, 4¼ hours) via Sparta (€2.60, one hour), five to Areopoli (€1.70, 30 minutes), two to Gerolimenas (€3.70, 1¼ hours), and one to the Diros Caves (€2.30, one hour).

ANEN Lines operates ferries to Kastelli–Kissamos on Crete (€15.60, seven hours) via Kythira (€7.10, 2½ hours), three times a week between June and September. The schedule is subject to constant change, so check with **Rozakis Travel** (☎ *2733 022 207, fax 2733 022 229;* e *rosakigy@otenet.gr)* before coming here to catch a boat.

## THE MANI

The Mani is divided into two regions, the Lakonian (inner) Mani in the south and Messinian (outer) Mani in the northwest below Kalamata.

### Lakonian Mani
☎ 2733

The Lakonian Mani is wild and remote, and its landscape is dotted with the dramatic stone-tower houses that are a trademark of the region. The houses were built as refuges from the clan wars of the 19th century. The best time to visit is in spring, when the barren countryside briefly bursts into life with a spectacular display of wild flowers.

The region's principal village is **Areopoli**, about 30km southwest of Gythio. There are a number of fine towers on the narrow, cobbled streets of the old town at the lower end of the main street, Kapetan Matepan.

Just south of here are the magnificent **Diros Caves** (admission €10.90; open 8am-5.30pm June-Sept, 8am-2.30pm Oct-May), where a subterranean river flows.

**Gerolimenas**, 20km further south, is a tiny fishing village built around a sheltered bay. **Vathia**, a village of towers built on a rocky peak, is 11km southeast of Gerolimenas. Beyond Vathia, the coastline is a series of rocky outcrops sheltering pebbled beaches.

Most of the accommodation in the Lakonian Mani is found in Areopoli.

GREECE

**Tsimova Rooms** (☎ 2733 051 301; singles/ doubles €22/36) has cosy rooms tucked away behind the Church of Taxiarhes on Kapetan Matepan.

**Pyrgos Kapetanakas** (☎ 2733 051 233, fax 2733 051 401; singles/doubles €30/45) occupies the tower house built by the powerful Kapetanakas family at the end of the 18th century. It's signposted to the right at the bottom of Kapetan Matepan.

**Nicola's Corner Taverna** (☎ 2733 051 366; Plateia Athanaton; mains €3-6.50) is a popular spot on the central square with a good choice of tasty taverna staples.

**Hotel Akrotenaritis** (☎ 2733 054 205; singles/doubles €18/35), in Gerolimenas, is a good budget option. Also in Gerolimenas, **Hotel Akrogiali** (☎ 2733 054 204, fax 2733 054 272; singles/doubles from €25/36) has a great setting overlooking the bay on the way into town. Both of these hotels have restaurants.

Areopoli is the focal point of the local bus network. There are four buses a day to Gythio and Sparta, two to Gerolimenas and Itilo, and one to Diros Caves. Crossing to the Messinian Mani involves changing buses at Itilo.

## Messinian Mani
☎ 2721

The Messinian Mani runs north along the coast from Itilo to Kalamata. The beaches here are some of the best in Greece, set against the dramatic backdrop of the Taygetos Mountains.

**Itilo**, the medieval capital of the entire Mani area, is split by a ravine that is the traditional dividing line between inner and outer Mani.

The picturesque coastal village of **Kardamyli**, 37km south of Kalamata, is a favourite destination for trekkers. It's well set up, with a network of colour-coded trails that crisscross the foothills of the Taygetos Mountains behind the village. Many of the walks incorporate the spectacular Vyros Gorge. If you plan to trek, strong, good-quality footwear is essential and make sure that you take plenty of water.

**Stoupa**, 10km south of Kardamyli, has a great beach and is a popular package destination in summer.

Kardamyli has a good choice of accommodation to suit all budgets, starting with several *domatia*.

**Olympia Koumounakou** (☎ 2721 073 623; singles/doubles €20/25) is a good place to try; it's signposted opposite the post office.

**Anniska Apartments** (☎/fax 2721 073 600; studios/apartments from €61.50/91.50) has a range of spacious, well-appointed studios and apartments. The studios sleep two people, while the larger apartments accommodate up to four people.

The popular **Taverna Perivolis** is one of nine tavernas around the village.

There are two buses a day from Kalamata to Itilo, stopping at Kardamyli and Stoupa.

## OLYMPIA Ολυμπία
☎ 2624

The site of ancient Olympia lies 500m beyond the modern town, surrounded by the foothills of Mt Kronion. There is a well-organised **municipal tourist office** (open 9am-9pm daily June-Sept, 8am-2.45pm Mon-Sat Oct-May) on the main street, which also changes money.

In ancient times, Olympia was a sacred place of temples, priests' dwellings and public buildings, as well as being the venue for the quadrennial Olympic Games. The first Olympics were staged in 776 BC, reaching the peak of their prestige in the 6th century BC. The city-states were bound by a sacred truce to stop fighting for three months and compete.

The **site** (admission €6 site only, €9 site & museum; open 8am-7pm daily Apr-Oct, 8am-5pm Mon-Fri, 8.30am-3pm Sat-Sun Nov-Mar) is dominated by the immense, ruined **Temple of Zeus**, to whom the games were dedicated. There's also a **museum** (admission €6), north of the archaeological site, which keeps similar hours.

There are three good camping grounds to choose from.

**Camping Diana** (☎ 2624 022 314), 250m west of town, is the most convenient. It has excellent facilities and a pool.

**Youth hostel** (☎ 2624 022 580; Praxitelous Kondyli 18; dorm beds €7) has free hot showers. There are two more good budget options around the corner on Stefanopoulou: **Pension Achilleys** (☎ 2624 022 562; Stefanopoulou 4; singles/doubles with shared bathroom €15/20) and **Pension Posidon** (☎ 2624 022 567; Stefanopoulou 9; singles/doubles with bathroom €18/28).

**Taverna To Steki tou Vangeli** (Stefanopoulou 13; mains €4-6.50) represents better value than most of the tavernas around town.

There are four buses a day to Olympia from Athens (€19.05, 5½ hours) and regular buses to Pyrgos, 24km away on the coast.

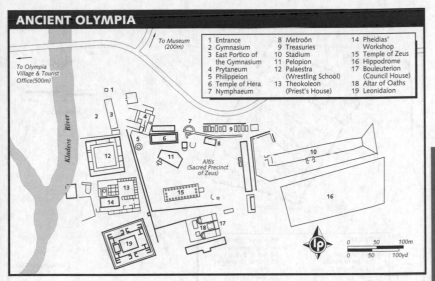

ANCIENT OLYMPIA

| | | |
|---|---|---|
| 1 Entrance | 8 Metroōn | 14 Pheidias' |
| 2 Gymnasium | 9 Treasuries | Workshop |
| 3 East Portico of | 10 Stadium | 15 Temple of Zeus |
| the Gymnasium | 11 Pelopion | 16 Hippodrome |
| 4 Prytaneum | 12 Palaestra | 17 Bouleuterion |
| 5 Philippeion | (Wrestling School) | (Council House) |
| 6 Temple of Hera | 13 Theokoleon | 18 Altar of Oaths |
| 7 Nymphaeum | (Priest's House) | 19 Leonidaion |

To Museum (200m)

To Olympia Village & Tourist Office (500m)

Kladeos River

Altis (Sacred Precinct of Zeus)

GREECE

# Central Greece

Central Greece has little going for it in terms of attractions – with the notable exceptions of Delphi and surroundings.

## DELPHI Δελφοί
## ☎ 2265 • pop 2400

Like so many of Greece's ancient sites, the setting at Delphi – overlooking the Gulf of Corinth from the slopes of Mt Parnassos – is stunning. The Delphic oracle is thought to have originated in Mycenaean times, when the earth goddess Gaea was worshipped here.

By the 6th century BC, Delphi had become the Sanctuary of Apollo and thousands of pilgrims came to consult the oracle, who was always a peasant woman of 50 years or more. She sat at the mouth of a chasm which emitted fumes. These she inhaled, causing her to gasp, writhe and shudder in divine frenzy. The pilgrim, after sacrificing a sheep or goat, would deliver a question, and the priestess' incoherent mumbling was then translated by a priest. Wars were fought, voyages embarked upon, and business transactions undertaken on the strength of these prophecies.

## Orientation & Information
The bus station, post office, OTE, National Bank of Greece and **tourist office** (☎ 2265

082 900; Vasileon Pavlou 44; open 7.30am-2.30pm Mon-Fri) are all on modern Delphi's main street, Vasileon Pavlou. The ancient site is 1km east of modern Delphi.

## Sanctuary of Apollo
The **Sacred Way** leads up from the entrance of the site to the **Temple of Apollo** (admission €6 site only, €9 site and museum, open 7.30am-7.15pm Mon-Fri, 8.30am-2.45pm Sat, Sun & public holidays). It was here that the oracle supposedly sat, although no chasm, let alone vapour, has been detected. The path continues to the theatre and stadium. Opposite this sanctuary is the **Sanctuary of Athena** (admission free) and the much-photographed **Tholos**, a 4th-century BC columned rotunda of Pentelic marble.

## Places to Stay & Eat
There are lots of hotels in the modern town, catering for the many tour groups that stop overnight.

**Hotel Tholos** (☎/fax 2265 082 268; Apollonos 31; singles/doubles with bathroom €15/30; open daily April-Nov, Fri & Sat only Dec-Mar) is great value for rooms with aircon and TV.

**Hotel Parnassos** (☎ 2265 082 321; Vasileon Pavlou & Frederikis 32; singles/doubles €30/38) is another good choice, and rates include buffet breakfast.

# ANCIENT DELPHI & SANCTUARY OF APOLLO

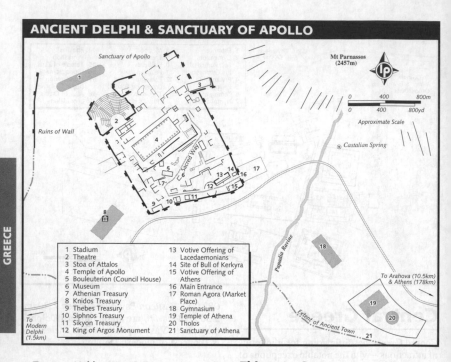

| | | |
|---|---|---|
| 1 | Stadium | 13 | Votive Offering of Lacedaemonians |
| 2 | Theatre | | |
| 3 | Stoa of Attalos | 14 | Site of Bull of Kerkyra |
| 4 | Temple of Apollo | 15 | Votive Offering of Athens |
| 5 | Bouleuterion (Council House) | | |
| 6 | Museum | 16 | Main Entrance |
| 7 | Athenian Treasury | 17 | Roman Agora (Market Place) |
| 8 | Knidos Treasury | | |
| 9 | Thebes Treasury | 18 | Gymnasium |
| 10 | Siphnos Treasury | 19 | Temple of Athena |
| 11 | Sikyon Treasury | 20 | Tholos |
| 12 | King of Argos Monument | 21 | Sanctuary of Athena |

**Taverna Vakhos** (☎ 2265 083 186; Apollonos 31; mains €4.80-10.50), next to the Hotel Tholos, turns out tasty taverna dishes such as lamb in lemon sauce with rice and potatoes (€5.60).

## Getting There & Away
There are five buses a day to Delphi from Athens (€10.20, three hours).

## METEORA Μετέωρα
☎ 2432
Meteora is an extraordinary place. The massive, sheer columns of rock that dot the landscape were created by wave action millions of years ago. Perched precariously atop these seemingly inaccessible outcrops are stunning monasteries that date back to the late 14th century. Each monastery is built around a central courtyard in the centre of which stands the main church.

Meteora is just north of the town of Kalambaka, on the Ioannina-Trikala road. The rocks behind the town are spectacularly floodlit at night. **Kastraki**, which is 2km from Kalambaka, is a charming village of red-tiled houses just west of the monasteries.

## Things to See
There were once monasteries on each of the 24 pinnacles, but only six are still occupied. They are **Megalou Meteorou** (Grand Me-teora; open 9am-1pm & 3pm-6pm Wed-Mon), **Varlaam** (open 9am-1pm & 3.30pm- 6pm Sat-Thur), **Agiou Stefanou** (open 9am-1pm & 3pm-5pm daily), **Agias Triados** (Holy Trinity; open 9am-5pm Fri-Wed), **Agiou Nikolaou** (open 9am-5pm daily) and **Agias Varvaras Rousanou** (open 9am-6pm Thur-Tues). Admission is €2 for each monastery; free for Greeks.

Meteora is best explored on foot, following the old paths where they exist. Allow a whole day to visit all of the monasteries, and take food and water. Women must wear skirts that reach below their knees, men must wear long trousers, and arms must be fully covered.

## Places to Stay & Eat
Kastraki is the best base for visiting Meteora. **Vrachos Camping** (☎ 2432 022 293), on the edge of the village, is excellent.

There are several **domatia** in town, charging from €20/30 for singles/doubles.

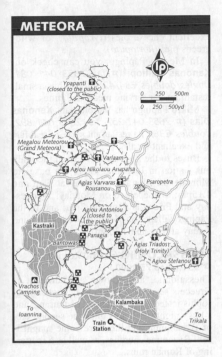

METEORA

Ypapanti
(closed to the public)

0    250    500m
0    250    500yd

Megalou Meteorou
(Grand Meteora)

Varlaam

Agiou Nikolaou Anapafsa

Agias Varvaras
Rousanou

Psaropetra

Agiou Antoniou
(closed to
the public)

Kastraki

Panagia

Bantovas

Agias Triados
(Holy Trinity)

Agiou Stefanou

Vrachos
Camping

Kalambaka

To
Ioannina

To
Trikala

Train
Station

**Hotel Sydney** *(☎/fax 2432 023 079; singles/doubles with bathroom €25/30)*, on the road into town from Kalambaka, has comfortable rooms.

In Kalambaka, **Koka Roka Rooms** *(☎ 2432 024 554; doubles with bathroom €30)*, is a popular travellers place; the taverna downstairs is good value. Telephone for a lift from the bus or train station.

### Getting There & Away

There are hourly buses to Trikala and two a day to Ioannina. Local buses shuttle constantly between Kalambaka and Kastraki; five a day continue to Metamorphosis.

Trikala is the region's major transport hub. It has eight buses a day which run to Athens (€18.20, 5½ hours).

There are trains between Kalambaka and Volos. These trains connect with services from Athens and Thessaloniki at Paleofarsalos.

# Northern Greece

Northern Greece covers the regions of Epiros, Thessaly, Macedonia and Thrace. It includes some areas of outstanding natural beauty, such as the Zagoria region of northwestern Epiros.

## IGOUMENITSA Ηγουμενίτσα

☎ 2665 • pop 6800

Igoumenitsa, opposite the island of Corfu, is the main port of northwestern Greece. Few people stay here any longer than it takes to buy a ticket out. The bus station is on Kyprou. To get there from the ferries, follow the waterfront (Ethnikis Antistasis) north for 500m and turn up El Venizelou. Kyprou is two blocks inland and the bus station is on the left.

If you get stuck for the night, you'll find signs for **domatia** around the port. The D-class **Egnatia** *(☎ 2665 023 648; Eleftherias 2; singles/doubles with bathroom €30/40)* has comfortable rooms.

**Alekos** *(☎ 2665 023 708; Ethnikis Andistasis 84; mains €3.5-5.50)*, 500m north of the Corfu ferry quay, does fine *mousakas* (€3.80) and other taverna favourites.

Bus services include nine buses a day to Ioannina (€6.20, two hours), and four a day to Athens (€28.45, 8½ hours).

There are international ferry services to the Italian ports of Ancona, Bari, Brindisi, Trieste and Venice. Ticket agencies are opposite the port.

Ferries to Corfu (€4.20, 1½ hours) operate every hour between 5am and 10pm.

## IOANNINA Ιωάννινα

☎ 2651 • pop 90,000

Ioannina is the largest town in Epiros, sitting on the western shore of Lake Pamvotis. In Ottoman times, it was one of the most important towns in the country.

The town centre is around Plateia Dimokratias where the main streets of the new town meet. All facilities of importance to travellers are nearby.

The **EOT office** *(☎ 2651 041 142; Dodonis 39; open 7.30am-2.30pm & 5.30pm-8.30pm Mon-Fri, 9am-1pm Sat)* is about 600m south of Plateia Dimokratias.

**Robinson Travel** *(☎ 2651 074 989; @ activities@robinson.gr; 8th Merarhias Gramou 10)* is an outfit that specialises in treks in the Zagoria region.

There are lots of Internet cafés in town, including **Armos Internet Café** *(2651 071 488; Harilaou Trikoupi 40)*, 300m west of Plateia Dimokratias.

GREECE

The **old town** juts out into the lake on a small peninsula. Inside the impressive fortifications lies a maze of winding streets flanked by traditional Turkish houses.

The **Nisi** (island) is a serene spot in the middle of the lake, with four monasteries set among the trees. Ferries (€0.80) to the island leave from just north of the old town. They run half-hourly in the summer and hourly in winter.

Most travellers end up staying either at the no-frills **Agapi Inn** (☎ 2651 020 541; Tsirigoti 6; doubles €18) near the bus station, or at the co-owned **Hotel Paris** (singles/doubles €20/30) next door.

There are several restaurants outside the entrance to the old town. **To Manteio Psistaria** is recommended.

Aegean Airlines and Olympic Airways both fly twice a day to Athens, and Olympic has a daily flight to Thessaloniki.

The main bus terminal is 300m north of Plateia Dimokratias on Zossimadon, the northern extension of Markou Botsari. Services include 12 buses a day to Athens (€24.85, seven hours), nine to Igoumenitsa, five to Thessaloniki and three to Trikala via Kalambaka.

## ZAGORIA & VIKOS GORGE
☎ 2653

The Zagoria (Ζαγόρα) region covers a large expanse of the Pindos Mountains north of Ioannina. It's a wilderness of raging rivers, crashing waterfalls and deep gorges. Here, snowcapped mountains rise out of dense forests and the remote villages that dot the hillsides are famous for their impressive grey-slate architecture.

The fairytale village of **Monodendri** is the starting point for treks through the dramatic **Vikos Gorge**, with its awesome sheer limestone walls. It's a strenuous 7½-hour walk from Monodendri to the twin villages of **Megalo Papingo** and **Mikro Papingo**. The trek is very popular and the path is clearly marked. Ioannina's EOT office has more information.

Other walks start from **Tsepelovo**, near Monodendri.

There are some wonderful places to stay, but none of them are particularly cheap.

The options in Monodendri include cosy **To Kalderimi** (☎ 2653 071 510; doubles €35). **Haradra tou Vikou** (☎ 2653 071 559)

specialises in fabulous *pittes* (pies). Try its excellent cheese pies (*tyropitta*), or wildgreens pies *(hortopitta)*.

In Megalo Papingo, you can check out **Xenonas Kalliopi** *(☎/fax 2653 041 081; singles/doubles €34/42)*. It also has a small restaurant-bar serving meals and pittes.

Mikro Papingo has the pleasant **Xenonas Dias** *(☎ 2653 041 257, fax 2653 041 892; doubles €36)*. Its restaurant serves breakfast and excellent meals.

Buses to the Zagoria leave from the main bus station in Ioannina. There are buses to Monodendri Monday to Friday at 6am and 4.15pm; to Tsepelovo on Monday, Wednesday and Friday at 6am and 3pm; and to the Papingo villages on Monday, Wednesday and Friday at 6am and 2.30pm.

## THESSALONIKI Θεσσαλονίκη
☎ 231 • pop 750,000

Thessaloniki, also known as Salonica, is Greece's second-largest city. It's a bustling, sophisticated place with good restaurants and a busy nightlife. It was once the second city of Byzantium, and there are some magnificent Byzantine churches, as well as a scattering of Roman ruins.

### Orientation

Thessaloniki is laid out on a grid system. The main thoroughfares – Tsimiski, Egnatia and Agiou Dimitriou – run parallel to Nikis, on the waterfront. Plateias Eleftherias and Aristotelous, both on Nikis, are the main squares. The city's most famous landmark is the White Tower (which is no longer white) at the eastern end of Nikis.

The train station is on Monastiriou, the westerly continuation of Egnatia beyond Plateia Dimokratias, and the airport is 16km to the southeast.

### Information

The **EOT office** *(☎ 231 027 1888; Plateia Aristotelous 8; open 8.30am-8pm Mon-Fri, 8.30am-2pm Sat)* can help with inquiries, or try the **tourist police** *(☎ 231 055 4871; Dodekanisou 4, 5th floor; open 7.30am-11pm daily)*.

There are numerous banks around the city centre, all with ATMs. The **National Bank of Greece** *(Tsimiski 11)* is open Saturday and Sunday for currency exchange; there are other branches elsewhere.

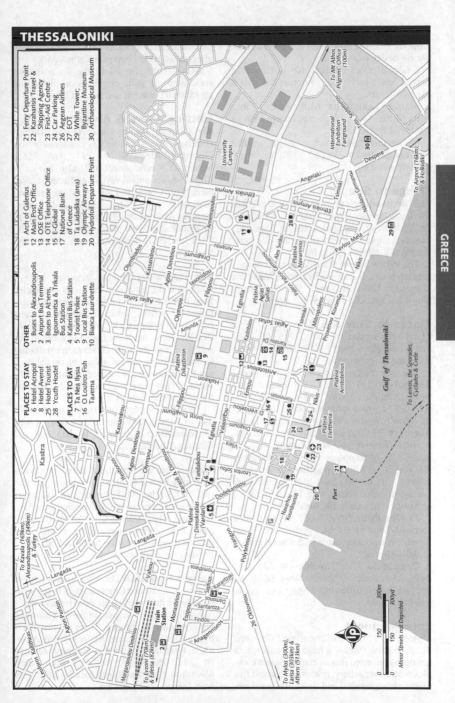

# THESSALONIKI

**PLACES TO STAY**
6 Hotel Acropol
8 Hotel Averof
25 Hotel Tourist
28 Ycuth Hostel

**PLACES TO EAT**
7 Ta Nea Ilysia
16 O Loutros Fish Taverna

**OTHER**
1 Buses to Alexandroupolis
2 Airport Bus Terminal
3 Buses to Athens, Igoumenitsa & Trikala Bus Station
4 Katerini Bus Station
5 Tourist Police
9 Local Bus Station
10 Bianca Laurdrette
11 Arch of Galerius
12 Main Post Office
13 OSE Office
14 OTE Telephone Office
15 E-Global
17 National Bank of Greece
18 Ta Ladadika (area)
19 Olympic Airways
20 Hydrofoil Departure Point
21 Ferry Departure Point
22 Karaharisis Travel & Shipping Agency
23 First-Aid Centre
24 Car Parking
26 Aegean Airlines
27 EOT
29 White Tower; Byzantine Museum
30 Archaeological Museum

GREECE

Gulf of Thessaloniki

To Mt Athos Pilgrims' Office (100m)

International Exhibition Fairground

To Airport (16km) & Helidiki

University Campus

To Levos, the Sporades, Cyclades & Crete

Kastra

To Kavala (169km), Alexandroupolis (349km) & Turkey

To Eezcni (70km) & Edessa (82km)

To Mylos (300m), Larisa (303km) & Athens (513km)

Train Station

Minor Streets not Depicted

0    150    300m
0    150    300yd

Send mail at the **main post office** *(Aristotelous 26)*, and make calls at the **OTE telephone office** *(Karolou Dil 27)*.

**E-Global** *(Vas Irakliou 40)* is the most central of the city's many Internet cafés. It's open 24 hours.

**Bianca Laundrette** *(Antoniadou)*, just north of the Arch of Galerius, charges €6 to wash and dry a load.

For medical attention you should try the **first-aid centre** *(☎ 231 053 0530; Navarhou Koundourioti 6)*.

## Things to See

The **archaeological museum** *(admission €4.40; open 8am-7pm Tues-Fri, 12.30pm-7pm Mon)*, at the eastern end of Tsimiski, houses a superb collection of treasures from the royal tombs of Philip II.

The **White Tower** is the city's most prominent landmark. It houses a **Byzantine Museum** *(admission free; open 8am-2.30pm Tues-Sun)*, which has splendid frescoes and icons.

## Places to Stay & Eat

The **youth hostel** *(☎ 231 022 5946; Alex Svolou 44; dorm beds €8)* is extremely basic and hard to recommend.

The best budget hotel in town is **Hotel Acropol** *(☎ 231 053 6170; Tandalidou 4; singles/doubles with shared bathroom €16/20.50)*, on a quiet side street off Egnatia. You'll find similar prices at the **Hotel Averof** *(☎ 231 053 8498; Leontos Sofou 24)*.

**Hotel Tourist** *(☎ 231 027 0501, fax 231 022 6865; Mitropoleos 21; singles/doubles €60/80.50)* is a big step up from these. Hotel Tourist is a fine old neoclassical hotel, which has comfortable rooms with TV and air-con, and prices include buffet breakfast.

**Ta Nea Ilysia** *(☎ 231 053 6996; Leotos Sofou 17; mains €4-6)*, opposite the Hotel Averof, is a popular place with a good choice of daily specials.

**O Loutros Fish Taverna** *(☎ 231 022 8895; M Koundoura 5; fish dishes €6-9)* has not lost its cult following despite its move to a new location.

## Entertainment

**Mylos** *(☎ 231 052 5968; Andreou Georgiou 56; admission free)* is a huge old mill which has been converted into an entertainment complex with an art gallery, restaurant, bar and live music club (classical and rock). To get there,

follow 26 Oktovriou southwest from Plateia Dimokratias; Andreou Georgiou is on the right after about 700m, opposite a small park.

Music bars abound in the Ta Ladadika area, with the main emphasis on music and all kinds of draught and bottled beer.

## Getting There & Away

**Air** Olympic Airways and Aegean Airlines both have seven flights a day to Athens (€96).

**Olympic Airways** *(☎ 231 036 8666; Navarhou Koundourioti 1-3)* also has daily flights to Ioannina, Lesvos and Limnos; three weekly to Corfu, Iraklio and Mykonos; and two weekly to Chios, Hania and Samos. **Aegean Airlines** *(☎ 231 028 0050; Venizelou 2)* also has two flights a day to Iraklio on Crete, and daily flights to Lesvos, Rhodes and Santorini.

**Bus** There are several bus terminals, most of them near the train station. Buses to Athens, Igoumenitsa and Trikala leave from Monastiriou 65 and 67; buses to Alexandroupolis leave from Koloniari 17; and buses to Litihoro (for Mt Olympus) leave from the Katerini bus station, Promitheos 10. Buses to the Halkidiki Peninsula leave from Karakasi 68 (in the eastern part of town; it's marked on the free EOT map). To get there, take local bus No 10 from Egnatia to the Botsari stop.

The **OSE** *(Aristotelous 18)* has two buses a day to Athens from the train station, as well as international services to İstanbul and Tirana (Albania).

**Train** There are nine trains a day to Athens, five of which are intercity express services (€27.60, six hours). There are also five trains to Alexandroupolis, two of which are express services (€16.20, 5½ hours). All international trains from Athens stop at Thessaloniki. You can get more information from the OSE office or from the train station.

**Ferry & Hydrofoil** There's a Sunday ferry to Lesvos, Limnos and Chios throughout the year. In summer there are at least three ferries a week to Iraklio (Crete), stopping in the Sporades and the Cyclades on the way. There are also daily hydrofoils to Skiathos, Skopelos and Alonnisos. **Karaharisis Travel & Shipping Agency** *(☎ 231 052 4544, fax 231 053 2289; Navarhou Koundourioti 8)* handles tickets for both ferries and hydrofoils.

GREECE

## Getting Around

There is no bus service from the Olympic Airways office to the airport. Take bus No 78 from the train station (€0.50). A taxi from the airport costs about €8.

## HALKIDIKI Χαλκιδική

Halkidiki is the three-pronged peninsula southeast of Thessaloniki. It's the main resort area of northern Greece, with superb sandy beaches right around its 500km of coastline. **Kassandra**, the southwestern prong of the peninsula, has surrendered irrevocably to mass tourism. The **Sithonia Peninsula**, the middle prong, is not as over-the-top and has some spectacular scenery.

## Mt Athos

Halkidiki's third prong is occupied by the all-male Monastic Republic of Mt Athos (also called the Holy Mountain), where monasteries full of priceless treasures stand amid an impressive landscape of gorges, wooded mountains and precipitous rocks.

Obtaining a four-day visitors permit involves a bit of work. Start early, because only 10 foreign adult males may enter Mt Athos per day and there are long waiting lists in summer. You can start the process from outside Thessaloniki, but you will have to pass through Thessaloniki anyway to pick up your reservation.

You must first book a date for your visit with the **Mount Athos Pilgrims' Office** (☎ 231 083 3733, fax 231 086 1611; Leoforos Karamanli 14; open 8.30am-1.30pm & 6pm-8pm Mon, Tues, Thur & Fri), just east of the International Exhibition Fairground in Thessaloniki. Call first and make a telephone booking.

Letters of recommendation are no longer required, but you must declare your intention to be a pilgrim. You need to supply a photocopy of your passport details and, if you are Orthodox, a photocopied certificate showing your religion.

You must then call at the Pilgrims' Office in person to collect the forms confirming your reservation. You can then proceed from Thessaloniki to the port of Ouranoupolis, which is the departure point for boats to Mt Athos, where you will be given your actual permit.

Armed at last with your permit, you can explore, on foot, the 20 monasteries and independent religious communities of Mt Athos. You can stay only one night at each monastery.

## MT OLYMPUS Ολυμπος Ορος
☎ 2352

Mt Olympus is Greece's highest and mightiest mountain. The ancients chose it as the abode of their gods and assumed it to be the exact centre of the earth. Olympus has eight peaks, the highest of which is Mytikas (2917m). The area is popular with trekkers, most of whom use the village of **Litohoro** as a base. Litohoro is 5km inland from the Athens-Thessaloniki highway.

The **EOS office** (☎ 2352 084 544; Plateia Kentriki; open 9am-1pm & 6pm-8.30pm Mon-Fri, 9am-1pm Sat) has information on the various treks and conditions.

The main route to the top takes two days with a stay overnight at one of the refuges on the mountain. Good protective clothing is essential, even in summer.

**Hotel Markisia** (☎ 2352 081 831; Dionysou 5; singles/doubles with bathroom €20.50/23.50) is a good, clean budget choice.

**Hotel Enipeas** (☎ 2352 084 328, fax 2352 081 328; Plateia Kentriki; doubles/triples €32.30/38.20) is a cheery place and has the best views of Olympus.

**Olympus Taverna** (Agiou Nikolaou) serves standard fare at reasonable prices.

There are four **refuges** (open May-Sept) on the mountain at altitudes ranging from 940m to 2720m.

There are eight buses a day to Litohoro from Thessaloniki (€6.10, 1½ hours), and three from Athens (€24.80, 5½ hours).

## ALEXANDROUPOLIS
Αλεξανδρούπολη
☎ 2551 • pop 37,000

Dusty Alexandroupolis doesn't have much going for it, but if you're going to Turkey or Samothraki, you may end up staying overnight here.

**Hotel Lido** (☎ 2551 028 808; Paleologou 15; singles/doubles without bathroom €16.20/22; singles/doubles with bathroom €22/27), one block north of the bus station, is a great budget option.

**Neraïda Restaurant** (☎ 2551 022 867; Plateia Polytehniou; mains €5-7) has a good range of local specialities.

GREECE

Olympic Airways and Aegean Airlines both have two flights a day to Athens (€79.55) from the airport which is 7km west of town. There are five trains and six buses (€20) a day to Thessaloniki. There's also a daily train and a daily OSE bus to İstanbul.

In summer there are at least two boats a day to Samothraki, dropping to one boat a day in winter. There are also hydrofoils to Samothraki and Limnos.

# Saronic Gulf Islands Νησιά του Σαρωνικού

The Saronic Gulf Islands are the closest island group to Athens. Not surprisingly, they are a very popular escape for residents of the congested capital. Accommodation can be hard to find between mid-June and September, and at weekends year-round.

## AEGINA Αίγινα
☎ 2297 • pop 11,000

Aegina is the closest island to Athens and is a popular destination for day-trippers. Many make for the lovely **Temple of Aphaia** (admission €4; open 8am-7pm daily Apr-Oct, 8am-5pm Nov-Mar), a well-preserved Doric temple 12km east of Aegina town. Buses from Aegina town to the small resort of **Agia Marina** can drop you at the site.

Most travellers prefer to stay in Aegina town, where the **Hotel Plaza** (☎ 2297 025 600; singles/doubles €25/28) has rooms overlooking the sea.

## POROS Πόρος
pop 4000

Poros is a big hit with the Brits, but it's hard to work out why. The beaches are nothing to write home about and there are no sites of significance. The main attraction is pretty Poros town, draped over the Sferia Peninsula. Sferia is linked to the rest of the island, known as Kalavria, by a narrow isthmus. Most of the package hotels are here. There are a few domatia in Poros town, signposted off the road to Kalavria.

The island lies little more than a stone's throw from the mainland, opposite the Peloponnese village of Galatas.

## HYDRA Ύδρα
☎ 2298 • pop 3000

Hydra is the island with the most style and is famous as the haunt of artists and jet-setters. Its gracious stone mansions are stacked up the rocky hillsides that surround the fine natural harbour. The main attraction is peace and quiet. There are no motorised vehicles on the island – apart from a garbage truck and a few construction vehicles.

Accommodation is expensive, but of a high standard.

**Pension Theresia** (☎ 2298 053 984, fax 2298 053 983; singles/doubles with bathroom €30/45) has clean, comfortable rooms with small communal kitchens. It's about 300m from the harbour on Tombazi.

**Hotel Miranda** (☎ 2298 052 230, fax 2298 053 510; e mirhydra@hol.gr; doubles with bathroom from €54) is a good spot for a minor splurge. It was once the mansion of a wealthy Hydriot sea captain.

## SPETSES Σπέτσες
☎ 2298 • pop 3700

Pine-covered Spetses is perhaps the most beautiful island in the group. It also has the best beaches, so it's packed with package tourists in summer. The **old harbour** in Spetses town is a delightful place to explore.

# Cyclades Κυκλάδες

The Cyclades, named after the rough circle they form around Delos, are quintessential Greek Islands with brilliant white villages, dazzling light and azure waters.

Delos, the most important historic island of the group, is uninhabited. The inhabited islands of the archipelago are Mykonos, Syros, Tinos, Andros, Paros, Naxos, Ios, Santorini (Thira), Anafi, Amorgos, Sikinos, Folegandros and the tiny islands of Koufonisi, Shinousa, Iraklia and Donousa, lying east of Naxos.

Some of the Cyclades, such as Mykonos, Ios and Santorini (Thira), have seized tourism, stuffing their coastlines with bars and their beaches with sun lounges. Others, such as Anafi, Sikinos and the tiny islands east of Naxos, are little more than clumps of rock, each with a village, secluded coves and curious tourists.

To give even the briefest rundown on every island is impossible in a single chapter.

For more detailed information, check out Lonely Planet's *Greek Islands* guide.

## History
The Cyclades enjoyed a flourishing Bronze Age civilisation (3000 to 1100 BC), more or less concurrent with the Minoan civilisation.

By the 5th century BC, the island of Delos had been taken over by Athens.

Between the 4th and 7th centuries AD, the islands, like the rest of Greece, suffered a series of invasions and occupations. During the Middle Ages they were raided by pirates – hence the labyrinthine character of their towns, which was meant to confuse attackers. On some islands the whole population would move into the mountainous interior to escape the pirates, while on others they would brave it out on the coast. Hence on some islands the hora is on the coast, and on others, it is inland.

The Cyclades became part of independent Greece in 1827.

## MYKONOS Μύκονος
**☎ 2289 • pop 6170**
Polished Greek island perfection, Mykonos is perhaps the most visited – and expensive – of the archipelago. It has the most sophisticated nightlife and is a mecca for gay travellers.

## Orientation & Information
There is no tourist office. The **tourist police** (*☎ 2289 022 482*) are at the port, in the same building as the **hotel reservation office** (*☎ 2289 024 540*), which has free tourist maps, the **Association of Rooms and Apartments** (*☎/fax 2289 026 860*) and the **camping information office** (*☎ 2289 022 852*).

**Island Mykonos Travel** (*☎ 2289 022 232;* e *islandmykonos@1net.gr*) on Taxi Square, where the port road meets the town, is a hectic but quite helpful agency with tourist and travel information. The **post office** is near the southern bus station. **Double Click** (*Florou Zouganeli*), which is off Taxi Square, has rather expensive Internet access.

## Things to See
Summer crowds consume the island's capital and port, shuffling through snaking streets of chic boutiques and blinding white walls with balconies of cascading flowers.

The most popular beaches are **Platys Gialos** (wall-to-wall sun lounges), the often nude

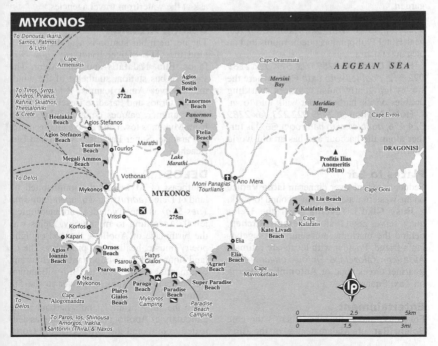

Paradise Beach and mainly gay **Super Paradise**, **Agrari** and **Elia**. The less squashy ones are **Panormos**, **Kato Livadi** and **Kalafatis**.

But wait, there's culture, too – the amazing World Heritage–listed ancient site on nearby **Delos** (see Delos, later).

## Places to Stay

**Paradise Beach Camping** (☎ 2289 022 852; ⓔ paradise@paradise.myk.forthnet.gr; camping per person/tent €7/3.50, sleeping bag area €7) is skin-to-skin mayhem in summer bursting with facilities as well as a party atmosphere.

**Mykonos Camping** (☎/fax 2289 024 578; ⓔ info.mykcamp.gr; camping per person/ tent €7/3.50), near Platys Gialos beach, also parties. Minibuses from both meet the ferries and buses jog regularly into town.

Rooms fill up quickly in high season so it's wise to go with the first domatia owner who accosts you. Outside July and August, rooms are cheap as chops.

Kalogera is a good street for mid-range lodgings such as **Hotel Philippi** (☎ 2289 022 294, fax 2289 024 680; singles/doubles/ triples €35/56/67) with spacious rooms and garden.

**Rooms Chez Maria** (☎ 2289 022 480; doubles/triples with bathroom €80/90), near Hotel Philippi, has quaint rooms and an elegant restaurant.

**Hotel Delos** (☎ 2289 022 517, fax 2289 022 312; doubles with bath €80), where the waves lap gently outside, offers sparkling doubles on the harbourfront walk into town.

**Hotel Apollon** (☎ 2289 022 223, fax 2289 024 456; doubles with bathroom €62) is further along the harbour and has an old-world charm.

## Places to Eat

Seduce someone over dinner in **Little Venice** on the western waterfront – it's bound to work.

Busy **Niko's Taverna**, near the Delos quay, serves good seafood. **Sesame Kitchen**, behind the maritime museum, is a vegetarian's friend. Popular with locals are intimate **Avra** (cnr Kalogera & Florou Zouganeli) for gourmet Greek food or **Antonini's Taverna** on Taxi Square.

## Entertainment

For house and Latin vibes, there's the chic **Bolero Bar**, off Malamatenias, or the flirty **Anchor Bar**, off Matogianni. **Rhapsody** in Little Venice is the place to chill.

For a huge night, it's **Space Dance** near the post office or **Cavo Paradiso**, 300m above Paradise Beach, world-famous for raves that attract top DJs. A 24-hour bus transports clubbers in summer.

**Porta**, **Kastro Bar**, **Icaros**, **Manto** and **Pierro's** are among popular gay spots.

## Getting There & Away

There are daily flights from Mykonos to Athens (€75) and to Santorini (Thira; €58). In summer, there are flights to and from Rhodes and Thessaloniki. Visit Island Mykonos Travel for schedules (see under Orientation & Information, earlier).

In winter, ferry services sleep most days and from July to September, the Cyclades are vulnerable to the meltemi, a fierce northeasterly wind that culls ferry schedules. Otherwise, there are daily ferries to Mykonos from Piraeus (€17). From Mykonos, there are daily ferries and hydrofoils to most Cycladic islands, three services weekly to Crete, and less-frequent services to the northeastern Aegean Islands and the Dodecanese. For schedules, ask at the waterfront travel agencies.

## Getting Around

The northern bus station is near the port, behind the OTE office. It serves Agios Stefanos, Elia, Kalafatis and Ano Mera. The southern bus station, southeast of the windmills, serves Agios Ioannis, Psarou, Platys Gialos, Ornos and Paradise Beach.

In summer, caïques (small fishing boats) from Mykonos town and Platys Gialos putter to Paradise, Super Paradise, Agrari and Elia Beaches.

## DELOS Δήλος

Southeast of Mykonos, the uninhabited island of Delos (admission €5; open 9am-3pm Tues-Sun) is the Cyclades' archaeological jewel. According to mythology, Delos was the birthplace of Apollo – the god of light, poetry, music, healing and prophecy. The island flourished as an important religious and commercial centre from the 3rd millennium BC, reaching its apex of power in the 5th century BC.

To the north of the island's harbour is the **Sanctuary of Apollo**, containing temples dedicated to him, and the **Terrace of the Lions**.

These proud beasts were carved in the 7th century or early 6th century BC using marble from Naxos to guard the sacred area. The original lions moved to the island's museum to avoid ageing; youthful replicas remain on the site. The **Sacred Lake** (dry since 1926) is where Leto supposedly gave birth to Apollo. The **museum** is east of this section.

South of the harbour is the **Theatre Quarter** where private houses were built around the **Theatre of Delos**. East of here are the **Sanctuaries of the Foreign Gods**. Climb up **Mt Kynthos** (113m) for a spectacular view of Delos and the surrounding islands.

Excursion boats leave Mykonos for Delos (€6 return, 30 minutes) between 9am and 12.50pm. To appreciate the site, invest in a guidebook or guided tour. **Meridian** (☎ 2289 024 702) offers a 3½-hour tour (€28.50).

## PAROS Πάρος
☎ 2284 • pop 9591
Paros is an attractive island with softly contoured and terraced hills that culminate in Mt Profitis Ilias. It has fine swimming beaches and is famous for its pure white marble from which the *Venus de Milo* was created.

### Orientation & Information
Paros' main town and port is Parikia, on the west coast. Agora, also known as Market St, is Parikia's main commercial thoroughfare running from the main square, Plateia Mavrogenous (opposite the ferry terminal).

There is no tourist office, but travel agencies oblige with information. The post office is on the waterfront, to the north of the pier.

Opposite the ferry quay, to the left, is Mcmphis.net Internet café, or there's funky **Cyber Cookies** *(Market St)*. An excellent website is Ⓦ www.parosweb.com.

### Things to See & Do
One of the most notable churches in Greece is Parikia's **Panagia Ekatontapyliani** *(Our Lady of the Hundred Gates; open 7am-9pm daily)* for its beautiful, ornate interior. Visitors must dress modestly (ie, no shorts).

On the northeast coast, **Naoussa** is still a sweet fishing village, despite a deluge in tourism, and there's good swimming nearby: **Kolimvythres** has Wild West rock formations; tiny **Monastiri** has a pumping beach bar; and **Santa Maria**, a dive-instruction centre.

**GREECE**

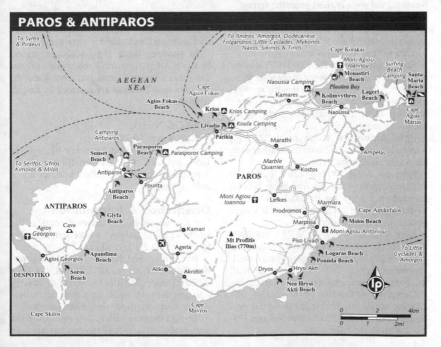

**PAROS & ANTIPAROS**

Take a bus to the peaceful inland villages of **Lefkes**, **Marmara** and **Marpissa** for walks through unspoilt hilly terrain and Kodak opportunities. The **Moni Agiou Antoniou** (Monastery of St Anthony), on a hill above Marpissa, offers soaring views.

You can visit the **marble quarries** by taking the bus to Marathi but the steep walk and marble powder may trouble those with respiratory conditions.

Less than 2km from Paros, the small island of **Antiparos** has fantastic beaches which has made it wildly popular. The chief attraction is its **cave** (admission €2; open 9.30am-3.30pm daily), which is considered to be one of Europe's best.

## Places to Stay

There's loads of camping on Paros but it's away from the action. **Koula Camping** (☎ 2284 022 081) is on Livadia beach. **Parasporas** (☎/fax 2284 022 268) and **Krios Camping** (☎ 2284 021 705) are near Parikia.

Head to Naoussa for **Naoussa Camping** (☎ 2284 051 565), or **Surfing Beach** (☎ 2284 052 491) on Santa Maria Beach. There's a bus service in summer between Parikia and Naoussa, and some owners greet the ferries.

Back in Parikia, Mike at **Rooms Mike** (☎ 2284 022 856; doubles/triples €30/45) is a brilliant host. Walk 50m left from the port and it's next to Memphis.net.

**Rooms Rena** (☎/fax 2284 021 427; singles/doubles/triples/quads with bathroom €29/38/44/55) is a friendly place with spotless rooms with balcony and fridge. To get there turn left from the pier, then right at the ancient cemetery.

**Hotel Argonauta** (☎/fax 2284 021 440; singles/doubles €53/65), on the main square, has a more traditional feel.

**Pension Sofia** (☎/fax 2284 022 085; doubles/triples €58/70) has been recommended by readers for its huge garden and fresh rooms. Turn left from the port; it's signposted from the harbourfront.

**Eleni Rooms** (☎ 2284 022 714, fax 2284 024 170; e info@eleni-rooms.gr; doubles/triples €55/75) has contemporary, well-appointed rooms. Turn left from the port, walk about 500m, and follow the signposts.

**Camping Antiparos** (☎/fax 2284 061 221; Agios Giannis Theologos Beach) is on a beach 1.5km north of Antiparos village. Follow the signs from the quay.

## Places to Eat

On Plateia Mavrogenous, trust **Zorba's** gyros for a quick fix, or **Restaurant Argonauta** for tasty Greek fare in cheery surrounds. **Ephesus**, on the street behind the yacht marina, is dip delicious.

## Entertainment

Mellow **Pirate** jazz-and-blues bar is tucked away in the old town. The far southern end of Parikia's waterfront has **Pebbles** bar for classical music, and **Mojo** and **Black Bart's** for upbeat vibes. Further along you'll find **The Dubliner** (three bars in one) and **Sex Club**, for dancing, not topless Playboy bunnies.

Pounda Beach has two rave clubs; **Pounda Beach Club** and **Viva Pounda**.

## Getting There & Away

There is one flight daily to and from Athens (€69.75). Paros is a major ferry hub with daily connections to Piraeus (€16), frequent ferries and daily catamarans to Naxos, Ios, Santorini (Thira) and Mykonos, and less-frequent ones to Amorgos. The Dodecanese and the northeastern Aegean Islands (via Syros) are also well serviced from here.

## Getting Around

The bus station, 100m left from the port, has frequent services to the entire island.

In summer there are hourly excursion boats to Antiparos from Parikia port, or you can catch a bus to Pounta and ferry it across. Beaches near Naoussa are serviced by caïque from Parikia.

## NAXOS Νάξος
☎ 2285 • pop 16,703
Naxos is the biggest and greenest of the Cyclades, but what it lacks in small-town allure, it makes up for with excellent beaches and a striking interior.

## Orientation & Information

Naxos town (hora), on the west coast, is the island's capital and port. Court Square is also known as Plateia Protodikiou.

Privately-owned **Naxos Tourist Information Centre** (NTIC; ☎ 2285 025 201, fax 2285 025 200; open 8.30am-11pm daily), directly opposite the port, offers help with accommodation, tours, luggage storage and laundry.

To find the post office, turn right from the port, walk 700m, cross Papavasiliou and take the left branch where the road forks. Reliable Internet access is at **Rental Centre** *(Court Square)* and the cool **M@trix Cyber Café**, off Court Square, towards the police station.

## Things to See & Do

Naxos town twists and curves up to a crumbling 13th-century **Kastro** and well-stocked **archaeological museum** *(admission €3; open 8.30am-3pm Tues-Sun).*

The town beach of **Agios Georgios** is a 10-minute walk from town; turn right from the port. Beyond it, wonderful sandy beaches as far as **Pyrgaki Beach** become progressively less crammed. **Agia Anna Beach** is a sublime 3km stretch.

A day trip to **Apollonas** on the north coast reveals a dramatic landscape. The **Tragaea** region is a vast Arcadian olive grove with tranquil villages in valleys and dome churches atop rocky crests.

**Filoti**, the largest settlement, perches on the slopes of **Mt Zeus** (1004m). It's a tough three-hour trail to the summit.

In Apollonas you'll find the mysterious 10.5m **kouros** (naked male statue), constructed circa 7th century, lying abandoned and unfinished in an ancient marble quarry.

The old village of **Apiranthos** is a gem, with paved marble streets and few tavernas.

There are a string of **minor islands** off the east coast of Naxos also known as the **Little Cyclades**. Only four are inhabited: Donousa, Shinousa, Iraklia and Ano Koufonisi. Intrepid visitors will find few amenities on these, but each has some *domatia*. They are served by

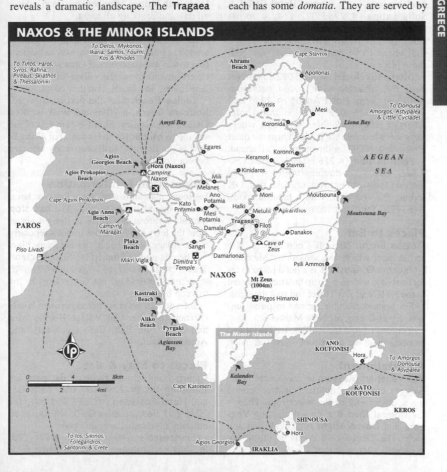

two to three ferries per week from Piraeus via Naxos, some of which continue to Amorgos.

## Places to Stay

**Camping Maragas** (☎/fax 2285 042 552; e maragas@naxos-island.com), on Agia Anna Beach 8km from town, is a lovely place with a café and bar and huge rooms available.

**Camping Naxos** (☎ 2285 023 500) is in a lonely spot, 1km south of Agios Georgios Beach.

Both Camping Maragas and Naxos have ferry pick-ups – or take the bus.

**Studios Stratos** (☎/fax 2285 025 898; *doubles/triples with bathroom €35/45)*, in the back streets around Agios Georgios, has immaculate, lovingly decorated rooms with mini kitchen. The combined **Hotel Galini & Sofia Latina** (☎ 2285 022 114; e info@ hotelgalini.com; *doubles with bathroom €50)*, next to the town hall, has great views. Call ahead to be met at the ferry for both these places.

**Dionyssos Hostel** (☎ 2285 022 331; *dorm beds €7, doubles with shared bathroom €30)* and pretty **Hotel Anixis** (☎ 2285 022 932, fax 2285 022 112; e info@hotel anixis.gr; *singles/doubles €40/50)*, where rates include breakfast, is found near the quiet Kastro; ask NTIC for directions or call ahead.

**Pension Irene** (☎ 2285 023 169; *doubles/ triples €30/40 • doubles/triples €36/50)* has two locations in town, one old, with OK rooms, and one new, with a fabulous pool. Ask NTIC for directions or call ahead.

## Places to Eat

**Picasso Bistro**, 20m off Court Square, is a stylish place which does sensational Mexican.

**Taverna O Apostolis** is a good place to try for ouzo and *mezedes*; go up the street adjacent to the NTIC and Zas Travel and spot the signs.

For upmarket ambience and inspired sunsets, try **El Greco**, off New Market St.

You can't avoid the waffles, ice cream and crepes around the waterfront – just surrender.

## Entertainment

The **Venetian Museum** by the Kastro holds twilight concerts. Nightlife clusters around the southern end of the waterfront. There's the tropical **Med Bar**, crowd-pleasing **Veggera** and **Day & Night** for Greek pop and rock. The **Ocean** club opens at 11pm, but goes wild after midnight.

## Getting There & Around

Naxos has six flights weekly to Athens (€70.40). There are daily ferries to Piraeus (€16.35) and good ferry and hydrofoil connections to most Cycladic islands. Boats go once a week to Crete, Thessaloniki and usually Rhodes, and to Samos two to three times per week. Check with travel agencies.

Buses travel to most villages regularly (including Apollonas and Filoti) and the beaches towards Pyrgaki. The bus terminal is in front of the port. Car and motorcycle rentals are off Court Square.

## IOS Ιος

☎ 2286 • pop 2000

In high season, Ios is the spoilt brat of the islands with little to offer beyond beach baking all day and drinking all night.

The island is reasonably popular with the older set – anyone over 25 – but the two groups tend to be polarised. The young stay in the hora (Ios town) and the others at Ormos port. Nonravers should avoid the village from June to September. The locals wish they could, too.

**Gialos Beach** near the port is crowded. **Koubara Beach**, a 20-minute walk west of Gialos, is less crazy. Stumble 1km east of the village to **Milopotas** to recover, but **Manganari** is the magnet, with four sandy crescent beaches on the south coast.

## Orientation & Information

Ios town, also known as 'the village' or hora, is 2km inland from the port. The **bus stop** *(Plateia Emirou)* in Ormos is straight ahead from the ferry quay. The bus trundles regularly to the village, otherwise it's a nasty, steep hike.

There is no EOT tourist office, but **Acteon Travel** (☎ 2286 091 343, fax 2286 091 088; e acteon@otenet.gr) has five offices in Ios to keep busy.

Internet access is scattered between hotels (Francesco's, Far Out Village Hotel), cafés and bars (Fun Pub, Café Cyclades), and Acteon Travel.

## Places to Stay & Eat

Clearly visible just right of the port are **Camping Ios** (☎ 2286 091 050; *tents €8)* and **Hotel Poseidon** (☎ 2286 091 091, fax 2286 091 969; *doubles €67)*, which has an enticing communal area and pool.

**Francesco's** (☎/fax 2286 091 223; e fragesco@otenet.gr; *dorm beds €15,* doubles with bathroom €50), in the village, is a lively meeting place with superlative views from its terrace bar.

Milopotas Beach parties hard from noon until midnight with up to 3000 people.

**Camping Stars** (☎ 2286 091 302; tents €7.50, bungalows with bathroom per person €19) has a pool, bar and live music.

**Far Out Camping Club** (☎ 2286 091 468; e camping@faroutclub.com; camping per person €8, bungalows & dorms per person €18) has tons of facilities and bungy jumping. Next door, **Far Out Village Hotel** (☎ 2286 092 305; doubles €82) is less hyper.

In Ormos, **Café Cyclades** does pricey Mexican. In the village, **The Nest** is the cheapest taverna for hungry backpackers, or try **Ali Baba's** near the gym for huge meals and funky ambience. **Lord Byron Taverna** and **Pithari** are cosy nooks for Greek fare. For decent seafood, try **Filippos** on the road between the port and Koubara Beach.

## Entertainment

At night, the village erupts with bars to explore and you'll have to elbow your way nicely to the other side. Perennial favourites

include **Red Bull**, **Slammers** and **Blue Note**. Opposite the central car park, **Sweet Irish Dreams** is a crowd pleaser with table dancing. For clubbing you could head to a place called **Scorpions**.

## Getting There & Around

Mercifully, Ios has daily connections to Piraeus (€16.50) and there are frequent hydrofoils and ferries to the major Cycladic islands. For schedules, visit Acteon Travel (see under Orientation & Information, earlier).

There are buses every 20 minutes between the port, the village and Milopotas Beach until early morning, and two to three per day to Manganari Beach (45 minutes).

## SANTORINI (THIRA)
Σαντορίνη (Θήρα)
☎ 2286 • pop 9360
Around 1450 BC, the volcanic heart of Santorini (Thira) exploded and sank, leaving an extraordinary landscape. Today, the startling sight of the submerged caldera almost encircled by sheer cliffs remains – this is certainly the most dramatic sights of all the islands. It's possible that the catastrophe destroyed the Minoan civilisation, but neither this theory nor the claim that the island was part of the lost continent of Atlantis has been proven.

## Orientation & Information
The capital, Fira, perches on top of the caldera on the west coast. The port of Athinios is 12km away.

The bus station and taxi station are located just south of Fira's main square Plateia Theotokopoulou.

There is no EOT tourist office or tourist police but there are several travel agencies on the square and the helpful **Dakoutros Travel** (☎ 2286 022 958, fax 2286 022 686), which is opposite the taxi station.

The post office is one block south of the taxi station. The best-value Internet café on the square is **PC Club**, above Santo Volcano Tours & Travel, or **Espresso Caffe**, up the steps opposite the taxi station.

## Fira
The shameless commercialism of Fira has not quite reduced its all-pervasive dramatic aura. The best of the town's museums is the exceptional **Museum of Prehistoric Thira**

*(admission free; open 8.30am-3pm Tues-Sun)*, which has wonderful displays of artefacts predominantly from ancient Akrotiri. To get there, walk south from the main square, past the bus station and take the next street on the right. The **Megaron Gyzi Museum** *(adult/student €2.50/1; open 10.30am-1.30pm & 5pm-8pm Mon-Sat, 10.30am-4.30pm Sun)*, behind the youth hostel and Catholic monastery, houses local memorabilia, including photographs of Fira before and after the 1956 earthquake.

### Around the Island
Excavations in 1967 uncovered the remarkably well-preserved Minoan settlement of **Akrotiri** with its remains of two- and three-storey buildings, and evidence of a sophisticated drainage system. Until a new shelter to protect the ruins is complete (around 2007), artefacts have been moved to the Museum of Prehistoric Thira. Without a guided tour, the site is just rubble. Dakoutros Travel conducts tours for €20.

**Moni Profiti Ilia**, a monastery built on the island's highest point, can be reached along a path from the site of **Ancient Thira**; the walk takes about one hour.

The flawless village of **Oia** (pronounced ee-ah), famed for its postcard sunsets, is less hectic than Fira and a must visit. Its caldera-facing tavernas are dreamy spots for brunch. Santorini's **beaches** of black volcanic sand sizzle – beach mats are essential. **Kamari**, **Perissa** and **Monolithos** get crowded but those near Oia are quieter. **Red Beach**, a 15-minute walk from Akrotiri, is very popular.

Of the surrounding islets, only **Thirasia** is inhabited. At **Palia Kameni** you can bathe in hot springs and on **Nea Kameni** you can clamber around on volcanic lava. A six-hour tour to these three islands by caïque or glass-bottomed boat costs €17. Tickets are available from most travel agencies.

### Places to Stay
You should beware the aggressive accommodation owners who meet boats and buses and claim that their rooms are in Fira town when they're actually in Karterados; a 20-minute walk or short bus ride into town. Ask to see a map to check their location. Dakoutros Travel can help with a range of accommodation in Fira (and Oia) and organises pick-ups from its office.

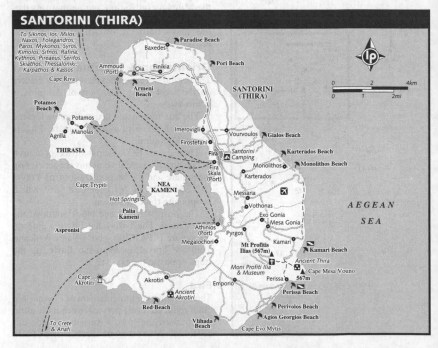

SANTORINI (THIRA)

**Santorini Camping** (☎ 2286 022 944; ⓔ santocam@olenel.gr; camping per person/ tent €6/3), 400m east of the main square, has a restaurant and swimming pool.

**Thira Hostel** (☎ 2286 023 864; dorm beds €11, doubles/triples with bathroom €35/40), 200m north of the square, is a spacious, run-down old monastery. Some may enjoy its decaying appeal! It also has a cheap restaurant.

**Pension Petros** (☎ 2286 022 573, fax 2286 022 615; doubles €60) is centrally located, 250m east of the square. Its owners meet the ferries.

**Hotel Olympia** (☎ 2286 022 213, fax 2286 022 498; doubles/triples €73/82) in Karterados has lovely rooms overlooking a pool.

**Hotel Hellas** (☎ 2286 023 555, fax 2286 023 840; doubles €79) at the top end of town, is roomy with relaxing rural and sea views and an edgeless pool.

**Astir Thira Hotel** (☎ 2286 022 585, fax 2286 022 525; ⓔ astir-h@hol.gr; doubles €120), about 500m from Fira on the main road, is an upmarket option with some caldera views and breakfast is included. Call ahead to be claimed at the ferry.

### Places to Eat
Effusive **Mama's Cyclades** up the top end of town past the youth hostel offers a hearty breakfast. On the square, **Lucky's Souvlakis** cares for the budget conscious. You'll find excellent-value meals at **Naoussa** on Erythrou Stavrou, which is not far from the cable-car station, and **Stani Taverna**, next to the Koo Club. **Koukoumavlos**, below the Orthodox cathedral, wins the fine-dining prize.

One must sunset-sip at bars overlooking the caldera; hang the expense!

### Entertainment
Bars and clubs are clustered along one street, Erythrou Stavrou. From the main square, facing north, turn left at George's Snack Corner, then take the first right.

**Koo Club**, **Enigma** and **Murphys** are all big. The dimly lit **Kira Thira Jazz Bar** is a cosy alternative. The **Dubliner Irish Pub**, next to the youth hostel, rocks till late.

### Getting There & Away
There are regular flights to Athens (€78.40), Rhodes (€80.40), Mykonos (€57.40) and Iraklio (Crete; €59.40). Book through the travel agencies on the main square.

There are daily ferries to Piraeus (€23.90), daily connections in summer to Mykonos, Ios, Naxos, Paros and Iraklio, and three ferries per week to Anafi, Sikinos, Folegandros, Sifnos, Serifos, Kimolos and Milos.

### Getting Around
Large ferries use Athinios port, where they are met by buses (€1.20) and taxis. Small boats use Fira Skala port, where the mode of transport is by donkey or by cable car (€3); otherwise it's a clamber up 600 steps.

There are daily boats from Athinios and Fira Skala to Thirasia and Oia. The islets surrounding Santorini (Thira) can be visited only on excursion from Fira.

Buses go frequently to Oia, Kamari, Perissa, Akrotiri, Ancient Thira and Monolithos. Port buses usually leave Fira, Kamari and Perissa 90 minutes to an hour before ferry departures.

# Crete Κρήτη

Crete, Greece's largest island, hosts a quarter of all visitors to the country. All of Crete's major towns are on the northern coast and it's here that the package-tourism industry thrives. You can escape the hordes by visiting the undeveloped western coast or by heading into the villages. The mountainous interior offers rigorous trekking and climbing. Crete is also the best place in Greece to buy high-quality, inexpensive leather goods.

For more detailed information, see Lonely Planet's Crete.

### History
Crete was the birthplace of Minoan culture, Europe's first advanced civilisation, which flourished from 2800 to 1450 BC. Very little is known of Minoan civilisation, which came to an abrupt end, possibly destroyed by Santorini's volcanic eruption.

Later, Crete passed from the warlike Dorians to the Romans, and then to the Genoese, who in turn sold it to the Venetians. Under the Venetians, Crete became a refuge for artists, writers and philosophers who fled Constantinople after it fell to the Turks. Their influence inspired the young Cretan painter Domenikos Theotokopoulos, who moved to Spain and there won immortality as the great El Greco.

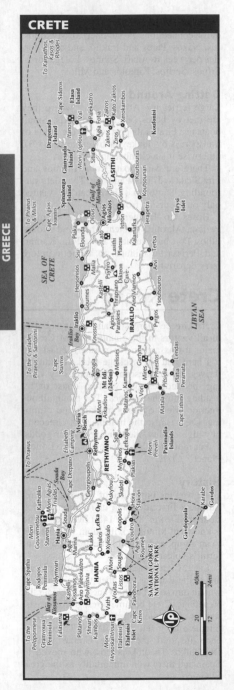

**CRETE**

The Turks finally conquered Crete in 1670. It became a British protectorate in 1898 after a series of insurrections and was united with independent Greece in 1913. There was fierce fighting during WWII when a German airborne invasion defeated Allied forces in the 10-day Battle of Crete. An active resistance movement drew heavy reprisals from the German occupiers.

## IRAKLIO Ηράκλειο
**☎ 281 • pop 127,600**

Iraklio, Crete's capital, is a noisy, polluted, unavoidable transport hub and it's the main connection to the Cyclades. Apart from the city's archaeological museum and proximity to Knossos, there's no reason to linger here.

### Information
There is no EOT tourist office but the **tourist police** (*☎ 281 028 3190; Dikeosynis 10; open 7am-10pm*) are helpful with maps and information.

Banks, travel agencies and Olympic Airways are on 25 Avgoustou. There's a central **post office** (*Plateia Daskalogiani*) and Internet access is available at **Cyber SportC@fe** (*25 Avgoustou*).

**Washsalon** (*Handakos 18*) laundrette also has luggage storage. A wash and dry will cost you €6.

### Archaeological Museum
Iraklio's archaeological museum (*adult/student €6/3; open 12.30pm-7pm Mon, 8am-7pm Tues-Sun*) has an outstanding collection, second only to the national museum in Athens.

### Places to Stay
Beware of taxi drivers who tell you that the pension of your choice is a dud; they're being paid commission by the big hotels.

**Rent Rooms Hellas** (*☎ 281 028 8851; Handakos 24; dorm beds €8; doubles/triples €27/34*) is the best budget choice and popular with backpackers. It's clean, with packed dorms, a rooftop bar and a bargain breakfast.

Near the old harbour and bus stations is a cluster of decent mid-range hotels.

**Hotel Lena** (*☎ 281 022 3280; Lahana 10; singles with bathroom €32, doubles without bathroom €33*) has large, dull rooms, while nearby **Ilaira Hotel** (*☎ 281 0227103; Epimenidou 1; singles/doubles €35/42*) has compact ones and nice views from the rooftop bar.

**Hotel Mirabello** (☎ *281 028 5052;* e *mirabhot@otenet.gr; Theotokopoulou 20; singles with shared bathroom €28, doubles with bathroom €46)* is clean and comfortable.

**Hotel Kastro** (☎ *281 028 4185;* e *info@kastro-hotel.gr; Theotokopoulou 22; singles/doubles with bathroom €55/75)* is remarkable value for its sleek, new, renovated interior. It won't be long before prices here take a hike.

### Places to Eat
There's a bustling, colourful **market** all the way along 1866 for self-caterers.

**Giakoumis Taverna** is the best of a bunch of cheap tavernas in the area around 1866.

**Ippokampos Ouzeri**, on the waterfront, offers a full range of well-priced *mezedes*.

**Pagopeion**, by Agios Titos church, is a super-cool café and bar with exceptional food at OK prices. (Check out the toilets!)

### Getting There & Away
It's easy to leave Iraklio. There are several flights a day to Athens and, in summer, daily

flights from Iraklio to Thessaloniki, and three flights a week to Rhodes and Santorini (Thira).

There are daily ferries to Piraeus (€24), as well as boats most days to Santorini (Thira) that continue on to other Cycladic islands. In summer, a boat sails twice weekly from Iraklio to Marmaris in Turkey, via Rhodes. For boat schedules, the **Skoutelis Travel Bureau** (☎ *281 028 0808, fax 281 033 2747; 25 Avgoustou 20)* seems friendly, or try some of the other agencies on this strip.

Iraklio has two bus stations. Bus Station Λ, just inland from the new harbour, serves eastern Crete (Agios Nikolaos, Ierapetra, Sitia, Malia and the Lasithi Plateau). The Hania and Rethymno terminal is opposite Bus Station A, across the street. Bus Station B, 50m beyond the Hania Gate, serves the southern route (Phaestos, Matala, Anogia). For more information, visit the **long-distance bus website** (w *www.ktel.org)*.

### Getting Around
In Iraklio, Bus No 1 travels to and from the airport (€0.60) every 15 minutes between 6am and 11pm. It stops at Plateia Eleftherias, across the road from the archaeological museum.

**GREECE**

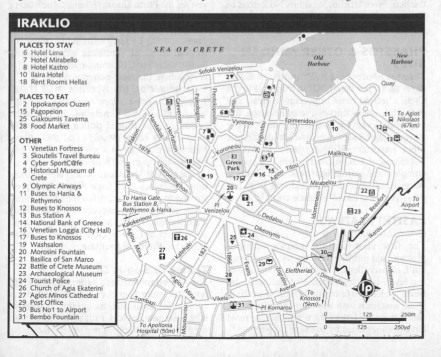

## IRAKLIO

**PLACES TO STAY**
6  Hotel Lena
7  Hotel Mirabello
8  Hotel Kastro
10  Ilaira Hotel
18  Rent Rooms Hellas

**PLACES TO EAT**
2  Ippokampos Ouzeri
15  Pagopeion
25  Giakoumis Taverna
28  Food Market

**OTHER**
1  Venetian Fortress
3  Skoutelis Travel Bureau
4  Cyber SportC@fe
5  Historical Museum of Crete
9  Olympic Airways
11  Buses to Hania & Rethymno
12  Buses to Knossos
13  Bus Station A
14  National Bank of Greece
16  Venetian Loggia (City Hall)
17  Buses to Knossos
19  Washsalon
20  Morosini Fountain
21  Basilica of San Marco
22  Battle of Crete Museum
23  Archaeological Museum
24  Tourist Police
26  Church of Agia Ekaterini
27  Agios Minos Cathedral
29  Post Office
30  Bus No1 to Airport
31  Bembo Fountain

SEA OF CRETE

Old Harbour

New Harbour

Quay

11  To Agios Nikolaos (67km)

To Airport

To Knossos (5km)

To Hania Gate, Bus Station B, Rethymno & Hania

To Apollonia Hospital (50m)

The car- and motorcycle-rental outlets are mostly along 25 Avgoustou.

## KNOSSOS Κνωσός

Five kilometres south of Iraklio, Knossos *(adult/concession €6/3; open noon-7pm Mon, 8am-7pm Tues-Sun Apr-Oct)*, is the most famous of Crete's Minoan sites and is the inspiration for the myth of the Minotaur. According to legend, King Minos of Knossos was given a bull to sacrifice to the god of Poseidon, but decided to keep it, as you would. This enraged Poseidon, who punished the king by causing his wife Pasiphae to fall in love with the animal. The result of this odd union was the Minotaur – half-man and half-bull – who lived in a labyrinth beneath the king's palace, munching on youths and maidens.

In 1900, the ruins of Knossos were uncovered by Arthur Evans. Although archaeologists tend to disparage Evans' reconstruction, the buildings – an immense palace, courtyards, private apartments, baths, lively frescoes and more – give a fine idea of what a Minoan palace might have looked like.

A whole day is needed to see the site and a guidebook is essential. Arrive early to avoid the jam. From Iraklio, local bus No 2 goes to Knossos (€0.80) every 10 minutes from Bus Station A; it also stops on 25 Avgoustou.

## PHAESTOS & OTHER MINOAN SITES

Phaestos *(Φαιστός; adult/concession €4/2; open 8am-7pm daily)*, 63km from Iraklio, is Crete's second-most important Minoan site and, while not as impressive as Knossos, it's still worth a visit for its stunning views of the surrounding Mesara plain and Mt Idi. Crete's other important Minoan sites are **Malia**, 34km east of Iraklio where there is a palace complex and adjoining town, and **Zakros**, 40km from Sitia, the smallest and least impressive of the island's palace complexes.

## LASITHI PLATEAU

Οροπέδιο Λασιθίου

The first view of this mountain-fringed plateau, laid out like an immense patchwork quilt, is marvellous. The plateau, 900m above sea level, is a vast expanse of orchards and fields, which was once dotted with some 1000 stone windmills with white canvas sails. Now, sadly, there are few of the originals left; most have been replaced by mechanical pumps.

The **Dikteon Cave** *(admission €4; open 8.30am-2.30pm Mon, 8am-7pm Tues-Sun)*, is where, according to mythology, the Titan Rhea hid the newborn Zeus from Cronos, his offspring-gobbling father.

The cave of stalagmites and stalactites is just outside the small village of Psyhro, which is the best place to stay. Try **Hotel Dias** *(☎ 2844 031 207; Agios Georgios; doubles with bathroom €16)*. On the main street, **Stavros** and **Platanos** tavernas serve decent food at OK prices.

There are daily buses to the area from Iraklio (€4.55, two hours) and three a week from Agios Nikolaos.

## RETHYMNO Ρέθυμνο
☎ 2831 • pop 24,000

Rethymno's gracious old quarter of crumbling Venetian and Turkish buildings radiates magic – and package tourists who crowd its long, sandy beachfront.

## Orientation & Information

Rethymno's bus station is at the western end of Igoumenou Gavriil. To reach the old quarter, follow Igoumenou east for 700m until you see the **Porto Guora** *(Ethnikis Andistasis)*, which is the remnant of a Venetian defensive wall and gate. Turn left and you're there. Those arriving by ferry will find the old quarter dead ahead. El Venizelou is the main strip by the waterfront. Running parallel behind it is Arkadiou, the main commercial street.

The **municipal tourist office** *(☎ 2831 029 148; open 8am-2.30pm Mon-Fri)* is on the beach side of El Venizelou, in the same building as the **tourist police** *(☎ 2831 028 156)*. **Ellotia Tours** *(☎ 2831 051 981; ⓔ elo tia@ret.forthnet.gr; Arkadiou 155)* will answer all transport and tour inquiries.

The **post office** *(Moatsou 21)* is in the new town, one block back from **Plateia Martyron** *(cnr Igoumenou Gavriil & Ethnikis Andistasis)*. There's 24-hour Internet access at **G@meNet-Café** opposite Plateia Martyron, or you could try upstairs at **Galero Café** *(Plateia Rimini)*, beside the **Rimondi fountain**.

## Things to See & Do

The **Venetian Fortress** *(admission €2.90; open 9am-6pm Tues-Sun)* affords great views across the town and mountains. Opposite is the **archaeological museum** *(admission €1.50; open 8.30am-3pm Tues-Sun)*.

The **historical and folk art museum** (*Vernardou; admission €3; open 9.30am-2.30pm & 6pm-9pm Mon-Sat)* proudly displays Cretan crafts.

**Happy Walker** (*☎/fax 2831 052 920; e hapwalk@hol.gr; w www.happywalker.nl; Tombazi 56)* is worth a visit for its programme of daily walks in the countryside (from €25 per person).

## Places to Stay
**Elisabeth Camping** (*☎ 2831 028 694; camping per person/tent €6.30/4.20)* is situated on Mysiria Beach, 4km east of town, and it is accessible by the bus that goes to and from Iraklio. From Hania, take the bus that services the beach hotels.

**Youth hostel** (*☎ 2831 022 848; e reservations@yhrethymno.com; Tombazi 45; dorm & roof beds €6)* is a well-run place with crowded dorms.

**Olga's Pension** (*☎ 2831 028 665; Souliou 57; singles/doubles/triples with bathroom €30/35/45)* is central with colourful, cosy rooms of intriguing taste and a wild rooftop garden.

**Garden House** (*☎ 2831 028 586; Nikiforou Foka 82; doubles/triples €35/50)* is a romantic, old, Venetian place which has average rooms but excellent ambience.

**Rent Rooms Sea Front** (*☎ 2831 051 981, fax 2831 051 062; e elotia@ret.forthnet.gr; Arkadiou 159; singles/doubles €24/35)* is ideally positioned with beach views and spacious rooms.

## Places to Eat
**Taverna Kyria Maria** (*Diog Mesologiou 20)* is tucked behind the Rimondi fountain under a lush canopy.

**Gounakis Restaurant & Bar** (*Koroneou 6)* has live Cretan music and reasonably priced food.

East of the Rimondi fountain, Arabatzoglou and Radamanthios have upmarket eateries of bewitching ambience. Check out the intimate **Avli**, cave-like **Castelo Taverna** and **Taverna Larenzo**.

## Getting There & Away
Ferries travel daily from Piraeus to Rethymno (€24). For schedules and other details, visit **ANEK** (*Arkadiou 250)* by the old Venetian harbour or Ellotia Tours (see Orientation & Information, earlier).

Buses depart regularly to Iraklio (€5.90, 1½ hours), Hania (€5.30, one hour), Agia Galini, Moni Arkadiou and Plakas.

## HANIA Χανιά
**☎ 2821 • pop 65,000**
Lovely Hania, the old capital of Crete, lures tourists in droves with its softly hued Venetian buildings and snug location near idyllic beaches and a glorious mountain interior.

## Orientation & Information
Hania is a place to amble wide-eyed for a couple of days, enjoying its vital signs and plotting side trips.

There is no EOT tourist office but you can try the **tourist police** (*2821 053 333; Kydonias 29; open 7.30am-2.30pm Mon-Fri)*, near Plateia 1866. Send your mail at the **central post office** (*Tzanakaki 3)*.

**Vranas Studios** (*Agion Deka)* has a comfortable Internet setup, or try **N@ftilos Internet Café** for cool ambience. It's next to the food market; walk up the steps off Mousouron.

**Laundry Express Fidias** (*Sarpaki)* is next to Pension Fidias; a wash and dry costs €6.

## Things to See & Do
The **archaeological museum** (*Halidon 30; admission €1.50; open 8.30am-3pm Tues-Sun)* used to be the Venetian Church of San Francesco, until the Turks made it into a mosque.

## Places to Stay
**Camping Hania** (*☎ 2821 031 138; camping per person/tent €5/3.50)* is 3km west of town on the beach. Jump on a Kalamaka bus from Plateia 1866.

**Pension Fidias** (*☎ 2821 052 494; Sarpaki 6; dorm beds/doubles/triples €8/15/21)*, behind the Orthodox Cathedral, is still the budget choice and renovations are planned.

**Vranas Studios** (*☎/fax 2821 058 618; Agion Deka; doubles €55-60, triples €70)* has superior, contemporary studios.

For rooms with character, wander through the ancient Venetian buildings around the old harbour. Friendly **Casa Dell Amore** (*☎ 2821 086 206; Theotokopoulou 52; doubles €45-50)* has cute, loft-style rooms of quirky design.

**Ifigenia II** (*☎ 2821 094 357, fax 2821 036 104; Angelou 18; doubles €35-40)* has a range of excitingly eccentric rooms, some with four-poster beds.

**Rooms for Rent George** (☎ 2821 088 715; Zambeliou 30; singles/doubles/triples €15/24/33) is an atmospheric relic.

## Places to Eat
The **food market** off Plateia Markopoulou is self-caterers' paradise.

**To Ayho Toy Kokkopa** (Agion Deka), beneath Vranas Studios, does crisp salads and sandwiches.

For alfresco dining, try romantic **Tsikoydadiko** in an ancient Venetian courtyard, or the preserved ruins at classy **Tholos Restaurant**; both serve local cuisine at reasonable prices.

**Suki Yaki** and **Chin Chin** offer a refreshing change with Thai and Chinese meals, respectively.

## Entertainment
Many restaurants play live Cretan music but **Café Kriti** is the authentic experience.

Harbour tavernas are packed at sunset. After dark, **Neorio Café**, **Bora Bora** and **Cocktails Galini** attract a younger crowd. For shots and dancing on the bar, it's **Nota-Bene**.

## Getting There & Away
If you must leave Hania, there are several flights a day to Athens and two flights a week to Thessaloniki.

There are daily ferries to Piraeus (€22) from the port of Souda, 10km east of town. The travel agencies on Halidon can help with all schedules and ticketing.

Frequent buses plough daily to Iraklio, Rethymno and Kastelli–Kissamos; buses run

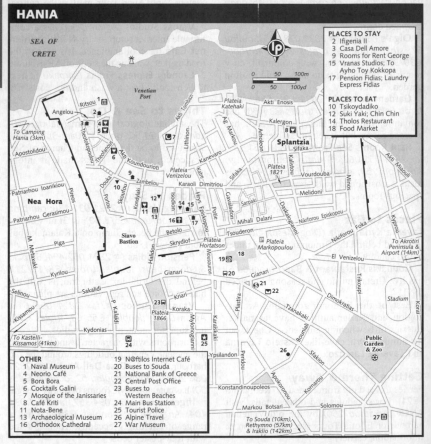

**HANIA**

PLACES TO STAY
2 Ifigenia II
3 Casa Dell Amore
9 Rooms for Rent George
15 Vranas Studios; To Ayho Toy Kokkopa
17 Pension Fidias; Laundry Express Fidias

PLACES TO EAT
10 Tsikoydadiko
12 Suki Yaki; Chin Chin
14 Tholos Restaurant
18 Food Market

OTHER
1 Naval Museum
4 Neorio Café
5 Bora Bora
6 Cocktails Galini
7 Mosque of the Janissaries
8 Café Kriti
11 Nota-Bene
13 Archaeological Museum
16 Orthodox Cathedral
19 N@ftilos Internet Café
20 Buses to Souda
21 National Bank of Greece
22 Central Post Office
23 Buses to Western Beaches
24 Main Bus Station
25 Tourist Police
26 Alpine Travel
27 War Museum

less-frequently to Paleohora, Omalos, Hora Sfakion and Elafonisi from the main bus station on Kydonias.

Buses for Souda (the port) leave frequently from outside the food market. Buses for the beaches west of Hania leave from the south-eastern corner of Plateia 1866.

## THE WEST COAST

This is Crete's least-developed coastline. At Falasarna, 16km west of Kastelli–Kissamos, there's a magnificent sandy beach and a few tavernas and *domatia*. There are buses to Falasarna in summer from Kastelli–Kissamos and Hania.

Further south, you can wade out to more beaches from the shallow waters surrounding superb Elafonisi islet. Travel agencies in Hania and Paleohora run excursions to the area.

## SAMARIA GORGE

Φαράγγι της Σαμαριάς

Samaria Gorge *(☎ 2825 067 179; admission €3.50; open 6am-3pm daily May–mid-Oct)* is one of Europe's most spectacular gorges. Rugged footwear, food, water and sun protection are essential for this strenuous six-hour trek, which is not recommended for inexperienced walkers. You can do the walk independently by taking the Omalos bus from the main bus station in Hania (€5, one hour, three daily) to the head of the gorge at Xyloskalo and walking the length of the gorge (16km) to Agia Roumeli, from where you take a boat to Hora Sfakion (€4.40, two daily) and then a bus back to Hania (€5.10; two hours; four daily). Too much? You could join one of the easier daily excursions from Hania that walk about 4km into the gorge. Check out the travel agencies on Halidon in Hania for information.

## LEFKA ORI Λευκά Όρη

Crete's rugged 'White Mountains' are south of Hania. **Alpine Travel** *(☎ 2821 050 939, fax 2821 053 309; e info@alpine.gr; Shopping Centre, Bldg C, 2nd floor, Bouniali 11-19)*, in Hania, offers excellent one- to 15-day trekking programmes from €58 per person, as well as trail advice.

**Trekking Plan** *(☎/fax 2821 060 861; e sales@cycling.gr, w www.cycling.gr)*, based in Agia Marina 8km west of Hania next to Santa Marina Hotel, has mountain biking, trekking and mountaineering tours.

## PALEOHORA & THE SOUTHWEST COAST

☎ 2823

Paleohora (Παλαιοχώρα), discovered by hippies back in the 1960s, is a relaxing, if overrated resort favoured by backpackers. There's a welcoming **tourist office** *(☎ 2823 041 507)* three blocks south of the bus stop. Some tour companies offer dolphin watching.

Further east, along Crete's southwest coast, are the resorts of Sougia, Loutro (the least developed) and Hora Sfakion.

**Camping Paleohora** *(☎ 2823 041 120; camping per person/tent €4/3)* is 1.5km northeast of town, near the pebble beach. There's also a restaurant and nightclub here.

**Homestay Anonymous** *(☎ 2823 042 098; singles/doubles/triples €12/17/20)*, in Paleohora, is a great place for backpackers with its warm service and communal kitchen.

**Oriental Bay Rooms** *(☎ 2823 041 076; doubles/triples with bathroom €36/39)* is comfy; it's at the north end of the pebble beach.

*Domatia* and tavernas dot the harbourfront. Readers recommend **Calypso** near the pebble beach. Near the sandy beach, try **The Third Eye** for vegetarian, or **The Small Garden** for international fare.

There are at least five buses daily between Hania and Paleohora (€5, 1¼ hours). No road links the coastal resorts but if you can't swim (kidding) daily boats from Paleohora to Elafonisi, Agia Roumeli and Hora Sfakion connect the resorts in summer.

Coastal paths lead from Paleohora to Sougia and from Agia Roumeli to Loutro. Both walks take a hefty six to seven hours.

## SITIA Σητεία

☎ 2843 • pop 9000

Back on the northeastern coast, package tourism gathers momentum as it advances eastwards, reaching a crescendo in Agios Nikolaos. Attractive Sitia, on a hotel-lined bay flanked by mountains, is an easy place to unwind and has good connections to the Dodecanese islands.

The main square, Plateia El Venizelou, is at the northern end of Karamanli.

The **municipal tourist office** *(open 9am-2.30pm & 5.30pm-8.30pm Mon-Fri)* is on the waterfront just before the town beach. **Tzortzakis Travel Agency** *(☎ 2843 025 080; e tzortzakis@sit.forthnet.gr; Kornarou 150)* is good for tickets and accommodation advice.

The **post office** (*Dimokratou*) is just off El Venizelou.

The ferry port is about 800m away, signposted from the square.

There is no shortage of *domatia* behind the waterfront but if you're desperate, the shabby **youth hostel** (☎ 2843 028 062; dorms €6) is 400m from the square on the road to Iraklio.

**Hotel Arhontiko** (☎ 2843 028 172; Kondylaki 16; doubles/triples €23/27.60) is a basic hotel, but it's immaculate. To find it, walk towards the ferry quay along El Venizelou, turn left up Filellinon and then right onto Kondylaki.

**Hotel Apollon** (☎ 2843 028 155, fax 2843 026 598; Kapetan Sifis 28; singles/doubles/triples €27.70/30.80/37) is in a central position, 150m up Kapetan Sifis from the harbourfront, on your right.

Just inland, **Kali Kardia** (*Foundalidhou 22*) and the harbourside **O Mixos** (*Kornarou 15*) are popular tavernas with the locals. At the port end of Kornarou, you'll find **Murphy's Irish Pub**.

At the time of writing, Sitia's domestic airport was closed for a runway extension. It normally receives one to two flights per week from Athens. There are daily ferries from Piraeus to Sitia (€24), three ferries per week to Rhodes and four to Karpathos. In summer, there's one ferry per week to Santorini (Thira). Visit Tzortzakis Travel Agency for tickets and schedules.

There are five buses daily to Ierapetra, and five to Iraklio, via Agios Nikolaos. In peak season, there are four buses daily to Vaï Beach.

## AROUND SITIA

The reconstructed **Moni Toplou** (*admission €2.50; open 9am-1pm & 2pm-6pm daily*), 15km from Sitia, houses some beautifully intricate icons and relics. To get there, take a Vaï bus from Sitia, get off at the fork for the monastery and plod the last 4km.

**Vaï Beach**, famous for its palm trees, is 26km from Sitia and worth the trip.

# Dodecanese
## Δωδεκάνησα

The Dodecanese are more verdant and mountainous than the Cyclades and have comparable beaches. Here, you get a sense of Greece's proximity to Asia. Ancient temples, massive crusader fortifications, mosques and imposing Italian-built neoclassical buildings stand juxtaposed, vestiges of a turbulent past.

There are 16 inhabited islands in the group; the most visited are Rhodes, Kos, Patmos and Symi.

## RHODES Ρόδος

According to mythology, the sun god Helios chose Rhodes as his bride and bestowed light, warmth and vegetation upon her. The blessing seems to have paid off, for Rhodes produces more flowers and sunny days than most Greek Islands.

The ancient sites of Lindos and Kamiros are legacies of Rhodes' importance in antiquity. In 1291, the Knights of St John, having fled Jerusalem under siege, came to Rhodes and established themselves as masters. In 1522, Süleyman I, sultan of the Ottoman Empire, staged a massive attack on the island and took Rhodes City. The island, along with the other Dodecanese islands, then became part of the Ottoman Empire.

In 1912 it was the Italians' turn and in 1944 the Germans took over. The following year Rhodes was liberated by British and Greek commandos. In 1948 the Dodecanese became part of Greece. These days, tourists rule.

### Rhodes City
☎ 2241 • pop 43,500

Rhodes' capital and port is Rhodes City, on the northern tip of the island. Almost everything of interest lies in the old town, enclosed within massive walls. The main thoroughfares are Sokratous, Pythagora, Agiou Fanouriou and Ipodamou, with a clump of spaghetti streets in between. The new town to the north is a monument to package tourism.

The main port, Commercial Harbour, is east of the old town, and north of here is Mandraki Harbour, the supposed site of the Colossus of Rhodes, a giant bronze statue of Apollo (built in 292–280 BC) – one of the Seven Wonders of the World. The statue stood for a mere 65 years before being toppled by an earthquake.

**Orientation & Information** The EOT tourist office (☎ 2241 023 255; e eot-rodos@otenet.gr; cnr Makariou & Papagou; open 8.30am-2.30pm Mon-Fri) is next door to the tourist police (☎ 2241 027 423; open 7.30am-9pm daily). In summer there is also a **municipal tourist office** (☎ 2241 035 945; Plateia Rimini; open 8am-9pm daily).

For ticketing and tour information, see **Triton Holidays** (☎ 2241 021 690; e info@tritondmc.gr; 1st floor, Plastira 9) in the new town. To get there turn left after the **National Bank of Greece** (Mandraki Harbour). In the old town, try **Castellania Travel** (☎ 2241 075 860; e castell@otenet.gr) which faces the clock tower in front of the Castellania Fountain. It's tucked in the right-hand back corner of the square.

Send mail at the **main post office** (Mandraki Harbour). There is a tiny Internet café in the old town, **Cosmonet** (Plateia Martyron Evreon), on the west corner of the square, or in the new town, **Minoan Internet Café** (Iroön Politehniou 13) has 20 computers.

**Things to See & Do** The old town is reputedly the world's finest surviving example of medieval fortification. The 12m-thick walls are closed to the public but you can take a **guided walk** (€6; 2.45pm Tues & Sat) along them starting in the courtyard of the Palace of the Knights.

**Odos Ippoton** (Avenue of the Knights) is lined with magnificent medieval buildings, the most imposing of which is the **Palace of the Knights** (Ippoton; admission €6; open 12.30pm-7pm Mon, 8am-7pm Tues-Sun), restored, but never used, as a holiday home for Mussolini.

The 15th-century Knight's Hospital now houses the **archaeological museum** (Plateia Mousiou; admission €4; open 8.30am-7pm Tues-Sun). It's a splendid building, restored

GREECE

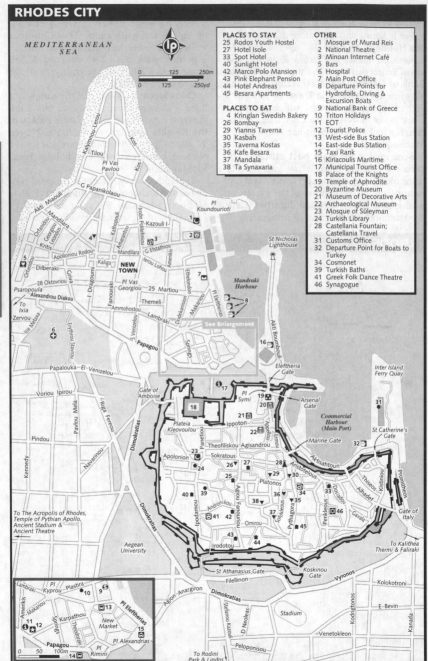

# RHODES CITY

**PLACES TO STAY**
25 Rodos Youth Hostel
27 Hotel Isole
33 Spot Hotel
40 Sunlight Hotel
42 Marco Polo Mansion
43 Pink Elephant Pension
44 Hotel Andreas
45 Besara Apartments

**PLACES TO EAT**
4 Kringlan Swedish Bakery
26 Bombay
29 Yiannis Taverna
30 Kasbah
35 Taverna Kostas
36 Kafe Besara
37 Mandala
38 Ta Synaxaria

**OTHER**
1 Mosque of Murad Reis
2 National Theatre
3 Minoan Internet Café
5 Bars
6 Hospital
7 Main Post Office
8 Departure Points for Hydrofoils, Diving & Excursion Boats
9 National Bank of Greece
10 Triton Holidays
11 EOT
12 Tourist Police
13 West-side Bus Station
14 East-side Bus Station
15 Taxi Rank
16 Kiriacoulis Maritime
17 Municipal Tourist Office
18 Palace of the Knights
19 Temple of Aphrodite
20 Byzantine Museum
21 Museum of Decorative Arts
22 Archaeological Museum
23 Mosque of Süleyman
24 Turkish Library
28 Castellania Fountain; Castellania Travel
31 Customs Office
32 Departure Point for Boats to Turkey
34 Cosmonet
39 Turkish Baths
41 Greek Folk Dance Theatre
46 Synagogue

by the Italians, with an impressive collection that includes the ethereal marble statue, the *Aphrodite of Rhodes*.

The 18th-century **Turkish Baths** *(Plateia Arionos; admission €1.50; open 11am-6pm Wed-Fri, 8am-6pm Sat)* – signposted from Ipodamou – offers a rare opportunity to bathe Turkish-style in Greece. Bring your own soap and towel.

**Places to Stay** The EOT can help with accommodation in the new town, but get there early; they're frantic in summer.

**Rodos Youth Hostel** *(☎ 2241 030 491; Ergiou 12; roof/dorm beds €6/8, doubles with/without bathroom €22/18)*, off Agio Fanouriou in the old town, has a lovely garden but lumpy mattresses. Ask about the new studios out the back.

**Sunlight Hotel** *(☎/fax 2241 021 435; Ipodamou 32; doubles/triples with bathroom €40/45)* is above sociable Stavros Bar; rooms have a fridge.

**Hotel Andreas** *(☎ 2241 034 156; e an dreasch@otenet.gr; Omirou 28D; rooms €33-59)* has small, pleasant rooms with varied facilities and terrific views from its terrace.

You'll find fresh, basic rooms at **Pink Elephant Pension** *(☎/fax 2241 022 469; e pinkelephantpension@yahoo.com; Timaxida; doubles €32-53)*, signposted off Irodotou, and **Spot Hotel** *(☎ 2241 034 737; e spothot@otenet.gr; Perikleous 12; singles/doubles/triples with bathroom €35/44/68)*.

**Hotel Isole** *(☎ 2241 020 682; e hotel isole@hotmail.com; Evdoxou 75; doubles with bathroom €47-73)* has cheerful rooms off a central lounge area and some remarkable views (check the attic!).

**Besara Apartments** *(☎/fax 2241 031 012; Sofokleous 11; 2-person/4-person apartments €25/35)* has large, self-contained apartments set around a lovely courtyard.

**Marco Polo Mansion** *(☎/fax 2241 025 562; e marcopolomansion@hotmail.com; Agiou Fanouriou 40-42; rooms €60-140)* is just the place to indulge yourself in one of its exotic theme rooms (featured in glossy magazines). Breakfast is included and there's a sophisticated café and courtyard downstairs.

**Places to Eat** Away from the venues with tacky photo menus, you'll find some good eateries.

You could check out **Kringlan Swedish Bakery** *(I Dragoumi 14)* in the new town for exceptional sandwiches and light snacks.

**Taverna Kostas** *(Pythagora 62)*, **Yiannis Taverna** *(Platanos)* and **Ta Synaxaria** *(Aristofanous)* are authentic Greek places with family service.

If you're tired of Greek food, there are some excellent options.

**Kasbah** *(Platanos 4)* serves some huge Moroccan-influenced meals in a refined atmosphere.

**Mandala** *(Sofokleous)* is very relaxed, with a healthy choice of stir-fries and pasta.

**Bombay** *(Agiou Fanouriou)* serves a tasty, rather than authentic version of Indian in enticing surrounds.

**Entertainment** The **Greek Folk Dance Theatre** *(☎ 2241 029 085; Andronikou; adult/concession €12/8; performances from 9.20pm Mon, Wed & Fri)* gives a first-rate show. Go Zorba!

The old town has some classy, less-chaotic bars for a cruisy night out, as well as leafy squares with live Greek music. In the new town, the drink-till-you-drop crowd goes bar hopping on Orfanidou in the city's northwest where there's a bar for every nationality.

## Around the Island

The **Acropolis of Lindos** *(admission €6, open 12.30pm-7pm Mon, 8am-7pm Tues-Sun)*, 47km from Rhodes City, is Rhodes' most important ancient city and is spectacularly perched atop a 116m-high rocky outcrop. Below the site is Lindos town, a tangle of streets with elaborately decorated 17th-century houses. It's beautiful but tainted by tourism. The bus to Lindos (€3.20) departs from Rhodes City's east-side station.

The extensive ruins of **Kamiros** *(admission €3; open 8.30am-7pm Tues-Sun)*, an ancient Doric city on the west coast, are well preserved, with the remains of houses, baths, a cemetery and a temple, but the site should be visited as much for its lovely setting on a gentle hillside overlooking the sea.

Between Rhodes City and Lindos the **beaches** are choked. If you prefer space, venture south to the bay of Lardos. Even further south, between Genardi and Plimmyri, you'll find good stretches of deserted sandy beach. Forget the southwestern coast; beaches tend to be pebbly and the sea choppy.

GREECE

## Getting There & Away

There are daily flights from Rhodes to Athens (€110) and Karpathos (€29). In summer there are regular flights to Iraklio, Mykonos, Santorini (Thira) and Kastellorizo. Contact Triton Holidays or Castellania Travel (see Orientation & Information under Rhodes City, earlier).

There are daily ferries from Rhodes to Piraeus (€29). Most sail via the Dodecanese north of Rhodes, but at least three times a week there is a service via Karpathos, Crete and the Cyclades. The EOT gives out a schedule. Kiriacoulis Maritime holds the hydrofoil schedules.

Excursion boats (€18 return) and hydrofoils (€12, one way) trip daily to Symi. Ferries travel less often (€8, one way). Similar services also run to Kos, Kalymnos, Nisyros, Tilos, Patmos and Leros.

Between April and October, there are regular boats from Rhodes to Marmaris in Turkey (€36, one way). There is an additional US$15 Turkish port tax each way.

From April to August, there are regular ferries to Israel (€100) via Cyprus (€71). Prices do not include foreign port tax. For information, contact Triton Holidays, Castellania Travel, or other travel agencies in the New Market area.

## Getting Around

There are frequent buses between the airport and Rhodes City's west-side bus station (€2). Or you could catch a taxi for about €13.

Rhodes City has two bus stations. The **west-side bus station**, next to the New Market, serves the airport, the west coast, Embona and Koskinou; the **east-side bus station** (*Plateia Rimini*) serves the east coast and the inland southern villages. The EOT has a schedule.

Car- and motorcycle-rental outlets compete for business in Rhodes City's new town on and around 28 Oktovriou – so try to bargain.

Cars are forbidden in most of the old town but there are small car parks around the periphery.

## KARPATHOS Κάρπαθος
☎ 2245 • pop 5323

Soothing Karpathos lies midway between Crete and Rhodes. It's a scenic, hype-free place with a cosy port.

The main port and capital of Karpathos is Pigadia.

Two main thoroughfares run parallel to the waterfront, Apodimon Karpathion and 28 Oktovriou. The bus stop is on the corner of Dimokratias and 28 Oktovriou. A booth on the harbourfront serves as municipal tourist office. There's no tourist police. **Possi Holidays** (*☎ 2245 022 627, fax 2245 022 252; Apodimon Karpathion*) can suggest local tours and handles travel arrangements. The Pavilion Hotel (see its entry, later in this section) has Internet access.

Karpathos has lovely **beaches**, particularly **Apella**, **Kyra Panagia**, **Lefkos** on the west coast and **Ammoöpi**, 8km south of Pigadia.

The northern village of **Olymbos** was isolated until 1980 when the first road and electricity arrived! Locals wear traditional outfits and the facades of houses are decorated with bright plaster reliefs.

Accommodation owners usually meet the boats.

**Christina's Rooms** (*☎ 2245 022 045; 28 Oktaviriou; doubles/triples with bathroom €27/30*), 20m from the bus stop, has large rooms and free Sunday dinners.

Ask for the 'traditional' room at **Elias Rooms** (*☎ 2245 022 446; e eliasrooms@hotmail.com; doubles/triples €303*).

**Pavilion Hotel** (*☎ 2245 022 059; e pavilion@inkarpathos.com; double studios €56.50*) has well-appointed studios; walk east on Apodimon Karpathion and turn left up Georgio Louziou to get there.

Head for **Taverna Karpathos** near the quay for fresh seafood or **Annemoussa** for decent Italian. There are also two nightclubs and a groovy lounge bar here.

Karpathos has two daily flights to Rhodes (€29) and three a week to Athens (€92.30).

There are three ferries a week to Rhodes (€14.50) and four to Piraeus (€26.30), via the Cyclades and Crete.

There are daily excursion boats from Pigadia to Apella and Kyra Panagia Beaches and the small port of Diafani; a free bus goes to Olymbos from Diafani. Local buses drop you at Lefkos and Ammoöpi Beaches.

## SYMI Σύμη
☎ 2246 • pop 2332

Symi town is extremely attractive, with pastel-coloured neoclassical mansions surrounding the harbour and hills. The island is swamped by day-trippers from Rhodes; it's worth staying over to enjoy Symi in cruise control.

The town is divided into Gialos, the harbour, and the tranquil horio above it, accessible by taxi, bus, or 360 steps from the harbour.

There is no tourist office or tourist police. The best source of information is the free and widely available English-language *Symi Visitor*, which includes maps of the town.

There is a tiny Internet café at Roloi Bar, in the street behind Vapori Bar.

Excursion boats to other parts of the island also run guided walks. **Kalodoukas Holidays** (☎ 2246 071 077; e information@ kalodoukas.gr) has a book of trails that you can do independently. An excellent website is w www.symivisitor.com.

Budget accommodation is scarce but digs in the village are cheaper; ask at Kalodoukas Holidays.

**Catherinettes Rooms & Studios** (☎/fax 2246 072 698; e marina-epe@rho.forth net.gr; doubles €54) in Gialos has airy rooms with ornate ceilings; prices include breakfast.

Located in the two streets opposite the excursion boats, **Hotel Albatros** (☎ 2246 071 829, fax 2246 072 257; e fabienne@ otenet.gr; doubles €50) and **Hotel Kokona** (☎ 2246 071 549, fax 2246 072 620; doubles €50) both have spotless, bright doubles.

From the ferry dock, the bulk of restaurants are to the left, past the central square. **Meraklis** is a cheap and cheery taverna. **Sunflower** offers excellent sandwiches and savoury vegetarian. **Tholos**, a five-minute walk past the clock tower, is a shaded, harbourside taverna with imaginative pickings.

Up in the Horio, **Kali Strata Bar** (Kali Strata) provides perfect sunset moments. A few steps up, **To Klima** creates Greek with a twist, while **Giorgio's Taverna** offers classics.

There are frequent ferries and hydrofoils between Rhodes and Kos that also call at Symi, as well as less-frequent services to Tilos, Nisyros, Kalymno, Leros and Patmos.

The bus and taxi stop is at the east end of the harbour, past the restaurants.

For tickets and tour information, see Kalodoukas Holidays in Gialos, or the horio. There's an ANEK booth opposite the quay.

## KOS Κως
☎ 2242 • pop 26,379

Kos is the birthplace of Hippocrates, the father of medicine, but that's as Greek as this place

gets. With its ruins and Turkish buildings on a backdrop of pretty palm-lined streets, neon cafés, pulsing clubs and tourist trains, Kos town exudes an aura of mini Las Vegas. It's well located for day trips to several islands and Turkey.

### Orientation & Information
Kos town, on the northeast coast, is the main town and port. The **municipal tourist office** (☎ 2242 024 460; e dotkos@hol.gr; open 8am-8.30pm Mon-Fri, 8am-3pm Sat), on the waterfront just past the police station, provides maps and accommodation information. The post office is on Vasileos Pavlou. The **tourist police** (☎ 2242 022 444) and regular police are housed together, just opposite the quay.

To get to the **bus station** (Kleopatras) walk 350m up Vasileos Pavlou from the harbourfront and turn right.

**Café Del Mare** (Megalou Alexandrou 4) is the best-equipped Internet café.

### Things to See & Do
The focus of the **archaeological museum** (Plateia Eleftherias; admission €3; open 8am-2.30pm Tues-Sun) is sculpture from excavations around the island. The **ancient agora**, with the ruins of the **Shrine of Aphrodite** and **Temple of Hercules**, is just off Plateia Eleftherias. It's free but has zero data.

On a pine-clad hill, 4km from Kos town, stand the extensive ruins of the renowned healing centre of **Asklipion** (admission €4; open 8.30am-6pm Tues-Sun), where Hippocrates practised medicine.

Further south is **Kefalos Bay** a long stretch of beach swamped in sun lounges and rippling with water sports.

### Places to Stay & Eat
**Kos Camping** (☎ 2242 023 910; camping per adult/tent €6/3.50) is 3km along the eastern waterfront, with good shade and a minimart. Hop on any of the buses from the harbourfront going to Agios Fokas.

**Pension Alexis** (☎ 2242 028 798, fax 2242 025 797; Irodotou 9; doubles/triples with shared bathroom €26/32) is a convivial place. It's noisy here, but Alexis is an admirable host. To find it, turn right from the port and walk about 300m to the port police, turn left and then take the first right.

**Hotel Afendoulis** (☎ *2242 025 321; Evripilou 1; doubles/triples with bathroom €36/ 45)* is a superior hotel with well-kept rooms in a quieter area. Turn left from the ferry, walk about 500m to Evripilou and turn right.

**Hotel Kamelia** (☎ *2242 028 983;* e *kam elia.hotel@hotmail.com; Artemisias 3; singles/ doubles/triples with bathroom €26.50/ 44/ 53)* has neat rooms with TV and garden views, and breakfast is included. To get there, turn left from the ferry, past the police, turn right up Korai, then left onto Artemisias.

Among the glut of uninspired tourist tavernas, **Filoxenia Taverna** *(cnr Pindou & Alikarnassou)* and **Barba's Grill**, opposite Hotel Afendoulis, are happy exceptions. Classy **Platanos**, by the Hippocrates tree, is top notch and top dollar.

## Entertainment
There are a dozen discos and clubs catering to the different music moods of the crowd around the streets of Diakon and Nafklirou. Head for **Kalua**, 400m past the ferry quay, for foam parties and dance mania.

## Getting There & Away
There are daily flights to Athens (€80.40) from Kos' international airport.

There are frequent ferries from Rhodes that continue on to Piraeus (€29.75), via Kalymnos, Leros and Patmos, and less-frequent connections to Nisyros, Tilos, Symi, Samos and Crete. Daily excursion boats visit Nisyros, Kalymnos, Patmos and Rhodes.

In summer, ferries depart daily for Bodrum in Turkey (€15 one way, €25 return). Port tax costs €10.

For tickets and scheduling information, visit the efficient **Exas Travel** (☎ *2242 029 900;* e *exas@exas.com; Antinavarhou Ioannini).*

## Getting Around
Next to the tourist office is a blue mini-train that leaves hourly for Asklipion (€3) and a mini-green train that does city tours (€2).

Buses for Agios Fokas leave from opposite the town hall on the harbourfront; all other buses (including those to Kefalos Bay) leave from the bus station on Kleopatras.

## PATMOS Πάτμος
☎ 2247 • pop 2663
Starkly scenic Patmos gets crowded duing summer but somehow remains remarkably tranquil. Orthodox and Western Christians have long made pilgrimages to this holy island for its World Heritage–listed sites. It entices the visitor to linger.

## Orientation & Information
The **tourist office** *(open 8am-1pm & 4pm-6pm Mon-Fri)*, post office and police station are in the white building at the island's port and capital of Skala. Buses leave regularly for the hora, 4.5km inland. **Blue Bay Hotel**, 200m left from the port (facing inland), has limited Internet access.

## Things to See & Do
The **Cave of the Apocalypse** *(admission free; open 8am-1.30pm Mon-Sat, 8am-1.30 pm Sun, 4pm-6pm Tues, Thur & Sun)* where St John wrote the divinely inspired *Book of Revelations*, is halfway between the port and hora. Take a bus or make the pilgrimage via the **Byzantine path**. To do this, walk up the Skala-Hora road and take the steps to the right 100m beyond the far side of the football field. The path begins opposite the top of the steps.

The **Monastery of St John the Theologian** *(admission monastery/treasury free/€5)*, which is open the same hours as the cave, exhibits monastic treasures: early manuscripts, embroidered robes, incredible carvings and an El Greco painting. Dress modestly (ie, no shorts) for the holy sites.

Patmos' coastline provides secluded coves, mostly with pebble beaches. The best is **Psili Ammos**, in the south, reached by excursion boat from Skala port.

## Places to Stay & Eat
**Stefanos Camping** (☎ *2247 031 821)* is on Meloi Beach, 2km northeast of Skala.

Try **Travel Point Holidays** (☎ *2247 032 801;* e *info@travelpoint.gr;* w *www.travel point.gr)*, an accommodation-finding service on the road to the hora, for budget pensions such as **Pension Maria Paskeledi** (☎ *2247 032 152, fax 2247 033 346; doubles/triples with bathroom €32/45)*.

**Hotel Delfini** (☎ *2247 032 060, fax 2247 032 061; doubles/triples €52/68)*, to the left of the port, has gentle views and rooms include breakfast.

There is a cluster of mid-range hotels about 700m to the right of the port, including one called **Hotel Australis** (☎ *2247 031 576,* *fax 2247 032 284; doubles/triples with bathroom €56/66),* with a prolific garden.

**Grigoris Taverna**, which is opposite the port's passenger-transit gate, is popular, or enjoy refined ambience and tangy Indonesian at **GiaGia**, next to Hotel Delfini. Further along, **Café Aman** offers excellent salads and pastas in a breezy setting.

### Getting There & Away
Frequent ferries travel between Patmos and Piraeus (€20.40), and to Rhodes (€17) via Leros, Kalymnos and Kos. Visit **GA Ferries**, inland from the central square, for schedules. In summer, there are daily Flying Dolphin hydrofoils to Leros, Kalymnos, Kos, Rhodes, Fourni, Ikaria, Agathonisi and Samos. See **Apollon Travel** on the waterfront, near the quay, for bookings.

# Northeastern Aegean Islands

There are seven major islands in this neglected group: Chios, Ikaria, Lesvos, Limnos, Samos, Samothraki and Thasos. The distance between them makes island hopping tricky but these neighbours reward exploration with wonderful hiking, crowd-free beaches and unique villages.

## SAMOS Σάμος
☎ 2273 • pop 32,000

Samos was an important centre of Hellenic culture and is reputedly the birthplace of the philosopher and mathematician Pythagoras. Lush and humid, its powerful mountains are skirted by forested hills.

### Orientation & Information
Samos has three ports: Vathy (Samos town), Karlovasi on the north coast and Pythagorio on the southeast coast.

Pretty Pythagorio, where you'll disembark if you've come from Patmos, is small and touristy. Its cordial **municipal tourist office** *(Lykourgou Logotheti)* is two blocks from the waterfront on the main street. Busy Vathy, 20 minutes away, is dreary but cheaper.

Vathy's useless EOT is in a side street one block north of the main square, Plateia Pythagorou. The competing travel agencies directly opposite the port help with travel, excursions, accommodation and luggage storage. Try **By Ship Travel** *(☎ 2273 025 065, fax 2273 028 570).*

**Diavlos NetCafé** *(Themistoklous Sofouli 160)* is on the waterfront, 250m from Plateia Pythagorou, next to the police station.

### Things to See & Do
Pythagorio's **Evpalinos Tunnel** *(adult/student €4/2, open 8.45am-2.45pm Tues-Sun),* built

GREECE

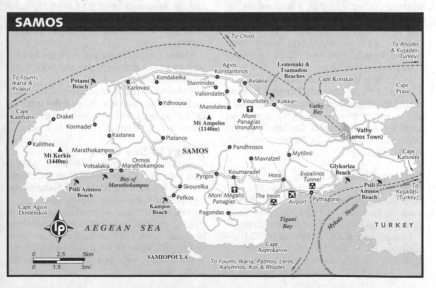

SAMOS

in the 6th century BC, is a 1km tunnel dug by political prisoners and used as an aqueduct to bring water from the springs of Mt Ampelos. Part of it can still be explored. It's 2km north of Pythagorio but there's no bus access.

Vathy's **archaeological museum** *(adult €3; open 8.30am-3pm Tues-Sun)*, by the municipal gardens, is first rate. The highlight is a 4.5m male kouros statue.

The captivating villages of **Vourliotes** and **Manolates** on the slopes of imposing Mt Ampelos, northwest of Vathy, provide excellent walking territory and there are many marked pathways.

Choice beaches, **Kampos** and **Psili Ammos**, are along the southwest coast in the Marathokampos area.

## Places to Stay & Eat

In Pythagorio, **Pension Sydney** *(☎ 2273 061 733; Pythagora; doubles with bathroom €30)* and **Pension Boulas** *(☎ 2273 061 277; Despoti Kyrillon; doubles with bathroom €29.50)*, both off Lykourgou Logotheti, offer simple, central rooms.

**Pythagoras Hotel** *(☎ 2273 028 601; e smicha@otenet.gr; doubles/triples/quads €26/33/36)* in Vathy is a friendly, great-value place with uplifting views. Facing inland, the hotel is 500m to the left of the quay. Call ahead for pick-up on arrival.

**Pension Vasso** *(☎/fax 2273 023 258; doubles/studios €35/75)*, where rooms include minikitchen, or **Hotel Samos** *(☎ 2273 028 377; e hotsamos@otenet.gr; singles/doubles €37/46.50)*, where room rates include breakfast, are two places to try for more modern facilities.

In Vathy, **La Casa** on the waterfront, 400m past the square, and **Taverna Petrino** behind Hotel Samos present tempting variety and attentive service. In Pythagorio, you could try Asian **Oriental Garden** *(Odyessa Orologa)*, or **Taverna Ta Platania** on leafy Plateia Irinis.

## Getting There & Away

There's a daily flight to Athens (€66.45) from the airport at Pythagorio, and three a week to Thessaloniki (€71.50). The travel agencies opposite the port handle tickets.

Ferries leave daily for Piraeus (€22.10) – most via Paros and Naxos, and some via Mykonos – and Ikaria, but only two a week visit Chios (€9.25). Daily hydrofoils ski to

Patmos (€11.68), carrying on to Leros, Kalymnos and Kos.

There are daily boats to Kuşadası (for Ephesus) in Turkey (€30, one way; plus port taxes for Greece €8.80 and Turkey €13).

## Getting Around

Pythagorio's **bus stop** *(Lykourgou Logotheti)* is on the main street, about 300m from the waterfront heading inland, on your left.

To get to Vathy's bus station, follow the waterfront and turn left onto Lekati, 250m south of Plateia Pythagorou (just before the police station).

You can get to most of the island's villages and beaches by bus, except Manolates. Agios Konstantinos, 4km away, is its closest bus stop.

## CHIOS Χίος

☎ 2271 • pop 54,000

Chios has not courted tourism because of its thriving shipping and mastic industries (mastic produces the resin used in chewing gum). The chief attraction lies in exploring its undulating interior and distinct villages.

## Orientation & Information

Chios town, the main port, is unattractive and noisy. It is, however, a good base for day trips to Turkey.

The **municipal tourist office** *(☎ 2271 044 389; e infochio@otenet.gr; Kanari 18; open 7am-10pm daily)* is on the main street that runs from the waterfront to Plateia Vounakiou, the main square.

Manos Centre, by the ferry dock, can help with transport arrangements and with some accommodation.

The **post office** *(Rodokanaki)* is one block back from the waterfront. Slick **Enter Internet Café** *(Aigaiou)* is visible upstairs on the southern waterfront; enter from the side street.

## Things to See & Do

Compelling **Philip Argenti Museum** *(admission free; open 8am-2pm Mon-Fri, 5pm-7.30pm Fri, 8am-12.30pm Sat)* contains the treasures of the wealthy Argenti family.

**Nea Moni** *(New Monastery; admission free; open 9am-1pm Tues-Sun)*, now World Heritage listed, is 14km west of Chios town and reveals some of the finest Byzantine art in the country, with mosaics dating from the 11th century.

The ghost village of **Anavatos**, 10km from Nea Moni and built on a precipitous cliff, bears testament to the tragedy of 1822, when the inhabitants perished during an uprising against Turkish rule.

**Pyrgi**, 24km southwest of Chios town, is one of Greece's most extraordinary villages. The facades of the town's dwellings are decorated with intricate grey and white geometric patterns and motifs.

The tiny medieval town of **Mesta**, 10km from Pyrgi and nestled within fortified walls, has two ornate churches and cobbled streets connected by overhead arches that lead to an enchanting square of tavernas laced with birdsong.

### Places to Stay
The tourist office gives out a practical accommodation guide for the town and villages.

**Chios Rooms** (☎ 2271 020 198; Leoforos Aigaiou; singles/doubles with shared bathroom €20/25, doubles with bathroom €30), on the waterfront at the opposite end of the harbour from the ferry dock, has bright, airy rooms in a building that oozes rustic charm.

**Hotel Kyma** (☎ 2271 044 500; e kyma@ chi.forthnet.gr; Evgenias Chandris 1; singles/ doubles/triples with bathroom €53/68/85), around the corner from Chios Rooms, has well appointed suites and prices include breakfast.

### Places to Eat
**Ouzeri Theodosiou**'s delectable *mezedes* are recommended by locals. It's 50m to the right of the ferry disembarkation point.

**Taverna Hotzas**, 15 minutes' walk from the town crush, has excellent food and ambience. To find it, walk up Kanari which becomes Aplotarias. At the fork, take Stefanou Tsouri, then turn right onto Kondyli G.

**Bella Visa** is a sleek place that serves sublime Italian. It's on the waterfront past Hotel Kyma.

### Getting There & Away
Moving on, there are daily flights from Chios to Athens (€62), three flights weekly to Thessaloniki (€60) and two to Lesvos (€28.30).

Ferries sail daily to Piraeus (€19.40), via Lesvos (€11.20), and once a week to Thessaloniki (€28), via Lesvos and Limnos.

There are two ferries per week to Samos (€10.25). In summer, there are daily boats to the wealthy island of Inousses to the east, and several to quiet Psara, west of Chios.

Daily boats travel to Çeşme in Turkey (€30, one way; Turkish port tax €8.80). The waterfront travel agencies handle bookings.

### Getting Around
There are two bus stations. Blue buses go regularly to local villages and Karfas and Kontari Beaches, and leave from the right side (coming from the waterfront) of Plateia Vounakiou, by the garden. Green long-distance buses to Pyrgi and Mesta leave from the station one block back to the left of Plateia Vounakiou. In summer, only one to two green buses per week go to Anavatos via Nea Moni.

**Rent a Car** (☎ 2271 029 300), just down from Hotel Kyma, quotes fair rates.

## LESVOS (MYTILINI)
Λέσβος (Μυτιλήνη)
Fertile Lesvos is the third-largest Greek island. It has always been a centre of philosophy and artistic achievement and still attracts creative types on sabbatical. Spoil yourself with its prized olive oil, ouzo, sardines and therapeutic hot springs.

An excellent source of information on the island is 🖳 www.greeknet.com.

### Mytilini
☎ 2251 • pop 23,970
The capital and main port, Mytilini, is a large, dreary working town. The **tourist police** (2251 022 776) are at the entrance to the quay. The **EOT** (☎ 2251 042 511; open 9am-1pm Sun-Fri), 50m up Aristarhou by the quay, offers brochures and maps, but is too busy for tourists! **Manos Centre** (☎ 2251 048 124; Kountourioti 47), 400m from the ferry on the waterfront, is the choice for travel arrangements.

**Things to See & Do** Mytilini's museums are exceptional. The neoclassical **archaeological museum** (admission €3; open 8.30am-7pm Tues-Sun) has a fascinating collection from Neolithic to Roman times. The **new archaeological museum** (same admission & hours) displays spectacular mosaics from ancient households. Both are on 8 Noemvriou, signposted from the ferry.

**Theophilos Museum** *(admission €2; open 9am-2.30pm & 6pm-8pm Tues-Sun)*, 4km from Mytilini in Varia village, is a shrine to the prolific folk painter, Theophilos.

Five kilometres from Mytilini are the **Loutra Yera hot springs** *(admission €2.50; open 7am-8pm daily)*.

**Places to Stay** Central, budget choices are **Arion Rooms** *(☎ 2251 042 650; Arionos 4; doubles €25)* for basic rooms with mythical frescoes and **Alkaios Rooms** *(☎/fax 2251 047 737; Alkaiou 16; doubles €24)* in an old mansion. To get there, face inland from the waterfront and take Alkaiou to the right of Therapon church; Arion is on the first left, Alkaios is another 100m straight ahead.

**Pelagia Koumniotou Rooms** *(☎ 2251 020 643; Terseti 6; doubles €25)* has pleasant rooms with mod cons. Terseti is 250m up 8 Noemvriou, past the museums, on your left.

**Getting There & Away** There are daily flights to Athens (€78) and to Thessaloniki (€80), five per week to Limnos (€36.25) and two per week to Chios (€28.25); but don't rush to leave.

In summer, there are daily boats to Piraeus (€24), some via Chios, Mykonos and Syros, and one boat per week to Thessaloniki (€28).

There are four ferries per week to Ayvalik in Turkey (€38 one way, €45 return, including taxes). Stop by Manos Centre for ticketing and schedules.

**Getting Around** Mytilini has two bus stations. For local buses, walk about 400m from the ferry to the harbour station where buses leave regularly for Loutra Yera and Varia.

For long-distance buses, walk 600m from the ferry along the waterfront to El Venizelou and turn right until you reach Agia Irinis park which is next to the station. There are regular services in summer to Mithymna, Petra, Agiasos, Skala Eresou, Mantamados and Agia Paraskevi.

For car hire, try **Samiotis Tours** *(Kountourioti 43)* on Mytilini's waterfront, or wait until you get to Mithymna for more competitive rates.

## Mithymna
☎ 2253 • pop 1333

The gracious, preserved town of Mithymna (known by locals as Molyvos) is 62km north of Mytilini. Cobbled streets canopied by flowering vines are lined with cosy tavernas and genteel stone cottages. You'll be tempted never to leave this scenic place.

**Orientation & Information** From the bus stop, walk straight ahead towards the town to a fork in the road. Take the right fork onto 17 Noemvriou, the main thoroughfare, or continue straight ahead to reach the colourful fishing port.

The **municipal tourist office** *(☎ 2253 071 347; open 9am-3.30pm daily)* is 50m from the bus stop. There are three Internet cafés and an open-air cinema along the port road.

**Things to See & Do** The noble **Genoese castle** *(admission €2; open 8am-7pm Tues-Sun)* hosts a drama festival in summer.

**Eftalou hot springs** *(admission €2.50; open 9am-1pm & 3pm-7pm Mon-Sat)*, 3km from town on the beach, is a tiny bathhouse with a whitewashed dome and steaming, pebbled pool.

**Mithymna Beach** gets crowded. Nearby Eftalou, **Skala Sykaminias** and **Petra** are better options.

**Places to Stay & Eat** There are over 50 *domatia* in Mithymna. Those nearest the port bars can ruin your sleep in high season, otherwise 17 Noemvriou is a good place to start. The tourist office also offers accommodation advice.

**Nassos Guest House** *(☎ 2253 071 432; e nassosguesthouse@hotmail.com; doubles with shared bathroom €29)* is an airy, friendly, traditional place with communal kitchen and rapturous views. To get there, head up 17 Noemvriou and take the second right (a sharp switchback).

At the end of the port road, elegant **Onap** has a varied, tempting menu. Next door, busy **Captain's Table** does Greek fare with flair. Upstairs at **Dilino** is ideal for breakfast.

**Entertainment** Head up the port road for action. For cruisy blues and nightcaps, drop by **Pirates Café**. **Café Del Mare** and **Christine's Bar** are good primers for a big night out at **Med Bar** dance club.

**Getting Around** In the summer, buses go regularly to Petra Beach and Eftalou. Excursion boats leave the port daily for Skala

Sykaminias. For more information, Faonas Travel at the port has schedules.

Competitive car- and scooter-hire outlets line the port road.

## Around the Island

East of Mithymna, the traditional picturesque villages surrounding **Mt Lepetymnos** (Sykaminia, Mantamados and Agia Paraskevi) are worth your time.

The southwestern beach resort of **Skala Esrou**, built over ancient Eresos, is the birthplace of sensuous Sappho (c. 630 BC), one of the great poets of ancient Greece.

It has become a popular destination for lesbians who come on a kind of pilgrimage to honour her.

Southern Lesvos is dominated by **Mt Olympus** (968m) and the very pretty day-trip destination of **Agiasos** which has good artisan workshops.

Local clubs, sponsored by the government, have established a network of gentle **walking trails** around the island that traverse olive groves and landscapes featuring water mills, stone bridges, and olive presses. The EOT in Mytilini has a map of the trails.

See Getting Around under Mytilini for transport information.

# Sporades Σποράδες

The Sporades group comprises the lush, pine-forested islands of Skiathos, Skopelos and Alonnisos, and far-flung Skyros, off Evia.

The main ports for these islands are Volos and Agios Konstantinos on the mainland.

## SKIATHOS Σκιάθος
☎ 2427 • pop 4100

Crowded and expensive with a happening nightlife, Skiathos has a universal beach-resort feel but no charm. There are loads of good beaches awash with water sports on the south coast, particularly Koukounaries.

## Orientation & Information

There is a tourist-information booth to the left as you leave the port. Harried travel agencies along the waterfront spit out tour and travel information.

Skiathos town's main thoroughfare is Papadiamanti, running inland opposite the port. Here you'll find the post office, **tourist police**

(☎ 2427 023 172) and Draft-Net Internet café. Internet Zone Café is up Evangelistrias, which is on your right just before you reach the post office. The bus stop is at the far end of the harbour; turn right from the ferry.

Nightlife sprawls along Politehniou; to find it, turn left off Papadiamanti and walk 70m up Evangelistrias.

## Places to Stay & Eat

There is a **Rooms to Let** bookings kiosk on the waterfront. Package-tour operators book accommodation solid for July and August when *domatia* owners drop value for money. Off peak, rooms are up to 50% cheaper.

**Camping Koukounaries** (☎ 2427 049 250; *camping per person/tent €6/3*) is 30 minutes away by bus at Koukounaries Beach.

**Hotel Karafelas** (☎ 2427 021 235, fax 2427 023 307; *singles/doubles with bathroom €30/53*), in town at the end of Papadiamanti on your left, has generous rooms with balconies.

**Hotel Marlton** (☎ 2427 022 552, ☎/fax 2427 022 878; *doubles/triples with bathroom €40/48*) is friendly and has fresh, pine-furnished rooms. To get there from Papadiamanti, turn right onto Evangelistrias and walk 50m.

**Pension Vasiliki** (☎ 2427 022 549, fax 2427 021 978; *doubles/triples with bathroom €45/55*) has rooms with TV and is in a quiet part of town off Evangelistrias, opposite Taverna Ilias. Follow the signs to the taverna.

On the waterfront, **Zio Peppe**'s yummy pizza cures hangovers. **Ta Psaradiki Ouzeri** by the fish market is the seafood winner.

On Papadiamanti, try reasonably priced **Niko's Café Bar**, or the slightly upmarket **Gerania**.

Scandinavian **Restaurant Bonaparte** *(Evangelistrias)*, left off Papadiamanti, offers pricier taste sensations.

## Getting There & Away

In summer, there are five flights per week from Athens to Skiathos (€69.35) and one a week to Skyros (€34.55).

There are frequent ferries to the mainland ports of Volos (€11) and Agios Konstantinos (€10.10), and frequent hydrofoils each day to Skopelos (€8.80) and Alonnisos (€12). In summer, there are two boats a week to Thessaloniki.

## Getting Around

Crowded buses ply the south-coast road between Skiathos town and Koukounaries every 20 minutes, stopping at all the beaches along the way.

Many of the south-coast beaches are only accessible by caïque from the port.

## SKOPELOS Σκόπελος
☎ 2424 • pop 5000

Skopelos has the appeal of a mountain-lake resort with its thick forests of scruffy pine and pebbled beaches of jade green.

## Orientation & Information

There is no tourist office or tourist police in Skopelos town, but **Thalpos Leisure & Services** (☎ 2424 022 947; e thalpos@ otenet.gr) on the waterfront is handy for accommodation and tours. It's a few doors past Pension Kir Sotos on the 1st floor.

The post office is elusive. Walk up the road opposite the port entrance, take the first sharp left, the first right, the first left, and it's on the right. To get to **Click & Surf Internet Café** (Doulidi) walk up the road opposite the port entrance, take the third left and walk a further 100m. The bus station is next to the port.

## Things to See & Do

Attractive **Skopelos town**, with its dazzling white, hillside homes, is a maze of narrow streets and stairways where the kissing balconies of cascading flowers and bright window shutters burst with colour. Take time to wander. You'll find stone churches with glittering interiors tucked around many corners.

**Glossa**, the island's other inland town, is quite ordinary but it's a pleasant drive there with marvellous views.

**Velanio Beach** is the island's nudie spot. Pebbled **Panormos Beach**, with its sheltered emerald bay surrounded by pine forest, is superb. The 2km stretch of **Milia Beach**, a few kilometres further on, is considered the island's best.

Thalpos Leisure & Services and **Madro Travel** (☎ 2424 022 145; e enquiries@ madrotravel.com) offer boat excursions and walking tours. Madro is at the end of the northern waterfront, about 70m before the church.

## Places to Stay

In high season, rooms are engulfed by package tourists so it pays to sift through the domatia owners who meet the boats. Thalpos Leisure & Services has an accommodation-finding service. Opposite the port entrance, the Rooms & Apartments Association of Skopelos has a brochure of domatia, but doesn't make bookings.

**Pension Kir Sotos** (☎ 2424 022 549, fax 2424 023 668; doubles/triples with bathroom €35/49), in the middle of the waterfront, has big rooms in an enchanting building. There's also a communal kitchen and courtyard.

**Pension Soula** (☎ 2424 022 930, 2424 024 631; doubles/studios from €24/27), a 10-minute walk out of town, is a welcoming place with airy rooms; you'll awake in rural bliss to donkeys braying and birdsong. To find it, walk left from the port and turn left at Hotel Amalia. Follow the road, bearing right after about 200m; it's on your right.

**Hotel Ionia** (☎ 2424 022 568, fax 2424 023 301, e hotelionia@vol.forthnet.gr; singles/doubles/triples with bathroom €35/60/70) has all mod cons, bright wall murals and a pool; prices include breakfast. Facing inland, take the road to the right of Pension Kir Sotos. It's a steep hike of about 300m. The road veers slightly right then bears left the last 120m; it's on your left.

## Places to Eat

**Zio Peppe**, on the waterfront, is the best place for a pizza fix.

**Taverna Fikinas** has imaginative dishes; follow the signs from the middle of the waterfront – getting there is a treasure hunt!

**The Garden**, on the road to Pension Soula (see Places to Stay, earlier), offers superb dining and service in an elegant garden.

## Entertainment

On the same strip as Click & Surf Internet Café (see Orientation & Information, earlier) you'll find the crowd-pleasing **Dancing Club Kounos**, **Panselinos** for Greek rembetika music, and **Metro Club** for Greek pop and rock.

For a sultry mood, it's **La Costa** bar, opposite the bus station, or the so-laid-back-it's-falling-over **Platanos Jazz Bar** at the northern end of the waterfront.

## Getting There & Away

In summer, there are daily ferries to Volos (€10.60) and Agios Konstantinos (€25.40) that also call at Skiathos. Flying Dolphin hydrofoils dash several times a day to Skiathos, Alonnisos, Volos and Agios Konstantinos. All boats leave from the same port, but in rough weather may depart from Agnontas Beach, southwest of town. Most hydrofoils also call in at Loutraki, the port below Glossa. For schedules and tickets, see **Kosifis Travel** opposite the port.

There are frequent buses from Skopelos town to Glossa, stopping at all beaches along the way.

## ALONNISOS Αλόννησος
☎ 2424 • pop 3000

Green, serene Alonnisos is the least visited of the Sporades. The area surrounding the island has been declared a marine park and has the cleanest waters in the Aegean.

The restful port village of Patitiri has two main thoroughfares; facing inland from the ferry quay, Pelasgon is to the left and Ikion Dolopon is to the far right.

There is no tourist office or tourist police but the post office, police and Internet access at Il Mondo Café are on Ikion Dolopon. The bus stop is on the corner of Ikion Dolopon and the waterfront.

The tiny hora, **Old Alonnisos**, is a few kilometres inland. Its streets sprout a profusion of plant life, alluring villas of eclectic design and dramatic vistas.

Alonnisos is ideal for walking. Waterfront travel agencies offer guided tours, or there's an excellent trail guide called *Alonnisos on Foot: A Walking & Swimming Guide* by Bente Keller & Elias Tsoukanas which is available at newsstands for €9.

**Patitiri Beach** is OK for a dip; **Kokkinokastro** and **Hrysia Milia**, on the east coast, are better.

The **Rooms to Let service** (☎/fax 2424 065 577), right of the quay, books accommodation all over the island.

**Camping Rocks** (☎ 2424 065 410) is a shady, basic site. It is a steep hike about 1.5km from the port; go up Pelasgon and take the first road on your left.

**Ikaros Camping** (☎ 2424 065 258) is smaller than Camping Rocks and is on the beach at the tiny fishing village of Steni Vala.

**Villa Gallini** (☎ 2424 065 573, fax 2424 065 094; doubles/triples with bathroom €45/72) has exceptional rooms, a pool and bar. It's 400m up Pelasgon on your left.

**Haravgi Hotel** (☎ 2424 065 090, fax 2424 065 189; doubles/studios €58/70) has sensational views over Patitiri and rooms have minikitchen. To get there take the first left up Pelasgon, and then turn left again.

**Fantasia House** (☎ 2424 065 186; doubles €35) in Old Alonnisos has sweet rooms and a verdant terrace. From the bus stop, it's on the road towards town.

In Patitiri, **To Kamaki Ouzeri** and **Kavari Ouzeri** on Ikion Dolopon offer delectably prepared fare. Get there early!

Cruisy **Café Dennis**, near the quay, and **Rahati** (signposted from Ikion Dolopon) with its moody interior and shady terrace, are the places to sip and lounge.

In the hora, **Azzurro** café has sublime views, and **Astrofengia**, signposted from the bus stop, serves scrumptious alternative fare.

There are daily ferries from Alonnisos to Volos, and two a week to Agios Konstantinos, via Skiathos and Skopelos. Flying Dolphin hydrofoils travel several times a day to Volos and Agios Konstantinos and between the islands.

The local bus runs to the hora every hour and to Steni Vala twice a day.

Car- and scooter-hire outlets are on Pelasgon and Ikion Dolopon, but only one main road spans the island! In summer, taxi boats leave Patitiri every morning for the east-coast beaches.

# Ionian Islands
Ιόνια Νησιά

The Ionian Islands stretch down the western coast of Greece from Corfu in the north to remote Kythira, which is off the southern tip of the Peloponnese.

## CORFU Κέρκυρα
pop 107,592

Corfu is the most important island in the group and has the largest population.

### Corfu Town
☎ 2661 • pop 36,000

The old town of Corfu, wedged between two fortresses, occupies a peninsula on the island's east coast. The narrow alleyways of high-shuttered tenements in mellow ochres and pinks are an immediate reminder of the town's long association with Venice.

**Orientation & Information** The town's old fortress (Palaio Frourio) stands on an eastern promontory, separated from the town by an area of parks and gardens known as the Spianada. The new fortress (Neo Frourio) lies to the northwest. Ferries dock at the new port, just west of the new fortress. The **long-distance bus station** (Avrami) is inland from the port.

The **EOT office** (☎ 2661 037 520; Rizospaston Voulefton) is between OTE and the post office, or try the **tourist police** (☎ 2661 030 265; Samartzi 4). All major Greek banks are in town, including the **National Bank of Greece** (cnr Voulgareos & Theotoki).

**Things to See** The **archaeological museum** (Vraili 5; admission €3; open 8.30am-3pm Tues-Sun) houses a collection of finds from Mycenaean to classical times. The star attraction is the pediment from the Temple of Artemis, decorated with gorgons.

The **Church of Agios Spiridon**, Corfu's most famous church, has an richly decorated interior. Pride of place is given to the remains of St Spiridon, displayed in a silver casket; four times a year it is paraded around town.

**Places to Stay & Eat** Near the fruit and vegetable market, **Hotel Hermes** (☎ 2661 039 268, fax 2661 031 747; G Markora 14; singles/doubles with shared bathroom €26.40/30.80, singles/doubles with private bathroom €30.80/38.15) has a certain shabby charm and is popular with backpackers.

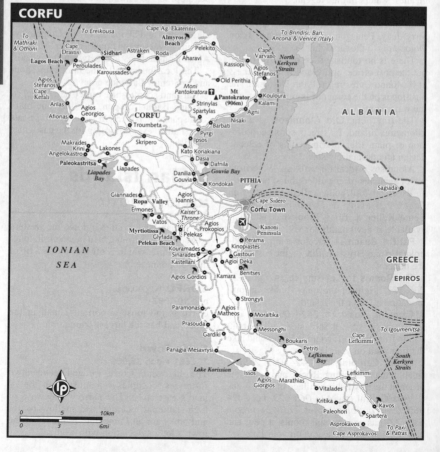

CORFU

**Hotel Konstantinopoulis** (☎ 2661 048 716, fax 2661 048 718; Zavitsianou 11; singles/doubles €52.80/70.50) has a great position overlooking the old harbour.

**Hrysomalis** (☎ 2661 030 342; Nikiforou Theotaki 6; mains €5), near the Spianada, is one of Corfu's oldest restaurants. It's a no-frills place that turns out excellent staples.

## Around the Island

Hardly anywhere in Corfu hasn't made a play for the tourist dollar, but the north is over the top. The only real attraction there is the view from the summit of **Mt Pantokrator** (906m), Corfu's highest mountain. There's a road to the top from the village of **Strinila**.

The main resort on the west coast is **Paleokastritsa**, built around a series of pretty bays. Further south, there are good beaches around the small village of **Agios Gordios**. Between Paleokastritsa and Agios Gordios is the hilltop village of **Pelekas**, supposedly the best place on Corfu to watch the sunset.

## Places to Stay

**Pink Palace** (☎ 2661 053 103/4, fax 2661 053 025; e pink-palace@ker.forthnet.gr; rooms from €22 per person), a huge complex of restaurants, bars and budget rooms that tumbles down a hillside outside Agios Gordios, is where most backpackers head. Rates include bed, breakfast and dinner. Debauchery is the main item on the menu for those who want to party hard.

## Getting There & Away

Three flights daily to Athens are offered by both **Olympic Airways** (☎ 2661 038 694; Polila 11, Corfu town) and **Aegean Airlines** (☎ 2661 027 100). Olympic also flies to Thessaloniki three times a week.

There are daily buses to Athens (€27.90, 11 hours) and Thessaloniki (€25.70, nine hours) from the Avrami terminal in Corfu town. Fares include the ferry to Igoumenitsa.

There are hourly ferries to Igoumenitsa (€4.10, 1½ hours) and a daily ferry to Paxoi. In summer, there are daily services to Patras (€17.90, 10 hours) on the international ferries that call at Corfu on their way from Italy.

## Getting Around

Buses for villages close to Corfu town leave from Plateia San Rocco. Services to other destinations leave from the station on Avrami.

## ITHAKI Ιθάκη
pop 3100

Ithaki (ancient Ithaca) is the fabled home of Odysseus, the hero of Homer's *Odyssey*, who pined for his island during his journeys to far-flung lands. It's a quiet place with some isolated coves. From the main town of Vathy you can walk to the **Fountain of Arethousa**, the fabled site of Odysseus' meeting with the swineherd Eumaeus on his return to Ithaki. Take water with you, as the fountain dries up in summer.

Ithaki has daily ferries to the mainland ports of Patras and Astakos, as well as daily services to Kefallonia and Lefkada.

## KEFALLONIA Κεφαλλονιά
pop 32,500

After years of drifting along in relative obscurity, quiet Kefallonia found itself thrust into the international spotlight following the success of Louis de Bernières' novel *Captain Corelli's Mandolin*.

Publicity reached fever pitch in the summer of 2001 with the release of the movie that starred Nicholas Cage, Penelope Cruz and John Hurt.

Visitors who come to the island's capital, Sami, hoping to wander the old Venetian streets depicted in the movie, will be disappointed to learn that it was all a cleverly constructed set. The originals were destroyed by a major earthquake in 1953.

Kefallonia is the largest of the Ionians, and tourism remains fairly low key outside the resort areas near the capital and on the beaches in the southwest. Public transport is very limited, apart from regular services between Argostoli and the main port of Sami, 25km away on the east coast.

There's an **EOT** (☎ 2671 022 248) on the waterfront in Argostoli.

**Kyknos Studios** (☎ 2671 023 398, fax 025 943, M Geroulanou 4; double studios €35.20), in Argostoli close to the main square, Plateia Vallianou, is a good place to check out.

**Hotel Melissani** (☎/fax 2674 022 464; singles/doubles €38.20/49.90), in Sami, is a pleasant older-style hotel offering such comforts as TV and fridge. It's signposted from the eastern end of the waterfront.

**Captain's Table** (☎ 2671 023 896; Rizospaston 3; mains €5-15), near Kyknos Studios, is one of Argostoli's top restaurants and the place to go for a splurge.

GREECE

**Delfinia** (☎ 2674 022 008; mains €4-10.50) is a popular waterfront spot favoured by local diners.

There is a daily flight to Athens from the airport, which is 9km south of Argostoli. There are daily ferries from Sami to Patras (€10, 2½ hours), as well as from Argostoli and the southeastern port of Poros to Kyllini in the Peloponnese. There are also ferry connections to the islands of Ithaki, Lefkada and Zakynthos.

## ZAKYNTHOS Ζάκυνθος
**pop 32,560**

Zakynthos, or Zante as it is also known, is a beautiful island surrounded by great beaches – so it's hardly surprising that the place is completely overrun by package groups. Its capital and port, Zakynthos town, is an imposing old Venetian town that has been painstakingly reconstructed after being levelled by an earthquake in 1953.

Some of the best beaches are around the huge **Bay of Laganas** in the south, which is where endangered loggerhead turtles come ashore to lay their eggs in August – at the peak of the tourist invasion. Conservation groups are urging people to stay away and the Greek government has declared this area a National Marine Park. There are regular ferries between Zakynthos and Kyllini in the Peloponnese.

# Italy

Tell people you're going to Italy and they'll sigh, even if they haven't been there. A place of myth, history, artistic achievement, romantic imagery and all manner of cliches, it stirs peoples hearts with both its simplicity and complexity. As Luigi Barzini wrote in *The Italians*: 'Italy is still a country of limitless opportunities. It offers stage settings for all kinds of adventures, licit or illicit loves, the study of art, the experience of pathos, the weaving of intrigues. It can be gay, tragic, mad, pastoral, archaic, modern, or simply *dolce*.' Many come to Italy to escape their daily lives and to feel more alive in the process. Soak up what's on offer – this is a country that understands, or seems to. However, if you're after efficient bureaucracy or sensitive urban planning outside of city centres, look elsewhere.

# Facts about Italy

## HISTORY

The traditional date for the founding of Rome by Romulus is 753 BC, but the country had already been inhabited for thousands of years. Palaeolithic Neanderthals lived in Italy during the last ice age more than 20,000 years ago, and by the start of the Bronze Age, around 2000 BC, the peninsula had been settled by several Italic tribes.

From about 900 BC the Etruscan civilisation developed, until these mysterious people dominated the area between the Arno and Tiber Valleys. After the foundation of Rome, Etruscan civilisation continued to flourish until the end of the 3rd century BC, when the Romans overwhelmed the last Etruscan city.

## The Roman Republic

The new Roman republic, after recovering from the invasion of the Gauls in 390 BC, began its expansion into southern Italy. Rome claimed Sicily following the Second Punic War against Hannibal in 241 BC, after his crossing of the Alps. Rome defeated Carthage in 202 BC and a few years later claimed Spain and Greece.

## Expansion & Empire

In the 1st century BC, under Julius Caesar, Rome conquered Gaul and moved into Egypt.

After Caesar's assassination by Brutus on the Ides of March in 44 BC, a power struggle began between Mark Antony and Octavius, leading to the deaths of Antony and Cleopatra in Egypt in 31 BC and the establishment of the Roman Empire in 27 BC. Octavius, who had been adopted by Julius Caesar as his son and heir, took the title of Augustus Caesar and became the first emperor. Augustus ruled for 45 years, a period of great

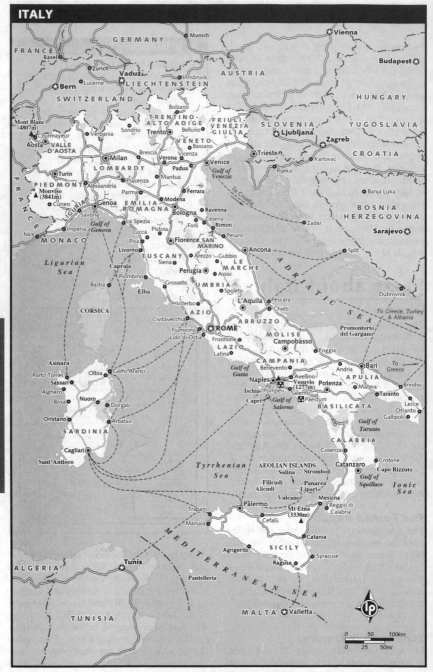

advancement in engineering, architecture, administration and literature.

## The Eastern & Western Empires

By the end of the 3rd century, the empire had grown to such an extent that Emperor Diocletian divided it between east and west for administrative purposes. His successor, Constantine, declared religious freedom for Christians and moved the seat of power to the eastern capital, Byzantium, which he renamed Constantinople. During the 4th century, Christianity was declared the official state religion and grew in power and influence.

By the early 5th century, German tribes had entered Rome, and in 476 the Western Roman Empire ended when the German warrior, Odoacer, deposed the emperor and declared himself ruler of Italy. The south and Sicily were dominated by Arab raiders until the Normans invaded in 1036.

## The City-States & the Renaissance

The Middle Ages in Italy were marked by the development of powerful city-states in the north. This was the time of Dante, Petrarch and Boccaccio, Giotto, Cimabue and Pisano.

In the 15th century the Renaissance, which began in Florence, spread throughout the country, fostering genius of the likes of Brunelleschi, Donatello, Bramante, Botticelli, da Vinci, Masaccio, Lippi, Raphael and Michelangelo.

By the early 16th century much of the country was under Spanish rule. This lasted until 1713 when, following the War of Spanish Succession, control of Italy passed to the Austrians. After the invasion by Napoleon in 1796 a degree of unity was introduced into Italy, for the first time since the fall of the Roman Empire.

## The Risorgimento

In the 1860s Italy's unification movement (The Risorgimento) gained momentum, and in 1861 the Kingdom of Italy was declared under the rule of King Vittorio Emanuele. Venice was wrested from Austria in 1866 and Rome from the papacy in 1870.

## Mussolini & WWII

In the years after WWI, Italy was in turmoil. In 1921 the Fascist Party, formed by Benito Mussolini in 1919, won 35 of the 135 seats in parliament. In October 1921, after a period of considerable unrest and strikes, the king asked Mussolini to form a government, whereupon he became prime minister with only 7% representation in parliament.

Mussolini formed the Rome-Berlin axis with Hitler in 1936 and Italy entered WWII as an ally of Germany in June 1941. After a series of military disasters and an invasion by the Allies in 1943, the king led a coup against Mussolini and had him arrested. After being rescued by the Germans, Mussolini tried to govern in the north, but was fiercely opposed by Italian partisans, who killed him in April 1945.

## The Italian Republic

In 1946, following a referendum, the constitutional monarchy was abolished and the republic established. Italy was a founding member of the European Economic Community in 1957 (forerunner of the European Union; EU) and was seriously disrupted by terrorism in the 1970s, thanks to the Red Brigades, who kidnapped and assassinated Prime Minister Aldo Moro in 1978.

In the decades following WWII, Italy's national government was dominated by the centre-right Christian Democrats, usually in coalition with other parties (excluding the Communists). Italy enjoyed significant economic growth in the 1980s, but the 1990s heralded a period of crisis for the country, both economically and politically.

## The 1990s to the Present

Against the backdrop of a severe economic crisis, the very foundations of Italian politics were shaken by a national bribery scandal known as *tangentopoli* (bribesville). Investigations eventually implicated thousands of politicians, public officials and businesspeople, and left the main parties in tatters after the 1992 elections, effectively demolishing the centre of the political spectrum.

After a period of right-wing government, elections in 1996 brought a centre-left coalition known as the Olive Tree to power. A programme of fiscal austerity was ushered in to guarantee Italy's entry into Europe's economic and monetary union (EMU), which occurred in 1998. The current (since 2001) prime minister is Silvio Berluschoni, a controversial (to put it mildly) right-wing politico, whose party, 'Forza Italia', has proved popular in many quarters with its desire to make Italian bureaucracy (at the expense of state welfare) more efficient. He also owns *a lot* of the Italian media, which is a sore point for a great many people.

## The Mafia

The 1990s saw Italy moving more decisively against the Sicilian Mafia (known in Sicily as *Cosa Nostra* – 'Our Thing'), prompted by the 1992 assassinations of prominent anti-Mafia judges Giovanni Falcone and Paolo Borsellino, which saw many Sicilians publicly protesting against the dishonourable conduct of the 'Men of Honour'. The testimonies of several *pentiti* (informers), led to important arrests – most notably of the Sicilian godfather, Salvatore 'Toto' Riina (serving a life sentence). The man believed to have taken power after Riina's arrest, Giovanni Brusca, was arrested in May 1996 and implicated in the aforementioned murders. He was imprisoned for 30 years in 1999. Subsequent high-profile arrests (such as Pietro Aglieri in 1997) have undoubtedly dented the Mafia's confidence, but this is an entrenched system, and the battle is both international and far from won.

## GEOGRAPHY

The boot-shaped country, incorporating the islands of Sicily and Sardinia, is bound by the Adriatic, Ligurian, Tyrrhenian and Ionian Seas, which all form part of the Mediterranean Sea. About 75% of the Italian peninsula is mountainous, with the Alps dividing the country from France, Switzerland and Austria, and the Apennines forming a backbone which extends from the Alps into Sicily. There are four active volcanoes: Stromboli and Vulcano (in the Aeolian Islands), Etna (Sicily) and Vesuvius (near Naples).

## CLIMATE

Italy lies in a temperate zone, but the climates of the north and south vary. Summers are uniformly hot, but are often extremely hot and dry in the south. Winters can be severely cold in the north – particularly in the Alps and the Po Valley – whereas they are mild in the south, Sicily and Sardinia.

## ECOLOGY & ENVIRONMENT

The countryside can be dramatically beautiful, but the long presence of humans on the peninsula has had a significant impact on the environment. Aesthetically the result is not always displeasing – much of the beauty of Tuscany, for instance, lies in the interaction of olive groves with vineyards, fallow fields and stands of cypress and pine. Centuries of tree clearing, combined with illegal building have also led to extensive land degradation and erosion. The alteration of the environment, combined with the Italians' passion for hunting, has led to many native animals and birds becoming extinct, rare or endangered. Under progressively introduced laws, many animals and birds are now protected.

There are over 20 national parks in Italy. Among the most important are the Parco Nazionale del Gran Paradiso and the Parco Nazionale dello Stelvio, both in the Alps, and the Parco Nazionale d'Abruzzo.

Central and southern Italy are sometimes subject to massive earthquakes. A series of quakes devastated parts of the Appenine areas of Umbria and the Marches in September 1997.

## GOVERNMENT & POLITICS

For administrative purposes Italy is divided into 20 regions, each of which have some degree of autonomy. The regions are then subdivided into provinces and municipalities.

The country is a parliamentary republic, headed by a president who appoints the prime minister. The parliament consists of a senate and chamber of deputies, which have equal legislative power. The national government is in Rome. Two-thirds of both houses are elected on the basis of who receives the most votes in their district (basically the same as the first-past-the-post system). The old (pre-1994) system produced unstable coalition governments, with 53 governments in 48 years between the declaration of the republic and the introduction of electoral reforms.

## ECONOMY

Italy is the fifth-largest economy in the world, thanks to the 1980s. However, the severe economic crisis of 1992–93 prompted a

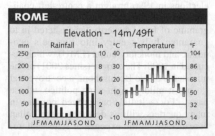

ROME
Elevation – 14m/49ft

succession of governments to pull the economy into line with Draconian measures, such as the partial privatisation of the huge public sector and reduced public spending.

Despite years of effort and the expenditure of trillions of lire for many years, a noticeable gap still exists between Italy's north and south. Italy's richest regions (Piedmont, Lombardy, Veneto and Emilia-Romagna) are northern, and its poorest (Calabria, Campania and Sicily) are southern.

## POPULATION & PEOPLE

The population of Italy is 57.8 million. Surprisingly, the country has the lowest birthrate in Europe. Foreigners may like to think of Italy as a land of passionate, animated people who gesticulate wildly, love to eat, drive like maniacs and hate to work. However, it takes more than a holiday to understand Italy's vigorous, remarkably diverse inhabitants. Overall, people remain fiercely protective of regional dialects and cuisine.

## ARTS
### Architecture, Painting & Sculpture

Italy has often been called a living museum and it's not necessary to enter a gallery to appreciate the country's artistic wealth – it is everywhere as you walk through Florence, Venice, Siena, Rome, Naples or Palermo. In the south of Italy and in Sicily, where Greek colonisation preceded Roman domination, there are important Greek archaeological sites such as the temples at Paestum, south of Salerno, and Agrigento in Sicily. Pompeii and Herculaneum give an idea of how ancient Romans actually lived.

Byzantine mosaics adorn churches found throughout Italy, most notably at Ravenna, in the Basilica of San Marco in Venice, and in Palermo.

The 15th and early 16th centuries in Italy saw one of the most explosions of artistic and literary achievement in recorded history – the Renaissance. Patronised mainly by the Medici family in Florence and the popes in Rome, painters, sculptors, architects and writers flourished and many artists of genius emerged. The High Renaissance (about 1490–1520) was dominated by three men: Leonardo da Vinci (1452–1519), Michelangelo Buonarroti (1475–1564) and Raphael (1483–1520).

The baroque period (17th century) was characterised by sumptuous, often fantastic architecture and richly decorative painting and sculpture. In Rome there are innumerable works by the great baroque sculptor and architect Gianlorenzo Bernini (1598–1680) and many works by Michelangelo Merisi da Caravaggio (1573–1610).

Neoclassicism in Italy produced the sculptor, Canova (1757–1822). Of the modern artists, Amedeo Modigliani (1884–1920) is perhaps the most famous. The early 20th century produced an artistic movement known as the Futurists, who rejected the sentimental art of the past and were infatuated by new technology, including modern warfare. Fascism produced its own style of architecture, characterised by the EUR satellite city and the work of Marcello Piacentini (1881–1960).

### Music

The realms of opera and instrumental music have seen Italian artists take a dominant place. Antonio Vivaldi (1675–1741) created the concerto in its present form. Verdi, Puccini, Bellini, Donizetti and Rossini, composers from the 19th and early 20th centuries, are all stars of the modern operatic era. Tenor Luciano Pavarotti (1935–) has recently had his crown as 'King of Mother's Day CD Sales' taken by Andrea Bocelli (1958–), who soared to international stardom in the 1990s.

### Literature

Before Dante wrote his *Divina Commedia* (Divine Comedy) and confirmed vernacular Italian as a serious medium for poetic expression, Latin was the language of writers. Among the greatest writers of ancient Rome were Cicero, Virgil, Ovid and Petronius.

A contemporary of Dante was Petrarch (1304–74). Giovanni Boccaccio (1313–75), author of the *Decameron,* is considered the first Italian novelist. *The Prince* by Machiavelli, a purely political work, has proved a lasting Renaissance work.

Italy's richest contribution to modern literature has been in the novel and short story. Southerner Carlo Levi based *Christ Stopped at Eboli* on his experiences in Basilicata. Leonardo Sciascia's taut writings on Sicilian themes posed as many questions as they appeared to answer. Umberto Eco's best-known work *The Name of the Rose* is a high-brow murder mystery of the first order.

ITALY

## Theatre

At a time when French playwrights ruled the stage, the Venetian Carlo Goldoni (1707–93) attempted to bring Italian theatre back into the limelight with the *commedia dell'arte*, the tradition of improvisational theatre. Sicilian Luigi Pirandello (1867–1936), author of *Six Characters in Search of an Author*, won the Nobel Prize in 1934. Modern Italian theatre's most enduring representative is actor/director Dario Fo, who won the Nobel Prize in 1998.

## Cinema

In the 1940s Roberto Rossellini produced the neorealist masterpiece *Rome Open City* starring Anna Magnani. Vittorio de Sica directed the 1948 classic *Bicycle Thieves*. Schooled with the masters of neorealism, Federico Fellini took the creative baton from them and carried it into the following decades, with films such as *La Dolce Vita*. Michelangelo Antonioni's career reached a climax with 1967's *Blow-up*. Bernardo Bertolucci's international hits include *Last Tango in Paris*, *The Last Emperor*, *Stealing Beauty* and *Besieged*. Franco Zeffirelli's most-recent film was *Tea with Mussolini* (1998). Other notable directors include the Taviani brothers, Giuseppe Tornatore, Nanni Moretti and Roberto Benigni, director of the Oscar-winning *Life is Beautiful* (1998). One recent film that proved wildly popular in Italy and abroad is Gabriele Muccino's *L'Ultimo Bacio* (2001), which tells the story of a group of young Italian men grappling with life's and love's big questions.

## SOCIETY & CONDUCT

It is difficult to make blanket assertions about Italian culture, because Italians have lived together as a nation for little over 100 years. Prior to unification, the peninsula was long subject to a varied mix of masters and cultures. This lack of unity contributed to the survival of local dialects and customs. Even today many Italians tend to identify more strongly with their region, or home town, than with the nation. An Italian is first and foremost a Tuscan or Sicilian, or even a Roman or Neapolitan.

In some parts of Italy, especially in the south, women might be harassed if they wear skimpy or see-through clothing. Modest dress is expected in all churches. Those that are major tourist attractions, such as St Peter's in Rome, strictly enforce dress codes (no hotpants, low-cut tops, bare shoulders or see-through garments – this goes for you too ladies).

## RELIGION

Around 85% of Italians profess to be Catholic. The remaining 15% includes about 800,000 Muslims, 500,000 evangelical Protestants, 200,000 Jehovah's Witnesses and smaller communities of Jews, Waldenses and Buddhists.

## LANGUAGE

English is most widely understood in the north, particularly in major centres such as Milan, Florence and Venice. Staff at most hotels and restaurants usually speak a little English, but you will be better received if you attempt to communicate in Italian.

Italian, a Romance language, is related to French, Spanish, Portuguese and Romanian. Modern literary Italian developed in the 13th and 14th centuries, predominantly through the works of Dante, Petrarch and Boccaccio, who wrote chiefly in the Florentine dialect. Although many dialects are spoken in everyday conversation, so-called standard Italian is the national language of schools, media and literature, and is understood throughout the country.

Many older Italians still expect to be addressed by the third-person formal, ie, *Lei* instead of *Tu*. It is not polite to use the greeting *ciao* when addressing strangers, unless they use it first; use *buongiorno* and *arrivederci*.

See the Language chapter at the back of this book for pronunciation guidelines and useful words and phrases.

# Facts for the Visitor

## HIGHLIGHTS

Coming up with a top 10 list for Italy is no easy task, given the wealth of must-see sights. Bearing that in mind, you could try the following:

1. Italian food and wine
2. Florence
3. Ancient ruins of Rome, Pompeii and Paestum
4. Venice
5. Siena
6. The Amalfi Coast
7. The Cinque Terre
8. The Aeolian Islands
9. The Dolomites
10. Palermo's mosaics and architecture

## SUGGESTED ITINERARIES

Depending on the length of your stay, you might want to see and do the following things:

**Two days**
 Visit Rome to see the Forum, the Colosseum, St Peter's Basilica and the Vatican museums.
**One week**
 Visit Rome and Florence, with detours in Tuscany to Siena and San Gimignano. Or visit Rome and Naples, with detours to Pompeii, Vesuvius and the Amalfi Coast.
**Two weeks**
 As above, plus Bologna, Verona, Ravenna and at least three days in Venice.
**One month**
 Visit Rome, Florence, Venice and Naples, and explore the north, centre and south in greater detail, with stays in Liguria, Tuscany, Umbria, the Dolomites, Campania, Apulia, Basilicata, Sicily and Sardinia.

## PLANNING
### When to Go

The best time to visit Italy is in the off season, particularly April to June and September to October, when the weather is good, prices are lower and there are fewer tourists. During July and August (the high season) it is very hot, prices are inflated, the country swarms with tourists, and hotels by the sea and in the mountains are usually booked out. Note that many hotels and restaurants in seaside areas close down for the winter months.

### Maps

Michelin map No 988 (1:1,000,000) covers the entire country. There is also a series of area maps at 1:400,000 – Nos 428 to 431 cover the mainland, No 432 covers Sicily and No 433 Sardinia.

If you're driving, note that Michelin's *Atlante Stradale e Turistico* (€18) is scaled at 1:300,000 and includes 74 town maps.

### What to Bring

A backpack is a big advantage in Italy, but if you plan to use a suitcase and portable trolley, be warned about endless flights of stairs at some train stations and in many smaller medieval towns, as well as petty thieves who prey on tourists who have no hands free because they are carrying too much luggage. A small pack (with a lock) for use on day trips and for sightseeing is preferable to a handbag or shoulder bag, particularly in southern cities,

where motorcycle bandits operate. A money-belt is essential in Italy, particularly in the south and Sicily, but also in major cities where groups of dishevelled-looking women and children prey on tourists with bulging pockets.

In the more mountainous areas the weather can change suddenly, even in high summer, so remember to bring at least one item of warm clothing. Most importantly, bring a pair of hardy, comfortable, worn-in walking shoes. In many cities, pavements are uneven and often made of cobblestones.

## TOURIST OFFICES
### Local Tourist Offices

There are three main categories of tourist office in Italy: regional, provincial and local. Their names vary throughout the country. Provincial offices are sometimes known as the Ente Provinciale per il Turismo (EPT) or, more commonly, the Azienda di Promozione Turistica (APT). The Azienda Autonoma di Soggiorno e Turismo (AAST) and Informazioni e Assistenza ai Turisti (IAT) offices usually have information only on the town itself. In some of the very small towns and villages the local tourist office is called a Pro Loco, and is often little more than a room with a desk. At most offices you should be able to get an *elenco degli alberghi* (list of hotels), a *pianta della città* (town map) and information on the major sights. Staff speak English in larger towns, but in the more out-of-the-way places it's Italian only. Tourist offices are generally open 8.30am to 12.30pm or 1pm and 3pm to 7pm Monday to Friday and on Saturday morning. Hours are usually extended in summer.

The Centro Turistico Studentesco e Giovanile (CTS) has offices all over Italy and specialises in discounts for students and young people, but is also useful for travellers of any age looking for cheap flights and sightseeing discounts. It is linked with the International Student Travel Confederation. You can get a student card here if you have documents proving that you are a student.

### Tourist Offices Abroad

Information about Italy can be obtained at **Italian State Tourist Offices** *(ENIT;* w *www .enit.it)* throughout the world, including:

**Australia**
 (☎ 02-9262 1666, fax 9262 5745) c/o Italian Chamber of Commerce, Level 26, 44 Market St, Sydney, NSW 2000

**Canada**
(☎ 416-925 4882, fax 925 4799) Suite 907, South Tower, 175 Bloor St East, Toronto, Ontario M4W 3R8
**UK**
(☎ 020-7355 1557, fax 7493 6695, e enit lond@globalnet.co.uk) 1 Princes St, London W1R 9AY
**USA**
*Chicago:* (☎ 312-644 0996, fax 644 3019, e enitch@italiantourism.com) Suite 2240, 500 North Michigan Ave, Chicago, IL 60611
*Los Angeles:* (☎ 310-820 1898, fax 820 6357, e enitla@earthlink.net) Suite 550, 12400 Wilshire Blvd, Los Angeles, CA 90025
*New York:* (☎ 212-245 5095, fax 586 9249, e enitny@italiantourism.com) Suite 1565, 630 Fifth Ave, New York, NY 10111

Sestante CIT (Compagnia Italiana di Turismo), Italy's national travel agency, also has offices throughout the world (known as CIT outside Italy). It can provide extensive information on Italy, as well as book tours and accommodation. It also makes train bookings. Offices include:

**Australia**
*Melbourne:* (☎ 03-9650 5510) Level 4, 227 Collins St, Melbourne, VIC 3000
*Sydney:* (☎ 02-9267 1255) Level 2, 263 Clarence St, Sydney, NSW 2000
**Canada**
*Montreal:* (☎ 514-845 9101, toll-free ☎ 800-361 7799) Suite 901, 666 Sherbrooke St West, Montreal, Quebec H3A 1E7
*Toronto:* (☎ 905-415 1060, toll-free ☎ 800-387 0711) Suite 401, 80 Tiverton Court, Markham, Ontario L3R 0G4
**France**
(☎ 01 44 51 39 51) 5 Blvd des Capucines, Paris 75002
**UK**
(☎ 020-8686 0677, 8686 5533) Marco Polo House, 3–5 Lansdowne Rd, Croydon, Surrey CR9 1LL
**USA**
(☎ 212-730 2121) Level 10, 15 West 44th St, New York, NY 10036

## VISAS & DOCUMENTS

EU citizens require only a national identity card or a passport to stay in Italy for as long as they like and since Italy is now a member of the Schengen Area, EU citizens can enter the country without passport controls.

Citizens of many other countries including the USA, Australia, Canada and New Zealand, do not need to apply for visas before arriving in Italy if they are entering the country as tourists only. If you are entering the country for any reason other than tourism, you should insist on having your passport stamped. Visitors are technically obliged to report to a *questura* (police headquarters) if they plan to stay at the same address for more than one week, to receive a *permesso di soggiorno* – in effect, permission to remain in the country for a nominated period up to the three-month limit. Tourists who are staying in hotels or youth hostels are not required to do this since proprietors need to register their guests with the police. A permesso di soggiorno only becomes a necessity (for non-EU citizens) if you plan to study, work (legally) or live in Italy.

## EMBASSIES & CONSULATES
### Italian Embassies & Consulates
Italian diplomatic missions abroad include:

**Australia**
*Embassy:* (☎ 02-6273 3333, fax 6273 4223, e ambital2@dynamite.com.au) 12 Grey St, Deakin, ACT 2601
*Consulate:* (☎ 03-9867 5744, fax 9866 3932, e itconmel@netlink.com.au) 509 St Kilda Rd, Melbourne, VIC 3004
*Consulate:* (☎ 02-9392 7900, fax 9252 4830, e itconsyd@armadillo.com.au) Level 45, Gateway, 1 Macquarie Place, Sydney, NSW 2000
**Canada**
*Embassy:* (☎ 613-232 2401, fax 233 1484, e ambital@italyincanada.com) Level 21, 275 Slater St, Ottawa, Ontario K1P 5H9
*Consulate:* (☎ 514-849 8351, fax 499 9471, e cgi@italconsul.montreal.qc.ca) 3489 Drummond St, Montreal, Quebec H3G 1X6
*Consulate:* (☎ 416-977 1566, fax 977 1119, e consolato.it@toronto.italconsulate.org) 136 Beverley St, Toronto, Ontario M5T 1Y5
**France**
*Embassy:* (☎ 01 49 54 03 00, fax 01 45 49 35 81, e ambasciata@amb-italie.fr) 7 rue de Varenne, Paris 75007
*Consulate:* (☎ 01 44 30 47 00, fax 01 45 25 87 50, e italconsulparigi@mailcity.com) 5 Blvd Emile Augier, Paris 75116
**New Zealand**
*Embassy:* (☎ 04-473 5339, fax 472 7255, e ambwell@xtra.co.nz) 34 Grant Rd, Thorndon, Wellington
**UK**
*Embassy:* (☎ 020-7312 2200, fax 7312 2230, e emblondon@embitaly.org.uk) 14 Three Kings Yard, London W1Y 4EH
*Consulate:* (☎ 020-7235 9371, fax 7823 1609) 38 Eaton Place, London SW1X 8AN

ITALY

**USA**
*Embassy:* (☎ 202-612 4400, fax 518 2154) 3000 Whitehaven St NW, Washington DC 20008
*Consulate:* (☎ 310-826 6207, fax 820 0727, ℮ cglos@conlang.com) Suite 300, 12400 Wilshire Blvd, West Los Angeles, CA 90025
*Consulate:* (☎ 212-7737 9100, fax 249 4945, ℮ italconsulnyc@italconsulnyc.org) 690 Park Ave, New York, NY 10021

## Embassies & Consulates in Italy

The headquarters of most foreign embassies are in Rome, although there are generally British and US consulates in other major cities. The following addresses and phone numbers are for Rome:

**Australia**
(☎ 06 85 27 21) Via Alessandria 215, 00198
**Canada**
(☎ 06 44 59 81) Via G B de Rossi 27, 00161
**France**
*Embassy:* (☎ 06 68 60 11) Piazza Farnese 67, 00186
*Consulate:* (☎ 06 68 80 21 52) Via Giulia 251, 00186
**Germany**
(☎ 06 49 21 31) Via San Martino della Battaglia 4, 00185
**New Zealand**
(☎ 06 441 71 71) Via Zara 28, 00198
**UK**
(☎ 06 42 20 00 01) Via XX Settembre 80a, 00187
**USA**
(☎ 06 4 67 41) Via Veneto 119a, 00187

For a complete list of all foreign embassies in Rome and other major cities throughout Italy, look in the local telephone book under *ambasciate* or *consolati,* or ask for a list at the tourist office.

## CUSTOMS

As of 1 July 1999, duty-free sales within the EU were abolished. Under the single market, goods bought in and exported within the EU incur no additional taxes, provided duty has been paid somewhere within the EU and the goods are for personal consumption.

Travellers coming from outside the EU, on the other hand, can import, duty-free: 200 cigarettes, 1L of spirits, 2L of wine, 60mls of perfume, 250mls of *eau de toilet,* and other goods up to a total value of €175; anything over this limit must be declared on arrival and the appropriate duty paid (it is advisable to carry all receipts).

## MONEY

A combination of travellers cheques and credit cards is the best way to take your money. If you buy travellers cheques in euro there should be no commission charged for cashing them. There are exchange offices at all major airports and train stations, but it is advisable to obtain a small amount of euro before arriving from a noneuro country to avoid problems and queues at the airport and train stations.

Major credit cards (eg, Visa, MasterCard and American Express), are widely accepted in Italy and can be used for purchases or payment in hotels and restaurants (although smaller places might not accept them). They can also be used to get money from ATMs *(bancomats)* or, if you don't have a PIN, over the counter in major banks, including Banca Commerciale Italiana, Cassa di Risparmio and Credito Italiano. If your credit card is lost, stolen or swallowed by an ATM, you can make a toll-free telephone call to have it cancelled. To cancel a MasterCard the number in Italy is ☎ 800-87 08 66 or make a reverse-charge call to St Louis is in the USA (☎ 314-275 66 90). To cancel a Visa card in Italy, phone ☎ 800-87 72 32. The toll-free emergency number to report a lost or stolen American Express (AmEx) card varies according to where the card was issued. Check with AmEx in your country or contact **American Express** (☎ 06 7 22 82) in Rome, which has a 24-hour card-holders' service.

The fastest way to receive money is through **Western Union** *(toll-free ☎ 800-01 38 39).* This service functions in Italy through the Mail Boxes Etc chain of stores, which you will find in the bigger cities. The sender and receiver have to turn up at a Western Union outlet with passport or other form of ID and the fees charged for the virtually immediate transfer depend on the amount sent.

## Currency

Italy's currency since 2002 is the euro. See the boxed text 'The Euro' in the introductory Facts for the Visitor chapter. A good website for exchange rates is Ⓦ www.oanda.com.

Remember that, as with other continental Europeans, Italians indicate decimals with commas and thousands with points.

## Costs

A *very* prudent traveller could get by on €45 per day, but only by staying in youth hostels, eating one meal a day (at the hostel), buying a sandwich or pizza by the slice for lunch and minimising the number of galleries and museums visited, since the entrance fee to most major museums is cripplingly expensive at around €4.50. You can save on transport costs by buying tourist or day tickets for city bus and underground services. When travelling by train, you can save money by avoiding the fast Eurostars, which charge a *supplemento rapido*. Italy's railways also offer a few cut-price options for students, young people and tourists for travel within a nominated period (see the introductory Getting Around section later in this chapter for more information).

Museums and galleries usually give discounts to students, but you will need a valid student card, which you can obtain from CTS offices if you have documents proving you are a student. Other discounts are offered to EU citizens aged between 18 and 25 (around 50%). EU citizens under 18 and over 65 years of age are generally admitted free of charge.

A basic breakdown of costs during an average day could be: accommodation €15 (youth hostel) to €40; breakfast (coffee and croissant) €1.75; lunch (sandwich and mineral water) €3.20; daily public transport ticket €6; entry fee for one museum €4.50 to €6.50; a sit-down dinner €8 to €25.

## Tipping & Bargaining

You are not expected to tip on top of restaurant service charges, but it is common practice among Italians to leave a small amount, say around 10%. In bars they will leave any small change as a tip. You can tip taxi drivers if you wish but it's not obligatory.

Bargaining is common throughout Italy in the various flea markets, but not normally in shops. You can try bargaining for the price of a room in a *pensione* (small hotel), particularly if you plan to stay for more than a few days or out of season.

## POST & COMMUNICATIONS
### Post

Stamps (*francobolli*) are available at post offices and authorised tobacconists (look for the official *tabacchi* sign: a big 'T', often white on black). Since letters often need to be weighed, what you get at the tobacconist's for international airmail will occasionally be an approximation of the proper rate. Main post offices in the bigger cities are generally open from around 8am to 6pm. Many open on Saturday morning, too.

Mail is divided into three zones: zone 1 (Italy, Europe and the Mediterranean Basin), zone 2 (Africa, Asia and the USA) and zone 3 (Oceania). *Posta Ordinaria* (ordinary post – not used much anymore) for letters and postcards up to 20g costs €0.41 (zone 1) and €0.52 (zones 2 and 3).

*Posta prioritaria* (priority post) for postcards and letters up to 20g costs €0.62 (zone 1) and €0.77 (zones 2 and 3). Using this service, mail is supposed to reach its destination within three days for Europe, five days for the Mediterranean Basin, five to six days for the USA, and eight days for South America, Canada, Africa, Asia, Australia and New Zealand.

Registered mail in Italy is known as *raccomandato*, insured mail as *assicurato* and express post as *postacelere*.

## Telephone & Fax

Italy's country code is ☎ 39. Area codes are an integral part of the telephone number, even if you're dialling a local number.

Local and long-distance calls can be made from public phones, or from a Telecom office. Italy's rates, particularly for long-distance calls, are among the highest in Europe. Most public phones accept only phonecards, sold in denominations of €2.50, €5 and €25 at tobacconists and newsstands, or from Telecom vending machines. Local calls from a public phone cost around €0.10 for three minutes. Off-peak hours for domestic calls are between 10pm to 8am. For international calls it's 10pm to 8am and all Sunday.

To make a reverse-charge (collect) call from a public phone, dial ☎ 170. For European countries call ☎ 15. All operators speak English. Numbers for this Home Country Direct service are displayed in the early pages of Italian phone books and include: Australia (☎ 172 10 61, Telstra), Canada (☎ 172 10 01, Teleglobe), New Zealand (☎ 172 10 64), UK (☎ 172 00 44) and USA (☎ 172 10 11, AT&T). For international directory inquiries call ☎ 176.

International faxes can cost €3.50 for the first page and €2 per page thereafter. You can transmit faxes from specialist fax/photocopy shops, post offices, Internet cafés and from some tabacchi.

## Email & Internet Access

Italy has a growing number of Internet cafés, where you can send and receive email or surf the Net for around €2 to €5 an hour.

## DIGITAL RESOURCES

There is an Italy page at Lonely Planet's website at ⓦ www.lonelyplanet.com. The following are just a few of the huge number of useful websites for travellers to Italy.

CTS at ⓦ www.cts.it has useful information (mostly in Italian) from Italy's leading student travel organisation; ⓦ www.beniculturali.com is a good cultural site that has museum information and online reservation options. Nature lovers can get Italian national park information at ⓦ www.parks.it.

The Vatican is represented at ⓦ www.vatican .va, which has detailed information about Vatican City, including virtual tours of the main monuments and the museums. If you're looking for train information, visit ⓦ www .fs-on-line.com, for details about timetables and services.

## BOOKS

For a more comprehensive guide to Italy, pick up a copy of Lonely Planet's *Italy*. If you want to concentrate on specific regions, pick up Lonely Planet's *Rome, Florence, Venice, Tuscany, Milan, Turin & Genoa* and *Sicily* guides. Also useful are the *Italian phrasebook, World Food Italy, Rome City Map* and *Florence City Map*. If you're a hiking enthusiast, a good companion is Lonely Planet's *Walking in Italy*.

For a potted history of the country, try the *Concise History of Italy* by Vincent Cronin. *A History of Contemporary Italy: Society and Politics 1943–1988* by Paul Ginsborg is well written and absorbing. Luigi Barzini's classic *The Italians* is a great introduction to Italian people and culture, while *Excellent Cadavers: The Mafia and the Death of the First Italian Republic* by Alexander Stille is a shocking and fascinating account of the Mafia in Sicily.

Interesting introductions to travelling in Italy include *A Traveller in Italy* by HV Morton, who also wrote similar guides to Rome and southern Italy.

## NEWSPAPERS & MAGAZINES

Major English-language newspapers available in Italy are the *Herald Tribune*, the English *Guardian*, the *Times* and the *Telegraph*. *Time* magazine, *Newsweek* and the *Economist* are available weekly.

## TIME

Italy is one hour ahead of GMT/UTC, and two hours ahead during summer. Daylight-saving time starts on the last Sunday in March, when clocks are put forward an hour. Clocks are put back an hour on the last Sunday in September. Remember to make allowances for daylight-saving time in your own country. Note that Italy operates on a 24-hour clock.

## LAUNDRY

Coin laundrettes, where you can do your own washing, can be found in most of the main cities and towns, although they are scarce in Italy's south. A load will cost around €3.10. Many camping grounds have laundry facilities.

## WOMEN TRAVELLERS

Italy is not a dangerous country for women, but women travelling alone may find themselves recipients of unwanted attention from men. Most of the attention falls into the nuisance category and it is best simply to ignore the catcalls, hisses and whistles. However, women touring alone should use common sense. Avoid walking alone in dark and deserted streets and look for centrally located hotels that are within easy walking distance of places where you can eat at night. In the south the often-persistent attention paid to women travelling alone can border on the very intrusive, particularly in the bigger cities. Women should never hitchhike alone.

## GAY & LESBIAN TRAVELLERS

Homosexuality is legal in Italy and generally well tolerated in major cities, although overt displays of affection might get a negative response in smaller towns and villages, particularly in the south. The age of consent for men and women is 16.

The national organisation for gays (men and women) is **Arcigay** (☎ 051 649 30 55, fax 051 528 22 26; ⓦ www.arcigay.it; *Via Don Minzoni 18*) in Bologna.

## DISABLED TRAVELLERS

The Italian travel agency CIT can advise on hotels that have special facilities. The UK-based **Royal Association for Disability and**

ITALY

**Rehabilitation** *(Radar;* ☎ *020-7250 3222;* Ⓦ *www.radar.org.uk; 12 City Forum, 250 City Rd, London EC1V 8AF)*, publishes a useful guide called *Holidays & Travel Abroad: A Guide for Disabled People.*

## SENIOR TRAVELLERS

Senior travellers who plan on using the train as their main mode of transport should look into the *Carta Argento* (€25), which gives the over-60s reductions of up to 40% on full-price train fares.

## DANGERS & ANNOYANCES

Theft is the main problem for travellers in Italy, mostly in the form of petty thievery and pickpocketing, especially in the bigger cities. Although not something you should be particularly worried about, a few precautions are necessary to avoid being robbed. Carry your valuables in a moneybelt and avoid flashing your dough in public. Pickpockets operate in crowded areas, such as markets and on buses headed for major tourist attractions.

Watch out for groups of kids that have a dishevelled look, as many can be lightning fast as they empty your pockets. Motorcycle bandits are a minor problem in Naples, Rome, Palermo and Syracuse. If you are using a shoulder bag, make sure that you wear the strap across your body and have the bag on the side away from the road.

Never leave valuables in a parked car – in fact, try not to leave anything in the car if you can help it.

It is a good idea to park your car in a supervised car park if you are leaving it for any amount of time. Car theft is a major problem in Rome and Naples.

## BUSINESS HOURS

Business hours can vary from city to city, but generally shops and businesses are open 8.30am to 1pm and 5pm to 7.30pm Monday to Saturday, and some are also open on Sunday morning. Banks are generally open 8.30am to 1.30pm and from 2.30pm to 4.30pm Monday to Friday, but hours vary between banks and cities. Large post offices are open 8am to 6pm or 7pm Monday to Saturday. Most museums close on Monday, and restaurants and bars are required to close for one day each week.

Opening times were liberalised under new trading hours laws that went into effect in April 1999, although Italians tend to value their time off and are not necessarily rushing to keep their shops open throughout the week.

## PUBLIC HOLIDAYS & SPECIAL EVENTS

Italy's national public holidays include: 6 January (Epiphany), Easter Monday, 25 April (Liberation Day), 1 May (Labour Day), 15 August (*Ferragosto* or Feast of the Assumption), 1 November (All Saints' Day), 8 December (Feast of the Immaculate Conception), 25 December (Christmas Day), and 26 December (Feast of St Stephen).

Individual towns also have public holidays to celebrate the feasts of their patron saints. Some of these are the Feast of St Mark in Venice on 25 April; the Feast of St John the Baptist on 24 June in Florence, Genoa and Turin; the Feast of St Peter and St Paul in Rome on 29 June; the Feast of St Rosalia in Palermo on July 15; the Feast of St Januarius in Naples on 19 September; and the Feast of St Ambrose in Milan on 7 December.

Annual events in Italy worth keeping in mind include:

**Carnevale** During the 10 days before Ash Wednesday, many towns stage carnivals (one last binge before Lent!). The one held in Venice is the best known, but there are also others, including at Viareggio in Tuscany and Ivrea near Turin.

**Holy Week** There are important festivals during this week everywhere in Italy, in particular the colourful and sombre traditional festivals of Sicily. In Assisi the rituals of Holy Week attract thousands of pilgrims.

**Scoppio del Carro** Literally 'Explosion of the Cart', this colourful event held in Florence in Piazza del Duomo on Easter Sunday features the explosion of a cart full of fireworks and dates back to the Crusades. If all goes well, it is seen as a good omen for the city.

**Corso dei Ceri** One of the strangest festivals in Italy, this is held in Gubbio (Umbria) on 15 May, and features a race run by men carrying enormous wooden constructions called *ceri*, in honour of the town's patron saint, Sant'Ubaldo.

### Emergency Services

Nationwide emergency numbers are *carabinieri* (police with military and civil duties) ☎ 112, police ☎ 113, fire brigade (Vigili del Fuoco) ☎ 115, Automobile Club d'Italia (ACI) ☎ 116, ambulance ☎ 118.

Il **Palio** On 2 July and 16 August, Siena stages this extraordinary horse race in the town's main piazza.

## ACTIVITIES
### Hiking
It is possible to go on organised treks in Italy, but if you want to go it alone you will find that trails are well marked and there are plenty of refuges in the Alps, in the Alpi Apuane in Tuscany and in the northern parts of the Apennines. The Dolomites provide spectacular walking and trekking opportunities. On Sardinia, head for the coastal gorges between Dorgali and Baunei. Sicily's Mt Etna is also a popular hiking destination.

### Skiing
The numerous excellent ski resorts in the Alps and the Apennines usually offer good skiing conditions from December to April.

### Cycling
This is a good option if you can't afford a car but want to see the more isolated parts of the country. Classic cycling areas include Tuscany and Umbria.

## ACCOMMODATION
The prices mentioned here are intended as a guide only. There is generally a fair degree of fluctuation throughout the country, depending on the season. Prices usually rise by 5% to 10% each year, although sometimes they remain fixed for years, or even drop.

### Camping
Facilities throughout Italy are usually reasonable and vary from major complexes with swimming pools, tennis courts and restaurants, to simple camping grounds. Average prices are around €6 per person and €6 or more for a site. Lists of camping grounds in and near major cities are often available at tourist information offices.

The Touring Club Italiano (TCI) publishes an annual book on all camping sites in Italy, *Campeggi e Villaggi Turistici* (€18). Free camping is forbidden in many of the more beautiful parts of Italy, although the authorities seem to pay less attention in the off season.

### Hostels
Hostels in Italy are called *ostelli per la gioventú* and are run by Associazione Italiana Alberghi per la Gioventú (AIG), which is affiliated with Hostelling International (HI). Prices, including breakfast, range from €10 to €15. Closing times vary, but are usually from 9am to 3pm or 5pm and curfews are around midnight. Men and women are often segregated, although some hostels also have family accommodation.

An HI membership card is not always required, but it is recommended that you have one. Membership cards can be purchased at major hostels, from CTS offices and from AIG offices throughout Italy. Pick up a list of all hostels in Italy, with details of prices, locations etc from the **AIG office** (☎ *06 487 11 52, fax 06 488 04 92; Via Cavour 44, Rome; open 9am-5pm Mon-Fri)*.

### Pensioni & Hotels
Establishments are required to notify local tourist boards of prices for the coming year and by law must then adhere to those prices (although they do have two legal opportunities each year to increase charges). If tourists believe they are being overcharged, they can make a complaint to the local tourist office. The best advice is to confirm hotel charges before you put your bags down, since many proprietors employ various methods of bill padding. These include a compulsory breakfast (up to €7.75 in the high season) and compulsory half or full board, although this can often be a good deal in some towns.

The cheapest way to stay in a hotel or pensione is to share a room with two or more people: the cost is usually no more than 15% of the cost of a double room for each additional person. Single rooms are uniformly expensive in Italy (from around €30) and quite a number of establishments do not even bother to cater for the single traveller.

There is often no difference between an establishment that calls itself a pensione and one that calls itself an *albergo* (hotel); in fact, some use both titles. *Locande* (similar to pensioni) and *alloggi*, also known as *affittacamere*, are generally cheaper, but not always.

### Rental Accommodation
Finding rental accommodation in the major cities can be difficult and time-consuming and you will often find the cost prohibitive, especially in Rome, Florence, Milan and Venice. Major resort areas, such as the Aeolian Islands and the Alps offer rental accommodation

ITALY

that's reasonably priced and readily available. Many tourist offices will provide information by mail, fax or email.

One organisation that organises expensive but charming villas and houses in Tuscany, Umbria, Veneto, the Amalfi Coast, Sicily and Rome is Cuendet. Write to **Cuendet & Cie spa** (☎ *0577 57 63 30, fax 0577 30 11 49;* W *www.cuendet.com; Strada di Strove 17, 53035 Monteriggioni, Siena).* CIT offices throughout the world also have lists of villas and apartments for rent in Italy.

## Agriturismo

This is basically a farm holiday and is becoming increasingly popular in Italy. Traditionally, the idea was that families rented out rooms in their farmhouses. For detailed information on all facilities in Italy contact **Agriturist** (☎ *06 685 23 42;* W *www.agriturist.it; Corso Vittorio Emanuele 101, 00186 Rome).* It publishes *Agriturist* (€14), which lists establishments throughout Italy.

## Refuges

Before you go hiking in any part of Italy, obtain information about refuges *(rifugi)* from the local tourist offices. Some refuges have private rooms, but many offer dorm-style accommodation, particularly those that are more isolated. Average prices are from €10 to €25 per person for B&B. A meal costs around the same as at a trattoria. The locations of refuges are marked on good hiking maps and most open only from late June to September. The alpine refuges of CAI (Italian Alpine Club) offer discounts to members of associated foreign alpine clubs.

## FOOD & DRINKS

Eating is one of life's great pleasures for Italians. Cooking styles vary notably from region to region and significantly between the north and south. In the north the food is rich and often creamy; in central Italy the locals use a lot of olive oil and herbs and regional specialities are noted for their simplicity, fine flavour and the use of fresh produce. As you go further south the food becomes hotter and spicier and the *dolci* (cakes and pastries) sweeter and richer.

Vegetarians will have no problems eating in Italy. Most eating establishments serve a selection of *contorni* (vegetables prepared in a variety of ways).

If you have access to cooking facilities, buy fruit and vegetables at open-air markets and salami, cheese and wine at *alimentari* or *salumerie* (a cross between a grocery store and a delicatessen). Fresh bread is available at a *forno* or *panetteria*.

Restaurants are divided into several categories. A *tavola calda* (literally 'hot table') usually offers inexpensive, pre-prepared meat, pasta and vegetable dishes in a self-service style. A *rosticceria* usually offers cooked meats, but also often has a larger selection of takeaway food. A pizzeria will of course serve pizza, but usually also a full menu. An *osteria* is likely to be either a wine bar offering a small selection of dishes, or a small *trattoria*. Many of the establishments that are in fact restaurants *(ristoranti)* call themselves trattoria and vice versa for reasons best known to themselves.

Most eating establishments charge a *coperto* (cover charge) of around €1 to €2, and a *servizio* (service charge) of 10% to 15%. Restaurants are usually open for lunch from 12.30pm to 3pm, but will rarely take orders after 2pm. In the evening, opening hours vary from north to south. In the north they eat dinner earlier, usually from 7.30pm, but in Sicily you will be hard-pressed to find a restaurant open before 8.30pm, and you'll be dining alone before about 9.30pm. Restaurants rarely stay open after 11.30pm.

A full meal will consist of an antipasto, which can vary from *bruschetta*, a type of garlic bread with various toppings, to fried vegetables, or *prosciutto e melone* (ham wrapped around melon). Next comes the *primo piatto,* a pasta dish or risotto, followed by the *secondo piatto* of meat or fish. Italians often then eat an *insalata* (salad) or contorni and round off the meal with dolci and *caffé,* often at a bar on the way home or back to work. In this chapter, we've costed eating out as a meal for one person with a first course, second course, some wine and a side dish or desert.

Italian wine is justifiably world-famous. Fortunately, wine is reasonably priced, so you will rarely pay more than €7.75 for a bottle of very drinkable wine and as little as €3.10 will still buy something of reasonable quality. Try the famous chianti and *brunello* in Tuscany, but also the *vernaccia* of San Gimignano, the *barolo* in Piedmont, the *lacrima christi* or *falanghina* in Naples and the *cannonau* in Sardinia. Beer is known as *birra* and the cheapest local variety is Peroni.

## ENTERTAINMENT

Italians have a great appreciation of entertainment, so visitors can indulge themselves with opera, theatre, classical music recitals, rock concerts and traditional festivals. Major entertainment festivals are also held, such as the Festival of Two Worlds in June/July at Spoleto, Umbria Jazz in Perugia in July, Rome's Estate Romana in July, and the Venice Biennale every odd-numbered year. Operas are performed in Verona and Rome throughout summer (for details see Entertainment under both cities) and at various times of the year throughout the country, notably at the opera houses in Milan and Rome.

## SPECTATOR SPORTS

Soccer *(calcio)* is the national passion and there are stadiums in all the major towns. If you'd rather watch a game than visit a Roman ruin, check newspapers for details of who's playing where, although tickets for the bigger matches can be hard to find. The Italian Formula One Grand Prix races are held at Monza, just north of Milan in September. The San Marino Grand Prix is held at Imola in May. Good luck finding a ticket, though.

## SHOPPING

Italy is synonymous with elegant, fashionable and high-quality clothing, leather goods, glass and ceramics. The problem is that most are very expensive. However, if you happen to be in the country during the summer sales in July and August and the winter sales in January and February, you can pick up some incredible bargains.

# Getting There & Away

## AIR

Although paying full fare to travel by plane in Europe is expensive, there are various discount options, including cut-price fares for students and people aged under 26. There are also stand-by fares, which are usually around 60% of the full fare. Several airlines offer cut-rate fares on legs of international flights between European cities. These are usually the cheapest fares available, but the catch is that they are often during the night or very early in the morning, and the days on which

you can fly are severely restricted. Some examples of high-season Alitalia fares at the time of writing are: Rome–Paris €311 return; Rome–London €271 return; and Rome–Amsterdam €311 return.

Another option is to travel on charter flights. Try **Charter Flight Centre** (☎ 020-7828 1090; W *charterflights.co.uk; 19 Denbigh St, London SW1)*, which specialises in such flights and also organises some regular scheduled flights.

Look in the classified pages of the London Sunday newspapers for information on other cheap flights. **STA Travel** (☎ *020-7361 6161, toll-free* ☎ *0870-160 05 99; 86 Old Brompton Rd, London SW7 3LQ)*, has occasional specials and can help with student fares. Within Italy, information on discount fares is available from CTS and Sestante CIT offices (see Tourist Offices in the Facts for the Visitor section, earlier in this chapter).

## LAND

If you are travelling by bus, train or car to Italy it will be necessary to cross various borders, so remember to check whether you require visas for those countries before leaving home.

### Bus

**Eurolines** (W *www.eurolines.com)* is the main international carrier in Europe, with representatives in Italy and throughout the continent. In Italy the main bus company operating this service is **Lazzi** (☎ *055 35 10 61; Piazza Adua 1, Florence* • ☎ *06 884 08 40; Via Tagliamento 27b, Rome)*. Buses leave from Rome, Florence, Milan, Turin, Venice and Naples, as well as numerous other Italian towns, for major cities throughout Europe including London, Paris, Barcelona, Madrid, Amsterdam, Budapest, Prague, Athens and Istanbul. Some ticket prices are Rome–Paris €82 (€148 return), Rome–London €116 (€179 return) and Rome–Barcelona €102 (€183 return).

### Train

Eurostar (ES) and Eurocity (EC) trains run from major destinations throughout Europe direct to major Italian cities. On overnight hauls you can book a *cuccetta* (known outside Italy as a couchette or sleeping berth, and worth booking!).

Travellers aged under 26 can take advantage of the Inter-Rail Pass, Eurail Pass Youth and Europass Youth. For price and also purchasing details, visit the website at **w** www .eurail.com.

You can book tickets at train stations or at CTS, Sestante CIT and most travel agencies. Eurostar and Eurocity trains carry a supplement (determined by the distance you are travelling and the type of train).

## Car & Motorcycle

Travelling with your own vehicle certainly gives you more flexibility. The drawbacks in Italy are that cars can be inconvenient in larger cities where you'll have to deal with heavy traffic, parking problems, the risk of car theft, the exorbitant price of petrol and toll charges on the autostrade.

If you want to rent a car or motorcycle, you will need a valid EU driving licence, an International Driving Permit, or your driving permit from your own country. If you're driving your own car, you'll need an international insurance certificate, known as a Carta Verde (Green Card), which can be obtained from your insurer.

## Hitching

Hitching is never safe in any country and we don't recommend it. Your best bet is to inquire at hostels throughout Europe, where you can often arrange a lift. **The International Lift Centre** (☎ 055 28 06 26) in Florence and **Enjoy Rome** (☎ 06 445 18 43) might be able to help organise lifts. Note that it is illegal to hitch on the autostrade.

## SEA

Ferries connect Italy to Spain, Croatia, Greece, Turkey, Tunisia and Malta. There are also services to Corsica (from Livorno) and Albania (from Bari and Ancona). See Getting There & Away under Brindisi (for ferries to/from Greece), Ancona (to/from Greece, Albania and Croatia), Venice (to/from Greece) and Sicily (to/from Malta and Tunisia).

# Getting Around

## AIR

Travelling by plane is expensive within Italy and it makes much better sense to use the efficient and considerably cheaper rail and bus services. The domestic airlines include Alitalia, Meridiana and Air One. The main airports are in Rome, Pisa, Milan, Bologna, Genoa, Turin, Naples, Catania, Palermo and Cagliari, but there are other, smaller airports throughout Italy. Domestic flights can be booked directly with the airlines or through Sestante CIT, CTS and other travel agencies.

Alitalia offers a range of discounts for students, young people and families, and for weekend travel.

## BUS

Numerous bus companies operate within Italy. It is usually necessary to make reservations only for long trips, such as Rome–Palermo or Rome–Brindisi. Otherwise, just arrive early enough to claim a seat.

Buses can be a cheaper and faster way to get around if your destination is not on major rail lines, for instance from Umbria to Rome or Florence, and in the interior areas of Sicily and Sardinia.

## TRAIN

Travelling by train in Italy is simple, relatively cheap and generally efficient. The Ferrovie dello Stato (FS) is the partially privatised state train system and there are many private train services throughout the country.

There are several types of trains: Regionale (R), which usually stop at all stations and can be very slow; interRegionale (iR), which run between the regions; intercity (IC) or Eurocity (EC), which service only the major cities; and Eurostar Italia (ES), which serves major Italian and European cities.

To go on the Intercity, Eurocity and Eurostar Italia trains, you have to pay a *supplemento,* an additional charge determined by the distance you are travelling and the type of train.

All tickets *must* be validated in the yellow machines at the entrance to all platforms at train stations.

It is not worth buying a Eurail or Inter-Rail pass if you are going to travel only in Italy. The FS offers its own discount passes for travel within the country. These include the Carta Verde for those aged between 12 and 26 years. It costs €26, is valid for one year, and entitles you to a 20% discount on all train travel. You can also buy a *biglietto chilometrico* (kilometric ticket), which is valid for two months and allows you to cover 3000km, with a maximum of 20 trips. It costs €181/117 for 1st/2nd class travel and you must pay the supplement if you catch an Intercity or Eurostar train. The main attraction of this ticket is that it can be used by up to five people, either singly or together.

Some examples of 2nd-class fares (including IC supplement) are Rome–Florence for €21.95 and Rome–Naples €16.53.

## CAR & MOTORCYCLE

Roads are generally good throughout the country and there is an excellent system of autostrade (freeways). The main north–south link is the Autostrada del Sole, which extends from Milan to Reggio di Calabria (called the A1 from Milan to Naples and the A3 from Naples to Reggio).

In Italy people drive on the right-hand side of the road and pass on the left. Unless otherwise indicated, you must give way to cars coming from the right. It is compulsory to wear seat belts if they are fitted to the car (front seat belts on all cars and back seat belts on cars produced after 26 April 1990). If you are caught not wearing your seat belt, you will be required to pay an on-the-spot fine of €30.

Wearing a helmet is compulsory for every motorcycle and moped rider and passenger – although you won't necessarily see this.

Some of the Italian cities, including Rome, Bologna, Florence, Milan and Turin have introduced restricted access to both private and rental cars in their historical centres. The restrictions, however, do not apply to vehicles with foreign registrations. *Motorini* (mopeds) and scooters (such as vespas) are able to enter the zones without any problems.

Speed limits, unless otherwise indicated by local signs, are: on autostrade 130km/h, on nonurban roads 110km/h; on secondary nonurban highways 90km/h; and in built-up areas 50km/h.

Petrol prices are high in Italy – around €1.05 per litre. Petrol is called *benzina,* unleaded petrol is *benzina senza piombo* and diesel is *gasolio.*

The blood-alcohol limit is 0.08% and there are now random breath tests.

## BOAT

*Navi* (large ferries) service the islands of Sicily and Sardinia, and *traghetti* (smaller ferries) and *aliscafi* (hydrofoils) service areas such as Elba, the Aeolian Islands, Capri and Ischia. The main embarkation points for Sicily and Sardinia are at Genoa, La Spezia, Livorno, Civitavecchia, Fiumicino and Naples.

**Tirrenia Navigazione** is the major company servicing the Mediterranean and it has offices throughout Italy. Most long-distance services travel overnight and all ferries carry vehicles (bicycles are free of charge).

## BICYCLE

Bikes are available for rent in many Italian towns – and cost around €10 a day or €60 a week. Bicycles can travel in the baggage compartment of some Italian trains (but not on the Eurostars or Intercity trains).

# Rome

**postcode 00100 • pop 2.65 million**
A phenomenal concentration of history, legend and monuments coexist in chaotic harmony in Rome, as well as an equally phenomenal concentration of people busily going about their everyday lives.

Rome's origins date to a group of Etruscan, Latin and Sabine settlements on the Palatine, Esquiline, Quirinal and surrounding hills, but it is the legend of Romulus and Remus (the twins raised by a she-wolf), which has captured the popular imagination. The myth says Romulus killed his brother during a battle over who should govern, and then established the city on the Palatine (Palatino), one of the famous Seven Hills of Rome. From the legend grew an empire that eventually controlled almost the entire world known to Europeans at the time.

In Rome there is visible evidence of the two great empires of the Western world: the Roman Empire and the Christian Church. On the one hand is the Forum and Colosseum, and on the other St Peter's and the Vatican. In between, in almost every piazza, lies so many layers of history that what you see is only the tip of the iceberg – this is exemplified by St Peter's Basilica, which stands on the site of an earlier basilica built by the Emperor Constantine over the necropolis where St Peter was buried.

## ORIENTATION

Rome is a vast city, but the historical centre is relatively small. Most of the major sights are west – and within walking distance – of the central train station, Stazione Termini. Lonely Planet's *Rome City Map* is handy to have, with detailed maps of central Rome and

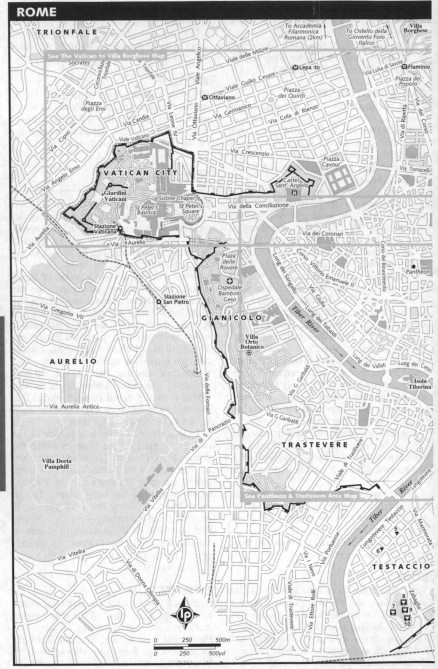

# ROME

See The Vatican to Villa Borghese Map

TRIONFALE

To Accademia
Filarmonica
Romana (2km)

To Ostello della
Gioventu Foro
Italico

Villa
Borghese

Socrates

Circonvallazione
Trionfale

Via Trionfale

Viale Angelico

Viale delle Milizie

Lepanto

Flaminio

Piazza
degli Eroi

Via Candia

Via Leone IV

Via Ottaviano

Viale Giulio Cesare

Ottaviano

Via Germanico

Piazza
dei Quiriti

Via Cola di Rienzo

Piazza
dei Quiriti

Via Luisa di Savoia

Piazza del
Popolo

Via di Ripetta

Via del Corso

Via Cipro

Viale Vaticano

Via Crescenzio

Via Tomacelli

VATICAN CITY

Giardini
Vaticani

Sistine Chapel

St Peter's
Basilica

St Peter's
Square

Castel
Sant' Angelo

Piazza
Cavour

Via Angelo Emo

Via della Conciliazione

Stazione
Vaticana

Via dei Coronari

Via Aurelia

Via Aurelia

Plaza
delle
Rovere

Corso Vittorio Emanuele II

Pantheon

Lung del Sangallo

Via Giulia

Lung dei Tebaldi

Corso del Rinascimento

Stazione
San Pietro

Ospedale
Bambino
Gesù

GIANICOLO

Tiber River

Via Gregorio VII

Villa
Orto
Botanico

Lung dei Vallati

Lung dei Cenci

AURELIO

Via G. Garibaldi

Isola
Tiberina

Via Aurelia Antica

Via delle Fornaci

Via G Garibaldi

Via di Trastevere

Villa Doria
Pamphili

Via di S Pancrazio

TRASTEVERE

River

Lungotevere

See Pantheon & Trastevere Area Map

Via Vitellia

Via Vitellia

Via di Donna Olimpia

Viale di Trastevere

Via Portuense

Tiber

Lungotevere Testaccio

Via Marmorata

5

6

TESTACCIO

Viale di Trastevere

Via Ettore Rolli

Viale dei Quattro Venti

7

8

9

10

Zabaglia

0    250    500m
0    250    500yd

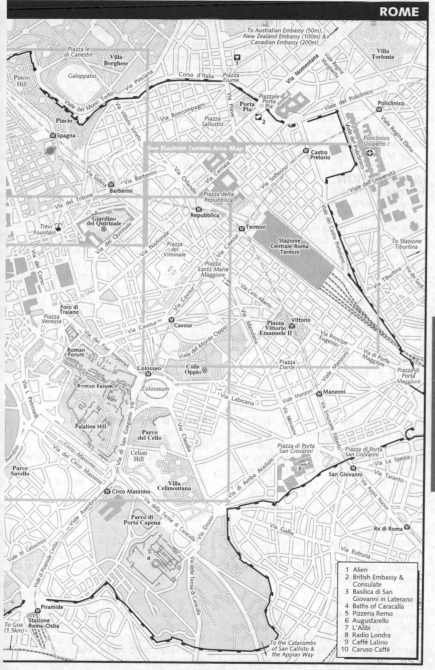

ROME

ITALY

To Australian Embassy (50m),
New Zealand Embassy (100m) &
Canadian Embassy (200m)

Piazza le
di Canestre

Villa
Borghese

Villa
Torlonia

Galoppatio

Pincio
Hill

Corso d'Italia

Piazza
Fiume

Via Nomentana

Via Regina Margherita

Pincio

Viale del Muro Torto

Via Pinciana

Via Boncompagni

Porta
Pia

Piazzale
Porta
Pia

Viale del Policlinico

Policlinico

Via Regina Siena

M Spagna

Via Vittorio Veneto

Piazza
Sallustio

Via Piave

Viale del Policlinico

Policlinico
Umberto I

Via Sistina

Via Barberini

Barberini

Via Orlando

Via Cernaia

See Stazione Termini Area Map

M Castro
Pretorio

Viale dell'Università

Via del Tritone

Piazza della
Repubblica

Via Solferino

Viale del Castro Pretorio

Trevi
Fountain

Giardino
del Quirinale

M Repubblica

Piazza della
Repubblica

To Stazione
Tiburtina

Via del Quirinale

Piazza
del
Viminale

M Termini

Stazione
Centrale-Roma
Termini

Via Nazionale

Via Cavour

Piazza
Santa Maria
Maggiore

Via Tiburtina

Via de Sardi

Foro di
Traiano

Via Cavour

Via Carlo Alberto

Piazza
Venezia

Via dei Fori Imperiali

M Cavour

Via Merulana

Piazza
Vittorio
Emanuele II

Vittorio

Via Principe
Eugenio

Via di Porta
Maggiore

Piazza di
Porta
Maggiore

Roman
Forum

Colosseo M

Colle
Oppio

Viale del Monte Oppio

Piazza
Dante

Viale Manzoni

Roman Forum

Colosseum

Via Labicana

Viale Manzoni

M Manzoni

Via Emanuele Filiberto

Palatine Hill

Parco
del Celio

Via Claudia

Celian
Hill

Parco
Savello

Circo Massimo

Via del Circo Massimo

Villa
Celimontana

Piazza di Porta
San Giovanni

3

Piazza di Porta
San Giovanni

San Giovanni

Via La Spezia

Via Taranto

M Circo Massimo

Viale Aventino

Parco di
Porta Capena

Via delle Terme di Caracalla

Via di Amba Aradam

Re di Roma M

Parco di
Porta Capena

4

Via delle Terme di Caracalla

Via Druso

Via Gallia

Via Eutruria

Appia Nuova

Piramide

Viale di Piramide Cestia

Stazione
Roma-Ostia

To Goa
(1.5km)

To the Catacombs
of San Callisto &
the Appian Way

1 Alien
2 British Embassy &
   Consulate
3 Basilica di San
   Giovanni in Laterano
4 Baths of Caracalla
5 Pizzeria Remo
6 Augustarello
7 L'Alibi
8 Radio Londra
9 Caffé Latino
10 Caruso Caffé

historical areas, a Metropolitana map and walking tour.

Plan an itinerary if your time is limited. Many of the major museums and galleries open all day until 7pm or 8pm. Many museums are closed on Monday, but it is a good idea to check.

The main bus terminus is in Piazza del Cinquecento, directly in front of the train station. Many intercity buses arrive and depart from the Piazzale Tiburtina, in front of the Stazione Tiburtina, accessible from Termini on the Metropolitana Linea B.

## INFORMATION
### Tourist Offices

There is an **APT tourist information office** (☎ 06 48 90 63 00; open 8am-9pm daily) at Stazione Termini. It's in the central causeway and has multilingual staff, as well as some 'roaming' staff who may approach you in the station (ID is visible).

There is a great **APT main office** (☎ 06 36 00 43 99; Via Parigi 5; open 9am-7pm Mon-Sat). Walk northwest from Stazione Termini, through Piazza della Repubblica. Via Parigi runs to the right from the top of the piazza, about a five-minute walk from the station. The office has information on hotels and museum opening hours and entrance fees. Staff can also provide maps and printed information about provincial and intercity bus services.

Another good source of information and assistance is **Enjoy Rome** (☎ 06 445 18 43, fax 06 445 68 90; W www.enjoyrome.com; Via Marghera 8a; open 8.30am-7pm Mon-Sat & 8.30am-2pm Sun), five minutes walk to the northeast of the station. It's a privately run tourist office that offers a free hotel-reservation service. The English-speaking staff can also organise alternative accommodation such as apartments. They have extensive up-to-date information about Rome and you can book great three-hour walking tours that cover all sorts of interests and are conducted by native-English speakers or art and history specialists.

## Money

Banks are open 8.45am to 1.30pm and usually from 2.45pm to 4pm Monday to Friday. You will find banks and exchange offices at Stazione Termini. There is also an exchange office (Banco di Santo Spirito) at Fiumicino

airport, to your right as you exit from the customs area.

Numerous other exchange offices are scattered throughout the city, including **American Express** (☎ 06 676 41; Piazza di Spagna 38) and **Thomas Cook** (☎ 06 482 81 82; Piazza Barberini 21).

Otherwise, go to any one of the dozens of banks in the city centre. Credit cards can also be used in automatic teller machines (ATMs), known as bancomats, to obtain cash 24 hours a day. You'll need a PIN from your bank.

## Post & Communications

The **main post office** (Piazza San Silvestro 19; open 8.30am-6.30pm Mon-Fri & 8.30am-1pm Sat) is off Via del Tritone. Fermo posta (poste restante) is available here, although the postcode is 00186.

The **Vatican post office** (☎ 06 69 88 34 06; Piazza di San Pietro (St Peter's Square); open 8.30am-6pm Mon-Fri & 8.30am-1pm Sat) offers a faster and more reliable service (no fermo posta though).

There is a small Telecom office at Stazione Termini, from where you can make international calls direct or through an operator. Another office is near the station, on Via San Martino della Battaglia opposite Hotel Lachea-Dolomiti. International calls can easily be made with a phonecard (scheda telefonica) from any public phone. These can be bought at tobacconists and newspaper stands.

## Email & Internet Access

There are dozens of Internet cafés scattered throughout the city. The biggest and most convenient is **easyEverything** (Via Barberini 2), which has hundreds of terminals, opens 24 hours daily and charges around €1 for 30 minutes, depending on the time of day.

## Travel Agencies

There is an office of Italy's national tourist agency, **Sestante CIT** (☎ 06 46 20 31 44; Piazza della Repubblica 65), where you can make bookings for planes, trains and ferries. The staff speak English and there's information on fares for students and young people, plus tours of Rome and surrounds.

The student tourist centre, **CTS** (☎ 06 462 04 31; W www.cts.it; Via Genova 16), off Via Nazionale, offers similar services. It can make hotel reservations, and focuses on the discount- and student-travel market.

## Bookshops

**Feltrinelli International** (☎ 06 482 78 78; Via Orlando 84) has literature and travel guides in several languages. **The Anglo-American Book Company** (☎ 06 679 52 22; Via della Vite 27), off Piazza di Spagna, has an excellent selection of literature and travel guides. The English-speaking **Economy Book & Video Center** (☎ 06 474 68 77; Via Torino 136), off Via Nazionale, has both new and second-hand books (travel guides included).

## Laundry

**Bolle Blu** (Via Palestra 59; open 8am-10pm daily) is a coin laundrette near the train station, and costs €3.10 for a 7kg wash (soap included). Near the Vatican, **Onda Blu** (Via degli Scipioni 35) keeps the same hours as Bolle Blu and charges €3.10 for a 16kg wash with soap.

## Medical & Emergency Services

Emergency medical treatment is available in the *pronto soccorso* (casualty section) at public hospitals, including **Ospedale San Gallicano** (☎ 06 588 23 90; Via di San Gallicano 25/a, Trastevere), which specialises in skin and venereal diseases; **Ospedale San Giacome** (☎ 06 362 61; Via Canova 29) near Piazza del Popolo; and **Policlinico Umberto I** (☎ 06 499 71; Via del Policlinico 155), which is close to Stazione Termini. Rome's paediatric hospital is **Bambino Gesú** (☎ 06 68 59 23 51; Piazza di Sant'Onofrio 4) on the Janiculum (Gianicolo) Hill. From Piazza della Rovere (on the Lungotevere near St Peter's) head uphill along Via del Gianicolo. The hospital is at the top of the hill.

There is a **24-hour pharmacy** (☎ 06 488 00 19; Piazza dei Cinquecento 51) near Stazione Termini. All pharmacies should post a list in their windows of others open at night nearby.

The **police headquarters** (questura; ☎ 06 468 61; Via San Vitale 11; open 24hr daily) is where thefts can be reported. Its **Foreigners Bureau** (Ufficio Stranieri; ☎ 06 46 86 29 77; Via Genova 2) is around the corner. For immediate police attendance call ☎ 113.

## Dangers & Annoyances

Thieves are active in the areas in and around Stazione Termini, at major sights such as the Colosseum and Roman Forum, and on crowded buses such as the No 64 from Stazione Termini to St Peters, although police activity seems to have reduced the problem in recent years. For more comprehensive information on how to avoid being robbed, see Dangers & Annoyances earlier in this chapter.

## THINGS TO SEE & DO

It would take years to explore every corner of Rome, months to begin to appreciate the incredible number of monuments, and weeks for a thorough tour of the city. You can, however, cover most of the important monuments in five days, or three at a minimum. Entry to various attractions is free for EU citizens aged under 18 and over 65, and half-price for EU citizens aged between 18 and 25 plus those from countries with reciprocal arrangements, teachers at state schools and many university students. Cumulative tickets represent good value for money, especially to full-fare payers. A good one to pick is the €20 ticket which covers the Museo Nazionale Romano, Colosseum, Palatine Hill, Baths of Caracalla and more. These tickets can be purchased at the sites they cover, or by calling ☎ 06 39 96 77 00. You can also visit the website Ⓦ www.archeorm.arti.beniculturali.it for details.

### Piazza del Campidoglio

Designed by Michelangelo in 1538, the piazza is on the Capitolino (Capitoline Hill), the most important of Rome's seven hills. Formerly the seat of the ancient Roman government, it is now the seat of Rome's municipal government. The facades of the three palaces that border the piazza were also designed by Michelangelo. A modern copy of the bronze equestrian statue of Emperor Marcus Aurelius stands at its centre; the original is now on display in the ground-floor portico of the Palazzo Nuovo (also called Palazzo del Museo Capitolino). This and the Palazzo dei Conservatori make up the **Musei Capitolini** (☎ 06 67 10 20 71; admission €6.20; open 9am-8pm Tues-Sun), well worth visiting for their collections of ancient Roman sculpture, including the famous *Capitoline Wolf*, an Etruscan statue dating from the 6th century BC.

Walk to the right of the Palazzo del Senato to see a panorama of the Roman Forum. Walk to the left of the same building to reach the ancient Roman **Carcere Mamertino**, where it's believed St Peter was imprisoned.

The **Chiesa di Santa Maria d'Aracoeli** is between the Campidoglio and the Monumento

Vittorio Emanuele II at the highest point of the Capitoline Hill. It is built on the site where legend says the Tiburtine Sybil told the Emperor Augustus of the coming birth of Christ.

## Piazza Venezia

This piazza is overshadowed by a neoclassical monument dedicated to Vittorio Emanuele II, often referred to by Italians as the *macchina da scrivere* (typewriter) due to its appearance. Built to commemorate Italian unification, the piazza incorporates the **Altare della Patria** and the tomb of the unknown soldier, as well as the **Museo del Risorgimento**. Also in the piazza is the 15th-century **Palazzo Venezia**, which was Mussolini's official residence and now houses a museum.

## Roman Forum & Palatine Hill

The commercial, political and religious centre of ancient Rome, the Roman Forum *(☎ 06 699 0110; admission to Forum free, to Palatine Hill with Colosseum €8; open 9am-1hr before sunset)*, stands in a valley between the Capitoline and Palatine (Palatino) hills. Originally marshland, the area was drained during the early republican era and became a centre for political rallies, public ceremonies and senate meetings. Its importance declined along with the empire after the 4th century, and the temples, monuments and buildings constructed by successive emperors, consuls and senators over a period of 900 years fell into ruin, eventually to be used as pasture.

The area was systematically excavated in the 18th and 19th centuries, and excavations are continuing. You can enter the Forum from Via dei Fori Imperiali, which leads from Piazza Venezia to the Colosseum.

As you enter the Forum, to your left is the **Tempio di Antonino e Faustina**, erected by the senate in AD 141 and transformed into a church in the 8th century. To your right are the remains of the **Basilica Aemilia**, built in 179 BC and demolished during the Renaissance, when it was plundered for its precious marble. The Via Sacra, which traverses the Forum from northwest to southeast, runs in front of the basilica. Towards the Campidoglio is the **Curia**, once the meeting place of the Roman senate and converted into a Christian church in the Middle Ages. The church was dismantled and the Curia restored in the 1930s. In front of the Curia is the **Lapis Niger**, a large piece of black marble that legend says

covered the grave of Romulus. Under the Lapis Niger is the oldest-known Latin inscription, dating from the 6th century BC.

The **Arco di Settimo Severo** was erected in AD 203 in honour of this emperor and his sons, and is considered one of Italy's major triumphal arches. A circular base stone beside the arch marks the *umbilicus urbis*, the symbolic centre of ancient Rome. To the south is the **Rostrum**, used in ancient times by public speakers and once decorated by the rams of captured ships.

South along Via Sacra is the **Tempio di Saturno**, one of the most important temples in ancient Rome. Eight granite columns remain. The **Basilica Giulia**, in front of the temple, was the seat of justice, and nearby is the **Tempio di Giulio Cesare** (Temple of Julius Caesar), which was erected by Augustus in 29 BC on the site where Caesar's body was burned and Mark Antony read his famous speech. Back towards the Palatine Hill is the **Tempio dei Castori**, built in 489 BC in honour of the Heavenly Twins, or Dioscuri. It is easily recognisable by its three remaining columns.

In the area southeast of the temple is the **Chiesa di Santa Maria Antiqua**, the oldest Christian church in the Forum. It is closed to the public. Back on Via Sacra is the **Case delle Vestali**, home of the virgins who tended the sacred flame in the adjoining **Tempio di Vesta**. If the flame went out, it was seen as a bad omen. The next major monument is the vast **Basilica di Costantino**. Its impressive design inspired Renaissance architects. The **Arco di Tito**, at the Colosseum end of the Forum, was built in AD 81 in honour of the victories of the emperors Titus and Vespasian against Jerusalem.

From here climb the Palatine, where wealthy Romans built their homes and legend says that Romulus founded the city. Archaeological evidence shows that the earliest settlements in the area were on the Palatine. Like the Forum, the buildings of the Palatine fell into ruin and in the Middle Ages the hill became the site of convents and churches. During the Renaissance, wealthy families established gardens here. The Farnese gardens were built over the ruins of the Domus Tiberiana.

Worth a look is the impressive **Domus Augustana**, which was the private residence of the emperors; the **Domus Flavia**, the residence of Domitian; the **Tempio della Magna Mater**, built in 204 BC to house a black stone connected with the Asiatic goddess Cybele; and the **Casa di Livia**, thought to have been the house of the wife of Emperor Augustus, and decorated with frescoes.

## Colosseum

Originally known as the Flavian Amphitheatre, Rome's best-known monument (☎ 06 700 42 61; admission with Palatine Hill €8; open 9am-1hr before sunset) was begun by Emperor Vespasian in AD 72 in the grounds of Nero's Golden House, and completed by his son Titus. The massive structure could seat 80,000 and featured bloody gladiatorial combat and wild beast shows that resulted in thousands of human and animal deaths.

In the Middle Ages the Colosseum became a fortress and was later used as a quarry for travertine and marble for the Palazzo Venezia and other buildings. Restoration works have been under way since 1992. Avoid having your photo taken with the muscly dudes dressed as gladiators unless you want to spend most of your time in Rome arguing about their extortionate demands for money.

## Arch of Constantine

On the west side of the Colosseum is the triumphal arch built to honour Constantine following his victory over his rival Maxentius at the battle of Milvian Bridge (near the present-day Zona Olimpica, northwest of the Villa Borghese) in AD 312. Its decorative reliefs were taken from earlier structures.

## Baths of Caracalla

The huge Terme di Caracalla complex (☎ 06 575 86 26; Viale delle Terme di Caracalla 52; admission €5; open 9am-1hr before sunset Tues-Sun & 9am-2pm Mon), covering 10 hectares, could hold 1600 people and included shops, gardens, libraries and entertainment. Begun by Antonius Caracalla and inaugurated in AD 217, the baths were used until the 6th century.

## Some Significant Churches

Down Via Cavour from Stazione Termini is the massive **Basilica di Santa Maria Maggiore**, built in the 5th century. Its main baroque facade was added in the 18th century, preserving the 13th-century mosaics of the earlier facade. Its bell tower is Romanesque and the interior is baroque. There are 5th-century mosaics decorating the triumphal arch and nave.

Follow Via Merulana to reach **Basilica di San Giovanni in Laterano**, Rome's cathedral. The original church was built in the 4th century, the first Christian basilica in Rome. Largely destroyed over a long period of time, it was rebuilt in the 17th century.

**Basilica di San Pietro in Vincoli**, just off Via Cavour, is worth a visit because it houses Michelangelo's *Moses* and his unfinished statues of Leah and Rachel, as well as the chains worn by St Peter during his imprisonment before being crucified, hence the church's name.

**Chiesa di San Clemente** (Via San Giovanni in Laterano), near the Colosseum, defines how history in Rome exists on many levels. The 12th-century church at street level was built over a 4th-century church that was, in turn, built over a 1st-century Roman house containing a temple dedicated to the pagan god Mithras.

**Santa Maria in Cosmedin**, northwest of **Circus Maximus**, is regarded as one of the finest medieval churches in Rome. It has a seven-storey bell tower and its interior is heavily decorated with Cosmatesque inlaid marble, including the beautiful floor. The main attraction for masses of tourists is, however, the **Bocca della Verità** (Mouth of Truth). Legend has it that if you put your right hand into the mouth and tell a lie, it will snap shut.

## Baths of Diocletian

Started by Emperor Diocletian, these baths (☎ 06 488 05 30; Viale E De Nicola 79; admission €5; open 9am-7.45pm Tues-Sun) were completed in the 4th century. The complex of baths, libraries, concert halls and gardens covered about 13 hectares and could house up to 3000 people. After the aqueduct that fed the baths was destroyed by invaders in AD 536, the complex fell into decay. Parts of the ruins are now incorporated into the Basilica di Santa Maria degli Angeli.

## Basilica di Santa Maria degli Angeli

Designed by Michelangelo, this church (open 7.30am-6.30pm Mon-Sat & 8am-7.30pm Sun) incorporates what was the great central hall and *tepidarium* (lukewarm room) of the original baths. During the following centuries

# PANTHEON & TRASTEVERE AREA

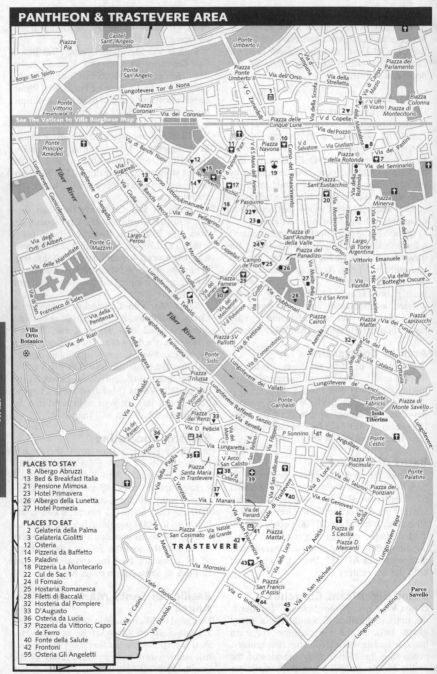

See The Vatican to Villa Borghese Map

ITALY

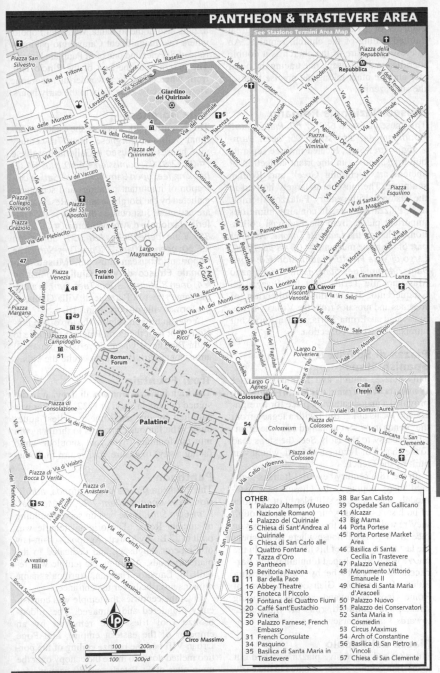

# PANTHEON & TRASTEVERE AREA

See Stazione Termini Area Map

ITALY

**OTHER**

1 Palazzo Altemps (Museo Nazionale Romano)
4 Palazzo del Quirinale
5 Chiesa di Sant'Andrea al Quirinale
6 Chiesa di San Carlo alle Quattro Fontane
7 Tazza d'Oro
9 Pantheon
10 Bevitoria Navona
11 Bar della Pace
16 Abbey Theatre
17 Enoteca Il Piccolo
19 Fontana dei Quattro Fiumi
20 Caffè Sant'Eustachio
29 Vineria
30 Palazzo Farnese; French Embassy
31 French Consulate
34 Pasquino
35 Basilica di Santa Maria in Trastevere

38 Bar San Calisto
39 Ospedale San Gallicano
41 Alcazar
43 Big Mama
44 Porta Portese
45 Porta Portese Market Area
46 Basilica di Santa Cecilia in Trastevere
47 Palazzo Venezia
48 Monumento Vittorio Emanuele II
49 Chiesa di Santa Maria d'Aracoeli
50 Palazzo Nuovo
51 Palazzo dei Conservatori
52 Santa Maria in Cosmedin
53 Circus Maximus
54 Arch of Constantine
56 Basilica di San Pietro in Vincoli
57 Chiesa di San Clemente

his work was drastically changed and little evidence of his design, apart from the great vaulted ceiling of the church, remains. An interesting feature of the church is a double meridian in the transept, one tracing the polar star and the other telling the precise time of the sun's zenith.

## Museo Nazionale Romano

This museum (☎ 06 683 37 59; Piazza Sant' Apollinare 44; admission €5; open 9am-7.45pm Tues-Sun), located in three separate buildings, houses an important collection of ancient art, including Greek and Roman sculpture. The museum is largely housed in the restored 15th-century Palazzo Altemps, near Piazza Navona. It contains numerous important pieces from the Ludovisi collection, including the Ludovisi Throne. Another part of the same museum (☎ 06 48 90 35 00; Largo di Villa Peretti 1; admission €6; open 9am-7.45pm Tues-Sun), is in the Palazzo Massimo alle Terme, just off Piazza dei Cinquecento. It contains a collection of frescoes and mosaics from the Villa of Livia, excavated at Prima Porta, and a knockout numismatic (coin) collection.

## Piazza di Spagna & Spanish Steps

This piazza, church and famous staircase (Scalinata della Trinitá dei Monti) have long provided a major gathering place for foreigners and locals alike. Built with a legacy from the French in 1725, but named after the Spanish Embassy to the Holy See, the steps lead to the church of Trinitá dei Monti, which was built by the French.

In the 18th century beautiful Italians gathered there, hoping to be chosen as artists' models, and there are still plenty of beauties of both sexes to cast your eye over, although they're well aware of this. To the right as you face the steps is the house where Keats spent the last three months of his life in 1821. In the piazza is the boat-shaped fountain of the Barcaccia, believed to be by Pietro Bernini, father of the famous Gian Lorenzo. One of Rome's most elegant and expensive shopping streets, Via Condotti, runs off the piazza towards Via del Corso.

## Piazza del Popolo

This vast and impressive piazza was laid out in the 16th century and redesigned in the early 19th century by Giuseppe Valadier. The piazza is also home to Santa Maria del Popolo, where two magnificent Caravaggio paintings (one of St Peter and one of St Paul) are housed. The piazza is at the foot of the Pincio Hill, from where there is a wonderful panoramic view of the city, especially in the early hours.

## Villa Borghese

This beautiful park was once the estate of Cardinal Scipione Borghese. His 17th-century villa houses the Museo e Galleria Borghese (☎ 06 32 81 01; admission €6.50, plus €1.03 booking fee; open 9am-9pm Tues-Sat), a collection of important paintings and sculptures gathered by the Borghese family. Reservations are essential. Just outside the park is the Galleria Nazionale d'Arte Moderna (☎ 06 32 29 81; Viale delle Belle Arti 131; admission €6.50; open 8.30am-7.30pm Tues-Sun). The important Etruscan museum, Museo Nazionale Etrusco di Villa Giulia (admission €4; open 8.30am-7.30pm Tues-Sun), is along the same street in Piazzale di Villa Giulia, in the former villa of Pope Julius III.

You can hire bicycles at the top of the Pincio Hill or near the Porta Pinciana entrance to Villa Borghese, where there is also a small amusement park that might excite the kids.

## Trevi Fountain

The high-baroque Fontana di Trevi was designed by Nicola Salvi in 1732. Its water was supplied by one of Rome's earliest aqueducts. The famous custom is to throw a coin into the fountain (over your shoulder while facing away) to ensure your return to Rome.

## Pantheon

The Pantheon (Piazza della Rotonda; admission free; open 8.30am-7.30pm Mon-Sat, 9am-6pm Sun), is the best preserved building of ancient Rome. The original temple was built in 27 BC by Marcus Agrippa, son-in-law of Emperor Augustus, and dedicated to the planetary gods. Although the temple was rebuilt by Emperor Hadrian, Agrippa's name remains inscribed over the entrance.

Over the centuries the temple was consistently plundered and damaged. The gilded-bronze roof tiles were removed by an emperor of the eastern empire, and Pope Urban VIII had the bronze ceiling of the portico melted down to make the canopy over the main altar of St Peter's and 80 cannons for

Castel Sant'Angelo. The Pantheon's extraordinary dome is considered the most important achievement of ancient Roman architecture. In 608 the temple was consecrated to the Virgin and all martyrs.

The Italian kings Vittorio Emanuele II and Umberto I and the painter Raphael are buried there.

## Piazza Navona

This vast and beautiful square, lined with baroque palaces, was laid out on the ruins of Domitian's stadium and features three fountains, including Bernini's masterpiece, the **Fontana dei Quattro Fiumi** (Fountain of the Four Rivers), in its centre. Take time to relax on one of the stone benches or the expensive cafés and watch the artists who gather in the piazza to work.

## Campo de' Fiori

This is a lively piazza where a flower and vegetable market is held every morning except Sunday. Now lined with bars and trattorias that get packed at night, the piazza was a place of execution during the Inquisition.

The **Palazzo Farnese** (Farnese Palace), in the piazza of the same name, is just off Campo de' Fiori. A magnificent Renaissance building, it was started in 1514 by Antonio da Sangallo, work was carried on by Michelangelo and it was completed by Giacomo della Porta. Built for Cardinal Alessandro Farnese (later Pope Paul III), the palace is now the French embassy. The piazza has two fountains, which were enormous granite baths taken from the Baths of Caracalla.

## Via Giulia

This elegant street was designed by Bramante, who was commissioned by Pope Julius II to create a new approach to St Peter's. It is lined with Renaissance palaces, antique shops and art galleries.

## Trastevere

You can wander through the narrow medieval streets of this area which, despite the many foreigners who live here, retains the air of a typical Roman neighbourhood. It is especially beautiful at night and is a wonderful area for bar-hopping or a meal.

Of particular note here is the **Basilica di Santa Maria in Trastevere**, in the lovely piazza of the same name. It is believed to be the oldest church dedicated to the Virgin in Rome. Although the first church was built on the site in the 4th century, the present structure was built in the 12th century and features a Romanesque bell tower and facade, with a mosaic of the Virgin. Its interior was redecorated during the baroque period, but the vibrant mosaics in the apse and on the triumphal arch date from the 12th century. Also take a look at the **Basilica di Santa Cecilia in Trastevere**.

## Gianicolo

The top of the Gianicolo (Janiculum), the hill between St Peter's and Trastevere, offers a stirring panoramic view of Rome.

## Catacombs

There are several catacombs in Rome, consisting of miles of tunnels carved out of volcanic rock, which were the meeting and burial places of early Christians in Rome. The largest are along Via Appia Antica, just outside the city and accessible Metropolitana Linea A to Colli Albani, then bus No 660. The **Catacombs of San Callisto** (admission €5; open 8.30am-noon & 2.30pm-5pm Thur-Tues Mar-Jan) and **Catacombs of San Sebastiano** (admission €5; open 8.30am-noon & 2.30pm-5pm Mon-Sat 10 Dec–10 Nov) are almost next to each other on Via Appia Antica. Admission to each is with a guide only.

## Vatican City

After the unification of Italy, the papal states of central Italy became part of the new kingdom of Italy, causing a considerable rift between church and state. In 1929, Mussolini, under the Lateran Treaty, gave the pope full sovereignty over what is now called the Vatican City.

The **tourist office** (☎ 06 69 88 16 62; Piazza San Pietro; open 8.30am-7pm Mon-Sat) is to the left of the basilica. Guided tours of the Vatican City gardens (€10) can be organised here. In the same area is the **Vatican post office** (☎ 06 69 88 34 06; open 8am-7pm Mon-Fri & 8.30am-6pm Sat), which is said to offer a much more reliable service than the normal Italian postal system.

The city has its own postal service, newspaper, radio station, train station and army of Swiss Guards kitted out in uniforms designed by Michelangelo.

ITALY

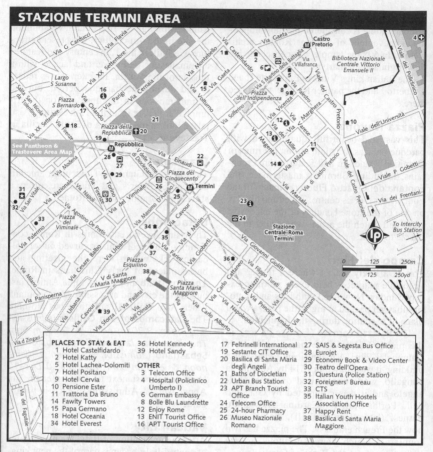

## STAZIONE TERMINI AREA

| PLACES TO STAY & EAT | 36 Hotel Kennedy | 17 Feltrinelli International | 27 SAIS & Segesta Bus Office |
| --- | --- | --- | --- |
| 1 Hotel Castelfidardo | 39 Hotel Sandy | 19 Sestante CIT Office | 28 Eurojet |
| 2 Hotel Katty | | 20 Basilica di Santa Maria | 29 Economy Book & Video Center |
| 5 Hotel Lachea-Dolomiti | OTHER | degli Angeli | 30 Teatro dell'Opera |
| 7 Hotel Positano | 3 Telecom Office | 21 Baths of Diocletian | 31 Questura (Police Station) |
| 9 Hotel Cervia | 4 Hospital (Policlinico | 22 Urban Bus Station | 32 Foreigners' Bureau |
| 10 Pensione Ester | Umberto I) | 23 APT Branch Tourist | 33 CTS |
| 11 Trattoria Da Bruno | 6 German Embassy | Office | 35 Italian Youth Hostels |
| 14 Fawlty Towers | 8 Bolle Blu Laundrette | 24 Telecom Office | Association Office |
| 15 Papa Germano | 12 Enjoy Rome | 25 24-hour Pharmacy | 37 Happy Rent |
| 18 Hotel Oceania | 13 ENIT Tourist Office | 26 Museo Nazionale | 38 Basilica di Santa Maria |
| 34 Hotel Everest | 16 APT Tourist Office | Romano | Maggiore |

**St Peter's Basilica & Square** The most famous church in the Christian world, **St Peter's** (San Pietro; open 7am-7pm daily Apr-Sept, 7am-6pm daily Oct-Mar) stands on the site where St Peter was buried. The first church on the site was built during Constantine's reign in the 4th century, and in 1506 work was started on a new basilica, designed by Bramante.

Although several architects were involved in its construction, it is generally held that St Peter's owes its grandeur and power to Michelangelo, who took over the project in 1547 at the age of 72 and was particularly responsible for the design of the dome. He died before the church was completed. The cavernous interior contains numerous treasures, including Michelangelo's superb Pietá,

sculpted when he was only 24 years old and the only work to carry his signature (on the sash across the breast of the Madonna). It's protected by bulletproof glass.

Bernini's huge, baroque Baldacchino (a heavily sculpted bronze canopy over the papal altar) stands 29m high and is an extraordinary work of art. Another point of note is the red porphyry disc near the central door, which marks the spot where Charlemagne and later emperors were crowned by the pope.

Entrance to Michelangelo's soaring dome is to the right as you climb the stairs to the atrium of the basilica. Make the entire climb on foot for €4, or pay €5 and you take the elevator for part of the way.

Dress rules and security are stringently enforced – no shorts, miniskirts or sleeveless tops, and be prepared to have your bags searched. Prams and strollers must be left in a designated area outside the basilica.

Bernini's **Piazza San Pietro** (St Peter's Square) is rightly considered a masterpiece. Laid out in the 17th century as a place for Christians of the world to gather, the immense piazza is bound by two semicircular colonnades, each of which is made up of four rows of Doric columns. In the centre of the piazza is an obelisk that was brought to Rome by Caligula from Heliopolis (in ancient Egypt). When you stand on the dark paving stones between the obelisk and either of the fountains, the colonnades appear to have only one row of columns.

The Pope usually gives a public audience at 10am every Wednesday in the Papal Audience Hall or St Peter's Square. You must make a booking, in person or by fax to the **Prefettura della Casa Pontifica** (☎ 06 69 88 46 31, fax 06 69 88 38 65), on the Monday or Tuesday before the audience between 9am and 1pm. Go through the bronze doors under the colonnade to the right as you face the basilica.

**Vatican Museums** From St Peter's follow the wall of the Vatican City (to the right as you face the basilica) to the museums (admission €10, free last Sun of month; open 8.45am-4.45pm Mon-Fri, 8.45am-1.45pm Sat & last Sun of month). The museums are closed Sunday and public holidays, but open on the last Sunday of every month (queues are always very long). Guided visits to the Vatican gardens cost €10 and can be booked by calling ☎ 06 69 88 44 66.

The Vatican museums contain an incredible collection of art and treasures collected by the popes, and you will need several hours (at least) to see the most important areas and museums. The Sistine Chapel comes towards the end of a full visit; otherwise, you can walk straight there and then work your way back through the museums.

The **Museo Pio-Clementino**, containing Greek and Roman antiquities, is on the ground floor near the entrance. Through the tapestry and map galleries are the **Stanze di Rafaello**, once the private apartments of Pope Julius II, decorated with frescoes by Raphael. Of particular interest is the magnificent **Stanza della Segnatura**, which features Raphael's masterpieces *The School of Athens* and *Disputation on the Sacrament*.

From Raphael's rooms, go down the stairs to the sumptuous **Appartamento Borgia**, decorated with frescoes by Pinturicchio, then go down another flight of stairs to the **Sistine Chapel**, the private papal chapel built in 1473 for Pope Sixtus IV. Michelangelo's wonderful frescoes of the *Creation* and *Last Judgment* have been superbly restored to their original brilliance. It took Michelangelo four years, at the height of the Renaissance, to paint the *Creation*; 24 years later he painted the extraordinary *Last Judgment*. The other walls of the chapel were painted by artists including Botticelli, Ghirlandaio, Pinturicchio and Signorelli. To best enjoy the frescoes on the ceiling, a pocket mirror is recommended so that you don't have to strain your neck.

## ORGANISED TOURS

**Enjoy Rome** (☎ 06 445 18 43, fax 06 445 68 90; ⓦ www.enjoyrome.com; Via Marghera 8a), offers excellent walking or bicycle tours of Rome's main sights from €13 (aged under 26) and €19 (over 26) per person and a bus tour for Pompeii. **ATAC** bus No 110 leaves daily every half-hour between 10am and 6pm (from 9am to 8pm in summer) from Piazza dei Cinquecento, in front of Stazione Termini, for a 90-minute tour of the city. Tickets cost €7.75 (€12.91 if you want to hop on and off). Night tours start at 8pm (9pm in summer). You can also do a basilica tour, which leaves every half-hour from 10.30am to 2.30pm (to 3pm in summer).

**Through Eternity Rome** (☎ 06 700 93 36, 06 347 336 52 98; ⓦ www.througheternity .com) has numerous walking tours from €20 per person with an emphasis on storytelling, plus it gets rave reviews from many travellers.

## SPECIAL EVENTS

Although Romans desert their city in summer, particularly in August when the weather is relentlessly hot, cultural and musical events take place. The Comune di Roma coordinates a diverse series of concerts, performances and events throughout summer under the general title Estate Romana (Roman Summer). The series usually features major international performers. Details are published in Rome's daily newspapers.

A jazz festival is held in July and August in the Villa Celimontana, which is a park on top of the Celian Hill (access from Piazza della Navicella).

ITALY

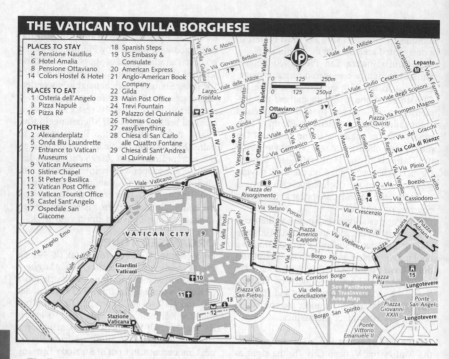

# THE VATICAN TO VILLA BORGHESE

**PLACES TO STAY**
4 Pensione Nautilus
6 Hotel Amalia
8 Pensione Ottaviano
14 Colors Hostel & Hotel

**PLACES TO EAT**
1 Osteria dell'Angelo
7 Pizza Napulè
16 Pizza Ré

**OTHER**
2 Alexanderplatz
5 Onda Blu Laundrette
7 Entrance to Vatican
  Museums
9 Vatican Museums
10 Sistine Chapel
11 St Peter's Basilica
12 Vatican Post Office
13 Vatican Tourist Office
15 Castel Sant'Angelo
17 Ospedale San
  Giacomo

18 Spanish Steps
19 US Embassy &
  Consulate
20 American Express
21 Anglo-American Book
  Company
22 Gilda
23 Main Post Office
24 Trevi Fountain
25 Palazzo del Quirinale
26 Thomas Cook
27 easyEverything
28 Chiesa di San Carlo
  alle Quattro Fontane
29 Chiesa di Sant'Andrea
  al Quirinale

The Festa de' Noantri is held in Trastevere in the last two weeks of July in honour of Our Lady of Mt Carmel.

At Christmas the focus is on the many churches of Rome, each setting up its own nativity scene. Among the most renowned is the 13th-century crib at Santa Maria Maggiore. During Holy Week, at Easter, the focus is again religious and events include the famous procession of the cross between the Colosseum and the Palatine on Good Friday, and the Pope's blessing of the city and the world in St Peter's Square on Easter Sunday.

The Spanish Steps become a sea of pink azaleas during the Spring Festival in April. Around mid-April, Italian Cultural Heritage Week sees many galleries, museums and tourist attractions open free of charge.

## PLACES TO STAY
### Camping
About 15 minutes from the centre by public transport is the **Village Camping Flaminio** (☎ 06 333 14 29; Via Flaminia Nuova 821; per person/tent €9.50/12). Tents and good bungalows are available for rent (although there's a fairly frustrating 4pm check-in and

10am check-out for bungalows). You can catch the Metropolitana Linea A from Termini station to Flaminio and change to the Prima Porta Linea, getting off at the Due Ponti station (request stop, so ring the bell), which is 100m from the camp site.

### Hostels
HI **Ostello della Gioventu Foro Italico** (☎ 06 323 62 67; e aig.sedenazionale@uni.net; Viale delle Olimpiadi 61; dorm bed €15) has over 300 beds and opens from 7am to midnight. Take Metropolitana Linea A to Ottaviano, then bus No 32 to Foro Italico. The head office of the **Italian Youth Hostel Association** (☎ 06 487 11 52; w www.ostellionline.org; Via Cavour 44, 00184 Rome; open 9am-5pm Mon-Fri) has information about the hostels in Italy. You can also join HI here.

### B&Bs
This type of accommodation in private houses is a relatively recent addition to Rome's accommodation options for budget travellers.
**Bed & Breakfast Italia** (☎ 06 68 80 15 13, fax 06 687 86 19; e info@bbitalia.it; Corso Vittorio Emanuele II 282; singles/doubles

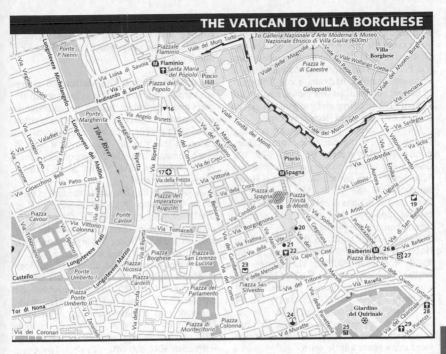

## THE VATICAN TO VILLA BORGHESE

per person per night without bath from €28/23, with bath €41/36) is one of several B&B networks and offers central rooms.

## Hotels & Pensioni

### North of Stazione Termini
To reach the pensioni in this area, head to the right as you leave the train platforms onto Via Castro Pretorio. The excellent and frequently recommended **Fawlty Towers** (☎ 06 445 48 02; Via Magenta 39; dorm bed €18, with bath €23) offers hostel-style accommodation and lots of information about Rome. Added bonuses are the sunny terrace and lack of curfew.

Nearby in Via Palestro are several reasonably priced hotels. **Hotel Cervia** (☎ 06 49 10 57, fax 06 49 10 56; e hotelcervia@wnt.it; Via Palestro 55; dorm bed €20, singles without bath €35) has tidy rooms and a ground floor location. **Hotel Katty** (☎ 06 444 12 16; Via Palestro 35; singles/doubles without bath €47/62, with bath €73/83-93) has basic rooms and some other, better ones, plus a friendly owner who'll chat your ear off. Around the corner is the clean and comfy **Pensione Ester** (☎ 06 495 71 23; Viale Castro Pretorio 25; doubles without bath €52).

**Hotel Positano** (☎ 06 49 03 60; e info@hotelpositano.it; Via Palestro 49; dorm bed €20, singles/doubles/triples with bath €70/105/140) is a flashier option, with very pleasant air-con rooms with TV, fridge and phone (not for dorms though).

Two good hotels, Lachea and Dolomiti, are in the same building, with the same charming management and good prices – **Hotel Lachea-Dolomiti** (☎ 06 495 72 56; e lachea@hotel-dolomiti.it, e dolomiti@hotel-dolomiti.it; Via San Martino della Battaglia 11; singles/doubles/triples without bath €47/68/73, with bath €68/104/124) has large, quiet, spotlessly clean rooms with all mod-cons.

**Papa Germano** (☎ 06 48 69 19; e info@hotelpapagermano.com; Via Calatafimi 14a; singles/doubles without bath €47/68, with bath 62/93) is one of the more popular two-star places in the area.

**Hotel Castelfidardo** (☎ 06 446 46 38, fax 06 494 13 78; e castelfidardo@italmarkey.it; Via Castelfidardo 31; singles/doubles/triples without bath €42/60/77, with bath €52/70/93) is a well-run and frequently recommended place with lovely rooms and a 5% discount for cash payments.

ITALY

**South of Stazione Termini** This area is a bit seedier, but prices remain the same. As you exit to the left of the station, follow Via Gioberti to Via G Amendola, which becomes Via F Turati. This street, and the parallel Via Principe Amedeo, harbours a concentration of budget pensioni, so you should easily find a room. The area improves as you get closer to the Colosseum and Roman Forum.

On Via Cavour, the main street running southwest from the piazza in front of Termini, is **Hotel Everest** (☎ 06 488 16 29; Via Cavour 47; singles/doubles with bath €80/120), with clean and pleasant rooms. **Hotel Sandy** (☎ 06 488 45 85; Via Cavour 136; dorm bed €18) has dorms with lockers, no curfew, not-great bathrooms and a party atmosphere for the young crowd.

Better-quality hotels in the area include **Hotel Oceania** (☎ 06 482 46 96, fax 06 488 5586; e hoceania@tin.it; Via Firenze 38; singles/doubles with bath €104/135) with a warm welcome and smart rooms. **Hotel Kennedy 2** (☎ 06 446 53 73, fax 06 446 54 17; e hotelkennedy@micanet.it; Via F Turati 62; singles/doubles with bath €88/155) has good rooms and a handy location, although some corners are a little worn.

**City Centre** On a square just off Via Vittorio Emanuele II, **Hotel Primavera** (☎ 06 68 80 31 09, fax 06 686 92 65; Piazza San Pantaleo 3; doubles with/without bath €115/95) has clean and plain doubles only available. The **Albergo Abruzzi** (☎ 06 679 20 21; Piazza della Rotonda 69; singles/doubles without bath €65/73-95) overlooks the Pantheon – which explains the noise. Rooms are adequate and bookings here are essential year-round.

**Pensione Mimosa** (☎ 06 68 80 17 53, fax 06 683 35 57; e hotelmimosa@tin.it; Via Santa Chiara 61; singles/doubles without bath €77/93, with bath €93/108), off Piazza della Minerva, has rooms of varying quality and a great location. Service varies, too, depending on who's at the front desk.

**Albergo della Lunetta** (☎ 06 686 10 80, fax 06 689 20 28; Piazza del Paradiso 68; singles/doubles/triples without bath €52/83/115, with bath €62/109/145) is a solid, decent choice. You'll definitely need to reserve in advance, or check for cancellations.

**Hotel Pomezia** (☎/fax 06 686 13 71; Via dei Chiavari 12; singles/doubles without

bath €50/85, with bath €105/205), is welcoming and well-kitted out, and includes breakfast in the rates, which can drop by 30% in the low season.

**Near St Peter's & the Vatican** Bargains are rare in this area, but it is comparatively quiet and reasonably close to the main sights. Bookings are a necessity, as rooms are often filled with people attending conferences and so on at the Vatican. The simplest way to reach the area is on the Metropolitana Linea A to Ottaviano. Bus No 64 from Termini stops at St Peter's.

A long-standing bargain in the area is **Pensione Ottaviano** (☎ 06 39 73 72 53; e gi .costantini@agora.stm.it; Via Ottaviano 6; dorm bed €18, doubles/triples without bath €62/70), near Piazza Risorgimento, with simple rooms and English-speaking staff. A classy new cheaper-end addition is **Colors Hostel & Hotel** (☎ 06 687 40 30; Via Boezio 31; dorm bed €18.50, doubles with/without bath €83/76). It has tidy rooms, great management and cooking facilities. **Pensione Nautilus** (☎ 06 324 21 18; Via Germanico 198; singles/doubles without bath €52/79, with bath €78/93) offers basic, tidy rooms, although things can seem a little dark at times. **Hotel Amalia** (☎ 06 39 72 33 56, fax 06 39 72 33 65; e hotelamalia@iol.it; Via Germanico 66; singles/doubles without bath €70/100, with bath €130/196-210) has quite swanky, sunny rooms and breakfast is included.

## PLACES TO EAT

Rome bursts at the seams with trattorias, pizzerias and restaurants – and not all of them are overrun by tourists or are frighteningly expensive. Eating times are generally from 12.30pm to 3pm and 8pm to 11pm. Most Romans head out for dinner about 9pm, so arrive earlier to claim a table. Prices in this guide reflect the cost per person for two courses with wine, plus a dessert or side dish.

Antipasto dishes in Rome are particularly good and many restaurants allow you to make your own mixed selection. Typical pasta dishes include *bucatini all'Amatriciana* (large, hollow spaghetti with a salty sauce of tomato and bacon), *penne all'arrabbiata* (penne with a hot sauce of tomatoes, peppers and chilli) and *spaghetti carbonara* (pancetta, eggs and cheese). Romans also love dishes prepared with offal – try *paiata* (pasta with veal intestines). *Saltimbocca alla Romana* (slices of veal and ham) is a classic meat dish, as is *straccetti con la rucola,* fine slices of beef tossed in garlic and oil and topped with fresh rocket. In winter you can't go past *carciofi alla Romana* (artichokes stuffed with garlic and mint or parsley).

Good options for cheap, quick meals are the hundreds of bars, where *panini* (sandwiches) cost €1.20 to €2.60 if taken *al banco* (at the bar), or takeaway pizzerias, usually called *pizza a taglio,* where a slice of freshly cooked pizza, sold by weight, can cost as little as €1.10. Bakeries are numerous and are another good choice for a cheap snack.

Try **Paladini** *(Via del Governo Vecchio 29)* for sandwiches, and **Il Fornaio** *(Via Baullari 6)* for mouth-watering pastries and bread.

There are numerous outdoor **markets**, notably the lively and colourful daily market in Campo de' Fiori. Other, cheaper food markets are held in Piazza Vittorio Emanuele, near the station, and off Viale delle Millizie, north of the Vatican. There's a well-stocked **24-hour supermarket** underneath the main concourse of Stazione Termini, which is handy for self-caterers.

## Restaurants, Trattorias & Pizzerias

The restaurants near Stazione Termini are generally to be avoided if you want to pay reasonable prices for halfway-decent food. The side streets around Piazza Navona and Campo de' Fiori harbour many budget trattorias and pizzerias, and the areas of San Lorenzo (to the east of Termini, near the university) and Testaccio (across the Tiber near Piramide) are popular local eating districts. Trastevere offers an excellent selection of rustic eating places hidden in tiny piazzas, and pizzerias where it doesn't cost the earth to sit at a table on the street.

**City Centre** The **Pizzeria La Montecarlo** *(☎ 06 686 18 77; Vicolo Savelli 12; meal about €11)* has paper sheets for tablecloths, a high turnover (queues form around 9.30pm) and a long list of tasty pizzas.

**Pizza Ré** *(☎ 06 321 14 68; Via di Ripetta 13; meal about €15)* gets packed despite its size (and with good reason) by lovers of Naples-style pizza. It's a swanky-looking place, too.

Wondering whether there are any great geniuses left in Rome? Yes, they're making pizza at **Pizzeria da Baffetto** *(☎ 06 686 16 17; Via del Governo Vecchio 114; pizza about €7),* a Roman institution. Expect to join a queue and share a table if you arrive after 9pm. Farther along the street is an **osteria** *(Via del Governo Vecchio 18; meal about €13),* where you can eat an excellent lunch in simple surrounds, with locals who know that it's best to arrive before 1pm if the tum's rumbling. Back along the street towards Piazza Navona is **Cul de Sac 1** *(☎ 06 68 80 10 94; Piazza Pasquino 73; meal about €15),* a wine bar which also has great meals, including hearty soups.

**Hostaria Romanesca** *(☎ 06 686 40 24; Piazza Capo de' Fiori; meal about €17)* is tiny, so arrive early in winter and get your fill of the generous pasta dishes. In summer there are numerous tables outside.

In cod we trust, and just off Campo de' Fiori is **Filetti di Baccalá** *(☎ 06 686 40 18; Largo dei Librari 88; meal about €9),* which serves only deliciously deep-fried cod fillets in cheap and cheerful surrounds.

In the Jewish quarter, just off Piazza delle Cinque Sole is **Hostaria dal Pompiere** *(☎ 06 686 83 77; Via Santa Maria de Caldari 38; meal about €22),* which has a tastefully subdued decor and some of the best *spaghetti alle vongole* you'll ever try.

**West of the Tiber** On the west bank of the Fiume Tevere (Tiber River), good-value restaurants are concentrated in Trastevere and the Testaccio district, past the Piramide metro stop. Many of the establishments around St Peter's and the Vatican are geared for tourists and can be very expensive. There are, however, some good options. Try **Pizza Napul'è** *(☎ 06 63 23 10 05; Viale Giulio Cesare 91; meal about €12)* or the handy and inexpensive **Osteria dell'Angelo** *(Via G Bettolo 24),* along Via Leone IV from the Vatican City, where you can gorge on cheap pasta for about €4 after a visit to the Vatican.

In Trastevere, try **Frontoni** *(Viale di Trastevere 54),* near Piazza Mastai, for fantastic panini. **D'Augusto** *(Piazza dei Renzi 15; meal about €15),* just around the corner from the Basilica di Santa Maria in Trastevere (turn right as you face the church and walk to Via della Pelliccia), is a very popular cheap eating spot. The food might be OK at best, but the atmosphere, especially in summer with tables outside in the piazza, is traditionally Roman. **Osteria da Lucia** *(Vicolo del Mattinato 2; meal about €20)* is more expensive, but the food is much better, the owners are lovely, and on sunny days you'll sit beneath the neighbours' washing.

For a good pizza dinner, try **Pizzeria da Vittorio** *(Via San Cosimato 14; meal about €15).* You'll have to wait for an outside table if you arrive after 8.30pm, but the atmosphere is great, and the bruschetta is worth trying too. Next door is **Capo de Ferro**, where the meals are about the same price and the same Trastevere atmosphere is available.

You won't find a cheaper, noisier, more chaotic pizzeria in Rome than **Pizzeria Remo** *(Piazza Santa Maria Liberatrice 44; meal about €10)* in Testaccio, when Friday and Saturday nights are filled with party types. **Augustarello** *(Via G Branca 98; meal about €15),* off the piazza, specialises in the very traditional Roman fare of offal dishes, which taste better than it sometimes sounds.

**Between Termini & the Forum** If you have no option but to eat near Stazione Termini, try to avoid the tourist traps offering overpriced full menus. **Trattoria da Bruno** *(☎ 06 49 04 03; Via Varese 29; meal about €18)* has good food and service, with what looks like a torture rack hanging from the ceiling. Just off Via Cavour is **Osteria Gli Angeletti** *(☎ 06 474 33 74; Via dell'Angeletto 3; meal about €17),* an excellent little restaurant with prices at the higher end of the budget range, but imaginative dishes that break out of the spag bog/gnocchi pesto/lasagne tourist-menu trap.

### Gelati
Both **Gelateria Giolitti** *(Via degli Uffici del Vicario 40)* near the Pantheon and **Gelateria della Palma** *(Via della Maddalena 20)* just around the corner have a huge selection of flavours and get big crowds – get the *fichi* (fig) or pistacchio at Della Palma dribbling down your chin. In Trastevere, **Fonte della Salute** *(Via Cardinale Marmaggi 2-6)* also has excellent gelati.

### ENTERTAINMENT
Rome's best entertainment guide is the weekly *Roma C'è* (€1.03), available at all newsstands. It has an English-language section. *La Repubblica* and *Il Messagero* are daily newspapers with cinema, theatre and concert listings.

*Wanted in Rome* is a fortnightly magazine for Rome's English-speaking community (€0.75). It has good cultural listings and is available at outlets including the **Economy Book & Video Center** *(Via Torino 136)*, and at newsstands in the city centre, including Largo Argentina.

### Cafés & Bars
Remember that prices skyrocket in bars as soon as you sit down, particularly near major tourist attractions. The same cappuccino taken at the bar will cost less – but passing an hour or so watching the world go by over a cappuccino, beer or wine in a beautiful location can be hard to beat, and despite what you may have heard, Italians do it too.

For great coffee head for **Tazza d'Oro** *(Via degli Orfani)* just off Piazza della Rotonda; and **Caffé Sant'Eustachio** *(Piazza Sant'Eustachio 82)*, where you might want to pipe up if you don't want any sugar in your espresso. Try the *granita di caffé* at either one in summer.

Campo de' Fiori is a popular spot to bar-hop and socialise for foreigners and locals alike. **Vineria** *(☎ 06 68 80 32 68; Campo de' Fiori 15)*, has a tempting selection of wine and beer, plus outdoor tables in warm weather. **Bar della Pace** *(Via della Pace 3-7)* is big with the trendy crew, and you can see why, as it's pretty damn schmick. **Bevitoria Navona** *(☎ 06 68 80 10 22; Piazza Navona 72)* has wine by the glass and makes for a charming early evening spot to have a drink (inside or out). In Trastevere, the slacker-alternative set chooses to hang at **Bar San Calisto** *(Piazza San Calisto)*, and it's easy to see why – drinks aren't extortionate and the clientele is frequently interesting for people watchers. Near Piazza Navona **Abbey Theatre** *(Via del Governo Vecchio 51)* is a popular and relatively intimate Irish pub, which means you can get Guinness and Kilkenny on tap. Also on Via del Governo Vecchio, at No 74, is the small-but-perfectly-formed **Enoteca Il Piccolo**, with a smattering of wines by the glass and a quiet, low-key atmosphere.

### Nightclubs
Among the more interesting and popular Roman live music clubs is **Radio Londra** *(☎ 06 575 00 44; Via di Monte Testaccio*

*67)*, in the Testaccio area. On the same street are the more sedate music clubs **Caruso Caffé** at No 36 and **Caffé Latino** at No 96, both generally offering jazz or blues, with some Latin DJ-ing thrown in for dancing. More jazz and blues can be heard at **Alexanderplatz** *(☎ 06 39 74 21 71; Via Ostia 9)* and **Big Mama** *(☎ 06 581 25 51; Via San Francesco a Ripa 18)* in Trastevere.

Roman discos are pants-wettingly expensive. Expect to pay up to €20 to get in, which may or may not include one drink. Popular stayers include **Alien** *(☎ 06 841 22 12; Via Velletri 13)*, for those who like the more mainstream end of house and techno, **Goa** *(☎ 06 574 82 77; Via Libetta 13)* with a groovy ethnic decor and glam crowd but a distant location near metro stop Garbatella, and **Gilda** *(☎ 06 679 73 96; Via Mario de' Fiori 97)*, which attracts a slightly older crowd. The best gay disco (according to many) is **L'Alibi** *(☎ 06 574 34 48; Via di Monte Testaccio 44)*.

## Cinema

There are a handful of cinemas in Trastevere that show English-language movies. There are daily shows at **Pasquino** *(☎ 06 580 36 22; Piazza Sant'Egidio)*, just off Piazza Santa Maria. **Alcazar** *(☎ 06 588 00 99; Via Merry del Val 14)* shows English-language films on Monday.

## Exhibitions & Concerts

From December to June, opera is performed at the **Teatro dell'Opera** *(☎ 06 48 16 02 55, toll-free ☎ 800 01 66 65; Piazza Beniamino Gigli)*. A season of concerts is held in October and November at the **Accademia di Santa Cecilia** *(☎ 06 68 80 10 44; Via della Conciliazione 4)* and the **Accademia Filarmonica Romana** *(Teatro Olimpia, Piazza Gentile da Fabriano 17)*.

## SHOPPING

It is probably advisable to stick to window-shopping in the expensive Ludovisi district, the area around Via Veneto. Many shops are in Via Sistina and Via Gregoriana, heading towards the Spanish Steps. Via Condotti and the parallel streets heading from Piazza di Spagna to Via del Corso are lined with very expensive clothing and footwear boutiques, as well as shops selling accessories. This is label heaven for the seriously fashion-conscious. Via del Corso itself offers good shopping, with

a mix of moderately expensive and cheaper high-street knock-off fashions.

It is cheaper, but not as interesting, to shop along Via del Tritone and Via Nazionale. There are some interesting second-hand clothes shops along Via del Governo Vecchio.

If clothes don't appeal, wander through the streets around Via Margutta, Via Ripetta, Piazza del Popolo and Via Frattina to look at the art galleries, artists' studios and antiquarian shops. Antique shops line Via Coronari, between Piazza Navona and Lungotevere di Tor di Nona.

Everyone flocks to the famous Porta Portese market every Sunday morning. Hundreds of stalls selling anything you can imagine (doll parts and broken typewriters anyone?) line the streets of the Porta Portese area parallel to Viale di Trastevere, near Trastevere. Take time to rummage through the piles of clothing and bric-a-brac and you will find some incredible bargains. Catch tram No 8 from Largo Argentina and get off near Ospedale San Gallicano on Viale di Trastevere (it's a 10-minute ride).

The market on Via Sannio, near Porta San Giovanni, sells new and second-hand clothes and shoes at bargain prices in the morning from Monday to Saturday.

## GETTING THERE & AWAY
### Air

The main airline offices are in the area around Via Veneto and Via Barberini, north of Stazione Termini. Qantas, British Airways and Alitalia are all on Via Bissolati. Cathay Pacific, Singapore Airlines and Thai International Airways are on Via Barberini. The main airport is Leonardo da Vinci, at Fiumicino (see Rome's Getting Around section, later).

### Bus

The main terminal for intercity buses is in Piazzale Tiburtina, in front of the Stazione Tiburtina. Catch the Metropolitana Linea B from Termini to Tiburtina. Buses connect with cities throughout Italy. Numerous companies, some of which are listed here, operate these services. For information about which companies operate services to which destinations and from where, go to the APT office, or Enjoy Rome (see Tourist Offices, earlier in this chapter). There are ticket offices for all of the companies at Tiburtina station. Cotral (also known as Linee Laziali) buses, which service Lazio, depart from numerous points throughout the city, depending on their destinations.

Some useful bus lines are:

**Cotral** (☎ 800 43 17 84) Via Volturno 65; services throughout Lazio

**Lazzi** (☎ 06 884 08 40) Via Tagliamento 27b; services to other European cities (with Eurolines) and northern and central Italy

**Marozzi** information at Eurojet (☎ 06 474 28 01), Piazza della Repubblica 54; services to Bari, Brindisi, Sorrento, the Amalfi Coast and Pompeii, as well as to Matera in Basilicata

**SAIS & Segesta** (☎ 06 481 96 76) Piazza della Repubblica 42; services to Sicily

**SENA** information at Picarozzi (☎ 06 440 44 95), Via Guido Mazzoni; services to Siena

**SULGA** information at Trioviaggi (☎ 06 440 27 38), Circumvallazione Nomentana, or Sulga Perugia (☎ 075 575 96 41); services to Perugia, Assisi and Romagna

## Train

Almost all trains arrive at and depart from Stazione Termini. There are regular connections to all major cities in Italy and throughout Europe. For train **timetable information** (☎ 848 88 80 88; open 7am-9pm), call or go to the information office at the station (English is spoken). Timetables can be bought at most newsstands in and around Termini and are particularly useful if you are travelling mostly by train. Services at Termini include telephones, money exchange (see Information earlier), tourist information, post office, shops and **luggage storage** (open 7am-midnight daily; €3.10 per piece first 5hr, €0.52 per hr per piece thereafter). Note that some trains depart from the stations at Ostiense and Tiburtina.

## Car & Motorcycle

The main road connecting Rome to the north and south is the Autostrada del Sole (A1), which extends from Milan to Reggio di Calabria. On the outskirts of the city it connects with the Grande Raccordo Anulare (GRA), the ring road encircling Rome. If you are entering or leaving Rome, use the Grande Raccordo and the major feeder roads that connect it to the city; it might be longer, but it is simpler and faster. If you're approaching from the north, take the Via Salaria, Via Nomentana or Via Flaminia exits. From the south, Via Appia Nuova, Via Cristoforo Colombo and Via del Mare (which connects Rome to the Lido di

Ostia) all provide reasonably direct routes into the city. The A12 connects the city to both Civitavecchia and Fiumicino airport.

Car rental offices at Stazione Termini in Rome include **Avis** (☎ 06 481 43 73), **Hertz** (☎ 06 474 03 89) and **Maggiore** (☎ 06 488 00 49). All have offices at both airports. **Happy Rent** (☎ 06 481 81 85; W www.happyrent .com; Via Farini 3), rents scooters (from €38 per day).

## Boat

Tirrenia and the Ferrovie dello Stato (FS) ferries leave for various points in Sardinia (see Sardinia's Getting There & Away section) from Civitavecchia. A Tirrenia fast ferry leaves from Fiumicino, near Rome, and Civitavecchia in summer only. Bookings can be made at the Sestante CIT, or any travel agency displaying the Tirrenia or FS sign. You can also book directly with **Tirrenia** (☎ 06 42 00 98 03; Via San Nicola da Tolentino 5, Rome); or at the Stazione Marittima (ferry terminal) at the ports. Bookings can be made at Stazione Termini for FS ferries.

## GETTING AROUND
## To/From the Airport

The main airport is **Leonardo da Vinci** (flight information ☎ 06 65 95 36 40) at Fiumicino. Access to the city is via the Leonardo Express train service (follow the signs to the station from the airport arrivals hall), which costs €8.78 one way. The train arrives at and leaves from platform Nos 25–29 at Termini. The trip takes 35 minutes. The first train leaves the airport for Termini at 6.37am and the last at 11.37pm. Another train makes stops along the way, including at Trastevere and Ostiense, and terminates at Stazione Tiburtina (€4.65). The trip takes about 50 minutes. A night bus runs every 45 minutes from Stazione Tiburtina to the airport from 12.30am to 3.45am, stopping at Termini at the corner of Via Giolitti about 10 minutes later. The airport is connected to Rome by an autostrade, accessible from the Grande Raccordo Anulare (ring road).

Taxis are prohibitively expensive from the airport (at least €45).

The other airport is **Ciampino**, which is used for most domestic and international charter flights. Blue Cotral buses (running from 6.50am to 11.40pm) connect with the Metropolitana (Linea A at Anagnina), where you can catch the subway to Termini or the

Vatican. But if you arrive very late at night, you could end up being forced to catch a taxi. A metropolitan train line, the FM4, connects Termini with the Ciampino airport and Albano Laziale. The airport is connected to Rome by Via Appia Nuova.

## Bus

The city bus company is **ATAC** (information in English ☎ 800 43 17 84; open 8am-6pm). Details on which buses head where are available at the ATAC information booth in the centre of Piazza dei Cinquecento. Another central point for main bus routes in the centre is Largo Argentina, on Corso Vittorio Emanuele south of the Pantheon. Buses run from 5.30am to midnight, with limited services throughout the night on some routes. A fast tram service, the No 8, connects Largo Argentina with Trastevere, Porta Portese and the suburb of Monte Verde.

Rome has an integrated public transport system, so you can use the same ticket for the bus, Metro, tram and the suburban railway. Tickets cost €0.77 and are valid for 75 minutes. They must be purchased *before* you get on the bus and validated in the orange machine as you enter. The fine for travelling without a ticket is €51, to be paid on the spot, and there is no sympathy for 'dumb tourists' or non-Italian speakers. Tickets can be purchased at any tobacconist, newsstand, metro station or at the main bus terminals. Daily tickets cost €3.10 and weekly tickets cost €12.40.

The new, private 'J' buses (☎ 800 07 62 87) cover some routes of interest to tourists (J2, J4, J5), and you can buy tickets on board, although they are more expensive than ATAC buses. Tickets cost €1 for 75 minutes, €2.45 per day and €9.30 per week. They can also be purchased at tobacconists and newsstands.

## Metropolitana

The Metropolitana (Metro) has two lines, A and B. Both pass through Stazione Termini. Take Linea A for Piazza di Spagna, the Vatican (Ottaviano) and Villa Borghese (Flaminio), and Linea B for the Colosseum, Circus Maximus and Piramide (for Testaccio and Stazione Ostiense). Tickets are the same as for city buses (see Bus earlier in this section). Trains run approximately every five minutes between 5.30am and 11.30pm (12.30am on Saturday).

## Taxi

Taxis are on radio call 24 hours a day in Rome. **Cooperativa Radio Taxi Romana** (☎ 06 35 70) and **La Capitale** (☎ 06 49 94) are two of the many operators. Major taxi ranks are at the airports, Stazione Termini and Largo Argentina in the historical centre (look for the orange-and-black taxi signs). There are surcharges for luggage (€1.03 per item), night service (€2.58), Sunday and public holidays (€1.03) and travel to/from Fiumicino airport (€7.23/5.94). The flagfall is €2.32 (for the first 3km), then €0.62 for every kilometre. There is a €2.58 supplement from 10pm to 7am, and €1.03 from 7am to 10pm on Sunday and public holidays.

## Car & Motorcycle

Negotiating Roman traffic by car is difficult enough, but you are in for enormous stress if you ride a motorcycle or vespa. Keep your wits about you and say a prayer. Pedestrians should watch out for motorcycles, which never seem to stop at red lights.

If your car goes missing after being parked illegally, check with the **traffic police** (☎ 06 676 91). It will cost about €100 to get it back, plus your parking fine.

A major parking area close to the centre is at the Villa Borghese. Entrance is from Piazzale Brasile at the top of Via Veneto. There is a supervised car park at Stazione Termini. There are large car parks at Stazione Tiburtina and Piazza dei Partigiani at Stazione Ostiense (both accessible to the centre of Rome by the Metro). A new car park at St Peter's station opened in 2002, and holds 144 cars (Metropolitana Linea A). See the preceding Getting There & Away section for information about car and scooter rental.

# Around Rome

## OSTIA ANTICA

The Romans founded this port city at the mouth of the Tiber in the 4th century BC and it became a strategically important centre of defence and trade. It was populated by merchants, sailors and slaves, and the ruins of the city provide a fascinating contrast to a place such as Pompeii. Ostia Antica was abandoned after barbarian invasions and the appearance of malaria, but Pope Gregory IV re-established the city in the 9th century.

The Rome APT office or Enjoy Rome can provide information about the ancient city, or call the ticket office on ☎ 06 56 35 80 99.

Of particular note in the excavated city (☎ 06 56 35 80 99; admission €4; open 8.30am-4pm Tues-Sun winter, to 6pm summer) are the mosaics of the **Terme di Nettuno** (Baths of Neptune); a **Roman theatre** built by Augustus; the **forum** and **temple**, dedicated to Jupiter, Juno and Minerva; and **Piazzale delle Corporazioni**, with the offices of Roman merchants, distinguished by mosaics depicting their trades.

To get to Ostia Antica take the Metropolitana Linea B to Magliana and then the Ostia Lido train (getting off at Ostia Antica). By car, take the SS8bis (aka Via del Mare) or Via Ostiense.

## TIVOLI
### postcode 00019 • pop 53,000
Set on a hill by the Anio River, Tivoli was a resort town of the ancient Romans and became popular as a summer playground for the Renaissance wealthy. Today it draws people for the terraced gardens and fountains of the Villa d'Este and the ruins of Villa Adriana, built by the Roman emperor Hadrian.

The local **tourist office** (☎ 0774 33 45 22) is in Largo Garibaldi near the Cotral bus stop.

### Things to See
Hadrian built his spectacular summer villa, **Villa Adriana** (☎ 0774 53 02 02; admission €6.20; open 9am-1hr before sunset daily), in the 2nd century AD. It was successively plundered by barbarians and Romans for building materials and many of its original decorations were used to embellish the Villa d'Este. However, enough remains to give an impression of the incredible size and magnificence of the villa. Give yourself about four hours to wander through the vast ruins.

Highlights include La Villa dell'Isola (the Villa of the Island) where Hadrian spent his pensive moments, the Imperial Palace and its Piazza d'Oro (Golden Square), and the floor mosaics of the Hospitalia.

The Renaissance **Villa d'Este** (admission €6.20; open 9am-1hr before sunset Tues-Sun) was built in the 16th century for Cardinal Ippolito d'Este on the site of a Franciscan monastery. The villa's wonderful gardens are decorated with numerous fountains, which are its main attraction.

### Getting There & Away
Tivoli is about 40km east of Rome and accessible by Cotral bus. Take Metropolitana Linea B from Stazione Termini to Ponte Mammolo; the bus leaves from outside the station every 20 minutes. The bus also stops near the Villa Adriana, about 1km from Tivoli. Otherwise, catch local bus No 4 from Tivoli's Piazza Garibaldi to Villa Adriana.

## TARQUINIA
### postcode 01016 • pop 15,300
Believed to have been founded in the 12th century BC and to have been the home of the Tarquin kings, who ruled Rome before the creation of the republic, Tarquinia was an important economic and political centre of the Etruscan League. The major attractions here are the painted tombs of its *necropoli* (burial grounds), although the town itself is quite pretty. There is a **IAT tourist information office** (☎ 0766 85 63 84; Piazza Cavour 1; open 9am-1pm Mon-Sat).

### Things to See
The 15th-century Palazzo Vitelleschi houses the **Museo Nazionale Tarquiniense** (admission €4 or €6.50 with Necropolis; open 8.30am-7.30pm Tues-Sun) and an excellent collection of Etruscan treasures, including frescoes from the tombs. Keep an eye out for a few red-and-black plates featuring acrobatic sex acts. There are also numerous sarcophagi found in the tombs. The **necropolis** (open 8.30am-6.30pm Tues-Sun) is a 15- to 20-minute walk away (or catch one of four daily buses). Ask at the tourist office for directions. The tombs are richly decorated with frescoes, although many have deteriorated.

### Places to Stay & Eat
Tarquinia has limited accommodation, so it is best visited as a day trip from Rome. If you must stay (especially at weekends), remember to book in advance. The nearest camp site is **Tusca Tirrenica** (☎ 0766 86 42 94; Viale Nereidi) 5km from the town and by the water. **Hotel San Marco** (☎ 0766 684 22 34, fax 0766 84 23 06; Piazza Cavour 10; singles/doubles with bath €52/68) is the closest spot to the sights and transport and has pleasing rooms.

For a meal try **Trattoria Arcadia** (Via Mazzini 6; meal about €15), a friendly joint with good *salsicce* (sausages), near the museum.

## Getting There & Away

To get there, take a Cotral bus (roughly every 45 minutes) to Civitavecchia from Via Lepanto in Rome, near the Metropolitana Linea A Lepanto stop, and change for a regular service to Tarquinia (every 45 minutes or so).

## CERVETERI

Ancient Caere was founded in the 8th century BC by the Etruscans, enjoying great prosperity as a maritime centre from the 7th to 5th centuries BC. The drawcards now are the tombs known as *tumoli*, great mounds with carved stone bases. Treasures taken from these tombs can be seen in the Vatican Museums, the Villa Giulia Museum and the Louvre. There is a **Pro Loco tourist office** *(Piazza Risorgimento 19).*

Once inside the main necropolis area, **Banditaccia** *(☎ 06 994 00 01; Via del Necropoli; admission €4.20; open 9am-7pm Tues-Sun summer; to 4pm winter),* it's a good idea to follow the recommended routes in order to see the best-preserved tombs. Banditaccia is accessible by local bus (summer only) from the main piazza in Cerveteri, but it is also a pleasant 3km walk west from the town.

Cerveteri is accessible from Rome by Cotral bus from Via Lepanto, outside the Lepanto stop on Metropolitana Linea A.

# Northern Italy

Italy's affluent north is capped by the Alps and bound by the beaches of Liguria and the lagoons of Venice, with the gently undulating Po River plain at its heart. Venice is the jewel in the crown, but gems are to be found throughout Piedmont, Lombardy, Emilia-Romagna and the Veneto.

## GENOA

**postcode 16100 • pop 628,800**

Genoa is aristocratic, seedy, grandiose and dingy. Still a busy port, and regional capital of Liguria, it retains an exuberance that its most famous son, Christopher Columbus (1451–1506), would surely recognise. From murky streets around the port to grand thoroughfares and noble palaces, Genoa, the once mighty maritime republic, is a compelling city worthy of its historical title, La Superba.

Recent events have, however, left a bloody mark as the city hit the headlines as host of

the G8 summit in the summer of 2001. Violent rioting culminated in police shooting dead a 23-year-old demonstrator.

## Orientation

Most trains stop at Genoa's two main stations, Principe and Brignole. The area around Brignole is closer to the city centre and a better bet for accommodation than Principe, which is closer to the port, an area that women travelling alone should avoid at night.

From Brignole walk straight ahead along Via Fiume to get to Via XX Settembre and the historical centre. Walking around Genoa is easier than using the local ATM bus service, but most useful buses stop outside both stations.

## Information

On the waterfront there is an **IAT information kiosk** *(☎ 010 24 87 11, fax 010 246 76 58; open 9am-1pm & 2pm-6pm daily)* opposite the aquarium. There are further branches at Stazione Principe *(open 9.30am-1pm & 2.30pm-6pm Mon-Sat),* Stazione Marittima, whose opening hours are based on ship arrival and departure times, and at the airport *(open 9.30am-12.30pm & 1.30pm-5.30pm Mon-Sat).* **Genova Informa** *(Piazza Matteotti; 9am-8pm daily)* also provides information.

The **main post office** *(Via Dante 4a),* is just off Piazza de Ferrari while the **Telecom office** *(Piazza Verdi; open 8am-9pm daily)* is to the left of Stazione Brignole as you approach it on foot. For Internet access try **Internet Point** *(Via di Ravecca 39)* where an hour online costs €6.20.

East of the city centre is **Ospedale San Martino** *(☎ 010 55 51; Via Benedetto XV).*

## Things to See & Do

Genoa claims to have the biggest historical centre in Europe and any tour of the city should start in the backstreets around the old port, which teem with activity, some of it nefarious, most of it entertaining. Search out the 12th-century, black-and-white marble **Cattedrale di San Lorenzo** and the huge **Palazzo Ducale** in Piazza Matteotti.

The palaces of the Doria family, one of the city's most important families in the 14th and 15th centuries, can be found in **Piazza San Matteo**. Further grand palaces line **Via Garibaldi**, several of which are open to the public and contain art galleries, including the 16th-century **Palazzo Bianco** and the

ITALY

17th-century **Palazzo Rosso**. Italian and Flemish Renaissance works are displayed in **Galleria Nazionale di Palazzo Spinola** *(Piazza Superiore di Pellicceria 1; admission €4; open 8.30am-7.30pm Tues-Sat, 1pm-8pm Sun)*.

Genoa's star attraction is, however, its **aquarium** *(Ponte Spinola; admission €11.60; open 9.30am-7.30pm Mon-Wed & Fri, 9.30am-10pm Thur, 9.30am-8.30pm Sat & Sun)*, on the waterfront. Europe's biggest, it is well worth a visit.

## Places to Stay

The HI **Ostello Genova** *(☎ 010 242 24 57; e hostelge@iol.it; Via Costanzi 120; B&B €13-18)* in Righi, is just outside Genoa. Evening meals cost €7.25. To get there catch bus No 40 from Stazione Brignole.

On the 3rd floor of a gracious old palazzo near Stazione Brignole, **Carola** *(☎ 010 839 13 40; Via Gropallo 4; singles/doubles/triples without bath €26/42/57, doubles/triples with bath €52/68)* offers simple rooms and a warm welcome. A few doors up at No 8, **Albergo Rita** *(☎/fax 010 87 02 07; singles/doubles/triples without bath €31/47/60, doubles/triples with bath €52/70)* has pleasant-enough rooms. Tucked away in the historic centre, **Hotel Major** *(☎ 010 247 41 74, fax 246 98 98; Via Garibaldi; singles/doubles without bath €31/41, with bath €41/52)* is a tight squeeze, but the owners are friendly.

Splash out a little at **Hotel Bel Soggiorno** *(☎ 010 54 28 80, fax 010 58 14 18; Via XX Settembre 19; singles/doubles with bath €73/93)*, where the rooms are all chintz and chandeliers.

One of the city's grandest establishments is the **Bristol Palace** *(☎ 010 59 25 41, fax 010 56 17 56; Via XX Settembre 35; singles/doubles with bath €171/243)*, which has all the trimmings.

## Places to Eat

Don't leave town without trying *pesto genovese*, *pansoti* (ravioli in walnut sauce), *farinata* (a Tuscan torte made with chickpea flour) and, of course, focaccia. Plenty of shops sell sandwiches and pizza by the slice in the Brignole and port areas. For seafood, head to the **Via Sottoripo arcades** on the waterfront; at No 113 you'll pay €5 for a bag of freshly fried calamari and zucchini.

The basic **Trattoria Da Maria** *(Vico Testa d'Oro 14; meal about €7)*, off Via XXV Aprile, is something of an institution, where good, cheap food is served in an amiably chaotic environment.

Hidden away in the old town, **La Santa** *(Vico degli Orefici 5; set menu €10.50)* specialises in Ligurian cooking.

## Entertainment

The Genoa Theatre Company performs at the **Politeama Genovese** *(☎ 010 839 35 89)* and the **Teatro di Genova** *(☎ 010 534 22 00)*. **Teatro della Tosse in Sant'Agostino** *(☎ 010 247 07 93; Piazza R Negri 4)* has a season of diverse shows from January to May. Opera buffs should head to **Teatro Carlo Felice** *(☎ 010 58 93 29)*, near Piazza De Ferrari.

## Getting There & Away

**Air** There are regular domestic and also international connections from **Cristoforo Colombo airport** *(☎ 010 601 54 10; Sestri Ponente)*, 6km west of the city. The **Volabus** *(☎ 558 24 14)* airport bus service (line No 100) leaves from Piazza Verdi, just outside Stazione Brignole, and also stops at Stazione Principe. Service is half-hourly from 5.30am to 11pm (€2.05, 25 minutes).

**Bus** There are buses for Rome, Florence, Milan and Perugia which leave from Piazza della Vittoria, south of Stazione Brignole. Eurolines coaches leave from the same piazza for Barcelona, Madrid and Paris. Book at **Geotravels** *(☎ 010 58 71 81)* in the piazza.

**Train** Genoa is connected by train to major cities. For train information call ☎ 848 88 80 88.

**Boat** The city's busy port is a major embarkation point for ferries to Sicily, Sardinia and Corsica. Major companies are **Corsica Ferries** *(☎ 019 21 55 11)* in Savona; **Moby Lines** *(☎ 010 254 15 13)* at Ponte Asserato for Corsica; **Tirrenia** *(☎ 199 12 31 99, 800 82 40 79)* at the Stazione Marittima, Ponte Colombo (for Sicily and Sardinia); and **Grandi Navi Veloci** and **Grandi Traghetti** *(☎ 010 58 93 31; Via Fieschi 17)* for Sardinia, Sicily, Malta and Tunisia. For more information, see the Getting There & Away sections under Sicily and Sardinia, and in the Corsica section in the France chapter.

## RIVIERA DI LEVANTE

The Ligurian coast from Genoa to La Spezia (on the border with Tuscany) is quite spectacular, rivalling the Amalfi Coast in its beauty. Summer here can be trying, so try to go in spring and autumn when the weather is more amenable to walking and the smaller crowds to sightseeing.

To explore the region, your best bet is to use either Santa Margherita Ligure in the north as a base or, further south, La Spezia. Tourist information is available in Santa Margherita at the **IAT tourist office** (☎ 0185 28 74 85, fax 0185 28 30 34; Via XXV Aprile 4) in the town centre, and in La Spezia near the waterfront at the **IAT tourist office** (☎ 0187 77 09 00, fax 0187 77 09 08; Via Mazzini 45).

### Things to See & Do

From pretty Santa Margherita Ligure you can explore the nearby resorts of **Portofino**, a haunt of the rich and famous, and **Camogli**, a fishing village turned resort town. The medieval Benedictine monastery of **San Fruttuoso** is a 2½-hour hilly walk from Camogli or Portofino, with sensational views along the way; you may want to catch the ferry back.

Farther south, there are the five tiny coastal villages of the **Cinque Terre** national park – Riomaggiore, Manorola, Corniglia, Vernazza and Montcrosso. All are easily reached by train from La Spezia. They are linked by a 12km path known as the Via dell'Amore (Lovers' Lane). The remarkable scenery is well worth the €3 toll.

### Places to Stay & Eat

Santa Margherita's **Nuova Riviera** (☎/fax 0185 28 74 03; e info@nuovariviera.com; Via Belvedere 10; singles/doubles with bath €75/90) is a lovely family-run hotel not far from the sea. Nearby, **Albergo Annabella** (☎ 0185 28 65 31; Via Costasecca 10; singles/ doubles without bath €43/75) has large, airy rooms.

The orderly and well-run **Ostello 5 Terre** (☎ 0187 92 02 15; e ostello@cdh.it; Via B Riccobaldi 21; dorm bed €19) in Manorola offers an evening meal for €11; be sure to book well ahead.

In La Spezia, **Albergo Parma** (☎ 0187 74 30 10, fax 0187 74 32 40; Via Fiume 143; singles/doubles without bath €25/42, with bath €32/57) has decent rooms opposite the station, while up a notch, the three-star **Hotel**

**Astoria** (☎ 0187 71 46 55, fax 0187 71 44 25; Via Roma 139; singles/doubles with bath €62/110) offers comfortable rooms and an abundant breakfast.

In Santa Margherita, **Caffè del Porto** (Via Bottaro 32; meal about €20) is a charming spot to while away the lunchtime torpor. The many good trattorias in La Spezia's include **La Tavernetta** (Via Fiume 57; meal about €18), and **I Gabbiani** (Molo Italia; meal around €15), a restaurant floating in the port.

### Getting There & Away

The entire coast is served by train and all points are accessible from Genoa. Buses leave from Santa Margherita's Piazza Martiri della Libertà for Portofino.

In the summer, **Servizio Marittimo del Tigullio** (☎ 0185 28 46 70) runs ferries from Santa Margherita to Portofino, San Fruttuoso and the Cinque Terre. From La Spezia there are numerous ferry routes along the coast, but for the Cinque Terre a cheaper option is a biglietto giornaliero Cinque Terre (a one-day rail pass; €5.20) valid for unlimited travel between Monterosso and La Spezia.

## TURIN

postcode 10100 • pop 898,400

More noted for its factories than its palaces, Turin is, in fact, a rather grand old city. Formerly the capital of Italy (until 1945) and seat of the House of Savoy, it feels like a place that was once great but that still counts. This is thanks to the Agnelli family, their industrial creation Fiat, and the most loved/ hated football team in Italy, Juventus. Towering buildings line the busy boulevards in this baroque city, which will host the Winter Olympics in 2006.

### Orientation & Information

The Porta Nuova train station is the point of arrival for most travellers. To reach the city centre, cross Corso Vittorio Emanuele II and walk straight ahead through the grand Carlo Felice and San Carlo piazzas until you come to Piazza Castello. If arriving on foot from the station, the spire of the Mole Antonelliana will be on your right as you enter Piazza Castello. There is a **tourist office** (☎ 011 53 51 81, fax 011 53 00 70; e info@turismotorino.org; Piazza Castello 161; open 9.30am-7pm Mon-Sat, 9.30am-3pm Sun) and there are also branches at the Porta Nuova train station

ITALY

(☎ 011 53 13 27, fax 011 561 70 95; open 9.30am-7pm Mon-Sat, 9.30am-3pm Sun) and the airport (☎ 011 567 81 24).

## Things to See

Museum enthusiasts should consider the *Torino Card*, a 48-hour pass valid for all public transport in the city and many of the city's museums. It costs €14.

Start at Piazza San Carlo, which is known as Turin's drawing room and is capped by the baroque churches of **San Carlo** and **Santa Cristina**. Nearby, the majestic **Piazza Castello** features the sumptuous **Palazzo Madama**, home to the **Museo Civico d'Arte Antica** and the 17th-century **Palazzo Reale** (Royal Palace) where the gardens were designed in 1697 by Louis le Nôtre, better known for his work at Versailles.

Not far away in the **Cattedrale di San Giovanni Battista**, west of the Palazzo Reale, lies one of the Catholic Church's great curiosities, the **Turin Shroud**, the linen cloth claimed to have been used to wrap the crucified Christ. Carbon dating seems to have scotched this theory, showing the cloth to be 13th century, but the faithful continue to come. The shroud is only brought out a few times a year, but there is a reasonable copy on display in the cathedral. For enthusiasts, the **Museo della Sindone** (*Museum of the Shroud; Via San Domenico 28; admission €5.50; open 9am-noon & 3pm-7pm daily*) will answer most questions.

Turin's enormous **Museo Egizio** (☎ 011 561 77 76; Via Accademia delle Scienze 6; admission €6.50; open 8.30am-7.30pm Tues-Sun) is considered one of the best museums of ancient Egyptian art after those in London and Cairo.

## Places to Stay & Eat

Turin has plenty of cheap, if a little rundown, accommodation.

In the hills east of the River Po there is **Campeggio Villa Rey** (☎ 011 819 01 17; Strada Superiore Val San Martino 27; per person/tent €3.65/6; open Mar-Oct) and **Ostello Torino** (☎ 011 660 29 39; Via Alby 1; dorm bed €12). To get to the hostel, catch bus No 52 from Porta Nuova station (No 64 on Sunday). An evening meal costs €8.

The one-star **Canelli** (☎ 011 54 60 78; Via San Dalmazzo 5b; singles/doubles without bath €14/19, singles/doubles/triples with bath €22/30/38) is reminiscent of a dusty university faculty building – all yellowing corridors and torn posters. Near the station the two-star **Bologna** (☎ 011 562 02 90, fax 011 562 01 93; Corso Vittorio Emanuele II 60; singles/doubles with bath €55/76) is deservedly popular. In a great location, **San Carlo** (☎ 011 562 78 46, fax 011 53 86 53; Piazza San Carlo 197; singles/doubles without bath €35/55, with bath €59/70) has rooms with old-world style. Up the luxury scale, **Dogana Vecchia** (☎ 011 436 67 52, fax 011 436 71 94; Via Corte D'Appello 4; singles/doubles with bath €83/104) continues to offer elegant rooms today as it did to the likes of Verdi and Mozart.

For a lunchtime bite try **La Grangia** (*Via Garibaldi 21; meal about €7*) and mingle with the city centre crowd. During the evening, the pizzas at **Pizzeria alla Baita dei 7 Nani** (*Via A Doria 5; pizza meal about €10*) are sought after. For gelati and chocolate you're spoiled for choice, but the ice cream at **Caffè Fiorio** (*Via Po 8*) was good enough for the father of Italian unification, Cavour.

## Getting There & Away

Turin is serviced by **Caselle international airport** (☎ 011 567 63 61), with flights to European and national destinations. **Sadem** (☎ 011 300 01 66) buses run to the airport every 45 minutes from the corner between Via Sacchi and Corso Vittorio Emanuele II, on the western side of Porta Nuova train station. Intercity, national and international buses terminate at the bus terminal on Corso Castelfidardo. Buses serve the Valle d'Aosta, most of the towns and ski resorts in Piedmont and major Italian cities. Regular trains connect with Milan, Aosta, Venice, Genoa and Rome.

## Getting Around

The city is well serviced by a network of buses and trams. A map of public-transport routes is available at the station information office.

# MILAN

**postcode 20100 • pop 1.3 million**

Milan, a self-styled sophisticated city, is all about money, looks and shopping. Capital of Italy's finance and fashion industries, this surprisingly scruffy city offers the best in Italian theatre, nightlife and clothes – and not a lot else.

Its origins are believed to be Celtic, but it was conquered by the Romans in 222 BC and became a major trading and transport centre. From the 13th century the city flourished under the rule of two powerful families: the Visconti, followed by the Sforza.

Milan closes down almost completely in August, when most of the city's inhabitants take their annual holidays.

## Orientation

From Milan's central train station (Stazione Centrale), it's easy to reach the centre of town on the efficient underground railway (known as the Metropolitana Milanese, or MM). The city of Milan is huge, but most sights are in the centre. Use the Duomo (cathedral) and the Castello Sforzesco as your points of reference; the main shopping areas and sights are around and between the two.

## Information

**Tourist Offices** The main branch of the **APT tourist office** (☎ 02 72 52 43 00, fax 02 72 52 43 50; Via Marconi 1; open 8.45am-1pm & 2pm-6pm Mon-Fri, 9am-1pm & 2pm-5pm Sat & Sun), is in Piazza del Duomo, where you can pick up the useful city guides *Hello Milano* and *Milano Mese*, and the excellent map *Milan is Milano*. The **branch office** (☎ 02 72 52 43 60; Stazione Centrale; open 9am-6.30pm Mon-Sat, 9am-12.30pm & 1.30pm-5pm Sun), near the Telecom office, has useful listings in English posted outside. There are also APT branches at Linate and Malpensa airports.

**Foreign Consulates** Diplomatic representation in Milan includes: **Australia** (☎ 02 77 70 42 17; Via Borgogna 2), **Canada** (☎ 02 675 81; Via Vittor Pisani 19), **France** (☎ 02 655 91 41; Via Mangili 1), the **UK** (☎ 02 72 30 01; Via San Paolo 7) and the **USA** (☎ 02 29 03 51; Via P Amedeo 2/10).

**Money** Banks in Milan open 8.30am to 1.30pm and 2.45pm to 3.45pm Monday to Friday. On Piazza Duomo, **Banca Ponti** at No 19 has an ATM, and there are exchange offices open daily at Stazione Centrale. There is an **American Express office** (☎ 02 720 03 694; Via Brera 3; open 9am-5.30pm Mon-Fri).

**Post & Communications** The **main post office** (Via Cordusio 4; open 8am-7pm

Mon-Fri, 8.30am-12pm Sat) is off Via Dante, near Piazza del Duomo. There are also post offices at the station and at Linate airport.

The somewhat squalid **Telecom office** (open 8am-9.30pm daily) on the upper level of Stazione Centrale, has international telephone directories, while the **office** (open 8am-9.30pm daily) in the Galleria Vittorio Emanuele II has Internet access (€0.10 for 70 seconds), a fax machine and phonecards.

The **Hard Disk Café** (Corso Sempione 44) was Milan's first Internet café and is one of Europe's biggest. **Terzomillennio** (Via Lazzaretto 2) is a more modest outfit, charging €1 for five minutes and €3.50 for half an hour.

**Bookshops** There's a good selection of English-language books at the **American Bookstore** (Via Campiero 16).

**Laundry** The **Lavanderia Self-Service** (Via Tadino 4; open 7.30am-9.30pm daily) charges €3.10 for a small load, and €6.10 for a mega-load of washing.

**Medical & Emergency Services** For an ambulance call ☎ 118. The public hospital, **Ospedale Maggiore Policlinico** (☎ 02 550 31; Via Francesco Sforza 35) is close to the centre, and there is an all-night **pharmacy** (☎ 02 669 07 35) in Stazione Centrale.

The **questura** (police headquarters; ☎ 02 622 61; Via Fatebenefratelli 11) is situated near the **Ufficio Stranieri** (Foreigners' Office; ☎ 02 622 61; Via Montebello 26) where English is spoken. For lost property call the **Milan City Council** (☎ 02 54 66 81 18; Via Friuli 30).

**Dangers & Annoyances** Milan's main shopping areas are popular haunts for groups of thieves, who are lightning-fast. They use a technique of waving cardboard or newspaper in your face to distract you while they head for your pockets or purse. Be particularly careful in the piazza in front of the Stazione Centrale.

## Things to See & Do

Start with the extraordinary **Duomo**, the city's unique landmark. Looking like the backdrop to an animated fairy tale, the cathedral was commissioned in 1386 to a lunatic French-Gothic design and finished 600 years later. The resulting spiky marble facade is an unforgettable mass of statues, pinnacles and

ITALY

ITALY

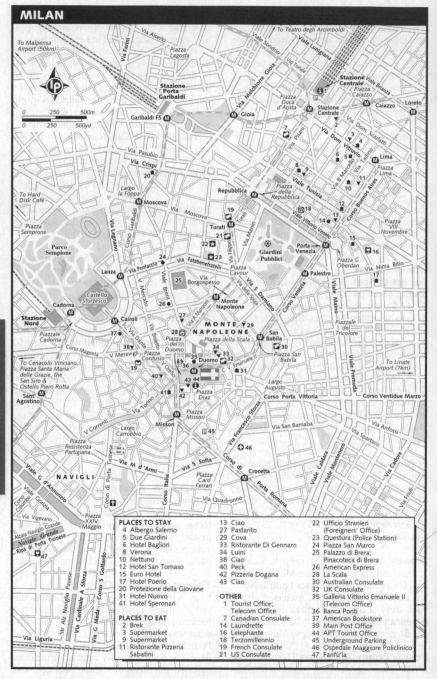

# MILAN

To Teatro degli Arcimboldi

To Malpensa
Airport (50km)

Piazza
Lagosta

Stazione
Porta
Garibaldi

Stazione
Centrale

Garibaldi FS Ⓜ

Ⓜ Gioia

Piazza
Duca
d'Aosta

Stazione
Centrale

Caiazzo

Loreto

Via Pasubio

Via Crispi

Largo
la Foppa

Repubblica

Piazza
della
Repubblica

Viale Tunisia

Piazza
Lima

Lima

To Hard
Disk Café

Ⓜ Moscova

Via Moscova

Piazza
Sempione

Parco
Sempione

Turati Ⓜ

Ⓜ
Porta
Venezia

Piazza
VIII-
Novembre

Lanza Ⓜ

Via Pontaccio

Via Fatebenefratelli

Giardini
Pubblici

Ⓜ Palestro

Castello
Sforzesco

Via
Borgospesso

Piazza
Cavour

Piazza G
Oberdan

Cadorna

Stazione
Nord

Ⓜ Cairoli

Monte
Napoleone

To Cenacolo Vinciano,
Piazza Santa Maria
delle Grazie, the
San Siro &
Ostello Piero Rotta

MONTE
NAPOLEONE

San
Babila

Ⓜ San
Babila

To Linate
Airport (7km)

Sant'
Agostino Ⓜ

Duomo

Galleria Vittorio
Emanuele II

Piazza San
Babila

Largo
Augusto

Corso Porta Vittoria

Corso Ventidue Marzo

Ⓜ Missori

Piazza
Missori

NAVIGLI

Piazza
Card
Ferrari

Piazza
Resistenza
Partigiana

Porta Romana

## PLACES TO STAY
4  Albergo Salerno
5  Due Giardini
6  Hotel Baglioni
8  Verona
9  Nettuno
12 Hotel San Tomaso
15 Euro Hotel
17 Hotel Poerio
20 Protezione della Giovane
31 Hotel Nuovo
41 Hotel Speronari

## PLACES TO EAT
2  Brek
3  Supermarket
9  Supermarket
11 Ristorante Pizzeria
   Sabatini

13 Ciao
27 Pastarito
29 Cova
33 Ristorante Di Gennaro
34 Luini
38 Ciao
40 Peck
42 Pizzeria Dogana
43 Ciao

## OTHER
1  Tourist Office;
   Telecom Office
7  Canadian Consulate
14 Laundrette
16 Lelephante
18 Terzomillennio
19 French Consulate
21 US Consulate

22 Ufficio Stranieri
   (Foreigners' Office)
23 Questura (Police Station)
24 Piazza San Marco
25 Palazzo di Brera;
   Pinacoteca di Brera
26 American Express
28 La Scala
30 Australian Consulate
32 UK Consulate
35 Galleria Vittorio Emanuele II
   (Telecom Office)
36 Banca Ponti
37 American Bookstore
39 Main Post Office
44 APT Tourist Office
45 Underground Parking
46 Ospedale Maggiore Policlinico
47 Fanfu'la

pillars. The view from the roof is also quite memorable (stairs €3.50, lift €5).

Back on solid ground, join the throngs and take a *passeggiata* (stroll) through the magnificent **Galleria Vittorio Emanuele II** to **La Scala**, the world's most-famous opera house, which is currently closed for a makeover. (See Entertainment later for more details.)

At the end of Via Dante is the immense **Castello Sforzesco** *(admission free; open 9.30am-5.30pm Tues-Sun)*, originally a Visconti fortress and entirely rebuilt by Francesco Sforza in the 15th century. Its museum collections include furniture, artefacts and sculpture, notably Michelangelo's unfinished *Pietà Rondanini*.

Nearby on Via Brera is the 17th-century Palazzo di Brera, home to the **Pinacoteca di Brera** *(admission €6.20; open 8.30am-7.15pm Tues-Sun)*. This gallery's vast collection includes Mantegna's masterpiece, the *Dead Christ*.

To view Leonardo da Vinci's *Last Supper* in the **Cenacolo Vinciano** *(☎ 02 89 42 11 46; Piazza Santa Maria delle Grazie 2; admission €6.50; open 8am-7.30pm Tues-Sun)* you'll need to phone to make a booking.

## Special Events
St Ambrose's Day (7 December) is Milan's major festival, with celebrations at the Fiera di Milano (MM1: stop Amendola Fiera).

## Places to Stay
**Hostels** The HI-run **Ostello Piero Rotta** *(☎/fax 02 39 26 70 95; Viale Salmoiraghi 1; dorm bed €16; closed 9am-3.30pm, curfew 12.30am)* is northwest of the city centre. Take the MM1 to the QT8 stop. **Protezione della Giovane** *(☎ 02 29 00 01 64; Corso Garibaldi 123; beds €22)* is run by nuns for single women aged 16 to 25 years. Prebooking is required.

**Hotels** Milan's hotels are among the most expensive and heavily booked in Italy, largely due to trade fairs held in the city, so book in advance. There are numerous budget hotels around Stazione Centrale, but the quality varies.

***Stazione Centrale & Corso Buenos Aires***
One of Milan's nicest one-star hotels is **Due Giardini** *(☎ 02 29 52 10 93, fax 02 29 51 69 33; Via B Marcello 47; singles/doubles with*

*bath €55/85)*, which has rooms overlooking a tranquil back garden (a rarity in central Milan). To get there turn right off Via D Scarlatti, which is to the left as you leave the station.

On busy Via Dom Vitruvio, off Piazza Duca d'Aosta, there are many hotels, some of them less than enticing. **Albergo Salerno** *(☎/fax 02 204 68 70; doubles with/without bath €77/60)* at No 18, is, however, a good option with clean, simple rooms.

**Nettuno** *(☎ 02 29 40 44 81; Via Tadino 27; singles/doubles/triples without bath €34/52/70, with bath €47/70/88)* is a modest outfit with some of the cheapest rates around. Near Piazza della Repubblica, you might be able to bargain the rates down at **Verona** *(☎ 02 66 98 30 91; Via Carlo Tenca 12; singles/doubles with bath €70/110)*, depending on the time of year.

Just off Corso Buenos Aires, the friendly **Hotel San Tomaso** *(☎ 02 29 51 47 47; e hotelsantomaso@tin.it; Viale Tunisia 6; singles/doubles/triples without bath €41/72/100, doubles with bath €82)* provides a TV and phone in every room. On the other side of Corso Buenos Aires, in a quiet(ish) street **Hotel Poerio** *(☎ 02 29 52 28 72; Via Poerio; singles without bath €31, singles/doubles with bath €42/62)* offers rooms at the basic end of the basic scale.

Closer to the centre, off Piazza G Oberdan, **Euro Hotel** *(☎ 02 20 40 40 10, fax 02 29 40 06 74; e eurohotel.viasirtori@tin.it; Via Sirtori 26; singles/doubles/triples €98/149/195)* provides modern rooms with shower, satellite TV and breakfast.

For some three-star comfort, try **Hotel Bagliori** *(☎ 02 29 52 68 84, fax 02 29 52 68 42; e hotelbagliori@tin.it; Via Boscovich 43; singles/doubles with bath €124/176)* with its pretty little walled garden.

***City Centre*** Right in the heart of things, near Piazza del Duomo (for which read handy but noisy), **Hotel Speronari** *(☎ 02 86 46 11 25, fax 02 72 00 31 78; Via Speronari 4; singles/doubles/triples without bath €47/73/88, with bath €62/104/130)* has decent-enough rooms.

**Hotel Nuovo** *(☎ 02 86 46 05 42, fax 02 72 00 17 52; Piazza Beccaria 6; singles/doubles without bath €31/51, doubles/triples with bath €93/124)*, just off Corso Vittorio Emanuele II and the Duomo, is a good deal with cheap rates and simple rooms.

## Places to Eat

There are plenty of fast-food outlets and sandwich bars in the station and Duomo areas, extremely popular during the lunchtime rush.

**Restaurants** If you're looking for a traditional trattoria, try the side streets south of the station and along Corso Buenos Aires.

***Around Stazione Centrale*** Anything but traditional, **Ciao outlet** *(Corso Buenos Aires 7; meal about €7)* is part of a self-service chain (there are a multitude of others, including those surrounding the Duomo and at Via Dante 5), but the food is pretty good and relatively cheap. The **Brek** chain is a similar but slightly more-expensive alternative.

**Ristorante Pizzeria Sabatini** *(☎ 02 29 40 28 14; Via Boscovich 54; pizza meal about €15)*, around the corner from Corso Buenos Aires, is a large and characterless place that nevertheless churns out tasty pizzas. Pasta is also available.

***City Centre*** The **Ristorante Di Gennaro** *(☎ 02 805 61 08; Via Santa Radegonda 14; pizza from €5)* is reputed to be one of the city's first pizzerias, and the pizzas and focaccias are good. **Pizzeria Dogana** *(☎ 02 805 67 66; cnr Via Capellari & Via Dogana; pizza from €5, meal about €26)* serves standard dishes within spitting distance of the Duomo.

Near La Scala, **Pastarito** *(☎ 02 86 22 10; Via Verdi 6; pasta meal about €10)* makes up for its lack of atmosphere with huge portions and reliable quality.

**Cafés & Sandwich Bars** The popular fast-food outlet **Luini** *(Via Santa Radegonda 16)*, just off Piazza del Duomo, is a meeting point for students skipping school. You won't, however, find many screaming teenagers in **Cova** *(Via Monte Napoleone 8)*, established in 1817 and one of Milan's grander tearooms. The best gourmet takeaway is **Peck** *(Via Spadari 7-9)*, a three-storey temple to luxury food.

**Self-Catering** There are two **supermarkets** at Stazione Centrale, one on the upper level and one on the western side, as well as those close by at Via D Vitruvio 32 and Via Casati 30.

## Entertainment

Music, theatre and cinema dominate Milan's entertainment calendar. The opera season at La Scala runs from 7 December through to July, but due to restoration work, performances are being staged at the modern **Teatro degli Arcimboldi** *(☎ 02 887 91; Viale dell' Innovazione)* in the city's northern reaches. The **box office** *(☎ 02 72 00 37 44)* has also been transferred, to the subterranean pedestrian passage in the Duomo underground station. The restoration project is due for completion in December 2004.

Nightlife of the pub/club variety is centred on, but not limited to, Brera and further south, Navigli. Try **Fanfù'la** *(Ripa di Porta Ticinese 37)*, which is fun and, on Friday nights, heaving. Alternatively, and in an altogether quieter area, **Lelephante** *(Via Melzo 22)* is a darkly coloured bar ideal for discussing the woes of the world.

For football fans a visit to the **San Siro**, official name Stadio Olympico Meazza, is nothing short of a pilgrimage. Home to AC Milan and Inter, ticket prices start at around €15. They can be bought at branches of Cariplo (AC Milan) and Banca Popolare di Milano (Inter) banks.

## Shopping

Looking good is an obsession, and power shopping is serious business in Milan; but it's not cheap. Hit the main streets behind the Duomo around Corso Vittorio Emanuele II for clothing, footwear and accessories, or dream on and window-shop for designer fashions in Via Monte Napoleone, Via della Spiga and Via Borgospesso.

The areas around Via Torino, Corso Buenos Aires and Corso XXII Marzo are less expensive. **Markets** are held around the canals (southwest of the centre), notably on Viale Papiniano on Tuesday and Saturday morning. A **flea market** *(Viale Gabriele d'Annunzio)* is held each Saturday, and there's an **antique market** *(Via Fiori Chiari)* in Brera every third Saturday of the month.

## Getting There & Away

**Air** Most international flights use **Malpensa airport**, about 50km northwest of Milan. Domestic and a few European flights use **Linate airport**, about 7km east of the city. For arrivals or departures for either airport call **flight information** *(☎ 02 74 85 22 00)*.

**Bus** Milan's stations are scattered throughout the city, although some international and national bus operators use Piazza Castello as a terminal. Check with the APT.

**Train** Regular trains go from Stazione Centrale to Venice, Florence, Bologna, Genoa, Turin and Rome, as well as major cities throughout Europe. For **timetable information** (☎ 848 88 80 88; open 7am-9pm) call or go to the busy office in Stazione Centrale (English is spoken). Regional trains stop at Stazione Porta Garibaldi and Stazione Nord in Piazzale Cadorna on the MM2 line.

**Car & Motorcycle** Milan is the major junction of Italy's motorways, including the Autostrada del Sole (A1) to Rome, the Milan–Turin (A4), the Milan–Genoa (A7) and the Serenissima (A4) for Verona and Venice, and the A8 and A9 north to the lakes and the Swiss border.

All these roads meet with the Milan ring road, known as the Tangenziale Est and Tangenziale Ovest (the east and west bypasses). From here follow the signs to the centre. The A4 in particular is an extremely busy road, where an accident can hold up traffic for hours. In winter all roads in the area become extremely hazardous because of rain, snow and fog.

## Getting Around

**To/From the Airport** STAM airport shuttle buses leave for Linate airport from Piazza Luigi di Savoia, on the east side of Stazione Centrale, every 30 minutes from 5.40am to 9.35pm (€1.81). You can also use the local ATM bus No 73 from Piazza San Babila (€1, 20 minutes).

For Malpensa airport, the Malpensa Shuttle and Malpensa Bus Express both depart from Piazza Luigi di Savoia every 20 minutes between 4.30am and 12.15am (€4.13 to €5.16 depending on which operator you use, 50 to 60 minutes). Buses link the airports hourly from 8am to 9.30pm.

The Malpensa Express train connects Malpensa airport with Cadorna underground station in the centre of Milan. Trains depart from Cadorna from 5.50am to 8.20pm, after which buses take over until 11.10pm. Tickets cost €9.30 and the journey takes 40 minutes.

**Bus & Metro** Milan's public transport system is extremely efficient, with underground (MM), tram and bus services. Tickets are €1,

valid for one underground ride and/or 75 minutes on buses and trams. You can buy tickets in the MM stations, as well as at authorised tobacconists and newsstands.

**Taxi** If you try to hail a taxi in the street it won't stop – head for the taxi ranks, all of which have telephones, or call a radio taxi company. Numbers include: ☎ 02 40 40, 02 52 51, 02 53 53, 02 83 83, 02 85 85.

**Car & Motorcycle** Entering central Milan by car is a hassle. The city is dotted with expensive car parks (look for the blue sign with a white 'P'). A cheaper alternative is to use one of the supervised car parks at the last stop on each MM line. In the centre there are private garages that charge around €3 per hour. If your car is clamped or towed away call the **Polizia Municipale** (☎ 02 772 72 59). Hertz, Avis, Maggiore and Europcar all have offices at Stazione Centrale.

## MANTUA

**postcode 24100 • pop 48,000**

Mantua is a pretty-enough town on the shores of Lake Superior. Closely associated with the Gonzaga family, who ruled from the 14th to 18th centuries, its sumptuous palaces were built on a grand scale. Popular with day trippers, the town is a traditional stronghold of Umberto Bossi's separatist *Lega Nord* party.

## Information

The **APT tourist office** (☎ 0376 32 82 53, fax 0376 36 32 92; ⓔ aptmantova@iol.it; Piazza Andrea Mantegna 6; open 8.30am-12.30pm & 3pm-6pm Mon-Sat, 9.30am-12.30pm Sun) is a 10-minute walk from the station along Corso Vittorio Emanuele, which becomes Corso Umberto 1.

## Things to See

**Piazza Sordello** is surrounded by impressive buildings, including the eclectic **cattedrale**, which combines a Romanesque tower, baroque facade and Renaissance interior. But the piazza is dominated by the massive **Palazzo Ducale** (admission €6.50; open 8.45am-7.15pm Tues-Sun), former seat of the Gonzaga family. The palace has some 500 rooms and 15 courtyards, but its showpieces are the Gonzaga apartments and art collection, and the **Camera degli Sposi** (Bridal Chamber), with frescoes by Mantegna.

Down by the lake the Gonzaga's lavishly decorated summer palace, **Palazzo del Tè** *(admission €8; open 9am-6pm Tues-Sun & 1pm-6pm Mon)* was completed in 1534.

## Places to Stay & Eat

You can pitch a tent 7km from town at **Agriturismo Facchini** *(☎ 0376 44 87 63; per person €6)* or a little closer at **Agricampeggio Corte Chiara** *(☎ 0376 39 08 04; per person/tent €6/6)*. In town, opposite the train station, **Albergo ABC** *(☎ 0376 32 33 47; Piazza Don Leoni 25; singles/doubles with bath €62/83)* has rooms with breakfast included. Further up the price scale **Due Guerrieri** *(☎ 0376 32 15 33, fax 0376 32 96 45; Piazza Sordello 52; singles/doubles with bath €67/104)* is centrally located.

For a casual pizza head for **Il Girasole** *(☎ 0376 22 58 80; pizza about €6)* in the elegant Piazza Erbe. **La Masseria** *(☎ 0376 36 53 03; Piazza Broletto 8; pizza €7, pasta €7.50)* has a good reputation and an interesting menu. For finer dining, **Ristorante Pavesi** *(☎ 0376 32 36 27; Piazza delle Erbe 13; set menu €34)* is your place.

## Getting There & Away

Mantua is accessible by train and bus from Verona (about 40 minutes), and by train from Milan and Bologna with a change at Modena.

## VERONA

postcode 37100 • pop 256,100

Verona is widely regarded as one of Italy's most beautiful cities, and justifiably so. Forever associated with Romeo and Juliet, the city was an important Roman centre long before the Della Scala (also known as the Scaligeri) family took the reins in the 13th and 14th centuries, a period noted for the savage family feuding on which Shakespeare based his tragedy.

## Orientation & Information

Buses leave for the historical centre from outside the train station (see Getting Around, later); otherwise, it's a 20-minute walk, heading right to leave the bus station, crossing the river and walking along Corso Porta Nuova to Piazza Brà.

The main **APT tourist office** *(☎ 045 806 86 80; e info@tourism.verona.it; Via degli Alpini 9; open 9am-6pm Mon-Sat, 9am-2pm Sun)*, faces Piazza Brà. There are also branches at the train station *(☎ 045 800 08 61;*

*open 9am-6pm Mon-Sat)* and airport *(☎ 045 861 91 63; open 11am-5pm Mon-Sat)* in the arrivals hall.

The **post office** *(Piazza Viviani)* is central, while Internet access is available at **Internet Train** *(☎ 045 801 33 94; Via Roma 19)* where 15 minutes costs €1.50.

## Things to See & Do

Piazza Brà's stunning pink marble Roman amphitheatre, known as the **Arena**, dates from the 1st century and is the third largest in existence. It is now Verona's opera house.

Walk along Via Mazzini to Via Cappello and **Casa di Giulietta** (Juliet's House), where the balcony overlooks a courtyard covered with lovers' graffiti. Further along the street is **Porta Leoni**, one of the gates to the old Roman Verona; **Porta Borsari**, the other city gate, is north of the Arena at Corso Porta Borsari.

**Piazza delle Erbe** The former site of the Roman forum, Piazza delle Erbe is lined with marble palaces and filled with market stalls selling the usual tourist tat. Just off the square is the elegant, and much quieter, **Piazza dei Signori**, flanked by the medieval town hall, the Renaissance **Loggia del Consiglio** and the Della Scala (Scaligeri) residence, partly decorated by Giotto and nowadays known as the **Governor's Palace**. Take a look at the **Duomo** *(Via Duomo)*, for its Romanesque main doors and Titian's glorious *Assumption*.

## Places to Stay & Eat

The excellent **Ostello Villa Francescatti** *(☎ 045 59 03 60, fax 045 800 91 27; Salita Fontana del Ferro 15; B&B €12.50)* offers an evening meal for €7.50. An HI or student card is necessary. To get there catch bus No 73 from the station.

**Pensione al Castello** *(☎/fax 045 800 44 03; Corso Cavour 43; singles/doubles without bath €52/83, with bath €88/99)* is a stone's throw from the river; the entrance is around the corner.

**Albergo Ciopeta** *(☎ 045 800 68 43; e ciopeta@iol.it; Vicolo Teatro Filarmonico 2; singles/doubles without bath €44/73)*, just off Piazza Brà, has air-conditioned rooms.

Hidden in a side street near Piazza delle Erbe, **Hotel Mazzanti** *(☎ 045 800 68 13, fax 045 801 12 62; Via Mazzanti 6; singles/doubles €61/98 with bath)* provides simple rooms, although some are a little poky.

Hotel All'Antica Porta Leona (☎ 045 59 54 99, fax 045 59 52 14, ⓔ htlanticaportaleona@ tiscalinet.it; Corticella Leoni 3; singles/doubles about €91/129) smacks of faded elegance.

Boiled meats are a Veronese speciality, as is the crisp Soave white wine. The Castello, Ciopeta and Mazzanti hotels all have reasonable restaurants. At the Mazzanti save room for the tiramisu, as it's devilishly good. To get away from the crowds, cross the river and try the **Trattoria All'Isolo** (☎ 045 59 42 91; Piazza dell'Isolo 5a; set menu €12) where they have an interesting boiled meat dish. For pizza on the hoof you'll find no bigger or better slice than at **Pizza Doge** (Via Roma 21b; pizza slice about €3.50).

## Entertainment

Verona hosts musical and cultural events throughout the year, culminating in a season of opera and drama from July to September at the **Arena** (tickets from €21.50). There is a lyric-symphonic season in winter at the 18th-century **Teatro Filarmonico** (☎ 800 28 80; Via dei Mutilati 4). For more information go online at Ⓦ www.arena.it, or ask at the tourist office. Booking is through the **box office** (☎ 045 800 51 51; Via Dietro Anfiteatro 6b), or website.

## Getting There & Away

The **Verona-Villafranca airport** (☎ 045 809 56 66) is 16km outside town and accessible by bus and train.

The main bus station is in the piazza in front of the train station, known as Porta Nuova. Buses leave for surrounding areas, including Mantua, Ferrara and Brescia.

Verona is on the Brenner Pass railway line to Austria and Germany, and is directly linked by train to Milan, Venice, Florence and Rome.

The city sits at the intersection of the Serenissima A4 (Milan–Venice) and the Brennero A22 autostrade.

## Getting Around

The APT airport bus (€4.20) departs from outside the train station every 20 minutes. Bus Nos 11, 12, 13 and 14 (Nos 91, 92 and 98 on Sunday), connect the station (bus stop A) with Piazza Brà, and Nos 72 and 73 go to Piazza delle Erbe.

If you arrive by car, there's a free car park situated in Via Città di Nimes (near the train station) – a good bet, as parking in the centre is limited.

## PADUA
postcode 35100 • pop 211,500

There is one compelling reason to come to Padua and, although thousands of pilgrims would disagree, it is not to visit the tomb of St Anthony. Rather it's to marvel at Giotto's recently restored frescoes in the Cappella degli Scrovegni (Scrovegni Chapel), considered by many one of the world's greatest works of figurative art. Masterpieces apart, Padua is a lively city thanks to its university, one of the oldest in Europe, and, as is the norm in these parts, it is porticoed and pretty.

## Orientation & Information

It's a 15-minute walk from the train station to the centre of town, or you can take bus Nos 3 or 8 along Corso del Popolo (which becomes Corso Garibaldi).

There is an **IAT tourist office** (☎ 049 875 20 77, fax 049 875 50 08; open 9.15am-6.30pm Mon-Sat, 9am-12.30pm Sun) at the station; another in the centre (☎ 049 876 79 27, fax 049 836 33 16; Galleria Pedrocchi; 9am-12.30pm & 3pm-7pm Mon-Sat), and a third in Piazza Del Santo (☎ 049 875 30 87; opening hours variable, Apr-Oct).

The **post office** (Corso Garibaldi 33) is on the main road from the station to the centre.

## Things to See

If you're planning a couple of days in the city the padovacard is a good investment. Giving significant reductions on museum entry and free transport, it is valid for one adult and one child under 12, and costs €13.

The **Cappella degli Scrovegni** (☎ 049 201 00 20; Ⓦ www.cappelladegliscrovegni.it; Piazza Eremitani 8; admission €11; open 9am-6pm Mon-Fri, 9am-1pm Sat) houses Giotto's emotionally charged frescoes. Painted between 1303 and 1305, the transcendent 38 panels depict the life of Christ. Booking is now required, and it's advisable to reserve a few days in advance. The ticket also gives access to the **Musei Civici agli Eremitani** (open 9am-6pm Tues-Sun winter, to 7pm spring to autumn) next door to the chapel.

Thousands of pilgrims arrive in Padua every year to visit the **Basilica di Sant'Antonio** (St Anthony's Basilica) in the hope that St Anthony, patron saint of Padua and of lost things, will help them find whatever it is they are looking for. The saint's gaudy tomb is in the basilica, along with artworks including

ITALY

the 14th-century frescoes and bronze sculptures by Donatello which adorn the high altar. Donatello's bronze equestrian statue, known as the *Gattamelata* (Honeyed Cat), is outside the basilica.

Nature lovers shouldn't miss Padua's botanical gardens, **Orto Botanico** *(Via Orto Botanico 15; admission €2.58; open 9am-1pm & 3pm-6pm Mon-Sat Apr-Oct, 9am-1pm Nov-Mar)*, which date from 1545 and contain many rare plants.

### Places to Stay & Eat

Padua has no shortage of budget hotels, but they fill up quickly in summer. The non-HI **Ostello della Città di Padova** *(☎ 049 875 22 19, fax 049 65 42 10; Via A Aleardi 30; dorm B&B €15.50)* is a five-minute bus ride from the station. Take bus No 3, 8 or 12 to Prato della Valle and then ask.

The shockingly pink **Junior** *(☎ 049 61 17 56; Via Faggin 2; singles/doubles with bath €37/70)* is in a flowery residential street and has simple rooms. The two-star **Sant'Antonio** *(☎ 049 875 13 93, fax 875 25 08; Via Santo Fermo 118; singles/doubles with bath €57/74)*, near the river, provides comfortable rooms with TV and phone. Not a stone's throw from the basilica, **Al Fagiano** *(☎/fax 049 875 00 73; Via Locatelli 45; singles/doubles/triples with bath €52/73/83)* offers large and airy rooms.

Fight through the lunchtime frenzy at **Dalla Zita** *(Via Gorizia 16; panini from €2.30)*, off Piazza Pedrocchi, where the menu of more than 100 sandwich fillings completely covers the walls. **Birroteca da Mario** *(Via Breda 3; pizza from €3.40)*, off Piazza della Frutta, is a good choice for a pub-style snack. **Trattoria al Pero** *(☎ 049 875 87 94; Via Santa Lucia 72; meal about €16)*, attracts a mix of locals and tourists and serves the most enormous plate of fried fish. Daily **food markets** are held in Piazza delle Erbe and Piazza della Frutta.

### Getting There & Away

Padua is directly linked by train to Milan, Venice and Bologna, and is easily accessible from most other major cities. Regular buses serve Venice, Milan, Trieste and surrounding towns. The **bus terminal** *(Piazzale Boschetti)* is off Via Trieste, near the train station. There is a large public car park in Prato della Valle, a massive piazza near the Basilica del Santo.

## VENICE
postcode 30100 ● pop 272,100

Venice is extraordinary. In no other city is fantasy and reality so artfully combined – picture delivery boats vying for space with gondolas or a €20 bill for afternoon tea in Piazza San Marco (St Mark's Square). Ever since Casanova set the romance myth rolling, travellers, writers and even dictators have been beguiled by La Serenissima (the Most Serene Republic); Byron waxed lyrical, Henry James commented, and Napoleon described San Marco's as the finest drawing room in Europe.

The secret to discovering its beauty is to *walk*. Parts of Dorsoduro and Castello see few tourists even in the high season (July to September), and it's here that you'll appreciate just how seductive Venice can be. It's easy to happily lose yourself for hours in the narrow winding streets between the Accademia and the train station, where the signs pointing to San Marco and the Rialto never seem to make any sense – but who's complaining?

The islands of the lagoon were first settled during the barbarian invasions of the 5th and 6th centuries AD, when the people of the Veneto sought refuge in this marshy region, gradually building the city on a raft of wooden posts driven into the subsoil. Following centuries of Byzantine rule, Venice evolved into a republic ruled by a succession of doges (chief magistrates) and enjoyed a period of independence that lasted 1000 years. It was the point where east met west, and the city grew in power to dominate half the Mediterranean, the Adriatic and the trade routes to the Levant. It was from Venice that Marco Polo set out on his voyage to China in 1271.

Today, Venice is increasingly being left to the tourists – the regular floods (caused by high tides) and sky-high property prices make it a difficult place to live. Most of the 'locals' live in industrial Mestre, which is linked to the city by the 4km-long bridge across the lagoon.

### Orientation

Venice is built on 117 small islands and has some 150 canals and 400 bridges. Only three bridges cross the Canal Grande (Grand Canal): the Rialto, the Accademia and, at the train station, the Scalzi. The city is divided into six *sestieri* (quarters): Cannaregio, Castello, San Marco, Dorsoduro, San Polo and Santa Croce. A street can be called a

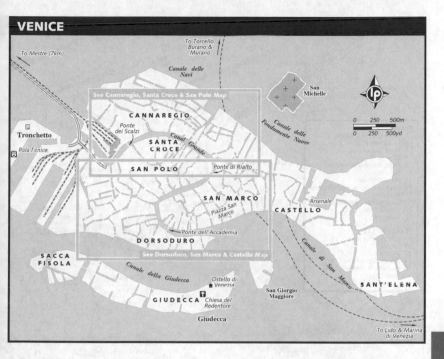

**VENICE**

calle, ruga or salizzada; a street beside a canal is a fondamenta; a canal is a rio; and a quay is a riva. The only square in Venice called a piazza is San Marco – all the others are called campo.

If all that isn't confusing enough, Venice also has its own style of street numbering. Instead of a system based on individual streets, each sestiere has a long series of numbers, so addresses become virtually meaningless to anyone who's not a Venetian postie. There are no cars in the city and all public transport is via the canals, on vaporetti (water buses). To cross the Grand Canal between the bridges, use a traghetto (basically a public gondola, but much cheaper). Signs will direct you to the various traghetto points. Of course, the other mode of transportation is a piedi (on foot).

To walk from the ferrovia (train station) to San Marco along the main thoroughfare, Lista di Spagna (whose name changes several times), will take a good half-hour – follow the signs to San Marco. From San Marco the routes to other main areas, such as the Rialto, the Accademia and the ferrovia, are well signposted but can be confusing, particularly in the Dorsoduro and San Polo areas.

The free tourist office map is not great so it's worth buying the yellow street-referenced Venezia map published by FMB.

## Information
**Tourist Offices** Central Venice has three **APT tourist office branches**: at the train station (open 8am-8pm daily); at Piazza San Marco 71f (open 9.45am-3.15pm Mon-Sat) and the Venice Pavilion (open 10am-6pm daily) on the waterfront next to the Giardini Ex Reali (turn right from San Marco). There are also offices at **Piazzale Roma** (open 8am-8pm daily), the Lido and airport. Pick up the useful guide Un Ospite di Venezia. For telephone information there is a central number, ☎ 041 529 87 11.

Visitors aged between 14 and 29 can buy a **Rolling Venice card** (☎ 899 90 90 90) for €2.58, which offers significant discounts on food, accommodation, shopping, transport and entry to museums. It is available from various outlets; check at the tourist offices for details. City planners have also introduced the Venice Card, a multipurpose pass for museums, public transport, car parks and restrooms. It comes in two forms, one costing €7

ITALY

## CANNAREGIO, SANTA CROCE & SAN POLO

**PLACES TO STAY**
5 Edelweiss Stella Alpina
6 Hotel Villa Rosa
7 Hotel Santa Lucia
8 Albergo Adua
9 Hotel Minerva & Nettuno
10 Hotel Rossi
13 Hotel Guerrini
14 Casa Gerotto; Alloggi Calderan
15 Al Gobbo
19 Locanda San Marcuola
20 Ostello Santa Fosca
27 Giorgione

**PLACES TO EAT**
17 Pizzeria all'Anfora
22 Sahara
23 Iguana
24 Standa Supermarket
26 Hosteria Ai Promessi Sposi
30 Rosa Salva
31 Cantina do Mori

and the other €16. For more information go online at W www.venicecard.it.

**Foreign Consulates** The **British consulate** (☎ 041 522 72 07) is in the Palazzo Querini near the Accademia, Dorsoduro 1051.

**Money** Most of the main banks have branches in the area around the Rialto and San Marco. The **American Express office** (☎ 041 520 08 44; Salizzada San Moisè 1471; open 9am-5.30pm Mon-Fri, 9.30am-12.30pm Sat & Sun) will exchange money without charging commission (exit from the western end of Piazza San Marco onto Calle Seconda dell'Ascensione). There's an ATM for card-holders. Additionally, there's a **Thomas Cook** (☎ 041 522 47 51; Piazza San Marco 141; open 9am-

7pm Mon-Sat, 9.30am-5pm Sun) and, at the train station, a **change office** (open 7am-9pm daily) on the main concourse opposite platform four.

**Post & Communications** The main **post office** (Salizzada del Fontego dei Tedeschi), near the Ponte di Rialto (Rialto Bridge) is on the main thoroughfare to the train station. Stamps are sold at windows No 1 to No 4 in the central courtyard.

There are several Telecom offices in the city, including those at the post office, near the Rialto and on Strada Nova.

Log on at **Nethouse** (☎ 041 277 11 90; Campo Santo Stefano 2967; open 24hr), which has 60 screens, printing and fax. Rates are €3 for 20 minutes or €9 per hour. **Netgate**

## CANNAREGIO, SANTA CROCE & SAN POLO

**OTHER**
1  Intercity Bus Station
2  Tourist Office
3  Tourist Office
4  Ponte dei Scalzi (Scalzi Bridge)
11 Park & Playground
12 Libreria Demetra
16 Speedy Wash
18 Museo Mocenigo
21 Paradiso Perduto
25 The Fiddler's Elbow
28 Ospedale Civile
29 SS Giovanni e Paolo

(☎ 041 244 02 13; *Calle dei Preti Crosera 3812, Dorsoduro; open 10.15am-8pm Mon-Fri, 10.15am-10pm Sat & 2.15pm-10pm Sun)* offers 11 minutes for €1.29 and one hour for €3.99.

**Bookshops** English-language guidebooks and general books on Venice are available at **Studium** *(cnr Calle de la Canonica)* behind the Basilica di San Marco, on the way from San Marco to Castello. **Libreria Demetra** *(Campo San Geremia 282, Cannaregio)* is open until midnight Monday to Friday.

**Laundry** At the self-service **Speedy Wash** *(Via Cannaregio 1520; open 9am-10pm daily)* you can wash 8kg for €4.50. Drying is a further €3.

**Medical & Emergency Services** If you need a hospital, there is the **Ospedale Civile** *(☎ 041 529 41 11; Campo SS Giovanni e Paolo).* The **questura** *(police headquarters; ☎ 041 271 55 11; Fondamenta di San Lorenzo 5056)* is in Castello. An emergency service in foreign languages is run by the carabinieri; call ☎ 112.

## Things to See & Do

Before you visit Venice's principal monuments, churches and museums, you should catch the No 1 vaporetto along the Grand Canal, lined with Gothic, Moorish, Renaissance and rococo palaces. Then you can stretch your legs by taking a long walk: start at **San Marco** and either delve into the tiny lanes of tranquil **Castello** or head for the

## DORSODURO, SAN MARCO & CASTELLO

PLACES TO STAY
2 Hotel Ai Tolentini
9 Foresteria Valdese
12 Locanda Silva; Locanda Canal
13 Hotel Noemi
14 Locanda Casa Petrarca
23 Casa Peron
24 Hotel Dalla Mora
26 Albergo Antico Capon
36 Hotel Galleria
55 Hotel ai Do Mori
61 Hotel Doni
62 Londra Palace

PLACES TO EAT
4 Bar ai Nomboli
5 Trattoria alla Madonna
6 Antica Carbonera
11 Cip Ciap
15 Pasticceria Marchini
19 Da Silvio
21 Arca
27 Mega 1 Supermarket
28 Bar DuChamp
29 Il Doge
30 L'Incontro
32 Osteria ai 4 Ferri
33 Gelati Nico
41 Vino Vino
47 Caffè Florian
52 Caffè Quadri
60 Al Vecio Penasa

**Ponte dell'Accademia** (Accademia Bridge) to reach the narrow streets and squares of **Dorsoduro** and **San Polo**.

Remember that most, but not all, museums are closed on Monday.

**Piazza & Basilica di San Marco** San Marco's dreamlike, 'can this be real' quality has you pinching yourself no matter how many times you visit. The piazza is enclosed by the basilica and the elegant arcades of the **Procuratie Vecchie** and **Procuratie Nuove**. While you're standing gob-smacked you might be lucky enough to see the bronze *mori* (Moors) strike the bell of the 15th-century **Torre dell'Orologio** (clock tower).

With its spangled spires, Byzantine domes and facade of mosaics and marble, the **Basilica**

**di San Marco** (St Mark's Basilica) is the Western counterpart of Constantinople's Santa Sophia. The elaborately decorated basilica was built to house the body of St Mark, stolen from its burial place in Egypt by two Venetian merchants and carried to Venice in a barrel of pork. The saint has been reburied several times in the basilica (at least twice the burial place was forgotten) and his body now lies under the high altar. The present basilica was built in the 11th century and is richly decorated with mosaics, marbles and sculpture, as well as a jumble of looted embellishments over the ensuing five centuries. The bronze horses prancing above the entrance are replicas of the famous statues liberated in the Sack of Constantinople in 1204. The originals can be seen in the basilica's **Galleria** (admission €1.55).

## DORSODURO, SAN MARCO & CASTELLO

| OTHER | | |
| --- | --- | --- |
| 1 Intercity Bus Station | | 39 Chiesa di Santa Maria della Salute |
| 3 Frari | | 40 Legatoria Piazzesi |
| 7 Ponte di Rialto (Rialto Bridge) | | 42 American Express |
| 8 Main Post Office; | | 43 Tourist Office; Venice Pavilion |
| Telecom Office | | 44 Libreria Nazionale Marciana |
| 10 Questura (Police Station) | | 45 Museo Archeologico |
| 16 Nethouse | | 46 Campanile (Bell Tower) |
| 17 Palazzo Grassi | | 48 Procuratie Nuove |
| 18 Netgate | | 49 Tourist Office |
| 20 Cafe Noir | | 50 Museo Correr |
| 22 Cafe Blue | | 51 Procuratie Vecchie |
| 25 Il Caffe | | 53 Thomas Cook |
| 31 Annelie Pizzi e Ricami | | 54 Torre dell'Orologio |
| 34 Galleria dell'Accademia | | (Clock Tower) |
| 35 British Consulate | | 56 Studium Bookshop |
| 37 Ponte dell'Accademia | | 57 Basilica di San Marco |
| (Accademia Bridge) | | 58 Palazzo Ducale |
| 38 Collezione Peggy Guggenheim | | 59 Ponte dei Sospiri |
| | | (Bridge of Sighs) |

Don't miss the **Pala d'Oro** *(admission €1.55)*, a stunning gold altarpiece decorated with silver, enamels and precious jewels. It is behind the basilica's altar.

The 99m freestanding **campanile** *(bell tower; admission to top €6)* dates from the 10th century, although it suddenly collapsed on 14 July 1902 and had to be rebuilt.

**Palazzo Ducale** The official residence of the doges and the seat of the republic's government, this palace *(admission €9.50; open 9am-7pm daily Apr-Oct, 9am-5pm daily Nov-Mar)*, also housed many government officials and the prisons. The original palace was built in the 9th century and later expanded, remodelled and given a Gothic tracery facade. Visit the **Sala del Maggior Consiglio** to see

the paintings by Tintoretto and Veronese. The ticket office closes 1½ hours before palace closing time and the admission ticket also covers entry to the nearby Museo Correr, Biblioteca Marciana and Museo Archeologico. For an additional €6 you can extend the ticket to cover the Palazzo Mocenigo (San Stae area), and Burano and Murano museums.

The **Ponte dei Sospiri** (Bridge of Sighs) connects the palace to the old dungeons. The bridge evokes romantic images, possibly because of its association with Casanova, a native of Venice who spent time in the cells.

**Galleria dell'Accademia** The Academy of Fine Arts *(admission €6.50; open 8.15am-7.15pm Tues-Sun, 8.15am-2pm Mon)* traces the development of Venetian art, and includes masterpieces by Bellini, Titian, Carpaccio, Tintoretto, Giorgione and Veronese.

For a change of pace, and style, visit the nearby **Collezione Peggy Guggenheim** *(admission €8; open 10am-6pm Wed-Fri, Sun & Mon, 10am-10pm Sat, early Apr–end Oct)* displayed in the former home of the American heiress. The collection runs the gamut of modern art from Bacon to Pollock, and the palazzo is set in a sculpture garden where Miss Guggenheim and her many pet dogs are buried.

**Churches**  Venice has many gorgeous churches, and most of them boast an art treasure or two. The **Chiesa del Redentore** (Church of the Redeemer) on Giudecca Island was built by Palladio to commemorate the end of the great plague of 1576, and is the scene of the annual Festa del Redentore (see Special Events, later). Longhena's **Chiesa di Santa Maria della Salute** guards the entrance to the Grand Canal and contains works by Tintoretto and Titian. Be sure to visit the great Gothic churches **SS Giovanni e Paolo**, with its glorious stained-glass windows, and the **Frari**, home to Titian's tomb and his uplifting *Assumption*. Entry to the latter is €2, or you can buy the Chorus Pass (€8), which gets you into 15 of the city's most famous churches.

**The Lido**  This thin strip of land, east of the centre, separates Venice from the Adriatic and is easily accessible by vaporetto Nos 1, 6, 14, 61 and 82. Once *the* most fashionable beach resort – and still very popular – it's almost impossible to find a space on its long beach in summer.

**Islands**  The island of **Murano** is the home of Venetian glass. Tour a factory for a behind-the-scenes look at its production, or visit the Glassworks Museum to see some exquisite historical pieces. **Burano**, still today a relatively sleepy fishing village, is renowned for its lace and pastel-coloured houses. **Torcello**, the republic's original island settlement, was abandoned due to malaria. Just about all that remains on the hauntingly deserted island is the Byzantine cathedral, its exquisite mosaics intact. Excursion boats travel to the three islands from San Marco (€15 return). Vaporetto No 12 goes to all three from Fondamenta Nuove.

**Gondolas**  Ask yourself what price for romance, and the rather alarming answer is €62

(€77.45 after 8pm) for a 50-minute ride. These are the official rates and are valid for the gondola (which can carry six people), not per person.

### Organised Tours

A popular new choice is to pick up an individual handheld audio-guide, which has commentaries on the city's major sights. They are available from the Pavilion tourist office (see Tourist Offices under Information earlier) and cost from €3.60 for an hour to €15.50 for two days. You'll have to leave your passport as a deposit until you return the guide. The **Associazione Guide Turistiche** *(☎ 041 520 90 38; Castello 5327)*, arranges group tours in various languages.

### Special Events

The major event of the year is Venice's famed Carnevale, held during the 10 days before Ash Wednesday, when Venetians don spectacular masks and costumes for what is literally a 10-day street party. At its decadent height in the 18th century, the Carnevale lasted for six months!

The Venice Biennale, a major exhibition of international visual arts, is held every odd-numbered year, and the Venice International Film Festival is held every September at the Palazzo del Cinema, on the Lido.

The Festa del Redentore (Festival of the Redeemer), held on the third weekend in July, features a spectacular fireworks display. The Regata Storica, a gondola race on the Grand Canal, is held on the first Sunday in September.

### Places to Stay

Venice is the most expensive city in Italy, so be prepared. The average cost of a basic single/double room without bath in a one-star hotel is around €45/70. Prices skyrocket in peak periods (Christmas, Carnevale, Easter etc), but do drop at other times of the year. It is always advisable to book in advance, but if you arrive with nothing lined up, try the **Associazione Veneziana Albergatori** *(☎ 800 84 30 06)* which runs a hotel-reservation office at the train station.

**Camping**  Litorale del Cavallino, northeast of the city on the Adriatic coast, has numerous camping grounds, many with bungalows. The tourist office has a full list. Try **Marina di Venezia** *(☎ 041 530 09 55, fax 041 96 60*

36; e camping@marinadivenezia.it; Via Montello 6, Punta Sabbioni; per person/tent €7.50/19; open mid-Apr–end Aug).

**Hostels** The HI **Ostello di Venezia** (☎ 041 523 82 11, fax 041 523 56 89; Fondamenta delle Zitelle 86; dorm bed €16) is on the island of Giudecca. It is open to members only, although you can buy a card there. Evening meals are available for €7.75 and curfew is 11.30pm. Take vaporetto No 41, 42 or 82 from the station and get off at Zitelle.

**Foresteria Valdese** (☎/fax 041 528 67 97; Castello 5170; dorm bed €20, doubles without bath €54, with bath €70) has a number of dormitory and double-room options. Follow Calle Lunga from Campo Santa Maria Formosa.

Students will feel at home at **Ostello Santa Fosca** (☎ 041 71 57 75; e cpu@iuav.unive.it; Cannaregio 2372; dorm bed €18, singles/doubles without bath €21), which is less than 15 minutes from the station through Campo Santa Fosca; check-in is between 5pm and 8pm daily.

**Hotels** Not surprisingly, bargain hotels are few and far between in Venice.

*Cannaregio* The two-star **Edelweiss Stella Alpina** (☎ 041 71 51 79, fax 041 72 09 16; e stelalpina@tin.it; Calle Priuli detta dei Cavalletti 99d; singles/doubles without bath €62/104, with bath €130/171), down the first street on the left after the Scalzi church, has decent rooms. The next street on the left is Calle della Misericordia, with two recommended hotels. **Hotel Santa Lucia** (☎ 041 71 51 80, fax 041 71 06 10; e hotelstlucia@libero.it; singles/doubles without bath €60/70, doubles/triples/quads with bath €110/140/170) at No 358 has a friendly owner and all rates include breakfast. At No 389, **Hotel Villa Rosa** (☎/fax 041 71 65 69; e villarosa@ve.nettuno.it; singles/doubles/triples/quads with bath €82/113/142/165) is pretty and pink with pleasant, well-furnished rooms.

On Lista di Spagna, the main drag, **Albergo Adua** (☎ 041 71 61 84, fax 041 244 01 62; singles/doubles without bath €70/75, with bath €100/114) at No 233a has simple rooms. Across the road at No 230, **Hotel Minerva & Nettuno** (☎ 041 71 59 68; e lchecchi@tin.it; singles/doubles without bath €50/61, with bath €58/92) has modest

rooms. **Hotel Rossi** (☎ 041 71 51 64, fax 041 71 77 84; e rossihotel@inter free.it; Calle de la Procuratie singles/doubles/ triples/quads with bath €65/89/ 108/126) is just off Lista di Spagna (via a Gothic archway) down a tiny side street. Rooms are clean and straightforward. On the same street, the two-star **Hotel Guerrini** (☎ 041 71 53 33, fax 041 71 51 14; singles/doubles with bath €140/150) has well-appointed rooms.

Around the corner, **Casa Gerotto and Alloggi Calderan** (☎/fax 041 71 53 61; Campo San Geremia 283; dorm bed €20, singles/doubles/triples without bath €36/62/83, with bath €46/88/108) has something for everyone in a pleasantly ramshackle atmosphere. **Al Gobbo** (☎ 041 71 50 01, fax 041 71 47 65; singles/doubles without bath €52/75, with bath €78/93), at No 312 in the same campo, is somewhat gloomy inside but has an enthusiastic owner. Recently opened and situated not two yards from the Grand Canal, **Locanda San Marcuola** (☎ 041 71 60 48, fax 041 275 92 17; e info@casanmarcuola.com; singles/doubles with bath €120/130) has classy rooms with Venetian decor.

For a multistar splurge the 15th-century **Giorgione** (☎ 041 522 58 10, fax 041 523 90 92; Calle Larga dei Proverbi 4587; doubles from €230), just off Campo dei SS Apostoli, has the lot.

*San Marco* Although this is the most touristy area of Venice, it has some surprisingly good-quality pensioni. **Hotel Noemi** (☎ 041 523 81 44; e info@hotelnoemi.com; Calle dei Fabbri 909; doubles with/without bath €139/ 87) is somewhat characterless but only a few steps from Piazza San Marco.

**Locanda Casa Petrarca** (☎ 041 520 04 30; Calle delle Schiavine 4386; singles without bath €44, doubles with/without bath €110/88) is run by a chatty English-speaking lady full of useful tips.

Just off Piazza San Marco and up some alarmingly steep stairs, **Hotel ai Do Mori** (☎ 041 520 48 17, fax 041 520 53 28; Calle Larga San Marco 658; doubles with/without bath €129/87) has some rooms with views of St Mark's Basilica.

*Castello* This atmospheric area is to the east of Piazza San Marco and is far less touristy. **Locanda Silva** (☎ 041 522 76 43, fax 041 528 68 17; Fondamenta del Rimedio 4423;

ITALY

*singles/doubles without bath €47/78, with bath €67/104)* has rather basic rooms and **Locanda Canal** (☎ 041 523 45 38, fax 041 241 91 38; *doubles with/without bath €110/83)*, next door at No 4422c, is much the same. To get there, head off from Campo Santa Maria Formosa towards San Marco.

**Hotel Doni** *(☎/fax 041 522 42 67; Calle del Vin 4656; singles/doubles without bath €50/80, doubles with bath €105)* gives pride of place to a room with an original fresco.

Live like a doge at the **Londra Palace** *(☎ 041 520 05 33, fax 041 522 50 32; Riva degli Schiavoni 4171; doubles from €370)* right on the waterfront.

***Dorsoduro, San Polo & Santa Croce*** Off Fondamenta Tolentini heading down from the station, **Hotel Ai Tolentini** *(☎ 041 275 91 40, fax 041 275 32 66; Corte dei Amai 197g; singles/doubles with bath €70/120)* has reasonable rooms and a helpful owner. At the characterful **Casa Peron** *(☎/fax 041 71 10 38; Salizzada San Pantalon 84; singles/ doubles without bath €45/70, with bath €85)* you may well be met by a huge green parrot. To get here from the station, cross Ponte dei Scalzi and follow the signs to San Marco and Rialto till you reach Rio delle Muneghette, then cross the wooden bridge. Nearby, **Hotel Dalla Mora** *(☎ 041 71 07 03, fax 041 72 30 06;* e *hoteldallamora@ libero.it; Santa Croce 42a; singles/doubles/ triples/quads with bath €57/88/108/129)* is on a small canal just off Salizzada San Pantalon and is justifiably popular.

In one of the liveliest squares in Venice, **Albergo Antico Capon** *(☎/fax 041 528 52 92; Campo Santa Margherita 3004b; singles/ doubles with bath €88)* provides airy rooms.

The pick of the one-stars **Hotel Galleria** *(☎ 041 523 24 89, fax 041 520 41 72;* e *galleria@tin.it; Dorsoduro 878a; singles/ doubles without bath €62/93, doubles with bath €104)* has elegant rooms in a 17th-century palace facing the Grand Canal at Ponte dell'Accademia.

***Mestre*** An economical but drab alternative to staying in Venice is to stay in Mestre. There are a number of good hotels as well as plenty of cafés and places to eat around the main square. If you're travelling by car, the savings on car-parking charges are considerable. The two-star **Albergo Roberta** *(☎ 041 92 93 55,*

*fax 041 93 09 83; Via Sernaglia 21; singles/ doubles with bath €68/104)* includes breakfast in the rates and the one-star **Albergo Giovannina** *(☎ 041 92 63 96, fax 041 538 84 42; Via Dante 113; singles without bath €36, doubles with bath €72)* is decent enough.

## Places to Eat

Wherever you choose to eat in Venice it will be expensive, but quality can vary greatly, so sniff around and be selective.

Bars serve a wide range of panini, *tramezzini* (sandwiches) and rolls with every imaginable filling. They cost from €2 if you eat them standing at the bar. Head for one of the many *bacari* (traditional wine bars), for wine by the glass *(ombra)* and interesting bite-sized snacks *(cicheti)*. The staples of the Veneto region's *cucina* are rice and beans. Try the *risi e bisi* (risotto with peas), followed by a glass of *fragolino*, the Veneto's fragrant strawberry wine.

**Restaurants** Avoid the tourist traps around San Marco and near the train station, where prices are high and the quality is poor.

***Cannaregio*** Tucked away down a tiny alleyway is **Hosteria Ai Promessi Sposi** *(☎ 041 522 86 09; Calle De L'Oca 4367; meal about €20)* where the mixed fish antipasti is a thing of wonder. It's all shuffling efficiency here as the old boys bring your food between sips. Winning a growing reputation is **Sahara** *(☎ 041 72 10 77; Fondamenta della Misericordia; meal about €19)* where you can feast on genuine Syrian grub. A few doors down, **Iguana** *(☎ 041 71 35 61; meal about €11)* represents Venice's Tex-Mex scene.

***Around San Marco & Castello*** The popular bar/osteria **Vino Vino** *(☎ 041 523 70 27; San Marco 2007; meal about €17)* is at Ponte Veste near Teatro La Fenice. Wine is sold by the glass. **Antica Carbonera** *(☎ 041 22 54 79; Calle Bembo; meal about €30)*, on the continuation of Calle dei Fabbri, is an old trattoria which offers atmosphere in return for euros. It isn't cheap. Just off Campo Santa Maria Formosa and over Ponte del Mondo Novo, **Cip Ciap** *(pizza slice €2.30)* provides welcome sustenance.

***Dorsoduro, San Polo & Santa Croce*** This is the best area for small, authentic trattorias and pizzerias. The pizzas are usually good at **Pizzeria all'Anfora** (☎ *041 524 03 25; pizza from €4.80*), across the Ponte dei Scalzi from the station at Lista dei Bari 1223.

**L'Incontro** (☎ *041 522 24 04; Rio Terrà Canal 3062a; meal about €26*), between Campo San Barnaba and Campo Santa Margherita, serves regional fare.

**Cantina do Mori** (*Sottoportego dei do Mori*), off Ruga Rialto, is a small, very popular wine bar that also serves sandwiches. The pricey **Trattoria alla Madonna** (☎ *041 21 01 67; Calle della Madonna 594; meal about €31*), two streets west of the Rialto, specialises in seafood.

The bustling **Arca** (☎ *041 524 22 36; Calle San Pantalon 3757; set menu €13, pizza from €5*), past Campo San Pantalon, has a warm and lively feel and opposite is **Da Silvio** (☎ *041 20 58 33; Calle San Pantalon 3748*), which offers more or less the same dishes at the same prices.

If you're looking for a typical osteria try **Osteria ai 4 Ferri** (☎ *041 520 69 78; Calle Lunga San Barnaba; meal about €17*), off Campo San Barnaba. You'll need to book.

**Cafés & Bars** If you can cope with paying at least €7 for a cappuccino, spend an hour or so sitting at an outdoor table in Piazza San Marco, listening to the orchestra at either **Caffè Florian** or **Caffè Quadri**. For a cheaper alternative, try Campo Santa Margherita's **Bar DuChamp**, a student favourite whose panini cost about €1.30 and there's Tetley on tap.

**Bar ai Nomboli** (*cnr Calle dei Nomboli & Rio Terrà dei Nomboli*), between Campo San Polo and the Frari, has a huge selection of sandwiches, while in the Castello area you can choose from an extensive range of cheap panini at the bar **Al Vecio Penasa** (*Calle delle Rasse 4585*).

**Gelati & Pastries** Some of the best gelati in Venice continue to be served at **Gelati Nico** (*Fondamenta Zattere ai Gesuati 922*). Join the locals along the fondamenta or take a seat at an outside table. **Il Doge** (*Campo Santa Margherita*) also has excellent ice cream. A popular place for cakes and pastries is **Pasticceria Marchini** (*Calle del Spezier 2769*), just off Campo Santo Stefano, where the display of goodies is, to put it mildly, tempting. **Rosa Salva** (*Campo SS Giovanni e Paolo*) is frequented by locals for its gelati and pastries.

**Self-Catering** For fruit and vegetables, as well as delicatessens, head for the **market** in the streets on the San Polo side of the Rialto Bridge, or on the Rio Terrà San Leonardo in Cannaregio. There's a **Mega 1** supermarket just off Campo Santa Margherita and a **Standa** supermarket on Strada Nova.

## Entertainment

The free weekly booklet *Un Ospite di Venezia* has entertainment listings, or you can buy a copy of the monthly *Venezia News* from newsagents for €2.07. The tourist office also has brochures listing events for the entire year.

Venice lost its opera house, the magnificent Teatro La Fenice, to a fire in January 1996. Reconstruction continues, and in the interim performances are held at **PalaFenice** (☎ *041 78 65 11*), a tentlike structure on the car-park island of Tronchetto.

Major art exhibitions are held at **Palazzo Grassi** (San Samuele vaporetto stop), and smaller exhibitions at various venues in the city throughout the year.

For less highbrow pursuits, in Cannaregio, **Paradiso Perduto** (*Fondamenta della Misericordia 2539; happy hour 6.30pm-7.30pm*) has live music and sangria. And where would Venice be without the Irish pub? We'll never know because **The Fiddler's Elbow** (*Corte dei Pali 3817*) does the job. In Dorsoduro, there's **Café Blue** (*Salizzada San Pantalon 3778*), a pub-like drinking den near trendy Campo Santa Margherita, or **Café Noir** (*Calle San Pantalon 3805*), a laid-back, student hang-out. On Campo Santa Margherita, **Il Caffè** is perennially popular.

## Shopping

For many visitors, Venice is synonymous with elaborate glassware. There are several workshops and showrooms in Venice, particularly in the area between San Marco and Castello and on the island of Murano. If you're interested in buying, shop around because quality and prices can vary dramatically.

Venice is a trinket box of jewellery, crystals, grotesque Carnevale masks and bronze lions. You'll find them in shops throughout the city. Lace is another characteristic product of the Venetian lagoon, produced mainly on the island of Burano and available in Venice at **Annelie Pizzi e Ricami** (*Calle Lunga San Barnaba 2748*). Marbled paper and luscious velvet fabrics are other Venetian specialities. Window-shop at Venice's oldest traditional papermaking establishment, **Legatoria Piazzesi** *(Campiello della Feltrina 2551c, San Marco)*, where the high quality is matched by the high prices.

For designer-label clothing, shoes, accessories and jewellery, head for the narrow streets between San Marco and the Rialto, particularly the Merceria and the area around Campo San Luca. Luxury items can be found in the area near La Fenice.

## Getting There & Away

**Air** Some 12km from Venice is **Marco Polo airport** *(☎ 041 260 61 11, flight info ☎ 041 260 92 60)* which services domestic and European flights. The Alilaguna service from St Mark's costs €9.81. From Piazzale Roma there are also **ATVO buses** *(☎ 041 520 55 30)* for €2.70 or the ACTV city bus No 5 for €0.77. The official rate for a water taxi from St Marks is €44.95.

**Bus** The ACTV buses *(☎ 899 90 90 90)* leave from Piazzale Roma for surrounding areas including Mestre and Chioggia, a fishing port at the southernmost point of the lagoon. Buses also go to Padua and Treviso. Tickets and information are available at the office in Piazzale Roma.

**Train** The train station, **Stazione Santa Lucia** *(☎ 848 88 80 88)*, is directly linked to Padua, Verona, Trieste, Milan and Bologna, and so is easily accessible for Florence and Rome. You can also head to major points in France, Germany, Austria, Switzerland, Slovenia and Croatia. The Venice Simplon *Orient Express* runs between Venice and London, via Innsbruck, Zurich and Paris, twice weekly. Ask at any travel agent or phone the headquarters in London *(☎ 020 7805 5100)*.

**Boat** You can catch ferries to Greece four times a week in winter and daily in summer from **Minoan Lines** *(☎ 041 240 71 01; Porto Venezia, Zona Santa Marta)*. High-season tickets cost from €72 one way.

## Getting Around

Once you cross the bridge from Mestre, cars must be left at the car park on the island of Tronchetto or at Piazzale Roma (cars are allowed on the Lido – take car ferry No 17 from Tronchetto). The car parks are not cheap at around €18 a day. A cheaper alternative is to leave the car at Fusina, near Mestre, and catch the vaporetto No 16 to Zattere and then the No 82 either to Piazza San Marco or the train station. Ask for information at the tourist office just before the bridge to Venice.

As there are no cars in Venice, vaporetti are the city's mode of public transport. From Piazzale Roma, vaporetto No 1 zigzags its way along the Grand Canal to San Marco and then to the Lido. There is the faster No 82 if you are in a hurry to get to St Mark's. The No 12 vaporetto leaves from Fondamenta Nuove for the islands of Murano, Burano and Torcello. A full timetable is available at vaporetto ticket offices (€0.50). A single ticket costs €3.10 (plus €3.10 for luggage), even if you only ride to the next station; a return is €5.16. A 24-hour ticket is €9.30 for unlimited travel, a 72-hour ticket is €18.08 (worthwhile) and a one-week ticket costs €30.99.

Water taxis are exorbitant, with a set charge of €13.94 for a maximum of seven minutes, then €0.25 every 15 seconds. It's an extra €4.13 if you phone for a taxi, and various other surcharges add up to make taking a gondola ride seem cheap.

## FERRARA

**postcode 44100 • pop 131,600**

Ferrara's wonderfully evocative medieval centre retains much of the character of its heyday when, as seat of the Este family (1260–1598), the town was a force to be reckoned with. The imposing **Castello Estense** attests to this and remains the dominant landmark in this charming town.

## Information

The **tourist information office** *(☎ 0532 20 93 70; @ infotur.comfe@fe.nettuno.it; open 9am-1pm & 2pm-6pm Mon-Sat, 9.30am-1pm & 2pm-5.30pm Sun)* is inside the **Castello Estense**.

## Things to See

The small historical centre encompasses medieval Ferrara, to the south of the **Castello Estense**. The castle – complete with moat and drawbridges – was begun by Nicolò II d'Este in 1385. It is partly open to the public and has a suitably chilling atmosphere.

The pink-and-white striped cathedral, the **Duomo**, dates from the 12th century, with

Gothic and Renaissance additions and an unusual triple facade. Its museum has a superb collection of Renaissance art. The Renaissance Palazzo dei Diamanti, along Corso Ercole I d'Este, contains the **Pinacoteca Nazionale** (☎ 0532 20 58 44; admission €4; open 9am-2pm Tues, Wed, Fri & Sat, 9am-7pm Thur, 9am-1pm Sun) and exhibitions of modern art.

The **Palazzo Schifanoia** (☎ 0532 20 99 88; Via Scandiana 23; admission €4.20; open 9am-6pm Tues-Sun) is one of the city's earliest major Renaissance buildings and another of the Este palaces. It features the 'Room of the Months', decorated with Ferrara's finest Renaissance frescoes.

### Special Events

Every May since 1289, Ferrara has celebrated the Palio, considered the oldest in Italy, which culminates in a horse race between the eight town districts. Less dramatic is the Buskers Festival held in August, which attracts street performers from all over the world.

### Places to Stay & Eat

Ferrara is a cheap alternative to Bologna, and can be used as a base for visiting Venice. Hidden in the cobbled streets, **Albergo Centro Storico** (☎ 0532 20 33 74; Via Vegri 15; singles/doubles without bath €26/36) has basic rooms. South of the cathedral is the modest **Pensione Artisti** (☎ 0532 76 10 38; Via Vittoria 66; singles without bath €21, doubles with/without bath €52/37). Better rooms are available at the two-star **Albergo Nazionale** (☎ 0532 20 96 04; Corso Porta Reno 32; singles/doubles with bath €42/63). Nearby **Hotel Corte Estense** (☎ 0532 24 21 68, fax 0532 24 21 76; e info@corteest ense.it; Via Correggiari 4/a; singles/doubles/triples with bath €73/124/166) has a beautiful internal courtyard and free parking for its guests.

**Pizzeria il Ciclone** (☎ 0532 21 02 62; Via Vignatagliata 11; pizza from €5.15, meal about €17) serves local specialities. Closer to the cathedral, **Il Brindisi** (☎ 0532 20 91 42; Via Adelardi 11; set menu from €10.30) claims to be the oldest **hosteria** in the world, dating back to the 15th century. Next door at **Pappagallo** (☎ 0532 20 47 96; meal about €8) meals are self-service. In the medieval quarter, **Locanda degli Eventi** (☎ 0532 76 13 47; Via Mayr Carlo 21; meal about €20) is a quaint local trattoria.

### Getting There & Away

Ferrara is on the Bologna–Venice train line, with regular trains to both cities. It is 40 minutes from Bologna and 1½ hours from Venice. Regular trains also run directly to Ravenna. Buses run from the train station to Modena (also in the Emilia-Romagna region).

## BOLOGNA
### postcode 40100 • pop 380,300

Bologna is vibrant, beautiful and red. And there can't be many cities where the predominant colour of the architecture so accurately reflects the traditional politics of its citizens. The regional capital of Emilia-Romagna, Bologna is home to the oldest university in Europe and its large student population gives the city much of its dynamism.

But it is food for which Bologna is most famous. Other than the eponymous spaghetti bolognese, known as *spaghetti al ragù*, the Bolognese have gifted the world with tortellini, lasagne and mortadella.

### Information

The main **IAT tourist office** (fax 051 23 14 54; Piazza Maggiore 1; open 9am-8pm daily) is complemented by branch offices at the train station (open 8.30am-7.30pm Mon-Sat) and airport (open 8am-8pm Mon-Sat, 9am-3pm Sun). All telephone queries are now dealt with by a centralised **Call Center** (☎ 051 24 65 41, lines open 9am-7pm Mon-Sat).

The **main post office** is in Piazza Minghetti.

Log on at the Internet café **Net Arena** (☎/fax 051 22 08 50; Via de' Giudei 3b) for €3.10 per hour.

### Medical & Emergency Services

In a medical emergency call ☎ 118, or **Ospedale Maggiore** (☎ 051 647 81 11). For the police go to the **questura** (police headquarters; ☎ 051 640 11 11; Piazza Galileo 7).

### Things to See & Do

The porticoed streets of Bologna are ideal for a stroll. The best starting point is the traffic-free centre formed by **Piazza Maggiore**, the adjoining **Piazza del Nettuno** and **Fontana del Nettuno** (Neptune's Fountain), sculpted in bronze by the French artist who became known as Giambologna, and **Piazza di Porta Ravegnana**, with its two leaning towers to rival Pisa's (originally there were 42).

ITALY

## BOLOGNA

**PLACES TO STAY**
3 Donatello
5 Accademia
9 Albergo Marconi
15 Albergo Panorama
20 Albergo Garisenda

**PLACES TO EAT**
6 Osteria Dell'Orsa
7 Diana
8 Pam Supermarket
10 Trattoria da Danio
11 Pizzeria La Bella Napoli
13 Mercato Ugo Bassi
14 Pizzeria Altero

**OTHER**
1 Tourist Office
2 Intercity Bus Terminal
4 Pinacoteca Nazionale
12 Basilica di San Francesco
16 Questura (Police Station)
17 Palazzo Comunale
18 Fontana del Nettuno
19 IAT Tourist Office
21 Net Arena
22 Le Due Torri (Leaning Towers)
23 Basilica di Santo Stefano
24 Main Post Office
25 Museo Civico Archeologico
26 Basilica di San Petronio
27 Basilica di San Domenico

The **Basilica di San Petronio** in Piazza Maggiore is dedicated to the city's patron saint, Petronius. It was here that Charles V was crowned emperor by the pope in 1530. The incomplete red-and-white marble facade displays the colours of Bologna, and the chapels inside contain notable works of art. The adjacent **Palazzo Comunale** (town hall) is a huge building combining several architectural styles in remarkable harmony. It features a bronze statue of Pope Gregory XIII (a native of Bologna, and the creator of the Gregorian calendar), an impressive staircase attributed to Bramante and Bologna's collection of art treasures.

The **Basilica di Santo Stefano** is a medieval religious complex of four churches (originally there were seven) and includes the

11th-century Chiesa del Crocefisso, which houses the bones of San Petronio.

The **Basilica di San Domenico**, erected in the early 16th century, houses the elaborate sarcophagus of St Dominic, the founder of the Dominican order. The chapel was designed by Nicoló Pisano and its shrine features figures carved by a young Michelangelo.

The **Museo Civico Archeologico, Pinacoteca Nazionale** and French Gothic **Basilica di San Francesco** are also well worth a visit.

### Places to Stay

Budget hotels in Bologna are difficult to come by and finding a single room can be a nightmare, so always book in advance.

A good option is the HI **Ostello Due Torri** (☎/fax 051 50 18 10; Via Viadagola 5; dorm *bed €12).* Take bus No 93 or 20b from Via Irnerio (off Via dell'Indipendenza south of the station), and ask the bus driver where to alight.

Right in the historic centre, **Albergo Garisenda** *(☎ 051 22 43 69, fax 051 22 10 07; Via Rizzoli 9, Galleria del Leone 1; singles/doubles/triples without bath €42/62/83)* has some rooms overlooking the two towers and the busy Via Rizzoli. Slightly further out, **Albergo Marconi** *(☎ 051 26 28 32; Via G Marconi 22; singles/doubles without bath €34/53, with bath €43/68)* provides functional but plain rooms. **Albergo Panorama** *(☎ 051 22 18 02; Via Livraghi 1; singles/doubles/triples/quads without bath €47/62/78/88)* has light and airy rooms. **Accademia** *(☎ 051 23 23 18, fax 051 26 35 90; Via delle Belle Arti 6; singles/doubles €82/113)* offers good two-star rooms and a grumpy owner. Closer to the station the three-star **Donatello** *(☎ 051 24 81 74, fax 051 24 47 76; Via dell'Indipendenza 65; singles/doubles €60/80)* gives discounts if there are no trade fairs on.

### Places to Eat

**Pizzeria La Bella Napoli** *(☎ 051 55 51 63; Via San Felice 40; pizza from €5)* serves popular and reasonably priced pizzas. A few doors away **Trattoria da Danio** *(☎ 051 55 52 02; Via San Felice 50a; meal about €15)* is a pearl, full of large locals who like their food. **Pizzeria Altero** *(Via Ugo Bassi 10; pizza slice from €1)* is the place for a quick lunchtime bite. For more of a pub feel, join the students at the **Osteria Dell'Orsa** *(☎ 051 23 15 76; Via Mentana 1G; panini from €4, mains about €7)* in the university quarter. **Diana** *(☎ 051 23 13 02; Via dell'Indipendenza 24a; meal about €36)* has waiters in white jackets.

Shop at **Mercato Ugo Bassi** *(Via Ugo Bassi 27; open Mon-Sat)*, a covered market offering all the local fare, or at supermarket **Pam** *(Via Marconi 28a).*

### Getting There & Away

Bologna's **Guiglielmo Marconi airport** *(☎ 051 647 96 15)* is northwest of the city.

On land, Bologna is a major transport junction and trains from all over the country stop here. National and international coaches to major cities depart from the terminal in Piazza XX Settembre, around the corner from the train station in Piazza delle Medaglie d'Oro. The city is linked to Milan, Florence and Rome by the A1 (Autostrada del Sole). The

A13 heads directly for Venice and Padua, and the A14 goes to Rimini and Ravenna.

### Getting Around

Traffic is restricted in the city centre, so it's best to park at one of the many public car parks outside the city walls. The bus system is efficient; to get to the city centre from the train station take bus No 25 or 27.

## RAVENNA
**postcode 48100 • pop 138,900**

Ravenna's exquisite mosaics, relics of the time it was capital of the Western Roman Empire and western seat of the Byzantines, are the big drawcards. But Ravenna is also the last resting place of Dante, who died here in 1321. Easily accessible from Bologna, this perfectly manicured, stress-free town, is worth a day trip at the very least.

### Information

There is an **IAT tourist office** *(☎ 0544 354 04, fax 0544 48 26 70; Via Salara 8; open 8.30am-6pm Mon-Sat, until 7pm Apr-Oct, 10am-4pm Sun).* For all things medical try **Ospedale Santa Maria delle Croci** *(☎ 0544 40 91 11; Via Missiroli 10).*

### Things to See

The pick of Ravenna's mosaics are found in the **Basilica di Sant'Apollinare Nuovo**, the **Basilica di San Vitale**, the **Mausoleo di Galla Placidia** (these are the oldest) and the **Battistero Neoniano**. These buildings are all in the town centre and an admission ticket to the four, as well as to the **Museo Arcivescovile**, costs €6. The mosaics in the **Basilica di Sant' Apollinare in Classe**, 5km away, are also notable. To get there take bus No 4 or 44 from the train station. **Dante's Tomb** is open to the public daily and is free.

### Special Events

Ravenna hosts a music festival from late June to early August, featuring world-renowned artists, while an annual theatre and literature festival is held in September in honour of Dante. In winter, opera and dance are staged at the **Teatro Alighieri** *(box office ☎ 0544 24 92 44; Piazza Garibaldi 5).*

### Places to Stay & Eat

The HI **Ostello Dante** *(☎ 0544 42 11 64; Via Aurelio Nicolodi 12; B&B €12.50, family* *rooms per person €14)* is 1km out of town. Take bus No 1 from Viale Pallavacini, to the left of the train station. **Al Giaciglio** *(☎/fax 0544 394 03; Via Rocca Brancaleone 42; singles/doubles without bath €30/42, with bath €36/51)* has very blue rooms and a restaurant with a set menu for €12.20. Two-star **Ravenna** *(☎ 0544 21 22 04, fax 0544 21 20 77; Via Maroncelli 12; singles/doubles with bath €42/62)*, provides anonymous rooms just outside the train station. In the heart of the city's historic centre, the three-star **Hotel Centrale Byron** *(☎ 0544 334 79, fax 0544 341 14; Via IV Novembre 14; singles/doubles with bath from €53/83)* offers all the mod cons and a chatty owner.

For a quick lunch, you could try the **Bizantino** self-service restaurant in the city's fresh-produce market in Piazza Andrea Costa. There is a fixed menu for €7.30, excluding drinks, but it is only open Monday to Friday. **Cá de Vén** *(☎ 0544 301 63; Via Corrado Ricci 24; meal about €25)* offers regional dishes and wine in monastic surroundings.

### Getting There & Away
Ravenna is accessible by train from Bologna, sometimes involving a change at Castel Bolognese. The trip takes around 1½ hours.

### Getting Around
Cycling is a popular way to get around, especially as there are no hills anywhere in sight. Rental is €7.75 per day or €1.03 per hour from COOP San Vitale, Piazza Farini, outside the station. The tourist office also has some bikes to lend in spring and summer. They don't charge, but phone ahead to check availability.

### SAN MARINO
**postcode 47890 • pop 28,000**
The world's oldest surviving republic, San Marino was founded in AD 300 by a stonemason said to have been escaping religious persecution; at least according to one legend. The tiny state (only 61 sq km) is an unashamed tourist trap but offers splendid views of the mountains and coast. You can wander along the city walls and visit the two fortresses.

The **tourist office** *(☎ 0549 88 29 98; Contrada Omagnano 20; open 8.30am-6.30pm daily)* is in the Palazzo del Turismo. San Marino is accessible from Rimini by bus.

# The Dolomites

The limestone Dolomites stretch across Trentino-Alto Adige and into the Veneto. Characterised by the reddish glow of the rock formations which jut into the sky like jagged teeth, this spectacular Alpine region is the Italians' favoured area for skiing and, in summer, hiking.

### Information
Information about Trentino-Alto Adige can be obtained in Trent (Trento) at the **APT del Trentino** *(☎ 0461 83 90 00, fax 0461 26 02 45; e info@trentino.to; Via Romagnosi 11)*; in Rome *(☎ 06 36 09 58 42, fax 06 320 24 13; Via del Babuino 20)*; and in Milan *(☎ 02 86 46 12 51, fax 02 72 00 21 88; Piazza Diaz 5)*. Bolzano's **tourist office** *(☎ 0471 30 70 00; e info@bolzano-bozen.it; Piazza Walther 8)* also has information on the region.

The **APT Dolomiti** *(☎ 0436 32 31/2/3, fax 0436 32 35)* at Cortina can provide details on trekking and skiing in the Veneto.

### Skiing
The Dolomites' numerous ski resorts range from expensive and fashionable Cortina d'Ampezzo in the Veneto to family-oriented resorts such as those in the Val Gardena in Trentino-Alto Adige. All the resorts have helpful tourist offices with information on facilities, accommodation and transport.

The high season is from Christmas to early January and from early February to April, when prices increase considerably. A good way to save money is to buy a *settimana bianca* (literally, 'white week'), package-deal that covers accommodation, food and ski passes for seven days. They are available from travel agencies throughout Italy.

If you want to go it alone, invest in a ski pass. Most resort areas offer their own passes for unlimited use of lifts at several resorts for a nominated period. Prices vary depending on the resort but expect to pay around €123 to €154 for six days.

The **Superski Dolomiti pass** *(w www.dolomitisuperski.com)*, which allows access to 464 lifts and 1220km of ski runs in 12 valleys for six days, costs €175.

The average cost of ski and boot hire in the Alps is around €15 a day for downhill and €10 for cross-country.

## Trekking

Without doubt, the Dolomites provide the most breathtaking opportunities for walking in the Italian Alps – from a half-day stroll with the kids to demanding treks that require mountaineering skills. The walking season runs from the end of June to the end of September. Alpine refuges *(rifugi)* usually close around 20 September.

Buy a map of the hiking trails with Alpine refuges marked. The best are the Tabacco 1:25,000 series, which are widely available at bookshops throughout the region. Lonely Planet's *Walking in Italy* outlines several treks in detail and the *Italy* guide also details some suggested hikes.

Hiking trails are generally well marked with numbers on red-and-white painted bands on trees and rocks along the trails, or by numbers inside different-coloured triangles for the Alte Vie (the four High Routes through the Dolomites that link a chain of rifugi and can take up to two weeks to walk – the APT in Trent has details).

Recommended hiking areas include:

**Alpe di Siusi** A vast plateau above the Val Gardena, at the foot of the spectacular Sciliar.
**Cortina area** Featuring the magnificent Parco Naturale de Fanes-Sennes-Braies.
**Pale di San Martino** Accessible from San Martino di Castrozza.

**Warning** Remember that even in summer the weather is extremely changeable in the Alps; although it might be sweltering when you set off, you should be prepared for very cold and wet weather on even the shortest of walks. Essentials include good-quality, worn-in walking boots, an anorak or pile/wind jacket, a lightweight backpack, a warm hat and gloves, a waterproof poncho, light food and plenty of water.

## Getting There & Away

The region has an excellent public transport network – the two principal bus companies are SAD (☎ 800 84 60 409) in Alto Adige and the Veneto, and Atesina in Trentino. There's a network of long-distance buses operated by a number of companies (eg, Lazzi, SITA, Sena, STAT and ATVO) connecting the main towns and ski resorts with major cities such as Rome, Florence, Venice, Bologna, Milan and Genoa. Information is available from tourist offices and *autostazioni* (bus stations) in the region. For long-distance travel information, try **Lazzi Express** (☎ *06 884 08 40; Via Tagliamento 27b)* in Rome, and (☎ *055 28 71 18; Piazza Stazione 47r)* in Florence. There is a **SITA office** (☎ *055 29 49 55; Via Santa Caterina da Siena 15)* in Florence.

## Getting Around

If you are planning to hike in the Alps during the warmer months, you'll find that hitching is no problem, especially near the resort towns. The areas around the major resorts are well serviced by local buses, and tourist offices will be able to provide information on routes. During winter, most resorts have 'ski bus' shuttle services from the towns to the main ski facilities.

## CORTINA D'AMPEZZO
### postcode 32043 • pop 6570

The ski resort for Italy's beautiful people, Cortina is excruciatingly fashionable and correspondingly expensive. It is also one of the best equipped and most picturesque resorts in the Dolomites. The area is very popular for trekking and climbing, with well-marked trails and numerous rifugi.

The **main APT tourist office** (☎ *0436 32 31/32/33)* has information on Cortina's accommodation options. **International Camping Olympia** (☎/*fax 0436 50 57; per person/ tent & car €7.50/9; open year round)* is 3.5km north of Cortina at Fiames. **Casa Tua** (☎ *0436 22 78;* ℮ *info@casatuacortina.com; Zuel 100; rooms per person €34 50)* in Cortina has varying rates, depending on the season. SAD buses connect Cortina with Bolzano, via Dobbiaco; ATVO with Venice, and Zani with Milan and Bologna.

## CANAZEI
### postcode 38032 • pop 1780

Set in the Fassa Dolomites, the resort of Canazei has more than 100km of trails and is linked to the challenging network of runs known as the **Sella Ronda**. Canazei also offers cross-country and summer skiing on Marmolada, which at 3342m is the highest peak in the Dolomites.

Spend a cheap night at the Marmolada **camping ground** (☎ *0462 60 16 60; per person/tent €7.75/7.75; open year-round)*, or contact the **APT tourist office** (☎ *0462 60 11 13, fax 0462 60 25 02; Via Roma 34)* for further details on accommodation. The resort is

ITALY

accessible by Atesina bus from Trent and SAD bus from Bolzano.

## VAL GARDENA

This is one of the most popular skiing areas in the Alps, due to its reasonable prices and first-class facilities. There are superb walking trails in the Sella Group and the Alpe di Siusi. The Vallunga, behind Selva, is great for family walks and cross-country skiing.

The valley's main towns are Ortisei, Santa Cristina and Selva, all offering plenty of accommodation and easy access to runs. Each town has a **tourist office** (Ortisei: ☎ 0471 79 63 28, fax 0471 79 67 49; Santa Cristina: ☎ 0471 79 30 46, fax 0471 79 31 98; Selva: ☎ 0471 79 51 22, fax 0471 79 42 45), which all have extensive information on accommodation and facilities. Staff speak English and will send details on request. The Val Gardena is accessible from Bolzano by SAD bus, and is connected to major Italian cities by coach services (Lazzi, SITA and STAT).

## SAN MARTINO DI CASTROZZA
**postcode 38058 • pop 700**

Located in a sheltered position beneath the Pale di San Martino, this resort is popular among Italians and offers good ski runs, as well as cross-country skiing and a toboggan run. The **APT office** (☎ 0439 76 88 67, fax 0439 76 88 14) will provide a full list of accommodation. **Hotel Suisse** (☎ 0439 680 87; Via Dolomiti 1; B&B from €30) is a pleasant one-star option. Buses travel regularly from Trent, Venice and Padua.

# Central Italy

Miraculously, the rolling green landscape and soft golden light of Tuscany, and rugged hill towns of Umbria and the Marches (Le Marche) seem virtually unchanged today. In each of the regions there is a strong artistic and cultural tradition and the smallest medieval town can harbour a masterpiece or two.

## FLORENCE
**postcode 50100 • pop 375,500**

Italy has been successfully selling itself on the back of Florence for centuries. And although everything they claim is true – it is a beautiful city with an artistic heritage unrivalled anywhere else in the world – it can also be disheartening. For most of the year, you're more likely to overhear conversations in English than in Italian, and, especially in summer, the heat, car fumes and crowds can be stifling. But, gripes apart, Florence remains one of the most enticing cities in Italy. Cradle of the Renaissance, home of Dante, Machiavelli, Michelangelo, the Medici and Carlo Collodi (the bloke who created Pinocchio), the wealth of history, art and culture continues to overwhelm.

Florence was founded as a colony of the Etruscan city of Fiesole in about 200 BC and later became the strategic Roman garrison settlement of Florentia. In the Middle Ages the city developed a flourishing economy based on banking and commerce, which sparked a period of building and growth previously unequalled in Italy. It was a major focal point for the Guelph and Ghibelline struggle of the 13th century, which saw Dante banished from the city. But Florence truly flourished in the 15th century under the Medici, reaching its cultural, artistic and political height as it gave birth to the Renaissance.

The Grand Duchy of the Medici was succeeded in the 18th century by the House of Lorraine (related to the Austrian Habsburgs). Following unification, Florence was the capital of the new kingdom of Italy from 1865 to 1871. During WWII parts of the city were destroyed by bombing, including all of the bridges except the Ponte Vecchio, and in 1966 a devastating flood destroyed or severely damaged many important works of art.

## Orientation

Whether you arrive by train, bus or car, the main train station, Santa Maria Novella, is a good reference point. Budget hotels and pensioni are concentrated around Via Nazionale to the east of the station, and Piazza Santa Maria Novella to the south. The main thoroughfare to the centre is Via de' Panzani and then Via de' Cerretani, about a 10-minute walk. You'll know you've arrived when you first glimpse the Duomo.

Once at Piazza del Duomo you will find Florence easy to negotiate, with most of the major sights within easy walking distance. Many museums are closed on Monday, but you won't waste your time by just strolling through the streets. Take the city ATAF buses for longer distances such as to Piazzale Michelangelo or the nearby suburb of Fiesole, both of which offer panoramic views of the city.

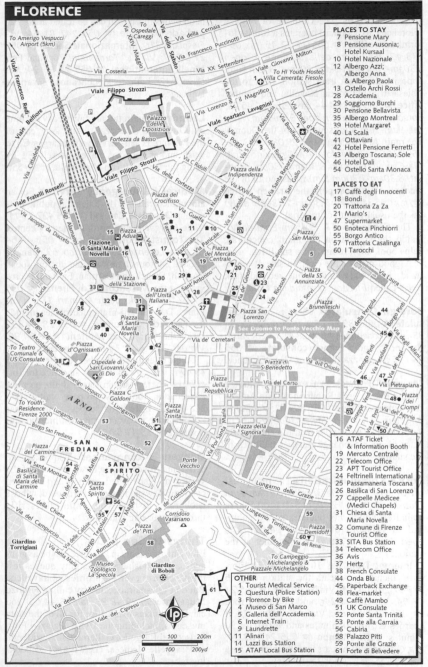

# FLORENCE

## PLACES TO STAY
7 Pensione Mary
8 Pensione Ausonia;
    Hotel Kursaal
10 Hotel Nazionale
12 Albergo Azzi;
    Albergo Anna
    & Albergo Paola
13 Ostello Archi Rossi
28 Accademia
29 Soggiorno Burchi
30 Pensione Bellavista
35 Albergo Montreal
39 Hotel Margaret
40 La Scala
41 Ottaviani
42 Hotel Pensione Ferretti
43 Albergo Toscana; Sole
46 Hotel Dali
54 Ostello Santa Monaca

## PLACES TO EAT
17 Caffè degli Innocenti
18 Bondi
20 Trattoria Za Za
21 Mario's
47 Supermarket
50 Enoteca Pinchiorri
55 Borgo Antico
57 Trattoria Casalinga
60 I Tarocchi

## OTHER
1 Tourist Medical Service
2 Questura (Police Station)
3 Florence by Bike
4 Museo di San Marco
5 Galleria dell'Accademia
6 Internet Train
9 Laundrette
11 Alinari
14 Lazzi Bus Station
15 ATAF Local Bus Station
16 ATAF Ticket
    & Information Booth
19 Mercato Centrale
22 Telecom Office
23 APT Tourist Office
24 Feltrinelli International
25 Passamaneria Toscana
26 Basilica di San Lorenzo
27 Cappelle Medicee
    (Medici Chapels)
31 Chiesa di Santa
    Maria Novella
32 Comune di Firenze
    Tourist Office
33 SITA Bus Station
34 Telecom Office
36 Avis
37 Hertz
38 French Consulate
44 Onda Blu
45 Paperback Exchange
47 Flea-market
49 Caffè Mambo
51 UK Consulate
52 Ponte Santa Trinità
53 Ponte alla Carraia
56 Cabiria
58 Palazzo Pitti
59 Ponte alle Grazie
61 Forte di Belvedere

ITALY

## Information

**Tourist Offices** The Comune di Firenze (Florence City Council) operates a **tourist information office** (☎ *055 21 22 45, fax 055 238 12 26; Piazza della Stazione 4; open 8.30am-7pm Mon-Sat, 8.30am-1.30pm Sun)*, opposite the main train station, next to the Chiesa di Santa Maria Novella; and another **office** (☎ *055 234 04 44, fax 055 226 45 24; Borgo Santa Croce 29r; open 9am-7pm Mon-Sat, 9am-2pm Sun)* southeast of the Duomo. The **main APT office** (☎ *055 29 08 32/33, fax 055 276 03 83; e infoturismo@provincia.fi.it; Via Cavour 1r; open 8.30am-6.30pm Mon-Sat, 8.30am-1.30pm Sun)* is just north of the Duomo. At the airport the **branch office** (*☎/fax 055 31 58 74; 7.30am-11.30pm daily)* has the usual wealth of material.

The **Consorzio ITA** (*8.45am-8pm daily)*, inside the station on the main concourse, helps book hotel rooms for a small fee.

A good map of the city, on sale at newsstands, is the one with the white, red and black cover called *Firenze: Pianta della Città.*

**Foreign Consulates** There is a **US consulate** (☎ *055 239 82 76; Lungarno Vespucci 38)*, a **UK consulate** (☎ *055 28 41 33; Lungarno Corsini 2)* and a **French consulate** (☎ *055 230 25 56; Piazza Ognissanti 2)* in Florence.

**Money** The major banks are concentrated around Piazza della Repubblica. The **American Express office** (☎ *055 509 81; Via Dante Alighieri 22r; open 9am-5.30pm Mon-Fri, 9.30am-12.30pm Sat)* is near the Duomo. Be wary of poor exchange rates at facilities in the station.

**Post & Communications** The **main post office** (*Via Pellicceria 3; open 8.15am-7pm Mon-Fri, 8.15am-12.30pm Sat)* is off Piazza della Repubblica. For phones, there is an unstaffed **Telecom office** (*Via Cavour 21r; open 7am-11pm daily)*, and another at the station.

**Internet Train** has 10 branches in Florence, including beneath the station (☎ *055 239 97 20)*, just off Via Nazionale (☎ *055 21 47 94; Via Guelfa 24r)* and in Santa Croce (☎ *055 263 85 55; Via dei Benci 36)*. It charges €1 for 10 minutes and €2.30 for 30 minutes. **Caffè Mambo** (☎ *055 247 89 94; Via G Verdi 49)* has a separate Internet area and charges €1.30 for 15 minutes.

**Bookshops** A selection of new and second-hand books in English can be found at the **Paperback Exchange** (☎ *055 247 81 54; Via Fiesolana 31r)*. **Internazionale Seeber** (☎ *055 21 56 97; Via de' Tornabuoni 70r)* and **Feltrinelli International** (☎ *055 21 95 24; Via Cavour 12r)* both stock publications in various languages.

**Laundry** Laundrettes are fairly easy to come by. **Onda Blu** (*Via degli Alfani 24r)*, east of the Duomo, is self-service and charges €3 to wash and €3 to dry. Save yourself €1 by using the laundrette on Via Guelfa at No 55r.

**Medical & Emergency Services** For an ambulance call ☎ 118. The main public hospital is **Ospedale Careggi** (☎ *055 427 71 11; Viale Morgagni 85)*, north of the city centre. The **Tourist Medical Service** (☎ *055 47 54 11; Via Lorenzo il Magnifico 59)* can be phoned 24 hours a day and the doctors speak English, French and German. First aid is provided at the **Misericordia di Firenze** (☎ *055 21 22 22; Vicolo degli Adimari 1)* just off Piazza Duomo. All-night pharmacies include the **Farmacia Comunale** (☎ *055 28 94 35)*, inside the station; and **Molteni** (☎ *28 94 90; Via dei Calzaiuoli 7r)* in the city centre.

At the **questura** (*police headquarters; ☎ 055 497 71; Via Zara 2)* there is an office for foreigners where you can report thefts etc. For information about lost property call ☎ 055 328 39 42. But if you suspect your car has been towed away, try the **municipal car pound** (☎ *055 41 57 81)*.

**Dangers & Annoyances** Pickpockets are active in crowds and on buses: beware of the groups of dishevelled women and children carrying newspapers and cardboard, whose trick is to distract you while others rifle through your bag and pockets.

## Things to See & Do

Enjoying the sights in Florence can be a 'grin-and-bear-it' business, as lengthy queues test the patience of even the heartiest of travellers. But don't despair, because by calling **Firenze Musei** (☎ *055 29 48 83, fax 26 44 06)* you can book tickets in advance for all of the state museums, including the Uffizi, Palazzo Pitti, Museo del Bargello, Galleria dell'Accademia and Cappelle Medicee. There is a €1.55 booking fee.

## DUOMO TO PONTE VECCHIO

**PLACES TO STAY**
1 Hotel Abaco
8 Hotel Pendini
15 Albergo Firenze
16 Pensione Maria
   Luisa de' Medici
22 Aily Home

**PLACES TO EAT**
6 Hosteria Il Caminetto
7 Gilli
13 Cantinetta da Verrazzano
17 Yellow Bar
19 Gelateria Vivoli
24 Trattoria Buzzino
25 Trattoria da Benvenuto
26 Angie's Pub
27 Fiaschetteria

**OTHER**
2 Battistero (Baptistry)
3 Misericordia di Firenze
4 Campanile (Bell Tower)
5 Duomo
9 Internazionale Seeber
10 Odeon
11 Main Post Office
12 Molteni Pharmacy
14 American Express
18 Museo del Bargello
20 Palazzo Vecchio
21 Loggia della Signoria
23 Galleria degli Uffizi
   (Uffizi Gallery)
28 Comune di Firenze
   Tourist Office
29 Internet Train
30 Chiesa di Santa Croce

**Duomo** With its nougat facade and sykline-dominating dome, the Duomo is one of Italy's most famous monuments, and the world's fourth-largest cathedral. Named the Cattedrale di Santa Maria del Fiore, the breathtaking structure was begun in 1294 by the Sienese architect Arnolfo di Cambio but took almost 150 years to complete.

The Renaissance architect Brunelleschi won a public competition in 1420 to design the enormous dome, the first of its kind since antiquity. The octagonal dome is decorated with frescoes by Vasari and Zuccari, and stained-glass windows by Donatello, Paolo Uccello and Lorenzo Ghiberti. The marble facade is a 19th-century replacement of the unfinished original, which was pulled down in the 16th century. For a bird's-eye view of Florence, climb to the top of the **cupola** (admission €6; open 8.30am-7pm Mon-Fri, 8.30am-5.40pm Sat).

Giotto designed and began building the graceful **campanile** (bell tower; admission €6; open 8.30am-7.30pm daily) next to the cathedral in 1334, but died before it was completed. Standing at 82m, the climb to the top is a tough one.

The Romanesque **battistero** (baptistry; admission €3, open noon-6pm Mon-Sat, 8.30am-1.30pm Sun), believed to have been built between the 5th and 11th centuries on the site of a Roman temple, is the oldest building in Florence. Dante was baptised here, and it is particularly famous for its gilded-bronze doors. The celebrated *Gates of Paradise* by Lorenzo Ghiberti face the Duomo to the east;

Ghiberti also designed the north door. The south door, by Andrea Pisano, dates from 1336 and is the oldest. Most of the doors are copies – the original panels are being removed for restoration and placement in the Museo dell'Opera del Duomo.

### Galleria degli Uffizi (Uffizi Gallery) The Palazzo degli Uffizi (admission €8; open 8.15am-6.50pm Tues-Sun), built by Vasari in the 16th century, houses the single greatest collection of Italian and Florentine art in existence. Bequeathed to the city by the Medici family in 1743, it contains some of the world's most-recognisable Renaissance paintings.

The gallery's inordinate number of masterpieces include 14th-century gems by Giotto and Cimabue; Botticelli's *Birth of Venus* and *Allegory of Spring* from the 15th century; and works by Filippo Lippi, Fra Angelico and Paolo Uccello. *The Annunciation* by Leonardo da Vinci is also here, along with Michelangelo's *Holy Family,* Titian's *Venus of Urbino* and renowned works by Raphael, Andrea del Sarto, Tintoretto and Caravaggio.

### Piazza della Signoria & Palazzo Vecchio Designed by Arnolfo di Cambio and built between 1298 and 1340, Palazzo Vecchio (admission €5.70; open 9am-7pm Tues, Wed & Sat, 9am-11pm Mon & Fri, 9am-2pm Thur, in summer, otherwise 9am-7pm Mon-Wed & Fri-Sat, 9am-2pm Thur) is the traditional seat of the Florentine government. In the 16th century it became the ducal palace of the Medici (before they moved to the Palazzo Pitti), and was given an interior facelift by Vasari. Visit the Michelozzo courtyard just inside the entrance and the lavishly decorated apartments upstairs.

The palace's turrets, battlements and bell tower form an imposing backdrop to Piazza della Signoria, scene of many pivotal political events in the history of Florence, including the execution of the religious and political reformer Savonarola; a bronze plaque marks the spot where he was burned at the stake in 1498. The **Loggia della Signoria**, which has recently been thoroughly cleaned up and stands at right angles to the Palazzo Vecchio, displays sculptures such as Giambologna's *Rape of the Sabine Women.* Cellini's famous *Perseus* has, however, been relocated to the Uffizi. The statue of *David* is a fine copy of Michelangelo's masterpiece; the original was installed on the site in 1504, and is now safely indoors in the Galleria dell'Accademia.

**Ponte Vecchio** This famous 14th-century bridge, lined with gold and silversmiths' shops, was the only one to survive Nazi bombing in WWII. Originally, the shops housed butchers, but when a corridor along the 1st floor was built by the Medici to link the Palazzo Pitti and Palazzo Vecchio, it was ordered that goldsmiths rather than noisome butchers should trade on the bridge.

**Palazzo Pitti** This immense and imposing palazzo was built for the Pitti family, great rivals of the Medici, who moved in a century later. The **Galleria Palatina** (Palatine Gallery; admission €6.50; open 8.15am-6.50pm Tues-Sun) has works by Raphael, Filippo Lippi, Titian and Rubens, hung in lavishly decorated rooms. The gallery and gloriously (some might say ridiculously) over-the-top **royal apartments** can be visited on the same ticket and keep the same hours. The palace also houses the **Museo degli Argenti** (Silver Museum), the **Galleria d'Arte Moderna** (Modern Art Gallery) and the **Galleria del Costume** (Costume Gallery; all three museums open 8.15am-1.50pm Tues-Sat).

Don't leave without visiting the Renaissance **Giardino di Boboli** (Boboli Gardens; admission €2), with grottoes, fountains, leafy walkways and panoramic city views.

**Museo del Bargello** The medieval **Palazzo del Bargello** (Via del Proconsolo 4; admission €4; open 8.15am-5pm Tues-Sun) should not be missed. With a bloody history as the seat of the chief magistrate and, later, as a police station, the palace now houses Florence's rich collection of sculpture. Here you'll marvel at Michelangelo's *Bacchus*, Donatello's bronze *David*, Giambologna's *Mercury* and works by Benvenuto Cellini.

**Galleria dell'Accademia** Arguably the most famous sculpture in the Western world, Michelangelo's *David* is housed in this gallery (Via Ricasoli 60; admission €6.50; open 8.15am-6.50pm Tues-Sun), as are four of the artist's unfinished *Slaves.* Early Florentine works are on show in the gallery upstairs.

**Museo di San Marco** This museum *(admission €4; open 8.15am-1.50pm Mon-Fri, 8.15am-6.50pm Sat, 8.15am-7pm Sun)*, pays homage to the work of Fra Angelico, who decorated many of the cells in this former Dominican convent with sublime frescoes and lived here from 1438 to 1455. Don't miss the peaceful cloisters (depicted in his *Annunciation*). The monastery also contains works by Fra Bartolomeo and Ghirlandaio, as well as the cell of the monk Savonarola.

**Basilica di San Lorenzo & Cappelle Medicee (Medici Chapels)** The basilica was built by Brunelleschi in the early 15th century for the Medici and includes his mathematically precise **Sagrestia Vecchia** (Old Sacristy), with sculptural decoration by Donatello. The cloister leads to the **Biblioteca Laurenziana**, the huge library built to house the Medici collection of some 10,000 manuscripts is entered via Michelangelo's flowing Mannerist stairway.

The **Cappelle Medicee** *(admission €6; open 8.15am-5pm Mon-Sat, 8.15am-5pm 1st, 3rd & 5th Sun of the month, otherwise 8.15am-1.50pm Sun)* are around the corner in Piazza Madonna degli Aldobrandini. The **Cappella dei Principi**, sumptuously decorated with marble and semiprecious stones, was the principal burial place of the Medici grand dukes. The incomplete **Sagrestia Nuova** was Michelangelo's first architectural effort, and contains his *Medici Madonna*, *Night & Day* and *Dawn & Dusk* sculptures, which adorn the Medici tombs.

**Other Attractions** The Tuscan Gothic **Chiesa di Santa Maria Novella** was constructed for the Dominican Order during the 13th and 14th centuries; its white-and-green marble facade was designed by Alberti in the 15th century. The church features Masaccio's *Trinity*, a masterpiece of perspective, and is decorated with frescoes by Ghirlandaio (who was perhaps assisted by a very young Michelangelo). **Cappella di Filippo Strozzi** has frescoes by Filippino Lippi, and those in the cloisters are by Paolo Uccello.

Head up to **Piazzale Michelangelo** for unparalleled views of Florence. To get there from the city centre, cross the Ponte Vecchio, turn left and walk along the river, then turn right at Piazza Giuseppe Poggi; if you're tired of walking, take bus No 13 from the station.

## Cycling

No churches and no museums is the promise of **I Bike Italy** *(☎ 055 234 23 71; W www.ibikeitaly.com)* on its single and two-day guided bike rides (and walking tours) in the countryside around Florence. It supplies all the gear and English-speaking guides. The Fiesole ride costs US$70, Chianti US$85 and Siena US$280 (two days; price includes meals and accommodation).

## Special Events

Major festivals include the Scoppio del Carro (Explosion of the Cart), held in front of the Duomo on Easter Sunday; and, on 24 June, the Festa di San Giovanni (Feast of St John, Florence's patron saint) and lively Calcio Storico, which features football matches played in 16th-century costume. Maggio Musicale Fiorentino, Italy's longest-running music festival, runs from April to June. For more information call the **Teatro Comunale** *(☎ 800 11 22 11)*.

## Places to Stay

Always ask the full price of a room before putting your bags down as hotels and pensioni in Florence are becoming increasingly expensive and are notorious for bill-padding, particularly in summer. Prices listed here are for high season.

**Camping** The **Campeggio Michelangelo** *(☎ 055 681 19 77, fax 055 68 93 48; Viale Michelangelo 80; per person/tent €7.50/4.80)* is near Piazzale Michelangelo. Take bus No 13 from the station. **Villa Camerata** *(☎ 055 60 14 51; Viale Augusto Righi 2-4; per person/tent €6/5)* is next to the HI hostel of the same name (see the following section). **Campeggio Panoramico** *(☎ 055 59 90 69, fax 055 591 86; Via Peramonda 1; per person/tent €8.50/14)*, in Fiesole, also has bungalows. Take bus No 7 from the station.

**Hostels** The HI **Ostello Villa Camerata** *(☎ 055 60 14 51, fax 055 61 03 00; Viale Augusto Righi 2-4; dorm bed €15; closed 9am-2pm)* is beautifully situated. Dinner costs €8 and there is a bar. Take bus No 17, which leaves from the right of the station as you exit the platforms and takes about a half-hour. It is open to HI members only and reservations can be made by mail (essential in summer).

The private **Ostello Archi Rossi** (☎ 055 29 08 04, fax 055 230 26 01; Via Faenza 94r; dorm bed €16) is another good option for a bed in a six- or nine-bed dorm. **Ostello Santa Monaca** (☎ 055 26 83 38; Via Santa Monaca 6; dorm bed €15.50) is a 20-minute walk from the station: go through Piazza Santa Maria Novella, along Via de' Fossi, across the Ponte alla Carraia, directly ahead along Via de' Serragli, and Via Santa Monaca is on the right. Further west, **Youth Residence Firenze 2000** (☎ 055 233 55 58; e euro pean@dada.it; Viale Raffaello Sanzio 16; doubles with bath from €62) lacks atmosphere and is not cheap, but its warm indoor pool is a big plus.

**Hotels** With more than 150 budget hotels in Florence, there is usually a room available somewhere, but, it is still a good idea to book. You should arrive by late morning to claim your room.

**Around the Station** Recently renovated **Pensione Bellavista** (☎ 055 28 45 28, fax 055 28 48 74; Largo Alinari 15; singles/doubles without bath €50/80, doubles with bath €90), at the start of Via Nazionale, has bright rooms and a loo with a view. **Albergo Azzi** (☎/fax 055 21 38 06; Via Faenza 56; singles without bath €42, doubles with/without bath €78/62) is one of three basic hotels in the same building; upstairs are **Albergo Anna** and **Paola**.

Across Via Nazionale, the easy to miss **Soggiorno Burchi** (☎ 055 41 44 54; Via Faenza 20; doubles with/without bath €60/50) is a private house with old-fashioned rooms. Nearby at the **Hotel Nazionale** (☎ 055 238 22 03, fax 055 238 17 35; Via Nazionale 22; singles/doubles without bath €47/75, with bath €57/85) some rooms have the dream view of the Duomo. A few doors up at No 24, **Pensione Ausonia** (☎ 055 49 65 47, fax 055 462 66 15; singles/doubles without bath €48/82, singles/doubles/triples/quads with bath €62/116/143/170) can cater to most requests and is run by a helpful couple; downstairs in their two-star **Hotel Kursaal** (☎ 055 49 63 24; doubles without bath €90), prices are the same except for the doubles without bath, and rooms have balcony, air-con and satellite TV. **Pensione Mary** (☎/fax 055 49 63 10; Piazza dell'Indipendenza 5; singles/doubles without bath €52/73, with

bath €68/93) is a little scruffy and the owner laid-back to the point of indifference.

Closer to the station, the two-star **Accademia** (☎ 055 29 34 51, fax 055 21 97 71; e info@accademiahotel.net; Via Faenza 7; singles/doubles with bath €90/150) is housed in an 18th-century palace, replete with magnificent stained-glass doors and carved wooden ceilings.

***Around Piazza Santa Maria Novella*** Via della Scala, which runs northwest off the piazza, is lined with pensioni. **La Scala** (☎ 055 21 26 29; singles without bath €52, doubles with/without bath €88/77) at No 21 is a cheerfully unpretentious place. A few doors down, at No 25, **Hotel Margaret** (☎ 055 21 01 38; singles without bath €50, doubles with/without bath €90/70, triples with bath €120) has newly refurbished rooms, as does **Albergo Montreal** (☎ 055 238 23 31, fax 055 28 74 91; singles/doubles without bath €40/60, doubles/triples/quads with bath €75/100/120) at No 43.

At **Sole** (☎/fax 055 239 60 94; Via del Sole 8; singles without bath €38, singles/doubles/triples with bath €46/77/104), ask for a quiet room as the street below can be noisy. **Albergo Toscana** (☎/fax 055 21 31 56; singles/doubles with bath €70/114), in the same building, has pretty rooms.

Moving north, the family-run **Hotel Pensione Ferretti** (☎ 055 238 13 28, fax 055 21 92 88; Via delle Belle Donne 17; singles/doubles/triples without bath €46/74/97, with bath €57/93/116) has comfortable rooms and a charming address. The much recommended **Hotel Abaco** (☎ 055 238 19 19, fax 055 28 22 89; Via dei Banchi 1; singles without bath €60, doubles with/without bath €85/70) offers 13th-century Florentine decor and double glazing; one room even has a fireplace.

**Ottaviani** (☎ 055 239 62 23, fax 055 29 33 55; Piazza Ottaviani 1; singles without/with bath €59/69, doubles without bath €59), just off Piazza Santa Maria Novella, has reasonable rates with breakfast included.

***The Duomo to Ponte Vecchio*** This area is a 15-minute walk from the station and is right in the heart of old Florence. One of the best deals in town is the small **Aily Home** (☎ 055 239 65 05; Piazza Santo Stefano 1; singles/doubles without bath €25/40), overlooking the river. **Albergo Firenze** (☎ 055 21 42 03, fax 055 21 23 70; Piazza dei Donati 4; singles/doubles with bath €62/83), just south of the Duomo, offers simple rooms, while those at **Pensione Maria Luisa de' Medici** (☎/fax 055 28 00 48; Via del Corso 1; doubles with/without bath €82/67) are large enough to cater for up to five people. Further east **Hotel Dali** (☎/fax 055 234 07 06; Via dell'Oriuolo 17; singles without bath €40, doubles with/without bath €75/60) has sunny rooms and free parking for guests.

Up several notches, the **Hotel Pendini** (☎ 055 21 11 70, fax 055 28 18 07; Via degli Strozzi 2; singles/doubles with bath €110/150, family suite €280) is just around the corner from Piazza della Repubblica. On the 4th floor, it has a distinctly chintzy feel. A family suite accommodates four.

***Villas*** Experience life in an old villa at **Bencistà** (☎/fax 055 591 63; Via Benedetto da Maiano 4; singles/doubles €160/176), about 1km from Fiesole in the hills overlooking Florence.

## Places to Eat
Tuscan cuisine is based on the quality of its ingredients and the simplicity of its recipes. At its most basic, how can you beat a thick slice of crusty bread drizzled with olive oil and downed with a glass of Chianti? Local specialities include *ribollita*, a very filling soup of vegetables and white beans, and *bistecca alla Fiorentina* (steak Florentine), usually served in slabs sufficient for two. At the time of writing the steak has become something of a political hot potato with EU lawmakers arguing over its legal status. A ban imposed following the mad cow disease scare technically means that it can not be served, however, you will find that this decree is not always followed. Use your judgment and buon appetito.

You can stock up on supplies at the **food market** (open 7am-2pm Mon-Sat) in San Lorenzo or at the **supermarket** on the western side of the train station, or east of Piazza Duomo at Via Pietrapiana 94.

**Restaurants – City Centre** A popular place for pizza is the **Yellow Bar** (☎ 055 21 17 66; Via del Proconsolo 39r; pizza meal about €10) which has plenty of seating but is still usually full. At **Trattoria Buzzino** (☎ 055 239 80 13; Via dei Leoni 8; meal €25, tourist menu €13) you'll be served hearty food, possibly by the waiter whose technique bears more than a passing resemblance to that of Basil Fawlty's hapless help Manuel. If, however, you're after a quieter affair, try **Trattoria da Benvenuto** (☎ 055 21 48 33; Via Mosca 16r; meal about €24) where the food and prices are reasonable. At No 35r on the same street, **Angie's Pub** has a huge list of panini from €2.50 and refreshingly cold beer and **Fiaschetteria** (Via dei Neri 17r; pasta from €3.50) offers good value for money.

At **Hosteria Il Caminetto** (☎ 055 239 62 74; Via dello Studio 34r; meal about €30), you can eat on the vine-covered terrace, but you'll pay for your proximity to the Duomo. On the other hand at **Enoteca Pinchiorri** (☎ 055 24 27 77; Via Ghibellina 87; meal about €93), you'll just pay, a lot, for its famed nouvelle cuisine.

**Restaurants – Around San Lorenzo** Tiny but popular **Mario's** (Via Rosina 2r; meal around €10; open lunch only), near the Mercato Centrale, serves delicious pasta. Around the corner at Piazza del Mercato Centrale 24, **Trattoria Za Za** (☎ 055 21 54 11; meal about €20) is another favourite, with outdoor seating and an imaginative menu. **Bondi** (Via dell'Ariento 85) specialises in focaccia and pizza slices from €1.55.

**Restaurants – in the Oltrarno** A bustling place popular with the locals is **Trattoria Casalinga** (☎ 055 21 86 24; Via dei Michelozzi 9r; meal about €16) where the food is great and the pace frenetic. **I Tarocchi** (☎ 055 234 39 12; Via de' Renai 16; pizza from €5, meal about €13) serves good pizza and huge portions of pasta. In trendy Piazza Santo Spirito, **Borgo Antico** (☎ 21 04 37; meal about €22) is a cool summer spot for alfresco dining.

**Cafés & Snack Bars** Perhaps the city's grandest café is the wonderfully intact *belle époque* **Gilli** (Piazza della Repubblica). If you can't resist the bountiful display of mouthwatering sweet and savoury delights, you'll save cash, if not calories, by both eating and drinking at the bar.

**Caffè degli Innocenti** (Via Nazionale 57), near the Mercato Centrale, has a good selection of panini and cakes for around €1.55 to €2.85. The streets between the Duomo and

**ITALY**

the Arno harbour many pizzerias where you can buy cheap takeaway pizza by the slice.

The **Cantinetta da Verrazzano** *(Via dei Tavolini 18r)* wine bar/café is a tight fit. All hanging hams and dark wood, this is the place to sip that Chianti.

**Gelati** South of Via Ghibellina, **Gelateria Vivoli** *(Via dell'Isola delle Stinche 7)* is widely considered the city's best. Don't be surprised to find a queue.

## Entertainment

Listings to look out for include the bimonthly *Florence Today* and the monthly *Florence Information*, which should be available at tourist offices. *Firenze Spettacolo*, the definitive monthly entertainment guide, is sold at newsstands for €1.55.

Concerts, opera and dance are performed year-round at the **Teatro Comunale** *(Corso Italia 16)*. For reservations contact the **box office** *(☎ 800 11 22 11)*.

Original language films are screened at the **Odeon** *(☎ 055 21 40 68; Piazza Strozzi; tickets €7.20)*, on Monday and Tuesday.

For a pint head to **The William** *(Via Magliabechi 7r)*, which is lively and loud, or across the river to the tiny **Cabiria** bar in Piazza Santo Spirito, itself a good place to hang out, especially in summer.

A more sedate pastime is the evening *passeggiata* (stroll) in Piazzale Michelangelo, overlooking the city.

## Shopping

The main shopping area is between the Duomo and the Arno, with boutiques concentrated along Via Roma, Via dei Calzaiuoli and Via Por Santa Maria, leading to the goldsmiths lining the Ponte Vecchio. Window-shop along Via de' Tornabuoni, where top designers such as Gucci, Ferragamo and Prada hawk their wares.

Smell the leather at the **open-air market** *(open Mon-Sat)* in the streets surrounding San Lorenzo where leather goods, clothing and jewellery are often cheap but sometimes of dodgy quality. You can bargain, but not if you use a credit card. The **flea market** *(Piazza dei Ciompi; open daily)*, off Borgo Allegri and north of Santa Croce, is not as extensive but there are often great bargains.

Florence is renowned for its beautifully patterned paper, which is stocked in the many *cartolerie* (stationer's shops) throughout the city and at the markets. Lovers of Florentine velvet cushions, tapestries and decorative tassels should head for **Passamaneria Toscana** *(Piazza San Lorenzo 12r)*.

## Getting There & Away

**Air** Florence is served by two airports, Amerigo Vespucci and Galileo Galilei. **Amerigo Vespucci** *(☎ 055 306 15, flight information ☎ 055 306 13 00/02)*, 5km northwest of the city centre, serves domestic and European flights. **Galileo Galilei** *(☎ 050 84 92 02)* is just under an hour away from Florence near Pisa, but is one of northern Italy's main international and domestic airports.

**Bus** The SITA bus station *(☎ 800 37 37 60; Via Santa Caterina da Siena 17)* is just west of the train station. Buses leave for Siena, San Gimignano and Volterra. **Lazzi** *(☎ 055 35 10 61; Piazza Adua 1)*, next to the station, runs services to Rome, Pistoia and Lucca.

**Train** Florence is on the main Rome–Milan line. Many of the trains are the fast Eurostars, for which booking is necessary. Regular trains also go to/from Venice (three hours) and Trieste (three hours). For train information ring ☎ 848 88 80 88.

**Car & Motorcycle** Florence is connected by the Autostrada del Sole (A1) to Bologna and Milan in the north and Rome and Naples to the south. The Firenze–Mare motorway (A11) links Florence with Prato, Pistoia, Lucca, Pisa and the Versilia coast, and a *superstrada* (dual carriageway) joins the city to Siena. Exits from the autostrade into Florence are well signposted, and either one of the exits marked 'Firenze nord' or 'Firenze sud' will take you to the centre of town. There are tourist information offices on the A1 both to the north and south of the city.

## Getting Around

**To/From the Airport** Regular trains to Pisa airport leave from platform five at Santa Maria Novella station daily from 6.46am to 5pm; journey time is 1½ hours. Check your bags in at the **air terminal** *(☎ 21 60 73)* near platform five, at least 15 minutes before train departure time.

You can get to Amerigo Vespucci airport by the Vola in Bus shuttle service which departs from the SITA coach depot in Via Santa Caterina da Siena every half-hour between 6am and 11.30pm. The journey takes about 25 minutes and tickets, which can be bought on the bus, cost €4.

**Bus** ATAF buses service the city centre and Fiesole. The terminal for the most useful buses is in a small piazza to the left as you go out of the station onto Via Valfonda. Bus No 7 leaves from here for Fiesole and also stops at the Duomo. Tickets must be bought before you get on the bus and are sold at most tobacconists and newsstands or from automatic vending machines at major bus stops (€1 for one hour, €1.80 for three hours, €4 for 24 hours).

**Car & Motorcycle** If you're spending the day in Florence, there are several car parks dotted around the city centre. A good choice is Fortezza da Basso, which costs €1.05 per hour. Further details are available from **Firenze Parcheggi** (☎ 055 500 19 94).

To rent a car, try **Hertz** (☎ 055 239 82 05; Via M Finiguerra 33r), or **Avis** (☎ 055 21 36 29; Borgo Ognissanti 128r). For bikes and scooters try **Alinari** (☎ 055 28 05 00; Via Guelfa 85r), or **Florence by Bike** (☎/fax 055 48 89 92; Via Zanobi 120/122r), which also runs bike tours.

**Taxi** You can find taxis outside the station, or call ☎ 055 4798 or ☎ 055 4390 to book one.

## PISA
**postcode 56100 • pop 92,000**
No city in Italy can lay claim to as beautiful a construction cock-up as Pisa. Its leaning tower is one of the must-see sights in Italy and a godsend to producers of tourist kitsch. Once a maritime power to rival Genoa and Venice, Pisa has an important university and was the home of Galileo Galilei (1564–1642). It was devastated by the Genoese in the 13th century, and its history eventually merged with that of Florence, its bigger neighbour up the River Arno. The city today retains its charm despite the many day-trippers.

### Orientation & Information
The focus for visitors is the Campo dei Miracoli, a 1.5km walk from the train station across the Arno. Bus No 3 will save you the sweat. The medieval town centre around Borgo Stretto is a kilometre or so from the station.

There are several **APT tourist information offices**: at the station (☎ 050 4 22 91; open 9am-7pm Mon-Fri, 9.30am-3.30pm Sun), the airport, and west of Campo dei Miracoli (☎ 050 56 04 64; Via Carlo Cammeo 2; 9am-6pm Mon-Sat, 10.30am-4.30pm Sun).

Internet access is available at **InternetSurf** (Via Carducci 5) near Campo dei Miracoli, where 15 minutes costs €0.50.

### Things to See & Do
The Pisans can justly claim that their **Campo dei Miracoli** (Field of Miracles) is one of the most beautiful squares in the world, whether by day or by night. A welcome expanse of well-kept lawns provides the perfect setting for the dazzling white marble cathedral, baptistry and bell tower – all of which lean to varying degrees.

The striped Pisan-Romanesque **cathedral** (admission €2), begun in 1063, has a graceful facade of tiered arches and a cavernous column-lined interior. The transept's bronze doors, facing the leaning tower, are by Bonanno Pisano, while the 16th-century bronze doors of the main entrance are by Giambologna. The cathedral's cupcake-like **battistero** (baptistry; admission €5), which was started in 1153 and took two centuries to complete, contains a pulpit sculpted by Nicola Pisano.

The campanile, better known as the **Leaning Tower** (Torre Pendente; admission €15), found itself in trouble from the start, because of the marshy nature of the land on which it was built. Its architect, Bonanno Pisano, managed to complete only three of the tower's eventual seven tiers before it started to tilt. It continued to lean by an average 1mm a year, and today is almost 4.1m off the perpendicular despite 11 years of ground-levelling work. It is now open to the public, but visits are limited to groups of 30 people, so entry times are staggered and waits inevitable.

To save on admission to the Campo's monuments and museums, you can choose from a number of ticket options; for example, entry to one museum and one monument costs €5, two museums and the cathedral €8. Admission to the Leaning Tower, however, is always separate.

After taking in the Campo dei Miracoli, wander down Via Santa Maria, along the

Arno and into the Borgo Stretto to explore the old city, which includes the impressive Piazza dei Cavalieri.

## Places to Stay & Eat

Pisa has a range of reasonably priced hotels. Many of the budget places double as residences for students during the school year, so it can sometimes be difficult to find a cheap room.

The non-HI **Ostello per la Gioventù** (*☎/fax 050 89 06 22; Via Pietrasantina 15; dorm bed €15*) is closed during the day between 9am and 6pm. Take bus No 3 from the station. **Albergo Serena** (*☎/fax 050 58 08 09; Via Cavaica 45; singles/doubles without bath €28/41*) is tucked away near Piazza Dante Alighieri and provides simple rooms. The three-star **Hotel di Stefano** (*☎ 050 55 35 59, fax 050 55 60 38; Via Sant'Apollonia 35; singles/doubles without bath €45/60, singles/doubles/triples/quads with bath €70/85/110/120*) offers tastefully decorated rooms and a lovely breakfast terrace. Just outside the station, **Albergo Milano** (*☎ 050 231 62, fax 050 442 37; Via Mascagni 14; singles/doubles without bath €37/47, doubles/triples/quads with bath €65/87/97*) is a modest but welcoming joint.

Splash out with a view of the Arno at the grand **Royal Victoria** (*☎ 050 94 01 11, fax 050 94 01 80; Lungarno Pacinotti 12; singles/doubles with bath €87/102*), which dates from 1839.

Being a university town, Pisa has a number of cheap eating places. For a whopping great pizza **Pizzeria Del Borgo** (*Vicolo del Tinti 15; pizza meal about €11.50*) just off Via Oberdan, is just the job; plus one of the waiters does impressions. **Antica Trattoria il Campano** (*☎ 050 58 05 85; Vicolo Santa Margherita; meal about €25*) serves Tuscan grub in a medieval atmosphere. In the same price range **Spaghetteria alle Bandierine** (*☎ 050 50 00 00; Via Mercanti 4; meal about €20*) has a rustic feel and continues to win plaudits for its seafood. Head to **La Bottega del Gelato** (*Piazza Garibaldi*) and join the queue for gelati, or for fruit try the open-air food **market** (*Piazza delle Vettovaglie*), off Borgo Stretto.

## Getting There & Away

The airport, with domestic and European flights, is only a few minutes away by train,

or by bus No 3 from the station. **Lazzi** (*☎ 050 462 88*) buses run to Florence via Lucca; somewhat surprisingly, there's an original Keith Haring mural opposite its office in Piazza Vittorio Emanuele. **CPT** (*☎ 050 50 55 11*) operates buses to Livorno via Tirrenia. Pisa is linked by direct train to Florence, Rome and Genoa. Local trains head for Lucca and Livorno.

## SIENA

**postcode 53100 • pop 54,000**

To bypass Siena would be to miss one of Italy's most captivating towns. Built on three hills and surrounded by medieval ramparts, its labyrinthine centre is jam-packed with majestic Gothic buildings in various shades of the colour known as burnt sienna; it's also usually crammed to bursting with visitors.

According to legend, Siena was founded by the sons of Remus (one of the founders of Rome). In the Middle Ages the city became a free republic, but its success and power led to serious rivalry with Florence, both politically and culturally. Painters of the Sienese School produced significant works of art, and the city was home to St Catherine and St Benedict.

Siena is divided into 17 *contrade* (districts) and each year 10 are chosen to compete in the Palio, a tumultuous horse race and pageant held in the shell-shaped Piazza del Campo on 2 July and 16 August.

### Orientation

Leaving the train station, cross the concourse to the bus stop opposite and catch bus No 3, 9 or 10 to Piazza Gramsci, then walk into the centre along Via dei Termini (it takes about 10 minutes to reach Piazza del Campo). Visitors' cars are not allowed into the medieval centre.

### Information

At the **APT office** (*☎ 0577 28 05 51, fax 0577 27 06 76; e aptsiena@siena.turismo .toscana.it; Piazza del Campo 56; open 8.30am-7.30pm Mon-Sat, 9am-3pm Sun*), grab the useful guide *Terre di Siena* and a map of the town.

The **post office** (*Piazza Matteotti 1*) is to the north of the centre, while to phone you can use the **Telecom offices** (*Via dei Termini 42 • Via di Città 113*).

Check your email at the **Internet Train** (*Via di Città 121*), which has 20 screens. For 15 minutes you'll pay €1.55, for one hour €5.16.

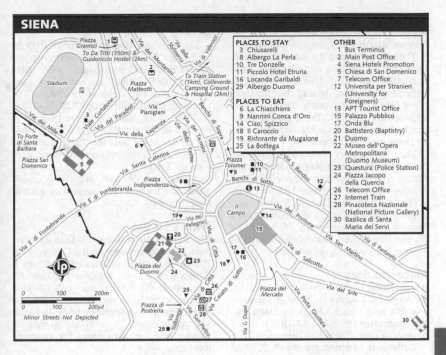

## SIENA

**PLACES TO STAY**
3  Chiusarelli
8  Albergo La Perla
10  Tre Donzelle
11  Piccolo Hotel Etruria
16  Locanda Garibaldi
29  Albergo Duomo

**PLACES TO EAT**
6  La Chiacchiera
9  Nannini Conca d'Oro
14  Ciao; Spizzico
18  Il Caroccio
19  Ristorante da Mugalone
25  La Bottega

**OTHER**
1  Bus Terminus
2  Main Post Office
4  Siena Hotels Promotion
5  Chiesa di San Domenico
7  Telecom Office
12  Universita per Stranieri
    (University for
    Foreigners)
13  APT Tourist Office
15  Palazzo Pubblico
17  Onda Blu
20  Battistero (Baptistery)
21  Duomo
22  Museo dell'Opera
    Metropolitana
    (Duomo Museum)
23  Questura (Police Station)
24  Piazza Jacopo
    della Quercia
26  Telecom Office
27  Internet Train
28  Pinacoteca Nazionale
    (National Picture Gallery)
30  Basilica di Santa
    Maria dei Servi

It's €6 to wash and dry up to 7kg at **Onda Blu** *(Via Casato di Sotto 17)*.

For an ambulance, call ☎ 118. The **public hospital** *(☎ 0577 58 51 11, Viale Bracci)* is just north of Siena at Le Scotte and the **questura** *(police headquarters; ☎ 0577 20 11 11; Via del Castoro 23)* is near the Duomo.

### Things to See

Siena's uniquely shell-shaped **Piazza del Campo** (known simply as Il Campo) has been the city's focus since the 14th century. The piazza's sloping base is formed by the nobly proportioned **Palazzo Pubblico** *(Town Hall; admission €6.50; open 10am-7pm daily mid-Mar–end Oct, 10am-5.30pm end Nov–mid-Feb, 10am-6.30pm rest of the year)*, which is also known as Palazzo Communale, considered one of Italy's most graceful Gothic buildings. Its Sienese art treasures include Simone Martini's *Maestà* and Ambrogio Lorenzetti's *Allegories of Good & Bad Government*. Paying an extra €5.50 you can enter the 102m-high **Torre del Mangia** (bell tower). A combined ticket costs €9.50.

The spectacular **Duomo** is another Gothic masterpiece, and one of the most enchanting cathedrals in Italy. Begun in 1196 and largely completed by 1215, extravagant plans for further construction were stymied by the arrival of the Black Death in 1348. Its black and white striped marble facade has a Romanesque lower section, with carvings by Giovanni Pisano, and the inlaid-marble floor features 56 panels depicting biblical stories. The marble and porphyry **pulpit** was carved by Nicola Pisano, father of Giovanni; other artworks include a bronze statue of St John the Baptist by Donatello, and statues of St Jerome and Mary Magdalene by Bernini.

A door in the north aisle leads to the **Libreria Piccolomini** *(admission €1.50)*, built by Pope Pius III to house the magnificent illustrated books of his uncle, Pope Pius II. It features frescoes by Pinturicchio and a Roman statue of the Three Graces.

The **Museo dell'Opera Metropolitana** *(Duomo Museum; admission €5.50; open 9am-7.30pm daily mid-Mar–Sept, 9am-6pm daily Oct, 9am-1.30pm daily Nov–mid-Mar)* is in Piazza del Duomo. Its many works of art formerly adorned the cathedral, including the *Maestà* by Duccio di Buoninsegna and the 12 marble statues by Giovanni Pisano, which once graced the Duomo's facade; other works include those by Ambrogio Lorenzetti, Simone Martini and Taddeo di Bartolo.

The **battistero** *(baptistry; admission €2.50; open 9am-7.30pm daily mid-Mar–Sept, 9am-6pm daily Oct, 10am-1pm & 2.30pm-5pm daily Nov–mid-Mar)* behind the cathedral, has a Gothic facade and is decorated with 15th-century frescoes. The highlight is the font by Jacopo della Quercia, with sculptures by Donatello and Ghiberti.

The 15th-century Palazzo Buonsignori houses the **Pinacoteca Nazionale** *(National Picture Gallery; admission €4; open 8.15am-7.15pm Tues-Sat, 8.30am-1.30pm Mon, 8.15am-1.15pm Sun)*, whose Sienese masterpieces include Duccio di Buoninsegna's *Madonna dei Francescani*, *Madonna col Bambino* by Simone Martini and a series of Madonnas by Ambrogio Lorenzetti.

### Places to Stay
It is always advisable to book in advance, but for August and during the Palio, it's imperative. For help with bookings try **Siena Hotels Promotion** *(☎ 0577 28 80 84; ✆ info@hotelsiena.com; Piazza San Domenico 2)*.

**Colleverde camping ground** *(☎ 0577 28 00 44, fax 0577 33 32 98; per person/tent €7.75/7.75; open late Mar-early Nov)* is 2km north of the historic centre at Strada di Scacciapensieri 47 (take bus No 3 from Piazza Gramsci).

**Guidoriccio hostel** *(☎ 0577 522 12; Via Fiorentina; B&B €16.50)* is about 3km out of the centre in Stellino. An evening meal costs €9. Take bus No 3 from Piazza Gramsci.

In the heart of the old town, **Tre Donzelle** *(☎ 0577 28 03 58, fax 0577 22 39 33; Via delle Donzelle 5; singles/doubles without bath €31/44, doubles with bath €57)* offers no-frills rooms. Nearby, the two-star **Piccolo Hotel Etruria** *(☎ 0577 28 80 88, fax 0577 28 84 61; Via delle Donzelle 3; singles without bath €39, singles/doubles/triples/quads with bath €44/73/96/119)* has large rooms and a 12.30am curfew. Space is of a premium at **Albergo La Perla** *(☎ 0577 471 44; Via delle Terme 25; singles/doubles with bath €50/65)* where it can get a little claustrophobic. Behind the town hall, **Locanda Garibaldi** *(☎ 0577 28 42 04; Via Giovanni Dupré 18; doubles/triples/quads with bath €70/89/108)* had a makeover recently so the rooms are in good nick. Its

small trattoria is reasonably priced with the set menu costing €15.

The three-star **Albergo Duomo** *(☎ 0577 28 90 88, fax 0577 430 43; Via Stalloreggi 38; singles/doubles/triples/quads with bath €104/130/171/186)* has quite pleasant rooms, some with views of the Duomo. The charming **Chiusarelli** *(☎ 0577 28 05 62, fax 0577 27 11 77; Viale Curtatone 15; singles/doubles with bath €73/109)* is well placed for drivers being near the Stadio Comunale car park, but it can get noisy on match days (usually Sunday).

Agriturismo is well organised around Siena. The tourist office can provide a list of establishments.

### Places to Eat
The ubiquitous self-service **Ciao** and fast food **Spizzico** are right on the Campo at No 77. For a more sophisticated meal, try **Il Caroccio** *(☎ 4 11 65; Via Casato di Sotto 32; meal about €30)* where the quality food is complemented by an enormous wine list. The **Ristorante da Mugalone** *(☎ 0577 28 32 35; Via dei Pellegrini 8; meal about €25)* is another good establishment for sampling local specialities.

Tiny **La Chiacchiera** *(☎ 0577 28 06 31, Costa di Sant'Antonio 4; meal about €18)*, off Via Santa Caterina, has a rustic feel with wooden stools and handwritten menus and is ideal for lunch.

There are several trattorias further north, in a quieter neighbourhood. **Da Titti** *(☎ 0577 480 87; Via di Camollia 193; meal about €15)* is one, serving standard Tuscan grub in simple surroundings.

Supermarket **La Bottega** *(Via di Città 152-6)* is centrally located, as is **Nannini Conca d'Oro** *(Banchi di Sopra 22)*, one of Siena's finest cafés and a good place to stock up on *panforte*.

### Getting There & Away
Regular Tra-In buses run from Florence to Siena, arriving at Piazza Gramsci. Buses also go to San Gimignano, Volterra and other points in Tuscany, and there's a daily bus to Rome. For Perugia, buses leave from the train station.

Siena is not on a main train line, so from Rome it is necessary to change at Chiusi and from Florence at Empoli, making buses a better alternative.

## SAN GIMIGNANO
**postcode 53037 • pop 7100**
In a region noted for its beauty, San Gimignano still manages to stand out. Characterised by its huge pockmarked towers, and in recent times by the sheer numbers of tourists, this tiny town is perched on a hill deep in the Tuscan countryside. Of an original 72 towers built as fortified homes for the town's 11th-century feuding families, 13 remain.

A veritable magnet for visitors, the best time to visit is during the week, preferably in deepest mid-winter. The Pro Loco **tourist information office** (☎ 0577 94 00 08; e prolocsg@ tin.it; Piazza del Duomo 1; open 9am-1pm & 3pm-7pm daily, to 6pm in winter) is in the town centre.

### Things to See & Do
Climb San Gimignano's tallest tower, **Torre Grossa**, off Piazza del Duomo, for a memorable view of the Tuscan hills. The tower is reached from within the **Palazzo del Popolo**, which houses the **Museo Civico**, featuring Lippo Memmi's 14th-century *Maestà*. The **Duomo**, known also as the Collegiata, has a Romanesque interior, frescoes by Ghirlandaio in the **Cappella di Santa Fina** and a particularly gruesome *Last Judgment* by Taddeo di Bartolo. The city's most-impressive piazza is **Piazza della Cisterna**, named for the 13th-century well at its centre.

### Places to Stay & Eat
San Gimignano offers few options for budget travellers. The nearest camping ground is **Il Boschetto di Piemma** (☎ 0577 94 03 52, fax 0577 94 19 82; per person/tent €4.70/5; open Easter-15 Oct), about 3km from San Gimignano at Santa Lucia. There is a bus service to the site. At the time of writing the youth hostel was closed with no scheduled reopening date, so for a cheap bed your best bet is the **Foresteria Monastero di San Girolamo** (☎ 0577 94 05 73; Via Folgore 32; B&B €25).

Hotels in town are expensive but there are numerous rooms for rent in **private homes**, and agriturismo is well organised in this area. For information, contact the tourist office. If you can afford a spacial treat, soak up the medieval ambience at **Hotel La Cisterna** (☎ 0577 94 03 28, fax 0577 94 20 80; Piazza della Cisterna 24; singles/doubles with bath €68/100).

For a plate of pasta and sip of the local wine, **Il Castello** (☎ 0577 94 08 78; Via del Castello 20; pastas about €5.50) is as good a spot as any. A fresh-produce **market** is held on Thursday morning in Piazza del Duomo.

### Getting There & Away
Regular buses link San Gimignano with Florence and Siena. They arrive at Porta San Giovanni (timetables are posted outside the tourist office). Enter through the Porta and continue straight ahead to reach Piazza del Duomo.

## CERTALDO
**postcode 50052 • pop 15,800**
Located in the Val d'Elsa between Florence and Siena, this small medieval town is definitely worth a visit. Giovanni Boccaccio, one of the fathers of the Italian language, was born here in 1313.

**Fattoria Bassetto** (☎ 0571 66 83 42; e bassetto@dedalo.com; dorm bed €21, room €36), 2km east of the town on the road to Siena, is in a former 14th-century Benedictine convent, surrounded by a garden with swimming pool.

# Umbria

Umbrians like to think of their hilly region as the green heart of Italy. Characterised by its many medieval hill towns, it is noted for its Romanesque and Gothic architecture. Towns such as Assisi, Gubbio, Spello, Spoleto, Todi and Orvieto are accessible by bus or train from Perugia, the region's capital.

## PERUGIA
**postcode 06100 • pop 158,200**
Perugia is a well-preserved medieval hill town that offers sweeping panoramas at every turn. Best known for its University for Foreigners, established in 1925, which attracts thousands of international students, the city is also famous for the Umbria Jazz Festival in July, and for chocolate.

Highlights, or lowlights, of Perugia's history, bloody even by medieval standards, include the vicious internal feuding of the Baglioni and Oddi families, wars waged against neighbours and the death of at least two popes. However, art and culture have thrived: it was the home of the painter Perugino, and Raphael, his student, also worked here.

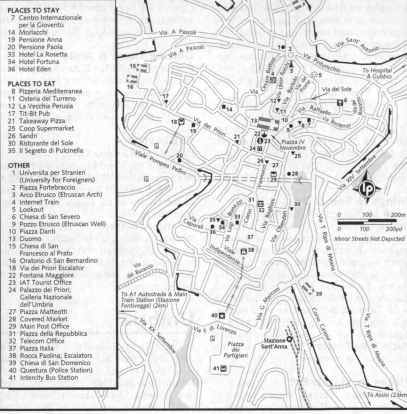

## PERUGIA

**PLACES TO STAY**
- 7 Centro Internazionale per la Gioventù
- 14 Morlacchi
- 19 Pensione Anna
- 20 Pensione Paola
- 33 Hotel La Rosetta
- 34 Hotel Fortuna
- 36 Hotel Eden

**PLACES TO EAT**
- 8 Pizzeria Mediterranea
- 11 Osteria del Turreno
- 12 La Vecchia Perusia
- 17 Tit-Bit Pub
- 21 Takeaway Pizza
- 25 Coop Supermarket
- 26 Sandri
- 30 Ristorante del Sole
- 35 Il Segreto di Pulcinella

**OTHER**
- 1 Universita per Stranieri (University for Foreigners)
- 2 Piazza Fortebraccio
- 3 Arco Etrusco (Etruscan Arch)
- 4 Internet Train
- 5 Lookout
- 6 Chiesa di San Severo
- 9 Pozzo Etrusco (Etruscan Well)
- 10 Piazza Danti
- 13 Duomo
- 15 Chiesa di San Francesco al Prato
- 16 Oratorio di San Bernardino
- 18 Via dei Priori Escalator
- 22 Fontana Maggiore
- 23 IAT Tourist Office
- 24 Palazzo dei Priori; Galleria Nazionale dell'Umbria
- 27 Piazza Matteotti
- 28 Covered Market
- 29 Main Post Office
- 31 Piazza della Repubblica
- 32 Telecom Office
- 37 Piazza Italia
- 38 Rocca Paolina; Escalators
- 39 Chiesa di San Domenico
- 40 Questura (Police Station)
- 41 Intercity Bus Station

## Orientation & Information

Perugia's hub is the old town's main drag, Corso Vannucci, running north-south from Piazza Italia, through Piazza della Repubblica and ending at Piazza IV Novembre and the Duomo.

The **IAT tourist office** (☎ 075 573 64 58, fax 075 573 93 86; ℮ info@iat.perugia.it; Piazza IV Novembre 3; open 8.30am-1.30pm & 3.30pm-6.30pm Mon-Sat, 9am-1pm Sun) is opposite the Duomo. The main **post office** is in Piazza Matteotti and **Internet Train** (Via Ulisse Rocchi 30) has cheap Internet access.

The monthly magazine Viva Perugia: What, Where, When (€0.52 at the newsstands) has events listings and other useful information for travellers.

## Things to See

Perugia's austere **Duomo** has an unfinished facade in red-and-white marble, while inside are frescoes and decorations by artists from the 15th to 18th centuries, as well as the Virgin Mary's wedding ring, which is unveiled every 30 July. The **Palazzo dei Priori**, nearby on Corso Vannucci, is a rambling 13th-century palace which houses the impressively frescoed **Sala dei Notari** and the **Galleria Nazionale dell'Umbria**, with works by Perugino and Fra Angelico. Between the two buildings, in Piazza IV Novembre, is the 13th-century **Fontana Maggiore**, designed by Fra Bevignate in 1278 and carved by Nicola and Giovanni Pisano.

At the other end of Corso Vannucci is the **Rocca Paolina** (Paolina Fortress), the ruins of a massive 16th-century fortress. Built by Pope Paul III over a medieval quarter formerly inhabited by some of Perugia's most powerful families, notably the Baglioni, the fortress was destroyed by the Perugians after Italian unification in 1860. A series of escalators pass through the underground ruins, which are often used to host exhibitions.

Raphael's fresco *Trinity with Saints*, some say his first, can be seen in the **Chiesa di San Severo**, on Piazza San Severo, along with frescoes by Perugino.

Etruscan remains in Perugia include the **Arco Etrusco** (Etruscan Arch), near the university, and the **Pozzo Etrusco** (Etruscan Well), near the Duomo.

## Places to Stay

Perugia has a good selection of reasonably priced hotels, but you could have problems if you arrive unannounced in July or August.

**Centro Internazionale per la Gioventù** (☎/fax 075 572 28 80; ℮ ostello@ostello .perugia.it; *Via Bontempi 13; dorm bed €12; closed 9.30am-4pm daily; closed mid-Dec–mid-Jan*) is a well-located non-HI place. Sheets (for the entire stay) are an extra €1.50. Its TV room has a frescoed ceiling and the terrace has some of Perugia's best views.

**Pensione Anna** (☎/fax 075 573 63 04; *Via dei Priori 48; singles/doubles without bath €30/46, with bath €40/62*), off Corso Vannucci, is full of character and antiques, while the two-star **Morlacchi** (☎/fax 075 572 03 19; *Via Tiberi 2; singles without bath €40, singles/doubles with bath €51/60*) nearby is a little smarter but similarly priced.

**Pensione Paola** (☎ 075 572 38 16; *Via della Canapina 5; singles/doubles without bath €28/42*) is down the escalator from Via dei Priori, and offers eight rooms with the use of a kitchen. Off the Piazza Italia end of Corso Vannucci, **Hotel Eden** (☎ 075 572 81 02, fax 075 572 03 42; *Via Cesare Caporali 9; singles/doubles with bath €36/57*) is excellent value with its blazingly white minimalist rooms. Around the corner at the elegant **Hotel Fortuna** (☎ 075 572 28 45, fax 075 573 50 40; *Via Bonazzi 19; singles/doubles with bath €79/114*) the rooms are wonderful. And, in a similar price-range, **La Rosetta** (☎/fax 075 572 08 41; *Piazza Italia 19; singles/doubles with bath €76/115*) provides palatial period-detailed rooms.

## Places to Eat

Being a student town, Perugia offers many budget eating options. Good places for pizza include **Tit-Bit Pub** (☎ 075 573 54 97; *Via dei Priori 105; pizza meal about €10*); **Il Segreto di Pulcinella** (☎ 075 573 62 84; *Via Larga 8; pizza from €5.50*); and **Pizzeria Mediterranea** (☎ 075 572 63 12; *Piazza Piccinino 11/12; pizza from €4.20*). There's also a tiny but popular **pizza takeaway** (*Via dei Priori 3*), near the Duomo.

**Osteria del Turreno** (☎ 075 572 19 76; *Piazza Danti 16; meal about €10*) serves panini as well as simple, hearty fare. **La Vecchia Perusia** (☎ 075 572 59 00; *Via Ulisse Rocchi 9; meal about €20*) is a little more pricey, specialising in local cuisine. For unforgettable panoramic views and an equally stunning antipasto spread, head for **Ristorante del Sole** (☎ 075 573 50 31; *Via Oberdan 28; meal about €25*).

**Sandri** (*Corso Vannucci 32*), by now a Perugian institution, has the best cakes in town, as well as free chocolate nibbles at the bar. To buy your own supplies of chocolate and other edibles there's a **Coop supermarket** (*Piazza Matteotti 15*), near the **covered market**.

## Getting There & Away

Perugia is not on the main Rome–Florence railway line, but there are some direct trains from both cities. Most services require a change, either at Foligno (from Rome) or Terontola (from Florence). Intercity buses leave from Piazza dei Partigiani (at the bottom of the Rocca Paolina escalators) for Rome, Fiumicino airport, Florence, Siena and towns throughout Umbria, including Assisi, Gubbio and nearby Lake Trasimeno. Timetables for trains and buses are available from the tourist office.

## Getting Around

The main train station is a couple of kilometres downhill from the historical centre. Catch any bus heading for Piazza Italia. Tickets cost €0.80 and can be bought from the ticket office on your left as you leave the station.

Most of the historical centre is closed to normal traffic, but tourists are allowed to drive to their hotels. It is probably wiser, however, not to do this, as driving in central Perugia is a nightmare. The solution is to park at one of the large car parks downhill, and take the pedestrian elevator up to the old

**ITALY**

centre. There is a supervised car park at Piazza dei Partigiani, from where you can catch the Rocca Paolina escalator to Piazza Italia, and there are two major car parks at the foot of the Via dei Priori escalator.

## ASSISI
### postcode 06081 • pop 25,500

Birthplace and spiritual home of the animal world's favourite saint, Assisi is a major port of call for millions of visitors who swarm to retrace the footsteps of St Francis. Somehow this small town perched halfway up Mt Subasio manages to cope while maintaining an air of tranquillity, particularly in the lanes off the central streets.

In September 1997, a strong earthquake rocked the town, causing considerable damage to the upper church of the Basilica di San Francesco (St Francis' Basilica), but five years on and it's business as usual, with little sign remaining of any damage.

The APT **tourist office** (☎ 075 81 25 34; e info@iat.assisi.pg.it; Piazza del Comune; open 8am-2pm & 3pm-6pm Mon-Fri, 9am-1pm & 3pm-6pm Sat, 9am-1pm Sun) has plenty of useful information.

## Things to See

If you're coming to Assisi to visit the religious sites, which you almost certainly are, look the part, as dress rules are applied rigidly – absolutely no shorts, miniskirts or low-cut dresses or tops are allowed.

The **Basilica di San Francesco** is composed of two churches, one built on top of the other. The lower church is decorated with frescoes by Simone Martini, Cimabue and a pupil of Giotto, and contains the crypt where St Francis is buried. The Italian Gothic upper church has a stone-vaulted roof, and was decorated by the great painters of the 13th and 14th centuries, in particular Giotto and Cimabue. The frescoes in the apse and entrance received the most damage in the 1997 earthquake.

The impressively frescoed 13th-century **Basilica di Santa Chiara** (St Clare's Basilica) contains the remains of St Clare, friend of St Francis and the founder of the Order of Poor Clares.

For spectacular views of the valley below, head to the massive 14th-century **Rocca Maggiore** fortress. You'll easily be able to spot the huge **Basilica di Santa Maria degli Angeli**, built around the first Franciscan

monastery. St Francis died in its **Cappella del Transito** in 1226.

## Places to Stay & Eat

Assisi is well geared for tourists and there are numerous budget hotels and *affittacamere* (rooms for rent). Peak periods, when you will need to book well in advance, are Easter, August and September, and the Feast of St Francis on 3 and 4 October. The tourist office has a full list of affittacamere and religious institutions.

The small HI **Ostello della Pace** (☎/fax 075 81 67 67; Via Valecchi 177; B&B €13) is on the bus line between Santa Maria degli Angeli and Assisi. The non-HI hostel **Fontemaggio** (☎ 075 81 36 36, fax 075 81 37 49; Via Eremo delle Carceri 8; dorm bed €18.50) also has camping facilities. From Piazza Matteotti, at the far end of town from the basilica, it's a 30-minute uphill walk along Via Eremo delle Carceri.

Heading into town from Piazza Matteotti you'll pass **Pensione La Rocca** (☎/fax 075 81 22 84; Vicolo della Fortezza; singles/doubles with bath €33.50/40) in a quiet corner. Some of its sunny rooms have views of the valley below. In the heart of town, the three-star **Dei Priori** (☎ 075 81 22 37, fax 075 81 68 04; e hpriori@tiscalinet.it; Corso Mazzini 15; singles/doubles with bath €77/114, superior doubles €150) has stylish carpeted rooms.

For a cheap slice of pizza, head for **Pizza Vincenzo**, just off Piazza del Comune at Via San Rufina 1a. A good self-service place in the same area is **Il Foro Romano** (Via Portico 23). **Il Pozzo Romano** (☎ 075 81 30 57; Via Santa Agnese 10; set menu €12.50), off Piazza Santa Chiara, serves simple dishes and is good value for money. To dine under ancient architraves try **Dal Carro** (☎ 075 81 33 07; Vicolo dei Nepis 2; set menu €12.50), off Corso Mazzini, where the pasta dishes win good reviews. If you want to splash out, the stylish **Medio Evo** (☎ 81 30 68; Via Arco dei Priori 4; meal about €30) is one of Assisi's top restaurants.

## Getting There & Away

Buses connect Assisi with Perugia, Foligno and other local towns, leaving from Piazza Matteotti. Buses for Rome and Florence leave from Piazzale dell'Unità d'Italia. Assisi's train station is in the valley, in the suburb of Santa Maria degli Angeli. It's on the same line as Perugia and a shuttle bus runs between Piazza Matteotti and the station.

## ANCONA
postcode 60100 • pop 98,100

Ancona, a largely unattractive and industrial port city in the Marches, is unlikely to be high on your wish list, but you may well find yourself here waiting for a ferry to Croatia, Greece or Turkey.

The easiest way to get from the train station to the port is by bus No 1. The main **APT office** (☎ 071 35 89 91, fax 071 358 99 29; e aptancona@tin.it; Via Thaon de Revel 4; open 9am-2pm & 3pm-6pm Mon-Fri, 9am-1pm & 3pm-6pm Sat, 9am-1pm Sun; opening hours shorter in winter) is out of the way. Stazione Marittima is home to a **branch office** (☎ 071 20 11 83), which opens in the summer months.

For postal matters go to the **main post office** (Largo XXIV Maggio; open 8.15am-7pm Mon-Sat) and for the Internet try **Internet Point** (Corso Carlo Alberto 82).

### Places to Stay & Eat
If you're stuck here, there are a couple of options for dining and accommodation. Many backpackers choose to bunk down at the ferry terminal, although the city has many cheap hotels. The relatively new **Ostello della Gioventù** (☎/fax 071 422 57; Via Lamaticci 7; dorm bed €12) is not far from the train station, while for a bite to eat the **Caffé Lombardo** (Corso Giuseppe Mazzini 130; sandwiches from €2.60) is a popular spot. **Osteria del Pozzo** (☎ 071 207 39 69; Via Bonda 2; meal about €16), just off Piazza del Plebiscito, also serves good food at reasonable prices.

### Getting There & Away
Buses depart from Piazza Cavour for towns throughout the Marches region. Rome is served by **Marozzi** (☎ 071 280 23 98). Ancona is on the Bologna–Lecce train line and thus easily accessible from major towns throughout Italy. It is also linked to Rome via Foligno.

Ferry operators have information booths at the ferry terminal, off Piazza Kennedy. Most lines offer discounts on return fares. Prices listed here are for one-way deck class in high season.

Companies include **Superfast** (☎ 071 207 02 40) to Patras in Greece (€78), **Minoan**

**Lines** (☎ 071 20 17 08) to Igoumenitsa and Patras (€68) and **Adriatica** (☎ 071 20 49 15) to Durrës in Albania (€86) and to Split in Croatia (€47).

## URBINO
postcode 61029 • pop 6000

This town in the Marches can be difficult to reach but, as the pride of the Marches, it is worth the effort. Birthplace of Raphael and Bramante, Urbino is still a centre of art, culture and learning.

The **IAT tourist office** (☎ 0722 26 13, fax 0722 24 41; Piazza Duca Federico 35; open 9am-1pm Mon-Sat) is conveniently situated in the centre of town.

To stock up on cash the **Banca Nazionale del Lavoro** (Via Vittorio Veneto) has an ATM, as do most banks spread about the town centre. There is a **main post office** (Via Bramante 18) and **Telecom offices** (Via Puccinotti 4 • Piazza San Francesco 1).

### Things to See
Urbino's main sight is the dominating **Palazzo Ducale** (admission €4.15; open 8.30am-7.15pm Tues-Sun, 8.30am-2pm Mon), designed by Laurana and completed in 1482. The best view is from Corso Garibaldi to the west, from where you can appreciate the size of the building and see its towers and loggias. Enter the palace from Piazza Duca Federico and visit the **Galleria Nazionale delle Marche**, featuring works by Raphael, Paolo Uccello and Verrocchio. Also visit the **Casa di Raffaello** (admission €2.60; Via Raffaello 5), where the artist Raphael was born, and the **Oratorio di San Giovanni Battista** (admission €1.55), with 15th-century frescoes by the Salimbeni brothers.

### Places to Stay & Eat
Urbino is a major university town and most cheap beds are taken by students during the school year. The tourist office has a full list of affittacamere. You could try **Pensione Fosca** (☎/fax 0722 32 96 22; Via Raffaello 61; singles/doubles without bath €21/35) with its simple rooms.

There are numerous bars around Piazza della Repubblica in the town centre and near the Palazzo Ducale which sell good panini. Go to **Pizzeria Galli** (Via Vittorio Veneto 19), for takeaway pizza by the slice, or sit down at **Ristorante Da Franco** (☎ 0722 24 92; Via

ITALY

del Poggio 1; meal about €10), which has a good value for money self-service section.

## Getting There & Away

There is no train service to Urbino, but it is connected by Soget and Bucci buses Monday to Friday to cities including Ancona, Pesaro and Arezzo. There is a bus link to the train station at the town of Fossato di Vico, on the Rome–Ancona line, or take a bus to Pesaro which is on the Bologna-Lecce line. There are also buses to Rome twice a day. All buses arrive at Piazza Mercatale, down Via Mazzini from Piazza della Repubblica. The tourist office has timetables for all bus services.

# Southern Italy

Although noticeably poorer than the north, the land of the *mezzogiorno* (midday sun) is rich in history and cultural traditions. The attractions of the area are straightforward: the people seem more passionate; myths, legends and history are intertwined; and the food is magnificent. Campania, Apulia and Basilicata are relatively untouristed in many parts and Naples is like no other city on earth.

## NAPLES

**postcode 80100 • pop 1.5 million**
Beautifully positioned on the Bay of Naples and overshadowed by Mt Vesuvius, the capital of the Campania region, is one of the most densely populated cities in Europe. Love it or hate it, Naples is a truly unforgettable city, with an energy that will either sweep you along or swamp you.

## Orientation

Both the Stazione Centrale and the main bus terminal are just off the vast Piazza Garibaldi. Naples is divided into *quartieri* (districts). The main shopping thoroughfare into the historical centre, Spaccanapoli, is Corso Umberto I, which heads southwest from Piazza Garibaldi to Piazza Bovio. West on the bay are Santa Lucia and Mergellina, both fashionable and picturesque and quite a contrast with the chaotic historical centre. In the hills overlooking the bay is the Vomero district, a natural balcony across the city and bay to Vesuvius.

## Information

**Tourist Offices** The **EPT office** (☎ 081 26 87 79; open 8am-8pm Mon-Sat, 8am-2pm Sun) at the train station, will make hotel bookings and has information on the region. Ask for *Qui Napoli* (Here Naples), published monthly in English and Italian, which lists events in the city, as well as information about transport and other services.

There's a good **AAST office** (☎ 081 552 33 28; open 9am-8pm Mon-Sat, 9am-3pm Sun) in Piazza del Gesù Nuovo. There is a student travel centre, **CTS** (☎ 552 79 60; Via Mezzocannone 25).

**Money** There are plenty of foreign-exchange booths throughout the city, which often offer lower rates than the banks. Banks with ATMs are plentiful, too. **Every Tour** (☎ 081 551 85 64; Piazza Municipio 5) is the agency for American Express.

**Post & Communications** The **main post office** (Piazza G Matteotti; open 8.15am-7pm Mon-Sat), is off Via Armando Diaz. There is a **Telecom office** (Via A Depretis 40; open 9am-1pm & 2pm-5.30pm Mon-Fri). **Aexis Telecom** (Piazza Gesù Nuovo 52; open 8am-10pm daily) has phones, faxes and Internet access (€3 per hour).

**Laundry** Near Montesanto metro station, **My Beautiful Laundrette** (Via Montesanto 2) charges €3.10 for a 6kg wash and €3.10 for drying.

**Medical & Emergency Services** For an ambulance call ☎ 081 752 06 96 or ☎ 112. Each city district has a Guardia Medica (after hours medical service); check in *Qui Napoli* for details. The **Ospedale Loreto-Mare** (☎ 081 254 27 01; Via A Vespucci) is on the waterfront, near the station. There's a **pharmacy** (open 8am-8pm daily) in the central station.

The **questura** (police station; ☎ 081 794 11 11; Via Medina 75) is just off Via A Diaz, and has an office for foreigners where you can report thefts and so on. To report a stolen car call ☎ 081 794 14 35.

**Dangers & Annoyances** The city's home-grown mafia, the Camorra, is a pervasive local force, but one that won't affect you as a tourist. However, the petty crime rate in Naples is very

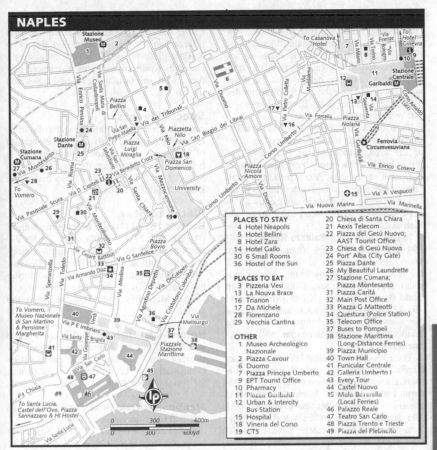

**NAPLES**

| PLACES TO STAY | |
| --- | --- |
| 4 | Hotel Neapolis |
| 5 | Hotel Bellini |
| 8 | Hotel Zara |
| 14 | Hotel Gallo |
| 30 | 6 Small Rooms |
| 36 | Hostel of the Sun |

| PLACES TO EAT | |
| --- | --- |
| 3 | Pizzeria Vesi |
| 13 | La Nouva Brace |
| 16 | Trianon |
| 17 | Da Michele |
| 28 | Fiorenzano |
| 29 | Vecchia Cantina |

| OTHER | |
| --- | --- |
| 1 | Museo Archeologico Nazionale |
| 2 | Piazza Cavour |
| 6 | Duomo |
| 7 | Piazza Principe Umberto |
| 9 | EPT Tourist Office |
| 10 | Pharmacy |
| 11 | Piazza Garibaldi |
| 12 | Urban & Intercity Bus Station |
| 15 | Hospital |
| 18 | Vineria del Corso |
| 19 | CTS |
| 20 | Chiesa di Santa Chiara |
| 21 | Aexis Telecom |
| 22 | Piazza del Gesú Nuovo; AAST Tourist Office |
| 23 | Chiesa di Gesú Nuovo |
| 24 | Port' Alba (City Gate) |
| 25 | Piazza Dante |
| 26 | My Beautiful Laundrette |
| 27 | Stazione Cumana; Piazza Montesanto |
| 31 | Piazza Carità |
| 32 | Main Post Office |
| 33 | Piazza G Matteotti |
| 34 | Questura (Police Station) |
| 35 | Telecom Office |
| 37 | Buses to Pompeii |
| 38 | Stazione Marittima (Long-Distance Ferries) |
| 39 | Piazza Municipio |
| 40 | Town Hall |
| 41 | Funicular Centrale |
| 42 | Galleria Umberto I |
| 43 | Every Tour |
| 44 | Castel Nuovo |
| 45 | Molo Beverello (Local Ferries) |
| 46 | Palazzo Reale |
| 47 | Teatro San Carlo |
| 48 | Piazza Trento e Trieste |
| 49 | Piazza del Plebiscito |

high, and bag-snatchers and pickpockets abound. Car theft is also a major problem. Keep your wits about you at night near the station, Piazza Dante, the area west of Via Toledo and as far north as Piazza Caritá.

Naples' legendary traffic means you need the power of prayer when crossing roads.

## Things to See & Do

If it's still available, a good investment is the **Napoli artecard** (☎ 800 60 06 01; ⓦ www.napoliartecard.com) which gives access to six museums at reduced rates and public transport for €13. You can buy it at the airport, train and metro stations, as well as at selected museums.

Spaccanapoli, the historic centre of Naples, is a great place to start your sight-

seeing. From the station and Corso Umberto I turn right onto Via Mezzocannone, which will take you to Via Benedetto Croce, the bustling main street of the quarter. To the left is spacious Piazza del Gesú Nuovo, with the 15th-century rusticated facade of **Chiesa di Gesú Nuovo** and the 14th-century **Chiesa di Santa Chiara**, restored to its original Gothic-Provençal style after it was severely damaged by bombing during WWII. The beautifully tiled **Chiostro delle Clarisse** (*Nuns' Cloisters; admission €3.10; open 9.30am-1pm & 2pm-5.30pm Mon-Fri, 9.30am-1pm Sat*) are also worth visiting.

The **Duomo** has a 19th-century facade but was built by the Angevin kings at the end of the 13th century, on the site of an earlier basilica. Inside is the **Cappella di San Gennaro**,

**ITALY**

which contains the head of St Januarius (the city's patron saint) and two vials of his congealed blood. The saint is said to have saved the city from plague, volcanic eruptions and other disasters. Every year the faithful gather to pray for a miracle, namely that the blood will liquefy and save the city from further disaster (see under Special Events, later) – if you're in town, don't miss it.

Turn off Via Duomo onto **Via dei Tribunali**, one of the more characteristic streets of the area, and head for Piazza Dante, through the 17th-century **Port'Alba**, one of the gates to the city. Via Roma, the most fashionable street in old Naples, heads to the left (becoming Via Toledo) and ends at Piazza Trento e Trieste and the **Piazza del Plebiscito**.

In the piazza is the **Palazzo Reale** (*☎ 081 794 40 21; admission €4.50; open 9am-8pm Thur-Tues)*, the former official residence of the Bourbon and Savoy kings, now a museum. Just off the piazza is the **Teatro San Carlo** (*☎ 081 797 21 11, box office ☎ 081 797 23 31; W www.teatrosancarlo.it)*, one of the most-famous opera houses in the world thanks to its perfect acoustics and lavish interior.

The 13th-century **Castel Nuovo** overlooks Naples' ferry port. The early-Renaissance triumphal arch commemorates the entry of Alfonso I of Aragon into Naples in 1443. It is possible to visit the **Museo Civico** (*☎ 081 795 20 03; admission €5.50; open 9am-7pm Mon-Sat)* in the castle. Situated southwest along the waterfront at Santa Lucia is the **Castel dell'Ovo**, originally a Norman castle, which is surrounded by a tiny fishing village, the **Borgo Marinaro**.

The **Museo Archeologico Nazionale** (*☎ 081 44 01 66; Piazza 17; admission €6.50; open 9am-8pm Wed-Mon)*, north of Piazza Dante, contains one of the most important collections of Greco-Roman artefacts in the world, mainly the rich collection of the Farnese family, and the art treasures discovered at Pompeii and Herculaneum. Don't forget to book a (free) tour to see the *gabinetto segreto* (secret cabinet), which may well leave your cheeks (facial) flushed.

Catch the Funicolare Centrale (funicular), on Via Toledo, to the relative tranquility of **Vomero** and the Certosa di San Martino, a 14th-century Carthusian monastery, rebuilt in

the 17th century in Neapolitan-baroque style. It houses the **Museo Nazionale di San Martino** *(Piazza San Martino 5; admission €6; open 8.30am-7.30pm Tues-Sun)*. The monastery's church is worth visiting, plus its terraced gardens, with spectacular views of Naples and the bay.

### Special Events
Neapolitans really get into the spirit of things, especially religious festivals. The celebration of St Januarius, the patron saint of the city, is held three times a year (the first Sunday in May, 19 September and 16 December) in the Duomo, and it's a must-see.

### Places to Stay
**Hostels** The HI Ostello Mergellina Napoli (*☎ 081 761 23 46; Salita della Grotta 23; dorm bed €13.50; open year-round)* is modern, safe and soulless, with breakfast included. Even with 200 beds, it fills up during busy periods. To get there take the Metropolitana to Mergellina and follow the sign to the hostel.

**Hotels** Most of the cheap hotels are near the station and Piazza Garibaldi in a rather unsavoury area. You can ask the tourist office at the station to recommend or book a room for you (let them know your budget though).

***Stazione Centrale Area*** The following are safe and offer decent accommodation.

**Hotel Zara** (*☎ 081 28 71 25; e hotelzar@ tin.it; Via Firenze 81; singles/doubles/triples without bath €26/47/73, doubles/triples with bath €57/83)* is clean, welcoming and has a kitchen.

**Hotel Ginevra** (*☎ 081 28 32 10, fax 081 554 17 57; e info@hotelginevra.it; Via Genova 116; singles/doubles/triples/quads without bath €25/40/66/65, with bath €40/50/70/80)*, near the station, is reliable and well-kept.

The **Casanova Hotel** (*☎ 081 26 82 87; Corso Garibaldi 333; singles/doubles without bath €18/39, with bath €26/52)* sounds like a brothel, but it's quiet, safe and friendly in a good way.

**Hotel Gallo** (*☎ 081 20 05 12, fax 081 20 18 49; Via Spaventa 11; singles/doubles/triples with bath €57/83/109)*, to the left of the train station, has nice clean rooms with breakfast.

**Around Spaccanapoli** The excellent **6 Small Rooms** (☎ 081 790 13 78; ⓔ info@ at6smallrooms.com; Via Diodato Lioy 18; dorm bed €15) is a friendly and sociable hostel, with cheery rooms, spacious kitchen (breakfast included) and great word-of-mouth from many travellers. Ask about the 'beer witch' if you're feeling thirsty.

**Hotel Bellini** (☎ 081 45 69 96, fax 081 29 22 56; Via San Paolo 44; singles/doubles with bath €42/68) has well-appointed rooms with TV, fridge and phone, and a central location.

**Hotel Neapolis** (☎ 081 442 08 15, fax 081 442 08 19; ⓔ informazioni@hotelneapolis .com; Via San Francesco del Giudice 13; singles/doubles/triples/quads with bath €73/ 114/124/145) is a swanky new hotel in the old quarter, with excellent rooms with all amenities, including personal computers.

**Stazione Marittima Area** The new **Hostel of The Sun** (☎/fax 081 420 63 93; ⓦ www .hostelnapoli.com; Via Melsurgo 15; dorm bed €16, doubles with/without bath €61/ 45) is close to the port, but on the 7th floor. It's tidy and laundry facilities are available.

**Vomero** Just near the funicular station, **Pensione Margherita** (☎ 081 556 70 44; Via D Cimarosa 29; singles/doubles with bath €32/58) is a decent place (some rooms have bay views). Initially you'll need a coin for the lift.

## Places to Eat
Naples is the home of pasta and pizza. A true Neapolitan pizza, topped with fresh tomatoes, oregano, basil and garlic, will leave other pizzas looking decidedly wrong. Try *calzone*, a stuffed version of pizza, or *mozzarella in carozza* (mozzarella deep-fried in bread), which is sold at street stalls, along with *misto di frittura* (deep-fried vegetables). Don't leave town without trying the *sfogliatelle* (light, flaky pastry filled with ricotta).

**Restaurants** There are numerous places to eat in and around Naples' centre.

**City Centre** Reputedly the best pizza in Naples (and therefore the world) is at **Da Michele** (☎ 081 553 92 04; Via Cesare Sersale 1; pizza €5-7). You can test this by taking a number and waiting for a bubbling,

sizzling masterpiece. **Trianon** (☎ 081 553 94 26; Via Pietro Colletta 46; pizza €5-10) near Via Tribunali, is also great, with a wider selection and marble-topped tables. **La Nouva Brace** (☎ 081 26 12 60; Via Spaventa 14; tourist menu €8.50) is very easy on the pocket, and has tasty local dishes, plus poetry (in dialect) on the walls. **Vecchia Cantina** (☎ 081 552 02 26; Via San Nicola alla Carita; meal about €12) has a convivial atmosphere with great pasta dishes (the pasta with zucchini is delicious – €4.50). **Pizzeria Vesi** (Via Tribunali 388; pizza €4.50-12) is a homy, good-value place in the old quarter, with locals flocking to enjoy both sit-down and takeaway delights.

**Mergellina & Vomero** Neapolitans often head for the area around Piazza Sannazzaro, southwest of the centre (handy to the HI hostel), for pizza. **Pizzeria da Pasqualino** (☎ 081 68 15 24; Piazza Sannazzaro 79; meal about €17) has outdoor tables (a tad noisy at times) and serves well-liked pizza, seafood and yummy tidbits for snackers. In Vomero, **Cantina di Sica** (☎ 081 556 75 20; Via Bernini 17; meal about €20) has excellent local dishes – try the *spaghetti alle vongole e pomodorini* (spaghetti with clams and cherry tomatoes).

**Food Stalls** Heavenly fried goodies are on offer at bargain prices at **Fiorenzano** (Piazza Montesanto). Naples has many **alimentari** (grocery shops) and **food stalls** scattered throughout the city.

## Entertainment
The monthly *Qui Napoli* and the local newspapers are the only real guides to what's on. In May the city organises Maggio dei Monumenti, with concerts and cultural events (mostly free) around town. Ask at the tourist office for details. The **Teatro San Carlo** (☎ 081 797 21 11, box office ☎ 081 797 23 31; ⓦ www.teatrosancarlo.it; tickets from €8) has year-round performances of opera, ballet and concerts and is definitely worth visiting.

There are a handful of good **bars** in Piazza Gesú Nuovo, which go off on weekend nights and then provide daytime coffee to ease the hangover.

**Vineria del Corso** (Via Paladino 8a) is a great little bar, with good lighting, charming decor and low-key electronica played at a polite volume. The wine list's good, too.

## Getting There & Away

**Air** Some 5km northeast of the city centre, **Capodichino airport** (☎ 081 789 61 11, ☎ 800 88 87 77; Viale Umberto Maddalena) has connections to most Italian and several European cities. Bus No 14 or 14R leaves from Piazza Garibaldi every 30 minutes for the airport (20 minutes).

**Bus** There are buses that leave from Piazza Garibaldi, just outside the train station, for destinations including Salerno, the Amalfi Coast, Caserta and Bari, Lecce and Brindisi in Apulia. Signage is limited, so you might have to ask at the booths to get the necessary information.

**Train** Naples is a major rail-transport centre for the south, and regular trains for most major Italian cities arrive and depart from the Stazione Centrale. There are over two dozen trains daily for Rome.

**Car & Motorcycle** Driving in Naples is not recommended. The traffic is chaotic, car and motorcycle theft is rife, and the street plan does not lend itself to easy navigation. However, the city is easily accessible from Rome on the A1. The Naples–Pompeii–Salerno road (A3) connects with the coastal road to Sorrento and the Amalfi Coast.

**Boat** Traghetti (ferries), aliscafi (hydrofoils) and navi veloci (fast ships) leave for Sorrento and the islands of Capri, Ischia and Procida from Molo Beverello, in front of Castel Nuovo. Some hydrofoils leave for the bay islands from Mergellina, and ferries for Ischia and Procida also leave from Pozzuoli. All operators have offices at the various ports from which they leave.

Hydrofoils cost around double the price of ferries but take half the time.

**Tirrenia** (☎ 199 12 31 99) operates ferries to Palermo and Cagliari while **Siremar** (☎ 081 580 03 40, 199 12 31 99) services the Aeolian Islands. Ferries leave from the Stazione Marittima on Molo Angioino, next to Molo Beverello (see the Getting There & Away sections under Sicily and Sardinia). **SNAV** (☎ 081 761 23 48) runs regular ferries and, in summer, hydrofoils to the Aeolian Islands.

## Getting Around

You can make your way around Naples by bus, tram, Metropolitana (underground) and funicular. City buses leave from Piazza Garibaldi in front of the central station bound for the centre of Naples and Mergellina. Tickets cost €0.77 for 1½ hours (€2.32 for 24 hours) and are valid for buses, trams, the Metropolitana and funicular services. Useful buses include No 14 or 14R to the airport; the R1 to Piazza Dante; the R3 to Mergellina; and No 110 from Piazza Garibaldi to Piazza Cavour and the archaeological museum. Tram No 1 leaves from east of Stazione Centrale for the city centre. To get to Molo Beverello and the ferry terminal from the train station, take bus No R2 or the M1.

The Metropolitana station is downstairs at the train station. Trains head west to Mergellina, stopping at Piazza Cavour, Piazza Amedeo and the funicular to Vomero, and then head on to the Campi Flegrei and Pozzuoli. Another line, still under construction in parts, will connect Piazza Garibaldi, the cathedral, Piazzas Bovio, Carita and Dante, the Museo Archeologico Nazionale and Piazza Vanvitelli.

The main funicular connecting the city centre with Vomero is the Funicolare Centrale in Piazza Duca d'Aosta, next to Galleria Umberto I, on Via Toledo.

The Ferrovia Circumvesuviana operates trains for Herculaneum, Pompeii and Sorrento. The station is about 400m southwest of Stazione Centrale, in Corso Garibaldi (take the underpass from Stazione Centrale). The Ferrovia Cumana and the Circumflegrea, based at Stazione Cumana in Piazza Montesanto, operate services to Pozzuoli, Baia and Cumae every 20 minutes.

## AROUND NAPLES

From Naples it's only a short distance to the **Campi Flegrei** (Phlegraean Fields) of volcanic lakes and mud baths, which inspired both Homer and Virgil in their writings. Unavoidably part of suburban Naples today, the area is dirty and overdeveloped, but still worth a half-day trip. The Greek colony of **Cumae** is certainly worth visiting, particularly to see the Cave of the Cumaean Sybil, home of one of the ancient world's greatest oracles. Also in the area is **Lake Avernus**, the mythical entrance to the underworld, and **Baia** with its submerged Roman ruins visible from a glass-bottomed boat.

Reached by CPTC bus from Naples' Piazza Garibaldi or by train from the Stazione Centrale is the wonderful **Palazzo Reale** (☎ 0823 44 74 47; admission €6.50; open 9am-7pm Tues-Sun) at Caserta, AKA Reggia di Caserta. Built in the 18th century under the Bourbon king Charles III, this imposing 1200-room palace is set in elegant gardens.

## Pompeii & Herculaneum

Buried under a layer of lapilli (burning fragments of pumice stone) during the devastating eruption of Mt Vesuvius in AD 79, **Pompeii** (☎ 857 53 47; Via Villa dei Misteri 2; admission €10, with Herculaneum €18 for 3 days; open 8.30am-7.30pm Apr-Oct & 8.30am-5pm Nov-Mar) provides a truly fascinating insight into the lives of ancient Romans. Once a resort town for wealthy Romans, the vast ruins include impressive temples, a forum, one of the largest-known Roman amphitheatres, and streets lined with shops and luxurious houses. Many of the site's original mosaics and frescoes are housed in Naples' Museo Archeologico Nazionale (see Things to See & Do under Naples, earlier). The exception is the Villa dei Misteri, where the frescoes remain in situ. Various houses and shops are closed, and details are provided at the entrance to the site. Bring a hat or umbrella, depending on the weather.

There are **tourist offices** (☎ 081 850 72 55; Via Sacra 1) in the new town, and just outside the excavations (toll free ☎ 800 01 33 50; Piazza Porta Marina Inferiore 12), near the Porta Marina entrance. Both offer information, notes on guided tours and a simple map.

Catch the Ferrovia Circumvesuviana train from Naples and get off at the Pompeii Scavi-Villa dei Misteri stop; the Porta Marina entrance is nearby.

**Herculaneum** (Ercolano; Corso Resina; admission €10, with Pompeii €18 for 3 days; open 8.30am-7.30pm, last entrance 6pm, Apr-Oct, 8.30am-5pm, last entrance 3.30pm, Nov-Mar) is closer to Naples and is also a good point from which to visit Mt Vesuvius. Legend says the city was founded by Hercules. First Greek, then Roman, it was also destroyed by the AD 79 eruption, buried under mud and lava. Most inhabitants of Herculaneum had enough warning and managed to escape. The ruins here are smaller and the

buildings, particularly the private houses, are remarkably well preserved. Here you can see better examples of the frescoes, mosaics and furniture that used to decorate Roman houses.

Herculaneum is also accessible on the Circumvesuviana train from Naples (get off at Ercolano Scavi; €1.55 one way). If you want to have a look into the huge crater of Mt Vesuvius, catch the **Trasporti Vesuviani bus** (☎ 081 739 28 33) from in front of the Ercolano Scavi train station or from Pompeii's Piazza Anfiteatro. The return ticket costs €3.10 from Ercolano and €5.16 from Pompeii. The first bus leaves Pompeii at 9.30am and takes 40 minutes to reach Herculaneum. You'll then need to walk about 1.5km to the summit, where you must pay €5.16 to be accompanied by a guide to the crater. The last bus returns to Pompeii from Herculaneum's Quota 1000 car park at 3pm, and there are only three buses to the crater (from Pompeii at 9.30am, 11am and 12.10pm).

## SORRENTO

**postcode 80067 • pop 17,450**

A resort town in a beautiful area, summer sees Sorrento overcrowded with middle-aged, middle-class, middle-brow tourists and the trinket shops that cater to them. However, it is handy to the Amalfi Coast and Capri, and pleasant out of season.

## Orientation & Information

The centre of town is Piazza Tasso, a short walk from the train station along Corso Italia. The very helpful **AAST tourist office** (☎ 081 807 40 33; ⊌ www.sorrento tourism.it; Via Luigi de Maio 35; open 8.45am-7pm Mon-Sat) is inside the Circolo dei Forestieri complex.

There is a **post office** (Corso Italia 210) and **Telecom telephone office** (Piazza Tasso 37). The **Deutsche Bank** (Piazza Angelina Laura) has an ATM.

Internet access is available at **Blu Online** (Via Fuorimura 20), near the train station, for €5 per hour.

For medical emergencies contact the **Ospedale Civile** (☎ 081 533 11 11).

## Places to Stay & Eat

Camping grounds include **Nube d'Argento** (☎ 081 878 13 44; fax 081 807 34 50; Via del Capo 21; camp site per person/tent €8.50/12), which is the closest to the action.

**ITALY**

Head south along Corso Italia, then follow Via Capo.

**Ostello delle Sirene** *(☎ 081 807 29 25; Via degli Aranci 156; dorm bed without bath €14, with bath €16)*, near the train station, is a good option, with breakfast included.

**Hotel Nice** *(☎ 081 878 16 50, fax 081 878 30 86; Corso Italia 257; singles/doubles with bath €52/65)* has pleasant rooms, but traffic noise is a problem.

**Pensione Linda** *(☎ 081 878 29 16; Via degli Aranci 125; singles/doubles with bath €26/47)* is a charming place with sweet service and bargain rates.

**Self-Service Angelina Lauro** *(☎ 081 807 40 97; Piazza Angelina Lauro 39; meal about €6)* offers a cheap feed. **Giardinello** *(☎ 081 878 46 16; Via dell'Accademia 7; pizza about €5-6)* has a good menu and friendly service, plus a nice courtyard for summer dining. The **supermarket** *(Corso Italia 223)* has plenty of groceries.

## Getting There & Away
Sorrento is accessible from Naples on the Circumvesuviana train line. SITA buses leave from outside the train station for the Amalfi Coast. Hydrofoils and ferries leave from the port, along Via de Maio and down the steps from the tourist office, for Capri and Napoli and Ischia. The tourist office hands out comprehensive timetables.

In summer, traffic is heavy along the coastal roads to Sorrento.

## CAPRI
**postcode 80073 • pop 7250**
This beautiful island, an hour by ferry from Naples, retains the mythical appeal that attracted Roman emperors, including Augustus and Tiberius, who built 12 villas here. Very popular in summer, Capri wears its jet-set exclusivity well, like a cashmere sweater jauntily tied over bronzed shoulders. A short bus ride takes you to Anacapri, the town uphill from Capri, which also has accommodation. The island, famous for its grottoes, is also a good place for walking. There are **tourist offices** at Marina Grande *(☎ 081 837 06 34; open 8.30am-8.30pm daily)*, where boats arrive; in Piazza Umberto I *(☎ 081 837 06 86; open 8.30am-8.30pm daily)* in the centre of town; and in Anacapri *(☎ 081 837 15 24; Piazza Vittoria 4)*. Online information can be found at **w** www.capri.it.

## Things to See & Do
There are boat tours of the grottoes, including the famous **Grotta Azzurra** (Blue Grotto). Boats leave from Marina Grande and a return trip costs €14.10 (which includes the cost of a motorboat to the grotto, rowing boat into the grotto and entrance fee). On Sunday and public holidays it's a ludicrous €30. It's cheaper to catch a bus from Anacapri (although the rowboat and entrance fee still cost €8.10). You can swim into the grotto before 9am and after 5pm, but do so only in company and when the sea is very calm. You can walk to most of the interesting points on the island. Sights include the **Giardini d'Augusto**, in the town of Capri, and **Villa Jovis** *(admission €2; open 9am-1hr before sunset daily)*, the ruins of one of Tiberius' villas, along the Via Longano and Via Tiberio. The latter is a one-hour walk uphill from Capri. The beautiful **Villa San Michele** *(☎ 081 837 14 01; Viale Axel Munthe; admission €5; open 9am-6pm daily May-Sept, 9.30am-5pm Mar-Apr & Oct, 10.30am-3.30pm Nov-Feb)* at Anacapri was the home of Swedish writer Dr Axel Munthe.

## Places to Stay & Eat
**Stella Maris** *(☎ 081 837 04 52, fax 081 837 86 62; Via Roma 27; singles/doubles without bath €45/80)*, just off Piazza Umberto I, is right in the noisy heart of town.

In Anacapri, there is the above-average **Loreley** *(☎ 081 837 14 40, fax 081 837 13 99; Via G Orlandi 16; singles/doubles with bath €67/108)*, with low-season reductions available.

In Capri, **La Cisterna** *(☎ 081 837 56 20; Via M Serafina 5; meal about €15)* is a good spot to assuage hunger pains. In Anacapri, **Il Saraceno** *(☎ 081 837 20 99; Via Trieste e Trento 18; meal about €17)* has a lovely family atmosphere and great home-made *limoncello* (lemon liqueur).

## Getting There & Away
Getting to Capri is no problem, as there are hydrofoils and ferries virtually every hour from Naples' Molo Beverello and Mergellina, especially in summer. The Naples daily *Il Mattino* has all sailing times.

Several companies make the trip. Try **Caremar** *(☎ 081 551 38 82)*, which runs ferries/fast ferries for €5.42/10.33 one way from Beverello; and **NLG** *(☎ 081 552 72 09)*, also in Beverello (hydrofoils €11 one way).

ITALY

## Getting Around

From Marina Grande, the funicular directly in front of the port takes you to the town of Capri, which is at the top of a steep hill some 3km from the port up a winding road. Tiny local buses connect the port with Capri, Anacapri and other points around the island. Tickets for the funicular and buses (buy on board) cost €1.30 each trip or €6.71 per daily ticket.

## AMALFI COAST

The 50km-stretch of the Amalfi Coast attracts the world's wealthy in summer and prices skyrocket. Nevertheless, it's a coastline and landscape of inspiring natural beauty, which is more than can be said for the summer hordes. Visit in spring or autumn and you'll find reasonably priced accommodation and a peaceful atmosphere.

There are **tourist information offices** in the individual towns, including in Positano (☎ 089 87 50 67; Via Saracino 2; open 8am-2pm Mon-Sat year-round & 3.30pm-8pm July-Aug), and Amalfi (☎ 089 87 11 07; Corso Roma 19; open 8.30am-1.30pm & 3pm-5.30pm Mon-Fri, 8.30am-12.30pm Sat), on the waterfront.

## Positano
postcode 84017 • pop 3900

This is the most beautiful and fashionable town on the coast, with corresponding prices for the most part.

**Villa delle Palme** (☎ 089 87 51 62; Via Pasitea 134; doubles with bath €78) is a very good English-speaking hotel, with the usual mod-con suspects in all rooms. Next door is the great pizzeria **Il Saraceno d'Oro** (pizza about €6), which is a cut above most of the tourist-trap joints in town.

## Around Positano

The hills behind Positano offer some great walks; the tourist office at Positano may have a brochure listing options, and you can buy walking guides in town. Visit **Nocelle**, a tiny, isolated village above Positano, accessible by walking track from the end of the road from Positano. Have lunch at **Trattoria Santa Croce** (☎ 089 81 12 60; meal about €20), which has panoramic views. It opens for lunch and dinner in summer, but at other times, telephone and check in advance. Nocelle is accessible by local bus from Positano, via Montepertuso.

On the way from Positano to Amalfi is the town of **Praiano**, which is not as scenic but has more budget options, including the only camping ground on the Amalfi Coast. **La Tranquillitá** (☎ 089 87 40 84; e contraq@ contraqpraiano.com; €13 per person per camp site, double bungalows €43 per person) has a pensione, bungalows and a small camping ground. Rates for the double bungalows include breakfast. The SITA bus stops outside.

## Amalfi
postcode 84011 • pop 5520

One of the four powerful maritime republics of medieval Italy, Amalfi is a popular tourist resort. It has an impressive **Duomo**, and nearby is the **Grotta dello Smeraldo**, a rival to Capri's Grotta Azzurra.

In the hills behind Amalfi is delightful **Ravello**, accessible by bus from Amalfi and worth a visit to see the magnificent 11th-century **Villa Rufolo** (admission €4; open 9am-6pm daily), once the home of popes and later of the German composer Wagner. The 20th-century **Villa Cimbrone** is set in beautiful gardens, which end at a terrace offering a spectacular view of the Gulf of Salerno. There are numerous walking paths in the hills between Amalfi and Ravello. Pick up *Strade e Sentieri* (€6.50), a guide to walks in the area.

**Places to Stay & Eat** The HI **Ostello Beato Solitudo** (☎/fax 089 82 50 48; Piazza G Avitabile 4; dorm bed €9.50) is in Agerola San Lazzaro, a village just 16km west of Amalfi. Regular buses leave from Amalfi throughout the day, the last departing at about 8.45pm.

For a room in Amalfi try **Pensione Proto** (☎ 089 87 10 03, fax 089 873 61 80; Via dei Curiali 4; singles/doubles without bath €44/70), which has clean, decent rooms. The delightful **Hotel Lidomare** (☎ 089 87 13 32, fax 089 87 13 94; e lidomare@amalfi coast.it; Largo Duchi Piccolomini 9; singles/doubles with bath €39/88) has romantic rooms and kind service. Just follow the signs from Piazza del Duomo.

**Pizzeria al Teatro** (Via E Marini 19; pizza about €7) offers good food in attractive surrounds. Follow the signs to the left from Via Pietro Capuana, the main shopping street off Piazza del Duomo. There's a **minimarket** next to Pensione Proto. The best pastries are nibbled at **Pasticceria Andrea Pansa** *(Piazza Duomo 40)*, an old-fashioned place with luxe charm.

## Getting There & Away

**Bus** The Amalfi Coast is accessible by regular SITA buses, which run between Salerno (a 40-minute train trip from Naples) and Sorrento (accessible from Naples on the Circumvesuviana train line). Buses stop in Amalfi at Piazza Flavio Gioia, from where you can catch a bus to Ravello.

**Car & Motorcycle** The narrow, spectacular and tortuous coastal road is clogged with traffic in summer – be prepared for delays. Things are quieter at other times. **Sorrento Rentacar** *(☎ 081 878 13 86; Corso Italia 210a, Sorrento)* rents scooters and cars.

**Boat** Hydrofoils and ferries also service the coast between April and mid-September daily, leaving from Salerno and stopping at Amalfi and Positano. There are also boats between Positano and Capri.

## PAESTUM
### postcode 84063

The sight that launched a 1000 postcards – the three Greek temples standing in fields of red poppies are well worth making an effort to visit. The **temples** *(admission €4.50; open 9am-1hr before sunset daily)*, just south of Salerno, are among the world's best-preserved monuments of the ancient Greek world and a Unesco World Heritage Site. A **tourist office** *(☎ 0828 81 10 16; open 9am-2pm daily)* and an interesting **museum** *(☎ 0828 81 10 23; admission €4.50; open 9am-7pm daily, closed 1st & 3rd Mon of month)* are at the site.

Paestum is accessible from Salerno by CSTP bus No 34 from Piazza della Concordia, or by train. Buses are frequent from Monday to Saturday and almost nonexistent on Sunday.

## MATERA
### postcode 75100 • pop 57,300

This ancient city of the Basilicata region still trades on haunting images of a peasant culture that existed until the 1960s. Its famous *sassi* (the stone houses built in the two ravines that slice through the city) were home to more than half of Matera's population until the 1950s, when the local government built a new residential area just out of Matera and relocated 15,000 people. The wards are now a Unesco World Heritage Site – a far cry from the days when Matera struggled against poverty and malaria. Francesco Rosi's excellent film *Cristo si é Fermato a Eboli* (Christ Stopped at Eboli) is a poignant illustration of what life was like in Basilicata.

There's a **tourist office** *(☎ 0835 33 19 83; Via de Viti De Marco 9; open 9am-1pm Mon-Sat & 4pm-6.30pm Mon & Thur)*, off the main Via Roma. **Itinera** *(☎/fax 0835 26 32 59; ℮ arrtir@tin.it)* can organise guided tours in English for up to 10 people (two to three hours) for €60. **Sassi Urban Network** *(SUN; ☎ 0835 31 98 06; Via Casalnuovo 15)* organises visits to the *sassi* churches (from €2.10) and also provides maps. Its information offices are to be found scattered all through the wards.

## Things to See

The two main *sassi* wards, known as **Barisano** and **Caveoso**, had no electricity, running water or sewerage until well into the 20th century. The oldest *sassi* are at the top of the ravines, and the dwellings that appear to be the oldest were established in the 20th century. As space ran out in the 1920s, the population turned troglodyte, and started moving into hand-hewn or natural caves. The *sassi* zones are accessible from Piazza Vittorio Veneto and Piazza del Duomo in the centre of Matera. Be sure to see the rock churches, **Santa Maria d'Idris** and **Santa Lucia alla Malve**, both with well-preserved Byzantine frescoes. The 13th-century Apulian-Romanesque **cathedral**, overlooking Sasso Barisano, is also worth a visit.

Parts of the wards have been restored and some people have moved back to the area. Excavations in Piazza Vittorio Veneto have revealed the ruins of parts of **Byzantine Matera**, including a castle and a rock church decorated with frescoes. Worth visiting is **Casa Grotta di Vico Solitario** *(☎ 0835 31 01 18; Piazza San Pietro Caveoso; admission €1.50)*, an authentic *sassi* dwelling (English brochures available).

## Places to Stay & Eat

Accommodation is best booked in advance. **Albergo Roma** *(☎/fax 0835 33 39 12; Via Roma 62; singles/doubles without bath €21/31)* has simple rooms but a central location.

**Sassi Hotel** (☎ *0835 33 10 09, fax 0835 33 37 33;* ✉ *hotelsassi@virgilio.it; Via San Giovanni Vecchio 89; dorm bed* €*15.50, singles/doubles with bath* €*52/78)* is the most atmospheric place to stay, as it's in – you guessed it – the *sassi.*

**L'Osteria** (☎ *0835 33 33 95; Via Fiorentini 58; meal about* €*14)* is a tiny place with mouth-watering local dishes. There's a **fresh produce market** near Piazza V Veneto, on Via A Persio.

## Getting There & Away

SITA buses connect Matera with Taranto and Metaponto. The town is on the private Ferrovie Apulo–Lucane train line, which connects with Bari, Altamura and Potenza. There are also three Marozzi buses a day between Rome and Matera (€30). Buses arrive in Piazza Matteotti, a short walk down Via Roma to the town centre. Buy tickets at **Biglietteria Manicone** (☎ *0835 332 86 21; Piazza Matteoti 3).*

## APULIA

The province of Apulia, the thin heel of the Italian peninsula, has long been dismissed as a rural backwater with endemic poverty, and it still retains a sense of isolation from the rest of Italy. Yet for centuries, the 400km-long coastline was fought over by virtually every major colonial power, from the Greeks to the Spanish – all intent on establishing a strategic foothold in the Mediterranean. Each culture left its distinctive architectural mark, still in evidence today, albeit often crumbling.

## Brindisi

postcode 72100 • pop 93,020

The highlight of no-one's trip to Italy, Brindisi swarms with travellers in transit, as this is the major embarkation point for ferries to Greece (bring a pack of playing cards!). Most backpackers gather at the train station or at either of the two ports. The train station and the old port are connected by Corso Umberto I – which becomes Corso Garibaldi (pedestrianised) – a five-minute walk. The new port, known as Costa Morena, is 7km from the train station, with free bus connections linking the two (see Boat under Getting There & Away, later).

There is a helpful **EPT tourist information office** (☎ *0831 56 21 26; Lungomare Regina Margherita 43).* Be mindful of your possessions (and not just around locals), especially in the area around the train station and the ports.

The best-value accommodation here is the non-HI **Babilonia Hostel** (☎ *0831 41 31 23;* ✉ *hostelbrandisi@hotmail.com; Via Brandi 2; dorm bed* €*12),* about 2km out of town and is definitely recommended if you have time to kill. Take bus No 3 from Via Cristoforo Colombo near the train station, or call and ask Francesco to pick you up. Turn left off Corso Umberto I onto Via S Lorenzo da Brindisi to get to the bog-standard but inexpensive **Hotel Venezia** (☎ *0831 52 75 11; Via Pisanelli 4; singles/doubles without bath* €*13/25).*

There's a **supermarket** *(Piazza Cairoli 30),* between the train station and the old port, plus a morning **market** in Piazza Mercato, behind the post office. **La Bruschetta** *(Via Colonne 30; meal about* €*21)* is a decent spot to grab a good lunch or dinner.

**Getting There & Away** Marozzi runs several buses a day to/from Rome's Stazione Tiburtina, leaving from Viale Arno. **Appia Travel** (☎ *0831 52 16 84; Viale Regina Margherita 8-9)* sells tickets (€34; nine hours). There are rail connections to major cities in northern Italy, as well as to Bari, Lecce, Ancona, Naples and Rome.

**Boat** Ferries leave Brindisi for Greek destinations including Corfu, Igoumenitsa, Patras and Kefallonia. Major ferry companies are **Hellenic Mediterranean Lines** *(HML,* ☎ *0031 52 85 31; Corso Garibaldi 8);* **Blue Star** (☎ *0831 51 44 84; Corso Garibaldi 65);* **Italian Ferries** (☎ *0831 59 08 40; Corso Garibaldi 96);* and **Med Link Lines** (☎ *0831 52 76 67; Corso Garibaldi 49).*

HML is the most expensive, but also the most reliable. HML also officially accepts Eurail and Inter-Rail passes, which means you pay only €12 to travel deck class. If you want to use your Eurail or Inter-Rail pass, it is important to reserve some weeks in advance in summer. Even with a booking in summer, you must still go to your boat company's embarkation office (ask them for details when you buy) to have your ticket checked.

Discounts are available for travellers under 26 years of age and holders of some Italian rail passes. Note that fares and services increase in July and August. Full prices in the 2002 high season for deck class were: HML to Corfu, Igoumenitsa, Kefallonia or Patras €46 (€37 return); Med Link to Patras €45 (€36 return); Blue Star to Corfu and Igoumenitsa €48.

Bicycles can be taken aboard free, but the average high-season fare for a motorcycle is €18 and for a car around €48. A good website for trip planning is W www.ferries.gr, which has details of fares and timetables from Brindisi to Greece in English. Be wary of any too-good-to-be-true offers from fly-by-night operators claiming your Eurail and Inter-Rail pass is accepted by them or invalid with anyone else. We get numerous letters from travellers who have been stung for two lots of ferry tickets.

The port tax is €6, payable when you buy your ticket. It is essential to check in at least two hours prior to departure. To get to the new port of Costa Morena from the train station take the free Portabagagli bus, which departs a handy two hours before boat departures.

## Lecce

**postcode 73100 • pop 97,450**
If baroque means 'architectural marzipan' to you, you're in for a sweet surprise in Lecce. The style here is so refined and particular to the city that Italians call it Barocco Leccese (Lecce baroque), and the city is known as the 'Florence of the South'. The numerous bars and restaurants are a pleasant discovery in such a small city, thanks to the students from Lecce's university.

There is a dozy **APT information office** (☎ 0832 24 80 92; Via Vittorio Emanuele 24) near Piazza Duomo. Take bus No 1, 2 or 4 from the station to the town centre, or a five-minute walk.

**Things to See & Do** The most famous example of Lecce baroque is the **Basilica di Santa Croce**. Artists worked for 150 years to decorate the building, creating an extraordinarily ornate facade. In the **Piazza del Duomo** are the 12th-century **cathedral** (completely restored in the baroque style by Giuseppe Zimbalo of Lecce) and its 70m-high **bell tower**; the **Palazzo del Vescovo** (Bishop's Palace); and the **Seminario**, with its elegant facade and baroque well in the courtyard. The piazza is particularly beautiful at night, when the lights really show the buildings at their best. In Piazza Sant'Oronzo are the remains of a **Roman amphitheatre**.

**Places to Stay & Eat** Camping facilities abound in the province of Salento. **Torre Rinalda** (☎ 0832 38 21 62, fax 0832 38 21 65; e info@torrerinalda.it; camp sites up to €33.50), near the sea at (you guessed it) Torre Rinalda, is accessible by STP bus from the terminal in Lecce's Via Adua. Given the prices it's best to be in a group.

Lecce's **Hotel Cappello** (☎ 0832 30 88 81; Via Montegrappa 4; singles/doubles with bath €28/44) is near the station and 'un buon mercato' (a good price). For a taste of faded glory, try **Grand Hotel** (☎ 0832 30 94 05; Viale Quarta 28; singles/doubles with bath €48/84) just near the train station.

**Ristorante Re Idomeneo** (Via Libertini 44; meal about €13) is near Piazza del Duomo and has hearty, inexpensive pasta dishes, beloved by locals. **Fiaschetteria** (Via d'Aragone 2; meal about €12) is just near Chiesa di San Matteo and serves tasty local dishes with excellent bread.

**Entertainment** For a small, seemingly sedate town, Lecce has some great little bars in its historic centre. Try **Caffe Letterario** (Via Paladini 46), where you can enjoy wine by the glass in colourful surrounds.

**Getting There & Away** STP buses connect Lecce with towns throughout the Salentine peninsula, leaving from Via Adua. Lecce is directly linked by Ferrovie dello Stato (FS) train to Brindisi, Bari, Rome, Naples and Bologna. The Ferrovie del Sud Est (FSE) runs trains to major points in Apulia.

# Sicily

Sicily is a land of Greek temples, Norman churches and fortresses, Arab domes, Byzantine mosaics and splendid baroque architecture. Its landscape, dominated by the volcano Mt Etna (3330m) on the east coast, ranges from fertile coast to mountains in the north to a vast, dry plateau at its centre.

With a population of about 5,070,000 people, Sicily has a mild climate in winter and a relentlessly hot summer. The best times to visit are in spring and autumn, when it's warm but quieter.

Most ferries from Italy arrive at Sicily's capital, Palermo, which is convenient as a jumping-off point. If you're short on time, spend a day in Palermo and then perhaps head for Taormina, Syracuse or Agrigento.

The Mafia remains a powerful force in Sicily, despite taking a hammering from the authorities throughout the 1990s. But the 'men of honour' are not interested in your travellers cheques, so you won't be in a *Godfather*-style shoot-out.

## Getting There & Away
**Air** There are flights from major cities in Italy and throughout Europe to Palermo and Catania. The easiest way to get information is from any Sestante CIT or Alitalia office.

**Bus & Train** Bus services from Rome to Sicily are operated by **Segesta/Interbus** (☎ *091 616 90 39, Palermo ☎ 616 79 19, Rome ☎ 06 481 96 76)*, which has departures from Rome's Piazza Tiburtina. Buses service Messina (€27, 9¼ hours), Catania (€30, 11 hours) Palermo (€35, 12 hours) and Syracuse (€32.50, 11½ hours).

One of the cheapest ways to reach Sicily is to catch a train to Messina. The cost of the ticket covers the 3km-ferry crossing from Villa San Giovanni (Calabria) to Messina.

**Boat** Sicily is accessible by ferry from Genoa, Livorno, Naples, Reggio di Calabria and Cagliari, and also from Malta and Tunisia. The main companies servicing the Mediterranean are **Tirrenia** (*Palermo ☎ 091 602 11 11, Rome ☎ 06 42 00 98 03)* and **Grimaldi** (*Palermo ☎ 091 58 74 04, Genoa ☎ 010 2 51 65)*, which runs Grandi Navi Veloci. Prices are determined by season and are highest from July to September. Timetables can change each year and it's best to check at a travel agency that takes ferry bookings. Book well in advance during summer, particularly if you have a car.

At the time of writing, high-season fares for a *poltrona* (airline-type chair on a ferry) were Genoa–Palermo (€100, 20 hours) and Livorno–Palermo (€94, 17 hours) with Grimaldi's Grandi Navi Veloci, and Naples–Palermo (€45, 9¾ hours) and Cagliari–Palermo (€39, 13½ hours) with Tirrenia.

**Virtu Ferries** (W *www.virtuferries.com)* serves Sicily-Malta. For information on ferries going from the mainland directly to Lipari, see Getting There & Away under Aeolian Islands later in this chapter.

## Getting Around
Bus is the most common (and often the most convenient) mode of public transport in Sicily. Numerous companies run services between Syracuse, Catania and Palermo, as well as to Agrigento and towns in the interior. The coastal train service between Messina and Palermo and Messina to Syracuse varies between efficient and reliable, to delayed and unpredictable.

## PALERMO
**postcode 90100 • pop 680,000**
An Arab emirate and later the seat of a Norman kingdom, Palermo was once regarded as the grandest and most beautiful city in Europe. Today, parts of it are in a remarkable state of decay, due to neglect and heavy bombing during WWII, yet enough evidence remains of its golden days to make Palermo one of the most fascinating cities in Italy. Thankfully, some much-needed EU funds are actually beginning to make it to the areas that need it too.

## Orientation
Palermo is a large but easily manageable city. The main streets of the historic centre are Via Roma and Via Maqueda, which extend from the central station to Piazza Castelnuovo, a vast square in the modern part of town.

## Information
**Tourist Offices** There is a main **APT tourist office** (☎ *091 58 38 47; Piazza Castelnuovo 34; open 8.30am 2pm & 2.30pm 6pm Mon Fri)*. There are branch offices at the Stazione Centrale (☎ *091 616 59 14)*, with the same opening hours as the main office, and at the airport (☎ *091 59 16 98; open 8am-midnight Mon-Fri, 8am-8pm Sat & Sun)*.

**Money** There is an **exchange office** (*open 8am-8pm daily)* at the Stazione Centrale. American Express is represented by **Ruggieri & Figli** (☎ *091 58 71 44; Via Emerico Amari 40)*, near the Stazione Marittima. Otherwise, there is no shortage of banks with ATMs in the city.

**Post & Communications** There is a **main post office** (*Via Roma 322; open 8.30am-6.30pm Mon-Sat)*, which also has a fax service. The main (and grotty) **Telecom telephone office** (*Piazza G Cesare; open 8am-9.30pm daily)* is opposite the station. You can use the Internet (€3.10 per hour), send faxes and make calls at **Aexis Telecom** (*Via Maqueda 347)*.

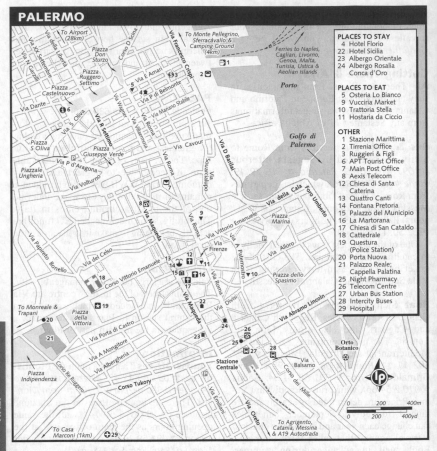

**PALERMO**

**Medical & Emergency Services** For an ambulance call ☎ 091 30 66 44. There is a public hospital, **Ospedale Civico** (☎ 091 666 11 11; Via Carmelo Lazzaro). A night pharmacy, **Lo Cascio** (☎ 091 616 21 17; Via Roma 1), is near the train station. The **questura** (police headquarters; ☎ 091 21 01 11; Piazza della Vittoria) is open 24 hours a day. You can also call the **Ufficio Stranieri** (Foreigners Office; ☎ 091 651 43 30; Piazza della Vittoria). If your car has been towed away, call ☎ 091 656 97 21 to find out where to collect it.

**Dangers & Annoyances** Contrary to popular opinion, Palermo is not a hotbed of thievery, but you will have to watch your valuables, which may attract pickpockets and bag snatchers. The historical centre can be a little dodgy at night, especially for women walking alone. Travellers might also wish to avoid walking alone in the area northeast of the station, between Via Roma and the port (although there is safety in numbers).

**Things to See**
The intersection of Via Vittorio Emanuele and Via Maqueda marks the **Quattro Canti** (four corners of historical Palermo). The four 17th-century Spanish baroque facades are each decorated with a statue. Nearby Piazza Pretoria has **Fontana Pretoria**, a beautiful fountain created by Florentine sculptors in the 16th century and once known as the Fountain of Shame because of its nude figures. Also in the piazza are the baroque **Chiesa di Santa Caterina** and the **Palazzo**

Splendid view towards Lykavittos Hill, the highest of Athens' eight hills

Stoa of Attalos, housing the Agora Museum, Athens, Greece

Backgammon, anyone?

Kalamata olives, Greece

Hearty late-night feasts are a staple of Greek life

Sunlight hits Florence's spectacular Cattedrale di Santa Maria del Fiore

Amalfi Coast, Italy

A Tuscan wine maker, Italy

Italian café chic, Siena

Your chariot awaits ouside Rome's Colosseum

**del Municipio** (town hall). Just off this piazza is Piazza Bellini and Palermo's famous church, **La Martorana** (☎ 091 616 1692; admission free; open 8am-1pm & 3.30-5.30pm Mon-Sat), with a beautiful Arab-Norman bell tower and Byzantine mosaics inside. Next to it is the Norman **Chiesa di San Cataldo** (admission free; open 9am-3.30pm Mon-Fri, 9am-1pm Sat & Sun), which mixes Arab and Norman styles. It's easily recognisable by its red domes, although the interior is very plain.

The huge **cattedrale** (☎ 091 33 43 76; Corso Vittorio Emanuele; admission free; open 7am-7pm Mon-Sat, 8am-1.30pm & 4pm-7pm Sun), although modified many times over the centuries, retains some vestiges of Norman architecture. At Piazza Indipendenza is **Palazzo Reale**, also known as the Palazzo dei Normanni, now the seat of the government. Step inside to see the **Cappella Palatina** (☎ 091 705 48 79; admission free; open 9am-11.45am & 3pm-4.45pm Mon-Fri, 9am-11.45am Sat, 9am-9.45am & noon-12.45pm Sun), a truly jaw-dropping example of Arab-Norman architecture, built during the reign of Roger II and lavishly decorated with Byzantine mosaics. King Roger's former bedroom, **Sala di Ruggero** (☎ 091 705 70 03; admission free; open 9am-noon Mon, Fri & Sat), is decorated with 12th-century mosaics. It is possible to visit the room only with a guide (free). Go upstairs from the Cappella Palatina.

Don't forget to take bus No 389 from Piazza Indipendenza to the nearby town of **Monreale** to see the magnificent mosaics in the world-famous 12th-century **Duomo** (☎ 091 640 44 13; admission free; open 8am-6pm daily), plus its **cloisters** (admission €4.50; open 9am-7pm Mon-Sat).

## Places to Stay

The best camping ground is **Trinacria** (☎/fax 091 53 05 90; Via Barcarello 25; per person/camp site per night €4.10/7.5), at Sferracavallo by the sea. Catch bus No 628 from Piazzale Alcide de Gasperi, which can be reached by bus No 101 or 107 from the station.

**Casa Marconi** (☎ 091 645 11 16, fax 091 657 03 10; e casamarconi@iol.it; Via Monfenera 140; singles & doubles with bath €26 per person) offers cheap, good-quality rooms. To get there, take bus No 246 from the station. Get off at Piazza Montegrappa; the hostel is a short walk from there.

Near the train station, the basic, anecdote-inducing **Albergo Orientale** (☎ 091 616 57 27; Via Maqueda 26; singles/doubles without bath €21/31), has a decaying palazzo courtyard entrance and no heating in winter. Lifestyles of the Rich & Famous it ain't, but it's cheap and close to the action. Around the corner is sweet and spotless **Albergo Rosalia Conca d'Oro** (☎ 091 616 45 43; Via Santa Rosalia 7; singles/doubles without bath €27/40), which is a tad more upmarket.

**Hotel Sicilia** (☎/fax 091 616 84 60; Via Divisi 99; singles/doubles with bath €39/62), on the corner of Via Maqueda, has decent rooms and friendly management, although it can get noisy.

**Hotel Florio** (☎/fax 091 609 08 52; Via Principe di Belmonte 33; singles/doubles with bath €45/65) is a new and appealing addition to Palermo's accommodation options, and it's in a nice part of town, too.

## Places to Eat

A popular Palermitan dish is pasta con le sarde (pasta with sardines, fennel, peppers, capers and pine nuts). Locals are late eaters and restaurants rarely open for dinner before 8.30pm.

**Osteria Lo Bianco** (Via E Amari 104; meal about €12), at the Castelnuovo end of town, serves tasty staples amid bright lights, wood panelling, plastic and warm smiles. The wonderful **Trattoria Stella** (Via Alloro 104) is in the La Kalsa quarter. Try the pesce spada (swordfish) and listen to the lilting Arabic-influenced songs coming out of the kitchen. **Hostaria da Ciccio** (Via Firenze 6; meal about €16) is worth trying, although it can seem a little quiet.

Palermo has numerous open-air markets, but the best two are the **Vucciria** held in the narrow streets between Via Roma, Piazza San Domenico and Via Vittoria Emanuele Monday to Saturday, and **Il Ballaro**, held in the Albergheria quarter, off Via Maqueda. There's a wealth of fruit and vegetables, seafood and dairy to choose from, and the atmosphere is unbeatable.

## Getting There & Away

**Air** The Falcone–Borsellino airport at Punta Raisi, 32km west of Palermo, serves as a terminal for domestic and European flights. For information on domestic and international flights, ring **Alitalia** (☎ 848 96 56 43).

**Bus** The main (intercity) terminal for destinations throughout Sicily and the mainland is in the area around Via Paolo Balsamo, to the right (east) as you leave the station. Offices for the various companies are all in this area, including **SAIS Trasporti** (☎ 091 616 11 41; Via Balsamo 16), **SAIS Autolinee** (☎ 091 616 60 28; Via Balsamo 18) and **Segesta** (☎ 091 616 90 39; Via Balsamo 26).

**Train** Regular trains leave from the Stazione Centrale for Milazzo, Messina, Catania, Syracuse and Agrigento as well as for nearby towns such as Cefalú. Direct trains go to Reggio di Calabria, Naples and Rome.

**Boat** The **Tirrenia office** (☎ 091 602 11 11) is at the port. Boats leave from the port (Molo Vittorio Veneto) for Sardinia and the mainland (see the introductory Sicily Getting There & Away section).

### Getting Around

Taxis to the airport cost upwards of €38. The cheaper option is to catch one of the regular blue Prestia e Comande buses, which leave from outside the station roughly every 45 minutes from 5am to 10.45pm. The trip takes one hour and costs €4.65. There's also a train service from the airport to Stazione Centrale between 5.40am and 10.40pm (€4.13). Most of Palermo's buses stop outside or near the train station. Bus No 101 or 107 runs along Via Roma from the train station to near Piazza Castelnuovo in a loop. Bus No 139 goes from the station past the port. You must buy tickets before you get on the bus; they cost €0.77 (for 1½ hours) or €2.58 (24 hours).

## AEOLIAN ISLANDS

Also known as the Lipari Islands, the seven islands of this archipelago just north of Milazzo are volcanic in origin. They range from the well-developed tourist resort of Lipari and the understated jet-set haunt of Panarea, to the rugged Vulcano, the spectacular scenery of Stromboli (and its fiercely active volcano), the fertile vineyards of Salina, and the solitude of Alicudi and Filicudi, which remain relatively undeveloped. The islands have been inhabited since the Neolithic era, when migrants sought the valuable volcanic glass, obsidian. The Isole Eolie (Aeolian Islands) are so named because the ancient Greeks believed they were the home of Aeolus, the god of wind. Homer wrote of them in the *Odyssey*.

### Information

The main **AAST tourist information office** (☎ 090 988 00 95; Via Vittorio Emanuele 202; open 8am-2pm Mon-Sat & 4.30pm-7.30pm Mon-Fri) for the islands is on Lipari. Other offices are open on Vulcano, Salina and Stromboli during summer.

### Things to See & Do

On **Lipari** visit the **castello** (citadel; admission €4.50; open 9am-1.30pm & 3pm-7pm Mon-Sat), with its archaeological park and museum. You can also go on excellent walks on the island. Catch a local bus from Lipari town to the hill-top village of Quattrocchi for a great view of Vulcano. The tourist office has information on boat trips and excursions to the other islands.

**Vulcano**, with its pungent sulphurous odour (you get used to it), is a short boat trip from Lipari. The main volcano, Vulcano Fossa, is still active, although the last recorded period of eruption was 1888–90. You can make the one-hour hike to the crater, or take a bath in the therapeutic hot muds.

**Stromboli** is the most spectacular of the islands. Climb the volcano (924m) at night to see the Sciara del Fuoco (Trail of Fire) – lava streaming down the side of the volcano, and the volcanic explosions from the crater. Many people make the trip (four to five hours) without a guide during the day, but at night you should go with a guided group. Contact **AGAI** (☎ 090 98 62 11; Piazza San Vincenzo), to organise a guide (they only depart if groups are large enough) or the privately owned **Strómbolania information office** (☎ 090 98 63 90; open 9am-noon & 3pm-8pm Easter-Sept) under the Ossidiana Hotel at Scari port, which can help organise climbs, plus other island tours.

### Places to Stay & Eat

Camping facilities are available on Salina and Vulcano. Most accommodation in summer is booked out well in advance on the smaller islands, particularly on Stromboli, and many places close during winter.

**Lipari** The best place to go for accommodation is Lipari, which has numerous budget hotels, *affittacamere* (private room rentals) and apartments. From here the other islands are easily accessible by regular hydrofoil. Accommodation touts at Lipari port are worth checking because offers are usually genuine. The island's camping ground, **Baia Unci** (☎ 090 981 19 09; e baiaunci@tin.it; €7.75/14 per person/camp site), is at Canneto, about 3km out of Lipari town.

**Diana Brown** (☎ 090 981 25 84, fax 090 981 32 13; e dbrown@netnet.it; Vico Himera 3; singles/doubles with bath €62/68) has great well-appointed rooms with a homy feel. She can also arrange excursions around the islands.

**Da Bartolo** (☎ 090 981 17 00; Via Garibaldi 53; meal about €25) is a good choice for seafood and pasta dishes. At **Nenzyna** (Via Roma 2; meal about €20) you'll find a tiny, aqua-coloured dining area where your seafood desires will be more than satisfied.

**Stromboli** Popular **Casa del Sole** (☎ 090 98 60 17; Via Soldato Cincotta; singles/doubles without bath €21/42), on the road to the volcano, has decent rooms and a good kitchen.

In splurge territory is **La Sirenetta** (☎ 090 98 60 25, fax 98 61 24; e lasirenetta@netnet.it; Via Marina 33; singles/doubles with bath €99/212, half-board €132), perfectly located at Ficogrande in front of **Strómbolicchio**, a towering rock rising out of the sea at San Vincenzo. The hotel has a panoramic terrace with a great restaurant.

**Vulcano** For a pleasant pensione try **Pensione La Giara** (☎ 090 985 22 29; Via Provinciale 18; B&B €58 per person with bath; closed late Oct–early Apr), which has good rooms and staggering discounts outside of August.

**Alicudi & Filicudi** If you want seclusion, head for Alicudi or Filicudi. The former offers **Ericusa** (☎ 090 988 99 02, fax 090 988 96 71; Via Regina Elena; doubles €62, half-board €60 per person) while Filicudi has the truly delightful **La Canna** (☎ 090 988 99 56, fax 090 988 99 66; e vianast@tin.it; Via Rosa 43; singles/doubles with bath €39/78; half-board €68 per person). There are restaurants at both these hotels.

### Getting There & Away
Ferries and hydrofoils leave for the islands from Milazzo (easily reached by train from Palermo and Messina) and all ticket offices are along Corso dei Mille at the port. SNAV runs hydrofoils (€10 one way). Siremar also has hydrofoils, but its ferries are half the price. If arriving at Milazzo by train, you will need to catch a bus to the port. Giunta buses from Milazzo stop at the port. SNAV also runs hydrofoils between the islands and Palermo (summer only).

You can travel directly to the islands from the mainland. Siremar runs regular ferries from Naples, and SNAV runs hydrofoils from Naples (see the Naples Getting There & Away section, earlier in this chapter), Messina and Reggio di Calabria. Occasionally the sea around the islands can be rough and sailings are cancelled, especially in winter.

### Getting Around
Regular hydrofoil and ferry services operate between the islands. Both Siremar and SNAV have booths at Lipari's port, where you can get full timetable information.

## TAORMINA
**postcode 98039 • pop 10,700**
Spectacularly located on a hill overlooking the sea and Mt Etna, Taormina was long ago discovered by the European jet set, which has made it one of the more expensive and touristy towns in Sicily. Its magnificent setting, its Greek theatre and the nearby beaches remain as seductive now as they were for the likes of Goethe and DH Lawrence. The **AAST tourist office** (☎ 0942 2 32 43; w www.taormina-ol .it; open 9am-2pm & 4pm-7pm Mon-Sat) in Palazzo Corvaja, just off Corso Umberto, has extensive information on the town.

### Things to See & Do
The **Greek theatre** (admission €4.50; open 9am-6.30pm daily) was built in the 3rd century BC and later greatly expanded and remodelled by the Romans. Concerts, theatre and festivals are staged here in summer and there are wonderful views of Mt Etna. From the beautiful **Villa Comunale** (also known as Trevelyan Gardens) there's a panoramic view of the sea. Along Corso Umberto is the **Duomo**, with a Gothic facade. The postcard-perfect local beach is **Isola Bella**, accessible by funivia (cable car), which costs €2.70 return.

Trips to Mt Etna can be organised through **CST** (☎ 0942 262 60 88; Corso Umberto 101).

ITALY

## Places to Stay & Eat

Bare-bones style **Campeggio San Leo** (☎ 0942 2 46 58; Via Nazionale; €4.20/ 14.50 per person/camp site per night) is accessible from the train station by the bus to Taormina – ask the driver to drop you off.

The tourist office has a list of affittacamere in Taormina. **Odyssey Youth Hostel B&B** (☎ 0942 2 45 33, fax 0942 2 32 11; w www .taorminaodyssey.it; Vicolo G Martino 2; dorm bed €15.50) is a friendly, small place, with pleasant rooms. To get here, follow the signs from Porta Messina along Via Cappuccini and head down Via Fontana Vecchia (about 10 minutes).

The HI **Ostello della Gioventu 'Ulisse'** (☎ 0942 2 31 93; Vicolo San Francesco di Paola 9; dorm bed €14.50) is reasonable enough, although restrictions on kitchen use and hot water plus a daytime lockout and curfew make it a bit of a pain, but rates include breakfast.

**Pensione Svizzera** (☎ 0942 2 37 90; e svizzera@tao.it; Via Pirandello 26; singles/ doubles/triples/quads with bath €52/72/ 108/120), on the way from the bus stop to the town centre, is a delightful place to treat yourself (or someone else).

**Gambero Rosso** (Via Naumachie 11; pizza €4.65-8) has smart service and nice outdoor seating. **Mamma Rosa** (Via Naumachie 10; pizza €5.20-7.20) has standard dishes and expensive seafood, but then again, eating in Taormina is rarely cheap! For a good, stiff drink **Arco Rosso** (Via Naumachie 7) can't be beaten.

There's a **Standa supermarket** (Via Apollo Arcagetta 19), near the Ulisse hostel and Porta Catania.

## Getting There & Away

Bus is the easiest way to get to Taormina. SAIS buses leave from Messina, Catania and also from the airport at Catania. Taormina is on the main train line between Messina and Catania, but the station is on the coast and regular buses will take you to Via Pirandello, near the centre; services are reduced on Sunday.

## MT ETNA

Dominating the landscape in eastern Sicily between Taormina and Catania, Mt Etna (3330m) is Europe's largest live volcano. It has four live craters at its summit and its slopes are littered with crevices and extinct cones. Eruptions of slow lava flows can occur, but are not really dangerous. Etna's most recent eruption was in 2001, which destroyed large parts of its surroundings. You can climb to the summit (about a seven-hour hike), but the handiest way is to take the 4WD minibus with **SITAS** (☎ 095 91 11 58) from the Rifugio Sapienza (the south side), or with **Le Betulle/STAR** (☎ 095 64 34 30) from Piano Provenzana (the north side). Both companies charge €38.

Mt Etna is best approached from Catania by **AST bus** (☎ 095 746 10 96), which departs from Via L Sturzo (in front of the train station) at about 8am, leaving from Rifugio Sapienza at about 4.45pm (€4.65 return). The private **Circumetnea train line** (☎ 095 54 12 50) circles Mt Etna from Catania to Giarre-Riposto. It starts from Catania just near Stazione Borgo, Via Caronda 352a (take a metro train from Catania's main train station, or any bus going up Via Etnea and get off at the metro stop named 'Borgo'). From Taormina, you can take an FS train to Giarre, where you can catch the Circumetnea.

In Catania, **Natura e Turismo** (NeT; ☎ 095 33 35 43; e natetur@tin.it; Via Quartararo 11) organises tours of the volcano with a volcanologist or expert guide.

A handy accommodation option in Catania is **Agora Hostel** (☎ 095 723 30 10; e agorahostel@hotmail.com; Piazza Curro 6; dorm bed €15.50, doubles without bath €48), which has regular parties and is close to La Pescheria market, making it good for self-caterers. The cheap dinners here get good reviews.

## SYRACUSE
**postcode 96100 • pop 125,700**

Once a powerful Greek city to rival Athens, Syracuse (Siracusa) is one of the highlights of a visit to Sicily. Founded in 743 BC by colonists from Corinth, it became a dominant sea power in the Mediterranean, prompting Athens to attack the city in 413 BC. Syracuse was the birthplace of the Greek mathematician and physicist Archimedes, and Plato attended the court of the tyrant Dionysius, who ruled from 405 to 367 BC.

## Orientation & Information

The main sights are in two areas: on the island of Ortygia and at the archaeological park 2km across town. There are two tourist information offices: an **AAT** (☎ 0931 46 42 55; Via Maestranza 33; open 8.30am-1.30pm & 2pm-5pm Mon-Fri, 8.30am-1.30pm Sat) on Ortygia, and an **APT** (☎ 0931 6 77 10; Via San Sebastiano 45; open 8.30am-1.30pm & 2pm-5pm Mon-Fri, 8.30am-1.30pm Sat).

## Ortygia

The island of Ortygia has eye-catching baroque palaces and churches. The **Duomo** was built in the 7th century on top of the Temple of Athena, incorporating most of the original columns in its three-aisled structure. The splendid **Piazza del Duomo** is lined with baroque palaces. Walk down Via Picherali to the waterfront and the **Fonte Aretusa** (Fountain of Arethusa), a natural freshwater spring. According to Greek legend, the nymph Arethusa, pursued by the river-god Alpheus, was turned into a fountain by the goddess Diana. Undeterred, Alpheus turned himself into the river that feeds the spring.

## Neapolis-Parco Archeologico

To get to this archaeological zone (☎ 0931 6 62 06; admission €4.50; open 9am-1hr before sunset daily), catch bus No 1 or 2 from Riva della Posta on Ortygia. The main attraction here is the 5th-century BC **Greek theatre**, its seating area carved out of solid rock. Nearby is the **Orecchio di Dionisio**, an artificial grotto in the shape of an ear that the tyrant of Syracuse, Dionysius, used as a prison. The impressive 2nd-century **Roman amphitheatre** is well preserved.

The excellent **Museo Archeologico Paolo Orsi** (☎ 0931 46 40 22; admission €4.50; open 9am-1pm Tues-Sat), about 500m east of the archaeological zone, off Viale Teocrito, contains Sicily's best-organised and most interesting archaeological collection.

## Places to Stay

Camping facilities are at **Agriturist Rinaura** (☎ 0931 72 12 24; €5/4 per person/camp site), about 4km from the city on the SS115, near the sea. Catch bus No 21 or 22 from Corso Umberto.

Fancy **Hotel Gran Bretagna** (☎ 0931 6 87 65, fax 0931 46 21 69; Via Savoia 21; singles/doubles/triples/quads with bath €69/96/120/140), just off Largo XXV Luglio on Ortygia, has lovely rooms.

**Hotel Aretusa** (☎/fax 0931 2 42 11; Via Francesco Crispi 75; singles/doubles without bath €27/42, with bath 32/48) is close to the train station and has clean, albeit spartan, rooms.

**Hotel Milano** (☎ 0931 6 69 81; Corso Umberto 10; singles/doubles without bath €19/37, with bath €37/66) has a little more on offer, such as TV and fridge, and is closer to Ortygia.

## Places to Eat

Ortygia is the best area for eating in Syracuse. Try **Pizzeria Nonna Margherita** (☎ 0931 6 53 64; Via Cavour 12; pizza €2.60-11.40), a casual place with great pizza – from simple, tasty Neapolitan to more elaborate affairs.

At **Pasticceria Tipica Catanese** (Corso Umberto 46) you can try scrumptious Sicilian sweets while planning your next trip to the dentist.

There is an open-air, fresh-produce **market** in the streets behind Riva della Poata, until 1pm Monday to Saturday. There are **alimentari** and **supermarkets** along Corso Gelone.

## Getting There & Away

**Interbus** (☎ 0931 6 67 10) buses leave from near the office at Via Trieste 28 (just behind Riva della Posta) for Catania, Palermo, Enna and surrounding towns. The service for Rome also leaves from here, connecting with the Rome bus at Catania. **AST** (☎ 0931 4 62 71) buses service the town and the surrounding area from Riva della Posta. Syracuse is easy to reach by train from Messina and Catania.

## AGRIGENTO

**postcode 92100 • pop 55,500**

Founded in approximately 582 BC as the Greek Akragas, Agrigento is today a pleasant medieval town, but the Greek temples in the valley below are the real reason to visit. The Italian novelist and dramatist Luigi Pirandello (1867–1936) was born here, as was the Greek philosopher and scientist Empedocles (c. 490–430 BC).

There's an **AAST tourist office** (☎ 0922 2 04 54; Via Cesare Battisti 15; open 9am-2pm Mon-Fri).

## Things to See & Do

Agrigento's **Valley of the Temples** (admission €4.50, with museum €6; Collina dei Templi open 8.30am-9pm, Tempio di Giove area open 8.30am-6.30pm) is one of the major Greek archaeological sights in the

**ITALY**

world. Its five main Doric temples were constructed in the 5th century BC and are in various states of ruin because of earthquakes and vandalism by early Christians. In an area known as the 'Collina dei Templi', you'll find the only temple to survive relatively intact – the **Tempio della Concordia**, which was transformed into a Christian church. The **Tempio di Giunone**, a short walk uphill to the east, has an impressive sacrificial altar.

The **Tempio di Ercole** is the oldest of the structures. Across the main road which divides the valley is the massive **Tempio di Giove**, one of the most imposing buildings of ancient Greece. Although now completely in ruins, it used to cover an area measuring 112m by 56m, with columns that were 18m high. **Telamoni**, colossal statues of men, were also used in the structure. The remains of one of them are in the fine **Museo Archeologico** *(admission €4.50, with temples €6; open 9am-1.30pm & 2pm-7.30pm Tues-Sat, 9am-1.30pm Sun & Mon)*, just north of the temples on Via dei Templi. Close by is the **Tempio di Castore e Polluce**, which was partly reconstructed in the 19th century. The temples are lit up at night. To get to the temples from the town, catch bus No 1, 2 or 3 from the train station.

### Places to Stay & Eat
The friendly **Bella Napoli** (☎ 0922 2 04 35; *Piazza Lena 6; singles/doubles/triples with bath €22/54/75)*, off Via Bac Bac at the end of Via Atenea, has clean, comfortable rooms. Good simple food can be had at **La Forchetta** *(Piazza San Francesco 9; meal about €13)*.

### Getting There & Away
Intercity buses leave from Piazza Rosselli, just off Piazza Vittorio Emanuele, for Palermo, Catania and surrounding towns.

# Sardinia

The second-largest island in the Mediterranean, Sardinia (Sardegna) was colonised by the Phoenicians and Romans, followed by the Pisans, Genoese and last but not least, the Spaniards. It is often said that the Sardinians (known on the island as Sardi) were never really conquered – they simply retreated into the hills. Despite this, their hospitality is noticeable.

The landscape of the island ranges from the 'savage, dark-bushed, sky-exposed land' described by DH Lawrence, to the beautiful gorges and valleys near Dorgali and the unspoiled coastline between Bosa and Alghero. Try to avoid the island in August, when the weather is hot and there are too many tourists.

### Getting There & Away
**Air** There are airports at Cagliari, Olbia, Alghero and Arbatax–Tortoli which link Sardinia with major Italian and European cities. For information contact Alitalia or the Sestante CIT, or CTS offices in all major towns.

**Boat** The island is accessible by ferry from Genoa, Livorno, Fiumicino, Civitavecchia, Naples, Palermo, Trapani, Bonifacio (Corsica) and Tunis. The departure points in Sardinia are Olbia, Golfo Aranci and Porto Torres in the north, Arbatax on the east coast and Cagliari in the south.

The main company, Tirrenia, runs a service between Civitavecchia and Olbia, Arbatax or Cagliari, and between Genoa and Porto Torres, Olbia, Arbatax or Cagliari. There are fast ferries between Fiumicino and Golfo Aranci/Arbatax and Civitavecchia and Olbia (both summer only). The national railway, Ferrovie dello Stato (FS), also runs a service between Civitavecchia and Golfo Aranci. **Moby Lines** (w www.mobylines.it, Italian only) and **Sardinia Ferries** (w www.sardiniaferries.com), which is also known as Elba and Corsica Ferries, both operate services from the mainland to Sardinia, as well as to Corsica and Elba. They depart from Genoa, Livorno, Civitavecchia and arrive at Olbia, Cagliari or Golfo Aranci. **Grandi Navi Veloci** (w www.gnv.it) runs a service between Genoa and Olbia (from June to September) or Porto Torres (year-round). Most travel agencies in Italy have brochures on the various companies' services.

Timetables change and prices fluctuate with the season. Prices for a poltrona on Tirrenia ferries in the 2002 high season were: Genoa to Cagliari (€54, 20 hours); Genoa to Porto Torres or Olbia (€46, 13 hours); Naples to Cagliari (€41, 16¼ hours); Palermo to Cagliari (€39, 13½ hours); Civitavecchia to Olbia (€25, eight hours); and Civitavecchia to Cagliari (€41, 14½ hours). The cost of taking a small car from Civitavecchia to Cagliari in the high season was €78. A motorcycle (over 200cc) costs €40 year-round for the same trip.

## Getting Around

**Bus** The two main bus companies are the state-run ARST, which operates extensive services throughout the island, and privately owned PANI, which links main towns.

**Train** The main FS train lines link Cagliari with Oristano, Sassari and Olbia. The private railways that link smaller towns throughout the island can be *very* slow. However, the *Trenino Verde* (little green train), which runs from Cagliari to Arbatax through the Barbagia, is a very relaxing and lovely way to see part of the interior (see Getting There & Away under Cagliari, later in this chapter).

**Car & Motorcycle** The best way to explore Sardinia properly is by road. Rental agencies are listed under Cagliari and some other towns around the island.

**Hitching** Away from the main towns, hitchhiking can be laborious because of light traffic. Women definitely should not hitchhike alone in Sardinia.

## CAGLIARI
**postcode 09100 • pop 163,000**
This attractive, friendly city offers a beautifully preserved medieval section, the delightful beach of Poetto, and salt lakes with a population of pink flamingoes.

## Orientation
If you arrive by bus, train or boat, you will find yourself at the port area of Cagliari. The main street along the harbour is Via Roma, and the old city stretches up the hill behind it to the castle. Most of the budget hotels and restaurants are in the area near the port, normally not a great place in most cities, but perfectly safe and pleasant here.

## Information
**Tourist Offices** There is an **AAST** information office (☎ 070 66 92 55; *Piazza Matteotti 9; open 8.30am-7.30pm Mon-Fri & 8.30am-1.30pm Sat*). There are also information offices at the airport and in the Stazione Marittima.

The **Ente Sardo Industrie Turistiche office** (*ESIT;* ☎ 070 6 02 31, 800 01 31 53; *Via*

*Goffredo Mameli 97; open 9am-6pm Mon-Sat*) has information on the whole island.

**Post & Communications** The **main post office** (☎ 070 6 03 11; *Piazza del Carmine 27*) is up Via La Maddalena from Via Roma. The **Telecom office** (*Via G M Angioj 6*) is north of Piazza Matteotti. You can use the Internet at **Web Travel Point** (☎ 070 65 93 07; *Via Maddalena 34*) for €2.60 for 30 minutes.

**Laundry** There's a **coin-operated laundry** (*Corso Vittorio Emanuele 232; open 9am-9pm*) that costs €3 per 7kg load (extra for drying).

**Medical & Emergency Services** For medical attention go to the **Ospedale San Giovanni di Dio** (☎ 070 66 32 37; *Via Ospedale*). For police help, go to the **questura** (*police headquarters;* ☎ 070 6 02 71; *Via Amat 9*).

## Things to See
The **Museo Archeologico Nazionale** (☎ 070 65 59 11; *Piazza Arsenale; admission €4; open 9am-8pm Tues-Sun*), in the Citadella dei Musei, has a fascinating collection of Nuraghic bronzes. These bronzes are objects found in stone constructions all over Sardinia (there are about 7000), a legacy of the island's native culture.

It's enjoyable to wander through the medieval quarter. The Pisan-Romanesque **Duomo** (☎ 070 66 38 37; *Piazza Palazzo*) was built in the 13th century and has an interesting Romanesque pulpit.

There are good sea and city views from **Bastione di San Remy** in Piazza Costituzione, in the town's centre. It once formed part of the fortifications of the old city.

The Pisan **Torre di San Pancrazio** (*Piazza Indipendenza; open 9am-5pm Tues-Sun*) is also worth a look. The **Roman amphitheatre** (*Viale Buon Cammino; open 9am-5pm Tues-Sun*) is considered the most important Roman monument in Sardinia. During summer opera is performed here.

A day on the **Spiaggia di Poetto**, east of the centre is well-spent and you can wander across to the salt lakes to see the flamingoes.

## Special Events
The Festival of Sant'Efisio, a colourful festival mixing the secular and the religious, is held annually for four days from 1 May.

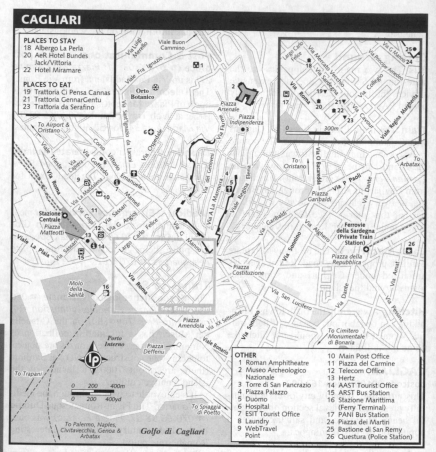

**CAGLIARI**

PLACES TO STAY
18  Albergo La Perla
20  AeR Hotel Bundes
    Jack/Vittoria
22  Hotel Miramare

PLACES TO EAT
19  Trattoria Ci Pensa Cannas
21  Trattoria GennarGentu
23  Trattoria da Serafino

OTHER
1  Roman Amphitheatre
2  Museo Archeologico
   Nazionale
3  Torre di San Pancrazio
4  Piazza Palazzo
5  Duomo
6  Hospital
7  ESIT Tourist Office
8  Laundry
9  WebTravel
   Point
10  Main Post Office
11  Piazza del Carmine
12  Telecom Office
13  Hertz
14  AAST Tourist Office
15  ARST Bus Station
16  Stazione Marittima
    (Ferry Terminal)
17  PANI Bus Station
24  Piazza dei Martiri
25  Bastione di San Remy
26  Questura (Police Station)

## Places to Stay & Eat

There are numerous hotels near the port.
Worth a stay is **AeR Hotel Bundes Jack/
Vittoria** (☎/fax 070 66 79 70; Via Roma 75;
singles/doubles with bath €43/63), with
lovely, spotless rooms and a warm welcome.
**Hotel Miramare** (☎/fax 070 66 40 21; Via
Roma 59; singles/doubles without bath
€32/42, with bath €37/47) has OK rooms.
**Albergo La Perla** (☎ 070 66 94 46; Via
Sardegna 18; singles/doubles/triples without bath €30/39/53) has a few different
retro decorating styles in evidence, but it's
decent.

Reasonably priced trattorias can be found
in the area behind Via Roma, particularly
around Via Sardegna and Via Cavour. **Trattoria da Serafino** (Via Lepanto 6; meal about
€12), on the corner of Via Sardegna, has
very good food at excellent prices. **Trattoria
GennarGentu** (☎ 070 67 20 21; Via Sardegna 60; meal about €13) is a friendly place.
Try the *spaghetti bottarga* (spaghetti with
dried tuna roe) for a true Sardinian flavour.
**Trattoria Ci Pensa Cannas** (Via Sardegna
37; meal about €12) is cheap and cheerful.
Via Sardegna also has **grocery shops** and
**bakeries**.

## Getting There & Away

**Air** Some 8km northwest of the city at Elmas
is **Cagliari's airport**. ARST buses leave regularly from Piazza Matteotti to coincide with
flight arrivals and departures. The **Alitalia
office** (☎ 070 24 00 79, 147 86 56 43) is at
the airport.

**Bus & Train** Departing from Piazza Matteotti are **ARST buses** (☎ *070 409 83 24, 800 86 50 42)* servicing nearby towns, the Costa del Sud and the Costa Rei. **PANI buses** (☎ *070 65 23 26)* leave from Stazione Marittima for towns such as Sassari, Oristano and Nuoro. The main train station is also in Piazza Matteotti. Regular trains leave for Oristano, Sassari, Porto Torres and Olbia. The private **Ferrovie della Sardegna** (FdS; ☎ *070 49 13 04)* train station is in Piazza della Repubblica. For information about the *Trenino Verde* which runs along a scenic route between Cagliari and Arbatax, contact ESIT (see Tourist Offices under Information earlier in this section), or the FdS directly (☎ *58 02 46)*. The most interesting and picturesque section of the route is between Mandas and Arbatax.

**Boat** Ferries arrive at the port adjacent to Via Roma. Bookings for Tirrenia can be made at the Stazione Marittima in the port area (☎ *070 66 60 65)*. See the introductory Sardinia Getting There & Away section for more details.

**Car & Motorcycle** For rental cars or motorcycles try **Hertz** (☎ *070 66 81 05; Piazza Matteotti 1)*, which also has a branch at the airport; or **Autonoleggio Cara** (☎ *070 66 34 71)*, which can deliver your scooter or bike to your hotel.

## CALA GONONE
**postcode 08022 • pop 1000**
This attractive seaside resort is an excellent base from which to explore the coves along the eastern coastline, as well as the Nuraghic sites and rugged terrain inland. Major points are accessible by bus and boat, but you'll need a car to explore.

## Information
There is a **Pro Loco office** (☎ *0784 9 36 96; Viale del Blu Marino)* where you can pick up maps, a list of hotels and information (generally from May to September). There is also a good **tourist office** (☎ *0784 9 62 43; Via Lamarmora 181; open 9am-1pm & 3.30pm-7pm Mon-Fri)* in nearby Dorgali. Also in Dorgali, **Coop Ghivine** (☎/fax *0784 9 67 21;* w *www.ghivine.com; Via Montebello 5)* organises excellent guided treks in the region from €30 per person.

## Things to See & Do
From Cala Gonone's tiny port, catch a boat (€7) to the **Grotta del Bue Marino** (admission €5.50)*, where a guide will take you on a 1km walk to see vast caves with stalagmites, stalactites and lakes. Sardinia's last colony of monk seals once lived here, but have not been sighted in years. Boats also leave for **Cala Luna**, an isolated beach where you can spend the day by the sea or take a walk along the fabulous gorge called **Codula di Luna**. However, the beach is packed with day-tripping tourists in summer. The boat trip to visit the grotto and beach costs around €18.

A **walking track** along the coast links Cala Fuili, about 3.5km south of Cala Gonone, and Cala Luna (about two hours, one way).

If you want to descend the impressive **Gorropu Gorge**, ask for information from the team of expert guides based in Urzulei – **Societá Gorropu** (☎ *0782 64 92 82, 0347 775 27 06;* e *francescomurru@virgilio.it)*. They also offer a wide range of guided walks in the area at competitive prices. It is necessary to use ropes and harnesses to traverse the Gorropu Gorge; however, when it doesn't rain too much, it is possible to walk for about 1km into the gorge from its northern entrance.

## Places to Stay
**Camping Gala Gonone** (☎ *0784 9 31 65, fax 0784 9 32 55;* w *www.campingcalagonone.it; Via Collodi; camp sites per person €15, 4-bed bungalows €110; open Apr-Oct)* has good-quality camping facilities, including a pool and restaurant.

Hotels include the attractive **Piccolo Hotel** (☎ *0784 9 32 32; Via Cristoforo Colombo 32; singles/doubles with bath €32/53)* near the port, and **Pop Hotel** (☎ *0784 9 31 85, fax 0784 9 31 58;* e *lfancel@box1.tin.it; singles/doubles with bath €57/93)*, which is right on the water and has a restaurant.

## Getting There & Away
Catch a PANI bus to Nuoro from Cagliari, Sassari or Oristano and then take an ARST bus to Cala Gonone (via Dorgali). If you are travelling by car, you will need a proper road map of the area.

## ALGHERO
**postcode 07041 • pop 40,600**
A highly popular tourist resort, Alghero is on the island's west coast, an area known as the

Coral Riviera. The town is a good base from which to explore the magnificent coastline linking it to Bosa in the south, and the famous Grotte di Nettuno (Neptune's Caves) on the Capocaccia to the north. The best time to visit is in spring or autumn, when the hordes are yet to arrive, or have long gone.

## Orientation & Information

The **train station** (*Via Don Minzoni*), is some distance from the centre, and is connected by a regular bus service to the centre of town.

The very helpful **AAST tourist office** (☎ *079 97 90 54; Piazza Porta Terra 9; open 8am-8pm Mon-Sat)* is near the port and just across the gardens from the bus station. The old city and most hotels and restaurants are in the area west of the tourist office.

There is a **main post office** (*Via XX Settembre 108*). There is a bank of **public telephones** (*Via Vittorio Emanuele*) at the opposite end of the gardens from the tourist office.

In an emergency ring the police on ☎ 113; for medical attention ring ☎ 079 98 71 61, or go to the **Ospedale Civile** (☎ *079 99 62 33; Via Don Minzoni*).

## Things to See & Do

The narrow streets of the old city and around the port are worth exploring. The most interesting church here is the **Chiesa di San Francesco** (*Via Carlo Alberto; open 9am-noon & 4pm-7pm daily*). The city's **cathedral** has been ruined by constant remodelling, but its bell tower remains a fine example of Gothic-Catalan architecture.

Near Alghero at the beautiful **Capocaccia** are the **Grotte di Nettuno**, accessible by boat (€10, hourly 8am to 7pm June to September, four daily April to May and October) from the port, or three times a day by the FS bus from Via Catalogna (€3.25 return, 50 minutes, 1 June to 30 September).

If you have your own transport, don't miss the **Nuraghe di Palmavera** (☎ *079 95 32 00; admission €2.05*), about 10km out of Alghero on the road to Porto Conte. The site features a ruined palace dating from around 1100 BC and about four dozen huts.

The coastline between Alghero and Bosa is picturesque. Rugged cliffs fall down to soli-

tary beaches, and near **Bosa** is one of the last habitats of the griffon vulture. The best way to see the coast is by car or motorcycle. If you want to rent a bicycle (from €9 per day) or motorcycle (from €70) to explore the coast, try **Cicloexpress** (☎ *079 98 69 50; Via Garibaldi*) at the port.

## Special Events

In summer Alghero stages the Estate Musicale Algherese (Alghero's Summer Music Festival) in the cloisters of the church of San Francesco, Via Carlo Alberto. A festival, complete with fireworks display, is held on 15 August for the Feast of the Assumption.

## Places to Stay & Eat

Finding a room in August without a reservation from months ago is a nightmare. At other times of the year you'll be fine. Camping facilities include **Calik** (☎/*fax 079 93 01 11; w www.campeggiocalik.it; open 1 Jun–30 Sept; camp site per person €12*) in Fertilia, which is about 6km out of town on the SS127bis. The HI **Ostello dei Giuliani** (☎/*fax 079 93 03 53; e ostellodeigiuliani@ ticalinet.it; Via Zara 1; dorm bed €10; open year-round*) is also in Fertilia and is in good condition. Take the hourly bus 'AF' from Via Catalogna to Fertilia. Breakfast is included in the rates and a meal costs €7.75.

In the old town is the excellent **Hotel San Francesco** (☎/*fax 079 98 03 30; e hotsfran@ tin.it; Via Ambrogio Machin 2; singles/ doubles with bath €43/75*), with a charming cloistered courtyard shared with the church of the same name.

A popular eating choice is stone-ceilinged **Trattoria Il Vecchio Mulino** (☎ *079 97 72 54; Via Don Deroma 7; meal about €12*), with a good range of pizza. For coffee, wine and cake, head to **Caffe Costantino** (*Piazza Civica 30*).

## Getting There & Away

Alghero is accessible from Sassari by train or bus. The main bus station is on Via Catalogna, next to the public park. **ARST** (☎ *079 95 01 79*) buses leave for Sassari and Porto Torres. **FdS buses** (☎ *079 95 04 58*) also service Sassari, Macomer and Bosa. **PANI buses** (☎ *079 23 69 83*) serve Cagliari, Nuoro and Macomer from Sassari.

# Malta

The islands of Malta, Gozo and Comino may look like tiny specks on the map, but you'll be amazed by how much they have to offer. Strategically placed in the Mediterranean, they have been occupied by several civilisations and have proved a tempting target for explorers and invaders. This tug of war has left Malta with an eclectic mix of influences and yet, strangely, it has managed to retain a certain individuality.

Its pleasant climate and scenic coastline has earned Malta a bucket-and-spade reputation but look beyond the beaches and there's 3000 years of history to explore. From prehistoric temples to baroque architecture you're never short of things to catch your eye or pique your interest.

Despite much development, especially in the tourist sector, Malta has kept a traditional outlook. The sense of family is still very strong and community spirit is at its best during the *festi* period when whole towns and villages join to pay homage to their patron saint.

The Maltese are a warm and friendly people and you'll feel at home in no time at all. Get caught up in the hustle and bustle of the Mediterranean lifestyle or escape to the quiet recesses of rural life on Gozo or Comino. It's your choice.

# Facts about Malta

## HISTORY

Malta has a fascinating history, and the island is crowded with physical and cultural reminders of the past. The islands' oldest monuments are the beautifully preserved megalithic temples built between 3800 and 2500 BC, which are the oldest surviving free-standing structures in the world.

From around 800 to 218 BC, Malta was colonised by the Phoenicians and, for the last 250 years of this period, by Phoenicia's principal North African colony, Carthage. The Maltese language (Malti) is Semitic in origin and is believed to be based on Phoenician. With watchful eyes painted on the prow, the colourful Maltese fishing boats – *luzzu* and *kajjik* – are scarcely changed from the Phoenician trading vessels that once plied the Mediterranean.

## At a Glance

- **Valletta** – stunning St John's Co-Cathedral
- **South Coast** – panoramic views from atop Dingli Cliffs, prehistoric temples of Ħaġar Qim overlooking the sea
- **Gozo** – bustling Victoria, picturesque Marsalforn and Ġgantija's megalithic temples in Xagħra
- **Comino** – uninhabited island home to the sparkling blue water of the Blue Lagoon

| | |
|---|---|
| **Capital** | Valletta |
| **Population** | 390,000 |
| **Official Language** | Malti, English |
| **Currency** | 1 Maltese lira (Lm) = 100 cents |
| **Time** | GMT/UTC+0100 |
| **Country Phone Code** | ☎ 356 |

Valletta, Sliema & St Julian's p438

Valletta p439

The Punic Wars saw the defeat of the Carthaginian general Hannibal in 208 BC, and Malta became part of the Roman Empire. In AD 60, St Paul – a prisoner en route to Rome – was shipwrecked on the island. According to local folklore he converted the islanders to Christianity.

Arabs from North Africa arrived in 870, but tolerated the local Christians. They brought citrus fruits and cotton and had an impact on Maltese customs and language. The Arabs were expelled in 1090 by the Norman King Roger of Sicily. For the next 400 years Malta's history was linked to Sicily, and its rulers were a succession of Normans, Angevins (French), Aragonese and Castilians (Spanish). The relatively small population of downtrodden islanders paid their taxes by trading, slaving and piracy, and were repaid by marauding North Africans (Berbers and Arabs) and Turks.

In 1530, the islands were given to the Knights of the Order of St John of Jerusalem by Charles V, Emperor of Spain; their rent was two Maltese falcons a year, one to be sent to the emperor and the other to the Viceroy of Sicily. The 12,000 or so local inhabitants were given no say in the matter.

The Order of St John was founded during the crusades to protect Christian pilgrims travelling to and from the Holy Land, and to care for the sick. The knights were drawn from the younger male members of Europe's aristocratic families; in other words, those who were not the principal heirs. The order comprised eight nationalities or *langues* (languages). In order to preserve their identity, the langues built magnificent palaces, called *auberges*. The eight langues – Italy, Germany, France, Provence, Castile, Aragón, Auvergne and England – correspond to the eight points of the Maltese Cross. It was a religious order, with the knights taking vows of celibacy, poverty and obedience, and handing over their patrimony. The Order of St John became extremely prestigious, wealthy and powerful as

a military and maritime force, and as a charitable organisation that founded and operated several hospitals.

As soon as they arrived in Malta, the knights began to fortify the harbour and to skirmish with infidels. In May 1565, an enormous Ottoman fleet carrying more than 30,000 men laid siege to the island. The 700 knights and 8000 Maltese and mercenary troops were commanded by a 70-year-old grand master, Jean de la Vallette. The Great Siege lasted for more than three months, with continuous and unbelievably ferocious fighting. After enormous bloodshed on both sides, help finally arrived from Sicily and the Turks withdrew.

The knights were hailed as the saviours of Europe. Money and honours were heaped upon them by grateful monarchs, and the construction of the new city of Valletta – named after the hero of the siege – and its enormous fortifications began. Malta was never again seriously threatened by the Turks.

Although the order continued to embellish Valletta, the knights sank into corrupt and ostentatious ways, largely supported by piracy. In 1798 Napoleon arrived, seeking to counter the British influence in the Mediterranean, and the knights, who were mostly French, surrendered to him without a fight.

The Maltese defeated the French in 1800 with the assistance of the British, and in 1814 Malta officially became part of the British Empire. The British decided to develop Malta into a major naval base. In WWII, Malta once again found itself under siege. Considered a linchpin in the battle for the Mediterranean, Malta was subjected to a blockade. In 1942 it suffered five months of day-and-night bombing raids, which left 40,000 homes destroyed and the population on the brink of starvation.

In 1947 the devastated island was given a measure of self-government. Malta's best-known leaders in the postwar period have been the leader of the Nationalist Party and prime minister, Dr George Borg Olivier, who led the country to independence in 1964; and Dominic Mintoff who, as prime minister and leader of the Maltese Labour Party, established the republic in 1974. In 1979 links with Britain were reduced further when Mintoff expelled the British armed services and signed agreements with Libya, the Soviet Union and North Korea. Domestic policy focused on state enterprises.

In 1987 the Nationalist Party assumed power under the prime ministership of Dr Eddie Fenech Adami, and it was returned by a landslide victory in 1992, when one of the party's main platforms was Malta's application to join the EU. However, the 1996 general election saw the Labour Party, led by Dr Alfred Sant, narrowly regain power. One of its main policies was to remove the country's application for full EU membership. In 1998, with the application suspended, Eddie Fenech Adami's Nationalist Party was returned to power. Negotiations for EU membership have since been going on in earnest. At the time of writing, Malta was awaiting an announcement from the European Commission outlining which applicant countries would be included in the first enlargement. Membership of the EU will be subject to a public referendum.

In recent decades, the Maltese people have achieved considerable prosperity, thanks largely to tourism, but increasingly because of shipping, trade and light industries.

## GEOGRAPHY

The Maltese archipelago consists of three inhabited islands: Malta (246 sq km), Gozo (67 sq km) and Comino (2.7 sq km). They lie in the middle of the Mediterranean, 93km south of Sicily, east of Tunisia and north of Libya.

The densely populated islands are formed of soft limestone – the golden building material used in all constructions. There are some low ridges and outcrops, but no major hills. The Victoria Lines escarpment traverses the island of Malta from the coast near Baar-ic-Cagaq almost to the bay of Fomm ir-Ri. The soil is generally thin and rocky, although in some valleys it is terraced and farmed intensively. There are few trees and, for most of the year, little greenery to soften the stony, sun-bleached landscape. The notable exception is Buskett Gardens, a lush valley of trees and orange groves protected by the imposing southern Dingli Cliffs. There is virtually no surface water and there are no permanent creeks or rivers. The water table is the main source of fresh water, but it is supplemented by several large desalination plants.

## CLIMATE

Malta enjoys a sunny climate with temperatures averaging 30°C in summer. Rainfall is low (only 580mm each year) and falls mainly between November and February. Whatever time of year you visit Malta you'll notice an almost constant wind – this is the hot sirocco wind blowing across from Africa.

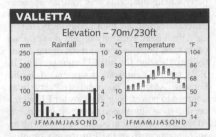

**VALLETTA**
Elevation – 70m/230ft
Rainfall / Temperature

## ECOLOGY & ENVIRONMENT

Malta's small surface area has been subjected to pressures of population, land use and development, a lack of protection for natural areas and more recently, a significant increase in pollution. The detrimental impact on the environment prompted the Maltese government to take action in 1990. Areas of ecological importance were identified and policies were drawn up to designate development zones across the islands. Hunting (of birds in particular) has been restricted, although it still remains very much part of the Maltese way of life.

## GOVERNMENT & POLITICS

Malta is an independent, neutral, democratic republic. The president has a ceremonial role and is elected by parliament. Executive power lies with the prime minister and the cabinet, the latter chosen from the majority party in the 65-member parliament.

There are two major parties: the Partit Tal-Haddiema, or Labour Party and the Partit Nazzjonalista, or Nationalist Party.

The official website for the Maltese government, Ⓦ www.gov.mt, is an excellent source of information.

## ECONOMY

The Maltese enjoy a good standard of living, low inflation and low unemployment. The economy is geared towards the rapidly expanding tourism industry, manufacturing and financial services.

## POPULATION & PEOPLE

The Maltese nation is made up of an eclectic mix of Mediterranean peoples. Malta has a population of around 360,000 with most people living in Valletta and its satellite towns; Gozo has just 30,000 residents, while Comino has only a handful.

## ARTS

If you are looking for handicrafts then you have certainly come to the right place. Handmade lace, glassware and silver filigree are among Malta's finest products. Lace-making is thought to have been introduced to the island in the 16th century when the knights arrived. There are plenty of stalls and shops selling traditional tablecloths and other such souvenirs in the more touristy areas.

Look out, too, for beautiful and intricate silver filigree – the art is thought to have been brought over to Malta from Sicily sometime during the 17th century. Maltese glassware is among the best in the world. The glassblowing industry has enjoyed increasing success and many pieces are exported internationally.

## SOCIETY & CONDUCT

Despite an easy blend of Mediterranean and British culture existing throughout the islands, there's still a strong feeling of tradition. The people remain fairly conservative in outlook and family values are held in high regard.

Females should cover up modestly in places of worship and men should opt for long trousers rather than shorts.

Smoking is permitted almost everywhere, although refrain from lighting up on public transport, unless of course you'd like to be ejected before your designated stop.

## RELIGION

Catholicism is the dominant religion and is still influential in many people's lives. This is most noticeable on Sundays when the majority of shops and businesses close down in order to mark the Sabbath. Abortion is illegal and divorce is frowned upon within the community.

## LANGUAGE

The official languages are Maltese (Malti) and English. Malti is an unusual language that has an Arabic grammar and construction, but has French, English, Italian, Spanish and Sicilian components. It is the only Semitic language to be written in the Latin alphabet. Most people speak English; French, German and Italian are also widely understood.

MALTA

See the Language chapter at the back of the book for pronunciation guidelines and useful words and phrases.

# Facts for the Visitor

## HIGHLIGHTS
The magnificent Hypogeum, a vast underground burial site in Paola, is an absolute must for anyone visiting Malta. You should also explore the medieval hill-top town of Mdina. Make sure you include a visit to neighbouring Gozo. Check out the striking megalithic temples at Ġgantija and enjoy the stunning coastline by taking a boat trip around the island. If you have time, take the ferry to Comino and make a healthy hike around the island or indulge in lazy sun-worshipping.

## PLANNING
### When to Go
Malta is a year-round destination, but try and avoid July and August when the island can get unbearably hot and is overrun with tourists. The season of *festi* runs from June to September – outside these months, accommodation costs can fall by up to 40%.

### Maps
There are plenty of maps available from bookshops and newsagencies but the best one to get hold of is the Insight Map Malta Fleximap which costs Lm3.45. Street signs are usually bilingual, but in less built-up areas they are in Malti only. Triq means street in Maltese.
   **Sapienzas Bookshop** (*☎ 21233621; 26 Republic St, Valletta*) is recommended.

### What to Bring
Bring light, cool clothing, a hat and plenty of sunscreen to protect you from the sun. Remember to bring something warm – it can become cool in the evenings. You'll probably find that you'll do lots of exploring on foot so comfortable shoes are a necessity.

## TOURIST OFFICES
### Local Tourist Offices
The **Malta Tourist Authority** (*MTA; Malta international airport: ☎ 216996073; open 24hrs daily • Valletta: ☎ 21237747; 1 City Arcade • Gozo: ☎ 21556114; Mġarr Harbour • Victoria:*

*☎ 21565171; Independence Square*) can provide a range of useful brochures, hotel listings and maps.

### Tourist Offices Abroad
The MTA has its main office in **London** (*☎ 020-7292 4900, fax 7734 1880; ⓦ www .visitmalta.com; Malta House, 36-38 Piccadilly, London, W1J 0LD*). See their website for other international representation. Maltese embassies and offices of Air Malta can also provide information.

## VISAS
Entry visas are not required for holiday visits of up to three months by nationals of Australia, Canada, the UK or the USA. Further information and useful links can be found on the MTA's official website.

## EMBASSIES & CONSULATES
### Maltese Embassies & Consulates
Malta has diplomatic missions located in the following countries:

**Australia** (*☎ 02 6290 1724*) 38 Culgoa Circuit, O'Malley, ACT 2606
**France** (*☎ 01 56597590*) 92, Ave des Champs-Elysees, Paris 75008
**Italy** (*☎ 06 687 99 47*) 12 Lungotevere Marzio, Rome 00186
**UK** (*☎ 020 7292 4800*) 36-38 Piccadilly, London W1J 0LD
**USA** (*☎ 202 462 3611*) 2017 Connecticut Ave, NW Washington, DC 20008

### Embassies & Consulates in Malta
The following countries have embassies in Malta:

**Australia** (*☎ 21338201*) Ta'Xbiex Terrace, Ta'X-biex MSD 11
**Canada** (*☎ 21233121*) 103 Archbishop St, Valletta
**Germany** (*☎ 2133157*) 5 Vilhena St, Floriana
**Tunisia** (*☎ 21345866*) 144/2 Tower Rd, Sliema
**UK** (*☎ 21233134*) 7 St Anne St, Floriana
**USA** (*☎ 21235960/65*) Development House, 3rd floor, St Anne St, Floriana

## CUSTOMS
Items for personal use are not subject to duty. One litre of spirits, 1L of wine and 200 cigarettes can be imported duty-free. Duty is charged on any gifts over Lm50 intended for local residents.

MALTA

## MONEY
### Currency
The Maltese lira is divided into 100 cents. There are one, two, five, 10, 25, 50 cent and Lm1 coins; and Lm2, Lm5, Lm10 and Lm20 notes. The currency is often referred to as the pound.

### Exchanging Money
Banks usually offer better rates of exchange than hotels or restaurants. There is a 24-hour bureau at the airport available to passengers only. Travellers arriving by ferry should note that there are no exchange facilities at the port. ATMs can be found in most towns and tourist areas.

### Exchange Rates

| country | unit | | Maltese lira |
|---------|------|---|--------------|
| Australia | A$1 | = | Lm0.25 |
| Canada | C$1 | = | Lm0.29 |
| euro zone | €1 | = | Lm0.42 |
| Japan | ¥100 | = | Lm0.36 |
| NZ | NZ$1 | = | Lm0.22 |
| UK | UK£1 | = | Lm0.65 |
| USA | US$1 | = | Lm0.44 |

### Costs
By European standards, Malta is good value, although prices are on the increase. In tourist areas you'll find that prices are typically higher. If you are travelling on a budget, reckon on around Lm10 per day. This will get you a hostel bed, a simple meal in a restaurant and plenty of snacks and drinks. Buying snacks from vendors or cooking your own meals will reduce costs.

### Tipping & Bargaining
Restaurants and taxis expect a 10% tip. Shops have fixed prices, but hotels and car hire agencies offer reduced rates in the low season (October to June). Taxi drivers are reluctant to negotiate, but make sure you agree on a firm fare before beginning your journey.

## POST & COMMUNICATIONS
### Post
Post offices are found in most towns and villages. It's worth noting that they are usually closed on Saturday afternoons, Sundays and public holidays. Local postage costs 6c; postcards or letters sent air mail to Europe cost 16c; to the USA 22c, and to Australia 27c.

### Telephone
Public telephones accept coins or phonecards. The latter can be bought at post offices and shops for Lm2, Lm3, Lm4 and Lm5. For local telephone inquiries, call ☎ 1182; for overseas inquiries, call ☎ 1152. Local calls cost 10c. The international direct dialling code is ☎ 00. International calls are discounted between 6pm and 8am weekdays and all day Saturday and Sunday.

To call Malta from abroad, dial the international access code ☎ 356 (the country code for Malta) and the number. There are no area codes in Malta; all numbers must now be preceded by ☎ 21 (note that some promotional brochures may not yet be updated).

### Email & Internet Access
Internet access is widely available throughout the islands, particularly in St Julian's and Sliema.

## DIGITAL RESOURCES
There's stacks of information on the MTA's official website (🕅 www.visitmalta.com) and also on the SearchMalta website at 🕅 www.searchmalta.com (the latter site provides details on services such as accommodation, car rental and leisure activities).

## BOOKS
For more detailed information on the Maltese islands check out Lonely Planet's *Malta*.

For a fascinating account of the Turkish siege of Malta in 1565, read *The Great Siege* by Ernle Bradford. Bradford's *Siege: Malta 1940–1943* covers the island's second major crisis. *The Kappillan of Malta* by Nicholas Monsarrat tells the story of a priest's experiences during WWII, interwoven with a potted history of Malta. For a well-illustrated study of Maltese architecture, you can try reader-recommended *5000 Years of Architecture in Malta* by Leonard Mahoney.

Many writers have spent time living here. Monsarrat lived on the island of Gozo for many years, while more recently Anthony Burgess spent time on Malta.

## NEWSPAPERS & MAGAZINES
The local English-language papers are the *Times*, the *Sunday Times*, the *Independent* and the *Independent on Sunday*. British, French, German and Italian newspapers are available on the evening of publication.

The hidden coves and sculpted coastline of Cala Gonone, on Sardinia's Gulf of Orosei

Lose yourself in the rolling hills of Tuscany

Italy's striking Dolomites

SCOTT DARSNEY

Gozo's inviting salt pans make a perfect spot to unwind, Malta

DUSHAN COORAY

Chefchouen, perched on the Rif Mountains, Morocco

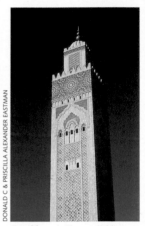

DONALD C & PRISCILLA ALEXANDER EASTMAN

Casablanca's Hassan II Mosque

DUSHAN COORAY

Just passing through, Meknès

DUSHAN COORAY

Kasbah des Oudaias and the city of Rabat in the distance, Morocco

## RADIO & TV

Two local TV stations broadcast in Malti, and all of the main Italian TV stations are received in Malta. Satellite and cable TV are widely available. The BBC World Service can be picked up on short-wave radio and some Maltese radio stations broadcast in English.

## TIME

Malta is one hour ahead of GMT/UTC.

## TOILETS

Small blocks of clean, Western-style public toilets are located throughout Malta. Paper is rarely provided, though, so stash some in your daypack or handbag.

## WOMEN TRAVELLERS

Malta remains a conservative society by Western standards and places firm belief in traditional family values. Women are primarily expected to be wives and mothers, although nowadays many women also work.

Men are friendly towards female travellers but never threatening or imposing. Normal caution should be observed but problems are unlikely. Note that the streets of Valletta are poorly lit and can be extremely quiet at night. Avoid walking alone if possible. The nightclub area in Paceville is hectic but it's not necessarily dangerous.

Dress conservatively if you are visiting churches or historical buildings – legs and shoulders should be covered modestly.

## GAY & LESBIAN TRAVELLERS

Homosexual sex was legalised in 1973. There are no predominantly gay areas in Malta but there are several openly gay and lesbian bars (see individual Entertainment entries, later).

For more information contact the **Malta Gay Rights Movement** (☎ 9949 9909). You can also visit ⓦ www.gaymalta.org.

## DISABLED TRAVELLERS

The **National Commission for Persons with Disability** (☎ 21487789, fax 21484609) can provide information on facilities and transportation. Wheelchair-bound travellers may experience problems in Valletta due to its narrow and uneven pavements, steep inclines and endless stone steps. The government is currently carrying out pavement modification to improve mobility. Many of the top-end hotels have disabled access and facilities, but public transport is not yet equipped.

## SENIOR TRAVELLERS

Malta is popular with the older generation. Those aged over 65 receive a discount at many of the listed attractions.

## TRAVEL WITH CHILDREN

Pharmacies are well stocked with baby gear including nappies, powdered milk and processed baby food. Kids might enjoy a harbour cruise (see Organised Tours under Valletta etc, later), or a visit to the **Mediterraneo Marine Park** (☎ 21372218) to see dolphins and sea lions; to get there take bus No 68 from Valletta. Older children might also enjoy the **Malta Experience**, an audiovisual presentation chronicling Malta's history and culture (see under Valletta, later).

## DANGERS & ANNOYANCES

Malta is pretty much crime free but normal precautions should be taken.

Taxi drivers will often try and overcharge unsuspecting tourists so make sure you agree on a reasonable price before you get into the vehicle. On arrival at the airport, ignore any taxi driver that tells you that the bus stop is miles away – they are just touting for business. Most towns and villages are well served by buses and are only a short (and cheap) ride from one another.

Be aware that hunting and trapping birds is a traditional pastime in Malta. It has recently been restricted but you may still see evidence of its existence.

### Emergency Services

For police emergencies call ☎ 191 and for medical emergencies call ☎ 196.

## BUSINESS HOURS

Shops are open between 9am and 1pm, and 3.30pm or 4pm and 7pm. Banks are open from 8.30am to 12.30pm or 12.45pm Monday to Friday; some banks also open in the afternoon. On Saturday they're open from 8.30am to noon. Summer hours are the same, although few banks are open in the afternoon.

Between 1 October and 30 June, offices are open from 8am to 1pm and 2.30pm or 3pm to 5.30pm Monday to Friday, and from

**MALTA**

8.30am to 1pm on Saturday; from July to September they are open 7.30am to 1.30pm Monday to Saturday.

## PUBLIC HOLIDAYS & SPECIAL EVENTS

There are fourteen national public holidays observed in Malta:

**New Year's Day** 1 January
**St Paul's Shipwreck** 10 February
**St Joseph's Day** 19 March
**Good Friday**
**Freedom Day** 31 March
**Labour Day** 1 May
**Commemoration of 1919 Independence Riots** 7 June
**Feast of Sts Peter & Paul, and Harvest Festival** 29 June
**Feast of the Assumption** 15 August
**Feast of Our Lady of Victories** 8 September
**Independence Day** 21 September
**Feast of the Immaculate Conception** 8 December
**Republic Day** 13 December
**Christmas Day** 25 December

Each village also has a *festa* (feast day) honouring their patron saint. You can't avoid getting caught up in the excitement as the whole community gets involved in the celebrations. Religious enthusiasm is apparent in the days leading up to and during the *festa* as families flock to the churches to give thanks. The streets are illuminated with thousands of lights and the festivities culminate in a huge procession. There are fireworks, marching brass bands and the villagers pay homage to a life-size statue of their patron saint. If there's a *festa* going on while you are there, don't miss it. The tourist office can supply you with details.

## ACTIVITIES
### Diving
Water babies are well catered for in Malta and Gozo. Conditions for diving are excellent and there are around 30 licensed diving schools to choose from. The MTA can provide listings. Visibility often exceeds 30m and there's a huge variety of marine life, including over 40 types of fish. The warm temperatures of the Mediterranean (with highs of 25°C in summer, falling only to 14°C in the winter) mean that diving is possible all the year-round.

Diving is strictly monitored by the Maltese government, and all divers must provide a medical certificate from either their own doctor or a local doctor (Lm3, available through dive centres). The minimum age for diving is 14 years. People wanting to dive unaccompanied will also need a local diving permit (Malta C-Card; Lm2), which is granted on presentation of a medical certificate, proof of qualification (minimum CMAS two-star) and two passport-sized photos.

A PADI open-water dive course will cost from Lm125. One escorted shore dive with equipment hire will cost about Lm15. **Maltaqua** (☎ 21571873; W www.maltaqua.com; St Paul's Bay), **Divecare** (☎ 21319994; St Julian's, Malta) and also **Calypso Diving** (☎ 21561757; W www.calypsodivers.com; Marina St, Marsalforn, Gozo) have been recommended by readers. Favourite dive spots include Ċirkewwa on Malta and Dwejra Blue Hole on Gozo.

### Horse Riding
There's plenty of scope for horse lovers with many riding schools providing lessons or pony treks. **Darmanin's Riding School** (☎ 2123 5649; Stables Lane, Marsa) charges Lm4 per hour for accompanied rides year-round.

### Walking
Distances on the Maltese islands are relatively small, so you can cover a lot of the islands on foot. Bear in mind that high temperatures in the summer months can make walking uncomfortable and unpleasant. Invest in a sunhat or sacrifice 15c for a more congenial bus ride.

### Swimming & Sunbathing
The best sandy beaches on Malta are Ġnejna Bay; **Ghajn Tuffiħea** and Golden Bay (bus Nos 47, 51 and 652); Paradise Bay (bus Nos 45, 48 and 645); Ramla Bay; Armier Bay (bus No 50); **Melliħea Bay** (bus Nos 44, 45 and 48); and also St George's Bay (bus Nos 64 and 67).

The best sandy beaches on Gozo are Ramla Bay (bus No 42) and Xlendi Bay (bus No 87). On Comino, the best beaches are Santa Maria Bay and San Niklaw Bay (private). They can get extremely crowded during high season.

### WORK
It is difficult for foreigners to work legally in Malta. Working without a permit is not encouraged.

MALTA

## ACCOMMODATION

Accommodation in Malta is plentiful and the MTA can provide listings. Camping is not permitted but you can easily find a cheap bed in a hostel (see Valletta, Sliema & St Julian's, later). Most places offer significantly reduced rates during off-peak periods and there are often reductions for stays of more than one night. The high season is generally June to September and some places also class the weeks over Christmas as high season. Another cheap option is to board with a local family. This can be arranged through the National Student Travel Service (NSTS); see Air in the Getting There & Away section, later, for contact details.

The NSTS is an associate member of Hostelling International (HI). It runs several hostels in Malta and also has agreements with certain guesthouses to provide cheap accommodation to hostellers. An HI-membership card is required in order to stay at any of the hostels in Malta. Cards can be obtained from the NSTS or from the main hostel, Hibernia House (see Places to Stay under Valletta, Sliema & St Julian's for contact details).

## FOOD

Malta is not well known for its cuisine but food fanatics won't be disappointed (neither will those on a budget). Most restaurants offer cheap pizzas and pastas and there's a good variety of vegetarian options on almost every menu. The national dish is *fenech* (rabbit), which is fried or baked in a casserole and is invariably cooked to perfection. Make sure you try the locally caught fish and seafood. There's plenty to choose from and portions are generous.

Other local favourites to look out for are *pastizzi*, the savoury pasties filled with cheese or mushy peas, and *bragioli*, which are spicy beef rolls.

Fresh produce is widely available from grocers and market stalls. Try the peppered Gozo cheese.

## DRINKS

Local beers are good. Cisk (pronounced *chisk*) is recommended and costs about 90c a pint. A good selection of wine is also available and the locally produced Pinot grigio (about Lm5 a bottle) is certainly worth a tipple. Ask your waiter for recommendations. Imported beers, wines and spirits can be bought everywhere.

## ENTERTAINMENT

There's plenty to do in the evenings with most bars and restaurants staying open until the early hours. Many restaurants don't open until 7pm and the Maltese tend to eat late so don't be surprised if things seem quiet in the early evening. If you are staying in the smaller towns there are often restaurants or bars with live music and a friendly local clientele to keep you entertained.

## SHOPPING

Shopaholics should be perfectly safe in Malta as there's little temptation (unless you have a weakness for lace, silver filigree or glassware of course). Other favourite handicrafts include hand-knitted clothing which can be picked up quite cheaply. Prices are always lower away from the main tourist areas.

# Getting There & Away

## AIR

Malta is well connected to Europe and North Africa. Scheduled prices aren't particularly good, but there are some excellent packages. Some bargains are available through **NSTS** (☎ 244983, fax 230330; e e@nsts.org; 220 St Paul St, Valletta), the representative in Malta for most student travel organisations and an associate member of Hostelling International (HI). **Air Malta** (☎ 21662211; w www.air malta.com) has scheduled flights to many destinations. See the website for details.

Air Malta has a series of agencies worldwide. They include:

**Australia** (☎ 02-9244 2111) World Aviation Systems, 403 George St, Sydney, NSW 2000
**Canada** (☎ 416-604 4112) Trans-Med Aviation Inc, 3323 Dundas Street West, Toronto M6P 2A6
**Egypt** (☎ 02-578 2692) Air Malta Office, Nile Hilton Commercial Centre, 34 Tahrir Square, Cairo
**UK** (☎ 020-8785 3199) Air Malta House, 314-316 Upper Richmond Rd, Putney, London SW15 6TU
**USA** (☎ 800 756 2582) World Aviation Systems, 300 N Continental Blvd, STE 610, Los Angeles

Other airlines servicing the country include Alitalia, KLM and Lufthansa. Avoid buying tickets in Malta if you can as prices are higher.

MALTA

You can often pick up a cheap charter flight from the UK during winter. Consult a travel agency to see what offers are available.

## SEA

Malta has regular sea links in summer with both Sicily (Palermo, Pozzallo, Syracuse and Catania) and northern Italy (Genoa and Livorno). Cars may be brought by ferry from Sicily and may be imported for up to three months.

The Italy–Malta ferry services change schedules frequently so it is best to confirm the information given here with a travel agency. **SMS Agency** (*☎ 21232211; 311 Republic St, Valletta*) has information about all of the services on offer.

**Virtú Ferries** (*☎ 21318854*) runs fast catamaran services to Sicily (Catania, Pozzallo and Licata). The journey to Catania takes three hours and costs Lm36 for an open return (a same-day return costs Lm24).

Other companies operate regular car-ferry services to Italian and Tunisian ports. The journey to Catania takes around 12 hours and a deck passenger is charged Lm20 (cars cost Lm35). You can book with **MA.RE.SI Shipping** whose head office is at SMS Agency (see earlier). **Grimaldi Ferries** (*☎ 21226873*) run between Malta and Salerno.

It is important to note that ferries do not have exchange facilities and there are none at Malta's port. Nor is there public transport the 500m from the port to the city of Valletta.

## DEPARTURE TAX

All passengers departing by sea are required to pay Lm4 departure tax which should be added by the travel agency when you buy your ticket.

# Getting Around

## BUS

Malta and Gozo are served by a network of buses run by the Malta Public Transport Authority (ATP). Most of Malta's services originate from the chaotic **City gate terminus** (*information ☎ 21250007*), situated just outside Valletta's city gates. The buses are bright yellow, many of them relics of the 1950s. Fares are cheap, ranging from 15c to 50c, depending on how many stages you pass through and whether it is an express service. Services

are regular and the more popular routes run until 11pm at night. Ask at the tourist office or an ATP kiosk for a free timetable.

Bus No 45 runs regularly from Valletta to Ċirkewwa to connect with the ferry to Gozo.

On Gozo, the bus terminus is located in Victoria, just south of Republic St. All services depart from here and cost 15c. Bus No 25 runs from the ferry port of Mġarr to Victoria.

## TAXI

Taxis are quite expensive. Some late-night fares will be unavoidable but make sure you establish a price in advance. From Valletta to St Julian's it's around Lm5. **Wembley Motors** (*☎ 21374141; St Andrews*) offers a 24-hour service.

## CAR & MOTORCYCLE

With low rental rates and cheap fuel it makes economic sense to hire a car but unless you're an extremely confident driver it's hardly worth the aggravation. Like the British, the Maltese drive on the left, but here the similarity stops. Indicators are rarely used, road rules are often ignored and with one of the highest accident rates in Europe, it can be an unnerving experience. Roads are confusingly signposted and parking can be difficult on Saturday and Sunday, and on holidays. All the car-hire companies are represented at the airport but rates vary so shop around. At the time of research **Hertz** (*☎ 21314636; 66 Gzira Rd, Gzira*) was offering a weekly summer rate of Lm72 for a small car (Lm58 a week in the low season). Local garages charge less. **La Ronde** (*☎ 21322962; Belvedere St, Gzira*) hires out motorcycles from Lm10 per day. Reductions are available with multiday rentals.

### Road Rules

The speed limits (64km/h on highways and 40km/h in urban areas) should slow you down but many drivers fail to observe them. Road conditions are invariably poor with lots of potholes and inadequate markings. There are no right of way rules at roundabouts and at intersections priority is given to whoever gets there first. Drink drivers are not tolerated and are subject to heavy fines.

### BICYCLE

Don't bother hiring a bicycle on Malta as the erratic driving, hills and daytime heat can make the experience extremely unpleasant.

Gozo is a better option for cyclists as it is much smaller and quieter. **Marsalforn Hotel** *(☎ 21556147)* hires out bicycles to suit all ages from Lm2 per day.

## HITCHHIKING
Hitchhiking is unusual and is frowned upon.

## BOAT
There's a regular ferry service between Ċirkewwa (Malta) and Mġarr (Gozo) that takes 30 minutes and runs every 45 minutes from 6am to 11.30pm (extended on Saturday and Sunday). It costs Lm5.75 return for a car with a driver and Lm1.75 for each additional passenger. You pay for your ticket on the return leg. All ferries are run by the **Gozo Channel Company** *(information ☎ 2155 6016)*. Many Maltese families head across to Gozo at the weekends so allow for delays.

If you'd like to travel between Valletta and Sliema, there is a **ferry service** *(☎ 2133 8981)*, which costs 35c one way. Ferries run from 7.30am to 6.15pm and depart from the Strand in Sliema.

If you want to explore Malta's impressive coastline at a slower pace one interesting option is to charter a yacht from **Captain Morgan Cruises** *(☎ 2134 3373)*.

## HELICOPTER
There is a regular helicopter service between Malta international airport and Gozo. Tickets cost Lm17 one way and Lm25 return (concessions are available). There are also tours by helicopter of the islands. Contact any travel agency for information and bookings.

## ORGANISED TOURS
There are lots of companies offering tours around the islands. Half-day tours cost around Lm4 but prices vary so shop around. If you're pushed for time they can be a good way to see the highlights but itineraries can often be rushed with little or no free time. A full-day trip around Malta will cost around Lm6. Day trips to Gozo and Comino are also available.

**Captain Morgan Cruises** *(☎ 21343373; Sliema)* runs sailing trips, cruises and jeep safaris. See the Valletta, Sliema & St Julian's section for information on harbour tours.

Day tours to Sicily are available from travel agencies. The journey takes 90 minutes by catamaran and the tour includes a visit to Mt Etna and Taormina. Prices begin at Lm36.

# Valletta, Sliema & St Julian's

Valletta, the city of the Knights of the Order of St John, is a settlement steeped in history and renowned for its architectural excellence. Commercial activity bustles around Republic St but wandering around the quiet back streets is where you'll really get a feel for everyday life. The city overlooks the impressive Grand Harbour to the southeast and Marsamxett Harbour to the northwest. To the southeast, the fortified peninsulas of Vittoriosa and Senglea, as well as Cospicua, are collectively known as the Three Cities.

The modern and fashionable areas of Sliema, St Julian's and Paċeville lie to the north of Valletta. Constantly being developed, they are crammed with high-rise hotels, apartment blocks, shops, restaurants, bars and nightclubs.

## Orientation
The eastern side of the island is intensively developed. Valletta and its surrounding suburbs have effectively merged to create a sprawling mass of industry, tourist facilities and residential homes. The airport is situated just southwest of the capital

The ferries from Italy dock in the Grand Harbour below Valletta. It's a steep 15-minute climb to the City Gate bus terminus.

## Information
Valletta's **local tourist office** *(☎ 237747; 1 City Arcade, Valletta)* can provide help with visitor inquiries.

The **post office** *(Castile Square; open 8.15am-4.30pm Mon-Fri, 8.15am-12.30pm Sat)* is near Auberge de Castile and there is no poste-restante service.

There are several banks in Valletta's main street, Republic St, including branches of the HSBC Bank at Nos 15 and 233. You can also change money at **Thomas Cook** *(☎ 2123 3629; 20 Republic St, Valletta ● ☎ 2134 0750; il-Piazzetta, Tower Rd, Sliema)*.

The **YMCA** *(☎ 21240680; 178 Merchants St, Valletta; open 10am-9pm Mon-Sat)* offers Internet access at 75c for half an hour. At the **Għall Kafé** *(☎ 21319694; 118 St George's Rd, Paċeville)* you'll pay 50c for 20 minutes. Multiuse cards can be purchased.

MALTA

# VALLETTA, SLIEMA & ST JULIAN'S

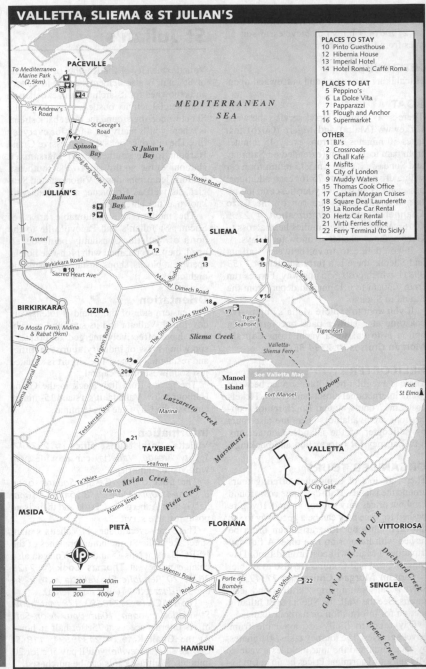

**PLACES TO STAY**
10 Pinto Guesthouse
12 Hibernia House
13 Imperial Hotel
14 Hotel Roma; Caffé Roma

**PLACES TO EAT**
5 Peppino's
6 La Dolce Vita
7 Papparazzi
11 Plough and Anchor
16 Supermarket

**OTHER**
1 BJ's
2 Crossroads
3 Ghall Kafé
4 Misfits
8 City of London
9 Muddy Waters
15 Thomas Cook Office
17 Captain Morgan Cruises
18 Square Deal Launderette
19 La Ronde Car Rental
20 Hertz Car Rental
21 Virtù Ferries office
22 Ferry Terminal (to Sicily)

MALTA

Most of the better hotels have a laundry service. For those that don't, the **Square Deal launderette** *(40 The Strand, Sliema)* charges a rather steep Lm2.50 per load.

## Things to See

A walk around the city walls is a good way to get your bearings. The views are spectacular and you'll get to see many of the city's highlights along the way. **St John's Co-Cathedral** *(St John's St; admission free but donations welcome)* dominates the centre of town with its grave exterior and impressive clock tower. Its baroque interior is breathtaking and the floor is covered with marble tombstones, marking the resting place of knights and dignitaries. The **museum** *(admission Lm1; open 9.15am-12.30pm & 1.30pm-4.15pm*

*Mon-Fri, 9.15am-12.30pm Sat)* houses a collection of tapestries and two magnificent works by the Italian painter, Caravaggio.

The **Grand Master's Palace** *(Republic St)* is now the seat of the Maltese parliament, and is open to the public when parliament is not in session. The corridors are lined with paintings of the Grand Masters and there is an exquisite fresco depicting the Great Siege. The **Armoury** is also worth a visit.

**Fort St Elmo** *(admission 50c; open 1.10pm-4.30pm Sat, 9am-4.30pm Sun)* was built in 1552 by the Knights of St John. It is shaped like a four-pointed star and its strategic location and design were vital to the islands' defence. Each month the Malta re-Enactment Society stages a military demonstration. Contact the tourist office for details.

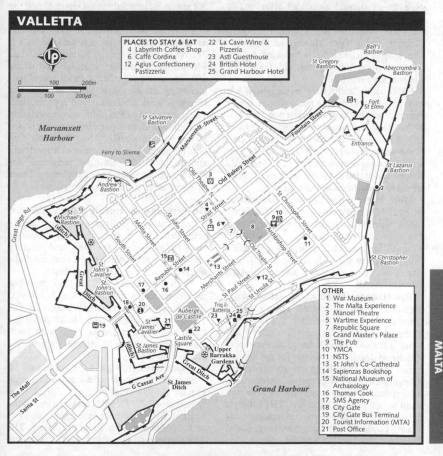

### VALLETTA

**PLACES TO STAY & EAT**
4 Labyrinth Coffee Shop
6 Caffé Cordina
12 Agius Confectionery Pastizzeria
22 La Cave Wine & Pizzeria
23 Asti Guesthouse
24 British Hotel
25 Grand Harbour Hotel

**OTHER**
1 War Museum
2 The Malta Experience
3 Manoel Theatre
5 Wartime Experience
7 Republic Square
8 Grand Master's Palace
9 The Pub
10 YMCA
11 NSTS
13 St John's Co-Cathedral
14 Sapienzas Bookshop
15 National Museum of Archaeology
16 Thomas Cook
17 SMS Agency
18 City Gate
19 City Gate Bus Terminal
20 Tourist Information (MTA)
21 Post Office

MALTA

Next to Fort St Elmo there is a small **war museum** *(admission Lm1; open 7.45am-2pm daily summer, 8.15am-5pm daily winter)* commemorating Malta's involvement in WWII. The museum is informative, yet moving, and should not be missed. It is here that the George Cross, which was presented to the Maltese people for their determination and bravery, is proudly displayed.

Another highlight is the **Manoel Theatre** *(☎ 21246389; 115 Old Theatre St; theatre tours Lm1.65; open 10am-1pm & 5pm-7pm Mon-Fri, 10am-noon Sat)*. It is one of the oldest theatres in Europe and was built by Grand Master Manoel de Vilhena in 1731. It has enjoyed a chequered past and during the latter half of the 19th century it served as a doss house for beggars. It has now been restored to its rightful glory and offers a full and varied programme of events. Theatre tours are available at 10.30am, 11.30am, 12.30pm and 4.30pm Monday to Saturday. The tour price includes admission to the museum (look out for the old fashioned wind-making machine).

Multimedia audiovisual experiences are springing up all the time but some are better than others. **The Malta Experience** *(☎ 2124 3776; Mediterranean Conference Centre, 103 Archbishop St; admission Lm3; open 11am-4pm Mon-Fri, 11am-1pm Sat & Sun)* provides a good introduction to the island's history and culture. Shows start every hour on the hour during opening times.

Much better is the **Wartime Experience** *(☎ 21227436; Embassy Cinema, Triq Santa Lucija; admission Lm2; screenings 10am, 11am, noon & 1pm daily)*, a poignant 45-minute film presentation depicting Malta's struggle against the odds during WWII. The history is clearly explained and the footage cleverly edited.

The **National Museum of Archaeology** *(Republic St; admission Lm1; open 7.45am-2pm daily mid-June–Sept; 8.15am-5pm Mon-Sat, 8.15am-4.15pm Sun Oct–mid-June)* is housed in the Auberge de Provence, which was designed by Cassar for the knights from Provence. The large airy rooms have a strangely calming effect and the information is comprehensive and easy to follow. The museum has a notable collection of Tarxien-style figurines – fat ladies with interchangeable heads. Look out for the Sleeping Lady, thought to date back to 3000 BC.

## Organised Tours
**Captain Morgan Cruises** *(☎ 21343373)* operates short harbour cruises for Lm6.25 throughout the day, and a variety of half- and full-day cruises around the islands, priced from Lm11.95. Boats leave from the Strand in Sliema and tickets can be purchased at any of the travel agencies on the waterfront. It also offers an underwater safari, with passengers seated in a glass observation keel, for Lm4.95. All tours are subject to weather conditions.

## Places to Stay
**Hostels** The main hostel is **Hibernia House** *(☎ 21333859, fax 21230330; Depiro St, Sliema; dorm beds Lm3.95)*. To get there, take bus No 62 or 67 to Balluta Bay, walk up St Francis St, turn right into Depiro St and the hostel is 200m on your left.

There are other hostels, or places which have hostel-price agreements with the NSTS. The NSTS offers a special hostelling package which includes airport welcome and transfers, seven overnight stays (with breakfast), including at least one night at Hibernia House, a week's bus pass and a phonecard. The package costs Lm75 for accommodation in eight-bed dorms (supplements apply for rooms with two beds). The NSTS must be notified seven days in advance of arrival date and flight details must be provided: for NSTS' contact details see the Getting There & Away section, earlier in this chapter.

**Guesthouses & Hotels** There's little distinction between a large guesthouse and a small hotel but in general the guesthouses tend to be family operated and slightly cheaper. It's advisable to ring ahead and make reservations at least a day in advance.

**Pinto Guesthouse** *(☎ 21313897; e info@pintohotel.com; Sacred Heart Ave, St Julian's; high season singles/doubles/triples, Lm8.50/13.50/15, low season Lm5.50/8/10.50)* has clean and spacious rooms, most with bathrooms. It is a steep 10-minute walk to this place from the bay.

**Imperial Hotel** *(☎ 21344093, Rudolph St, Sliema; e imperial@waldonet.net.mt; high season singles/doubles Lm16.50/27, low season Lm10.70/15.40)* is tucked away in the heart of Sliema but once inside you can't fail to be impressed with its grand decor. The facilities include a pool and courtyard garden.

MALTA

**Hotel Roma** *(☎ 2131587; Ghar Il-Lembi St, Sliema; rooms Lm10-14)* has bright cheery rooms with good facilities and a café and restaurant downstairs.

**Asti Guesthouse** *(☎ 21239506; 18 St Ursula St; Lm5.50 year-round)*, in Valletta, was once a convent. Rooms are quite basic but very good value.

**Grand Harbour Hotel** *(☎ 21246003; 47 Battery St, Valletta; Lm9.90 per person)* has small but pleasant rooms. There are no reductions off season. The hotel overlooks the Grand Harbour and has a rooftop sundeck.

**British Hotel** *(☎ 21239711;* e *info@brit ishhotel.com; 40 Battery St, Valletta; singles/ twins Lm12/18 year-round)* is a family-run place next door. The inland rooms are a bit dark and soulless but all have bathrooms.

**Kappara Hotel** *(☎ 21387297)*, a men-only gay hotel, has excellent facilities including a bar situated in a WWII bomb shelter. For more information contact the hotel.

## Places to Eat

There are lots of cheap restaurants, cafés and bars in Sliema, Paċeville and around St Julian's Bay. Prices are fairly standard – around Lm2 for a pizza and Lm2.50 for pasta.

Fight your way through the huge portions on the kitsch menu at **Paparazzi** *(☎ 2137 4966)*. Overlooking Spinola Bay it's a great place to people-watch while you polish off one of their potent cocktails.

**Peppino's**, just over the road, is popular with both locals and tourists. The excellent food and welcoming atmosphere make it a haunt that should not be bypassed lightly. A meal for two, with wine costs around Lm15.

**La Dolce Vita** *(☎ 21337036; 159 St George's Rd; open 11am-11pm)*, back on the same side of the road as Paparazzi, is where you'll find the best place to go for fresh fish. It has a balcony for outside dining and is frequented by locals. Try the swordfish at Lm5.75.

**Plough and Anchor** *(☎ 21334725; 1 Main St, St Julian's)* has good cheap pub grub and a cosy bar downstairs crammed with maritime paraphernalia. The restaurant upstairs has a more extensive menu.

**La Cave Winecellar & Pizzeria** *(☎ 2124 3677; Castile Square; pizzas Lm2-3)* is situated beneath the Castille Hotel in Valletta. The wine list is as long as your arm and the pizza *calzones* are huge.

**Caffe Cordina** *(☎ 21234385; 244/5 Republic St)* is the place to go for a daytime snack in Valletta. Indoor and outside dining allows you to enjoy their famous sweets and coffees whatever the weather.

**Labyrinth** *(44 Strait St)*, also in Valletta, is a coffee shop with some good lunchtime choices. The basement supper club has a wider menu and often has live jazz.

While you're on the move, treat yourself to a delicious savoury *pastizzi* or jammy cake from **Agius Confectionery Pastizzeria** *(273 St Paul St)* – they're only 5c each.

## Entertainment

You'll find little going on after dark in Valletta so if you crave a bit of nightlife head to Paċeville. It is jam-packed at the weekends and all bars and clubs stay open until late. Wander until you find something to your taste (or quiet enough to get in the door). For jazz and blues head for **BJ's** *(Ball St)*. Drinks are fairly cheap and the atmosphere is nice and chilled. For shooters and cocktails check out **Crossroads**, a lively bar, open until 4am at weekends, with a good variety of loud music. **Misfits** has DJs at weekends and is popular with the young and trendy. During the week it's a lot more laidback and holds jazz, film and alternative nights. **Muddy Waters** is favoured by the student crowd and has live bands and drinks promotions on Thursday nights.

Raise a glass in memory of the late Oliver Reed in his favourite drinking spot, simply named **The Pub** *(136 Archbishop St, Valletta)*. It has a good selection of beers and cheap snacks.

There are several gay and lesbian bars. **City of London** *(Balluta St, St Julian's)* is packed at weekends (everyone is welcome) and there's a great party atmosphere.

## Getting Around

Bus No 8 leaves from outside the departures hall at Malta international airport terminal about every half hour and goes to the Valletta City Gate bus terminus. The journey costs 15c. Taxis operate on official rates – book one at the designated booth. To Sliema or St Julian's it costs Lm8.

## AROUND VALLETTA

The town of Paola could be swiftly passed through were it not for the magnificent

**MALTA**

**Hypogeum** (☎ 21825579; admission Lm3; open 8.30am-4pm daily), a complex of underground burial chambers. The number of daily visitors has recently been restricted in order to preserve this Unesco National World Heritage Site. Tickets should be purchased as soon as you arrive in Malta as there is often a waiting period of several days. At the time of writing, tickets were only available directly from the Hypogeum. Take bus No 8, 11 or 27 from Valletta. Admission includes a short film and fascinating tour around the chambers.

While you are in Paola, take the time to visit the **Tarxien Temples** (admission Lm1). These megalithic temples are thought to have been erected in 3000 BC.

For accommodation you could try the **University Residence** (☎ 21436168, fax 21434963; Triq R.M.Bonnici; Lija bus No 40 from Valletta; dorm beds per night Lm6, min 2-night stay).

# Around Malta

## NORTH COAST
**Buġibba** is the traditional name for St Paul's Bay but it could just as easily be called 'Package Resort Central'. Crammed full of hotels, bars and restaurants it gets bombarded by tourists in summer. It's fine if you want a couple of weeks of pure hedonism, but there are much nicer places to plump for with lots more to offer. Catch bus No 43, 44, 45, 49 or 58 from Valletta.

Much of the rest of the north coast is exposed and uninhabited.

You can stay in **Crystal Hotel** (☎ 2157 3022, fax 21571975; 100 Triq Il Halel; Buġibba bus No 49 from Valletta or No 70 from Sliema; dorm bed per night Lm5.50, min 3-night stay).

## WEST COAST
Solitude can be difficult to find in the summer months but if you are desperate for some peace and quiet the west coast is your best option. The best access is by private boat.

## MOSTA
Mosta is a bustling little market town but has little to recommend apart from its **church**. It was designed by Maltese architect Giorgio Grognet de Vassé and work began in 1833.

Twenty-seven years later the church was complete, resplendent with what is thought to be the largest unsupported dome in Europe. It was struck by three enemy bombs during WWII but miraculously, the damage was minimal and no-one was hurt. To get there take bus No 49 or 58 from Valletta.

## MDINA & RABAT
Mdina, once the capital of Malta, is perched on an easily defendable, rocky outcrop in the southwest of Malta. Thanks to its geographical attributes, it has been a fortified city for over 3000 years and was the islands political centre before the knights arrived and chose to settle around the Grand Harbour. Affectionately nicknamed The Silent City, you can spend hours wandering around the quiet, narrow streets. Despite the small honey pots of tourist bustle that have inevitably developed, the city has retained its historical charm.

The name Mdina comes from the Arabic term for 'walled city'. Rabat is the sprawling town settlement outside the walls to Mdina's south.

## Things to See & Do
Mdina's main piazza is dominated by the **cathedral**. It is not as impressive as St Paul's in Valletta but still worth visiting to see the marble tombstones covering the floor and the huge fresco of St Paul's Shipwreck. The adjacent **museum** (admission Lm1; open 9am-4.30pm Mon-Fri, 9am-2pm Sat) has an impressive marble hall.

The **Mdina Experience** (☎ 21454322; 7 Mesquita Square; admission Lm1.60; open 10.30am-4.30pm Mon-Fri, 10.30am-2pm Sat) is the local version of Valletta's Malta Experience.

Alternatively, you can wander around the **Mdina Dungeons** (Vilhena Palace, St Publius Square; admission Lm1.50). The restored dungeons have waxwork dummies depicting torture methods throughout the ages. It might prove popular with gore-obsessed adolescents but unfortunately has little else going for it.

Your time would be far better spent in Rabat where you can visit **St Paul's Church** and **St Paul's grotto** (a cave where St Paul is said to have preached during his stay on the island). Further down the road you will find **St Paul's Catacombs** (admission Lm1; open daily), a series of rock-cut tombs thought to date back to the 3rd century.

Far more interesting are the nearby **St Agatha's Catacombs** *(admission 50c; open 9am-5.30pm Mon-Fri, 9am-1pm Sat July-Sept, 9am-noon & 1pm-5pm Mon-Fri, 9am-1pm Sat Oct-June)*, an underground complex of burial chambers boasting some amazing Byzantine frescoes. Wait by the entrance to the museum for the next guided tour. The tunnels are quite low in some places and movement can be restricted but don't let this put you off – the tour is fascinating.

## Places to Eat
For a relaxing lunch or a quick afternoon drink you can't go far wrong with the **Fontanella Tea Garden** *(1 Bastion St)*. Built into the fortifications, it offers fantastic views from the outside terrace.

Unobtrusive **Medina** *(7 Holy Cross St)* is one of Malta's best restaurants. The menu offers Italian, French and Maltese dishes and a meal for two with wine will set you back around Lm20.

There are plenty of places to eat and drink in Rabat but you can't beat **Baron snack bar** *(light lunch mains around Lm3.50)* for the interesting local clientele and cheap, simple food and snacks.

## Getting There & Away
Catch bus No 80 or 81 from Valletta to reach Mdina and Rabat.

## SOUTH COAST
The views are fantastic from the top of **Dingli Cliffs**, although the nearby stone quarries provide a noisy, industrial soundtrack in the background.

Further inland you can see a good example of cart ruts, an interesting topographical feature that repeatedly occurs across the island. These ruts have been dated back to prehistoric times but their origin remains a mystery. British visitors have nicknamed this collection **Clapham Junction**, after a notoriously complicated London train station.

To the southeast, you'll find the village of Qrendi and the nearby prehistoric temples of **Hagar Qim** *(admission Lm1; open daily)* and **Mnajdra**. Built between 3600 and 3000 BC these megalithic structures have been partially restored to give an idea of what they once may have looked like. Unfortunately, Mnajdra, the more interesting of the two, has been defaced by vandals and was closed to

the public at the time of writing. It is not known when it will be reopened.

## EAST COAST
Marsaxlokk is a tiny fishing village and a charming place to spend a couple of hours. The natural harbour is crammed with colourful fishing boats and there are a couple of good fish restaurants where you can sample the local fare.

Take bus No 27 or 30 from Valletta to get there. Buses run from 6.30am to 7.30pm every half hour, more frequently on Sunday, and cost 15c.

# Gozo

The island of Gozo is much smaller and quieter than Malta and life slips by at a slower pace. Fewer tourists venture over to Gozo and if they do, it is often on a day trip. The sights can be packed into one day but we recommend spending several days there – traipse round the sights, visit the beach, take a boat trip or simply relax.

## VICTORIA (RABAT)
Victoria is the commercial centre of Gozo, a busy town located in the middle of the island. There are no hotels around here but plenty of other facilities. Victoria's quite helpful **tourist office** *(☎ 2156 5171; Independence Square)* can provide information on anything you might need. The square is a hive of activity with open-air cafés, treasure-trove craft shops and traders peddling their fresh produce. The bus station is just south of Republic St, about 10-minutes' walk from the Citadel. All bus routes originate and terminate here.

Victoria is built on a hill, crowned by the **Citadel** (also known as Il-Kastell, or Citadella). A stroll around the Citadel offers breathtaking views across the island but beware of the well-worn steps and walkways. The **Cathedral of the Assumption** was built between 1697 and 1711 and was designed by Lorenzo Gafa. Its elegant design is marred only by the fact that funds ran out before completion and the structure remained flat-topped. This can not be detected from inside due to an elaborate trompe l'oeil painted on the ceiling. The illusion is impressive.

The archaeological and folklore **museums** display good collections, but if you are pushed

MALTA

for time, you don't need to feel like you've missed out – the museums in Valletta are much better.

## MARSALFORN

Marsalforn is built around a picturesque cove and is the favoured choice for tourists in the summer months. Just to the east of the cove you'll find some interesting salt pans and strangely eroded cliffs.

You can change money at the **HSBC Bank** (*open 8am-12.45pm Mon-Fri Nov–mid-June, 8am-11.30am mid-June–Oct*) on the harbour front.

Gozo is an excellent place for diving and there are several dive shops dotted around (see Activities in the Facts for the Visitor section, earlier, for more information). You can also book boat trips at the kiosk on the harbour front. This is the best way to enjoy the breathtaking coastline and see features such as the **Azure Window** and the **Inland Sea**. A half-day tour of Gozo and Comino costs Lm6 per person. You can hire cars at **Smugglers Rent-A-Car** (*☎ 21551005; 22 Marina St*) for Lm12 per day in high season (minimum three-day rental period). There are several supermarkets and grocery shops.

### Places to Stay

**Atlantis Hotel** (*☎ 21554685; e info@atl antisgozo.com; Qolla St; inland rooms per person low/high season Lm6/14*) is family-run and has comfortable rooms. Cars and jeeps can be hired and there are excellent leisure facilities available.

**Marsalforn Hotel** (*☎ 21556147; B&B per person Lm7*) is a bright-green and white guesthouse situated on a road junction. Bicycles can be hired here. If you are travelling with a group it will work out much cheaper if you hire an apartment. The hotel also has spacious **self-catering flats** that sleep up to six people, costing Lm18/15 per night in high/low season. Prices can vary a great deal according to availability so book in advance. Contact Joseph & Maria Bugeja (*☎ 2155 3630; e bugejajoe @vol.net.mt*) for details.

### Places to Eat

The restaurants clustered around the harbour serve decent, cheap food but they are nothing to write home about. **Il-Kartell** (*☎ 21556918; Marina St*), on the west side of the bay, is rather better. It is housed in a couple of ren-

ovated boatsheds and serves great fish dishes at reasonable prices.

**Il-Forno** (*☎ 21565140; 25 Marina St*), on the opposite side of the bay, is another good choice. It is the oldest building in Marsalforn and serves appetising home-cooked food, including Maltese specialities. There's live music and a good selection of wines.

### Getting there & Away

Marsalforn is a 4km walk from Victoria, or you can catch bus No 21 from the main terminus.

## XAGĦRA

For such a small town there's a lot to see in Xagħra. To the south of the main street you'll find **Ta'Kola Windmill** (*admission Lm1; open 7.45am-2pm daily mid-June–Sept, 8.15am-5pm Mon-Sat, 8.15am-4pm Sun Oct–mid-June*). You can climb to the top of the tower to see the original mechanical fittings from the 18th century or wander around the small museum. Admission includes entrance to Ġgantija.

Close by are the megalithic temples of **Ġgantija** (*open 8.30am-4.30pm Mon-Sat, 8.30am-3pm Sun*). The route to the temples is well signposted, although you can always follow the trail of other holidaymakers if you get lost. These megalithic temples date back to 3000 to 3600 BC and are the largest of their kind in Malta – the walls are over 6m high. Little is known about the people who built them but evidence of sacrificial offerings have been discovered on this site.

**Xerri's Grotto** (*☎ 21552733; admission 50c; open daily*) and **Nino's Cave** (*admission 35c; open daily*) are located to the north of the main street. These underground caves boast an astounding collection of stalactites and stalagmites. Access is gained through private houses and they are open at the owner's discretion (usually 9am to 6pm in summer).

It's not far from here to one of the best beaches on Gozo. **Ramla Bay** has a beautiful sandy beach that is perfect for sunbathing. It gets crowded in summer so you'll need to get there early to get a good spot. Follow the signposts from the town. There's a small car park and a café serving drinks and snacks.

### Places to Stay & Eat

**Xagħra Lodge** (*☎ 21562362; e xagħra lodge@waldonet.net.mt; Dun Gorg Preca St; rooms per person high/low season Lm10/8*) has comfortable guesthouse accommodation. Facilities include a swimming pool, bar and Chinese restaurant.

**Oleander's** (☎ 21557230; open noon-3pm & 7pm-10pm Tues-Sat) is situated on the main square and is a great place to go for lunch or dinner. Pastas, steaks and Maltese dishes are all reasonably priced.

# Comino

While staying on Gozo you should hop across to the neighbouring island of Comino. It is more or less uninhabited and perfect for getting away from the hustle and bustle. It is only 2.5km by 1.5km in size so it is impossible to get lost. The main attraction is the **Blue Lagoon**, a sheltered cove with a clean sandy beach and sparkling blue water. You can hike around the whole of Comino in a few hours but don't forget to protect yourself against the sun as the island is extremely exposed.

**Comino Hotel** (☎ 21529821; ⓦ *www.com inohotels.com*) runs a frequent ferry service between Mġarr Harbour and Comino, costing Lm2. Pay at the reception before you return to Gozo.

# Morocco

Morocco is not the first place you'd think of as Mediterranean, but with mainland Spain only 35 minutes away, it's easier to get here from Europe than it is from the rest of Africa! Ever-popular with backpackers, the country has a lot to offer the independent traveller. Its greatest charm lies in the labyrinths of its imperial cities – Fès, Marrakesh, Mcknès and Rabat. The countryside is often breathtaking.

This chapter covers the main destinations accessible to travellers, concentrating on the Mediterranean and Atlantic coasts, the Rif, the Middle Atlas and Marrakesh. For full coverage of the country, check out the latest edition of Lonely Planet's *Morocco*.

## Facts about Morocco

### HISTORY

Most modern Moroccans are the descendants of Berber settlers who came to the region thousands of years ago. Their independent spirit has outlived countless conquerors over the centuries and produced one of Africa's most colourful cultures.

The Berbers were well established by the time the Phoenicians and the Romans started showing an interest in North Africa. Both faded away before the arrival of Islam in the 7th century, when Arab armies took over the whole North African coast and much of Spain.

Tribal divisions soon reasserted themselves, however, and the Berbers, having adopted Islam, developed their own brand of Shi'ism, known as Kharijism. By 829 the Kharijites had established a stable Idrissid state with its capital at Fès, dominating all of Morocco.

This unity was short lived and by the 11th century the region had fragmented. Out of the chaos emerged the Almoravids, who overran Morocco and Muslim Spain (Al-Andalus) and founded Marrakesh. They were supplanted by the Almohads, who raised Fès, Marrakesh and Rabat to heights of splendour before crumbling as Christian armies regained Spain. The successive Merenid dynasty revitalised the Moroccan heartland, but it too collapsed after Granada fell to the Christians in 1492 and Muslim refugees poured into Morocco.

## At a Glance

- **Rif Mountains** – spectacular scenery and the tranquil town of Chefchaouen
- **Fès** – the cultural and spiritual capital of Morocco
- **Rabat** – a 17th-century medina and ancient fortifications overlooking the sea
- **Casablanca** – cosmopolitan boulevards, French colonial and traditional Moroccan architecture, stunning Hassan II Mosque
- **Marrakesh** – lively, eye-opening Place Djemaa el-Fna

| | |
|---|---|
| **Capital** | Rabat |
| **Population** | 30 million (approx) |
| **Official Language** | Arabic |
| **Currency** | 1 dirham (Dh) = 100 centimes |
| **Time** | GMT/UTC+0000 |
| **Country Phone Code** | ☎ 212 |

Morocco managed to retain its independence until France took over much of the country in 1912, handing Spain a token zone in the north. Rabat was made the capital and Casablanca developed as a major port.

By 1934 the last opposition from Berber mountain tribes had been crushed, but Moroccan resistance moved into political channels with the Istiqlal (independence) party. After WWII, violent opposition resurfaced and in 1953 the French exiled Sultan Mohammed V;

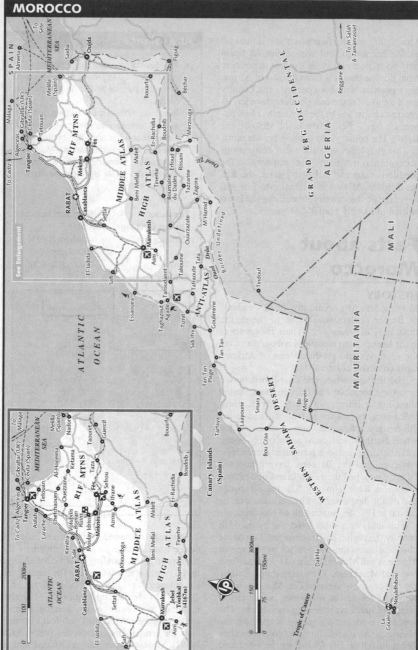

this only succeeded in further stoking Moroccan discontent and he was allowed to return in 1955. Independence was granted the following year.

The Spanish withdrew around the same time but still retained the coastal enclaves of Ceuta and Melilla. Sultan Mohammed V became a king, succeeded by his son Hassan II, who despite moves towards democracy and several coup attempts retained all effective power until his death in July 1999. The new king, Mohammed VI, has adopted a reformist agenda, vowing to tackle the huge developmental problems in Morocco, and achieved huge popularity as well as breaking tradition with his highly publicised marriage in 2002.

The disputed territory of Western Sahara, however, remains a problem. The situation dates back to the 1975 'Green March', when 350,000 unarmed Moroccans marched into the colony shortly before the Spanish withdrew; the Polisario Front, which had been struggling for years against Spanish rule, turned to fight its new overlords, supported by Algeria. In 1991 the United Nations brokered a cease-fire on the understanding that a referendum on the territory's future would be held in 1992. The vote has still not taken place, largely due to a dispute over voter eligibility, and looks unlikely to happen in the near future.

## GEOGRAPHY

One of Africa's most geographically diverse areas, Morocco is spectacularly beautiful. It is traversed by four mountain ranges: the Rif, the Middle Atlas, the High Atlas and the Anti-Atlas. Certain peaks of the High Atlas remain snow-capped all year and are among the highest in Africa.

Between the mountain ranges themselves, and between these ranges and the Atlantic Ocean, are plateaus and plains. Fed by melting snow, they are fertile and well watered; on many of the plains further south, however, agriculture is tenuous except along certain river courses.

## CLIMATE

The geological variety is mirrored by wide-ranging climatic conditions.

Weather in the coastal regions is generally mild, but can become cool and wet, particularly in the north. Average temperatures in Tangier and Casablanca range from 12°C (54°F) in winter to 25°C (77°F) and above in

RABAT
Elevation – 83m/272ft

summer. Rainfall is highest in the Rif and northern Middle Atlas, where only the summer months are dry. The Atlantic coast remains agreeable year-round, cooled by sea breezes.

The rainy season is from November to January, but can go on as late as April; however, recent years have been typified by drought, relieved slightly by rains in 2002. Drought years seem to rotate on a two-year cycle, with devastating effects on agriculture.

In winter the mountains can get as cold as -20°C (without taking the wind-chill factor into account), with snow often blocking mountain passes. Take enough warm clothing to cope with an unwelcome night stuck in an unheated bus.

## ECOLOGY & ENVIRONMENT

Deforestation and soil erosion are major problems in some areas. Nevertheless, springtime can see blazes of colourful wildflowers and there are still pine and cedar forests in the north and rolling wooded parkland towards the south.

Many larger 'African' mammals (eg, Barbary lion) have become extinct, though wild boar, large wild sheep (*mouflon*) and macaque monkeys can be seen in the Atlas.

Thanks to its diverse climate and habitats and its importance as a migratory pit stop, Morocco has much to offer the bird-watcher. More than 300 species have been recorded, including huge concentrations of migrating storks, hawks and eagles in spring and autumn, colourful bee-eaters and rollers, majestic bustards and graceful cranes.

## GOVERNMENT & POLITICS

Morocco is ruled by King Mohammed VI, who came to the throne in July 1999. During his father King Hassan II's reign, the country's constitution was considerably modernised with the introduction of an elected lowered chamber and a system of multiparty politics.

The government is now a coalition, with the socialist Abderrahmane Youssoufi as prime minister; the next election is in late 2002.

A consummate populist, Mohammed VI has been quick to build on these developments, accelerating the release of political prisoners and apologising for political disappearances in the past. However, while the climate of fear that existed under Hassan II has disappeared, a few political detentions continue and insulting the king remains a broadly interpreted criminal offence. The government has a dialogue with pressure groups such as Amnesty International.

Despite these democratic moves, Morocco remains essentially an absolute monarchy. The king retains the right to appoint his prime minister and approve all ministers subsequently chosen; the major ministries of justice, foreign affairs and internal affairs remain firmly in royal hands. The 275-seat upper house consists of deputies indirectly elected from local and regional government, professional bodies and trade unions.

## ECONOMY

The mainstays of Morocco's economy are agriculture, mining, tourism, manufacturing, and remittances from Moroccans abroad.

Morocco is the world's third-largest exporter of phosphates and tourism is now a major foreign exchange earner. However, the country is still largely dependent on agriculture, and a series of drought years has greatly restricted its promising economic growth.

Years of IMF-imposed austerity measures, followed by continued public spending cuts and massive privatisation, have made the economy leaner and fitter, but not without serious social costs, such as rising unemployment.

The economic hope for Morocco is the March 2000 free trade agreement with the European Union (EU), which will remove all trade barriers between the two by 2012. The payoff for Europe should be a clampdown on the flow of drugs and access to new markets. Huge EU investment in Morocco's infrastructure and development is planned, but much economic modernisation is needed.

## POPULATION & PEOPLE

The population is estimated to be 30 million and growing at around 1.8% per annum. The largest city is Casablanca, with a population of around five million.

The bulk of the population is made up of Arab and Berber peoples who have intermarried over the centuries. Morocco once hosted a large population of Jews, but the vast majority left after the foundation of Israel in 1948. Trade with trans-Saharan Africa brought a population of black Africans into Morocco, many of whom originally came as slaves.

## ARTS

Music and architecture are arguably the highest forms of culture in Morocco. The former is drawn from many traditions, from classics of the Arab-Andalucían heritage through to the more African rhythms of Berber music. *Raï*, a fusion of traditional, tribal and modern Western popular forms, began in Algeria and has become very popular in Morocco, as has Egyptian pop music. Cheap cassettes are easily obtained throughout the country.

Little in Europe can prepare you for the visual feast of the great mosques and *medersas* (Koranic schools) that bejewel major Moroccan cities. Moroccan monuments are virtuoso pieces of geometric design and harmony, and the skills are still practised today.

## SOCIETY & CONDUCT

Despite extensive Westernisation, Morocco remains a largely conservative Muslim society. As a rule, a high degree of modesty is demanded of both sexes in dress as well as behaviour, and even in the liberal cities scant clothing will stand out a mile. Women in particular are well advised to keep their shoulders and upper arms covered and to opt for long skirts or trousers.

You should always ask permission before taking photographs – urban Moroccans usually have no problem with this, but women generally do *not* want to be photographed. Respect their right to privacy.

If invited into a Moroccan home, it is customary to remove your shoes before stepping onto the carpet. Food is served in common dishes and eaten with the right hand – the left hand is used for personal hygiene and should not be used to eat with or to touch any common source of food or water, or to hand over money or presents.

All mosques and religious buildings in active use are off limits to non-Muslims. Cemeteries are pretty much no-go areas, too: don't take shortcuts through them.

## RELIGION

All but a tiny minority of the population is Sunni Muslim, but in Morocco, Islam is far from strictly orthodox. The worship of local saints and holy people *(marabouts)* is still common, a resurgence of pre-Islamic traditions. The whitewashed *koubba* (tomb) of the *marabout* is a common sight all over north Africa.

Where these local saints have accumulated many followers, prosperous individuals have endowed the *koubba* with educational institutions known as *zawiyyas*, which offer an alternative to orthodox *medersas*.

## LANGUAGE

Arabic is the official language, but French and Berber are widely spoken. Spanish is spoken in former Spanish-held territory (particularly the north, where it can be hard to get by without it) and some English in the main tourist centres. Arabic and French are taught in schools and French is important in university education and commerce.

Although many Moroccans speak many different languages passably, don't expect much beyond Moroccan Arabic and French or Spanish outside main cities and tourist spots.

Spoken Moroccan Arabic *(darija)* is considerably different from the Middle Eastern variety. Pick up a copy of Lonely Planet's *Moroccan Arabic phrasebook* for more detailed coverage. Various Berber dialects are spoken in the countryside, particularly in the mountains.

See the Language Chapter at the back of this book for pronunciation guidelines and useful words and phrases.

# Facts for the Visitor

## HIGHLIGHTS

The imperial cities of Fès, Marrakesh, Meknès and Rabat are the best places to discover the characteristic medieval vibe of the medina, packed with all the arts, crafts, monuments, sights and smells of traditional Morocco. For a glimpse of modern Islam, don't miss the amazing Hassan II Mosque in Casablanca.

Elsewhere you can explore the breathtaking Rif Mountains around Chefchaouen, experience the sedate and seedy sides of Tangier and Tetouan, expose yourself to some sun in the relaxed Spanish enclaves, or just bask on the Atlantic beaches at Asilah and Larache.

## SUGGESTED ITINERARIES

Depending on how much time you have, you might want to do the following:

**One week**
Visit three of the imperial cities (Fès, Marrakesh, Meknès and Rabat).
**Two weeks**
Visit Casablanca, the imperial cities, Chefchaouen and Ceuta, Tetouan or Tangier.
**Three to four weeks**
Visit everywhere listed in this chapter.

## PLANNING
## When to Go

The most pleasant times to explore Morocco are during spring (April to May) and autumn (September to October). Midsummer can be very enjoyable on the coast but viciously hot in the interior, it is also the high season, so prices especially for accommodation are higher, but there are more services, such as ferries, for travellers. During winter it gets surprisingly cold across the northwest.

### Maps

The best option is the Michelin No 959 *Morocco* (scale 1:1,000,000). In Rabat, the **Cartography Division of the Conservation & Topography Department** *(☎ 295034, fax 295549; Blvd Hassan II)*, 4km from the city centre, stocks a range of maps, including topographical sheets (useful for hiking). Unfortunately, you must make an official request for any maps you want, a process that can take days.

### What to Bring

Bring any special medication you need. It's a good idea to use sun protection (eg, a hat, sunglasses and sunscreen) year-round. A sleeping bag can be useful in winter. Also bring your own contraceptives – you can get hold of condoms and even the pill, but quality is dubious and availability uncertain.

## TOURIST OFFICES
## Local Tourist Offices

The national tourist body, **ONMT** *(head office: ☎ 730562; W www.tourism-in-morocco .com; Rue al-Abtal, Rabat)*, has offices (usually called Délégation Régionale du Tourisme) in the main cities. A few cities also have local offices known as *syndicats d'initiative*; these are often less helpful than ONMT offices, but all have brochures and simple maps.

## Tourist Offices Abroad
The ONMT maintains offices in Australia (Sydney), Belgium (Brussels), Canada (Montreal), France (Paris), Germany (Düsseldorf), Italy (Milan), Japan (Tokyo), Portugal (Lisbon), Spain (Madrid), Sweden (Stockholm), Switzerland (Zürich), the UK (London) and the USA (New York and Orlando).

## VISAS
Most visitors to Morocco need no visa and on entry are granted leave to remain in the country for 90 days. Exceptions include nationals of Israel, South Africa and Zimbabwe. Visa requirements can change, so check with the Moroccan embassy in your country or a reputable travel agent before travelling.

Entry requirements for Ceuta and Melilla are the same as for Spain (see that chapter).

### Visa Extensions
If the 90 days you are entitled to are insufficient, the simplest thing to do is leave (eg, go to the Spanish enclaves) and come back a few days later. Your chances improve if you re-enter by a different route.

People on visas may, however, prefer to try for an extension (this may take up to two weeks). Go to the nearest police headquarters, or Préfecture, with your passport, four photos, proof of sufficient funds and preferably a letter from your embassy requesting a visa extension on your behalf.

## EMBASSIES & CONSULATES
### Moroccan Embassies & Consulates
**Australia** (☎ 02-9922 4999) Suite 2, 11 West St, North Sydney, NSW 2060
**Canada** (☎ 613-236 7391) 38 Range Rd, Ottawa, Ontario, K1N 8J4
**France** (☎ 01 45 20 69 35) 5 Rue Le Tasse, Paris 75016
**Germany** (☎ 030-20 61 24 0) Niederwallstrasse 39, 10117 Berlin
**Japan** (☎ 03-478 3271) Silva Kingdom 3, 16-3, Sendagaya, Shibuya-ku, Tokyo 151
**Netherlands** (☎ 70-346 9617) Oranjestraat 9, 2514 JB, The Hague
**Spain** (☎ 91 563 1090) Calle Serrano 179, 28002 Madrid
**Tunisia** (☎ 01-782 775) 39 Avenue du 1er Juin, Mutuelleville, Tunis

**UK** (☎ 020-7581 5001) 49 Queen's Gate Gardens, London SW7 5NE
**USA** (☎ 202-462 7979) 1601 21st St NW, Washington, DC 20009

## Embassies & Consulates in Morocco
Most embassies are in Rabat but there are some consulates in Tangier and Casablanca. Embassies in Rabat (area code ☎ 037) include:

**Algeria** (☎ 765474) 46-8 Ave Tariq ibn Zayid
**Canada** (☎ 672880) 13b Rue Jaafar as-Sadiq, Agdal
**France** (☎ 689700) 3 Rue Sahnoun
  *Service de Visas* (☎ 702404) Rue Ibn al-Khatib
**Germany** (☎ 709662) 7 Rue Madnine
**Japan** (☎ 631782) 39 Ave Ahmed Balafrej Souissi
**Netherlands** (☎ 733512) 40 Rue de Tunis
**Spain** (☎ 768989) 3-5 Rue Madnine
  *Consulate* (☎ 704147) 57 Rue du Chellah
**Tunisia** (☎ 730636) 6 Ave de Fès
**UK** (☎ 720905) 17 Blvd de la Tour Hassan
**USA** (☎ 762265) 2 Ave de Marrakesh

## CUSTOMS
You can import up to 200 cigarettes and 1L of spirits duty-free.

## MONEY
The unit of currency is the dirham (Dh), equal to 100 centimes. The importation or exportation of local currency is prohibited; there's not much of a black market and little reason to use it.

The Spanish enclaves of Ceuta and Melilla now use the euro.

### Exchange Rates

| country | unit | | dirham |
|---|---|---|---|
| Australia | A$1 | = | Dh6.20 |
| Canada | C$1 | = | Dh7.35 |
| euro zone | €1 | = | Dh10.26 |
| Japan | ¥100 | = | Dh8.83 |
| New Zealand | NZ$1 | = | Dh5.13 |
| UK | UK£1 | = | Dh16.78 |
| USA | US$1 | = | Dh11.66 |

### Exchanging Money
Banking services are generally quick and efficient; many banks have separate bureaus de change, but it is becoming more difficult to change travellers cheques – the branches of the Banque Populaire or the BMCI are your best bet.

Australian, Canadian and New Zealand dollars are not quoted in banks and are not usually accepted.

**Credit and Debit Cards** Major credit cards are widely accepted in the main tourist centres, although their use often attracts a surcharge. American Express is represented by the travel agency Voyages Schwartz, which can be found in Rabat, Casablanca and Tangier.

Automated teller machines *(guichets automatiques;* ATM*)* are now a common sight; many accept Visa, MasterCard, Electron, Cirrus, Maestro and InterBank. BMCE and Crédit du Maroc ATMs are a good bet.

## Costs

Moroccan prices are refreshingly reasonable. With a few small tips here and there, plus entry charges to museums and the like, you can get by on US$15 to US$20 a day if you stay in cheap hotels, eat at cheap restaurants and are not in a hurry. Hot showers, the occasional splurge and a taxi or two can take this up to US$30 or US$35 a day.

If you're under 26, an international student card can get you big reductions on internal (and some international) flights and international rail fares departing from Morocco.

## Tipping & Bargaining

Tipping and bargaining are integral parts of Moroccan life. Practically any service can warrant a tip, but don't be railroaded. A few dirham for a service willingly rendered can, however, make your life a lot easier. Between 5% and 10% of a restaurant bill is about right.

When souvenir hunting, decide beforehand how much you are prepared to spend on an item (to get an idea of prices, visit the Ensemble Artisanal in any major city), but be aware that carpet vendors often start with hugely inflated prices. Wait until the price has been reduced considerably before making your first (low) offer, then approach your limit slowly.

# POST & COMMUNICATIONS

## Post

The Moroccan post is fairly reliable and offers poste restante. Take your passport to claim mail. There's a small charge for collecting letters.

Outgoing parcels are inspected by customs at the post office so don't turn up with a sealed parcel. There are nifty flat-pack boxes available.

## Telephone & Fax

The telephone system in Morocco is good. Private *téléboutiques* are widespread and efficient; attendants sell phonecards *(télécartes)* and provide change. They are marked on maps throughout this chapter. Phonecards for public phones are available from kiosks and some post offices.

A three-minute call to the USA will cost about US$1.50 and a three-minute call to Europe at least US$2. For international calls, there is a 20% reduction between 8pm and 8am weekdays and throughout the weekend.

Reverse charge (collect) calls to most countries are possible. A list of toll-free numbers connecting you to a relevant operator can be found in the Moroccan phone book (Annuaire des Abonnés au Téléphone).

When calling overseas from Morocco, dial ☎ 00, the country code and then the city code and number. Morocco's country code is ☎ 212.

Many *téléboutiques* have fax machines. Prices per page vary but you can expect to pay about Dh50 to Europe and Dh70 to North America and Australia.

## Email & Internet Access

Internet cafés have sprung up all over Morocco. See entries for each town.

One hour on the Internet costs between Dh5 and Dh15. Access is fairly reliable, though connections are better in the north and usually quicker in the morning.

# DIGITAL RESOURCES

There are numerous Internet sites about Morocco. Four: Ⓦ www.mincom.gov.ma, Ⓦ www.marweb.com, Ⓦ www.morocco.com and Ⓦ www.i-cias.com/mor.htm, will get you started.

# BOOKS

See Lonely Planet's *Morocco* for more detailed information on the country.

*The Moors: Islam in the West* by Michael Brett & Werner Forman details Moorish civilisation at its height, with superb colour photographs. *The Conquest of Morocco* by Douglas Porch examines the takeover of Morocco by Paris.

*Doing Daily Battle* by Fatima Mernissi is a collection of interviews with Moroccan women giving a valuable insight into their lives. A number of Western writers have connections with Morocco, including long-time Tangier resident Paul Bowles, who died in 1999.

## NEWSPAPERS & MAGAZINES
Foreign press is available at central newsstands in the major centres. News magazines such as *Newsweek* and *Time* are fairly easy to find, along with the *Herald Tribune*, some UK papers, including the *International Guardian*, and their continental European equivalents. The French press is the most up-to-date and by far the cheapest.

## RADIO & TV
Local radio is in Arabic and French, and you can pick up Spanish broadcasts in most parts of the country. Midi 1 (97.5 FM) is a good French language station covering northern Morocco. The BBC broadcasts into the area on short-wave frequencies 15,070MHz and 12,095MHz from about 8am to 11pm.

Satellite and digital television provide numerous foreign channels, including CNN, NBC and Canal+. The government-owned stations TVM and 2M broadcast in Arabic and French.

## TIME
Moroccan time is GMT/UTC all year, so in summer Morocco is two hours behind European time and one hour behind UK time.

## LAUNDRY
You're better off doing it yourself – most hotels will do it for you, but it takes time. Establishments called *pressings* are actually dry-cleaners, and can be very expensive.

## TOILETS
Public toilets are few and far between, so use the toilets in cafés and hotels – you'll need your own paper, a tip (Dh0.50 to Dh1.50) for the attendant, stout-soled shoes and a nose clip. They are mostly of the 'squatter' variety.

## WOMEN TRAVELLERS
Although a certain level of sexual harassment is almost the norm, Morocco can be less problematic than overtly macho countries such as Italy and Spain. Harassment is generally of the leering, verbal variety. In the bigger cities especially, female travellers will receive hopeful greetings from every male over the age of 13! Ignore them entirely. Women will save themselves a great deal of grief by dressing modestly and avoiding anything skin-tight. It's also wise not to walk around alone at night, as after dark all 'good' Moroccan women are at home.

## GAY & LESBIAN TRAVELLERS
Homosexual acts are officially illegal in Morocco – in theory you can go to jail and/or get fined. However, although not openly admitted or shown, male homosexuality remains relatively common. Male homosexuals are advised to be discreet; aggression towards gay male travellers is not unheard of.

Gay women shouldn't encounter any particular problems, though it's commonly believed by Moroccans that there are no lesbians in their country.

## DANGERS & ANNOYANCES
Morocco's era as a hippy paradise is long past. Plenty of fine *kif* (dope) is grown in the Rif Mountains, but drug busts are common and Morocco is not a good place to investigate prison conditions! The majority of shakedowns and rip-offs in Morocco are drug-related; a common ploy is to get you stoned, sell you a piece the size of a house brick and turn you over to the police (or threaten to).

Those disembarking (and embarking) the ferry in Tangier should expect some hassle from touts and hustlers trying to pull you one way or the other (usually to a hotel/ferry ticket office where they get commission). Ceuta and Melilla are far more pleasant ports of entry.

On the more popular tourist routes you may come across professional hitchhikers and people pretending that their cars have broken down. Once you stop to assist them various scams unfold.

Morocco has its share of pickpockets and thieves but they're not a major problem.

### Guides
A few years ago the Brigade Touristique (tourist police) was set up in the principal tourist centres to clamp down on Morocco's notorious *faux guides* (false guides) and hustlers. Anyone convicted of operating as an unofficial guide faces jail and/or a huge fine.

This has reduced, but not eliminated, the problem of the *faux guides*. You'll still find plenty hanging around the entrances to the

## Emergency Services

The national emergency number is ☎ 19 for police and ☎ 15 for ambulance or fire. Dial ☎ 177 for highway emergency service.

big city medinas and outside bus and train stations. Friendly overtures are the usual ploy to get your attention; the more direct line 'one mosquito better than thousand mosquitoes' is a Tangier favourite! Most will go away if you ignore them and don't stop, but some can be persistent and even unpleasant – stay calm and polite, and head for a café or taxi.

If you end up with one of these people remember their main interest is the commission gained from certain hotels or on articles sold to you in the *souqs*.

Official guides can be engaged through tourist offices and hotels at the fixed price of Dh120 per half day (plus tip). It's worth taking a guide in the larger medinas; their local knowledge is extensive and they'll save you from being hassled by others. If you don't want a shopping expedition included in your tour, make this clear beforehand.

## BUSINESS HOURS

Banking hours are usually 8.30am to 11.30am and 2.30pm to 4.30pm weekdays, with Friday lunch lasting from 11.15am to 3pm. During Ramadan hours are 9am to 3pm. In some tourist areas exchange offices keep longer hours and open over the weekend. Post offices generally keep similar hours, but don't close until around 6pm. *Téléboutiques* are open until around 10pm, Internet cafés often later. Many museums and some monuments are closed on Tuesday.

## PUBLIC HOLIDAYS & SPECIAL EVENTS

All banks, post offices and most shops are shut on the main public holidays. Major secular holidays are:

**New Year's Day** 1 January
**Independence Manifesto** 11 January
**Labour Day** 1 May
**Feast of the Throne** 30 July
**Allegiance of Wadi-Eddahab** 14 August
**Anniversary of the King's and People's Revolution** 20 August
**Anniversary of the Green March** 6 November
**Independence Day** 18 November

In addition to secular holidays there are many national and local Islamic holidays and festivals, all tied to the lunar calendar.

Probably the most important is the Aïd al-Fitr, held at the end of the month-long Ramadan fast, which is fairly strictly observed by most Muslims. The festivities generally last four or five days, during which just about everything grinds to a halt.

Another important Muslim festival is Aïd al-Adha, which marks the end of the Islamic year. Again, most things shut down for four or five days. The third main religious festival, known as Mawlid an-Nabi (or simply Mouloud), celebrates the birthday of the Prophet Mohammed.

Local festivals, mostly in honour of *marabouts* (saints) and known as *moussems* or *amouggars*, are common among the Berbers and usually held in the summer months.

## ACTIVITIES
### Surfing & Windsurfing

With thousands of kilometres of Atlantic coastline, Morocco has some great surfing spots – the Oudayas Surf Club in Rabat is a good place for information.

### Trekking

The area around Chefchaouen offers some good trekking opportunities, although most travellers head straight for the High Atlas. Early spring is the best time to go.

## ACCOMMODATION
### Camping

You can camp anywhere in Morocco if you have permission from the landowner. There are also many official sites, where you'll pay around Dh10 per person plus Dh10 to pitch a tent, with extra charges applicable for vehicles, electricity and hot water.

### Hostels

There are hostels (*auberges de jeunesse*) in Casablanca, Chefchaouen, Fès, Meknès, Rabat and Tangier. If you're travelling alone, they are among the cheapest places to stay. The Moroccan Ministry of Youth and Sports also has reception centres in many major cities, which can be booked by travellers: beds at **Centres d'Acceuil** (*info & reservations:* ☎ 037-670192, *fax 037-670175; 6 Rue Soumaya, Rabat*) cost Dh50, and advance booking is essential.

## Hotels

Cheap, unclassified hotels of varying quality tend to be clustered in the medinas of most cities. Singles/doubles cost from Dh20/40; showers are often cold, but there are always *hammams* (bath houses) nearby.

For a little more, you can often find better unclassified or one-star hotels outside the medinas. In one-star hotels, singles/doubles with shower start at around Dh60/120; rooms in two-star places start at around Dh150/200. Prices can include breakfast, which is hardly ever a good deal – coffee and a croissant is Dh7 to Dh10 in a café.

The extra star in the three-star category (from Dh200/250) should get you a TV and a telephone. Five-star hotels (from Dh1000 a double) range from sterile modern cubes to former palaces.

Prices given here are for high season and include tax; always check the price you are quoted is TTC (all taxes included).

## FOOD

At its best, Moroccan food is superb. Influenced by Berber, Arabic and Mediterranean (particularly Spanish and French) traditions, the cuisine features a sublime use of spices and fresh local produce.

Restaurant food, particularly in the tourist zones, can be variable; head for the places full of locals and you won't go far wrong. Typical dishes include *tajine*, a meat and vegetable stew cooked slowly in an earthenware dish, and couscous, fluffy steamed semolina served with tender meat and vegetables. The preparation of couscous is very laborious and many restaurants only serve it on Fridays, the day it's traditionally eaten.

*Harira*, a thick soup made from lamb stock, lentils, chickpeas, onions, tomatoes, fresh herbs and spices, is usually eaten as a first course in the evening, but is substantial enough to make a meal on its own. In a cheap restaurant a bowl costs around Dh5.

Salads are served everywhere, the nicest being the traditional *salade marocaine* made from finely diced green peppers, tomatoes and red onion. *Brochettes* (skewered meat barbecued over hot coals) or roast chicken are other staples, served with crispy (if you're lucky) french fries. Fish dishes also make an excellent choice in coastal areas.

*Pastilla*, a Fès speciality, is a rich and delicious dish made from pigeon meat, lemon-flavoured eggs, almonds, cinnamon, saffron and sugar, encased in layer upon layer of very fine *ouarka* pastry.

Vegetarians shouldn't have any problems – fresh fruit and vegetables are widely available, as well as a range of pulses such as lentils and chickpeas. When ordering couscous or *tajine*, ask for your dish to be served *sans viande* (without meat).

Coffee and croissants (around Dh8) make a good, cheap breakfast. Even cheaper is a breakfast of *bessara* (pea soup with spices and olive oil), fresh bread and mint tea. You'll find stalls near the markets in most towns.

Morocco is full of patisseries which produce excellent French and Moroccan pastries. This is where the locals head in the early evening.

If you're on a tight budget, you can eat well for as little as Dh50 per day. A three-course meal in a medium-priced restaurant will cost around Dh80 (without drinks); if you want to treat yourself in a traditional Moroccan palace restaurant or a smart French joint, expect to pay upwards of Dh150 per person.

## DRINKS

Morocco is full of cafés, but many are serious, all-male preserves – female travellers may prefer to patronise the patisseries.

Mint tea, the legendary 'Moroccan whisky', is everywhere. It's made with Chinese gunpowder tea, fresh mint and copious sugar. It usually comes in elegant Moroccan teapots, but may just be served by the glass. English tea is usually served black and known as *thé Lipton*. Coffee is served in the French style: short black or large milky white. *Qahwa ness-ness* is half coffee, half milk served in a glass.

Fruit juices, especially fresh orange, are also common; however, the French *jus* is often used to refer to smoothie-like fruit concoctions, which are popular and frequently delicious.

It's not advisable to drink tap water in Morocco, though in major cities you should be all right. Bottled water is available everywhere and costs Dh5 for a big bottle (more in restaurants). Water taken from streams in the mountains should be treated with purification tablets.

Beer is easy to find in the *villes nouvelles* (new towns). The local Stork or Flag brands typically cost from Dh11 to Dh15 in bars (more than double that in fancy hotels). Imported beer is very expensive. Reasonably palatable Moroccan wines can be had for around Dh35 in liquor shops; the whites and rosés are better than the reds.

## ENTERTAINMENT

As a Muslim country, Morocco isn't big on nightlife. The major cities have some good cinemas (movies dubbed into French), but any bars, discos and nightclubs are usually male preserves and tend to be dubious, expensive or both. Many hotels and restaurants provide traditional music to accompany dinner; the real thing, however, is best heard at the annual festivals and *moussems*.

## SHOPPING

Moroccan crafts are famous for their variety and quality. Items to look for include traditional carpets and flatweave rugs, ceramics, chased brass and copperware, painted woodwork, leatherwork and jewellery; Fès, Rabat and Tetouan are particularly noted for their *souqs* (markets).

Look around before buying. All the major cities have a government-run Ensemble Artisanal where you can look at good-quality items and check the upper-range prices. See the Tipping & Bargaining section earlier.

Morocco has a tradition of perfume making and in the bigger cities you'll find perfumeries selling excellent copies (Dh50 for 20ml) of all the famous names.

# Getting There & Away

## AIR

Morocco is well served by air travel options from Europe, the Middle East and West Africa. The main entry point is Mohammed V airport, 30km southeast of Casablanca. International flights also land at Tangier, Marrakesh and Fès. Air France and RAM are the major carriers; other airlines operating to Morocco include Alitalia, British Airways, Gulf Air, Iberia, KLM and Lufthansa.

### Europe & the UK

Charter flights to Morocco can be found from cities such as Paris, Amsterdam, Brussels and Düsseldorf, costing around UK£200; tickets are generally returns and are not usually valid for more than one month.

In the high season, scheduled flights (valid for one month) between London and Casablanca are as much as UK£350. It is much cheaper to fly to Málaga (as little as UK£69 one way) and then catch a ferry.

There are no cheap one-way flights out of Morocco. Expect to pay around Dh5000 for a standard fare to Northern Europe.

### North America & Australasia

RAM and TWA have direct flights from New York to Casablanca (around US$800); fares from other US and Canadian cities (via Europe) will cost at least an extra US$200. It may be more economical to fly to Paris, Amsterdam or London and continue from there. There are no direct flights between Australia or New Zealand and Morocco – head for a European destination first.

## LAND

### Europe

**Bus** Eurolines and the Moroccan national bus line Compagnie des Transports Marocains (CTM) operate buses between Morocco and many European cities. A one-way/open return ticket from London to Marrakesh costs UK£102/177 (UK£81/141 under 25s). These fares usually include the cost of the ferry. Regular buses to Paris and other European cities run from major Moroccan terminals; one-way tickets start at Dh450 (Málaga), rising to Dh1200 (Paris).

The land border between Morocco and Algeria was closed in 1994 and at the time of writing looked set to remain so.

**Train** Trains offer couchettes and the option of breaking your trip along the way, although for the price of a ticket from London to Paris you could fly to Málaga. A one-way/return ticket to Algeciras via the Eurostar, valid for two months, costs UK£207/308 – 30% less for under-26s. These tickets don't usually include the ferry fare. Heading the other way, one-way tickets from Casablanca to London start around Dh2000, less with a student card.

The Moroccan rail system is part of the Inter-Rail network. A two-zone ticket giving unlimited travel in France, Belgium, the Netherlands, Spain and Morocco for one month costs UK£265 (UK£189 if under 26); the cheapest single-zone pass, covering Spain

MOROCCO

and Morocco, costs UK£169/119 for 12 days. However, you need to have lived in Europe for six months.

The Eurail Pass (US$486 for 15 days) will get you as far as Algeciras, but doesn't cover Morocco.

## SEA
### Spain
The main operators are Trasmediterranea, Limadet, Buquebus and Euroferrys. The most popular route is Algeciras–Tangier; others include Algeciras/Málaga–Ceuta, Almeria/Málaga–Melilla, Gibraltar–Tangier and Tarifa–Tangier. Hydrofoils are commonly used between Spain and Spanish Morocco; the Tangier runs use ferries.

**Algeciras–Tangier** There's a ferry roughly every hour between 7am and 10pm in high season; the crossing takes 2½ hours. Adult one-way fares are €26.77 (Dh250); children under 12 travel at half-price. A normal car costs €69.38 (Dh648).

**Algeciras & Málaga–Ceuta** There are up to 17 hydrofoils (35 minutes) per day between Algeciras and Ceuta. One-way fares are around €20; cars cost from €32.

Buquebus usually runs a Málaga–Ceuta hydrofoil (€30; cars €90; 90 minutes) twice daily in summer.

**Almeria & Málaga–Melilla** Trasmediterranea has six overnight services a week between Almeria or Málaga and Melilla. The crossings take 6½ to eight hours and 7½ to 10 hours respectively; the cheapest one-way fare is €26.31; cars cost €69.50 and cabin space is available from €43.76 per person.

**Gibraltar–Tangier** FRS runs five weekly services. The voyage (70 minutes) costs UK£18 (Dh260) one way, cars UK£46 (Dh730).

**Tarifa–Tangier** FRS offers up to six daily services (35 minutes) in high season. Fares are €21 (Dh200) one-way, cars €69 (Dh645).

# Getting Around

## AIR
RAM has a good internal network; if you're under 22 or a student under 31, you are enti-

tled to at least 25% (and often up to 60%) off all fares. The standard one-way fare between Casablanca and Tangier is Dh813.

## BUS
There is a good network of bus routes all over the country; departures are frequent and the tickets are cheap.

CTM (Compagnie des Transports Marocains) is really the only national company, though other companies such as SATAS can be just as good. On major intercity routes CTM runs 1st- and 2nd-class services; there are more of the former, so you'll often pay the higher fare (about 25% more) unless you're very flexible about departure times. Advance booking is advisable, especially in smaller towns with few services. In many places, CTM has its own terminal.

Some examples of 1st-class CTM fares are:

| from | to | fare (Dh) |
| --- | --- | --- |
| Casablanca | Fès | 80 |
| Casablanca | Tangier | 110 |
| Tangier | Fès | 80 |

There is an official baggage charge on CTM buses (Dh5 per pack). On other lines baggage handlers usually ask for Dh3 to Dh5.

## TRAIN
Morocco has one of the most modern rail systems in Africa, with a choice of 1st or 2nd class and *ordinaire* or *rapide* trains. Most trains are now *rapide*, but there are still a few cheaper *ordinaire* services on overnight routes. Couchettes are available on long-distance night trains between Marrakesh and Tangier. There are refreshment trolleys and sometimes buffet cars on longer journeys.

The TNR (shuttle trains) between Rabat, Casablanca and Mohammed V international airport are particularly fast (Casablanca to Rabat in 55 minutes) and comfortable. Second-class fares are roughly comparable to bus fares.

Timetables are prominently displayed in train stations, and a free book of timetables, *Indicateur Horaires*, is sometimes available at stations.

Supratours runs luxury buses in conjunction with trains to destinations not on the rail network; useful ones include Tetouan and Nador.

## CAR & MOTORCYCLE

You drive on the right in Morocco. An International Driving Permit is officially required, but most national licences are sufficient. Main roads are in decent condition, but many secondary roads are not so hot: some mountain roads can be blocked by snow in winter, and desert roads are sometimes awash with sand drifts.

The traffic-accident rate in Morocco is high; night driving can be particularly hazardous since cars, bicycles and donkeys may travel without lights.

The expanding motorway network now stretches from Casablanca to Tangier and from Rabat to Fès. Tolls are payable (Dh8 minimum) and the speed limit on the motorway is 120km/h – elsewhere it's 100km/h (40 to 60km/h in built-up areas).

You should give way to traffic entering a roundabout from the right. It's compulsory for drivers and passengers to wear seatbelts.

There are frequent police and customs roadblocks, especially around the ports. Always stop; often you'll be waved through, but have your licence and passport handy.

Most towns have paid-parking areas. They give some peace of mind and cost a few dirham for a few hours or Dh10 overnight.

Leaded, unleaded and diesel are the most widely available types of fuel; all are much cheaper in the Spanish enclaves.

### Rental

You'll find all the major companies in Moroccan cities, plus plenty of local companies. Renault 4s and Fiat Unos are cheapest (around Dh1400, plus 20% tax, for three days with unlimited kilometres; insurance is extra). You may be asked to leave a deposit of at least Dh3000 if not paying by credit card, and you need to be at least 21 years old. Shop around and always haggle for discounts.

### BICYCLE

Distances are great, roads are narrow and dusty, and you'll need to carry all supplies (including spare parts, food and lots of drinking water), but the rewards can justify the effort. You can transport bikes on trains (minimum charge Dh20) and buses, but pack them well.

### HITCHING

Hitching in Morocco is possible, but it demands a thick skin and considerable diplomatic expertise because of aggressive hustlers; negotiate petrol money in advance. Women should never hitch alone.

### LOCAL TRANSPORT

Most cities have reasonable and useful local bus networks. A ride costs about Dh2.50.

*Petits taxis* (small taxis used in cities) are equally useful and cheap; most drivers use the meter without question. Fares around a town shouldn't be more than Dh10, but rise by about 50% after 8pm. *Petits taxis* won't leave the city limits or take more then three passengers.

*Grands taxis* (larger, long-distance taxis) work a little like buses. Usually ageing Mercedes, they take six or even seven passengers to a fixed destination for a standard fare and leave when full. They are quicker than buses and can leave more frequently, but are more expensive and often less comfortable!

# The Mediterranean Coast & the Rif

## TANGIER
☎ 039

Sadly, most people's first impression of Tangier is as an unpleasant port of entry plagued by touts and hustlers. The Brigade Touristique (see Dangers & Annoyances section earlier) has done a lot to alleviate the hassle that gave the city its dubious image, but travellers are often inclined not to stick around for the time it takes to learn the ins and outs of this deceptively vibrant city.

Historically, Tangier has been prized for millennia as a strategic site commanding the Strait of Gibraltar. Settled as a trading port by the ancient Greeks and Phoenicians, Tangier has been occupied by Romans, Vandals, Byzantines, Arabs, Berbers, Fatimids, Almoravids, Almohads, Merenids, Portuguese, Spanish, British and French, all of whom left their mark in some way.

The defining moment in Tangier's history, however, was the period known as the 'Inter-Zone years', when the city and surrounding countryside were declared an international zone controlled by the resident diplomatic agents of France, Spain, Britain, Portugal, Sweden, Netherlands, Belgium, Italy and the USA.

# CENTRAL TANGIER

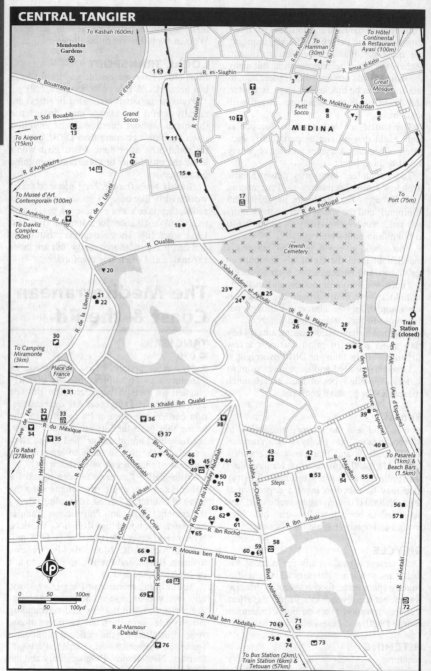

To Kasbah (600m)

Mendoubia
Gardens

To Hôtel
Continental
& Restaurant
Ayasi (100m)

R. des Almohades
R. du Commerce
To
Hamman
(30m)

R. Jemaa el-Kébir

Great
Mosque

R. es-Siaghin

R. d'Italie

R. Bouarraqia

R. Touahine

Ave Mokhtar Ahardan

Petit
Socco

Grand
Socco

R. Sidi Bouabib

MEDINA

To Airport
(15km)

R. d'Angleterre

To Museé d'Art
Contemporain (100m)

R. de la Liberté

To Dawliz
Complex
(50m)

R. Amérique du Sud

R. du Portugal

To
Port
(75m)

R. Oualiliis

Jewish
Cemetery

R Salah Eddine el-Ayoubi

To Camping
Miramonte
(3km)

(R de la Plage)

Place de
France

Train
Station
(closed)

Ave des FAR

Ave d'Espagne

Ave des FAR

R. de la Liberté

R Khalid ibn Qualid

Ave de Fés

R. du Méxique

R. Ahmed Chaouki

Blvd Pasteur

To Rabat
(278km)

Ave du Prince Héritier

al-Alhass

R. el-Moutanabi

R du Prince du Moulay Abdallah

R al-Jabha el-Ouatania

R. Magellan

R.

To Pasarela
(1km) &
Beach Bars
(1.5km)

Steps

R Omar Ibn

R. de la Croix

R ibn Rochd

R ibn Jubair

R Sorolla

R Moussa ben Noussair

Blvd Mohammed V

R al-Antaki

R al-Mansour
Dahabi

R Allal ben Abdallah

To Bus Station (2km),
Train Station (6km) &
Tetouan (57km)

0    50    100m
0    50    100yd

## CENTRAL TANGIER

**PLACES TO STAY**
5 Hôtel Mamora
6 Hôtel Olid
8 Pension Palace
22 Hôtel El Minzah
25 Pension Atou
26 Pension Talavera
27 Pension Le Détroit
39 Hôtel l'Marsa
40 Hôtel Biarritz
41 Hôtel Excelsior
42 Hôtel El Muniria &
Tanger Inn
53 Hôtel Ibn Batouta
54 Hôtel Magellan
55 Hôtel Nabil
56 Hôtel El Djenina
57 Youth Hostel

**PLACES TO EAT**
2 Restaurant Mamounia Palace
3 Cafe Tingis
4 Restaurant Andalus
7 Restaurant Ahlan
11 Restaurant Economique
20 Restaurant Populaire Saveur
23 Sandwich Genève
24 Sandwich Cervantes
28 Restaurant Africa

45 Restaurant Romero
47 Le Petit Prince
48 Trattoria La Miranda
64 Casa Pepé (Liquor Store)
65 Porte du Nord

**OTHER**
1 BMCE Bank (ATM)
9 Church of the Immaculate
Conception
10 Spanish Church
12 Hammam
13 Mosque
14 Cinéma Rif
15 Covered Market
16 Musée de la Fondation
Lorin
17 American Legation Museum
18 Covered Market
19 Dean's Bar
21 British Airways
29 Public Showers
30 French Consulate
31 Royal Air Maroc
32 Negrescu English Bar
33 Espace Net
34 Pilo Bar
35 Trou dans le Mur Bar
36 Paname Bar

37 BMCE (Late Bank & ATMs)
38 Les Ambassadeurs Bar
43 Church
44 Budget
46 Tourist Office
49 Telephone & Fax Office;
Cyber Espace Pasteur
50 Limadet Boat Ticket Office
51 Trasmediterranea Office
52 Iberia Airlines
58 Téléboutique
59 Crédit du Maroc
60 Le Palace Disco (Hôtel
Tanjah-Flandria)
61 Voyages Schwartz (American
Express)
62 Avis
63 Librairie des Colonnes
66 Paris Pressing (Laundry)
67 The Pub
68 Cinéma Goya
69 Chico's Pub
70 Banque Populaire
71 Wafabank
72 Club Internet 3000
73 Main Post Office
74 Hertz
75 Cady Loc (Car Rental)
76 London's Bar

During this time Tangier became a fashionable resort, renowned for its high-profile gay scene and popular with artists, writers, bankers, exiles and all kinds of dodgy characters, as well as being an infamous haven for paedophiles. The zone was abolished with independence in 1956, but many places (and people!) retain a certain louche nostalgia.

### Orientation

Like many large Moroccan towns, Tangier is divided between the convoluted, hectic streets of the old medina and the wide, ordered boulevards of the ville nouvelle. The modern shops and offices and most of the restaurants and better hotels are in the latter area, while the medina has markets, craft shops, cheaper hotels and smaller restaurants. The tiny square known as the Petit Socco is the heart of the medina; the larger Grand Socco lies between the two halves of town.

### Information

**Tourist Offices** The Délégation Régionale du Tourisme (☎ 948050; 29 Blvd Pasteur) can arrange official guides and offers a limited range of brochures.

**Money** There are plenty of banks along Blvd Pasteur and Blvd Mohammed V, most with ATMs and some with change booths.

**Post & Communications** The main post office (Blvd Mohammed V) has poste restante (c/o Tangier Principale 90000). The parcel counter is around the back of the building.

Internet services are available all over town for about Dh10 an hour. Try **Club Internet 3000** (☎ 945106; Rue al-Antaki) or **Espace Net** (16 Rue du Méxique) which charges Dh8 per hour.

**Bookshops** The **Librairie des Colonnes** (☎ 936955; 54 Blvd Pasteur) has a good selection of French literature and some English novels. **Librairie Dar Baroud** at the Hotel Continental stocks a good range of English books on Morocco and translations of Moroccan authors.

### Things to See

In the heart of the medina the **Petit Socco**, with its cafés and restaurants, is the focus of activity. In the days of the international zone this was the sin and sleaze centre, but it now looks largely harmless.

Heading north from the Petit Socco, Rue des Almohades takes you to the **kasbah,** built on the highest point of the city. You enter from Bab el-Assa at the end of Rue ben Raissouli in the medina. The gate opens onto a large courtyard leading to the 17th-century **Dar el-Makhzen** *(admission Dh10; open daily),* the former sultan's palace. It's now a museum housing beautiful craftwork.

The **American Legation Museum** *(admission free; open Mon-Fri),* a fascinating reminder that Morocco was the first country to recognise US independence, houses an excellent collection of paintings and prints. Knock on the door.

The **Musée de la Fondation Lorin** *(44 Rue Touahine; admission free; open daily except Sat)* documents Tangier's local history from 1890 to 1960, and is well worth a look.

In the ville nouvelle, the **Musée d'Art Contemporain** *(Rue d'Angleterre; admission Dh10; open Wed-Mon)* displays work by modern Moroccan artists.

## Places to Stay

**Camping & Hostels** About 3km west of the centre, **Camping Miramonte** *(☎ 943738; sites per adult/tent/car Dh15/10/10)* overlooks Jew's Bay. Turn left off Ave Hassan II on to Rue des USA, then take the first right (it's a Dh10 *petit taxi* ride).

The **Youth Hostel** *(☎ 946127; 8 Rue al-Antaki; members/others Dh30/33, showers Dh5)* offers decent dorm beds, but there have been complaints from women travellers.

**Hotels** There are numerous small hotels in the medina, particularly between the Petit Socco and the port area, but the European-style places in the ville nouvelle are generally more comfortable, with most offering substantial discounts out of season.

*Medina Area* There are plenty of cheap *pensions,* though many are now filled with West African refugees; prices start at Dh30. Not all have showers, but there are several *hammams* around the Petit Socco and one at 80 Rue des Almohades.

Ave Mokhtar Ahardan has countless options: **Pension Palace** *(☎ 936128)* and **Hôtel Olid** *(☎ 931310)* are both OK at Dh40 per person (Dh10 for a hot shower).

Opposite the Olid, **Hôtel Mamora** *(☎ 934 105; singles/doubles Dh305/352)* is surprisingly upmarket and offers some beautiful views over the Great Mosque. However, **Hôtel Continental** *(☎ 931024, fax 931143; 36 Dar Baroud; singles/doubles Dh339/420 including breakfast)* rules the roost in this price range. Perched above the port, it was used for some scenes in the film of Paul Bowles' *The Sheltering Sky,* and still oozes character.

*Ville Nouvelle* Rue Salah Eddine el-Ayoubi houses an overflow of cheapies from the medina, all similarly priced; there are public showers at the end of the road. **Pension Atou** *(☎ 936333; no showers)* and **Pension Talavera** *(☎ 931474)* are about the cheapest at Dh30 per person; **Pension Le Détroit** *(☎ 934838)* charges a little more but is still a good choice.

The stretch of Ave des FAR leading into Rue al-Antaki is packed with hotels of various categories. **Hôtel L'Marsa** *(☎ 932339; 92 Ave des FAR; per person Dh50, showers Dh5)* and **Hôtel Excelsior** *(☎ 066 564787; 17 Rue Magellan; singles/doubles Dh50/80, showers Dh10)* are reasonable value at the bottom end of the scale; nearby, **Hôtel Magellan** *(☎ 372319; 16 Rue Magellan; singles/doubles Dh40/80)* is a great cheap option with excellent views.

Directly opposite each other on Rue Magellan, hotels **El Muniria** *(☎ 935337; Dh130/150)* and **Ibn Batouta** *(☎ 939311; rooms Dh150-250)* couldn't be more different. William Burroughs wrote *The Naked Lunch* at the Muniria, which is quiet and slightly run-down but still full of character; its neighbour, by contrast, is modern and lively, boasting satellite TV and a resident crowd of touts and hangers-on, as well as suspiciously variable room prices!

**Hôtel Biarritz** *(☎ 932473; 102 Ave des FAR)* and **Hôtel Nabil** *(☎ 375407; 11 Rue Magellan)* also seem to be in direct competition, both charging Dh205/232 for singles/doubles. There's not much in it, so go for the best views.

For a bit more cash, **Hôtel El Djenina** *(☎ 942244, fax 942246; 8 Rue al-Antaki; singles/doubles with TV Dh249/295)* has nicely furnished rooms with en suite.

*The* top-end hotel in Tangier is **El Minzah** *(☎ 935885; ⓔ elminzah@tangeroise.net.ma; 85 Rue de la Liberté; singles/doubles from*

*Dh1200/1500)*, a grand reminder of the 1930s; don't forget your souvenir underpants!

## Places to Eat
**Medina Area** For really cheap food and self-catering head to the covered market and food stalls close to the Grand Socco. Numerous small cafés and restaurants here and around the Petit Socco offer cheap traditional fare.

Just down the hill from Hôtel Continental, the unsigned **Restaurant Ayasi** *(7 Rue Dar el-Baroud)* serves *bessara* in the morning and fish, chicken and *tajines* later on. On the eastern side of the Grand Socco, tiny **Restaurant Economique** offers *harira*, *bessara* and *brochettes* all day.

**Restaurant Ahlan** *(Ave Mokhtar Ahardan)* is a popular spot for lunch. Nearby, just north of the Petit Socco, **Restaurant Andalus** *(7 Rue du Commerce)* is a pleasant hole-in-the-wall serving cheap meals such as liver (Dh35) and swordfish (Dh45).

**Restaurant Mamounia Palace** *(☎ 935099; Rue es-Siaghin)* offers full 'Moroccan feasts' tour-group style (Dh120 a throw).

To watch the world go by over coffee or mint tea, try the pleasantly faded **Cafe Tingis** *(Petit Socco)*.

**Ville Nouvelle** Filled rolls are available for around Dh10 from **Sandwich Cervantes** and **Sandwich Genève**, opposite each other on Rue Salah Eddine el-Ayoubi.

There are several restaurants further down where the road meets Ave des FAR, most with set menus around Dh45. **Restaurant Africa** *(☎ 935436; 83 Rue Salah Eddine el-Ayoubi)* is as good as any, and happens to be licensed.

The unique **Restaurant Populaire Saveur** *(☎ 336326; Rue Oualili)* is a real experience: while the almost compulsory set menus are a tad pricy at Dh100/150, the food is excellent (especially the seafood *tajine*) and there are copious extras. Not least of these is the service, which is friendly, personal and delightfully eccentric!

Western-style food is also well represented. **Trattoria La Miranda** *(☎ 931643; 30 Rue Ahmed Chaouki)* is a good place for pasta (Dh50-70); however, the meat and fish dishes are expensive (Dh110) and it can be a bit quiet. For Spanish-style fish, try **Restaurant Romero** *(☎ 932277; 12 Rue Prince Moulay Abdallah; mains Dh50-75)*, which has a wide-ranging menu and stays open until 3.30am.

There are innumerable cafés and patisseries around Place de la France and down Blvd Pasteur; try the cakes at **Le Petit Prince** *(34 Blvd Pasteur)* or a fancy mint tea at the high-class **Porte du Nord** *(☎ 370545; Rue ibn Rochd)*.

The well-stocked liquor shop **Casa Pepé** *(9 Rue ibn Rochd)* also offers a decent delicatessen counter.

## Entertainment
Tangier has a bit more nightlife than many other Moroccan towns its size, although much of it is a bit seedy and not advisable for women travellers.

**Bars** Some particularly lively and colourful local bars include **Trou dans le Mur** *(Hole in the Wall; Ave du Prince Héritier)*, the **Paname** *(15 Blvd Pasteur)* and **Les Ambassadeurs** *(Rue du Prince du Moulay Abdallah)*.

Britons will find themselves nominally well catered for: **The Pub** *(☎ 934789; 2 Rue Sorolla)*, **London's** *(Rue al-Mansour Dahabi)* with live music most nights, **Chico's Pub** *(10 Rue de Sorolla)* and **Negrescu English Bar** *(Rue du Méxique)* offer a varied range of drinking opportunities.

The **Pilo** *(Ave de Fès)*, just past the intersection with Rue du Méxique, is a relaxed place, with excellent tapas and good views of the twilight zone outside.

The much-reduced European gay population still frequents some of the beach bars south of town. Popular places include the **Macumba**, **Miami Beach** and **Coco Beach**.

Some remnants of Tangier's seedy Inter-Zone days have survived: the tiny **Tanger Inn** *(Rue Magellan; open 9pm-late)*, next to the Hôtel El Muniria, and the famous **Dean's Bar** *(Rue Amérique du Sud)* still attract the occasional curious traveller, but on many nights calling them 'quiet' would be charitable!

**Nightclubs** The three most popular nightclubs in town are **Pasarela**, down by the beach on Ave des FAR, the **Olivia Valere** in the Ahlan Hôtel, about 5km along the road to Rabat, and **Le Palace** disco in Hôtel Tanjah-Flandria. Entry to all these clubs is around Dh100; drinks start at Dh40.

**Cinemas** Most of the cinemas in Tangier show a straightforward mixture of Bollywood and Hong Kong pulp; for Western

MOROCCO

releases, try **Cinéma Goya** *(Rue du Prince du Moulay Abdallah)* or the screens in the **Dawliz** complex north of the medina. Both cost Dh20.

## Getting There and Away

**Air** Daily flights to Casablanca (Dh813 one way) are available with **RAM** *(☎ 979501, fax 932681)*, plus direct flights to Amsterdam, Brussels, London, Madrid and Paris. Regional Airlines flies to Málaga, Iberia flies to Madrid and British Airways flies to London.

**Bus** Most CTM buses leave from the CTM office near the port entrance. Others (and some 2nd-class services) leave from the *gare routière* on Place Jamia el-Arabia, an Dh8 *petit taxi* ride away. Most non-CTM buses also leave from here, covering hundreds of destinations.

Regular CTM departures include Casablanca (Dh110), Fès (Dh85), Rabat (Dh83), and Tetouan (Dh13.50).

**Train** Tangier's only functional train station, Tangier Morora, is about 5km southeast of town; a *petit taxi* costs about Dh13. Trains south from Tangier split at Sidi Kacem to Rabat (Dh89.50, five hours), Casablanca (Dh116.50, six hours) and also Marrakesh (Dh188.50, nine to 10 hours), or to Meknès (Dh79.50, four hours) and Fès (Dh95.50, five hours). The only cheap *ordinaire* service south (Marrakesh Dh142.50, Fès Dh71) leaves at 10.30pm.

**Taxi** *Grands taxis* leave from the bus station; there are frequent departures to Tetouan (Dh20), Asilah (Dh20) and Fnideq (Dh25).

**Car** Most car rental firms have offices on or around Blvd Mohammed V and Rue Allal ben Abdellah.

**Boat** If you're heading to Spain or Gibraltar by boat, you can buy tickets from virtually any travel agency (there are plenty on Ave des FAR; the Limadet and Trasmediterranea offices are on Rue du Prince du Moulay Abdallah). It is possible to get them from the port itself, but the entrance is a hot spot for touts and the whole process can turn into a real hassle – be firm and make sure you know what you're doing.

## Getting Around

Few local bus services in Tangier are any use to the traveller; local departures, such as they are, leave from outside Mohammed V Mosque on Rue de Belgique.

*Petits taxis* are metered and cost under Dh10 around town.

## CEUTA
## ☎ 956

Ceuta is one of the two remaining Spanish-run towns on Moroccan soil, the other being Melilla (see later in this chapter). About 70% of their inhabitants are Spanish; both are administered as city provinces of Spain, but are waiting to be granted full autonomous status on an equal footing with the other provinces. Morocco occasionally campaigns for their return, but Spain's increasing importance as a trading partner has prevented these tiny enclaves from becoming a serious point of contention.

The main function of the cities is to supply Spanish troops stationed there. The principal trade is in tax-free goods; however, Morocco's Free Trade Agreement with the EU may remove the need to smuggle goods out to the rest of Africa, seriously affecting the local economy.

Known as Sebta in Morocco, Ceuta offers a couple of days' distraction but it's not cheap. If you're heading for Morocco, you could catch an early fast-ferry from Algeciras and go straight through to Tangier, Tetouan or Chefchaouen.

## Information

Both Ceuta and Melilla keep Spanish time and use the euro.

Plenty of banks line Paseo de Revellín and its continuation, Calle Camoens; the BBVA on Plaza de los Reyes is your best bet for travellers cheques. There's no need to buy dirham here – you can do so at the border as long as you have cash.

The **tourist office** *(☎ 501401; open Mon-Sat)*, beside the dock near the end of Avenida Muelle Cañonero Dato, has a list of places to stay.

The **main post office** *(correos y telégrafos; Plaza de España)* can handle most postal requirements.

**Indy Net** *(☎ 524076; 6 Calle Isabel Cabral)*, the only Internet café in town, charges €3 per hour.

There are plenty of public phones, which accept coins, phonecards and credit cards. Direct overseas dialling is cheaper than in Morocco. Note that calls into both enclaves require the international dialling code for Spain (☎ 34), not Morocco; the area code is also necessary within the towns themselves.

## Things to See & Do

The **Museo de la Legión** *(Paseo de Colón)* is dedicated to and run by the Spanish Legion and holds a staggering array of military paraphernalia. Entry is free and includes a guided tour.

Opened in May 1995, the **Maritime Park** *(Parque Marítimo del Mediterráneo)* is a huge complex on the seafront, complete with manufactured beach, pools, restaurants, bars and casino.

## Places to Stay & Eat

Finding accommodation in Ceuta can be tricky, especially during the annual carnival in mid-March, so it's worth trying to book in advance. Not everywhere is signed; look out for the blue or green F (for *fondas*, or inn), HR (for *hostal-residencia*) and CH (for *casas de huéspedes*, or boarding house) signs close to the entrances.

There aren't many genuinely cheap places in town; **Pensión Revellín** *(☎ 516762; 2 Paseo de Revellín; singles/doubles €7.20/13.20, showers €1.80)* just about fits the bill.

Up the street, **Pensión La Bohemia** *(☎ 510615; 16 Paseo de Revellín; per person €20)* is much more pleasant but, on the other hand, more expensive.

Also nearby, **Hostal Central** *(☎ 516716; 15 Paseo del Revellín; singles/doubles €24/45)* is excellent value; the small en suite rooms come with TVs, and the staff speak some English.

Up towards the top end, **Gran Hotel Ulises** *(☎ 514540; 5 Calle Camoens; singles/doubles €37/56)* is a good choice.

There are plenty of eating and drinking options around town, including two Chinese restaurants and an Irish pub, as well as the ubiquitous *bocadillos* (sandwiches) and tapas. **Cafetería La Campana** *(13 Calle Real)* does a good breakfast; to mix with a lively Spanish set, try the tiny **Méson Planta Baja** bar *(19 Tte. Pacheco)* in the evening.

More expensive places can be found on the stretch of road between McDonald's and

the Maritime Park, but they're not always as fun as the cheaper lot around Calle Real. On the other side of the yacht harbour, **Club Nautico** *(☎ 514440; Calle Edrisis; mains from €6)* is good for a civilised fish dinner.

## Getting There & Away

**Morocco** The No 7 bus runs every ten minutes or so between Plaza de la Constitución and the *frontera* (€0.54). If you arrive by ferry and want to head for the border, there's a stop just up from the tourist office on Calle Edrisis.

Once through the border, there are plenty of *grands taxis* to Tetouan (Dh20) and to nearby Fnideq (Dh5), where you can easily find taxis or buses to Tangier (whatever the touts say!).

**Mainland Spain** The ferry terminal is 800m west of the centre. There are frequent fast-ferries (hydrofoils) as well as cheaper ferries to Algeciras. Two hydrofoil services per day head to Málaga in high season.

If you can afford to travel in style, there are regular helicopter flights between Málaga and Ceuta year-round (€100 each way).

## TETOUAN
☎ 039

Set against the dramatic backdrop of the Rif Mountains, Tetouan was originally settled by Arab-Berber and Jewish refugees from Muslim Andalucía in the 16th century, and was subsequently occupied by the Spanish during the protectorate years. Even as a sprawling urban zone, the city retains a distinctly Spanish air, especially around the classic whitewashed medina.

Tetouan can sometimes have an intimidating atmosphere, particularly at night; while much of the former hassle has disappeared, it's still a place to be on your guard.

## Information

The **tourist office** *(☎ 961916; 30 Ave Mohammed V)* has helpful staff who speak English.

There are plenty of banks along Ave Mohammed V.

There's copious Internet access around town at Dh10 an hour – check out **Magic Internet** *(Rue 10 Mai)*, **Cyber Primo** *(Place Moulay el-Mehdi)* or the stylishly ultraviolet **Cyber Élégance** *(☎ 711843; Rue du P Sidi Mohammed)*.

MOROCCO

# TETOUAN

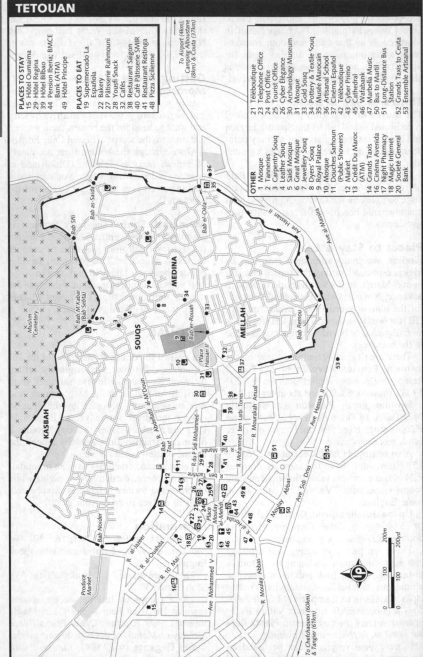

**PLACES TO STAY**
15 Hôtel Oumaima
29 Hôtel Regina
39 Hôtel Bilbao
44 Pension Iberia; BMCE Bank (ATM)
49 Hôtel Principe

**PLACES TO EAT**
19 Supermercado La Española
22 Bakery
27 Pâtisserie Rahmouni
28 Yousfi Snack
32 Cafés
38 Restaurant Saigon
40 Café Pâtisserie SMIR
41 Restaurant Restinga
48 Pizza Sicilienne

**OTHER**
1 Mosque
2 Tanneries
3 Carpentry Souq
4 Leather Souq
5 Saïdi Mosque
6 Great Mosque
7 Jewellery Souq
8 Dyers' Souq
9 Royal Palace
10 Mosque
11 Douches Sarhoun (Public Showers)
12 Market
13 Crédit Du Maroc (ATM)
14 Grands Taxis
16 Cinéma Avenida
17 Night Pharmacy
18 Magic Internet
20 Société General Bank

21 Téléboutique
23 Telephone Office
24 Post Office
25 Tourist Office
26 Cyber Elégance
30 Archaeology Museum
31 Mosque
33 Gold Souq
34 Pottery & Textile Souq
35 Musée Marocain
36 Cinéma Español
37 Artisanal School
42 Téléboutique
43 Cyber Primo
45 Cathedral
46 Wafabank
47 Marbella Music
50 Bus to Martil
51 Long-Distance Bus Station
52 Grands Taxis to Ceuta
53 Ensemble Artisanal

## Things to See

The bustling Unesco Heritage **medina** is the main point of interest for visitors, and is best entered through Bab er-Rouah. Outside, **Place Hassan II**, the grand main square linking the old and new parts of the city, is the focus for all kinds of local activity!

Just inside the eastern gate of Bab el-Okla, the excellent **Musée Marocain** *(admission Dh10; open Wed-Mon)* has well-presented exhibits of everyday Moroccan and Andalucían life. The small **Archaeology Museum** *(admission Dh10; open Mon-Fri)*, off Place al-Jala, has a good collection originating largely from the Roman ruins of Lixus, near Larache.

Outside Bab el-Okla is the **Artisanal School** *(admission Dh10; open Mon-Fri)*, where children learn traditional crafts. The building itself is worth a visit.

## Places to Stay

The nearest camping ground is **Camping Alboustane** *(☎ 688822)* on the beach at Martil, 8km away.

There are plenty of cheap, basic *pensions*, although some of the ones around Place Moulay el-Mehdi are best avoided. **Hôtel Bilbao** *(7 Ave Mohammed V; singles/doubles Dh31/52)* is one of the cheapest options; **Pension Iberia** *(☎ 963679; 5 Place Moulay el-Mehdi; singles/doubles Dh60/80, showers Dh5)* is a bit better and has some nice views.

**Hôtel Príncipe** *(☎ 962795; 20 Rue ben Tachfine; singles/doubles Dh60/74, with shower Dh70/100)* is OK, although some of the en suites are barely functional.

**Hôtel Oumaima** *(☎ 963473; Rue 10 Mai; singles/doubles Dh200/236)* is getting a bit tatty but has decent rooms with en suite and phone; **Hôtel Regina** *(☎ 962113; Rue Sidi Mandri; singles/doubles Dh205/246)* has more character and low-season discounts.

## Places to Eat

There are plenty of cheap eats in and around the medina; in the ville nouvelle, **Yousfi Snack** *(Rue ben Tachfine)* is a good bet for a munch, and **Supermercado La Española** *(Rue 10 Mai)* has plenty of supplies (including booze).

**Restaurant Saigon** *(Rue Mohammed ben Larbi Torres)* is good value and has friendly, if slightly scatty, service. Two courses and a drink should cost around Dh35. The licensed

**Restaurant Restinga**, which is just off Ave Mohammed V, is also good.

For those with more Italian tastes, **Pizza Sicilienne** *(☎ 993184; Rue al-Horuba)* serves its namesake for around Dh25. Watch out for the rowdy pool hall next door!

**Café Pâtisserie SMIR** *(Ave Mohammed V)* was shrouded in scaffolding when we visited but still served excellent pastries, as does the local branch of **Pâtisserie Rahmouni** *(10 Rue ben Tachfine)*.

## Shopping

Tetouan is a good place to buy music, especially of the modern Arabic variety. The slick staff at **Marbella Music** *(☎ 712237; Rue Moulay Abbas; tapes Dh15)* are particularly obliging and helpful to the clueless.

## Getting There & Away

**Bus** The **long-distance bus station** *(cnr Rue Sidi Mandri & Rue Moulay Abbas)* has CTM buses to Casablanca (Dh105), Chefchaouen (Dh16.50), Fès (Dh70), Rabat (Dh80) and Tangier (Dh13). Numerous other companies have buses to these and other destinations, including Marrakesh (Dh130).

Local buses to Martil (Dh2.50) leave from Rue Moulay Abbas.

**Taxi** *Grands taxis* to Chefchaouen (Dh25) and Tangier (Dh20) leave from Rue al-Jazeer. *Grands taxis* for the Ceuta border (Dh20) leave from Ave Sidi Driss, down the steps opposite the bus station.

## CHEFCHAOUEN
☎ 039

Nestled on the slopes of the Rif Mountains, this picturesque town is deservedly popular with travellers. The air is cool and clear and the atmosphere relaxed – while the people are well aware of its touristic appeal, any hassle is friendly and unpressured.

The town, originally called Chaouen, was founded in 1471 after a huge influx of Muslim and Jewish refugees from Andalucía, who gave the town its unique Hispanic look of whitewashed houses. Surprisingly, the striking pale blue that the town is so famous for only dates back to the 1930s.

## Information

The post office is on the main street, Ave Hassan II. There are various banks around

MOROCCO

# CHEFCHAOUEN

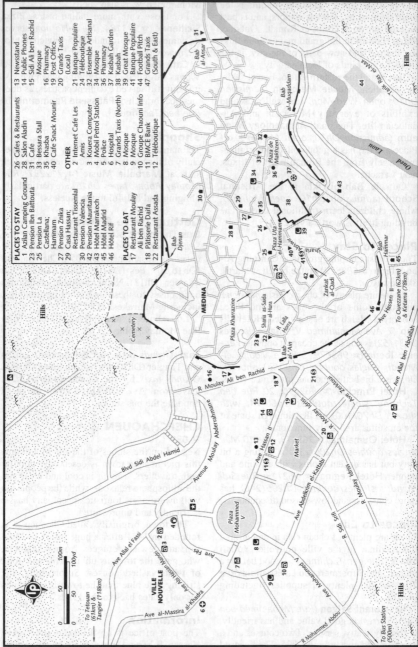

town, but not many ATMs; Banque Populaire kiosk on Plaza Uta el-Hammam changes travellers cheques (Dh10.70 commission per cheque).

Good Internet access is available at **Groupe Chaouni Info** for Dh10 an hour; **Kouera Computer** (☎ 987284; Ave Abi Hassan Mandri) is slower but cheaper, and also has a Playstation!

## Things to See & Do
The old **medina** is easy to navigate – all the painted streets are dead ends. The centre of activity is the **Plaza Uta el-Hammam**, a spacious cobbled area full of cafés, which is dominated by the 15th-century **kasbah** (entry to museum & gardens Dh10) and the **Great Mosque**. This is also where you will undoubtedly be offered kif, in a very friendly manner of course!

A lively **market** is held in the new town on Mondays and Thursdays.

The mountains around the town provide some excellent **trekking**. Contact the president of the **Association Randonnée et Culture** at Casa Hassan (☎ 986153).

## Places to Stay
The pleasant **Azilan camping ground** (☎ 986979; per person sleeping out Dh10) is situated north of town, a steep 30-minute walk up the hill.

There's a great range of cheap hotels in the medina, many with roof terraces where you can sleep in nice weather. Receptionists often seem to sleep for most of the morning, so be gentle with them!

The cheapest options are the very basic **Pension Ibn Battouta** (☎ 986044; 31 Rue Abi Khancha; per person Dh20, showers Dh5) and the popular **Pension Mauritania** (☎ 986184; 15 Rue Kadi Alami; singles/doubles Dh25/40, showers Dh5).

**Pension La Castellana** (☎ 986295; 4 Rue Bouhali; terrace Dh15, singles/doubles Dh30/60) is a popular choice even out of season, largely thanks to its wonderful roof terrace.

**Pension Valencia** (☎ 62-147119; Rue Hassan I; per person Dh30, terrace Dh20) is similarly well endowed up top, but the inside rooms are less desirable.

**Pension Znika** (☎ 986624; Rue Znika; per person Dh35) is another good option, with hot showers included.

Outside the medina, **Hôtel Marrakech** (☎ 987113; Ave Hassan II; singles/doubles Dh50/80, with bath Dh80/120) offers a variety of rooms and has a popular terrace and restaurant.

Nearby on Ave Hassan II, **Hôtel Rif** (☎ 986982; singles/doubles Dh60/90, with bath Dh97/140) and also **Hôtel Madrid** (☎ 987496, fax 987498; singles/doubles Dh180/261, double with 4-poster & TV Dh298) cater for more upscale tastes. Both have excellent views; the Madrid also has some luxury rooms and probably the only power showers in Morocco!

**Casa Hassan** (☎ 986153, fax 988196; 22 Rue Targui; half-board doubles from Dh350) is still the discerning choice in town, with some fantastically characterful traditional rooms.

## Places to Eat
Produce can be bought from the market or various transient sellers around the medina; the local goats' cheese is excellent. Snack stalls also appear sporadically on Plaza Uta el-Hammam or just outside Bab al-'Ain.

The clusters of small restaurants and cafés on Plaza Uta el-Hammam are frequented by just about everyone in town at some point. They're all pretty much of a muchness, with Moroccan and Spanish dishes going for around Dh25; **Cafe Snack Mounir** is worth a look.

**Restaurant Assada** (dishes around Dh18), near Bab al-'Ain to the north, is a tiny local spot offering good-value standards. Outside the medina, up the hill from the Bab al-'Ain, the popular **Restaurant Moulay Ali ben Rachid** is also a good option.

For a bit of extra money there are some excellent set menus at **Salon Aladin** (set menu Dh45) and at its new rival **Khasba** (☎ 883397; set menu Dh43), off Place Uta el-Hammam; the Aladin is a quiet, relaxed upstairs space away from the square, while Khasba is a more flamboyant, overfriendly spot at street level (it's a favourite with touts and dealers). The hands-down winner in this class, however, is **Restaurant Tissemlal** (set menu Dh50) at Casa Hassan (see Places to Stay), which has just a touch of inspiration in its decor and menu.

Many hotels also have terrace restaurants, which are expensive but offer superb views free of charge.

Pâtisserie Daifa (☎ 988433; Ave Hassan II), outside Bab al-'Ain, does good pastries and bread.

## Getting There & Away

**Bus** The bus station is a 15-minute downhill walk southwest of the old town. Many of the CTM and other buses are through services and often arrive already full, so it's a good idea to book a seat in advance.

If you're not having any luck getting a bus to Fès (Dh50, four hours), try for one to Meknès (Dh45, three hours) and take a local bus or *grand taxi* from there.

In addition to the numerous buses to Tetouan (Dh15, one hour) and Tangier (Dh33, two hours), there are departures to Fnideq (near the Ceuta border), Rabat, Casablanca and Nador (Dh86, eight hours).

**Taxi** *Grands taxis* going northwest to Tetouan (Dh25) and occasionally Tangier (Dh50) leave from just off Plaza Mohammed V. Taxis heading south and east leave from Ave Allal ben Abdallah.

## MELILLA
☎ 952

Spanish Melilla is smaller and more out of the way than its sister Ceuta (see earlier in this chapter) and has more of a Moroccan flavour to it, even amid the imposing colonial architecture. High unemployment has hit the Moroccan population here particularly hard; you may encounter the odd hustler.

## Information

In the Palicio de Congresos y Exposiciones you'll find a well-stocked **tourist desk** (☎ 675444; Calle Fortuny) .

Most of the banks are on Avenida de Juan Carlos I Rey, and you can buy and sell dirham. There's a Banque Populaire on the Moroccan side of the border (cash exchanges only); local moneychangers don't offer great rates.

**Locutorio Fon-net** (☎ 680974; Calle Ejército Español) has telephones and Internet access for €1 an hour.

## Things to See

The medieval fortress of **Melilla la Vieja** is pretty quiet these days but still very impressive, and offers some great views. Inside the walls, tucked away in the maze of winding Castilian streets, are the **Iglesia de la Con-**cepción, the **Museo Municipal** and the **Museo Militar**. The main entrance is through the massive **Puerta de la Marina**.

## Places to Stay & Eat

Be warned – accommodation in Melilla is expensive.

Cheapest by far is **Pensión del Puerto** (☎ 681270; 1 Calle Santiago; per person €10) off Avenida General Macías.

It's a big jump to **Hostal Rioja** (☎ 682709; 10 Calle Ejército Español; singles/doubles (€19/28, plus €3 in summer), the next step up. Perhaps the best option is the friendly **Hostal Cazaza** (☎ 684648; 6 Calle Primo de Rivera; singles/doubles €23/35), which has nice rooms with TV, bathroom and balcony.

There are plenty of good snack stops along Calle Castelar, not far from the Mercado Municipal. **Anthony Pizzeria** (1 Calle Cándido) is still a popular spot for Italian food; for proper Spanish munch, try the €6.01 set menu at **Cafe Central**, by the entrance to the Parque Hernandez.

In the evening head to **La Onubense** and **La Cervecería**, opposite each other on Calle O'Donell, for some excellent tapas (and maybe a beer or two).

## Getting There & Away

**Morocco** The No 2 bus (marked Aforos) runs between Plaza de España and the *frontera* (€0.48) every 30 minutes from 7.30am to 10pm. On the Moroccan side there are frequent buses (Dh2.30) and *grands taxis* (Dh10) to Nador, the major transport hub for the region, until about 8pm.

**Mainland Spain** Trasmediterranea runs daily ferries to Málaga and Almería. Buy your tickets at its office on Plaza de España or in the ferry terminal. Spanish rail and coach tickets can be booked at travel agents in town. There are also several flights to Málaga.

# The Middle Atlas

## MEKNÈS
☎ 055

Meknès is perhaps the most underrated of the imperial cities, generally receiving less attention than its larger neighbours. However, the city was Alawite sultan Moulay Ismail's capital for 55 years in the 17th century, and still houses an enormous palace complex. Unfortunately, an earthquake in 1755 severely damaged Meknès, and little was done to restore it until the onset of mass tourism revealed its economic potential. It's now a relaxed and pleasant alternative (or antidote!) to the hustle and bustle of Fès.

## Information

The Oued Boufekrane (Boufekrane River) divides the new town from the old.

The **tourist office** (☎ 524426) is next to the main post office, facing Place de France.

Banks with ATMs are concentrated in the ville nouvelle. There is a BMCE **bureau de change** on Ave des FAR.

Internet cafés are very cheap, if not always fast, at Dh5 an hour. Try **NetWhyNot** on Ave Mohammed V or **Cyber Paris** and **Easy-Everything**, either side of Pizza Fongue.

## Things to See

Entry to most sights is Dh10.

At the very heart of the old town is busy Place el-Hedim that faces **Bab el-Mansour**, one of the most impressive monumental gateways in Morocco. To the north of the square are the **medina** and the major *souqs*; to the east you'll find the old and new **mellahs** (Jewish quarters).

Enter the medina through the arch next to the **Dar Jamaï** museum (closed for restoration) along the main covered street you'll find the beautiful 14th-century **Medersa Bou Inania** *(open daily)* and the **Great Mosque**.

To visit the **Imperial City**, start from Bab el-Mansour and follow the road through the gate around to the small **Koubbat as-Sufara'**, where foreign ambassadors were formally received. Beside it is the entrance to an enormous underground granary.

Opposite and a little to the left, through another gate, is the **Mausoleum of Moulay Ismail** *(admission free; open Sat-Thur)*, one of the few Islamic monuments that's open to non-Muslims in Morocco.

From the mausoleum, the road follows the walls of the **Dar el-Makhzen** (Royal Palace) to reach the **Agdal basin**, a grand artificial lake, and the spectacular **Heri es-Souani** granaries and stables *(open daily)*.

## Places to Stay

**Camping Agdal** (☎ 555396; *camp sites per person/tent Dh20/10*) is in a lovely place near the Agdal basin, a long way from the ville nouvelle.

The **youth hostel** (☎ 524698; *dorm beds Dh30*) is close to posh Hotel Transatlantique, about 1km from the ville nouvelle centre.

There are dozens of cheap hotels along Rue Dar Smen and Rue Rouamzine in the medina. **Hôtel Regina** (☎ 530280; *singles/doubles Dh60/90*) and **Hôtel Maroc** (☎ 530075; *singles/doubles Dh60/120*) are both reasonable and have pleasant courtyards.

In the ville nouvelle, **Hôtel Toubkal** (☎ 522218; *Rue Mohammed V; singles/ doubles Dh50/100*) is cheap but very basic, with dubious electricity supply; **Hôtel Touring** (☎ 522351; *34 Ave Allal ben Abdallah; singles/doubles Dh75/117*) is a slightly better option.

**Hôtel Majestic** (☎ 522035; *19 Ave Mohammed V; singles/doubles Dh146/172*) is a good mid-range choice with a nice roof terrace; it's currently being refurbished, so avoid the third floor! The quirky **Hôtel Excelsior** (☎ 521900; *57 Ave des FAR; singles/ doubles Dh120/140*) is also worth a look.

Next door, **Hôtel Akouas** (☎ 515967, fax 515994; *27 Rue Amir Abdelkader; singles/ doubles Dh308/375*) tops the comfort league with rooms of varying quality and a decent bar, restaurant and terrace.

**Hôtel Transatlantique** (☎ 525050; *Rue el-Merinyne; rooms from Dh600*) is the grand old man of the hotels here, but is some way out of town.

## Places to Eat

As usual, there are plenty of simple restaurants in the medina, particularly along Rue Dar Smen. The aptly named **Restaurant Économique** at No 123 is good, as is **Snack Bounania**, in its own courtyard located near the *medersa*.

There's an excellent view and more expensive traditional fare at **Collier de la Colombe** (*67 Rue Driba; set menu Dh75*), near the imperial city.

The ville nouvelle has some cheap eats and lots of rotisseries, mainly along and around Ave Mohammed V. **Restaurant Marhaba** (☎ 521632), a tiny tiled place, does a decent *tajine* for Dh30. **Pizza Fongue** (*Zankat Accra; Dh20*) is another good option.

Classier and far more Western, **Pizzeria Le Four** (☎ 520857; *11 Rue Ibn Khaldoun; pizza from Dh40*) is licensed and popular

MOROCCO

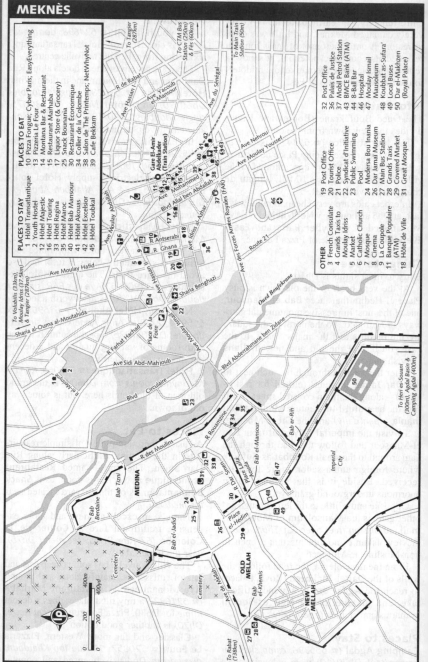

# MEKNÈS

**PLACES TO STAY**
1 Hôtel Transatlantique
2 Youth Hostel
12 Hôtel Majestic
16 Hôtel Touring
33 Hôtel Regina
35 Hôtel Maroc
40 Hôtel Bab Mansour
41 Hôtel Akouas
42 Hôtel Excelsior
45 Hôtel Toubkal

**PLACES TO EAT**
10 Pizza Fongue; Cyber Paris; EasyEverything
13 Pizzeria Le Four
14 Montana Bar & Restaurant
15 Restaurant Marhaba
17 Liquor Store (& Grocery)
25 Snack Bounania
30 Restaurant Economique
34 Collier de la Colombe
38 Salon de Thé Printemps; NetWhyNot
39 Cafe Bekkam

**OTHER**
3 French Consulate
4 Grands Taxis to Moulay Idriss
5 Market
6 Catholic Church
7 Mosque
8 Cinema
9 La Coupole
11 Banque Populaire (ATM)
18 Hôtel de Ville
19 Post Office
20 Tourist Office
21 Police
22 Syndicat d'Initiative
23 Public Swimming Pool
24 Medersa Bou Inania
26 Dar Jamaï Museum
27 Main Bus Station
28 Grands Taxis
29 Covered Market
31 Great Mosque
32 Post Office
36 Palais de Justice
37 Mobil Petrol Station
43 BMCE Bank (ATM)
44 8-Ball Bar
46 Hospital
47 Moulay Ismail Mausoleum
48 Koubbat as-Sufara'
49 Local Buses
50 Dar el-Makhzen (Royal Palace)

with travellers; 14% tax is added. Across the road, the **Montana** (☎ 520568; mains from Dh45) has more Western staples and a bar downstairs.

For breakfast or coffee, join the lively mixed crowds at **Cafe Bekkam** or **Salon de Thé Printemps**, in shopping precincts either side of Ave Mohammed V.

There is a **market** and a **liquor shop** in the ville nouvelle.

## Entertainment

Most of the bars in town are attached to hotels and restaurants – **La Coupole** (☎ 522483; Rue Ghana) and **Pizzeria Le Four** are two of the better (but quieter) places, or men could try the **8-Ball** if they're feeling tough!

The best discos are in **Hôtel Bab Mansour** and **Hôtel Akouas**.

## Getting There & Away

**Bus** The **CTM bus station** is on Ave des FAR; the **main bus station** (where CTM buses also stop) is just outside Bab el-Khemis. Destinations include Fès (one hour), Rabat (2½ hours), Casablanca (four hours), Chefchaouen (five hours), Tangier (six hours) and Marrakesh (seven hours).

Local buses and *grands taxis* to the same destinations also leave from here.

**Train** Head for the more convenient **El-Amir Abdelkader station**, parallel to Ave Mohammed V. All trains to Fès (Dh16.50, one hour), Rabat (Dh55.50, 2½ hours), Casablanca (Dh81, 3½ hours), and Marrakesh (Dh153.50, seven hours) stop here.

## AROUND MEKNÈS

About 33km from Meknès, the **Volubilis** site (*Oualili in Arabic; admission Dh20; open sunrise-sunset daily*) contains the best-preserved Roman ruins in Morocco. Dating largely from the 2nd and 3rd centuries AD, the site was actually originally settled by Carthaginian traders in the 3rd century BC. It is noted for its mosaic floors, many of which have been left *in situ*.

To get there, take a *grand taxi* (Dh7 per person) or bus (Dh6) from Place de la Foire in Meknès and hop out at the turn-off to Moulay Idriss. From there it's a pleasant half-hour walk. Going back, you can hitch or walk to Moulay Idriss and wait for a bus or taxi. If you have a group, you could hire a *grand taxi*

for a half-day trip – don't pay more than Dh300.

## FÈS
☎ 055

Fès is the oldest of Morocco's imperial cities, founded shortly after the Arabs swept across North Africa following the death of the Prophet Mohammed. Its magnificent buildings reflect a rich heritage of Arab-Berber imagination and artistry – while Rabat and Marrakesh are more important on paper, Fès is still widely seen as the cultural and spiritual capital of Morocco.

The medina of Fès el-Bali (Old Fès) is one of the largest medieval cities in the modern world. Its narrow, winding alleys and covered bazaars are crammed with workshops, restaurants, mosques, *medersas*, markets and tanneries; the exotic smells, the hammering of metal workers, the call of the muezzin and the jostling crowds are an unforgettable experience.

### History

Fès was founded in AD 789 by Idriss I on the right bank of the Oued Fès; his son, Idriss II, extended the city onto the left bank in 809, completing what is now known as Fès el-Bali.

The earliest settlers were mainly Muslim refugees from Córdoba and Kairouan. Both groups brought their own traditional skills and crafts, with the result that Fès quickly became a renowned centre of Islamic intellectual and architectural development.

The city reached its height under the Merenids, who took it from the Almohads in 1250 and erected a new quarter, Fès el-Jdid. Fès remained the capital throughout their rule; with the rise of the Saadians in the 16th century, however, its privileged status was largely lost. A renaissance came in the 19th century under the Alawite ruler Moulay Abdallah, and in 1916 the French began building the ville nouvelle southwest of the two ancient cities.

### Orientation

Fès consists of three distinct parts. The original walled city of Fès el-Bali is in the east; southwest is the French-built ville nouvelle with most of the restaurants and hotels, and the Merenid walled city of Fès el-Jdid lies between the two.

MOROCCO

# FÈS

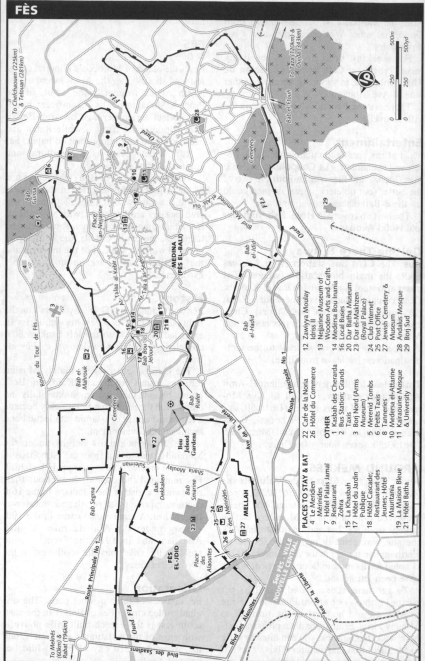

To Chefchaouen (225km) & Tetouan (281km)

To Taza (120km) & Oujda (343km)

500m
500yd

Bab el-Ftouh

Cemetery

Bab Guissa

Oued Fès

Place an-Neijarine

MEDINA
(FÈS EL-BALI)

Av. Talaa al-Kebir

Av. Tala a as-Seghir

Bab el-Jdid

Bab el-Hadid

Oued Fès

Route du Tour de Fès

Bab el-Mahrouk

Bab Bou Jeloud

Cemetery

Bou Jeloud Gardens

Route Principale No 1

Bab Riafer

Bab Segma

Bab Dekkaken

Bab Smarine

Sharia Moulay Suleiman

R. des Mérinides

MELLAH

Place des Alaouites

FÈS EL-JDID

Route Principale No 1

Oued FÈS

To Meknès (60km) & Rabat (196km)

Blvd des Saadiens

Ave. de la Liberté

Blvd des Alaouites

See FÈS - VILLE NOUVELLE CENTRAL

## PLACES TO STAY & EAT
4 Le Meridien Mérinides
7 Hôtel Palais Jamaï
9 Restaurant Zohra
15 La Khasbah
17 Hôtel du Jardin Publique
18 Hôtel Cascade; Restaurant des Jeunes; Hôtel Mauritania
19 La Maison Bleue
21 Hôtel Batha

22 Cafe de la Noria
26 Hôtel du Commerce

## OTHER
1 Kasbah des Cherarda
2 Bus Station; Grands Taxis
3 Borj Nord (Arms Museum)
5 Merenid Tombs
8 Petits Taxis
10 Medersa el-Attarine
11 Kairaouine Mosque & University

12 Zawiyya Moulay Idriss II
13 Nejjarine Museum of Wooden Arts and Crafts
14 Medersa Bou Inania
16 Local Buses
20 Dar Batha Museum
23 Dar el-Makhzen (Royal Palace)
24 Club Internet
25 Post Office
27 Jewish Cemetery & Museum
28 Andalus Mosque
29 Borj Sud

## Information

The **ONMT office** (☎ 623460; Place de la Résistance) is in the ville nouvelle. Official guides are available here or through hotels at Dh120/150 for a half/full day.

Plenty of unofficial guides hang around and will guide you for a lot less – they can be useful, especially in stopping other would-be guides bothering you.

The main post office is located in the ville nouvelle, as are most banks with ATMs.

Internet cafés all over town charge from Dh7 to Dh15 an hour. **Club Internet** (Rue des Mérinides) has good fast connections for Dh10 per hour; **SIBED** (☎ 941383; Rue Arabie Saoudite) stays open until midnight and charges Dh8 per hour.

## Things to See

**Fès el-Bali** The old **medina** is an incredible maze of twisting alleys, arches, mosques, shrines, fountains, workshops and markets, and keeps most travellers busy for the duration of their stay. Unfortunately, most of the religious sites are closed to non-Muslims; entry to the exceptions costs Dh10.

The most convenient entry point is **Bab Bou Jeloud**; close by is the **Medersa Bou Inania**, built by the Merenid sultan Bou Inan between 1350 and 1357. The carved woodwork is magnificent; sadly it is closed until summer 2003 for renovations.

In the guts of the city, you can only take a peek into the **Kairaouine Mosque**, one of the largest mosques in Morocco. Founded between AD 859 and 862 for Tunisian refugees, it has one of the finest libraries in the Muslim world.

Nearby, the **Medersa el-Attarine** (open daily), built by Abu Said in 1325, displays some beautiful Merenid craftsmanship.

On the boundary between Fès el-Bali and Fès el-Jdid, the **Dar Batha museum** (Place de Batha; open Wed-Mon) was built as a palace over 100 years ago, and now houses historical and artistic artefacts from ruined or decaying medersas as well as Fassi embroidery, tribal carpets and ceramics.

**Fès el-Jdid** Built by the Merenids in the 13th century, Fès' 'other' walled city is not as lively or interesting as Fès el-Bali. It contains the old Jewish quarter (mellah) and a couple of mosques and synagogues (one housing a **museum**).

The **Dar el-Makhzen** (Royal Palace) has 80 hectares of grounds but is closed to the public.

At the northern end of the main street, Sharia Moulay Suleiman, is the enormous **Bab Dekkaken**, formerly the main entrance to the royal palace. Between it and Bab Bou Jeloud are the **Bou Jeloud Gardens**, through which flows the Oued Fès, the city's main water source.

**Borj Nord & Merenid Tombs** For a spectacular view of Fès, walk or take a taxi up to the Borj Nord fortress and the Merenid tombs, where you can see the whole of Fès sprawled at your feet. The 16th-century Borj Nord, built by the Saadian sultan Ahmed al-Mansour, houses the **Arms Museum** (open Wed-Mon). The tombs, mostly ruins, are dramatic against the city backdrop; sunrise and sunset are spectacular but don't come alone.

## Places to Stay

**Camping & Hostels** The shady **Camping Diamant Vert** (☎ 608369; sites per person/ tent Dh20/15), 6km south off the Ifrane road, sits in a valley with a clean stream. Take bus No 17 to 'Ain Chkef from Place de Florence.

**Camping International** (☎ 731439, fax 731554; bus No 38 from Place Atlas; sites per adult/child Dh40/30), 3km down the Sefrou road, has more extensive facilities.

The **youth hostel** (☎ 624085; 18 Rue Abdeslam Serghini; dorm beds/doubles for members Dh45/55, for nonmembers Dh50/60) in the ville nouvelle is a lovely quiet little place with its own courtyard, TV, hot showers and tortoise! Rates include breakfast.

**Hotels – Medina** The most colourful hotels are around Bab Bou Jeloud. They are basic and not all have showers, but there are copious hammams.

**Hôtel du Jardin Publique** (☎ 633086; singles/doubles Dh40/60), outside the gate, has large, clean rooms. Inside the gate, **Hôtel Mauritania** (singles/doubles Dh50/80) is OK; **Hôtel Cascade** (☎ 638442; singles/doubles Dh50/100) is popular and well touted, but the fantastic roof terraces are better than the rooms! With the medina crowds right outside, these places can get noisy.

Fès el-Jdid doesn't offer the full-on medina experience, but it is central and relatively quiet. The best place is probably **Hôtel du**

MOROCCO

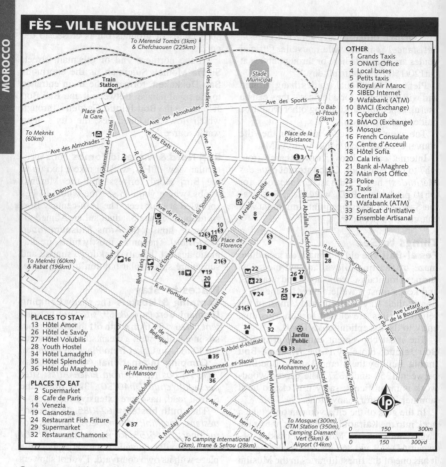

## FÈS – VILLE NOUVELLE CENTRAL

To Merenid Tombs (3km)
& Chefchaouen (225km)

Train
Station

Place de
la Gare

To Meknès
(60km)

Ave des Almohades

Ave des Almohades

R de Damas

Ave Mohammed el-Hayani

R Chenguit

Blvd des Saadiens

Ave des Etats Unis

Ave de France

R du Soudan

Ave Mohammed el-Korri

Stade
Municipal

Ave des Sports

Place de la
Résistance

R Arabie Saoudite

Blvd Abdallah Chefchaouni

To Bab
el-Ftouh
(3km)

Blvd ben Jerrah

Blvd Tariq Ibn Ziad

R d'Espagne

To Meknès (60km)
& Rabat (196km)

R du Portugal

R Hassan II

Ave Hassan II

Place de
Florence

R Moham
meg Diouri

R du Ravin

See Fès Map

Ave Letard
de la Bouralliére

Jardin
Public

R Abdel el-Khattabi

Place Ahmed
el-Mansoor

R de
Belgique

R Moulay
Slimane

R Allal Ben Abdullah

Ave Mohammed es-Slaoui

Ave Youssef ben Tachfine

Place
Mohammed V

Blvd Mohammed V

Ave Abdelaziz Boutaleb

Ave Slaoui Zerktouni

To Mosque (300m),
CTM Station (350m),
Camping Diamant
Vert (5km) &
Airport (14km)

To Camping International
(2km), Ifrane & Sefrou (28km)

**OTHER**
1  Grands Taxis
3  ONMT Office
4  Local buses
5  Petits taxis
6  Royal Air Maroc
7  SIBED Internet
9  Wafabank (ATM)
10 BMCI (Exchange)
11 Cyberclub
12 BMAO (Exchange)
15 Mosque
16 French Consulate
17 Centre d'Acceuil
18 Hôtel Sofia
20 Cala Iris
21 Bank al-Maghreb
22 Main Post Office
23 Police
25 Taxis
30 Central Market
31 Wafabank (ATM)
33 Syndicat d'Initiative
37 Ensemble Artisanal

**PLACES TO STAY**
13 Hôtel Amor
26 Hôtel de Savôy
27 Hôtel Volubilis
28 Youth Hostel
34 Hôtel Lamadghri
35 Hôtel Splendid
36 Hôtel du Maghreb

**PLACES TO EAT**
2  Supermarket
8  Cafe de Paris
14 Venezia
19 Casanostra
24 Restaurant Fish Friture
29 Supermarket
32 Restaurant Chamonix

0      150      300m
0      150      300yd

**Commerce** (*Place des Alaouites; singles/doubles Dh40/60*).

The only medina mid-range choice is **Hôtel Batha** (*☎ 741077, fax 741078; Place de Batha; singles/doubles with bath Dh190/240*), overlooking the Batha museum. There's a bar, restaurant and pool.

Near the Merenid tombs, **Le Meridien Mérinides** (*☎ 645226, fax 645225; rooms from Dh1100*) offers a sweeping panorama of the old medina; the swimming pool and restaurants make good spots for a sunset drink.

The cash-burner of choice here is **Hôtel Palais Jamaï** (*☎ 634331, fax 635096; e sales@palais-jamai.co.ma; Bab Guissa; rooms from Dh2100*), the former pleasure dome of a late-19th-century grand vizier. It's set in a lush Andalucían garden.

For the same kind of money you can forfeit facilities such as swimming pools for personalised service in a beautifully restored *riad* (lavish old-style townhouse), as at **La Maison Bleue** (*☎ 636052, fax 740686; W www.maisonbleue.com; 2 Place de Batha; suites Dh1685-Dh2835*).

**Hotels – Ville Nouvelle** Near the student area, **Hôtel de Savoy** and **Hôtel Volubilis** charge the same (*singles/doubles Dh50/70*) and are both reasonable; rooms facing the road can be noisy.

**Hôtel du Maghreb** (*☎ 621567; 25 Ave Mohammed es-Saloui; singles/doubles Dh60/100*) is slightly better; showers are included.

The three-star **Hôtel Amor** (*☎ 622724; 31 Rue Arabie Saoudite; singles/doubles Dh164/*

198) has bright, clean rooms with bathroom, as well as a restaurant and bar; it's worth it just for the Mr Men shower curtains!

In the same price range, **Hôtel Lamadghri** (☎ 620310; 10 Rue Abasse El Mssadi; rooms with shower/bath Dh154/200) is light and quiet, with a pleasant courtyard.

One step closer the top end, **Hôtel Splendid** (☎ 622148, fax 654892; 9 Rue Abdelkrim el-Khattabi; singles/doubles Dh281/342) goes a bit overboard on the 'traditional' trappings, but the rooms are great and it has a superb pool and terrace.

## Places to Eat
There are multiple eating options in the popular Bab Bou Jeloud area: you can get a filled roll from a snack stall for about Dh10, or try one of the tourist-oriented terrace restaurants for a larger feed. The **Restaurant des Jeunes** and the pushy **La Khasbah** do meals around Dh50.

In the ville nouvelle there are a number of food shops on Blvd ben Jerrah; you'll find countless snack bars along Ave de France and around Place de Florence, as well as a few cheap eats around Blvd Mohammed V and the central market. The popular **Venezia** (Ave de France; Dh12-20) is one of the best.

For something more substantial, **Restaurant Chamonix** (set menu Dh50), near the market, offers the usual, plus pizza. Nearby, **Restaurant Fish Friture** (Blvd Mohammed V) serves cheap seafood and pizza from Dh40.

The sparky **Casanostra** (☎ 932841; 16 Rue Arabie Saoudite; dishes around Dh40) is a good approximation of a cheap Western pizza/pasta joint; the service is friendly and it's popular with Moroccan families.

If you're prepared to spend more, try the **Al Fassia** restaurant (meals Dh390) in Hôtel Palais Jamaï. Several other traditional restaurants set in centuries-old buildings offer less expensive alternatives; **Restaurant Zohra** (☎ 637699; 3 Derb Ain Nass Blida; set menus from Dh70) is the cheapest and least touristy.

There's a multitude of cafés and patisseries in the ville nouvelle, particularly along Ave Hassan II/Ave de la Liberté – **Cafe de Paris** has a nice salon de thé, but you can basically take your pick. For sheer tranquillity, however, the **Cafe de la Noria** in the Bou Jeloud Gardens is unbeatable.

There are **supermarkets** near the train station and opposite the central market.

## Entertainment
There are a few bars scattered around the ville nouvelle. The European-looking **Cala Iris** (Ave Hassan II) is a good place to start, as are the hotel bars.

Some of the bigger hotels have nightclubs: try the discos in the **Sofia** and **Mérinides** hotels.

## Getting There & Away
**Air** Fès airport (☎ 674712) is at Saiss, 15km to the south. RAM (☎ 625516; 54 Ave Hassan II) has regular flights to Casablanca (45 minutes) and Paris (three hours).

**Bus** The CTM buses (☎ 732384) originate at the **bus station** (Place Baghdadi) near Bab Bou Jeloud, and call in at the ville nouvelle terminus half an hour later.

There are daily buses to Tangier (Dh80, six hours), Marrakesh (Dh130, nine hours), Casablanca (Dh80, five hours) via Rabat (Dh50, four hours) and Meknès (Dh15, one hour).

Cheaper buses run more regularly and reservations can be made.

**Train** The train station is in the ville nouvelle, 10 minutes' walk from the town centre. There are daily departures to Tangier (Dh95.50, five hours), Marrakesh (Dh171, 7½ hours), and Casablanca (Dh97, 4½ hours) via Rabat (Dh72, 3½ hours) and Meknès (Dh16.50, one hour).

**Taxi & Car** Grands taxis to Meknès (Dh15), Rabat (Dh60) and Casablanca (Dh100) leave from the bus station.

Most car-rental agencies are located in the ville nouvelle, especially on Ave Hassan II.

## Getting Around
Fès has good local bus services (around Dh2), although they are like sardine cans at times. Useful routes include:

**No 9** Place de l'Atlas – Ave Hassan II – Dar Batha
**No 12** Bab Bou Jeloud – Bab Guissa – Bab el-Ftouh
**No 16** train station – airport
**No 47** train station – Bab Bou Jeloud

Red petits taxis are metered: expect to pay about Dh10 from the train station to Bab Bou Jeloud. Only grands taxis go out to the airport (Dh80).

## AROUND FÈS

Set against jagged mountain bluffs and rich farmland, the picturesque Berber town of **Sefrou** makes a fine contrast to the intensity of Fès, just 28km away. Accommodation options are limited, but it's worth a quick trip. The town boasts a small walled **medina** and **mellah**, with a lively market on Thursday; the best points of entry/exit are Bab Taksebt, Bab Zemghila and the Bab Merba. You can go and see a **waterfall** about 1.5km to the west of town.

Sadly the hustle endemic to Fès has now started to spread to Sefrou – expect some (mostly friendly) attention from local guides and bolshie children.

Regular buses (Dh5) and *grands taxis* (Dh8) between Fès and Sefrou drop off at Place Moulay Hassan, in front of the Bab M'Kam and Bab Taksebt, and pick up just around the corner.

# North Atlantic Coast

## ASILAH
☎ 039

The small port of Asilah has enjoyed a disproportionately tumultuous history. Settled by the Carthaginians and taken over by the Romans, it came under Portuguese and Spanish control in the 15th and 16th centuries. Early last century, Asilah became the residence of the bandit Er-Raissouli, who effectively controlled northeastern Morocco until he was imprisoned in 1925.

Unfortunately, the proximity of Tangier has rubbed off slightly on Asilah, bringing a number of touts into the tourist trade; the hassle is generally friendly though.

### Things to See

The 15th-century Portuguese **ramparts** are still intact; access is limited, but the views are excellent.

The **Palais de Raissouli**, **Hassan II International Center** and **El Kamra** tower are the focus of the annual **Cultural Moussem** in early August; the latter venues also house art exhibitions throughout the year.

Several decent **beaches** stretch north of the town, while **Paradise Beach**, a local favourite, is 3km south.

### Places to Stay

**Camping As-Saada** and **Camping Echrigui** are a few hundred metres north of town. Both are secure, have decent facilities and fill up in summer.

There is not much budget accommodation in Asilah, although touts will try and steer you into the medina. **Hôtel Marhaba** (☎ 417144; Rue Abdel M ben Ali; per person Dh50, showers Dh5) is simple, clean and has a great roof terrace.

**Hôtel Sahara** (☎ 417185; 9 Rue Tarfaya; singles/doubles Dh98/126, showers Dh5) has a good range of rooms, although they pack the beds in a bit. Prices drop about Dh25 out of season.

**Hôtel Mansour** (☎ 417390, fax 416272; 56 Ave Mohammed V; singles/doubles Dh195/240) is a quiet, friendly place; it's much cheaper in winter.

If you have a little bit of spare cash, stay at the fantastically stylish Spanish-run **Hôtel Patio de la Luna** (☎ 416074; 12 Plaza Zelaya; singles/doubles Dh200/300).

### Places to Eat

Fish is a good option here! There's a whole line of restaurants and cafés along Ave Hassan II with main courses around Dh30, or some more expensive places across from Bab Kasaba: **Casa García** (☎ 417465), **Restaurante Oceano Casa Pepe** (☎ 417395) and **Restaurant de la Place** (☎ 417326) all offer dishes for around Dh50.

### Getting There & Away

The best way to reach Asilah is by bus (Dh10) or *grand taxi* from Tangier (Dh20) or Larache (Dh12). Regular buses leave for Rabat, Casablanca, Fès and Meknès. There are trains, but the station is 1.5km to the north of town.

## LARACHE
☎ 039

Larache is a big working town, but often almost entirely devoid of tourists, making it a more relaxed place than Asilah. At one time the town was completely walled; the kasbah and ramparts are now mostly in ruins, but the old **medina**, a fortress known as **Casbah de la Cigogne** and a Spanish-built citadel housing the **archaeological museum** (admission Dh10; open Wed-Mon) are still largely intact.

While the town is still worth a wander, particularly along the seafront on Ave Moulay Ismail and Rue de Casablanca, most people come to Larache to visit the Roman ruins of **Lixus** *(admission free)*. Situated about 3½km north of town, on a hillock overlooking the Loukkos estuary and the Tangier–Larache highway, the scattered and overgrown remains of an amphitheatre, temples, mosaics and the public baths are strangely impressive.

There are a number of reasonable beaches north of town.

## Information

The post office and many of the banks are on Blvd Mohammed V; only Banque Populaire changes travellers cheques (with commission). There are several Internet cafés around town, charging Dh10 an hour.

## Places to Stay

There are plenty of cheap hotels in central Larache. **Pension Atlas** *(☎ 912014; 154 Rue 2 Mars; singles/doubles Dh25/50, showers Dh5)*, in the medina, is easy to find and has small, moderately clean rooms.

In the ville nouvelle, **Pension Amal** *(☎ 912788; 10 Ave Abdallah ben Yassine; singles/doubles Dh40/65, showers Dh6)* is very clean and good value; one street down, **Pension Palmera** *(☎ 500641; 8 Passage beni Mellal; singles/doubles Dh30/60, showers Dh5)* is cheaper and not as spotless, but has a 'proper' Western toilet.

**Hôtel Hay Essalam** *(☎ 916822; 9 Ave Hassan II)* is excellent mid-range value, with immaculate en suite singles/doubles (some with TV and balcony) for Dh116/133 and rooms without facilities for Dh90/116.

The faded **Hôtel España** *(☎ 913195, fax 915628; 3 Ave Hassan II; singles/doubles without bath Dh122/163, with en suite Dh204/245)* is still clinging on to its former grandeur. Rooms have TV and phone.

At the top end is **Hôtel Riad Larache** *(☎ 912626, fax 912629; 88 Ave Mohammed ben Abdallah; singles/doubles Dh239/314)*, set in extensive grounds, which has a range of traditionally furbished rooms and suites (from Dh680). Prices include breakfast.

Prices tend to rise by 10% in summer.

## Places to Eat

Numerous snack stalls and carts appear in the area around Ave Hassan II and the medina every evening, offering a variety of very cheap Moroccan and Spanish-style food. It's even possible to find *churros* (the Spanish dunking doughnuts) in the late afternoon.

There are plenty of decent restaurants around Place de la Libération, most serving mains for about Dh25; **Restaurant Comercial** has a pleasant upstairs seating area.

Patisserie-wise, **Salon de Thé Lacoste** *(Ave Mohammed ben Abdallah)* and **Le Sourire** *(Ave Hassan)*, next to Hôtel España, are both top-notch. **Café Central** *(Place de la Libération)* is a popular place for coffee.

## Getting There & Away

Larache is most easily reached by bus, but booking is not always possible on the way out, so turn up in the morning and get the first available service.

CTM buses run to Fès (Dh89) via Meknès (Dh61), Tangier (Dh29) and Casablanca (Dh82) via Rabat (Dh56). There are also non-CTM buses to these destinations and Tetouan (Dh20), Ceuta (Dh25) and Asilah (Dh10).

*Grands taxis* to Asilah (Dh12) leave from outside the bus station.

## Getting Around

For the beach or the Lixus ruins, catch bus No 4 or 5 opposite the Casbah de la Cigogne, or take a *petit taxi* (around Dh15, but you may have to haggle).

## RABAT
☎ 037

Rabat's current role as Morocco's capital began during the French protectorate, but its history goes back 2500 years. The Phoenicians and the Romans both had short-lived interests in the area, but the city itself only came to prominence under the Almohad Sultan Yacoub al-Mansour in the 12th century. He used the kasbah as a base for campaigns in Spain, and built the magnificent Almohad Bab Oudaia and the unfinished Tour Hassan. However, the city rapidly declined after his death in 1199.

In the early 17th century, the Muslims expelled from Spain resettled the city and neighbouring Salé, ushering in the colourful era of the Sallee Rovers. These corsairs plundered thousands of merchant vessels returning to Europe from Asia, West Africa and the Americas, spawning a whole clutch of popular legends.

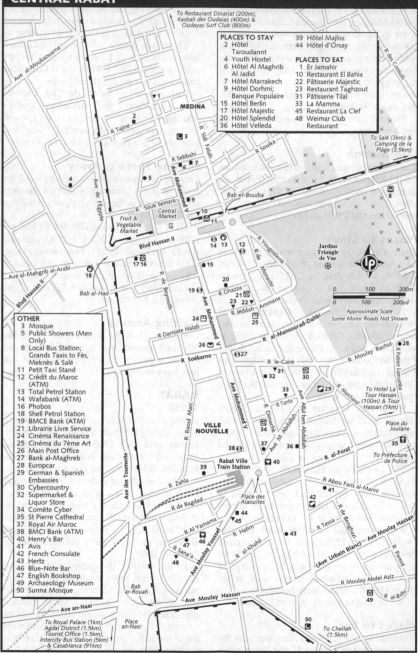

# CENTRAL RABAT

To Restaurant Dinarjat (200m),
Kasbah des Oudaias (400m) &
Oudayas Surf Club (800m)

**PLACES TO STAY**
2  Hôtel
   Taroudannt
4  Youth Hostel
6  Hôtel Al Maghrib
   Al Jadid
7  Hôtel Marrakech
9  Hôtel Dorhmi;
   Banque Populaire
15 Hôtel Berlin
17 Hôtel Majestic
20 Hôtel Splendid
36 Hôtel Velleda

39 Hôtel Majliss
44 Hôtel d'Orsay

**PLACES TO EAT**
1  Er Jamahir
10 Restaurant El Bahia
22 Pâtisserie Majestic
23 Restaurant Taghzout
31 Pâtisserie Tilal
33 La Mamma
45 Restaurant La Clef
48 Weimar Club
   Restaurant

To Salé (3km) &
Camping de la
Plage (3.5km)

MEDINA

Bab el-Bouiba

Jardins
Triangle
de Vue

0     100    200m
0     100    200yd
Approximate Scale
Some Minor Roads Not Shown

Bab al-Had

Bab al-Had

VILLE
NOUVELLE

Rabat Ville
Train Station

Place des
Alaouites

Bab
ar-Rouah

**OTHER**
3  Mosque
5  Public Showers (Men
   Only)
8  Local Bus Station;
   Grands Taxis to Fès,
   Meknès & Salé
11 Petit Taxi Stand
12 Crédit du Maroc
   (ATM)
13 Total Petrol Station
14 Wafabank (ATM)
16 Phobos
18 Shell Petrol Station
19 BMCE Bank (ATM)
21 Librairie Livre Service
24 Cinéma Renaissance
25 Cinéma du 7ème Art
26 Main Post Office
27 Bank al-Maghreb
28 Europcar
29 German & Spanish
   Embassies
30 Cybercountry
32 Supermarket &
   Liquor Store
34 Comète Cyber
35 St Pierre Cathedral
37 Royal Air Maroc
38 BMCI Bank (ATM)
40 Henry's Bar
41 Avis
42 French Consulate
43 Hertz
46 Blue-Note Bar
47 English Bookshop
49 Archaeology Museum
50 Sunna Mosque

To Hotel La
Tour Hassan
(100m) & Tour
Hassan (1km)

Place du
Joulane

To Préfecture
de Police

To Chellah
(1.5km)

Place
an-Nasr

To Royal Palace (1km),
Agdal District (1.5km),
Tourist Office (1.5km),
Intercity Bus Station (5km)
& Casablanca (91km)

MOROCCO

French rule brought capital status and a new sense of respectability; independence brought the newly wealthy middle class. Casablanca may be the economic heavyweight, but Rabat is the serious older brother, maintaining a definite air of French sophistication and maturity. It's a relaxed place, even in the *souqs*, and it's worth staying a few days.

## Information
**Tourist Office** Rabat's **ONMT office** (☎ 730562; *Rue al-Abtal; bus No 3 from Blvd Hassan II*) is inconveniently located in Agdal, west of the city.

**Money** The banks are concentrated along Ave Mohammed V and Ave Allal ben Abdalla. The majority have exchange booths and ATMs. There's a useful BMCE bureau at Rabat Ville train station.

**Post & Communications** The parcel ('Colis postaux') and EMS ('Poste Rapide') offices are to the right of the **main post office** (*cnr Rue Soekarno & Ave Mohammed V*).

*Téléboutiques* can be found all over town; **Phobos** (*Blvd Hassan II*) also has Internet access. There are numerous Internet cafés, all charging Dh10 an hour. Among the best are **Comète Cyber** (*4 Rue Tihama*), which stays open until 1am, and also the friendly **Cybercountry** (☎ 261195; *Rue le Caire; open 9am-11pm*).

**Bookshops** Reasonable English-language books are available at the **English Bookshop** (☎ 706593; *7 Rue Al Yamama*).

**Librairie Livre Service** (*Ave Allal ben Abdallah*) has a small English-language section, a wide range of French books, and Internet access.

## Things to See
The 17th-century **medina** is a far cry from the dense medieval mazes of Fès or Tangier, but it's definitely worth exploring, as it's hard to get lost! There are some excellent carpet shops and jewellery shops. Follow Rue Souika, then head north up Rue des Consuls (where there's an informal morning carpet *souq* on Tuesday and Thursday) to get to the **Kasbah des Oudaias** (ancient fortifications) overlooking the Atlantic Ocean. The main entry is the impressive **Almohad Bab Oudaia**, built in 1195.

The kasbah houses a palace built by Moulay Ismail that now contains the **Museum of Moroccan Arts** (*admission Dh10; open daily*).

Southeast of the medina, past the dazzling white of the French **St Pierre Cathedral**, is Rabat's most famous landmark, the **Tour Hassan**. This incomplete minaret is the last remnant of the great mosque begun by Yacoub al-Mansour, which was levelled by the 1755 earthquake. On the same site is the **Mausoleum of Mohammed V**, the present king's grandfather.

The impressive **Bab ar-Rouah**, Gate of the Winds, guards the southern entrance to the ville nouvelle near the Royal Palace. Further on, beyond the city walls, is the **Chellah** (*admission Dh10; open daily*), a former Berber city turned Merenid necropolis, which also encompasses the remains of the ancient Roman city of **Sala**.

Rabat's **Archaeology Museum** (*23 Rue al-Brihi; admission Dh10; open Wed-Mon*) is interesting, but the marvellous Roman bronzes are sometimes away on loan.

For more active pursuits, there's the King's own **Oudayas Surf Club** (☎ 260683), perched in a stylish clubhouse above the Atlantic west of the kasbah.

## Places to Stay
**Camping & Hostels** There's not much shade at **Camping de la Plage** (*sites per person/2-person tent/car/camper vans Dh15/22/12/30*) but it's pretty friendly. It's at Salé beach and is well signposted. It's Dh15 for power and water, plus Dh10 per hot shower.

The **Youth Hostel** (☎ 725769; *43 Rue Marassa; dorm beds Dh30*), opposite the medina walls, is pleasant enough. Cold showers are included, but there are no cooking facilities.

**Hotels** There are countless cheap deals in the medina, particularly around the central market and off Ave Mohammed V. **Hôtel Al Maghrib Al Jadid** (☎ 732207; *2 Rue Sebbahi; singles/doubles Dh60/100*) and its annexe **Hôtel Marrakech** are good traveller-oriented places, with clean, very pink rooms! Hot showers are Dh7.50. Slightly further away, **Hôtel Taroudannt** (☎ 720521; *18 Rue Tajine; singles/doubles Dh45/80, showers Dh7*) could be cleaner but has a pleasant internal courtyard.

**Hôtel Dorhmi** (☎ 723898; 313 Ave Mohammed V; singles/doubles Dh80/120, showers Dh7) has comfortable rooms with huge beds and a nice terrace.

In the ville nouvelle, check out **Hôtel Berlin** (☎ 703435; 261 Ave Mohammed V; singles/doubles Dh60/92, showers Dh6), which is a reasonable option, tucked away above a decent Chinese restaurant.

A bit more expensive is **Hôtel Velleda** (☎ 769531; 106 Ave Allal ben Abdallah; singles/doubles Dh126/162), a nicely furnished place on the 4th floor (use the lift). Most of the rooms have bathrooms, small balconies and good views.

**Hôtel Splendid** (☎ 723283; 8 Rue Ghazza; basic singles/doubles Dh102/124, with en suites Dh157/183) has some great rooms with en suite and a lovely courtyard. Prices are due to rise, however.

The friendly three-star **Hôtel d'Orsay** (☎ 202277; 11 Ave Moulay Youssef; singles/doubles Dh211/264), near the train station, has nice rooms with good facilities.

Looking out over the medina walls, **Hôtel Majestic** (☎ 722997; 121 Blvd Hassan II; singles/doubles Dh232/275, TV Dh10) is a classy middle-bracket choice. It has large, well-equipped en suite rooms, some with balconies.

Trying hard to make an impact in the four-star category, **Hôtel Majliss** (☎ 733726, fax 733731; 6 Rue Zahla; singles/doubles Dh480/628) is friendly and characterful, if too close to the train station. Undisputed king of the top end is the luxurious **Hôtel La Tour Hassan** (☎ 704201, fax 725408; 26 Rue Chellah; rooms from Dh2000).

## Places to Eat

For self-caterers the grocery stalls around the market are a good bet, although foodstuffs are cheaper from the stalls along Rue Souika. There is a supermarket and liquor shop on Rue Dimachk.

There are plenty of good, cheap places to eat in the medina; you should be able to get a decent meal for as little as Dh20.

**Er Jamahir** (215 Ave Mohammed V; mains Dh12-18) is a tiny locals' place; look out for the cut-out of a chef with a *tajine*.

The pleasant Moroccan-style **Restaurant El Bahia** (☎ 734504; Blvd Hassan II; mains around Dh35, 10% service charge) is built into the walls of the medina.

If you have more to spend try **Restaurant Dinarjat** (☎ 704239; 6 Rue Belgnaoui; about Dh200 per person), a 17th-century mansion in the heart of the medina. The experience is sometimes better than the food.

There are plenty of restaurants in the ville nouvelle. **Restaurant Taghzout** (Rue Jeddah Ammane) is an excellent cheap option frequented by locals, offering fish dishes and *tajine* for Dh25.

**Restaurant La Clef** (☎ 701972; Ave Moulay Youssef) has a good selection of Moroccan standards for around Dh50, as well as some French dishes and a Dh65 set menu.

For the die-hard Europeans, **La Mamma** (☎ 707329; 6 Rue Zankat Tanta) has good authentic pizzas for Dh50 and does deliveries, while the stylish **Weimar Club Restaurant** (☎ 732650; 7 Rue Sana'a; dishes around Dh50) in the Goethe Institut serves excellent German/French cuisine.

There are numerous cafés along and around Ave Mohammed V – **Pâtisserie Majestic** (Ave Allal ben Abdallah) and **Pâtisserie Tilal** (8 Rue le Caire) are both excellent. In the southeast corner of the Kasbah des Oudaias, the quiet and shady **Café Maure** overlooks the estuary to Salé.

## Entertainment

The two main cinemas are **Cinéma Renaissance** (Ave Mohammed V; Dh20/25), which shows mainstream Western releases, and **Cinéma du 7ème Art** (Rue Allal ben Abdallah), with an eclectic programme and has a very popular garden café.

At night central Rabat is generally a quiet and sensible place, without much riotous nightlife. Some cafés double as bars, such as **Henry's** (Ave M Abdallah), but close early. The **Blue-Note** (Rue Al Yamama) is a typically dark hideout for Moroccan males, but may be worth a look.

## Getting There & Away

**Bus**  The bus station is inconveniently situated 5km from the centre of town. Take local bus No 30 or a *petit taxi* (Dh20) to the centre.

CTM offers a comprehensive service; cheaper non-CTM buses are also available for most destinations.

**Train**  Conveniently located in the centre of town, **Rabat Ville train station** (Ave Mohammed V) has 22 trains to Casablanca

MOROCCO

(Dh29.50, 50 minutes); half are shuttle services linking Rabat with Mohammed V airport (Dh55, two hours) via Casa Port. There are also frequent departures to Tangier (Dh89.50, five hours) and Fès (Dh72, five hours) via Meknès (Dh55.50, 2½ hours).

**Taxi** *Grands taxis* for Casablanca (Dh27) leave from outside the *gare routière* (Inter-city bus station). Taxis for Fès (Dh55), Meknès (Dh40) and Salé (Dh3) leave from near the bus terminal on Blvd Hassan II.

**Car** The following are among the car-rental agencies in Rabat:

**Avis** (☎ 769759) 7 Rue Abou Faris al-Marini
**Budget** (☎ 705789) train station, Ave Mohammed V
**Europcar** (☎ 722328) 25 Rue Patrice Lumumba
**Hertz** (☎ 709227) 46 Ave Mohammed V

## Getting Around
The No 16 bus leaves from the **main local city bus station** *(Blvd Hassan II)* for Salé and No 3 goes to Agdal. Bus Nos 30 and 17 run past Rabat's intercity bus station; they leave from a stop just inside Bab al-Had.
*Petits taxis* can usually be found around the station, but their meters go round pretty fast.

## AROUND RABAT
The town of **Salé** is worlds away from Rabat. Left to its own devices since the demise of the corsairs, the Morocco of yesteryear just about lives on, spared from the tourist hordes. There's not much to see but it's a quiet, pleasant place to spend some time.

In the 13th century the Merenid sultan built the walls and gates that stand today and a canal between the Oued Bou Regreg and the Bab Mrisa to allow safe access for shipping. Salé became the principal seaport through which the sultanate at Fès traded with the outside world until the end of the 16th century.

The only real point of interest in Salé is the beautiful 14th-century Merenid **medersa** *(admission Dh10)* next to the Grand Mosque in the medina.

*Grands taxis* to Rabat (Dh2.50) leave from Bab Mrisa; bus No 16 also links the two. You can catch small boats across the river below Bab Bou Haja.

## CASABLANCA
☎ 022
Casablanca is by far Morocco's largest city and its industrial centre. Although its history goes back many centuries (including over 200 years of Portuguese occupation), it had declined into insignificance by the mid-1880s, and only reached its current size and status under French rule.

The key to this renaissance was the decision of the French resident-general, Lyautey, to develop the city as a commercial centre. It was largely his ideas that gave Casablanca its wide boulevards, public parks, fountains and imposing Mauresque civic buildings (a blend of French colonial and traditional Moroccan styles), as well as firmly establishing it at the heart of Morocco's economic well-being.

Amid the 1930s architecture, the Art Deco touches and the very Western pedestrian precincts, cosmopolitan Morocco is alive, well and totally fashionable. Casablanca has ingrained 'attitude', its own style and a gritty edge that gives it a very different air from Rabat or Tangier; as a city, it remains an excellent barometer of liberal Islam.

## Information
**Tourist Offices** The **ONMT office** *(☎ 271177; 55 Rue Omar Slaoui; open Mon-Fri)* is generally helpful. There's also a **syndicat d'initiative** *(98 Blvd Mohammed V; open daily)* nearer the centre of town.

**Money** Most of the principal banks have branches on Ave des FAR or Blvd Mohammed V, many with ATMs and change bureaus. The **Crédit du Maroc** *(Blvd Mohammed V)* and **Banque Populaire** *(Ave des FAR)* will change travellers cheques. There are independent exchange counters and banks with ATMs at Mohammed V international airport.

American Express is represented by **Voyages Schwartz** *(☎ 222947; 112 Rue Prince Moulay Abdallah; open Mon-Sat)*.

**Post & Communications** The **main post office** *(Place Mohammed V)* services poste restante. The parcel office is just left of the main entrance.

**Email & Internet Access** There are plenty of Internet cafés scattered around town, charging between Dh10 and Dh15 an hour.

# CENTRAL CASABLANCA

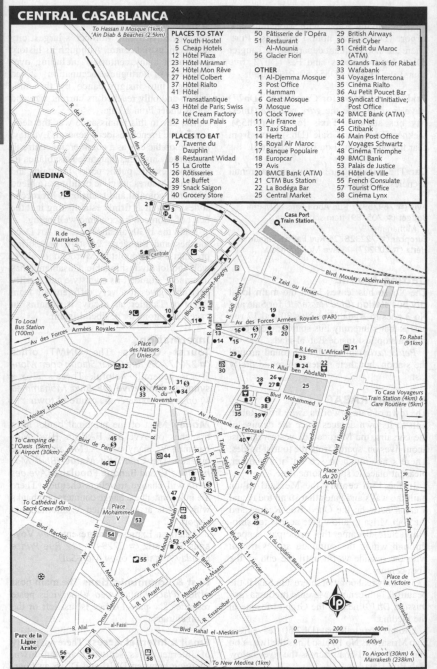

**PLACES TO STAY**
2 Youth Hostel
5 Cheap Hotels
12 Hôtel Plaza
23 Hôtel Miramar
24 Hôtel Mon Rêve
27 Hôtel Colbert
37 Hôtel Rialto
41 Hôtel Transatlantique
43 Hôtel de Paris; Swiss Ice Cream Factory
52 Hôtel du Palais

**PLACES TO EAT**
7 Taverne du Dauphin
8 Restaurant Widad
15 La Grotte
26 Rôtisseries
28 Le Buffet
39 Snack Saigon
40 Grocery Store
50 Pâtisserie de l'Opéra
51 Restaurant Al-Mounia
56 Glacier Fiori

**OTHER**
1 Al-Djemma Mosque
3 Post Office
4 Hammam
6 Great Mosque
9 Mosque
10 Clock Tower
11 Air France
13 Taxi Stand
14 Hertz
16 Royal Air Maroc
17 Banque Populaire
18 Europcar
19 Avis
20 BMCE Bank (ATM)
21 CTM Bus Station
22 La Bodéga Bar
25 Central Market
29 British Airways
30 First Cyber
31 Crédit du Maroc (ATM)
32 Grands Taxis for Rabat
33 Wafabank
34 Voyages Intercona
35 Cinéma Rialto
36 Au Petit Poucet Bar
38 Syndicat d'Initiative; Post Office
42 BMCE Bank (ATM)
44 Euro Net
45 Citibank
46 Main Post Office
47 Voyages Schwartz
48 Cinéma Triomphe
49 BMCI Bank
53 Palais de Justice
54 Hôtel de Ville
55 French Consulate
57 Tourist Office
58 Cinéma Lynx

Euro Net *(51 Rue Tata)* is a good option, while **First Cyber** *(☎ 492017; 62 Rue Allah ben Abdellah)* also sells mobile phones.

## Things to See
The stunning **Hassan II Mosque** is Casablanca's principal landmark, overlooking the ocean just north of the medina. The third biggest religious monument in the world, it's hard to believe it was built as recently as 1993! Unusually, it's open to non-Muslims: there are guided tours in various languages every day except Friday (Dh100 per person; Dh50 for students).

The central **ville nouvelle** around Place Mohammed V has some of the best examples of Mauresque architecture: the *hôtel de ville* (town hall), the *palais de justice* (law courts) and the post office are all impressive edifices in their own right, and the sadly neglected **Cathédrale du Sacré Cœur** is still an extraordinary sight. Contrary to expectations, Casablanca has some wonderful architecture, so try to look around you occasionally!

Casablanca's **beaches**, such as they are, are west of town along Blvd de la Corniche and beyond, in the suburb of 'Ain Diab. It's a trendy area and crowded in summer. Take bus No 9 from Place Oued al-Makhazine, just west of Place des Nations Unies.

## Places to Stay
**Camping & Hostels** Bus No 31 runs past **Camping de l'Oasis** *(☎ 253367; sites per person, tent & car Dh15)*, which is about 5km southwest of town.

The **Youth Hostel** *(☎ 220551, fax 226777; 6 Place Ahmed El Bidaoui; dorm beds/doubles/triples Dh45/120/180)* is in the medina, just off Blvd des Almohades. It's clean and comfortable; showers and breakfast are included.

**Hotels** There are a number of small hotels in the medina, particularly around Rue Centrale; most cost around Dh45, but unless you're a *hammam* junkie the ville nouvelle options are much better.

The cheap places tend to be near the main market, around Rue Allal ben Abdallah. **Hôtel Miramar** *(☎ 310308; 22 Rue Léon L'Africain; singles/doubles Dh62/76, shower Dh6)* is about the cheapest, if not the nicest, and is conveniently close to the CTM bus station.

Nearby, **Hôtel Mon Rêve** *(☎ 311439; 7 Rue Chaoui)* charges the same and also has sizeable triples for Dh110; showers cost Dh7. There's no hot water in the rooms.

**Hôtel Colbert** *(☎ 314241; 38 Rue Chaoui; singles/doubles Dh68/83, with en suite Dh84/100)*, opposite the market, is well liked by travellers, offering a choice of rooms with or without bathroom (hot showers cost Dh10). **Hôtel Rialto** *(☎ 275122; 9 Rue Salah ben Bouchaib; singles/doubles Dh84/120)* is generally an amenable place, but the showers are not always as clean as they could be.

South of the centre, **Hôtel du Palais** *(☎ 276121; 68 Rue Fahrat Hachad; singles/doubles Dh140/200)* has gone slightly up-market, with a corresponding hike in prices. It's still reasonable value in this range, however, and now has hot water!

Built in 1936, the characterful **Hôtel Plaza** *(☎ 297698; 18 Blvd Houphouet-Boigny; singles/doubles with en suite & breakfast Dh284/365)* has rooms with balconies and sea views, as well as cheaper rooms without bathrooms. It also has a bar.

The three-star **Hôtel de Paris** *(☎ 274275, fax 298069; 2 Rue Ech-Cherif Amziane; singles/doubles Dh372/440)*, in the pedestrian zone off Rue Prince Moulay Abdallah, has comfortable, traditionally decorated rooms with heating, phone and TV. If you run into him, long-time employee Aziz is a good source of tourist information.

Slightly away from the central top-end places but far more fun, **Hôtel Transatlantique** *(☎ 294551, fax 294792; 79 Rue Chaoui; singles/doubles Dh770/925)* has an outrageous Art Deco lobby, two restaurants, various bars and a nightclub. The rooms are a slight anticlimax but come with all the trimmings.

## Places to Eat
Fresh food is cheapest in the medina, but there is also a good delicatessen in the central **market**. There are a few cheap restaurants around the clock tower entrance to the medina, including the very popular **Restaurant Widad**, which serves decent Moroccan dishes.

Outside the medina, the best place for good, cheap food is along Rue Chaoui, where there are plenty of good *rôtisseries* and restaurants offering meals for around Dh25.

**Snack Saigon** *(Rue Salah ben Bouchaib)* is a tiny place that serves proper Moroccan

MOROCCO

standards to a mainly local crowd; marked prices are between Dh15 and Dh30, but can fluctuate.

Despite its vaguely South Pacific decor, **La Grotte** (*Rue Léon L'Africain*) serves good honest *tajines* (Dh30) and pizza (Dh25) to a varied set of mainly young locals.

There are a number of reasonable restaurants along Blvd Mohammed V; **Le Buffet** (☎ 222344; 99 Blvd Mohammed V; mains Dh70-80) is popular with local couples and has an excellent set menu for Dh75.

If you want seafood head to the popular **Taverne du Dauphin** (☎ 221200; 115 Blvd Houphouet-Boigny) in the medina wall. Mains start around Dh50, but 20% tax is added, so if you don't fancy a full meal, try the bar for a relaxed drink or snack.

**Restaurant Al-Mounia** (☎ 222669; 95 Rue du Prince Moulay Abdallah; mains from Dh110) is still a very pleasant spot for traditional Moroccan cuisine, including vegetarian dishes, but prices seem to be increasing rapidly.

The city centre is filled with French-style cafés. **Pâtisserie de l'Opéra** (50 Blvd du11 Janvier) is a tranquil and very women-friendly place, while **Glacier Fiori** (☎ 261967; Rue Omar Slaoui) is popular with businessmen for a quiet read of *L'Opinion* over a morning coffee.

For delicious home-made ice cream visit the **Swiss Ice Cream Factory** (*Rue Ech-Charif Amziane*). It's a women-friendly spot deservedly popular with the young and trendy.

There are plentiful options for self-caterers, such as the **grocery shop** on Ave Houmane el-Fetouaki.

## Entertainment

**Bars & Nightclubs** Central Casablanca has a large red-light district and plenty of seedy bars and cabaret places, so it can be hard to find a 'normal' place for a drink or a dance – apparently even the sailors' bars in the port can be friendlier than some local dives! Women should be particularly cautious here after dark.

**Au Petit Poucet**, next to the restaurant of the same name, is a die-hard relic of 1920s France (complete with chain-smoking male clientele) and less forbidding than most. Saint-Exupéry, the French author and aviator, used to spend time here between mail flights.

**La Bodéga** (☎ 541842; 129 Rue Allal ben Abdallah) is a Spanish-style tapas bar and restaurant. It's expensive but women-friendly and good fun, with regular live music.

The trendiest clubs and bars are to be found in the wealthy beachside suburb of 'Ain Diab, west of town.

**Cinema** The spanking new **Cinéma Triomphe** (*Rue Prince Moulay Abdallah*), a prestige project in an impressive modern building, has recently opened for business, showing the usual dubbed mainstream fare. Its main rival is **Cinéma Lynx** (☎ 220229; 50 Ave Mers Sultan; tickets from Dh20); for those less concerned with repertoire, **Cinéma Rialto** (*Rue Salah ben Bouchaib*) is a classic Art Deco building.

## Getting There & Away

**Air** From Casablanca's Mohammed V airport (30km southeast of the city), there are regular connections to Western Europe, the rest of Africa and the Middle East.

Internally, you can get to any destination directly from Casablanca with RAM. There are eight weekly flights to Fès (Dh842, 45 minutes) and at least six to Tangier (Dh827, 50 minutes).

**Bus** The flash **CTM bus station** (☎ 449224; Rue Léon L'Africain) has daily departures to Fès (five hours) and Meknès (four hours), Rabat (one hour), Tangier (six hours) and Tetouan (five hours).

CTM also operates **international buses** (☎ 458000) to Belgium, France, Germany, Italy and Spain from Casablanca.

Ouled Ziane is the bus station for almost all non-CTM services – unfortunately, it's some distance from the city centre. Take a taxi (Dh10), or catch bus No 10 from Blvd Mohammed V.

**Train** Most long-distance departures to destinations across the country leave from Casa Voyageurs station, 4km east of the city. A *petit taxi* costs Dh10, or catch local bus No 30.

Shuttle trains to Mohammed V Airport (via Casa Voyageurs, Dh30, 38 minutes) and north to Rabat (Dh29.50, 50 minutes) leave from the central Casa Port station.

**Taxi & Car** *Grands taxis* to Rabat (Dh27) leave from Blvd Hassan Seghir, near the

CTM bus station; there's also a rank on Ave des FAR.

Most international car rental firms have offices on Ave des FAR and/or in Mohammed V airport.

## Getting Around

Shuttle trains (TNR) run from Mohammed V airport to Casa Voyageurs and Casa Port (Dh25, 24 minutes). A *grand taxi* to the airport costs Dh150 (Dh200 after 8pm).

Useful local bus routes include:

**No 9** From the terminal to 'Ain Diab and the beaches
**No 10** From Place de la Concorde to Ouled Ziane bus station via Blvd Mohammed V
**No 15** From the terminal to the Hassan II Mosque
**No 30** From Blvd Ziraoui to Casa Voyageurs train station via Ave des FAR and Blvd Mohammed V

There's no shortage of *petits taxis* in Casablanca. Expect to pay Dh5 for a ride within the city centre with the meter on.

# The High Atlas

## MARRAKESH
☎ 044 • pop 900,000

Basking in the clear African light of the south, Marrakesh has an entirely different feel from its sister cities to the north. It remains unmistakably more African than cosmopolitan Casablanca, more Moroccan than sanitised Rabat, and more Berber than proud and aloof Fès.

Positioned on an important crossroads, Morocco's fourth-largest city is still regarded as the southern capital, attracting merchants and traders from the surrounding plains, High Atlas and the Sahara. Just as the colour blue is synonymous with Fès, green with Meknès and white with Rabat, red is Marrakesh's colour. A local Berber legend has it that when the minaret of the Koutoubia Mosque was planted in the city's heart, it poured so much blood that all the walls, houses and roads turned this colour. At dusk, in the last rays of the setting sun, you could almost believe the blood is flowing again as the city's ramparts turn crimson.

## Orientation

The old city and the ville nouvelle are roughly the same size. It takes about 30 minutes to walk from the centre of the ville nouvelle to Place Djemaa el-Fna, the main square in the heart of the old city.

The medina walls enclose an unusual amount of open space. It is not until you have penetrated beyond the large and irregularly shaped Place Djemaa el-Fna, the medina's focal point, that you reach the traditional maze of *souqs* and twisting alleys. Most of the budget hotels are clustered in the narrow streets to the east and southeast of Place Djemaa el-Fna. The *souqs* and principal religious buildings lie to the north, and the palaces to the south. To the southwest rises the city's most prominent landmark, the minaret of the Koutoubia Mosque.

## Information

**Tourist Offices** The main **ONMT office** (☎ 436131, fax 436057; Place Abdel Moumen ben Ali, Gueliz; open Mon-Sat) is in the ville nouvelle. There is also a separate medina **tourist office** (open Mon-Fri) south of the Koutoubia.

**Money** Most banks will change cash or travellers cheques and there's no shortage of ATMs. **Crèdit du Maroc** (open 8.45am-1pm & 3pm-6.45pm Mon-Sat) offers after-hours exchange facilities at its branches in the ville nouvelle (215 Ave Mohammed V) and the medina (Rue de Bab Agnaou).

American Express in Marrakesh is represented by **Voyages Schwartz** (☎ 433321; 2nd floor, Immeuble Moutaouakil, 1 Rue Mauritanie; open 9am-12.30pm & 3pm-6.30pm Mon-Fri, Sat 9am-12.30pm) in the ville nouvelle.

**Post & Communications** The main **post office** (Place du 16 Novembre; open 8.30am-6.30pm Mon-Fri, 8.30am-11.30am Sat) is in the ville nouvelle. Limited services are available after hours. There's also a useful **post and telephone office** (Place Djemaa el-Fna) on the medina's main square.

The many Internet cafés in the medina and the Gueliz area charge a standard Dh10 per hour.

**Travel Agencies** Most travel agencies, and Royal Air Maroc, are on or near Ave Mohammed V, west of Place du 16 Novembre in Gueliz. including **Menara Tours** (☎ 446654, fax 446107; W www.menara-tours.ma; 41

MOROCCO

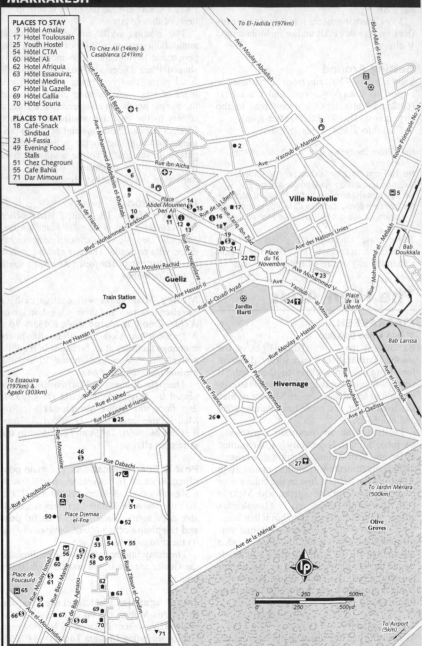

# MARRAKESH

**PLACES TO STAY**
9   Hôtel Amalay
17  Hotel Toulousain
25  Youth Hostel
54  Hôtel CTM
60  Hôtel Ali
62  Hotel Afriquia
63  Hôtel Essaouira;
    Hotel Medina
67  Hôtel la Gazelle
69  Hôtel Gallia
70  Hôtel Souria

**PLACES TO EAT**
18  Café-Snack
    Sindibad
23  Al-Fassia
49  Evening Food
    Stalls
51  Chez Chegrouni
55  Cafe Bahia
71  Dar Mimoun

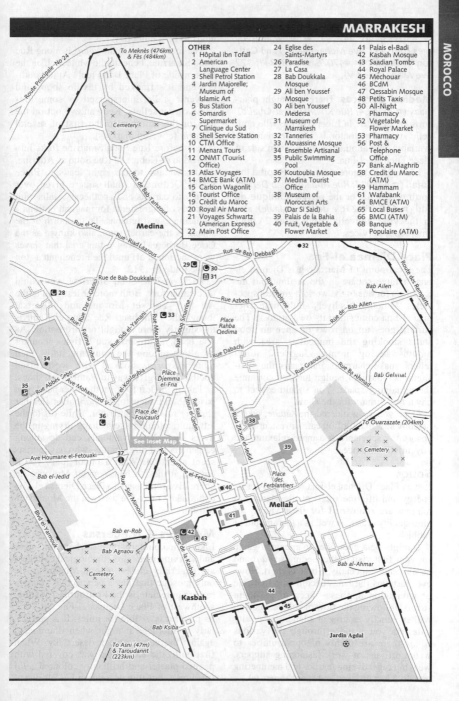

# MARRAKESH

**OTHER**
1 Hôpital ibn Tofaïl
2 American Language Center
3 Shell Petrol Station
4 Jardin Majorelle; Museum of Islamic Art
5 Bus Station
6 Somardis Supermarket
7 Clinique du Sud
8 Shell Service Station
10 CTM Office
11 Menara Tours
12 ONMT (Tourist Office)
13 Atlas Voyages
14 BMCE Bank (ATM)
15 Carlson Wagonlit
16 Tourist Office
19 Crèdit du Maroc
20 Royal Air Maroc
21 Voyages Schwartz (American Express)
22 Main Post Office
24 Eglise des Saints-Martyrs
26 Paradise
27 La Casa
28 Bab Doukkala Mosque
29 Ali ben Youssef Mosque
30 Ali ben Youssef Medersa
31 Museum of Marrakesh
32 Tanneries
33 Mouassine Mosque
34 Ensemble Artisanal
35 Public Swimming Pool
36 Koutoubia Mosque
37 Medina Tourist Office
38 Museum of Moroccan Arts (Dar Si Said)
39 Palais de la Bahia
40 Fruit, Vegetable & Flower Market
41 Palais el-Badi
42 Kasbah Mosque
43 Saadian Tombs
44 Royal Palace
45 Mechouar
46 BCdM
47 Qessabin Mosque
48 Petits Taxis
50 All-Night Pharmacy
52 Vegetable & Flower Market
53 Pharmacy
56 Post & Telephone Office
57 Bank al-Maghrib
58 Credit du Maroc (ATM)
59 Hammam
61 Wafabank
64 BMCE (ATM)
65 Local Buses
66 BMCI (ATM)
68 Banque Populaire (ATM)

Rue de Yougoslavie), **Atlas Voyages**
(☎ 430333, fax 447963; W www.atlasvoy
ages.com; 131 Ave Mohammed V) and **Carlson Wagonlit** (☎ 447076, fax 432341; 122
Ave Mohammed V).

**Medical Services** There is a night pharmacy (☎ 389564; Rue Khalid ben el-Oualid),
north of Place de la Liberté in the ville nouvelle, where a doctor is also permanently
available, and another on the western side of
Place Djemaa el-Fna.

For anything more serious, try **Hôpital Ibn
Tofaïl** (☎ 448011; Rue Abdelouahab Derraq)
north of Gueliz, or the private **Clinique du
Sud** (☎ 447999; 2 Rue de Yougoslavie), also
in the ville nouvelle. Both offer 24-hour
emergency services.

## Place Djemaa el-Fna

The focal point of Marrakesh is Djemaa el-
Fna, a huge square in the medina and the
backdrop for one of the world's greatest spectacles. Although it's lively all the time, Djemaa el-Fna comes into its own at dusk. The
curtain goes up on rows of open-air food
stalls smoking the immediate area with
mouth-watering aromas. Jugglers, story-
tellers, snake charmers, musicians, the occasional acrobat and benign lunatics consume
the remaining space. You should expect to
pay a few dirham for the show.

Once you've wandered the square, take a
balcony seat in a rooftop café or restaurant to
absorb the spectacle at a more relaxing and
voyeuristic distance.

## Souqs

Just as Place Djemaa el-Fna is famous for its
energy and life, the souqs of the Marrakesh
medina are renowned for their variety of
high-quality crafts, as well as a fair amount of
rubbish.

It might be a good idea to engage a guide
for your first visit to the medina's souqs and
monuments, especially if time is short. However tortuous the lanes become the first rule
of navigation applies – keep to the main
streets, following the flow of people, and you
will eventually emerge at a landmark or city
gate. As you wander through the various
souqs there are plenty of opportunities to
watch artisans at work fashioning slippers,
weaving rugs, dyeing textiles and hammering
metals. Most artisans and shopkeepers take a

break between 1.30pm and 3pm. Friday also
tends to be a quiet day.

The main access to the souqs is along Rue
Souq Smarrine, beneath the white arch on the
eastern side of Place Bab Fteuh. At its southern end it's flanked by textile shops and
souvenir stalls, interspersed by some big-
name carpet sellers. Keep an eye out for the
left for the entrance to the first of several
qissaria (covered markets).

Just before Rue Souq Smarrine forks into
Rue Souq el-Kebir and Rue Souq al-Attarine,
a narrow lane to the right leads to Place
Rahba Qedima, a small square given over
mainly to carpets and apothecary stalls with
all kinds of ingredients for magical potions –
including caged iguanas. To the north of the
square is the carpet souq, also known as the
Criée Berbère. It was in this area that slaves
were auctioned off until the French put a stop
to the trade in 1912.

Back on Rue Souq Smarrine, you could
take either fork. Both more or less lead to the
Ali ben Youssef Mosque and Medersa,
though the right-hand Rue Souq el-Kebir is
the slightly more straightforward option. As
you head northwards you'll first encounter
jewellers among the souvenir stalls, then
more qissaria, stocked with westernised
goods, which give way to leatherwork shops.

Taking the left fork, on the other hand, you
pass the entrance to the babouche (leather
slipper) souq on your right, while off to the
left multicoloured skeins hang drying in the
dyers souq. You eventually end up among
carpenters and blacksmiths, who pay tourists
scant attention. With a bit of luck, you'll
emerge at the Ali ben Youssef Mosque. An
alternative route back to Place Djemaa el-Fna
could take you to the west via the Mouassine
Mosque.

## Mosques & Medersas

Like their counterparts elsewhere, mosques
and working medersas (theological colleges)
are generally closed to non-Muslims. The
only mosque that has a perspective you can
really appreciate is the **Koutoubia Mosque**,
southwest of Place Djemaa el-Fna. At 70m,
its minaret is visible for miles. It is particularly memorable at night when illuminated
against the velvety-black desert sky. When
first built, the Koutoubia was covered with
painted plaster and brilliantly coloured zellij
(tilework), but this decoration has all disap-

peared. What can still be seen, however, are the decorative panels, which are different on each face and practically constitute a textbook of Islamic design.

The largest of the mosques inside the medina is the **Ali ben Youssef Mosque**, first built in the second half of the 12th century. It's the oldest surviving mosque in Marrakesh, but the building itself is fairly recent. Next door is the **Ali ben Youssef Medersa** (admission Dh20; open 9am-6pm daily) of the same name. Although undergoing a painstaking restoration, it is a beautiful and still peaceful and meditative place with some absolutely stunning examples of stucco decoration.

The other big mosque in the medina is the **Mouassine Mosque**, built in the 16th century by the Saadians on land formerly occupied by the Jewish community. Its most notable features are the three huge doorways and the elaborate fountain to the northeast. The fountain has three sections: two arched bays for animals and one for humans.

## Palaces

The most famous of the city's palaces is the **Palais el-Badi** (admission Dh10; open 8.30am-11.45am & 2.30pm-5.45pm daily), south of Place Djemaa el-Fna. Built by Ahmed al-Mansour between 1578 and 1602, at the time of its construction it was reputed to be one of the most beautiful in the world (and was known as 'the Incomparable'). It included marble from Italy and other precious building materials from as far away as India. Unfortunately, the palace is now largely a ruin, having been plundered by Moulay Ismail in 1696 for its materials, which were used to build his new capital at Meknès. The easiest way to get to the palace is to take Ave Houmane el-Fetouaki south from the Koutoubia Mosque to Place des Ferblantiers. Go through the large gate and turn right.

The **Palais de la Bahia** (admission Dh10; open 8.30am-11.15am & 2.30pm-5.45pm Sat-Thur, 8.30am-11.30am & 3pm-5.45pm Fri) was built towards the end of the 19th century as the residence of Si' Ahmed ben Musa, the Grand Vizier of Sultan Moulay al-Hassan I. Upon Bou Ahmed's death it was ransacked, but much has since been restored. It's a rambling structure with fountains, elaborate reception rooms, living quarters, pleasure gardens and numerous secluded, shady courtyards. To get here from the Palais el-Badi,

take the road heading northeast from Place des Ferblantiers and you'll soon come to the entrance on your right.

Farther north of the Palais de la Bahia and again off to the right (it's signposted), the **Dar Si Said** (admission Dh10; open 9am-11.45am & 2.30pm-5.45pm Mon, Wed, Thur, Sat & Sun, 9am-11.30am & 3pm-5.45pm Fri), which now houses the Museum of Moroccan Arts, is well worth a visit. The museum has one of the finest collections in the country, including jewellery, carpets, oil lamps, pottery and leatherwork.

## Museum of Marrakesh

Inaugurated in 1997, the Omar Benjelloun Foundation's museum (adult/child Dh30/10; open 9.30am-6pm daily) is housed in a beautifully restored 19th-century riad with some very impressive zellij work. Not only does the house have a glorious central courtyard with fountains around which galleries display artworks, it also allows the visitor an insight into household features such as the original hammam.

## Saadian Tombs

Alongside the Kasbah Mosque is this necropolis (admission Dh10; open 8.30am-11.45am & 2.30pm-5.45pm daily), started by the Saadian sultan Ahmed al-Mansour in the late 1500s. Unlike the Palais el-Badi, another of al-Mansour's projects, the tombs escaped Moulay Ismail's depredations – possibly because he was superstitious about plundering the dead. Instead he sealed the tombs and, as a result, they still convey some of the opulence and superb artistry that must also have been lavished on the palace.

The tombs are signposted down a narrow alleyway at the southern edge of the Kasbah Mosque.

## Jardin Majorelle & Museum of Islamic Art

Now owned by the French couturier Yves Saint-Laurent, these lush gardens (admission gardens Dh20, museum Dh15; open 8am-noon & 2pm-5pm daily, 8am-noon & 3pm-7pm summer) provide a wonderful haven. They were designed by the French painter Jacques Majorelle, who lived here from 1922 to 1962. Among the cacti, bamboo and cascades of bougainvillaea is a deep-blue villa, now housing the museum. It contains one of those Moroccan collections you'd love to scoop up and take home to decorate your house with. Exhibits, including carpets, wedding curtains, jewellery, manuscripts and belts are labelled in Arabic and French.

## Organised Tours

Menara Tours (see Travel Agencies earlier) offers day trips to the Ourika Valley (from Dh270); Asni, Ouirgane and Tahanaoute (from Dh270); Telouet in the High Atlas (from Dh500); and the Cascades d'Ouzoud (waterfalls; from Dh400). Another agency with a good reputation is **Pampa Voyages** (☎ 431052, fax 446455; W www.pampa maroc.com; 213 Ave Mohammed V). It specialises in longer tailor-made tours into the Atlas Mountains and the Drâa Valley. Among other things, it can organise excursions into the desert with camels and bivouacs.

While Hôtel Ali (see Places to Stay) is no longer the trekking centre it once was, it remains your best bet for information on the High Atlas. You can arrange treks (Dh350 per person per day) or join an organised tour through its associated travel agency **Sahara Expedition** (☎ 427977, fax 427972; W www .saharaexpe.ma; Angle Ave el-Mouahidine & Rue Bani Marine).

## Special Events

If you're in Marrakesh in June (the dates change), inquire about the two-week Festival of Folklore (information ☎ 446114). The performances take place principally in the Palais el-Badi.

## Places to Stay

**Hostels** The **youth hostel** (☎ 447713; Rue Mohammed el-Hansali; dorm beds Dh40; open 8am-9am & 1pm-10pm daily) is not far from the train station, so it could be a first stop. It's also spotless, has hot showers for Dh5 and boasts a kitchen. However, there's an 11.30pm curfew and for the same price you can stay closer to the action in a medina budget hotel. You'll need your HI membership card.

**Hotels – Medina** There are dozens of budget hotels in the lanes immediately south of Place Djemaa el-Fna between Rue de Bab Agnaou and Rue Riad Zitoun el-Qedim. Many have rooms set around cheerful little courtyards, and roof terraces for soaking up the sun and views. Apart from that, its clean-

liness and the shower situation, there's often not much between them. The best places fill up quickly, so it's worth calling ahead. Some spots will let you sleep on the terrace for around Dh25 if you're really stuck.

**Hôtel Essaouira** (☎ 443805, fax 426323; 3 Derb Sidi Bouloukat; singles/doubles Dh50/80) is among the most appealing. It has a tiled central courtyard, terrace café and basic but clean rooms. Bathroom facilities are limited, and hot showers cost Dh5. Follow the signs from Rue Riad Zitoun el-Qedim.

**Hôtel Afriquia** (☎ 442403; 45 Derb Sidi Bouloukat; singles/doubles/triples Dh50/ 100/150; doubles with bathroom Dh150) is larger than many budget hotels. Plus points include a lovely, tree-filled courtyard and the psychedelically tiled and tiered terrace affording panoramic views.

**Hôtel la Gazelle** (☎ 441112, fax 445537; 12 Rue Bani Marine; singles/doubles Dh70/ 120) lies southwest of the main budget-hotel area. It's a spruce, friendly little place and from the terrace there are fine views to the square, Koutoubia Mosque and mountains.

**Hôtel Souria** (☎ 067 482131; e hotel souria@yahoo.fr; 17 Rue de la Recette; doubles Dh120), near the Hôtel el-Atlal, is delightfully homey – the female owners even invite you to share their small kitchen. Prices are slightly above average, but you get a tidy little room, either around a cool and tranquil courtyard or on the terrace. Hot showers here cost Dh10.

**Hôtel Ali** (☎ 444979, fax 440522; e hot elali@hotmail.com; Rue Moulay Ismail; dorm beds or roof terrace sleeping Dh40, singles/doubles/triples Dh100/150/200) is a stalwart of the budget scene and much favoured by trekking groups. Regulars swear by its cheap rates and friendly and efficient service, not to mention its sweeping views over the square and Koutoubia Mosque to the Atlas from the terrace. It's got everything the traveller needs: Internet, exchange (cash and travellers cheques), restaurant, café, bicycle rental, laundry service and baggage store. In addition, car rental, tours and trekking are available through the affiliated Sahara Expedition (for details see Organised Tours, earlier). There's even a wide range of accommodation options, from rooms with bathroom and air-con (some with a semi-private terrace or balcony), to basic dorm beds or a mattress on the roof. Rates include a dull breakfast.

**Hôtel Gallia** (☎ 445913, fax 444853; e hotelgalliamarrakech@menara.co.ma; 30 Rue de la Recette; singles/doubles Dh230/360) is one of the medina's most appealing hotels. It has two lovely courtyards and the entire place is scrubbed from top to toe daily. Most rooms have air-con, while the central heating is welcome in winter. Rates include an excellent breakfast. Needless to say, you'll need to book (by fax) several weeks in advance.

**Hotels – Ville Nouvelle** The ville nouvelle is short of cheap hotels. The few that exist can be found around Ave Mohammed V, west of Place du 16 Novembre.

**Hôtel Toulousain** (☎ 430033, fax 431446; 44 Rue Tariq ibn Ziad; singles/doubles Dh110/160, with bathroom Dh150/190) is your best option. It's a nice quiet place around two courtyards, one of them home to a venerable banana palm. Rooms on the 1st floor are more airy. Prices include breakfast; hot showers cost Dh5.

**Hôtel Amalay** (☎ 448685, fax 431554; 87 Ave Mohammed V; singles/doubles Dh339/415) makes up for lack of character with its friendly welcome and handy location. It also boasts air-con in the rooms (those on the front can be noisy), plus a bar and restaurant.

## Places to Eat

**Medina** The liveliest, cheapest and most entertaining place to eat remains Place Djemaa el-Fna. By the time the sun sets, much of the square is taken over by stalls, each specialising in certain dishes and vying for your custom – the busiest are usually the best. You can eat your fill for Dh25 or less and wash it down with a Dh2.50 orange juice from a nearby juice stand.

At lunchtime, before the stalls on Place Djemaa el-Fna itself get going, you'll find much the same fare in the qissaria on the square's northern side. Here several vendors sharing a central kitchen will do you a meal for under Dh20.

**Chez Chegrouni** (4-6 Place Djemaa el-Fna; salads Dh5, mains around Dh40) is probably the best budget restaurant on the square. It's best known for its excellent tajines, including a melt-in-the-mouth lamb version. At busy times you squeeze up at tres-

tle tables inside or on a small roadside terrace; get here early for a front-row seat.

**Chez Bahia** (Rue Riad Zitoun el-Qedim; tajine Dh15) dishes up some of the cheapest tajines in town. To fill up, try a pastilla (sweet or savoury pies) or some of the bight-sized flaky-pastry triangles known as briouat.

**Hôtel Ali** (☎ 444979; Rue Moulay Ismail; set menus from Dh50, buffet Dh60 or Dh50 for hotel guests) is a major hang-out for travellers stocking up on the Ali's no-nonsense fodder. If you fancy a real pig-out, wait until 6.30pm, when you can load your plate as many times as you like from the buffet of Moroccan fare, vegetables, salad, fruit and dessert.

**Dar Mimoun** (☎ 443348; 1 Derb ben Amrane; salads Dh25, mains around Dh50-60; set menus from Dh120; open 9am-11pm daily), with its lovely salons around a leafy courtyard, offers the riad experience at affordable prices. The selection of Moroccan salads is a meal in itself. You can also have breakfast here.

**Ville Nouvelle** There is any number of inexpensive places to eat in the ville nouvelle. You'll find a good selection on or around Ave Mohammed V and Blvd Mohammed Zerktouni.

For bottom-rung local food, head for a group of hole-in-the-wall places on Rue ibn Aicha, where a solid meal of rotisserie chicken or brochettes (skewered meat), chips and salad will cost around Dh25 to Dh30.

**Café-Snack Sindibad** (3 Ave Mohammed V; mains Dh25-35) looks a bit down-at-heel, but the food – everything from pizzas and salads to couscous, kefta and tajines – is as cheap and tasty as ever.

**Al-Fassia** (☎ 434060; 232 Ave Mohammed V; mains around Dh100, lunch set menu Dh154) is one of the few Moroccan-style restaurants in the ville nouvelle dishing up quality local cuisine. It's a very attractive place with a cool, peaceful garden and a cushioned pavilion. The lunchtime set menu offers excellent value.

**Self-Catering** You'll find plenty of stalls selling fresh produce in the souqs. Alternatively, try the **markets** on Ave Mohammed V or on the eastern side of Place Djemaa el-Fna.

The **Somardis supermarket** (Rue ibn Aicha), in the ville nouvelle, is a reasonable places to stock up on supplies which are hard to get elsewhere – such as breakfast cereals and cheese.

## Entertainment

**Bars & Clubs** The majority of bars are dire, male-oriented places filled with prostitutes. One reasonable option, particularly if you get a table outside, is the top-floor bar of **Hôtel Tachfine** (*Blvd Mohammed Zerktouni*), offering stunning views.

If you want to party on, there are some decent nightclubs, many attached to hotels, in the ville nouvelle. Entry varies from Dh80 to Dh150, which includes the first drink. Most offer the standard fare of Arab pop interspersed with techno, club, dance etc. Dress smartly. Most places don't get going until around 1am. **La Casa** (*☎ 448226; Ave Président Kennedy; open 7pm-1.30am daily*), in Hôtel el-Andalous, starts out as a tapas bar/restaurant before the DJ cranks up the music at 9.30pm and everyone hits the dance floor. **Paradise** (*☎ 339100; Ave de France; entry Dh150; open 10.30pm-4am daily*) is the biggest and most expensive but also the prettiest of the city-centre nightclubs.

**Folkloric Shows** The only folkloric show of any real interest is **Chez Ali** (*☎ 307730; dinner & show Dh400; 8pm-11pm nightly*), out on the Safi road, which offers a sampler of traditional singing and dancing and ends up with an enactment of a *fantasia* (musket-firing cavalry charge). You can buy tickets (including transport and dinner) through hotels or tour agencies.

## Getting There & Away

**Air** Ménara airport (*☎ 447865*) is 6km southwest of Marrakesh. **Royal Air Maroc** (*☎ 446444, fax 446002; 197 Ave Mohammed V*) has several flights daily to and from Casablanca (Dh828, 40 minutes), as well as international flights to Geneva, London and Paris. Other carriers include British Airways and Air France.

**Bus** The **main bus station** (*☎ 433933*) is just outside the city walls by Bab Doukkala, a 20-minute walk or roughly Dh15 taxi ride from Place Djemaa el-Fna. The majority of

buses leave between 4am and 5pm. It's advisable to get tickets for early-morning departures the day before. You can also buy tickets at the **CTM booking office** (*☎ 044 448328; Blvd Mohammed Zerktouni*) in Gueliz. This is also the arrival and departure point for its international buses, including Paris (Dh1100) and Madrid (Dh800), both twice weekly.

Buses run to dozens of towns, including Rabat (Dh80, six hours, every half hour 5am to midnight) via Casablanca (Dh44, four hours), Meknès (from Dh100, six hours, at least three daily), Fès (from Dh103, eight hours, at least six daily) and Tangier (Dh150, 11 hours, 8am daily).

**Train** The **train station** (*☎ 446569; Ave Hassan II*) lies on the western side of Gueliz. Take a taxi or city bus (Nos 3, 8, 10 and 14, among others; Dh3) into the centre. There are eight trains to Casablanca (2nd-class *rapide* Dh76, three hours) and Rabat (Dh100, four hours).

There are six direct trains to Fès (Dh171, eight hours) via Meknès (Dh154, seven hours). Overnight trains to Tangier (Dh143) leave once daily; if you want a couchette (Dh193), it's advisable to book at least two days in advance.

## Getting Around

**To/From the Airport** A taxi to/from the airport (6km) should be Dh50, but you'll need to establish the fare before getting in. Bus No 11 runs irregularly to Place Djemaa el-Fna.

**Bus** Local buses (*☎ 335272*), charging Dh3 for all fares, run from Place de Foucauld, near Place Djemaa el-Fna, to the following places:

Nos 1 & 20 Ave Mohammed V–Gueliz
Nos 3 & 10 Bab Doukkala–main post office–train station–Douar Laskar
No 8 Bab Doukkala–main post office–train station–Douar Laskar
No 11 Ave Ménara–airport
No 14 train station

**Taxi** The creamy-beige *petits taxis* that dart around town cost between Dh5 and Dh10 per journey. The drivers are all supposed to use their meters, but you may need to insist.

# Portugal

Spirited yet unassuming, Portugal has a dusty patina of faded grandeur; the quiet remains of a far-flung colonialist realm. Even as the country flows towards the economic mainstream of the European Union (EU) it still seems to gaze nostalgically over its shoulder and out to sea.

For visitors, this far side of Europe offers more than beaches and port wine. Beyond the crowded Algarve, one finds wide appeal: a simple, hearty cuisine based on seafood and lingering conversation, an enticing architectural blend wandering from the Moorish to Manueline to surrealist styles, and a changing landscape that can occasionally lapse into impressionism. Like the *emigrantes* (economically inspired Portuguese who eventually find their way back to their *roots*), *estrangeiros* (foreigners) who have tasted the real Portugal can only be expected to return.

## Facts about Portugal

### HISTORY

The early history of Portugal goes back to the Celts who settled the Iberian Peninsula around 700 BC. A subsequent pattern of invasion and reinvasion was established by the Phoenicians, Greeks, Romans and Visigoths.

In the 8th century the Moors crossed the Strait of Gibraltar and commenced a long occupation that introduced Islamic culture, architecture and agricultural techniques to Portugal. The Moors were ejected in the 12th century by powerful Christian forces in the north of the country who mobilised attacks against them with the help of European Crusaders.

In the 15th century Portugal entered a phase of conquest and discovery inspired by Prince Henry the Navigator. Explorers such as Vasco da Gama, Ferdinand Magellan and Bartolomeu Diaz discovered new trade routes and helped create an empire that, at its peak, extended to Africa, Brazil, India and the Far East. This period of immense power and wealth ended in 1580 when Spain occupied the Portuguese throne. The Portuguese regained it within 90 years, but their imperial momentum had been lost.

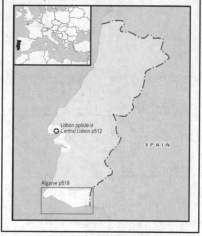

Lisbon pp508-9
Central Lisbon p512

SPAIN

Algarve p518

At the close of the 18th century Napoleon mounted several invasions of Portugal, but was eventually trounced by the troops of the Anglo-Portuguese alliance.

A period of civil war and political mayhem in the 19th century culminated in the abolition of the monarchy in 1910 and the founding of a democratic republic.

A military coup in 1926 set the stage for the dictatorship of António de Oliveira Salazar, who clung to power until his death in 1968. General dissatisfaction with his regime and a ruinous colonial war in Africa led to the so called Revolution of the Carnations, a peaceful military coup on 25 April 1974.

PORTUGAL

The granting of independence to Portugal's African colonies in 1974–75 produced a flood of nearly a million refugees into the country. The 1970s and early 1980s saw extreme swings between political right and left, and strikes over state versus private ownership.

Portugal's entry into the EU in 1986 and its membership of the European Monetary System in 1992 secured some stability, although the 1990s were troubled by recession, rising unemployment and a continuing backwardness in agriculture and education.

Expo '98 triggered vast infrastructure projects and launched Portugal into a new era of economic success, and is set to be boosted again when the country hosts the European football championships in 2004.

## GEOGRAPHY & GEOLOGY
Portugal is about twice the size of Switzerland, just 560km from north to south and 220km from east to west.

## CLIMATE
Midsummer heat is searing in the Algarve, but tolerable elsewhere. Sun-seekers receive a warm welcome in Portugal; there's an average 12 hours of sunshine a day during a typical Algarve summer (six hours in winter).

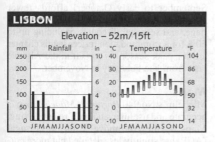

## ECOLOGY & ENVIRONMENT
Portugal has 12 *parques naturais* (natural parks), nine nature reserves and several other protected areas. The government's **Instituto da Conservação da Natureza** *(ICN; Information Division;* ☎ *213 523 317; Rua Ferreira Lapa 29-A, Lisbon)* manages them all, though information is best obtained from each park's headquarters.

## GOVERNMENT & POLITICS
Portugal has a Western-style democracy based on the Assembleiada República, a single-chamber parliament with 230 members and an elected president. The two main parties are the Socialist Party (Partido Socialista; PS) and also the right-of-centre Social Democratic Party (Partido Social Democrata; PSD). Other parties include the Communist Party (PCP) and the new Left Bloc (BE). In April 2002 the PSD, under Durão Barroso, commenced a four-year term of office.

## ECONOMY
After severe economic problems in the 1980s, Portugal tamed inflation to around 2% thanks largely to infrastructure investment and privatisation, but the shaky early days of life in the euro currency zone have seen the country's annual growth rate dip to around 1.5% and inflation rise to almost 3%. Agriculture plays a decreasing role compared with industry and services (eg, telecommunications, banking and tourism). Portugal benefits from low labour costs, a young population and massive EU funding.

## POPULATION & PEOPLE
Portugal's population of 10 million does not include the estimated three million Portuguese living abroad as migrant workers.

## ARTS
### Music
The best-known form of Portuguese music is the melancholy, nostalgic songs called *fado,* popularly considered to have originated with the yearnings of 16th-century sailors. Much on offer to tourists in Lisbon is overpriced and far from authentic. The late Amália Rodrigues was the star of Portuguese *fado*; her recordings are available in most Portuguese record shops.

### Literature
In the 16th century, Gil Vicente, master of farce and religious drama, set the stage for Portugal's dramatic tradition. Later in that century Luís de Camões wrote *Os Lusíadas,* an epic poem celebrating the age of discovery (available in translation as *The Lusiads*). Camões is considered Portugal's national poet.

Two of Portugal's finest 20th-century writers are poet-dramatist Fernando Pessoa (1888–1935), author of the 1934 *Message*; and the 1998 Nobel Prize-winning novelist José Saramago, whose novels (notably *Baltasar and Blimunda* and *The Year of the*

PORTUGAL

*Death of Ricardo Reis)* weave together the real and imaginary. Others to try are Eça de Queiroz *(The Maias)* and Fernando Namora *(Mountain Doctor)*. A contemporary Portuguese 'whodunnit', close to the political bone, is *The Ballad of Dog's Beach* by José Cardoso Pires.

### Architecture
Unique to Portugal is Manueline architecture, named after its patron King Manuel I (1495–1521). It symbolises the zest for discovery of that era and is characterised by boisterous spiralling columns and nautical themes.

### Crafts
The most striking Portuguese craft is the decorative blue and white *azulejo* tiles based on Moorish techniques of the 15th century. Superb examples are to be seen all over the country. Lisbon has its own *azulejo* museum.

## SOCIETY & CONDUCT
Despite prosperity and foreign influence, the Portuguese have kept a firm grip on their culture. Folk dancing remains the pride of villages everywhere, and local festivals are celebrated with gusto. TV soccer matches, a modern element of male Portuguese life, ensure the continuation of the traditional long lunch break.

The Portuguese tend to be very friendly but socially conservative: win their hearts by dressing modestly outside of the beach resorts, and by greeting and thanking them in Portuguese. Shorts and hats are considered offensive inside churches.

## RELIGION
Portugal is 99% Roman Catholic, with fewer than 120,000 Protestants and about 5000 Jews.

## LANGUAGE
Like French, Italian, Spanish and Romanian, Portuguese is a Romance language, derived from Latin. It's spoken by over 10 million people in Portugal and 130 million in Brazil, and is the official language of five African nations. Nearly all turismo staff speak English. In Lisbon and the Algarve it's easy to find English-speakers, but they are rare in the countryside, and among older folk. In the north, you'll find returned emigrant workers who speak French or German.

See the Language Guide at the back of this book for pronunciation guidelines and useful words and phrases. For more, pick up Lonely Planet's *Portuguese phrasebook*.

# Facts for the Visitor

## HIGHLIGHTS
In Lisbon don't miss the Museu Calouste Gulbenkian, and Europe's largest Oceanarium. In the Algarve see some of the region's finest beaches near Lagos.

## SUGGESTED ITINERARIES
Depending on the length of your stay, you might want to see and do the following:

**Two days**
Lisbon
**One week**
Devote four or five days to Lisbon and Sintra and a couple of days in the Algarve.
**Two weeks**
As for one week, with more time in the Algarve (including one or two days each in Tavira, Lagos and Sagres).

## PLANNING
### When to Go
Peak tourist season is June to early September. Going earlier (late March or April) or later (late September to early October) affords fewer crowds, milder temperatures, spectacular foliage, and seasonal discounts, including up to 50% for accommodation (prices in this chapter are for peak season). Tourism in the Algarve lasts from late February to November.

### Maps
Michelin's No 940 *Portugal; Madeira* map is accurate and useful even if you're not driving. Maps by the Automóvel Club de Portugal (ACP) are slightly less detailed but more current. For maps and information on the national and natural parks visit the information offices at or near each park, although even here trekkers will find little of use.

Topographic maps are published (and sold) by two mapping agencies in Lisbon: the civilian **Instituto Português de Cartográfia e Cadastro** (☎ *213 819 600*, fax *213 819 697*; ✉ *ipcc@ipcc.pt; Rua Artilharia Um 107*), and the military **Instituto Geográfico do Exército** (☎ *218 505 300*, fax *218 532 119*; ✉ *igeoe@igeoe.pt; Avenida Dr Alfredo Bensaúde*).

## TOURIST OFFICES
### Local Tourist Offices

Called *postos de turismo* or just *turismos*, local tourist offices are found throughout Portugal and offer information, maps and varying degrees of assistance.

### Tourist Offices Abroad

Portuguese tourist offices operating abroad under the administrative umbrella of Investimentos, Comércio e Turismo de Portugal (ICEP) include:

**Canada** Portuguese Trade & Tourism Commission (☎ 416-921-7376, fax 921-1353, ℮ iceptor@idirect.com), Suite 1005, 60 Bloor St West, Toronto, Ontario M4W 3B8

**Spain** Oficina de Turismo de Portugal (☎ 91 761 7230, fax 570 2270, ℮ turismo-portugal@icep.net), Paseo de la Castellana 141-17D, 28046 Madrid

**UK** Portuguese Trade & Tourism Office (☎ 020-7494 1441, fax 7494 1868, ℮ iceplondt@ aol.com), 22–25a Sackville St, London W1X 1DE

**USA** Portuguese National Tourist Office (☎ 212-354 4403, fax 764 6137, ℮ tourism@portugal.org), 4th floor, 590 Fifth Ave, New York, NY 10036-4704

## VISAS & DOCUMENTS
### Visas

No visa is required for any length of stay by nationals of EU countries. Those from Canada, Israel, Australia, New Zealand and the USA can stay up to 60 days in any half-year without a visa. Others, including South African nationals, need visas (and should try to get them in advance) unless they're spouses or children of EU citizens.

Portugal is a signatory of the Schengen Convention on the abolition of mutual border controls (see Visas in the introductory Facts for the Visitor chapter), but unless you're a citizen of the UK, Ireland or a Schengen country, you should check visa regulations with the consulate of each Schengen country you plan to visit. You must apply in your country of residence.

Outside Portugal, visa information is supplied by Portuguese consulates. In Portugal, contact the **Foreigners Registration Service** (*Serviço de Estrangeiros e Fronteiras;* ☎ 213 585 545; *Rua São Sebastião da Pedreira 15, Lisbon; open 9am-noon & 2pm-4pm Mon-Fri*) for information.

## EMBASSIES & CONSULATES
### Portuguese Embassies & Consulates

Portuguese embassies abroad include:

**Australia** (☎ 02-6290 1733) 23 Culgoa Circuit, O'Malley, ACT 2606
**Canada** (☎ 613-729-0883) 645 Island Park Dr, Ottawa, Ont K1Y 0B8
**France** (☎ 01 47 27 35 29) 3 Rue de Noisiel, 75116 Paris
**Ireland** (☎ 01-289 4416) Knocksinna House, Foxrock, Dublin 18
**Spain** (☎ 91 561 78 00) Calle Castello 128, 28006 Madrid
**UK** (☎ 020-7235 5331) 11 Belgrave Square, London SW1X 8PP
**USA** (☎ 202-328 8610) 2125 Kalorama Rd NW, Washington, DC 20008

### Embassies & Consulates in Portugal

Foreign embassies in Portugal include:

**Australia**
   *Embassy:* (☎ 213 101 500) Avenida da Liberdade 200, Lisbon
**Canada**
   *Embassy & Consulate:* (☎ 213 164 600) Avenida da Liberdade 196, Lisbon
   *Consulate:* (☎ 289 803 757) Rua Frei Lourenço de Santa Maria 1, Faro
**France**
   *Embassy:* (☎ 213 939 100) Santos o Velho 5, Lisbon
**Ireland**
   *Embassy:* (☎ 213 929 440) Rua da Imprensa à Estrela 1, Lisbon
**Spain**
   *Embassy:* (☎ 213 472 381) Rua do Salitre 1, Lisbon
   *Consulate:* (☎ 281 544 888) Avenida Ministro Duarte Pacheco, Vila Real de Santo António
**UK**
   *Embassy:* (☎ 213 924 000) Rua de São Bernardo 33, Lisbon
   *Consulate:* (☎ 282 417 800) Largo Francisco A Maurício 7, Portimão
**USA**
   *Embassy:* (☎ 217 273 300) Avenida das Forças Armadas, Lisbon

New Zealand has an honorary consul only in **Lisbon** (☎ *213 509 690; open 9am-1pm Mon-Fri*); the nearest embassy is to be found in **Rome** (☎ *39-6-440 29 28*). See the Italy chapter for more details.

PORTUGAL

## CUSTOMS

The duty-free allowance for travellers over 18 years old from non-EU countries is 200 cigarettes or 50 cigars, 1L of spirits or 2L of wine. EU nationals can import 800 cigarettes, 200 cigars, 10L of spirits, 20L of fortified wine or 110L of beer – assuming they can carry it all.

Duty-free shopping at Portuguese airports is no more, but see Taxes & Refunds later in this chapter for information about sales-tax refunds.

## MONEY
### Currency

In January 2002 the euro, subdivided into 100 cêntimos, became the official unit of currency in Portugal. Prices are written with the € sign in front of the figure, eg, one euro 50 cêntimos is €1.50. See the boxed text 'The Euro' in the introductory Facts for the Visitor chapter.

There is no limit on the importation of currency. If you leave Portugal with more than €12,470 you must prove that you brought in at least this much.

### Exchanging Money

Portuguese banks can change most foreign cash and travellers cheques but charge a commission of around €12.50. Better deals for travellers cheques are at private exchange bureaus in Lisbon, Porto and tourist resorts.

Better value (and handier) are the 24-hour Multibanco ATMs at most banks. Exchange rates are reasonable and normally the only charge is a handling fee of about 1.5% to your home bank. Few tourist centres have automated cash-exchange machines.

Major credit cards – especially Visa and MasterCard – are widely accepted by shops, hotels and a growing number of guesthouses and restaurants.

### Costs

Portugal remains one of the cheapest places to travel in Europe. On a rock-bottom budget – using hostels or camping grounds, and mostly self-catering – you can squeeze by on US$20 to US$25 a day. With bottom-end accommodation and cheap restaurant meals, figure around US$30. Travelling with a companion and taking advantage of the off-season discounts (see When to Go earlier in this section), two can eat and sleep well for US$60 to US$70 per day. Outside major tourist areas, and in low season, prices dip appreciably.

Concessions are often available on admission fees, etc, if you're over 65, under 26 or hold a student card.

### Tipping & Bargaining

A reasonable restaurant tip is 10%. For a snack, a bit of loose change is sufficient. Taxi drivers appreciate 10% of the fare, and petrol station attendants €0.50 to €1.

Good-humoured bargaining is acceptable in markets but you'll find the Portuguese tough opponents! Off season, you can sometimes bargain down the price of accommodation.

### Taxes & Refunds

IVA is a sales tax levied on a wide range of goods and services; in most shops it's 17%. Tourists from non-EU countries can claim an IVA refund on goods from shops belonging to the Global Refund network. The minimum purchase for a refund is €60 in any one shop. The shop assistant fills in a cheque for the refund (minus an administration fee). When you leave Portugal you present goods, cheque and your passport at customs for a cash, postal-note or credit-card refund.

This service is available at Lisbon and Faro airports (postal refund only at Faro). If you're leaving overland, contact customs at your final EU border point, or call **Global Refund** (☎ 218 463 025) in Lisbon.

## POST & COMMUNICATIONS
### Post

Postcards and letters up to 20g cost €0.28 within Portugal, €0.46 to Spain, €0.54 to European destinations and €0.70 worldwide. For delivery to North America or Australasia allow eight to 10 days; to Europe four to six.

For parcels, 'economy air' (or surface airlift, SAL) costs about a third less than airmail and usually arrives a week or so later. The main post offices in Lisbon are open into the evening and at weekends but charge €0.32 for each item claimed. Most major towns have a post office with *posta restante* service.

Addresses in Portugal are written with the street name first, followed by the building address and often a floor number with a symbol, eg, 15-3. An alphabetical tag on the address, eg, 2-A, indicates an adjoining entrance or building. R/C (*rés do chão*) means ground floor.

## Telephone

Aside from a few assistance numbers, domestic numbers have nine digits, all of which must be dialled from any location.

Local calls from public coin telephones start at €0.20, but the machines are often broken, especially in big cities, swallowing your cash without allowing you a call. It's easier to buy a PT (Portugal Telecom) phonecard (in €3, €6 or €9 denominations) or a discount card, such as the onicard, offering the option of dialling from any fixed-line phone. Both are available from newsagents, tobacconists, post or telephone offices.

Domestic charges drop by 50% from 9pm to 9am on weekdays, and all day Saturday and Sunday. International charges drop by around 10% to 25% from 9pm to 9am, and 20% to 50% during the weekend. Hotels typically charge over *three times* the economy rate!

A three-minute direct-dial (IDD) evening/weekend call from Portugal using an onicard costs about €0.51 within the EU, €0.42 to the USA or Canada, and €0.87 to Australia or New Zealand.

To call Portugal from abroad, dial the international access code, then ☎ 351 (the country code for Portugal) and the number. From Portugal, the international access code is ☎ 00. For operator help or to make a reverse-charge (collect) call from Portugal, dial ☎ 171. For domestic inquiries, dial ☎ 118; for numbers abroad, dial ☎ 177. Multilingual operators are available.

For more information on telephoning in Europe, see the Telephones Appendix at the back of this book.

## Fax

Post offices operate a domestic and international service called Corfax, costing €2.70 for the first page sent within Portugal and €4.25 for international destinations. Some private shops offer much cheaper services.

## Email & Internet Access

Many towns have a branch of the Instituto Português da Juventude or IPJ, a state-funded youth-centre network. Most of these offer free Internet access during certain hours. Some municipal libraries also have free access. Some newer youth hostels have access for around €2.50 per hour. Internet cafés in the bigger towns charge €1.50 to €4 per hour.

## DIGITAL RESOURCES

Three useful websites on Portugal to check out are: **A Collection of Home Pages about Portugal** (Ⓦ *www.well.com/user/ideamen/ portugal.html*), **Portugal.com** (Ⓦ *www.por tugal.com*) and also **Portugal Info** (Ⓦ *www .portugalinfo.net*).

## BOOKS

Rose Macaulay's *They Went to Portugal* and *They Went to Portugal Too* follow a wide variety of visitors from medieval times to the 19th century. Marion Kaplan's *The Portuguese: The Land and Its People* offers a fine overview of Portugal and its place in the modern world.

Walkers and car tourers should pack the *Landscapes of Portugal* series by Brian & Aileen Anderson, including books on the Algarve, Sintra/Estoril and the Costa Verde. More detailed is *Walking in Portugal* by Bethan Davies and Ben Cole.

## NEWSPAPERS & MAGAZINES

Portuguese-language newspapers include the dailies *Diário de Notícias, Público* and *Jornal de Notícias*, and weeklies *O Independente* and *Expresso*. For entertainment listings, check local dailies or seasonal cultural-events calendars from tourist offices.

English-language newspapers published in Portugal include *The News*, with regional editions featuring local news and classified pages, and *Anglo-Portuguese News*. Newspapers and magazines from abroad are widely available in the major cities and tourist resorts.

## RADIO & TV

Portuguese radio is represented by the state-owned stations *Antena 1, 2* and *3*, by *Rádio Renascença* and by a clutch of local stations. BBC World Service is at 12.095MHz or 15.485MHz short-wave, but reception is poor.

Portuguese TV includes state-run channels RTP-1 (or Canal 1) and RTP-2 (or TV2) and two private channels, SIC and TVI. Soaps (*telenovelas*) take up the lion's share of broadcasting time.

## TIME

Portugal conforms to GMT/UTC, as does Britain. Clocks are advanced an hour on the last Sunday in March and go back on the last Sunday in October.

PORTUGAL

## LAUNDRY

There are *lavandarias* everywhere, most specialising in dry-cleaning *(limpeza à seco)*. They'll often do wash-and-dry *(lavar e secar)*, too, although it may take a day or two. Expect €7.50 to €12.50 for a 5kg load.

## TOILETS

The rare public toilets are of the sit-down variety, generally clean and usually free. Coin-operated toilet booths are increasingly common in bigger cities. Most people, however, go to the nearest café for a drink or pastry and use the facilities there.

## WOMEN TRAVELLERS

Outside Lisbon an unaccompanied foreign woman is an oddity, and older people may fuss over you as if you were in need of protection. Women travelling on their own or in small groups report few hassles, although in Lisbon women should be cautious after dark. Hitching is not recommended for solo women.

## GAY & LESBIAN TRAVELLERS

In this mostly Catholic country, there is little understanding or acceptance of homosexuality. But Lisbon has a flourishing gay scene, with an annual Gay Pride Festival (around 28 June) and a **Gay & Lesbian Community Center** *(Centro Comunitário Gay e Lésbico de Lisboa;* ☎ *218 873 918; Rua de São Lazaro 88; open 5pm-9pm daily)*. For information on gay-friendly bars, restaurants and clubs in Lisbon, check the websites Ⓦ www.ilga-portugal.org and Ⓦ www.portugalgay.pt.

## DISABLED TRAVELLERS

The **Secretariado Nacional de Rehabilitação** *(*☎ *217 936 517, fax 217 965 182; Avenida Conde de Valbom 63, Lisbon)* publishes the Portuguese-language *Guia de Turismo* with sections on barrier-free accommodation, transport, shops, restaurants and sights in Portugal. It's available at its offices or at Turintegra.

Turintegra, part of the **Cooperativa Nacional Apoio Deficientes** *(CNAD;* ☎*/fax 218 595 332; Praça Dr Fernando Amado, Lote 566-E, 1900 Lisbon)* keeps a keener eye on developments and arranges holidays and transport for disabled travellers.

## SENIOR TRAVELLERS

Travellers 60 and over can receive discounts of up to 50% at many of Portugal's attractions.

### Emergency Services

The national emergency number is ☎ 112 for police, fire and medical emergencies anywhere in Portugal. See Car & Motorcycle in the Getting Around section later in this chapter for information regarding roadside assistance in the event of breakdown.

Domestic rail travel is half-price for senior travellers on weekdays and those with a Railplus Card (to qualify you have to be a holder of a senior citizens railcard at home) can benefit from up to 25% off the price of journeys across international borders. In the UK, passes are available from larger stations. (See also Cheap Tickets in the Train section of the introductory Getting Around chapter.)

## DANGERS & ANNOYANCES

The most widespread crime against foreigners is theft from rental cars, followed by pickpocketing, and pilfering from camping grounds. On the increase are armed robberies, mostly in the Algarve, Estoril Coast and parts of Lisbon. But with the usual precautions (use a money belt or something similar, bag your camera when not in use and don't leave valuables in cars or tents) there's little cause for worry. For peace of mind take out travel insurance.

Avoid swimming on beaches that are not marked as safe: Atlantic currents are notoriously dangerous (and badly polluted near major cities).

## BUSINESS HOURS

Most banks are open 8.30am to 3pm weekdays. Most museums and other tourist attractions are open 10am to 5pm weekdays but are often closed at lunchtime and all day Monday. Shopping hours generally extend from 9am to 7pm on weekdays, and 9am to 1pm on Saturday. Lunch is given lingering and serious attention between noon and 3pm.

## PUBLIC HOLIDAYS & SPECIAL EVENTS

Public holidays in Portugal include:

**New Year's Day** 1 January
**Carnival** Shrove Tuesday; February/March
**Good Friday and the following Saturday**
  March/April
**Liberty Day** 25 April

**May Day** 1 May
**Corpus Christi** May/June
**National Day** 10 June
**Feast of the Assumption** 15 August
**Republic Day** 5 October
**All Saints' Day** 1 November
**Independence Day** 1 December
**Feast of the Immaculate Conception** 8 December
**Christmas Day** 25 December

A couple of Portugal's most interesting cultural events include the **Festa do Santo António** *(Festival of St Anthony)*, which fills the streets of Lisbon on 13 June, and the **Algarve Folk Music and Dance Festival**, held at different locations during September.

## ACTIVITIES

Off-road cycling (BTT; *bicyclete tudo terrano,* all-terrain bicycle) is booming in Portugal, with bike trips on offer at many tourist destinations (see Setúbal in Around Lisbon and Tavira in The Algarve sections, later in this chapter).

Despite some fine rambling country, walking is not a Portuguese passion. Some parks are establishing trails, though, and some adventure travel agencies offer walking tours (see the Lisbon and Monchique sections later in this chapter).

Popular water sports include surfing, windsurfing, canoeing, white-water rafting and water-skiing. For information on local specialists see the sections for Lagos, Sagres and Tavira.

The Instituto Português da Juventude (see Travel Agencies in the Lisbon section for contact details) offers holiday programmes for 16 to 30-year-olds (visitors, too), including BTT, canoeing and rock climbing. Private organisations offering activites are listed under individual town sections. (See also Organised Tours, later in this chapter.)

## COURSES

**Interlingua in Portimão** *(☎/fax 282 416 030;* e *interlingua@mail.telepac.pt)* runs a two-hour fun course in Portuguese language basics for €20. Longer courses are offered by **Centro de Línguas** *(☎/fax 282 761 070;* e *cll@mail.telepac.pt)* in Lagos; **Cambridge School** *(☎ 213 124 600, fax 213 534 729;* e *cambridge@mail.telepac.pt)* in Lisbon; Lisbon-based **IPFEL** *(☎ 213 154 116, fax 213 154 119;* e *instituto@ipfel.pt)*; and **CIAL– Centro de Línguas** *(☎ 289 807 611)* in Faro.

## ACCOMMODATION

Most tourist offices have lists of accommodation to suit a range of budgets, and can help you find and book it. Although the government uses stars to grade some types of accommodation, criteria seem erratic.

## Camping

Camping is popular, and easily the cheapest option. The multilingual, annually updated *Roteiro Campista* (€4.90), sold in larger bookshops, contains details of nearly all Portugal's camping grounds. Depending on facilities and season, most prices per night run to about €1 to €3 per adult, €1.50 to €3 for a small tent and €1 to €3 per car. Many camping grounds close in the low season.

## Hostels

Portugal has 41 *pousadas da juventude* (youth hostels), all part of the Hostelling International (HI) system. Low rates are offset by segregated dorms, midnight curfews and partial daytime exclusion at most of them.

In the high season, dorm beds cost €9.50 to €15, and most hostels offer basic doubles for €23 to €30 (without bath) or €26.50 to €42 (with bath). Bed linen and breakfast are included. Many hostels have kitchens where you can do your own cooking, plus TV rooms and social areas.

Advance reservations are essential in summer. Most hostels will call ahead to your next stop at no charge, or you can pay €1.50 per set of bookings (with three days' notice) through the country's central HI reservations office, **Movijovem** *(☎ 213 524 072, fax 213 596 001;* e *reservas@movijovem.pt; Avenida Duque d'Ávila 137, Lisbon).*

If you don't already have a card from your national hostel association, you can pay a €2 supplement per night (and have a one- or six-night or a year-long 'guest card').

## Private Rooms

Another option is a private room *(quarto particular)*, usually in a private house, with shared facilities. Home-owners may approach you at the bus or train station; otherwise watch for 'quartos' signs or ask at tourist offices. Rooms are usually clean, cheap (€25 to €50 for a double in summer) and free from hostel-style restrictions. A variant is a rooming house *(dormida)*, where doubles are about €25. You may be able to bargain in the low season.

## Guesthouses

The most common types of guesthouse, the Portuguese equivalent of B&Bs, are the *residencial* and the *pensão*. Both are graded from one to three stars, and the best are often cheaper and better run than some hotels. High-season *pensão* rates for a double start from around €30; a *residencial*, where breakfast is normally included, is a bit more. Many have cheaper rooms with shared bathrooms.

## Hotels

The government grades hotels with one to five stars. For a high-season double expect €55 up to as much as €250. *Estalagem* and *albergaria* refer to upmarket inns. Prices drop spectacularly in low season. Breakfast is usually included.

## Other Accommodation

Pousadas de Portugal are government-run former castles, monasteries or palaces, often in spectacular locations. For details contact tourist offices, or **Pousadas de Portugal** (☎ 218 442 001, fax 218 442 085; *Avenida Santa Joana Princesa 10, 1749 Lisbon*).

Private counterparts are operated under a scheme called Turismo de Habitação and a number of smaller schemes (often collectively called 'Turihab'), which allow you to stay in anything from a farmhouse to a manor house; some also have self-catering cottages. The tourist offices can tell you about local Turihab properties.

A double in the high season costs a minimum of €82 and up to €182 in a Pousada de Portugal, but between €60 and €100 in a Turihab property.

## FOOD

Eating and drinking get serious attention in Portugal. Fast-food is largely ignored in favour of leisurely dining.

The line between snacks and meals is blurred. Bars and cafés offer snacks or even a small menu. For full meals try a *casa do pasto* (a simple, cheap eatery), *restaurante*, *cervejaria* (bar-restaurant) or *marisqueira* (seafood restaurant). Lunchtime typically lasts from noon to 3pm, evening meals from 7pm to 10.30pm.

The *prato do dia* (dish of the day) is often a bargain at around €4.50; the *ementa turística* (tourist menu) rarely is. A full portion or *dose* is ample for two decent appetites; a *meia dose* (half-portion) is a quarter to a third cheaper. The *couvert* – the bread, cheese, butter, olives and other titbits at the start of a meal – costs extra.

Common snacks are *pastéis de bacalhau* (codfish cakes), *prego em pão* (meat and egg in a roll) and *tosta mista* (toasted cheese and ham sandwich). Prices start around €1.20.

Seafood offers exceptional value, especially *linguado grelhado* (grilled sole), *bife de atum* (tuna steak) and the omnipresent *bacalhau* (dried cod) cooked in dozens of ways. Meat is hit-or-miss, but worth sampling are local *presunto* (ham), *borrego* (roast lamb) and *cabrito* (kid). Main-dish prices start around €5.

Cafés and *pastelarias* (pastry shops) offer splendid desserts and cakes – try a delicious *pastel de nata* (custard tart).

Local markets offer fresh seafood, vegetables and fruit. Big cities have grocery shops *(minimercadoes)* and many now have vast *hipermercados*.

## DRINKS

Coffee is a hallowed institution with its own nomenclature. In Lisbon, a small black espresso is known as a *bica*, and elsewhere simply as a *café*. Half-and-half coffee and milk is *café com leite*. For coffee with lots of milk at breakfast, ask for a *galão*. Tea *(chá)* comes with lemon *(com limão)* or with milk *(com leite)*. Fresh orange juice is common. Mineral water *(água mineral)* is carbonated *(com gás)* or still *(sem gás)*.

Local beers *(cerveja)* include Sagres (in the south). A 20cL draught is called *um imperial*; *uma garrafa* is a bottle.

Portuguese wine *(vinho)* offers great value in all varieties: red *(tinto)*, white *(branco)* and semi-sparkling young *(vinho verde)*, which is usually white. The rarer red isn't quite as good. Restaurants often have quaffable *vinho da casa* (house wine) for as little as €1.99 per 350mL jug. For under €5 a bottle you can please the most discerning taste buds.

## ENTERTAINMENT

Portugal has many local festivals and fairs, often centred on saints' days and featuring music, dance, fireworks, parades, handicraft fairs or animal markets. See Public Holidays & Special Events earlier in this chapter.

*Fado,* the melancholy Portuguese equivalent of the blues (see Music under Facts about

Portugal), is offered in *casas de fado* in Lisbon. More conventional bars, pubs and clubs abound in Lisbon and the Algarve.

Some bigger towns sponsor summer cultural programmes, especially music (rock, jazz and classical) and dance. Ask at tourist offices for free what's-on publications, or see the local newspapers for listings.

Cinemas cost around €4 a ticket, with prices often reduced once weekly to lure audiences from their homes. Foreign films are usually subtitled.

## SPECTATOR SPORTS

Football (soccer) dominates the sporting scene. The season lasts from August to May and most villages and towns have a team. The two best are Lisbon's Benfica and Sporting. Ask the tourist office about forthcoming matches. The fever will peak in 2004 when Portugal hosts the European football championships.

Bullfighting remains popular despite pressure from international animal-rights activists. The season runs from March to October. Portuguese rules prohibit a public kill, although bulls are often dispatched in private afterwards. In Lisbon, bullfights are held at Campo Pequeno on Thursday.

## SHOPPING

Leather goods, especially shoes and bags, are good value, as are textiles, such as lace and embroidered linen. Handicrafts range from inexpensive pottery and basketwork to substantial purchases such as Arraiolos rugs, filigree jewellery and made-to-order *azulejos*.

# Getting There & Away

## AIR

BA and TAP Air Portugal have daily direct flights from London to Lisbon; they also go to Faro. On most days there are direct links to Lisbon from Paris, Frankfurt, Amsterdam, Brussels and Madrid.

From the UK, high-season London–Faro return fares start about UK£110 with no-frills carrier **Go** (☎ 0870 607 6543). Charter fares to Lisbon or Faro start about UK£180. **TAP Air Portugal** (☎ 0845-601 0932) offers youth/student fares for year-long trips, but the best deals are with agencies such as

**Trailfinders** (☎ 020-7937 1234) and **STA Travel** (☎ 020-7361 6161).

France has frequent Portugal connections at reasonable prices. **TAP Air Portugal** (☎ 08 02 31 93 20) and **Air France** (☎ 08 20 82 08 20) have youth/student fares but you're better off with agencies like **usit Connection** (☎ 01 43 29 69 50) or **Wasteels** (☎ 01 43 62 30 20).

For prices from Portugal, ask youth travel agencies **Tagus** (Lisbon; ☎ 213 525 986) or **Wasteels** (Lisbon; ☎ 218 869 793). **TAP Air Portugal** (☎ 808 205 700) and **BA** (☎ 808 200 125) can be contacted at local rates from anywhere in Portugal.

## LAND
## Bus

Portugal's main Eurolines agents are **Intercentro** (Lisbon; ☎ 213 571 745) and **Intersul** (Faro; ☎ 289 899 770), serving central and southern Portugal respectively.

UK-based **Busabout** (☎ 020-7950 1661) is a Europe-wide 'hop-on, hop-off' coach network with stops at hostels and camping grounds, and passes that let you travel as much as you want within a set period. Its Portugal stops are in Lisbon and Lagos.

**Spain** Spanish connections of **Eurolines** (Madrid; ☎ 915 063 360) are as follows: Madrid–Lisbon (€35.45), Seville–Lisbon (€31.25) and Barcelona–Lisbon (€71.92), all at least three times weekly.

Spanish operators with Portugal links include **ALSA** (Madrid; ☎ 902 42 22 42), with twice-daily Madrid–Lisbon services; and **Damas** (Huelva; ☎ 959 25 69 00), running twice daily from Seville to Faro via Huelva, jointly with the Algarve line EVA. Three times weekly, **Transportes Agobe** (☎ 958 63 52 74) runs from Granada via Seville and the Algarve to Lisbon.

**The UK & France** A variety of bus services are available from **Eurolines** (UK; ☎ 08705-143219 • France; ☎ 083 669 52 52) in London (Victoria coach station) via the Channel ferry, with a 7½-hour stopover and change of coach in Paris. These include five to Lisbon (42 hours), both UK£82/€134 one way from London/Paris.

The independent line **IASA** (Paris; ☎ 01 43 53 90 82) runs services between Paris and Lisbon. A one-way/return fare to Lisbon is €84/152.

## Train

**Spain** The main rail route is Madrid–Lisbon on the *Talgo Lusitânia*. The nightly express takes 9½ hours, and a 2nd-class reserved seat costs €46.28 for a sleeper berth €65.51.

There are no direct southern trains: from Seville you can ride to Huelva (three daily), catch a bus for Ayamonte, change buses to cross the border to Vila Real de Santo António then catch one of the frequent trains to Faro and Lagos.

The daily Paris–Lisbon train (see the following UK & France entry) goes via Salamanca, Valladolid, Burgos, Vitória and San Sebastian.

**The UK & France** In general, it's only worth taking the train if you can use under-26 rail passes such as Inter-Rail (see Rail Passes in the introductory Getting Around chapter at the beginning of this book).

All services from London to Portugal go via Paris, where you change trains (and stations) for the *TGV Atlantique* to Irún in Spain (change trains again). From Irún there is an express service to Madrid, changing there to the overnight *Lusitânia* to Lisbon. Change at Lisbon for the south of Portugal.

Buying a one-way, 2nd-class, adult/youth London–Lisbon ticket (seat only) for the cheapest route, via the channel ferry, costs UK£102/87; allow at least 30 hours. Tickets for this route are available from bigger train stations or from **Trains Europe** (☎ 020-8699 3654). The Eurostar service to Paris via the Channel Tunnel cuts several hours off the trip but bumps up the cost. Ring **Rail Europe** (☎ 08705-848848) for details.

## Car & Motorcycle

The quickest routes from the UK are by ferry via northern Spain: from Portsmouth to Bilbao with **P&O Stena Line** (☎ 08706-003300), or, between March and November, from Plymouth to Santander with **Brittany Ferries** (☎ 08705-360360).

Alternatively, motor through France via Bordeaux, and through Spain via Burgos and Salamanca.

## DEPARTURE TAX

Airport taxes for return flights between Portugal and other European countries range from about €17 for Spain to UK£22/€34 for the UK.

# Getting Around

## AIR

Flights within Portugal are poor value unless you have a youth/student card. Both **PGA Portugália Airlines** *(Lisbon; ☎ 218 425 559)* and **TAP Air Portugal** *(☎ 808 205 700)* have many daily Lisbon–Faro links, for €102.08; Portugália offers a 50% youth discount. TAP has a daily Lisbon–Faro service connecting with its international arrivals and departures at Lisbon.

## BUS

A welter of regional bus companies together operate a network of comfortable, direct intercity *expressos,* fast regional *rápidas,* and *carreiras,* which stop at every crossroad. Local weekend services can thin out to nothing, especially when school is out.

An express service for Lisbon–Faro (under five hours) costs €14. A youth card should get you discounts of about 20%.

## TRAIN

Caminhos de Ferro Portugueses (CP), the state railway company, operates three main services: *rápido* or *intercidade* (IC on timetables), *interregional* (IR) and *regional* (R). *Intercidade* and *interregional* tickets cost at least twice the price of regional services, with reservations either mandatory or recommended. If you can match your itinerary and pace to a regional service, rail travel is cheaper, if slower, than by bus. The IC fare for Lisbon–Faro is €11.30

Children aged four to 11 and adults over 65 travel at half-price. Youth-card holders get 30% off *regional* (R) and IR services (except at weekends). There are also family discounts. One-/two-/three-week tourist tickets *(bilhetes turísticos)* at €100/170/250 are good for 1st-class travel, but worthwhile only if you're practically living on Portuguese trains.

Frequent train travellers may want to buy the *Guia Horário Oficial* (€1.75), with all domestic and international timetables, from ticket windows at most stations.

## CAR & MOTORCYCLE

**ACP** *(Automóvel Clube de Portugal; head office: ☎ 213 180 100, fax 213 180 227; Rua Rosa Araújo 24, Lisbon; emergency help numbers for southern Portugal: ☎ 219 429*

*103)*, Portugal's representative for various foreign car, motorcycle and touring clubs, provides medical, legal and breakdown assistance for members. **ACP Insurance** (☎ *217 991 200*) can advise members on car and motorcycle insurance. But anyone can get road information and maps from its head office (see earlier).

Petrol is pricey, eg, €0.89 and up for 1L of 95-octane unleaded fuel *(sem chumbo)*, which is readily available.

### Road Rules

There are indeed rules, though Portuguese drivers are among Europe's most accident-prone. Although city driving (and parking) is hectic, rural roads have surprisingly little traffic. EU subsidies have paid for major upgrades of the road system, and there are now long stretches of motorway, some of them toll roads.

Driving is on the right. Speed limits for cars and motorcycles are 50km/h in cities as well as public centres, 90km/h on normal roads and 120km/h on motorways (but 50, 70 and 100km/h for motorcycles with sidecars). Drivers and front passengers in cars must wear seat belts. Motorcyclists and passengers must wear helmets, and motorcycles must have headlights on day and night.

Drink-driving laws here are strict, with a maximum legal blood-alcohol level of 0.02%.

### Car Rental

Portugal has dozens of local car-rental firms, many offering lower daily rates than international firms. To rent a small car for a week in the high season, budget for about UK£200 from the UK or at least €225 from Portugal (with tax, insurance and unlimited mileage). However, fly-drive packages from international firms or TAP Air Portugal can be good value. You must be at least 25 years of age and have held your licence for over a year (some companies allow younger drivers at higher rates).

### BICYCLE

A growing number of towns have bike-rental outfits (€7.50 to €17.50 a day). If you're bringing your own machine, pack plenty of spares. Bicycles can no longer be taken with you on trains, though most bus lines will accept them as accompanied baggage, subject to space and sometimes for an extra fee.

### LOCAL TRANSPORT

Except in Lisbon there's little reason to take a municipal bus. Lisbon's underground system is handy for getting around the city centre and out to Parque das Nações (see that entry in the Lisbon section for details), the former Expo site.

Taxis are good value over short distances, especially for two or more people, and are plentiful in towns. Most are metered and the clock starts at €1.50, plus €1.75 for luggage, and increases at around €0.35 per kilometre. Fares increase by around 20% at night, at weekends and if your trip leaves the city limits.

Enthusiasts for stately progress shouldn't miss the trams in Lisbon, an endangered species, and the *elevadores* (funiculars and elevators) of Lisbon. Commuter ferries cross the Rio Tejo all day to/from Lisbon.

### ORGANISED TOURS

**Gray Lines** (☎ *213 522 594, fax 213 560 668; Avenida Praia da Vitória 12-B, Lisbon)* organises multiday coach tours throughout Portugal, through local agents or upper-end tourist hotels. **Miltours** (☎ *289 890 600; Veríssimo de Almeida 14, Faro)* has day trips in the Algarve and elsewhere.

Among unusual offerings made by UK agencies are an art and history tour in May by **Martin Randall Travel** (☎ *020-8742 3355)* and wine tours by **Arblaster & Clarke** (☎ *01730-893344)*. The UK agency **Explore Worldwide** (☎ *01252-760000)* offers hiking holidays in Portugal, while **Ramblers Holidays** (☎ *01707-331133)* offers more sedate walking tours. For contact details of the adventure-travel specialists within Portugal, see Activities under Facts for the Visitor in this chapter.

# Lisbon

**pop 720,000**
Although it has the crowds, noise and traffic of a capital city, Lisbon's low skyline and breezy position beside the Rio Tejo (River Tagus) lend it a small, manageable feel. Its unpretentious atmosphere, pleasant blend of architectural styles and diverse attractions appeal to a wide range of visitors. Furthermore, Lisbon (Lisboa to the Portuguese) is one of Europe's most economical destinations.

# LISBON

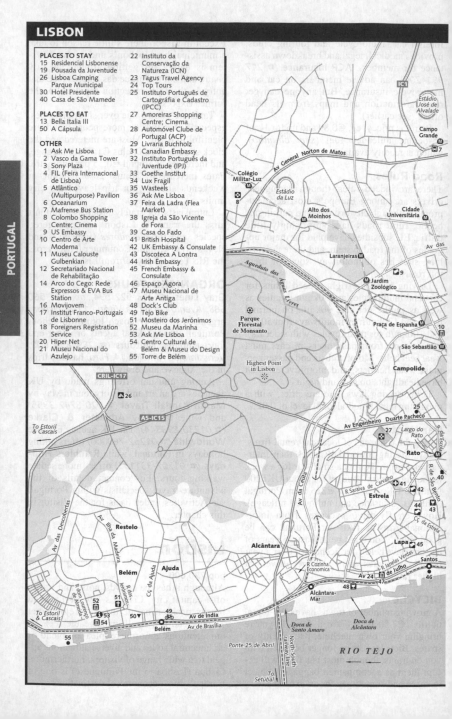

**PLACES TO STAY**
15 Residencial Lisbonense
19 Pousada da Juventude
26 Lisboa Camping
   Parque Municipal
30 Hotel Presidente
40 Casa de São Mamede

**PLACES TO EAT**
13 Bella Italia III
50 A Cápsula

**OTHER**
1 Ask Me Lisboa
2 Vasco da Gama Tower
3 Sony Plaza
4 FIL (Feira Internacional
   de Lisboa)
5 Atlântico
   (Multipurpose) Pavilion
6 Oceanarium
7 Mafrense Bus Station
8 Colombo Shopping
   Centre; Cinema
9 US Embassy
10 Centro de Arte
   Moderna
11 Museu Calouste
   Gulbenkian
12 Secretariado Nacional
   de Rehabilitação
14 Arco do Cego: Rede
   Expressos & EVA Bus
   Station
16 Movijovem
17 Institut Franco-Portugais
   de Lisbonne
18 Foreigners Registration
   Service
20 Hiper Net
21 Museu Nacional do
   Azulejo

22 Instituto da
   Conservação da
   Natureza (ICN)
23 Tagus Travel Agency
24 Top Tours
25 Instituto Português de
   Cartográfia e Cadastro
   (IPCC)
27 Amoreiras Shopping
   Centre; Cinema
28 Automóvel Clube de
   Portugal (ACP)
29 Livraria Buchholz
31 Canadian Embassy
32 Instituto Português da
   Juventude (IPJ)
33 Goethe Institut
34 Lux Fragil
35 Wasteels
36 Ask Me Lisboa
37 Feira da Ladra (Flea
   Market)
38 Igreja da São Vicente
   de Fora
39 Casa do Fado
41 British Hospital
42 UK Embassy & Consulate
43 Discoteca A Lontra
44 Irish Embassy
45 French Embassy &
   Consulate
46 Espaço Ágora
47 Museu Nacional de
   Arte Antiga
48 Dock's Club
49 Tejo Bike
51 Mosteiro dos Jerónimos
52 Museu da Marinha
53 Ask Me Lisboa
54 Centro Cultural de
   Belém & Museu do Design
55 Torre de Belém

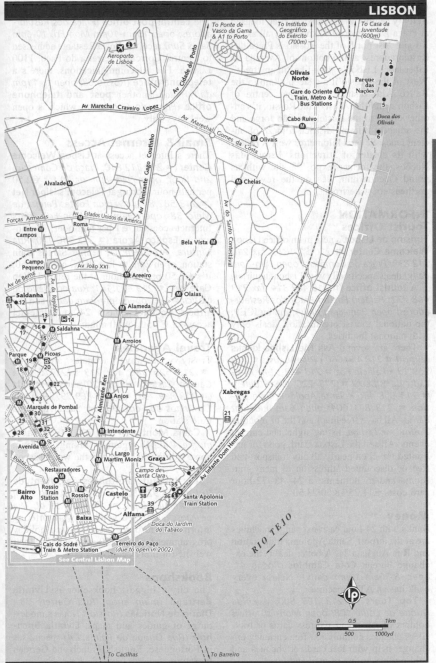

## ORIENTATION

Activity centres on the Baixa district, focused at Praça Dom Pedro IV, known by all as the Rossio. Just north of the Rossio is Praça dos Restauradores, at the bottom of Avenida da Liberdade, Lisbon's park-like 'main street'. West of the Rossio it's a steep climb to the Bairro Alto district, traditional centre of Lisbon's nightlife. East of the Rossio, it's another climb to the Castelo de São Jorge and the adjacent Alfama district, a maze of ancient lanes. Several kilometres west is Belém with its cluster of attractions. Parque das Nações, the former Expo '98 site with its grand Oceanarium, lies on the revamped northeastern waterfront.

## INFORMATION
### Tourist Offices

**Turismo de Lisboa**'s new main office **Lisboa Welcome Center** (☎ *210 312 810, fax 210 312 899; Praça do Comércio; open 9am-8pm daily)* deals specifically with Lisbon inquiries.

A **tourist office** (☎ *213 463 314, fax 213 468 772; Palácio Foz on Praça dos Restauradores; open 9am-8pm daily)*, run by ICEP, the national tourist organisation, deals only with national inquiries.

There are several **Ask Me Lisboa** kiosks *(airport ☎ 218 450 660 • Rua Augusta ☎ 213 259 13 • Palácio Foz ☎ 213 463 314 • Mercado da Ribeira ☎ 213 225 128 • Belém ☎ 213 658 435 • Santa Apolónia train station ☎ 218 821 604; open 6am-midnight daily)*. All have free maps and the bi-monthly *Follow me Lisboa*, listing sights and current events. All sell the Lisboa Card, good for unlimited travel on nearly all city transport and free or discounted admission to many museums and monuments; a 24-/48-/72-hour card costs €11.25/18.50/23.50.

## Money

Banks with 24-hour cash-exchange machines are at the airport, Santa Apolónia train station and Rua Augusta 24. A better deal is the exchange bureau **Cota Câmbios** *(Rossio 41; open 8.30am-10pm daily)*. Nearly every bank has an ATM machine.

**Top Tours** (☎ *213 108 800; Avenida Duque de Loulé 108; open Mon-Fri)* offers holders of American Express cards or travellers cheques commission-free currency exchange, help with lost cards or cheques and holding/forwarding of mail and faxes.

## Post & Communications

The **central post office** *(Praça dos Restauradores; open 10am-10pm Mon-Fri, 10-6pm Sat & Sun)* receives Posta Restante addressed to Central Correios, Terreira do Paço, 1100 Lisboa. For telecommunications, there's a **telephone office** *(Rossio 68; open to 11pm daily)*, and another **post and telephone office** *(Praça do Comércio)*, which is open weekdays only.

## Email & Internet Access

There's Internet access at **Lisboa Welcome Center** (☎ *210 312 810; Praça do Comércio, 2nd floor; open 9am-8pm daily)* for €2.50 per half-hour. **Portugal Telecom's Hiper Net** (☎ *213 582 841; Avenida Fontes Pereira de Melo 38; open 9am-9pm Mon-Fri)* offers Internet access at €1 per half-hour; 30 minutes at **Espaço Ágora** (☎ *213 940 170; Rua Cintura, Armazém 1)*, behind Santos train station, open 2pm to 1am daily, costs €1.50. It's €2.50 per half-hour at the relaxed **Web Café bar** (☎ *213 421 181; Rua do Diário de Notícias 126; open 4pm-2am daily)* and the airport **PostNet** boasts 24-hour Internet access at €1.50 for 30 minutes.

## Travel Agencies

Trusty youth-travel agencies are **Tagus** (☎ *213 525 986, fax 213 532 715; Rua Camilo Castelo Branco 20)*; and **Wasteels** (☎ *218 869 793, fax 218 869 797; Rua dos Caminhos do Ferro 90)*, by Santa Apolónia train station.

**Cabra Montêz** (☎ *918 200 143;* e *cabra montez@ip.pt)* organises biking, walking, horse riding and karting in the wider Lisbon area.

The **Instituto Português da Juventude** *(IPJ;* ☎ *218 920 800, fax 218 920 808;* e *ipj .infor@mail.telepac.pt,* w *www.sej.pt; Via de Moscavide)* is a youth network offering information resources, courses and holiday programmes for 16- to 30-year-olds. See their website for more details.

## Bookshops

The city's biggest bookseller is **Livraria Bertrand** *(main shop; Rua Garrett 73)*. **Diário de Notícias** *(Rossio 11)* has a modest range of guides and maps. **Livraria Buchholz** *(Rua Duque de Palmela 4)* specialises in Portuguese, English, French and German literature.

## Cultural Centres

The hours that the library at the **British Council** *(☎ 213 924 160; Rua de São Marçal 174; open 2pm-6.30pm Mon-Sat)* opens in the morning seem to vary, so it's best to turn up in the afternoon. The **Institut Franco-Portugais de Lisbonne** *(☎ 213 111 400; Avenida Luís Bivar 91)* has cultural events and a library open weekdays 1pm to 8pm. The library at the **Goethe Institut** *(☎ 218 824 511; Campo dos Mártires da Pátria 37)* is open Tuesday to Friday 11am to 7pm (Wednesday 3pm to 8pm).

## Laundry

Head to self-service **Lava Neve** *(Rua da Alegria 37; open 10am-1pm Mon-Sat & 3pm-7pm Mon-Fri)* to do your washing.

## Medical & Emergency Services

The **British Hospital** *(☎ 213 955 067, 213 976 329; Rua Saraiva de Carvalho 49)* has English-speaking staff.

## Dangers & Annoyances

Take normal precautions against theft, particularly on rush-hour transport. At night avoid wandering alone in the Alfama and Cais do Sodré districts. A tourist-oriented, **multilingual police office** *(☎ 213 466 802; Praça dos Restauradores)* is in the Foz Cultura building beside the ICEP tourist office.

## THINGS TO SEE & DO
### Baixa

The Baixa district, with its imposing squares and straight streets, is ideal for strolling. From the Rossio, ascend at a stately pace by funicular or lift into the surrounding hilly districts.

## Castelo de São Jorge

The castle, dating from Visigothic times, has been tarted up and commands superb views. Take bus No 37 from Rossio, or tram No 28, which clanks up steep gradients and incredibly narrow streets from Largo Martim Moniz.

## Alfama

Though increasingly gentrified and full of tourist restaurants, this ancient district below the castle is a fascinating maze of alleys. The terrace at **Largo das Portas do Sol** provides a great viewpoint.

The **Casa do Fado** *(Largo do Chafariz de Dentro 1; adult/concession €2.50/1.25; open 10am-1pm & 2pm-5.30pm daily)* offers an excellent audiovisual look at *fado's* history.

## Belém

In this quarter, 6km west of Rossio, don't miss **Mosteiro dos Jerónimos** *(Jerónimos Monastery; admission to cloisters €3, free Sun morning; open 10am-5pm Tues-Sun)*, which dates from 1496, a soaring extravaganza of Manueline architecture and the city's finest sight.

Sitting obligingly in the river a 10-minute walk away from Mosteiro dos Jerónimos is the Manueline **Torre de Belém**, *the* tourist icon of Portugal; the tower's admission and opening times are the same as for the monastery.

Beside the monastery is the **Museu da Marinha** *(Maritime Museum; admission €3; open 10am-6pm Tues-Sun, to 5pm winter)*, a collection of nautical paraphernalia. The brilliant **Museu do Design** *(adult/student €3/1.50; open 11am-7.15pm daily)* is in the Centro Cultural de Belém, opposite.

To reach Belém take the train, or bus No 43, from Cais do Sodré, or tram No 15 from Praça da Figueira.

## Other Museums

The **Museu Calouste Gulbenkian** *(open 2pm-6pm Tues, 10am-6pm Wed-Sun)* is considered Portugal's finest museum. Allow several hours to view its treasures, including paintings, sculptures and jewellery. Adjacent to it, **Centro de Arte Moderna** *(open 2pm-6pm Tues, 10am-6pm Wed-Sun)* exhibits a cross section of modern Portuguese art. Entry to each costs €3 (free to students, children and seniors, and to all on Sunday). The handiest metro station is São Sebastião.

One of Lisbon's most attractive museums is the **Museu Nacional do Azulejo** *(National Azulejos Museum; admission €2.50; open 2pm-6pm Tues, 10am-6pm Wed-Sun)* in the former convent of Nossa Senhora da Madre de Deus. Take bus No 104 from Praça do Comércio (Monday to Friday) or No 59 from Rossio (Saturday and Sunday).

The **Museu Nacional de Arte Antiga** *(Antique Art Museum; Rua das Janelas Verdes; bus No 40 or 60 or tram No 15 from Praça da Figueira; adult/student €3/1.50, admission free Sun morning; open 2pm-6pm Tues, 10am-6pm Wed-Sun)* houses the national collection of works by Portuguese painters.

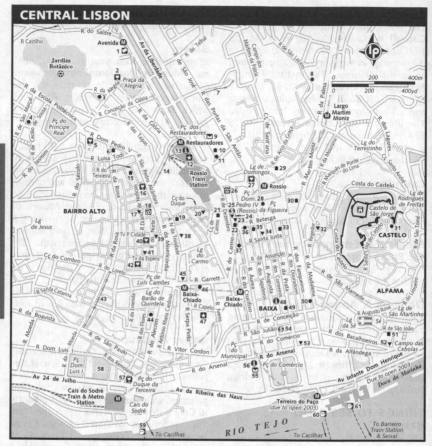

## CENTRAL LISBON

## Parque das Nações

The former site for Expo '98, which is a revitalised 2km-long waterfront area in the northeast, has a range of attractions, notably a magnificent **Oceanarium** *(adult/senior & child under 16 €9.50/8.50; open 10am-7pm daily)*, which is Europe's largest. Take the metro to Oriente station, which is an equally impressive Expo project.

## ORGANISED TOURS

**Carris** *(☎ 966 298 558)* offers tours by either open-top bus (€13) or tram (€16) that start from Praça do Comércio.

**Transtejo** *(☎ 218 820 348)* runs cruises on the Rio Tejo for €15/8 per adult/senior & child that leave from the Terreiro do Paço ferry terminal.

## PLACES TO STAY
## Camping

**Lisboa Camping Parque Municipal** *(☎ 217 623 100; Parque Florestal de Monsanto; bus No 43 from Cais do Sodré)* is 6km northwest of Rossio.

## Hostels

The **pousada da juventude** *(☎ 213 532 696; Rua Andrade Corvo 46)* is central. The closest metro station is Picoas, or take bus No 46 from Santa Apolónia station or Rossio. The newer **casa da juventude** *(☎ 218 920 890; Via de Moscavide)* is 1km north of Gare do Oriente. Take bus No 44 from Praça dos Restauradores or Oriente to the Avenida da Boa Esperança roundabout; the hostel is 250m down the road. Reservations are essential at both hostels.

## CENTRAL LISBON

| PLACES TO STAY | | 45 | Café A Brasileira | 28 | Carris Kiosk |
|---|---|---|---|---|---|
| 6 | Pensão Londres | 52 | Solar do Vez | 31 | Largo das Portas do Sol |
| 10 | Pensão Imperial | 53 | Martinho da Arcada | 36 | Diário de Notícias |
| 15 | Pensão Globo | | | 37 | Elevador de Santa Justa |
| 19 | Pensão Duque | | OTHER | 40 | Adega Machado (Casa de Fado) |
| 21 | Hospedaria Bons Dias | 1 | Spanish Embassy | 42 | Adega do Ribatejo (Casa de |
| 22 | Pensão Santo Tirso | 2 | Hot Clube de Portugal | | Fado) |
| 29 | Pensão Residencial Gerês | 3 | Lava Neve | 43 | Elevador da Bica |
| 30 | Pensão Residencial Alcobia | 4 | British Council | 44 | Fabrica Sant'Ana |
| 33 | Pensão Norte | 5 | Pavilhão Chinês Bar | 46 | Livraria Bertrand |
| 35 | Pensão Arco da Bandeira | 7 | Elevador de Lavra | 47 | Police Sation |
| 49 | Pensão Prata | 8 | Gay & Lesbian Community | 48 | Ask Me Lisboa |
| 51 | Pensão São João da Praça & | | Centre | 50 | Santos Ofícios |
| | Sé Guest House | 9 | Central Post & Telephone | 54 | 24-Hour Cash Exchange |
| | | | Office | | Machine |
| PLACES TO EAT | | 11 | ABEP Ticket Kiosk | 55 | Post and Telephone Office |
| 17 | Stravaganza | 12 | Tourist Police Post | 56 | Lisboa Welcome Center |
| 20 | Restaurante O Sol | 13 | ICEP National Tourist Office & | 57 | Ó Gilíns Irish Pub |
| 23 | Café Nicola | | Turismo de Lisboa | 58 | Mercado da Ribeira; Ask Me |
| 24 | Pingo Doce Supermarket | 14 | Elevador da Glória | | Lisboa |
| 32 | São Cristóvão | 16 | Solar do Vinho do Porto | 59 | Cais do Sodré Car Ferry |
| 34 | Nilo | 18 | Web Café | | Terminal |
| 38 | Cervejaria da Trindade | 25 | Cota Câmbios | 60 | Cais de Alfândega Ferry |
| 39 | Restaurante Sinal Vermelho | 26 | Telephone Office | | Terminal |
| 41 | Restaurante A Primavera | 27 | A Ginjinha | 61 | Terreiro do Paço Ferry Terminal |

## Hotels & Guesthouses

In the high season – and for central hotels at any time – advance bookings are imperative.

**Baixa & Restauradores** There are adequate doubles at **Pensão Santo Tirso** (☎ 213 470 428; Praça Dom Pedro IV 18, 3rd floor; doubles around €40), as is the case at **Pensão Prata** (☎ 213 468 908; Rua da Prata 71, 3rd floor; doubles with/without bath €30/25) and **Pensão Arco da Bandeira** (☎ 213 423 478; Rua dos Sapateiros 226, 4th floor).

Slightly pricier are **Pensão Duque** (☎ 213 463 444; Calçada do Duque 53) and **Pensão Norte** (☎ 218 878 941; Rua dos Douradores 159, 2nd floor).

More salubrious, with doubles around €35 to €40, are **Pensão Imperial** (☎ 213 420 166; Praça dos Restauradores 78, 4th floor) and friendly **Hospedaria Bons Dias** (☎ 213 471 918; Calçada do Carmo 25, 5th floor). Rates at old-fashioned **Pensão Residencial Alcobia** (☎ 218 865 171, fax 218 865 174; Poço do Borratém 15; doubles with/without bath €45/38) include breakfast. Brighter **Pensão Residencial Gerês** (☎ 218 810 497, fax 218 882 006; Calçada do Garcia 6; rooms €45) offers rates without breakfast.

**Bairro Alto & Rato** Near the Elevador da Glória is pleasant **Pensão Globo** (☎ 213 462 279; Rua do Teixeira 37; doubles without bath from €30). **Pensão Londres** (☎ 213 462 203, fax 213 465 682; Rua Dom Pedro V 53; doubles from around €40) has spacious rooms, the upper ones with great views. Elegant, old **Casa de São Mamede** (☎ 213 963 166, fax 213 951 896; Rua Escola Politécnica 159; doubles €80) has rooms with bath and breakfast.

**Marquês de Pombal & Saldanha** The **Residencial Lisbonense** (☎ 213 544 628; Rua Pinheiro Chagas 1; doubles with bath €40) offers bright doubles with breakfast. A three-star hotel with four-star facilities is **Hotel Presidente** (☎ 213 173 570, fax 213 520 272; Rua Alexandre Herculano 13; doubles €102).

**Alfama** Behind the cathedral, popular **Pensão São João da Praça** (☎ 218 862 591, fax 218 880 415; Rua São João da Praça 97, 2nd floor) and its 1st-floor neighbour, genteel **Sé Guest House** (☎ 218 864 400), have doubles from €45 to €65, including breakfast.

## PLACES TO EAT

There are dozens of restaurants and cafés in the Baixa (best for lunchtime bargains) and Bairro Alto (pricier evening venues). A trendier restaurant and bar zone is riverside **Doca de Santo Amaro**, near Alcântara-Mar station. The main market, **Mercado da Ribeira**, is near Cais do Sodré station and the most centrally located supermarket is **Pingo Doce** just off the Rossio on Rua de Dezembro.

### Baixa & Alfama

Minimalist **Nilo** (☎ 213 467 014; Rua dos Correeiros 217) is one of many reasonably priced places along Rua dos Correeiros. **Restaurante O Sol** (☎ 213 471 944; Calçada do Duque 23; set meals around €5) serves vegetarian cuisine in a great location.

Among several restaurants with outdoor seating in lower Alfama, **Solar do Vez** (☎ 218 870 794; Campo das Cebolas 48; mains €6-8) has an appealing simplicity. **São Cristóvão** (☎ 218 885 578; Rua de São Cristóvão 30; mains €4-5) dishes up aromatic Cape Verdean dishes.

For coffee or a meal, try Art Deco **Café Nicola** (☎ 213 460 579; Rossio 24) or 18th-century **Martinho da Arcada** (☎ 218 879 259; Praça do Comércio 3). The literary pedigree of Art Nouveau **Café A Brasileira** (☎ 213 469 547; Rua Garrett 120) is symbolised by the bronze figure of Fernando Pessoa outside.

### Bairro Alto & Saldanha

Tiny **Restaurante A Primavera** (☎ 213 420 477; Travessa da Espera 34; mains €7-10) has a family ambience. **Restaurante Sinal Vermelho** (☎ 213 461 252; Rua das Gáveas 89; mains €8.50-11.50) is one of Lisbon's best (with great desserts).

Chic **Stravaganza** (☎ 213 468 868; Rua do Grémio Lusitano 18) offers innovative Italian dishes – try spaghetti Mafioso (€8.50). Converted convent **Cervejaria da Trindade** (☎ 213 423 506; Rua Nova da Trindade 20-C; mains from €7) is adorned with azulejos.

Bright and cheerful **Bella Italia III** (☎ 213 528 636; Avenida Duque d'Ávila 40-C) is a pastelaria-cum-restaurant, with pizzas and half-portions of Portuguese fare for under €5.

### Belém

A row of attractive restaurants with outdoor seating in Belém includes **A Cápsula** (☎ 213 648 768; Rua Vieira Portuense 72), serving classics such as pork Alentejana (€7.50).

## ENTERTAINMENT

For listings, pick up the free bi-monthly Follow me Lisboa or Lisboa Step By Step from the tourist office, or Público from a newsstand.

### Music & Bars

Many casas de fado (which are also restaurants) produce pricey, inferior fado and have a minimum charge of around €16. In Bairro Alto, try the professional **Adega Machado** (☎ 213 224 640; Rua do Norte 91) or simpler **Adega do Ribatejo** (☎ 213 468 343; Rua Diário de Notícias 23).

**Hot Clube de Portugal** (☎ 213 467 369; Praça da Alegria 39; open 10pm-2am Tues-Sat) is part of a thriving live jazz scene.

**Ó Gilíns Irish Pub** (☎ 213 421 899; Rua dos Remolares 8-10; open 11am-2am) has live music Friday and Saturday evenings.

Clubs come and go. Stalwart **Lux Fragil** (☎ 218 820 890; Avenida Infante Dom Henrique, Cais da Pedra à Santa Apolónia; open midnight-5am) remains. Riverside options include: **Dock's Club** (☎ 213 950 856; Rua da Cintura do Porto de Lisboa 226; open to 6am Tues-Sat).

The African music scene (predominantly Cape Verdean) centres around Rua de São Bento; **Discoteca A Lontra** (☎ 213 691 083; Rua de São Bento 155; open to 4am Tues-Sun) is popular.

For a taste of real – though hardly undiscovered – Lisbon sip a sticky glass of ginjinha (cherry liquor) outside **A Ginjinha** (Largo de Domingos; open 9am-10.30pm), by the Rossio. Peruse the lengthy port wine list at snooty **Solar do Vinho do Porto** (☎ 213 475 707; Rua de São Pedro de Alcântara 45; open 2pm-midnight Mon-Sat); or for cocktails in quirky surrounds ring the bell at **Pavilhão Chinês** (☎ 213 424 729; Rua Dom Pedro V 89; 6pm-2am Mon-Sat, from 9pm Sunday).

### Cinemas

Lisbon has many cinemas, including multiscreen ones at **Amoreiras** (☎ 213 878 752) and **Colombo** (☎ 217 113 222) shopping complexes. Tickets cost €4 (€3.50 Monday).

## SPECTATOR SPORTS

Lisbon's football teams are Benfica and Sporting. Ask the tourist office about fixtures and tickets. Bullfights are staged at Campo Pequeno between April and October. Tickets are available at **ABEP ticket agency** (Praça dos Restauradores).

## SHOPPING

For azulejos, try posh **Fabrica Sant'Ana** (Rua do Alecrim 95) or **The Museu Nacional do**

Azulejo. **Santos Ofícios** *(Rua da Madalena 87)* has an eclectic range of Portuguese folk art. On Tuesday and Saturday, visit the **Feira da Ladra** *(Campo de Santa Clara)*, a huge open-air market in the Alfama.

## GETTING THERE & AWAY
### Air
Lisbon is connected by daily flights to Faro and many European centres (see the introductory Getting There & Away and Getting Around sections of this chapter). For arrival and departure information call ☎ 218 413 700.

### Bus
A dozen different companies, including **Renex** *(☎ 222 003 395)*, operate from Gare do Oriente. The **Arco do Cego terminal** is the base for **Rede Expressos** *(☎ 707 223 344)* and **EVA** *(☎ 213 147 710)*, whose networks cover the whole country.

### Train
**Santa Apolónia station** *(☎ 218 816 121)* is the terminus for all international services (trains also stop en route at the better-connected Gare do Oriente). Cais do Sodré station is for Belém, Cascais and Estoril. Rossio station serves Sintra.

Barreiro station, across the river, is the terminus for southern Portugal; connecting ferries leave frequently from the pier at Terreiro do Paço.

The north-south railway line, over the Ponte de 25 Abril, goes to suburban areas and will eventually carry on further to southern Portugal.

### Ferry
Cais da Alfândega is the terminal for several ferries, including to Cacilhas (€0.55), a transfer point for some buses to Setúbal. A car (and bike) ferry runs from Cais do Sodré terminal.

## GETTING AROUND
### To/From the Airport
The AeroBus runs every 20 minutes from 7.45am to 8.45pm, taking 30 to 45 minutes between the airport and Cais do Sodré, including a stop by the ICEP tourist office. A ticket for €2.30/5.50 is good for one/three days on all buses, trams and funiculars. Local bus Nos 44, 45 and 83 also run near the ICEP tourist office; No 44 links the airport with Gare do Oriente too. A taxi into town is about €10, plus €1.75 if your luggage needs to go in the boot (trunk).

### Bus & Tram
Two-journey bus and tram tickets are €0.93 from Carris kiosks, most conveniently at Praça da Figueira and the Santa Justa Elevador, or €0.90 per ride from the driver. A one-/four-/seven-day Passe Turístico, valid for trams, buses and the metro, costs €2.55/9.25/13.10.

Buses and trams run from 6am to 1am, with some night services. Pick up a transport map, *Planta dos Transportes Públicas da Carris*, from tourist offices or Carris kiosks.

Wheelchair users can call the **Cooperativa Nacional Apoio Deficientes** *(☎ 218 595 332)* for assistance to hire adapted transport.

The clattering, antediluvian trams *(eléctricos)* are an endearing component of Lisbon; try No 28 to Alfama from Largo Martim Moniz.

### Metro
The metro is useful for hops across town and to the Parque das Nações. Individual tickets cost €0.55; a *caderneta* of 10 tickets is €4.50. A day ticket *(bilhete diário)* is €1.40. The metro operates from 6.30am to 1am. Beware of rush-hour pickpockets.

### Taxi
Lisbon's plentiful taxis are best hired from taxi ranks. Some at the airport are less than scrupulous. From the Rossio to Belém is around €5 and to Castelo de São Jorge about €3.50.

### Car & Bicycle
Car rental companies in Lisbon include **Avis** *(☎ 800 201 002)*, **Europcar** *(☎ 218 410 163)* and the cheaper **Rupauto** *(☎ 217 933 258, fax 217 931 768)*. **Tejo Bike** *(☎ 218 871 976)*, 300m east of Belém, rents bikes for €4 an hour to ride along the waterfront.

# Around Lisbon

## SINTRA
**pop 20,000**
If you take only one trip from Lisbon, make it Sintra. Beloved by Portuguese royalty and English nobility, its thick forests and startling architecture provide a complete change from Lisbon. The **tourist office** *(☎ 219 231 157, fax*

PORTUGAL

*219 235 176; Praça da República 23)*, in the historic centre, sells tourist day passes (€7).

At weekends and during the annual July music festival, expect droves of visitors. In the high season book accommodation in advance.

### Things to See

The Manueline and Gothic **Palácio Nacional de Sintra** *(☎ 219 106 840; adult/student €3/1.50; open 10am-5pm Thur-Tues)*, dominates the town with its twin chimneys and Moorish origins.

One of Sintra's best museums is the **Museu do Brinquedo** *(☎ 219 242 172; Rua Visconde de Monserrate; adult/concession €3/1.50; open 10am-6pm Tues-Sun)*, with 20,000 toys from around the world.

An easy 3km climb from the centre leads to ruined **Castelo dos Mouros** *(open 9am-6pm daily)* providing fine views. Twenty minutes futher on is the exuberantly romantic **Palácio da Pena** *(☎ 219 105 340; open 10am-4pm Tues-Sun)*, built in 1839. Cars are prohibited; Stagecoach bus No 434 (€3) runs regularly from the station via the tourist office. Rambling **Monserrate Gardens** *(☎ 219 237 300; open 10am-5pm daily)* are 4km from town. A ticket for all three costs €5/3.50 for adult/concession.

En route to the gardens is an extraordinary, mystical mansion, **Quinta da Regaleira** *(☎ 219 106 650; adult/concession €9.98/4.99; open 10am-6pm daily, to 3.30pm winter)*. Visits must be pre-arranged.

The theme park **Sintrolândia** *(Granja do Marquês, 5km northeast of Sintra)*, which promises to be a huge tourism and leisure complex, was not yet open at the time of writing. Ask at the tourist office for the latest information.

### Places to Stay

The best camping ground is **Camping Praia Grande** *(☎ 219 290 581)*, on the coast 11km from Sintra and linked by frequent buses. A **pousada da juventude** *(☎ 219 241 210)* is at Santa Eufémia, 4km from the centre; it's essential to make a reservation.

**Residencial Adelaide** *(☎ 219 230 873; Rua Guilherme Gomes Fernandes 11; doubles from €25)*, a 10-minute walk from the station, has reasonable doubles. The tourist office has a list of private rooms at a similar price. Across the tracks is friendly **Piela's** *(☎ 219 241 691; Rua João de Deus 70; rooms €25-50)*, which

is due to move in 2003 to Avenida Desiderio Cambournac 1–3.

### Places to Eat

Close to the tourist office is **Tulhas** *(☎ 219 232 378; Rua Gil Vicente 4-6)*, whose hits include bacalhau with cream €6.75. Simple **A Tasca do Manel** *(☎ 219 230 215; Largo Dr Vergílio Horta 5; mains around €6)* serves standards. **Restaurante Parreirinha** *(☎ 219 231 207; Rua João de Deus 41; mains €6-7)* has great grilled fish. Cavernous, classy **Xentra** *(☎ 219 240 759; Rua Consiglieri Pedroso 2-A; snacks €2-3, mains around €8)* has a similarly elegant bar (until 2am).

### Getting There & Away

The Lisbon–Sintra railway terminates in Estefânia, 1.5km northeast of the historic centre. Sintra's bus station, and another train station, are a further 1km east in the newtown district of Portela de Sintra. Frequent shuttle buses run to the historic centre from the bus station.

Trains run every 15 minutes from Lisbon's Rossio station. Buses run regularly from Sintra to Estoril and Cascais.

### Getting Around

A taxi to Palácio da Pena or Monserrate Gardens costs around €10 return. Horse-drawn carriages are a romantic alternative: expect to pay €55 to Monserrate and back. Old trams run from Ribeira de Sintra (1.5km from the centre) to Praia das Maças, 12km to the west.

## CASCAIS

**pop 30,000**

Cascais, *the* beach resort west of Lisbon, is packed in summer. The **tourist office** *(☎ 214 868 204; Rua Visconde de Luz 14)* has accommodation lists and bus timetables; there's also a **tourist police post** *(☎ 214 863 929)*.

**Ciber Forum** *(☎ 214 868 311; Rua da Bela Vista 126; open to 8pm daily, to 11pm Fri & Sat)* has Internet access at €2.50 per half-hour and a courtyard café.

### Things to See & Do

Two kilometres east of Cascais, **Estoril** is an old-fashioned resort with Europe's biggest **casino** *(open 3pm-3am daily)*. Praia Tamariz beach (beside the train station) has an ocean swimming pool.

The sea roars into the coast at **Boca do Inferno** (Hell's Mouth), 2km west of Cascais. Spectacular **Cabo da Roca**, Europe's westernmost point, is 16km from Cascais and Sintra (served by buses from both towns). Wild **Guincho** beach, 3km from Cascais, is a popular surfing venue.

**Transrent** (☎ 214 864 566; Centro Commercial Cisne, Avenida Marginal) rents cars, motorcycles and bicycles.

### Places to Stay & Eat
**Camping Orbitur do Guincho** (☎ 214 871 014, fax 214 872 167) is 7km from Cascais near Guincho beach. **Residencial Avenida** (☎ 214 864 417; Rua da Palmeira 14; doubles without bath €30) is another option. The tourist office can recommend **private rooms** from around €30. Fairytale **Casa da Pergola** (☎ 214 840 040, fax 214 834 791; Avenida Valbom 13; doubles from €92) has a beautiful garden.

A **Económica** (☎ 214 833 524; Rua Sebastião J C Melo 35; mains €5-7) serves standards. Try the octopus rice (€5.50) at **A Tasca** (Rua Afonso Sanches 61).

### Getting There & Away
Trains run frequently to Estoril and Cascais from Cais do Sodré station in Lisbon.

### SETÚBAL
pop 110,000
This refreshingly untouristy city, an easy 50km south of Lisbon, has fine beaches and seafood restaurants, and is a good base for exploring nearby Parque Natural da Arrábida and Reserva Natural do Estuário do Sado.

The **tourist office** (☎/fax 265 534 402; Praça do Quebedo) is a five-minute walk east from the **bus terminal** (Avenida 5 de Outubro). There's also a **regional tourist office** (☎ 265 539 130, fax 265 539 127; Travessa Frei Gaspar 10).

The **Instituto Português da Juventude** (IPJ; ☎ 265 534 431; Largo José Afonso) has free Internet access for limited periods on weekdays. **Sobecome** (☎ 265 521 150; Avenida Luisa Todi 333, 1st floor; open 10am-2am daily) charges €2.50 for 30 minutes.

### Things to See
The town's main cultural attraction is the 15th-century **Igreja de Jesus** (Praça Miguel Bombarda), with early Manueline decoration

inside. The **Galeria da Pintura Quinhentista** (admission free; open 9am-noon & 2pm-5pm Tues-Sat) around the corner displays a renowned collection of 16th-century paintings.

Good **beaches** west of town include Praia da Figueirinha (accessible by bus in the summer). Across the estuary at Tróia is a more developed beach, plus the ruins of a Roman settlement. On the ferry trip across you may see some of the estuary's 30 or so bottle-nosed dolphins.

### Activities
**SAL** (☎ 265 227 685) organises walks from €5 per person. For jeep safaris, hiking and biking in the Serra da Arrábida, or canoe trips through the Reserva Natural do Estuário do Sado, contact **Planeta Terra** (☎ 919 471 871; Praça General Luís Domingues 9). **Vertigem Azul** (☎ 265 238 000; Avenida Luísa Todi 375) offers dolphin-spotting and canoeing trips.

### Places to Stay & Eat
A municipal **camping ground** (☎ 265 522 475) is 1.5km west of town. The **pousada da juventude** (☎ 265 534 431; Largo José Afonso) has doubles with bath, as well as dorm beds.

Crumbling **Residencial Todi** (☎ 265 220 592; Avenida Luísa Todi 244; doubles with/without bath €20/15) is basic. **Pensão Bom Regresso** (☎ 265 229 812; Praça de Bocage 48; doubles €25) overlooks the square. **Residencial Bocage** (☎ 265 543 080, fax 265 543 089; Rua São Cristovão 14; doubles €44.90) is smarter.

Cheaper restaurants east of the regional tourist office include **Triângulo** (☎ 265 233 927; Rua Arronches Junqueiro 72). Seafood places line the western end of Avenida Luísa Todi; friendly **Casa do Chico** (☎ 265 239 502; Avenida Luísa Todi 490) is less touristy than most. Popular **Restaurante Antóniu's** (☎ 265 523 706; Rua Trabalhadores do Mar 31) is also recommended.

### Getting There & Away
Buses leave frequently from Lisbon's Gare do Oriente and also from Cacilhas, a short ferry ride from Lisbon's Cais de Alfândega. Ferries shuttle across the estuary to Tróia regularly; the tourist office has the latest timetable.

PORTUGAL

# The Algarve

Boisterous and full of foreigners, the Algarve is about as far from traditional Portugal as one can get. The focus is on Albufeira and Lagos, with sun, sand and golf (and surfing along the western coast) as the drawcards, but there are other attractions: the forested slopes of Monchique, the fortified village of Silves and windswept, historic Sagres. The district capital and largest town is Faro.

## Information

Expat-oriented, English-language newspapers with entertainment information include the *Algarve News,* and *Algarve Resident.*

**Dangers & Annoyances** Theft is a problem in the Algarve. Don't leave anything valuable in your vehicle, tent or on the beach.

Swimmers should be aware of dangerous currents, especially on the western coast. Beaches are marked by coloured flags: red means no bathing, yellow means wading but no swimming, green means anything goes.

## Shopping

Few souvenirs are made in the Algarve, but woollens (cardigans and fishing pullovers) and Moorish-influenced ceramics are good value. Algarviana is a local *amaretto* (bitter almond liqueur), and the bottled waters of Monchique are sold everywhere.

## Getting Around

Rede Expressos and EVA together run an efficient network of bus services throughout the Algarve. The IP1/EO1 superhighway, to run the length of the coast, is nearly complete. Bicycles, scooters and motorcycles can be rented everywhere; see town listings.

## LAGOS
### pop 20,000

This tourist resort has some of the Algarve's finest beaches. Of the two **tourist offices,** the new municipal **Posto de Informação** (☎ 282 764 111; Largo Marquês de Pombal; 10am-6pm Mon-Sat) is the more convenient, the other **tourist office** (☎ 282 763 031; open 9.30am-12.30pm & 2pm-5.30pm Mon-Fri; sometimes Sat & Sun) is 1km northeast of the centre, at the Situo São João roundabout. The **pousada da juventude** (see Places to Stay, later) offers Internet access at €1.50 per half-hour.

## Things to See & Do

In the old town, the **municipal museum** houses an assortment of exhibits from archaeological finds to ecclesiastical treasures. The adjacent **Igreja de Santo António** has some intricate baroque woodwork.

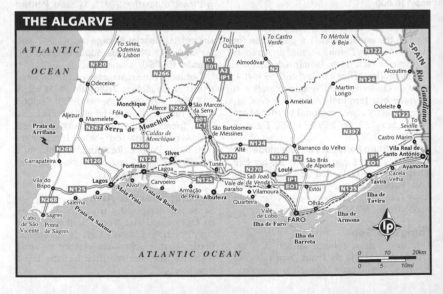

THE ALGARVE

The beach scene includes **Meia Praia**, a vast expanse of sand to the east; and to the west **Praia da Luz** and the smaller and more secluded **Praia do Pinhão**.

**Blue Ocean** (☎ 282 782 718) organises diving, kayaking and snorkelling safaris. On the seaside promenade, local fishermen offer motorboat jaunts to the nearby grottoes. For horse riding in the Algarve interior ring **Tiffany's** (☎ 282 697 395).

### Places to Stay

The camping ground is **Trindade** (☎ 282 763 893), 200m south of the Lançarote gate in the town walls. The **pousada da juventude** (☎ 282 761 970; Rua Lançarote de Freitas 50) is another worthwhile choice.

**Residencial Marazul** (☎ 289 769 749; Rua 25 de Abril 13; doubles from €55) has smart rooms. **Private rooms** are plentiful, for around €35 to €50.

### Places to Eat

Unassuming **A Gamba** (☎ 282 760 453; Rua Conselheiro Joaquim Machado 5) serves good traditional fare for around €5-7. A local favourite is **Restaurante Bar Barros** (☎ 282 762 276; Rua Portas de Portugal 83), where creamy grilled scabbard fish is €6.73. **Mullens** (☎ 282 761 281; Rua Cândido dos Reis 86) is a wood-panelled pub with good food.

### Getting There & Away

Bus and train services depart frequently for other Algarve towns and around six times daily to Lisbon; by train, change at Tunes for Lisbon.

### Getting Around

You can rent bicycles, mopeds and motorcycles from **Motoride** (☎ 289 761 720; Rua José Afonso 23), or agents in town. Expect to pay about €5 a day for a mountain bike or €30 for a motorbike.

## SAGRES
**pop 2500**

Sagres is a small, windy fishing port perched on dramatic cliffs in Portugal's southwestern corner. The **tourist office** (☎ 282 624 873; Rua Comandante Matoso; open Mon-Fri, & Sat morning) is just beyond Praça da República. **Turinfo** (☎ 282 620 003; Praça da República; open daily) rents cars and bikes, books hotels and arranges jeep and fishing trips.

### Things to See & Do

In the **fort**, on a wide, windy promontory, Henry the Navigator established his school of navigation and primed the explorers who later founded the Portuguese empire.

You can hire windsurfers at sand-dune fringed **Praia do Martinhal**; another option is the beach at the village of **Salema**, 17km east.

No Sagres visit would be complete without a trip to **Cabo de São Vicente** (Cape St Vincent), 6km to the west. A solitary lighthouse stands on this barren cape, Europe's most southwestern point.

### Places to Stay & Eat

**Parque de Campismo Sagres** (☎ 282 624 351) is 2km from town, off the Vila do Bispo road. Many folk rent **rooms** for about €25 a double. Good-value traditional dishes can be had at **Restaurante A Sagres** before the village, and at **cafés** in Praça da República.

### Getting There & Away

Frequent buses run daily to Sagres from Lagos (45 to 65 minutes), fewer on Sunday. Three continue out to Cabo de São Vicente on weekdays.

## MONCHIQUE
**pop 6840**

This quiet highland town in the forested Serra de Monchique offers a quiet alternative to the discos and beach life on the coast.

### Things to See & Do

Monchique's **Igreja Matriz** has an amazing Manueline portal, its stone seemingly tied in knots! Follow the brown pedestrian signs up from the bus station, around the old town's narrow streets. **Caldas de Monchique**, 6km south, is a revamped but still charming hot-spring hamlet. Some 8km west is the Algarve's 'rooftop', the 902m **Fóia** peak atop the Serra de Monchique, with terrific views through a forest of radio masts.

Monchique's **tourist office** (☎ 289 911 189) is in the square where the bus stops. Ring **Alternativtour** (☎ 282 420 800) for bike and walking tours. For horse riding in the mountains contact **Casa Sesmaria** (☎ 282 912 511; experienced riders only).

### Places to Stay & Eat

**Residencial Estrela de Monchique** (☎ 282 913 111; Rua do Porto Fundo 46; doubles

€50) is central. **Restaurante A Charrete** (☎ 282 912 142; Rua Dr Samora Gil 30) is the best in town – try the hearty beans with cabbage (€6.98).

## Getting There & Away
Over a dozen buses run daily from Lagos to Portimão, from where five to nine services run daily to Monchique.

## SILVES
**pop 10,500**
Silves was the capital of Moorish Algarve, rivalling Lisbon for influence. Times are quieter now, but the huge castle is well worth a visit.

The **tourist office** (☎ 289 442 255; Rua 25 de Abril; open Mon-Fri & Sat morning) is closed out of season.

### Places to Stay & Eat
Try **Residencial Sousa** (☎ 282 442 502; Rua Samoura Barros 17; doubles €30) or **Residencial Ponte Romana** (☎ 282 443 275; doubles €30) beside the old bridge.

**Restaurante Rui** (☎ 282 442 682; Rua C Vilarinho 27), Silves' best fish restaurant, serves a memorable *arroz de marisco* (shellfish rice; €23.50 for two). For cheaper meals, try the **riverfront restaurants** opposite the old bridge.

### Getting There & Away
Silves train station is 2km from town; trains from Lagos (35 minutes) stop nine times daily (from Faro, change at Tunes), to be met by local buses. Six buses run daily to Silves from Albufeira (40 minutes).

## FARO
**pop 45,000**
Pleasantly low-key Faro is the main transport hub and commercial centre of the Algarve. The **tourist office** (☎ 289 803 604; Rua da Misericórdia) has leaflets on just about every Algarve community.

### Things to See & Do
The palm-clad **waterfront** around Praça de Dom Francisco Gomes has pleasant cafés. Faro's beach, **Praia de Faro** (Ilha de Faro) is 6km southwest of the city; take bus No 16 from opposite the bus station. Less crowded is the unspoilt **Ilha Desserta** in the nature park **Parque Natural da Ria Formosa** (☎ 917 811 856; lagoon tours available). Access is

by ferry June to mid-September from Cais da Porta Nova.

At Estói, 12km north of Faro, the romantically ruined **Estói Palace** has a surreal garden of statues, balustrades and *azulejos*; take the Faro–São Brás de Alportel bus that goes via Estói.

### Places to Stay & Eat
The **municipal camping ground** (☎ 289 817 876; Praia de Faro) is big and cheap. The **pousada da juventude** (☎ 289 826 521; Rua da Polícia de Segurança Pública 1) has dorm beds and rooms.

**Residencial Adelaide** (☎ 289 802 383, fax 289 826 870; Rua Cruz dos Mestres 7; doubles from €45) is a friendly budget *pensão*. Aptly-named, friendly **Pensão Residencial Centro** (☎ 289 807 291; Largo Terreiro do Bispo 10; doubles €40) is spotless.

Lively **Sol e Jardim** (☎ 289 820 030; Praça Ferreira de Almeida 22) serves good grilled squid (€7.49). **A Velha Casa** (☎ 289 824 719; Rua do Pé da Cruz 33; mains €6-7) has good charcoal-grilled meat and fish.

### Getting There & Away
Faro airport has both domestic and international flights (see the introductory Getting There & Away section of this chapter).

From the bus station, just west of the centre, there are at least a six daily express coaches to Lisbon (about four hours) and frequent buses to other coastal towns.

The train station is a few minutes' walk west of the bus station. Four trains run daily to Lisbon (Barreiro), and about a dozen to Albufeira and ten to Portimão.

### Getting Around
The airport is 6km from the centre. The Aero-Bus runs into town in summer only (free to those with airline tickets). Bus Nos 14 and 16 run into town until 9pm (but infrequently in winter). A taxi costs about €7.50.

## TAVIRA
**pop 12,000**
Tavira is one of the Algarve's oldest and handsomest towns. The **tourist office** (☎ 281 322 511; Rua da Galeria 9) dispenses information. Bicycles and scooters can be rented from **Loris Rent** (☎ 964 079 233) next door. For walking or biking call **Exploratio** (☎ 919 338 226). To sail contact **Clube Náutico**

*(☎ 281 326 858)*. Jose Salvador Rocha organises diving trips *(☎ 939 017 329)*. **Cyber Café**, opposite the bus station, *(☎ 281 325 375; Rua dos Pelames 1)* has Internet access for €2 per half-hour.

## Things to See & Do
In the old town the **Igreja da Misericórdia** has a striking Renaissance doorway and interior *azulejos*. From there, it's a short climb to the **castle** dominating the town.

**Ilha da Tavira**, 2km from Tavira, is an island beach connected to the mainland by ferry. Walk 2km along the river to the ferry terminal at Quatro Águas or take the (summer only) bus from the bus station.

For a look at the old Algarve, take a bus to nearby **Cacela Velha**, an unspoilt hamlet 8km from Tavira. Another worthwhile day trip is to the fishing centre of **Olhão**, 22km west of Tavira.

## Places to Stay & Eat
Ilha da Tavira has a **camping ground** *(☎ 281 324 455)*, which is open July to September, when ferries operate (dates vary, so check these). **Pensão Residencial Lagoas** *(☎ 281 322 252; Rua Almirante Cândido dos Reis 24; doubles €38)* has character and a pretty roof terrace; centrally located **Residencial Imperial** *(☎ 281 322 234; Rua José Pires Padinha 24; doubles €40)* provides breakfast; and smart **Pensão Residencial Princesa do Gilão** *(☎ 281 325 171; Rua Borda de Água de Aguiar 10; rooms €60)* overlooks the river.

Budget restaurants on riverside Rua Dr José Pires Padinha include **A Barquinha** *(☎ 281 322 843)* at No 142. **Cantinho do Emigrante** *(☎ 281 323 696; Praça Dr Padinha 27)* also has good-value fare. **Restaurante Bica** *(☎ 281 332 483)*, below Residencial Lagoas, has delicious specials such as sole with orange €10.

Good seafood lunches are up for grabs in Olhão, in the many restaurants that line Rua 5 de Outubro.

## Getting There & Away
Some 15 trains and at least six express buses run daily between Faro and Tavira (30 to 50 minutes).

**PORTUGAL**

# Slovenia

Slovenia (Slovenija) is one of the most over-looked gems in all of Europe. The wealthiest nation of former Yugoslavia, Slovenia – an Alpine country – has much more in common with its Central European neighbours than with the Balkan countries it split from in a 10-day war in 1991. The two million Slovenes were economically the most well-off among the peoples of what was once Yugoslavia, and the relative affluence and orderliness of this nation is immediately apparent. Many of its cities and towns bear the imprint of the Habsburg Empire and the Venetian Republic, and the Julian Alps are reminiscent of Switzerland.

Fairy-tale Bled Castle, breathtaking Lake Bohinj, the scenic caves at Postojna and Škocjan, the lush Soča Valley, the coastal towns of Piran and Koper and thriving Ljubljana are great attractions. All are accessible at much less than the cost of similar places in Western Europe. The amazing variety that is packed into one small area makes this country truly a 'Europe in miniature'. An added bonus is that Slovenia is a nation of polyglots, and communicating with these friendly, helpful people is never difficult.

# Facts about Slovenia

## HISTORY

The early Slovenes settled in the river valleys of the Danube Basin and the eastern Alps during the 6th century AD. Slovenia was brought under Germanic rule in 748, initially by the Frankish empire of the Carolingians, who converted the population to Christianity, and then as part of the Holy Roman Empire in the 9th century. The Austro-German monarchy took over control in the early 14th century and ruled (as the Habsburg Empire from 1804) right up until the end of WWI in 1918 – with only one brief interruption.

Over those six centuries, the upper classes became totally Germanised, though the peasantry retained their Slovenian identity. The Bible was translated into the vernacular during the Reformation in 1584, but Slovene did not come into common usage as a written language until the early 19th century.

In 1809, in a bid to isolate the Habsburg Empire from the Adriatic, Napoleon set up the Illyrian Provinces (Slovenia, Dalmatia and part of Croatia) with Ljubljana as the capital. Though the Habsburgs returned in 1814, French reforms in education, law and public administration endured. The democratic revolution that swept Europe in 1848 also brought increased political and national consciousness among Slovenes and, following WWI and the dissolution of the Austro-Hungarian Empire,

SLOVENIA

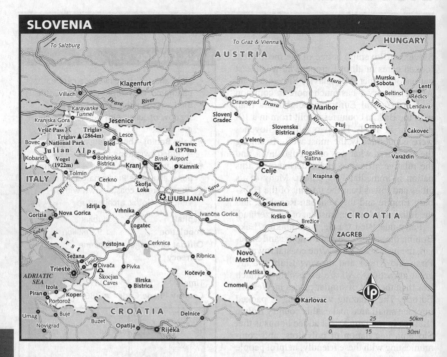

Slovenia was included in the Kingdom of Serbs, Croats and Slovenes.

During WWII much of Slovenia was annexed by Germany, with Italy and Hungary taking smaller bits of territory. The Slovenian Partisans fought courageously from mountain bases against the invaders, and Slovenia joined the Socialist Federal Republic of Yugoslavia in 1945.

Moves by Serbia in the late 1980s to assert its leading role culturally and economically among the Yugoslav republics was a big concern to Slovenes. When Belgrade abruptly ended the autonomy of Kosovo (where 90% of the population is ethnically Albanian) in late 1988, Slovenes feared the same could happen to them. For some years, Slovenia's interests had been shifting to the capitalist west and north; the Yugoslav connection, on the other hand, had become not only an economic burden but a political threat as well.

In the spring of 1990, Slovenia became the first Yugoslav republic to hold free elections and shed 45 years of communist rule; in December the electorate voted by 88% in favour of independence. The Slovenian government began stockpiling weapons, and on 25 June 1991 it pulled the republic out of the Yugoslav Federation. Slovenia took control of the border crossings and a 10-day war ensued. Resistance from the Slovenian militia was determined and, as no territorial claims or minority issues were involved, the Yugoslav government agreed to a truce brokered by the European Community (EC).

Slovenia got a new constitution in late December 1991, and on 15 January 1992 the EC formally recognised the country. Slovenia was admitted to the UN in May 1992 and is currently negotiating to become a member of the EU. Accession is expected to be granted in January 2004.

## GEOGRAPHY

Slovenia is wedged between Austria and Croatia and shares much shorter borders with Italy and Hungary. With an area of just 20,256 sq km, Slovenia is the smallest country in Eastern Europe, about the size of Wales or Israel. Much of the country is mountainous, culminating in the northwest with the Julian Alps and the nation's highest peak, Mt Triglav (2864m). From this jagged knot, the main Alpine chain continues east along the Austrian border, while the Dinaric Range runs southeast along the coast into Croatia.

Below the limestone plateau of the Karst region lying between Ljubljana and Koper is Europe's most extensive network of karst caverns, which gave their name to other such caves around the world.

The coastal range forms a barrier isolating the Istrian Peninsula from Slovenia's corner of the Danube Basin. Much of the interior east of the Alps is drained by the Sava and Drava Rivers, both of which empty into the Danube. The Soča flows through western Slovenia into the Adriatic.

## CLIMATE

Slovenia is temperate with four distinct seasons, but topography creates three individual climates. The northwest has an alpine climate with strong influences from the Atlantic as well as abundant precipitation. Temperatures in the Alpine valleys are moderate in summer but cold in winter. The coast and western Slovenia, as far north as the Soča Valley, have a Mediterranean climate with mild, sunny weather much of the year, though the *burja*, a cold and dry northeasterly wind from the Adriatic, can be fierce at times. Most of eastern Slovenia has a continental climate with hot summers and cold winters.

Most of the rain falls in March and April and again in October and November. January is the coldest month with an average temperature of -2°C and July the warmest (21°C).

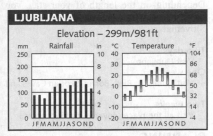

## ECOLOGY & ENVIRONMENT

Slovenia is a very green country – over half its total area is covered in forest – and is home to 2900 plant species; Triglav National Park is particularly rich in indigenous flowering plants. Common European animals (deer, boar, chamois) abound, and rare species include *Proteus anguinus*, the unique 'human fish' that inhabits pools in karst caves.

## GOVERNMENT & POLITICS

Slovenia's constitution provides for a parliamentary system of government. The National Assembly, which has exclusive jurisdiction over passing of laws, consists of 90 deputies elected for four years by proportional representation. The 40 members of the advisory Council of State are elected for five-year terms by regions and special-interest groups. The head of state, the president, is elected directly for a maximum of two five-year terms. Executive power is vested in the prime minister and the 15-member cabinet.

In parliamentary elections in November 2000, a centrist alliance of the Liberal Democrats, the People's Party, Social-Democrats and the Democratic Party of Pensioners of Slovenia garnered more than two-thirds of the vote, seating 62 MPs. Liberal Democrat Party leader Janez Drnovšek, prime minister from the first elections in 1992, again was elected head of government. Milan Kučan – a former Communist, elected as Slovenia's first president in November 1992, received a second five-year term in 1997. The most recent presidential elections were held during November 2002.

## ECONOMY

Slovenia has emerged as one of the strongest economies of the former socialist countries of Eastern Europe in the years since independence. Inflation has dropped, employment is on the rise and the per-capita GDP has hovered around US$10,000 for the past few years.

For many Slovenes, however, the economic picture remains unclear. Real wages continue to grow – but faster than inflation, which puts Slovenia's international competitiveness at a disadvantage. Inflation rocketed up to 200% after independence and has steadily declined since; it is currently at 8.4%. The official unemployment rate is around 8%.

## POPULATION & PEOPLE

Slovenia was the most homogeneous of all the Yugoslav republics; about 88% of the population are Slovenes. About 5% of the population is considered Croat, Serbian or Bosnian (mostly recent immigrants) and small ethnic enclaves of Italians (3000) and Hungarians (8500) still live in border areas. Some towns are officially bilingual; you'll see Italian in Piran, Koper and Portorož, and Magyar (Hungarian) in Murska Sobota and

Lendava. There are some 2300 Roma (Gypsies), mostly in the northeast.

## ARTS

Slovenia's best-loved writer is the Romantic poet France Prešeren (1800–49), whose lyric poetry set new standards for Slovenian literature and helped to raise national the consciousness. Disappointed in love, Prešeren wrote sensitive love poems but also satirical verse and epic poetry.

Many notable bridges, squares and buildings in Ljubljana and elsewhere in Slovenia were designed by the architect Jože Plečnik (1872–1957), who studied under Otto Wagner in Vienna.

Postmodernist painting and sculpture has been more or less dominated since the 1980s by the multimedia group Neue Slowenische Kunst (NSK) and the five-member artists' cooperative IRWIN. Avante-garde dance is best exemplified by Betontanc, an NSK dance company that mixes live music and theatrical elements (called 'physical theatre' here) with sharp political comment.

Since WWII, many Slovenian folk traditions have been lost, but compilations by the trio Trutamora Slovenica (available at music shops in Ljubljana) examine the roots of Slovenian folk music. Folk groups – both 'pure' and popular – to watch out for include the Avseniki, Ansambel Lojzeta Slaka, the Alpski Kvintet led by Oto Pestner, and the Roma band Šukar.

Popular music runs the gamut from Slovenian *chanson* (best exemplified by Vita Mavrič) and folk to jazz and techno. Three punk groups from the late 1970s and early 1980s, Pankrti, Borghesia and Laibach, hailed from Slovenia.

Literature is extremely important to Slovenes; the last census marked a 99.6% literacy rate. Popular fiction writers include Drago Jančar and Boris Pahor. *Afterwards: Slovenian Writing 1945–1995*, edited by Andrew Zawacki, showcases the talents of the modern Slovenian *literati* (available in English at all large Ljubljana bookshops).

## RELIGION

About 70% of Slovenes consider themselves Roman Catholic, but churches are hardly full on Sunday. Most weddings are now civil ceremonies. Yugoslav immigrants have brought a small Muslim population of about 5%.

## LANGUAGE

Slovene is a South Slavic language written in the Roman alphabet and closely related to Croatian and Serbian. It is grammatically complex with lots of cases, genders and tenses and has something that is very rare in linguistics: singular, dual and plural forms. It's one *miza* (table) and three or more *mize* (tables) but two *mizi*.

Virtually everyone in Slovenia is able to speaks at least one other language: Croatian, Serbian, German, English and/or Italian. English is definitely the preferred language of the young.

See the Language section at the end of the book for pronunciation guidelines and useful words and phrases. Lonely Planet's *Eastern Europe phrasebook* contains a chapter on Slovene.

# Facts for the Visitor

## HIGHLIGHTS

Ljubljana, Piran and Koper have outstanding architecture; the hill-top castles at Bled and Ljubljana are impressive. The Škocjan and Postojna Caves are among the world's foremost underground wonders. The Soča Valley is indescribably beautiful in spring, while the frescoed Church of St John the Baptist is in itself worth the trip to Lake Bohinj.

## SUGGESTED ITINERARIES

Depending on the length of your stay, you might want to see and do the following in Slovenia:

**Two days**
  Visit Ljubljana
**One week**
  Visit Ljubljana, Bled, Bohinj, Škocjan Caves and Piran
**Two weeks**
  Visit all the places covered in this chapter

## PLANNING
## When to Go

Snow can linger in the mountains as late as June, but May and June are great months to be in the lowlands and valleys when everything is fresh and in blossom. (April can be a bit wet though.) In July and August, hotel rates go up and there will be lots of tourists, especially on the coast, but all the youth hostels are open. September is an excellent month to visit as the days are long and the weather still warm, and it's the best time for hiking and climbing. October and November can be quite rainy, and winter (December to March) is definitely for skiers.

## Maps

The Geodesic Institute of Slovenia (Geodetski Zavod Slovenije; GZS), the country's principal cartographic agency, produces national (1:300,000), regional (1:50,000) and topographical maps of the entire country (64 sheets at a scale of 1:50,000) as well as city plans. The Alpine Association of Slovenia (Planinska Zveza Slovenije; PZS) has some 30 different hiking maps, with scales as large as 1:25,000.

## TOURIST OFFICES
## Local Tourist Offices

Located in the World Trade Centre, the **Slovenian Tourist Board** (STO; ☎ 01-589 18 40, fax 589 18 41; ⓦ www.slovenia-tourism.si; Dunajska cesta 156) is the umbrella organisation for tourist offices in Slovenia. It handles requests for information in writing or you can check out its excellent website.

The best office for face-to-face information in Slovenia is the **Ljubljana Tourist Information Centre** (TIC). Most of the destinations that are described in this chapter have some form of tourist office but if the place you're visiting doesn't, seek some assistance at a branch of one of the big travel agencies (eg, Kompas or Globtour) or from museum or from hotel staff. You can find comprehensive sites on most towns in this chapter on the Internet by typing in the city name, such as ⓦ www .ljubljana.si or ⓦ www.ptuj.si.

## Tourist Offices Abroad

The Slovenian Tourist Board maintains tourist offices in the following countries:

**Austria** (☎ 01-715 4010, fax 713 8177) Hilton Center, Landstrasser Hauptstrasse 2, 1030 Vienna
**Croatia** (☎ 01-457 2118, fax 457 7921, ⓔ kompas-zagreb@zg.tel.hr) Hotel Esplanade, Mihanovičeva 1, 10000 Zagreb
**Germany** (☎ 089-2916 1202, fax 2916 1273, ⓔ slowenien.fva@t-online.de) Maximiliansplatz 12a, 80333 Munich
**Hungary** (☎ 1-269 6879, fax 268 1454, ⓔ tourism.and.travel@kompas.hu) Rakoczi ut 14, 1072 Budapest

**Italy** (☎ 022 951 1187, fax 022 951 4071, ⓔ slovenia@tin.it) Galeria Buenos Aires 1, 20124 Milan
**Netherlands & Belgium** (☎ 010-465 3003, fax 465 7514, ⓔ kompasnl@euronet.nl) Benthuizerstraat 29, 3036 CB Rotterdam
**Switzerland** (☎ 01-212 6394, fax 212 5266, ⓔ adria.slo@bluewin.ch) Löwenstrasse 54, 8001 Zürich
**UK** (☎ 020-7287 7133, fax 7287 5476, ⓔ slovenia@cpts.fsbusiness.co.uk) 49 Conduit St, London W1S 2YS
**USA** (☎ 212-358 9686, 358 9025, ⓔ slotouristboard@sloveniatravel.com) 345 East 12th St, New York, NY 10003

In addition, the Kompas travel agency has representative offices in many cities around the world, including:

**Canada** (☎ 514-938 4041) 4060 Ste-Catherine St West, Suite 535, Montreal, Que H3Z 2Z3
**France** (☎ 01-53 92 27 80) 14 Rue de la Source, 75016 Paris
**USA** (☎ 954-771 9200) 2929 East Commercial Blvd, Suite 201, Ft Lauderdale, FL 33306

## VISAS & DOCUMENTS

Passport-holders from Australia, Canada, Israel, Japan, New Zealand, Switzerland, USA and EU countries do not require visas for stays in Slovenia of up to 90 days; those from the EU as well as Switzerland can also enter on a national identity card for a stay of up to 30 days. Citizens of other countries requiring visas (including South Africans) can get them at any Slovenian embassy or consulate. They cost the equivalent of €20 for a single entry and €40 for multiple entries.

## EMBASSIES & CONSULATES
## Slovenian Embassies & Consulates

Slovenia has diplomatic representation in the following countries; the website ⓦ www.gov .si/mzz/eng contains further listings.

**Australia** (☎ 02-6243 4830) Advance Bank Centre, Level 6, 60 Marcus Clark St, Canberra, ACT 2601
**Austria** (☎ 01-586 1309) Nibelungengasse 13, 1010 Vienna
**Canada** (☎ 613-565 5781) 150 Metcalfe St, Suite 2101, Ottawa, Ontario K2P 1P1
**Croatia** (☎ 01-631 1000) Savska cesta 41/IX, 10000 Zagreb
**Germany** (☎ 030-206 1450) Hausvogteiplatz 3-4, 10117 Berlin

SLOVENIA

Hungary (☎ 1-438 5600) Cseppkő ut 68, 1025 Budapest
Italy (☎ 068 091 4310) Via Leonardo Pisano 10, 00197 Rome
UK (☎ 020-7495 7775) Suite 1, Cavendish Court, 11-15 Wigmore St, London W1H 9LA
USA (☎ 202-667 5363) 1525 New Hampshire Ave NW, Washington, DC 20036

## Embassies & Consulates in Slovenia

Selected countries that have representation in Ljubljana (area code ☎ 01) appear in the following list. Citizens of countries not listed here should contact their embassies in Vienna or Budapest.

Albania (☎ 432 23 24) Ob Ljubljanici 12
Australia (☎ 425 42 52) Trg Republike 3/XII
Austria (☎ 479 07 00) Prešernova cesta 23
Bosnia-Hercegovina (☎ 432 40 42) Kolarjeva 26
Canada (☎ 430 35 70) Miklošičeva cesta 19
Croatia (☎ 425 62 20) Gruberjevo nab 6
France (☎ 426 45 25) Barjanska 1
Germany (☎ 251 61 66) Prešernova cesta 27
Hungary (☎ 512 18 82) ul Konrada Babnika 5
Ireland (☎ 308 12 34) temporary office at Grand Hotel Union, Miklošičeva cesta 1
Netherlands (☎ 420 14 61) Palača Kapitelj, Poljanski nasip 6
Romania (☎ 505 82 94) Podlimbarskega 43
Slovakia (☎ 425 54 25) Tivolska cesta 4
South Africa (☎ 200 63 00) Pražakova ul 4
UK (☎ 200 39 10) Trg Republike 3/IV
USA (☎ 200 55 00) Prešernova cesta 31

## CUSTOMS

Travellers are allowed to bring in the usual personal effects, a couple of cameras and electronic goods for their own use, as well as 200 cigarettes, a generous 4L of spirits and 1L of wine.

## MONEY
## Currency

Slovenia's currency, the tolar, is abbreviated as SIT. Prices in shops and restaurants, and train and bus fares are always in tolars, but because of inflation, a few hotels, guesthouses and even camping grounds use the euro. For that reason, some accommodation and a few other items are listed in this book in euros. You are always welcome to pay in tolars, though.

Money includes coins of one, two, five and 10 tolars and the banknotes are in denominations of 10, 20, 50, 100, 200, 500, 1000, 5000 and 10,000 tolars.

## Exchange Rates

Conversion rates for major currencies at the time of publication are listed below:

| country | unit | | tolar |
|---------|------|---|-------|
| Australia | A$1 | = | 135.65 SIT |
| Canada | C$1 | = | 155.21 SIT |
| euro zone | €1 | = | 228.88 SIT |
| Japan | ¥100 | = | 192.05 SIT |
| NZ | NZ$1 | = | 116.81 SIT |
| UK | UK£1 | = | 355.39 SIT |
| USA | US$1 | = | 237.10 SIT |

## Exchanging Money

**Cash & Travellers Cheques** It is simple to change cash at banks, travel agencies, any *menjalnica* (private exchange bureau) and certain post offices. Slovenia recently had a problem with travellers-cheque fraud, so it's difficult to exchange them, even at banks, but restaurants and hotels will still accept them.

There's no black market and exchange rates vary little, but watch out for a commission *(provizija)* of up to 3% tacked on by some tourist offices, hotels and travel agencies.

**ATMs & Credit Cards** Visa, MasterCard/ Eurocard and American Express credit cards are widely accepted at most restaurants, shops, hotels, car-rental firms and travel agencies; Diners Club less so.

Automated teller machines (ATMs) linked to Cirrus or Plus now blanket Slovenia; their locations are noted in the Information sections of the individual destinations. Clients of Visa can get cash advances in tolars from any A Banka branch; MasterCard and Eurocard can be used any branch of **Nova Ljubljanska Banka** *(☎ 01-425 01 55; Trg Republike 2, Ljubljana)*; and **American Express** *(☎ 01-431 90 20; Trubarjeva, Ljubljana).*

## Costs

Slovenia remains much cheaper than neighbouring Italy and Austria, but don't expect the low prices you'd see in Eastern European countries like Hungary or Bulgaria.

If you stay in private rooms or at guesthouses, eat at medium-priced restaurants and travel 2nd class on the train or by bus, you should get by for under US$40 a day. Staying at hostels or college dormitories, eating takeaway at lunch and at self-service restaurants at night will cut costs considerably.

Travelling in a little more style and comfort – occasional restaurant splurges with bottles of wine, an active nightlife, staying at small hotels or guesthouses with 'character' – will cost about US$65 a day.

## Tipping & Bargaining

Tipping isn't customary in Slovenia, but no-one's going to complain if you leave your change at the table in a restaurant.

Unlike some of its Eastern European neighbours, bargaining is not commonplace in Slovenia. You can try it at street markets, but you run the risk of offending someone.

## Taxes & Refunds

A 'circulation tax' (prometni davek) not unlike Value-Added Tax (VAT) applies to the purchase of most goods and services here. Visitors can claim refunds on total purchases of 15,000 SIT or more (certain tobacco products and spirits are exempt) through Kompas MTS, which has offices at Brnik airport and some two dozen border crossings. Ask for a DDV-VP form at the time of purchase.

Most towns and cities levy a 'tourist tax' on overnight visitors of between 150 SIT and 300 SIT per person per night (less at camping grounds), which is included in the prices listed in this chapter.

## POST & COMMUNICATIONS
## Post

Poste restante is sent to the main post office in a city or town (in the capital, it goes to the branch at Slovenska cesta 32, 1101 Ljubljana) where it is held for 30 days. American Express card-holders can have their mail addressed c/o Atlas Express, Trubarjeva cesta 50, 1000 Ljubljana.

Domestic mail costs 31 SIT for up to 20g and 56 SIT for up to 100g. Postcards are 31 SIT. For international mail, the base rate is 95 SIT for 20g or less, 221 SIT for up to 100g and 83 SIT to 107 SIT for a postcard, depending on the size. Then you have to add on the airmail charge: 30 SIT for every 10g. An aerogramme is 125 SIT.

## Telephone

The easiest place to make long-distance calls and send faxes and telegrams is from a post office or telephone centre; the one at Trg Osvobodilne Fronte (Trg OF) near the train and bus stations in Ljubljana is open 24 hours.

Public telephones on the street do not accept coins; they require a phonecard (telefonska kartica) available at all post offices and some newsstands.

Phonecards cost 700/1000/1700/3500 SIT for 25/50/100/300 pulses. A local one-minute call absorbs one pulse, and a three-minute call from Slovenia will cost about 126 SIT to most of Western Europe, the USA, Canada and Croatia; 162 SIT to Eastern Europe; 342 SIT to Australia; and 486 SIT to Japan, South Africa and New Zealand. International rates are 20% cheaper between 7pm and 7am Monday to Saturday, and all day Sunday.

The international access code in Slovenia is ☎ 00. The international operator or directory inquiries can be reached on ☎ 115. To call Slovenia from abroad dial the international access code, ☎ 386 (Slovenia's country code), the area code (without the initial zero, eg, 1 in Ljubljana) followed by the number.

## Email & Internet Access

There is now an Internet café in almost every town in Slovenia. Ljubljana has 11 places to check your email. If you can't find an Internet café (in Ptuj, for example), try the local university or library. They will usually let travellers log on to the Internet for free or at little cost.

## DIGITAL RESOURCES

The official Slovenian tourist information website is Ⓦ www.slovenia-tourism.si. You can find information on accommodation, traffic conditions, the different regions etc.

The site Ⓦ www.matkurja.com is a comprehensive overview of Slovenian websites, including resources for travellers. Many sites are in English.

See the Digital Resources section in the Ljubljana section for more useful websites.

## BOOKS

Books can be expensive in Slovenia. Lonely Planet's Slovenia is the only complete and independent English-language guide to this country. Discover Slovenia, published annually by the Cankarjeva Založba bookshop in Ljubljana (3500 SIT), is a colourful and easy introduction available in seven languages, including English, German, and French, and Zoë Brân's After Yugoslavia, part of the Lonely Planet Journeys series, retraces the author's 1978 trip through the former Yugoslavia.

SLOVENIA

## NEWSPAPERS & MAGAZINES

Slovenia publishes four daily newspapers, the most widely read being *Delo* (Work), *Večer* (Evening) and *Slovenske Novice* (a tabloid with Slovenian news). The entertainment and culture magazine *Ljubljana Life* is published monthly and is available in hotels and at the TIC. There are no local English-language newspapers, though the *International Herald Tribune*, *Guardian International*, *Financial Times* and *USA Today* are available in the afternoon on the day of publication at hotels and department stores in Ljubljana.

## RADIO & TV

News, weather, traffic and tourist information in English, German and Italian follows the Slovene-language news, on Radio Slovenija 1 during the weekends in July and August. Also in July and August, Radio Slovenija 1 and 2 broadcast a report on the weather, including conditions on the sea and in the mountains, in the same languages. There's a nightly news bulletin in English and German at 10.30pm throughout the year on Radio 1. Most Slovene hotels have English- or German-language cable channels.

## TIME

Slovenia is one hour ahead of GMT/UTC. The country goes onto summer time (GMT/UTC plus two hours) on the last Sunday in March when clocks are advanced by one hour. On the last Sunday in October they're turned back one hour.

## LAUNDRY

Commercial laundrettes are rare in Slovenia. The best places to look for do-it-yourself washers and dryers are hostels, college dormitories and camping grounds, and there are a couple of places in Ljubljana that will do your laundry reasonably quickly (see Laundry under Information in the Ljubljana section).

## PHOTOGRAPHY

Film is plentiful and fairly inexpensive in Slovenia. A roll of 24 exposures costs about 900 SIT.

## WOMEN TRAVELLERS

Women are unlikely to encounter problems while travelling in Slovenia. Crime is low and harassment is rare. There is a **women's crisis helpline** (☎ 080 11 55) for emergencies.

---

### Emergency Services

In the event of an emergency call ☎ 113 for the police and ☎ 112 for the fire, first aid or ambulance services.

The automobile assistance (AMZS) information number is ☎ 530 53 00. For road emergency and towing services ring ☎ 1987. These numbers can be dialled nationwide.

---

## GAY & LESBIAN TRAVELLERS

The gay association **Roza Klub** (☎ 01-430 47 40; Kersnikova ul 4, Ljubljana), organises a disco every Sunday night at Klub K4 in Ljubljana. Roza Klub is made up of a gay branch of the S/vKUC (Student Cultural Centre), Magnus, as well as a lesbian branch, LL (the same contact details as Roza Klub).

The **GALfon** (☎ 01-432 40 89) is a hotline and source of general information for gays and lesbians. It operates daily from 7pm to 10pm. The **Slovenian Queer Resources Directory** (Ⓦ www.ljudmila.org/siqrd) leaves no stone unturned.

Gay and lesbian travellers should encounter no major problems in Slovenia.

## DISABLED TRAVELLERS

Slovenia's government is currently working on making public spaces more accessible to the disabled, but it's still a pretty tough go. A group that looks after the interests and special needs of physically challenged people is the **Zveza Paraplegikov Republike Slovenije** (ZPRS; ☎ 01-432 71 38) in Ljubljana.

## SENIOR TRAVELLERS

Senior citizens may be entitled to discounts in Slovenia on things like museum admission fees, provided they show proof of age.

## DANGERS & ANNOYANCES

Slovenia is hardly a violent or dangerous place. Police say that 90% of all crimes reported involve theft so travellers should take the usual precautions. Bike theft is fairly common in Ljubljana.

## BUSINESS HOURS

Shops, groceries and department stores open 7.30am or 8am to 7pm on weekdays and to 1pm on Saturday. Bank hours are generally 8am to 4.30pm or 5pm on weekdays (often with a lunch break) and till noon on Saturday.

Main post offices are open 7am to 8pm on weekdays, till 1pm on Saturday and occasionally 9am to 11am on Sunday.

## PUBLIC HOLIDAYS & SPECIAL EVENTS

Public holidays in Slovenia include two days at New Year (1 and 2 January), National Culture Day (8 February), Easter Sunday and Monday (March/April), Insurrection Day (27 April), two days for Labour Day (1 and 2 May), National Day (25 June), Assumption Day (15 August), Reformation Day (31 October), All Saints' Day (1 November), Christmas (25 December) and Independence Day (26 December).

Though cultural events are scheduled throughout the year, the highlights of the Slovenian summer season (July and August) are the International Summer Festival in Ljubljana; the Piran Musical Evenings; the Primorska Summer Festival at Piran, Koper, Izola and Portorož in July; and Summer in the Old Town in Ljubljana, with three or four cultural events a week taking place.

## ACTIVITIES
### Skiing

Skiing is by far the most popular sport in Slovenia, and every fourth Slovene is an active skier. The country has many well-equipped ski resorts in the Julian Alps, especially Vogel (skiing up to 1840m) above Lake Bohinj, Kranjska Gora (1600m), Kanin (2300m) above Bovec, and Krvavec (1970m), north-east of Kranj.

All these resorts have multiple chairlifts, cable cars, ski schools, equipment rentals and large resort hotels.

### Hiking

Hiking is almost as popular as skiing in Slovenia, and there are approximately 7000km of marked trails and 165 mountain huts. Visitors can experience the full grandeur of the Julian Alps in the Triglav National Park at Lake Bohinj, and for the veteran mountaineer there's the Slovenian Alpine Trail, which crosses all the highest peaks in the country.

### Kayaking, Canoeing & Rafting

The best white-water rafting is on the Soča, one of only half a dozen rivers in the European Alps whose upper waters are still unspoiled. The centre is at Bovec.

### Fishing

Slovenia's rivers and Alpine lakes and streams are teeming with trout, grayling, pike and other fish. The best rivers for angling are the Soča, the Krka, the Kolpa and the Sava Bohinjka near Bohinj. Lake fishing is good at Bled and Bohinj.

### Cycling

Mountain bikes are available for hire at Bled and Bohinj. You can also rent bikes on the coast and in Ljubljana.

## WORK

Employment of foreigners in Slovenia is among the most restricted in Europe. Even foreign businesses have difficulty obtaining working visas for their employees. This is likely to change when Slovenia is accepted into the EU, expected 1 January 2004. Legislation will be changed to reflect that in the more liberalized EU countries.

## ACCOMMODATION
### Camping

In summer, camping is the cheapest way to go, and you'll find there are convenient camping grounds all over the country. You don't always need a tent as some camping grounds have inexpensive bungalows or caravans. Two of the best camping grounds are Zlatorog on Lake Bohinj and Jezero Fiesa near Piran, though they can be very crowded in summer. It is forbidden to camp 'rough' in Slovenia.

### Hostels & Student Dormitories

Slovenia has only a handful of 'official' hostels, including two in Ljubljana and excellent ones in Bled and Piran, but many others aren't open year-round. You'll find that some college dormitories accept travellers in the summer months.

### Private Rooms & Apartments

Private rooms arranged by tourist offices and travel agencies can be inexpensive, but a surcharge of up to 50% is often levied on stays of less than three nights. You can often bargain for rooms without the surcharge by going directly to any house with a sign reading 'sobe' (rooms).

### Pensions & Guesthouses

A small guesthouse (called a penzion or gostišče) can be good value, though in July and

August you may be required to take at least one meal and the rates are higher.

## Farmhouses

The agricultural cooperatives of Slovenia have organised a unique program to accommodate visitors on working farms. Prices are about 3500 SIT per night for bed and breakfast (30% more if less than a two-night stay) to about 5000 SIT per night with full-board during high season (July, August and around Christmas). Contact the **Association of Tourist Farms of Slovenia** (☎ 03-491 64 80; ℮ ztks@siol.net). Bookings can be made through **ABC Farm & Countryside Holidays** (☎ 01-507 61 27, fax 519 98 76; Ul Jožeta Jame 16, Ljubljana).

## Hotels

Hotel rates vary according to the time of year, with July and August the peak season and May/June and September/October the shoulder seasons. In Ljubljana, prices are constant all year. Many hotels in Slovenia includes breakfast in the price, and many offer free admission or discounts to the spa in town.

## FOOD

Slovenian cuisine is heavily influenced by the food of its neighbours. From Austria, there's *klobasa* (sausage), *zavitek* (strudel) and *Dunajski zrezek* (Wiener schnitzel). *Njoki* (potato dumplings), *rižota* (risotto) and the ravioli-like *žlikrofi* are obviously Italian, and Hungary has contributed *golaž* (goulash), *paprikaš* (chicken or beef 'stew') and *palačinke* (thin pancakes filled with jam or nuts and topped with chocolate). And then there's that old Balkan stand-by, *burek*, a greasy, layered cheese, meat or even apple pie served at takeaway places everywhere.

No Slovenian meal can be considered complete without soup, be it the very simple *goveja juha z rezanci* (beef broth with little egg noodles), *zelenjavna juha* (vegetable soup) or *gobova juha* (mushroom soup). There are several types of Slovenian dumplings called *štruklji* that are made with various types of local cheese.

Also try the baked delicacies, including *potica* (walnut roll) and *gibanica* (pastry filled with poppy seeds, walnuts, apple and/ or sultanas and cottage cheese and topped with cream). Traditional dishes are best tried at an inn (*gostilna* or *gostišče*).

Many restaurants have set lunches for 900 to 1600 SIT. These can be great value, as some are upmarket restaurants where dinner can cost three or four times as much.

## DRINKS

Wine-growing regions of Slovenia are Podravje in the east, noted for such white wines as Renski Rizling (a true German Riesling), Beli Pinot (Pinot Blanc) and Traminec (Traminer); Posavje in the southeast (try the distinctly Slovenian light-red Cviček); and the area around the coast, which produces a hearty red called Teran made from Refošk grapes. *Vinska cesta* means 'wine road', and wherever you see one of these signs, you'll find wineries and vineyards open for tasting. They cover the area around Maribor, where it's said that every house has its own vineyard.

*Žganje* is a strong brandy or *eau de vie* that is distilled from a variety of fruits, but most commonly plums. The finest brandy is Pleterska Hruška, made from pears.

## SPECTATOR SPORTS

For skiing enthusiasts, World Cup slalom and giant slalom events are held at Kranjska Gora in late December. In early January, women's World Cup skiing takes place in Maribor.

## SHOPPING

Slovenia isn't famous for its handicrafts, but there are some beautiful things available, especially antiques. Every Sunday, the **antique flea market** takes place along the Ljubljanica River. You'll find furniture, stamps, art, knickknacks and every imaginable item. Most of the best craft stores, including **Dom** and **365,** and the best antique shops can be found on Mestni trg (square) near the Town Hall.

# Getting There & Away

## AIR

Slovenia's national air carrier, **Adria Airways** (in Ljubljana ☎ 01-231 33 12, at Brnik airport ☎ 04-202 51 11; ⓦ www.adria.si) has nonstop flights to Ljubljana from cities including Amsterdam, Brussels, Copenhagen, Frankfurt, İstanbul, London, Moscow, Munich, Ohrid, Paris, Sarajevo, Skopje, Split, Tirana, Vienna and Zürich. You can check out the website for the schedules. From May to October, Adria flies to Dublin, Manchester and Tel Aviv.

Lufthansa flies from Frankfurt and Munich and Swiss from Zürich.

## LAND
### Bus

Buses from Ljubljana serve a number of international destinations, including the following cities and towns: Belgrade (7100 to 7400 SIT, three daily); Frankfurt (17,550 SIT, daily at 7.30pm); Munich (7900 SIT, daily at 7.30pm); Rijeka (2880 SIT, daily at 7.40pm); Split (7140 SIT, daily at 7.40pm); Trieste (2110 SIT, daily at 6.25am) and Zagreb (2570 SIT, three daily).

**Italy** Nova Gorica is the easiest departure point from Slovenia to Italy, as you can catch up to five buses a day to/from the Italian city of Gorizia or simply walk across the border at Rožna Dolina. Take one of 17 daily buses (2020 SIT). Koper also has good connections with Italy – some 17 buses a day on weekdays go to/from Trieste, 21km to the northeast. There's also a daily bus from Trieste to Ljubljana (2110 SIT, daily at 6.25am).

**Hungary** There is no direct bus that links Ljubljana to Budapest. Instead, take one of up to five daily buses to Lendava; the Hungarian border is 5km to the north. The first Hungarian train station, Rédics, is only 2km beyond the border.

### Train

The main train routes into Slovenia from Austria are Vienna/Graz to Maribor and Ljubljana and Salzburg to Jesenice. Tickets cost 8000 SIT from Ljubljana to Salzburg (four hours) and 11,558 SIT to Vienna (six hours). But it's cheaper to take a local train to Maribor (1380 SIT) and buy your ticket on to Vienna from there. Similarly, from Austria you should only buy a ticket as far as Jesenice or Maribor, as domestic fares are much lower than the international fares.

There are three trains a day between Munich and Ljubljana (12,806 SIT, seven hours). Take the EuroCity *Mimara* via Salzburg or the *Lisinski* express, which leaves at 11.30pm (a sleeping carriage is available). A 1000 SIT supplement is payable on the *Mimara*. Seat reservations (600 SIT) are available on both.

Two trains a day travel from Trieste to Ljubljana (4400 SIT, three hours) via the towns of Divača and Sežana. From Croatia it's Zagreb to Ljubljana (2500 SIT, 2½ hours) via Zidani Most, or Rijeka to Ljubljana (2099 SIT, 2½ hours) via Pivka. The InterCity *Drava* and *Venezia Express* trains link Ljubljana with Budapest (9900 SIT, eight hours, two daily) via northwestern Croatia and Zagreb respectively. Three trains a day go to Belgrade (8000 SIT).

### Border Crossings

Slovenia maintains some 150 border crossings with Italy, Austria, Hungary and Croatia, but only 26 are considered international or interstate crossings. The rest are minor crossings only open to Slovenian citizens or others with special permits.

### SEA

From late March to November on Friday, Saturday and Sunday, the *Prince of Venice*, a 39m Australian-made catamaran seating some 330 passengers, sails between Izola and Venice (return ticket 15,000/13,500/9500 SIT high/shoulder/off season). The boat departs from Izola at 8am and returns at 5.30pm. There's an additional sailing on Tuesday and Saturday in July and August. The price of the boat trip includes a sightseeing tour in Venice. From Izola there are frequent buses to Portorož, Piran and Koper. Another catamaran, the *Marconi*, links Trieste with Piran (see Cruises in the Piran section).

### DEPARTURE TAX

A departure tax of 2700 SIT is levied on all passengers leaving Slovenia by air, though this is almost always included in your airline ticket price.

# Getting Around

## BUS

Except for long journeys, the bus is preferable to the train in Slovenia. Departures are frequent. In some cases you don't have much of a choice; travelling by bus is the only practical way to get from Ljubljana to Bled and Bohinj, the Julian Alps and much of the coast.

In Ljubljana you can buy your ticket with seat reservation (600 SIT, depending on the destination) the day before, but many people simply pay the driver on boarding. The one time you really might need a reservation is Friday afternoon, when many students travel from Ljubljana to their homes or people leave the city for the weekend. There is a 220 SIT charge for each bag placed underneath the bus.

Useful footnotes that you might see on the Slovenian bus schedules include: *vozi vsak dan* (runs daily); *vozi ob delavnikih* (runs on working days – Monday to Friday); *vozi ob sobotah* (runs on Saturday); and *vozi ob nedeljah in praznikih* (runs only on Sunday and holidays).

### TRAIN
Slovenske Železnice (SŽ; Slovenian Railways) operates on just over 1200km of track. The country's most scenic rail routes run along the Soča River from Jesenice to Nova Gorica via Bled (Bled Jezero station) and Bohinjska Bistrica (89km) and from Ljubljana to Zagreb (160km) along the Sava River.

On posted timetables in Slovenia, *odhod* or *odhodi vlakov* means 'departures' and *prihod* (or *prihodi vlakov*) is 'arrivals'. If you don't have time to buy a ticket, seek out the conductor who will sell you one for an extra charge of 200 SIT.

### CAR & MOTORCYCLE
Even though it's a small country, having your own wheels will help if you're planning some outdoor activities, as the buses don't run frequently off the beaten path. The use of seat belts in the front seats is compulsory in Slovenia, and a new law requires all vehicles to have their headlights on throughout the day outside built-up areas. Speed limits for cars are 50km/h in built-up areas, 90km/h on secondary roads, 100km/h on main highways and 130km/h on motorways.

Tolls are payable on several motorways, but they're not terribly expensive. For example, Ljubljana to Postojna will cost 440 SIT. Petrol remains relatively cheap: 187.00/195.20 SIT per litre for 95/98 octane (both unleaded). Diesel costs 154.60 SIT.

Slovenia's automobile club, the **Avto Moto Zveza Slovenije** (*AMZS;* ☎ *01-530 53 00*), may be a helpful contact.

The permitted blood-alcohol level for motorists is 0.05% or 0.5g/kg of blood (the level is zero for professional drivers) and the law is strictly enforced. Anything over that could earn you a fine of 25,000 SIT and one to three demerit points.

### Car Rental
Car rentals from international firms like Avis, National, Budget and Kompas Hertz vary widely in price, but expect to pay from about 14,750/73,920 SIT a day/week with unlimited mileage, collision damage waiver, theft protection and personal accident insurance for a compact (like a Ford Fiesta). Add 20% VAT.

Some car-rental agencies have minimum-age rules (21 or 23 years) and/or require that you've had a valid licence for one or even two years. Three international chains are **Kompas Hertz** (☎ *01-231 12 41; Miklošičeva ul 11*), **National** (☎ *01- 588 44 50; Baragova ul 5*) and **Avis** (☎ *01- 430 80 10; Čufarjeva ul 2*). They also have counters at the airport. Two excellent smaller agencies, with more competitive rates, are **ABC Rent a Car** (☎ *04-236 79 90; open 24hr*) at Brnik airport and **Avtoimpex** (☎ *01- 519 72 97; Celovška cesta 252*) in Ljubljana.

### HITCHING
Hitchhiking is legal everywhere except on motorways and some major highways and is generally easy; even young women do it. But hitching is never a totally safe way of getting around and, although we mention it as an option, we don't recommend it.

# Ljubljana

☎ 01 • pop 280,000

Ljubljana (Laibach in German) is by far the largest and most populous city in Slovenia. However, in many ways the city, the name of which almost means 'beloved' *(ljubljena)* in Slovene, doesn't feel like an industrious municipality of national importance but a pleasant, self-contented town with responsibilities only to itself and its citizens. The most beautiful parts of the city are the Old Town below the castle and the embankments designed by Plečnik, along the narrow Ljubljanica River.

Ljubljana began as the Roman town of Emona, and legacies of the Roman presence can still be seen throughout the city. The Habsburgs took control of Ljubljana in the 14th century and later built many of the pale-coloured churches and mansions that earned the city the nickname 'White Ljubljana'. From 1809 to 1814 Ljubljana was the capital of the Illyrian Provinces, Napoleon's short-lived springboard to the Adriatic.

Despite the patina of imperial Austria, contemporary Ljubljana has a vibrant Slavic air all its own. It's like a little Prague without the hordes of tourists but with all the facilities you'll need. Almost 50,000 students attend Ljubljana University's 20 faculties and three art academies, so the city always feels young.

## Orientation

The tiny bus station and renovated train station are opposite each other on the square Trg Osvobodilne Fronte (known as Trg OF) at the northern end of the town centre (called Center).

## Information

**Tourist Offices** The Ljubljana **Tourist Information Centre** (TIC; ☎ 306 12 15, fax 306 12 04; e pcl.tic-lj@ljubljana.si; Stritarjeva ul 2; open 8am-8pm Mon-Fri, 10am-6pm Sat, Sun & holidays in summer; to 6pm daily low season) is in the historical Kresija building southeast of Triple Bridge. The **branch office** (☎/fax 433 94 75; open 9am-9pm daily in summer, 10am-5.30pm Mon-Fri Oct-May) is at the train station. The TIC is worth visiting to pick up free maps and brochures, organise sightseeing trips or inquire about accommodation options.

The main office of the **Alpine Association of Slovenia** (☎ 134 30 22; W www.pzs.si; Dvoržakova ul 9) is in a small house set back from the street. It can help plan trekking or hiking trips anywhere in the country, including the Julian Alps.

**Money** There are more than 50 ATMs in Ljubljana. Many are in the Center, including an **A Banka** (Trg Osvobodilne Fronte 2) opposite the train station and another one at Slovenska 58 (where card-holders can get cash advances). There are branches of Banka Koper outside the Globtour agency in the Maximarket passageway connecting Trg Republike with Plečnikov trg and at Cigaletova ul 4.

You can get cash advances on MasterCard at **Nova Ljubljanska Banka** (Trg Republike 2; open 8am-5pm Mon-Fri, 9am-noon Sat). Next to the SKB Banka on Trg Ajdovščina is a currency exchange machine that changes the banknotes of 18 countries into tolar at a good rate. **Hida exchange bureau** (Pogarčarjev trg 1; open 7am-7pm Mon-Fri, 7am-2pm Sat) is inside the Seminary building near the open-air market.

**Post & Communications** Poste-restante mail will only be held for 30 days at the **post office** (☎ 426 46 68; Slovenska cesta 32; postal code 1101; open 7am-8pm Mon-Fri, 7am-1pm Sat). Make international telephone calls or send faxes from here or the **main post office** (Pražakova ul 3; same hours).

To mail a parcel you must go to the **special customs post office** (Trg OF 5; open 24hr) opposite the bus station. Do not seal your package until after it has been inspected; the maximum weight is about 15kg, depending on the destination.

**Email & Internet Access** Internet access is free at **Klub K4 Café** (☎ 431 70 10; Kersnikova ul 4). **Cyber Café** (Slovenska cesta 10) sells drinks and has five terminals for 200/400/600 SIT for 15/30/60 minutes; students pay half price.

**Kavarna Čerin** (☎ 232 09 90, Trubarjeva 52) is a full-service café with free Internet access (and peanuts) for the purchase of a drink. Hotel Turist (see Places to Stay later in this section) has an Internet connection, free for guests, 220 SIT per 20 minutes for all others (available 24 hours).

**Digital Resources** Useful websites for Ljubljana include:

- W www.ljubljana.si City of Ljubljana
- W www.uni-lj.si Ljubljana University (check out the Welcome page with practical information in English for foreign students)
- W www.geocities.com/ljubljanalife The English-language magazine for expatriates and visitors

**Travel Agencies** Backpackers and students should head for the **ZMT Infopoint** (☎ 438 03 12; Kersnikova ul 6), which sells ISIC cards, **Mladi Turist** (☎ 425 92 60; Salendrova ul 4), the office of the Slovenian Youth Hostel Association, or **Erazem Travel Office** (☎ 433 10 76; Trubarjeva cesta 7).

There is also an **American Express** representative (☎ 431 90 20; Trubarjeva 50) in the city centre.

**Bookshops** Ljubljana's largest bookshop is **Mladinska Knjiga** (Slovenska cesta 29). It has an extensive collection of books in English. There's also **DZS** (☎ 200 80 42; Mestni tri 26). **Kod & Kam** (Trg Francoske Revolucije 7) is excellent for travel guides and maps, especially if you plan to go hiking.

**SLOVENIA**

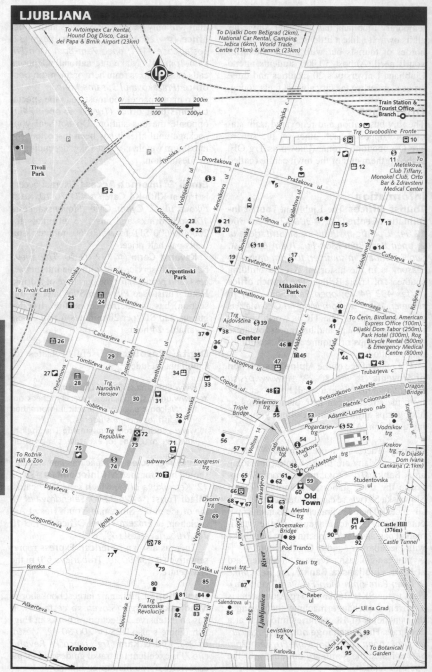

# LJUBLJANA

To Avtoimpex Car Rental,
Hound Dog Disco, Casa
del Papa & Brnik Airport (23km)

To Dijaški Dom Bežigrad (2km),
National Car Rental, Camping
Ježica (6km), World Trade
Centre (11km) & Kamnik (23km)

Train Station &
Tourist Office
Branch

Trg Osvobodilne Fronte

To
Metelkova,
Club Tiffany,
Monokel Club, Orto
Bar & Zdravstveni
Medical Center

Tivoli
Park

Pražakova ul

To Tivoli Castle

Argentinski
Park

Miklošičev
Park

Komenskega ul

To Cerin, Birdland, American
Express Office (100m),
Dijaški Dom Tabor (250m),
Park Hotel (300m), Rog
Bicycle Rental (500m)
& Emergency Medical
Centre (800m)

Trg
Ajdovščina

Center

Trg
Narodnih
Herojev

To Rožnik
Hill & Zoo

Trg
Republike

subway

Dragon
Bridge

Prešernov
trg

Triple
Bridge

Plečnik Colonnade
Adamič-Lundrovo nab

Pogačarjev
trg

Vodnikov
trg

Krekov
trg
To Dijaški
Dom Ivana
Cankarja (2.1km)

Kongresni
trg

Študentovska
ul

Dvorni
trg

Old
Town

Mestni
trg

Shoemaker
Bridge

Pod TranČo

Castle Hill
(376m)

Castle Tunnel

Stari trg

To Rožnik

Rimska c

Reber
ul

Ul na Grad

Trg
Francoske
Revolucije

Turjaška ul

Novi trg

Salendrova ul

Breg

Aškerčeva c

Levstikov
trg

Zoisova c

Karlovška c

Gornji trg

To Botanical
Garden

**Krakovo**

SLOVENIA

## LJUBLJANA

| PLACES TO STAY | 12 | Kompas Cinema | 52 | Hida Exchange Bureau; |
|---|---|---|---|---|
| 40 Hotel Turist; Klub Central | 14 | Avis | | Seminary |
| 46 Grand Hotel Union | 15 | Kinoteka Cinema | 54 | Tourist Information Centre (TIC) |
| 80 Pri Mraku | 16 | Kompas Hertz Car Rental | 55 | Prešeren Monument |
| | 17 | Banka Koper | 56 | Chemoexpress Laundry |
| PLACES TO EAT | 18 | A Banka | 58 | Robba Fountain |
| 5 Burek Stand | 20 | K4 Café; Roza Klub; | 59 | Town Hall |
| 13 Burek Stand | | University Student Centre | 60 | Vinoteka Movia |
| 19 Evropa Café | 21 | ZMT Infopoint | 61 | DZS Bookshop |
| 35 Quick | 22 | Adria Airways | 62 | Bicycle Rentals |
| 38 Šestica | 23 | Lufthansa Ticket Office | 63 | 365 |
| 44 Napoli | 24 | National Gallery | 64 | Maček |
| 53 Ribca | 25 | Church of Sts Cyril & | 66 | Filharmonija |
| 57 Zvezda Café | | Methodius | 69 | Ljubljana University |
| 65 Žibila | 26 | Museum of Modern Art | 70 | Ursuline Church of the Holy |
| 67 Ljubljanski Dvor | 27 | US Embassy | | Trinity |
| 68 Burja | 28 | National Museum | 71 | Brewery Pub |
| 77 Prema | 29 | Opera House | 72 | Maximarket Department Store |
| 79 Foculus | 30 | Parliament Building | | & Supermarket; Banka Koper |
| 87 Pri Viteza | 31 | Jazz Club Gajo | 73 | Globtour Agency |
| 88 Najboljski Gyros | 32 | Mladinska Knjiga Bookshop | 74 | Nova Ljubljanska Banka |
| 94 Špajza | 33 | Post Office (Poste Restante) | 75 | UK Embassy; Australian |
| 95 Pri sv Florianu; Moro | 34 | Komuna Cinema | | Consulate |
| | 36 | Kompas Travel Agency; | 76 | Cankarjev Dom |
| OTHER | | Holidays' Pub | 78 | Cyber Cafe |
| 1 Tivoli Recreation Centre & | 37 | Cankarjeva Založba Bookshop | 81 | Ilirija Column |
| Zlati Klub | 39 | SKB Banka | 82 | Križanke Booking Office |
| 2 Ilirija Swimming Pool | 41 | Tour As | 83 | Križanke Theatre |
| 3 Alpine Association of Slovenia | 42 | Patrick's Irish Pub | 84 | Kod & Kam Bookshop |
| 4 City Bus Ticket Kiosks | 43 | Salon | 85 | National & University Library |
| 6 Main Post Office | 45 | Art Nouveau Bank Buildings | 86 | Mladi Turist |
| 7 Canadian Consulate | 47 | Union Cinema | 89 | Dom |
| 8 City Airport Buses | 48 | Franciscan Church | 90 | Castle Tower |
| 9 Post Office (Customs) | 49 | Erazem Travel Office | 91 | Ljubljana Castle |
| 10 Bus Station | 50 | Produce Market | 92 | Pentagonal Tower |
| 11 A Banka | 51 | Cathedral of St Nicholas | 93 | Church of St Florian |

The best places to buy English and other foreign-language newspapers and magazines are the newsstands in the lobby of the **Grand Hotel Union** (*Miklošičeva cesta 1*) and in the basement of the **Maximarket department store** (*Trg Republike*).

**Laundry** The student dormitory **Dijaški Dom Kam** (*Kardeljeva ploščad 14*), north of the Center in Bežigrad, has washing machines and dryers that you can use (Building C), as does **Camping Ježica** (*Dunajska cesta 270*).

**Chemoexpress** (*Wolfova ul 12; open 7am-6pm Mon-Fri*) near Prešernov trg is an old-style laundry and dry cleaner.

**Left Luggage** The 24-hour left-luggage office (*garderoba*; 400 SIT per piece) at the train station is on platform No 1. There is a smaller *garderoba* (open 5.30am to 8.15pm) inside the bus station.

**Medical Services** In a medical emergency, dial ☎ 112, or go to the **emergency medical centre** (☎ 232 30 60; *Bohoričeva 9*). If you need to see a doctor, try the **Zdravstveni dom Center** (☎ 472 37 00; *Metelkova 9*).

### Things to See & Do

The most picturesque sights of old Ljubljana are along the banks of the Ljubljanica, a tributary of the Sava that curves around the foot of Castle Hill.

Opposite the tourist information centre and the Kresija building is the celebrated **Triple Bridge**. In 1931, Jože Plečnik added the side bridges to the original central span, which dates from 1842. On the northern side of the bridge is Prešernov trg with its pink **Franciscan church** (1660), a **statue** (1905) of poet France Prešeren and some wonderful Art Nouveau buildings. A lively pedestrian street, **Čopova ul**, runs northwest.

SLOVENIA

On the southern side of the bridge in Mestni trg, the baroque **Robba Fountain** stands in front of the **Town Hall** (Magistrat; 1718). Italian sculptor Francesco Robba designed this fountain in 1751 and modelled it after one in Rome. Enter the town hall to see the double Gothic courtyard. South of Mestni trg is **Stari trg**, full of atmosphere day and night. Northeast are the twin towers of the **Cathedral of St Nicholas** (1708), which contains impressive frescoes. Behind the cathedral is Ljubljana's colourful open-air **produce market** (closed Sunday) and an arch-fronted **colonnade** along the riverside designed by Plečnik.

**Ljubljana Castle** has finally been renovated, so you can now climb the 19th-century Castle Tower to the west, view the exhibits in the Gothic chapel and the **Pentagonal Tower** (open Tues-Sun). There's a new virtual **museum** (adult/child 700/400 SIT; open 10am-9pm daily). Študentovska ul, opposite the Vodnik statue in the market square, offers a panoramic path to the castle, or try Reber ul between Stari trg 17 and 19. You can take the tram, which leaves Prešernov trg (next to the Triple Bridge) daily during the winter at 20 past the hour from 10am to 3pm, and May to September from 10am to 8pm. The train costs 500/350 SIT for adults/children and students.

Near the now-closed Municipal Museum is the 1941 **National & University Library** (Gosposka ul 14), designed by Plečnik, and north on Gosposka ul is the main building (1902) of **Ljubljana University** (Kongresni trg 12), which was formerly the regional parliament. The elegant **Filharmonija** (Philharmonic Hall), at No 10 on the southeastern corner of the square, is home to the Slovenian Philharmonic Orchestra. The **Ursuline Church of the Holy Trinity** (1726), with an altar by Robba, faces Kongresni trg to the west.

Walk west along Šubičeva ul to several fine museums. The **National Museum** (Muzejska ul 1; adult/child 500/300 SIT; open 10am-6pm Tues-Sun), built in 1885, has prehistory and natural history collections. The highlight is a Celtic *situla*, a kind of pail, from the 6th century BC sporting a fascinating relief.

The **National Gallery** (Prešernova cesta 24; adult/child 700/500 SIT, free Sat afternoon; open 10am-6pm Tues-Sun) displays European portraits and landscapes from the 17th to 19th centuries, as well as copies of medieval frescoes. The gallery's north wing has a permanent collection of European

paintings from the Middle Ages to the 20th century and is used for temporary exhibits.

Diagonally opposite the National Gallery is the **Museum of Modern Art** (Cankarjeva ul 15; adult/senior 1000/500 SIT, children free; open 10am-6pm Tues-Sun) where a part of the International Biennial of Graphic Arts is held summers of odd-numbered years.

The Serbian Orthodox **Church of Sts Cyril & Methodius** (open 3pm-6pm Tues-Sat), opposite the Museum of Modern Art, is worth visiting to see the beautiful modern frescoes. The subway from the Museum of Modern Art leads to Ljubljana's green lung, **Tivoli Park**.

## Activities

The **Tivoli Recreation Centre** (☎ 431 51 55; Celovška cesta 25) in Tivoli Park has bowling alleys, tennis courts, an indoor swimming pool, a fitness centre and a roller-skating rink. In summer, there's minigolf. The **Zlati Klub** at this centre has several saunas, a steam room, warm and cold splash pools and even a small outside pool surrounded by high walls so you can sunbathe in the nude (mixed sexes, but Friday mornings 9am-1pm are women only).

The outdoor **Ilirija pool** (Celovška cesta 3; open 9am-11am Mon-Fri, 6.30pm-10pm Tues-Thur, 10am-8pm Sat & Sun in summer) is opposite the Tivoli hotel.

## Organised Tours

Guided tours (€5.50, half-price for students, pensioners and children) of Ljubljana are available in Slovene and English from in front of the Town Hall at Mestni trg 1. Tours leave at 5pm daily from 1 June to 30 September and at 11am Sunday from 1 October to 31 May.

## Places to Stay

**Camping** Some 6km north of Center on the Sava is **Camping Ježica** (☎ 568 39 13; Dunajska cesta 270; bus No 6 or 8; tent or caravan sites per adult/child low season €6/5, high season €8/6; bungalow singles/doubles/triples €25/40/50), a shady camping area open year-round with a restaurant and swimming pool that accommodates 300 people.

**Hostels & Student Dormitories** Three student dormitories (dijaški dom) are open to foreign travellers in July and August. Most central is **Dijaški Dom Tabor** (☎ 234 88 40, fax 234 88 55; e ssljddta1s@guest.arnes.si; Vidovdanska ul 7; singles 4000 SIT, doubles or triples per bed 2900/3400 SIT members/ nonmembers) across from the Park Hotel and affiliated with Hostelling International (HI). Rates include breakfast.

**Dijaški Dom Bežigrad** (☎ 534 28 67; e dd .lj-bezigrad@guest.arnes.si; Kardeljeva pl 28; bus No 6; singles/shared per person 3800/ 3300 SIT, breakfast 460 SIT) another HI member, is in the Bežigrad district 2km north of the train and bus stations. The Bežigrad has 50 rooms available in July and August.

**Dijaška Dom Ivana Cankarja** (☎ 474 86 00; e dd.lj-ic@guest.arnes.si; Polanski cesta 26; accommodation per person €10-14, including breakfast €12-15) is just east of the town centre (10% less for students).

**Private Rooms & Apartments** The TIC has about 40 **private rooms** on its list, but just a handful are in Center. Most of the others would require a bus trip up to Bežigrad. Prices range from 3500 SIT for singles and 5000 SIT for doubles. It also has eight apartments and one studio – four of which are central – for one to four people costing from 9700 SIT to 16,700 SIT. Whether you're looking for an apartment for one day or several months, try **Tour As** (☎ 434 26 60; e info@apartmaji.si; Mala ul 8) by Hotel Turist.

**Hotels** The best deal for location and quality is **Pri Mraku** (☎ 433 40 49; e mrak@daj-dam .si; Rimska cesta 4, singles/doubles 13,950/ 19,200 SIT). For 8450 SIT per person, up to four people can have a 5th-floor room with shared bathroom. The Mraku also has an excellent restaurant.

The 122-room **Park Hotel** (☎ 433 13 06, fax 433 05 46; e hotel.park@siol.net; Tabor 9; singles/doubles from €37/50) is where most people usually end up, as it's the city's only large budget hotel close to Center and the Old Town. It's pretty depressing, but the price is right and rates include breakfast. Students with cards get a 20% discount.

**Bit Center Hotel** (☎ 548 00 55, fax 548 00 56; w www.bit-center.net; Litijska 57; bus No 9 from the railway station; singles/ doubles or triples 5490/8190 SIT, breakfast 800 SIT), one small step up from a hostel, is also a possibility. Hotel guests get a 50% discount on sauna and health-club services, available in the same building.

A reasonable alternative in the town centre is the three-star **Hotel Turist** (☎ 234 91 30,

fax 234 91 40; e info@hotelturist.si; Dalmatinova; 15 singles/doubles from €66/90).

## Places to Eat

**Restaurants** There are several excellent restaurants in Ljubljana that are relatively good value. **Šestica** (Slovenska cesta 40; lunch menus 1000-1400 SIT, mains 1100-2000 SIT) is a 200-year-old stand-by with a pleasant courtyard.

If you're in the mood to try horse meat, visit **Pri Vitezu** (Breg 4), a pricey but highly rated restaurant along the Ljubljanica.

**Pri sv Florijanu** (☎ 351 22 14; Gornji trg 20; set lunch 1690 SIT) has creative modern Slovenian food, including a great vegetable soup and leek risotto. The set lunch is good value. **Moro**, the happening new Moroccan themed bar and restaurant, is downstairs.

The capital abounds in Italian restaurants and pizzerias. Among the best in town are **Ljubljanski Dvor** (Dvorni trg 1) on the west bank of the Ljubljanica and **Foculus** (Gregorčičeva ul 3; small/large pizzas 800/1100 SIT) next door to the Glej Theatre. Other pizza-pasta places include **Napoli** (Prečna ul 7) off Trubarjeva cesta and **Čerin** (Trubarjeva 52), which also has Internet access in its next-door Kavarna Čerin.

**Špajza** (Gornji trg 28) is popular with locals. **Casa del Papa** (☎ 434 31 58; Celovška 54) serves Latin-influenced lunch and dinner in a Hemingway-inspired setting.

The delicious vegetarian restaurant **Vegodrom** (☎ 459 17 50, Maistrova 10) also serves Indian cuisine like samosas and palak paneer.

**Cafés** For coffee and cakes you might try the elegant **Evropa Café** (Gosposvetska cesta 2) on the corner of Slovenska cesta or the trendy **Zvezda Café** (Wolfova 14).

**Self-Service & Fast Food** For hamburgers, to-go coffee and other fast food visit **Quick** (Cankarjeva cesta 12; open 6.30am-11pm Mon-Sat, 4pm-10pm Sun), with a play area for kids. For a quick and tasty lunch, try **Ribca** (Pogačarjev trg), a seafood bar below the Plečnik Colonnade. **Najboljski Gyros** (Stari trg 19; open 9am-1am Mon-Thurs, noon-1am Fri & Sat) sells gyros, pizzas and crepes, all under 1000 SIT.

There are **burek stands** (about 500 SIT) at several locations in Ljubljana. The one at Kolodvorska ul 20 is open 24 hours.

**Self-Catering** In the basement of the Maxi-market shopping arcade, the **supermarket** *(Trg Republike; open 9am-8pm Mon-Fri, to 3pm Sat & Sun)* has about the largest selection in town. The best places for picnic supplies are the city's many delicatessens, including **Žibila** *(Kongresni trg 9)* and **Burja** *(Kongresni trg 11)*. For healthy snacks and vegetarian food, try **Prema** *(Gregorčičeva 9)*.

## Entertainment
Ask the TIC for its monthly programme of events in English – it is called *Where to? in Ljubljana* – or check out *Ljubljana Life*, the English-language monthly magazine available at the TIC and in hotels and restaurants.

**Pubs & Bars** A fun place to try Slovenian wine is **Vinoteka Movia** *(Mestni trg 2)*, a wine bar next to the Town Hall. Pleasant and congenial places for a *pivo* (beer) or glass of *vino* (wine) include **Salon** *(Trubarjeva cesta 23)*, **Patrick's Irish Pub** *(Prečna ul 6)* and **Holidays' Pub** *(Slovenska cesta 36)* next to the Kompas travel agency. Along the river, the most popular bar for locals and tourists is **Maček** *(Cankarjevo nab 19)*.

**Clubs** Two of the most popular conventional clubs are **Klub Central** *(Dalmatinova ul 15)* next to the Turist Hotel and **Hound Dog** *(Trg Prekomorskih Brigad 4)* in the Hotel M, both populated by a young crowd. The student hang-out **K4** *(Kersnikova ul 4)* has a disco every night, open until the wee hours on Friday and Saturday nights and until around midnight on other nights. A popular place is **Metelkova mesto** (along Metelkova cesta near Maistrova ul), where squatters have turned former Yugoslav army barracks into the hippest spot in town, with several nightclubs and bars.

**Gay & Lesbian Venues** A popular spot for both gays and lesbians on Sunday night is **Roza Klub** *(open 10pm-4am)* at K4. At the Metelkova squat, there's a café/pub for gays called **Club Tiffany**. **Monokel Club** *(open Thur-Mon)* is a popular spot for lesbians in the same building.

**Rock & Jazz** Ljubljana has a number of excellent rock clubs with canned or live music including **Orto Bar** *(Grablovičeva ul 1)* and the **Brewery Pub** *(Plečnikov trg 1)*. For jazz,

you cannott beat the **Jazz Club Gajo** *(Beethovnova ul 8)* near the Parliament building. **Birdland** *(Trubarjeva cesta 50)* also has a jam session on Wednesday night and occasional jazz concerts on the weekend.

**Classical Music, Opera & Dance** Ljubljana is home to two orchestras. Concerts are held in various locations all over town, but the main venue – with up to 700 cultural events every year – is **Cankarjev Dom** *(Trg Republike)*. The **ticket office** *(☎ 241 71 00; open 10am-2pm & 4.30pm-8pm Mon-Fri, 10am-1pm Sat & 1hr before performances)*, is in the basement of the nearby Maximarket mall. Tickets will cost anywhere between 1500 SIT and 3000 SIT with gala performances worth as much as 6000 SIT. Also check for any concerts performed at the beautiful **Filharmonija** *(Kongresni trg 10)*.

At the ticket office of the **Opera House** *(☎ 425 48 40; Župančičeva ul 1; open 2pm-5pm Mon-Fri, 6pm-7pm Sat & 1hr before performances)* you can also buy ballet tickets.

For tickets to the Ljubljana Summer Festival and anything else that is staged at the Križanke, go to the **booking office** *(☎ 252 65 44; Trg Francoske Revolucije 1-2; open 10am-2pm & 4.30pm-8pm Mon-Fri, 10am-1pm Sat & 1hr before performances)* behind the Ilirija Column.

**Cinemas** For first-run films, try the **Komuna** *(Cankarjeva cesta 1)*, **Kompas** *(Miklošičeva cesta 38)* or **Union** *(Nazorjeva ul 2)*. All three generally have three screenings a day. The **Kinoteka** *(Miklošičeva cesta 28)* shows art and classic films. Cinema tickets generally cost around 800 SIT, and there are discounts usually available for the first session on weekday screenings.

## Getting There & Away
**Bus** You can reach virtually anywhere in the country by bus from the capital. The timetable in the shed-like **bus station** *(☎ 090 42 30; Trg OF)* lists all routes and times.

Some sample destinations and one-way fares are: Bled (1220 SIT, hourly); Bohinj (1730 SIT, hourly); Jesenice (1310 SIT, hourly); Koper (2200 SIT, eight a day); Maribor (2370 SIT, 10 a day); Murska Sobota (3570 SIT, five a day); Novo Mesto (1390 SIT, hourly); Piran (3370 SIT, seven a day); Postojna (1120 SIT, 25 a day) Ptuj (connect in Maribor); and Rogaška Slatina (1950 SIT, daily at 9.30am).

**Train** All domestic and international trains arrive at and depart from the station (☎ 291 33 32; Trg OF 6). Local trains leave Ljubljana regularly for Bled (680 SIT, 51km); Jesenice (800 SIT, 64km); Koper (1380 SIT, 153km); Maribor (1380 SIT, 156km); Murska Sobota (2100 SIT, 216km); and Novo Mesto (950 SIT, 75km).

There is a 260 SIT surcharge on domestic InterCity train tickets. For more details on international trains to/from Ljubljana, see the introductory Getting There & Away section of this chapter.

## Getting Around

**To/From the Airport** The city bus from lane No 28 leaves every hour for Brnik airport (680 SIT), 23km to the northwest, hourly at 10 minutes past the hour Monday to Friday and weekends on odd hours. There's also an **airport shuttle** (☎ 040-887 766) for about 2500 SIT. A taxi will cost between 5000 SIT and 6500 SIT. Brnik is about 40 to 45 minutes from the city centre.

**Bus** Ljubljana's bus system (☎ 582 24 60) is excellent and very user-friendly. There are 22 lines; five (Nos 1, 2, 3, 6 and 11) are considered to be main lines. These start to operate at 3.15am and run until midnight, while the rest run from 5am to 10.30pm.

You can either pay on board the bus (230 SIT) or use the tiny yellow plastic tokens (170 SIT) that are available from the bus station, newsstands, tobacconists, post offices and the two kiosks on the pavement in front of Slovenska cesta 55. An all-day ticket is also available for 660 SIT.

**Taxi** You can call a taxi on one of 10 numbers: ☎ 9700 to 9709. Flag fall is 150 SIT, and rates are 100 to 300 SIT per kilometre, depending on time of day. A taxi from the bus or train station to downtown runs at about 700 SIT, and 2000 SIT to outlying hotels.

**Bicycle** Visitors can rent bicycles from **Rog** (☎ 520 03 10; open 8am-7pm Mon-Fri, 8am-noon Sat), next to Rozmanova ul 1. From June to the end of September, you can also rent bikes near **Café Maček** (☎ 041-696 515) on Cankarjevo nab.

# Julian Alps

Slovenia shares the Julian Alps in the northwestern corner of the country with Italy. The tri-peaked Mt Triglav (2864m), the country's highest summit, is climbed regularly by thousands of weekend warriors, but there are countless less ambitious hikes on offer in the region. Lakes Bled and Bohinj make ideal starting points – Bled with its comfortable resort facilities, Bohinj right beneath the rocky crags themselves. Most of this spectacular area falls within the boundaries of the Triglav National Park, which was established in 1924.

## BLED
☎ 04 • pop 5400

Bled, a fashionable resort at just over 500m, is set on an idyllic, 2km-long emerald-green lake with a little island and church in the centre and a dramatic castle towering overhead. Trout and carp proliferate in the clear water, which is surprisingly warm and a pleasure for swimming or boating. To the northeast, the highest peaks of the Karavanke Range form a natural boundary with Austria, and the Julian Alps lie to the west. Bled has been a favourite destination for travellers for decades. All in all, it is beautiful but be warned that it can get very crowded – and pricey – in season.

## Orientation

Bled village is at the northeastern end of the lake below Bled Castle. The bus station is also here on Cesta Svobode, but the main Lesce–Bled train station is about 4km to the southeast. In addition there's Bled Jezero, a branch-line train station northwest of the lake, not far from the camping ground.

## Information

**Tourist Offices** Beld **tourist office** (☎ 574 11 22, fax 574 15 55; ⓦ www.bled.si; Cesta Svobode 15; open 9am-7pm Mon-Sat, 9am-3pm Sun Apr-Oct; 9am-5pm Mon-Sat, 9am-2pm Sun Nov-Mar) is next to the Park Hotel. In July and August the office stays open till 10pm Monday to Saturday and to 8pm on Sunday. Ask for the useful booklet Bled Tourist Information (300 SIT), available in English or German, which is reproduced on the town's useful website.

In Triglav shopping centre, **Kompas** (☎ 574 15 15; Ljubljanska cesta 4) sells some good

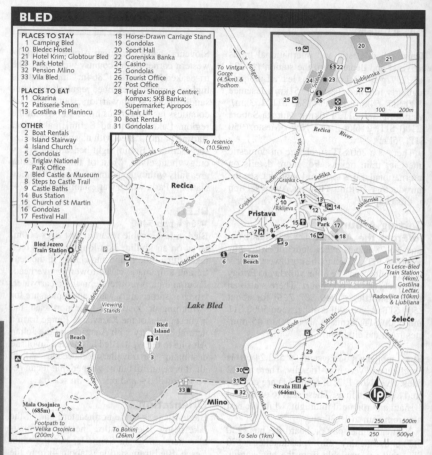

## BLED

**PLACES TO STAY**
1 Camping Bled
10 Bledec Hostel
21 Hotel Krim; Globtour Bled
23 Park Hotel
32 Pension Mlino
33 Vila Bled

**PLACES TO EAT**
11 Okarina
12 Patisserie Šmon
13 Gostilna Pri Planincu

**OTHER**
2 Boat Rentals
3 Island Stairway
4 Island Church
5 Gondolas
6 Triglav National
Park Office
7 Bled Castle & Museum
8 Steps to Castle Trail
9 Castle Baths
14 Bus Station
15 Church of St Martin
16 Gondolas
17 Festival Hall

18 Horse-Drawn Carriage Stand
19 Gondolas
20 Sport Hall
22 Gorenjska Banka
24 Casino
25 Gondolas
26 Tourist Office
27 Post Office
28 Triglav Shopping Centre;
Kompas; SKB Banka;
Supermarket; Apropos
29 Chair Lift
30 Boat Rentals
31 Gondolas

hiking maps. The **Triglav National Park office** (☎ 578 02 00; Kidričeva cesta 2; open 7am-3pm Mon-Fri) is located on the lake's northern shore.

**Email & Internet Access** Internet access is available at the **Bledec Hostel** at a cost of 500 SIT for 30 minutes. In the Triglav shopping centre, **Apropos** (Ljubljanska cesta 4; open 8am-midnight Mon-Sat) charges 1000 SIT for one hour, 500 SIT for 30 minutes.

**Money** Gorenjska Banka (Cesta Svobode 15; open 9am-11.30am & 2pm-5pm Mon-Fri, 8am-11am Sat), in the Park Hotel shopping complex, has an ATM for MasterCard/Cirrus holders. **SKB Banka** ATM (Ljubljanska cesta 4; open 8.30am-noon & 2pm-5pm Mon-Fri)

accepts all cards. Kompas and the tourist office change money.

**Post & Communications** The post office (Ljubljanska cesta 10; open 7am-7pm Mon-Fri, to noon Sat) is also in the centre of town.

## Things to See

There are several trails to **Bled Castle** (adult/child 700/400 SIT; open 9am-8pm daily May-Sept, 9am-5pm Oct-Apr), the easiest is the one south from behind Bledec Hostel at Grajska cesta 17. The castle was the seat of the Bishops of Brixen (South Tirol) for over 800 years. Atop a steep cliff 100m above the lake, it offers magnificent views in clear weather. The **museum** presents the history of the area and allows a peep into a small 16th-century chapel. The expensive restaurant serves drinks on a terrace with a magnificent view.

Bled's other striking feature is tiny **Bled Island** (Blejski Otok) at the western end of the lake. The tolling 'bell of wishes' echoes across the lake from the tall white belfry rising above the dense vegetation. It's said that all who ring it will get their wish; naturally it chimes constantly. Underneath the present baroque church are the foundations of what was a pre-Romanesque chapel, unique in Slovenia. Most people reach the island on a *pletna*, a large gondola hand-propelled by a boatman. The price (1800 SIT per person) includes a half-hour visit to the island, church and belfry. If there are two or three of you it would be cheaper and more fun to hire a rowing boat (2000 SIT an hour for up to four) from the Castle Baths on the shore below the castle, in Mlino on the southern lakeshore or in front of the **Casino** *(Cesta Svobode 15)*.

## Hiking

An excellent half-day hike from Bled features a visit to the most impressive **Vintgar Gorge** *(adult/child 500/300 SIT; open daily May–Oct)*, 4.5km to the northwest. Head northwest on Prešernova cesta then north on Partizanska cesta to Cesta v Vintgar. This will take you to Podhom, where signs point the way to the gorge entrance. A wooden footbridge hugs the rock wall for 1600m along the Radovna River, crisscrossing the raging torrent four times over rapids, waterfalls and pools before reaching **Šum Waterfall**.

From there a trail leads over Hom Hill (834m) east to the ancient pilgrimage **Church of St Catherine**. The trail then leads due south through Zasip and back to Bled. From late June to mid-September an Alpetour bus makes the run from Bled's bus station to Vintgar daily, or take the hourly Krnica bus to Spodnje Gorje which is 1km from the entrance; in summer there are two daily buses from Spodnje Gorje to the gorge entrance.

## Places to Stay

**Camping** At the western end of the lake **Camping Bled** *(☎ 575 20 00; adult/child low season 1250/875 SIT, high season 1840/1290 SIT; open Apr–mid-Oct)* is in a quiet valley about 2.5km from the bus station. The location is good and there's even a beach, tennis courts, a large restaurant and a supermarket, but it fills up very quickly in summer.

**Hostels** The **Bledec Hostel** *(☎ 574 52 50; Grajska cesta 17; beds low/high season with ISIC/IYHF card €14/15, without card €17/19)* has a total of 55 beds in 13 rooms. Self-service laundry facilities are available for 800 SIT. Breakfast is included.

**Private Rooms** Finding a private room in Bled is easy. Travel agencies have extensive lists, and there are lots of houses around the lake with *'sobe'* or *'Zimmer frei'* signs indicating rooms to rent. **Kompas** *(☎ 574 15 15; e kompas.bled@siol.net; Ljubljanska cesta 4 singles €14-21, doubles €18-34, 2-person apartments €24-38)* is a good place to start. Rooms or apartments are also available from the tourist office or **Globtour Bled** *(☎ 574 41 86, fax 574 41 85; Ljubljanska cesta 7)* at Krim Hotel. All charge similar prices.

**Hotels** Most of Bled's hotels are pretty expensive affairs. Among the cheapest is the 212-bed **Hotel Krim** *(☎ 579 70 00, fax 574 37 29; e hotelkrim@hotel-krim.si; Ljubljanska cesta 7; singles/doubles high season €48/68)* in the town centre.

Central **Park Hotel** *(☎ 579 30 00; e info@gp-hoteli-bled.si; Cesta Svobode 15; singles/doubles €91/98 low season, €107/114 high season)* has attractive rooms, some with a wonderful lake view.

Across from the boat rentals and just a little way out of town, is the attractive **Pension Mlino** *(☎ 574 14 04, fax 574 15 06; Cesta Svobode 45; doubles summer 6600 SIT, off season 4400 SIT)*.

For a splurge and a little history, check out **Vila Bled** *(☎ 579 15 00; Cesta Svobode 26; e vilabled@robas.si; singles/doubles low season €95/135, high season €115/155)*, a grand resort hotel that was once Tito's summer home. It's been a hotel since the 80s, and includes tennis courts, a private boathouse, and Communist-era artwork.

## Places to Eat

Bled's best choice for an affordable meal is the homy **Gostilna Pri Planincu** *(Grajska cesta 8; meals from 2000 SIT)*, which is just a stone's throw from the bus station. The menu includes some excellent dishes such as mushroom soup and grilled chicken with fries and salad.

**Okarina** *(☎ 574 14 58; Riklijeva cesta 9)* has top-rate Indian cuisine with an assortment of vegetarian dishes as well as offering its Slovenian specialities.

**Patisserie Šmon** *(Grajska 3)* offers scrumptious desserts and coffee.

There's a **supermarket** in the Triglav shopping centre.

A few miles out of town in Radovljica is **Gostilna Lečtar** *(☎ 537 48 00; Linhartov trg 2; closed Tuesday)*. This traditional restaurant is one of the most famous in Slovenia, and Radovljica is a charming small town with frescoed buildings. Take the main highway towards Ljubljana and you'll see signs for Radovljica.

## Getting There & Around

If you're coming from Ljubljana, take the bus not the train. The train from Ljubljana will leave you at the Lesce-Bled station, 4km southeast of Bled while the bus takes you to the town centre. There are buses to Ljubljana (hourly), Bohinj (hourly starting at 7.20am), Radovljica (every 30 minutes) and Kranjska Gora via Lesce (eight daily). One bus a day from July to mid-September goes to Bovec via Kranjska Gora and the heart-stopping Vršič Pass.

Lesce-Bled train station handles up to 20 trains a day from Ljubljana (55 minutes). About eight cross the Austrian border, continuing on to Germany. There are six trains daily to Jesenice, six to Nova Gorica, 10 to Bohinj, and one a day at 6.14am during the summer to Skofja Loca.

**Kompas** *(☎ 574 15 15; Ljubljanska cesta)* rents out bicycles and mountain bikes for 4700/1500/2200 SIT per hour/half-day/day.

## BOHINJ
☎ 04

Bohinj is a larger and much less developed glacial lake, 26km southwest of Bled. It is exceedingly beautiful, with high mountains that rise directly from the basin-shaped valley. There are secluded beaches for swimming just off the trail along the northern shore and there are many hiking possibilities, including an ascent of Mt Triglav.

## Orientation

There is no town called Bohinj; the name actually refers to the entire valley, its settlements and the lake. The largest town in the Bohinj area is Bohinjska Bistrica (population 3080), 6km east of the lake. The main settlement on the lake is Ribčev Laz at the southeastern corner. All in a row just up from the bus stop, are the post office, tourist office, a supermarket, a pizzeria and the Alpinum travel agency.

About 1km north across the Sava Bohinjka River and at the mouth of the Mostnica Canyon sits the town of Stara Fužina. The Zlatorog Hotel is situated at Ukanc at the western end of the lake near the camping ground and the cable car, which takes visitors up Mt Vogel and to the ski lifts (1922m).

## Information

There's a helpful and very efficient **tourist office** *(☎ 572 33 70, fax 572 33 30; ⓦ www .bohinj.si; Ribčev Laz 48; open 7.30am-8pm daily July–mid-Sept, 8am-6pm Mon-Sat, 9am-3pm Sun mid-Sept–Jun)*. Its website contains much useful information.

The tourist office can change money but there's a 3% commission. There's an ATM at the post office next door. There are braches of **Gorenjska Banka** at Trg Svobode 2b and in Bohinjska Bistrica.

The **post office** *(Ribčev Laz 47; open 8am-6pm Mon-Fri, 8am-noon Sat)* is open during the listed hours but with a couple of half-hour breaks during the day.

**Alpinum travel agency** *(☎ 572 34 41; Ribčev Laz 50)* organises sporting activities in Bohinj and rents rooms.

## Things to See & Do

The **Church of St John the Baptist**, on the northern side of the Sava Bohinjka across the stone bridge from Ribčev Laz, has exquisite 15th-century frescoes and can lay claim to being the most beautiful and evocative church in Slovenia. The **Alpine Dairy Museum** *(adult/child 400/300 SIT)*, at house No 181 in Stara Fužina about 1.5km north of Ribčev Laz, has a small but interesting collection related to Alpine dairy farming in the Bohinj Valley, once the most important such centre in Slovenia. If you have time, take a walk over to **Studor**, a village a couple of kilometres to the east renowned for its *kozolci* and *toplarji*, single and double hayracks that are unique to Slovenia.

Sporting equipment is available to rent from **Alpinsport kiosk** *(☎ 572 34 86; Ribčev Laz 53)*, just before the stone bridge to the church. Canoes & kayaks cost from 800/3100 SIT per hour/day. It also organises **guided mountain tours** (4600 SIT) and **canoe trips** (3600 SIT)

A swell time: surfers head for the beaches north of Sagres, Portugal

Strolling through the Old Quarter in Lagos, Portugal

On parade in Lisbon, Portugal

Heights of Maribor, Slovenia

Boating on the tranquil waters of Lake Bled, Slovenia

JEFF GREENBERG

Floodlit fountain near Atocha station, Madrid, Spain

ELLIOT DANIEL

Madrid's speedy Metro

SUNA KANGA

Flamenco at Los Gallos, Madrid

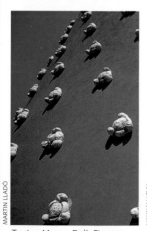

MARTIN LLADÓ

Teatre-Museu Dalí, Figueres

HANNAH LEVY

The eye-like Hemisferic at the City of Arts & Sciences, Valencia

on the Sava, as well as 'canyoning' through the rapids of the Mostnica Gorge stuffed into a neoprene suit, life jacket and helmet starting at 7900 SIT.

The **Vogel cable car** *(adult/child return 1000/700 SIT)*, above the camping ground at the western end of Lake Bohinj about 5km from Ribčev Laz, will whisk you 1000m up into the mountains. It runs every half-hour year round except in November, from 8am to 6pm (till 8pm in July and August). From the upper station (1540m) you can scale **Mt Vogel** in a couple of hours for a sweeping view of the surrounding region.

## Savica Waterfall

An hour's hike west of the Zlatorog Hotel at Ukanc is the **Savica Waterfall** *(adult/child 300/150 SIT)*, the source of the Sava River, which gushes from a limestone cave and falls 60m into a narrow gorge. It costs 500 SIT for the car park, but the receipt can be redeemed for a drink at the restaurant.

## Places to Stay

**Autocamp Zlatorog** *(☎ 572 34 82, fax 572 34 83; camp sites per person 1100-2100 SIT; open year-round)* caters mostly to camper vans, but its location on the lake near the Zlatorog Hotel can't be beaten.

The tourist office can arrange **private rooms** *(singles/doubles with shower low season 1920/3200 SIT, July & August to 2400/4000 SIT)* in neighbouring villages. There is usually a 30% surcharge for if you are staying fewer than three days.

## Places to Eat

**Pizza Center** *(Ribčev Laz 50)*, next to the Alpinum travel agency, is very popular year-round.

For a truly different lunch, try **Planšar** *(Stara Fužina 179)* opposite the Alpine Dairy Museum. It specialises in home-made dairy products, and you can taste a number of local specialities for about 700 SIT.

There's a **Mercator supermarket** *(Ribčev Laz 49; open 7am-7pm Mon-Fri, 7am-5pm Sat)* for self-caterers.

## Getting There & Around

There are hourly buses between Ribčev Laz and Ljubljana via Bled, Radovljica, Kranj and Bohinjska Bistrica. There are also about six local buses a day to Bohinjska Bistrica. All of these buses stop near the post office on Triglavska cesta in Bohinjska Bistrica and in Ribčev Laz (500m from the TIC towards Pension Kristal) before carrying on to Zlatorog Hotel in Ukanc. The closest train station is at Bohinjska Bistrica, which is on the Jesenice to Nova Gorica line.

Mountain bikes and helmets can be rented from **Alpinsport kiosk** *(☎ 572 34 86; Ribčev Laz 53)* for 800/3100 SIT per hour/day.

## KRANJSKA GORA
☎ 04 • pop 1530

Known primarily for the best skiing in Slovenia, Kranjska Gora is also a worthy summer and off-season sporting ground. Climbing, fishing, ice-skating, hiking, bicycling – it's all here.

The Kranjska Gora **tourist office** *(☎ 588 17 68; e turisticno.drustvo.kg@siol.net; Tičarjeva 2; open 8am-8pm Mon-Sat, 9am-6pm Sun; off-season to 3pm Mon-Fri, to 6pm Sat & 1pm Sun)* has useful handouts and sells maps and guides to surrounding areas.

A good ski school and rental place is **Bernik** *(☎ 588 14 70; e sport@s5.net; Borovška cesta 88a)*.

## Places to Stay & Eat

For **private rooms**, you can contact the tourist office. A decent, well-priced hotel that's in the centre of town is the **Hotel Prisank** *(☎ 588 41 70; e info@htp-gorenjka.si; Borovška 93; depending on season singles 5100-9400 SIT, doubles 7200-13,500 SIT)*.

**Pizzeria Pino** *(☎ 588 15 64; Borovška 75)* sells good meat and vegetarian pizzas for 700 to 1200 SIT.

There is also the **Mercator supermarket** *(Borovška 92)* in the same street.

## HIKING MT TRIGLAV

The Julian Alps are among the finest hiking areas in Central and Eastern Europe. None of the 150 mountain huts *(planinska koča or planinski dom)* is more than five hours' walk from the next. The huts in the higher regions are open from July to September, and in the lower regions from June to October. You'll never be turned away if the weather looks bad, but some huts on Triglav get very crowded at weekends, especially in August and September. A bed for the night should cost about 2500 SIT per person. Meals are also available, so you don't need to carry a lot of gear. Leave most of your things below, but warm clothes, sturdy boots and good physical condition are indispensable.

The best months for hiking are August to October, though above 1500m you can encounter winter conditions at any time. Keep to the trails that are well marked with a red circle and a white centre, rest frequently and never *ever* try to trek alone.

For good information about the mountain huts and detailed maps, contact the **Alpine Association of Slovenia** (see the Information section under Ljubljana) or the TICs in Bled, Bohinj, Kranjska Gora (all excellent places to start a mountain-hut hike) or Ljubljana. You will also be able to pick up a copy of the 1:20,000 *Triglav* map or the 1:50,000-scale *Julijske Alpe – Vzhodni Del* (*Julian Alps – Eastern Part*), which is published by the Alpine Association and available at bookshops and tourist offices.

The *Dnevnik S Slovenske Planinske Poti*, a mountain hut 'passport', is a booklet published by the Alpine Association and available at any Triglav area tourist office. Hikers can bring this booklet with them to any of the 150 huts and try to collect as many stamps as possible.

# Soča Valley

## BOVEC & KOBARID
☎ 05 • pop 1775 & 1460

The Soča Valley, defined by the bluer-than-blue Soča, stretches from the Triglav National Park to Nova Gorica and is one of the most beautiful and peaceful spots in Slovenia. Of course it wasn't always that way. During much of WWI, this was the site of the infamous Soča (or Isonzo) Front, which claimed the lives of an estimated one million people and was immortalised by the American writer Ernest Hemingway in his novel *A Farewell to Arms*. Today visitors flock to the town of Kobarid to relive these events at the award-winning **Kobarid Museum** (☎ 389 00 00; Gregorčičeva ul 10; adult/student & child 700/500 SIT) or, more commonly, head for Bovec, 21km to the north, to take part in some of the best whitewater rafting in Europe. The season lasts from April to October.

In Bovec, the people to see for any sort of water sports are **Soča Rafting** (☎ 389 62 00; e soca.rafting@arctur.si), 100m from the Alp Hotel (across from the post office) or **Bovec**

**Rafting Team** (☎ 388 61 28; Trg Golobarskih Žrtev) in the small kiosk opposite the Martinov Hram restaurant. Rafting trips on the Soča lasting about 1½ hours start at 7000 SIT (students receive a discount). The cost of the trip includes all necessary safety equipment and gear. A kayak costs from 4500 SIT for four hours including equipment; a two-person canoe is 5500 SIT per person. There are kayaking lessons in summer (eg, a two-day intensive course for beginners costs 24,000 SIT without equipment).

In Kobarid, the **tourist office** in the Kobarid Museum and, in Bovec, the **Avrigo Tours agency** (☎ 388 60 22; Trg Golobarskih Žrtev 47), next to the Alp hotel, can organise **private double rooms** from 2500 SIT per person.

There are four camping grounds in Bovec – the closest is **Polovnik** (☎ 388 60 69) – and there is one in Kobarid – **Koren** (☎ 388 53 12).

### Getting There & Away
There are up to six buses between Kobarid and Bovec and to Tolmin daily. Other destinations include Ljubljana (two to five buses daily), Nova Gorica (four to six) and Cerkno (up to five). In July and August there's a daily bus to Ljubljana via the Vršič Pass and Kranjska Gora. From Bled there are three trains every day to Most na Soči (55 minutes) from where you can catch regular buses to Kobarid and Bovec (45 minutes).

# Karst Region

## POSTOJNA
☎ 05 • pop 8200

Vying with Bled as the top tourist spot in Slovenia, **Postojna Cave** (adult/student & child 2400/1200 SIT) continues to attract the hordes. The electric train ride into the cave (to breeze through the less attractive parts) makes a visit seem a bit like Disneyland. Visitors get to see about 5.7km of the cave's over 20km on a 1½-hour tour in Slovenian, English, German or Italian. About 4km are covered by an electric train that will shuttle you through colourfully lit karst formations along the so-called Old Passage; the remaining 1700m is on foot. The tour ends with a viewing of a tank full of *Proteus anguinus*, the 'human fish' inhabiting Slovenia's karst caves. Dress warmly as the cave is a constant 9.5°C (with 95% humidity) all year.

From May to September, tours leave on the hour between 9am and 6pm daily. In March, April and October there are tours at 10am, noon, 2pm and 4pm with an extra daily one at 5pm in April and additional tours on the weekend in October at 11am, 1pm, 3pm and 5pm. Between November and February, tours leave at 10am and 2pm on weekdays, with extra ones added at noon and 4pm on the weekend and public holidays.

If you have the chance, visit the **Predjama Castle**, an awesome 16th-century fortress perched in the gaping mouth of a hill-top cavern 9km northwest of Postojna. As close as you'll get from Postojna by local bus (and during the school year only) though, is Bukovje, a village about 2km north of Predjama. Visiting the castles and the moderately impressive caves costs 1300/650 SIT for adults/students and children. A taxi from Postojna plus an hour's wait at the castle costs 12,000 SIT.

## Orientation & Information

Postojna Cave is about 2km northwest of the town's bus station while the train station is 1km southeast of the centre. The caves are well signposted from the town centre and taxis are available from the bus and train stations.

The **tourist office** (☎ 726 51 83; Jamska cesta 9; ℮ td.tic.postojna@siol.net; open 8am–6pm Mon-Fri, to 7pm in summer, 8am-noon Sat year-round) is in the shopping centre beneath the Hotel Jama.

**Kompas** (☎ 726 42 81; ℮ info@kompas-postojna.si; Titov trg 2a) can arrange **private rooms** from 2800 SIT per person.

## Getting There & Away

Postojna is a day trip from Ljubljana or a stopover on the way to/from the coast or Croatian Istria; almost all buses between the capital and the coast stop here. There are direct trains to Postojna from Ljubljana (one hour, 67km, 21per day) and Koper (1½ hours, 86km, 13 per day) but the bus station is closer to the caves.

## ŠKOCJAN CAVES
☎ 05

Škocjan Caves (adult/student/child 1700/1000/800 SIT), which some travellers consider a highlight of their visit, are close to the village of Matavun, 4km southeast of Divača (between Postojna and Koper). They have

been heavily promoted since 1986 when they were first entered on Unesco's World Heritage List. There are seven two-hour tours a day at 10am, and 11.30am and on the hour from 1pm to 5pm from June to September. Tours leave at 10am, 1pm and 3.30pm in April, May and October. There's a daily tour at 10am and an extra one at 3pm on Sunday and holidays from November to March.

These caves are in located in more natural surroundings than the Postojna Cave but are tough to reach without your own transport. From the train station at Divača (there are up to a dozen trains daily to/from Ljubljana), you can follow a path leading southeast through the village of Dolnje Ležeče to Matavun. The driver of any bus heading along the highway to or from the coast will let you off at the access road (there are huge signs announcing the caves) if you ask in advance. From where the bus drops you, walk the remaining 1.5km to the caves' entrance.

## LIPICA
☎ 05 ● pop 130

The famous Lipizzaner horses of the imperial Spanish Riding School in Vienna have been bred here since the 18th century and now perform at numerous equestrian events around the world. You can tour the 311-hectare **Lipica Stud Farm** (☎ 739 15 80, fax 734 63 70; ℮ lipica@siol.net; adult/student & child €6/2; open year-round); there are between four and nine tours a day, depending on the season. A tour combined with an exhibition (€12/4), in which the snow-white creatures go through their paces is available at 3pm Tuesday, Friday and Sunday from May to October but Friday and Sunday only in April. If you've made prior arrangement, you can ride the horses all year or take a riding lesson (€17 to €60, depending on the season and length).

There are several expensive hotels available on the premises, or try the **Pension Risnik** (☎ 763 00 08; Kraška cesta 24; accommodation per person 2200 SIT) in nearby Divača.

For dinner, try the excellent Italian cuisine at **Gostilna Malovec** (☎ 763 12 25; Kraška cesta 30a).

Lipica is 10km southwest of Divača and 10km south of Sežana, which are both on the main train line from Trieste to Ljubljana. From Monday to Friday there are five buses a day from Sežana to Lipica.

# The Coast

## KOPER
☎ 05 • pop 24,000

Koper, only 21km south of Trieste, is an industrial port town with a quaint city centre. The town's Italian name, Capodistria, recalls its former status as capital of Istria under the Venetian Republic in the 15th and 16th centuries. After WWII, the port was developed to provide Slovenia with an alternative to Italian Trieste and Croatian Rijeka. Once an island but now firmly connected to the mainland by a causeway, the Old Town's medieval flavour lingers despite the industry, container ports, high-rise buildings and motorways beyond its 'walls'. This administrative centre is the largest town on the Slovene coast and makes a good base for exploring the region.

## Orientation

The bus and train stations are combined in a modern structure about a kilometre southeast of the Old Town at the end of Kolodvorska cesta. There's a left luggage facility open 5.30am to 10pm that costs 400 SIT.

## Information

**Tourist Offices** You will find the **tourist office** (*☎/fax 627 37 91; Ukmarjev trg 7; open 9am-9pm Mon-Sat, 9am-1pm Sun June-Sept; 9am-2pm & 5pm-7pm Mon-Fri, 9am-1pm Sat Oct-May*) opposite the marina.

**Money** The fairly central **Nova Ljubljanska Banka** (*Pristaniška ul 45; open 8.30am-noon, 3.30pm-6pm Mon-Fri*) has an ATM. There are also a couple of private exchange offices on Pristaniška ul, including **Maki** (*open 8am-7pm Mon-Fri, to 1pm Sat*). The ATM on the southeastern corner of Titov trg takes Visa, MasterCard, Maestro and Cirrus. The ATM at the post office accepts MasterCard and Cirrus.

**Post & Communications** The **post office** (*Muzejski trg 3; open 8am-7pm Mon-Fri, 8am-noon Sat*) is near the regional museum.

**Email & Internet Access** Travellers can use the five computers at **PINA** (*Gregorčičeva ul 6, 3rd floor*), a cultural and educational centre, for free. The computers are available on weekdays 10am to 2pm and 6pm to 10pm, and 6pm to 10 pm on Saturday.

## Things to See

From the stations you enter Prešernov trg through the **Muda Gate** (1516). Walk past the bridge-shaped **Da Ponte Fountain** (1666), into Župančičeva ul and then right onto Čevljanka ul. This leads to Titov trg, the medieval central square. Most of the things to see in Koper are clustered here.

The 36m-high **City Tower** (1480), which you can climb daily in summer, stands beside the **Cathedral of St Nazarius**, dating mostly from the 18th-century. The lower portion of the cathedral's facade is Gothic, and the upper part is Renaissance. North is the sublime **Loggia** (1463), now a café and gallery, and to the south is the 1452 **Praetorian Palace** (free guided visits 10.15am and 5pm), both good examples of Venetian Gothic style. On the narrow lane behind the cathedral is a 12th-century Romanesque baptistry called the **Carmine Rotunda**. Trg Brolo to the east of the cathedral contains several more old Venetian buildings, including **Brutti Palace**, now a library, at No 1 and the **Fontico**, a 14th-century granary, at No 4.

The **Koper Regional Museum** (*Kidričeva ul 19; adult/student & child 350/250 SIT; open 8am-3pm Mon-Fri, 8am-1pm Sat year-round, 6pm-8pm Mon-Fri in summer*) is in the Belgramoni-Tacco Palace. It contains old maps and photos of the port and coast, an Italianate sculpture garden and paintings from the 16th to 18th centuries, and copies of medieval frescoes.

## Places to Stay

The closest camping grounds are **Adria** (*☎ 652 83 23*), at Ankaran about 10km to the north by road, and **Jadranka** (*☎ 640 23 00*) at Izola 8km to the west.

Both the tourist office and **Kompas** (*☎ 627 15 81; Pristaniška ul*) opposite the vegetable market have private rooms for about 2700 to 3100 SIT per person, depending on the category and season. Apartments for three/four people start at 10,000/16,000 SIT. Most of the rooms are in the new town beyond the train station.

In July and August the **Dijaški Dom Koper** (*☎ 627 32 52; Cankarjeva ul 5; beds per person 3500 SIT*), an official hostel in the Old Town east of Trg Brolo, rents out 380 beds in triple rooms. The rest of the year only three beds are available. An HI card will get you a 10% discount.

SLOVENIA

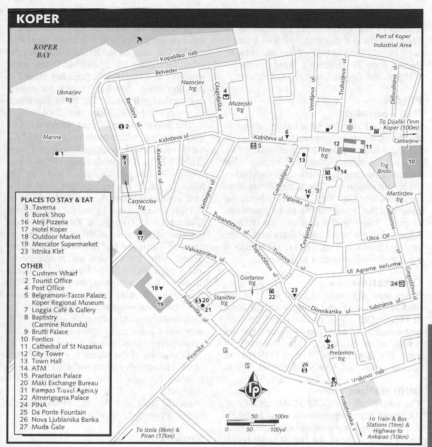

**KOPER**

KOPER BAY

*KOPER BAY*

Port of Koper
Industrial Area

Kopališko nab

Belveder

*Ukmarjev trg*

Nazorjev trg

Glagoljaška ul

Muzejski trg

To Dijaški Dom
Koper (100m)

Marina

Kidričeva ul

Kidričeva ul

Titov trg

Trg Brolo

Carpacciov trg

Martinzev trg

Župančičeva ul

Ulica OF

Valvazorjeva ul

Ul Agrarne Reforme

Gortanov trg

Staničev trg

Dimnikarska ul

Sabinjeva ul

Pristaniška

Prešernov trg

Vojkovo nab

Kolodvorska c

To Izola (8km) &
Piran (17km)

To Train & Bus
Stations (1km) &
Highway to
Ankaran (10km)

**PLACES TO STAY & EAT**
3  Taverna
6  Burek Shop
16 Atrij Pizzeria
17 Hotel Koper
18 Outdoor Market
19 Mercator Supermarket
23 Istrska Klet

**OTHER**
1  Customs Wharf
2  Tourist Office
4  Post Office
5  Belgramoni-Tacco Palace;
   Koper Regional Museum
7  Loggia Café & Gallery
8  Baptistry
   (Carmine Rotunda)
9  Brutti Palace
10 Fontico
11 Cathedral of St Nazarius
12 City Tower
13 Town Hall
14 ATM
15 Praetorian Palace
20 Maki Exchange Bureau
21 Kompas Travel Agency
22 Almerigogna Palace
24 PINA
25 Da Ponte Fountain
26 Nova Ljublanska Banka
27 Muda Gate

0    50    100m
0    50    100yd

SLOVENIA

The only hotel in the Old Town is the reno-vated **Hotel Koper** (☎ *610 05 00, fax 610 05 94; e koper@terme-catez.si; Pristaniška ul 3; singles/doubles off season 10,700/17,200 SIT, July & Aug 13,000/20,800 SIT*), with its business-like facilities.

### Places to Eat
For fried dough on the go, head for the **burek shop** (*Kidričeva ul 8*). **Pizzeria Atrij** (*Triglavska ul 2; open to 10pm daily*) has a courtyard out the back.

One of the most colourful places for a meal in Koper is **Istrska Klet** (*Župančičeva ul 39; mains around 1200 SIT*), in an old palace. This is a good place to try Teran, the hearty red (almost purple) wine from the Karst and coastal wine-growing areas.

**Taverna** (*Pristaniška ul 1; lunch 850/1000 SIT*), in a 15th-century salt warehouse oppo-site the marina, has some decent fish dishes and lunch menus.

The large shopping centre and outdoor **market** (*Pristaniška ul; open 7am-2pm*) is open most days and contains a **Mercator supermarket** and various **food shops**.

### Getting There & Away
There are buses almost every 20 minutes on weekdays to Piran (17km) and Portorož via Izola, and every 40 minutes on weekends. Buses also leave every hour or 90 minutes for Ljubljana (2400 SIT, 2¼ hours) via Divača and Postojna. You can also take the train to Ljubljana (1700 SIT, 2¼ hours), which is much more comfortable.

Up to 17 buses a day depart for Trieste (600 SIT) during the week. Destinations in Croatia include Buzet (three or four buses a day), Poreč (three or four), Pula (one or two); Rijeka (one at 10.10am), Rovinj (one at 3.55pm) and Zagreb (two).

## PIRAN
☎ 05 • pop 4400

Picturesque Piran (Pirano in Italian), sitting at the tip of a narrow peninsula, is everyone's favourite town on the Slovenian coast. It's a gem of Venetian Gothic architecture with narrow little streets, but it can be mobbed at the height of summer. The name derives from the Greek word for 'fire', *pyr*, referring to the ones lit at Punta, the very tip of the peninsula, to guide ships to the port at Aegida (now Koper). Piran's long history dates back to the ancient Greeks, and remnants of the medieval town walls still protect it to the east.

## Orientation

Buses stop just south of Piran Harbour and next to the library on Tartinijev trg, the heart of Piran's Old Town. Piran charges an exorbitant amount of money to park inside the city centre, so go to the car park just south of town. It's 1600 SIT for 24 hours (3400 SIT to park in town), and there's a shuttle into Piran.

## Information

The **tourist office** (☎ 673 25 07, fax 673 25 09; Stjenkova ul) opposite the Piran Hotel essentially rents out rooms and keeps very brief hours. Instead head for the **Maona travel agency** (☎ 673 12 91; e maona@siol.net; Cankarjevo nab 7; open Apr-Oct), where the helpful and knowledgeable staff can organise accommodation, an endless string of activities and boat cruises. During the months when the office is closed, ask at the agency in nearby Portorož (see that section later in the chapter).

**Banka Koper** (Tartinijev trg 12; open 8.30am-noon & 3pm-5pm Mon-Fri, to noon Sat) changes cash and has an ATM.

There's a **post office** (Cankarjevo nab 5; open 8am-7pm Mon-Fri, 8am-noon Sat) on the harbourfront.

## Things to See & Do

The exhibits of Piran's **Maritime Museum** (Cankarjevo nab 3; adult/student 500/400 SIT; open 9am-noon & 3pm-6pm Tues-Sun), in a 17th-century harbourside palace, focus on the three 'Ss' that have shaped Piran's development over the centuries: the sea, sailing and salt-making (at Sečovlje just southeast of Portorož). The antique model ships are first-rate; other rooms are filled with old figureheads, weapons and votive folk paintings placed in the pilgrimage church at Strunjan for protection against shipwreck. The **Piran Aquarium** (Tomšičeva ul 4) is closed until 2004.

The **Town Hall** and **Court House** stand on Tartinijev trg, which contains a statue of the local violinist and composer Giuseppe Tartini (1692–1770). A short distance to the northwest is Prvomajski trg (also known as Trg Maja 1) and its baroque **cistern**, used in the 18th century to store the town's fresh water.

Piran is dominated by the tall tower of the **Church of St George**, a Renaissance and baroque structure on a ridge above the sea north of Tartinijev trg. It's wonderfully decorated with frescoes and has marble altars and a large statue of the George slaying the dragon. The free-standing **bell tower** (1609) was modelled on the campanile of San Marco in Venice; the octagonal **Baptistry** from the 17th century next to it contains altars, paintings and a Roman sarcophagus from the 2nd century, later used as a baptismal font.

To the east of the church is a 200m stretch of the 15th-century **town walls**, which can be climbed for superb views of Piran and the Adriatic.

During July and August, **Piran Musical Evenings** are held on Tartini trg.

## Cruises

Maona and other travel agencies in Piran and Portorož can book you on any number of cruises – from a loop that takes in the towns along the coast to day-long excursions to Venice, Trieste, Rovinj or Brioni National Park in Croatia.

From late-May to October, the large catamaran *Marconi* sails down the Istrian Coast in Croatia as far as the Brioni Islands and the national park there. All-day excursions cost €54/29 return for adults/children aged four to 12; lunch is extra. To Rovinj the cost is €27/18. The boat leaves at 10am and returns at about 6.45pm except in September when it departs and returns 20 minutes earlier. At 8.35pm (6.50pm in September) on the same days, the *Marconi* heads for Trieste (35 minutes, one way €16/12 for adults/children) and returns the following morning at 9am.

## PIRAN

**GULF OF TRIESTE**

Bathing Area

Prešernovo nabrežje

Adamičeva

Trail to Beaches, Fiesa, Hotel Fiesa & Camping Jezero Fiesa (700m)

Vegova Bonifacijeva ul

Židovski trg

Gregorčičeva ul

Trg 1 Maja

Verdijeva ul

Prešernovo nab

Obzidna ul

Kosovelova ul

Tomažičev trg

Tartinijev trg

Kajuhova ul

Stjenkova ul

Tomažičeva ul

IX Korpusa

Ul Svobode

Roznanova

**PIRAN BAY**

Bathing Area

Kidričeva nab

Marina

Leninova ul

Cankarjevo nabrežje

Town Walls

Bidovčeva ul

Gortanova ul

**Piran Harbour**

Trg Bratsva

Bolniška ul

Customs Wharf

Županičeva

Tomažičeva ul

Grudnova ul

Dantejeva ul

To Car Park (200m) & Portorož (5km)

**PLACES TO STAY**
4 Val Hostel
23 Piran Hotel

**PLACES TO EAT**
3 Pizzerias & Pubs
6 Bife Ivo
7 Pavel
8 Delfin
27 Neptun
29 Mercator Supermarket

**OTHER**
1 Punta Lighthouse
2 Church of St Clement
5 Cistern
9 Fruit Market
10 Church of St George
11 Bell Tower
12 Baptistry
13 Church of St Francis & Monastery
14 Church of St Peter
15 Tartini Memorial
16 Venetian House
17 Town Hall
18 Court House
19 Bus Stop
20 Banka Koper
21 Piran Aquarium
22 Tourist Office (Rooms)
24 Cafe Teater
25 Maritime Museum
26 Post Office
28 Maona Travel Agency
30 Customs Office
31 Bus Stop

0   50   100m
0   50   100yd

**SLOVENIA**

## Places to Stay

**Camping** The closest camping ground is **Camping Jezero Fiesa** (☎ 674 62 30, fax 674 64 26; open June-Sept) at Fiesa, 4km by road from Piran (but less than a 1km walk on the coastal trail east of the Church of St George). It's in a quiet valley by two small ponds, and close to the beach, but can be crowded.

**Private Rooms & Hostels** The **tourist offices** (☎ 674 70 15; w www.portoroz.si) in Piran and Portorož as well as the **Maona travel agency** (☎ 674 64 23; e maona@siol.net) can arrange private rooms and apartments throughout the year. Single rooms cost 3100 to 3800 SIT, depending on the category and the season, while doubles are 4600 to 6600 SIT and triples 5800 SIT to 7700 SIT.

Apartments for two are 6200 SIT to 7700 SIT. They usually levy a 50% surcharge for rooms if you stay fewer than three nights.

A very central, relatively cheap place is the **Val Hostel** (☎ 673 25 55, fax 673 25 56; e yhostel.val@siol.net; Gregorčičeva ul 38a; beds off-season per person €16, summer & holidays €18; open year-round) at Vegova ul. It has 56 beds with shared shower; breakfast is included in the rates.

**Hotels** Not in Piran itself, but definitely one of the nicest places to stay on the coast is **Fiesa** (☎ 671 22 00, fax 671 22 23; e hotel.fiesa@amis.net; singles/doubles €35/52, July & Aug €50/89). The hotel is a pleasant, four-storey, 22-room place overlooking the sea near the Jezero Fiesa camping ground.

With a position right at the edge of the water is the **Piran Hotel** (☎ *676 21 00, fax 676 25 22;* e *recepcija.piran@hoteli-piran.si; Kidričeva nab 4; singles/doubles low season from €41/66, high season €58/98),* which has recently refurbished rooms. Sitting on your private balcony during sunrise makes the higher-priced, sea-view rooms worth it.

### Places to Eat
Piran has plenty of seafood restaurants along Prešernovo nab, but you do pay for location. Two good ones are **Bife Ivo** and **Pavel**. You can also try the local favourites: **Delfin** *(Kosovelova ul 4)* near Prvomajski trg or the more expensive **Neptun** *(Župančičeva ul 7)* behind Maona travel agency.

**Cafe Teater**, just south of the Piran Hotel, offers six beers on tap and light snacks. There are also several pizzerias along Prešernovo nab near the Punta lighthouse including **Flora** and **Punta**. **Mercator supermarket** *(open 7am-8pm Mon-Fri, 7am-1pm Sat, 7am-11am Sun)* is opposite Trg Bratsva 8.

### Getting There & Away
The local bus company I&I links Piran with Portorož and Lucija (bus No 1); with Portorož and Fiesa (bus No 2; mid-June to August only); with Strunjan and Portorož (bus No 3); and with Portorož, Sečovlje and Padna (bus No 4). Schedules vary, but bus No 1 (210 SIT) runs about every 10 to 15 minutes.

Other destinations that can be reached from Piran include Ljubljana via Divača and Postojna (six to 10 a day) and Nova Gorica (one or two). Six buses head for Trieste on weekdays, and there are two daily departures for Zagreb. One bus daily heads south for Croatian Istria at 4.25pm, stopping at the coastal towns of Umag, Poreč and Rovinj.

### PORTOROŽ
☎ 05 • pop 2950
The 'Port of Roses' is essentially a solid strip of high-rise hotels, restaurants, bars, travel agencies, shops, discos, beaches with turnstiles, parked cars and tourists. It's not to everyone's taste, but it does have the best beaches in Slovenia and tons of places to stay and eat. The **tourist office** (☎ *674 02 31, fax 674 82 61;* w *www.portoroz.si; Obala 16; open 9am-9pm high season)* is also the TIC for Piran. It has information on the Primorska Summer Festival, a celebration of music and dance that takes place in Portorož, Piran, Koper and Izola throughout July.

The **post office** *(K Stari cesta 1; open 8am-7pm Mon-Fri, 8am-noon Sat)* is opposite the now empty Palace Hotel (1891).

Try at either the tourist office or **Kompas** (☎ *617 80 00;* e *portoroz@kompas.si; Obala 41)* for private accommodation.

The beaches at Portorož, including the main one accommodating 6000 bodies, are 'managed' so you'll have to pay anywhere from 300 to 800 SIT to use them. They are open 9am to dusk in season. You can rent cabin space, umbrellas and chaise lounges, and there's a variety of activities to spend more money on, including water skiing, paragliding and water bike rentals.

# Eastern Slovenia

## MARIBOR
☎ 02 • pop 96,900
Maribor straddles the Drava River, but everything you'll want to access is on the northern side, between the train station and 'Lent,' the old town.

### Information
**Tourist Offices** The **tourist office** (☎ *234 66 11, fax 234 66 13;* e *matic@maribor.si; Partinzanska cesta 47; open 9am-6pm Mon-Fri, 9am-1pm Sat)* is across from the train station. It can arrange private accommodation and has a wealth of information on the *vinska cestas* (wine routes) in the area.

**Money** There's an ATM in the train station. **Nova KBM Banka** has an ATM opposite Maribor Castle on Slovenska ul. **Ljubljanska Banka** *(Ventrinjska 2; open 9am-1pm & 3pm-5pm Mon-Fri)* exchanges cash with no commission.

**Post & Communications** The main **post office** *(Partinzanska cesta 54)* is next to the train station. The exchange desk is open 7am to 7pm Monday to Saturday and 9am to 1pm Sunday for cash transactions only.

**Email & Internet Access** If you don't mind the smoke, **Kibla multimedijski center** offers free Internet access. Enter the Narodni Dom building at Kneza Koljca ul 9 and go through the first door on the left.

## Things to See and Do

Maribor is the second largest city in Slovenia, industrial but with a charming pedestrian city centre, largely free of tourists. Although not readily available outside the country, some connoisseurs say Slovenian wines equal French or Italian. The 2,400-year-old viticulture tradition in this region is most evident in the hills around Maribor. The city is also the starting point for winery tours of the surrounding area. There's no public transport in these areas, so you'll need a rental car (see the Getting There & Around section later).

The oldest living grapevine, **Stara Trta** (Vojašniška 8), has been continuously producing wine for over 400 years. Across from the castle in Trg Svobode is the **Vinag** wine cellar, a 20,000-sq-metre cellar that can store seven million litres of wine.

Enjoy the 'green treasure' Pohorje area on a day trip using local bus No 6, which departs from the train station. The bus drops you at the Pohorje cable car, which will take you to areas for hiking and skiing.

The **Lent Festival** takes over Maribor for two weeks in the end of June and start of July.

## Places to Stay

HI hostel **Dijaski Dom 26 Junij** (☎ 480 17 10; Zeleznikova ul 12; bus No 3; accommodation per person 2700 SIT) is only open July and August.

A fairly central and inexpensive hotel is **Club VIP** (☎ 229 62 00, fax 229 62 10; Tomšičeva 10; singles/doubles €36/55). To take advantage of the free entry into the Fontana spa, try the pleasant, central **Orel Hotel** (☎ 250 67 00, fax 251 84 97; e orel@ termemb.si; Grajski trg 3a; singles/doubles 12,000/19,000 SIT).

## Places to Eat

**Bolarič deli** (Juličeva ul 3; light meals 450-900 SIT open 7am-7pm Mon-Fri, to 1pm Sat) is the cheapest place around. Decent pizza can be found at **Verdi** (Dravska ul), next to the river. Around the corner is **Grill Ranca** (Vojašniška ul 4), serving Balkan favourites.

The **Mercator supermarket** (open 7am-8pm Mon-Fri, 7am-6pm Sat, 8am-11am Sun) is a few steps away from the bus station.

## Getting There & Away

Ten buses a day go to Ljubljana, starting at 5am and ending at 5.50pm. This is the best jump-off point for Rogaška Slatina (three daily) or Ptuj (20 daily). Take local bus No 6 to get to the Pohorje cable car.

Trains link Maribo to many cities in neighbouring countries: Vienna (7489 SIT, four hours, two a day); Graz (2358 SIT, one hour, two a day); and Zagreb (3100 SIT, three hours, two a day at 12.10pm and 7.55pm); Budapest (7000 SIT, seven hours, two daily at 9.10am and 3.20pm; change at Pragersko). Trains also go to Ljubljana (2½ hours, eight daily).

## Getting Around

To follow the vinska cesta, try **Avis** (☎ 228 79 10; Partizanska cesta 24; open 8am-4pm Mon-Fri, to noon Sat).

If you want to get around the area without a car, you can rent bicycles at **Café Promenada** (☎ 613 13 10; Lackova u 45).

## PTUJ

☎ 02 • pop 19,100

Charming and compact Ptuj is Slovenia's version of an Italian hill town. It's first incarnation was as Poetovio, a Roman village. Remnants of its Roman past still dot the town, and there's a hill-top castle with a magnificent museum.

## Information

The helpful Ptuj **tourist office** (☎ 779 60 11; w www.ptuj.si; Slovenski trg 3; open 8am-5pm Mon-Fri, to 1pm Sat) also opens a branch at No 14 during the summer.

## Things to See & Do

The hill-top castle features the **Ptuj Regional Museum** (adult/child 600/300 SIT; open 9am-5pm winter, to 6pm in summer, to 8pm Sat & Sun July & Aug), with exhibits on musical instruments, weaponry, the Kurentovanje Festival and Ptuj's history. Call ahead to arrange an English-speaking guide (250 SIT).

About 1.5km from the centre of town is **Terme Ptuj** (☎ 782 72 11; Pot v Toplice 9; adult/child 1800/1200 SIT), a giant spa complex with four swimming pools, water slides, massage treatments and eight tennis courts.

The **library** (Prešernova ul 33-35) is in the building complex known in the 1700s as the Small Castle. You can also check your email for free for up to one hour on the 2nd floor. The ornate **Town Hall** (Mestni trg 1) was built in 1907 to resemble the earlier late-Gothic version. The **Town's Tower** (Slovenski trg) stands in front of the **Provost's Church**. The tower was mentioned as early as 1376 in city documents, and has been rebuilt many times down through the centuries.

Every February for the 10 days surrounding Mardi Gras, Ptuj hosts the **Kurentovanje Festival**, a district-wide party that attracts visitors from all over the world.

## Places to Stay & Eat

The TIC arranges **private accommodation** starting at around 3500 SIT per person.

The **Terme Ptuj camping ground** (☎ *782 72 11; adult/child €8.60/6.10*) offers free access to the spa complex. It also has **apartments** *(singles/doubles/rooms for up to 6 people €40/65/82)*.

The central **Garni Hotel Mitra** (☎/*fax 774 21 01;* ℮ *fredi@zerak.com; Prešernova ul 6; singles/doubles/triples 7700/11,000/13,500 SIT)* offers pleasant rooms.

A great place to try Slovenian seafood dishes is **Ribič** (☎ *771 46 71; Dravska ul 9)*. It serves fresh fish for 4000 SIT per kilo and a host of Slovene specialities.

There's an **open-air market** *(Novi trg; open 7am to 3pm daily)* for self-caterers.

## Getting There & Away

Ptuj is on the line to many European destinations. There are trains to Munich (10 hours, two per day), Venice (eight hours, one daily), Zagreb (three hours, five a day) and Ljubljana (2½ hours, 11 a day). By bus, you can get to Maribor (680 SIT, 40 minutes, at least hourly), Rogaška Slatina (3.10pm daily) and Ljubljana (2½ hours, 11 daily).

## THERMAL SPAS

Slovenia was once a Roman protectorate, and this is evident in Slovenian devotion to spa culture. Nearly every town in this chapter boasts a spa, and there are a multitude of spas off the beaten track as well. The famous healing properties of the region's thermal waters have brought visitors to Slovenia for centuries. For information about spas in Slovenia, contact the **Slovenian Spas Community** (☎ *03-544 21 11;* ₩ *www.terme-giz.si).*

## Rogaška Slatina

The most famous and oldest spa town in Slovenia, Rogaška Slatina is past its heyday as the premier spot to 'take the waters', but it's in beautiful surroundings and has several good spas.

In the middle of the town there's a **tourist office** (☎ *03-811 50 13;* ℮ *tic.rogaska@siol .net; Zdravliški trg 1)* near several hotels and spas. A good bet for a bed is the **Zdravliški Dom** (☎ *03-811 20 00; doubles from €35)*.

To get to Rogaška Slatina, take either the bus or train to Celje and transfer. The bus drops you off next to the town centre, which is pedestrian-only, and the train stops about 200m away.

# Spain

Spain is a land of majesty and madness, where ghosts of a legendary past stalk the earth and seemingly every day is devoted to a frenzied, unrelenting quest for bliss. The clashes and combinations that shaped Spain's chequered history have given rise to a culture painted in the brightest of colours and steeped in the most vivacious of traditions.

Indeed, Spaniards approach life with such exuberance that visitors have to stop and stare. In almost every city, the nightlife will outlast the foreigners. And just when the bewildered traveller appears to have come to terms with the pace, they are surrounded by the beating drums of a fiesta, with day and night turning into a blur of dancing, laughing, eating and drinking.

This apparently single-minded pursuit of joy actually arises from a syncretic blend of influences – reflected by the wealth of Spain's historical sights. Long a meeting point (and battleground) for many civilisations, the country brims over with remnants of a glorious past. Fascinating prehistoric displays beckon the traveller at archaeological museums in Madrid. Tarragona's seaside amphitheatre is among several reminders of the classical period. After Roman times, the Moorish era left the most powerful cultural and artistic legacy, focused on Granada's Alhambra, Córdoba's mosque and Seville's *alcázar* (fortress) but apparent in monuments throughout much of the country. Christian Spain saw the construction of hundreds of impressive castles, cathedrals, monasteries, palaces and mansions, which today stand as romantic, mist-kissed tributes to the Middle Ages.

The rise of the Spanish empire engendered the flowering of Spain's devotion to the arts, evident today in its abundance of world-class museums. These include Madrid's Prado and Thyssen-Bornemisza museums, Figueres' idiosyncratic Dalí museum, and Barcelona's mesmerising Picasso and Miró galleries.

Spain's cultural pluralism is mirrored in its very geography, among the most diverse in Europe. The landscape varies from soaring mountains to arid plains to idyllic beaches – often within just a few kilometres. Holidaymakers enjoy the uncanny predictability of sunshine on the Mediterranean coast from April to October. More active beachgoers take advantage of the chillier surf strips of western Andalucía and, elsewhere, hikers and climbers enjoy good summer weather and spectacular scenery in the mountains of Andalucía.

All these facets combine to render Spain one of Europe's most sublime, inspiring destinations. It doesn't matter how high your expectations are for the country: they will be surpassed.

## At a Glance

- **Beaches** – isolated spots on Menorca and the Costa de la Luz, and the famed (and more crowded) Costa Brava and Costa Blanca
- **Madrid** – Spain's capital, filled with museums, parks and buzzing nightlife
- **Barcelona** – stylish, dynamic with heaps to do: Gaudí monuments, medieval Barri Gòtic and fiestas
- **Seville** – home of the Alcázar and a hub for flamenco, bullfighting and fiestas
- **Granada** – showcase of Andalucía's Muslim past, backed by snowcapped Sierra Nevada

| | |
|---|---|
| **Capital** | Madrid |
| **Population** | 40 million |
| **Official Language** | Spanish (Castilian) |
| **Currency** | euro |
| **Time** | GMT/UTC+0100 |
| **Country Phone Code** | ☎ 34 |

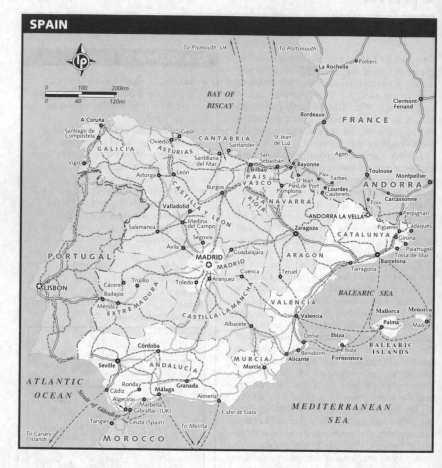

SPAIN

# Facts about Spain

## HISTORY
### Ancient History

Located at the crossroads between Europe and Africa, the Iberian Peninsula has long been a target for invading peoples and civilisations. From around 8000 to 3000 BC pioneers from North Africa known as the Iberians crossed the Strait of Gibraltar and settled the peninsula. Around 1000 BC Celtic tribes entered northern Spain, while Phoenician merchants were establishing trading settlements along the Mediterranean coast. They were followed by Greeks and Carthaginians, who arrived around 600 to 500 BC.

The Romans arrived in the 3rd century BC but took two centuries to subdue the peninsula. Although Christianity came to Spain during the 1st century AD, it was initially opposed by the Romans leading to persecution and martyrdom. In AD 409 Roman Hispania was invaded by Germanic tribes, and by 419 the Christian Visigoths, another Germanic people, had established a kingdom that lasted until 711, when the Moors – Muslim Berbers and Arabs from North Africa – crossed the Strait of Gibraltar and defeated Roderic, the last Visigoth king.

### Muslim Spain & the Reconquista

By 714 the Muslim armies had occupied the entire peninsula, apart from some northern mountain regions. Muslim dominion was to last almost 800 years in parts of Spain. In Islamic Spain (known as 'al-Andalus') arts and sciences prospered, new crops and agricultural techniques were introduced, and palaces, mosques, schools, gardens and public baths were built.

In 722 a small army under the Visigothic leader Pelayo inflicted the first defeat on the Muslims (known to Christians as *moros*, or Moors) at Covadonga in northern Spain. This marked the beginning of the Reconquista, the spluttering reconquest of Spain by the Christians. By the early 11th century, the frontier between Christian and Muslim Spain stretched from Barcelona to the Atlantic.

In 1085 Alfonso VI, king of León and Castile, took Toledo. This prompted the Muslim leaders to request help from northern Africa, which arrived in the form of the Almoravids. They recaptured much territory and ruled it until the 1140s. The Almoravids were followed by the Almohads, another North African dynasty, which ruled until 1212. But by the mid-13th century, the Christians had taken most of the peninsula except for the state of Granada.

In the process the kingdoms of Castile and Aragón emerged as Christian Spain's two main powers, and in 1469 they were united by the marriage of Isabel, princess of Castile, and Fernando, heir to Aragón's throne. Known as the Catholic Monarchs, they united Spain and laid the foundations for the Spanish golden age. They also revived the notorious Inquisition, which expelled and executed thousands of Jews and other non-Christians. In 1492 the last Muslim ruler of Granada surrendered to them, which marked the completion of the Reconquista.

## The Golden Age

Also in 1492, while searching for an alternative passage to India, Christopher Columbus stumbled on the Bahamas and claimed the Americas for Spain. This sparked a period of exploration and exploitation that was to yield Spain enormous wealth while destroying the ancient American empires. For three centuries, gold and silver from the New World were used to finance the rapid expansion and slow decline of the Spanish empire.

In 1516 Fernando was succeeded by his grandson Carlos, of the Habsburg dynasty. Carlos was elected Holy Roman Emperor in 1519 and ruled over an empire that included Austria, southern Germany, the Netherlands, Spain and the American colonies. He and his successors were to lead Spain into a series of expensive wars that ultimately bankrupted the empire. In 1588 Sir Francis Drake's English fleet annihilated the mighty Spanish Armada. The Thirty Years' War (1618–48) saw Spain in conflict with the Netherlands, France and England. By the reign of the last Habsburg monarch, Carlos II (1655–1700), the Spanish empire was in decline.

## The 18th & 19th Centuries

Carlos II died heirless. At the end of the subsequent War of the Spanish Succession (1702–13), Felipe V, grandson of French king Louis XIV, became the first of Spain's Bourbon dynasty. A period of stability, enlightened reforms and economic growth ensued, ended by events following the French Revolution of 1789.

When Louis XVI was guillotined in 1793, Spain declared war on the French republic, but then turned to alliance with France and war against Britain, in which the Battle of Trafalgar (1805) ended Spanish sea power. In 1807–08 French troops entered Spain and Napoleon convinced Carlos IV, the Spanish king, to abdicate. In his place Napoleon installed his own brother Joseph Bonaparte. The Spaniards retaliated with a five-year war of independence. In 1815 Napoleon was defeated by Wellington, and a Bourbon, Fernando VII, was restored to the Spanish throne.

Fernando's reign was a disastrous advertisement for monarchy: the Inquisition was re-established, liberals and constitutionalists were persecuted, free speech was repressed, Spain entered a severe recession and the American colonies won their independence. After Fernando's death in 1833 came the First Carlist War (1834–39), fought between conservative forces led by Don Carlos, Fernando's brother, and liberals who supported the claim of Fernando's daughter Isabel (later Isabel II) to the throne. In 1868 the monarchy was overthrown during the Septembrina Revolution and Isabel II was forced to flee. The First Republic was declared in 1873, but within 18 months the army had restored the monarchy, with Isabel's son Alfonso XII on the throne. Despite political turmoil Spain's economy prospered in the second half of the 19th century, fuelled by industrialisation.

The disastrous Spanish-American War of 1898 marked the end of the Spanish empire. Spain was defeated by the USA and lost its last overseas possessions – Cuba, Puerto Rico, Guam and the Philippines.

## The 20th Century

The early 20th century was characterised by military disasters in Morocco and growing instability as radical forces struggled to overthrow the established order. In 1923, with Spain on the brink of civil war, Miguel Primo de Rivera made himself military dictator, ruling until 1930. In 1931 Alfonso XIII fled the country, and the Second Republic was declared.

Like its predecessor, the Second Republic fell victim to internal conflict. The 1936 elections split the nation in two, with the Popular Front (an uneasy alliance of leftist parties) on one side and the right-wing Nationalists (an alliance of the army, Church and the fascist-style Falange Party) on the other.

Nationalist plotters in the army rose against the government in July 1936. During the subsequent Spanish Civil War (1936–39), the Nationalists, led by General Francisco Franco, received heavy military support from Nazi Germany and fascist Italy, while the elected Republican government received support only from Russia and, to a lesser degree, from the International Brigades, made up of foreign leftists.

By 1939 Franco had won and an estimated 350,000 Spaniards had died. After the war, thousands of Republicans were executed, jailed or forced into exile. Franco's 35-year dictatorship began with Spain isolated internationally and crippled by recession. It wasn't until the 1950s and 1960s, when the rise in tourism and a treaty with the USA combined to provide much-needed funds, that the country began to recover. By the 1970s Spain had the fastest-growing economy in Europe.

Franco died in 1975, having named Juan Carlos, grandson of Alfonso XIII, his successor. King Juan Carlos is widely credited with having overseen Spain's transition from dictatorship to democracy. The first elections were held in 1977, a new constitution was drafted in 1978, and a failed military coup in 1981 was seen as a futile attempt to turn back the clock. Spain joined the European Community in 1986 and celebrated its return to the world stage in style in 1992, with Expo '92 in Seville and the Olympic Games in Barcelona.

## Spain Today

In 1996 the centre-right Partido Popular (Popular Party; PP), led by José María Aznar, won a plurality in parliament and began a programme of economic decentralisation and liberalisation. In 1997 Spain became fully integrated in the North Atlantic Treaty Organisation (NATO), and in 1999 it met the criteria for launching the new European currency, the euro.

By the time of the 2000 general election, Spain enjoyed the fastest-growing economy in the EU. The torrid economic pace gained widespread support for Aznar's policies, leading to an absolute majority in both parliamentary houses for his PP. Aznar has since continued his programme of labour-market reform and promotion of competition.

Spain assumed the rotating presidency of the EU moments before 1 January 2002, thus presiding over the Euro zone's official transition to the new cash currency.

## GEOGRAPHY & ECOLOGY

Spain is probably Europe's most geographically diverse country, with landscapes ranging from the near-deserts of Almería to the rugged mountains of the Pyrenees.

The country covers 84% of the Iberian Peninsula and spreads over nearly 505,000 sq km, more than half of which is high table-land, the *meseta*. This is supported and divided by several mountain chains. The main ones are the Pyrenees, along the border with France; the Cordillera Cantábrica, backing the northern coast; the Sistema Ibérico, from the central north towards the middle Mediterranean coast; the Cordillera Central, from north of Madrid towards the Portuguese border; and three east-west chains across Andalucía, one of which is the highest range of all – the Sierra Nevada.

The major rivers are the Ebro, Duero, Tajo (Tagus), Guadiana and Guadalquivir, each draining a different basin between the mountains and all flowing into the Atlantic Ocean (except for the Ebro, which reaches the Mediterranean Sea).

## CLIMATE

The *meseta* and Ebro basin have a continental climate: scorching in summer, cold in winter, and always dry. Madrid regularly freezes from December through February, and temperatures climb above 30°C in July

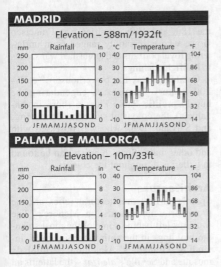

**MADRID**

Elevation – 588m/1932ft

**PALMA DE MALLORCA**

Elevation – 10m/33ft

and August. The Guadalquivir basin in Andalucía is only a little wetter and positively broils in high summer, with temperatures in Seville that kill people every year. This area doesn't get as cold as the *meseta* in winter.

The Pyrenees and the Cordillera Cantábrica backing the Bay of Biscay coast bear the brunt of cold northern and northwestern airstreams. Even in high summer you never know when you might get a shower. The Mediterranean coast and Balearic Islands get a little more rain than Madrid, and the southern coast can be even hotter in summer. The Mediterranean also provides Spain's warmest waters (reaching 27°C or so in August), and you can swim as early as April or even late March in the southeast.

In general there are pleasant or hot temperatures just about everywhere from April to early November (plus March in the south, but minus a month at either end on the northern and northwestern coasts). Snowfalls in the mountains start as early as October and some snow cover lasts all year on highest peaks.

## FLORA & FAUNA

The brown bear, wolf, lynx and wild boar all survive in Spain, although only the boar exists in healthy numbers. Spain's high mountains harbour the goat-like chamois and Spanish ibex (the latter is rare) and big birds of prey such as eagles, vultures and the lammergeier. The marshy Ebro delta and Guadalquivir estuary are important for waterbirds, among them the spectacular greater flamingo. Many of Spain's 5500 seed-bearing plants occur nowhere else in Europe because of the barrier of the Pyrenees. Spring wildflowers are magnificent in many country and hilly areas.

The conservation picture has improved by leaps and bounds in the past 25 years and Spain now has 25,000 sq km of protected areas, including 10 national parks. But overgrazing, reservoir creation, tourism, housing developments, agricultural and industrial effluent, fires and hunting all still threaten plant and animal life.

## GOVERNMENT & POLITICS

Spain is a constitutional monarchy. The 1978 constitution restored parliamentary government and grouped the country's 50 provinces into 17 autonomous communities, each with its own regional government. Since 1996 Spain has been governed by the right-of-centre Partido Popular (PP), led by José María Aznar, which unseated long-standing centre-left PSOE party led by Felipe González. With a strong mandate from the people in the 2000 elections, the PP enjoys popularity never before experienced by a conservative party in democratic Spain.

Spain's government has long been embroiled in a campaign against the Basque separatist movement of ETA. Although ETA's support and funding has dried up somewhat in recent years, it has pressed on with its agenda, most recently detonating two car bombs in Madrid on 1 May 2002.

## ECONOMY

Spain experienced an amazing economic turnabout in the 20th century, raising its living standards from the lowest in Western Europe to a level comparable to the rest of the continent. Recession hit in the early 1990s, though an initially slow recovery sped up by the end of the decade. At 15%, unemployment in the country remains among the highest in Western Europe.

Service industries employ over six million people and produce close to 60% of the country's GDP. The arrival of over 50 million tourists every year brings work to around 10% of the entire labour force. Industry accounts for about one-third of both workforce and GDP, but agriculture accounts for only 4% of GDP compared with 23% in 1960, although it employs one in 10 workers.

SPAIN

## POPULATION & PEOPLE

Spain's population of 40 million is descended from the many peoples who have settled here over the millennia, among them Iberians, Celts, Romans, Jews, Visigoths, Berbers and Arabs. The biggest cities are Madrid (three million), Barcelona (1.5 million), Valencia (746,610) and Seville (702,520). Each region proudly preserves its own unique culture, and some – Catalunya for example – display a fiercely independent spirit.

## ARTS
### Cinema

Early Spanish cinema was hamstrung by a lack of funds and technology, and perhaps the greatest of all Spanish directors, Luis Buñuel, made his silent surrealist classics *Un Chien Andalou* (1928) and *L'Age d'Or* (1930) in France. However, he returned to Spain to make *Tierra sin Pan* (Land Without Bread; 1932), a film about rural poverty in the Las Hurdes area of Extremadura.

Franco's regime saw strict censorship, but satirical and uneasy films like Juan Antonio Bardem's *Muerte de un Ciclista* (Death of a Cyclist; 1955) and Luis Berlanga's *Bienvenido Mr Marshall* (Welcome Mr Marshall; 1953) still managed to appear. Carlos Saura, with films like *Ana y los Lobos* (Anna and the Wolves; 1973), and Victor Erice, with *El Espiritu de la Colmena* (Spirit of the Beehive; 1973) and *El Sur* (The South; 1983), looked at the problems of young people scarred by the Spanish Civil War and its aftermath.

After Franco, Pedro Almodóvar broke away from this serious cinema dwelling on the past with humorous films set amid the social and artistic revolution of the late 1970s and 1980s, notably *Mujeres al Borde de un Ataque de Nervios* (Women on the Verge of a Nervous Breakdown; 1988). In 1995 Ken Loach produced a moving co-production on the Spanish Civil War, *Tierra y Libertad* (Land and Freedom).

### Painting

The golden age of Spanish art (1550–1650) was strongly influenced by Italy, but the great Spanish artists developed their talents in unique ways. The giants were Toledo-based El Greco (originally from Crete) and Diego Velázquez, perhaps Spain's most revered painter. Both excelled with insightful portraits. Francisco Zurbarán and Bartolomé Esteban Murillo were also prominent. The genius of the 18th and 19th centuries was Francisco Goya, whose versatility ranged from unflattering royal portraits and anguished war scenes to bullfight etchings.

Catalunya was the powerhouse of early-20th-century Spanish art, engendering the hugely prolific Pablo Picasso (born in Andalucía), the colourful symbolist Joan Miró, and Salvador Dalí, who was obsessed with the unconscious and weird. Works by these and other major Spanish artists can be found in galleries throughout the country.

### Architecture

Spain's earliest architectural relics are the prehistoric monuments on Menorca. The Muslims left behind some of the most splendid buildings in the entire Islamic world, including Granada's Alhambra, Córdoba's mosque and Seville's *alcázar* – the latter is an example of *mudéjar* architecture, the name given to Moorish work done throughout Christian-held territory.

The first main Christian architectural movement was Romanesque, in the north in the 11th and 12th centuries. Surviving manifestations include countless lovely country churches and several cathedrals. Later came the many great Gothic cathedrals of the 13th to 16th centuries, as well as Renaissance styles and the austere work of Juan de Herrera, responsible for El Escorial (see the Around Madrid section). Spain then followed the usual path to baroque (17th and 18th centuries) and neoclassicism (19th century) before Catalunya produced its startling modernist (roughly Art Nouveau) movement around the turn of the 20th century, of which Antoni Gaudí's Sagrada Família church is the most stunning example. More recent architecture is likely to excite only specialists.

### Literature

One of the earliest works of Spanish literature is the *Cantar de mío Cid* (Song of My Cid), an anonymous epic poem describing the life of El Cid, an 11th-century Christian knight. Miguel de Cervantes' novel *Don Quixote de la Mancha* is the masterpiece of the literary flowering of the 16th and 17th centuries, as well as one of the world's great works of fiction. The playwrights Lope de Vega and Pedro Calderón de la Barca were also leading lights of the age.

SPAIN

La Sagrada Família, Barcelona

Escape the crowds on Menorca's beaches, Spain

The Blue Mosque, İstanbul, Turkey

Facade of the Celsus Library, Ephesus, Turkey

Whirling dervish, Turkey

Shop till you drop at the Grand Bazaar, İstanbul

İstiklal Caddesi, İstanbul's fashionable shopping street, Turkey

Ölüdeniz, Turkey

National Museum of Belgrade

Church belltower, Montenegro

Historic Kotor lies at the head of the huge Kotor Fjord, Yugoslavia

The next high point, in the early 20th century, grew out of the crisis of the Spanish-American War that spawned the intellectual 'Generation of '98'. Philosophical essayist Miguel de Unamuno was prominent, but the towering figure was poet and playwright Federico García Lorca, whose tragedies *Bodas de Sangre* (Blood Weddings) and *Yerma* (Barren) won international acclaim before he was murdered in the Civil War for his Republican sympathies.

Camilo José Cela, author of the civil-war-aftermath novel *La Familia de Pascal Duarte* (The Family of Pascal Duarte), won the 1989 Nobel Prize for literature. Juan Goytisolo is probably the major contemporary writer; his most approachable work is his autobiography, *Forbidden Territory*. In the past 25 years there has been a proliferation of women writers – particularly feminists – among whose prominent representatives are Adelaide Morales, Ana María Matute and Rosa Montero.

## SOCIETY & CONDUCT

Most Spaniards are economical with etiquette, but this does not signify unfriendliness. They're gregarious people, on the whole very tolerant and easy-going towards foreigners. It's not easy to give offence. However, obviously disrespectful behaviour, including excessively casual dress in churches, won't go down well.

### Siesta

Contrary to popular belief, most Spaniards do not sleep in the afternoon. The siesta is generally devoted to a long, leisurely lunch and lingering conversation. Then again, if you've stayed out until 5am...

### Flamenco

Getting to see real, deeply emotional flamenco can be hard, as it tends to happen semispontaneously in little bars. Andalucía is its traditional home. You'll find plenty of clubs there and elsewhere offering flamenco shows; these are generally aimed at tourists and are expensive, but some are good. Your best chance of catching the real thing is probably at one of the flamenco festivals in the south, usually held in summer.

## RELIGION

Only about 20% of Spaniards are regular churchgoers, but Catholicism is deeply ingrained in the culture. As the writer Unamuno said, 'Here in Spain we are all Catholics, even the atheists'.

Many Spaniards have a deep-seated scepticism of the Church; during the Civil War, churches were burnt and clerics shot because they represented repression, corruption and the old order.

## LANGUAGE

Spanish, or Castilian *(castellano)*, as it is often and more precisely called, is spoken by just about all Spaniards, but there are also three widely spoken regional languages. Catalan (another Romance language, closely related to Spanish and French) is spoken by about two-thirds of people in Catalunya and the Balearic Islands and half the people in the Valencia region; Galician (another Romance language that sounds like a cross between Spanish and Portuguese) is spoken by many in the northwest; and Basque (of mysterious, non-Latin origin) is spoken by a minority in the País Vasco and Navarra.

English isn't as widely spoken as many travellers seem to expect. In the principal cities and tourist areas it's not too difficult to find people who speak at least some English, though generally you'll be better received if you at least try to communicate in Spanish.

See the Language chapter at the back of the book for pronunciation guidelines and useful words and phrases.

# Facts for the Visitor

## HIGHLIGHTS
### Beaches

It's still possible to have a beach to yourself in Spain, although summertime makes the task tricky. Such gems as the beaches of Cabo Favàritx in Menorca and some of the secluded coves on Cabo de Gata in Andalucía are bound to be quiet. There are also good, relatively uncrowded beaches on the Costa de la Luz, between Tarifa and Cádiz.

### Museums & Galleries

Spain is home to some of the world's finest art galleries. The Prado in Madrid has few rivals, and there are outstanding art museums in Seville, Barcelona, Valencia and Córdoba. Fascinating smaller galleries, such as the Dalí museum in Figueres, also abound. Tarragona has an excellent archaeological museum.

SPAIN

## Buildings

Don't miss Andalucía's Muslim-era gems – Granada's Alhambra, Seville's *alcázar* and Córdoba's Mezquita – or Gaudí's amazing La Sagrada Família in Barcelona.

For even more exciting views, and loads of medieval ghosts, visit the ruined castle in Morella, Valencia province.

## Scenery

Outstanding mountain scenery and highly picturesque villages characterise parts of Andalucía, such as the Alpujarras. On the coast, the stark, hilly Cabo de Gata, Andalucía, stands out.

## SUGGESTED ITINERARIES

If you want to whiz around as many places as possible in a limited time, the following itineraries might suit you:

**Two days**
Fly to Madrid, Barcelona or Seville, or nip into Barcelona overland from France.

**One week**
Spend two days each in Barcelona and Madrid and one in Seville, allowing two days for travel.

**Two weeks**
Spend more time in the places above, plus visit Toledo and Granada or Córdoba

**One month**
As above, plus some of the following: side trips from the cities mentioned above; a visit to Mallorca and Formentera.

## PLANNING
## When to Go

For most purposes the ideal months to visit Spain are May, June and September (plus April and October in the south). At these times you can rely on good weather, yet avoid the extreme heat and crush of Spanish and foreign tourists in July and August, when temperatures may climb to 45°C in parts of Andalucía and Madrid is unbearably hot and almost deserted.

The summer overflows with festivals, including Sanfermines (think Pamplona's running of the bulls) and Semana Grande all along the northern coast (dates vary from place to place), but there's no shortage of excellent festivals during the rest of the year.

Winter brings unceasing rains (except when it snows) to the north. Madrid regularly freezes from December through February. At these times Andalucía is the place to be, with temperatures reaching the mid-teens in most places and there's good skiing in the Sierra Nevada.

## Maps

Some of the best maps are published by Michelin, which produces a 1:1,000,000 *Spain & Portugal* map and six 1:400,000 regional maps. The country map doesn't show railways, but the regional maps do.

## What to Bring

You can buy anything you need in Spain, but some articles, such as sunscreen, are more expensive than elsewhere. Books in English tend to be expensive and hard to find outside main cities.

A pair of strong shoes and a towel are essential. A moneybelt or shoulder wallet can be useful in big cities. Bring sunglasses if glare gets to you. If you want to blend in, pack more than T-shirts, shorts and runners (sneakers) – Spaniards are quite dressy, and many tourists look like slobs to them.

## TOURIST OFFICES

Most towns and large villages of any interest have an *oficina de turismo* (tourist office). These will supply you with a map and brochures with basic information on local sights, attractions, accommodation, history etc. Staffs are generally helpful and often speak some English. A **nationwide phone line** *(☎ 901 30 06 00; open 9am-6pm daily)* offers information in English.

## Tourist Offices Abroad

Spain has tourist information centres in 29 countries, including the following:

**Canada** (☎ 416-961 3131; e toronto@tour spain.es) 2 Bloor St W, 34th floor, Toronto, Ontario M4W 3E2

**France** (☎ 01 45 03 82 57; e paris@tourspain .es) 43 Rue Decamps, 75784 Paris, Cedex 16

**Portugal** (☎ 01-21 354 1992; e lisboa@tour spain.es) Avenida Sidónio Pais 28 3 Dto, 1050-215 Lisbon

**UK** (☎ 020-7486 8077, brochure request ☎ 090-6364 0630 at UK£0.60 a minute; e londres@ tourspain.es) 22–23 Manchester Square, London W1M 5AP

**USA** (☎ 212-265 8822; e oetny@tourspain.es) 666 Fifth Ave, 35th floor, New York, NY 10103

## VISAS & DOCUMENTS

Citizens of EU countries can enter Spain with their national identity card or passport. UK citizens must have a full passport, not just a British visitor passport. Non-EU nationals must take their passport.

EU, Norway and Iceland citizens do not need a visa. Nationals of Australia, Canada, Israel, Japan, New Zealand, Switzerland and the USA need no visa for stays of up to 90 days but must have a passport valid for the whole visit. This 90-day limit applies throughout the EU, so don't overstay your time in the EU even if Spain is only part of your trip. South Africans are among nationalities that do need a visa.

It's best to obtain the visa in your country of residence. Single-entry visas are available in flavours of 30-day and 90-day, and there's a 90-day multiple-entry visa, too, although if you apply in a country where you're not a resident the 90-day option may not be available. Multiple-entry visas will save you a lot of time and trouble if you plan to leave Spain (say to go to Gibraltar or Morocco), and then re-enter it.

Spain is one of the Schengen Area countries; the others are Portugal, Italy, France, Germany, Austria, the Netherlands, Belgium, Luxembourg, Sweden, Finland, Denmark and Greece. A visa for one Schengen country is valid for the others as well. Compare validity, prices and permitted entries before applying. Schengen countries theoretically have done away with passport control on travel between them.

### Stays of Longer than 90 Days

Nationals of the EU, Norway and Iceland planning to stay in Spain more than 90 days are supposed to apply during their first month in the country for a residence card. This is a lengthy and complicated procedure; if you intend to subject yourself to the ordeal, consult a Spanish consulate before you go to Spain, as you'll need to take certain documents with you.

Other nationalities on a Schengen visa are flat out of luck when it comes to extensions. For stays of longer than 90 days you're supposed to get a residence card. This is a nightmarish process, starting with a residence visa issued by a Spanish consulate in your country of residence; be sure to start the process well in advance.

## EMBASSIES & CONSULATES
### Spanish Embassies & Consulates

Spanish embassies include:

**Australia** (☎ 02-6273 3555; ℮ embespau@mail .mae.es) 15 Arkana St, Yarralumba, ACT 2600
*Consulates in Brisbane, Melbourne, Perth and Sydney*
**Canada** (☎ 613-747 2252; ℮ spain@DocuWeb .ca) 74 Stanley Ave, Ottawa, Ontario K1M 1P4
*Consulate in Montreal* (☎ 514-935 5235)
*Consulate in Toronto* (☎ 416-977 1661)
**France** (☎ 01 44 43 18 00; ℮ ambespfr@mail .mae.es) 22 Avenue Marceau, 75381 Paris, Cedex 08
**Portugal** (☎ 01-347 2381; ℮ embesppt@mail .mae.es) Rua do Salitre 1, 1250 Lisbon
**UK** (☎ 020-7235 5555; ℮ espemblon@espem blon.freeserve.co.uk) 39 Chesham Place, London SW1X 8SB
*Consulates in Belfast, Edinburgh, Liverpool and Manchester*
**USA** (☎ 202-452 0100) 2375 Pennsylvania Ave NW, Washington, DC 20037
*Consulates in Albuquerque, Atlanta, Baltimore, Boston, Chicago, Cincinnati, Corpus Christi, Dallas, El Paso, Honolulu, Houston, Kansas City, Los Angeles, Miami, New Orleans, New York, Saint Louis, San Antonio, San Diego, San Francisco and Seattle*

### Embassies & Consulates in Spain

Some 70 countries have embassies in Madrid, including:

**Australia** (☎ 91 441 93 00) Plaza del Descubridor Diego de Ordás 3-28003, Edificio Santa Engrácia 120
**Canada** (☎ 91 431 43 00) Calle de Núñez de Balboa 35
**France** (☎ 91 423 89 00) Calle de Salustiano Olózaga 9
**Germany** (☎ 91 557 90 00) Calle de Fortuny 8
**Ireland** (☎ 91 576 35 00) Paseo de la Castellana 36
**Japan** (☎ 91 590 76 00) Calle de Serrano 109
**Morocco** (☎ 91 563 10 90) Calle de Serrano 179
*Consulate* (☎ 91 561 21 45) Calle de Leizaran 31
**New Zealand** (☎ 91 523 02 26) Plaza de la Lealtad 3
**Portugal** (☎ 91 561 78 00) Calle de Pinar 1
*Consulate* (☎ 91 445 46 00) Calle Martínez Campos 11
**UK** (☎ 91 700 82 00) Calle de Fernando el Santo 16
*Consulate* (☎ 91 308 52 01) Edificio Colón, Calle del Marqués Ensenada 16
**USA** (☎ 91 587 22 00) Calle de Serrano 75

SPAIN

## CUSTOMS

From outside the EU you are allowed to bring in duty-free one bottle of spirits, one bottle of wine, 50mL of perfume and 200 cigarettes. From within the EU you can bring 2L of wine *and* 1L of spirits, with the same limits on the rest. Duty-free allowances for travel between EU countries were abolished in 1999.

## MONEY
## Currency & Exchange Rates

Like in the rest of the Eurozone, Spain's currency for everyday transactions is now the euro (€). See Money in the introductory Facts for the Visitor chapter for more information on this sparkly new medium of exchange, including exchange rates.

Banks mostly open 8.30am to 2pm Monday to Friday and 8.30am to 1pm Saturday and tend to give better exchange rates than do the currency-exchange offices. Travellers cheques attract a slightly better rate than cash. ATMs accepting a wide variety of cards are common.

## Costs

Spain is one of Western Europe's more affordable countries. If you are particularly frugal, it's possible to scrape by on €20 to €30 a day. This would involve staying in the cheapest possible accommodation, avoiding eating in restaurants or going to museums or bars, and not moving around too much. Places such as Madrid, Barcelona and Seville will place a greater strain on your moneybelt.

A more reasonable budget would be €50 a day. This would allow you €20 for accommodation, €20 for meals, €2 for public transport and €5 for entry fees to museum, sights or entertainment...and a bit left over for a drink or two and intercity travel.

Remember that students (and sometimes seniors) are entitled to discounts of up to 50% on admission fees and about 30% on transportation.

## Tipping & Bargaining

In restaurants, prices include a service charge, and tipping is a matter of personal choice – most people leave some small change, and 5% is plenty. It's common to leave small change in bars and cafés. The only places in Spain where you are likely to bargain are markets and, occasionally, cheap hotels, particularly if you're staying for a few days.

## Consumer Taxes & Refunds

In Spain, VAT (value-added tax) is known as *impuesto sobre el valor añadido* (IVA). On accommodation and restaurant prices, there's a flat IVA of 7%, which is usually, but not always, included in quoted prices. To check, ask if the price is 'con IVA' (with VAT).

On retail goods, alcohol, electrical appliances etc IVA is 16%. Visitors are entitled to a refund of IVA on any item costing more than €90 that they are taking out of the EU. Ask the shop for a Europe Tax-Free Shopping Cheque when you buy, then present the goods and cheque to customs when you leave. If they can't offer a cheque, at least get an official receipt with the business's address and a description of the item purchased. Customs stamps the cheque and you then cash it at a booth with the 'Cash Refund' sign. There are booths at all main Spanish airports; at the border crossings at Algeciras, Gibraltar and Andorra; and at similar refund points throughout the EU.

## POST & COMMUNICATIONS
## Post

Main post offices in provincial capitals are usually open about 8.30am to 8.30pm Monday to Friday and about 9am to 1.30pm Saturday. Stamps are also sold at *estancos* (tobacco shops with the 'Tabacos' sign in yellow letters on a maroon background). A standard airmail letter or card costs €0.25 within Spain, €0.50 to the rest of Europe, and €0.75 to the rest of the world.

Mail to/from Europe normally takes up to a week, and to North America, Australia or New Zealand around 10 days, but there may be some unaccountable long delays.

Poste-restante mail can be addressed to you at either *poste restante* or *lista de correos*, the Spanish name for it, at the city in question. It's a fairly reliable system, although mail may well arrive late. Unfortunately, American Express (AmEx) no longer offers free client mail service.

Common abbreviations used in Spanish addresses are 1, 2, 3 etc, which mean 1st, 2nd and 3rd floor, and 's/n' *(sin número)*, which means that the building has no number.

## Telephone & Fax

Area codes in Spain are an integral part of the phone number; all numbers are nine digits long, without area codes.

Blue public pay phones are common and easy to use. They accept coins, phonecards *(tarjetas telefónicas)* and, in some cases, credit cards. Phonecards come in 1000 and 2000 ptas denominations and are available at main post offices and *estancos*. (At the time of research prices were still given in pesetas. Future new cards should be in denominations of €5, €10 and €20.) A one-minute call from a pay phone costs €0.06 within a local area, €0.13 to other places in the same province, €0.16 to other provinces, or €0.18 to another EU country or the USA. Australia and Asia can be reached for €0.93 per minute. Plans are under way to equalise international rates.

Provincial and interprovincial calls, except those to mobile phones, are around 50% cheaper between 8pm and 8am and all day Saturday and Sunday; local and international calls are around 10% cheaper between 6pm and 8am and all day Saturday and Sunday.

International reverse-charge (collect) calls are simple to make: from a pay phone or private phone, dial ☎ 900 99 00 followed by ☎ 61 for Australia, ☎ 44 for the UK, ☎ 64 for New Zealand, ☎ 15 for Canada, and for the USA ☎ 11 (AT&T) or ☎ 14 (MCI).

Most main post offices have a fax service, but you'll often find cheaper rates at shops or offices with 'Fax Público' signs.

### Email & Internet Access

Internet-access points have sprouted up everywhere in major Spanish cities and towns. Larger cities even sport 24-hour Internet cafés. Charges for an hour online range anywhere from €0.50 to €4.

## DIGITAL RESOURCES

There are thousands of websites devoted to travelling in Spain, and a search on Ⓦ www .google.com will bring up many useful ones. Spain's official tourist site is at Ⓦ www.tour spain.es. The British embassy maintains an excellent Web page at Ⓦ www.britishem bassy.org.uy/dslc/Websites.htm, with a list of links to Spanish press and cultural sites. For cultural and practical information on the country (eg, lists of festivals, the types of accommodation) check out Ⓦ www.okspain .org. Although Ⓦ www.spainview.com is primarily aimed at journalists and editors, it offers links to a wealth of information on the country.

## BOOKS

*The New Spaniards* by John Hooper is a fascinating account of modern Spanish society and culture. For a very readable and thorough, but not overlong, survey of Spanish history pick up *The Story of Spain* by Mark Williams.

Classic accounts of life and travel in Spain include Gerald Brenan's *South from Granada* (1920s), Laurie Lee's *As I Walked Out One Midsummer Morning* (1930s), George Orwell's *Homage to Catalunya* (the Civil War) and James Michener's *Iberia* (1960s). Among the best of more recent books are *Homage to Barcelona* by Colm Toíbín; *Spanish Journeys* by Adam Hopkins; and *Cities of Spain* by David Gilmour.

Of foreign literature set in Spain, Ernest Hemingway's Civil War novel *For Whom the Bell Tolls* is a must. *The Sun Also Rises* is partly set in Pamplona.

If you're planning in-depth travels in Spain, get a hold of Lonely Planet's *Spain*.

## NEWSPAPERS & MAGAZINES

The major daily newspapers in Spain are solidly liberal *El País*, conservative *ABC*, and *El Mundo*, which specialises in breaking political scandals. There's also a welter of regional dailies, some of the best coming out of Barcelona and Andalucía.

International press, such as the *International Herald Tribune*, *Time* and *Newsweek*, and daily papers from Western European countries reach major cities and tourist areas on the day of publication; elsewhere they're harder to find and arrive a day or two later.

## RADIO & TV

Hundreds of radio stations inhabit the FM band. You'll hear a substantial proportion of British and American music. The national pop/rock station, RNE 3, has admirably varied programming.

Spaniards are Europe's greatest TV watchers after the British, but they do a lot of watching in bars and cafés, which makes it more of a social activity. Most TVs receive six channels: two state-run (TVE1 and La2), three privately run (Antena 3, Tele 5 and Canal5), and one regional channel. Apart from news, TV seems to consist mostly of game and talk shows, sports, soap operas, sitcoms, and English-language films dubbed into Spanish.

SPAIN

## PHOTOGRAPHY & VIDEO

Main brands of film are widely available and processing is fast and generally efficient. A roll of print film (36 exposures, 100 ISO) costs around €4 and can be processed for around €10, though there are often better deals if you have two or three rolls developed together. The equivalent in slide film is around €6 plus the same for processing. Nearly all pre-recorded videos in Spain use the PAL image-registration system common to Western Europe, South Asia and Australia. These won't work on most video players in France, North America and Japan.

## TIME

Spain is one hour ahead of GMT/UTC from the last Sunday in September to the last Sunday in March and two hours ahead in summer.

## LAUNDRY

Self-service laundrettes are rare. Laundries *(lavanderías)* are common but not particularly cheap. They will usually wash, dry and fold a load for €8 to €10.

## TOILETS

Public toilets are not very common in Spain. The easiest thing to do is head for a café. It is polite to buy something in exchange for using their toilets.

## WOMEN TRAVELLERS

As almost everywhere, women should be ready to ignore stares, catcalls and unnecessary comments. However, Spain has one of the lowest incidences of reported rape in the developed world, and physical harassment is relatively infrequent.

The **Asociación de Asistencia a Mujeres Violadas** *(☎ 91 574 01 10; Calle de O'Donnell 42 bajo, Madrid; open 10am-2pm & 4pm-7pm Mon-Fri, recorded message at other times)* offers advice and help to rape victims and can provide details of similar centres in other cities, though only limited English is spoken.

## GAY & LESBIAN TRAVELLERS

Attitudes towards gays and lesbians are pretty tolerant, especially in the cities. Madrid, Barcelona, Sitges, Ibiza and Cádiz all have active gay and lesbian scenes. A good source of information on gay and lesbian places and organisations throughout Spain is **Coordinadora Gai-Lesbiana** *(☎ 93 298 00 29, fax 93 298 06 18; W www.cogailes.org; Carrer de Finlandia 45, E08014 Barcelona)*. In Madrid, the equivalent is called **Cogam** *(☎/fax 91 522 45 17, toll-free throughout Spain ☎ 900 601 601 6pm-10pm daily; Calle del Fuencarral 37, 28004 Madrid)*.

## DISABLED TRAVELLERS

Spain is an increasingly wheelchair-friendly country to visit. Spanish tourist offices in other countries can provide a basic information sheet with some useful addresses, and give information on accessible accommodation in specific places. **Inserso** *(☎ 91 347 88 88; Calle de Ginzo de Limea 58, 28029 Madrid)* is the government department for the disabled, with branches in all of Spain's 50 provinces.

You'll find some wheelchair–accessible accommodation in main centres, but many budget establishments lack lifts and ramps. Most of Hostelling International-affiliated youth hostels are suitable for use by those who require wheelchairs.

## SENIOR TRAVELLERS

Veterans of life will find Spain a welcoming and accessible destination. There are reduced prices for people over 60, 63 or 65 (depending on the place) at some attractions and occasionally on transport.

## USEFUL ORGANISATIONS

The travel agency **TIVE** *(☎ 91 543 74 12, fax 91 544 00 62; Calle de Fernando El Católico 88, Madrid)* has offices in major cities throughout Spain. It specialises in discounted tickets and travel arrangements for students and young people.

## DANGERS & ANNOYANCES

In large cities, keep valuables close and wear a moneybelt or neck pouch. Always beware of pickpockets and bag-snatchers. Muggings have been on the rise recently in Barcelona, so take extra care in that city.

It's a good idea to take your car radio and any other valuables with you any time you leave your car, leaving nothing at all visible within. In youth hostels, don't leave your belongings unattended, as theft is common.

## LEGAL MATTERS

Spaniards no longer enjoy liberal drug laws. No matter what anyone tells you, it is not

## Emergency Services

The emergency number for the police, medical and fire services is ☎ 112. You can also call the police direct on ☎ 091. See Car & Motorcycle in the introductory Getting Around section later in this chapter for information regarding roadside breakdown assistance.

legal to smoke dope in public bars. There is a reasonable degree of tolerance when it comes to people having a smoke in their own home, but not in hotel rooms or guesthouses.

If arrested in Spain you have the right to an attorney and to know the reason you are being held. You may also request a phone call.

## BUSINESS HOURS

Generally, people work Monday to Friday from 9am to 2pm and then again from 4.30pm or 5pm for another three hours. Shops and travel agencies are usually open these hours on Saturday, too, though some may skip the evening session. Museums all have their own unique opening hours; major ones tend to open for something like normal business hours (with or without the afternoon break), but often have their weekly closing day on Monday, not Sunday.

## PUBLIC HOLIDAYS & SPECIAL EVENTS

Spain has at least 14 official holidays a year, some observed nationwide, some very local. When a holiday falls close to a weekend, Spaniards like to make a *puente* (bridge), taking the intervening day off, too. The following holidays are observed virtually everywhere:

**New Year's Day** 1 January
**Epiphany or Three Kings' Day** (when children receive presents) 6 January
**Good Friday** before Easter Sunday
**Labour Day** 1 May
**Feast of the Assumption** 15 August
**National Day** 12 October
**All Saints' Day** 1 November
**Feast of the Immaculate Conception** 8 December
**Christmas** 25 December

The two main periods when Spaniards go on holiday are Semana Santa (the week leading up to Easter Sunday) and the month of August. At these times accommodation in resorts can be scarce and transport heavily booked, but other cities are often half-empty.

## Fiestas & Festivals

Spaniards indulge their love of colour, noise, crowds and partying at innumerable local fiestas and *ferias* (fairs); even small villages will have at least one, probably several, during the year. Many fiestas are based on religion. Local tourist offices can always supply detailed information.

Among festivals to look out for are *carnaval*, a time of fancy-dress parades and merrymaking celebrated around the country about seven weeks before Easter (wildest in Cádiz and Sitges); Valencia's week-long mid-March party, Las Fallas de San José, with all-night dancing and drinking, first-class fireworks and processions; Semana Santa, with its parades of holy images and huge crowds, notably in Seville; Seville's Feria de Abril, a week-long party held in late April, a kind of counterbalance to the religious peak of Semana Santa; Sanfermines, with the running of the bulls, in Pamplona in July; Semana Grande, another week of heavy drinking and hangovers, all along the northern coast during the first half of August; and Barcelona's week-long party, the Festes de la Mercè, around 24 September.

## ACTIVITIES
### Surfing & Windsurfing

Tarifa, Spain's southernmost point, is a windsurfer's heaven, with constant breezes and long, empty beaches.

### Skiing

Skiing in Spain is cheap, and facilities and conditions are good. The season runs from December to May. The most accessible resorts are in the Sierra Nevada (very close to Granada), the Pyrenees (north of Barcelona) and in the ranges north of Madrid. Contact tourist offices in these cities for information. Affordable day trips can be booked through travel agents.

### Cycling

Bike touring isn't as common as in other parts of Europe because of deterrents such as the often-mountainous terrain and summer heat. It's a more viable option on the Balearic Islands than on much of the mainland, although plenty of people get on their bikes in spring and autumn in the south. Mountain biking is increasingly popular, and areas such as Andalucía and Catalunya have many good

SPAIN

tracks. Finding bikes to rent is a hit-and-miss affair, so if you're set on the idea it's best to bring your own.

## Hiking

Spain is a trekker's paradise, so much so that Lonely Planet has published a guide to some of the best treks in the country, *Walking in Spain*. See also the Mallorca section of this chapter. Walking country roads and paths, between settlements, can also be highly enjoyable and a great way to meet the locals.

Two organisations publish detailed close-up maps of small parts of Spain. The CNIG covers most of the country in 1:25,000 (1cm to 250m) sheets, most of which are recent. The CNIG and the Servicio Geográfico del Ejército (SGE; Army Geographic Service) each publish a 1:50,000 series; the SGE's tends to be more up to date, as the maps were published in the mid-1980s. Also useful for hiking and exploring some areas are the *Guía Cartográfica* and *Guía Excursionista y Turística* series published by Editorial Alpina. The series combines information booklets in Spanish (or sometimes Catalan) with detailed maps at scales ranging from 1:25,000 to 1:50,000, well worth their price (around €4). You may find CNIG, SGE and Alpina publications in local bookshops, but it's more reliable to get them in advance from specialist map or travel shops such as Altaïr and Quera in Barcelona.

## COURSES

The best place to take a language course in Spain is generally at a university. It can also be fun to combine study with a stay in one of Spain's most exciting cities, such as Barcelona, Madrid or Seville. There are also hundreds of private language colleges throughout the country; the **Instituto Cervantes** (☎ 020-7235 0353; 102 Eaton Square, London SW1 W9AN; in Spain ☎ 91 436 76 00; ☎ informa@cervantes.es; Palacio de la Trinidad, Calle Francisco Silvela 82, Madrid) can send you lists of these and of universities that run courses. Some Spanish embassies and consulates also have information.

Other courses available in Spain include art, cookery and photography. Spanish tourist offices can help with information.

## WORK

EU, Norway and Iceland nationals are allowed to work in Spain without a visa, but if they plan to stay more than three months, they are supposed to apply within the first month for a residence card (see Visas & Documents earlier in this chapter). Virtually everyone else is supposed to obtain, from a Spanish consulate in their country of residence, a work permit and, if they plan to stay more than 90 days, a residence visa. These procedures are even more difficult.

That said, quite a few people do manage to work in Spain one way or another – though with Spain's unemployment rate running at around 15%, don't rely on it. Teaching English is an obvious option. A TEFL certificate will be a big help. Another possibility is gaining summer work in a bar or restaurant in a tourist resort.

## ACCOMMODATION
## Camping

Spain has more than 800 camping grounds. Facilities and settings vary enormously and grounds are officially rated from 1st class to 3rd class. You can expect to pay around €4 each per person, car and tent. Tourist offices can direct you to the nearest camping ground. Many are open all year, though quite a few close from around October to Easter. With certain exceptions (such as many beaches and environmentally protected areas) it is legal to camp outside camping grounds. You'll need permission to camp on private land.

## Hostels

Spain's youth hostels *(albergues juveniles)* are often the cheapest place to stay for lone travellers, but two people can usually get a double room elsewhere for a similar price. With some notable exceptions, hostels are only moderate value. Many have curfews or are closed during the day, or they lack any cooking facilities (if so they usually have a cafeteria). They can be short on privacy and are often heavily booked by school groups. Most are members of the country's Hostelling International (HI) organisation **Red Española de Albergues Juveniles** (REAJ; ☎ 91 347 77 00, fax 91 401 81 60; Calle de José Ortega y Gasset 71, 28006 Madrid).

Prices often depend on the season or whether you're under 26; typically you pay €10 or more. Some hostels require HI membership; others may charge more if you're not a member. You can buy HI cards for €15 at virtually all hostels.

## Pensiones, Hostales & Hotels

Officially, all the establishments are either hotels (from one to five stars), *hostales* (one to three stars) or *pensiones*. In practice, there are all sorts of overlapping categories, especially at the budget end of the market. In broad terms, the cheapest are usually *fondas* and *casas de huéspedes*, followed by *pensiones*. All these normally have shared bathrooms and singles/doubles for €10/15 to €20/25. Some hostales and *hostal-residencias* come in the same price range, but others have rooms with bathrooms costing anywhere up to €65 or so. A double in a three-star hotel will cost you over €100. The luxurious state-run *paradores*, often converted historic buildings, cost upwards of €200.

Room rates vary by season. It is noted where seasonal variations are particularly large in the individual city sections. July and August, Semana Santa and sometimes Christmas and New Year are the highest seasons. At other times prices in many places go down by 5% to 25%. In many cases you have to add 7% IVA.

## FOOD

It's a good idea to reset your stomach's clock in Spain, unless you want to eat alone or with other tourists. Most Spaniards start the day with a light breakfast *(desayuno)*, perhaps coffee with a *tostada* (piece of buttered toast) or *pastel* (pastry). *Churros con chocolate* (long, spiral-shaped deep-fried doughnuts with thick hot chocolate) are a delicious start to the day and unique to Spain.

Lunch *(almuerzo* or *comida)* is usually the main meal of the day, eaten between about 1.30pm and 4pm. The evening meal *(cena)* is usually lighter and may be eaten as late as 10pm or 11pm. It's common (and a great idea!) to go to a bar or café for a snack around 11am and again around 7pm or 8pm.

Spain has a huge variety of local cuisines. Seafood as well as meat is prominent almost everywhere. One of the most characteristic dishes, from the Valencia region, is *paella* – rice, seafood, the odd vegetable and often chicken or meat, all simmered up together, traditionally coloured yellow with saffron. Another dish, of Andalucían origin, is *gazpacho*, a soup made from tomatoes, breadcrumbs, cucumber and/or green peppers, eaten cold. *Tortillas* (omelettes) are an inexpensive stand-by and come in many varieties. *Jamón serrano* (cured ham) is a treat for meat-eaters.

## Cafés & Bars

If you want to follow Spanish habits, you'll be spending plenty of time in cafés and bars, almost all of which offer a range of tapas. These saucer-sized minisnacks are part of the Spanish way of life and come in infinite varieties, from calamari rings to potato salad to spinach with chickpeas to a small serving of tripe. A typical tapa costs €0.50 to €2 (although sometimes they will come free with your drinks), but check before you order because some are a lot dearer. A *ración* is a meal-sized serving of these snacks; a *media ración* is a half *ración*.

The other popular snacks are *bocadillos*, long filled white bread rolls. Spaniards eat so many *bocadillos* that some cafés sell nothing else. Try not to leave Spain without sampling a *bocadillo de tortilla de patata*, a roll filled with potato omelette.

You can often save 10% to 20% by ordering and eating food at the bar rather than at a table.

## Restaurants

Throughout Spain there are plenty of restaurants serving good, simple food at affordable prices, often featuring regional specialities. Many restaurants offer a *menú del día* – the budget traveller's best friend. For around €5 to €10 you typically get a starter, a main course, dessert, bread and wine – often with a choice of two or three dishes for each course. The *plato combinado* is a near relative of the menú. Such 'combined plates' may include steak and egg with chips and salad, or fried squid with potato salad. You'll pay more for your meals if you order à la carte but the food will be better.

## Vegetarian Food

Finding vegetarian fare can be a headache. It's not uncommon for 'meatless' food to be flavoured with meat stock. But in larger cities and important student centres there's a growing awareness of vegetarianism, so that if there isn't a vegetarian restaurant, there are often vegetarian items on menus. A good vegetarian snack at almost any place with *bocadillos* or sandwiches is a *bocadillo* (or sandwich) *vegetal*, which has a filling of salad and, often, fried egg (*sin huevo* means 'without egg').

## Self-Catering

Every town of any substance has a *mercado* (food market). These are fun and of great value. Even big eaters should be able to put together a filling meal of bread, *chorizo* (spiced sausage), cheese, fruit and a drink for €3 or less. If you shop carefully you can eat three healthy meals a day for as little as €5.

## DRINKS
Coffee in Spain is strong. Addicts should specify how they want their fix: *café con leche* is about 50% coffee, 50% hot milk; *café solo* is a short black; *café cortado* is a short black with a little milk.

The most common way to order a beer (*cerveza*) is to ask for a *caña*, which is a small draught beer. *Corto* and *zurrito* are other names for this. A larger beer (about 300mL) is often called a *tubo*, or (in Catalunya) a *jarra*. All these words apply to draught beer (*cerveza de barril*) – if you just ask for a *cerveza* you're likely to get bottled beer, which is more expensive.

Wine (*vino*) comes in white (*blanco*), red (*tinto*) or rosé (*rosado*). *Tinto de verano*, a kind of wine shandy, is good in summer. There are also many regional grape specialities, such as *jerez* (sherry) in Jerez de la Frontera and *cava* (a sparkling wine) in Catalunya. *Sangría*, a sweet punch made of red wine, fruit and spirits, is refreshing and very popular with tourists.

The cheapest drink is, of course, water. To specify tap water (which is safe to drink almost everywhere), ask for *agua del grifo*.

## ENTERTAINMENT
Spain has some of the best nightlife in Europe; wild and *very* late nights, especially on Friday and Saturday, are an integral part of the Spain experience. Many young Spaniards don't even think about going out until midnight or so. Bars, which come in all shapes, sizes and themes, are the main attractions until around 2am or 3am. Some play great music that will get you hopping before you move on to a disco till 5am or 6am. Discos are generally expensive (think covers of €15 to €30), but not to be missed if you like to splurge. Spain's contributions to modern dance music are *bakalao* and *makina*, kinds of frenzied (150bpm to 180bpm) techno.

The live-music scene is less exciting. Spanish rock and pop tends to be imitative, though the bigger cities usually offer a reasonable choice of bands. See the earlier Society & Conduct section for information on flamenco.

Cinemas abound and are good value, though foreign films are usually dubbed into Spanish. To see a film in its original language, look for the 'VO' marking (for *versión original*).

## SPECTATOR SPORTS
The national sport is *fútbol* (soccer). The best teams to see for both crowd support and skill level are usually Real Madrid and FC Barcelona, although the atmosphere can be electric anywhere. The season runs from September to May.

Bullfighting is enjoying a resurgence despite continued pressure from international animal-rights activists. It's a complex activity that's regarded as much as an art form as a sport by aficionados. If you decide to see a *corrida de toros* visit from March to October. Madrid, Seville and Pamplona are among the best places to catch a bullfight.

## SHOPPING
Many of Spain's best handicrafts are fragile or bulky and inconvenient unless you're going straight home. Pottery comes in a great range of attractive regional varieties. Some lovely rugs and blankets are made in places like the Alpujarras and Níjar in Andalucía. There's some pleasing woodwork available, too, such as Granada's marquetry boxes and chess sets. Leather jackets, bags and belts are quite good value in many places.

# Getting There & Away

## AIR
Spain has many international airports, including Madrid, Barcelona, Seville, Málaga, Almería, Alicante, Valencia, Palma de Mallorca, Ibiza and Maó (Menorca). In general, the cheapest destinations are Málaga, the Balearic Islands, Barcelona and Madrid.

### Australia
In general, the best thing to do is to fly to London, Paris, Frankfurt or Rome, then make your way overland. Alternatively, some flight deals to these centres include a couple of short-haul flights within Europe, and Madrid and Barcelona are usually acceptable destinations for these. Some round-the-world (RTW) fares include stops in Spain. STA Travel should be

able to help you out with a good price. Generally speaking, a return fare to Europe for under A$1700 is too good to pass up.

## The USA & Canada
Return fares to Madrid from Miami, New York, Atlanta or Chicago range from US$700 to US$850 on Iberia or Delta. From the west coast or Canada you are usually looking at about US$100 more. Sales can slash prices down to US$500 or even lower.

## The UK
Scheduled flights to Spain are generally expensive, but with the huge range of charter, discount and low-season fares, it's often cheaper to fly than to take a bus or train. Check the travel sections of *TNT* or *Time Out* magazines or the weekend newspapers. Sample destinations from London include Madrid (UK£110 in low season with short notice), Barcelona (UK£130), Ibiza (UK£119) and Málaga (UK£110).

## Leaving Spain
For northern Europe, check the ads in local English-language papers in tourist centres like the Costa del Sol, the Costa Blanca and the Balearic Islands. You may pick up a one-way fare to London for under €90. The youth and student travel agency TIVE (see Useful Organisations earlier in the Facts for the Visitor section of this chapter) and the general travel agency Halcón Viatges, both with branches in most main cities, have some good fares. Generally you're looking at around €95 to €110 one way to London, Paris or Amsterdam, and at least €300 to the USA.

Departure taxes on flights out of Spain, which vary, are factored directly into tickets.

## LAND
### Bus
There are regular bus services to Spain from all major centres in Europe, including Lisbon, London and Paris. In London, **Eurolines** (☎ 0870-514 3219) has services at least three times a week to Barcelona (UK£90 one way, 23 to 25 hours), Madrid (UK£80 one way, at least 27 hours) and Málaga (UK£80 one way, 34 hours). Tickets are sold by major travel agencies, and people under 26 and senior citizens qualify for a 10% discount. There are also bus services to Morocco from some Spanish cities.

### Train
Reaching Spain by train is more expensive than by bus unless you have a rail pass, though fares for those under 26 come close to the bus price. Normal one-way fares from London (using the ferry across the Channel, not Eurostar) to Madrid (via Paris) are under UK£110. For more details, contact the **Rail Europe Travel Centre** (☎ 08705-848 848) in London or a travel agent. See the introductory Getting Around chapter for more on rail passes and train travel through Europe.

### Car & Motorcycle
If you're driving or riding to Spain from England, you'll have to choose between going through France (check visa requirements) or taking a direct ferry from England to Spain (see the following section). The cheapest way is to take one of the shorter ferries from England to France, then a quick drive down through France.

## SEA
### The UK
There are two direct ferry services. **Brittany Ferries** (☎ 0870 536 0360 in Britain) runs Plymouth–Santander ferries twice weekly from about mid-March to mid-November (24 hours), and a Portsmouth–Santander service (30 hours), usually once a week, in other months. **P&O European Ferries** (☎ 08702 424 999 in Britain) runs Portsmouth–Bilbao ferries twice weekly, on Monday and Thursday, almost year-round (35 hours). Prices on all services are similar: one-way passenger fares range from about UK£50 in winter to UK£90 in summer (cabins extra); a car and driver costs from UK£160 to UK£275, or you can take a vehicle and several passengers for UK£250 to UK£400.

### Morocco
Ferry services between Spain and Morocco include Algeciras–Tangier, Algeciras–Ceuta, Gibraltar–Tangier, and from Málaga–Melilla, Almería–Melilla and Almería–Nador. Those to and from Algeciras are the fastest, cheapest and most frequent, with over 20 ferries a day to Ceuta (€13, 1½ hours) and 14 to Tangier (€14, 2½ hours). Hydrofoils make the same trip in half the time for about 75% more. Taking a car to Ceuta/Tangier costs €60/70.

You can buy tickets at Algeciras' harbour, but it's more convenient to go to one of the many agencies on the waterfront. The price doesn't vary, so just look for the place with the shortest queue.

Don't buy Moroccan currency until you reach Morocco, as you will get ripped off in Algeciras.

# Getting Around

Students and seniors are eligible for discounts of 30% to 50% on almost all types of transportation within Spain.

## AIR

Spain has three main domestic airlines: **Iberia** (☎ 902 40 05 00), **Air Europa** (☎ 902 40 15 01) and **Spanair** (☎ 902 13 14 15). They and a couple of smaller airlines compete to produce some fares that can make flying worthwhile if you're in a hurry, especially for longer or return trips.

The return fare between Madrid and Barcelona can be as high as €150. To Palma de Mallorca, Santiago de Compostela or Málaga you are looking at around €200 return. All these fares can be cut in half if you comply with certain restrictions.

Among travel agencies, **TIVE** (see Useful Organisations, earlier in this chapter) and **Halcón Viatges** (see Travel Agencies in the Barcelona section later in this chapter) are always worth checking for fares. There are some useful deals if you're under 26 (or, in some cases, over 63).

## BUS

Spain's bus network is operated by dozens of independent companies and is more extensive than its train system, serving remote towns and villages as well as the major routes. The choice between bus and train depends on the particular trip you're taking; for the best value, compare fares, journey times and frequencies each time you move. Buses to/from Madrid are often cheaper than (or barely different from) cross-country routes. For instance Seville to Madrid costs €15, while the shorter Seville–Granada trip is €15.50.

Many towns and cities have one main bus station where most buses arrive and depart, and these usually have an information desk giving information on all services. Tourist offices can also help with information but don't sell tickets or list prices, as a rule.

## TRAIN

Trains are mostly modern and comfortable, and late arrivals are now the exception rather than the rule. The main headache is deciding which compartment on which train gives you the best value.

RENFE, the national railway company, runs numerous types of train, and travel times can vary a lot on the same route. So can fares, which may depend not just on the type of train but also the day of the week and time of day. RENFE's website (W www.renfe.es) is an excellent resource for schedule and fare information.

*Regionales* are all-stops trains (think cheap and slow). *Cercanías* provide regular services from major cities to the surrounding suburbs and hinterland, sometimes even crossing regional boundaries.

Among long-distance *(largo recorrido)* trains, the standard daytime train is the *diurno* (its night-time equivalent is the *estrella*). Quicker is the InterCity (mainly because it makes fewer stops), while the *Talgo* is fastest and dearest.

Best of all is the AVE high-speed service that links Madrid and Seville in just 2½ hours. The *Talgo 200* uses part of this line to speed down to Málaga from Madrid. The *Euromed* is an AVE-style train that speeds south from Barcelona to Valencia and Alicante. A *Tren Hotel* is a 1st-class sleeper-only express.

There's also a bewildering range of accommodation types, especially on overnight trains (fares quoted in this chapter are typical 2nd-class seat fares). Fortunately ticket clerks understand the problem and are usually happy to go through a few options with you. The cheapest sleeper option is usually a *litera*, a bunk in a six-berth 2nd-class compartment.

You can buy tickets and make reservations at stations, RENFE offices in many city centres and travel agencies that display the RENFE logo.

### Train Passes

Rail passes are valid for all RENFE trains, but Inter-Rail users have to pay €9.50 supplements on Talgo and InterCity services, and on the high-speed AVE service between Madrid and Seville. All pass-holders making reservations for long-distance trains pay a fee of about €5.

RENFE's Tarjeta Turística (also known as the Spain Flexipass) is a rail pass for non-

Europeans, valid for three to 10 days' travel in a two-month period. In 2nd class, three days costs US$155, and 10 days is US$365. It can be purchased from agents outside Europe, or at a few main train stations and RENFE offices in Spain.

## CAR & MOTORCYCLE

If you're driving or riding around Spain, consider investing €5 in the *Michelin Atlas de Carreteras España Portugal*. It's a handy atlas with detailed road maps as well as maps of all the main towns and cities. Most travel stores and petrol stations will carry it.

Spain's roads vary enormously but are generally quite good. Fastest are the *autopistas*, multilane freeways between major cities. On some, mainly in the north, you have to pay hefty tolls (from the French border to Barcelona, for example, it's about €12). Minor routes can be slow going but are usually more scenic. Petrol is relatively expensive, at around €0.85 for a litre of unleaded.

The head office of the Spanish automobile club is **Real Automovil Club de España** (*RACE;* ☎ *91 434 11 22;* ✉ *inforace@race.es; Avenida Ciudad de Barcelona 132, Madrid*). For the RACE's 24-hour, nationwide, on-road emergency service, call toll free ☎ 900 11 22 22.

### Road Rules

Driving in Spain is not too bad, and locals show respect for the rules. Speed limits are 120km/h on the autopistas, 90km/h or 100km/h on other country roads and 50km/h in built-up areas. The maximum allowable blood-alcohol level is 0.05%. Seat belts must be worn, and all motorcyclists must always wear a helmet and keep headlights on day and night.

Trying to find a parking spot in larger towns and cities can be a nightmare. Spanish drivers park anywhere to save themselves the hassle of a half-hour search, but *grúas* (tow trucks) will tow your car if given the chance. The cost of bailing out a car can be as high as €100.

Remember that Spanish cities do not have US-style parking meters at every spot. Instead, if you park in a blue zone from around 8am to 8pm, you have to obtain a ticket from a street-side meter, which may be several blocks away. You then display the ticket from your dashboard until your time runs out (expiration time is written on the ticket).

### Rental

Rates vary widely from place to place. The best deals tend to be in the major tourist areas, including at their airports. At Málaga airport you can rent a small car for under €120 a week. More generally, you're looking at up to €50 for a day with unlimited kilometres, plus insurance, damage waiver and taxes. Hiring for several days can bring the average daily cost down a great deal – a small car for a week might cost under €140. Local companies often have better rates than the big firms.

### BICYCLE

See Cycling in the Activities section earlier in this chapter.

### HITCHING

Although we don't recommend it, it's still possible to thumb your way around parts of Spain, but large doses of patience and common sense are necessary. Women should avoid hitching alone at any time. Hitching is illegal on autopistas and difficult on the major highways. Your chances are better on minor roads, although the going on these can still be painfully slow.

### BOAT

For information on ferries to, from and between the Balearic Islands, see that section of this chapter.

### LOCAL TRANSPORT

In many Spanish towns you will not need to use public transport, as transport terminals and accommodation are centralised and within walking distance of most tourist attractions.

Most towns in Spain have an effective local bus system. In larger cities, these can be complicated, but tourist offices can tell you which buses you need. Barcelona and Madrid both have efficient underground systems that are faster and easier to use than the bus systems.

Taxis are still pretty cheap. If you split a cross-town fare between three or four people, it can be a decidedly good deal. Rates vary slightly from city to city: in Barcelona, they cost €1.30 flag fall, plus about €1 per kilometre; in Madrid they're a bit more expensive (€1.35 flag fall). There are supplements for luggage and airport trips.

SPAIN

# Madrid

**pop 3 million**
One of the most appealing aspects about Madrid is that, despite being the country's capital, there is a friendly neighbourhood feel about the place. Right in the city centre you find quaint family-owned shops, bars packed with locals and an overall lack of the stress levels on the street that you find in most cities this size. There is also plenty to do and see, including a remarkable collection of museums and galleries, beautiful parks and gardens, and a vibrant nightlife with, reputedly, more bars per square metre than any other city in Europe.

## ORIENTATION
The most interesting part of Madrid lies between Parque del Retiro in the east and Campo del Moro in the west. These two parks are more or less connected by Calle de Alcalá and Calle Mayor, which meet in the middle at Puerta del Sol. Calle Mayor passes the historic main square, Plaza Mayor, on its way from Puerta del Sol to the Palacio Real in front of Campo del Moro.

The main north-south thoroughfare is Paseo de la Castellana, which runs (changing names to Paseo de los Recoletos and finally Paseo del Prado) all the way from Chamartín train station in the north to Madrid's other big station, Atocha.

## INFORMATION
### Tourist Offices
The **Oficina Municipal de Turismo** (☎ 91 588 16 36, fax 91 366 54 77; e munemadrid @infoturismo.es; Plaza Mayor 3; metro Sol; open 10am-8pm Mon-Sat, 10am-2pm Sun) is conveniently situated in the city's emblematic main square. The additional tourist information offices include those located at **Chamartín train station** (☎ 91 315 99 76; open 8am-8pm Mon-Sat, 8am-2pm Sun), **Barajas airport** (☎ 91 305 86 56; open 8am-8pm daily), and **Mercado Puerta de Toledo** (☎ 91 364 18 76; Ronda de Toledo 1; open 9am-8pm Mon-Sat, 9am-2pm Sun). There is also a multilingual local information hotline on ☎ 010.

## Money
Large banks like Caja de Madrid usually have the best rates, but check commissions first.

Banks are generally open 8.30am to 2pm weekdays and, during the winter months, to 1pm on Saturday. **American Express** (☎ 91 527 03 03; open 24 hr; ☎ 900 99 44 26 for replacing lost travellers cheques; Plaza de las Cortes 2; metro Banco de España; open 9am-5.30pm Mon-Fri, 9am-noon Sat) is reasonably priced.

If you're desperate, there are plenty of *bureaux de change* around Puerta del Sol and Plaza Mayor, which have the predictable rip-off rates but are often open until midnight.

## Post & Communications
The **main post office** (☎ 91 521 6500; Plaza de la Cibeles; metro Banco de España) is in gigantic Palacio de Comunicaciones. **Poste restante** (lista de correos; open 8am-9.30pm Mon-Fri, 8.30am-2pm Sat) is at windows 17 to 20. Don't forget your passport.

**Telefónica** (☎ 91 522 39 14; Gran Vía 30; metro Gran Vía; open 10am-10pm daily) has phone books for the whole country and cabins where you can make calls in relative peace.

## Email & Internet Access
Internet connections are available at dozens of cafés, as well as at such Net centres as **Navegaweb**, part of the 'Telefónica' centre (see earlier), which charges €1.80 an hour; **WEC** (☎ 91 429 16 90; Calle de Atocha 45; metro Antón Martín; open 10am-10pm daily) at €2.40 an hour; and **ONO** (☎ 91 547 47 71; Gran Vía 59; metro Gran Vía; open 24hr), with varying rates depending on the time.

## Travel Agencies
For cheap travel tickets try **Viajes Zeppelin** (☎ 91 542 51 54; Plaza de Santo Domingo 2; metro Santo Domingo). If you are aged under 25 or a student, check out **TIVE** (☎ 91 543 74 12; Calle de Fernando el Católico 88; metro: Moncloa) or the **Instituto de la Juventud** (☎ 91 347 77 00; Calle de José Ortega y Gasset 71; metro Lista) – both open 9am to 1pm Monday to Friday.

## Bookshops
**La Casa del Libro** (☎ 91 521 21 13; Gran Vía 29-31) is massive and the largest of the three branches in town, with a good selection of books in English and other languages. For more English books, as well as videos and a children's section, go to **Booksellers** (☎ 91 442 79 59; Calle de José Abascal 48; metro

*Alonso Cano)*. **Desnivel** *(☎ 91 429 97 40; Plaza Matute 6; metro Huertas)* specialises in walking, climbing and adventure guides, and has a large selection of maps.

## Laundry

Laundrettes are hard to find. Two still in business are **Lavomatique** *(Calle de Cervantes 1; metro Antón Martín; open 9am-8pm Mon-Sat)* and **Lavandería Alba** *(☎ 91 522 44 63; Calle del Barco 26; metro Gran Vía; open 9am-9pm Mon-Sat)*.

## Medical & Emergency Services

If you have a minor medical problem and speak some Spanish (or are good at gesticulating), ask a pharmacist's advice. There are several 24-hour pharmacies, including **Farmacia del Globo** *(☎ 91 369 20 00; Plaza de Antón Martín 46; metro Antón Martín)*. For more serious problems, head for the nearest emergency health centre – **Casa de Socorro** *(☎ 91 588 96 60; Calle Navas de Tolosa 10; metro Callao)* is the most convenient if you are in the centre. You can also get help at the **Anglo-American Medical Unit** *(☎ 91 435 18 23; Calle del Conde de Aranda 1; metro Retiro)*. For an ambulance, call ☎ 061, or Cruz Roja on ☎ 91 522 22 22.

In the case of an emergency see the boxed text 'Emergency Services' near Dangers & Annoyances in the Facts for the Visitor section earlier in this chapter.

## THINGS TO SEE & DO
## Museo del Prado

The city is elite among Europe's art capitals with three major museums, including the Prado *(☎ 91 330 29 00; Paseo del Prado s/n; adult/student €3/1.50, admission free 2.30pm-7pm Sat & all day Sun; open 9am-7pm Tues-Sat, 9am-2pm Sun & holidays)*, the best-known and largest of the trio. The main emphasis is on Spanish, Flemish and Italian art from the 15th to 19th centuries, and one of its strengths lies in the generous coverage given to certain individual geniuses, such as three of the Spanish greats, Goya, Velázquez and El Greco.

Of Velázquez' works, it's *Las Meninas* that most people come to see. This masterpiece depicts maids of honour attending the daughter of King Felipe IV, and Velázquez himself painting portraits of the queen and king (through whose eyes the scene is witnessed). It takes pride of place in room 12 on the 1st floor, the focal point of the Velázquez collection.

Virtually the whole southern wing of the 1st floor is given over to Goya. His portraits, in rooms 34 to 38, include the pair *Maja Desnuda* and *Maja Vestida*; legend has it that the woman depicted here is the Duchess of Alba, Spain's richest woman in Goya's time. Goya was supposedly commissioned to paint her portrait by her husband and ended up having an affair with her, so painted an extra portrait for himself. In room 39 are Goya's great war masterpieces, crowned by *El Dos de Mayo 1808* (2 May 1808) and, next to it, *Los Fusilamientos de Moncloa*, also known as *El Tres de Mayo 1808* (3 May 1808), in which he recreates the pathos of the hopeless Madrid revolt against the French. There are more Goya works in rooms 66 and 67 on the ground floor.

Other well-represented artists include El Greco, the Flemish masters Hieronymus Bosch and Peter Paul Rubens, and the Italians Tintoretto, Titian and Raphael.

Entry to the Prado is free on selected national holidays. Tickets include entrance to the Casón del Buen Retiro, a subsidiary a short walk to the east, that contains the Collection's 19th-century works.

## Centro de Arte Reina Sofía

Opposite Atocha station, this museum *(☎ 91 467 50 62; Calle Santa Isabel 52; adult/student €3/1.50, admission free 2.30pm-7pm Sat & Sun; open 10am-9pm Mon & Wed-Sat, 10am-2.30pm Sun)* houses a superb collection of predominantly Spanish modern art. The exhibition focuses on the period 1900 to 1940 and includes, in room 7, Picasso's famous *Guernica*, his protest at the German bombing of the Basque town of Guernica during the Spanish Civil War in 1937.

*Guernica* was painted in Paris. Picasso insisted that it stay outside Spain until Franco and his cronies were gone and democracy had been restored. It was secretly brought to Spain in 1981 and moved here from the Casón del Buen Retiro in 1992.

The museum also contains further works by Picasso, while room 9 is devoted to Salvador Dalí's surrealist work and room 13 contains a collection of Joan Miró's late works, characterised by their remarkable simplicity.

SPAIN

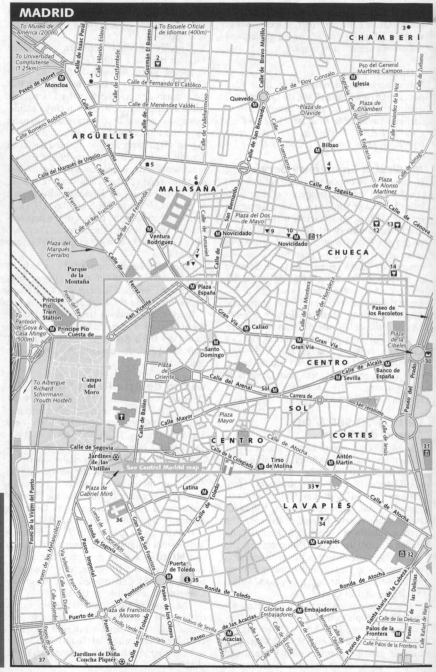

# MADRID

To Museo de
América (200m)

To Universidade
Complutense
(1.25km)

Paseo de Moret
**Moncloa** Ⓜ

Calle de Isaac Peral

Calle Hilarión Eslava

To Escuele Oficial
de Idiomas (400m)

Calle de Gaztambide

Calle de Guzmán El Bueno

Calle de la Princesa

Calle de Fernando El Católico

Calle de Menéndez Valdés

Calle de Vallehermoso

Calle de Bravo Murillo

**CHAMBERÍ** 3●

Pso del General
Martínez Campos

**Quevedo** Ⓜ

Calle de Eloy Gonzalo

Engracia

**Iglesia** Ⓜ

Plaza de
Chamberí

Plaza de
Olavide

Calle de San Bernardo

Calle de Fuencarral

**Bilbao** Ⓜ

Calle Fernández de la Hoz

Calle de Santa Engracia

Calle de Almagro

Calle de Zurbano

Calle Romero Robledo

**ARGÜELLES**

Calle del Marqués de Urquijo

Calle de Tutor

Calle de Ferraz

Calle del Rey Francisco

Calle de Luisa Fernanda

📱5

Calle de Luisa Fernanda

6
●
**MALASAÑA**

**Ventura
Rodríguez** Ⓜ

Calle de

Plaza del
Marqués de
Cerralbo

**Parque
de la
Montaña**

Calle de San Bernardo

Calle de Sagasta

4▼

Plaza de
Alonso
Martínez

Calle de Génova

Calle de Amaniel

Plaza del Dos
de Mayo

San Bernardo

**Novidado** Ⓜ

7▼

8▼

▼9

10▼
▼

**Novidado** Ⓜ

🏛11

12

13

**CHUECA**

14

Paseo del Rey

Ferraz

San Vicente

Cuesta de

Calle de Bailén

**Príncipe
Pío
Train
Station**

To
Panteón
de Goya &
Casa Mingo
(500m)

**Príncipe Pío** Ⓜ
Cuesta de

To Albergue
Richard
Schirrmann
(Youth Hostel)

**Campo
del
Moro**

Plaza
de
Oriente

Ⓜ **Plaza
España**

Gran Vía

**Callao** Ⓜ

**Santo
Domingo**

Calle de la Montera

Calle de Hortaleza

Gran Vía

**Gran Vía** Ⓜ

Calle de Alcalá

**Sevilla** Ⓜ

**CENTRO**

Banco de
España

Paseo de
los Recoletos

Plaza
de la
Cibeles

30

Calle del Arenal

**Sol** Ⓜ

Carrera de

San Jerónimo

**SOL**

Paseo del Prado

Calle Mayor

Plaza
Mayor

**CENTRO**

Calle de Atocha

Calle de la Colegiata

Calle de Segovia

**Jardines
de las
Vistillas**

See Central Madrid map

Plaza de
Gabriel Miró

**Latina** Ⓜ

**Tirso
de Molina** Ⓜ

**CORTES**

**Antón
Martín** Ⓜ

Calle de Jesús

31
🏛

Paseo de la Virgen del Puerto

Cuesta de las Descalzas

Ronda de Segovia

Gran Vía de San Francisco

36

Calle de Toledo

33▼

**LAVAPIÉS**

▼
34

Calle de Atocha

**Lavapiés** Ⓜ

🏛32

Paseo de los Melancólicos

Vía Inferior al paseo imperial

Paseo Imperial

Calle Juan Duque

Calle Alejandro

Puerto de

Calle de Toledo

**Puerta
de Toledo** Ⓜ

🄵35

Ronda de Toledo

Ronda de Atocha

las Delicias

Santa María de la Cabeza

Calle de las Delicias

Paseo de las Delicias

Paseo de la Virgen del Puerto

Calle Juan Duque

Plaza de Francisco
Morano

Pasillo Verde
Ferroviario

Paseo de los Pontones

Paseo de los Olmos

San Isidro de Sevilla

de las Acacias

Glorieta de
Embajadores Ⓜ

**Embajadores** Ⓜ

**Palos de la
Frontera** Ⓜ

Calle Palos de la Frontera

Calle Rafael de Riego

37

**Jardines de Doña
Concha Piquer**

Calle de Toledo

Paseo
Acacias

Calle de Embajadores

Calle de
Bernardo

Paseo de

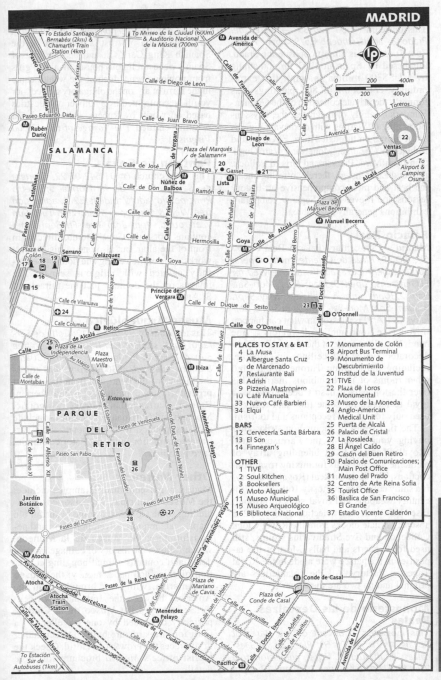

# MADRID

To Estadio Santiago
Bernabéu (2km) &
Chamartín Train
Station (4km)

To Museo de la Ciudad (600m)
& Auditorio Nacional
de la Música (700m)

Avenida de
América

Calle de Francisco Silvela

Calle de Diego de León

Calle de Cartagena

Calle de Ardemans

Los Toreros

Paseo Eduardo Data

Rubén
Dario

Calle de Juan Bravo

Diego de
León

Avenida de

Ventas

22

To
Airport &
Camping
Osuna

SALAMANCA

Plaza del Marqués
de Salamanca

Calle de José

Núñez de
Balboa

Ortega y ● Gasset

20

Lista

● 21

Calle de Alcalá

Calle de Don Balboa

Ramón de la Cruz

Calle de Alcántara

Plaza de)
Manuel Becerra

Calle de

Calle del Príncipe

Calle de Peñalver

Ayala

Calle de Alcalá

Manuel Becerra

Plaza de
Colón

Serrano

Velázquez

Calle de

Hermosilla

Goya

Calle de Alcalá

GOYA

17 ⚓ 18
19
● 16

Calle de Goya

Calle Fuente del Berro

Calle de Vilanueva

Principe de
Vergara

Calle del Duque de Sesto

Calle del Doctor Esquerdo

15

24

Calle Columela

Retiro

Calle de O'Donnell

23

O'Donnell

Calle de Alcalá

25

Plaza de la
Independencia

Plaza
Maestro
Villa

Av México

Ibiza

Calle de
Montalbán

Paseo Salón del Estanque

Estanque

PARQUE

DEL

RETIRO

Paseo de Venezuela

29

C de Alfonso XII

Paseo San Pablo

26

Jardín
Botánico

Paseo del Duque

Paseo del Urugay

28

27

Atocha

Atocha

Atocha
Train
Station

Avenidade la Ciudadde Barcelona

Paseo de la Reina Cristina

Plaza de
Mariano
de Cavia

Conde de Casal

Plaza del
Conde de Casal

Menéndez
Pelayo

Avenida de la Ciudad de Barcelona

Pacifico

To Estación
Sur de
Autobuses (1km)

| PLACES TO STAY & EAT | |
|---|---|
| 4 | La Musa |
| 5 | Albergue Santa Cruz de Marcenado |
| 7 | Restaurante Bali |
| 8 | Adrish |
| 9 | Pizzeria Mastropiero |
| 10 | Café Manuela |
| 33 | Nuevo Café Barbieri |
| 34 | Elqui |

| BARS | |
|---|---|
| 12 | Cervecería Santa Bárbara |
| 13 | El Son |
| 14 | Finnegan's |

| OTHER | |
|---|---|
| 1 | TIVE |
| 2 | Soul Kitchen |
| 3 | Booksellers |
| 6 | Moto Alquiler |
| 11 | Museo Municipal |
| 15 | Museo Arqueológico |
| 16 | Biblioteca Nacional |
| 17 | Monumento de Colón |
| 18 | Airport Bus Terminal |
| 19 | Monumento de Descubrimiento |
| 20 | Institud de la Juventud |
| 21 | TIVE |
| 22 | Plaza de Toros Monumental |
| 23 | Museo de la Moneda |
| 24 | Anglo-American Medical Unit |
| 25 | Puerta de Alcalá |
| 26 | Palacio de Cristal |
| 27 | La Rosaleda |
| 28 | El Ángel Caído |
| 29 | Casón del Buen Retiro |
| 30 | Palacio de Comunicaciones; Main Post Office |
| 31 | Museo del Prado |
| 32 | Centro de Arte Reina Sofia |
| 35 | Tourist Office |
| 36 | Basílica de San Francisco El Grande |
| 37 | Estadio Vicente Calderón |

SPAIN

## Museo Thyssen-Bornemisza

This museum (☎ 91 420 39 44; Paseo del Prado 8; adult/student €5/3; open 10am-7pm Tues-Sun) is almost opposite the Prado. Purchased by Spain in 1993 for something over US$300 million (a snip), this extraordinary collection of 800 paintings was formerly the private collection of the German-Hungarian family of magnates, the Thyssen-Bornemiszas. Starting with medieval religious art, it moves on through Titian, El Greco and Rubens to Cézanne, Monet and Van Gogh, then from Miró, Picasso and Gris to Pollock, Dalí and Lichtenstein, thereby offering one of the best and most comprehensive art-history lessons you'll ever have. Separate temporary exhibitions generally cost more.

## Palacio Real

Madrid's 18th-century Palacio Real (☎ 91 542 00 59; Plaza de Oriente; metro Opera; adult/student €6/3, admission free Wed for EU citizens; open 9.30am-6pm Mon-Sat, 9am-2.30pm Sun & holidays May-Sept; 9.30am-5pm Mon-Sat, 9am-2pm Sun & holidays Oct-Apr) is a lesson in what can happen if you give your interior decorators a free hand. You'll see some of the most elaborately decorated walls and ceilings imaginable, including the sublime Throne Room (and other rooms of more dubious merit). This over-the-top palace hasn't been used as a royal residence for some time and today is used only for official receptions and tourism.

The first series of rooms you strike after buying your ticket is the Farmacia Real (Royal Pharmacy), an unending array of medicine jars and stills for mixing royal concoctions. The Armería Real (Royal Armoury) is a shiny collection of mostly 16th- and 17th-century weapons and royal suits of armour. Elsewhere are a good selection of Goyas, 215 absurdly ornate clocks from the Royal Clock Collection and five Stradivarius violins, still used for concerts and balls. Most of the tapestries in the palace were made in the Royal Tapestry Factory. All the chandeliers are original and no two are the same.

## Monasterio de las Descalzas Reales

This monastery (Convent of the Barefoot Royals; ☎ 91 542 00 59; Plaza de las Descalzas; adult/student €5/4, admission free Wed for EU citizens; open 10.30am-12.45pm Tues-Sat, 4pm-5.30pm Tues-Thur & Sat, 11am-1.45pm Sun & holidays) was founded in 1559 by Juana of Austria, daughter of the Spanish King Carlos I, and became one of Spain's richest religious houses thanks to gifts from noblewomen. Much of the wealth came in the form of art; on the obligatory guided tour you'll be confronted by a number of tapestries based on works by Rubens and a wonderful painting entitled The Voyage of the 11,000 Virgins.

## Panteón de Goya

This little church (☎ 91 542 07 22; Glorieta de San Antonio de la Florida 5; metro Príncipe Pío; adult/student €2/1, admission free Wed & Sun; open 10am-2pm Tues-Sun year-round, 4pm-8pm Tues-Fri Sept-June) contains not only Goya's tomb, directly in front of the altar, but also one of his greatest works – the entire ceiling and dome – beautifully painted with religious scenes. The images on the dome depict the miracle of St Anthony.

## Museo Arqueológico

This museum (☎ 91 577 79 12; Calle de Serrano; adult/student €3/1.50, admission free Sun & 2.30pm-8.30pm Sat; open 9.30am-8.30pm Tues-Sat, 9.30am-2pm Sun) traces the history of the peninsula from the earliest prehistoric cave paintings to the Iberian, Roman, Carthaginian, Greek, Visigothic, Moorish and Christian eras. Exhibits include mosaics, pottery, fossilised bones and a partial reconstruction of the prehistoric Altamira cave paintings.

## Other Museums

Madrid is museum mad. Examples include: the **Museo Municipal**, with assorted art, including some Goyas, and some beautiful old maps, scale models, silver, porcelain and period furniture; the **Museo de la Moneda**, which follows the history of coinage in great detail and contains a mind-boggling collection of coins and paper money; the **Museo de América**, with stuff brought from the Americas between the 16th and 20th centuries; and even the **Museo de la Ciudad**, perfectly described by one traveller as 'a must for infrastructure buffs!', which rather dryly traces the growth of Madrid. Check the tourist office's Madrid brochure for more details.

SPAIN

## Real Jardín Botánico

The ideal way to end a cultural overdose day is a stroll through this beautiful eight-hectare botanical garden *(admission €1.50; open 10am-dark daily)* next door to the Prado.

## Parque del Retiro

This is another great place to bench-sit or stroll. Time it right and you may catch a puppet show during the summer.

Walk along **Paseo de las Estatuas**, a path lined with statues originally from the Palacio Real. It ends at a lake overlooked by a **statue of Alfonso XII**. There are rowing boats for rent at the northern end when the weather is good.

Perhaps the most important, and certainly the most controversial, of the park's other monuments is **El Ángel Caído** (The Fallen Angel). First-prize winner at an international exhibition in Paris in 1878, this is said to be the first statue in the world dedicated to the devil.

You should also visit some of the park's gardens, such as the exquisite **La Rosaleda** *(rose garden)*, and the **Chinese Garden** on a tiny island near the Fallen Angel. The all-glass **Palacio de Cristal** in the middle of the park frequently stages modern-art exhibitions.

## Campo del Moro

This stately garden is directly behind the Palacio Real, and the palace is visible through the trees from just about all points. A couple of fountains and statues, a thatch-roofed pagoda and a carriage museum provide artificial diversions, but nature is the real attraction.

## El Rastro

If you get up early on a Sunday morning, you'll find the city almost deserted, until you get to **El Rastro** *(metro Latina)*. The market spreads along and between Calle de Ribera de Curtidores and Calle de los Embajadores. It is one of the biggest flea markets you're ever likely to see, where you find almost anything, from hippie threads to the kitchen sink. It's also said to be the place to go if you want to buy your car stereo back. Watch your pockets and bags.

## ORGANISED TOURS

You can pick up a **Madrid Vision bus** *(☎ 91 779 18 88)* around the centre of Madrid up to 10 times a day. A full return trip costs €9.60 and you can hop on and off at any of 20 clearly marked stops. Taped commentaries in four languages, including English, are available,

and the bus stops at several major monuments, including the Prado and near Plaza Mayor. **Descubre Madrid** is a walking tour with several itineraries available. Check at the tourist office at Plaza Mayor 3 for exact times and routes.

## SPECIAL EVENTS

Madrid's major fiesta celebrates its patron saint, San Isidro Labrador, throughout the third week of May. There are free music performances around the city and one of the country's top bullfight seasons at the Plaza Monumental de las Ventas. The Malasaña district, already busy enough, has its biggest party on 2 May, and the Fiesta de San Juan is held in the Parque del Retiro for the seven days leading up to 24 June. The city now sashays through the hottest months and there are plenty of people around to enjoy the consecutive festivals of La Paloma, San Cayetano and San Lorenzo in August. The last week of September is Chamartín's Fiesta de Otoño (Autumn Festival), about the only time you would go to Chamartín other than to catch a train.

## PLACES TO STAY

Finding a place to stay in Madrid is never really a problem. However, it is obviously wise to book ahead. In general, you won't have to leave credit card details.

## Camping

There is one camping ground within striking distance of central Madrid. To reach **Camping Osuna** *(☎ 91 741 05 10; Avenida de Logroño; camp sites per person €5, the same price per tent/car)*, which is near the airport, take metro No 5 or bus No 101 to Canillejas (the end of the line), from where it's about 500m.

## Hostels

There are two HI youth hostels in Madrid. **Albergue Richard Schirrman** *(☎ 91 463 56 99; metro El Lago, bus No 33 from Plaza Ópera; dorm beds for under/over 26 €8/12)* is in the Casa de Campo park. B&B is available. This is a seedy area at night, so try and time your arrival during the day.

**Albergue Santa Cruz de Marcenado** *(☎ 91 547 45 32; Calle de Santa Cruz de Marcenado 28; metro Argüelles, bus Nos 1, 61 & Circular; dorm beds for under/over 26 €8/12)*, has rooms for four, six and eight people. B&B costs the same as in Albergue

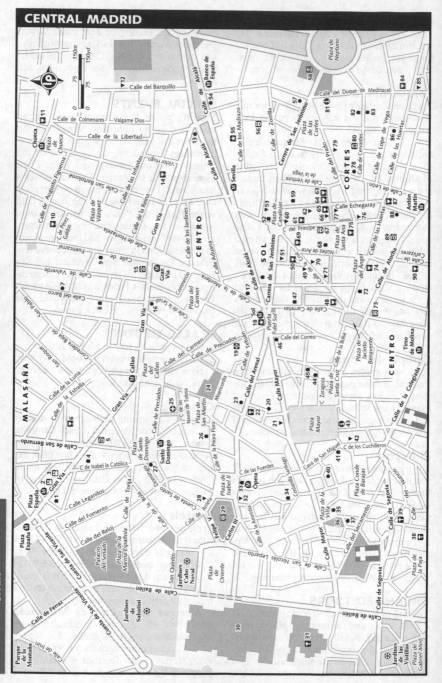

# CENTRAL MADRID

## CENTRAL MADRID

| PLACES TO STAY | | | | | |
|---|---|---|---|---|---|
| 1 | Hostal Residencia Buenos Aires | 70 | La Trucha | 19 | El Corte Inglés Department Store |
| 4 | Hostal El Pinar | 71 | Las Bravas | 20 | Chocolatería de San Ginés |
| 8 | Hotel Laris | 76 | El Salón de Prado | 22 | Iglesia de San Ginés |
| 9 | Hostal Ginebra | 77 | Cervecería La Cañita | 23 | Jamoneria Ferpal |
| 17 | Hostal Centro Sol | 79 | Tocorora | 24 | Monasterio de las Descalzas Reales |
| 26 | Hostal Paz | 85 | Maceira | 25 | Casa de Socorro (Emergency Health Centre) |
| 33 | Hostal Oriente | | | 27 | Viajes Zeppelin |
| 34 | Hostal Mairu | **BARS & CLUBS** | | 29 | Teatro Real |
| 41 | Hostal La Macarena | 6 | Morocco Disco | 30 | Palacio Real |
| 44 | Hostal Santa Cruz | 10 | Cruising | 31 | Catedral de Nuestra Señora de la Almudena |
| 45 | Hostal Comercial | 11 | Rimmel | 35 | Torre de los Lujanes |
| 46 | Hostal Riesco | 14 | Bar Cock | 36 | Ayuntamiento |
| 47 | Hostal El Pilar | 48 | Torero | 37 | Casa de Cisneros |
| 52 | Hotel Asturias | 50 | Alhambra | 38 | Iglesia de San Andrés |
| 59 | Hotel Santander | 61 | O'Neills | 39 | Iglesia de San Pedro |
| 68 | Hostal Rodriguez | 63 | Carbones | 40 | Mercado de San Miguel |
| 72 | Hostal Persal | 64 | Los Gabrieles | 43 | Tourist Office |
| 82 | Hostal Dulcinea | 65 | Viva Madrid | 54 | RENFE Train Booking Office |
| 83 | Hostal Gonzalo | 69 | Suristán | 55 | Police Station |
| | | 74 | Café Central | 56 | Teatro de la Zarzuela |
| **PLACES TO EAT** | | 75 | Cervecería Alemana | 57 | American Express |
| 12 | El Pepinillo de Barquillo | 84 | Los Gatos | 58 | Museo Thyssen-Bornemisza |
| 21 | Comme Bio | 87 | Café Populart | 67 | Teatro de la Comedia |
| 28 | Restaurante La Paella Real | 90 | Casa Patas | 73 | Teatro Calderón |
| 32 | Café del Real | | | 78 | Lavomatique |
| 42 | Restaurante Sobrino de Botín | **OTHER** | | 80 | Casa de Lope de Vega |
| 49 | La Casa del Abuelo | 2 | Princess Cinema | 81 | Tourist Office |
| 51 | Museo del Jamón | 3 | Renoir Cinema | 86 | Convento de las Trinitarias |
| 53 | La Finca de Susana | 5 | ONO | 88 | Desnivel |
| 60 | Ducados Café | 7 | Lavandería Alba | 89 | WEC |
| 62 | El Jaraíz | 13 | Edificio Metropolis | | |
| 66 | La Trucha | 15 | Telefónica/Internet Centre | | |
| | | 16 | La Casa del Libro | | |
| | | 18 | Police Station | | |

Richard Schirrman. This is one of the few Spanish hostels in HI's International Booking Network.

## Hostales & Hotels

There is an excellent range of accommodation in Madrid. At the budget end, hostales and *pensiones* tend to cluster in three or four parts of the city and the price-to-quality ratio is fairly standard. In August you may get a better deal because of the heat, although the city doesn't empty as it once did, due to the influx of visitors and air-con systems.

**Around Plaza de Santa Ana** Santa Ana is cleaned up and humming, so budget places are starting to disappear. Close to Sol and within walking distance of the Prado museum and Atocha train station, there are countless bars, cafés and restaurants here attracting every class of clientele.

Just off the square, **Hostal Rodriguez** (☎ 91 522 44 31; *Nuñez de Arce 9, 3rd floor;*

*doubles with/withouth bath €40/37)* has clean and comfortable rooms.

West off the square, **Hostal Persal** (☎ 91 369 46 43, fax 91 369 19 52; e *hostalpersal@mad.servicom.es; Plaza del Ángel 12; singles/doubles €60/75)* provides understated luxury with pleasant comfortable en suite rooms and all the extras, including TV, phone and a bumper breakfast.

There are small but cute rooms at **Hostal El Pilar** (☎ 91 531 26 26; *Calle Carretas, 13; doubles from €44)*; try for one overlooking the church.

In the same price bracket, **Hostal Gonzalo** (☎ 91 429 27 14, fax 91 420 20 07; *Calle de Cervantes 34; singles/doubles €35/43)* is in sparkling nick. Rooms have shower and TV. The staff will take a few euros off the bill if you stay at least three days. Across the road **Hostal Dulcinea** (☎ 91 429 93 09, fax 91 369 25 69; e *donato@teleline.es; Calle de Cervantes 19; singles/doubles €36/42)* has well-maintained if simply furnished rooms.

SPAIN

### Around Puerta del Sol & Plaza Mayor

You can't get more central than Plaza Puerta del Sol. This and Plaza Mayor, Madrid's true heart, are not major budget accommodation areas but, if you're euro-economising, there are a few good options tucked away among the cafés, bars and souvenir shops.

The pick of the cheaper bunch is **Hostal Comercial** (☎ 91 522 66 30; Calle Esparteros 12; singles/doubles €30/35) with bath, TV and balcony. Right on the square, **Hostal Riesco** (☎ 91 522 26 92; Calle de Correo 2, 3rd floor; singles/doubles €33/41) is a natty little place but may require earplugs on a Saturday night. **Hostal Santa Cruz** (☎ 91 522 24 41; Plaza de Santa Cruz 6; singles/doubles from €24/36) is bright and smart, in a prime location. A great old building, **Hotel Asturias** (☎ 91 429 66 76, fax 91 429 49 36; e ast urias@chh.es; Calle Sevilla 2; singles/doubles €78/103) combines upmarket convenience with old-world chintz, with the added plus of a lively bar, popular with the locals.

There's a cosy overstuffed sofa feel at **Hotel Santander** (☎ 91 429 95 51, fax 91 369 10 78; Calle Echegaray 1; doubles with bath €60) and this street is buzzing with plenty of bar choices. Just off Plaza Mayor in a tastefully revamped old building, **Hostal La Macarena** (☎ 91 365 92 21, fax 91 366 61 11; Cava de San Miguel 8; singles/doubles €57/73) has excellent rooms with bath, TV and phone – pricey but worth it. **Hostal Centro Sol** (☎ 91 522 15 82, fax 91 522 57 78; Carrera de San Jerónimo 5; singles/doubles €46/54) offers smallish rooms but all the extras, like TV, phone, heating, air-con, minibar, even a hair-dryer.

### Around Gran Vía

The hostales on and around Gran Vía tend to be a little more expensive, so it's worth shopping around.

A good budget choice is **Hostal El Pinar** (☎ 91 547 32 82; Calle de Isabel la Católica 19; singles/doubles without bath from €19/31), which has a certain old-fashioned charm. **Hostal Residencia Buenos Aires** (☎ 91 542 01 02, fax 91 542 24 66; Gran Vía 61; doubles from €48) is shiny smart with all mod cons, plus a cafeteria.

Calle de Fuencarral is similarly choked with hostales and pensiones, especially at the Gran Vía end. **Hostal Ginebra** (☎ 91 532 10 35; Calle de Fuencarral 17; singles/doubles with bath €32/40) is a reliable choice not far

from Gran Vía. All rooms have TV and phone, and some have a private balcony.

**Hotel Laris** (☎ 91 521 46 80, fax 521 46 85; Calle del Barco 3; doubles €63) has been handsomely reformed and provides guests with all the extras.

### Around Ópera

The tiny **Hostal Paz** (☎ 91 547 30 47; Calle Flora 4; singles/doubles €20/30) looks pretty grim from the outside but the cheap rooms inside are reasonable, if a little cramped. Quietly tucked away, **Hostal Mairu** (☎ 91 547 30 88; Calle del Espejo 2; singles/doubles with bath from €22/33) is simple but well priced and some rooms include a small fridge. **Hostal Oriente** (☎/fax 91 548 03 14; Calle del Arenal 23; singles/doubles from €33/51) is a pleasant mid-range choice.

### Rental

Many of the hostales mentioned above will do a deal on long stays. You can also check the rental pages of *Segundamano* magazine or notice boards at universities, the Escuela Oficial de Idiomas and cultural institutes like the British Council or Alliance Française.

## PLACES TO EAT

Madrid heaves with an infinite number of bars and restaurants, ranging from intimate tapas bars shoe-horned into tiny spaces to cavernous old *mesones* (taverns) with smoke-blackened walls, antique furniture as well as lip-smacking traditional food. Around Santa Ana it doesn't seem to matter that the sea is more than a pebble's throw away: there are plenty of excellent seafood restaurants around. One of the best is **Maceira** (☎ 91 429 42 93; Calle de Jesús 7; metro Antón Martín; open lunch only), tucked away from the main tourist hubbub. Splash (or slurp) your *pulpo a la gallega* (octopus in paprika and oil) down with a crisp white Ribeiro.

In **La Casa del Abuelo** (☎ 91 432 28 40; Calle de la Victoria 14; metro Sol), on a back-street southeast of Puerta del Sol, you can sip a *chato* (small glass) of the heavy El Abuelo red wine while munching on heavenly king prawns, grilled or with garlic. Next, duck around the corner to **Las Bravas** (☎ 91 532 26 20; Callejón de Álvarez Gato; metro Sol) for a *caña* (glass of draught beer) and the best *patatas bravas* (fried potatoes with spicy tomato sauce) in town.

**La Trucha** (☎ 91 532 08 90; Calle de Núñez de Arce 6; metro Sol; open Tues-Sat) is one of Madrid's great bars for tapas. It's off Plaza de Santa Ana, and there's another at Calle de Manuel Fernández y González 3. You can eat at the bar or in the restaurant.

For crusty old men in flat caps, check out the all-time local **Cervecería La Cañita** (☎ 91 429 04 61; Calle Echegaray 20; metro Sol), which serves tasty tapas from €2. A few doors away **El Jaraíz** (☎ 91 369 48 10; Calle Echegaray 12) is upmarket smart, serving trendy tapas such as Roquefort and dates accompanied by giant goblets of wine. Something of an institution is the **Museo del Jamón**, a Miss Piggy nightmare with hundreds of hams swinging from the ceiling. There are 10 branches in town, including one at Carrera de San Jerónimo 6.

Everything Cuban is still pretty cool and **Tocorora** (☎ 91 369 40 00; Calle del Prado 3; metro Antón Martín) is top banana with black beans, tamales, fried yucca, avocado salad and umpteen makes of rum.

**La Finca de Susana** (☎ 91 369 35 57; Calle de Arlabán 4; metro Sevilla) simply hums with young couples and atmosphere, and dishes up Spanish-with-a-twist fare for around €12.

Vegetarians often have to make do with a plate of chips and salad in Spain, but Madrid offers a few safe ports. **Elqui** (☎ 91 168 04 62; Calle de Buenavista 18; metro Antón Martín; open for lunch until 4pm Tues-Sun, dinner Fri & Sat) is a self-service buffet style restaurant for piling up your plate. **Comme Bio** (☎ 91 354 63 00; Calle Mayor 30; metro Sol) is excellent and inexpensive, with a health-food shop out front where you can stock up on muesli bars to go.

### Around Plaza Mayor

You know you're getting close to Plaza Mayor when you see signs in English saying 'Typical Spanish Restaurant' and 'Hemingway Never Ate Here'. Nevertheless, when the sun's shining (or rising), there's not a finer place to be than at one of the outdoor cafés in the plaza.

Calle de la Cava San Miguel and Calle de Cuchilleros are packed with mesones that are fun for a little tapas hopping, if you don't mind paying a little more. The splendid **Restaurante Sobrino de Botín** (☎ 91 366 42 17; Calle de los Cuchilleros 17; metro Sol;

set menu €30) is one of Europe's oldest restaurants (established in 1725), with loads of atmosphere despite the tourists.

### Other Areas

Just about anywhere you go in central Madrid, you can find cheap restaurants with reasonable, filling food.

**Casa Mingo** (☎ 91 547 79 18; Paseo de la Florida 34; metro Príncipe Pío), near the Panteón de Goya, is a bustling great place for chicken and cider. A full roast bird, salad and bottle of cider – enough for two – comes to around €12.

If you're after paella at all costs, head for **Restaurante La Paella Real** (☎ 91 542 09 42; Calle de Arrieta 2; metro Opera; paella for two from €23) just off Plaza de Oriente, which does a whole range of rice-based dishes. For more unconventional dishes (and decor), try **El Pepinillo de Barquillo** (☎ 91 310 25 46; Calle del Barquillo 42; metro Chueca), with its giant pickle hanging from the ceiling and dishes that range from snails and spaghetti to vegie plates with panache.

In the Malasaña area a couple of blocks from Plaza del Dos de Mayo, **La Musa** (☎ 91 448 75 58; Calle Manuela Malasaña 18; metro Bilbao) is stylish and arty, dishing up nouvelle-style Spanish food at affordable prices. For more mainstream fare, head for **Pizzeria Mastroplero** (Calle de San Vicente Ferrer 34) on the corner of Calle del Dos de Mayo. This is a justifiably popular Argentine-run joint where you can get pizza by the slice.

The Plaza de España area is a good hunting-ground for non-Spanish food, though prices tend to be higher. **Restaurante Bali** (☎ 91 541 91 22; Calle de San Bernardino 6; metro Plaza España) has spicy Indonesian food at around €20 for two people, while the **Adrish**, across the street at No 1, is a good Indian restaurant, but typically spiced down for the Spanish palate.

### Cafés

Madrid has many fine places for a coffee and light bite, ranging from sumptuously elegant with chandeliers and palms, to small and smoky refuges for writing that epic love letter. Historic, elegant **El Salón del Prado** (☎ 91 429 33 61; Calle del Prado 4; metro Antón Martín) also has chamber music concerts on Thursday nights. There's a crumbling romantic feel about **Nuevo Café**

Barbieri (☎ 91 527 36 58; Calle del Ave María 45; metro Lavapiés), with its Art Deco light fixtures and red velvet decor. Local artists exhibit at **Café Manuela** (☎ 91 531 70 37; San Vicente Ferrer 11; metro Tribunal), which also has a piano, board games and Belle Époque detailing. **Café del Real** (Plaza de Isabel II; metro Ópera) has a cosy touch of faded elegance – good for breakfast and busy at night, too. In the centre, **Ducados Café** (☎ 91 360 00 89; Plaza de Canalejas 3; metro Sol) has bare brick and beams, and serves up Tex-Mex and a good tosta (bite-size toast with topping) choice along with head-spinning cocktails, and coffees.

## ENTERTAINMENT

A copy of the weekly Guía del Ocio (€1 at newsstands) will give you a good rundown of what's on in Madrid. Its comprehensive listings include music gigs, art exhibitions, TV, cinema, and theatre. It's very handy even if you can't read Spanish.

### Bars

The epicentres of Madrid's nightlife are the Santa Ana–Calle de las Huertas area and the Malasaña-Chueca zone north of Gran Vía. The latter can be a bit druggy late at night.

The bars on Plaza de Santa Ana are where el todo Madrid seem to start their evening out. **Cervecería Alemana** (☎ 91 429 70 33; Plaza de Santa Ana 6) appeals to travellers as well with its beer served in steins and low-key feel. There's not much elbow-room at **Viva Madrid** (☎ 91 429 36 40; Calle de Manuel Fernández y González 7) at weekends, but take a look at its tiles and heavy wooden ceilings. On the same street, **Carbones** (open until 4am) is a busy place with good mainstream music on the jukebox. **Los Gabrieles** (☎ 91 429 62 61; Calle Echegaray 17) is a dazzling tiled bar with a huge history, most famously serving as a meeting point for the beautiful people of Spain's movida.

**Café Populart** (☎ 91 429 84 07; Calle de las Huertas 22) often has music, generally jazz or blues. For more jazz with your drinks, **Café Central** (☎ 91 369 41 43; Plaza del Ángel 10) is another good choice. Just at the bottom of Huertas is the amiable **Los Gatos** (☎ 91 429 30 67; Calle de Jesús 2), a lively local haunt.

In Malasaña, **Cervecería Santa Bárbara** (Plaza de Santa Bárbara 8) is a classic Madrid drinking house and a good place to kick off a night out. If you fancy some salsa with your cerveza head for **El Son** (☎ 91 308 04 29; Calle Fernando V1 21), a Latino music bar.

Irish pubs are very popular in Madrid: two good ones are **O'Neill's** (☎ 91 521 20 30; Calle Principe 12) and **Finnegan's** (☎ 91 310 05 21; Plaza de las Salesas 9).

Calle de Pelayo Campoamor is lined with an assortment of bars, graduating from hi-octane rock bars at the northern end to the gay bar centre at the southern Chueca area. **Rimmel** (Calle de Luis de Góngora 4) and **Cruising** (☎ 91 521 51 43; Calle de Pérez Galdós 5) are among the more popular gay haunts. The latter has a dark room and puts on occasional shows.

Raising many a schoolgirl titter, the quaintly named **Bar Cock** (☎ 91 532 67 37; Calle de la Reina 16) once served as a discreet salon for high-class prostitution. The ladies in question have gone but this popular bar is still plush and atmospheric.

### Live Music & Discos

If you like the skirt-swirling Spanish sound, head for **Alhambra** (☎ 91 521 07 08; Calle Victoria 9) in Santa Ana, which gathers speed at around 11pm. **Morocco** (☎ 91 531 31 77; Calle del Marqués de Leganés 7) in Malasaña is still a popular stop on the Madrid disco circuit. It gets going about 1am.

Near Plaza de Santa Ana, Calle de la Cruz has a couple of good dance spaces; try to pick up fliers for them before you go – they may save you queuing. **Suristán** at No 7 is a buzzing nightclub dedicated to world music with a colourful, multiethnic clientele and modest cover charge. **Torero** at No 26 has Latin music upstairs and disco house downstairs.

**Soul Kitchen** (Calle Fernandez de los Rios 67) has recently re-opened, and is bigger and badder than ever with the latest hip-hop, reggae and house tracks.

Madrid's not the best where authentic flamenco is concerned, although **Casa Patas** (☎ 91 369 04 96; Calle de Cañizares 10) hosts recognised masters of flamenco song, guitar and dance. Bigger flamenco names also play some of Madrid's theatres – check listings.

### Cinemas

With tickets around €5, cinemas are reasonably priced. Films in their original language (with Spanish subtitles) are usually marked VO (versión original). A good part of town for these is on and around Calle de Martín de los Heros and Calle de la Princesa, near Plaza de España. The **Renoir, Alphaville** and **Princesa** complexes here all screen VO movies.

## Classical Music, Theatre & Opera

There's plenty happening, except in the height of summer. The city's grandest stage, **Teatro Real** (☎ 91 516 06 06; Plaza de Isabel 11), is the scene for opera. If you can't get into the Teatro Real, the **Teatro Calderón** (☎ 91 369 14 34; Calle de Atocha 18) plays second fiddle. The beautiful old **Teatro de la Comedia** (☎ 91 521 49 31; Calle del Príncipe 14), home to the Compañía Nacional de Teatro Clásico, stages gems of classic Spanish and European theatre. The **Centro Cultural de la Villa** (☎ 91 575 60 80), under the waterfall at Plaza de Colón, stages everything from classical concerts to comic theatre, opera and even classy flamenco. Also important for classical music is the **Auditorio Nacional de Música** (☎ 91 337 01 40; Avenida del Príncipe de Vergara 146; metro Cruz del Rayo).

## SPECTATOR SPORTS

Spending an afternoon or evening at a football (soccer) match provides quite an insight into Spanish culture. Tickets can be bought on the day of the match, starting from around €15, although big games may be sold out. Real Madrid's home is the huge **Estadio Santiago Bernabeu** (metro Santiago Bernabeu). Atlético Madrid plays at **Estadio Vicente Calderón** (metro Pirámides).

Bullfights take place most Sundays between March and October – more often during the festival of San Isidro Labrador in May – and in the height of summer. Madrid has Spain's largest bullring, the **Plaza de Toros Monumental de Las Ventas** (☎ 91 726 48 00; metro Ventas), and a second bullring by metro Vista Alegre. Tickets are best bought in advance, from agencies or at the rings, and cost up to €12.

## SHOPPING

If you're self-catering, follow the shopping baskets to the nearest market. In the centre, **Mercado San Miguel** (Plaza de San Miguel) has a good choice of fruit and veg. Pick up your deli items from the mouthwatering display at **Jamonería Ferpal** (Calle Arenal 7). For big-time shopping, El Corte Inglés has a

branch on Calle de Preciados with a good size supermarket, albeit pricey. The cheaper hypermarkets are on the outskirts of town. Forgetting food, the most famous market is **El Rastro** (see Things to See & Do earlier in this Madrid section).

For more serious retail therapy, head for Calle de Serrano, a block east of Paseo de la Castellana. Calle del Almirante, off Paseo de Recoletos, has a wide range of engaging, less mainstream shops. For guitars and other musical instruments, hunt around the area near the Palacio Real. For leather, try the shops on Calle del Príncipe and Gran Vía, or Calle de Fuencarral for shoes. For designer clothing, go to the Chueca area.

## GETTING THERE & AWAY
### Air

Scheduled and charter flights from all over the world arrive at Madrid's **Barajas airport** (☎ 902 35 35 70), 16km northeast of the city. With nowhere in Spain more than 12 hours away by bus or train, domestic flights are generally not good value unless you're in a burning hurry. Nor is Madrid the budget international flight capital of Europe. That said, you *can* find bargains to popular destinations such as London, Paris and New York. To get an idea of domestic fares, see the Getting Around section earlier in this chapter. See also Travel Agencies under Information earlier in this Madrid section.

Airline offices in Madrid include:

**Air France** (☎ 91 330 04 12, bookings ☎ 90 111 22 66) Torre de Madrid, Plaza de España 18
**American Airlines** (☎ 91 453 14 00) Calle de Orense 4
**British Airways** (☎ 91 387 43 00 or ☎ 902 11 13 33) Calle de Serrano 60
**Iberia** (☎ 91 587 75 36, bookings ☎ 902 40 05 00) Calle de Velázquez 130
**Lufthansa** (☎ 902 22 01 01) Calle del Cardenal Marcelo Spinola 2

### Bus

There are eight bus stations dotted around Madrid, serving many different bus companies. Tourist offices can tell you which one you need for your destination. Most buses to the south, and some to other places (including a number of international services), use the **Estación Sur de Autobuses** (☎ 91 468 42 00; Calle de Méndez Álvaro; metro Méndez Álvaro).

## Train

**Atocha train station**, south of the centre, is used by most trains to/from southern Spain and many destinations around Madrid. Some trains from the north also terminate here, passing through **Chamartín**, the other main station (in the northern part of the city), on the way.

There is a main booking office of **RENFE** (☎ 91 328 90 20; Calle de Alcalá 44; open 9.30am-8pm Mon-Fri).

For information on fares to Madrid from other towns, see the Getting There & Away entries under those towns.

## Car & Motorcycle

Madrid is surrounded by two ring-road systems, the older M-30 and the M-40, considerably further out (a third, the M-50, is under construction). Roads in and out of the city can get pretty clogged at peak hours (around 8am to 10am, 4pm to 5pm and 8pm to 9pm) and on Sunday night.

Car-rental companies in Madrid include **Avis** (☎ 91 547 20 48), **Atesa** (☎ 902 10 01 01), **Europcar** (☎ 91 541 88 92) and **Hertz** (☎ 91 542 58 03). All these have offices at the airport, in the city centre and often at the main train stations. Highway robbery on hire cars leaving the airport is a problem, so be careful.

You can rent motorbikes from **Moto Alquiler** (☎ 91 542 06 57; Calle del Conde Duque 13), but it's pricey, starting at €35 per day for a 50cc Vespa. Rental is from 8am to 8pm and you have to leave a refundable deposit of around €300 on your credit card.

## GETTING AROUND
### To/From the Airport

The metro runs right into town from the airport, at the upper level of the T2 terminal. Alternatively, an airport bus service runs to/from an underground terminal in Plaza de Colón every 12 to 15 minutes. The trip takes 30 minutes in average traffic and costs €2.50. Note that a taxi between the airport and city centre should cost no more than €20. This is a common rip-off route.

## Bus & Metro

In general, the very efficient underground (metro) system is faster and easier than city buses for getting around central Madrid. Trains run from 6.30am to 1.30am.

Bus route maps are available from tourist offices. Night owls may find the 20 bus lines, running from midnight to 6am, useful. They run from Puerta del Sol and Plaza de la Cibeles.

A single ride on the metro costs €0.95. A 10-ride Metrobus ticket (€5) can be used on buses and the metro.

## Taxi

Madrid's taxis are inexpensive by European standards. They're handy late at night, although in peak hours it's quicker to walk or get the metro. Flag fall is €1.35, after which you are charged according to time, so avoid rush-hour traffic.

## Car & Motorcycle

There's little point subjecting yourself to Madrid's traffic just to move from one part of the city to another, especially during peak hours. Most on-street parking spaces in central Madrid are designated for people with special permits, but almost everybody ignores this – ignoring the 12,000-plus parking tickets slapped on vehicles every day. But you risk being towed if you park in a marked no-parking or loading zone, or if you double-park. There are plenty of car parks across the city, costing about €1.75 an hour.

## AROUND MADRID
### El Escorial

The extraordinary 16th-century monastery-palace complex of San Lorenzo de El Escorial (adult/student €6/3 with an additional €1 for a guided tour; open 10am-6pm Tues-Sun Apr-Sept, 10am-5pm Tues-Sun Oct-Mar) lies one hour northwest of Madrid, just outside the town of the same name.

El Escorial was built by Felipe II, king of Spain, Naples, Sicily, Milan, the Netherlands and large parts of the Americas, to commemorate his victory over the French in the battle of St Quentin (1557) and as a mausoleum for his father Carlos I, the first of Spain's Habsburg monarchs. Felipe began searching for a site in 1558, deciding on El Escorial in 1562. The last stone was placed in 1584, and the next 11 years were spent on decoration. El Escorial's austere style, reflecting not only Felipe's wishes but also the watchful eye of architect Juan de Herrera, is loved by some, hated by others. Either way, it's a quintessential monument of Spain's golden age.

Almost all visitors to El Escorial make it a day trip from Madrid.

**Information** You can get information on El Escorial from tourist offices in Madrid, or from the local **tourist office** (☎ *91 890 53 13; Calle de Floridablanca 10; open 10am-2pm & 3pm-5pm Mon-Fri, 10am-2pm Sat)* close to the monastery.

**Things to See** Above the monastery's main gateway, on its western side, stands a **statue of San Lorenzo** holding a symbolic gridiron, the instrument of his martyrdom (he was roasted alive on one). Inside, across the Patio de los Reyes, stands the restrained **basílica**, a cavernous church with a beautiful white-marble crucifixion by Benvenuto Cellini, sculpted in 1576. At either side of the altar stand bronze statues of Carlos I and his family (to the left), and Felipe II with three of his four wives and his eldest son (on the right).

The route you have to follow leads first to the **Museo de Arquitectura**, detailing in Spanish how El Escorial was constructed, and the **Museo de Pintura**, with 16th- and 17th-century Spanish, Italian and Flemish fine art. You then head upstairs to the richly decorated **Palacio de Felipe II**, in one room of which the monarch died in 1598; his bed was positioned so that he could watch proceedings at the basílica's high altar. Next you descend to the **Panteón de los Reyes**, where almost all Spain's monarchs since Carlos I, and their spouses, lie in gilded marble coffins. Three empty sarcophagi await future arrivals. Backtracking a little, you find yourself in the **Panteón de los Infantes**, a larger series of chambers and tunnels housing the tombs of princes, princesses and other lesser royalty.

Finally, the **Salas Capitulares** in the southeast of the monastery house a minor treasure trove of El Grecos, Titians, Tintorettos and other old masters.

When you emerge, it's worth heading back to the entrance, where you can gain access to the **biblioteca** (library), once one of Europe's finest and still a haven for some 40,000 historical and valuable books.

**Getting There & Away** The Herranz bus company has a service every 10 minutes from 10am to 11pm from No 3 bus stop at the Moncloa metro station in Madrid to San Lorenzo de El Escorial (€2.50 one way). Only about 10 buses run on Sunday and during holidays.

Up to 20 sluggish *cercanías* trains (line C-8a) serve El Escorial from Atocha station (via Chamartín) in Madrid (€3). Local buses will take you the 2km from the train station up to the monastery.

## Toledo
**pop 69,450**

The narrow, winding streets of Toledo, perched on a small hill above the Río Tajo, are crammed with museums, churches and other monumental reminders of a splendid and turbulent past. As the main city of Muslim central Spain, Toledo was the peninsula's leading centre of learning and the arts in the 11th century. Until 1492, Christians, Jews and Muslims coexisted peaceably here. El Greco lived here from 1577 to 1614, and many of his works can still be seen in the city.

Toledo is packed with tourists during the day. Try to stay here overnight, when you can really appreciate its spark and soul.

**Information** The main tourist office (☎ *925 22 08 43, fax 925 25 26 48)* is just outside Toledo's main gate, the Puerta Nueva de Bisagra, at the northern end of town. A smaller information office is open in the *ayuntamiento* (town hall), across from the cathedral.

**Things to See** As well as the historical sights, Toledo's tourist shops are fun, many reflecting the city's swashbuckling past with suits of armour and swords for sale. Toledo is also famous for its marzipan; try **Santo Tomé** (Calle Santo Tomé 5).

The **cathedral** (Cardenal Cisneros; open 10.30am-6.30pm daily), in the heart of the Old City, is stunning. You could easily spend an afternoon here, admiring the glorious stone architecture, stained-glass windows, tombs of kings in the Capilla Mayor and art by the likes of El Greco, Velázquez and Goya. You have to buy a ticket (€4.80) to enter four areas – the **Coro**, **Sacristía**, **Capilla de la Torre** and **Sala Capitular**, which contain some of the finest art and artisanship.

The **alcázar** (Calle Cuesta de Carlos V, 2; admission €2, free Wed; open 9.30am-2pm Tues-Sun), Toledo's main landmark, was fought over repeatedly from the Middle Ages through to the Spanish Civil War, when it was besieged by Republican troops. Today it's a military museum.

The **Museo de Santa Cruz** (Calle de Cervantes 3; admission €1.20; 10am-6.30pm

*Tues-Sat, 10am-2pm Sun)* contains a large collection of furniture, faded tapestries, military and religious paraphernalia, and paintings. Upstairs is an impressive collection of El Grecos, including the masterpiece *La Asunción* (Assumption of the Virgin).

In the southwest of the Old City, the queues outside an unremarkable church, the **Iglesia de Santo Tomé** *(Plaza del Conde; admission €1.20; open 10am-6pm daily, later in summer)* indicate there must be something special inside. That something is El Greco's masterpiece *El Entierro del Conde de Orgaz*. The painting depicts the burial of the Count of Orgaz in 1322 by San Esteban (St Stephen) and San Agustín (St Augustine), observed by a heavenly entourage, including Christ, the Virgin, John the Baptist and Noah.

The so-called **Casa y Museo de El Greco** *(Calle de Samuel Leví; admission €1.20; open 10am-2pm, 4pm-6pm Mon-Sat, 10am-2pm Sun)*, in Toledo's former Jewish quarter, contains the artist's famous *Vista y Plano de Toledo*, plus about another 20 of his more minor works.

To the north lies one of the city's most visible sights, **San Juan de los Reyes**, the Franciscan monastery and church founded by Fernando and Isabel. The prevalent late Flemish-Gothic style is tarted up with lavish Isabelline ornament and counterbalanced by mudéjar decoration. Outside hang the chains of Christian prisoners freed after the fall of Granada in 1492.

**Places to Stay & Eat** Toledo's HI hostel, **Residencia Juvenil de San Servando** *(☎ 925 22 45 54, fax 925 21 39 54; beds under/over 26 €10/13, including breakfast)*, is beautifully located in the Castillo de San Servando. Cheap accommodation in the city is not easy to come by, especially from Easter to September. **La Belviseña** *(☎ 925 22 00 67; Cuesta del Can 5; rooms per person €10)* is basic but among the best value. Pleasant **Pensión Segovia** *(☎ 925 21 11 24; Calle de los Recoletos 2; singles/doubles €14.42/19.43)* has simple clean rooms.

Appealing new **La Posada de Zocodover** *(☎ 925 22 15 71; Calle Condonerias 6; doubles with bath €37.30)* has just seven exquisite rooms that get snapped-up fast. Comfy and chic, **Hotel Santa Isabel** *(☎/fax 925 25 31 36; Calle de Santa Isabel 24;*

*singles/doubles €28/42)* is well placed near the cathedral, yet is away from the tourist hordes.

Among the cheap lunch spots, **El Delfín** *(☎ 925 21 38 14; Calle Taller del Moro 1; set menu €6)* is acceptable, if unexciting. Similarly priced with spaghetti and macaroni on the menu is **Los Tercios** *(☎ 925 22 05 50; Plaza Solarejo 2)*, on a shady plaza.

If you just want to sip a drink and people-gaze, **Cafe Bar Tolsedo** *(Plaza de Zocodover)* has tables on the bustling square and serves good basic tapas, such as spicy *patatas bravas*. An unpretentious tavern-style restaurant, **La Campana Gorda** *(☎ 925 21 01 46; Calle Hombre de Palo 13)* specialises in roast meats and fish, and football on the TV.

**Getting There & Around** To reach most major destinations from Toledo, you need to backtrack to Madrid (or at least Aranjuez). Toledo's **bus station** *(☎ 925 22 36 41; Avenida de Castilla-La Mancha)* has buses for €3.66 every half-hour from about 6am to 10pm from Madrid (Estación Sur). The Aisa line has a service from Toledo to Cuenca at 5.30pm, Monday to Friday.

Trains from Madrid (Atocha) are more pleasant than the bus, but there are only nine of them daily. The first from Madrid departs at 7.05am, the last from Toledo at 8.58pm (€4.81 one way). Toledo's train station is 400m east of the Puente de Azarquiel on the Calle Paseo de la Rosa *(☎ 902 24 02 02)*.

Bus No 5 links the train and bus stations with Plaza de Zocodover.

## Segovia

The first thing you'll notice when you arrive is the 1st-century AD Roman **aqueduct** stretching over 800m away from the old town's eastern end. Its 163 arches reach up to 29m high, all without the aid of mortar.

At the heart of the old city is the 16th-century Gothic **cathedral** *(admission €2)* on pretty Plaza Mayor. Its sombre interior is anchored by an imposing choir and enlivened by about 20 chapels. A remarkable Romanesque doorway from the original church is housed in the Capilla del Cristo del Consuelo.

Rapunzel towers, turrets topped with slate witch's hats and a deep, dark moat render the **alcázar** *(admission €3)* a most memorable monument. A 15th-century fairy-tale castle, perched on a craggy cliff top at the old city's western end – it was virtually destroyed by fire in 1862. The current structure is an evocative, over-the-top reconstruction of the original. Climb the Torre de Juan II for some magnificent views.

Both the **main tourist office** (☎ 921 46 03 34; *Plaza Mayor*) and the **branch tourist office** (☎ 921 46 29 14; *Plaza del Azuguejo*), beside the aqueduct, are open daily.

**Places to Stay & Eat** About 2km along the road to La Granja is **Camping Acueducto** (☎ 921 42 50 00; €4 per person or car; open Apr-Sept). Hotels to try include **Pensión Aragón** (☎ 921 46 09 14; Plaza Mayor 4; singles/doubles/quads €13/24/26), the more pleasant **Hostal Plaza** (☎ 921 46 03 03, fax 921 46 03 05; Calle del Cronista Lecea 11; singles/doubles €34/40), **Hostal Juan Bravo** (☎ 921 43 55 21; Calle de Juan Bravo 12), with similar prices, and close to the aqueduct is spick-and-span **Hostal Don Jaime** (☎ 921 44 47 87; Calle de Ochoa Ondategui 8; singles/doubles €25/41).

Simple **Bar Ratos** (Calle de los Escuderos; bocadillos €3) makes generously stuffed sandwiches. **Cueva de San Esteban** (Calle de Valdeláguila 15; set lunch €6) has delicious lunch menús. Sample Segovia's speciality – *cochinillo asado* (roast suckling pig) at **Mesón José María** (Calle del Cronista Lecea 11; suckling pig ración €5.50), a favourite among Segovians.

For meatless fare, try **La Almuzara** (Marqués del Arco 3; vegie plato combinado €7; open for lunch Wed-Sun, dinner Tues-Sun), which has a warm, arty ambience.

**Getting There & Away** Up to 30 buses daily run to Madrid (€5, 1½ hours); others serve Ávila and Salamanca. The bus station is 500m south of the aqueduct, just off Paseo Ezequiel González. Trains to Madrid leave every two hours (€4.50, 1¾ hours). The station is southeast of town; take bus No 2 from there to the centre.

## Ávila

Impressive Ávila is one of the world's best-preserved walled cities. Constructed during the 11th and 12th centuries, its imposing *muralla* (rampart) consists of no fewer than eight monumental gates and 88 towers. The cathedral forms a central bulwark in the eastern wall. Buses to Madrid leave up to eight

times on weekdays, down to three on weekends (€5.50, 1½ hours). There are up to 30 trains a day to Madrid (€5.50, 1½ hours).

# Catalunya

Many Catalans bristle at the idea of being lumped together with 'ordinary' Spaniards, maintaining that their corner of the universe is a little closer to heaven. And with its soaring peaks, tranquil coastal resorts, sleepy small towns and exuberant capital, modern-day Catalunya may well lay claim to being its own world. Whether or not one sympathises with Catalan separatists, one must admit that the region offers a culture and also a lifestyle that sets it apart from the rest of Spain.

## BARCELONA
**pop 1.5 million**
Until the 1990s, Barcelona remained a well-kept secret among Western backpackers. The 1992 Olympic Games served as the town's coming-out party, stylishly introducing this first-class city to the world. Today, folks come from all corners of the globe to marvel at Barcelona's transcendent modernist architecture, to visit its top-shelf museums and to roam the streets of its old quarter.

No-one should come to Barcelona and miss the visionary creations of Antoni Gaudí, including the Sagrada Família church and Parc Güell. Visitors can further indulge their souls by spending entire days admiring the works of Pablo Picasso and Joan Miró and spending entire nights in debauched frenzy, winding their way through the city's myriad bars and clubs. And whether it's midday or midnight, Barcelona's famed street, La Rambla, presents a never-ending stream of hawkers, musicians, beggars, backpackers and villains – nonstop entertainment for both the privileged and destitute alike.

## Orientation
Barcelona's main square, Plaça de Catalunya, is a good place to get your bearings. The main tourist office is right here, and La Rambla extends southwards from the plaza. Most travellers base themselves in Barcelona's old city (Ciutat Vella), the area bordered by the harbour Port Vell (south), Plaça de Catalunya (north), Ronda de Sant Pau (west) and Parc de la Ciutadella (east).

# BARCELONA

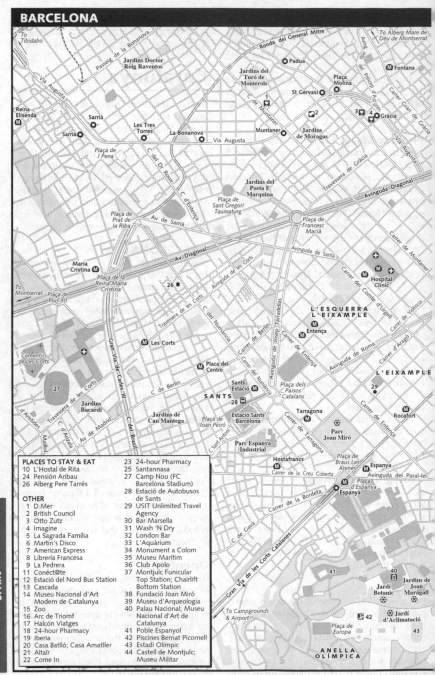

**PLACES TO STAY & EAT**
10 L'Hostal de Rita
24 Pensión Aribau
26 Alberg Pere Tarrés

**OTHER**
1 D.Mer
2 British Council
3 Otto Zutz
4 Imagine
5 La Sagrada Família
6 Martin's Disco
7 American Express
8 Librería Francesa
9 La Pedrera
11 Conéct@te
12 Estació del Nord Bus Station
13 Cascada
14 Museu Nacional d'Art Modern de Catalunya
15 Zoo
16 Arc de Triomf
17 Halcón Viatges
18 24-hour Pharmacy
19 Iberia
20 Casa Batlló; Casa Amatller
21 Altaïr
22 Come In

23 24-hour Pharmacy
25 Santannasa
27 Camp Nou (FC Barcelona Stadium)
28 Estació de Autobusos de Sants
29 USIT Unlimited Travel Agency
30 Bar Marsella
31 Wash 'N Dry
32 London Bar
33 L'Aquàrium
34 Monument a Colom
35 Museu Marítim
36 Club Apolo
37 Montjuïc Funicular Top Station; Chairlift Bottom Station
38 Fundació Joan Miró
39 Museu d'Arqueologia
40 Palau Nacional; Museu Nacional d'Art de Catalunya
41 Poble Espanyol
42 Piscines Bernat Picornell
43 Estadi Olímpic
44 Castell de Montjuïc; Museu Militar

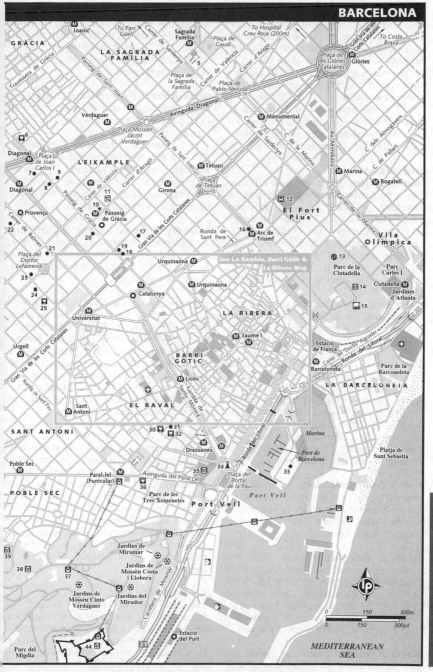

BARCELONA

GRÀCIA

Joanic

To Parc
Güell

Carrer de Sardenya

LA SAGRADA
FAMÍLIA

Sagrada
Família

Plaça de
Gaudí

To Hospital
Creu Roja (200m)

Gran Via de les
Corts Catalanes

To Costa
Brava

Plaça de
les Glòries
Catalanes

Glòries

Passeig de Sant Joan

5

Carrer de València

Carrer d'Aragó

Travessera de Gràcia

Plaça de
la Sagrada
Família

Plaça de
Pablo Neruda

Verdaguer

Avinguda Diagonal

Monumental

Plaça Mossèn
Jàcint Verdaguer

Carrer de Sardenya

C de la Marina

Av. Meridiana

6

Diagonal

Plaça
de Joan
Carles I

L'EIXAMPLE

Carrer d'Aragó

Passeig de Sant Joan

Tetuan

Marina

Bogatell

7

9

Carrer de València

Girona

Plaça
de Tetuan

Carrer de la Marina

Diagonal

8

Passeig de Gràcia

11

Carrer de Balmes

22

Provença

10

Passeig
de Gràcia

El Fort
Pius

12

20

17

Gran Via de les Corts Catalanes

Ronda de
Sant Pere

16

Arc de
Triomf

Vila
Olímpica

21

19
18

Plaça del
Doctor
Lefamendí

Urquinaona

See La Rambla, Barri Gòtic &
La Ribera Map

13

23

Urquinaona

Parc de la
Ciutadella

Parc
Carles I

24

Catalunya

14

Ciutadella

Jardines
d'Atlanta

25

LA RIBERA

15

Universitat

Urgell

BARRI
GÒTIC

Jaume I

Estació
de França

Carrer del "Doctor" Aiguader

Ronda del Litoral

Gran Via de les Corts Catalanes

Barceloneta

Parc de la
Barconeleta

Ronda de Sant Pau

Liceu

Rambla de
Santa Mònica

LA DARCELONEIA

SANT ANTONI

Sant
Antoni

EL RAVAL

30

31
32

SANT ANTONI

Marina

Platja de
Sant Sebastià

Drassanes

Ronda del Litoral

Port de
Barcelona

Poble Sec

35

34

33

POBLE SEC

Paral·lel
(Funicular)

36

Avinguda del Paral·lel

Parc de les
Tres Xemeneies

Plaça del
Portal
de la Pau

Port Vell

Port Vell
Port Vell

39

38

37

Jardins de
Miramar

Jardins de
Mossèn Costa
i Llobera

Carretera de Miramar

Jardins de
Mössèn Cinto
Verdaguer

Jardins del
Mirador

Estació
del Port

Parc del
Migdia

44

21

MEDITERRANEAN
SEA

0        150        300m
0        150        300yd

SPAIN

La Rambla, the city's best-known boulevard, runs through the heart of the old city down to the harbour. On the eastern side is the medieval quarter (Barri Gòtic), and on the west the seedy Barri Xinès. North of the old city is the gracious neighbourhood of L'Eixample, where you'll find the best of Barcelona's modernist architecture.

One of the best maps of Barcelona is Lonely Planet's very own *Barcelona* City Map. Other good maps are available from the tourist office (see Information following).

## Information

**Tourist Offices** The main tourist office in town is the **Centre d'Informació Turisme de Barcelona** (☎ *906 30 12 82;* ⓦ *www .barcelonaturisme.com; Plaça de Catalunya 17-S; open 9am-9pm daily)*, which is actually underground. Ask here for city maps, lists of attractions and handy discount cards (such as the Barcelona Card and ArTicket) that let you into select locations for reduced admission fees.

Handy offices are located at Estació Sants, the main train station, and at the EU passengers arrivals hall at the airport and both open daily (mornings only on Sunday and holidays).

**Money** Banks usually have the best rates for both cash and travellers cheques. Banking hours are usually 8am to 2pm Monday to Friday. The two **American Express offices** *(Passeig de Gràcia 101; La Rambla dels Capuxtins 74; open 9.30am-6pm Mon-Fri, 10am-noon Sat)* offer reasonable rates. For after-hours money emergencies, currency-exchange booths throng La Rambla.

**Post & Communications** The **main post office** *(Plaça d'Antoni López; open 8am-9.30pm Mon-Sat)* is open for most services, including poste restante *(lista de correos)*, during the listed hours.

**Email & Internet Access** There are dozens of places to check your emails. Both **EasyEverything** *(La Rambla)*, at €0.50 to €2 an hour, and **Conéct@te** *(Carrer d'Aragó 283)*, at €1.50 an hour, are open 24 hours, although you might not want to wander too close to unshowered Internet users at 4am.

**Travel Agencies** Youth and student air, train and bus tickets can be purchased at **USIT**

**Unlimited** (☎ *93 412 01 04; Ronda de l'Universitat 16)*. There's a branch in the **Turisme Juvenil de Catalunya office** *(Carrer de Rocafort 116-122)*. **Halcón Viatges** (☎ *902 30 06 00; Carrer de Pau Claris 108)* is a reliable chain of travel agents.

**Bookshops** In the Barri Gòtic, **Quera** *(Carrer de Petritxol 2)* specialises in maps and guides. **Próleg** *(Carrer de la Dagueria 13)* is a good women's bookshop.

In L'Eixample, **Altaïr** *(Carrer de Balmes 71)* is a superb travel bookshop. **Librería Francesa** *(Passeig de Gràcia 91)* has French-language books and **Come In** *(Carrer de Provença 203)* is good for novels and books on Spain, as well as dictionaries.

**Laundry** Two good self-service laundrettes are **Lavomatic** *(Carrer del Consolat de Mar 43-45)* and **Wash 'N Dry** *(Carrer Nou de la Rambla 19)*. Cleaning and drying a large load should cost about €6.

**Emergency** The **Guàrdia Urbana** *(City Police;* ☎ *092; La Rambla 43)* has a station opposite Plaça Reial. For an ambulance or emergency medical help call ☎ 061. **Hospital Creu Roja** (☎ *93 300 20 20; Carrer del Dos de Maig 301)* has an emergency room. For 24-hour tourist assistance in English, call ☎ 93 344 13 00. There are 24-hour pharmacies at Carrer d'Aribau 62, Passeig de Gràcia 26 and La Rambla 98.

**Dangers & Annoyances** Watch your pockets, bags and cameras on the train to and from the airport, on La Rambla, in Barri Gòtic south of Plaça Reial and in Barri Xinès – especially at night. These last two areas have been somewhat cleaned up in recent years but pickpockets, bag-snatchers and intimidating beggars still stalk the unsuspecting. In addition, be wary when walking in deserted areas, even strolling in parks during the daytime, as violent muggings of foreigners have been on the rise recently.

## La Rambla

The best way to introduce yourself to Barcelona is by a leisurely stroll from Plaça de Catalunya down La Rambla, the magnificent boulevard of a thousand faces. This long strip, shaded by leafy trees and varied buildings, is an ever-changing blur of activity, lined with newsstands, bird and flower stalls and cafés. It's populated by artists, buskers, human statues, shoe-shine merchants, beggars and a constant stream of people promenading and just enjoying the sights.

About halfway down La Rambla is the wonderful **Mercat de la Boqueria**, which is worth visiting just for the sights and sounds, but is also a good place to stock up on fresh fruit, vegetables, nuts, bread and pastries. Just off La Rambla, further south, **Plaça Reial** used to be a seedy square of ill repute, but it's now quite pleasant, with numerous cafés and bars and a couple of music clubs. Just off the other side of La Rambla is Gaudí's moody **Palau Güell** *(Carrer Nou de la Rambla 3-5; admission €3; open 10am-6.30pm Mon-Sat)*, a house built by Gaudí in the late 1880s for his patron, the industrialist Eusebi Güell.

Down at the end of La Rambla stands the **Monument a Colom**, a statue of Columbus atop a tall pedestal. A small lift will take you to the top of the monument (admission €1.80). Just west, in the beautiful 14th-century Royal Shipyards, is the **Museu Marítim** *(admission €5.50; open 10am-7pm daily)*, with an impressive array of boats, models, maps and more. If you like boats and the sea, you won't be disappointed.

### Barri Gòtic

The Gothic Quarter's centrepiece is its serene **cathedral** *(open 8.30am-1.30pm daily, 4pm-7.30pm Mon-Fri, 5pm-7.30pm Sat & Sun)*. Be sure to visit the lovely, verdant cloister. Each Sunday at noon, crowds gather in front of the cathedral to dance the Catalan national dance, the *sardana*. East of the cathedral is the fascinating **Museu d'Història de la Ciutat** *(City History Museum; admission €3.50; open 10am-2pm & 4pm-8pm Tues-Sat, 10am-2pm Sun, no afternoon break June-Sept)*, composed of several buildings around **Plaça del Rei**, the palace courtyard of the medieval monarchs of Aragón. From the royal chapel, climb the Mirador del Rei Martí for good views. The museum also includes a remarkable subterranean walk through excavated portions of Roman and Visigothic Barcelona.

A few minutes' walk west of the cathedral, **Plaça de Sant Josep Oriol** is a sometime hang-out for bohemian musicians and buskers. The plaza is surrounded by cafés and towards the end of the week becomes an outdoor art and craft market in summer.

### Waterfront

For a look at the modern face of Barcelona, take a stroll along the once-seedy waterfront. From the bottom of La Rambla you can cross the Rambla de Mar footbridge to the **Moll d'Espanya**, a former wharf in the middle of the old harbour, Port Vell. There you'll find **L'Aquàrium** *(admission €11; open 9.30am-9pm or later daily)*, one of Europe's best (and more expensive) aquariums. Northeast of Port Vell, on the far side of the fishing-oriented La Barceloneta area, the city **beaches** begin. Along the beachfront, after 1.3km you'll reach the **Vila Olímpica**, site of the 1992 Olympic village, which is fronted by the impressive **Port Olímpic**, a large marina with dozens of overpriced, touristy bars and restaurants. Don't come here to hobnob with locals.

### La Sagrada Família

Gaudí's life masterpiece *(cnr Carrer de Sardenya & Carrer de Mallorca; metro Sagrada Família; admission €6, with tour €9; open 9am-8pm daily Apr-Sept, 9am-6pm daily Oct-Mar)* is Barcelona's most famous building and can stir the soul. Construction began in 1882 and is proceeding at a suitably otherworldly pace. The church is not yet half-built, and it's anyone's guess whether it will be finished by 2082. Some feel that it should not be completed but rather left as a monument to the master, whose career was cut short when he was hit by a tram in 1926.

Today there are eight towers, all over 100m high, with 10 more to come – the total representing the 12 Apostles, four Evangelists and the Virgin Mary, plus the tallest tower (170m) standing for her son. Although La Sagrada Família is effectively a building site, the awesome dimensions and its extravagant yet careful sculpting make it Barcelona's greatest highlight. The northeastern Nativity Facade was done under Gaudí's own supervision; the very different northwestern Passion Facade has been built since the 1950s.

You can climb high inside some of the towers by spiral staircases for a vertiginous overview of the interior and a panorama to the sea, or you can opt out and take a lift for €2 some of the way up.

### Passeig de Gràcia

Many of Barcelona's finest modernist buildings are along the aptly named Passeig de

**SPAIN**

# LA RAMBLA, BARRI GÒTIC & LA RIBERA

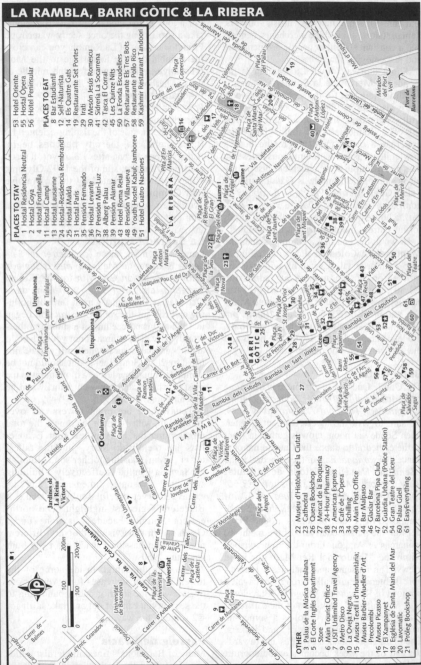

**PLACES TO STAY**
1 Hostal Residencia Neutral
2 Hostal Goya
4 Hostal Fontanella
11 Hostal Campi
13 Hostal Lausanne
24 Hostal-Residencia Rembrandt
25 Hostal Maldà
31 Hostal Paris
35 Pension Fernando
36 Pension Levante
37 Pension Mari-Luz
38 Alberg Palau
39 Pension Palau
43 Hotel Roma Reial
48 Pension Villanueva
49 Youth Hostel Kabul; Jamboree
51 Hotel Cuatro Naciones

53 Hotel Oriente
55 Hostal Òpera
56 Hotel Peninsular

**PLACES TO EAT**
8 Bar Estudiantil
12 Self-Naturista
14 Els Quatre Gats
19 Restaurante Set Portes
29 Irati
30 Mesón Jesus Romescu
41 Sidreria La Socarrena
42 Tasca El Corral
45 Les Quinze Nits
50 La Fonda Escudellers
57 Restaurante Els Tres Bots
58 Restaurante Pollo Rico
59 Kashmir Restaurant Tandoori

**OTHER**
3 Palau de la Música Catalana
5 El Corte Inglés Department Store
6 Main Tourist Office
7 USIT Unlimited Travel Agency
9 Metro Disco
10 La Oveja Negra
15 Museu Tèxtil d'Indumentària; Museu Barbier-Mueller d'Art Precolombí
16 Museu Picasso
17 El Xampanyet
18 Església de Santa Maria del Mar
20 Lavomatic
21 Pròleg Bookshop

22 Museu d'Història de la Ciutat
23 Cathedral
26 Quera Bookshop
27 Mercat de la Boqueria
28 24-Hour Pharmacy
32 American Express
33 Café de l'Opera
34 Schilling
40 Main Post Office
44 Bar Malpaso
46 Glaciar Bar
47 Barcelona Pipa Club
52 Guàrdia Urbana (Police Station)
54 Gran Teatre del Liceu
60 Palau Güell
61 EasyEverything

Gràcia in L'Eixample. Gaudí's beautifully coloured **Casa Batlló** *(Passeig de Gràcia 43)* beckons onlookers from afar, while his grey-stone **La Pedrera** *(Passeig de Gràcia 92; admission €6; open 10am-8pm daily, guided visits 6pm Mon-Fri, 11am Sat & Sun)* ripples around the corner of Carrer de Provença. Don't miss its surreal roof, which features some truly bizarre chimney pots.

Next door to Casa Batlló is **Casa Amatller** *(Passeig de Gràcia 41)*, by another leading modernist architect, Josep Puig i Cadafalch. Check here for tickets to the Ruta del Modernism, which allows sightseers access to over 50 modernist highlights throughout the city.

### La Ribera

East of the Barri Gòtic lies La Ribera, home to some outstanding museums and more modernist works. Smack-dab in its centre is the **Museu Picasso** *(Carrer de Montcada 15-19; admission €4.50, free first Sun of month; open 10am-8pm Tues-Sat, 10am-3pm Sun)*, housed in a medieval mansion. It's home to the most important collection of Picasso's work in Spain – more than 3000 pieces, including paintings, drawings, engravings and ceramics. The museum concentrates on Picasso's Barcelona periods (1895–1900 and 1901–04) early in his career, and shows how the precocious Picasso learned to handle a whole spectrum of subjects and treatments before developing his own forms of expression. There are also two rooms devoted to Picasso's 1950s series of interpretations of Velázquez' masterpiece *Las Meninas* (see the Museo del Prado entry under Things to See & Do in the Madrid section, earlier).

The **Museu Textil i d'Indumentària** *(Textile & Costume Museum; combined ticket with Museu Barbier-Mueller d'Art Precolombí €3.50; open 10am-8pm Tues-Sat, 10am-3pm Sun)*, opposite the Museu Picasso, has a fascinating collection of tapestries, clothing and other textiles from centuries past and present. The entry fee includes admission to the **Museu Barbier-Mueller d'Art Precolombí** *(open 10am-8pm Tues-Sat, 10am-3pm Sun)*, which holds one of the most prestigious collections of pre-Columbian art in the world.

At the southern end of Carrer de Montcada is the **Església de Santa Maria del Mar**, probably the most stonily Gothic of Barcelona's churches.

A modernist high point is Montaner's **Palau de la Música Catalana** *(Carrer de Sant Pere 11)* concert hall, a marvellous concoction of tile, brick, sculpted stone and stained glass. Guided tours are given at 6am Monday to Friday and at 11am Saturday and Sunday.

### Parc de la Ciutadella

As well as being ideal for a picnic or stroll, this large park *(open 8am-9pm daily)* east of the Ciutat Vella has some specific attractions. The headliners are the monumental **cascada** (waterfall), a dramatic combination of statuary, rocks, greenery and thundering water created in the 1870s, with the young Gaudí lending a hand, and the **Museu Nacional d'Art Modern de Catalunya** *(admission €3; open 10am-7pm Tues-Sat, 10am-2.30pm Sun)*, with a good collection of 19th- and early-20th-century Catalan art. At the southern end of the park is Barcelona's **zoo** *(admission €10; open 10am-5pm daily winter, longer hours as the weather gets nicer)*, famed for its still-kicking albino gorilla.

### Parc Güell

This man-meets-nature marvel *(admission free; open 9am-6pm winter, up to 9pm summer)* in the north of the city is where Gaudí turned to landscape gardening. It's a strange, enchanting place where the artist's passion for natural forms took flight to the point where the artificial seems almost less contrived than does the natural.

The main, lower gate, flanked by buildings with the appearance of Hansel and Gretel's gingerbread house, sets the mood, with its winding paths and carefully tended flower beds, skewed tunnels with rough stone columns resembling tree roots, and the famous dragon of broken glass and tiles. The house in which Gaudí lived most of his last 20 years has been converted into the **Casa-Museum Gaudí** *(admission €3; open 10am-8pm daily Apr-Sept, 10am-6pm Sun-Fri Oct-Mar)*. The simplest way to Parc Güell is to take the metro to Lesseps and then walk 10 to 15 minutes; follow the signs heading northeast along Travessera de Dalt, then left up Carrer de Larrard.

### Montjuïc

This hill overlooking the city from the southwest is home to some of Barcelona's best museums and attractions, some fine parks and the main 1992 Olympic sites. In good weather, it's well worth a hike or funicular ride, if only for the views.

On the northern side, the impressive Palau Nacional houses the **Museu Nacional d'Art de Catalunya** *(admission €4.50; open 10am-7pm Tues-Sat, 10am-2.30pm Sun)*, with a great collection of Romanesque frescoes, woodcarvings and sculpture from medieval Catalunya.

Nearby is the **Poble Espanyol** *(Spanish Village; adult/child 7-14 years & student €7/3.50, free after 9pm Sun & Tues-Thur; open 9am-8pm Mon, 9am-2am Tues-Thur, 9am-4am Fri & Sat, 9am-midnight Sun)*, by day a tour group's paradise with craft workshops, souvenir shops and creditable copies of famous Spanish architecture. After dark it becomes a nightlife jungle, featuring bars and restaurants galore.

Downhill eastwards of the Palau Nacional, the **Museu d'Arqueologia** *(admission €2.50; open 9.30am-7pm Tues-Sat, 10am-2.30pm Sun)* has a good collection from Catalunya and the Balearic Islands.

Above the Palau Nacional is the Anella Olímpica (Olympic Ring), where you can swim in the Olympic pool, the **Piscines Bernat Picornell** *(limited tickets €8; open 7am-midnight Mon-Fri, 7am-9pm Sat, 7.30am-4.30pm Sun)* and wander into the main **Estadi Olímpic** *(admission free; open 10am-6pm daily)*.

The **Fundació Joan Miró** *(admission €7; open 10am-7pm or 8pm Tues, Wed, Fri & Sat, 10am-9.30pm Thur, 10am-2.30pm Sun & holidays)*, a short distance downhill eastwards of the Estadi Olímpic, is one of the best modern-art museums in Spain. Aside from many works by Miró, there are both permanent and changing exhibitions of other modern art.

At the top of Montjuïc is the **Castell de Montjuïc**, with a military museum *(€2.50 includes castle admission; open 9.30am-4.30pm Tues-Sun Nov–mid-Mar, 9.30am-7pm mid-Mar–Oct)* and great views. It was used as a political prison up to the France era.

To get to Montjuïc you can either walk or take a bus from Plaça d'Espanya (Espanya metro station). Bus No 61 from here links most of the main sights and ends at the foot of a chairlift (€3.50) up to the castle. A funicular railway (€1.50) from Parallel metro station also runs to the chairlift.

## Tibidabo

At 542m, this is the highest hill in the wooded range that forms the backdrop to Barcelona. It's a good place for long walks along winding roads, some fresh air and, if the air's clear, 70km views. At the top are the **Temple del Sagrat Cor**, a church topped by a giant Christ statue, and the **Parc d'Atraccions** *(admission €17)*, a somewhat kitschy funfair. A short distance along the ridge is the 115m-high **Torre de Collserola** *(observation deck €4.50; open 11am-2.30pm Wed-Fri winter, up to 8pm summer, 11am-6pm or 8pm Sat & Sun)* telecommunications tower, with a hair-raising external glass lift that skyrockets you 560m above sea level.

The fun way to Tibidabo is to take the U7 suburban train from Plaça de Catalunya to Avinguda de Tibidabo (€1, 10 minutes), then hop on the *tramvia blau* (€2) across the road, which will take you up to the foot of the Tibidabo funicular railway. The funicular climbs to the church at the top of the hill for €2. All these run every 30 minutes from at least 9am to 9.30pm. The funicular and amusement park are open weekends only outside of the summer months (June to September).

## Organised Tours

The **Bus Turístic** (☎ 93 423 18 00) service covers two circuits (24 stops) linking virtually all the major tourist sights. Tourist offices and many hotels have leaflets explaining the system. Tickets, available on the bus, are €14 for one day's unlimited rides, €18 for two consecutive days. Service is about every 20 minutes from 9am to 9.30pm. Tickets entitle you to substantial discounts on entry fees and tickets to more than 20 sights along the route.

A **walking tour** (€7) of the Ciutat Vella on Saturday and Sunday mornings departs from the Centre Oficina d'Informació de Turisme de Barcelona on Plaça de Catalunya (English at 10am, Spanish and Catalan at noon).

## Special Events

Barcelona's biggest festival is the Festes de la Mercè, several days of merrymaking around 24 September, including *castellers* (human-castle builders), giants, and *correfocs* – a parade of firework-spitting dragons and devils. Through the year, the city is apt to go nuts at the drop of a hat. Tourist offices can help but can't predict soccer victories over Real Madrid.

## Places to Stay

Finding a place to sleep isn't particularly cheap or easy between Semana Santa and October. Unless you're willing to canvass hostels, it's wise to book ahead.

**Camping** The closest camping ground to Barcelona is **El Toro Bravo** (☎ 93 637 34 62, fax 93 637 21 15), on Carretera C-246. **La Ballena Alegre** (☎ 93 658 05 04, fax 93 658 05 75), 2km further, is also pleasant, and there are several more camping grounds down that highway. All charge upwards of €20 per site. Ask at the tourist office for transportation information.

**Hostels** A handful of places in Barcelona provide dormitory accommodation. For two people they're not great value, but they're certainly good places to meet other travellers. All require you to rent sheets (€1 to €3) if you don't have them (or a sleeping bag).

Grungy, happy **Youth Hostel Kabul** (☎ 93 318 51 90; Plaça Reial 17; dorm beds €12-18) is a rough-and-ready place with no curfew and a party-hearty atmosphere. This is where youth come from all over Western Europe to get some...exposure to Spanish culture. No card is needed. Security is slack, but there are safes available for your valuables. Bookings are not taken.

Not as loud or social is the III **Alberg Palau** (☎ 93 412 50 80; Carrer del Palau 6; dorm beds €13; open 7am-midnight daily), with just 40 places. Rooms resemble university dorms; the rates include breakfast and kitchen use. No card is needed.

**Alberg Mare de Déu de Montserrat** (☎ 93 210 51 51, fax 93 210 07 98; Passeig Mare de Déu del Coll 41-51; dorm beds for ISIC or IYTC card holders & under 25s/all others €15/20, including breakfast), with 180 beds, is the biggest and most comfortable hostel, but it's 4km north of the centre. A hostel card is needed. It's closed during the day and you can't get in after 3am. The hostel is a 10-minute walk from Vallcarca metro or a 20-minute ride from Plaça de Catalunya on bus No 28.

The HI **Alberg Pere Tarrés** (☎ 93 410 23 09, fax 93 419 62 68; Carrer de Numància 149; metro Les Corts; dorm beds €14-16), about a five-minute walk from the metro, has 90 beds, which range in price depending on age and hostel-card possession. It has a kitchen, but it's closed during the day and you can't get in after 2am.

**Pensiones & Hostales** Most of the cheaper options are scattered through the old city on either side of La Rambla. Generally, the areas closer to the port and on the western side of La Rambla are seedier and cheaper, and as you move north towards Plaça de Catalunya standards (and prices) rise.

**Hostal Maldà** (☎ 93 317 30 02; Carrer del Pi 5; singles/doubles €9/18), upstairs in an arcade, is about as cheap as you'll find. It's a rambling family-run establishment that shelters cosy rooms and an adorable little kitten. Rambling **Hostal Paris** (☎ 93 301 37 85, fax 93 412 70 96; Carrer del Cardenal Casañas 4; singles from €22, doubles with bath €40) caters to backpackers. It can be slightly dingy and more than a bit unfriendly, but it's central and reasonable. The simple dorm-style **Pensión Mari-Luz** (☎ 93 317 34 63; Carrer del Palau 4; beds €12-15, doubles €36-40) is brighter and more sociable.

**Pensión Alamar** (☎ 93 302 50 12; Carrer de la Comtessa de Sobradiel 1; singles/doubles €18/36) is fantastic value. It's a good place for lone travellers to meet other wanderers in a tranquil setting. **Hostal Levante** (☎ 93 317 95 65, fax 93 317 05 26; Ⓦ www.hostallevante.com; Baixada de Sant Miquel 2; singles/doubles €24/46, with bath €27/52) is a plain family-run place in a quiet location. Ask about apartments for longer stays.

If you want a nice double on Plaça Reial, head to **Pensión Villanueva** (☎/fax 91 301 50 84; Plaça Reial 2; singles €12-18, doubles €20-35); rates depend on the season.

**Hostal Fontanella** (☎/fax 93 317 59 43; Via Laietana 71; singles/doubles €26/41, with bath €32/55) is a warm, immaculate place, with 10 smallish rooms. An excellent deal is the friendly **Hostal Campi** (☎/fax 93 301 35 45, fax 93 301 41 33; ⓔ hcampi@ terra.es; Carrer de la Canuda 4; singles/ doubles €20/38, doubles with bath €45), with roomy doubles.

Up near Plaça de Catalunya is the solid **Hostal Lausanne** (☎ 93 302 11 39; Avinguda del Portal de l'Àngel 24, 1st floor; singles/doubles from €22/42), with good security and slightly dingy rooms (the doubles are spiffier). **Hostal-Residencia Rembrandt** (☎/fax 93 318 10 11; Carrer Portaferrissa 23;

singles/doubles €25/42, doubles with bath €42) offers rooms ranging from acceptable to stylish. Reservations are accepted only for stays of longer than three nights.

Busy **Hostal Ópera** (☎ 93 318 82 01; Carrer de Sant Pau 20; singles/doubles €31/50) offers spotless, bright rooms with bath. **Pensión Fernando** (☎/fax 93 301 79 93; Carrer de Ferran 4; beds €15, doubles with/without bath €51/36) is a friendly place with a sunny rooftop terrace.

A few cheapies are spread strategically across L'Eixample, north of Plaça de Catalunya. **Hostal Goya** (☎ 93 302 25 65, fax 93 412 04 35; e goya@cconline.es; Carrer de Pau Claris 74; singles/doubles €27/45, with bath €32/55) has several beautifully renovated rooms. **Pensión Aribau** (☎ 93 453 11 06; Carrer d'Aribau 37; singles/doubles €28/42, doubles with bath €50) offers reasonable rooms. The singles come with TV, while many doubles have shower, TV, toilet and even a fridge.

A leafier location is **Hotel Residencia Neutral** (☎/fax 93 487 68 48; Rambla de Catalunya 42; doubles with bath €45), a happy, bustling place.

**Hotels** Once-grand **Hotel Peninsular** (☎ 93 302 31 38, fax 93 412 36 99; Carrer de Sant Pau 34; singles/doubles €45/65) offers bare rooms that don't quite live up to the impressive foyer and central atrium. Higher up the scale, but good value, is **Hotel Roma Reial** (☎ 93 302 03 66; Plaça Reial 11; singles/doubles €50/65), which offers mod cons but tiny rooms.

If you want to be right on La Rambla, try **Hotel Cuatro Naciones** (☎ 93 317 36 24, fax 93 302 69 85; La Rambla 40; doubles €76). A century ago this was Barcelona's top hotel; today its rooms are merely adequate. For a lot more flair, head to **Hotel Oriente** (☎ 93 302 25 58, fax 93 412 28 19; La Rambla 45-47; e horiente@husa.es; singles/doubles €86/125), which offers beautiful, spacious quarters.

## Places to Eat

They don't want you to find them, but supermarkets do exist in Barcelona. A convenient one in the old quarter is **Dia**, right next to Pensión Alamar (see its entry under Pensiones & Hostales in Places to Stay earlier).

The greatest concentration of cheaper restaurants is within walking distance of La Rambla. There are a few good-value places on Carrer de Sant Pau, west off La Rambla. **Kashmir Restaurant Tandoori** (Carrer de Sant Pau 39; most dishes €5) does tasty curries and biryanis. **Restaurante Pollo Rico** (Carrer de Sant Pau 31; chicken dishes or omelette €5) serves tasty main dishes with chips, bread and wine. **Restaurante Els Tres Bots** (Carrer de Sant Pau 42; set menu €6) is grungy but cheap, with a good selection of Spanish staples.

There are lots more places in Barri Gòtic. **Self-Naturista** (Carrer de Santa Anna 13; set menu €6.50), a bright self-service vegetarian restaurant, does tasty, fresh dishes. **Mesón Jesús Romescu** (Carrer dels Cecs de la Boqueria 4; set menu €11) is a cosy, homey place that serves piping-hot Spanish dishes.

Carrer de la Mercè, running roughly west from the main post office, is a good place to find little northern Spanish cider houses. **Tasca El Corral** (Carrer de la Mercè 19) and **Sidrería La Socarrena** (Carrer de la Mercè 21) are both worth checking. A Basque favourite is **Irati** (Carrer del Cardenal Cassanyes 17; tapas around €4). Enjoy a range of mouthwatering tapas and a *zurrito* of beer or six.

For something a bit more upmarket, **Les Quinze Nits** (Plaça Reial 6) and **La Fonda Escudellers** (Carrer dels Escudellers) are two stylish bistro-like restaurants under the same management, with a big range of good Catalan and Spanish dishes at reasonable prices. This results in long queues in summer and on the weekend. Three courses with wine and coffee will cost about €20 at either.

Carrer dels Escudellers, Plaça Reial and La Rambla itself also have a couple of good night-time takeaway felafel joints at around €2.50 a serving.

To impress your date, head for **Restaurante Set Portes** (☎ 93 319 30 33; Passeig d'Isabel II 14; paella €16), a classic dating from 1836 and specialising in paella. It's essential to book. Another famous institution is **Els Quatre Gats** (Carrer Montsió 3), Picasso's former hang-out. The standard café fare costs about 50% more than it should, but it's worth it for the bohemian ambience.

L'Eixample has a few good restaurants to offer as well. **Bar Estudiantil** (Plaça de la Universitat; plats combinats €4) does economical combination plates (eg, chicken, chips and eggplant). It's open until late into the night and is a genuine student hang-out.

**L'Hostal de Rita** (*Carrer d'Aragó 279; set menu €7, mains €5-8*), a block east of Passeig de Gràcia, is an excellent, ultrapopular mid-range restaurant with a four-course lunch menú and à-la-carte mains available.

## Entertainment

Barcelona's entertainment bible is the weekly *Guía del Ocio* (€1 at newsstands). Its excellent listings (in Spanish) include theatre, films, music and art exhibitions. Gay and lesbian options have their own special section, labelled 'El Ambiente'.

The tourist office can provide information on current festivals, concerts and other performances.

**Bars** Barcelona's multifarious bars are at their busiest from about 11pm to 2am or 3am, especially Thursday to Saturday.

**Café de l'Òpera** (*La Rambla 74*), opposite the Liceu opera house, is the liveliest place on a very lively street. It gets packed with all and sundry at night. **Glaciar** (*Plaça Reial 3*) is busy with a young crowd of foreigners and locals. Tiny **Bar Malpaso** (*Carrer d'En Rauric 20*), just off Plaça Reial, plays great Latin and African music. Another hip low-lit place with a more varied (including gay) clientele is the relaxed **Schilling** (*Carrer de Ferran 23*).

**El Xampanyet** (*Carrer de Montcada 22*), near the Museu Picasso, is a small place specialising in *cava* (Catalan sparkling wine) and good tapas.

West of La Rambla, **La Oveja Negra** (*Carrer de les Sitges 5*) is a noisy, barn-like tavern with a young crowd. Hidden away on a side street is **Bar Marsella** (*Carrer de Sant Pau 65*), specialising in absinthe (*absenta* in Catalan), a potent but mellow beverage with supposed narcotic qualities.

If by 2.30am you still need a drink and don't want to get funky at a disco, your best bet is **London Bar** (*Carrer Nou de la Rambla 36; open until about 5am Mon-Sat*), which sometimes has live music.

Lesbian bars are clustered in Sarrià, north of the city centre. Try friendly, intimate **D.Mer** (*Carrer de Plató 13*) or the more girly **Imagine** (*Carrer de Marià Cubí 4*). Gay men can try **Santannasa** (*Carrer de Aribau 27*), which sports a cute dance floor.

**Live Music & Discos** Many music places have dance space, and some discos have bands around midnight or so, to pull in some clientele before the real action starts about 3am. If you go for the band, you can normally stay for the disco at no extra cost and avoid bouncers' whims about what you're wearing, your measurements etc. Count on €2 to €6 for a beer in any of these places. Cover charges can be anything from zero to €25, which may include a drink.

**Barcelona Pipa Club** (*Plaça Reial 3; cover €7*) has jazz Thursday to Saturday around midnight (ring the bell to get in). **Jamboree** (*Plaça Reial 17; cover €9*) has jazz and funk, and a disco later, from about 1.30am. **Club Apolo** (*Carrer Nou de la Rambla 113; cover around €15*) has live world music several nights a week, followed by live salsa or a varied disco.

Manhattanites might feel comfortable at chic **Otto Zutz** (*Carrer de Lincoln 15*). Wear your bestest, blackest outfit.

**Mirablau** (*Plaça Dr Andrau; open until 5am*), at the foot of the Tibidabo funicular, is a bar with great views and a small disco floor.

The two top gay discos are **Metro** (*Carrer de Sepúlveda 185*) and **Martin's** (*Passeig de Gràcia 130*). Metro attracts some lesbians and straights as well as gay men; Martin's is strictly boys only.

**Cinemas** For films in their original language (with Spanish subtitles), check listings for those marked VO (*versión original*). A ticket is usually €5 or more, but many cinemas reduce prices on Monday or Wednesday. Check the *Guía del Ocio* for cinema listings.

**Classical Music & Opera** The Gran Teatre del Liceu (☎ 93 485 99 00; ⓦ www .liceubarcelona.com; La Rambla 51-59) opera house, gutted by fire in 1994, is still being rebuilt but is open for business. Call or check the website for information on opera, dance and concerts.

There are other fine theatres, among them the lovely **Palau de la Música Catalana** (☎ 93 295 72 00; ⓦ www.palaumusica.org; Carrer de Sant Francesa de Paula 2), the city's chief concert hall.

## Getting There & Away

**Air** Barcelona's airport, 14km southwest of the city centre at El Prat de Llobregat, caters to international as well as domestic flights. It's not a European hub, but you can often dig up specials and cheap youth fares.

**SPAIN**

Airlines include **Iberia** (☎ 902 40 05 00; Passeig de Gràcia 30), **Spanair** (24hr ☎ 902 13 14 15) and **Air Europa** (☎ 902 40 15 01); the latter two airline offices are at the airport.

**Bus** The station for virtually all domestic and international buses is the **Estació del Nord** (☎ 93 265 65 08; Carrer d'Alí Bei 80; metro Arc de Triomf; information desk open 7am-9pm daily). A few international buses leave from Estació d'Autobuses de Sants, beside Estació Sants train station.

Several buses a day go to most main Spanish cities, including Madrid (€22, seven to eight hours), Valencia (€24, 4½ hours) and Granada (€54, 13 to 15 hours). Buses run several times a week to London, Paris (€80) and other European cities.

**Train** Virtually all trains travelling to and from destinations within Spain stop at **Estació Sants** (metro Sants-Estació); many international trains use **Estació de França** (metro Barceloneta).

For some international destinations you have to change trains at Montpellier or the French border. There are direct trains daily to Paris, Zürich and Milan.

Daily trains run to most major cities in Spain. To Madrid there are seven trains a day (€42, 6½ to 9½ hours), to Valencia 10 (€32, as little as three hours on high-speed Euromed train) and to Granada (€46, eight hours).

Tickets and information are available at the stations or from the RENFE office in **Passeig de Gràcia metro/train station** (Passeig de Gràcia; open 7am-10pm Mon-Sat, till 9pm Sun).

**Car & Motorcycle** Tolls on the A-7 autopista to the French border are over €12. The N-II to the French border and the N-340 southbound from Barcelona are toll-free but slower. The fastest route to Madrid is via Zaragoza on the A-2 (around €20), which heads west off the A-7 south of Barcelona, then the toll-free N-II from Zaragoza.

## Getting Around
**To/From the Airport** Trains link the airport to Estació Sants and Catalunya station on Plaça de Catalunya every half-hour. They take 15 to 20 minutes and a ticket is €2. The A1 Aerobús does the 40-minute run between Plaça de Catalunya and the airport every 15 minutes, or every half-hour at weekends. The fare is €3.50. A taxi from the airport to Plaça de Catalunya is around €15 to €20.

**Bus, Metro & Train** Barcelona's metro system spreads its tentacles around the city in such a way that most places of interest are within a 10-minute walk of a station. Buses and suburban trains are needed only for a few destinations.

A single metro, bus or suburban train ride costs €1, but a T-1 ticket, valid for 10 rides, costs only €5.50, while a T-DIA ticket gives unlimited city travel in one day for €4.

**Car & Motorcycle** While traffic flows smoothly thanks to an extensive one-way system, navigating can be frustrating. Parking a car is also difficult and, if you choose a parking garage, quite expensive (over €20 per day). It's better to ditch your car and rely on public transport.

**Taxi** Barcelona's black-and-yellow taxis are plentiful, reasonably priced and especially handy for late-night transport. Flag fall is €1.30, after which it's about €1 per kilometre.

## MONESTIR DE MONTSERRAT
Unless you are on a pilgrimage, the prime attraction of Montserrat, 50km northwest of Barcelona, is its incredible setting. The Benedictine Monastery of Montserrat sits high on the side of an 1236m-high mountain of truly weird rocky peaks, and it's best reached by cable car. The monastery was founded in 1025 to commemorate an apparition of the Virgin Mary on this site. Pilgrims still come from all over Christendom to pay homage to the Black Virgin (La Moreneta), a 12th-century wooden sculpture of Mary, regarded as Catalunya's patroness.

Montserrat's **information centre** (☎ 93 877 77 77; open 10am-6pm daily) is to the left along the road from the top cable-car station. It has a couple of good free leaflets and maps on the mountain and monastery.

## Things to See & Do
If you are making a day trip to Montserrat, come early. Apart from the monastery, exploring the mountain is a treat.

The two-part **Museu de Montserrat** (admission €4; open 10am-6pm Mon-Fri, 9.30am-6.30pm Sat & Sun), on the plaza in front of the monastery's basilica, has an excellent collection ranging from an Egyptian mummy to art by El Greco and Picasso.

Opening times for when you can file past the image of the Black Virgin, high above the main altar of the 16th-century basílica, vary according to season. The Montserrat Boys' Choir (Escolania) sings in the basilica Monday to Sunday at 1pm and 7pm, except in July. The church fills up quickly, so try to arrive early.

You can explore the mountain above the monastery on a web of paths leading to small chapels and some of the peaks. The Funicular de Sant Joan (€3.50 return) will lift you up the first 250m from the monastery.

### Places to Stay & Eat
There are several accommodation options (all ☎ 93 877 77 01) at the monastery. The cheapest rooms are in the Cel.les Abat Olibia (*double apartments high season €23-25*), blocks of simple apartments, with showers, for up to 10 people. Overlooking Plaça de Santa Maria is the luxurious and excellent-value Hotel Abat Cisneros (*singles/doubles €24/44, high season €41/76*).

The Cisneros offers probably the finest dining on the mountain. Its delicious four-course Catalan menú costs about €18. Otherwise, restaurant options are bland and uninspiring. Snack bars and cafeterias line the road approach to the monastery, and a few shops by the basilica offer cheap snacks.

### Getting There & Away
Trains run from Plaça d'Espanya station in Barcelona to Aeri de Montserrat up to 18 times a day (most often on summer weekdays), a 1½-hour ride. Return tickets for €20 include the cable car between Aeri de Montserrat and the monastery.

There's also a daily bus to the monastery leaving from Estació d'Autobuses de Sants in Barcelona at 9am (plus 8am in July and August) for €10 return. It returns at 5pm.

## COSTA BRAVA
The Costa Brava ranks with Spain's Costa Blanca and Costa del Sol among Europe's most popular holiday spots. It stands alone, however, in its spectacular rugged scenery and proximity to northern Europe, both of which have sent prices skyrocketing in the area.

The main jumping-off points for the Costa Brava are the inland towns of Girona ('Gerona' in Castilian) and Figueres. Both are on the A-7 autopista and the toll-free N-II highway, which connect Barcelona with France. Along the coast, the most appealing resorts are (from north to south) Cadaqués, L'Escala (La Escala), Tamariu, Llafranc, Calella de Palafrugell and Tossa de Mar.

Tourist offices along the coast are very helpful, with information on accommodation, transport and other things. There are branches in Girona (☎ 972 22 65 75), Figueres (☎ 972 50 31 55), Palafrugell (☎ 972 30 02 28) and Cadaqués (☎ 972 25 83 15).

### Coastal Resorts & Islands
The Costa Brava (Rugged Coast) is all about picturesque inlets and coves. Beaches tend to be small and scattered. Some longer beaches at places like L'Estartit and Empúries are worth visiting off-season, but there has been a tendency to build tall buildings wherever engineers think it can be done. Fortunately, in many places it just can't.

Cadaqués, about one hour's drive east of Figueres at the end of an agonising series of hairpin bends, is perhaps the most picturesque of all Spanish resorts. It's haunted by the memory of former resident Salvador Dalí, whose name adorns several establishments. Cadaqués is short on beaches, so people spend a lot of time sitting at waterfront cafés or wandering along the beautiful coast. About 10km northeast of Cadaqués is Cap de Creus, a rocky peninsula with a single restaurant atop a craggy cliff. This is paradise for anyone who likes to scramble around rocks risking life and limb with every step.

Further down the coast, past L'Escala and L'Estartit, is Palafrugell, itself a few kilometres inland with little to offer, but near three gorgeous beach towns that have to be seen to be believed. The most northerly of these, Tamariu, is also the smallest, least crowded and most exclusive. Llafranc is the biggest and busiest, and has the longest beach. Calella de Palafrugell, with its truly picture-postcard setting, is never overcrowded and always relaxed. If you're driving down this coast, it's worth stopping at some of these towns, particularly out of season.

For a spectacular stretch of coastline, take a drive north from Tossa de Mar to San Feliu de Guíxols. There are 360 curves in this 20km stretch of road, which, with brief stops to take in the scenery, can take a good two hours.

SPAIN

Among the most exciting attractions on the Costa Brava are the **Illes Medes**, off the coast from the package resort of L'Estartit. These seven islets and their surrounding coral reefs, with a total land area of only 21.5 hectares, have been declared a natural park to protect their extraordinarily diverse flora and fauna. Almost 1500 different life forms have been identified on and around the islands. You can arrange glass-bottom boat trips and diving.

## Museums & Historical Attractions

When you have had enough beach for a while, make sure you put the **Teatre-Museu Dalí** *(Plaça Gala i Salvador Dalí; admission €9; open 9am-7.15pm daily July-Sept, 10.30am-5.15pm daily June, 10.30am-5.15pm Tues-Sun Oct-May)*, in Figueres, at the top of your list. This 19th-century theatre was converted by Dalí himself and houses a huge and fascinating collection of his strange creations. Queues are long on summer mornings.

**Girona** sports a lovely though tiny medieval quarter centred on a Gothic cathedral. For a stroll through antiquity, check out the ruins of the Greek and Roman town of **Empúries**, 2km from L'Escala.

## Places to Stay & Eat

Most visitors to the Costa Brava rent apartments. If you are interested in renting your own pad for a week or so, contact local tourist offices in advance for information. Seaside restaurants in the coastal towns provide dramatic settings but often at high prices.

**Figueres** Reasonable rooms with bath can be found at **Pensión Isabel II** *(☎ 972 50 47 35; Carrer de Isabel II 16; singles/doubles €21/26)*. A little grungier but still solid is **Pensión Mallol** *(☎ 972 50 22 83; Carrer de Pep Ventura 9; singles/doubles €15/25)*. Avoid sleeping in Figueres' Parc Municipal – people have been attacked here at night.

**Restaurant Versalles** *(Carrer de la Jonquera; platos combinados €5)* is at a sociable location away from the noise and high prices of the main plaza.

**Girona** Eight kilometres south of town is **Camping Can Toni Manescal** *(☎ 972 47 61 17)*. **Alberg de Joventut** *(☎ 972 21 80 03; Carrer de Ciutadans 9; beds €12)* offers standard HI fare. **Pensión Viladomat** *(☎ 972*

20 31 76; Carrer dels Ciutadans 5; doubles €31)* has comfortable rooms.

Dine on Girona's own Rambla for good people-watching. **Arts Café** *(La Rambla 23)* offers a mellow atmosphere and a good range of cheap snacks.

**Cadaqués** At the top of the town as you head towards Cabo de Creus is **Camping Cadaqués** *(☎ 972 25 81 26, fax 972 159 383)*. A room in town is probably better value. **Hostal Marina** *(☎ 972 25 81 99; Carrer de Riera 3; singles/doubles €19/36, high season €25/49)* has fresh, bright rooms.

**Around Palafrugell** There are camping grounds at all three of Palafrugell's satellites, all charging similar hefty rates. In Calella de Palafrugell, try **Camping Moby Dick** *(☎ 972 61 43 07)*; in Llafranc, **Camping Kim's** *(☎ 972 30 11 56)*; and in Tamariu, **Camping Tamariu** *(☎ 972 62 04 22)*.

Hotel and pensione rooms are relatively thin here, as many people come on package deals and stay in apartments. In Calella de Palafrugell, the friendly **Hostería del Plancton** *(☎ 972 61 50 81; rooms €15; open June-Sept)* is one of the best deals on the Costa Brava. **Residencia Montaña** *(☎ 972 30 04 04; Carrer de Cesàrea 2; rooms €52, July-Aug €88)*, in Llafranc, is not a bad deal as long as you stay away during the high season. In Tamariu, **Hotel Sol d'Or** *(☎ 972 62 01 72; Carrer de la Riera 18; doubles with bath €45)* is near the beach.

Numerous food stalls and cafés cluster in all three towns.

## Getting There & Away

A few buses run daily from Barcelona to Tossa del Mar, L'Estartit and Cadaqués for a couple of euros, but for the small resorts near Palafrugell you need to get to Girona first. Girona and Figueres are both on the railway connecting Barcelona to France. The dozen or so trains daily from Barcelona to Portbou at the border all stop in Girona, and most in Figueres. The fare from Barcelona to Girona is €5, to Figueres €6.

## Getting Around

There are two or three buses a day from Figueres to Cadaqués and three or four to L'Escala. Figueres' bus station is across the road from the train station.

# TARRAGONA

| PLACES TO STAY | PLACES TO EAT |
| --- | --- |
| 7  Hostal Noria | 6  Jerónimo |
| 20  Hotel Lauria | 8  Les Voltes |
| 22  Habitaciones | 9  Can Llesques |
| Mariflor | 16  Café & Restaurant |
| | Cantonada |
| | 17  Restaurant Bufet |
| | El Tiberi |
| | 18  Mesón Andaluz |
| | 19  Viena |

**OTHER**
1  Cathedral
2  Entrance to Cathedral, Cloister;
   Museu Diocesà
3  Entrance to Passeig Arqueològic
4  Main Tourist Office
5  Museu Casa Castellarnau
10  Museu Arqueològic
11  Museu de la Romanitat
12  Regional Tourist Office
13  Market
14  Post Office
15  Roman Forum
21  Roman Amphitheatre

Several buses daily run to Palafrugell from Girona (where the bus station is behind the train station), and there are buses from Palafrugell to Calella de Palafrugell, Llafranc and Tamariu. Buses go to most other coastal towns (south of Cadaqués) from Girona.

## TARRAGONA
### pop 115,150

Tarragona's relaxed, backwards-gazing nature makes a perfect contrast to the frenetic, modern city life of Barcelona. Founded in 218 BC, the town was for a long time the capital of much of Roman Spain, and Roman structures figure among its most important attractions. A medieval cathedral and 17th-century British additions to the old city walls provide evocative representations of other historical periods.

And Tarragona's archaeological museum is one of the most interesting in Spain.

For those who don't want to be too *tranquilo*, Tarragona's large student population and constant stream of travellers ensures a lively beach scene. Spain's answer to Disneyland, Port Aventura, is just a few kilometres south of town.

## Orientation & Information

Tarragona's main street is Rambla Nova, which runs approximately northwest from a cliff top overlooking the Mediterranean. A couple of blocks east, parallel to Rambla Nova, is Rambla Vella, which marks the beginning of the old town.

The town's **main tourist office** (☎ 977 25 07 95; *Carrer Major 39; open Mon-Sat &*

SPAIN

*Sun morning)* and **regional tourist office** *(Carrer de Fortuny 4; open Mon-Sat)* offer maps and lists of accommodation.

## The Old City & Around

The **Museu d'Història de Tarragona** *(admission to each site €2; open 9am-8pm Tues-Sat, 10am-2pm Sun)* comprises four separate Roman sites around the city, plus the 14th-century noble mansion now serving as the **Museu Casa Castellarnau** *(Carrer dels Cavallers 14)*. A good place to start is the **Museu de la Romanitat** *(Plaça del Rei)*, which includes part of the vaults of the Roman circus, where chariot races were held. Nearby is the well-preserved **Roman amphitheatre**, where gladiators battled each other (or unlucky souls were thrown to wild animals) to the death. On Carrer de Lleida, a few blocks west of Rambla Nova, are remains of a **Roman forum**. The **Passeig Arqueològic** *(open until midnight)* is a peaceful walkway along the old city walls, which are a combination of Roman, Iberian and 17th-century British efforts.

Tarragona's **Museu Arqueològic** *(Plaça del Rei 5; admission €2.50, free Tues; open daily)* gives further insight into the city's rich history. The carefully presented exhibits include frescoes, mosaics, sculpture and pottery dating back to the 2nd century BC.

The **cathedral** *(open daily)* sits grandly at the highest point of Tarragona, overlooking the old town. Some parts of the building date back to the 12th century AD. It's open for tourist visits during the week for hours that vary with the season (longest in summer). Entrance is through the beautiful cloister with the excellent Museu Diocesà.

Platja del Miracle is the main city beach. It is reasonably clean but can get terribly crowded in summer. Several other beaches dot the coast north of town, but in good weather you will never be alone.

## Port Aventura

Port Aventura *(☎ 902-20 22 20; ☒ www.universalmediterranea.com; adult/child 5-12 years €31/23, after 7pm €22; open 10am-8pm daily Semana Santa–mid-June & mid-Sept–Dec, 10am-midnight daily mid-June–mid-Sept, closed Jan–Semana Santa)*, 7km west of Tarragona, near Salou, is Spain's biggest and most involved funfair-adventure park. Themed rides and other attractions are

sure to entice the kids and teenagers, although the faux-cultural areas reflect the plastic insipidity of American amusement-park influence. Hair-raising experiences include a virtual submarine and the Dragon Khan, claimed to be Europe's biggest roller coaster.

Trains run to Port Aventura station, a 1km walk from the site, several times a day from Tarragona and also Barcelona ((8 return).

## Places to Stay

**Camping Tàrraco** *(☎ 977 29 02 89)* is near Platja Arrabassada, off the N-340 road 2km northeast of the centre. There are more, better camping grounds on Platja Larga, a couple of kilometres further on. A good option is **Camping Playa Large** *(☎ 977 207 952; sites €3-4 per person)*.

If you intend to stay in Tarragona in summer, call ahead to book a room. **Hostal Noria** *(☎ 977 23 87 17; Plaça de la Font 53; singles/doubles €17/29)* is decent value but is often full. **Habitaciones Mariflor** *(☎ 977 23 82 31; Carrer del General Contreras 29; singles/doubles €13/24, high season €17/3)* occupies a drab building near the train station but has clean rooms at good prices.

The three-star **Hotel Lauria** *(☎ 977 23 67 12; Rambla Nova 20; singles/doubles €40/57)* is a worthwhile splurge with a wonderful location, a pool and delightfully airy rooms, some with views of the Mediterranean.

## Places to Eat

For solid Catalan food, head for the stylish **Restaurant Bufet El Tiberi** *(Carrer de Martí d'Ardenya 5; buffet €9-10; closed Sun evening & Mon)*, which offers an all-you-can-eat buffet. Nearby is a backstreet local favourite, **Mesón Andaluz** *(Carrer de Pons d'Icart 3; set menu €9)*, with a good three-course menú.

**Jerónimo** *(Plaça de la Font 6; meat platter €15)* is the place to dig into porcine delights. Carnivores will enjoy the mixed meat and sausage platter. If cheese is your thing, try a *taula de formatges* at **Can Llesques** *(Carrer de Natzaret 6; cheese platter €7-8)*, which is a pleasant spot looking onto Plaça del Rei.

**Café Cantonada** *(Carrer de Fortuny 23)* is a popular place for tapas; next door, **Restaurant Cantonada** *(dishes from €5)* has pizza and pasta. Rambla Nova has several good places, either for a snack or a meal. **Viena**

(Rambla Nova 50; sandwiches from €1) has good croissants and a vast range of *entrepans* (sandwiches).

Tucked under the vaults of the former Roman circus, **Les Voltes** (Carrer de Trinquet Vell 12; set menu €9) is a little overpriced, but the menú is decent value.

### Getting There & Away

The train station is southwest of the old town, on the coast. Over 20 regional trains a day run from Barcelona to Tarragona (€4, one to 1½ hours). There are about 12 trains daily from Tarragona to Valencia (€11.50, two to 3½ hours). To Madrid (€40, six hours) there are four trains each day via Zaragoza.

The bus station is on Avinguda Roma, just off Plaça Imperial Tarraco. Buses run to regional cities, such as Barcelona (€3) and throughout Spain, including Madrid (€23).

# Balearic Islands

### pop 878,630

The Balearic Islands of Mallorca, Menorca, Ibiza and Formentera share a language – Catalan – but in other ways they are quite different, ranging from the culture and sophistication of the grand old city of Palma (Mallorca) to the hedonistic foam-soaked fun of an Ibizan disco.

Despite the annual invasion of several million tourists, the islands have maintained strong links with their cultural identity and their past. Beyond the bars and beaches are Gothic cathedrals, Stone Age ruins and Moorish remains, as well as simple fishing villages, endless olive groves and orange orchards.

Most place names and addresses are given in Catalan. High-season prices are quoted here. Out of season, you will often find things are much cheaper and accommodation especially can be as much as half the rates quoted below. However, as many places close from October to May, always double-check before turning up with your bags.

### Getting There & Away

**Air** Scheduled flights from the major cities on the Spanish mainland are operated by several airlines, including Iberia, Air Europa and Spanair.

Standard one-way fares from Barcelona are not great value, hovering around €49 to Palma de Mallorca and more to the other islands. At the time of writing, the cheapest return fare available was €83 with Spanair. Cheap charter flights to the mainland are increasingly rare.

Interisland flights are expensive (given the flying times involved), with Palma to Maó or Ibiza costing €87/137 one way/return.

**Boat** The major ferry company for the islands is **Trasmediterránea** (information & ticket purchases ☎ 902 45 46 45; ⓦ www .trasmediterranea.es), with offices in (and services between) Barcelona (☎ 93 295 90 00), Valencia (☎ 96 367 65 12), Palma de Mallorca (☎ 971 40 50 14), Maó (☎ 971 36 60 50) and Ibiza city (☎ 971 31 51 00).

Duration time of the services varies dramatically, depending on the type of ferry. The maximum time is given here, but always check whether there is a faster ferry (such as a catamaran) available. At the time of writing, the fast-ferry service from Palma was out of service for an indefinite period. Scheduled services are: Barcelona-Palma/Palma-Barcelona (eight hours, up to 13 services weekly); Palma-Maó/Maó-Palma (four hours, two services weekly); Palma-Valencia/Valencia-Palma (eight hours, seven services weekly); Palma-Ibiza/Ibiza-Palma (five hours, two services weekly). Prices quoted below are the one-way fares during summer; low- and mid-season fares are considerably cheaper.

Fares from the mainland to any of the islands are €45.50 for a Butaca Turista (seat) and €63 for the same class on a catamaran; a berth in a cabin ranges from €80 (four-share) to €162 (single cabin) per person. Taking a small car costs €126, or there are economy packages (Paquete Ahorro) available.

Interisland services (Palma–Ibiza city and Palma-Maó) both cost €25 for a Butaca Turista, and €69 for a small car. Ask, too, about economy packages.

Another company, **Balearia** (☎ 902 16 01 80; ⓦ www.balearia.com), operates three daily ferries from Dénia (on the coast between Valencia and Alicante) to Ibiza (from €44 one way, three hours). There are also services between Valencia and Palma (from €46 one way, six hours) and between Ibiza and Palma (€35, two hours).

**Iscomar** (☎ 902 11 91 28) has from one to four daily car ferries (depending on the season) between Ciutadella on Menorca and Port d'Alcúdia on Mallorca, as well as between

Palma and Dénia and Ibiza and Dénia. **Cape Balear** (☎ 902 10 04 44) operates up to three daily fast ferries to Ciutadella from Cala Ratjada (Mallorca) in summer for around €48 return. The crossing takes 75 minutes.

## MALLORCA

Mallorca is the largest of the Balearic Islands. Most of the five million annual visitors to the island are here for the three *s* words: sun, sand and sea. There is, however, far more to see, including the capital city Palma, with its medina-like backstreets, flanked by sunbaked ochre buildings and fanciful Gaudí/ Gothic cathedral. West of the city, the shoreline bubbles up into low, rocky hills while, at Cala Major, grand old mansions and Miró's house are a world away from the thumping nightlife of the Brit resorts.

### Orientation & Information

Palma de Mallorca is on the southern side of the island, on a bay famous for its brilliant sunsets. The Serra de Tramuntana mountain range, which runs parallel with the northwestern coastline, is trekkers' heaven. Mallorca's best beaches are along the northern and eastern coasts, along with most of the big tourist resorts.

All of the major resorts have at least one tourist office. Palma has four, including the **main tourist office** (☎ 971 71 22 16, fax 971 72 12 51; ⓦ www.balearia.com; Plaça de la Reina) Other locations include Plaça d'Espanya (☎ 971 75 43 29), Carrer Sant Domingo 11 (☎ 971 72 40 90) and at the airport. Palma has several Internet centres, including **Big Byte** (☎ 971 71 17 54; Carrer Apuntadores 6; open 10am-midnight daily) at €2.50 an hour.

### Things to See & Do

Overlooking Palma and its port, like a grand old dame, is the enormous **cathedral** (Plaça Almoina; admission €3.50). It houses an excellent museum, and some of the interior features were designed by Antoni Gaudí.

In front of the cathedral is the **Palau Almudaina** (admission €3), the one-time residence of the Mallorcan monarchs. Inside is a collection of tapestries and artworks. It's not really worth the entry fee unless this is seriously your thing. Instead, visit the rich and varied **Museu de Mallorca** (Carrer Portella 5; admission €2; open 10am-2pm & 5pm-7pm Tues-Sat, Sun morning).

Also near the cathedral are the interesting **Museu Diocesáno** and the **Banys Árabs** (Arab Baths; Carrer Can Sera 7; open 9.30am-8pm daily), the only remaining monument to the Muslim domination of the island. Also worth visiting is the collection of the **Fundació Joan Miró** (Carrer Joan de Saridakis 29; open 10am-6pm Tues-Sat, Sun morning) housed in the artist's one-time home and studio, 2km west of the centre in Cala Major.

Mallorca's northwestern coast is a world away from the high-rise tourism on the other side of the island. Dominated by the Serra de Tramuntana mountains, it's a beautiful region of olive groves, pine forests and small villages with stone buildings; it also has a rugged and rocky coastline.

There are a couple of highlights for drivers: the hair-raising road down to the small port of **Sa Calobra** and the amazing trip along the peninsula leading to the island's northern tip, **Cap Formentor**.

If you don't have your own wheels, take the **Palma to Sóller train** (for details see Getting Around later in this section). It's one of the most popular and spectacular excursions on the island. Sóller is also the best place to base yourself for trekking. It is a relatively easy three-hour return walk from here to the beautiful, if heritaged, village of **Deiá,** where Robert Graves, poet and author of *I Claudius,* lived most of his life. The tourist office's *Hiking Excursions* brochure covers 20 of the island's better walks or, for more detailed information, get a copy of Lonely Planet's *Walking in Spain.*

Most of Mallorca's best beaches have been consumed by tourist developments, although there are exceptions. The lovely **Cala Mondragó** on the southeastern coast is backed by just a couple of hostales while, a little further south, the attractive port town of **Cala Figuera** and nearby **Cala Santanyi** beach have both escaped many of the ravages of mass tourism. There are also some good quiet beaches near the popular German resort of **Colonia San Jordi**, particularly **Ses Arenes** and **Es Trenc**, both a few kilometres back up the coast towards Palma.

### Places to Stay

**Palma** The cluttered 19th-century charm of **Hostal Pons** (☎ 971 72 26 58; Carrer Vi 8; singles/doubles €16/32) overcomes its limitations (spongy beds, only one bathroom).

## PALMA DE MALLORCA

**PLACES TO STAY**
9  Hotel Born
12  Hostal Pons
13  Hotel Palau Sa Font
16  Hostal Apuntadores
17  Hotel Ritzi

**PLACES TO EAT**
3  Restaurant Celler Sa Premsa
4  Sa Pastanga
6  Cafeteria Verona
11  Bar Bosch
14  Bar Dia
18  Abaco

**OTHER**
1  Bus Station; Airport Bus
2  Tourist Office
5  Mercat de l'Olivar
7  Iglesia Santa Magdalena
8  Hospital
10  Teatro Principal
15  Big Byte
19  American Express
20  Tourist Office
21  Post Office
22  Main Tourist Office
23  Ayuntamiento

24  Iglesia Santa Eulália
25  Basílica de Sant Francesc
26  Banys Árabs (Arab Baths)
27  Museu de Mallorca
28  Museu Diocesáno
29  Cathedral
30  Palau Almudaina

---

**Hostal Apuntadores** (☎ 971 71 34 91; e apuntadores@ctv.es; Carrer Apuntadores 8; dorm beds €14, singles/doubles €21/33, doubles with bath €37) has a 7th-floor terrace with a view of the city, and a lively downstairs bar-restaurant where you can get cheap meals and chat with other travellers. Next door, **Hostal Ritzi** (☎ 971 71 46 10; doubles without bath €23, with shower only €34, with bath & shower €49) needs a lick of paint, but is very central, with good security and satellite TV in the communal sitting room.

The superb **Hotel Born** (☎ 971 71 29 42, fax 971 71 86 18; e hotel_born@hotmail .com; Carrer Sant Jaume 3; singles/doubles up to €65/91) in a restored 18th-century palace has a classic Mallorcan patio. Even older, the 14th-century **Hotel Palau Sa Font** (☎ 971 71 22 77, fax 971 71 26 18; e info@ pauausafont.com; Carrer Apuntadores 38; singles/doubles from €90/132) is German-owned and has cutting-edge modern decor and class.

**Other Areas** After Palma, you should head for the hills. In Deiá, there is the exquisite **S'Hotel D'es Puig** (☎ 971 63 94 09, fax 971 63 92 10; e puig@futurnet.es; singles/ doubles with breakfast €69/103) in the middle of the village, while **Hostal Miramar** (☎ 971 63 90 84; singles/doubles with breakfast €29/57), overlooking the town, is very good value. In nearby Fornalutx, said to be the prettiest village on the island, **Cán Verdera** (☎ 971 63 82 03, fax 971 63 81 09; e canverdera@ctv.es; doubles up to €168)

**SPAIN**

is serious splurge time, housed in an old stone building with original beams, new pool and great views. Beside the train station in Sóller, the down-to-earth **Hotel El Guía** (☎ 971 63 02 27; singles/doubles with breakfast €44/65) has pleasant rooms.

If you want to stay on the southeastern coast, the large **Hostal Playa Mondragó** (☎ 971 65 77 52; Cala Mondragó; rooms per person €11) has B&B rates. At Cala Figuera, **Hostal Cán Jordi** (☎ 971 64 50 35; singles/doubles from €24/33) is justifiably popular.

You can also sleep cheaply at several quirky old monasteries around the island with prices typically under €18 per person. The tourist offices have a list (see Orientation & Information earlier in this section).

### Places to Eat

For Palma's best range of eateries, wander through the maze of streets between Plaça de la Reina and the port. Carrer Apuntadores is lined with restaurants, including seafood and Italian, and an inexpensive takeaway **Bar Dia** (☎ 971 71 62 64) at number 18. Around the corner is the incredible **Abaco** (☎ 971 71 59 11; Carrer Sant Joan 1), the bar of your wildest dreams (with the drinks bill of your darkest nightmares).

For the cost-conscious, **Cafeteria Verona** (☎ 971 71 28 34; Carrer Convento de Santa Magdalena; set menu €6; open lunch only) is a check-cloth, bistro-style place serving inexpensive local and international food. Up the road **Bar Bosch** (☎ 971 72 11 31; Plaça Rei Joan Carlos) is a prime people-watching spot and is good for sandwiches and snacks.

Rumbling tummies should head for **Restaurant Celler Sa Premsa** (☎ 971 72 35 29; Plaça del Bisbe Berenguer de Palou 8; set menu €9), a cavernous, atmospheric place with enormous portions of stolid local fare. For vegetarian food, try **Sa Pastanga** (☎ 971 71 44 47; Carrer Sant Elies 6; set menu €9), serving simple delicious dishes.

### Getting Around

Bus No 25 runs every 20 minutes between the airport and Plaça Espanya in central Palma (€2.50, 20 minutes). Alternatively, a taxi will cost around €14.

Most parts of the island are accessible by bus from Palma. Buses generally depart from or near the bus station at Plaça Espanya – the tourist office has details. Mallorca's two train lines also start from Plaça Espanya. One goes to the inland town of Inca and the other goes to Sóller (€2.50 one way, or €4.50 for the Parada Turística), both highly picturesque jaunts; check at the tourist office for times.

The best way to get around the island is by car – it's worth renting one just for the drive along the northwestern coast. There are about 30 rental agencies in Palma (and all the big companies have reps at the airport). If you want to compare prices, check the many harbourside offices along Passeig Marítim.

## IBIZA

Once a hippie hideaway, now more mainstream 'hip', Ibiza ('Eivissa' in Catalan) is best known for its extraordinary clubbing scene. The flip side is very different, particularly in the rural villages in the south. Here the countrywomen still wear long black skirts and wide straw hats and – forget the nudist beaches – the only traffic stoppers are the goatherds.

### Orientation & Information

The capital, Ibiza (Eivissa) city, is on the southeastern side of the island. This is where most travellers arrive (by ferry or air; the airport is to the south) and it's also the best base. The next largest towns are Santa Eulària des Riu on the eastern coast and Sant Antoni de Portmany on the western coast, the latter best avoided unless you are seriously into discos and getting drunk. Other big resorts are scattered around the island.

In Ibiza city, the **tourist office** (☎ 971 30 19 00, fax 971 30 15 62; e promocio@cief .es) is opposite the Estación Marítima. There are numerous cafés where you can go online but not many, aside from **Wash and Dry.Com** (☎ 971 39 48 22; Avinguda Espanya 53), where you can do a load of washing as well.

### Things to See & Do

Shopping seems to be a major pastime in Ibiza city. The port area of **Sa Penya** is crammed with funky and trashy clothes boutiques and arty-crafty market stalls. From here you can wander up into **D'Alt Vila**, the atmospheric old walled town, with its upmarket restaurants, galleries and the **Museu d'Art Contemporani**. There are fine views from the walls and from the **cathedral** at the top, and the **Museu Arqueològic** next door is worth a visit.

The heavily developed **Platja de ses Figueretes** beach is a 20-minute walk south of Sa Penya – you'd be better off taking the half-hour bus ride (€1.50) south to the beaches at **Ses Salines**.

Away from the coach tours, Ibiza has numerous unspoiled and relatively undeveloped beaches. On the northeastern coast, **Cala de Boix** is the only black-sand beach on the islands, while further north are the lovely beaches of **S'Aigua Blanca**. On the northern coast near Portinatx, **Cala Xarraca** is in a picturesque, secluded bay and, near Port de Sant Miquel, is the attractive **Cala Benirras**. On the southwestern coast, **Cala d'Hort** has a spectacular setting overlooking two rugged rock-islets, Es Verda and Es Verdranell.

## Places to Stay

**Ibiza City** There are several hostales in the streets around the port, although in midsummer cheap beds are scarce. On the waterfront **Hostal-Restaurante La Marina** (☎ 971 31 01 72, fax 971 31 48 94; Carrer Barcelona 7; singles/doubles €55/75) has sunny doubles with harbour views.

One of the best choices is **Casa de Huéspedes La Peña** (☎ 971 19 02 40; Carrer de la Virgen 76; doubles around €30; open June-Oct) at the far end of Sa Penya. There are 13 simple and tidy doubles with shared bathrooms. **Hostal Parque** (☎ 971 30 13 58; Plaça del Parque 4; singles/doubles with bath €48/72) has a revamped new look, but is on one of the liveliest squares so can be noisy. If you can afford it, the delightful **La Ventana** (☎ 971 39 08 57; Sa Carrossa 13; doubles up to €125) has wrought-iron four-poster beds, simple yet stylish decor and fantastic terrace views of the old castle walls.

**Other Areas** One of the best of Ibiza's camping grounds is **Camping Cala Nova** (☎ 971 33 17 74), 500m north of the resort town of Cala Nova and close to a good beach.

If you want luxury, with a pool, sauna, gymnasium and sun terrace, **Can Curreu** (☎ 971 33 52 80, fax 971 33 52 80; e cur reu@ibiza-hotels.com; doubles from €195) near Santa Eulais is a gorgeous small hotel. For sand between the toes, **Pensión Sa Plana** (☎ 971 33 50 73; doubles with breakfast from €45) is near the S'Aigua Blanca beaches and has a pool. Or you could stay by the black-sand beach at Cala Boix, at the cliff-top **Hostal Cala Boix** (☎ 971 33 52 24; rooms per person €17), with breakfast included in the rates.

## Places to Eat

Start your evening out with a drink at one of the bars lining the lively Plaça del Parque. **Herry's Bar** does a great tomato and olive oil *tostada* tapa. For something more substantial, **L'Absinthe** across the way, is woody and rustic, with some innovative salads and pasta dishes. Carnivorous folk may prefer the meaty menu and tapas at around €3 at **Viejo Almacen** (☎ 971 31 44 32; Azara 5). Hang out with the local fishermen at no-frills **La Estrella** (Plaça San Antonio Riquer; sandwiches, hot dogs, burgers €2.50-3), or eat Andalucían-style fare at **La Oliva** (☎ 971 30 57 52; Calle Santa Cruz), which has a pretty patio and excellent fish soup.

A hip place for a coffee and coñac is **Café Libro Azul** (☎ 971 39 23 80; Calle Cayetano Soler), which doubles as a bookshop and plays suitably laid-back jazz.

Just within the old town walls, **El Portalón** (☎ 971 30 39 01; Plaça Desamparados 1) serves classy French cuisine, while the heady views from **Plaça del Sol** on the square of the same name are in surprising contrast to the down-to-earth menu, which includes filled baked potatoes, as a very welcome change from chips.

## Entertainment

Ibiza's summer nightlife is renowned. At night, wander the fashion-catwalk of cobbled streets where designer chic couples and seriously studded swingers dodge the outrageous PR performers hired by the discos to attract dusk-to-dawn clubbers. Dozens of bars keep Ibiza city's port area jumping until the early hours – particularly on Carrer de Barcelona and Carrer de Garijo Cipriano. After they wind down, you can continue on to one of the island's world-famous discos – if you can afford the around €30 entry, that is. There's a handy 'Discobus' service that operates nightly from midnight until 6am doing circuits between the major discos, bars and hotels in Ibiza city, Platja d'en Bossa, San Rafael and San Antonio. The big names are **Pacha**, on the northern side of Ibiza city's port; **Privilege** and **Amnesia**, both 6km out on the road to Sant Antoni; **El Divino**, across the water from the town centre (hop on one

**SPAIN**

of its boats); and **Space**, south of Ibiza city in Platja d'En Bossa.

## Getting Around

Buses run between the airport and Ibiza city hourly (€1.50); a taxi costs around €12. Buses to other parts of the island leave from the series of bus stops along Avenida d'Isidoro Macabich. Pick up a timetable from the tourist office (see Orientation & Information earlier in this section).

If you want to get to some of the more secluded beaches you will need to rent wheels. In Ibiza city, **Autos Isla Blanca** (☎ 971 31 54 07; Carrer de Felipe II) will hire out a Renault Twingo for €103 for three days all-inclusive, or a scooter for around €28 a day.

## FORMENTERA

A short boat ride south of Ibiza, Formentera is the smallest and least developed of the four main Balearic Islands. That said, the island is attracting an increasing number of package tourists, particularly from Germany, so it lacks the tranquillity that made it such a hippie haven some thirty years ago. There are some excellent short walking and cycling trails, however, and most of the time it is still possible to spread a towel out on the beach without kicking sand over your neighbour.

## Orientation & Information

Formentera is about 20km from east to west. Ferries arrive at La Savina on the northwestern coast; the **tourist office** (☎ 971 32 20 57, fax 971 32 38 25; W www.illadeformen tera.es) is behind the rental agencies you'll see when you disembark. Three kilometres south is the island's pretty capital, Sant Francesc Xavier, where you'll find several banks, a pharmacy and a good-sized supermarket for your picnic supplies. From here, the main road runs along the middle of the island before climbing to the highest point (192m). At the eastern end of the island is the Sa Mola lighthouse. Es Pujols is 3km east of La Savina and is the main tourist resort where most of the hostales are located (and the only place with any nightlife to speak of).

## Things to See & Do

Some of the island's best and most popular beaches are the beautiful white strips of sand along the narrow promontory, which stretches north towards Ibiza. A 2km walking trail leads from the La Savina–Es Pujols road to the far end of the promontory, from where you can wade across a narrow strait to **S'Espalmador**, a privately owned uninhabited islet with beautiful, quiet beaches. If you don't fancy the paddle, there are regular boat rides. Along Formentera's southern coast, **Platja de Migjorn** is made up of numerous coves and beaches. Tracks lead down to these off the main road. On the western coast is the lovely **Cala Saona** beach.

The tourist office's *Green Tours* brochure outlines 19 excellent walking and cycling trails in five languages that take you through some of the island's most scenic areas.

## Places to Stay & Eat

Camping is not allowed on Formentera. Sadly, the coastal accommodation places mainly cater to German and British package-tour agencies and are overpriced and/or booked out in summer. In Es Pujols you could try **Hostal Tahiti** (☎ 971 32 81 22; singles/doubles €58/72; open May-Sept), with B&B available. One of the few hotels open year-round **Hostal Bellavista** (☎ 971 32 70 16; singles/doubles €54/66) has sea views and a handy terrace bar. If you prefer peace and quiet, you are better off in Es Caló. **Fonda Rafalet** (☎ 971 32 70 16; singles/doubles in Aug €39/58; open Apr-Oct) has good rooms on the waterfront or, across the road, there is the tiny and simple **Casa de Huéspedes Miramar** (☎ 971 32 70 60; rooms per person €30; open May-Sept).

Perhaps the best budget bet is to base yourself in one of the small inland towns and bike it to the beaches. In Sant Ferrán de ses Roques (1.6km south of Es Pujols), the popular **Hostal Pepe** (☎ 971 32 80 33; singles/doubles €24/37) offers rooms with bath and the price includes breakfast. Aside from the inevitable tourist-orientated restaurants serving overpriced egg-and-chip style food, there are some excellent seafood restaurants on the island. Many of the hostales also have bars/restaurants typically serving fairly uninspired but inexpensive meals. In Es Pujols, **S'Avaradero** on the seafront (☎ 971 32 90 43; Avenida Miramar 32-36) serves great seafood and Argentinean-style meat dishes. Also on the beach, **Bar Restaurant Flipper** (☎ 971 18 75 96; Playa Mitjorn, Arenals) is good for fresh fish and typical island dishes. Try the *arroz a la marinera* for a real taste of Formentera.

Wind up the evening with a blast of good music at the **Blue Bar** (☎ *971 18 70 11; Playa Mitjorn km 8)*, open until 4am. For tapas and local wine, **Bar Sa Barraca** (☎ *971 32 80 27; Avenida Miramar, Es Pujols)* is good while, among the plethora of pizzerias, **El Gatto E La Volpe** (☎ *971 32 91 00; Carretera Punta Prima, Es Pujols)* is better than most.

## Getting There & Away
There are 20 to 25 ferries daily between Ibiza city and Formentera. The trip takes around half an hour and prices between the various companies are fiercely competitive, but cost around €10 one way.

## Getting Around
A string of rental agencies lines the harbour in La Savina. Bikes start at €5 a day (€6 for a mountain bike) and scooters start at €17 and head up to €25 for more powerful motorbikes. A regular bus service connects all the main towns.

## MENORCA
Although Menorca is the second largest Balearic island, it is the least overrun. In 1993, the island was declared a Biosphere Reserve by Unesco, with the aim of preserving important environmental areas, such as the Albufera d'es Grau wetlands and its unique collection of archaeological sites.

## Orientation & Information
The capital, Maó (Mahón in Spanish), is at the eastern end of the island. Its busy port is the arrival point for most ferries and Menorca's airport is 7km southwest. The main road runs down the middle of the island to Ciutadella, Menorca's second-largest town, with secondary roads leading north and south to the resorts and beaches.

The **main tourist office** (☎ *971 36 37 90,* fax *971 35 45 30;* ⓦ *www.caib.es; Plaça de S'Esplanada 40)* is in Maó. There is a second **tourist office** (☎ *971 38 26 93; Plaça la Catedral s/n)* in Ciutadella. During the summer there is an additional office at the airport. There are **post offices** in Maó (*Carrer del Bon Aire)* and Ciutadella (*Pio V1 4)*.

## Things to See & Do
Maó and Ciutadella are both harbour towns, and from either place you'll have to commute to the beaches. Maó absorbs most of the tourist

traffic. While you're here, you can take a boat cruise around its impressive harbour and sample the local gin at the **Xoriguer distillery** *(open 8.30am-7pm Mon-Fri, 9am-1pm Sat)*. Ciutadella, with its smaller harbour and historic buildings, has a more distinctively Spanish feel about it. Follow all the shopping baskets to the colourful market on Plaça Llibertat, surrounded by lively tapas bars.

In the centre of the island, the 357m-high **Monte Toro** has great views of the whole island and, on a clear day, you can see as far as Mallorca.

With your own transport and a bit of footwork, you'll be able to discover some of Menorca's off-the-beaten-track beaches. North of Maó, a drive across a lunar landscape leads to the lighthouse at **Cabo de Favàritx**. If you park just before the gate to the lighthouse and climb up the rocks behind you, you'll see a couple of the eight beaches that are just waiting for scramblers like yourself to grace their sands.

On the northern coast, the picturesque town of **Fornells** is on a large bay popular with windsurfers. Further west, at the beach of Binimella, you can continue to the unspoilt **Cala Pregonda**, which is a good 20-minute walk from the nearest parking spot.

North of Ciutadella is **La Vall** (*€4.50 per car)*, another stretch of untouched beach backed by a private nature park. On the southern coast are two good beaches either side of the Santa Galdana resort – Cala Mitjana to the east and Macarella to the west. Menorca's beaches aren't its only attractions. The interior of the island is liberally sprinkled with reminders of its rich and ancient heritage. Pick up a copy of the tourist office's *Archaeological Guide to Menorca*.

## Places to Stay & Eat
Menorca's two **camping grounds** *(open summer only)* are near the resorts of **Santa Galdana** (☎ *971 37 30 95)*, about 8km south of Ferreries, and **Son Bou** (☎ *971 37 26 05)*, south of Alaior.

Maó and Ciutadella both have a handful of good budget options. In Maó, **Hostal Orsi** (☎ *971 36 47 51; Carrer de la Infanta 19; singles/doubles with bath €21/42)* is run by a Glaswegian and an American, who are a mine of information. It's bright, clean and well located. If you are not euro-economising, **Hotel del Almirante** (☎ *971 36 27 00,* fax *36 27 04;*

@ *hotel.almirante@menorca.net; singles/
doubles €52/83)* is a magnificent Georgian-
style mansion and a former residence of Nelson's second-in-command at Trafalgar. The
potted aspidistras say it all.

In Ciutadella **Hostal Oasis** *(☎ 971 38 21
97; Carrer Sant Isidre 33; doubles only €42)*
has homey rooms around a central courtyard
and restaurant, so lots of atmosphere, but it
can be noisy at night.

Ciutadella's port is also lined with restaurants and you won't have any trouble finding
somewhere to eat. **Cappuccino Menorca**
*(☎ 971 35 66 20; Moll de Llevant)* is a classy
place for a light meal, cocktail or coffee.
After dinner, check out **Jazzbah**, a hip little
music bar. In Maó port, **Latitud 40** *(☎ 971 36
41 76; Moll de Llevant 265)* is a popular bar-
restaurant with the boating fraternity if
you're looking for a job scrubbing decks.
**Casanova** *(☎ 971 35 41 69; Puerto de
Mahon 15)* is a good pizza place.

### Getting Around
From the airport, a taxi into Maó costs around
€7.50; there are no buses.

**TMSA** *(☎ 971 36 03 61)* runs six buses a
day between Maó and Ciutadella *(€3.50)*,
with connections to the major resorts on the
southern coast. In summer there are also daily
bus services to most of the coastal towns
from both Maó and Ciutadella.

If you're planning to hire a car, rates vary
seasonally from around €24 to €48 a day;
during the summer, minimum hire periods
sometimes apply. In Maó, places worth trying include **Autos Valls** *(☎ 971 36 84 65;
Plaça d'Espanya 13)* and **Autos Isla** *(☎ 971
36 65 69; Avinguda de Josep Maria
Quadrado 28)*. **Just Bicicletas** *(☎ 971 36 47
51; Andén de Llevant 35-36)* hires out mountain bikes *(€6 per day)*. At **Motos Gelabert**
*(☎ 971 36 06 14; José Anselmo Clavé)* you
can rent a scooter from €15 a day.

# Valencia

Although perhaps best known for the package
resorts of the Costa Blanca, to which people
flock in summer, this region also includes
Spain's lively third-largest city, Valencia. If
you penetrate inland, mountains buckle towards the rough and ready interior where
there are some rare undiscovered secrets.

## VALENCIA
**pop 746,610**
Valencia is a vibrant city, its old quarter
brimming with gracious baroque-fronted
houses and its streets buzzing with life until
the early hours – especially during the country's wildest party: Las Fallas de San José
(mid-March), an exuberant blend of fireworks, music, all-night partying and over 350
*fallas*, giant sculptures that all go up in
flames on the final night.

### Orientation
The action part of the city is oval, bounded by
the old course of the Turia River and the sickle-
shaped inner ring road of Calles Colón, Játiva
and Guillem de Castro. These trace the walls of
the old city, demolished in 1865 as – believe it
or not – a job-creation project that dismantled
one of the Mediterranean coastline's major
monuments.

Within the oval are three major squares:
Plazas del Ayuntamiento, de la Reina (also
known as Plaza de Zaragoza) and de la Virgen.

### Information
There is a **main tourist office** *(☎ 963 98 64
22, fax 963 98 64 21; @ touristinfo.valen
cia@turisme.m400.gva.es; Calle Paz 48; open
10am-6.30pm Mon-Fri, 10am-2pm Sat)* in
the centre. Three smaller ones are at the train
station, town hall and Teatro Principal.

Among several Internet cafés in town is
**Jump** *(☎ 963 80 50 34; Calle Albacete 8)*,
just south of the Plaza del Ayuntamiento; it
charges €1.50 an hour.

### Things to See & Do
Located in the dried-up bed of the city's
Turia River, the aesthetically stunning, ultra-
modern **Ciudad de las Artes y las Ciencias**
*(information & reservations ☎ 902 100 031)*
includes a planetarium, IMAX cinema and
laser show, interactive science museum,
aquarium and open-air auditorium.

The **Museo de Bellas Artes** *(Fine Arts
Museum; admission free; open 10am-
2.15pm & 4pm-7.30pm Tues-Sat, 10am-
7.30pm Sun)* ranks among Spain's best, with
works by El Greco, Goya, Velázquez, Ribera
and Ribalta.

The **Instituto Valenciano de Arte Moderno** *(IVAM; admission €2, free Sun)*, beside
Puente de las Artes, houses an impressive permanent collection of 20th-century Spanish art.

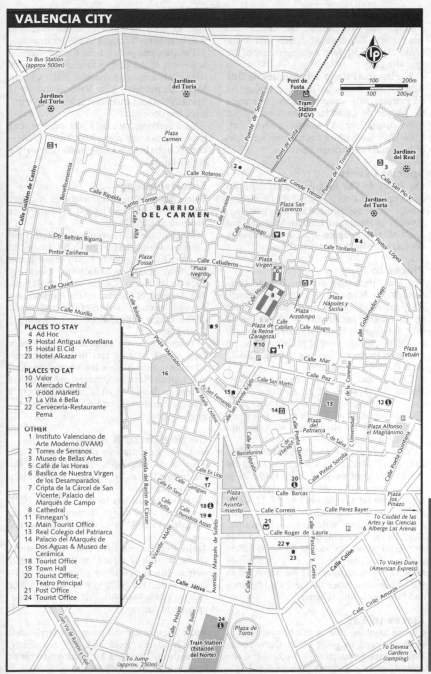

# VALENCIA CITY

**PLACES TO STAY**
4  Ad Hoc
9  Hostal Antigua Morellana
15 Hostal El Cid
23 Hotel Alkazar

**PLACES TO EAT**
10 Valor
16 Mercado Central
   (Food Market)
17 La Vita é Bella
22 Cervecería-Restaurante
   Pema

**OTHER**
1  Instituto Valenciano de
   Arte Moderno (IVAM)
2  Torres de Serranos
3  Museo de Bellas Artes
5  Café de las Horas
6  Basílica de Nuestra Virgen
   de los Desamparados
7  Cripta de la Cárcel de San
   Vicente; Palacio del
   Marqués de Campo
8  Cathedral
11 Finnegan's
12 Main Tourist Office
13 Real Colegio del Patriarca
14 Palacio del Marqués de
   Dos Aguas & Museo de
   Cerámica
18 Tourist Office
19 Town Hall
20 Tourist Office;
   Teatro Principal
21 Post Office
24 Tourist Office

Valencia's cathedral boasts three magnificent portals – one Romanesque, one Gothic and one baroque. Climb the Miguelete bell-tower (admission €1.50) for a sweeping view of the sprawling city.

The baroque **Palacio del Marqués de Dos Aguas** *(Calle del Poeta Querol)* is fronted by an extravagantly sculpted facade. It houses the **Museo de Cerámica** *(admission €2.50; open 10am-2pm & 4pm-8pm Tues-Sat, 10am-2pm Sun)*, which has a superb selection of local and international ceramics.

## Special Events
**Las Fallas de San José** in mid-March is an exuberant, anarchic swirl of fireworks, music, festive bonfires and all-night partying. If you're in Spain then, head for Valencia, but don't plan on sleeping – accommodation is booked up months in advance.

## Places to Stay
The nearest camping ground, **Devesa Gardens** *(☎/fax 961 61 11 36; open year-round)*, is 13km south of Valencia near El Saler beach. **Alberge Las Arenas** *(☎/fax 963 56 42 88; Calle Eugenia Viñes 24; open year-round)* is within squinting view of Malvarrosa beach and offers Internet connection; take bus No 32 from Plaza del Ayuntamiento.

Central and near the covered market, **Hostal El Cid** *(☎ 963 92 23 23; Calle Cerrajeros 13; singles/doubles without bath €12/24, doubles with bath €32)* is a steep stair climb but excellent value with satellite TV, bath and air-con.

Near Plaza del Ayuntamiento, **Hotel Alkazar** *(☎ 963 51 55 51; Calle Mosén Femades 11; singles/doubles with bath €48/52)* is very pleasant and comfortable. **Hostal Antigua Morellana** *(☎/fax 963 91 57 73; Calle en Bou 2; doubles with bath €42)* in a renovated 18th-century building has cosy rooms. North of the cathedral, the owner of **Ad Hoc** *(☎ 963 91 91 40, fax 963 91 36 67; e adhoc @nixo.net; Calle Boix 4; singles/doubles €89/110 with discounts at weekends)* is in the art business, hence the stencilled ceilings and fabulous colour scheme.

## Places to Eat
Choose anything from a full-blown meal to a simple tapa at good-value **Cervecería-Restaurante Pema** *(☎ 963 56 22 14; Calle Mosén Femades 3; lunch menu €6.50)*.

**La Vita é Bella** *(☎ 963 52 21 31; Calle En Llop 4)* is an outstanding Italian restaurant with crisp pizza crust and to-die-for tiramasu.

For authentic paella, head for Las Arenas, just north of the port, where a long line of restaurants serves up the real stuff. Chocoholics are pandered to at **Valor** *(Plaza de la Reina 20)*, where chocolate is served in cups, thick and delicious.

And everyone, not only self-caterers, can have fun browsing around the bustling **Mercado Central**, Valencia's *modernista*-style covered market.

## Entertainment
Valencia's nightlife is legendary, as is its gay community – the third largest in Spain, after Madrid and Barcelona.

Much of the action centres on Barrio del Carmen, which has everything from hip designer bars to gloomy heavy-metal hangouts. For serious sophistication, check out **Café de las Horas** *(Calle Conde de Almodóvar 1)*, north of the Plaza de la Virgen, with its plush baroque interior, or the programme of the **Teatro Principal** *(☎ 963 51 00 51; Calle Barcas 15)*.

Younger groovers head for the university 2km east (€3.50 by taxi from the centre). Along Avenida Blasco Ibáñez and particularly around Plaza de Xuquer there are scores of dusk-to-dawn bars and discos. **Finnegan's** *(Plaza de la Reina)*, an Irish pub, draws the English-speakers.

## Getting There & Away
**Bus** The bus station *(☎ 963 49 72 22; Avenida de Menéndez Pidal)* is beside the old riverbed. Bus No 8 connects it to Plaza del Ayuntamiento.

Major destinations include: Madrid (€18 to €20, up to 12 daily), Barcelona (€18, up to 12 daily) and Alicante (€12.50, 2¼ hours).

**Train** Express trains run from **Estación del Norte** *(☎ 963 52 02 02, ☎ 902 24 02 02)* to/from Madrid (€37, 3½ hours, up to 10 daily), Barcelona (€29 to €32, three to four hours, 12 daily) and Alicante (€9, two hours, up to eight daily).

**Boat** Regular car and passenger ferries that go to Mallorca, Ibiza and, less frequently, Menorca are operated by **Trasmediterránea** *(reservations ☎ 902 45 46 45)*.

## Getting Around
EMT (☎ 963 52 83 99) buses run until about 10pm, with night services continuing on seven routes until around 1am.

The smart high-speed tram is a pleasant way to get to the beach, the paella restaurants of Las Arenas and the port. Metro lines primarily serve the outer suburbs.

# INLAND VALENCIA
## Morella
pop 2720

Perched on a hill top, crowned by a castle and completely enclosed by a wall over 2km long, the fairy-tale town of Morella, in the north of the Valencia region, is one of Spain's oldest continually inhabited towns.

The **tourist office** (☎/fax 964 17 30 32; open 10am-2pm & 4pm-7pm daily) is just behind the Torres de San Miguel, which flank the main entrance gate.

**Things to See & Do** Morella's **castle**, although in ruins, remains imposing and gives breathtaking views of the town and surrounding countryside. You can visit the **castle grounds** (admission €2; open 10.30am-7.30pm daily).

The old town is easily explored on foot. Four small **museums** (admission for each museum €1-2), set in the towers of the ancient walls, have displays on local history, folklore, photography and the 'age of the dinosaurs' – with fossils of dinosaurs found in the region.

**Places to Stay & Eat** The cheapest option is friendly **Fonda Moreno** (☎ 964 16 01 05; Calle de San Nicolás 12; doubles €35), which has six quaint and basic doubles. Its upstairs restaurant does a hearty menú for €6.

Freshly refurbished **Hostal El Cid** (☎ 964 16 01 25; Puerta de San Mateo 2; singles/ doubles €21/37) has spruced up rooms with bath and good views.

**Hotel Cardenal Ram** (☎ 964 17 30 85; Cuesta de Suñer 1; singles/doubles €37.50/ 59), occupying a 16th-century cardinal's palace, has rooms with all facilities.

**Restaurante Vinatea** (☎ 964 16 07 44; Calle Blasco de Alagón 17; set menu €6; open Tues-Sun) does excellent tapas, plus a menú that is rich in local dishes.

**Getting There & Away** The bus company **Autos Mediterráneo** (☎ 964 22 05 36) runs two buses daily, from Monday to Saturday to/from both Castellón and Vinarós.

## Guadalest
A spectacular route runs west from just south of Calpe (see its individual entry later in this section) to the inland town of **Alcoy**, famous for its Moros y Cristianos fiesta in April. About halfway to Alcoy, stop at the old Muslim settlement of **Guadalest**, dominated by the Castillo de San José and besieged nowadays by coach parties from the coast.

## Elche (Elx)
pop 198,190

Just 20km southwest of Alicante, Elche is famed for its extensive palm groves, planted by the Muslims, but, aside from these, it's a fairly dreary town, only warranting a day trip.

Visit the **Huerto del Cura** (€2; open 9am-6pm daily), with its tended lawns, colourful flower beds and a freakish eight-pronged palm tree. The gardens are opposite the hotel of the same name. Try and visit to coincide with the annual festival, the **Misteri d'Elx**. This extraordinary two-part medieval mystery play and lyric drama is performed in the Basílica de Santa María on 14 and 15 August (with public rehearsals the three previous days).

# ALICANTE
pop 283,240

Alicante (Alacant) is an underrated city with most tourists heading straight for the Costa Blanca beaches. Yet there's an appealing faded grandeur about the place, particularly around the old quarter, overlooked by the majestic limestone cathedral. The nightlife is also equal to that of any self-respecting Andalucían city, particularly during the Fiesta de Sant Joan, 24 June, when Alicante stages its own version of Las Fallas (see Special Events under the Valencia city section earlier in this chapter).

Alicante has five tourist offices but the most central is the **main tourist office** (☎ 965 20 00 00; e turismo@alicante-ay to.es; Rambla de Méndez Núñez 23; open 10am-7pm Mon-Fri, 10am-2pm Sat). You can connect to the Internet at **Up Internet** (☎ 965 20 05 77; Angel Lozano 10; open 10am-2am daily) for €1.50 an hour.

## Things to See & Do
The **Castillo de Santa Bárbara** (admission free), a 16th-century fortress, overlooks the

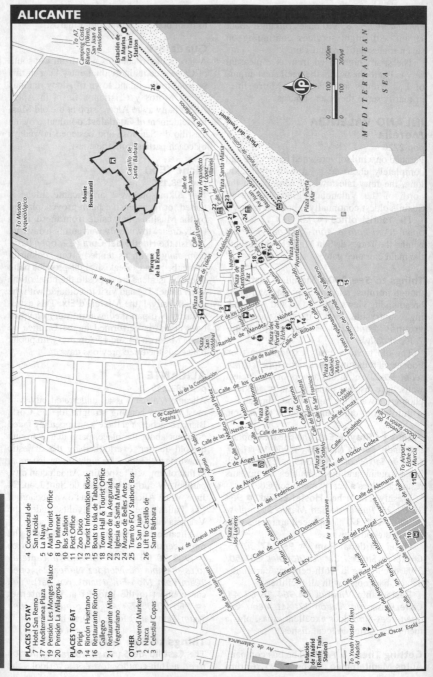

# ALICANTE

**PLACES TO STAY**
7 Hotel San Remo
17 Mediterranea Plaza
19 Pensión Les Monges Palace
20 Pensión La Milagrosa

**PLACES TO EAT**
9 Piripi
16 Rincón Huertano
Restaurante Rincón
Gallego
21 Restaurante Mixto
Vegetariano

**OTHER**
1 Covered Market
2 Nazca
3 Celestial Copas
4 Concatedral de
San Nicolás
5 La Naya
6 Main Tourist Office
8 Up Internet
10 Post Office
12 Zoo Disco
13 Tourist Information Kiosk
15 Boats to Isla de Tabarca
18 Town Hall & Tourist Office
22 Museo de la Asegurada
23 Iglesia de Santa María
24 Museo de Belles Artes
25 Tram to FGV Station; Bus
to San Juan
26 Lift to Castillo de
Santa Bárbara

city. Take the lift (€2.50 return), reached by a footbridge opposite Playa del Postiguet, or walk either via Avenida Jaime II or Parque de la Ereta.

The **Museo de la Asegurada** *(Plaza Santa María; admission free; open 10am-2pm & 5pm-9pm June-Sept; 10am-2pm & 4pm-8pm Oct-May; closed Sun & Mon afternoon)* houses an excellent collection of modern art, including works by Dalí, Miró and Picasso.

The **Museo Arqueológico** *(Plaza Gómez Ulla s/n; adult/student €6/3; open 10am-2pm & 5pm-9pm June-Sept; 10am-2pm & 4pm-8pm Oct-May; closed Sun & Mon afternoon)* houses an excellent collection of Roman and medieval antiquities. The emphasis is on local painters at the **Museo de Bellas Artes** *(Calle Gravina; admission free; open 10am-2pm & 5pm-9pm June-Sept; 10am-2pm & 4pm-8pm Oct-May; closed Sun & Mon afternoon)*, which has recently moved to this suitably cyc-catching 18th-century mansion.

**Playa del Postiguet** This is the closest beach to Alicante. Larger and less crowded beaches are at **Playa de San Juan**, easily reached by bus Nos 21 and 22.

Most days, **Kontiki** *(☎ 965 21 63 96)* runs boat trips (€13 return) to popular **Isla de Tabarca**, where there's good snorkelling and scuba diving from quiet beaches.

## Places to Stay
About 10km north of Alicante, **Camping Costa Blanca** *(☎ 965 63 06 70; outside Campello, 200m from the beach)* has a good pool. Alicante's youth hostel, **La Florida** *(☎ 965 11 30 44; Avenida de Orihuela 59)*, 2km west of the centre, is open year-round but has limited spaces during the winter months.

At the outstanding **Pensión Les Monges Palace** *(☎ 965 21 50 46, fax 965 14 71 89; Calle de Monges 2)* rooms range from €22 for a single with washbasin and shower to €78 for a luxurious double with jacuzzi.

**Pensión La Milagrosa** *(☎ 965 21 69 18; Calle de Villavieja 8; rooms per person €15)* has clean, basic rooms and a small guest kitchen. **Hotel San Remo** *(☎ 965 20 95 00; Calle Navas; singles/doubles €39.50/54)* on a busy shopping street has pleasant rooms with full bathroom. **Mediterránea Plaza** *(☎ 965 21 01 88, fax 965 20 67 50; Plaza del Ayuntamiento 6; doubles €104)* is a sparkling new marble-clad hotel on this historic city plaza.

## Places to Eat
**Restaurante Rincón Gallego** *(☎ 965 14 00 14; Plaza del Ayuntamiento 7; daily menu €11.50)* is popular with locals and has a vast choice of traditional Galícian *raciones*. Nearby, **Restaurante Mixto Vegetariano** *(Plaza de Santa María 2; set menu €6)* is a simple hole-in-the-wall place with vegetarian menús. **Rincón Huertano** *(☎ 965 14 04 57; Plaza Portal de Elche 4)* serves old-style traditional cuisine, such as rice and snails.

Highly regarded **Piripi** *(☎ 965 22 79 40; Calle Oscar Esplá 30)* is the place to go for stylish tapas or fine rice and seafood dishes. Expect to pay about €30 a head for a three-course meal.

## Entertainment
Alicante's nightlife zone clusters around the cathedral, where there is a good choice of early evening bars. Later on, look out for **Celestial Copas**, **La Naya**, **Nazca** and **Zoo** discos. In summer, the disco scene at Playa de San Juan is thumping. There are also hundreds of discos in the coastal resorts between Alicante and Dénia.

## Getting There & Away
There are daily services from the bus station on Calle de Portugal to Almería (€16, 4½ hours), Valencia (€12, 2¼ hours), Barcelona (€28, eight hours), Madrid (€31.50, 4¼ hours) and towns along the Costa Blanca.

From the train station on Avenida de Salamanca, there's a frequent service to Madrid (€28, four hours), Valencia (€8.50 to €19, two hours) and also Barcelona (€39, around five hours).

From Estación de la Marina, the Ferrocarriles de la Generalitat Valenciana (FGV) station at the northeastern end of Playa del Postiguet, a narrow-gauge line follows an attractive coastal route northwards as far as Dénia (€6) via Playa de San Juan (€1), Benidorm (€3) and Calpe (€4).

## COSTA BLANCA
The Costa Blanca (White Coast), one of Europe's most popular tourist regions, has its share of concrete jungles, particularly around Benidorm, which resembles a Las Vegas skyline from a distance. But if you're looking for a rollicking nightlife, good beaches and a suntan, you won't be disappointed. There are a couple of interesting places to visit as well.

**SPAIN**

Keep in mind that accommodation is just about impossible to find during the coach-tour circuit months of July and August.

## Xàbia
### pop 24,650
In contrast to the comparatively Spanish resort of Dénia, 10km northwest, over two-thirds of annual visitors to Xàbia (Jávea) are foreigners, so it's not the greatest place to brush up your Spanish. This laid-back resort is in three parts: the old town (3km inland), the port and the beach zone of El Arenal, lined with pleasant bar-restaurants. It's best visited early in the tourist season.

**Camping Xàbia** (☎ 965 79 10 70) is about 1km from El Arenal. The port area is pleasant and has some reasonably priced *pensiones*. In the old town, **Hostal Levante** (☎ 965 79 15 91; Calle Maestro Alonso 5; singles/doubles €15/30, rooms with shower/bath €28/36) has basic rooms.

## Calpe
Calpe (Calp), 22km northeast of Benidorm, is dominated by the Gibraltaresque **Peñon de Ilfach** (332m), a giant molar protruding from the sea. The climb towards the summit is popular – while you're up there, enjoy the seascape and decide which of Calpe's two long sandy beaches you want to laze on.

**Camping Ilfach** and **Camping Levante**, both on Avenida de la Marina, are a short walk from Playa Levante. **Pensión Céntrica** (☎ 965 83 55 28; Plaza de Ilfach; double rooms with washbasin €22) just off Avenida Gabriel Miró, is squeaky clean.

## Benidorm
### pop 57,230
Benidorm succumbed to cheap package tourism (nearly five million visitors annually) several decades ago. About the only things going for it these days are the 5km of (crowded) white beaches and a high-spirited nightlife with more karaoke bars per square metre than anywhere else in Spain.

Almost everyone here is on a package deal and there's no truly budget accommodation. **Hostal Santa Faz** (☎ 965 85 40 63; Calle Sant Faz 18; singles/doubles €42/60) has attractive rooms with full bathroom. Deprived Brits may want to stop by the oldest chippy in Benidorm, **Ray's** (San Vicente 4), which has been serving fish and chips for over 20 years.

# Andalucía

The stronghold of the Muslims in Spain for nearly eight centuries, Andalucía is an incomparably beautiful province, peppered with Moorish reminders of the past: the magnificent Alhambra in Granada, the timeless elegance of Córdoba's Mezquita and the whitewashed villages nestling in ochre hills. Seville, is one of Spain's most exciting cities.

Away from the cities and resorts, Andalucía is relatively untainted by tourists. Its scenery ranges from semideserts to lush river valleys to gorge-ridden mountains. Its long coastline stretches from the remote beaches of Cabo de Gata, past the crowds of the Costa del Sol, to come within 14km of Africa at Tarifa before opening up to the Atlantic Ocean with the long sandy beaches of the Costa de la Luz. A couple of good websites on Andalucía are ⓦ www .andalucia.org and ⓦ www.andalucia.com.

## SEVILLE
### pop 702,520
It's hard to describe Seville without slipping into superlative overdose. If you want to inhale some authentic ¡Olé! essence, this is the place. Seville is a Spanish cliche of flamenco, tapas bars, strolling guitarists and bullfights. If this wasn't enough, there is the marvellous exuberance of the people. Seville's air of contentment is well founded. An important and prosperous centre in Muslim times and later in the 16th and 17th centuries, the city took the world stage more recently when it hosted its Expo in 1992. Although the architectural legacy and infrastructure from this Expo come nowhere near matching that of Seville's 1929 World's Fair, the hi-tech new bridges and few remaining pavilions add an upbeat modern dimension to the city.

Seville is quite an expensive place, so it's worth planning your visit carefully. In July and August, the city is stiflingly hot and it's a two-hour drive to the nearest beach. The best time to come is during the unforgettable Easter week and April *feria* (see Special Events later in this section), though rooms then (if you can get one) cost close to double the regular rates.

## Information
The **main tourist office** (☎ 954 22 14 04, fax 954 22 97 53; ⓔ otsevilla@turismo-anda luz.com; Avenida de la Constitución 21; open

*9am-7pm Mon-Fri, 10am-7pm Sat, 10am-2pm Sun)* is always extremely busy, so you might try the other **tourist offices** *(☎ 954 23 44 65; Paseo de las Delicias 9; open 8.30am-2.45pm Mon-Fri* • *☎ 954 50 56 00; Calle de Arjona 28; open 8am-8.45pm Mon-Fri, 8.30am-2.30pm Sat & Sun)*. Pick up a copy of the monthly freebie *The Tourist*, which includes a map of Seville and lots of restaurants and what's-on type of info in English.

Seville has heaps of public Internet/email services. A typical rate is €2.50 an hour. One reasonably central place is **Cibercenter** *(☎ 954 22 88 99; Calle Julio César 9; open 10am-10pm Mon-Sat, 4pm-10pm Sun)*. **Librería Beta** *(Avenida de la Constitución 9 & 27)* has guidebooks and novels in English. **Lavandería Roma** *(Calle de Castelar 2C; open Mon-Sat)* will wash, dry and fold a load of washing for €6.

## Things to See & Do

**Cathedral & Giralda** Seville's massive cathedral *(Calle Alemanes; adult/student & pensioner €6/1.50, admission free Sun; open 11am-5pm Mon-Sat, 2.30pm-6pm Sun)*, one of the biggest in the world, was built on the site of Muslim Seville's main mosque between 1401 and 1507. The structure is primarily Gothic, although most of the internal decoration is in later styles. The adjoining tower, La Giralda, was the mosque's minaret and dates from the 12th century. The puff-you-out climb to the top is worth it for the stunning panoramic views of the city. One highlight of the cathedral's lavish interior is Christopher Columbus' supposed tomb inside the southern door (no-one's 100% sure that his remains didn't get mislaid somewhere in the Caribbean). The four crowned sepulchre-bearers represent the four kingdoms of Spain at the time of Columbus' sailing. The entrance to the cathedral and La Giralda is the Puerta del Perdón on Calle Alemanes.

**Alcázar** Seville's alcázar *(admission €5, students & pensioners free; open 9.30am-5pm Tues-Sat, 9.30am-1.30pm Sun & holidays)*, a residence of Muslim and Christian royalty for many centuries, was founded in AD 913 as a Muslim fortress. It has been adapted by Seville's rulers almost every century since, making it a mishmash of styles but adding to its fascination. The highlights are the **Palacio de Don Pedro**, exquisitely decor-

ated by Muslim artisans for the Castilian King Pedro the Cruel in the 1360s, and the large, immaculately tended **gardens**, the perfect place to ease your body and brain after some intensive sightseeing.

**Walks & Parks** To appreciate fully the **Barrio de Santa Cruz**, the old Jewish quarter immediately east of the cathedral, you need to head for the tangle of narrow streets and plazas east of the main Calle Mateus Gago artery. There's no better place to get lost. A more straightforward walk is along the **riverbank**, where the 13th-century Torre del Oro contains a small, crowded maritime museum. Nearby is Seville's famous bullring, the **Plaza de Toros de la Real Maestranza**, one of the oldest in Spain (begun in 1758). Interesting tours (€3) are given in English and Spanish about every 20 minutes from 9.30am to 2pm and 3pm to 6pm or 7pm daily (bullfight days 10am to 3pm).

South of the centre is **Parque de María Luisa** with its maze of paths, tall trees, flowers, fountains and shaded lawns. Be sure to seek out the magnificent **Plaza de España** with its fountains, canal and a dazzling semicircle of *azuelejo* (ceramic tile) clad buildings.

**Museums** The **Archivo de las Indias** *(admission free; open 10am-1pm Mon-Fri)*, beside the cathedral, houses over 40 million documents dating from 1492 through to the decolonisation of the Americas. At the time of writing, it was temporarily closed for refurbishment.

The **Museo de Bellas Artes** *(Plaza del Museo; adult/student €1.50/1, EU citizens free; open Tues-Sun)* has an outstanding, beautifully housed collection of Spanish art, focusing on Seville artists such as Bartolemé Esteban Murillo and Francisco Zurbarán.

## Organised Tours

River cruises by **Cruceros Turísticos** *(€12, one hour)* operate at least hourly from 11am to 7pm from the Torre del Oro. There are also night cruises with open bar for €24. A daily walking tour of the city leaves from the main tourist office on Avenida de la Constitución at 2.45pm daily and costs €9/6 per adult/student. You can also buy a special **tapas route** coupon book for €27, which lists the best-known bars. It works out cheaper to go *solo*.

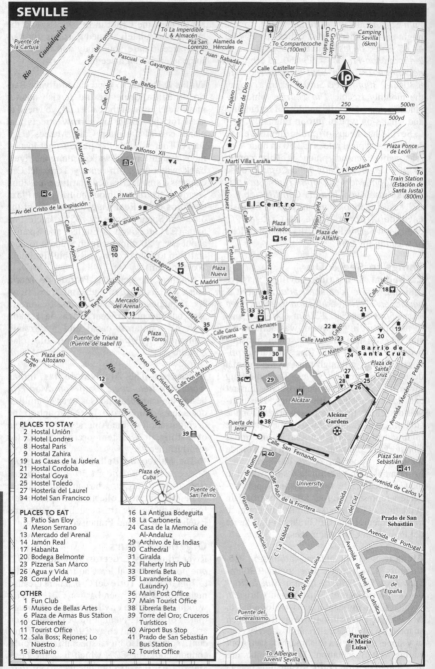

# SEVILLE

**PLACES TO STAY**
2 Hostal Unión
7 Hotel Londres
8 Hostal Paris
9 Hostal Zahira
19 Las Casas de la Judería
21 Hostal Cordoba
22 Hostal Goya
26 Hostel Toledo
27 Hostería del Laurel
34 Hotel San Francisco

**PLACES TO EAT**
3 Patio San Eloy
4 Meson Serrano
13 Mercado del Arenal
14 Jamón Real
17 Habanita
20 Bodega Belmonte
23 Pizzeria San Marco
26 Agua y Vida
28 Corral del Agua

**OTHER**
1 Fun Club
4 Museo de Bellas Artes
6 Plaza de Armas Bus Station
10 Cibercenter
11 Tourist Office
12 Sala Boss; Rejones; Lo
Nuestro
15 Bestiario

16 La Antigua Bodeguita
18 La Carbonería
24 Casa de la Memoria de
Al-Andaluz
29 Archivo de las Indias
30 Cathedral
31 Giralda
32 Flaherty Irish Pub
33 Librería Beta
35 Lavandería Roma
(Laundry)
36 Main Post Office
37 Main Tourist Office
38 Librería Beta
39 Torre del Oro; Cruceros
Turísticos
40 Airport Bus Stop
41 Prado de San Sebastián
Bus Station
42 Tourist Office

SPAIN

## Special Events

The first of Seville's two great festivals is Semana Santa, the week leading up to Easter Sunday. Throughout the week, long processions of religious brotherhoods, dressed in strange penitents' garb with tall, pointed hoods, accompany sacred images through the city, watched by huge crowds. The Feria de Abril, a week in late April, is a welcome release after this solemnity: the festivities involve six days of music, dancing, horse-riding and traditional dress on a site in the Los Remedios area west of the river, plus daily bullfights and a general city-wide party.

## Places to Stay

Summer prices given here can come down substantially from October to March.

Camping Sevilla (☎ 954 51 43 79; €3 per person), 6km out on the N-IV towards Córdoba, has good rates for two people with a car and tent, and runs a shuttle bus to/from Avenida de Portugal in the city.

Seville's hostel, Albergue Juvenil Sevilla (☎ 955 05 65 00; Calle Isaac Peral 2; bus No 34; beds for under/over 26 €8.50/11.50 with breakfast), has 277 places, all in twins or triples. It's about 10 minutes south by bus from opposite the main tourist office. Accommodation in Barrio de Santa Cruz includes basic, no-frills Hostal Toledo (☎ 954 21 53 35; Calle Santa Teresa 15; doubles from €26) and the more spacious, central and more costly Hostal Goya (☎ 954 21 11 70; Calle Mateos Gago 31; singles/doubles from €37/47). Freshly refurbished with light wood and a lick of paint, Hostal Cordoba (☎ 954 22 74 98; Calle Farnesio 12; singles/doubles €30/60) is well priced. Costing lots more, Hostería del Laurel (☎ 954 22 02 95; e host-laurel@ eintec.es; Plaza de los Venerables 5; singles/doubles €64/90) is a fabulous, cosy hotel. Bright and cheery Hotel San Francisco (☎ 954 50 15 41; Alvarez Quintero 38; singles/doubles from €55/68) is close to the cathedral, and delightful Las Casas de la Judería (☎ 954 41 51 50, fax 954 42 21 70; e jude ria@zoom.es; Callejón de Dos Hermanas 7; singles/doubles from €88/132) is justifiably pricey. The rooms are in small Andalucían-style houses set around patios and fountains.

The area north of Plaza Nueva is well situated for shops, as well as the sights. No-frills Hostal Unión (☎ 954 22 92 94; Calle Tarifa 4; singles/doubles €27/36) has nine good

clean rooms. Hotel Londres (☎ 954 50 27 45; Calle Pedro Martir 1; singles/doubles €38/48) is in a gracious old house with a tiled lobby and pleasant rooms. A few doors down, Hostal Paris (☎ 954 22 98 61, fax 95 421 96 45; singles/doubles €38/52) has a light, cheery interior. Located bang in the centre of one of the city's most attractive pedestrian streets Hotel Zahira (☎ 954 22 10 61, fax 954 21 30 48; Calle San Eloy 43; singles/doubles €32/45) is sparkling clean and comfortable.

## Places to Eat

Barrio de Santa Cruz provides a wonderful setting for restaurants, although expect to pay slightly more. The cool courtyard at Corral del Agua (☎ 954 22 48 42; Callejodel Agua 6; fish dishes around €9) is an ideal summer spot for enjoying excellent fish dishes. On the corner, Agua y Vida (☎ 954 56 04 71; Callején del Agua 8; tapas €1.50) has a good choice of tapas, including spinach and chickpeas as a rare vegan option. In the same area Pizzeria San Marco (☎ 954 56 43 90; Calle Mesón del Moro 6; open Tues-Sun) was once a Moorish bathhouse and does popular pizzas and pastas for around €5. Bullfighting is the decor theme at Bodega Belmonte (☎ 954 21 40 14; Calle Mateos Gago 24) and you'll find interesting bits of the beast on the menu. Calle Santa María La Blanca has several places with outdoor tables. At Casa Fernando there's plenty of sandwich choice for under €1.50.

West of Avenida de la Constitución, Jamón Real (☎ 954 56 39 98; Calle Pastor y Landero) specialises in Extremadura cuisine, such as migas (fried breadcrumbs) with pork and ham for €5. Further north, bright, busy Patio San Eloy (☎ 954 22 11 48; Calle de San Eloy 9; tapas €1.50) is known for its fino (sherry) bar and montaditos (multitiered sandwiches). Meson Serrano (☎ 954 21 82 99; Calle Alfonso XII 8) has an outside tiled terrace, excellent tapas and more substantial fare. Cuban and vegetarian cuisine is the deal at Habanita (☎ 606 71 64 56; Calle Golfo 3) in the buzzy Alfafa district due north.

Mercado del Arenal (Calle Pastor y Landero) is the main food market in the centre and also has stalls selling bread and drinks for one-stop picnic planning.

## Entertainment

Seville's nightlife is among the liveliest in Spain. On fine nights throngs of people block the streets outside popular bars. As in most places in Spain, the real action begins around midnight on Friday and Saturday.

**Drinking & Dancing** Until about 1am, Plaza Salvador has several popular watering-holes, including **La Antigua Bodeguita** at No 6 with outdoor barrel tables for checking out the crowd.

There are some hugely popular bars around the cathedral, including **Flaherty Irish Pub** (Calle Alemanes 7) with regular, live Celtic music. The crowds from about midnight around Calle de Adriano, west of Avenida de la Constitución, have to be seen to be believed. Busy music bars around here include **Bestiario** (Calle Zaragoza s/n), which is more spacious and modern than some. Nearby on Calle García Vinuesa and Calle Dos de Mayo are some quieter *bodegas* (traditional wine bars), some with good tapas, that attract an older crowd.

Plaza de la Alfalfa is another good area; there are some great tapas bars east along Calle Alfalfa and at least five throbbing music bars north on Calle Pérez Galdós. The **Fun Club** (Alameda de Hércules 86; open Thur-Sun) is a small, busy dance warehouse – live bands play some nights here. Several good pub-like bars line the same street a little further north. **El Corto Maltés** is a more laid-back drinking den, while **Tetería Platea** at No 87 is a Moroccan-style teahouse with lots of kick-back space and Arabic music.

In summer there's a lively scene along the eastern bank of the Río Guadalquivir, which is dotted with temporary bars. On the far bank, **Sala Boss**, **Rejones** and **Lo Nuestro**, side by side on Calle del Betis, all play good music year-round, attracting an interesting mix of students and travellers.

**Flamenco** Seville is arguably Spain's flamenco capital and you're most likely to catch a spontaneous atmosphere (of unpredictable quality) in one of the bars staging regular nights of flamenco with no admission fee. These include the sprawling **La Carbonería** (Calle Levíes 18), thronged nearly every night from about 11pm to 4am. More orientated towards tourists with classes available for the intrepid is the new **Casa de la Memoria de Al-Andaluz** (☎ 954 56 06 70; Calle Ximenez de Enciso 28), with flamenco at 9pm that costs €11.

## Spectator Sports

The bullfighting season runs from Easter to October, with fights most Sundays about 6.30pm, and every day during the Feria de Abril and the preceding week. The bullring is on Paseo de Cristóbal Colón. Tickets start at around €9 or €18, depending on who's doing the fighting.

## Getting There & Away

**Air** There's quite a range of domestic and international flights at **Seville airport** (☎ 954 44 90 00). **Air Europa** (☎ 954 44 91 79) flies to Barcelona from €95.

**Bus** Buses to Madrid, Portugal and Andalucía west of Seville leave from the **Plaza de Armas bus station** (☎ 954 90 80 40). Numerous daily buses run to/from Madrid (€15, six hours); to/from Lisbon there are eight direct buses a week (€30, eight hours). Daily buses run to/from places on the Algarve, such as Faro, Albufeira and Lagos.

Buses to other parts of Andalucía and eastern Spain use **Prado de San Sebastián bus station** (☎ 954 41 71 11). Daily services include nine or more each to Córdoba (€9, 1¾ hours), Granada (€15.50, three hours) and Málaga (€13.50, 2½ hours).

**Train** Seville's Santa Justa train station is 1.5km northeast of the centre on Avenida Kansas City. To/from Madrid, there are 18 superfast AVE trains each day, covering the 471km in just 2½ hours and costing €62.50 in the cheapest class (turista); a few other trains take 3¼ to 3¾ hours for €52.

Other daily trains include about 20 to Córdoba (€7 to €9, 45 minutes with AVE trains to 1¼ hours) and three or more each to Granada (€17, three hours) and Málaga (€13, 2½ hours). For Lisbon (€99, 16 hours) you must change at Madrid.

## Getting Around

The airport is 7km from the centre, off the N-IV Córdoba road. **Amarillos Tour** (☎ 902 21 03 17) runs buses to/from Puerta de Jerez in the city at least nine times daily (€2). Bus No C1, in front of Santa Justa train station, follows a clockwise circuit via Avenida de Carlos V, close to Prado de San Sebastián bus station and the city centre; No C2 does the same route anticlockwise. Bus No C4, south down Calle de Arjona from Plaza de Armas bus station, goes to Puerta de Jerez in the centre; returning, take No C3.

# CÓRDOBA

**pop 314,030**

Roman Córdoba was the capital of Baetica province, covering most of Andalucía. Following the Muslim invasion in AD 711 it soon became the effective Islamic capital on the peninsula, a position it held until the Cordoban Caliphate broke up after the death of its ruler Al-Mansour in 1002. Muslim Córdoba at its peak was the most splendid city in Europe and its Mezquita (Mosque) is one of the most magnificent of all Islamic buildings. From the 11th century Córdoba was overshadowed by Seville and in the 13th century both cities fell to the Christians in the Reconquista.

Córdoba's Moorish legacy lives on in the winding alleys, archways and flower-filled patios of the old quarter. The best time to visit is from about mid-April to mid-June, when the weather is warm – but not too warm – and the city stages most of its annual festivals.

## Orientation

Immediately north of the Río Guadalquivir is the old city, a warren of narrow streets surrounding the Mezquita. Around 500m north of here is Plaza de las Tendillas, the main square of the modern city.

## Information

The helpful **regional tourist office** (☎ 957 47 12 35; Calle de Torrijos 10; open 9.30am-6pm Mon-Fri, 10am-7pm Sat, 10am-2pm Sun Mar-Oct; open until 6pm Mon-Fri Nov-Feb) faces the Mezquita. The **municipal tourist office** (☎ 957 20 05 22; Plaza de Judá Leví) is a block west of the Mezquita.

Connect to the Internet at **Ch@t Is** (☎ 957 48 50 24; Calle Claudio Marcelo 15; open 10am-10pm) near the Plaza de las Tendillas for €1.80 an hour.

## Things to See & Do

The inside of the famous **Mezquita** (admission €6.50; open 10am-7.30pm Mon-Sat, 2pm-7.30pm Sun & holidays Apr-Sept; 10am-5.30pm Mon-Sat, 2pm-5.30pm Sun & holidays Oct-Mar), begun by the emir Abd ar-Rahman I in AD 785 and enlarged by subsequent generations, is a mesmerising sequence of two-tier arches amid a thicket of columns. From 1236 the mosque was used as a church

and in the 16th century a cathedral was built right in its centre – somewhat wrecking the effect of the original Muslim building, in many people's opinion.

The Judería, Córdoba's medieval Jewish quarter northwest of the Mezquita, is an intriguing maze of narrow streets and small plazas. Don't miss the beautiful little **Sinagoga** (Calle Judíos; admission €0.30, EU citizens free; open 10am-7pm Tues-Sun), one of Spain's very few surviving medieval synagogues. Nearby are the **Casa Andalusí** (Calle Judíos 12; admission €2.50; open 10.30am-8pm Mon-Sat), a commercialised, yet still interesting, 12th-century house with exhibits on Córdoba's medieval Muslim culture, and the **Museo Taurino** (Bullfighting Museum; Plaza de Maimónides; admission €3; open 10am-2pm & 5.30pm-7.30pm Tues-Sat), celebrating Córdoba's legendary matadors such as El Cordobés and Manolete.

Southwest of the Mezquita stands the **Alcázar de los Reyes Cristianos** (Castle of the Christian Monarchs; admission €2; open 10am-2pm & 5.30pm-7.30pm Tues-Sat), with large and lovely gardens.

The **Museo Arqueológico** (Plaza de Jerónimo Páez 7; admission €1.50, EU citizens free; open 9am-8pm Wed-Sat, 3pm-8pm Tues) is also worth a visit. On the southern side of the river, across the **Puente Romano**, is the **Torre de la Calahorra** (admission €3.50; open 10am-2pm & 4.30pm-8.30pm daily) with a museum highlighting the intellectual achievements of Islamic Córdoba, with excellent models of the Mezquita and Granada's Alhambra.

## Places to Stay

Most people look for lodgings close to the Mezquita. Córdoba's excellent youth hostel, **Albergue Juvenil Córdoba** (☎ 957 29 01 66; bed for under/over 26 €10/13), is perfectly positioned on Plaza de Judá Leví. It has no curfew and breakfast is included in the rates.

Many Córdoba lodgings are built around charming patios. One such place is friendly and central **Hostal Deanes** (☎ 957 29 37 44; fax 957 42 17 23; Calle Deanes 6; singles/doubles €24/31), which has the added plus of a tapas bar styled for the locals, rather than tourists. There are some good places to the east, away from the tourist masses. **Hostal La Fuente** (☎ 957 48 78 27, fax 957 48 78 27; @ terra.es; Calle San Fernando 51;

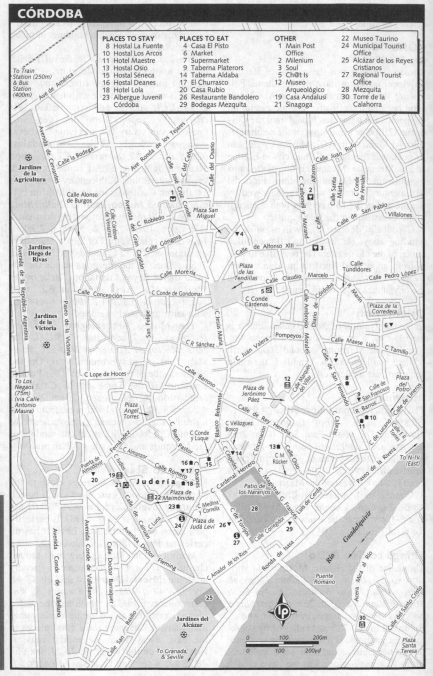

# CÓRDOBA

| PLACES TO STAY | PLACES TO EAT | OTHER | 22 Museo Taurino |
|---|---|---|---|
| 8 Hostal La Fuente | 4 Casa El Pisto | 1 Main Post Office | 24 Municipal Tourist Office |
| 10 Hostal Los Arcos | 6 Market | | 25 Alcázar de los Reyes Cristianos |
| 11 Hotel Maestre | 7 Supermarket | 2 Milenium | |
| 13 Hostal Osio | 9 Taberna Platerors | 3 Soul | 27 Regional Tourist Office |
| 15 Hostal Séneca | 14 Taberna Aldaba | 5 Ch@t Is | |
| 16 Hostal Deanes | 17 El Churrasco | 12 Museo Arqueológico | 28 Mezquita |
| 18 Hotel Lola | 20 Casa Rubio | 19 Casa Andalusí | 30 Torre de la Calahorra |
| 23 Albergue Juvenil Córdoba | 26 Restaurante Bandolero | 21 Sinagoga | |
| | 29 Bodegas Mezquita | | |

singles/doubles €24/42) has compact rooms around a large patio. Pretty **Hostal Osio** (☎/fax 957 48 51 65; e hostalosio@iespana .es; Calle Osio 6; singles/doubles €20/40) has two patios, pine furnishings and good views – try for room 10 overlooking the adjacent convent. **Hostal Los Arcos** (☎ 957 48 56 43 or ☎ 957 486 011; Calle Romero Barros 14; singles/doubles with bath €20/31) has rooms similarly set around a pretty patio. **Hotel Maestre** (☎ 957 47 24 10, fax 957 47 53 95; Calle Romero Barros 4; singles/doubles €29/48) is a small bright hotel with a dash of Spanish chic. The management also runs a cheaper hostal next door.

Just north of the Mezquita, the charming **Hostal Séneca** (☎/fax 957 47 32 34; Calle Conde y Luque 7; singles/doubles without bath €25/32, with bath €31/39) has rooms with rates that include breakfast. It's advisable to phone ahead.

Lord it up at fabulous **Hotel Lola** (☎ 957 20 03 05, fax 957 42 20 63; e hotel@hotelco nencantolola.com; Calle Romero 3; doubles from €108) with its very charming típico Córdoban decor.

## Places to Eat
Handy **Taberna Aldaba** (☎ 957 48 60 06; Velázquez Bosco 8) near the Mezquita has good tapas deals, such as four plus a cerveza for €7. **Restaurante Bandolero** (Calle de Torrijos 6; media raciones €2.50-5), across from the great mosque, provides media raciones and à la carte; expect to pay up to €10 for three courses with drinks. **Casa Rubio** (☎ 957 42 08 53; Puerta Almodóvar 5) in the Judería serves tasty tapas, such as fried aubergine slices with honey, and good main dishes for around €5. **El Churrasco** (☎ 957 29 08 19; Calle Romero 16; set menu €20) is one of Córdoba's very best restaurants. The food is rich and service attentive.

**Taberna Platerors** (☎ 957 47 00 42; Calle de San Francisco 6; raciones €3) is a large patio tavern and restaurant serving solid home-style Córdoban fare. There's a general food **market** on Calle de San Fernando. For gourmet products and olive-oil and fino tasting, head for **Bodegas Mezquita** (Corregidor Luis de la Cerda 13). **Casa El Pisto** (Taberna San Miguel; Plaza San Miguel 1; media raciones €2.50-5; open Mon-Sat) is a particularly atmospheric old watering-hole with a good range of tapas, media ración and ración.

## Entertainment
Córdoba's livelier bars are scattered around the north and west of town. **Casa El Pisto** (see the preceding Places to Eat section) is one. **Soul** (Calle Alfonso XIII 3; open until 3am daily) attracts a studenty/arty crowd and **Milenium** (Calle Alfaros 33) may have live bands a couple of nights a week. **Magister** (Calle Morería) brews its own tasty beer (around €1.50 a glass). Just beyond the Jardines de la Victoria, **Los Negaos** (Calle Magistral Seco de Herrara 6) has weekly concerts; look for the flyers around town.

## Getting There & Away
The train station on Avenida de América, and the **bus station** (☎ 957 40 40 40; Plaza de las Tres Culturas) behind it, are about 1km northwest of Plaza de las Tendillas. At least 10 buses a day run to/from Seville (€8) and five or more to/from Granada (€9.50), Madrid (€10) and Málaga (€9.50), among many other destinations.

About 20 trains a day run to/from Seville (€6.50 to €13, 45 minutes to 1¼ hours). Options to/from Madrid range from several AVEs (€36.50 to €43, 1¾ hours) to a middle-of-the-night estrella service (€23, 6¼ hours).

## GRANADA
pop 243,340
From the 13th to 15th centuries, Granada was capital of the last Muslim kingdom in Spain and the finest city on the peninsula. Today it has the greatest Muslim legacy in the country and one of the most magnificent buildings on the continent – the Alhambra. Southeast of the city, the Sierra Nevada mountain range (mainland Spain's highest and the location of Europe's most southerly ski slopes) and the Alpujarras valleys, with their picturesque, mysterious villages, are well worth exploring if you have time to spare.

## Information
Granada has a **main tourist office** (☎ 958 24 71 28; Plaza de Mariana Pineda 10; open 9.30am-7pm Mon-Fri, 10am-2pm Sat). The more central **regional tourist office** (☎ 958 22 10 22; Corral del Carbón, Calle Libreras 2) opens the same hours but is tiny and usually crowded.

**Navegaweb** (Calle Reyes Católicos 55; open 10am-11pm daily) offers Internet access for a reasonable €1.05 an hour.

# GRANADA

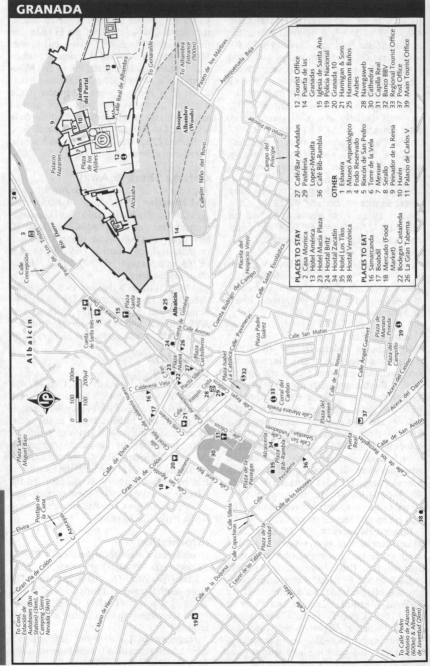

**PLACES TO STAY**
2 Casa Morisca
13 Hotel América
23 Hotel Macía Plaza
24 Hostal Britz
34 Hostal Zacatín
35 Hotel Los Tilos
38 Hostal Verónica

**PLACES TO EAT**
16 Samarcanda
17 Boabdil
18 Mercado (Food Market)
22 Bodegas Castañeda
26 La Gran Taberna
27 Café/Bar Al-Andalus
29 Pastelería Lopez-Mezquita
36 Café Bib-Rambla

**OTHER**
1 Eshavira
3 Museo Arqueológico
4 Fodo Reservado
5 Rincón de San Pedro
6 Torre de la Vela
7 Mexuar
8 Serallo
9 Peinador de la Reina
10 Harén
11 Palacio de Carlos V
12 Tourist Office
14 Puerta de las Granadas
15 Iglesia de Santa Ana
19 Policía Nacional
20 Granada 10
21 Hannigan & Sons
25 Hammam Baños Árabes
28 Navegaweb
30 Cathedral
31 Capilla Real
32 Banco BBV
33 Regional Tourist Office
37 Post Office
39 Main Tourist Office

SPAIN

## Things to See

**Alhambra** One of the greatest accomplishments of Islamic art and architecture, the Alhambra *(adult/EU citizen €7/5; open 8.30am-8pm daily Mar-Apr, 8.30am-6pm daily Nov-Feb)* is simply breathtaking. Much has been written about its fortress, palace, patios and gardens, but nothing can really prepare you for what you will see. It is becoming increasingly essential to book in advance, whatever the time of year. You can reserve via any branch of the Banco Bilbao Viscaya (BBV), including the Granada branch on Plaza Isabel la Católica or by calling ☎ 902 22 44 60 from within Spain and paying by credit card. Alternatively check out **W** www.decompras.bbv.es for choosing the time and day you wish to visit.

The **Alcazaba** is the Alhambra's fortress, dating from the 11th to the 13th centuries. There are spectacular heady views from the tops of the towers. The **Palacio Nazaries** (Nasrid Palace), built for Granada's Muslim rulers in their 13th- to 15th-century heyday, is the centrepiece of the Alhambra. The beauty of its patios and intricacy of its stucco and woodwork, epitomised by the Patio de los Leones (Patio of the Lions) and Sala de las Dos Hermanas (Hall of the Two Sisters), are stunning. Don't miss the **Generalife**, the soul-soothing palace gardens – a great spot to relax and contemplate the Alhambra from a little distance.

**Other Attractions** Explore the narrow, hilly streets of the **Albaicín**, the old Moorish quarter across the river from the Alhambra and head for the **Mirador de San Nicolas** – a steep climb, but worth it for the views. On your way, stop by the **Museo Arqueológico** *(Archaeological Museum; Carrera del Darro)* at the foot of the Albaicín. Another enjoyable area for strolling is around **Plaza de Bib-Rambla**, looking in at the **Capilla Real** *(Royal Chapel; Calle Oficios)*, in which Fernando and Isabel, the Christian conquerors of Granada in 1492, are buried. Next door to the chapel is Granada's **cathedral**, which dates in part from the early 16th century.

Pamper yourself with a visit to the new Arab baths, **Hammam Baños Árabes** *(☎ 958 22 99 78; Calle Santa Ana 16; open 10am-midnight daily)*, which offer a range of treatments and an on-going cultural programme in fabulous surroundings.

## Places to Stay

**Camping Sierra Nevada** *(☎ 958 15 00 62; Avenida de Madrid 107; open year-round)*, 200m from the Estación de Autobuses, is the closest camping ground to the centre. Granada's modern youth hostel, **Albergue de Juventud** *(☎ 958 27 26 38 or ☎ 958 00 29 00; Calle Ramón y Cajal 2; dorm beds for under/over 26 yrs €13/17)* is 1.7km west of the centre and a 600m walk southwest of the train station. Most of the year, bed and breakfast is offered at the listed rate.

Right on bustling Plaza Nueva (well placed for the Alhambra and Albaicín), **Hostal Britz** *(☎/fax 958 22 36 52; Cuesta de Gomérez 1; singles/doubles €17/26.50, doubles with bath €37)* provides bright comfortable rooms, some with balconies. Across the square, the tastefully renovated **Hotel Macía Plaza** *(☎ 958 22 75 36, fax 958 28 55 91; **e** maciaplaza@maciahoteles.com; singles/doubles €42/63)* has very pleasant rooms. For a night to remember, **Casa Morisca** *(☎ 958 22 11 00, fax 958 21 57 96; **e** casamorisca@terra.es; Cuesta de la Victoria 9; doubles from €108)* has Alhambra views and fabulous Moorish-inspired decor with central patio, wooden ceilings and rich tilework.

The Plaza Bib-Rambla area is another with plenty of choice. Good value, no frills **Hotel Los Tilos** *(☎ 958 26 67 12; Plaza Bib-Rambla; singles/doubles with bath & breakfast €41/62)* overlooks a daily flower market and has superb views from a 4th-floor terrace. **Hostal Zacatín** *(☎ 958 22 11 55; Calle Ermita 11; singles/doubles €20/29)* is a hospitable, simple place. South of the cathedral **Hostal Verónica** *(☎ 958 25 81 45; Calle Angel 17; singles/doubles €19.50/35.50)* is small and friendly.

**Hotel América** *(☎ 958 22 74 71, fax 958 22 74 70; Calle Real de Alhambra 53; doubles with breakfast €110; open Mar-Oct)* has a magical position within the walls of the Alhambra; you need to reserve well ahead.

## Places to Eat

Popular **Bodegas Castañeda** *(☎ 958 22 32 22; Calle Almireceros 1)* is an unpretentious local bar-restaurant serving classic tapas and interesting quasi-international fare. Nearby **Café/Bar Al-Andalus** *(☎ 958 22 67 30; Calle Elivira; meat mains around €6)* has good cheap Arabic food, such as felafel in pitta bread and kebabs.

**SPAIN**

La Gran Taberna *(☎ 958 22 88 46; Plaza Nueva 12)* is a traditional-style *bodega* with untraditional inexpensive tapas such as trout with cottage cheese.

Most of the *teterías* (Arabic-style teahouses) are located on a picturesque pedestrian street (Calle Calderería Nueva) west of Plaza Nueva, and are expensive but can be enjoyable. The **Samarcanda** around the corner *(☎ 958 21 00 14; Calle Calderería Vieja 3)* has tasty Lebanese dishes.

**Café Bib-Rambla** *(Plaza Bib-Rambla)* is great for a breakfast of chocolate and *churros* (spiral-shaped doughnuts). **Boabdil** *(☎ 958 22 81 36; Hospital de Peregrines 2; daily menu from €5)* is a kitchen-sink-informal restaurant with good basic food.

For fresh fruit and vegies, there is the large covered **mercado** *(market; Calle San Agustín)*. Indulge in a home-made meringue at **Pastelería Lopez-Mezuíta** *(Reyes Católicos 39)*, one of the best cafés and cake shops in town.

## Entertainment

Nightlife in the Albaicín centres on Carrera del Darro, with several bars and clubs within a few doors of each other, including **Rincón de San Pedro** *(Carrera del Darro 12)* and **Fodo Reservado** *(Santa Inés 4)*, just around the corner.

For foot-tapping live jazz, head for **Eshavira** *(Postigo de la Cuna 2)*, where there is the occasional impromptu flamenco evening. Those suffering from draught-Guinness deprivation should check out **Hannigan & Sons** Irish pub *(Cetti Meriem 1)*. With a tad more sophistication than most, **Granada 10** *(Calle Cárcel Baja)* near the cathedral attracts a smarter set, while **Cool** *(Calle Dr. Guirao)* is the city's largest disco with three massive dance floors.

In the evening, coaches of tourists descend on the Sacromonte caves to see overpriced and contrived flamenco shows. The impromptu flamenco that you find at the annual *ferias* and fiestas is far more rewarding.

## Getting There & Away

Granada's **bus station** *(☎ 958 18 54 80; Carretera de Jáen s/n)* is 3km northwest of the centre. Catch a No 3 bus to reach the centre. At least nine daily buses serve Madrid (€12, five to six hours), and others run to Barcelona, Valencia and destinations across Andalucía.

The **train station** *(☎ 958 27 12 72; Avenida de Andaluces)* is about 1.5km west of the centre. Of the two trains daily to Madrid, one takes 9½ hours overnight (€22), the other six hours (€23). To Seville, there are three trains a day (from €15, three hours). For Málaga and Córdoba, you have to change trains in Bobadilla. There's one train daily to Valencia and Barcelona.

## COSTA DE ALMERÍA

The coast east of Almería city in eastern Andalucía is perhaps the last section of Spain's Mediterranean coast where you can have a beach to yourself (not in high summer, admittedly). This is Spain's sunniest region – even in late March it can be warm enough to strip off and take in the rays.

The most useful **tourist offices** are in Almería (☎ 950 62 11 17), San José (☎ 950 38 02 99) and Mojácar (☎ 950 47 51 62).

### Things to See & Do

The **alcazaba**, an enormous 10th-century Muslim fortress, is the highlight of Almería city. In its heyday the city was more important than Granada.

The best thing about the region is the wonderful coastline and semidesert scenery of the **Cabo de Gata** promontory. All along the 50km coast from El Cabo de Gata village to Agua Amarga, some of the most beautiful and empty beaches on the Mediterranean alternate with precipitous cliffs and scattered villages. Roads or paths run along or close to this whole coastline. The main village is laid-back **San José**, with excellent beaches, such as **Playa de los Genoveses** and **Playa de Mónsul** within 7km heading southwest. **Mojácar**, 30km north of Agua Amarga, is a white town of Muslim origin, with cube-shaped houses perched on a hill 2km from the coast. Although a long resort strip, Mojácar Playa is still a pretty place and it's not hard to spend time here, especially if you fancy a livelier summer beach scene than Cabo de Gata offers.

### Places to Stay & Eat

**Almería** The oldest hotel in town and still family-run, **La Perla** *(☎ 950 23 88 77, fax 950 27 58 16; Plaza del Carmen 7; doubles from €48)* still exudes a certain old-world charm.

**Cabo de Gata** In high summer it's a good idea to ring ahead about accommodation, as some places fill up. In San José there is

**Camping Tau** (☎ 950 38 01 66; open Apr-Sept) and the friendly non-HI youth hostel **Albergue Juvenil de San José** (☎ 950 38 03 53; Calle Montemar s/n; bunk beds €8.50; open Apr-Sept). **Hostal Bahía** (☎ 950 38 03 07; Calle Correo; singles/doubles €35/42) has attractive rooms with bath. **Restaurante El Emigrante** across the road does good fish and meat mains for around €6 to €9.

**Mojácar** The better-value places are mostly up in the old town. **Hostal La Esquinica** (☎ 950 47 50 09; Calle Cano 1; singles/doubles €20/24) is cheap and cheerful. Charming **Hostal Mamabel's** (☎ 950 47 24 48; Calle Embajadores 5; doubles from €60) has eight big rooms with sea views and bath (one circular!), and a good restaurant. Newer **Hotel Simon** (☎ 950 47 87 69, fax 950 47 87 69; e hotelsimon@interbook.net; Cruce de la Fuente; doubles with bath from €40) has a slick, high standard. **Restaurante El Viento del Desierto** (Plaza del Frontón; mains €5-6) is good value and serves the best steamed mussels in town. **Tito's Beach Bar** (☎ 950 61 50 30; Paseo del Mediterráneo 2) has good music and an excellent Mexican restaurant with garden Margarita Bar next door.

### Getting There & Away
Almería has an international and domestic airport and is accessible by bus and train from Madrid, Granada and Seville, and by bus only from Málaga, Valencia and Barcelona. Buses run from Almería bus station to El Cabo de Gata village and (except nonsummer Sundays) to San José. Mojácar can be reached by bus from Almeriá, Murcia, Granada and Madrid.

## MÁLAGA
pop 534,200
Although Málaga is still largely ignored by the sun and sand seekers who head straight for the Costa del Sol, the city is well worth a visit. There's plenty to see and savour here, ranging from some Moorish monuments to arguably the best fried fish in Spain.

### Orientation
Málaga is situated at the mouth of the Guadalmedina River. The central thoroughfare is the Alameda Principal, which continues eastward as the tree-lined Paseo del Parque and westward as Avenida de Andalucía.

### Information
The **main tourist office** (☎ 952 21 34 45; Pasaje Chinitas 4; open 10am-6.30pm Mon-Fri, 10am-2pm Sat) is located in one of the city's most historic areas. The **municipal tourist office** (☎ 952 60 44 10; Avenida de Cervantes 1) is near the park. There are additional information kiosks near the train station and in the centre. **Ciber Málaga Café** (Avenida de Andalucía 11) is open from 10am until late and offers Internet access for €2.50 an hour.

### Things to See & Do
The historic core of the city lies around the cathedral: a web of narrow cobbled streets lined with faded ochre-coloured buildings, interspersed with small squares, old-fashioned shops, tapas bars and cafés.

The city's history is colourfully diverse. A **Roman amphitheatre** is currently under excavation but can be plainly viewed near the Alcazaba's main entrance on Calle Alcazabilla. The **Alcazaba** fortress and palace (☎ 952 21 60 05; admission free; open 9am-8pm Tues-Sun summer, 9am-7pm Tues-Sun winter) dates from the 8th century and has recently undergone extensive restoration. The cherry on the cake is the hill-top **Castillo Gibralfaro** (admission free; open 9am-7pm daily). It's quite a hike, but well worth it for the views. The **cathedral** (admission €1.80; open Mon-Sat 10am-6.45pm) has a peculiar lopsided look with one unfinished tower but is being restored and the entrance is magnificent. Check it out from one of the pavement cafés across the way. After a succession of delays, and a fire, the long-awaited **Picasso Museum** is scheduled to open in October 2003. Meanwhile, art buffs can make do with the house where Picasso was born, **Casa Natal** (☎ 952 06 02 15; Plaza de la Merced 15; open 11am-2pm & 5pm-8pm Mon-Sat, Sun morning).

### Places to Stay
Málaga is short on accommodation, so book ahead. The picturesque small **Hotel Venecía** (☎ 952 21 36 36; Alameda Principal 9; singles/doubles €58/72) is in a great central location. A cheaper option is **Pensión Córdoba** (☎ 952 21 44 69; Calle Bolsa 9; singles/doubles without bath €18/28), a humble friendly place. **Hotel Carlos V** (☎ 952 21 51 20; Calle Císter 10; singles/doubles €24/46)

SPAIN

near the cathedral has been refurbished. The smartest by far is **Hotel Larios** (*☎ 952 22 22 00; Marquées de Larios 2; doubles from €81*) with its steel, grey and beige interior.

## Places to Eat

For affordable eats, head for the tapas bars. A good place to start is the spit 'n' sawdust **Antigua Casa de Guardia** (*☎ 952 21 46 80; Alameda Principal 18*), the oldest bar in town; try the fresh prawns. The nearby **Restaurante El Compá** (*☎ 952 06 07 10; Calle La Bolsa 7*) is fronted by an excellent tapas bar, while the restaurant specialises in rice and fish dishes. Málaga's most famous tapas bar is the tiny **Bar Logueno** (*Marín García s/n*), where tapas start at €1.50 and there are 75-plus varieties to choose from. For that special seafood moment, **El Morata** (*☎ 952 29 26 45; Calle Paseo Pedregal 13*) is just one of several excellent fish restaurants in the Pedregalejo area, 4.5km east of the centre.

## Entertainment

Serious party time starts late around Plaza de la Merced and Calle Granada. **ZZ Pub** (*Calle Tejón y Rodriguez*) has live music on Monday and Thursday. **Warner Bar** (*Plaza de los Martinez*) is good for a little frenetic air punching, while **Doctor Funk** (*Calle José Denis Belgrano 19*), just off Calle Granada, is a heaving reggae club shoe-horned into a small smoky space. There are several *teterías* (Arabic-style teahouses) in town, including **Barrakis** (*Calle Horno*) near the Plaza de la Constitucíon, housed in a former 14th-century Arab bakery.

## Getting There & Away

Málaga airport has a good range of domestic as well as international flights. Trains and buses run every half-hour from the airport to the city centre The city is also linked by train and bus to all major Spanish centres. The bus and train stations are around the corner from each other, 1km west of the city centre.

## TORREMOLINOS
### pop 43,610

Torremolinos is trying hard to shed its image as a spam-and-chips resort by pumping money into landscaping and more upmarket tourist facilities and restaurants. Surprisingly, there is still a relatively untainted old part of town with local bars frequented by old men who play dominoes and drink *anís*.

The **tourist office** (*☎ 952 37 95 12; Plaza de la Independencia; open 9am-1.30pm Mon-Fri*) is in the centre. From July to September there are additional tourism booths on the beachfront.

## Things to See & Do

If you're travelling family-style, there's no shortage of laid-on entertainment. **Tivoli World** (*☎ 952 44 28 48; Arroyo de la Miel; admission €4; open 10am-6pm daily*) is the Costa del Sol's biggest theme park with tiny-tot rides, as well as concerts, restaurants and bars. A better than average aquarium, **Sea Life** (*☎ 952 56 01 50; Benalmádena Port; adult/child €8/5; open 10am-8pm*) has an educational 'touch pool' for young children. Other attractions around town include an equestrian show, birds of prey exhibition, water park and various sea-sports. Pick up the respective flyers at the tourist office.

## Places to Stay & Eat

For basic comforts in the old part of town, **Hostal Castilla** (*☎ 952 38 10 50; Calle Manila 3; singles/doubles with shared bath €18/36*) is good value. Nearer to the beach, **Hotel Cabello** (*☎ 952 38 45 05; Calle Chiriva; singles/doubles €55/60*) is located in the former fishing village of La Carihuela. The best seafood restaurants are here, too, including **El Roqueo** (*☎ 91 238 49 46; Carmen 35*) – try the *gambas pil-pil* (prawns in chilli sauce). Back in town, a rare vegetarian restaurant, **Albahaca** (*☎ 952 05 12 06; Calle Doña Maria Barrabino 11*), offers a four-course menu for €6.

## Getting There & Away

Trains to/from Málaga and Fuengirola run every half-hour from 6am to 10.30pm stopping at the airport. The bus station is on Calle Hoyo and there are services to all the major Costa del Sol resorts, as well as to Ronda, Cádiz and Granada, several times a day.

## FUENGIROLA
### pop 50,260

Fuengirola is a speedy 18km via autovia from Torremolinos and, despite the annual tide of tourists who come here to sun-flop on the beach, remains essentially a Spanish working town. It is not a pretty place, having suffered from greedy developers and political corruption, but the beach is pleasant enough, and there's a vast choice of shops, restaurants and bars.

Fuengirola's annual fair at the beginning of October is one of the biggest and best on the Costa del Sol. Aside from then, accommodation is plentiful, although the faceless high-rise hotels on the beachfront tend to be block-booked in advance by tour companies. Hostales include the spick-and-span **Hostal Italia** (☎ 952 47 4193, fax 952 47 11 40; Calle de la Cruz 1; singles/doubles €39/26) near the main plaza, and the new **Hostal Santa Fe** (☎ 952 47 41 81; singles/doubles/triples €21/30/36) in Los Boliches. There are plenty of budget restaurants and bars here, mainly crammed into the pedestrian quarter, east of the church square. Bar **Tu Casa** (☎ 952 46 3332; Calle Marconi 22) attracts a lively crowd of resident and visiting expats and holds regular pool tournaments.

### Getting There & Away
There are half-hourly trains to Málaga, with stops including Torremolinos and the airport. There are also regular buses to Marbella, Mijas and major Andalucían cities leaving the main bus station on Calle Alfonso X111.

## MARBELLA
**pop 110,850**
Marbella is this Costa's classiest resort. The inherent wealth glitters most brightly along the Golden Mile, a tiara of star-studded clubs, restaurants and hotels that stretches from Marbella to Puerto Banus, where black-tinted-window Mercs slide along a quayside of jaw-dropping luxury yachts.

The main **tourist office** is on Glorieta Fontanilla (☎ 952 77 14 42; open 9.30am-9pm Mon-Fri, 10am-2pm Sat). A second **tourist office** (☎ 952 82 35 50; open 9am-9pm Mon-Fr, 9am-2pm Sat) is located on the northern side of Plaza de los Naranjos.

### Things to See & Do
The old part of Marbella around the Plaza de los Naranjos is very pretty, duly reflected by the drink prices at the pavement cafés. Nearby on the Plaza de la Iglesia is the 16th-century **Iglesia de Nuestra Señora de la Encarnación** and, a few paces east, the **Museo del Grabado Español Contemporáneo** (☎ 952 82 50 35; Calle Hospital Bazán; admission €2.50; open 10am-2pm & 5.30-8.30pm Mon-Fri) houses works by Picasso, Miró and Dalí. There's a

**Bonsai Museum** (☎ 952 86 29 26; adult/child €3/2.50; open 10.30am-1.30pm & 4pm-7pm daily) in Parque de la Represa.

### Places to Stay & Eat
The old town has several reasonable hostales. Cheery **Hostal La Luna** (☎ 952 82 57 78; Calle Luna 7; singles/doubles €30/40) has balconied rooms and a pretty patio. Equally good value is **Hostal La Pilarica** (☎ 952 77 42 52; Calle San Cristóbal 31; singles/doubles €21/36). Definitely in the splash-your-cash category is the **Castillo de Monda** (☎ 952 45 71 42, fax 952 45 73 36; doubles from €110), a restored Moorish castle that crowns the whitewashed *pueblo* of Monda, 14km north of Marbella.

The self-important but excellent **Finca Besaya** (☎ 952 86 56 30; Urb. Rio Verde Alto; dinner only) has a classy fixed price menu for €42. For more affordable eats, head for the tapas bars in the old town. **Quernecia** (Calle Tetuan 9) is always packed with locals – a good sign. Tapas cost from €1.50, and include small taster dishes of paella and couscous.

### Getting There & Away
The **bus station** (☎ 952 76 44 00; Calle Trapiche) is a good half-hour hike from the hub of town, although some buses still stop in Calle Ricardo Soriano in the centre. Buses from the station run a regular service to Málaga, Fuengirola, La Línea, Algeciras, Cádiz, Seville and Granada.

## RONDA
**pop 34,210**
One of the prettiest and most historic towns in Andalucía, Ronda is a world apart from the nearby Costa del Sol. The town straddles the savagely deep El Tajo gorge, at the heart of some lovely hill country that's dotted with white villages.

The **regional tourist office** (☎ 952 87 12 72; Plaza de España 1) has lots of interesting information on the area.

### Things to See & Do
Ronda is a pleasure to wander around, but during the day you'll have to contend with busloads of day-trippers from the coast.

The **Plaza de Toros** (1785) is considered the home of bullfighting and is a mecca for aficionados; inside is the small but fascinating **Museo Taurino** (admission €2.50).

SPAIN

Vertiginous cliff-top views open out from the nearby Alameda del Tajo park.

The 18th-century **Puente Nuevo** (New Bridge), an amazing feat of engineering, crosses the gorge to the originally Muslim old town (La Ciudad), which is littered with ancient churches, monuments and palaces. At the **Casa del Rey Moro** (Calle Santo Domingo 17; admission €4; open daily), you can climb down a Muslim-era stairway cut inside the rock right to the bottom of the gorge. Try not to miss the **Iglesia de Santa María la Mayor**, a church whose tower was once the minaret of a mosque; the **Museo del Bandolero** (Calle Armiñán 29), dedicated to the banditry for which central Andalucía was once renowned; or the beautiful **Baños Arabes** (Arab Baths; open Wed-Sun).

## Places to Stay & Eat

**Camping El Sur** (☎ 952 87 59 39) is a good small site 2km out on the Algeciras road.

Pleasant **Hotel Morales** (☎/fax 952 87 15 38; Calle Sevilla 51; singles/doubles €21/39) has attractive rooms with bath and also friendly informative owners.

**Alavera de los Baños** (☎/fax 952 87 91 43; e alavera@ctv.es; singles/doubles with breakfast €42/58) is a small German-run hotel next to the 13th-century Arab baths. There are some excellent old-style tapas bars among the nondescript international restaurants, including **Marisquería Paco** (Plaza del Socorro), good for seafood, and **Bodega La Giralda** (Calle Nueva 19), a great spot for wine downed with olives, cheese and chorizo tapas.

## Getting There & Away

Several buses run daily to Seville (€7.50, 2½ hours), Málaga (€6.50, two hours) and Cádiz. One goes to Algeciras (€6) Monday to Friday. The bus station is on Plaza Concepción García Redondo.

A few direct trains go to Granada (€11, 2¼ hours), Málaga (€7, two hours), Algeciras, Córdoba and Madrid. For Seville, and further trains to/from the above destinations, change at Bobadilla or Antequera. The station is on Avenida de Andalucía.

## ALGECIRAS
pop 105,070

Algeciras, an unattractive industrial and fishing town between Tarifa and Gibraltar, is the major port linking Spain with Morocco. Keep your wits about you, and ignore offers from the legions of money-changers, drug-pushers and ticket-hawkers. The **tourist office** (☎ 956 57 26 36; Calle Juan de la Cierva; open 9am-2pm Mon-Fri) is near the ferry port.

If you need a room, there's loads of budget accommodation in the streets behind Avenida de la Marina, the street the port is on. Beware early-hours market noise, though. Friendly **Hostal González** (☎ 956 65 28 43; Calle José Santacana 7; singles/doubles €15/24) has good, clean rooms with bath.

## Getting There & Away

**Bus** About 400m inland from the port, **Comes** (Calle San Bernardo) runs frequent buses to/from La Línea, and several daily to/from Tarifa, Cádiz and Seville. **Portillo** (Avenida Virgen del Carmen 15), 200m north of the port, runs buses to/from Málaga, the Costa del Sol and Granada. **Bacoma**, inside the port, runs buses to/from Barcelona, Valencia, France, Germany and Holland.

**Train** Direct daily trains run to/from Madrid and Granada, passing through Ronda and through Bobadilla, where you can change for Málaga, Córdoba and Seville.

**Boat** Frequent ferries to/from Tangier, in Morocco, and Ceuta, the Spanish enclave on the Moroccan coast, are operated **EuroFerrys** (☎ 956 65 11 78), **Trasmediterránea** (☎ 902 45 46 45) and other companies. Usually at least 20 daily go to Tangier and 40 or more to Ceuta. From late June to September there are ferries almost around the clock. Buy your ticket in the port or at agencies on Avenida de la Marina – prices are the same. To Tangier, adults pay €14 one way (2½ hours). To Ceuta, it's €13 by ferry (1½ hour). Cars cost €69. **Buquebus** (☎ 902 41 42 42) crosses to Ceuta in about 30 minutes for €17.50 (cars €58.50).

## CÁDIZ, TARIFA & THE COSTA DE LA LUZ

The historic port of Cádiz has a well-aged atmosphere with backstreets flanked by magnificent 18th-century buildings interspersed with elegant squares fringed by lofty palm trees. The best time to visit is during the February **Carnaval**, close to Rio in terms of outrageous exuberance. Ninety kilometres to its southeast is the attractive, laid-back and windy Tarifa, which is perched at continental Europe's most southerly point and with a lively windsurfing scene. Between the two places stretch the long, sandy beaches of the Costa de la Luz (Coast of Light), where stuck-in-a-time-warp villages, such as Los Caños de Meca, Zahara de los Atunes and Bolonia have fairly plentiful mid-range accommodation – they're unfortunately a little hard to reach without your own wheels.

### Things to See & Do

**Cádiz** On attractive Plaza de Mina the **Museo de Cádiz** *(open 9am-2pm Wed-Sat, 2.30pm-8pm Tues, 9.30am-2.30pm Sun)* has a magnificent collection of archaeological remains, as well as a fine art collection. The **Castillo de Santa Catalina** *(open daily)* dates from 1598 and the large 18th-century **cathedral** *(admission €1.50; open 9am-8pm Wed-Sat, 2.30pm-8pm Tues, 9.30am-2.30pm Sun)* is the city's most striking landmark. The city's lively central market is on Plaza de las Flores, the former site of a Phoenician temple. From Cádiz you can easily visit the historic sherry-making towns of El Puerto de Santa María and Jerez de la Frontera by bus or train (or boat, to El Puerto).

**Tarifa** A 10km-long beach much beloved of windsurfers, **Playa de los Lances** stretches northwest from Tarifa. For **windsurf rental** and classes try places along here, such as **Club Mistral** at the Hurricane Hotel or **Spin Out Surf Base** in front of Camping Torre de la Peña II (€48 for two hours' tuition). In Tarifa town, enjoy exploring the winding old streets and visit **Castillo de Guzmán**, the castle dating from the 10th century.

### Places to Stay & Eat

Cádiz's excellent independent youth hostel **Quo Qádiz** *(☎/fax 956 22 19 39; Calle Diego Arias 1; beds per person from €6)* has accommodation with rates that include breakfast. **Hostal Bahía** *(☎ 956 25 90 61; Calle Plocia 5; singles/doubles €41/52)* is a winner, just off the bustling main square. Plaza de San Juan de Dios and the Plaza de Mina areas are full of varied places to eat.

In Tarifa, a good choice is bright and central **Hostal Alborada** *(☎ 956 68 11 40; Calle San José 52; doubles with bath €37.50)*. There are plenty of eating options on and near the central Calle Sancho IV El Bravo.

### Getting There & Away

The main bus station is on Plaza de Hispanidad, near Plaza de España. There are regular buses to/from Algeciras (€8, 2¾ hours), Seville (€9, 1½ hours), Cordoba (€15, 4½ hours), Málaga (€14.50, five hours), as well as to Ronda and Tarifa. Up to 15 daily trains chuff to/from Seville (€8, two hours), with others heading for Córdoba and beyond.

# Gibraltar

**pop 27,030**

The British colony of Gibraltar occupies a huge lump of limestone, almost 5km long and over 1km wide, near the mouth of the Mediterranean. Gibraltar has certainly had a rocky history: it was the bridgehead for the Muslim invasion of Spain in AD 711 and Castile didn't finally wrest it from the Muslims until 1462. In 1704 an Anglo-Dutch fleet captured Gibraltar. Spain gave up military attempts to regain it from Britain after the failure of the Great Siege of 1779–83, but after 300 years of concentrated Britishness, both Britain and Spain are now talking about joint Anglo-Spanish sovereignty – much to the ire of the Gibraltarians.

Gibraltar is like 1960s Britain on a sunny day. It's old-fashioned and safe, attracting coachloads of day trippers from the Costa del Sol who come to be reassured by the helmet-wearing policemen, double-decker buses, bangers and mash, and Marks & Spencer.

### Information

To enter Gibraltar you need a passport or EU national identity card. EU, US, Canada, Australia, New Zealand, Israel, South Africa and Singapore passport-holders are among those who do *not* need visitor's visas for Gibraltar, but anyone who needs a visa for Spain should have at least a double-entry Spanish visa if they intend to return to Spain from Gibraltar.

Gibraltar has a helpful tourist office right at the border. There is also a **main tourist office** *(☎ 45000; Duke of Kent House, Cathedral Square; open 9am-5.30pm Mon-Fri)* and another office located at Casemates *(☎ 74982; open 9.30am-5.30pm Mon-Fri, 10am-4pm Sat & Sun)*.

The currency is the Gibraltar pound or pound sterling. Change any unspent Gibraltar pounds before you leave. You can always use

**SPAIN**

euros. At the time of writing, the exchange rate is €1 to £0.70.

To phone Gibraltar from Spain, the telephone code is ☎ 9567; from other countries dial the international access code, then ☎ 350 and the local number.

## Things to See & Do

Central Gibraltar is nothing special – you could almost be in Bletchley or Bradford – but the **Gibraltar Museum** *(Bomb House Lane; admission £2; open 10am-6pm Mon-Fri, 10am-2pm Sat)* has an interesting historical, architectural and military collection, and includes a Muslim-era bathhouse.

The large **Upper Rock Nature Reserve** *(admission £7/1.50 adult/vehicle; open 9.30am-7pm daily)*, covering most of the upper rock, has spectacular views and several interesting spots to visit.

The rock's most famous inhabitants are its colony of **Barbary macaques**, the only wild primates (apart from *Homo sapiens* football supporters) in Europe. Some of these hang around the **Apes' Den** near the middle cable-car station, others can often be seen at the top station or Great Siege Tunnels.

Other attractions include **St Michael's Cave**, a large natural grotto renowned for its stalagmites and stalactites and the **Great Siege Tunnels**, a series of galleries hewn from the rock by the British during the Great Siege to provide new gun emplacements. Worth a stop on the way down to the town from here are the **Gibraltar, a City under Siege** exhibition and the **Tower of Homage**, part of Gibraltar's 14th-century Muslim castle.

From about April to September, several boats make daily **dolphin-watching trips** of about two hours (£12 to £15 per person) from Watergardens Quay or adjacent Marina Bay.

## Places to Stay

**Emile Youth Hostel** *(☎ 51106; Montagu Bastion, Line Wall Rd; dorm beds £12)* has 43 places in two- to eight-person rooms and rates include a continental breakfast.

**Queen's Hotel** *(☎ 74000; 1 Boyd St; singles/doubles with bath £39/46)* offers a 20% student discount. All rates include English breakfast. **Cannon Hotel** *(☎/fax 51711; 9 Cannon Lane; singles/doubles £42/48)* has decent rooms with bath. Rates include an English breakfast.

## Places to Eat

Most pubs do British pub meals. The **Star Bar** *(Parliament Lane)* has a traditional Sunday roast for £4.95. At **The Market Tavern** *(1 Waterport Market Place)* you can have a choice of four different breakfasts (including Scottish and vegetarian).

For a restaurant meal, the chic **House of Sacarello** *(57 Irish Town; specials £5.75-6.10)* is a good bet, with tasty soups around £2 and some excellent daily specials. The Indian food at **Maharajah** *(5 Tuckey's Lane)* is spicy and good.

## Getting There & Away

**GB Airways** *(☎ 79300, in the UK ☎ 0345-222111)* flies daily to/from London. Return fares from London range from around £175 to £400, depending on the season.

There are no regular buses to Gibraltar, but La Línea bus station is only a five-minute walk from the border.

To take a car into Gibraltar you need an insurance certificate, registration document, nationality plate and driving licence. You do *not* have to pay a fee, despite what con artists might try to tell you. Many park their vehicles in La Línea and walk across the border.

## Getting Around

The frequent bus Nos 3, 9 and 10 run direct from the border into town.

All of Gibraltar can be covered on foot, but there are other options. Weather permitting, the **cable car** *(£5/7 one way/return)* leaves its lower station on Red Sands Rd every few minutes from 9.30am to 5.15pm Monday to Saturday. For the Apes' Den, disembark at the middle station.

# Turkey

Turkey is Asia's foothold in Europe, the only country that bridges both continents. It has thousands of kilometres of Mediterranean coastline and the tourism boom of the 1990s put it on the map for everyone from package holidaymakers to villa-renters.

With a famously hospitable people, hundreds of spectacular historic ruins, varied countryside and excellent food, Turkey has lots to offer, especially if you take in a few of the more off-the-beaten-track destinations.

## Facts about Turkey

### HISTORY

By 7000 BC a Neolithic city, one of the oldest ever recorded, was already established at Çatal Höyük, near Konya. The greatest of the early civilisations of Anatolia (Asian Turkey) was that of the Hittites, a force to be reckoned with from 2000 to 1200 BC with their capital at Hattuşa, east of Ankara.

After the collapse of the Hittite empire, Anatolia splintered into several small states and it wasn't until the Graeco-Roman period that parts of the country were reunited. Later, Christianity spread through Anatolia, carried by the apostle Paul, a native of Tarsus (near Adana).

### Byzantine Empire & the Crusades

In AD 330 the Roman emperor Constantine founded a new imperial city at Byzantium (modern İstanbul). Renamed Constantinople, this strategic city became the capital of the Eastern Roman Empire and was the centre of the Byzantine Empire for 1000 years. During the European Dark Ages, the Byzantine Empire kept alive the flame of western culture although it was occasionally threatened by the empires of the east (Persians, Arabs, Turks) and west (the Christian powers of Europe).

The Byzantine Empire's decline came with the arrival of the Seljuk Turks and their defeat of the Byzantine forces at Manzikert, near Lake Van, in August 1071. The Seljuks overran most of Anatolia, and established a provincial capital at Konya. Their domains included today's Turkey, Iran and Iraq.

With significantly reduced territory, the Byzantines endeavoured to protect Constan-

## At a Glance

- **İstanbul** – architectural treasures, bustling Grand Bazaar, sailing up the Bosphorus
- **Çanakkale** – historical Troy and haunting Gallipoli
- **Behramkale** – beautiful hilltop village, the ruins of the Temple of Athena and sea views of the island of Lesbos
- **Selçuk** – splendid ruins of Ephesus, the ancient capital of Roman Asia
- **Dalyan** – elegant Lycian tombs, the ruined city of Kaunos, the Sultaniye hot springs

| | |
|---|---|
| **Capital** | Ankara |
| **Population** | 68 million |
| **Official Language** | Turkish |
| **Currency** | Turkish lira |
| **Time** | GMT/UTC+0200 |
| **Country Phone Code** | ☎ 90 |

tinople and reclaim Anatolia but the Fourth Crusade (1202–04) proved disastrous for them when a combined Venetian and crusader force took and plundered Constantinople. They eventually regained the ravaged city in 1261.

### Ottoman Empire

A Mongol invasion of the late 1200s put an end to Seljuk power, but new small Turkish states soon arose in western Anatolia. One,

TURKEY

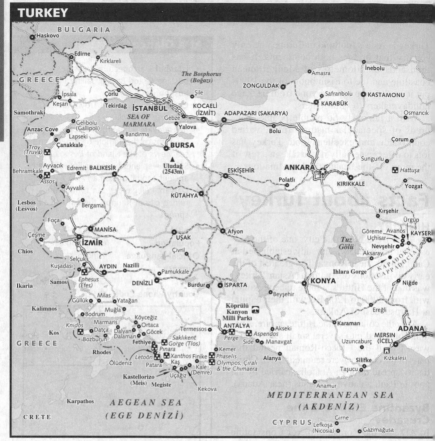

headed by Osman (1258–1326), grew into the Ottoman Empire, and in 1453 Constantinople finally fell to the Ottoman sultan Mehmet II (the Conqueror).

A century later, under Süleyman the Magnificent, the Ottoman Empire reached the peak of its power, spreading deep into Europe, Asia and North Africa. Ottoman success was based on military expansion. When their march westwards was stalled at Vienna in 1683, the rot set in and by the 19th century the great European powers had begun to covet the sultan's vast domains.

Nationalist ideas swept through Europe after the French Revolution, and in 1829 the Greeks won their independence, followed by the Serbs, the Romanians and the Bulgarians. Italy took Tripolitania in North Africa from

Turkey, and in 1913 the Ottomans lost both Albania and Macedonia.

The Turks emerged from WWI stripped of their last non-Turkish provinces – Syria, Palestine, Mesopotamia (Iraq) and Arabia. Most of Anatolia itself was to be parcelled out to the victorious Europeans, leaving the Turks virtually nothing.

## Mustafa Kemal Atatürk

At this low point, Mustafa Kemal, the father of modern Turkey, took over. Atatürk, as he was later called, had made his name by repelling the Anzacs in their heroic but futile attempt to capture Gallipoli during WWI.

Rallying the remnants of the Turkish army during the Turkish War of Independence that followed WWI, he pushed the last of the weak

**TURKEY**

Ottoman rulers aside and out-manoeuvred the Allied forces. The Turks finally won in 1923 by pushing the invading Greeks into the sea at Smyrna (İzmir). In the ensuing population exchange over a million Greeks left Turkey and nearly half a million Turks moved in.

After renegotiation of the WWI treaties a new Turkish republic, reduced to Anatolia and part of Thrace, was born. Atatürk then embarked on a rapid modernisation programme: establishing a secular democracy, introducing the Latin script and European dress, and adopting equal rights for women (at least in theory). The capital was also moved from İstanbul to Ankara. Such sweeping changes did not come easily and some of the battles (eg, over women's head covering) are still being fought today.

Relations with Greece improved in 1930 but were soured again after WWII by the conflict over Cyprus, particularly after the Greek-led anti-Makarios coup and subsequent Turkish invasion of the island in 1974. (For more information see the Cyprus chapter, earlier in this book.)

## Modern Turkey

Since Atatürk's death, Turkey has experienced three military coups and a lot of political turbulence. During the 1980s and 90s it was also wracked by the conflict with the PKK (Kurdistan Workers Party), led by Abdullah Öcalan, which wanted the creation of a Kurdish state in Turkey's southeastern corner. This conflict led to an estimated 35,000 deaths and huge population shifts inside the country. In 1999 Öcalan was sentenced to death, a sentence which was being reviewed by the European Court of Human Rights at the time of writing.

In February 2001 the Turkish economy collapsed in spectacular fashion. One of the few sectors of the economy to stay in good shape was tourism, which was then knocked for six by the events of 11 September and the ensuing wariness about travel. However, Turkey is not only strategically positioned but also the only Muslim member-state of NATO, so by late 2001 the IMF was pumping in funds to refloat the economy. It remains to be seen how quickly tourism can recover.

## GEOGRAPHY

The Dardanelles, the Sea of Marmara and the Bosphorus strait divide Turkey into Asian and European parts but Eastern Thrace (European Turkey) makes up only 3% of the 788,695-sq-km land area. The remaining 97% is Anatolia, a vast plateau rising eastward towards the Caucasus Mountains. Turkey's 6000km-long coastline is almost entirely given over to tourism except where mountains come too close to the sea to squeeze in even a tiny hotel.

## CLIMATE

The Aegean and Mediterranean coasts have mild, rainy winters and hot, dry summers. In İstanbul, the summer temperatures average around 28°C to 30°C; the winters are chilly but usually above freezing, with rain and perhaps a dusting of snow. The Anatolian plateau can be boiling hot (although less humid than the coast) in summer and freezing in winter.

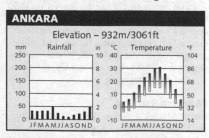

### ANKARA
Elevation – 932m/3061ft

## ECOLOGY & ENVIRONMENT

Turkey's embryonic environmental movement is making slow progress, and you may well be shocked by the amount of discarded litter and half-built properties disfiguring the west in particular.

Recently, the biggest environmental rows have been over Turkey's programme for building large dams. One such scheme that would have drowned the historic town of Hasankeyf in southeastern Turkey seems to have been derailed, but white-water rafting on the Çoruh River around Yusufeli in northeastern Turkey looks likely to vanish for the sake of a dam.

## FLORA & FAUNA

Turkey has a network of national parks protecting some of its most spectacular scenery and, with it, the bird and animal life. But the speed of development in the west is rapidly eliminating all the remaining wildlife; you'll see many more birds, for example, in eastern Turkey than in the west.

## GOVERNMENT & POLITICS

In theory Turkey is a multiparty democracy on the Western European model, although in practice it has proved more of a semidemocracy with the military wielding considerable power behind the scenes. There have been 57 governments since the republic's creation in 1923.

During the 1990s no one political party was able to win absolute control of parliament in elections based on proportional representation.

In 1999 an unlikely coalition government made up of representatives of the right-wing MHP (National Unity Party), the right-of-centre ANAP (Motherland Party) and the left-wing DSP (Democratic Socialist Party) came to power. To most people's amazement it managed to cling to power despite presiding over the worst economic disaster in the Republic's history. At the time of writing the prime minister was veteran left-winger Bulent Ecevit, while the president was Ahmet Necdet Sezer.

In June 2002 ill health prevented the elderly prime minister from working effectively. With support ebbing away from him, he was finally forced to call elections for November 2002. The popular Foreign Minister İsmael Cem defected from the DSP to set up a new political party focused on getting Turkey into the European Union as quickly as possible. However, opinion polls suggested that the new AK Party, a religious party dominated by Recep Tayyip Erdoğan, was likely to win the majority of votes. It remains to be seen what will be the outcome of what could be a hugely important election.

## ECONOMY

In 2001 the Turkish economy imploded in Argentinian-style. The value of the Turkish lira slumped from TL650,000 to US$1 to TL1,600,000 although it has since stabilised at around TL1,300,000. An IMF restructuring programme involving fixed exchange rates had to be abandoned and another hastily drawn up. Over a million people lost their jobs, the economy contracted by 9.4% (the worst such contraction since WWII), and there is little to suggest it has since recovered.

The tragedy of 11 September also hit the vital tourism industry, and rumours of possible war with Iraq continued to cast a shadow over it at the time of writing.

## POPULATION & PEOPLE

Turkey's roughly 68 million people are predominantly Turks, with a large Kurdish minority (perhaps 12 million) and much smaller groups of Laz, Hemsin, Arabs, Jews, Greeks and Armenians. The Laz and Hemsin people are natives of the northeastern corner of Turkey on the Black Sea coast, while Arab influence is strongest in the Hatay area abutting Syria. Southeastern Turkey is pretty solidly Kurdish, although the problems of the last 20 years have led many to head west in search of a better life.

## ARTS

Islam discourages images of humans or animals, so the Ottomans produced little sculpture or portraiture. Instead artists concentrated on calligraphy, architecture, tiles, jewellery, carpet-making, textiles and glass-making.

Ottoman literature and court music were mostly religious and both can sound pompous and lugubrious to Western ears. Folk music was livelier and has since undergone a major revival. Some modern Turkish 'pop' music draws on folk music traditions.

As with all else, Atatürk changed Turkey's cultural picture, encouraging painting, sculpture, Western music (he loved opera), dance and drama. Recently Ottoman arts like papermarbling and Karagöz shadow-puppet plays have been enjoying a resurgence, seen as traditions worthy of preservation. It goes without saying that carpet-weaving continues to be a Turkish passion.

## SOCIETY & CONDUCT

As a result of Atatürk's reforms, republican Turkey has largely adapted to a modern Westernised lifestyle, at least on the surface. In the big cities and coastal resorts you will not feel much need to adapt to fit in. In smaller towns and villages, however, you may find people warier and more conservative. There is also a small but growing group of 'born again' Muslims who may make you feel uncomfortable, especially about alcohol, skimpy clothing and anything pertaining to religion.

To keep everyone smiling, try to remember that public drunkenness is not particularly acceptable in Turkey and that most people prefer women to keep their legs, upper arms and neckline covered except on the beach. Be particularly careful when going into a mosque: women should cover their heads and shoulders; both men and women should cover their legs and remove their shoes.

## RELIGION

Turkey is 99% Muslim, overwhelmingly Sunni, with small groups of Shiites and larger groups of Alevis mainly in the east. Most Turks are fairly relaxed about their religion; many women uncover their heads and many men drink alcohol (although almost no one touches pork).

## LANGUAGE

Turkish is the official language and almost everyone understands it. It was been written in the Latin script since Atatürk rejected Arabic in 1928. In big cities and tourist areas, many locals will speak passable English, French, German or Japanese – or all of these.

See the Language Chapter at the back of this book for pronunciation guidelines and useful words and phrases.

# Facts for the Visitor

## HIGHLIGHTS

The must-see sights of İstanbul include Topkapı Palace, Aya Sofya (Hagia Sofia), the Blue Mosque, the Turkish & Islamic Arts Museum and the Basilica Cistern.

Heading down the Aegean from İstanbul, top places to stay include Çanakkale for the Gallipoli battlefields and the ruins of Troy; and Selçuk, for excursions to the ruins at Ephesus, Priene, Miletus and Didyma. Along

TURKEY

the Mediterranean coast, particularly inviting small resorts include **Dalyan, Kaş** and **Olympos**, perfect bases for exploring local Graeco-Roman and Lycian archaeological sites.

Turkey's **best beaches** are at Pamucak (near Ephesus), Ölüdeniz, Bodrum, Patara, Antalya, Side and Alanya.

Inland, Turkey's premier attraction is the spectacular landscape of **Cappadocia** where the village of Göreme makes a popular base.

## SUGGESTED ITINERARIES

Most people come primarily to see İstanbul, the Aegean and Mediterranean coasts and Cappadocia. With limited time, consider these itineraries:

**Two days**
Explore İstanbul or Selçuk/Ephesus.
**One week**
Tour İstanbul and the Aegean coast to Bodrum or Marmaris.
**Two weeks**
Continue along the coast to Antalya or Alanya, then return to İstanbul via Cappadocia.
**One month**
Follow the above itinerary, spending longer in each destination and relaxing for four days on a *gület* (yacht).

## PLANNING
## When to Go

In general, spring (April/May) and autumn (September/October) have the most pleasant weather. The heat and crowds of July and August can be pretty unbearable, especially in İstanbul.

## Maps

The excellent free map of Turkey provided by the tourist offices shows the location of most attractions. The Bartholomew Euromap of Turkey in two sheets at 1:800,000, is also excellent but many locally produced maps are not worth the paper they're printed on.

## What to Bring

It's worth packing mosquito repellent (from April to September); sunblock; sunglasses; a universal sink plug; sandals; and reading matter. Women should bring their favoured sanitary protection.

## TOURIST OFFICES
## Local Tourist Offices

Local tourist offices can rarely do much more than hand out brochures and sketch maps.

## Tourist Offices Abroad

Turkey has tourist offices in the following countries:

**Australia** (☎ 02-9223 3055, ℮ turkish@ozemail.com.au) Room 17, Level 3, 428 George St, Sydney NSW 2000
**Canada** (☎ 613-230 8654) Suite 801, Constitution Square, 360 Albert St, Ottawa Ontario K1R 7X7
**UK** (☎ 020-7629 7771, ℮ TTO@cityscape.co.uk) 1st floor, 170–73 Piccadilly, London W1V 9DD
**USA** (☎ 212-687 2194, ℮ tourny@idt.net) 821 UN Plaza, New York, NY 10017

## VISAS & DOCUMENTS

Nationals of the following countries don't need a visa to visit Turkey for up to three months: Belgium, Denmark, Finland, France, Germany, the Netherlands, Japan, New Zealand, Norway, Sweden and Switzerland. Although nationals of Australia, Austria, Canada, Greece, Ireland, Israel, Italy, Portugal, Spain, the UK and the USA need a visa, this is just a sticker which you buy on arrival at the airport or at an overland border; join the queue to buy your visa before the one for immigration. At the time of writing British citizens paid UK£10, Australians US$20 and citizens of Canada and the USA a hefty US$45. You *must* pay in hard currency cash.

The standard visa is valid for three months and usually allows for multiple entries.

## Student & Youth Cards

Fewer museums seem to be giving discounts to holders of International Student Identity Cards (ISICs) although it's probably still worth brandishing them hopefully.

## EMBASSIES & CONSULATES
## Turkish Embassies Abroad

Turkey has embassies in the following countries:

**Australia** (☎ 02-6295 0227) 60 Mugga Way, Red Hill ACT 2603
**Canada** (☎ 613-789 4044) 197 Wurtemburg St, Ottawa, Ontario KIN 8L9
**France** (☎ 01 53 92 71)16 Ave de Lamballe, 75016 Paris
**Germany** (☎ 49-228 95 38 30) Utestr 47, 53179 Bonn 2
**Ireland** (☎ 1-668 5240) 11 Clyde Rd, Ballsbridge, Dublin 4
**Netherlands** (☎ 70-360 4912) Jan Evenstraat 2514 BS, The Hague

New Zealand (☎ 4-472 1290) 15–17 Murphy St, Level 8, Wellington
UK (☎ 020-7393 0202) 43 Belgrave Square, London SW1X 8PA
USA (☎ 202-659 8200) 1714 Massachusetts Ave, NW Washington, DC 20036

## Foreign Consulates in Turkey

Most embassies are in Ankara but countries with consulates in İstanbul (☎ code 0212) include:

Australia (☎ 257 7050) Tepecik Yolu 58, Etiler, İstanbul
France (☎ 293 2460) İstiklal Caddesi 8, Taksim, İstanbul
Germany (☎ 334 6100) İnönü Caddesi 16-18, Taksim, İstanbul
Greece (☎ 245 0596) Ağahamam Turnacıbaşı Sokak 32, Beyoğlu, İstanbul
Ireland (☎ 246 6025) Cumhuriyet Caddesi 26/A, Harbiye, İstanbul
Netherlands (☎ 251 5030) İstiklal Caddesi 393, Beyoğlu, İstanbul
New Zealand (☎ 327 2211) Yeşilgimen Sokak 75, İhlamur, Beşiktaş, İstanbul
UK (☎ 293 7546) Meşrutiyet Caddesi 34, Beyoğlu, İstanbul
USA (☎ 229 0075) Şehit Halil İbrahim Caddesi 23, İstiniye, İstanbul

## CUSTOMS

Two hundred cigarettes, 50 cigars or 200g of tobacco, one litre of liquor and four litres of wine can be imported duty-free. Duty-free items can be bought both on arrival and departure from Turkey's international airports.

It's strictly illegal to buy, sell or export antiquities. Customs officers spot-check luggage and will want proof that you have permission before letting you leave with an antique carpet.

## MONEY
### Currency

The Turkish lira (TL) comes in coins of 25,000, 50,000, 100,000 and 250,000 lira, and notes (bills) of 100,000, 250,000, 500,000, one million, five million, 10 million and 20 million lira. Hopes that the zeros could be lopped off these unwieldy denominations once inflation was under control have been abandoned in the wake of the economic crisis. Prices in this section are quoted in more stable US dollars.

### Exchange Rates

During 2001 the Turkish lira devalued steadily in line with inflation. At the time of writing, however, it had regained some of its value. Check exchange rates shortly before your visit and be prepared for fluctuations.

| country | unit | | Turkish lira |
| --- | --- | --- | --- |
| Australia | A$1 | = | TL908,100 |
| Canada | C$1 | = | TL1,050,800 |
| euro zone | €1 | = | TL1,648,200 |
| Japan | ¥100 | = | TL13,600 |
| New Zealand | NZ$1 | = | TL792,800 |
| UK | UK£1 | = | TL2,621,700 |
| USA | US$1 | = | TL1,670,000 |

### Exchanging Money

It's easy to change major currencies in most exchange offices, post offices (PTTs), shops and hotels although banks may make heavier weather of it. Cashing even major travellers cheques is less easy (post offices in tourist areas are a good bet) and the exchange rate is usually slightly lower. Places that don't charge a commission usually offer a worse exchange rate instead.

Major foreign currencies are readily accepted in shops, hotels and restaurants in main tourist areas.

**Credit Cards & ATMs** Visa and MasterCard/Access are quite widely accepted by hotels, restaurants, carpet shops etc although not by *pensions* and local restaurants. You can also get cash advances on these cards. American Express (AmEx) cards are rarely useful.

Automated Teller Machines (ATMs) readily dispense Turkish lira to Visa, MasterCard, Cirrus, Maestro and Eurocard-holders; there's hardly a town that lacks a machine. Provided that your home banking card only requires a four-digit PIN number, it's perfectly possible to get around Turkey with nothing else, provided you remember to draw out money in the towns to tide you through the villages and keep some cash in reserve.

### Security

Although Turkey is one of Europe's safest countries, you must still take precautions. Wear a money belt under your clothing and beware of pickpockets and purse-snatchers on buses, at markets and other crowded places. Be especially careful in İstanbul and when staying in hostels. See also Dangers & Annoyances, later in this section.

## Costs

Turkey is still relatively cheap, especially away from İstanbul and the coast. It's still possible to travel on as little as US$15 to US$20 per person per day if you use buses or trains, stay in *pensions* and eat only one restaurant meal daily. For US$20 to US$35 per day you can upgrade to one- and two-star hotels, eat most meals in restaurants and manage some of the heftier monument admission fees. On more than US$50 per person per day you can luxuriate in three- and four-star hotels, take the occasional flight and dine out constantly. Costs are lowest in small towns off the tourist trail, but Cappadocia, Selçuk, Pamukkale and Olympos still offer bargain prices.

Unfortunately since the economic crisis, frequent price increases have become a fact of life in Turkey. The prices given here should be treated as guidelines only.

## Tipping & Bargaining

Leave waiters and bath attendants around 10% of the bill; a hotel porter US$0.50 to US$1; and a cinema usher a few coins. You might round up your taxi fare but there's no need to tip *dolmuş* (minibus) drivers.

It's wise to bargain for souvenirs. Even if the establishment has set prices, it's still worth trying if you're buying several items or shopping in the low season. In tourist areas hotel prices tend to be fixed; elsewhere it's worth bargaining if you visit between October and late May or plan to stay more than one night.

## Taxes & Refunds

Value-added tax (VAT) is included in the price of most items and services: look for signs saying *KDV dahil* (VAT included). Some hotels and shops discount the price if you agree to forego the official receipt.

If you buy an expensive item, such as a carpet, ask the shopkeeper for a *KDV iade özel fatura* (special VAT refund receipt). Get it stamped as you clear customs, then try to get a refund at a bank in the airport departure lounge. Alternatively, you can mail the receipt and one distant day a cheque may conceivably arrive.

## POST & COMMUNICATIONS
## Post

Turkish *postanes* (post offices) are indicated by black-on-yellow 'PTT' signs. Postcards to Europe cost US$0.30; to Australia, New Zealand and the USA US$0.45. Letters to Europe cost US$0.45; to Australia, New Zealand and the USA US$0.55.

If you have mail addressed to you care of poste restante in a major city, the address should include Merkez Postane (central post office) or the name of the local post office at which you wish to retrieve it.

## Telephone

Phoning home from Turkey is surprisingly expensive, mainly because of taxes; it costs around UK£1 to phone Britain for one minute, US$3 to phone the USA and even more to call Australia. The cheapest rates operate from 10.30pm to 7am and from 7am on Sunday to 7am on Monday; it's also slightly cheaper to phone on Saturday or after 8pm on weekdays. Hotels often levy some exorbitant surcharges, even on local calls. Wherever possible, try to make collect (reverse-charge) calls, although this facility is not currently available to New Zealand.

Everywhere in Turkey has an area telephone code; we list these beneath the relevant place names in this chapter. To call from one town to the next you will need the area code including the initial '0'. Note that İstanbul has two codes: ☎ 0212 for the European side and ☎ 0216 for the Asian side.

When calling from outside Turkey, dial ☎ 00 and then the country code (☎ 90), followed by the area code (minus the zero) and the seven-digit subscriber number.

These days almost all Türk Telekom's public telephones require telephone cards which can be bought at telephone centres or at some shops. If you're only going to make one call, it's easier to look for a booth saying 'köntörlü telefon' where the cost of your call will be metered.

The Turks just love mobile *(cep)* phones. However, note that calling a mobile costs roughly three times the cost of calling a land line. If you set up a roaming facility with your home phone provider you should be able to connect your own mobile to the Turkcell or Telsim network. At the time of writing US-bought mobile phones couldn't be used in Turkey.

## Fax

It's easiest and cheapest to send and receive faxes at your hotel. Telephone centres have faxes but will tie you up in paperwork.

## Email & Internet Access

Turkish post offices offer Internet access but you're better off using one of the ubiquitous Internet cafés. Many *pensions* will also let you use their Internet connection for a small fee.

## DIGITAL RESOURCES

The Turkey Home Page (Ⓦ www.turkey.org/) has news, arts and cultural features, lists of coming events and links to dozens of Turkey-related websites. The *Turkish Daily News* site (Ⓦ www.turkishdailynews.com) is also useful. For public transport info (but no fares), try Ⓦ www.neredennereye.com.

## BOOKS
### Lonely Planet

Lonely Planet's *Turkey* offers details about the entire country. LP also publishes a *Turkish phrasebook* and a *Turkey World Food* guide.

### Travel

Jeremy Scal's *A Fez of the Heart* and Tim Kelsey's *Dervish* are very readable accounts of recent travels in Turkey.

### History & Politics

For a good factual account of the making of modern Turkey look for *Turkey Unveiled* by Nicole and Hugh Pope.

## NEWSPAPERS & MAGAZINES

The dull-as-ditchwater *Turkish Daily News* is the local English-language paper. In major tourist areas you'll find many day-old European and US newspapers and magazines.

## RADIO & TV

Most hotels and *pensions* in tourist areas subscribe to cable or satellite TV services that offer programmes in English, French and German, as well as all the myriad Turkish channels.

TRT (Turkish Radio & Television) provides short news broadcasts in English on the radio each morning and evening.

## TIME

Turkey is on Eastern European Time, two hours ahead of GMT/UTC. When it's noon in Turkey, it's 11am in Paris and Frankfurt, 10am in London, 5am in New York and 2am in Los Angeles. In summer/winter it's 5/7pm in Perth and Hong Kong, 7/9pm in Sydney and 9/11pm in Auckland. From late March to late September, Turkey observes daylight-saving time when clocks are turned ahead one hour.

## LAUNDRY

Laundrettes are beginning to appear in the larger cities, but most people get their washing done in their hotel or *pension* for around US$3.50 a load.

## TOILETS

Although most hotels and public facilities have familiar Western toilets, you'll also see enough traditional hole-in-the-ground models to be able to join in the 'healthy' debate over which is the more hygienic. The Turkish custom is to wash yourself with water from a jug or a pipe attached to the toilet using the left hand. Doesn't appeal? Then always carry toilet paper and don't forget to place it in the bin provided to avoid inadvertently flooding the premises.

Almost all public toilets require payment of about US$0.20.

## WOMEN TRAVELLERS

Things may be changing but Turkish society is still basically sexually segregated, especially once you get away from the big cities and tourist resorts. Although younger Turks are questioning the old ways and some women now hold positions of authority (there's even been a woman prime minister), foreign women still find themselves being hassled, supposedly because Turkish men are unaccustomed to brazen Western ways. Mostly it's just silliness but serious assaults do occasionally occur. Travelling with a male usually improves matters, as does travelling with another female.

Turkish women ignore men who speak to them in the street. Wearing a headscarf, a skirt that comes below the knees, a wedding ring and sunglasses makes you less conspicuous. Away from beach resorts you should certainly avoid skimpy tops and brief shorts.

## GAY & LESBIAN TRAVELLERS

Although not uncommon in a culture that traditionally separates men and women, overt homosexuality is not socially acceptable except in a few small pockets of İstanbul and some resorts. Laws prohibiting 'lewd behaviour' can be turned against homosexuals if required, so be discreet. Some *hammams* are known to be gay meeting places.

TURKEY

For more information, contact Turkey's own gay and lesbian support group, LAMBDA İstanbul, on @ lambda@lambdaistanbul.org.

## DISABLED TRAVELLERS
Turkey is a nightmare for disabled travellers. Obstacles lurk everywhere; ramps, wide doorways and properly equipped toilets are almost unheard-of. Crossing most streets is for the young and agile only; everyone else does so at their peril. You must plan your trip very carefully and budget to patronise mostly luxury hotels, restaurants and transport.

## TRAVEL WITH CHILDREN
Turks adore children so bringing yours along should prove a bonus provided you're careful about hygiene. Disposable nappies are readily available; not so pre-prepared baby food. Cappadocia, in particular, can be recommended as a paradise for children of all ages who generally love the opportunities offered by the troglodyte lifestyle.

## SENIOR TRAVELLERS
Age should prove no barrier to enjoying a holiday in Turkey, a country where elderly people are held in great respect and whose prime minister is in his late-70s. Some museums and other attractions offer discounted admission to people aged over 60.

## DANGERS & ANNOYANCES
Although Turkey is one of the safest countries in the region, the number of ne'er-do-wells seems to be on the increase so take precautions. Wear a money belt under your clothing and be wary of pickpockets on buses, at markets and other crowded places. Keep an eye out for anyone suspicious lurking near ATM machines. And remember that a Western passport can be a valuable commodity.

### Emergency Services
The national emergency number is ☎ 155 for police, ☎ 156 for Jandarma (Gendarmerie), ☎ 112 for ambulance, ☎ 141 for a doctor (after hours) and ☎ 110 in the case of fire.

You're likely to be connected to Turkish-speaking operators only if you ring any of these numbers, so your best bet is to find an English-speaking local, such as hotel staff, to act as an intermediary.

In İstanbul, single men are sometimes lured to a bar (often near İstiklal Caddesi) by new Turkish 'friends'. The man is then made to pay an outrageous bill. Drugging is also becoming a serious problem, especially for lone men. Sometimes the person in the seat next to you on the bus buys you a drink, slips a drug into it and then makes off with your luggage. However, it can also happen in hostels, *pensions* and especially in bars so be a tad wary of whom you befriend, especially when you're new to the country.

## BUSINESS HOURS
Most banks, museums and offices are open 8.30am to noon and 1.30pm to 5pm Monday to Friday. In tourist areas food and souvenir shops are often open virtually around the clock.

## PUBLIC HOLIDAYS & SPECIAL EVENTS
National Turkish holidays include:

**New Year's Day** 1 January
**Children's Day** 23 April
**Youth & Sports Day** 19 May
**Victory Day** 30 August
**Republic Day** 29 October
**Atatürk's Death** 10 November

Turkey also celebrates all the main Islamic holidays of which the most important are the month-long **Ramazan** and, two months later, **Kurban Bayramı**. Since these holidays are celebrated according to the Muslim lunar calendar, they take place around 11 days earlier each year. For the next few years both holidays will occur during the winter.

On **Anzac Day** (25 April) huge crowds descend on Çanakkale to attend the dawn services in memory of the failed Anzac landings of WWI. In June crowds assemble to watch oil-covered men wrestling in a field at Kırkpınar near Edirne. The International İstanbul Music Festival in late June/early July takes place in a variety of atmospheric venues around town. Then from 10 to 17 December the dervishes whirl at the Mevlâna Festival in Konya.

## ACTIVITIES
Popular activities include hiking and trekking in the Kaçkar Mountains and other national parks. With the opening of the 500km Lycian Way from Fethiye to Antalya, Turkey also has its first waymarked national trail.

All sorts of water sports, including diving, water-skiing, rafting and kayaking, are available in the Aegean and Mediterranean resorts. You can also try tandem paragliding at Ölüdeniz (for details see that section under The Mediterranean Coast, later in this chapter).

Skiing is becoming more popular, with the best facilities at Uludağ, near Bursa, and on Mt Erciyes, near Kayseri.

Those of a lazier disposition may want to take a *gület* (yacht) trip along the coast, stopping off to swim in bays along the way.

The laziest 'activity' of all consists of paying a visit to a *hammam*, or Turkish bath, where you can get yourself scrubbed and massaged for a fraction of what it would cost in most Western countries. The sexes were always segregated in traditional Turkish baths and this remains the case if you frequent one of the inland baths. Along the coast, however, mixed bathing has become the norm – along with inflated prices – in response to the perceived preferences of Westerners.

## LANGUAGE COURSES

A great place to learn Turkish is **Dilmer** (☎ 252 5154; *İnönü Caddesi, Prof Dr Tarık Zafer Tunaya Sokak 18, Taksim, İstanbul*). One and two month courses are available (morning, afternoon and evening) at a variety of levels. Another possibility is **International House** (☎ 282 9064; *Nispetiye Caddesi, Güvercin Durağı, Erdölen İşhani 38, Kat 1, Levent, İstanbul*).

## WORK

The most lucrative work (up to US$200 a week) involves nannying for the wealthy city elite, a job mainly offered to English-speaking women who must be prepared for long hours and demanding employers. Otherwise there is some work available for qualified teachers of English (whose employers should be able to arrange a work permit).

Most travellers work illegally for subsistence wages in *pensions*, bars and carpet shops, leaving the country every three months to renew their visas.

## ACCOMMODATION
### Camping

Camping facilities are dotted about Turkey, although not perhaps as frequently as you might hope. Some hotels and *pensions* will also let you camp in their grounds and use their facilities for a small fee (US$2 to US$4). A few resorts boast well-equipped European-style camp sites.

## Hostels

Given that *pensions* are so cheap, Turkey has no real hostel network, although a few places now claim to be affiliated to the IYHA. Some are real hostels with dormitories, others little different from the cheapest *pensions*.

## Pensions & Hotels

Tourist areas usually boast lots of small family-run *pensions*, some of them offering self-catering facilities, and most offering services such as tours and book exchanges.

There are also plenty of cheap hotels, although the very cheapest will be too basic for many tastes and not really suitable for lone women.

The price of most hotels is fixed by the local authorities and should be on display in the reception area; often you'll be offered a cheaper price although it should *never* be more. One- and two-star hotels (US$15 to US$40 a double) offer reasonable comfort and private bathrooms at excellent prices; three-star places can be quite luxurious.

## FOOD

It is not without reason that Turkish food is regarded as one of the world's greatest cuisines. No-one need fear going hungry.

Kebabs are, of course, the mainstay of restaurant meals and you'll find *lokantas* (restaurants) selling a wide range of kebabs everywhere you go. Try the ubiquitous *durum döner kebab* – lamb packed onto a vertical revolving spit, sliced off and tucked into bread and rolled up in *pide* bread. Laid on a bed of *pide* bread and with a side serving of yogurt, *döner kebab* becomes delicious *İskender kebab*, a primarily lunch-time delicacy.

For a quick, cheap fill you could hardly better a freshly-cooked *pide* or Turkish pizza topped with cheese or meat.

For vegetarians a meal of *mezes* (hors d'oeuvres) can be an excellent way to ensure a varied diet. Most restaurants will be able to rustle up at least *beyaz peynir* (white sheep's milk cheese), *börek* (flaky pastry stuffed with white cheese and parsley), *kuru fasulye* (dried beans) and *patlıcan tava* (fried aubergine).

In this chapter, the suggested price of a 'meal' should be taken to cover a soup or starter followed by a main dish and a soft drink. For more information on Turkish cuisine, look out for Lonely Planet's *World Food Turkey* guide.

## DRINKS
The Turkish liquor of choice is *rakı*, a fiery aniseed drink like Greek *ouzo*; do as the Turks do and cut it by half with water if you don't want to suffer ill effects. Turkish wine, both red and white, is worth the occasional splurge. You can buy Tuborg or Efes Pilsen beers everywhere, although outside the resorts you may need to find a Tekel store to buy wine.

Not a day will pass without your being offered a glass of *çay*. Turkish tea is grown on the eastern Black Sea coast and served in tiny tulip-shaped glasses with copious quantities of sugar. If it's too strong for you, ask for the milder but wholly chemical *elma çay* (apple tea).

If offered a tiny cup of traditional Turkish *kahve* (coffee), order it *sade* (no sugar), *orta* (medium-sweet) or *çok şekerli* (very sweet) and take care not to swig the grains.

Good bottled water is sold everywhere.

## ENTERTAINMENT
İstanbul, Ankara and İzmir have opera, symphony, ballet and theatre, and most Turkish towns have at least one cinema, often showing films in the original language. In summer, resorts like Bodrum throb to the sound of innumerable clubs and discos.

## SPECTATOR SPORTS
Turks are fanatical football-lovers (soccer) and if you can get to a match – especially with one of İstanbul's biggies, Galatasaray, Fenerbahçe or Beşiktaş – you're guaranteed to have a good time.

## SHOPPING
Clothes, jewellery, handicrafts, woollen socks, leather apparel, carpets, tiles, meerschaum pipes, brass and copperware can all be good buys provided you bargain well.

# Getting There & Away

You can get in and out of Turkey across the borders of eight countries.

## AIR
The cheapest air fares are almost always to İstanbul; to reach other Turkish airports, even Ankara, you usually have to transit at İstanbul.

Turkish Airlines and European carriers fly to İstanbul from all the European capitals. One-way full-fare tickets from London to İstanbul can cost as much as US$425; it's usually advisable to buy an excursion ticket (from US$300) even if you don't plan to use the return portion. If you're planning a two- or three-week stay, it's also worth inquiring about cheaper charter flights.

Turkish Airlines offers flights to İstanbul from New York from about US$625/649 one way/return. From Los Angeles fares start at US$757/740 one way/return.

The cheapest flights to İstanbul from Sydney or Melbourne (Australia) are on Egypt Air via Singapore and Cairo; one-way/return fares start at A$985/1695. Japanese Airlines, Malaysian Airlines and also Singapore Airlines offer fairly competitive fares.

Fares to İstanbul from Auckland (New Zealand) start from NZ$1440/2400 one way/return with Air New Zealand.

Turkish Airlines offers daily nonstop flights to İstanbul from Athens (1½ hours) and Tel Aviv (two hours) as well as to Bangkok, Karachi, Singapore, Tokyo and many Middle Eastern cities.

The US$12 departure tax is included in the price of your air ticket.

## LAND
### Western Europe
At the time of writing there were no direct trains between Western Europe and Turkey. Instead one train a day heads from İstanbul to Bucharest (17 hours) and then onto Budapest (31 hours), with connections to elsewhere in Europe. There have been reports of long delays and hassle, especially of women, at the Bulgarian border.

Despite the appeal of train journeys, getting to Turkey overland is usually cheaper and faster by bus. Several Turkish bus lines, including Ulusoy, Varan and Bosfor offer reliable, comfortable services between İstanbul and major European cities like Frankfurt, Munich and Vienna for around US$70 one way. These services travel via Greece and the ferry to Italy, thereby avoiding any hassle at the Bulgarian border.

## Greece

Most people travel between Greece and Turkey by boat via the Aegean islands (see the following Sea section for more details). If you're planning to travel from the mainland, note that the daily Thessaloniki–İstanbul passenger train takes 16 to 18 hours to cover the 850km, with a change of train (and a delay) at the border. The bus does the journey in greater comfort in little more than half the time.

## SEA

**Turkish Maritime Lines** (TML; ☎ 464 8864) runs car ferries from İzmir to Venice weekly from May to mid-October. The fares start at US$160 one way with reclining seat; mid-price cabins are priced from US$340 per person.

Private ferries link Turkey's Aegean coast and the Greek islands, which are in turn linked by air or boat to Athens. Services are usually daily in summer, several times a week in spring and autumn and perhaps just once a week in winter. In summer expect daily boats connecting Lesbos–Ayvalık, Chios–Çeşme, Samos–Kuşadası, Kos–Bodrum, Rhodes–Marmaris, Rhodes–Bodrum, Rhodes–Fethiye and Kastellorizo–Kaş. The cheapest and most frequent ferries are Samos–Kuşadası and Rhodes–Marmaris; the most expensive and hassley is the Lesbos–Ayvalık ferry.

There are daily services to Turkish (Northern) Cyprus from Taşucu (near Silifke), and less frequent services from Alanya.

# Getting Around

## AIR

**Turkish Airlines** (Türk Hava Yolları, THY) links all the country's major cities, but domestic flights fill up rapidly so try to book in advance. Smoking is prohibited on domestic flights.

A one-way ticket from İstanbul to Ankara (50 minutes) or Kayseri (for Cappadocia; one hour) costs US$76.

## BUS

Turkish buses go just about everywhere cheaply, comfortably and without permitting any smoking. Kamil Koç, Metro, Ulusoy and Varan are the premium companies, offering greater speed and comfort for slightly higher fares. They have a better safety record than most companies, an important consideration in a country where traffic accidents claim hundreds of lives every year.

A town's *otogar* (bus terminal) is often on the outskirts, but the bigger bus companies usually have free *servis* minibuses to ferry you into the centre and back again. Most *otogar*s have an *emanet* (left-luggage room) with a small charge. Don't leave valuables in unlocked luggage.

Local routes are usually operated by midibuses or *dolmuşes*, minibuses that sometimes run to a timetable but more usually set off when they're full.

## Fez Bus

Fez Bus (☎ 516 9024; W www.feztravel.com; Aybıyık Caddesi, Sultanahmet, İstanbul) is a 'hop-on, hop-off' bus service linking the main resorts of the Aegean and the Mediterranean with İstanbul and Cappadocia. The Turkish Delight pass (covering İstanbul–Gallipoli Bergama–Selçuk–Köceğiz–Fethiye–Olympos–Cappadocia–İstanbul) costs from US$174.

## TRAIN

Turkish State Railways (TCDD) has a hard time competing with the long-distance buses for speed and comfort although trains are usually a bit cheaper than buses. Unfortunately, the stations are not always in the city centre. Only the special express trains, such as the *Fatih* and *Başkent*, are faster than the bus.

*Ekspres* and *mototren* services often have only one class; if they have 2nd class it costs 30% less. Return fares are cheaper than two singles. These trains are a little slower than buses, but they are sometimes more pleasant because you can get up and move around. On *yolcu* and *posta* trains you could grow old and die before reaching your destination.

Sleeping-car trains linking İstanbul, İzmir and Ankara are good value; the cheaper *örtülü kuşetli* carriages have four, simple beds per compartment.

## CAR & MOTORCYCLE

**Türkiye Turing ve Otomobil Kurumu** (TTOK, Turkish Touring & Automobile Association; ☎ 0212-282 8140; Oto Sanayi Sitesi Yanı, Seyrantepe, 4 Levent, İstanbul) can help with questions and problems.

Carnets (permits to import cars) are not required for stays of less than three months, but details of your car are stamped in your passport to ensure it leaves the country with you. An International Driving Permit is handy if your licence is from a country likely to seem obscure to a Turkish police officer.

Car mechanical services are easy to find, reasonably competent and cheap. The most common and so most easily serviced models are Fiat, Renault, Mercedes, Volkswagen and Toyota.

In the major cities plan to park your car and use public transport – traffic is terrible and parking almost impossible.

Turkey has a very high motor-vehicle accident rate, so always drive defensively and avoid driving at night.

### Rental

All the main car rental companies are represented in İstanbul, Ankara and İzmir, but car hire in Turkey is pricey (budget around US$35 a day) and driving is hazardous.

### BICYCLE

The countryside is varied and beautiful, and road surfaces acceptable if a bit rough. Turkish drivers regard cyclists as a curiosity and/ or a nuisance.

### HITCHING

Because of the extensive, cheap bus system, hitching is not common in Turkey. Women should never hitchhike, especially alone; if you absolutely must do it, do it with another woman or (preferably) a man, don't accept a ride in a vehicle that has only men in it, and expect some hassles.

### BOAT

**Turkish Maritime Lines** (☎ TML; 0212-249 9222; information ☎ 244 0207; Rıhtım Caddesi, Karaköy, İstanbul) operates a car ferry service year-round between İstanbul and İzmir, departing İstanbul every Friday afternoon and arriving the next morning in İzmir. In the other direction it departs from İzmir every Sunday afternoon, arriving in İstanbul on Monday morning. Fares range from US$17 for a reclining seat to US$164 for a luxury cabin, plus US$28 for a car.

### ORGANISED TOURS

Most independent travellers find tours around Turkey expensive, especially since many of them park you in a carpet shop for an hour or so. In general, it's faster and cheaper to make

your own travel arrangements. Be particularly careful if booking a tour out of İstanbul; some of these are ludicrously expensive compared with doing it yourself especially if you end up travelling on the same bus services and staying in the same *pensions*.

Visitors who want to see the Gallipoli battlefield sites in a hurry may need to take a tour; see the Çanakkale section under The Aegean Coast later in this chapter for details. If you're on a whistlestop tour of Cappadocia you may also need to take a tour to see all the sights quickly; see Göreme in the Cappadocia section later in this chapter for details of some good local operators.

# İstanbul

☎ 0212 (European side), ☎ 0216 (Asian side)
• pop 12 million

With 3000 years of colourful history, İstanbul, formerly Constantinople, has plenty to show for itself. This city is more than a step back in time; after dark, a plethora of bars and fine restaurants will satiate the most energetic of souls. İstanbul has theatres and galleries – and it's a shopper's paradise.

## HISTORY

Late in the 2nd century AD, the Roman Empire conquered the small city-state of Byzantium, which was renamed Constantinople in AD 330 after Emperor Constantine moved his capital there.

The city walls kept out barbarians for centuries as the western part of the Roman Empire collapsed before invasions of Goths, Vandals and Huns. When Constantinople fell for the first time it was to the misguided Fourth Crusade in 1204. Bent on pillage, the Crusaders abandoned their dreams of Jerusalem, instead ravaging Constantinople's churches, shipping out the art and melting down the silver and gold. By the time the Byzantines regained the city in 1261 it was a mere shadow of its former glory.

The Ottoman Turks attacked in 1314, but then withdrew. Finally, in 1453, after a long and bitter siege, the walls were breached just north of Topkapı Gate. Mehmet II, the Conqueror, marched to Aya Sofya (Hagia Sofia) and converted the church into a mosque. Apart from a tiny enclave on the Black Sea, the Byzantine Empire had ended.

As capital of the Ottoman Empire the city experienced a new golden age. During the glittering reign of Süleyman the Magnificent (1520–66), the city was graced with many beautiful new buildings. Even during the empire's long decline, the capital retained much of its charm. Occupied by Allied forces after WWI, it came to be thought of as the decadent capital of the sultans, just as Atatürk's armies were shaping a new republican state.

When the Turkish Republic was proclaimed in 1923, Ankara became the new capital. Nevertheless, İstanbul remains the centre for business, finance, journalism and the arts.

## ORIENTATION

The Bosphorus strait, between the Black and Marmara Seas, divides Europe from Asia. European İstanbul is divided by the Haliç (Golden Horn) estuary into the 'newer' quarter of Beyoğlu in the north and Old İstanbul in the south; the Galata Bridge spans the two.

Sultanahmet, the heart of Old İstanbul, has many tourist sites, cheap hotels as well as restaurants. Divan Yolu runs west through Sultanahmet, past the Grand Bazaar (Kapalı Çarşı) and İstanbul University to Aksaray, a major traffic intersection.

Eminönü, north of Sultanahmet at the southern end of Galata Bridge, is the terminus of a tram and many bus lines and ferries. Sirkeci train station, the terminus for the European trains, is 100m east of Eminönü.

Karaköy, at the northern end of Galata Bridge, is another ferry terminus. Up the hill from Karaköy is the southern end of Beyoğlu's pedestrian mall, İstiklal Caddesi. At the northern end of the street is Taksim Square, heart of 'modern' İstanbul, with many fancy hotels and airline offices.

İstanbul's *otogar* is at Esenler, about 10km west of the city.

### Maps

Lonely Planet offers an *İstanbul City Map*. The İstanbul tourist offices also supply an excellent free map of the city showing all the important attractions.

## INFORMATION

### Tourist Offices

There are **tourist offices** in the international arrivals hall at Atatürk airport *(☎ 573 4136)*; in Sirkeci station *(☎ 511 5888)*; and also in Sultanahmet *(☎ 518 8754)*.

### Money

Ubiquitous ATMs spit out Turkish liras upon insertion of your credit or bank cash card; **Yapı Kredi** seems best, **İş Bankası** least good because it lets you remove so little at a time. Exchange offices are cheapest outside the Grand Bazaar (Kapalı Çarşı), but are also plentiful in Sultanahmet, Sirkeci and Taksim. Most are open 9am to 9pm.

### Post & Telephone

For poste restante go to **Merkez Postane** *(main PTT; Sehinşah Pehlevi Sokak; tram Sirkeci)*, just west of Sirkeci station. For much of the year a PTT booth also opens in Sultanahmet Meydanı (Sultanahment Square).

All phone numbers in this section use the ☎ 0212 area code unless indicated otherwise.

### Email & Internet Access

You can check your email at several hostels and cafés in Cankurtaran/Sultanahmet, including the Orient Youth Hostel and Mavi Guesthouse (see Places to Stay); and at **Yağmur Cybercafe** *(☎ 292 3020; Şeyh Bender Sokak 18/2, Asmalımescit, Tünel; tram Tünel)*. Expect to pay around US$1 an hour.

### Travel Agencies

Divan Yolu in Sultanahmet boasts several travel agencies that sell cheap air and bus tickets but you will need to shop around for the best deals. **Marco Polo** *(☎ 519 2804; ⓔ marco_polo@superonline.com; Divan Yolu 54)* can make air reservations for you while you wait, while others like **Backpackers Travel** *(☎ 638 6343; ⓦ www.backpackerstravel.net; Yeni Akbıyık Caddesi 22)* will have to use an intermediary.

### Bookshops

**Aypa** *(☎ 516 0100; Mimar Mehmetağa Caddesi 19, Sultanahmet)*, just down the hill from the Blue Mosque, has a good selection.

The best shops are on or near İstiklal Caddesi, including **Robinson Crusoe** *(☎ 293 6968; İstiklal Caddesi 389)*; **Homer** *(☎ 249 5902; Yeni Çarşı Caddesi 28)*; and **Pandora** *(☎ 243 3503; Büyükparmakkapı Sokak 3)*.

### Laundry

In Sultanahmet, try the **Hobby Laundry**, in the Yücelt Interyouth Hostel or the cheaper **Star Laundry** *(Akbıyık Caddesi 18)* opposite the Orient Youth Hostel.

TURKEY

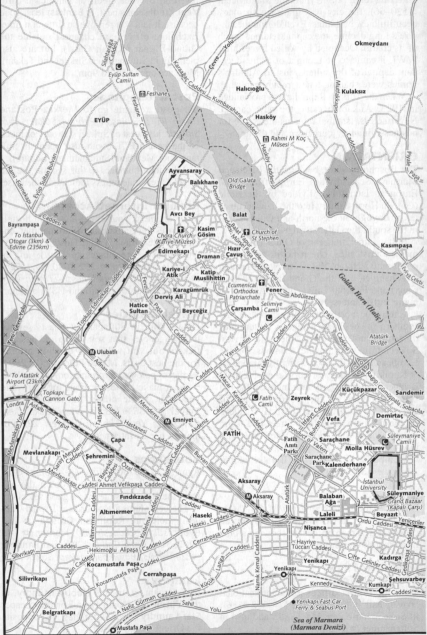

# İSTANBUL

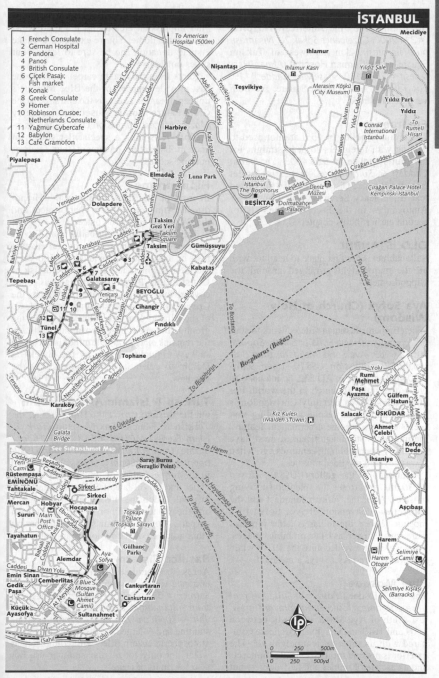

İSTANBUL

Key:
1 French Consulate
2 German Hospital
3 Pandora
4 Panos
5 British Consulate
6 Çiçek Pasajı;
  Fish market
7 Konak
8 Greek Consulate
9 Homer
10 Robinson Crusoe;
   Netherlands Consulate
11 Yağmur Cybercafe
12 Babylon
13 Cafe Gramofon

## Medical Services

In an emergency the **American Hospital** (☎ 311 2000; Güzelbahçe Sokak 20, Nişantaşı; bus Nişantaşı), 2km northwest of Taksim Square, or the **German Hospital** (Alman Hastanesi; ☎ 293 2150, Sıraselviler Caddesi 119; bus Taksim), near Taksim Square, are both very well regarded.

## Emergency

The ordinary **police** (☎ 155) are not used to dealing with foreigners so head straight for the **tourist police** (☎ 527 4503; Yerebatan Caddesi 6, Sultanahmet) across the street from the Basilica Cistern. See also the boxed text 'Emergency Services' near Dangers & Annoyances in the Facts for the Visitor section earlier in this chapter.

## OLD İSTANBUL

Sultanahmet is the first place to head to, with all the major sights arranged around the Hippodrome.

## Aya Sofya (Church of Holy Wisdom)

When Emperor Justinian ordered work to start on Aya Sofya (Hagia Sofia or Sancta Sophia; ☎ 522 0989; Aya Sofya Meydanı; tram Sultanahmet; admission US$10; open 9am-4.30pm Tues-Sun) in AD 532, he intended to create the grandest church in the world. For 1000 years it was certainly Christendom's largest church and despite scaffolding that seems to have become a permanent feature, the interior is still magnificent; it must have been truly overwhelming centuries ago when it was covered in gilded mosaics.

Climb up to the **gallery** (US$10; closed 11.30am-1pm) to see the splendid surviving mosaics. After the Turkish conquest and the subsequent conversion of Aya Sofya to a mosque (hence the minarets), the mosaics were covered over, as Islam prohibits images. They were not revealed until the 1930s when Atatürk declared Aya Sofya a museum.

## Blue Mosque

The Blue Mosque (Mosque of Sultan Ahmet I; Hippodrome; closed during prayer times), just south of Aya Sofya, was built between 1609 and 1619 and is light and delicate compared with its squat ancient neighbour. The exterior is notable for its six slender minarets and a cascade of domes and half-domes, but it's inside where you'll find the luminous blue impression created by the tiled walls and painted dome. You're expected to make a small donation and be sure to leave your shoes outside.

Rents from the **Arasta** carpet shops to the east provide support for the Blue Mosque's upkeep. Near the Arasta is the entrance to the **Great Palace Mosaic Museum** (Büyüksaray Mozaik Müzesi; admission US$2; open 9am-4.30pm Tues-Sun), a spectacular stretch of ancient Byzantine pavement that features hunting scenes.

## Hippodrome

In front of the Blue Mosque is the Hippodrome (Atmeydanı) where chariot races and the Byzantine riots took place.

The **Obelisk of Theodosius** is an Egyptian column from the temple of Karnak that rests on a Byzantine base and has 3500-year-old hieroglyphics. The 10m-high **Obelisk of Constantine Porphyrogenitus** was once covered in bronze, subsequently stolen by the Crusaders. The base rests at the former level of the Hippodrome, several metres below the ground. Between these two monuments are the remains of a **spiral column** of intertwined snakes originally erected by the Greeks at Delphi to celebrate their victory over the Persians.

## Turkish & Islamic Arts Museum

On the western side of the Hippodrome, the Turkish & Islamic Arts Museum (Türk ve İslam Eserleri Müzesi; ☎ 518 1805; Hippodrome; tram Sultanahmet; admission US$2; open 9.30am-5.30pm Tues-Sun) is housed in the former palace of İbrahim Paşa, grand vizier and son-in-law of Süleyman the Magnificent. Inside, the most spectacular exhibits are the wonderful floor-to-ceiling Turkish carpets, but don't miss the fascinating ethnographic collection downstairs either.

## Basilica Cistern

Across the tram lines from Aya Sofya is the entrance to the Basilica Cistern (Yerebatan Sarnıçı; ☎ 522 1259; Yerebatan Caddesi 13; tram Sultanahmet; admission US$2.75; open 9am-4.30pm daily), which was built by Constantine and enlarged by Justinian. This vast, atmospheric cistern filled with columns held water not only for regular summer use but also for times of siege.

## Topkapı Palace

Just northeast of Aya Sofya is sprawling Topkapı Palace (*Topkapı Sarayı;* ☎ *512 0480; Soğukçeşme Sokak; tram Sultanahmet; admission US$10; open 9.30am-5pm Wed-Mon*), the opulent palace of the sultans from 1462 until they moved to Dolmabahçe Palace in the 19th century. Topkapı is not just a palace but a collection of courtyards, houses and libraries, with a 400-room harem.

In the vast First Court, where the crack troops known as janissaries once gathered, is **Aya İrini** (the Church of Divine Peace), dating from around AD 540.

Buy your ticket at the Middle Gate (Orta Kapı) leading to the Second Court.

Within the Second Court are exhibits of priceless porcelain, silverware and crystal, arms and calligraphy. Right beside the Imperial Council Chamber (Kubbealtı) is the entrance to the intriguing **harem** (*admission: palace admission plus US$10; 9.30am-noon & 1pm-3.30pm Wed-Mon*), a succession of sumptuously decorated rooms that served as the sultan's family quarters.

On show in the Third Court are the sultan's ceremonial robes and the **Imperial Treasury** (*admission: palace admission plus US$10*), with its incredible wealth of gold and gems. The **Sacred Safekeeping Rooms** hold a solid-gold casket containing the Prophet Mohammed's cloak and other Islamic relics.

In the Fourth Court, beautiful tiled kiosks offer fine views of the city.

## İstanbul Archaeology Museum

Down the hill from the First Court to the west of Topkapı Palace is the **İstanbul Archaeology Museum** (*İstanbul Arkeoloji Müzesi;* ☎ *520 7740; Osman Hamdi Bey Yokuşu; tram Gülhane; admission US$3.40; open 9.30am-5pm Tues-Sun*). The main building houses an outstanding collection of Greek and Roman statuary, including the magnificent sarcophagi from the royal necropolis at Sidon in Lebanon, while a separate building on the same site (the Museum of the Ancient Orient) houses Hittite and other older archaeological finds. Also in the grounds is the graceful Tiled Pavilion (Çinili Köşk), built on the orders of Sultan Mehmet the Conqueror in 1472 and one of İstanbul's oldest Turkish buildings. Although it houses a museum of Turkish tile work you'll be lucky to find it open.

## Covered Market (Grand Bazaar)

Just north of Divan Yolu, near İstanbul University, is the Covered Market, or Grand Bazaar (*Kapalı Çarşı;* Ⓦ *www.mygrandbazaar.net; tram Universite; open 8.30am-6.30pm Mon-Sat*), a labyrinthine medieval shopping mall of some 4500 shops. It's a fun place to wander around and get lost – which you certainly will!

## Chora Church

Near Edirnekapı is the marvellous **Chora Church** (*Kariye Müzesi;* ☎ *523 3009; Kariye Camii Sokak; admission US$10; open 9am-4.30pm Thur-Tues*), a Byzantine building with the best 14th-century mosaics east of Ravenna as well as some glorious frescoes. Built in the 11th century, it was restored and converted to a mosque, and is now a museum. To get there, take an Edirnekapı bus along Fevzi Paşa Caddesi.

## Eminönü

Near Galata Bridge's southern end looms the large **Yeni Cami** (New Mosque), built between 1597 and 1663. Beside it the **Egyptian Bazaar** (*Mısır Çarşısı*), full of spice and food vendors, is worth a wander.

## DOLMABAHÇE PALACE

Cross the Galata Bridge and follow Necatibey Caddesi along the Bosphorus from Karaköy eastwards and you'll come to the grandiose **Dolmabahçe Palace** (☎ *236 9000; Dolmabahçe Caddesi; bus Kabataş; admission Selamlik US$4, Haremlik US$4, or combined ticket US$7; open 9am-3pm Tues, Wed & Fri-Sun*) right on the waterfront. The palace was built between 1843 and 1856 as home for some of the last Ottoman sultans, but was guaranteed its place in the history books when Atatürk died there on 10 November 1938.

Visitors are taken on guided tours of the two main buildings: the Selamlik (or men's apartments) and Haremlik (or family apartments). Both are stuffed to the gills with over-elaborate furniture and fittings, and as the tour is also very rushed not everyone will want to put aside the two hours required to see both parts. If you decide to opt for just one part, better make it the Haremlik.

Any bus heading out of Karaköy along the Bosphorus shore road will take you to Dolmabahçe.

TURKEY

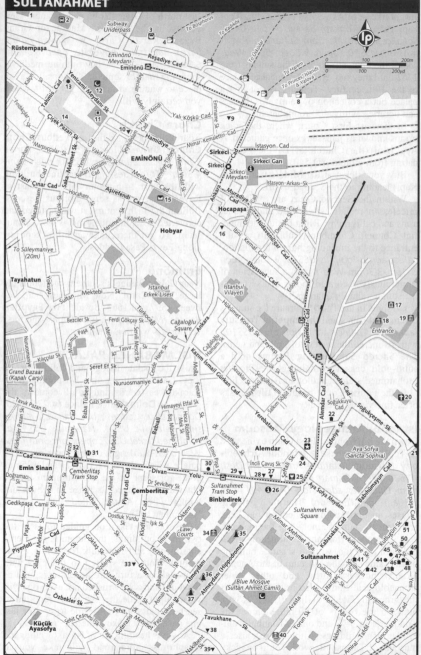

# SULTANAHMET

## SULTANAHMET

| | | | | | |
|---|---|---|---|---|---|
| **PLACES TO STAY** | | 38 | Buhara 93 | 18 | Museum of the Ancient |
| 22 | Yücelt Interyouth Hostel; | 39 | Doy Doy | | Orient |
| | Hobby Laundry | | | 19 | İstanbul Archaeology |
| 41 | Side Hotel & Pension | **OTHER** | | | Museum |
| 42 | İstanbul Hostel | 1 | Zindan Han | 20 | Aya İrini |
| 43 | Sultan Hostel | 2 | City Buses | | (Church of Divine Peace) |
| 46 | Orient Youth Hostel | 3 | Seabus | 21 | Imperial Gate; Topkapı Palace |
| 47 | Hanedan Guest House | 4 | Boğaz Ferry; | 23 | Tourist Police |
| 48 | Sebnem Hotel | | Bosphorus Tour | 24 | Basilica Cistern |
| 49 | Alp Guest House | 5 | Eminönü Ferry Port | | (Yerebatan Sarniçi) |
| 50 | Hotel Empress Zoe | 6 | Sirkeci Ferry Port | 25 | The Sultan Pub |
| 51 | Mavi Guesthouse | 7 | Harem (Car Ferry) | 26 | Tourist Office |
| | | 8 | Yalova, Çınarcık & Adalar | 30 | Marco Polo |
| **PLACES TO EAT** | | | (Princes' Islands) Ferry | 31 | Çemberlitaş Hamamı |
| 9 | Borsa Fast Food | 11 | Tomb of Valide Sultan | 32 | Çemberlitaş |
| 10 | Ali Muhiddin Hacı Bekir | | Turhan Hatice | 34 | Turkish & Islamic Arts |
| | Confectionery | 12 | Yeni Cami | | Museum |
| 16 | Hocapaşa | 13 | Main Entrance to Egyptian | 35 | Obelisk of Theodosius |
| | Restaurants | | Bazaar (Mısır Çarşısı) | 36 | Spiral Column |
| 27 | Pudding Shop | 14 | Egyptian Bazaar | 37 | Obelisk of Constantine |
| | (Lale Restaurant) | | (Mısır Çarşısı) | | Porphyrogenitus |
| 28 | Can Restaurant | 15 | Central Post Office | 40 | Great Palace Mosaic Museum |
| 29 | Sultanahmet Köftecisi | 17 | Tiled Pavilion | 44 | Backpackers Travel |
| 33 | Yeni Birlik Lokantası | | (Çinili Kösk) | 45 | Star Laundry |

## BEYOĞLU

The heart of Beyoğlu is İstiklal Caddesi, a pedestrian street served by a picturesque restored tram (US$0.30). The famed **Pera Palas Oteli**, patronised by the likes of Agatha Christie and Atatürk, is off to the west and near the big Galatasaray Lisesi (high school) are the colourful **Fish Market** (Balık Pazar) and **Çiçek Pasajı** (Flower Passage), an assortment of fish-and-beer restaurants where a fun night out is normally guaranteed.

**Taksim Square**, with its huge hotels, is the hub of modern İstanbul.

## THE BOSPHORUS

The shores of the Bosphorus north of İstanbul are home to some beautiful old Ottoman buildings, including **Rumeli Castle** *(Rumeli Hisarı; admission US$2; opening hours 9.30am-5pm Thur-Tues)*, the huge castle built by Mehmet the Conqueror on the European side to complete his stranglehold on Constantinople. To get there, take any bus or *dolmuş* going north along the European shore to Bebek, Emirgan, Yeniköy or Sarıyer.

In summer a ferry ride up the Bosphorus is *de rigueur* for all İstanbul visitors and is likely to prove a highlight of your trip. Organised excursion ferries depart from Eminönü daily at 10.35am and 12.35pm and 2.10pm each weekday, and stop at Beşiktaş, Kanlıca,

Yeniköy, Sarıyer, Rumeli Kavağı and Anadolu Kavağı (1¾ hours). Extra trips are added on Sunday and holidays.

The weekday return fare is US$5, half price on Saturday and Sunday. Hold on to your ticket as you need it to re-board the boat for the return trip.

## PLACES TO STAY

Camping aside, the best place to head for accommodation to suit all budgets is the Sultanahmet/Cankurtaran district.

## PLACES TO STAY – BUDGET
### Camping

Camping in İstanbul is hardly convenient and costs about as much as staying in a cheap hotel, on top of which you must pay fares in and out of the centre.

**Ataköy Mokamp** *(☎ 559 6000; Ataköy Sahil Yolu, Bakırköy; tent sites US$11)* has camping facilities. To get there, take bus No 81 from Eminönü.

### Hostels

İstanbul's hostels charge around US$8 for a bed in summer, less in winter. In high summer even the hostels fill up (with the inevitable problems of noise and over-stretched facilities), and roof space becomes available for around US$5.

**TURKEY**

**Yücelt Interyouth Hostel** (☎ 513 6150; Caferiye Sokak 6/1, Sultanahmet), a little way from the other hostels, is a big, brash place with lots of facilities including a mini-gym and laundry.

**İstanbul Hostel** (☎ 516 9380; W www .istanbul-hostel.com; Kutlugün Sokak), in Cankurtaran, is immaculately clean, and shows movies in its basement bar.

**Mavi Guesthouse** (☎ 516 5878; W www .maviguesthouse.com; Kutlugün Sokak 3) is small and welcoming. Rates include breakfast, and the cosy ground-floor lounge is a plus.

One block over is Akbıyık Caddesi, with lots of places to stay, eat and drink.

**Orient Youth Hostel** (☎ 518 0789; W www .hostels.com/orienthostel; Akbıyık Caddesi 13) is a popular place with some newly decorated rooms, a top-floor café with marvellous Bosphorus views and a basement bar that features belly-dancers and water-pipes.

**Sultan Hostel** (☎ 516 9260; W www.sul tanhostel.com; Terbıyık Sokak 3), just around the corner, is used as a base by Fez Bus. It also boasts Marmara views from its roof.

## PLACES TO STAY – MID-RANGE

Many Cankurtaran pensions are gradually upgrading into classy small hotels.

**Side Hotel & Pension** (☎/fax 517 6590; W www.sidehotel.com; Utangaç Sokak 20; singles/doubles in pension from US$20/35, in hotel from US$40/50) is one of those places where you arrive knowing no one and leave with a whole bunch of new friends. To find it, head down from Aya Sofya and you'll come to Utangaç Sokak on the right. The tariff includes breakfast.

Three small places in Adliye Sokak, a turn-off from Akbıyık Caddesi, are likely to be quieter than those right on it. **Hanedan Guest House** (☎ 516 4869; singles/doubles with shower US$25/35) is simplest but has a small roof-top café. **Alp Guest House** (☎ 517 9570; Adliye Sokak 4; singles/doubles with shower US$35/50) has pleasingly decorated rooms, but smartest is **Sebnem Hotel** (☎ 517 6623; W www.sebnemhotel.com; singles/doubles with shower from US$45/55), across the road, with comfortable rooms.

**Hotel Empress Zoe** (☎ 518 2504; W www .emzoe.com; Akbıyık Caddesi, Adliye Sokak 10; singles/doubles with shower from US$55/70) has tiny, stylish rooms although you must navigate a spiral staircase to access them.

## PLACES TO EAT

Once a legend among travellers, the **Pudding Shop**, aka Lale Restaurant, is now just one of a string of cheapish restaurants along Divan Yolu opposite the Hippodrome. At any of them a typical, if unmemorable, kebab meal costs around US$4 to US$6. Worth trying is the **Can Restaurant** but the **Sultanahmet Köftecisi** is famed for its delicious grilled meatballs with salad, bread and a drink for US$3 or less.

**Yeni Birlik Lokantası** (Üçler Sokak 46; open 8am-3pm; meals US$3-5) is favoured by lawyers and a good place to find a choice of stews at lunch-time. From the southwestern end of the Hippodrome, walk up Üçler Sokak one block to find it.

**Doy Doy** (Sifa Hamamı Sokak 13; meals US$3.50) is a long-time favourite, downhill from the southeastern end of the Hippodrome. Offering cheap, simple Turkish staples, it's usually busy with locals and travellers. Across the road **Buhara 93** (Nakilbent Sokak 15/A) has similarly cheap and appetising meals.

The Kumkapı neighbourhood on the shoreline 800m south of Beyazıt along Tiyatro Caddesi boasts dozens of good seafood restaurants. On summer evenings the whole place turns into one big party. A meal of fish and rakı is likely to cost US$14 to US$22 but you need to check the price of everything before eating. For a cheaper lunch, US$1 buys you a delicious fish sandwich from a boat moored near the Galata Bridge.

Although there's a reasonable selection of places to eat in Sultanahmet, for a bigger choice you must head across town to Beyoğlu. Hop on a bus to Taksim Square (T4 from the Hippodrome) and start walking along İstiklal Caddesi and you'll be spoilt for choice, from the takeaway döner places right at the start of the street to the flashier, more Westernised bar-cafés at the Tünel end.

**Konak** (İstiklal Caddesi 259), near the big Galatasaray Lisesi (high school), is a great place to tuck into an İskender kebab beneath plaster ceilings and chandeliers that hint at the area's past glory. A meal with cold drink will cost around US$4, a pide even less.

### Self Catering

Every Wednesday you can pick up what you need at the Akbıyık Caddesi street market. The Egyptian Bazaar and surrounding streets sell dried fruit, pulses, fish and more.

## ENTERTAINMENT
### Turkish Baths
İstanbul's most interesting historical *hammams* (Turkish baths) are pretty touristy, with prices to reflect their non-Turkish clientele. The best one to try if you're a first-timer is the beautiful **Çemberlitaş Hamamı** *(Vezirhan Caddesi 8; tram Çemberlitaş; admission US$18; open 6am-midnight daily)*, just off Divan Yolu beside the Çemberlitaş monument. There are separate baths for men and women in a building possibly designed by the great Sinan himself. Prices would be outrageous anywhere else in Turkey but service is experienced and hassle-free.

### Bars & Clubs
Near the Basilica Cistern are a group of bars. Bunker-style **Bodrum** really fires up and **Gila** attracts *some* locals and has awesome views of Aya Sofya, but **The Sultan Pub** is better for a quiet drink (and good for women travellers). The Orient and Yücelt hostels also have popular, smoky **bars**.

Cross to Beyoğlu to party with the wealthier of İstanbul's youth. Ritzy **Cafe Gramofon**, at the southern end of İstiklal Caddesi, has live jazz (it's also a comfortable environment for women). **Pano** wine bar, opposite the British Consulate, is so popular you may have to queue to get in.

At **Babylon** *(☎ 292 7368; Şehbender Sokak 3, Beyoğlu; tram Tünel)* big name bands occasionally play to rapturous audiences.

But Beyoğlu can be seedy. Ignore touts who try to encourage you onto their turf – it'll only end in tears.

## GETTING THERE & AWAY
### Air
Most people fly into İstanbul's Atatürk International Airport, Turkey's international flight hub. Most foreign airlines have their offices near Taksim, or north of it, along Cumhuriyet Caddesi.

### Bus
**İstanbul Otogar** *(Uluslararası İstanbul Otogarı; ☎ 658 0036)* at Esenler is a monster of a place, with 168 ticket offices and buses leaving for all parts of Turkey and beyond. To get to it from Sultanahmet take the tram to Aksaray, switch to the metro and get out at Otogar.

Buses depart for Ankara (US$12 to US$24, six hours) roughly every 15 minutes, day and night; buses for most other cities depart at least every hour. Heading east to Anatolia, you might want to board at the smaller **Harem Otogar** *(☎ 0216-333 3763)*, to the north of Haydarpaşa on the Asian shore, which is accessible via ferry from Karaköy, but the choice of service there is more limited.

### Train
**Sirkeci** *(☎ 520 6575)* is the station for services to Edirne, Greece and Eastern Europe. **Haydarpaşa** *(☎ 0216-336 4470)*, on the Asian shore, is the terminus for trains to Anatolia, Syria and Iran. From Sirkeci there are three express trains a day to Edirne (US$3, 6½ hours). The nightly *Bosfor Expresi* goes to Bucharest (US$26, 18 hours) and Budapest (US$95, 32 hours).

From Haydarpaşa there are seven express trains a day to Ankara (US$10 to US$28, seven to 10 hours), the fastest being sleeper only.

### Boat
For information on car ferries to İzmir, see Boat in the introductory Getting Around section earlier in this chapter.

Yenikapı, south of Aksaray Square, is the dock for *hızlı feribot* (fast car ferries) across the Sea of Marmara. Heading for Bursa, take a Yalova ferry or catamaran, which will get you to Yalova in less than an hour for US$35 (car and driver). The voyage to Bandırma takes less than two hours and costs US$70 (car and driver) or US$12 (pedestrian/passenger).

## GETTING AROUND
### To/From the Airport
The fastest way into town from the airport is by taxi. During the day *(gündüz)* it costs US$10 to Sultanahmet (20 minutes), US$12 to Taksim (30 minutes) and US$8 to the *otogar* (20 minutes). Fares are higher at night *(gece)*.

A cheaper, slower alternative is the Havaş airport bus (US$2, 30 to 60 minutes), which goes to Taksim Square via Aksaray. Buses leave every 30 minutes from 5am to 11.30pm.

Many Divan Yolu travel agencies and Sultanahmet hostels book minibus transport from hotels to the airport for about US$4 a head. Unfortunately, this option only works going *from* town to the airport and not vice versa.

### Bus
City buses are crowded but useful. The destinations and intermediate stops are indicated

at the front and side of the bus. On most routes you must have a ticket (US$0.50) before boarding; stock up on tickets in advance from the white booths near major stops or nearby shops.

### Train

To get to Sirkeci station, take the *tramvay* (tram) from Aksaray or Sultanahmet, or any bus for Eminönü. Haydarpaşa station is connected by ferry to Karaköy (US$0.60, at least every 30 minutes).

Every 20 minutes suburban trains from Sirkeci (US$0.40) run along the southern walls of Old İstanbul and head west along the Marmara shore. There's a handy station in Cankurtaran for Sultanahmet.

### Underground

The Tünel, İstanbul's ancient underground train, mounts the hill from Karaköy to Tünel Square and İstiklal Caddesi (US$0.50, every 10 or 15 minutes from 7am to 9pm).

### Tram

The useful *hızlı tramvay* (fast tram) network has three lines. The first runs between Eminönü and Aksaray via Divan Yolu and Sultanahmet; the second runs west from Aksaray to the *otogar*. A third line runs from Taksim to 4 Levent. Another restored tram trundles along İstiklal Caddesi to Taksim. All tram tickets cost US$0.50.

### Taxi

İstanbul has 60,000 yellow taxis, all of them with meters even if not every driver wants to run them. From Sultanahmet to Taksim costs around US$5; to the *otogar* around US$10.

### Boat

The cheapest and nicest way to travel any distance in İstanbul is by ferry. Short ferry hops cost US$0.60, longer ones US$1.20.

The main ferry docks are at the mouth of the Golden Horn (Eminönü, Sirkeci and Karaköy) and at Kabataş, just before the Dolmabahçe Palace.

# Around İstanbul

Since İstanbul is such a vast city, few places are within easy day-trip reach. However, if you make an early start it would be possible to see the sites of Edirne in Thrace (Trakya), the only bit of Turkey that is geographically within Europe. The fast ferry link means that you can also just about make Bursa and back in a day although it's much better to plan an overnight stay.

## EDİRNE

☎ 0284  •  pop 115,000

Edirne is a surprisingly pleasant, under-visited town with several fine old mosques. If you're passing through, have a look at the **Üçşerefeli Cami**, the **Eski Cami** and especially the **Selimiye Camii**, the finest work of master architect Sinan. The impressive **Beyazıt II Camii** complex is on the outskirts. There are several good, cheap hotels a few blocks from the **tourist office** (*☎/fax 225 1518; Hürriyet Meydanı 17*) in the town centre.

Buses from İstanbul run every 20 minutes (US$5, three hours, 235km).

## BURSA

☎ 224  •  pop 1 million

Sprawling at the base of Uludağ mountain, Turkey's biggest winter sports centre, Bursa was the Ottoman capital before İstanbul. It retains several fine mosques and pretty neighbourhoods from early Ottoman times, but its biggest attractions are the thermal springs in the village-like suburb of Çekirge. Bursa's wonderful covered market should also delight anyone who finds İstanbul's version too touristy.

### Orientation & Information

The city centre, with its banks and shops, is along Atatürk Caddesi between the Ulu Cami (Grand Mosque) to the west and the main square, Cumhuriyet Alanı, commonly called Heykel (Statue), to the east. The **PTT** is on the southern side of Atatürk Caddesi opposite the Ulu Cami. Çekirge, with its hot springs, is about 6km west of Heykel.

Bursa's *otogar* is an inconvenient 10km north of the centre on the Yalova road.

The **tourist office** (*☎ 251 1834; Orhangazi Altgeçidi subway, Ulu Cami Parkı*) is opposite the Koza Han (Silk Market).

### Things to See & Do

The largest of Bursa's beautiful mosques is the 20-domed **Ulu Cami** (*Grand Mosque; Atatürk Caddesi*), built in 1399. Northeast of Ulu Cami is the **bedesten** or covered bazaar where you'll find the **Karagöz shop** (☎ 221 8727) with details of puppet shows. The **Koza Han** (*Silk Market*) is worth wandering through, too.

Northwest of Ulu Cami is the **Muradiye Complex**, with decorated tombs dating from the 14th and 15th centuries. Continue on to the **mineral baths** in the suburb of Çekirge. To rejuvenate at **Eski Kaplıca**, beside the Kervansaray Termal Hotel, will set you back US$5; another US$5 for a scrub or a limp-wristed massage.

About a kilometre east of Heykel you'll find the early Ottoman **Yeşil Cami** (Green Mosque), built in 1424, and its beautifully tiled **Yeşil Türbe** (*Green Tomb; admission free; open 8.30am-5.30pm*). Nearby is the **Turkish & Islamic Arts Museum** (*admission US$0.75; open 8.30am-noon & 1pm-5pm Tues-Sun*), which was closed for restoration at the time of writing.

On a clear day it's worth going up **Uludağ**. From Heykel take bus Nos 3/B or 3/C or a *dolmuş* east to the *teleferik* (cable car) up the mountain (US$3 return).

## Places to Stay

The centre of town has a motley bunch of places to stay. You're better off forking out a bit more and staying in Çekirge where you'll also get free mineral baths. **Öz Yeşilyayla Termal Otel** (☎ 239 6496; *Selvi Sokak 6; singles/doubles with shared bathroom US$15/20*) is straight from the 1950s – everything creaks as you walk across the floor. There's free use of the basement mineral baths.

**Boyugüzel Termal Otel** (☎/fax 233 9999; *Selvi Sokak; singles/doubles with shower US$20/30*), right next door, is smart and modern and throws 30 minutes in the mineral bath downstairs into the room price.

In the centre, **Otel Güneş** (☎ 222 1404; *İnebey Caddesi 75; singles/doubles with shared bathroom US$5/8*), in an old wooden building, is clean and simple, if somewhat cramped.

**Hotel Çeşmeli** (☎ 224 1511; *Gümüşçeken Caddesi 6; singles/doubles with shower US$19/30*), just north of Atatürk Caddesi, is better – friendly, fairly quiet and very clean.

**Hotel Efehan** (☎ 225 2260; *Gümüşçeken Caddesi 34; singles/doubles with shower US$20/30*) has immaculate decor. Rooms come with mod cons such as hair-drier, TV and minibar.

## Places to Eat

Bursa was the birthplace of the *İskender kebab* although the quality of kebabs seems to be going downhill.

**Kebapçı İskender** (*Ünlü Caddesi 7; full meals US$6*), just east of Heykel, dates back to 1867 and is beginning to show its age, although the *İskender kebab* is still tasty. **Adanur Hacıbey**, opposite, costs the same but is less fancy.

**Çiçek Izgara** (*Belediye Caddesi 15; open 11am-3.30pm & 5.30pm-9pm daily; full meals US$2.50*), near the half-timbered Belediye in the flower market, is bright, modern, super-popular and good for lone women.

**Çınar Izgara** (*Atatürk Caddesi, Ulucami Yanı; full meals US$4*) is housed in what was the old toilet block of the Ulu Cami and has pictures of old Bursa on the walls. Service is attentive and the food is tasty.

For a jolly evening of seafood and drinks, head straight for Sakarya Caddesi, off Altıparmak Caddesi. **Arap Şükrü** (☎ 221 1453; *Sakarya Caddesi 6; meals US$10*) is usually reliable and the calamares (US$2) and grilled mackerel (US$3.50) are most enjoyable.

## Getting There & Away

The fastest way to get to İstanbul is to take the hourly bus to Yalova (US$2, one hour), then a catamaran or fast car ferry to İstanbul's Yenikapı docks (US$5, one hour, at least seven a day). Be sure to get a bus that departs at least 1½ hours before the scheduled boat departure.

*Karayolu ile* (by road) buses to İstanbul take four hours and drag you all around the Bay of İzmit. Those designated *feribot ile* (by ferry) take you to Topçular, east of Yalova, and then by car ferry to Eskihisar, a much more pleasant way to go.

## Getting Around

There are no *servis* buses to the *otogar* so you must take a bus (US$0.30, 45 minutes, 10km) between the *otogar* and the city centre. A taxi costs US$5.

City buses (BOİ; US$0.30) have stops marked on the front. The best place to pick them up is on Atatürk Caddesi just before Heykel. Many *dolmuşes* wait in front of Ulu Cami Parkı, although the Çekirge *dolmuş* waits at the northeasterly end of Feraizcizade Sokak.

# The Aegean Coast

While the coastal scenery of the Aegean Coast is not as spectacular as that of the Mediterranean, this is the part of Turkey that was once Asia Minor and it is studded with fantastic historic sites, including the ruins of Troy, Ephesus and Pergamum (Bergama). This is also where you come to see the battlefield sites at Gallipoli.

## ÇANAKKALE
☎ 286  •  pop 60,000

Çanakkale makes a good base for visiting Troy and Gallipoli (Gelibolu), across the other side of the Dardanelles. The defence of the straits during WWI led to a Turkish victory over Anzac (Australian and New Zealand) forces on 18 March 1916, now a big local holiday. But even more people flock to town on 25 April for Anzac Day, when a dawn service commemorates the anniversary of the Allied landings on the peninsula in 1915.

The **tourist office** (☎ 217 1187), all the cheap hotels and a range of restaurants are located close to the ferry pier, near the town's landmark clock tower.

### Things to See

Built by Sultan Mehmet the Conqueror in 1452, the **Ottoman castle** now houses an **Army Museum** (admission US$0.75; open 9am-noon & 1.30pm-5pm Tues-Wed & Fri-Sun). Just over 2km south of the ferry pier on the road to Troy, the **Archaeological Museum** (admission US$0.75; open 9am-5pm daily) holds artefacts found at Troy and Assos.

### Places to Stay

In summer camping is available at **Mocamp Trova** (☎ 232 8025; Güzelyalı Beach), 15km south of Çanakkale, off the road to Troy.

Except on Anzac Day, Çanakkale has accommodation to fit all pockets. Unfortunately the stresses and strains of 25 April result in more complaints from readers about Çanakkale hotels than about anywhere else in the country. Do yourself a favour and check prices carefully before settling in.

**Anzac House** (☎ 213 5969; ⓔ www.anzac house.com; Cumhuriyet Bulvarı; dorm beds US$5, singles/doubles US$9/14) provides clean, simple budget accommodation although some of the rooms are windowless boxes.

**Hotel Efes** (☎ 217 3256; Aralık Sokak 5; dorm beds US$5, singles/doubles with shower US$10/14), behind the clock tower, is bright, cheerful and female-run.

**Hotel Kervansaray** (☎ 217 8192; Fetvane Sokak 13; singles/doubles without shower US$5/9) is inside a quaint old pasha's house. The rooms are very basic, but there's an inviting courtyard and garden.

**Yellow Rose Pension** (☎/fax 217 3343; Yeni Sokak 5; dorm beds US$4, singles/doubles US$6/12) offers simple rooms 50m southeast of the clock tower in an attractive house on a quiet side street.

**Otel Anafartalar** (☎ 217 4454; İskele Meydanı; singles/doubles with shower US$25/34) is a high-rise, waterfront hotel with fine views of the straits if you can bag a front room.

### Places to Eat

**Trakya Restaurant** (Cumhuriyet Meydanı; meals US$5), across the road from Anzac House, can fill you up with pide and other staples 24 hours a day. **Gülen** (Cumhuriyet Meydanı; meals US$5) has cheerier decor and does a decent İskender kebab as well as a range of pides.

In summer it's fun to dine at one of the long-lived waterfront restaurants – **Rıhtım**, **Yeni Entellektüel** or **Çekic**. All of them specialise in fish, but be sure to check the prices to avoid nasty shocks.

### Getting There & Away

There are hourly buses to Çanakkale from İstanbul (US$11, six hours, 340km), with equally frequent onward buses to İzmir (US$8, five hours, 340km).

## GALLIPOLI

Always the first line of defence for İstanbul, the Dardanelles defences proved their worth in WWI. Atop the narrow, hilly peninsula, Mustafa Kemal (Atatürk) and his troops fought off a superior but badly commanded force of Anzac and British troops. After nine months and horrendous casualties, the Allied forces were withdrawn. For most people a visit to the battlefields and war graves of Gallipoli (now a national park) is a moving experience.

If time is tight the easiest way to see the sights is on a minibus tour from Çanakkale with **Troyanzac Tours** (☎ 217 5849) or **Hassle Free Tours** (☎ 213 5969) for about US$20 per person. **Down Under Travel**

(☎ 814 2431; Eceabat) also comes in for lots of praise from readers. With time on your hands, it's cheaper to take a ferry from Çanakkale to Eceabat and a *dolmuş* to Kabatepe and follow the heritage trail described in a booklet sold at the visitors centre there.

Most people use Çanakkale as a base for exploring Gallipoli but you could also stay at Eceabat on the Thracian side of the straits. **TJs Hostel** (☎ 814 2940; e tjs_tours@mail .excite.com; Cumhuriyet Caddesi 5, Eceabat; bed with shower US$5) gets particularly fond reviews from its guests.

Hourly car ferries cross the straits from Çanakkale to Eceabat and from Lapseki to Gallipoli (US$0.50). More frequent private ferries (US$0.30) cross to Kilitbahir from in front of Çanakkale's Hotel Bakır.

## TROY

According to Homer, Paris abducted the beautiful Helen from her husband, Menelaus, King of Sparta, and whisked her off to Troy, thus precipitating the Trojan War. After 10 years of carnage failed to end the war, Odysseus came up with the idea of filling a wooden horse with soldiers and leaving it outside the west gate for the Trojans to wheel inside the walls.

Despite the romantic story you shouldn't get too excited about Troy (Truva; admission US$7; open 8.30am-5pm daily Nov-May, 8am-7.30pm daily Jun-Oct) as there's little left to see. Nor are most people thrilled with the tacky imitation 'Trojan Horse'.

It's estimated that nine successive cities have been built on this same site: Troy I goes right back to the Bronze Age; legendary Troy is thought to be Troy VI; most of the ruins you see are Roman ones from Troy IX. You may want to take one of the tours offered in Çanakkale to get more out of Troy.

In summer frequent *dolmuşes* run from Çanakkale (US$1.50, 30km). Walk straight inland from the ferry pier to Atatürk Caddesi, and turn right towards Troy; the *dolmuş* stop is at the bridge.

## BEHRAMKALE (ASSOS)

☎ 286

Behramkale, 19km southwest of Ayvacık, consists of a beautiful hilltop village, with the ruins of a **Temple of Athena** (admission US$0.75; open 8am-5pm Tues-Sun) looking across the water to Lesbos (Lesvos) in Greece; and a small *iskele* (port), 2km further on. Both

get overcrowded in summer, especially at weekends. Visit in the low season if you can.

**Çakır Camping** (☎ 721 7048; US$5 per site) is right on the beach but there are other possibilities in the olive groves nearby.

In Behramkale itself **Dolunay Pansiyon** (☎ 721 72710) and other *pensions* can put you up for around US$12.50 a head. The lovely port hotels charge around US$45/60 per singles/doubles with half-board in summer and are all fairly similar. These places fill up quickly so phone ahead: **Behram** (☎ 721 7016), **Kervansaray** (☎ 721 7093), **Assos Şen** (☎ 721 7076) and **Nazlıhan** (☎ 721 7385).

Infrequent *dolmuşes* (US$1.50) go to Behramkale from Ayvacık (not to be confused with nearby Ayvalık). Ayvacık is linked by bus to Çanakkale and Ayvalık.

## AYVALIK

☎ 266 • pop 30,000

Inhabited by Ottoman Greeks until 1923, this small fishing port and beach resort is the departure point for ferries to Lesbos.

The *otogar* is 1.5km north of the town centre, the **tourist office** (☎/fax 312 2122) 1km south, opposite the marina. Offshore is **Alibey Island** (Cunda), lined with open-air fish restaurants and linked by ferries and a causeway to the mainland.

## Places to Stay & Eat

**Taksiyarhis Pansiyon** (☎ 312 1494; Mareşal Çakmak Caddesi 71; beds US$7), a renovated Ottoman house, is the most interesting place to stay. It's five minutes' walk east of the PTT behind the former Taxiarkhis church and is often full in summer. Breakfast is US$2.50.

**Bonjour Pansiyon** (☎ 312 8085; Fevzi Çakmak Caddesi, Çeşme Sokak 5; singles/ doubles with shower US$12/20; open May-Sept) is in the fine, restored house of a French ambassador to the sultan.

**Chez Beliz Pansiyon** (☎ 312 4897; Mareşal Çakmak Caddesi 28; beds from US$10; open May-Nov) boasts a gorgeous garden, an exuberant hostess and excellent food.

**Hüsnü Baba'nin Yeri** (Tenekeciler Sokaği 16; meals US$4), off İnönü Caddesi in a shady alley, doesn't look much but offers excellent *mezes* to wash down with *rakı*. Sea urchins anyone? In season only, of course.

**Kardeşler** (meals US$10-12) on the waterfront is pricier but good for seafood and great views. **15 Kardeşler** (Talatpaşa Caddesi;

meals US$4.50), in the street behind, offers cheaper soup and kebab suppers.

## Getting There & Away

There are frequent direct buses from İzmir to Ayvalık (US$3.50, three hours, 240km). Coming from Çanakkale (US$5, 3½ hours, 200km) the buses will probably drop you on the main highway to hitch to the centre.

Daily boats operate to Lesbos from late May to September (US$40/50 one way/return). There's at least one boat a week even in winter.

## BERGAMA

☎ 232 • pop 46,900

From the 3rd century BC to the 1st century AD, Bergama (formerly Pergamum) was a powerful and cultured kingdom. A line of rulers beginning with a general under Alexander the Great ruled over this small but wealthy kingdom, famous now for its extensive ruins.

The **tourist office** (☎ 633 1862; İzmir Caddesi 57) is midway between the otogar and the market. Taxis waiting here charge US$4 to the acropolis, US$8 total to wait and bring you back down.

## Things to See

The **Asclepion** (Temple of Asclepios; admission US$4; open 8.30am-5.30pm daily), 3.5km from the city centre, became a famous medical school with a library that rivalled that of Alexandria in Egypt. The **Acropolis** (admission US$4; open 8.30am-5.30pm daily), a hill-top site 6km from the city centre, has a spectacular sloping theatre. If you're a walker, follow the pretty path marked by dots down through the ruins to get back to town. The excellent **Archaeology & Ethnography Museum** (admission US$2; open 8.30am- 5.30pm daily) contains finds from both sites.

## Places to Stay & Eat

**Pension Athena** (☎ 633 3420; İmam Çıkmazı 5; beds with/without shower US$7/5), in an old Ottoman house, is run by natural-born host Aydın Şengül. A feast of a breakfast is US$2. It's at the Acropolis end of town.

**Böblingen Pension** (☎ 633 2153; Asklepion Caddesi 2; singles/doubles with shower US$10/20), spotless and family-run, is at the start of the road to the Asclepion. Prices include breakfast.

**Anıl Hotel** (☎ 631 3031; Hatuniye Caddesi 4; singles/doubles with shower US$37/ 50) has cheerful modern rooms. Ask for a quieter one at the back.

**Meydan Restaurant** (İstiklal Meydanı; meals US$5), near the Basilica (Red Hall) on the main street, serves meals on a vine-shaded terrace.

**Sağlam 3 Restaurant** (Cumhuriyet Meydanı 29; meals US$4) serves a range of kebab, while **Sağlam 2** (İstiklal Meydanı 3; meals US$3) offers cheaper soups and pides, with live music upstairs to round off the evening.

## Getting There & Away

Buses shuttle between Bergama and İzmir every half-hour in summer (US$3, two hours, 100km). Fairly frequent buses also connect Bergama with Ayvalık (US$2.50, 1¾ hours, 60km).

## İZMİR

☎ 232 • pop 2.5 million

Turkey's third-largest city, İzmir (once Smyrna) was the birthplace of Homer in about 700 BC. Today it's the main transport hub for the Aegean coast but a good place to skip on a short trip. It's spread out and baffling to find your way around, its sites are relatively minor and its hotels overpriced.

## Orientation & Information

Central İzmir is a web of plazas linked by streets that aren't at right angles to each other. Instead of names the back streets have numbers. You'll go mad without a map – the tourist office supplies a good one free.

Budget hotels cluster near Basmane train station, a district sometimes called Çankaya. To the southwest, Anafartalar Caddesi winds through the bazaar to the waterfront at Konak, the commercial and governmental centre. Atatürk Caddesi (Birinci Kordon) runs northeast from Konak along the waterfront past Cumhuriyet Meydanı with an equestrian statue of Atatürk, the main PTT and luxury hotels.

At Atatürk Caddesi's northern end is the harbour, Alsancak İskelesi, and the smaller, mostly suburban Alsancak train station. İzmir's flashy new otogar is 6km northeast of the town centre.

The tourist office (☎ 484 2147; Gaziosmanpaşa Bulvarı 1/C, Cumhuriyet Meydanı) is next to the Turkish Airlines office (☎ 484 1220; Büyük Efes Oteli, Gaziosmanpaşa Bulvarı 1/F, Cumhuriyet Meydanı).

## Things to See

Since most of old İzmir was destroyed by earthquakes there's little to see here. However, it does boast the remains of an extensive 2nd-century AD Roman **agora** *(admission US$1.40; open 8.30am-noon & 1pm-5pm daily)*, right inside the sprawling, atmospheric **bazaar**. It's also worth taking a bus to the hilltop **Kadifekale** fortress where women still weave kilims on horizontal looms. The **Archaeology & Ethnography museums** *(combined admission US$2.75; open 9am-noon & 1pm-5pm Tues-Sun)* are both quite interesting although it's rare for both to be open.

## Places to Stay

Decent mid-range places are scarce and İzmir has more than its fair share of seedy dives. For the cheapest places to stay, walk out of the front of Basmane train station, turn left, cross the main road and walk up shady Anafartalar Caddesi, the bazaar area.

**Otel Hikmet** *(☎ 484 2672; 945 Sokak No 26; singles/doubles US$3.50/5.50)*, near the Hatuniye Camii, is clean and dirt-cheap.

**Otel Antik Han** *(☎ 489 2750; Anafartalar Caddesi 600; singles/doubles with shower US$20/30)*, in a restored house in the bazaar, is another good choice. Rooms have TVs, ceiling fans and plenty of character but can be noisy because of nearby music-halls.

**Hotel Baylan** *(☎ 483 1426; 1299 Sokak No 8; singles/doubles with shower US$35/ 55)* is a professionally managed and comfortable two-star place. To find it, cross the road outside the station, turn left and then immediately right.

## Places to Eat

For bargain basement meals, especially at lunchtime, head straight into the bazaar and take your pick of what's cooking.

**Gönlibel** *(Anafartalar Caddesi 878; full meals US$4)* is clean, cheap and handy for Basmane station. Try the delicious *kiremitte tavuk* (chicken baked on a tile) for just US$2.

**Dört Mevsim Et Lokantası** *(1369 Sokak 51/A; meals US$5-6)* is an excellent place with an open *ocakbaşı* grill, a full range of kebabs and welcoming service.

For something more Westernised, hit the waterfront café-bars, great places for hanging out with an atmosphere that's reminiscent of Thessaloniki (Greece).

## Getting There & Away

**Air** Turkish Airlines offers nonstop flights to İstanbul (US$82, 50 minutes) and Ankara, with connections to other destinations.

**Bus** Many bus companies have ticket offices around Dokuz Eylül Meydanı, near Basmane station. They usually provide a *servis* (free minibus) to the *otogar*. From İzmir there are frequent buses to Selçuk (US$1.75, one hour, 80km) Çanakkale (US$8, five hours, 340km) and Pamukkale (US$4, four hours, 260km), as well as many to other destinations.

**Train** The evening *Mavi Tren* (US$10, 14 hours) hauls sleeping cars from Basmane train station to Ankara; or you can take the *İzmir Express* for US$8.

For İstanbul, take the *Marmara Express* to Bandırma (US$2), then a fast ferry.

**Boat** For details of summer-only ferry services from İzmir to Venice, and of the ferry service linking İstanbul and İzmir see Sea in the Getting There & Away section and Boat in the Getting Around section respectively; both are near the start of this chapter.

## Getting Around

**To/From the Airport** A Havaş bus (US$2.50, 30 minutes, 25km) departs for Adnan Menderes airport from outside the Turkish Airlines office 1½ hours before every Turkish Airlines' departure.

Trains (US$0.50) run every hour from Alsancak train station to the airport; some south-bound trains from Basmane also stop at the airport. A taxi can cost up to US$30.

**Bus** There is a local bus terminal right beside Konak Meydanı. Local bus tickets cost US$0.40 and must be bought before boarding. Catch bus No 33 to Kadifekale or bus Nos 601, 603 and 605 to the *otogar*.

## ÇEŞME

☎ 0232  •  pop 100,000

A beach resort in its own right, Çeşme is mainly a stopping-off point between Chios (Greece) and Turkey. If you're staying it has a small **Genoese fortress** *(admission US$2; open 8.30am-noon & 1pm-5pm daily)*; a ludicrously overpriced **hammam**; and a choice of **boat excursions**. There's a decent beach 6km away at **Ilıca**.

## Places to Stay

**Barınak Pansiyon** (☎ 712 6670; *Kutludağ Sokak 62; singles/doubles with shower US$ 11/17)* and **Sahil Pansiyon** (☎ 712 6934; *Kutludağ Sokak 64; singles/doubles with shower US$12/17)* are both good value but only open from May to November.

Right by the harbour, **Hotel Ertan** (☎ 712 6795; *Cumhuriyet Meydanı; singles/doubles with shower US$20/25)* gets good reports even if the rooms look fairly ordinary.

## Getting There & Away

To get to Çeşme from İzmir (US$2, 1¼ hours, 85km) you have to take a bus from Üçkuyular rather than the main İzmir *otogar* (bus No 605 will get you there from Konak).

In summer there are daily ferries to Chios (US$30 one way, US$40 same-day return trip).

## SELÇUK & EPHESUS
☎ 232

Selçuk is an easy hour's bus trip south of İzmir. Almost everybody comes here to visit the splendid Roman ruins of Ephesus; in its heyday only Athens was more magnificent, and in Roman times this was Asia's capital.

## Orientation & Information

Although touristy, Selçuk is a backwater compared with coastal playpens like Kuşadası and so is more attractive for most backpackers. Most of the *pensions* are on the quieter western side of the highway (Atatürk Caddesi) behind the museum, but others are on the eastern side along with the *otogar*, restaurants and train station. There's a **tourist office** (☎/fax 892 1328) in the park across from the *otogar*.

Ephesus is a 3km, 35-minute walk west from Selçuk's *otogar* along a shady road – turn left (south) at the Tusan Motel. Frequent *dolmuşes* to Pamucak and Kuşadası pass the Ephesus turn-off (US$0.50, five minutes).

## Things to See

**Ephesus** *(admission US$10; open 8am-5pm daily, 8.30am-7pm in summer)* first flourished as a centre for worship of the Anatolian goddess later identified with Diana/Artemis. The **Arcadian Way** through Ephesus was the main street to the port, which has long been silted up. The immense **Great Theatre** holds 24,000 people. The **Temple of Hadrian**, the **Celsus Library**, the **Marble Way** (where the rich lived), the **Terraced Houses** *(Yamaç*

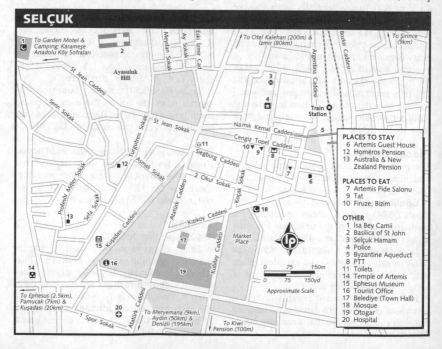

**SELÇUK**

PLACES TO STAY
6 Artemis Guest House
12 Homeros Pension
13 Australia & New Zealand Pension

PLACES TO EAT
7 Artemis Pide Salonu
9 Tat
10 Firuze; Bizim

OTHER
1 İsa Bey Camii
2 Basilica of St John
3 Selçuk Hamam
4 Police
5 Byzantine Aqueduct
8 PTT
11 Toilets
14 Temple of Artemis
15 Ephesus Museum
16 Tourist Office
17 Belediye (Town Hall)
18 Mosque
19 Otogar
20 Hospital

*Evleri; admission US$20)* and the **Fountain of Trajan** are still in amazingly good shape, or under painstaking restoration. A centre for early Christianity, Ephesus was also visited by St Paul.

Selçuk's main site is the excellent **Ephesus Museum** *(admission US$2; open 8.30am-noon & 12.30pm-4.30pm)*, with its priceless collection of artefacts from the Roman period. Above Selçuk, visit the **Basilica of St John** *(admission US$2; open 8am-6pm)*, said to be built over his tomb. Between Ephesus and Selçuk, the foundations of the **Temple of Artemis** are all that remain of one of the Seven Wonders of the Ancient World.

## Places to Stay
**Garden Motel & Camping** *(☎ 892 1163; tent site for two US$7)* is west of Ayasuluk Hill, with tent sites in an idyllic location amid fruit orchards.

Selçuk has almost 100 small *pensions* mostly charging US$7 per person with perhaps another US$2 for breakfast. They're modest, friendly places, and in some cases it's possible to sleep on the roof or camp in the garden for US$2 to US$3 per person.

**Homeros Pension** *(☎ 892 3995; Asmalı Sokak 17)* has some simple *pension* rooms across the road from slightly more expensive, beautiful, individually decorated rooms. There's a good roof terrace.

**Australia & New Zealand Pension** *(☎ 892 1050;* **w** *www.anzturkishguesthouse.com; Profesör Mitler Sokak 17)*, has a dormitory and comfortable rooms with showers set around a courtyard, and excellent meals on its roof terrace.

**Artemis Guest House** *(Jimmy's Place; ☎ 892 6191;* **w** *www.artemisguesthouse .com; 1012 Sokak 2)*, in the newer part of town, offers a multitude of services for travellers, including a library of information to put the official tourist offices to shame.

**Kiwi Pension** *(Alison's Place; ☎ 891 4892;* **w** *www.kiwipension.com; Kubilay Caddesi 8)* is a spotless place just south of the centre. Its lovely swimming pool is one kilometre away in an orange orchard.

If you have more to spend, **Otel Kalehan** *(☎ 892 6154; singles/doubles with shower & air-con US$30/50)*, on the main road beside the Shell station, has pleasantly decorated rooms in three buildings set around a pool and garden.

## Places to Eat
**Artemis Pide Salonu** *(Cengiz Topel Caddesi; meals US$1.50-2.50)*, a half-block south of the tea garden, is a great place for hit-and-run type meals.

On the next block, **Firuze** and **Bizim** are a bit simpler, with slightly lower prices. Also popular is the **Tat** *(meal with wine around US$6)*.

In a lovely location opposite the İsa Bey Camii **Karameşe Anadolu Köy Sofraları** *(☎ 892 0466; meals US$5)* serves OK kebabs amid picturesque water and greenery.

## Getting There & Away
Selçuk's hassley *otogar* is opposite the tourist office. Buses from İzmir (US$1.75, one hour, 80km) usually drop you on the main highway nearby.

Frequent minibuses head for Kuşadası (US$0.90, 30 minutes, 20km) and the beach at Pamucak (US$0.75, 10 minutes, 7km) from the *otogar*.

## KUŞADASI
☎ 256 • pop 37,100
Kuşadası is a shameless tourist trap and you'll probably want to whip through to catch a boat out to Samos (Greece). If you do decide to stay, there are several attractions nearby and a raging nightlife.

The **tourist office** *(☎ 614 1103)* is beside the pier near the ferry offices.

## Things to See & Do
The 16th-century **castle** on the island in the harbour aside, Kuşadası is short on sights, although it does make a good base for visits to the ancient cities of **Priene**, **Miletus** and **Didyma** *(admission to each site US$1)* to the south. If you're pushed for time a tour of the ancient cities from the *otogar* costs around US$20.

## Places to Stay
Coming from the harbour walk up Barbaros Hayrettin Caddesi, turn right towards the Akdeniz Apartotel, and take Yıldırım Caddesi, the road to the left of the Akdeniz, or Aslanlar Caddesi, the road to the right, to reach most of the *pensions* and cheap hotels.

**Hotel Liman** *(Mr Happy's; ☎ 614 7770; fax 614 6913;* **e** *hasandegirmenci@usa.net; Kıbrıs Caddesi, Buyral Sokak 4; singles/ doubles with shower & air-con US$15/20)* is down by the harbour and could hardly be handier for the ferry to Samos. The attractive, modern building has a lift and tiled bathrooms; the sea-facing doubles are definitely the best rooms but there's also a good-value, five-bed family room.

**Golden Bed Pension** *(☎/fax 614 8707;* W *www.kusadasihotels.com/goldenbed; Aslanlar Caddesi, Uğurlu 1 Çıkmazı 4; singles/ doubles with shower US$8/10)* is tucked away in a quiet cul-de-sac, at the top of a steep hill – it will pay for a taxi to the *pension*. This *pension* is spotlessly clean and has a terrific rooftop terrace with a bar overlooking the town. It's a friendly, peaceful retreat that would suit solo women travellers.

**Sezgin's Guesthouse** *(☎ 514 4225, fax 612 2046;* W *www.sezginhotel.com; Aslanlar Caddesi 68; doubles with shower & with/ without air-con US$18/12)* has lots to offer backpackers, including a laundry, movies in several languages and Internet access. It also offers a swimming pool and garden bar.

**Düsseldorf Pansiyon** *(☎ 614 9473; Yıldırım Caddesi 61; singles/doubles US$4/ 7.50)* is a very simple *pension*, which is run by an elderly couple, in a fine old building in the old part of town. Breakfast in the garden costs US$1.30.

**Hotel Sammy's Palace** *(☎ 612 2588, fax 612 9991;* W *www.hotelsammyspalace.com; Kıbrıs Caddesi 14; dorm beds US$5, singles/ doubles with shower US$12/16)* is up the hill as you come in on the ferry from Samos – chances are if that's the way you're arriving someone touting for Sammy's will already have met you in Greece. Some rooms have air-con. Breakfast is US$2 extra.

**Stella Traveller's Inn** *(☎ 614 1632, fax 612 9012; Bezirgan Sokak 44; dorm beds US$6, singles/doubles with shower US$12/ 24)* used to be a package-holiday hotel with fabulous views over the harbour. It has now been reincarnated as a backpackers place, complete with pool and restaurant.

## Places to Eat

Kuşadası is fish-and-chips and 'full English breakfast' country. For something more Turkish cut into the Kaleiçi district behind the harbour and try **Avlu** *(Cephane Sokak; meals US$3)*, with indoor and outdoor tables and tasty soups and stews.

Good seafood places facing the harbour charge US$15 to US$25 for a fish dinner,

depending on the fish and the season. Try **Toros** *(Balıkı Limanı; meals US$10-15)* for friendly service and excellent sea bream.

For drinks and snacks, the Kaleiçi district shelters several charming café-bars, a million miles more sophisticated than the crass offerings of Barlar Sokak (Bar Lane).

## Getting There & Away

Kuşadası's *otogar* is 1.5km southeast of the centre on the bypass at the southern end of Kahramanlar Caddesi. Direct buses depart for far-flung parts of the country, or you can transfer at İzmir (US$2.50, every 30 minutes) or Söke. In summer there are frequent buses to Bodrum (US$4, two hours) and Denizli (for Pamukkale; US$6, three hours).

For Selçuk (US$0.90, 30 minutes) pick up a minibus on Adnan Menderes Bulvarı.

In summer three boats sail daily to Samos (US$30/35/55 one way/same-day return/open return). In winter there may be only one or two boats per week.

## PAMUKKALE
☎ 258

Way inland east of Selçuk, Pamukkale is renowned for the brilliant white ledges with pools (travertines) that flow over the plateau edge. Sadly, in recent years the water supply has dried up and you can only swim in odd corners here and there. Behind this natural wonder lie the extensive ruins of Roman Hierapolis, an ancient spa town.

## Travertines & Hierapolis Ruins

As you climb the hill above Pamukkale village you pay to enter the **travertines and Hierapolis** *(admission US$3; open ticket valid from 9am-9am next day)*. The ruins of Hierapolis, including a theatre, a colonnaded street with public toilet and a vast necropolis, are very spread out; allow at least half a day to do them justice.

You can swim amid sunken Roman columns at **Pamukkale Termal** *(US$3)* on top of the ridge and visit **Hierapolis Archaeology Museum** *(admission US$0.75; open 9am-noon & 1pm-5pm Tues-Sun)*, which contains some spectacular sarcophagi and friezes from Hierapolis and nearby Afrodisias.

## Places to Stay

Over 60 *pensions* and hotels lurk below the travertines in Pamukkale village. For cheerful service and decent rooms, good bargains are **Kervansaray Pension** (☎ 272 2209; e ker vansaray2@superonline.com; singles/doubles with shower US$12/18) and the nearby **Aspawa** (☎ 272 2094; e aspawa@mail.koc .net.tr; singles/doubles US$8/12). Breakfast is included in the room rates at both places. **Weisse Burg Pension** (☎ 272 2064; singles/ doubles US$6/12) comes recommended by readers. An excellent breakfast costs US$2, dinners are US$5.

**Meltem Motel** (☎ 272 2413; e meltem motel@superonline.com; dorm beds/singles/ doubles US$4/5/8) is big and popular with backpackers. It has its own pool and a rooftop terrace.

**Koray Motel** (☎ 272 2300; w www.koray hotel.com; Fevzi Çakmak Caddesi 27; doubles with shower US$20), a few streets south, has a poolside restaurant and bar, and tour services.

### Places to Eat
Eating in your *pension* or hotel is usually the best idea. Of Pamukkale's restaurants, the **Gürsoy** (meals US$4-6), opposite the Yörük Motel, has the nicest terrace, but the **Han** (meals US$4-6), around the corner, offers best value for money.

### Getting There & Away
Frequent buses run from İzmir to Denizli (US$4, four hours, 260km). There are also regular buses from Denizli to Konya (US$10, seven hours, 440km).

Municipal buses and *dolmuşes* make the half-hour trip between Pamukkale and Denizli every 30 minutes or so (US$0.50).

## BODRUM
☎ 252 • pop 30,000
Bodrum (formerly Halicarnassus) is the site of the Mausoleum, the monumental tomb of King Mausolus and another of the Seven Wonders of the Ancient World. By some miracle Bodrum has managed to avoid the urban sprawl that has so damaged Kuşadası and Marmaris – in spring and autumn it's still a delightful place to stay.

### Orientation & Information
The *otogar* is 500m inland on Cevat Sakir Caddesi from the Adliye Camii, a mosque in the town centre. The **PTT** and several banks are on Cevat Sakir. The **tourist office** (☎ 316 1091) is beside the Castle of St Peter.

### Things to See
There's little left of the **Mausoleum** (admission US$2; open 8am-noon & 12.30pm-5pm Tues-Sun) although the Castle of St Peter, built in 1402 and rebuilt in 1522 by the Crusaders, using stones from the tomb, makes up for its shortcomings. The castle houses the **Museum of Underwater Archaeology** (admission US$7; open 8am-noon & 1pm-5pm Tues-Sun), containing finds from the oldest Mediterranean shipwreck ever discovered (admission US$2; open 10am-11am & 2pm-4pm); and a model of a Carian princess' tomb (admission US$2; open 10am-noon & 2pm-4pm).

Westward past the marina and over the hill, **Gümbet** has a nicer beach than Bodrum but is solid package-holiday territory; you may prefer less developed **Ortakent**. **Gümüşlük**, to the west of the Bodrum peninsula, is the least spoilt of the many smaller villages nearby. Hourly *dolmuşes* run there (US$1).

### Places to Stay
The narrow streets north of Bodrum's western harbour have pleasant family-run *pensions*, generally charging around US$18 to US$25 per doubles in the high season. Those behind the western bay tend to be quieter than those on the eastern bay because they're further from the famously noisy Halikarnas Disco. Few places stay open in winter.

Two quiet, modern places are tucked away down a narrow alley which begins between Neyzen Tevfik 84 and 86: **Yenilmez** (☎ 316 2520; Menekşe Çıkmazı 30; doubles with shower US$18) and **Menekşe** (☎ 316 5890; Menekşe Çıkmazı 34; doubles with shower US$18).

**Emiko Pension** (☎/fax 316 5560; Atatürk Caddesi, Uslu Sokak 11; beds with shower US$5) is spotless, quiet and is run by a Japanese woman.

Türkkuyusu Sokak starts just north of the Adliye Camii and passes several good *pensions*, mostly with shady courtyards. **Şenlik Pansiyon** (☎ 316 6382; Türkkuyusu Sokak 115; beds with showers from US$6) could do with new mattresses but stays open when other places close. **Sedan** (☎ 316 0355; Türkkuyusu Sokak 121; doubles with/ without shower US$24/16), just behind it, is a family-run place with some newer rooms.

**Su Otel** (☎ 316 6906; Turgutreis Caddesi, 1201 Sokak; singles/doubles with shower & air-con US$40/65) is a colourful oasis set around a charming, flower-filled courtyard, with a swimming pool; the rooms are decorated with local crafts.

## Places to Eat

The small streets east of the Adliye Camii harbour several cheap eateries where you can grab a *döner kebab* for less than US$2 at a streetside buffet. Otherwise, continue eastward to Kilise Meydanı, a plaza filled with open-air restaurants. At either **Nazilli** or **Karadeniz** a *pide* topped with meat or cheese should cost only US$3. **Vida** *(meals US$5)*, just around from Karadeniz, does an excellent tomato soup for US$0.75.

In warm weather, check out Meyhaneler Sokak (Taverna St), off İskele Caddesi. Wall-to-wall tavernas serve food, drink and live music to rapturous crowds for US$10 to US$15; **İbo** seems particularly good and offers *mezes* such as stuffed vine leaves and octopus salad.

**Yağhane** *(☎ 313 4747; meals around US$20)*, on the western bay, is housed in an old olive-oil factory. At the time of writing it was the 'in' place with the upmarket yachting clientele. Alternatively, head for the serial fish restaurants lining the eastern bay, making sure to check all prices before ordering.

## Getting There & Away

Bodrum **airport** *(☎ 523 0129)* is actually nearer to Milas and has few flights. Havaş buses meet arrivals and charge US$4.50 for the Bodrum run. The taxi fare is US$32.

Bodrum offers frequent bus services to Antalya (US$10, 11 hours, 640km), Fethiye (US$6, 4½ hours, 265km), İzmir (US$10, four hours, 250km), Kuşadası and Selçuk (US$4, three hours) and Marmaris (US$5, three hours, 165km).

In summer daily hydrofoils and boats link Bodrum with Kos *(one way/day return from US$14/18 )*; in winter services shrink to three times weekly. In summer there are also boats to Datça, Knidos, Marmaris and Rhodes; check with the ferry offices near the castle.

# The Mediterranean Coast

Turkey's Mediterranean coastline winds eastward for more than 1200km from Marmaris to Antakya on the Syrian border. From Marmaris to Fethiye the gorgeous 'Turquoise Coast' is perfect for boat excursions, with many secluded coves for swimming. The rugged peninsula between Fethiye and Antalya and the Taurus Mountains east of Antalya are wild and beautiful. Further east you pass through fewer resorts and more workaday cities. The entire coast is liberally sprinkled with impressive ruins.

## MARMARİS

☎ 252 • pop 22,700

Like Bodrum, Marmaris sits on a beautiful bay at the edge of a hilly peninsula. Unlike Bodrum, however, Marmaris has succumbed to unplanned, haphazard development, which has robbed it of much of its charm – although you may still want to drop by to sample the nightlife and the shopping and to hop on a boat to Rhodes.

## Orientation & Information

İskele Meydanı (main square) and the **tourist office** *(☎ 412 1035)* are by the ferry pier northeast of the castle. The **PTT** *(Fevzipaşa Caddesi)* is in the bazaar, which is mostly a pedestrian precinct. Hacı Mustafa Sokak, aka Bar St, runs inland from the bazaar; action here keeps going until the early hours.

The *otogar* is 2km north of town, off the road to Bodrum.

## Things to See & Do

The small **castle** *(admission US$0.75; open 8am-noon & 1pm-5pm Tues-Sun)* has a few unexciting exhibition rooms but offers fine views of Marmaris.

Wooden boats along the waterfront offer tours of outlying beaches and islands. Before picking your boat, check carefully what the excursion costs, where it goes, whether lunch is included and, if so, what's on the menu. A day's outing usually costs around US$16 to US$20 per person.

The most popular excursions are to **Dalyan** and **Kaunos** or to the bays around Marmaris, but you can also take longer, more serious boat trips to Datça and ruins at Knidos. It's also worth asking about boats heading for **Cleopatra's Island**, which offers silky-soft sand and water as warm as a Jacuzzi.

## Places to Stay

Unlike Kuşadası and Bodrum, Marmaris lacks a network of small, welcoming *pensions*.

Indeed, almost all the cheaper places have been squeezed out by the relentless growth of hotels serving the package-holiday market. The cheapies that remain may be fairly central but are often noisy and uninspiring. There are several moderately priced hotels a short walk from İskele Meydanı.

The **Interyouth Hostel** (*☎/fax 412 7823; Tepe Mahallesi, 42 Sokak 45*) is deep in the bazaar. In season it's a good travellers' hangout with lots of services and atmosphere. Out of season, it charges more than some of the cheaper hotels for grim rooms without shower.

Otherwise, to find the cheapest accommodation stroll along the waterfront to Abdi İpekçi Park and turn inland just past the park, then left at the first street and right past Ayçe Otel. **Maltepe Pension** (*☎ 412 1629; rooms with shower US$20*), across a wooden footbridge, is serviceable. The **Özcan Pension** (*☎ 412 7761; Çam Sokak 3*), next door, is bigger but similarly priced.

**Hotel Aylin** (*☎ 412 8283; 1. Sokak 4; singles/doubles with shower from US$5/9*) offers reasonably comfortable rooms even at times of year when most places close.

**Hotel Begonya** (*☎ 412 4095; Hacı Mustafa Sokak 71; singles/doubles with shower US$20/35*) is potentially delightful, with a breakfast courtyard filled with plants. But Hacı Mustafa is wall-to-wall bars – good news if you're up for a big night, not so great if you're keener on your beauty sleep.

## Places to Eat

Marmaris has literally hundreds of restaurants. For the cheapest fare, head for the PTT in the bazaar. Just inland from it are several good, cheap restaurants including **Sofra** (*36. Sokak 23; meals US$3.50*) and **Liman Restaurant** (*40. Sokak 32; meals US$5*). Both places heave with happy diners at lunchtime.

Cut inland from the Atatürk statue along Ulusal Egemenlik Bulvarı and turn right opposite the Tansaş shopping centre to find **Kırçiçeği Pide-Pizza Çorba ve Kebap Salonu** (*Yeni Yol Caddesi 15; meals US$3*), which is always crowded with locals, tucking into soups and filling *pides*.

The **waterfront restaurants** beyond the tourist office have pleasant outdoor dining areas but prices are higher than those inland and the extra pays for the setting, not the food. Assume you'll spend between US$10 and US$20 per person for a full meal with wine.

**Kartal Restaurant & Terrace Bar** (*☎ 412 3308; Eski Cami Sokak; meal with drinks US$12-18*) is in the attractive castle area; follow the signs from the waterfront to find it.

## Getting There & Away

The nearest airports are Bodrum and Dalaman.

Marmaris *otogar* has frequent buses and minibuses to Antalya (US$9.50, seven hours, 590km), Bodrum (US$4, three hours, 165km), Dalyan (via Ortaca; US$2, two hours), Datça (US$3, 1¾ hours, 75km), and Fethiye (US$4, three hours, 170km).

Car ferries run to Rhodes daily in summer (less frequently in winter; US$32/50 one way/return).

## DATÇA
**☎ 0252 • pop 6100**

Marmaris not your scene? Then why not jump on a bus west to Datça, a smaller, quieter reminder of what Marmaris might have been like in its heyday with the added bonus of a spectacular ride to reach it? Datça has no specific sites although there's a nice outdoor cinema by the harbour, and in summer you can take boat trips to Knidos or the Greek islands of Rhodes and Symi. Old Datça, a picturesque hamlet of cobbled streets and old stone houses on the eastern outskirts, is an even quieter place to stay.

### Places to Stay

**Tuna Pansiyon** (*☎ 712 3931; İskele Caddesi; singles/doubles with shower US$10/13*) has clean, comfortable rooms, some with sea-facing balconies. **Huzur Pansiyon** (*☎ 712 3364; Yat Liman Mevii; singles/doubles with shower US$13/20*) is similar but much closer to the harbour with its bars and restaurants.

**Hotel Club Dorya** (*☎ 712 3593; singles/doubles with shower US$25/42*) is right on the promontory at the far end of Datça. The gardens and views are great, but the rooms could do with brightening up.

**Dede Pansiyon** (*☎/fax 712 3951; W www.nisanyan.net; Old Datça; singles/doubles with shower & air-con US$17/34*) consists of half a dozen individually decorated rooms set in a pretty garden with its own pool.

### Getting There & Away

Regular buses ply back and forth between Marmaris and Datça (US$3, 1¾ hours, 90km). Minibuses from Datça to Karaköy pass the junction to Old Datça regularly (US$0.30). It's a five-minute walk into the village.

## KÖYCEĞİZ
☎ 252 • pop 7,600

In early spring Köyceğiz smells sweetly of orange blossom, a reminder that this quiet town on the edge of a placid lake still has a farming life beyond tourism. It makes a pleasant alternative to Dalyan if you want to visit Kaunos, wallow in the mud baths and laze on İstuzu beach.

### Places to Stay & Eat
Tango Pansiyon (☎ 262 2501; W www.tango pension.com; Ali İhsan Kalmaz Caddesi; dorm beds US$5, singles/doubles with shower US$12/16) has clean, pleasant rooms and a range of activities, from moonlight cruises to short treks. If it's full, the same people run Samba Pension, nearby.

Hotel Kaunos (☎ 262 4288; singles/ doubles with shower US$5/10) has a decent waterfront location but rather faded rooms.

Hotel Alila (☎/fax 262 1150; Emeksiz Caddesi; singles/doubles with shower US$14/24) is newer and altogether more cheerful, with a fine pool and an inviting dining room.

Çiçek Restaurant (meals US$5) on the main square is good for people-watching while you eat standard fare, but Colıba (Emeksiz Caddesi; meals US$5) exhibits more flair in both its menu and decor.

### Getting There & Away
There are hourly dolmuşes from Ortaca (US$0.75, 25 minutes) or Muğla (US$1.50, one hour).

## DALYAN
☎ 252

Set on the banks of a placid river and backed by a cliff-face cut with elegant Lycian tombs, Dalyan was always too good to remain undiscovered by tour operators and some people now feel it has become a bit too touristy. Still, İztuzu beach, a short boat hop along the river, is a gorgeous place to sun yourself (as well as being one of the few remaining nesting grounds of the carretta carretta, or sea turtle). The same boat trips (US$5.50) usually take in a visit to the ruined city of Kaunos (Caunos; admission US$2; open 8.30am-5.30pm daily) and the Sultaniye hot springs (admission US$0.75) on the shores of Köyceğiz Lake.

### Places to Stay & Eat
Dalyan Camping (tent sites US$4) is 500m southwest of the dolmuş stand.

There's a cluster of places in Yalı Sokak, northwest of Maraş Caddesi, past the school.

Hotel Caria (☎ 284 2075; doubles with shower US$20) has comfortable rooms with balconies and a gorgeous, river-facing roof terrace.

Çınar Sahil Pansiyon (☎ 284 2117), across the road, is more casual about its welcome but has an equally inviting location.

Hotel Dönmez (☎ 284 2107; doubles with shower US$17), close by, has the added benefit of a swimming pool.

Most Dalyan restaurants serve a predictable menu of mezes, kebabs and fish but Metin Pide & Pizza Restaurant (Sulungur Sokak; meals US$2) rustles up excellent Italian-style pizzas.

It's a shameless tourist trap but you could also try the Ley Ley Restaurant (☎ 384 4660; Dalyan Yolu; meals US$8-10), which looks out over storks nesting.

### Getting There & Away
From Dalaman airport or Marmaris, take a bus to Ortaca and change for a minibus to Dalyan (US$0.50, 30 minutes).

## GÖCEK
☎ 252

About 23km east of Dalaman is the pretty yachting harbour and fishing port of Göcek, on a bay at the foot of the mountains. It has a few cheap pensions (and pricier hotels) overlooking the waters. There's nothing much here to do except cruise the outlying islands but it's a good, quiet place to unwind.

### Places to Stay
Küçükkargı Ormaniçl Dinlenme Yeri (2-person tent US$3), 10km east of Göcek, has camping facilities in woodland overlooking a lovely bay.

Taştepe (☎ 645 1372; Atatürk Caddesi; doubles with shower US$8) has fairly simple rooms, but those facing the harbour are very inviting. Pension Tufan's (☎ 645 1334; doubles with shower US$10) has similarly appealing harbour-facing front rooms.

### Getting There & Away
Hourly minibuses for Göcek (US$1) depart from behind Fethiye's Yeni Cami.

## FETHİYE

☎ 252 • pop 48,200

Despite its picture-postcard harbour backdrop, Fethiye still has much more of the feel of a living town than big resorts like Kuşadası and Marmaris. It can be very hot and crowded in summer but is still worth a visit and makes a good base for visiting the beautiful **Saklıkent Gorge** and the ruins at **Tlos** and **Pınara**. The beach at **Calış**, 5km northeast of the centre, is many kilometres long, and backed by hotels.

### Orientation & Information

Fethiye's *otogar* is 2km east of the centre. Karagözler *dolmuşes* ply up and down the main street, taking you past the government buildings, the PTT and several banks, before skirting the bazaar district, curving around the bay past the **tourist office** (☎/fax 614 1527), and cutting up by the marina on the western side of the town.

### Things to See & Do

Of ancient Telmessos, little more remains than the ruins of a theatre and several Lycian sarcophagi dating from about 400 BC. The picturesque rock-cut **Tomb of Amyntas** (admission US$2; open 8am-7pm) makes a perfect vantage point for watching the sun set over the harbour.

Most people succumb to the **'12 Island'** boat tour, which mixes swimming, cruising and sightseeing; prices start at around US$8 per person. Don't miss the **hammam** (open 7am-midnight) in the bazaar either.

*Dolmuşes* run to the nearby Ottoman Greek 'ghost town' of **Kaya Köy** (admission US$2), abandoned after the population exchange of 1923.

### Places to Stay

Most of the better *pensions* are uphill from the yacht marina along Fevzi Çakmak Caddesi; take a Karagözler *dolmuş* along the harbour road to reach them. **Yıldırım** (☎ 614 3913), **Pınara** (☎ 614 2151) and **İrem** (☎ 614 3985) all charge around US$16/30 for singles/doubles with shower and breakfast.

**İdeal Pension** (☎ 614 1981; W www.ide alpension.com; Zafer Caddesi 1; singles/doubles with shower US$5/10), a street back from the harbour road, has great views from its terrace and a range of backpacker services: laundry, Internet access, book exchange etc.

**Ferah Pension** (Monica's Place; ☎ 614 2816; W www.backpackingeurope.com; 2 Karagözler Mahallesi, Ordu Caddesi 2; dorm beds US$5, doubles with/without shower US$12/10) has nicer rooms but is a little further from the centre. Dinners are said to be impressive. Breakfast is US$2 extra.

**Cennet Pansiyon** (☎ 614 2230; 2 Karagözler Mahallesi; doubles with shower US$7) has a pleasant waterside location. An on-site restaurant makes up for the rather remote position.

### Places to Eat

Side by side on Tütün Sokak are two local favourites – **Sedir Restaurant** and **Şamdan Restaurant** – both serving excellent pizza for around US$3.50. In Eski Cami Geçidi Likya Sokak look out for the popular **Meğri** (meals US$5) with a wide range of piping hot meals.

Right opposite the post office **Birlik Lokantası** (Atatürk Caddesi; meals US$4) serves up big portions of *İskender kebab*.

Near the *hammams*, **Café Oley** (Eski Meğri Sokak 4; meals US$5) offers such unexpected delights as smoked salmon sandwiches for anyone kebabed out.

### Getting There & Away

If you're heading for Antalya, note that the *yayla* (inland) route is shorter and cheaper (US$6) than the *sahil* (coastal) route (US$8). The midibuses that ply the coastal route also serve Patara, Kınık (for Xanthos; US$2), Kalkan (US$2) and Kaş (US$3). Minibuses to local destinations leave from behind the big white Yeni Cami in the town centre.

A summer hydrofoil service links Rhodes (Greece) and Fethiye on Tuesday and Thursday (one-way/same-day return/open-return fares US$50/75/95).

## ÖLÜDENİZ

☎ 252

Over the mountains to the south of Fethiye, lovely **Ölüdeniz** (Dead Sea) has proved a bit too beautiful for its own good and now has far too many hotels catering for the package holiday market backed up behind the sands. Still, the lagoon itself remains tranquillity incarnate (admission US$0.50; open 8am-8pm) and along its banks you'll find moderately priced bungalows and camping areas. This is a good place to try **tandem paragliding** for a cool US$100.

## Places to Stay & Eat

**Ölüdeniz Camping** (☎ 617 0048; treehouse beds/tents US$1.75/3, bungalows from US$8) is probably the most popular choice although there are several similar camping grounds further around the lagoon near the Hotel Meri.

**Hotel Meri** (☎ 617 0001; W www.hotelmeri.com; doubles with shower from US$74) is the oldest and most appealing of Ölüdeniz's hotels, not least because it has gardens and a pool of its own.

When it comes to eating, you may well feel disinclined to venture further than the **cafés** attached to the camping grounds.

## Getting There & Away

Frequent *dolmuşes* to Ölüdeniz (US$1, 30 minutes, 17km) run from behind Fethiye's Yeni Cami.

## PATARA
☎ 0242

Patara's main claim to fame is its superb 20km beach, one of the best in Turkey. However, there are also extensive **ruins** (admission US$7; open 7.30am-7pm daily May-Oct; 8am-5.30pm Nov-Mar) here.

## Places to Stay

All the places to stay and most places to eat are in Gelemiş village, 1.5km inland from the beach. All these places to stay charge US$7 for a bed with shower.

**Flower Pension** (☎ 843 5164) is one of the furthest inland but has the plus of a host who's particularly welcoming.

**St Nicholas Pension** (☎ 843 5024) is a bit more central and offers services like a terrace restaurant and canoe hire.

**Golden Pension** (☎ 843 5162), opposite, has a restaurant. Some rooms have fans.

## Getting There & Away

Midibuses plying the Fethiye–Antalya main road will drop you 2km from Gelemiş village (3.5km from the beach, signposted 'Patara').

## AROUND PATARA

From Patara (or Fethiye) it's easy to visit two of Turkey's Unesco-listed World Heritage Sites, both of them atmospheric ruins. The **Letoön** (admission US$2), just off the Fethiye–Antalya highway near Kumluova, boasts excellent mosaics, a good theatre and a sacred pool used in the worship of the goddess Leto.

With its Roman theatre and Lycian pillar tombs, **Xanthos** (admission US$2), a few kilometres southeast of Letoön above the village of Kınık, is among the most impressive sites along this part of the coast, even though many of its best sculptures are now in the British Museum (London).

## KALKAN
☎ 242

Once a quaint fishing village but now a rather Disneyfied, upmarket tourist resort, Kalkan is 11km east of the Patara turn-off. Its narrow streets lined with pretty houses tumble down a steep hillside to a marina with plenty of open-air restaurants.

## Places to Stay

**Kalamaki Pension** (☎ 844 3649; doubles with shower US$24) is a popular choice with an excellent rooftop restaurant.

**Balıkçı Han** (☎ 844 3075; doubles with shower US$34) was designed to look like an older building and is very atmospheric.

**Daphne Pansiyon** (☎ 844 3547; Kocakaya Caddesi; singles/doubles with shower US$12/25), near the mosque on the road down to the harbour, is nicely decorated and throws in breakfast on its roof terrace.

**Patara Stone House** (☎ 844 3076; singles/doubles with shower US$13/25) is almost hidden beneath a veil of bougainvillea, right on the waterfront. **Çetinkaya Pension** (☎ 844 3307; doubles with shower US$10), nearby, seems especially friendly.

## Getting There & Away

Hourly buses connect Kalkan with Kaş (US$1, 35 minutes, 29km) and Patara (US$0.50, 25 minutes, 15km).

## KAŞ
☎ 242  •  pop 8000

Kaş is another of those places that seems to have everything: a picturesque quayside, pleasant restaurants, excellent shops, a scattering of Lycian tombs and a big Sunday **market**. Even the **tourist office** (☎ 836 1238), on the main square, is better informed than most.

## Things to See & Do

Apart from enjoying the town's ambience and few small pebble beaches, you can walk west a few hundred metres to the well-preserved **theatre**. Lycian **sarcophagi** are dotted about the streets, and tombs cut into the cliffs above the town.

The most popular boat trip sails around **Kekova** island and out to beautiful **Kaleköy** (Simena), passing over Lycian ruins beneath the sea. You'll pay around US$10 per person in a glass-bottomed boat.

Other excursions take in Patara, Xanthos and the wonderful 18km-long **Saklıkent Gorge**, where you can eat trout on platforms over an ice-cold river.

## Places to Stay
**Kaş Camping** (☎ 836 1050; tent sites US$5) is in an olive grove just west of town.

Kaş' quietest places to stay are all on the western side of town and rise in price (and quality) the nearer you get to the sea. Yenicami Caddesi, just south of the otogar, has lots of small, family-run pensions, including **Orion Hotel** (☎/fax 836 1286); **Anıl Motel** (☎ 836 1791), **Hilal** (☎ 836 1207) and **Santoşa** (☎ 836 1714). In high season a bed with shower in any of these places are likely to cost US$10 including breakfast.

Turn right at Ay Pansiyon and follow the signs to one of Kaş' best places to stay. **Kale Otel** (☎ 836 4074; Kilise Mevkii; singles/doubles with shower & air-con US$20/33) is immaculately clean, with a lawn overlooking the sea, lovely rooms and great breakfasts. It's often very busy with German groups. **Hotel Korsan Karakedi** (☎ 836 1887; Yeni Cami Sokak 7; singles/doubles with shower US$10/23), up the hill behind it, offers a warm welcome to compensate for lumpy bedding.

**Ateş Pension** (☎ 836 1393; e atespension@superonline.com; doubles with shower US$10), one more street back, rambles across two buildings but has a good rooftop terrace.

## Places to Eat
**Corner Cafe**, at the PTT end of İbrahim Serin Caddesi, serves juices or a vegetable omelette for US$1, and yogurt with fruit and honey for US$1.75. **Cafe Merhaba**, across the street, is good for cakes, coffee and it has Western newspapers.

**Sympathy Restaurant** (☎ 836 2418; Uzunçarşı Gürsöy Sokak 11; meals around US$8) offers excellent cooking, including a fine spread of mezes, in a cosy atmosphere.

**Mercan Restaurant** (meals US$12-18) is popular because of its waterside location but if you order fish, its worth checking to be sure you receive the variety you've ordered.

For cheaper eats, cut up Atatürk Bulvarı and try either **2000 Restaurant** or **Kervan Restaurant**, both busiest at lunchtime.

## Getting There & Away
Frequent midibuses connect Kaş with Kalkan (US$1, 35 minutes, 29km) and Kale (Demre; US$1.30, one hour, 45km).

## KALE (DEMRE)
☎ 0242  •  pop 13,600
Set on an alluvial plain covered in greenhouses, Kale (ancient Myra) is famous for a generous 4th-century bishop who, according to legend, gave anonymous gifts to dowryless girls, thus enabling them to marry. He was later canonised as St Nicholas, the original Father Christmas (Noel Baba in Turkish). The restored 3rd-century **Church of St Nicholas** (admission US$4; open 8am-5.30pm daily) supposedly holds his tomb but it is more interesting for the remains of Byzantine frescoes and mosaic floors.

About 2km inland from the church is a rock face honeycombed with ancient **Lycian tombs**, right next to a large **Roman theatre** (admission US$7; open 8am-5.30pm daily).

## Getting There & Away
Frequent midibuses ply up and down the coastal road, connecting Kale with Kaş and the turn-off for Olympos.

## OLYMPOS & ÇİRALİ
☎ 0242
After climbing into the mountains, the switchback coastal road reaches a turn-off marked for Olympos. From here it's just over 8km down a winding unpaved road to the village and a further 3.5km along an ever-worsening road to **ancient Olympos** (admission US$7), a wild, abandoned place where ruins peek out from forest copses, rock outcrops and riverbanks. You have to pay the admission fee for the ruins to access the beach from Olympos, although your ticket should be valid for a week.

Most people come here to stay in the treehouses lining the road from the beach. If that's not your thing, there are normal pensions and hotels at neighbouring Çirali.

## Chimaera

According to legend, the Chimaera (Yanartaş), a natural eternal flame, was the hot breath of a subterranean monster. Easily sighted by mariners in ancient times, it is today a mere glimmer of its former fiery self but no less exotic for all that.

To find the Chimaera, follow the signs 3km east down a neighbouring valley. A half-hour climb leads to the flames.

## Places to Stay & Eat

**Olympos** Lining the road to the Olympos ruins are assorted treehouse-cabin-bar complexes where prices of around US$5 per person in a treehouse or US$7 in a cabin include breakfast and dinner.

**Kadir's** (☎ 892 1250), the granddaddy of them all and still the most visually inviting, offers rustic, ramshackle charm with Internet connections but is furthest from the beach.

**Bayram's** (☎ 892 1243; W www.bayrams .com) doesn't look quite so pretty but is the sort of place where you arrive for a day and find yourself staying a week.

**Türkmen** (☎ 892 1249) is popular with holidaying Turkish families, while **Orange** (☎ 892 1242) and **Şaban** (☎ 892 1265) also get good reviews.

**Çirali** A separate turn from the Fethiye–Antalya highway less than a kilometre east of the Olympos turn-off leads to the more conventional *pensions* and hotels at Çirali. Or you can get there by walking a kilometre along the beach from Olympos.

**Olympos Lodge** (☎ 825 7171; e olimpos lodge@superonline.com; singles/doubles with shower US$87/134) is a delightful place with a well-tended garden right by the beach.

**Sima Peace Pension** (☎ 825 7245; singles/ doubles with shower US$10/15) is a pleasing group of wooden chalets set around a garden.

## Getting There & Away

Buses and midibuses playing the Fethiye-Antalya road will drop you at the Olympos or Çirali turn-offs. In summer *dolmuşes* wait to run you down to Olympos (US$0.50); if you don't want to walk the seven kilometres to Çirali you may need to ring a *pension* to collect you, or take a taxi.

The nicest way to get from Olympos to Fethiye or vice versa is on a three- or four-day 'blue cruise' on a *gület* (wooden yacht), calling in at bays along the way. Prices for three-day cruises start from around US$100.

## ANTALYA
☎ 242 • pop 509,000

A bustling, modern town, Antalya has more than just its lovely harbour setting to boast about and so avoids that soullessness that tends to come over resorts that live only for tourism. It's fun to kick around in **Kaleiçi**, the old restored Ottoman town which spreads back from a beautiful marina and the sea-facing Karaalioğlu Parkı.

Pebbly Konyaaltı beach spreads out to the west of town, sandy Lara beach to the east. Both are solidly backed with package-holiday hotels – you'd do best to wait until Olympos for a swim.

## Orientation & Information

The *otogar* is 4km north of the centre on the D650 highway to Burdur. The city centre is at Kalekapısı, a major intersection marked by a landmark clock tower. To get into Kaleiçi, head south down the hill from the clock tower.

The **tourist office** (☎/fax 241 1747; Cumhuriyet Caddesi 91) and the **Turkish Airlines** office (☎ 243 4383) are in the same building 600m west of Kalekapısı in the Özel İdare Çarşısı building. The **PTT** is around the corner in Güllük Caddesi. The **Owl Bookshop** (☎ 243 5718; Akarçeşme Sokak 21) is one of Turkey's best second-hand bookshops.

## Antalya Museum

Antalya Museum (Cumhuriyet Caddesi; tram Müze; admission US$7; open 9am-6pm Tues-Sun) houses the spectacular finds from nearby Perge, Aspendos and Side, as well as a truly wonderful ethnographic collection. Get there on the tramvay (US$0.30) from Kalekapısı.

## Kaleiçi

Heading down from the clock tower you'll pass the **Yivli Minare** (Grooved Minaret), which rises above an old mosque. Further into Kaleiçi the **Kesik Minare** (Truncated Minaret) is built on the site of a ruined Roman temple.

Just off Atatürk Caddesi the monumental **Hadrian's Gate** (Hadriyanüs Kapısı) was built for the Roman emperor's visit in AD 130.

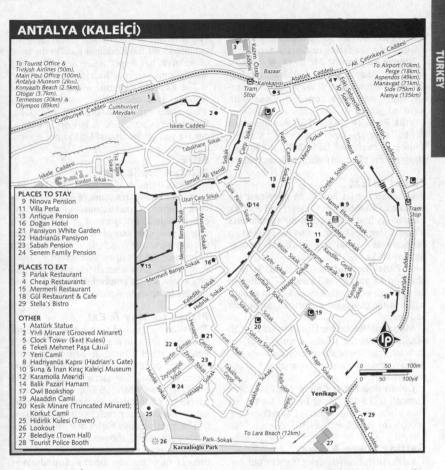

## ANTALYA (KALEİÇİ)

To Tourist Office &
Turkish Airlines (50m),
Main Post Office (100m),
Antalya Museum (2km),
Konyaaltı Beach (2.5km),
Otogar (3.7km),
Termessos (30km) &
Olympos (89km)

To Airport (10km),
Perge (18km),
Aspendos (49km),
Manavgat (71km),
Side (75km) &
Alanya (135km)

**PLACES TO STAY**
9  Ninova Pension
11 Villa Perla
13 Antique Pension
16 Doğan Hotel
21 Pansiyon White Garden
22 Hadrianüs Pansiyon
23 Sabah Pension
24 Senem Family Pension

**PLACES TO EAT**
3  Parlak Restaurant
4  Cheap Restaurants
15 Mermerli Restaurant
18 Gül Restaurant & Cafe
29 Stella's Bistro

**OTHER**
1  Atatürk Statue
2  Yivli Minare (Grooved Minaret)
5  Clock Tower (Saat Kulesi)
6  Tekeli Mehmet Paşa Camii
7  Yeni Camii
8  Hadriyanüs Kapısı (Hadrian's Gate)
10 Suna & İnan Kıraç Kaleiçi Museum
12 Karamolla Mesridi
14 Balık Pazari Hamam
17 Owl Bookshop
19 Alaaddin Camii
20 Kesik Minare (Truncated Minaret);
   Korkut Camii
25 Hidirlik Kulesi (Tower)
26 Lookout
27 Belediye (Town Hall)
28 Tourist Police Booth

---

The **Suna & İnan Kıraç Kaleiçi Museum** (☎ 243 4274; Kocatepe Sokak; admission US$0.75; open 9am-noon & 1pm-6pm Thur-Tues Oct-May; 9am-noon & 2pm-7.30pm Thur-Tues June-Sept) houses a fine collection of pottery together with rooms set up to show important events in Ottoman family life.

## Places to Stay

Kaleiçi is full of *pensions* and more seem to open (and close) every year.

**Pansiyon White Garden** (☎ 241 9115; Hesapçı Geçidi 9; doubles with shower with/without air-con US$18/15) is a spotless family-run place with a pleasant courtyard bar-restaurant.

**Senem Family Pension** (☎ 247 1752; Zeytingeçidi Sokak 9; singles/doubles with shower & air-con US$15/18), near the Hıdırlık Kulesi, offers clean, simple rooms and an inviting roof terrace.

**Sabah Pension** (☎ 247 5345; Hesapçı Sokak 60/A; singles/doubles with shower US$10/16) is a popular backpackers place, offering tours, car hire and evening meals.

**Hadrianüs Pansiyon** (☎ 244 0030; Zeytin Sokak 4/A-B; singles/doubles with shower US$10/20) is a series of old, mostly unrestored buildings around a large walled garden. **Antique Pension** (☎ 242 4615; e antique@ixir.com; Paşa Camii Sokak 28; singles/doubles with shower US$10/17) is equally old but has had the necessary makeover.

For a bit more money Kaleiçi has many other lovely places, including the **Doğan Hotel** (☎ 247 4654; w www.doganhotel.com;

*Mermerli Banyo Sokak 5; singles/doubles with shower US$20/30),* a beautifully rebuilt house with a sea-facing restaurant-terrace.

**Ninova Pension** *(☎ 248 6114;* W *www.ni nova.com; Hamit Efendi Sokak 9; singles/ doubles with shower US$25/40)* has comfortable rooms in a restored house with secluded garden.

**Villa Perla** *(☎ 248 9793;* e *villaperla@ hotmail.com; Hesapçı Sokak 26; singles/ doubles with shower US$50/70)* is a lovely, idiosyncratic place furnished with antiquities.

### Places to Eat

Eski Sebzeciler İçi Sokak, an alley near the junction of Cumhuriyet Caddesi and Atatürk Caddesi, is lined with **open-air restaurants** where a *tandır kebab* (mutton cooked in earthenware), salad and drink can cost as little as US$4.

At **Parlak Restaurant** *(meals US$5-10),* a block up Kazım Özalp/Sarampol Caddesi on the left, skewered chicken and lamb kebabs sizzle in the courtyard as patrons down *rakı* and beer.

**Mermerli Restaurant** *(meals US$7-10),* perched above the southeastern side of the harbour, can't be beaten for sunset views of the bay. Prices are lower than at most harbour restaurants.

**Gül Restaurant & Cafe** *(Kocatepe Sokak 1; meals US$5-10; closed Sunday lunch)* is a cosy place offering a plate of appetisers big enough for three for US$2.50.

### Getting There & Away

Turkish Airlines offers daily flights from Antalya to Ankara and İstanbul. The airport is 10km east of the city centre; the airport bus costs US$2, a taxi about US$10.

From the *otogar,* buses head for Alanya (US$3, 2½ hours, 115km), Göreme (US$12, 10 hours, 485km), Konya (US$12, six hours, 349km), Manavgat/Side (US$2, 1¾ hours, 65km) and Olympos (US$2, 1½ hours, 79km).

## AROUND ANTALYA

Between Antalya and Alanya there are several spectacular Graeco-Roman ruins. **Perge** *(admission US$10),* east of Antalya near Aksu, boasts a 12,000-seat stadium and a 15,000-seat theatre. **Aspendos** *(admission US$10),* 47km east of Antalya, has Turkey's best-preserved ancient theatre, dating from the 2nd century AD and still used for performances

during the Aspendos Festival every June/July. **Termessos** *(admission US$0.75),* high in the mountains off the Korkuteli road to the west of Antalya, has a spectacular setting but demands some vigorous walking and climbing.

The **Köprülü Kanyon,** 96km northeast of Antalya, is a deservedly popular spot for white-water rafting. **Medraft** *(☎ 248 0083; Cumhuriyet Caddesi 76/6, Işlk Apt, Antalya)* can fix you up for around US$55 per person.

## SİDE

☎ 242 • pop 18,000

No doubt because of its fine sandy beaches, Side, four kilometres south of Manavgat, has been overrun by tourists and is now a tawdry, overcrowded caricature of its former self unless you visit out of season. Impressive ancient structures include a **Roman bath** *(admission US$3; open 8am-noon & 1pm-5pm daily),* now a small museum; the old **city walls;** a huge **amphitheatre** *(US$5);* and seaside **temples** to Apollo and Athena.

### Places to Stay & Eat

The village is packed with *pensions* and hotels, which fill up in summer. Inland, **Pettino's Pension** *(☎ 753 3608;* e *pettino@superon line.com; beds with shower US$8)* offers rooms in a wooden house; air-con costs US$5 extra. **Trio's** *(meals US$7),* opposite, is a friendly place that pads out the standard kebab menu with surprises such as curried chicken.

**The Beach House Hotel** *(☎ 753 1607; singles/doubles with shower US$10.50/21)* offers pleasant rooms, some with sea views. The owners also run the nearby **Soundwaves Restaurant** *(meals around US$15),* which offers such delicacies as garlic prawns and onion steak.

**Side Hotel** *(☎ 753 3824; Şarmaşık Sokak 25; singles/doubles with shower US$15/20)* offers comfortable rooms right by the western beach, perfect for a longer stay.

### Getting There & Away

Frequent mini-buses connect Side with Manavgat *otogar* (US$0.30) where there are onward buses to Antalya (US$2, 1¾ hours, 65km) and Alanya (US$2, one hour, 63km).

## ALANYA

☎ 242 • pop 110,100

Alanya is as close as Turkey gets to a no-go zone for independent travellers. It's not that there's a shortage of hotels – far from it, there are hundreds of them. However, most are firmly closed in winter and block-booked to package-holiday companies in summer. You may still want to stop by to take in the ruins of a magnificent Seljuk castle perched high on a hill above town.

The *otogar* is 3km west of the centre; to get into town take a bus from the road leading to the sea (US$0.20) outside the *otogar* and get off at the roundabout by the Küyülarönü Camii. Downhill lies the old waterfront area with trendy shops and good food; uphill above the harbour are the few remaining cheap hotels.

The **tourist office** (*☎/fax 513 1240*) is on the western side of the promontory.

### Things to See & Do

Alanya's crowning glory is the Seljuk **castle** (*admission US$10; open 8am-7pm daily*), a fortress built in 1226 under the reign of Alaeddin Keykubad I, high up above the modern town; take a bus up and the stroll back down to take advantage of the views. It's also worth visiting the **Kızıl Kule** (*Red Tower; admission US$2; open 8am-noon & 1.30pm-5.30pm Tues-Sun*), down by the harbour and also built in 1226.

There are good beaches to the east and west but they're solidly backed with high-rise hotels.

### Places to Stay

Sadly, cheap accommodation has virtually disappeared as *pensions* give way to accommodation for package holidaymakers. A couple of places linger on in noise-ridden İskele Caddesi, above the harbour. The first is **Baba Hotel** (*☎ 513 1032; İskele Caddesi 6; singles/doubles without shower US$6/12*), with mundane rooms.

**Hotel Temiz** (*☎ 513 1016; İskele Caddesi 12; singles/doubles with shower US$15/24*), a little further towards the Kızıl Kule (Red Tower), is more expensive but infinitely more comfortable and welcoming.

**Hotel Kaptan** (*☎ 513 4900; İskele Caddesi; singles/doubles with shower & sea views US$51/66*) has modern rooms and spotless bathrooms.

**Club Hotel Bedesten** (*☎ 512 1234; doubles with shower US$54*) is Alanya's finest offering, right up on the hill with spectacular views.

### Places to Eat

These days to get a cheap bite you have to head well inland to the bazaar and beyond. Otherwise the waterfront restaurants, especially long-lived **Mahperi** (*meals US$8-12*), are worth frequenting for evening meals. Or you could try the **Ottoman House Restaurant** (*Kültür Caddesi; meals US$10-15*) where a big plate of *mezes* as a main course costs US$5.

### Getting There & Away

There are frequent buses to Alanya from Antalya (US$3, 2¾ hours, 115km) and also Manavgat (US$2, one hour, 63km).

### THE EASTERN COAST

East of Alanya the coast sheds some of its touristic freight. About 7km east of **Anamur** there is a wonderful 13th-century castle right on the beach, with *pensions* and camping grounds nearby. The ghostly ruins of Byzantine **Anemurium** are 8.5km west of the town. **Silifke** has a Crusader castle and a ruined Roman temple. From **Taşucu**, 11km southwest of Silifke, boats and hydrofoils depart daily for Girne (Kyrenia) in Northern Cyprus. **Kızkalesi** (Maiden's Castle) is a growing holiday resort with a striking Crusader castle offshore.

### ANTAKYA (HATAY)
☎ 0326

The biblical Antioch, Antakya was vilified as the Roman empire's most depraved city. Undeterred, St Peter dropped by to preach here and you can visit the ancient **St Peter Church** (*St Pierre Kilisesi; cost US$3.50; 8.30am-noon & 1.30pm-4.30pm Tues-Sun*), 3km east of the centre. The magnificent Roman mosaics in the **Antakya Museum** (*admission US$3.50; open 8am-noon & 1.30pm-5pm Tues-Sun*) more than justify the long detour.

### Places to Stay

**Jasmin Hotel** (*☎ 212 7171; İstiklal Caddesi 14; doubles US$6.50*) is about the best choice for basic rooms. **Divan Oteli** (*☎ 215 1518; İstiklal Caddesi 62; singles/doubles with shower US$10/20*) is up a step in quality.

**Onur Hotel** (*☎ 216 2210; İstiklal Sokak 10; singles/doubles with shower US$31/44*), on the edge of the bazaar, is quiet at night and has comfortable, modern rooms.

# Central Anatolia

İstanbul may be exotic and intriguing, the coast's pretty and relaxing, but it's the Anatolian plateau which is Turkey's heartland, as Atatürk acknowledged when he moved the capital to Ankara in 1923.

## ANKARA
☎ 312 • pop 4 million
Despite being the capital of Turkey, no one could call Ankara an exciting city. Nevertheless, due to its central location, and because most of the embassies are here, there's a good chance you'll at least pass through.

### Orientation & Information
Ankara's hisar (citadel) crowns a hill a kilometre east of Ulus Meydanı (Ulus Square), the heart of Old Ankara, with several medium-priced hotels. Nearby Opera Meydanı (Opera Square) has lots of cheap hotels. The newer Ankara lies further south, around Kızılay Meydanı (Kızılay Square) and Kavaklıdere.

Atatürk Bulvarı is the city's main north-south axis. Ankara's mammoth *otogar* is 6.5km southwest of Ulus Meydanı and 6km west of Kızılay Meydanı. The Havaş bus terminal is next to Ankara Garı (train station), 1.4km southwest of Ulus Meydanı.

The **tourist office** (☎/fax 231 5572; Gazi Mustafa Kemal Bulvarı 121) is opposite Maltepe Ankaray station. The main **PTT** (Atatürk Bulvarı) is just south of Ulus Meydanı, although there's a handy branch beside Ankara Garı. There are branches of the main banks with ATM machines in Ulus.

### Things to See
The **Anatolian Civilisations Museum** (Anadolu Medeniyetleri Müzesi; ☎ 329 3160; Hisarparkı Caddesi; admission US$8 Mon, US$5.50 Tues-Sun; open 8.30am-5pm daily) is Ankara's most worthwhile attraction. With the world's richest collection of Hittite artefacts, it's an essential supplement to visiting central Turkey's Hittite sites. The Phyrgian collection is equally spectacular. It's uphill from Ulus Meydanı, next to the citadel which you can explore afterwards.

North of Ulus Meydanı, on the eastern side of Çankırı Caddesi (the continuation of Atatürk Bulvarı), are some Roman ruins, including the

**Column of Julian**, erected in AD 363 and the **Temple of Augustus & Rome**. On the western side of Çankırı Caddesi are remains of the **Roman Baths** (admission US$0.75; open 8.30am-noon & 1pm-5pm).

The **Anıt Kabir** (Mausoleum of Atatürk; admission free; open 9am-5pm daily), 2km west of Kızılay Meydanı, is the monumental tomb of the founder of modern Turkey.

### Places to Stay
Ulus has numerous budget and mid-range hotels.

Along the eastern side of Opera Meydanı, on the corner of Sanayi Caddesi and Tavus Sokak, are a row of small, cheap hotels.

**Otel Mithat** (☎ 311 5410; Tavus Sokak 2; singles/doubles with shower US$9/14) is probably comfortable, despite it's minimalist decor. Breakfast costs US$1.50 extra.

**Ferah Oteli** (☎ 309 1174; Denizciler Caddesi 58; singles/doubles with shower US$6/12), one street back, is a quieter choice. Some back rooms have fine city views.

**Hotel Oğultürk** (☎ 309 2900; Rüzgarlı Eşdost Sokak 6; singles/doubles with shower US$45/65), a three-star place north of Ulus, discounts its prices when it's quiet and welcomes single women.

**Hotel Spor** (☎ 324 2165; Rüzgarlı Plevne Sokak 6; singles/doubles with shower US$18/25), one street west, is spotless and welcoming, another good choice for women.

**Angora House Hotel** (☎ 309 8380; Kalekapısı Sokak 16-68; singles/doubles with shower from US$40/55), tucked inside the citadel, is Ankara's only really individual hotel and well worth the cost. An advance booking is advisable.

### Places to Eat
**Kebabistan** (Atatürk Bulvarı 3; meals US$3-5), at the southeast corner of Ulus above the courtyard of a block of offices and shops, offers a full range of kebab lunches and dinners. **Akman Boza ve Pasta Salonu**, underneath, does the dessert and coffee afterwards.

**Uğrak Lokantası** (Çankırı Caddesi, Ulus; meals US$4-5) has a mouth-watering array of desserts, like stuffed quince (US$1), to round off a tasty soup and stew meal.

For more choice, head straight for Kızılay and you'll find lots of stalls selling things such as stuffed baked potatoes. **Köşk** (Tuna Caddesi, İnkılap Sokak 2; meals US$4-5)

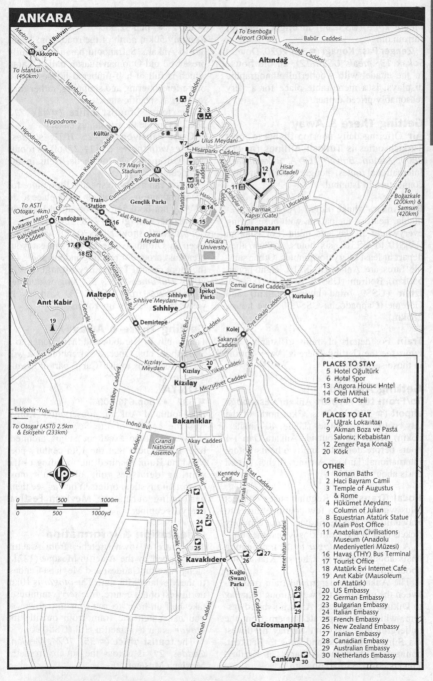

# ANKARA

To Esenboğa Airport (30km)
Babür Caddesi
Altındağ Caddesi
Altındağ

Metro Line
Ö/ Özal Bulvarı
Akköprü

To İstanbul
(450km)

İstanbul Caddesi

Çankırı Caddesi

Hippodrome

Kültür

Ulus

Kazım Karabekir Caddesi

Hipodrom Caddesi

19 Mayıs Stadium

Ulus

Cumhuriyet Bul

Ulus Meydanı
Hisarparkı Caddesi

Sanayi Caddesi

Hisar (Citadel)

Anafartalar Caddesi

To Boğazkale
(200km) &
Samsun
(420km)

Train Station

Gençlik Parkı

Talat Paşa Bul

Tandoğan

Celal Bayar Bul

To ASTİ
(Otogar, 4km)

Ankaray Metro

Bahçelievler Caddesi

Maltepe

Gazi Mustafa Kemal Bul

Opera Meydanı

Ankara University

Samanpazarı

Hasırcılar Sk

Kınacılar Sk

Parmak Kapısı (Gate)

Ulucanlar

Anıt Kabir

Maltepe

Anıt Kabir

Genlik Caddesi

Akdeniz Caddesi

Abdi İpekçi Parkı
Cemal Gürsel Caddesi

Sıhhiye Meydanı
Sıhhiye
Sıhhiye

Demirtepe

Ziya Gökalp Caddesi

Kurtuluş

Kızılay Meydanı
Kızılay
Kızılay

Kolej
Sakarya Caddesi

Tuna Caddesi

Çankırı Sk

Atatürk Bul

Yüksel Caddesi

Mesrutiyet Caddesi

Eskişehir-Yolu

To Otogar (ASTİ) 2.5km
& Eskişehir (233km)

İnönü Bul

Bakanlıklar

Necatibey Caddesi

Grand National Assembly

Akay Caddesi

Dikmen Caddesi

Atatürk Bul

Kennedy Cad

Esat Caddesi

Tunalı Hilmi Caddesi

Güvenlik Caddesi

Kavaklıdere

Kuğlu (Swan) Parkı

İran Caddesi

Nenehatun Caddesi

Cinnah Caddesi

Gaziosmanpaşa

Çankaya

0    500    1000m
0    500    1000yd

## PLACES TO STAY
5 Hotel Oğultürk
6 Hotel Spor
13 Angora House Hotel
14 Otel Mithat
15 Ferah Oteli

## PLACES TO EAT
7 Uğrak Lokantası
9 Akman Boza ve Pasta
Salonu; Kebabistan
12 Zenger Paşa Konaği
20 Kösk

## OTHER
1 Roman Baths
2 Haci Bayram Camii
3 Temple of Augustus
& Rome
4 Hükümet Meydanı;
Column of Julian
8 Equestrian Atatürk Statue
10 Main Post Office
11 Anatolian Civilisations
Museum (Anadolu
Medeniyetleri Müzesi)
16 Havaş (THY) Bus Terminal
17 Tourist Office
18 Atatürk Evi Internet Cafe
19 Anıt Kabir (Mausoleum
of Atatürk)
20 US Embassy
22 German Embassy
23 Bulgarian Embassy
24 Italian Embassy
25 French Embassy
26 New Zealand Embassy
27 Iranian Embassy
28 Canadian Embassy
29 Australian Embassy
30 Netherlands Embassy

TURKEY

offers excellent *İskender kebab* (US$3) and *İnegöl köfte* (US$2.50) in bright, cheerful surroundings.

**Zenger Paşa Konağı** (☎ *311 7070; Doyran Sokak 13; meals US$6-12)*, an old house in the citadel with wonderful ethnographic displays, is a memorable place for a very reasonably priced dinner.

## Getting There & Away

**Air** Offering daily nonstop flights to most Turkish cities is **Turkish Airlines** (☎ *419 2800; Atatürk Bulvarı 167/A, Bakanlıklar)*. International routes, though, usually require a connection in İstanbul.

**Bus** Ankara's huge *otogar* (ASTİ) is the vehicular heart of the nation, with buses going everywhere all day and night. For İstanbul (US$10 to US$18, six hours, 450km) they depart at least every 15 minutes. Other sample fares are Antalya (US$10, eight hours, 550km), Bodrum (US$12, 12 hours, 785km), İzmir (US$9, nine hours, 600km) and Göreme (Cappadocia; US$7.50, five hours, 285km).

**Train** For details of trains to İstanbul and İzmir see the Getting There & Away entries in those sections.

## Getting Around

**To/From the Airport** Ankara's **Esenboğa airport** (☎ *398 0100)* is 33km north of the city centre. Havaş buses (US$3, 40 minutes, 33km) depart from outside Ankara Garı 1½ hours before domestic and two hours before international Turkish Airlines flights. A taxi costs about US$25.

**Local Transport** Regular buses connect Ulus with Kızılay; a few continue direct to Kavaklıdere and Çankaya. You can buy tickets (US$0.50) from kiosks near the stops.

A taxi from the *otogar* to the train station costs about US$3; to Ulus or Kızılay it's about US$2.50.

The Ankaray underground train runs between the *otogar* in the west through Kızılay to Dikimevi in the east. Ankara's metro system, which is a separate system from the underground, runs from Kızılay northwest via Sıhhiye, Maltepe and Ulus to Batıkent, connecting with the Ankaray at Kızılay. Tickets cost US$0.50 on both.

## SAFRANBOLU
☎ 0372 • pop 32,500

Roughly 50km north of the road from İstanbul to Ankara, Safranbolu has a beautifully preserved old Ottoman quarter called **Çarşı**, which is full of half-timbered houses. It's a place for pottering and shopping, rather than looking at specific sites.

The town's **tourist office** (☎/*fax 712 3863)* is inside the *arasta*, or bazaar.

**Çarşı Pansiyon** (☎ *725 1079; singles/ doubles with shower US$14/27)* offers rooms with Ottoman-style low beds, right in the town centre.

If you can afford to spend a little more for accommodation, Safranbolu is the place to do it. Why not book into the beautiful **Havuzlu Asmazlar Konağı** (☎ *725 2883; singles/ doubles with shower US$30/50)* where you sleep in Ottoman-style rooms and eat your breakfast around a relaxing indoor pool? Or the more central **Tahsin Bey Konağı** (☎ *712 2065; Hükümet Sokak 50; singles/doubles with shower from US$17/35)* with lovely views from the upstairs rooms?

## Getting There & Away

Take a bus to Karabuk and then change to a Safranbolu bus. Once at Safranbolu you will need a local bus to the 'Çarşı' part of town.

## KONYA
☎ 332 • pop 611,000

Due south of Ankara, conservative Konya was the capital of the Seljuk Turks and showcases some excellent Seljuk architecture. It was here that the 13th-century poet Mevlana Rumi inspired the founding of the whirling dervishes, one of Islam's most important mystical orders. You can see them performing during the **Mevlana Festival** every December.

## Orientation & Information

The centre of town stretches from Alaettin Hill, topped by the Alaettin Mosque (1221), along Alaettin Caddesi and Mevlana Caddesi to the Mevlana Museum. The *otogar* is 10km northwest of the centre; free *servis* minibuses take half-an-hour to run you into town, or you can catch the tram from outside the *otogar* as far as Alaettin Hill (US$0.30).

The **tourist office** (☎ *351 1074; Mevlana Caddesi 21)* is across the square from the Mevlana Museum.

## Things to See

Mevlana's **tomb** *(Mevlana Müsezi; admission US$4; open 9am-5pm daily, 10am-5pm Mon)* is topped by a brilliant turquoise-tiled dome. It's a powerful place to visit, very popular with pilgrims; you should be especially careful about dressing modestly when you go inside.

It's also worth visiting two outstanding Seljuk seminaries near Alaettin Hill: the **Büyük Karatay Museum** *(admission US$ 0.75; open 9am-noon & 1pm-5 pm daily)*, a ceramics museum; and the **İnceminare Medresesi** *(Seminary of the Slender Minaret; admission US$0.75; open 9am-noon & 1pm-5pm)*, a museum of wood and stone carvings.

## Places to Stay & Eat

**Hotel Ulusan** *(☎ 351 5004; Kurşuncular Sokak 2; singles/doubles with shared bathroom US$6/12)*, immediately behind the PTT, is first choice, with clean, simple rooms.

**Mavi Köşk** *(☎ 350 1904; Bostan Çelebi Sokak 13; singles/doubles with shower US$9/11)* and **Derviş** *(☎/fax 351 1688; Bostan Çelebi Sokak 11/D; singles/doubles US$10/15)*, side by side near the Mevlana Museum, are also good, cheap choices.

**Kök & Esra Otel** *(☎ 352 0671; Yeni Aziziye Caddesi, Kadılar Sokak 28; singles/doubles with shower US$10/15)* is a step up in quality, with comfortable, if rather idiosyncratically decorated rooms.

**Sifa Restaurant** *(Mevlana Caddesi 29; meals US$6)* specialises in Konya's very own *tandir kebab*, a melt-in-your-mouth version of lamb. **Dilayla Restaurant** *(Mevlana Caddesi, Altın Çarşışı Biţiği; meals US$4)*, nearby, is smaller but similar and stays open when other places close.

## Getting There & Away

There are frequent buses from Konya to Nevşehir (US$6, 3½ hours, 236km) and Pamukkale (US$10, seven hours, 450km).

# Cappadocia

Cappadocia, the region between Ankara and Malatya, and between Aksaray and Kayseri, is famous for its fantastic natural **rock formations**. Over the centuries people have carved houses, churches, fortresses, even complete underground cities, into the soft, eerily eroded volcanic stone. The attractions include the Göreme valleys; the pretty Ihlara Gorge with a stream flowing through it; and the huge underground cities at **Kaymaklı** and **Derinkuyu** *(admission US$7; open 8am-5pm daily)*.

## Information

Ürgüp, Avanos and Uçhisar have plenty of hotels and *pensions*, but Göreme is most attractive to low-budget travellers.

Good daily tours (around US$30) of local highlights including Ihlara Gorge are offered by **Ötuken Voyage** *(☎ 271 2757)*, **Neşe Tour** *(☎ 271 2525)* and **Zemi Tour** *(☎ 271 2576)* in Göreme. **Kirkit Voyage** *(☎ 511 3259; W www.kirkit.com)* in Avanos; and **Argeus** *(☎ 341 4688; W www.argeus.com.tr)* in Ürgüp are experienced, professional travel agents with more varied programmes, including horse-riding and cycling tours.

## GÖREME

☎ 0384 • pop 2000

The Göreme landscape is one of Turkey's most amazing sights. Over the centuries a thick layer of volcanic tufa has been eroded into fantastic, eerie shapes, dubbed fairy chimneys by the locals. Early Christians carved chambers and vaults into the chimneys for use as churches, stables and homes. Blow your budget and view all this drama from above in a hot-air balloon with **Kapadokya Balloons** *(☎ 271 2755; e fly@kapadokyaballoons.com; US$230)*.

## Göreme Open-Air Museum

Medieval frescoes can be seen in the rock-hewn monastery, nunnery and cave churches of **Göreme Open Air Museum** *(admission US$7, plus Karanlık Kilisesi US$10; open 8am-5.30pm daily, to 4.30pm Nov-Apr)*. Some date from the 8th century, though the best are from the 10th to 13th centuries. The churches are tiny so try to visit when the adjacent coach party is not looking too full. Don't miss the **Tokalı church**, across the road from the main entrance but with some of the best frescoes.

## Places to Stay

You can camp at the **Dilek** or **Berlin** camp grounds *(tent sites US$6)*, side by side amid wonderful rock formations on the road that lead to the Open Air Museum.

Göreme has some of Turkey's best-value *pensions*, often offering the chance to try out the troglodyte lifestyle. In most, a dorm bed costs US$3.50, a bed in a room with/without shower costs US$7/5.

**Köse Pension** (☎ 271 2294; Ⓦ www.kose pension.com), near the PTT, is a very popular choice, with a gorgeous swimming pool, a book exchange and good home-cooked food for vegetarians and meat-eaters alike.

**Kelebek** (☎ 271 2531; Ⓦ www.kelebek hotel.com), right up in the old village, boasts spectacular views, great food and also a wide range of rooms, including a cave honeymoon suite, complete with its own Jacuzzi (for US$60).

**Paradise** (☎ 271 2248), tucked in amid fairy chimneys just off the Open Air Museum road, is also popular with backpackers.

**Flintstones** (☎ 271 2555), along the road leading to the Pigeon Valley, is quiet and secluded with a pleasant swimming pool.

**Shoestring Cave Pension** (☎ 271 2450) has simple cave rooms set around a pleasant courtyard. Its meals get good reviews.

**Tuna Caves** (☎ 271 2236), off the road leading up to the old village, tends to get extremely busy.

**Cave Hotel Melek** (☎ 271 2463; doubles US$10, with shower US$16) offers clean, simple rock-cut rooms in a quiet location.

**Ottoman House** (☎ 271 2616; doubles with shower US$15) boasts of offering luxury at affordable prices in a modern building.

### Places to Eat

Best of Göreme 's restaurants is the **Orient** (meals from US$5), as you head up the hill towards Uçhisar; the steaks (US$4) are especially well regarded. Also popular is the **Local**, handily placed on the corner of the road leading up to the Open Air Museum and offering very tasty 'Ottoman' specials. Along the main road to Avanos, **Sedef** and **Sultan** offer a wide choice of mezes, while **Tardelli** majors in pizzas and pides. **Mercan** and **SOS** tend to have the lowest prices.

### Getting There & Away

Although you can fly from İstanbul to Kayseri and then travel down to Göreme, most people arrive on the overnight bus from İstanbul (US$15, 11 hours, 725km) or Antalya (US$13, 10 hours, 485km).

Half-hourly dolmuşes connect Göreme with Nevşehir via Uçhisar (US$0.50). There are also buses to Avanos and Ürgüp.

## UÇHISAR

Between Göreme and Nevşehir is picturesque Uçhisar, built around a **rock citadel** (admission US$1; opening hours 8am to sunset daily), which afford panoramic views from its summit. There are many more places to stay here, although most only open from May to September.

## AVANOS
☎ 0384 • pop 12,000

On the northern bank of the sweeping Kızılırmak (Red River), Avanos is known for its pottery. Best value among the pensions is **Kirkit Pansiyon** (☎ 511 3148; doubles US$8, with shower US$10); from the northern end of the bridge, walk east and bear left at the first alley.

**Venessa Pansiyon** (☎ 511 3840; Hafızağa Sokak 20; beds with shower US$10) is a beautifully restored old house with its own private underground city.

**Sofa Motel** (☎ 511 5186; singles/doubles with shower US$20/35), moving up the price and comfort scale, is near the northern end of the bridge. Its tastefully decorated rooms are popular with groups, so book head.

### Getting There & Away

Two buses an hour link Nevşehir with Avanos (US$0.45).

## ÜRGÜP
☎ 0384 • pop 13,500

Despite being a bigger town, Ürgüp still has plenty of appeal, with old sandstone buildings, cobbled streets and a stone hill shot through with rooms and passages. For wine buffs, it also boasts Cappadocia's best wineries. The helpful **tourist office** (☎/fax 341 4059; Kayseri Caddesi) is downhill in the park.

### Places to Stay & Eat

**Hotel Elvan** (☎ 341 4191; Dutlu Cami Mahallesi, Barbaros Hayrettin Sokak 11; doubles with shower US$15-25) has homey rooms arranged around a courtyard.

**Asia Minor Hotel** (☎ 341 4645; İstiklal Caddesi; doubles with shower US$40) has stylish rooms and a pleasant garden. **Hitit Hotel** (☎ 341 4481; İstiklal Caddesi) is marginally cheaper, with an equally inviting garden, but more mundane rooms.

**Esbelli Evi** (☎ 341 3395; Ⓦ www.esbelli .com.tr; singles/doubles with shower US$70/

85), behind Club Ürgüp on the one-way system out of town, was created out of a group of lovely rock-cut rooms in a warren of inviting courtyards. Advance reservation is advisable.

Where Esbelli led, others have since followed and Ürgüp now boasts some of the finest boutique hotels around, mostly clustered together in the Esbelli Mahallesi. **Ügüp Evi** (☎ 341 3173), **Elkepi Evi** (☎ 341 6000), **Kayadam Pansiyon** (☎ 341 6673) and **Yunak Everli** (☎ 341 6920) are all guaranteed to offer memorable stays for prices not dissimilar to Esbelli's.

**Sömine Restaurant** (meals US$8-14) is the town's most prominent eatery right on the main square, with indoor and outdoor tables. Ürgüp-style kebabs baked on tiles are a speciality. The **Ocakbaşı** (meals US$15) beside the *otogar* offers better food – especially grills and *mezes* – if in a less immediately inviting setting.

### Getting There & Away
There are hourly buses to Ürgüp from Nevşehir and every two hours from Göreme (US$0.75).

## IHLARA GORGE
☎ 0382
A once remote, beautiful canyon full of rock-cut churches dating back to Byzantine times (admission US$3.50), Ihlara is now a mainstay of the day-trip excursions run out of Cappadocia. If you have the time, you're better off staying and walking the entire 16km length of the gorge.

### Places to Stay & Eat
Ihlara village is 40km southeast of Aksaray. **Anatolia Pansiyon** (☎ 453 7440; camping US$3 per person, doubles with shower US$16) offers comfortable rooms on the road running along the top of the gorge. **Akar Pansiyon** (☎ 453 7018; doubles with shower US$16), on the road towards Aksaray, has a handy shop close by. There are more inviting camp sites and simple restaurants in the gorge itself, near the village of Belisırma.

### Getting There & Away
Several daily buses connect Ihlara with Aksaray (US$0.75).

## KAYSERİ
☎ 0352 • pop 425,000
In the shadow of Mt Erciyes, Kayseri, a conservative but fast modernising town, was once the capital of Cappadocia and boasts many ancient buildings tucked away behind the ugly high-rises.

### Things to See
Near the **tourist office** (☎ 222 3903) is the beautiful **Hunat Hatun mosque**, **tomb** and **seminary**. Opposite, behind the massive 6th-century city walls, is the **Ulu Cami** (Great Mosque), begun by the Seljuks in 1136. Also inside the walls is the ancient **Vezirhanı**, once a caravanserai. Further out are the **Gıyasiye ve Sifaiye Medreseleri** (Twin Seminaries) in Mimar Sinan Park, a Seljuk hospital now housing a **medical museum** (admission US$0.75). Don't miss the beautifully decorated 18th-century **Güpgüpoğlu Konağı** (admission US$0.75; open 8am-5pm Tues-Sun).

### Places to Stay & Eat
**Hunat Oteli** (☎ 232 4319; Zengin Sokak 5; beds without shower US$7), behind the Hunat Mosque, is the cheapest choice but no less friendly for that.

**Hotel Sur** (☎ 222 4367; Talas Caddesi 12; singles/doubles with shower US$20/30), tucked in behind the walls, offers more comfortable rooms.

**Hotel Turan** (☎ 222 5537; Turan Caddesi 8; singles/doubles with shower US$18/28) is right in the heart of the shopping centre with some sizeable rooms.

**Beyaz Saray** (Millet Caddesi 8) boasts a mouth-watering *İskender kebab* (US$3), as does the older **İskender Kebab Salonu** across the road.

### Getting There & Away
A *dolmuş* to Kayseri from Ürgüp costs US$2, a bus from Göreme costs US$3.

# Yugoslavia Југославија

The Federal Republic of Yugoslavia, consisting of Serbia and Montenegro, occupies the heart of the Balkans astride major land and river routes from Western Europe to Asia Minor. It is a region with a tumultuous history.

## Facts about Yugoslavia

### HISTORY
The original inhabitants of the region were the Illyrians, followed by the Celts, who arrived in the 4th century BC. The Roman conquest of Moesia Superior (Serbia) began in the 3rd century BC and under Augustus the empire extended to Singidunum (Belgrade) on the Danube. In AD 395 Theodosius I divided the empire and what is now Serbia passed to the Byzantine Empire.

During the 6th century, Slavic tribes (Serbs, Croats and Slovenes) crossed the Danube and occupied much of the Balkan Peninsula. In 879 Sts Cyril and Methodius converted the Serbs to the Orthodox religion.

An independent Serbian kingdom appeared in 1217 with a 'Golden Age' during Stefan Dušan's reign (1346–55). After Stefan's death Serbia declined and, at the Battle of Kosovo on 28 June 1389, the Turks defeated Serbia, ushering in 500 years of Islamic rule. A revolt in 1815 led to de facto Serbian independence from the Turks. Autonomy for Serbia was recognised in 1829 and independence was achieved in 1878.

On 28 June 1914, Austria-Hungary used the assassination of Archduke Ferdinand by a Serb nationalist as a pretext to invade Serbia, sparking WWI. After the war, Croatia, Slovenia, Vojvodina, Serbia, Montenegro and Macedonia formed the Kingdom of Serbs, Croats and Slovenes under the king of Serbia. In 1929 the country became Yugoslavia.

On 25 March 1941 Yugoslavia joined the Tripartite Alliance, a Nazi-supported fascist military pact. This sparked a military coup. Peter II was installed as king and Yugoslavia abruptly withdrew from the Alliance. Livid, Hitler ordered immediate invasion and Yugoslavia was carved up between Germany, Italy, Hungary and Bulgaria.

## At a Glance

- **Belgrade** – medieval gates; Orthodox churches; Turkish baths
- **Novi Sad** – smart city streets; outdoor café culture; baroque Petrovaradin Citadel
- **Budva** – barren coastal mountains and lovely beaches
- **Durmitor National Park** – pretty mountain lakes with activities galore
- **Cetinje** – subject of songs and epic poems; monasteries, palaces and mansions

| | |
|---|---|
| **Capital** | Belgrade |
| **Population** | 11 million (2002 est.) |
| **Official Language** | Serbia & Montenegro – Serbian (Serbo-Croatian), Kosovo – Albanian |
| **Currency** | 1 Yugoslav dinar (DIN) = 100 paras |
| | 1 euro (€) = 100 cents |
| **Time** | GMT/UTC+0100 |
| **Country Phone Code** | ☎ 381 |

Almost immediately the Communist Party, under Josip Broz Tito, declared an armed uprising, laying the basis for a future communist Yugoslavia. In 1945 the Communist Party won control of the national assembly, abolished the monarchy and declared Yugoslavia

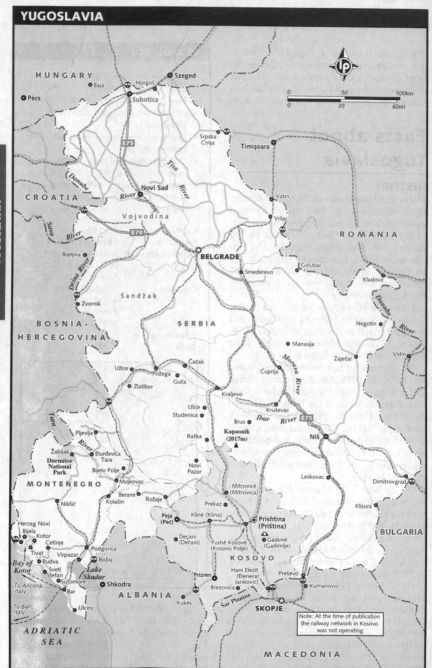

YUGOSLAVIA

Note: At the time of publication the railway network in Kosovo was not operating

a federal republic. Serbia's size was reduced with Bosnia-Hercegovina, Montenegro and Macedonia being granted republic status within this 'second' Yugoslavia. The Albanians of Kosovo and Hungarians of Vojvodina were denied republic status as their national homelands were outside Yugoslavia.

Tito broke with Stalin in 1948 and, as a reward, received US$2 billion in economic and military aid from the USA and UK between 1950 and 1960. Growing regional inequalities led, however, to increased tension as Slovenia, Croatia and Kosovo demanded greater autonomy.

In 1986 the Serbian Academy of Sciences called on Serbia to reassert its hegemony. When Slobodan Milošević took over as Communist Party leader in Serbia, Milošević espoused a vision of a 'Greater Serbia' that horrified Slovenia and Croatia. On 25 June 1991 Slovenia and Croatia declared their independence, leading to an invasion of Slovenia by the federal army. Consequently the then European Community (EC), imposed a weapons embargo on Yugoslavia.

On 15 January 1992 the EC recognised the independence of both Croatia and Slovenia, prompting both Macedonia and Bosnia-Hercegovina to demand recognition of their own independence. Montenegro alone voted to remain in Yugoslavia. On 27 April 1992 a 'third' Yugoslav federation was declared by Serbia and Montenegro. The new constitution made no mention of 'autonomous provinces', infuriating Albanians in Kosovo, long brutally repressed by Serbia. Violence in Kosovo erupted in January 1998, largely provoked by the federal army and police. The West provided a storm of protest but little else other than another arms embargo. In March 1999 peace talks in Paris failed when Serbia rejected a US-brokered peace plan. In a reply to resistance in Kosovo, Serbian forces moved to empty the country of its Albanian population. Hundreds of thousands fleeing into Macedonia and Albania galvanised America and NATO into action. Not wishing to enter into a potentially disastrous land war, they embarked on a 78-day bombing campaign. On 12 June 1999 Serbian forces withdrew from Kosovo.

In the September 2000 federal presidential elections the opposition, led by Vojislav Koštunica, declared victory, a claim denied by Milošević. Hundreds of thousands of opposition supporters occupied the streets and a

## Watch this space.

By the time you read this chapter it could be in the wrong part of the book, it should be under 'S' for Serbia and Montenegro. There's still a lot of wrangling and politicking to be done before the parliaments of Serbia and Montenegro agree to dump the name (and constitution) of Yugoslavia. So to be safe, and accurate, we've decided to wait until it's official.

general strike was called. Meanwhile, Yugoslavia's constitutional court annulled the election and pronounced that Milošević should remain as president. On 5 October opposition supporters occupied parliament and the state TV station. The following day Russia recognised Koštunica's presidency thus persuading Milošević that his days had ended.

Koštunica immediately restored ties with Europe, acknowledged Yugoslav atrocities in Kosovo and, in November, Yugoslavia rejoined the UN. In December, Milošević's party was soundly defeated in Serbian parliamentary elections. In April 2001 Milošević was arrested for misappropriating state funds and abusing his position. In June he was extradited to the Netherlands to stand trial at the international war crimes tribunal. It's likely that other extraditions will follow.

In April 2002 Serbia and Montenegro agreed to replace the federation with a union of Serbia and Montenegro. The deal was brokered under heavy EU pressure seeking to prevent further regional violence. Montenegro also put a three-year hold on any independence referendum. At the time of writing the constitutional detail still has to be written, wrangled over and ratified by parliament. Until then the name Yugoslavia still lives.

## GEOGRAPHY

Mountains and plateaus account for the lower half of this 102,350-sq-km federation. Serbia covers 77,651 sq km and Montenegro 13,812 sq km. Yugoslavia's interior and southern mountains belong to the Balkan Range while the coastal range is an arm of the Dinaric Alps. Most rivers flow north into the Danube. Down south, rivers have cut deep canyons into the plateau.

Yugoslavia's only coastline is the scenically superb 150km Montenegrin coast. The Bay of Kotor is southern Europe's only real fjord and Montenegro's magnificent Tara Canyon is Europe's largest.

## CLIMATE

The north has a continental climate with cold winters and hot, humid summers. The coastal region has hot, dry summers and relatively cold winters with heavy snowfall inland.

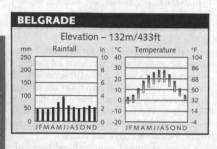

**BELGRADE**

Elevation – 132m/433ft

## GOVERNMENT & POLITICS

Yugoslavia has a presidential parliamentary system with federal power vested in a parliament headed by a prime minister Dragiša Pešić and president Vojislav Koštunica. Serbia and Montenegro also have their own parliaments, prime ministers and presidents who wield political power. In the new union, Serbia and Montenegro will be semi-independent states with foreign affairs, customs and defence controlled federally.

## ECONOMY

Conflict, sanctions and disruption of trade links have devastated the economy over the 20 years or so. The old Yugoslav economy was based on the whole federation with states specialising in certain industries. Now each has to survive on its own.

Hyperinflation, the highest in European history, was a constant problem. At one point in Yugoslavia's economic history, it was cheaper to use banknotes to paper walls than to buy wallpaper. The dinar has now become quite stable; inflation in 2001 was 40%, it is expected at 26% for 2002 and 10% is targeted for 2003.

The country's agricultural production is mainly on the northern plain. Vojvodina and Kosovo have most of the mineral resources, including coal and petroleum, hence the strategic importance of those former autonomous regions to Serbia. Yugoslavia is largely self-sufficient in fuel.

## POPULATION & PEOPLE

The last published figures came from the 1991 census with no figures yet released from the April 2002 census. The population is made up of Serbs (62%), Montenegrins (5%), Albanians (estimated at 17%), Hungarians (3%) and Slavic Muslims (3%), plus Croats, Roma, Slovaks, Macedonians, Romanians, Bulgarians, Turks and Ukrainians. War has altered those figures, especially with some 400,000 refugees in Serbia and Montenegro.

About 23% of Vojvodina's population is Hungarian, concentrated around Subotica. There are large Slavic Muslim and Albanian minorities in Montenegro and southern Serbia; Belgrade has an estimated Muslim population of 10,000.

## ARTS
### Literature

Bosnian-born Nobel Prize winner Ivo Andric's novel *Bridge on the Drina* foresaw the region's disasters of the early 1990s. Milorad Pavic's novel *Dictionary of the Khazars* is a novel written in the form of a dictionary. Further books worthy of perusal are *In the Hold* by Vladimir Arsenijević, *Words are Something Else* by David Albahari, *Petrija's Wreath* by Dragoslav Mihailović and *Fear and its Servant* by Mirjana Novaković.

### Cinema

The award-winning film *Underground*, by Sarajevo-born director Emil Kusturica, is worth seeing. Told in a chaotic, colourful style, the film deals with Yugoslav history. *Tockovi*, by Djordje Milosavljevic, is a black comedy where the hero wanders into lonely motel on a stormy night and gets stuck with a group of people who think he's a mass murderer. Bosnian director Danis Tanovic's *No Man's Land* superbly deals with an encounter between a Serb and Bosnian soldier stuck in a trench on their own during the Bosnian war.

### Music

Serbia's vibrant dances are similar to those of Bulgaria with musicians using bagpipes, flutes and fiddles.

*Blehmuzika*, or brass music greatly influenced by Turkish and Austrian military music, has become the national music of Serbia with an annual festival at Guča in August.

Momcilo Bajagic is popular with the younger generation whose music fuses street poetry and jazz with traditional elements. Djorde Balašević appeals to a wider audience, again combining traditional elements with modern motifs. Darkwood Dub, combining fusion and rock with electronic music, and Eyesburn, who blends hard rock with reggae sampling, are two popular current bands.

## SOCIETY & CONDUCT
All nationalities are very hospitable to visitors despite recent history. Respect should be shown for all religious establishments and customs. Dress appropriately and learning some basic words will open doors and create smiles.

## RELIGION
Serbs and Montenegrins are predominantly Orthodox, Hungarians are Roman Catholic and Albanians are predominantly Muslim.

## LANGUAGE
Serbian is the common language. Through working abroad, many Yugoslavs have German as a second language and most educated people often know English and French. Hungarians in Vojvodina use the Latin alphabet, Montenegrins and Serbians use both Latin and Cyrillic. (See the Croatian & Serbian language section at the back of this book.)

# Facts for the Visitor

## HIGHLIGHTS
There's a wealth of castles, including the baroque Petrovaradin Citadel at Novi Sad, Belgrade's Kalemegdan Citadel and Smederevo, and the old Montenegrin capital of Cetinje which will please romantics. Of the beach resorts, Budva is chic but Kotor more impressive with its fjord and medieval walled town. Montenegro's Tara Canyon and Durmitor National Park stack up to any similar sights in the world.

## SUGGESTED ITINERARIES
Depending on time available and where you arrive you might visit the following:

**Two days**
    Visit either Belgrade, Novi Sad or Budva, Cetinje and Kotor
**One week**
    Visit all of the above
**Two weeks**
    Visit all areas covered in this chapter

## PLANNING
### When to Go
Avoid the Montenegrin coast during July and August when accommodation becomes both expensive and scarce. The ski season is generally December to March.

### Maps
The Freytag & Berndt map *Yugoslavia, Slovenia, Croatia* shows former Yugoslavia with the new countries. The *Savezna Republika Jugoslavija Autokarta* map shows new borders and some town maps. *Plan Grada Beograd* is a detailed Belgrade city map. The latter two are free from the Tourist Organization of Belgrade.

## TOURIST OFFICES
There are tourist offices in Belgrade, Novi Sad and Niš. Elsewhere, travel agencies may help with information.

## VISAS & DOCUMENTS
A visa is only required for Serbia, not for Montenegro. You will need an initial hotel booking to accompany your application. The Ministry of Foreign Affair's website at W www.mfa.gov.yu gives details.

Serbia has been trialling granting 30-day visas at Belgrade airport and border posts; this may become permanent. Please note, crossings between Serbia and Kosovo or Montenegro are not through border posts (see the boxed text 'Border Crossings' in the Getting There & Away section later in this chapter).

## EMBASSIES & CONSULATES
### Yugoslav Embassies
Yugoslavia has embassies in the following countries:

**Australia** (☎ 02-6290 2630, fax 6290 2631, e yuembau@ozemail.com.au) 4 Bulwarra Close, O'Malley, ACT 2606
**Canada** (☎ 613-233 6289, fax 233 7850, W www.yuemb.ca) 17 Blackburn Ave, Ottawa, Ontario, K1A 8A2
**France** (☎ 01 40 72 24 24, fax 01 40 72 24 11, e pariz@compuserve.com) 54 rue de la Faisanderie 75116, Paris
**UK** (☎ 020-7235 9049, fax 7235 7090, W www.yugoslavembassy.org.uk) 28 Belgrave Square, London, SW1X 8QB
**USA** (☎ 202-332 0333, fax 332 3933, W www.yuembusa.org) 2134 Kalorama Rd NW, Washington DC, 20008

## Embassies & Consulates in Yugoslavia

The following countries have representation in Belgrade:

**Albania** (☎ 306 5350) Bulevar Mira 25A
**Australia** (☎ 624 655) Cika Ljubina 13
**Bulgaria** (☎ 361 3980) Birčaninova 26
**Canada** (☎ 306 3000) Kneza Miloša 75
**France** (☎ 302 3500) Pariska 11
**Germany** (☎ 361 4255) Kneza Miloša 74–6
**Hungary** (☎ 444 0472) Brigada (Krunska Proleterskih) 72
**Romania** (☎ 361 8327) Kneza Miloša 70
**UK** (☎ 645 087) Resavska (Generala Ždanova) 46
**USA** (☎ 361 9344) Kneza Miloša 50

# MONEY

## Currency

Montenegro has adopted the euro and the dinar is not accepted. Serbia, however, retains the dinar, which is used for most transactions, although some hotels may want payment in euros or US dollars. Some international train journeys may require part payment in dinar and part in euros. The euro is quite readily accepted in Serbia as many Serbians work in Western Europe.

## Exchange Rates

Conversion rates for major currencies at the time of publication are listed below.

| country | unit | | euro | | dinar |
|---|---|---|---|---|---|
| Australia | A$1 | = | €0.61 | = | 37.81 |
| Canada | C$1 | = | €0.71 | = | 44.20 |
| euro zone | €1 | | | = | 62.43 |
| Japan | ¥100 | = | €0.87 | = | 54.39 |
| NZ | NZ$1 | = | €0.51 | = | 32.10 |
| UK | £1 | = | €1.58 | = | 98.73 |
| USA | US$1 | = | €1.09 | = | 67.83 |

## Exchanging Money

Until the expected global banking agreements are made, few banks deal with travellers cheques or credit cards. So come with euros in cash. Many exchange offices in Serbia will readily change these and other hard currencies into dinars and back again when you leave. Look for their large blue diamond signs hanging outside.

## Tipping & Bargaining

It's common to round up restaurant bills to a convenient figure; taxi drivers will expect the same. Prices are fixed in shops and generally also in markets but you might be successful in bargaining.

# POST & COMMUNICATIONS

## Post

Parcels should be taken unsealed to a main post office for inspection. Allow time to check the repacking and complete the transaction.

You can receive mail, addressed poste restante, in all towns for a small charge.

## Telephone & Fax

The international access code for outgoing calls is ☎ 99. To call Yugoslavia from outside dial the international access code, ☎ 381 (country code), area code (without the initial zero) and the number.

In Serbia you can use a phonecard (100, 300 or 500 DIN) to make a call from a public phone. A phone call to Europe/Australia/North America costs 42/76/76 DIN per minute. In Montenegro the highest-value phonecard (€1.70) doesn't give enough time (Europe/Australia/North America €0.90/1.64/1.64 per minute), so use the post office. Press the *i* button on Serbian and Montenegrin public phones for dialling commands in English.

Faxes can be sent from any large hotel or from post offices, which in Serbia charge 172/236/236 DIN per page when sending to Europe/Australia/North America.

## Email & Internet Access

Internet cafés are widespread in Yugoslavia with fast connections.

# DIGITAL RESOURCES

There are several informative websites for visitors to check out, including Ⓦ www.serbia-tourism.org.yu, Ⓦ www.beograd.org.yu and Ⓦ www.visit-montenegro.com.

# BOOKS

Rebecca West's *Black Lamb & Grey Falcon* is a classic portrait of prewar Yugoslavia. Former partisan and dissident Milovan Djilas' fascinating books about Yugoslav history and politics are published in English.

Titles dealing with the turbulence of the 1990s include *Yugoslavia: Death of a Nation* by Laura Silber and Allan Little, Misha Glenny's book *The Fall of Yugoslavia* (1998) and *Yugoslavia's Bloody Collapse* by Christopher Bennett (1996). *The Death of Yugoslavia* by Laura Silber (published November 2002) continues the account.

## NEWSPAPERS & MAGAZINES
Some foreign-language magazines are available but it can be hard to find newspapers. Try the newsstands in Belgrade's Kneza Mihaila.

## RADIO & TV
The liberalisation of Serbia has permitted an independent media. Studio B, the independent radio and TV station, closed several times under Milosevic, is flourishing along with another 13 stations, including three state-owned channels all offering sport, movies, politics, news programmes, debates and foreign-made series. CNN, Eurosport and MTV are also available with the right equipment. Many FM and AM radio stations cater to all tastes.

## TOILETS
Restaurant and hotel toilets are a somewhat cleaner option than public toilets, which are few and far between.

## WOMEN TRAVELLERS
Other than the cursory interest shown by men towards solo women travellers, travel is hassle-free and easy.

## GAY & LESBIAN TRAVELLERS
Homosexuality has been legal in Yugoslavia since 1932. For more information, contact **Arkadia** *(Brace Baruh 11, 11000 Belgrade)* or the website W www.gay-serbia.com.

## DISABLED TRAVELLERS
There are very few facilities in the region for those with disabilities. Wheelchair access could be problematic in Belgrade with its numerous inclines but most hotels will have lifts.

## DANGERS & ANNOYANCES
Travel nearly everywhere is safe but avoid southeastern Serbia where there is still Serb-Albanian tension.

Many Yugoslavs are chain-smokers who can't imagine that they might inconvenience nonsmokers. The 'No smoking' signs are routinely ignored.

It's fine to discuss politics if you're also willing to listen. Check with the police before photographing any official building that they're guarding.

---

### Emergency Services
In an emergency you can dial ☎ 92 for police, ☎ 93 for the fire service and ☎ 94 for the ambulance. For motoring assistance in Belgrade call ☎ 987 and in Serbia and Montenegro (ie, outside Belgrade) the number for motoring assistance is ☎ 011 9800.

---

## BUSINESS HOURS
Banks keep long hours, often 7am to 7pm weekdays and 7am to noon Saturday. On weekdays many shops open from 7am, close from noon to 4pm but reopen until 8pm. Department stores, supermarkets and some restaurants generally stay open all day. Most government offices are closed on Saturday; although shops stay open until 2pm many other businesses close at 3pm.

## PUBLIC HOLIDAYS & SPECIAL EVENTS
Public holidays in Serbia and Montenegro include New Year (1 and 2 January), Orthodox Christmas (6 and 7 January), Constitution Day, Serbia (28 March), Constitution Day of Federal Republic of Yugoslavia (27 April), International Labour Days (1 and 2 May), Victory Day (9 May) and Uprising Day, Montenegro (13 July). If 28 March or 13 July fall on a Sunday, the following Monday or Tuesday is a holiday. Orthodox churches celebrate Easter between one and five weeks later than other churches.

Belgrade hosts a film festival (FEST) in February, a jazz festival is held in August, an international theatre festival (BITEF) in mid-September and a festival of classical music in October. Every August Novi Sad hosts the Exit music festival, which attracts bands from all over Europe to play on various stages within the Petrovaradin Citadel. Niš hosts a jazz and blues festival within its citadel in mid-July. There is an annual festival of brass-band music at Guča near Čačak in the last week of August. Budva has a summer festival in July and August and Herceg Novi hosts the Suncale Skale music festival in July.

## ACTIVITIES
Serbia's main skiing resorts are Zlatibor and Kopaonik while Montenegro's is Žabljak. The ski season is from December to March, while resorts become popular hiking areas in

summer. For white-water rafting the Tara River in Montenegro's Durmitor National Park is the most popular river in the country.

## ACCOMMODATION

For hostel accommodation contact Ferijalni Savez Beograd (see the Belgrade Places to Stay section for details). Hostels exist in Belgrade, Palić (Subotica), Kladovo (east Serbia), Kopaonik (southern Serbia) and at Sutomore and Bijela (southern Montenegro).

Hotels can be pricey, Belgrade hotels are reasonable for a capital, Montenegrin hotels outside the coast and Žabljak are iniquitously expensive.

Private rooms (along the coast, seldom inland and not in Belgrade), which are organised through travel agencies, are best. In summer you can camp along the Montenegrin coast at a few organised camping grounds. An overnight bus or train will always save you a night's accommodation.

## FOOD

The cheapest snack is *burek*, a greasy pie made with *sir* (cheese), *meso* (meat), *krompiruša* (potato) or *pecurke* (mushrooms); with yogurt it makes a good breakfast filler. *Čevapčići* (grilled kebabs of spiced minced meats) are popular everywhere, as is the universal pizza. A good midday meal of soup or *čevapčići* should cost about 120 DIN/€2.

### Regional Dishes

Yugoslavia's regional cuisines range from spicy Hungarian goulash in Vojvodina to various grilled meats. A speciality of Vojvodina is *alaska čorba* (fiery riverfish stew). In Montenegro, try *kajmak* (cream from boiled milk which is salted and turned into cheese).

Serbia is famous for grilled meats, such as *čevapčići*, *pljeskavica* (a large, spicy hamburger steak) and *ražnjići* (a pork or veal shish kebab with onions and peppers). All together they become a *mešano meso* (mixed grill). *Duveč* is grilled pork cutlets with spiced stewed peppers, zucchini and tomatoes in rice cooked in an oven – absolutely delicious.

Other popular dishes are *musaka* (aubergine and potato layered with minced meat), *sarma* (cabbage stuffed with minced meat and rice), *kapama* (stewed lamb, onions and spinach with yogurt) and *punjena tikvica* (zucchini stuffed with minced meat and rice).

For vegetarians there's pizza or a *Srpska salata* (Serbian salad) of raw peppers, onions and tomatoes, seasoned with oil, vinegar and maybe chilli. Also ask for *gibanica* (cheese pie), *zeljanica* (cheese pie with spinach) or *pasulj prebranac* (cooked and spiced beans). *Šopska salata* is also very popular, consisting of chopped tomatoes, cucumber and onion, topped with grated soft white cheese.

## DRINKS

*Pivo* (beer) is universally available. Nikšićko *pivo* (both light and dark), brewed at Nikšić in Montenegro, is terribly good. Yugoslav cognac is called *vinjak*, many people distil their own plum brandy and Montenegrin red wine is a good drop.

Coffee is usually served Turkish-style, 'black as hell, strong as death and sweet as love'; superb espresso and cappuccinos are found in many cafés. For anything other than herbal teas (camomile or hibiscus) ask for Indian tea.

# Getting There & Away

You must fill out a currency declaration form on arrival and show it on departure, otherwise you'll have problems.

## AIR

JAT (Yugoslav Airlines) have regional services throughout Europe. Montenegro Airlines fly from Podgorica to Budapest, Frankfurt and Zürich. Other airlines such as Lufthansa and Aeroflot fly to Belgrade.

### Border Crossings

Visitors flying into Kosovo can only legally first enter Serbia via Macedonia as there are no immigration facilities at the crossings between Kosovo and Serbia or Montenegro. While you can enter Serbia without a check, problems will arise at hotels or leaving the country – there'll be no entry stamp in your passport, which means you're there illegally.

Similarly if you drive into Kosovo from Albania or Macedonia and are driving on to Serbia, you'll have to go via Macedonia to buy the necessary insurance at the border post.

## LAND
### Train
International trains from Belgrade call at Novi Sad and Subotica for destinations in the north and west, and Niš for those going east. Montenegro has no international services. Reservations are recommended and a student card will get you a reduction on some trains. Eurail and Inter-Rail passes are accepted and sold at Belgrade train station.

Sample services from Belgrade are:

| destination | cost (DIN) | duration (hours) | frequency |
| --- | --- | --- | --- |
| Bucharest | 1799 | 14 | daily |
| Budapest | 2311 | 7 | daily |
| İstanbul | 5787 | 26 | daily |
| Ljubljana | 1731 | 10 | daily |
| Moscow | 6423 | 50 | daily |
| Munich | 4940 | 17 | daily |
| Sofia | 1250 | 11 | daily |
| Thessaloniki | 1933 | 16 | daily |
| Vienna | 3518 | 11 | daily |
| Zagreb | 1110 | 7 | daily |

### Car & Motorcycle
Drivers from Britain, Spain, Germany and some other countries need an international driving licence, otherwise visitors can use their national licences. Vehicles need a third-party insurance recognised in Yugoslavia plus insurance (from €80 a month) bought at the border. For details contact **Auto-Moto Savez Jugoslavije** (Yugoslav Automotive Association; ☎ 011 9800; W www.amsj.co.yu; Ruzveltova 18, Belgrade). For travel into Kosovo see the boxed text 'Border Crossings' earlier. Traffic police are everywhere so drive carefully and stick assiduously to speed limits.

### Sea
A ferry service operates between Bar and Italy (see Bar in the Montenegro section later).

### Departure Tax
There is a departure tax of 600 DIN when leaving Yugoslavia by air.

# Getting Around

## AIR
JAT flies from Belgrade to Tivat and Podgorica (Montenegro) several times daily. The company also runs inexpensive buses between airports and city centres. Montenegro Airlines also flies daily between Podgorica and Belgrade.

## BUS
Buses are necessary for travel to Novi Pazar in Serbia, for the Montenegrin coast and getting to Žabljak.

## TRAIN
Jugoslovenske Železnice (JŽ) provides adequate railway services from Belgrade serving Novi Sad, Subotica, Niš, and the highly scenic line down to Bar. There are four classes of train: *ekspresni* (express), *poslovni* (rapid), *brzi* (fast) and *putnicki* (slow), so make sure you have the right ticket.

## Car Hire
Most of the well-known outfits, VIP, Hertz, Europcar and Net Rent a Car all have offices at Belgrade airport. The typical cost for a small car is €55 a day.

# Serbia Србија

The dominant role of Serbia (Srbija) in Yugoslavia was underlined by its control of two formerly autonomous provinces, Vojvodina and Kosovo, and the federal capital being Belgrade.

## BELGRADE БЕОГРАД
☎ 011 • pop 2 million (est. 2002)
Belgrade (Beograd) is strategically situated on the southern edge of the Carpathian Basin where the Sava River joins the Danube. Destroyed and rebuilt 40 times in its 2300-year history, Belgrade is well on its way to being a European capital. It is a lively, vibrant city with fine restaurants, shops, bars and street cafés, and chic crowds.

## History
The Celtic settlement of Singidunum was founded in the 3rd century BC on a bluff overlooking the confluence of the Sava and Danube Rivers. The Romans arrived in the 1st century AD and stayed here until the 5th century. Much of Kneza Mihaila is built over the main Roman street. The Slavic name Beograd (White City) first appeared in a papal letter in 878.

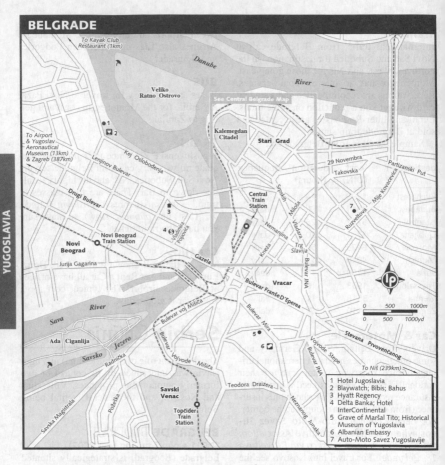

**BELGRADE**

To Kayak Club
Restaurant (1km)

*Danube*

*River*

Veliko
Ratno Ostrovo

See Central Belgrade Map

●1
◻2

To Airport
& Yugoslav
Aeronautical
Museum (13km)
& Zagreb (387km)

Kalemegdan
Citadel

Stari Grad

Kej Oslobodenja

Lenjinov Bulevar

29 Novembra

Takovska

Partizanski Put

Mije Kovacevica

Drugi Bulevar

Central
Train
Station

Sindjih

Milosa

Ruzveltova

7

◻3

Vladimira Popovica

Nemanjina

Vladara

Novi Beograd
Train Station

Novi
Beograd

4 ◒

Kneza

Trg
Slavija

Bulevar JNA

Jurija Gagarina

Gazela

Vracar

Bulevar Franše D'Eperea

Bulevar voj Mišića

Sava

*River*

Bulevar Mira

5 ●

6 ◻

Voivode Stepe

Stevana  Prvovenčanog

Ada  Ciganlija

Savsko

Jezero

Bulevar – Vojvode – Mišića

Bulevar JNA

To Niš (239km)

Radnička

Savski
Venac

Teodora Draizera

Savska Magistrala

Požeška

Topčider
Train
Station

Nemanjog Junaka

0      500      1000m
0      500      1000yd

1  Hotel Jugoslavia
2  Blaywatch; Bibis; Bahus
3  Hyatt Regency
4  Delta Banka; Hotel
   InterContinental
5  Grave of Maršal Tito; Historical
   Museum of Yugoslavia
6  Albanian Embassy
7  Auto-Moto Savez Yugoslavije

YUGOSLAVIA

The Serbs made Belgrade their capital in 1403 after being pushed north by Turks who captured the city in 1521. In 1842 the city became the Serbian capital and in 1918 the capital of the Kingdom of Serbs, Croats and Slovenes, later Yugoslavia.

## Orientation

The train station and the two adjacent bus stations are on the southern side of the city. From the train station, travel in an easterly direction along Milovana Milovanovića and up Balkanska to Terazije, the heart of modern Belgrade. Kneza Mihaila, Belgrade's lively pedestrian boulevard, runs northwest through the old town from Terazije to the Kalemegdan Citadel overlooking the Sava and Danube Rivers.

## Information

**Tourist Offices** The friendly, helpful **Tourist Organization of Belgrade** (☎ 635 622, fax 635 343; Terazije Passage; open 9am-8pm Mon-Fri, 9am-4pm Sat) is in the underpass near Kneza Mihaila. (Note the public toilets here for future reference.) There's also a **tourist office** (☎ 601 555; open 8am-8pm daily) located at Belgrade airport.

**Money** Most travellers cheques can be cashed at **Atlas Bank** (☎ 302 4000; Emilijana Josimovića 4), and AmEx travellers cheques at the **Astral Banka** (cnr Maršala Birjuzova & Pop Lukina). There are many private exchange offices in Belgrade, just look out for the large blue diamond sign.

Currently the only ATM machine catering for foreign-issued cards is in the foyer of the **Hotel InterContinental** *(Vladimira Popovića 10)*, which accepts Visa cards. In the same foyer **Delta Banka** *(open 6.30am-10pm daily)* cashes travellers cheques.

**Post & Communications** For phone calls there's the **central post office** *(Zmaj Jovina 17; open 7am-8pm daily)* and the **telephone centre** *(Takovska; open 7am-midnight Mon-Fri, 7am-10pm Sat & Sun)* in the **Main Post Office** by Sveti Marko church.

Changes to seven-digit numbers should be completed by 2003 but be aware that some numbers listed may change.

**Email & Internet Access** Better to use in the daytime, **IPS** *(Makedonska 4; open 24hr)* charges 80 DIN an hour. At night Belgrade's young commandeer the terminals to play the latest game. **Plato Cyber Club** *(Akademski plato 1; open 24hr)* charges 35 DIN an hour and has a huge, separate game section.

**Travel Agencies** The main office for **JAT** *(☎ 642 773, fax 642 534;* w *www.jat.co.yu; Srpskih Vladara 18)* deals with just its own services, while **Putnik** *(☎ 323 2911, fax 323 4461;* w *www.putnik.co.yu; Terazije 27)* offers a wide range of domestic and international transport and tour services.

**Bas Turist** *(☎ 638 555, fax 784 859; BAS bus station)* and, across the street, **Turist Biro Lasta** *(☎ 641 251, fax 642 473; Milovana Milovanovića 1)* and **Putnik** *(Milovana Milovanovića; open 7am-7pm)* all sell tickets for buses. **KSR Beograd Tours** *(☎ 641 258, fax 687 447; Milovana Milovanovića 5; open Mon-Sat)* has train information and tickets at train station prices but without the crowds. The helpful staff speak good English.

**Jolly Travel** *(☎ 323 2393, fax 334 1843;* w *www.jolly.co.yu; Kneza Miloša 9)* offers sightseeing tours of Belgrade from €50 to €55 for two people. It offers car hire and books airline tickets and hotels.

**Bookshops** There are two good shops for English books and magazines. **Plato Bookshop** *(off Kneza Mihaila)* is the smaller of the two Plato bookshops. The **International Press Service Bookshop** *(IPS; ☎ 328 1859; Trg Republike 5)*, in the basement of the building, stocks foreign magazines, videos and CDs.

**Libraries** At the Kalemegdan end of the street, the **City Library** *(Kneza Mihaila; open 8am-8pm Mon-Fri, 2pm-8pm Sat)* has books in foreign languages. Also of interest are the foundations of a large Roman atrium in the basement plus a small exhibition of remains.

**The British Council** *(Terazije 8; open 11am-4pm Mon, Wed & Fri, 2pm-7pm Tues & Thur)* has a range of newspapers, magazines and books.

**Laundry** While your hotel laundry will cope with your usual washing, **Express Dry Cleaners** *(☎ 322 3479; Majke Jevrosime 53)* will charge you 150 DIN to dry-clean trousers or 300 DIN for a jacket.

**Left Luggage** The BAS bus station **left-luggage room** *(open 6am-10pm daily)* charges 40 DIN per piece. The train station **left-luggage office** *(open 24hr)* charges 10 DIN per piece.

**Medical & Emergency Services** Two handy pharmacies are the **Prvi Maj** *(☎ 324 0533; Srpskih Vladara 9; open 24hr)*; and the **Sveti Sava** *(☎ 643 170; Nemanjina 2; open 24hr)*.

**Boris Kidrič Hospital** *(☎ 643 839; Pasterova 1)* has a **Diplomatic Section** *(consultations 300 DIN; open 7am-7pm Mon-Fri)*. At other times, go to any of the clinics in **Klinički Centar** *(Pasterova; open 24hr)*.

**Things to See & Do**
From the train station take tram No 1, 2 or 13 heading northwest to **Kalemegdan Citadel**. This area has been fortified since Celtic times, with the Roman settlement of Singidunum on the flood plain below. Much of what is seen today dates from the 17th century, but there are also medieval gates, Orthodox churches, Muslim tombs and Turkish baths.

The large **Military Museum** *(☎ 360 4149; Kalemegdan; admission 20 DIN; 10am-5pm daily)* presents a complete military history of Yugoslavia. Some of the exhibits are quite recent but the guidebook in English (30 DIN) only takes you up to the 1980s. Proudly displayed are captured Kosovo Liberation Army (KLA) weapons and bits of a downed American stealth fighter. Outside are a number of bombs and missiles contributed to the collection by NATO in 1999 and a line-up of old guns and tanks, some quite rare.

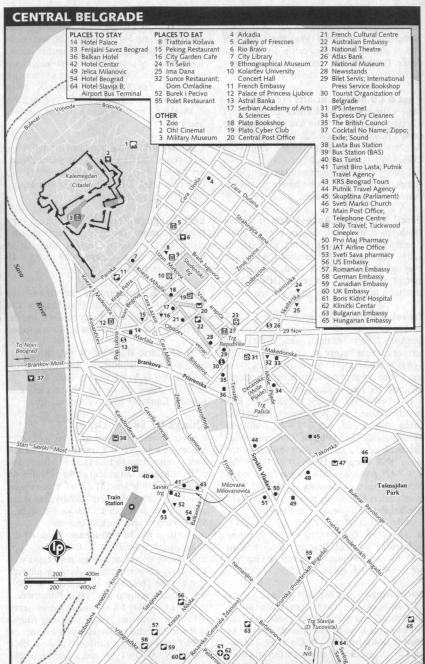

# CENTRAL BELGRADE

**PLACES TO STAY**
14  Hotel Palace
33  Ferijalni Savez Beograd
36  Balkan Hotel
42  Hotel Centar
49  Jelica Milanovic
54  Hotel Beograd
64  Hotel Slavija B;
    Airport Bus Terminal

**PLACES TO EAT**
8  Trattoria Košava
15  Peking Restaurant
16  City Garden Cafe
24  Tri Šeširi
25  Ima Dana
32  Sunce Restaurant;
    Dom Omladine
52  Burek i Pecivo
55  Polet Restaurant

**OTHER**
1  Zoo
2  Oh! Cinema!
3  Military Museum
4  Arkadia
5  Gallery of Frescoes
6  Rio Bravo
7  City Library
9  Ethnographical Museum
10  Kolarčev University
    Concert Hall
11  French Embassy
12  Palace of Princess Ljubice
13  Astral Banka
17  Serbian Academy of Arts
    & Sciences
18  Plato Bookshop
19  Plato Cyber Club
20  Central Post Office

21  French Cultural Centre
22  Australian Embassy
23  National Theatre
26  Atlas Bank
27  National Museum
28  Newsstands
29  Bilet Servis; International
    Press Service Bookshop
30  Tourist Organization of
    Belgrade
31  IPS Internet
34  Express Dry Cleaners
35  The British Council
37  Cocktail No Name; Zippo;
    Exile; Sound
38  Lasta Bus Station
39  Bus Station (BAS)
40  Bas Turist
41  Turist Biro Lasta; Putnik
    Travel Agency
43  KRS Beograd Tours
44  Putnik Travel Agency
45  Skupština (Parliament)
46  Sveti Marko Church
47  Main Post Office;
    Telephone Centre
48  Jolly Travel; Tuckwood
    Cineplex
50  Prvi Maj Pharmacy
51  JAT Airline Office
53  Sveti Sava pharmacy
56  US Embassy
57  Romanian Embassy
58  German Embassy
59  Canadian Embassy
60  UK Embassy
61  Boris Kidrič Hospital
62  Klinički Centar
63  Bulgarian Embassy
65  Hungarian Embassy

YUGOSLAVIA

Stari Grad is the oldest part of Belgrade, with several museums, especially the **National Museum** (☎ 624 322; Trg Republike; admission 50 DIN, free Sun; open 10am-5pm Tues, Wed, Fri & Sat; noon-8pm Thur; 10am-2pm Sun) with archaeological exhibits. There's a modern art gallery on the 3rd floor displaying just a fraction of a very large collection of national and European art, including some from Pablo Picasso and Claude Monet. Nadežeta Petrović (1873–1915), one of Serbia's first women artists, is well represented.

A few blocks away is the **Ethnographical Museum** (☎ 328 1888; Studentski Trg 13; admission 40 DIN; open 10am-5pm Tues-Fri, 9am-5pm Sat, 9am-1pm Sun), with a comprehensive collection of Serbian costumes and folk art. Detailed explanations are provided in English. Nearby is the **Gallery of Frescoes** (☎ 621 491; Cara Uroša 20; admission 50 DIN; 10am-5pm Mon-Wed, Fri & Sat, noon-8pm Thur, 10am-2pm Sun) with full-size replicas (and some originals) of paintings from churches and monasteries.

What could be a memorable museum is the **Palace of Princess Ljubice** (☎ 638 264; Kneza Sime Markovića 8; admission 30 DIN; open 10am-5pm Tues-Fri, 10am-4pm Sat & Sun), a Balkan-style palace (1831) with period furnishings. At present it's just a formal arrangement of furniture, carpets and paintings let down by the lack of human detail.

Behind the Main Post Office is **Sveti Marko Serbian Orthodox Church** (built from 1932 to 1939) with four tremendous pillars supporting a towering dome. Inside is the grave of the emperor Dušan (1308–55).

Take trolleybus No 40 or 41 south from Kneza Miloša to visit the white marble **grave of Maršal Tito** (Bulevar Mira; admission free; open 9am-2pm Tues-Sat). It's adjacent to an official residence that Tito never lived in, due to ill health. In 1999 the Milošević family moved in; Slobodan has since changed address but Mrs M has refused to move out. Between this well-guarded house and Tito's grave is the **Historical Museum of Yugoslavia** (admission free; 10am-5pm Tues-Sun). During our visit it was hosting a semipermanent display of artworks presented to Tito by grateful workers' organisations, toadying minions and friendly countries.

At the airport is the exceptional **Yugoslav Aeronautical Museum** (☎ 670 992; Belgrade International Airport; admission 300 DIN; open 8.30am-2.30pm Tues-Fri, 11am-3.30pm Sat & Sun), especially so if you are an aircraft buff. It has examples of many of the aircraft that flew with or against the Yugoslav air force, including a Hurricane, Spitfire and Messerschmitt from WWII, Russian MiG fighters and still more bits of that American stealth fighter.

**Ada Ciganlija**, an island park in the Sava River, is just the place to escape the bustle of Belgrade. In summer you can swim in the river (naturists 1km upstream), rent a bicycle or just stroll among the trees. Many small cafés overlooking the beach sell cold beer at reasonable prices.

## Places to Stay

Inquiries and bookings for youth hostels should be made through the helpful **Ferijalni Savez Beograd** (☎ 324 8550, fax 322 0762; ⓦ www.hostels.org.yu; 2nd floor, Makedonska 22). You need HI membership, an international student card or you can join (300 DIN) when booking.

There are two hostels in Belgrade. **Hotel Slavija B** (☎ 450 842; Svetog Save 1-9; rooms per person including breakfast US$11.50) offers singles and doubles with bathrooms to budget travellers. This special price is only available through Ferijalni Savez Beograd.

**Jelica Milanovic** (☎ 323 1268; Krunska 8; rooms per person with shared/private bathroom €7.50/9; open July & Aug) is college accommodation only available during holidays. No food is available here.

Belgrade is full of state-owned, B-category hotels and their prices include breakfast. **Hotel Centar** (☎ 644 055, fax 657 838; Savski trg 7; singles/doubles 680/1360 DIN), opposite the train station, has basic and spartan accommodation in an annexe at the back of the hotel. **Hotel Beograd** (☎ 645 199, fax 643 746; Nemanjina 6; singles/doubles 1522/2044 DIN), visible from the train station, has time-worn rooms with bathrooms. **Balkan Hotel** (☎ 687 466, fax 687 581 Prizrenska 2; singles/doubles 1600/2250 DIN) is a useful central hotel that's not as worn out as some. The rooms have bathrooms, the staff is helpful but the breakfast is rather unimaginative.

**Hotel Palace** (☎ 185 585, fax 184 458; Topličin venac 23; singles/doubles US$71/92) is a previously state-owned hotel. Now privately owned and renovated, the quality

YUGOSLAVIA

and prices have gone up in the world. The top-floor Panorama restaurant gives views over the city.

If you want to go overboard, the **Hyatt Regency** (☎ 301 1234, fax 311 2234; e admin@hyatt.co.yu; Milentija Popovića 5; rooms US$220 plus 20% tax), in dull Novi Beograd, will charge you heavily for the privilege. If you fancy a splash out on a buffet breakfast it'll set you back 1075 DIN.

## Places to Eat

Belgraders do very well for fast food with kiosks and cafés offering burek, čevapčići, pastries, hot dogs and some inventive pizza. Those around Trg Republika are open 24 hours. You can fill up for under 100 DIN.

A great place for a breakfast burek near the train station is the **Burek i Pecivo** (Nemanjina 5; open 5am-1pm Mon-Fri, 5am-11am Sat), near the Hotel Beograd. Belgrade has some top-class cafés and the best cappuccino in town can be sipped at **City Garden Cafe** (Vuka Karadžića).

**Sunce Restaurant** (☎ 324 8474; Dečanska 1; buffet 249 DIN; open 9am-9pm Mon-Sat) is a rarity – a vegetarian restaurant. The many-item buffet is an all-you-can-eat variety.

For inexpensive seafood try the **Polet Restaurant** (Njegoševa; meals 140-300 DIN; open 11am-11pm daily) and its corba (spicy fish soup) for 60 DIN. Portions are large and the service is attentive.

For local colour visit the atmospheric cobbled street of Skadarska with open-air evening performances in summer. **Tri Šeširi** (Three Hats; ☎ 324 7501; Skadarska 29; dishes 300-460 DIN; open lunch & dinner daily) offers meat and more meat dishes plus a nightly band playing those stirring Serbian folk songs.

**Ima Dana** (☎ 323 4422; Skadarska 38; meals 250-350 DIN; open 11am-5pm, 7pm-1am daily) does a lovely pike dish for 1000 DIN a kilo, although the size of serving is up to you. It also has a resident band performing the songs composed in Skadarska during the 19th century when this area was the Bo-hemian part of the Balkans.

**Trattoria Košava** (Kralja Petra 6; dishes 300-400 DIN; 9am-1am Mon-Fri, noon-1am Sat & Sun) is a light, airy Italian-style restaurant reportedly doing the best osso bucco ever. Downstairs, a small café offers snacks and yummy cakes.

**Peking Restaurant** (Vuka Karadžića 2; dishes 275-410 DIN; open 11am-midnight Mon-Sat, 2pm-midnight Sun) does some good but expensive Chinese food if you're hankering for a change, and even kajmak if you're not. **Bahus** (☎ 602 971; open 10am-midnight daily) is an expensive restaurant where you'd wine and dine your favourite or where you'd want to impress someone that paying twice the price of other barges is of no consequence. However the food is rather fine and a 1kg lobster will cost 4000 DIN.

If you're out Zemun way then a cheap place to eat alongside the Danube is the **Kayak Club restaurant** (Ivo Lola Ribar; buffet 199 DIN; open 2pm-6pm Thur-Sun) with an all-you-can-eat buffet.

## Entertainment

Party life in Belgrade revolves around the many barges and boats moored on the Sava and Danube Rivers. Along Kej Oslobođenja, adjacent to Hotel Jugoslavia, there's a strip of a kilometre of some 20 barges. Bus Nos 15, 84 and 706 will get you to this place from central Belgrade.

**Blaywatch** (open 11am-1am daily) is a play on the TV series Baywatch and the Serbian blay which means 'to do nothing'. This is where those with the youth, clothes and money come to flaunt it. **Bibis** (open 10am-2am daily) is a much more agreeable place, popular in winter, selling cheaper drinks and also snacks; the beer comes in large pottery mugs decorated with a green kangaroo.

On the western bank of the Sava River is another 1.5km strip of floating bars, restaurants and discos. Here you'll find **Cocktail No Name** playing pop and 80s music, **Zippo** for Serbian folk music, **Exile** pounding out techno and nearby **Sound** playing house and disco. Getting there is by walking over the Brankov Most or by tram No 7, 9 or 11.

Back on land there's the interesting **Oh! Cinema!** (☎ 328 4000; Kalemegdan Citadel) café/bar overlooking the Danube and zoo. It's a favourite place to hang out through summer nights with live music, probably giving insomnia to the tigers below.

**Rio Bravo** (Kralja Petra 54; open 11am-2am Mon-Fri, 5pm-2am Sat & Sun) has live bands at the weekend and recorded music other nights. There are four venues offering different music and this is the place for jazz and 1920s Chicago music.

For a mix-and-match evening among the clubs the best place to wander is down Strahinjića Bana, four blocks northeast of Studentski trg.

The **Bilet Servis** (☎ 625 365; Trg Republike 5; 9am-8pm Mon-Fri, 9am-3pm Sat) has a counter for event tickets and the English-speaking staff will quite happily search for something for you.

In winter there's opera at the elegant **National Theatre** (☎ 620 946; Trg Republike; box office open 10am-2pm Tues-Sun, 10am-3pm performance days). **Belgrade Philharmonia** concerts take place in the **Kolarčev University** (☎ 630 550; Studentski trg 5; box office open 10am-noon & 6pm-8pm daily) usually every Wednesday and Friday, except in July and August. In October it hosts a festival of classical music.

Concerts also take place in the **Serbian Academy of Arts & Sciences** (☎ 334 2400; Kneza Mihaila 35; admission free; concerts 6pm Mon & Thur), which also presents exhibitions. When we visited there was a display of military and civil uniforms; coal miners even had a dress uniform in communist times. **Dom Omladine** (☎ 322 0127; Makedonska 22) has nonclassical music concerts, film festivals and multimedia events.

The **French Cultural Centre** (Kneza Mihaila 31; open noon-6pm Mon-Fri, 11am-3pm Sat) often shows free films and videos.

For the latest Hollywood blockbuster the **Tuckwood Cineplex** (☎ 323 6517; Kneza Miloša 7; tickets 100-200 DIN) shows films in either English or with English subtitles.

### Getting There & Away
**Bus** Frequent buses to many places around Yugoslavia leave from both bus stations. Posted destinations are in Cyrillic only and it's easier to buy your ticket from a ticket agency. Sample services are Niš (435 DIN, three hours), Podgorica (850 DIN, nine hours), Budva (900 DIN, 12 hours) and Novi Pazar (275 DIN, three hours) for Kosovo.

**Train** Information regarding international trains is covered in the introductory Getting There & Away section earlier. Overnight trains with couchettes or sleepers run from Belgrade to Bar (1100 DIN, nine to 11 hours); a sleeper supplement costs 2000 DIN.

There are four trains a day to Novi Sad (120 DIN, two hours), two to Subotica (155 DIN,

3½ hours) and four to Niš (300 DIN, five hours). All trains to Subotica call at Novi Sad and international trains also call at both places.

**Train Station** Ticket counters are numbered; international tickets are sold at Nos 11 and 12 and regular tickets at Nos 7 to 20. Sleeper and couchette reservations are made at Nos 19 and 20 and information is at Nos 23 and 24. Timetables are in the Latin alphabet. There is a **tourist bureau** (open 7am-9.30pm daily), an **exchange bureau** and a **sales counter** (☎/fax 658 868; open 9am-4pm Mon-Sat) for Eurail passes located at the track end of the station.

### Getting Around
**To/From the Airport** Surcin airport is 18km west of Belgrade. Ignore taxi drivers who'll meet you in the airport; they overcharge. Instead go outside and look for a fare from 450 to 600 DIN to Belgrade.

The JAT bus (30 DIN; airport to town hourly 5am to 9pm, town to airport hourly 7am to 8pm) is the best transport between town (Hotel Slavija B, Trg Slavija) and the airport via the train station.

**Public Transport** Private buses and state-owned buses, trams and trolleybuses charge 10 DIN for any journey.

**Taxi** Belgrade's taxis are in plentiful supply and flag fall is 40 DIN. A trip around the town centre should cost around 150 DIN. Check that the meter is running. If not, point it out to the driver.

## VOJVODINA ВОЈВОДИНА
Vojvodina (21,506 sq km) was an autonomous province until annexed by Serbia in 1990. Slavs settled here in the 6th century, Hungarians in the 10th century and Serbs in 1389 following their defeat by the Turks. The region was under Turkish rule from the 16th century until the Habsburgs cleared them out in the late 17th century. Again, it became a refuge for Serbs leaving the Turkish-controlled lands farther south. The region remained a part of Hungary until 1918. This low-lying land of many rivers merges imperceptibly into the Great Hungarian Plain and Romania's Banat. Numerous canals crisscross this fertile plain that provides much of Yugoslavia's wheat, corn and crude oil.

## Novi Sad Нови Сад
☎ 021 • pop 270,000 (est. 2002)

Novi Sad, capital of Vojvodina, is a modern
city situated at a strategic bend of the
Danube. The city developed in the 18th century when a powerful fortress was constructed on a hill top, overlooking the river,
to hold the area for the Habsburgs. Novi
Sad's attractions are simply wandering the
pedestrian streets, such as Dunavska, with
their string of smart boutiques and outdoor
cafés, and visiting Petrovaradin Citadel.

### Orientation & Information
The adjacent
train and intercity bus stations are at the end
of Bulevar Oslobođenja, on the northwestern
side. It's a 20-minute walk to the city centre,
otherwise catch bus No 11A to the city bus
station. Then ask directions to the **tourist office** (☎ 421 811; Dunavska 27) in a quaint old
part of town. The **telephone centre** (open
24hr) is next to the **main post office**.

It's easier to buy domestic and international
train tickets from **KSR Beograd Tours** (☎ 27
445, fax 27 423; Svetozara Miletića 4) than
at the train station. **Atlas Bank** (☎ 421 600;
Futoška 2) or the **Micro Finance Bank** (☎ 58
942; Bulevar Cara Lazara 7b) will cash euro
or US-dollar travellers cheques.

Novi Sad plays host to the Exit Festival,
held in August, attracting music bands from
all over Europe.

### Things to See & Do
The main museum,
**Muzej Vojvodine** (☎ 26 555; Dunavska 35 &
37; admission 20 DIN; open 9am-7pm Tues-
Fri, 9am-2pm Sat & Sun), is in two buildings.
No 35 covers Vojvodina history from Palaeolithic times to the late 19th century and No 37
takes the story to 1945 with an emphasis on
WWI and WWII. The collection is impressive in its thoroughness and, although captioned in Serbian, the main explanatory
panels are in English.

Across the Danube River is the majestic
**Petrovaradin Citadel**, the 'Gibraltar of the
Danube', built between 1699 and 1780 and
designed by French architect Vauban. Stairs
beside the large church in the lower town
lead up to the fortress. The citadel contains a
small **museum** (☎ 432 055; admission 30
DIN; open 9am-5pm Tues-Sun Apr-June,
9am-5pm July-Mar) and a **planetarium**
(☎ 433 038; admission 40 DIN; shows 7pm
Thur, 5pm Sat & Sun). The chief pleasure is
simply to walk the walls and enjoy the splendid view. Have a close look at the clock
tower. The hour hand is the longer one so
that the clock would be easy to read from the
river.

### Places to Stay & Eat
On the Danube the
large **autocamp** (☎ 368 400, fax 366 801;
Ribarsko Ostrvo; bungalows per double/
triple 1400/1745 DIN) has basic, well-used

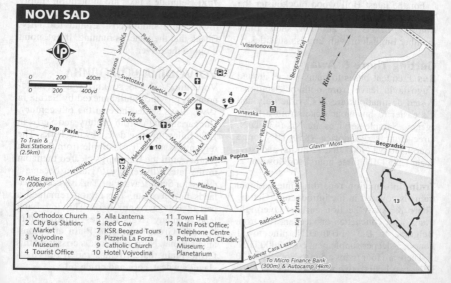

**NOVI SAD**

| | |
|---|---|
| 1 Orthodox Church | 5 Alla Lanterna | 11 Town Hall |
| 2 City Bus Station; | 6 Red Cow | 12 Main Post Office; |
|   Market | 7 KSR Beograd Tours |   Telephone Centre |
| 3 Vojvodine | 8 Pizzeria La Forza | 13 Petrovaradin Citadel; |
|   Museum | 9 Catholic Church |   Museum; |
| 4 Tourist Office | 10 Hotel Vojvodina |   Planetarium |

bungalow accommodation. Breakfast is not included but there are two restaurants onsite. There's a small zoo, a children's playground and beaches on the Danube. Take bus No 4 from the train station or city centre to Liman and then walk towards the river or take a taxi ride for 80 DIN.

The oldest, most appealing and central of Novi Sad's hotels is **Hotel Vojvodina** (☎ 622 122, fax 615 445; Trg Slobode 2; singles/ doubles 1600/2200 DIN). With an attractive pastel facade, it's conveniently located but expensive for rooms with bathroom and breakfast.

**Alla Lanterna** (☎ 622 002; Dunavska 27; meals 240-290 DIN; open 8am-midnight) is a pizza/pasta place with bags of atmosphere. Maybe it's something to do with the internal wall decorations that must have taken several truckloads of pebbles. In warm weather the café sprawls onto the pedestrian street.

**Pizzeria La Forza** (Katolicka Porta 6; pasta dishes 150-180 DIN; open 8am-11pm Mon-Sat, 3pm-11pm Sun) is a bright and cheery spot for a quick bite with a good selection of filling pasta.

The **Red Cow** (cnr Dunavska & Zmaj Jovina) is a trendy Irish pub that's just the place for a refreshing Guinness or draught Nikšić or an evening out.

**Getting There & Away** Novi Sad is served by frequent local trains to Belgrade (120 DIN, two hours) and Subotica (112 DIN, 1½ hours), plus international trains.

## Subotica Суботица
☎ 024 • pop 150,000 (est. 2002)
At 10km from the border at Kelebija, Subotica is a useful transit point to/from Szeged (Hungary); it's also worth a day trip from Belgrade. The train station is just a short walk from the town centre.

**Micro Finance Bank** (Lenjina Park 8) cashes travellers cheques and there's a **currency exchange office** (open 8am-7pm Mon-Fri, 8am-1pm Sat) in the old town hall.

The train station has a **left-luggage office** (37.50 DIN per item; open 24hr) and an **exchange office**.

**Things to See** The imposing Art Nouveau **town hall** (Trg Republike), built in 1910, contains an excellent **historical museum** (open 9am-2pm Tues-Sat) on the 1st floor (captions

in Serbian and Hungarian) displaying regional life and a mammoth skull. Check to see whether the exquisitely decorated council chambers are open. The dark varnished wood, green baize cloth and high-backed chairs give a succinct air of petty municipal power.

An equally exquisite piece of architecture is the amazingly beautiful Art Nouveau **Modern Art Gallery** (Trg Lenina 5; open 7am-1pm Mon, Wed & Fri, 7am-6pm Tues & Thur, 9am-noon Sat).

**Places to Stay & Eat** The only hotel in Subotica is **Hotel Patria** (☎ 554 500, fax 551 762; Đure Đakovica; singles/doubles 1800/ 2800 DIN), where rooms come with bath and breakfast. Avis has a desk here (see also Rental under Car & Motorcycle in the introductory Getting Around chapter) and the hotel can organise local excursions. There's a youth hostel **Zorka** (☎ 754 418; Palić; per person €6, full board €12) by the lake at Palić for budget accommodation.

There is a dearth of restaurants in the town centre but the **Pizza Vento** (Borisa Kidriča 2; pizzas 160-200 DIN; open 7am-midnight) is a relaxing spot for a decently large pizza and a beer. Go to **Lipa** (Đure Đakovica 13, burek 60 DIN; open 24hr), a bakery and burek shop, for an excellent cheese and mushroom burek and yogurt for breakfast. **Ravel Nušićeva** (Trg Republike; open 9am-10pm daily) does the best line in squidgy cakes and some excellent coffee.

**Getting There & Away** There are two local trains a day to/from Szeged, Hungary (155 DIN, 1¾ hours), and other international trains. Trains to Belgrade (155 DIN, 3½ hours) also call at Novi Sad. Five daily buses serve Szeged and Subotica (€2.50, 1½ hours) but the train is more convenient.

## SMEDEREVO СМЕДЕРЕВО
**Smederevo Fortress** (admission 10 DIN; open daylight hours) is a triangular fort with 25 towers and a water moat fronting the Danube. An inner citadel overlooks the river. Built by despot Djuradj Brankovic, it served as his capital from 1428 to 1430. The fortifications were never really tested in battle and the only damage has been wrought by time and the massive explosion of an ammunition train in WWII.

The **Smederevo Museum** (admission 10 DIN; open 10am-5pm Mon-Fri, 10am-3pm

*Sat & Sun)* is a 'history of the town' museum with artefacts dating from Roman times and some interesting frescoes. A half-hourly bus service (130 DIN, 1½ hours) from Belgrade makes this a pleasant day trip.

## NIŠ НИШ
**☎ 018 • pop 300,000 (est. 2002)**

Niš lies at the junction of several international road and rail routes. It was settled in pre-Roman times and flourished during the time of local boy made good, Emperor Constantine (280–337 AD). Turkish rule lasted from 1386 until 1877 despite several Serb revolts, of which the Ćele Kula is a gruesome reminder (for details see its entry in the Things to See section, later).

### Orientation & Information
Just north of the river is Tvrđava Citadel and to the west is the main market area and the bus station. The train station is to the west on Dimitrija Tucovića.

The helpful **Tourist Organisation of Niš** (*☎ 523 455; Gen Milojka Lešjanina 26)* has some basic tourist literature in English.

The **Micro Finance Bank** *(☎/fax 547 845; Lole Ribara 19)* will cash euro or US-dollar travellers cheques.

The **Web Caffe** *(Kultur Centre, 3rd floor, Pobede; open 9am-midnight Mon-Sat, noon-midnight Sun)* is a central Internet café charging 90 DIN an hour.

**KSR Beograd** *(☎ 523 808; Trg Oslobođenja 9)* sells train tickets in a more relaxed and helpful atmosphere than the train station.

### Things to See
**Tvrđava** *(Jadranska; admission free; always open)* is a citadel built by the Turks in 1396 on the site of a Roman fortress. It's a large open area, bounded by a defensive stone wall; even the small **mosque** seems to be an empty shell.

The macabre **Ćele Kula** *(Tower of Skulls; Brače Taskovića; admission 60 DIN; open 9am-4pm Tues-Sat, 10am-2pm Sun)* was erected by the Turks in 1809 as a warning to would-be Serbian rebels. During 1809 a force under the Duke of Resava trying to liberate Niš attacked a larger Turkish force. The Serbs suffered heavily. The Duke rushed the Turkish defences and fired his pistol into their powder magazine. The resulting exploion reportedly wiped out 4000 Serbs and ~,000 Turks. When the battle was won all

the dead Serbs were beheaded, scalped and their skulls embedded in this short square tower. Only 58 remain.

**Mediana** *(Sofia rd; admission site free, museum 20 DIN; open 9am-4pm Tues-Sat 10am-2pm Sun)*, on the eastern outskirts of Niš, is the remains of a 4th-century Roman palace complex possibly belonging to the emperor Constantine the Great. Archaeological digging has revealed a palace, forum and a large grain storage area with some large, almost intact, pottery vessels.

### Places to Stay & Eat
**Niš Hotel** *(☎ 24 643, fax 23 779; Voždova 12; singles/doubles 1550/2230 DIN)* is probably the best-value hotel in town. The rooms are large and have bathrooms.

**Casablanca** *(☎ 40 750; Jeronimova 26; dishes 180-350 DIN; open noon-1am)* has a varied menu with Mexican, French, Italian and Greek dishes accompanied on most nights with a similar mix in music.

**Tramvaj** *(Tramway; Pobedina 9)* is an intriguing small café in the centre of town that has an Isle of Man (UK) tram as its servery, while customers gather on slatted tram benches. The Tramvaj does a very nice aromatic coffee.

# Montenegro
# Црна Гора

From an interior with Alpine-type scenery to giddy-deep canyons, coastal fjords, and a sparsely vegetated and highly folded limestone mountain range that plummets down to an azure Adriatic sea, the 13,812-sq-km **Republic of Montenegro** *(Crna Gora)* has got the works.

North of Podgorica, both railway and road run through the Moraca Canyon, while 40km west of Mojkovac is the 1.3km deep Tara Canyon. Other striking features are the winding Bay of Kotor, the largest fjord in southern Europe, and the vast, beautiful and ecologically significant Lake Skadar. Of historical interest are the old towns of Budva, Cetinje and the walled cities of Kotor and Herceg Novi.

Montenegro is a very popular holiday spot; June to September is the high season, peaking in July and August. Quoted accommodation prices are for the high season.

## History

Only tiny Montenegro kept its head above the Turkish tide that engulfed the Balkans for over four centuries from the 14th century. From 1482 Montenegro was ruled from Cetinje by *vladike* (bishops). With the defeat of the Turks in 1878, Montenegrin independence was assured and later recognised by the Congress of Berlin. Nicola I Petrovic, Montenegro's ruler, declared himself king in 1910 but was evicted by the Austrians in 1916; following WWI Montenegro was incorporated into Serbia. During WWII Montenegrins fought valiantly in Tito's partisan army and afterwards the region was rewarded with republic status within Yugoslavia.

Montenegro has been in the Yugoslav federation through its several incarnations, but recently with a burgeoning independence movement. Under the proposed new union with Serbia, Milo Đukanović, President of Montenegro has put any independence moves on hold.

## Getting There & Away

You can enter Montenegro by road from Croatia, Serbia and Albania, or by ship from Italy. Crossing into Albania at Božaj requires a €20 taxi ride from Podgorica, walking over the border and catching an onward taxi. Similarly it's a €15 taxi ride from Herceg Novi to the Croatian border or catch the one daily bus to the border.

The only international rail connections are through Serbia. A main rail line runs from Belgrade to Bar where ferries connect for Italy.

## PODGORICA ПОДГОРИЦА

☎ 081 ● pop 170,000 (est. 2002)

Podgorica is a place to arrive in, do your business and leave. Don't stay here. The cheapest hotel charges foreigners €50, twice the price as for a local. It's far better to go south and stay at the cheaper private rooms and apartments on the coast.

## Orientation & Information

The train and bus stations (including a post office branch) are adjacent in the eastern part of the town. The hub of the town centres around Slobode. **Atlas Bank** (☎ 248 870; *Stanka Dragojevića 4-6; open 8am-4pm Mon-Fri, 8am-1pm Sat*) will cash AmEx and Thomas Cook travellers cheques and the **Podgorica Bank** (*Novaka Miloševa 8a; open*

*7am-8pm Mon-Sat*) will give cash advances up to €500 on Visa cards.

You'll find an Internet café, **Internet cg** (*Vučedolska 13; open 9am-9pm Mon-Sat*), off Slobode, that charges €1.80 an hour.

**JAT** (☎ 244 248, fax 245 065; *Ivana Milutinovica 20*) has an airport transfer bus (€1.50) leaving from its office 1½ hours before every flight and returning after each arrival. **Montenegro Airlines** (☎ 224 406, fax 246 207; @ officepg@mgx.cg.yu; *Slobode 23*) flies to Frankfurt, Zürich and Budapest.

## Places to Eat

There are some cheap eating places around the bus and train stations, and some pleasant cafés in Bokeška.

**Pizzeria Leone** (*Njegoševa 42; pizzas €3.15-4.20; open 8am-midnight Mon-Sat, 3pm-midnight Sun*) caters for the Montenegrin's love of Italian food and serves the excellent local Nikšić beer.

## Getting There & Away

There are five buses to Belgrade (€14, nine hours), five to Žabljak (€6, four hours) and many to Budva (€3.25, 1½ hours). A 7.30am bus leaves on Sunday and Wednesday for İstanbul for €100.

You can fly to Belgrade for €46.50 or take the scenic train route (€8 plus €9 sleeper supplement, eight hours). There are frequent trains to Bar and two daily trains to Nikšić (€1.60, two hours).

## LAKE SKADAR & VIRPAZAR

A causeway carries road and rail from Podgorica to Bar over the western edge of the 44km-long Lake Skadar. The biggest lake in the Balkans, it's one of the largest bird sanctuaries and remaining pelican habitats in Europe. Jutting westward from the causeway is the 400-year old Turkish castle of Lesendro. Chat to **Gorbis travel agency** (☎ 081-230 624; @ gorbis@cg.yu; *Slobode 47*) in Podgorica about trips on the lake.

Alternatively nose around Virpazar, south of the causeway, where in summer there are likely to be sightseeing boats. You'll also find one of Montenegro's finest restaurants here, the 100-year-old **Pelican Restaurant** (*Virpazar; dishes €5-10; open 8am-midnight daily*). It's the service that provides the ambience and dessert is always on the house. For starters try the *dalmatinsko varvo*, a potato, onion and spinach pie followed by a fish salad of perch, eel or trout – all from the lake. Weekend evenings, May to September, there's live music. The Pelican also offers **accommodation** *(doubles €20 with shared bathroom)*.

## BAR БАР
☎ 085

Backed by a precipitous coastal range, Bar is a would-be modern city and Yugoslavia's only port. There's little to attract a visitor to Bar except as a convenient transport centre.

The ferry terminal in Bar is 300 metres from town centre but the bus and train stations are about 2km southeast of the centre.

Tourist information is very limited and your best bet is to try **Montenegro Tourist** *(☎ 311 133; Obala 13 Jula)* by the ferry terminal.

### Places to Stay & Eat
Visitors with time or their own transport will be able to choose from a whole range of places with 'sobe', 'zimmer' or 'private room' signs all along the coast. **Adria Tours** *(☎ 313 621; Novo Pristanište 65; full board singles/doubles €15/29)*, two kilometres northwest at Šušanj, can arrange accommodation.

**Hotel Topolica** *(☎ 311 013, fax 312 731; e htpkorali@cg.yu; B-grade singles/doubles including breakfast €16.85/25.60)*, a four-storey socialist relic, is the only hotel in town. The B-grade section at the back comes with private bathrooms and shabby furniture. If you ask you can get a room with a sea view.

Places to eat are limited with drinks-only cafés and bars outnumbering restaurants. **Pizeria Bell** *(Vladimira Rolovic, Podkovica C; pizza €3, pasta €4-5; open 7am-11pm daily)*, just up the street from the ferry terminal, is a small cosy pizza/pasta joint that's open year-round.

### Getting There & Away
Four trains a day travel to/from Belgrade (€8, nine hours). The couchette supplement is €9, making this cheap accommodation plus transport.

There are two daily buses to Ulcinj (€1.80, 1½ hours) and frequent buses to Budva (€2, 45 minutes) and Kotor (€3.20, three hours).

**Montenegro Lines** *(☎ 312 336; Obala 13 Jula)* sails at 10pm on Tuesday, Thursday and Saturday to Bari (Italy). In summer it's a daily service. Deck passage (10 hours) costs

€40 and a bunk from €13. For ferries to Ancona (Italy) chat to **Mecur** *(☎ 313 617, fax 313 618; e mercur@Eunet.yu; Obala 13 Jula)*. The Thursday service takes 16 hours and costs €46 for a deck seat.

In midsummer, transport to/from Bar is very crowded as Serbians head for the beach.

## ULCINJ УЛЦИЊ
☎ 085

Founded by the Greeks, Ulcinj gained notoriety as a North African pirate base between 1571 and 1878. There was even a market for slaves from whom the few resident black families are descended. The Turks held the area for over 300 years and today there are many Muslim Albanians in Ulcinj. Many Kosovars fled here as refugees in 1999 and come today as holiday makers. The busy season is July and August when Ulcinj bulges at the seams with several thousand extra people.

### Orientation & Information
Buses from Bar stop on the edge of town. Walk into town by turning right onto 26 Novembar at the first major junction. Mala Plaža (Small Beach) is below the old town at the end of 26 Novembar. Velika Plaža (Great Beach), Ulcinj's famous 12km stretch of unbroken sand, begins about 5km southeast of town (take the Ada bus or a minibus in season).

**intron cyber caffe** *(26 Novembar; open 9am-2pm daily)* is up a side alley opposite Caffe Montenegro; one hour costs €2.50.

### Things to See
The ancient **ramparts** of old Ulcinj (Stari Grad) overlook the sea, but most of the buildings inside were shattered by earthquakes in 1979 and later reconstructed. The **museum** *(open 7am-noon Mon-Fri)*, containing Montenegrin and Turkish artefacts, is by the upper gate. You can walk among the houses and along the wall for the view.

### Places to Stay
The camping ground **Tomi** is east of Milena and adjacent to Velika Plaža; it's open May to September. Farther on (100 metres), there's a sign to **HTP Velika Plaža** *(☎ 413 145; Ada Rd)*, which has a variety of accommodation. Inappropriately named **houses** *(per person with shared bathroom €3)* have two beds with just enough walk-around space; **bungalows** *(per person with private*

bathroom €5) take three people and provide more space; and **pavilions** *(per person with private bathroom €8)* are larger still and also take three people. Out-of-season prices are 20% less. There are restaurants onsite and breakfast/lunch/dinner costs €3/6/4.

The many private rooms and apartments can be booked through a travel agency like **Real Estate Tourist Agency** *(☎ 421 609, fax 421 612;* W *www.realestate.cg.yu; 26 Novembar).* It can offer accommodation in **private rooms** *(from €10, no meals)* or in a **hotel** *(doubles from €42 plus breakfast/ half-board/full board €4/9/12).*

Of the many hotels the **Albatros** *(☎ 423 628, fax 423 263;* e *info@hoteli-albatros .cg.yu; A-category singles/doubles €37.90/ 58.30, B-category €29.30/45.10)* is a pleasant modern hotel, 15 minutes' walk uphill from Mala Plaža. Rooms have private bathrooms and the price includes full board. It has a sauna, fitness room and swimming pool.

### Places to Eat
There are some chic eating places like the **Restaurant Teuta** *(038 137; Stari Grad; dishes €13-25; open 8am-late daily)* in the Old Town if your budget can stand it. You're paying for good food and a rooftop view over the town and sea. Down on the seafront is a string of restaurants all specialising in seafood; try the **Marinero** *(Obala Borisa Kidriča; dishes €15; open 7am-late daily)* for coffee or a full meal.

There are also numerous inexpensive cafés around town offering *čevapčići.* **Gallo Nero** *(☎ 315 245; 26 Novembar; dishes €5-12; open 10am-late daily)* has the best food in Ulcinj, matched by excellent service. You can come here for a snack or a full-blown meal.

### Getting There & Away
Buses to Bar (€1.60, 45 minutes) run every couple of hours in season. There's only one bus, late in the day, to Podgorica so go via Bar. Many minibuses and buses ply the road to Ada (and Velika Plaža) from the market place or the main post office for €1.50 in season.

### BUDVA БУДВА
☎ 086
Budva is Yugoslavia's top beach resort. A series of fine beaches punctuate the coastline to Sveti Stefan, with high barren coastal mountains forming a magnificent backdrop.

The modern bus station (no left-luggage office) is about 1km from the Old Town. The main square is at the end of Mediteranska by the harbour, where **JAT** *(☎ 41 641; Mediteranska 2)* has an office. Its bus (€2) runs between Tivat airport and the office, leaving 1½ hours before each flight.

### Things to See
Budva's big tourist-puller is its old **walled town**. Levelled by two earthquakes in 1979, it has since been completely rebuilt as a tourist attraction. It's so picturesque it seems almost contrived. Budva's main beach is pebbly and average. **Mogren Beach** is better, follow the coastal path northwards for 500m from the Grand Hotel Avala.

About 5km southeast of Budva is the former village of **Sveti Stefan**, an island now linked to the mainland and a luxury hotel complex. Admission is €3.75 so settle for the long-range picture-postcard view.

### Places to Stay & Eat
If you have a tent with you, try **Autocamp Avala** *(☎ 451 205; open June-Sept)* at Boreti, 2km on the road to Bar, or the manager may help you find a private room nearby.

There's a whole string of private rooms, apartments and hotels along this coastal strip, you could just look out for signs that say 'sobe', 'zimmer' or 'rooms'. The very helpful **Globtour** *(☎ 451 020, fax 52 827;* e *glob tourbd@cg.yu; Mediteranska 23)* can arrange for you **private rooms** *(half-board/full board €7.50/10).*

There's the very pleasant B-grade **Hotel Mediteran** *(☎ 51 423; Bečiči; rooms per person €27),* booked by **Maestral Tours** *(☎/fax 52 250; Mediteranska 23),* which is about 2km south along the coast. This rambling holiday hotel has several restaurants, an English pub and a private part of the beach.

The handiest hotel for the old part of the city is the modern **Hotel Mogren** *(☎ 452 041, fax 51 750; singles/doubles €40.90/66.40)* just outside the northern gate of the Old Town. Rates are very high during the peak season but the rooms are well equipped and quite large; some have balconies overlooking the Old Town.

Budva has no shortage of expensive bars and restaurants in the Old Town or along the harbourside. Probably the best is the **Restaurant Jadran** *(☎ 451 028; Slovenska obala 10;*

*dishes €5-10; open 8am-late daily)*, with some very appetising fish dishes. It's a circular restaurant with nautical junk and an outside patio overlooking the floodlit Old Town.

### Getting There & Away
There are frequent buses to Podgorica (€3.25, 1½ hours) via Cetinje (€2, 35 minutes), Kotor (€1.70, 30 minutes) and Bar (€2, one hour). There are also eight buses daily to Belgrade (€15, 12 hours) and one to Žabljak (€8, four hours).

## KOTOR КОТОР
☎ 082
Kotor is a big secret. Not only is the town at the head of southern Europe's deepest fjord, but it also has a walled medieval city that is Unesco listed.

### Orientation & Information
Four kilometres of walls encircle the Old Town (another Stari Grad) built over a thousand years from the 9th century. The main access is via an 18th-century gate fronting onto the harbour. Within is an entanglement of small streets and lanes linking squares where the main aristocratic families had mansions. Six Romanesque churches date from the 12th and 13th centuries, St Tripun's Cathedral (1166) being the most important. Also significant is a 6th-century clock tower.

For information on accommodation try **Mercur Intours** *(☎ 325 113, fax 325 137; Stari Grad, opposite the main entrance)* and **Meridian Travel Agency** *(☎ 11 188, fax 11 226; e travel@cg.yu; Stari Grad)*; both have helpful English-speaking staff.

Within the Old Town **IDK Computers** *(Stari Grad; open 2pm-midnight summer, 5pm-midnight rest of year)* charges €2 per hour for Internet access.

### Things to See & Do
The major attraction by far is wandering around the Old Town, popping into the old churches, dawdling for coffee at the pavement cafés and people-watching. Energetic? Then slog up the steep winding path to the old fortifications on the mountainside above Kotor. You'll be rewarded with stunning views of Kotor fjord.

Kotor has a proud maritime history and the **Maritime Museum** *(Stari Grad; admission €1; open 7am-7pm Mon-Sat & 9am-5pm*

*Sun May-Sept, 7am-3pm Mon-Fri & 9am-noon Sat & Sun Oct-Apr)* covers much of it over its three storeys of displays. A leaflet in English is available.

If you have transport then travel to Cetinje via a string of hairpin bends over the mountains. The views here are marvellous. Alternatively drive around the fjord and see all the little stone harbours cuddling braces of small boats against the waves.

### Places to Stay and Eat
For **private rooms** *(per person from €8)* and **hotels** *(doubles half-board €34.60)* contact the information booth outside the main entrance to the city or try a travel agency (see Orientation & Information earlier).

**Hotel Rendezvous** *(☎ 16 796; Stari Grad; singles/doubles €20/40)* is a private hotel above a small bar. For its price it's the best value within the Old Town. The rooms, although small, are quite acceptable and with private bathrooms. It can be a bit noisy at night.

**Bastion Restaurant** *(Stari Grad; dishes €5-8; open 10am-late)* is a small, almost unannounced, restaurant near St Mary's church in the northeastern part of the Old Town. It's a very popular lunchtime venue and you may need to wait for a table. Although rather pricey the food is fresh, hot and tasty.

**Pizzeria Giardino** *(Stari Grad; meals €3.50-5; open 9am-late)* is probably the best value restaurant within the Old Town. The pizza marinara was one of the best we tasted in Montenegro.

### Getting There & Away
The bus station is south of the Old Town. Frequent buses ply to Podgorica (€4.50, two hours), Herceg Novi (€2, one hour) and Budva (€1.50, 30 minutes). If you are driving, the shortest way to Herceg Novi is via the ferry at Lepetane (€3.50 per car, every half hour).

## AROUND KOTOR
**Perast** is a small waterside village about 30km from Kotor. The interest here is the small island in the fjord called **Lady of the Rock**. It's an artificial island created by the locals over 550 years by taking and dropping stones on the site every July 22. An underwater rock helped the work start and a later sinking of 87 captured ships loaded with rocks made island-creating a little easier.

Between mid-May and mid-October boats regularly ply between the island and Perast for €1 return; just ask on the waterfront. A hourly minibus service connects with Kotor for €1.

## HERCEG NOVI ХЕРЦЕГ НОВИ
☎ 088

Herceg Novi is another walled town, a day trip from Kotor or Budva, that's also the nearest town to the Croatian border.

**Private accommodation** *(per person €5-8)* and **hotels** *(singles/doubles including break-fast from €25/36)* can be arranged through **Gorbis** *(☎ 26 085; Njegoševa 64)*, which is also a ticketing agency. There are many small restaurants and bars around the old citadel. The bus station is on the main highway with a frequent bus service to Kotor (€1, one hour).

## CETINJE ЦЕТИНЊЕ
☎ 086

Cetinje, perched on a high plateau above Budva, is the old capital of Montenegro, and is subject of songs and epic poems. Much re-mains of old Cetinje, from museums to palaces, mansions and monasteries. At the start of the 20th century all the large states of Europe had embassies here. Short hikes can be made in the hills behind Cetinje Monastery.

From the bus station turn left and then right and you will find the main square, Balšica Pazar. There is a big wall map in the square to help you get oriented.

There are no banks here for changing money.

### Things to See & Do

The most imposing building in Cetinje is the former parliament, which is now the **National Museum of Montenegro** *(Novice Cerovic; admission €1.50; open 9am-5pm daily in season, 9am-2.30pm Mon-Fri off season)*. It houses exhibits showing Mon-tenegro from 60,000 BC to the modern day. On display are many old books, some copies of frescoes, 44 captured Turkish flags and the coat (three bullet holes in the back) of Duke Danlo, last prince-bishop, who was killed in Kotor in 1860.

Adjacent is the 1832 residence of the prince-bishop Petar II Petrovic Njegoš, also a museum and known as **Biljarda Hall** *(admission €1.50; open 9am-5pm in season, 9am-2pm off season)* for the billiard table installed in 1840. The Hall houses a fascinating relief

map of Montenegro created by the Austrians in 1917 for tactical planning purposes.

The **Royal Court** *(admission €2; open 9am-3pm Mon-Fri off season, 9am-5pm daily in season)* is the former residence (1871) of Nicola Petrović I, the last king of Montenegro. Although looted during WWII, sufficient furnishings, many stern portraits and period weapons remain to give a picture of the times.

Twenty kilometres away on the summit of **Mt Lovcen** (1749m), the 'Black Mountain' that gave Montenegro its Italian name, is the mausoleum of Petar II Petrovic Njegoš, a revered poet and ruler. Take a taxi and then climb 461 steps to the mausoleum with its sweeping view of the Bay of Kotor, moun-tains, coast and, on a clear morning, Italy.

**Cetinje Monastery** Founded in 1484, re-built 1785, Cetinje Monastery *(€0.50; open 8am-7pm daily May-Oct, groups only Nov-Apr)* contains a copy of the *Oktoih* or *Octoe-chos* (Book of the Eight Voices), printed near here in 1494 – it's one of the oldest collec-tions of liturgical songs in a Slavic language. For the curious, or devout, the monastery has a portion of the true cross and the mummified right hand of St John the Baptist. The latter, important as the hand that baptised Christ, is set in a bejewelled casket with a little glass window. It takes some imagination to conjure it as a hand.

The museum houses a collection of por-traits, vestments, ancient hand-written texts and gifts from Russian churches.

### Places to Stay & Eat

For a **private room** *(€5 per person)* ask at **Al-liance Tours** *(☎ 31 157; ℮ alliance@cg.yu; Njegoševa 32; open Mon-Sat)* next to the post office; Alliance also sells airline tickets and has tourist information. **Petar Marti-novic** *(☎ 31 809; Bajova Pivljanina 19; beds €7.50-10)* offers accommodation without meals. The rooms in this corner house are quite comfortable; the more expensive ones have bathrooms.

Otherwise, the only hotel is the **Grand Hotel** *(☎ 31 876, fax 31 213; Njegoševa; singles/doubles €25.57/40.92)*, a modern overrated 'five-star' hotel where rooms come with bathroom and breakfast. It has a swim-ming pool and there's a disco on Friday and Sunday nights.

YUGOSLAVIA

There is not a glut of eating options in Cetinje. **Restoran Korzo** *(Njegoševa; mains €3-5; open 8am-11pm daily)* next to the post office has a big mixed grill speciality that is popular locally. Next to the Royal Court, **Gradska Kafana** *(dishes €4-6; open 7am-11pm daily)*, has an expansive courtyard for al fresco dining.

## Getting There & Away
With a frequent bus services from Kotor (€2, 45 minutes) and Budva (€2, 35 minutes), Cetinje is an easy day trip.

## DURMITOR NATIONAL PARK
☎ 0872

Durmitor National Park is a popular hiking and mountaineering area just west of the ski resort **Žabljak**, the highest town in Yugoslavia (1450m).

Some 18 mountain lakes dot the Durmitor Range and you can walk around the largest, **Crno jezero** *(Black Lake)*, 3km from Žabljak, in an hour or two and take a swim in summer. The rounded mass of Meded (2287m) rises directly behind the lake surrounded by a backdrop of other peaks, including Savin kuk (2313m), which can be climbed in eight hours there and back. The 1.3km-deep **Tara Canyon** that cuts dramatically into the earth for about 80km is best seen from a rock promontory at Curevac, a €4 taxi ride away.

Durmitor enjoys two tourist seasons, June to September and December to March. Be prepared as the weather is very changeable, even in summer.

## Orientation & Information
Žabljak town centre is around the junction of the Nikšić road from the south and the Đurdevica Tara bridge road. Here there's a tourist information centre, taxi stand and bus stop. Adjacent is the Hotel Žabljak, Ski Centar Durmitor and a supermarket. The **bus station**, on the Nikšić road, is at the southern end of town.

The **Tourist Information Centre** *(☎ 61 659; town centre; open 8am-8pm daily in season, 8am-3pm off season)* has maps and some fine books but the attendant doesn't speak English. For more information go to Sveti Đordije (see its entry in the following Places to Stay & Eat section) where the owner speaks English, German and Italian.

The **Durmitor National Park office** *(☎ 61 474, fax 61 346; next to Hotel Durmitor;*

*open 7am-2pm Mon-Fri)* sells good maps of the park and has a small exhibition of local fauna and flora.

## Places to Stay & Eat
**Sveti Đordije** *(☎/fax 61 367; Njegoševa)*, just opposite the turn-off to Hotel Jezera, is a tourist agency that can arrange **private rooms** *(per person with shared bathroom from €6.50, 4-person apartment €34)*. Out of season there's a 20% discount; half-board costs an extra €7.50 per person.

The Tourist Information Centre in the town centre arranges accommodation in **private rooms** *(winter season €5-7.50, summer season €4-6)*. **Ski Centar Durmitor** *(☎ 61 144, fax 61 579; town centre)* is happy to book hotel accommodation for you.

The **Planinka** *(☎ 61 344; town centre; singles/doubles half-board €20/30)* and **Hotel Jezera** *(☎ 61 103, fax 61 579; Njegoševa; singles/doubles €25/40 B&B)* are modern ski hotels with good amenities, restaurants and bars.

**Hotel Žabljak** *(☎ 61 300; town centre; singles/doubles €18/26)* has reasonable rooms with bathrooms; rates include breakfast. Out of season it may be the only hotel open.

On a hill top five minutes' walk beyond the national park office is **Autocamp Ivando**, which is just a fenced-off field. People around here rent **private rooms** *(€6 per person)* but bring your own sleeping bag. Set right in the middle of the forest, Ivan-do is a perfect base for hikers.

**National Restaurant** *(☎ 61 337; dishes €5-8.50; open 8am-late daily)*, behind the city council offices; is a new restaurant-bar. Try its kačamak with sour milk (like yogurt) if you're hungry. We had it for lunch, didn't need an evening meal and even next day's breakfast was a struggle. On a cold winter's day a glass or two of *loza* (grappa) is very warming.

All the hotels have **restaurants** open to nonresidents.

## Activities
In winter there's skiing, snowboarding, motor-sledging or having fun with a dog-drawn team. In summer there's rafting trips down the steep forested Tara Gorge and over countless foaming rapids. These begin at Splavište near the Đurđevica Tara bridge. There's also horse riding, hiking, cycling, mountaineering and paragliding.

The **Sports Association** (☎ *069 477 681*) rents out motor sledges (from €20/35 per half/one hour). **Ski Centar Durmitor** arranges ski passes (€6.15/35.79 per day/week), ski lessons (€3.07/17.90 for one/seven lessons) and equipment rental (€3.07/17.90 per day/week).

**Rafting** is a group activity but individuals can join by prior arrangement. **Sveti Đordije** offers two-/three-day trips for €200/250 per person including transfers, accommodation and food. A one-day trip with food, transfers and accommodation costs €80. The minimum group size is eight. Ski Centar Durmitor organises trips for groups of 25.

Sveti Đordije also organises summer day tours around the Durmitor area. Typically these are for six to eight people (individuals

may join) and cost €30 per person. The day trip includes a visit to the **Piva Monastery**, near the Bosnian border, which has remarkable frescoes.

The **Durmitor National Park office** also offers rafting trips for €150 for a group of 10, although individuals can join. It has horses for hire for €25/50 for a half/whole day, including an English-speaking guide.

## Getting There & Away

There's a 4.30am and 4pm bus to Belgrade (€12.25, 10 hours) and also services to Podgorica (€6.10, 5½ hours), Nikšić (€5, 2½ hours) and Mojkovac (€3.50, 3½ hours). At Mojkovac you can connect with Bar-Belgrade trains. There is one daily direct bus from Belgrade to Žabljak (750 DIN, 10 hours).

YUGOSLAVIA

# Appendix – Telephones

## Dial Direct

You can dial directly from public telephone boxes from almost anywhere in Europe to almost anywhere in the world. This is usually cheaper than going through the operator. In much of Europe, public telephones accepting phonecards are becoming the norm and in some countries coin-operated phones are difficult to find.

To call abroad simply dial the international access code (IAC) for the country you are calling from (most commonly ☎ 00 in Europe but see the following table), the country code (CC) for the country you are calling, the local area code (usually dropping the leading zero if there is one) and then the number. If, for example, you are in Italy (international access code ☎ 00) and want to make a call to the USA (country code ☎ 1), San Francisco (area code ☎ 415), number ☎ 123 4567, then you dial ☎ 00-1-415-123 4567. To call from the UK (☎ 00) to Australia (☎ 61), Sydney (☎ 02), number ☎ 1234 5678, you dial the following: ☎ 00-61-2-1234 5678.

## Home Direct

If you would rather have somebody else pay for the call, you can, from many countries, dial directly to your home country operator and then reverse charges; you can also charge the call to a phone company credit card. To do this, simply dial the relevant 'home direct' or 'country direct' number to be connected to your own operator. For the USA there's a choice of AT&T, MCI or Sprint Global One home direct services. Home direct numbers vary from country to country – check with your telephone company before you leave, or with the international operator in the country you're ringing from. From phone boxes in some countries you may need a coin or local phonecard to be connected with the relevant home direct operator.

In some places (particularly airports), you may find dedicated home direct phones where you simply press the button labelled USA, Australia, Hong Kong or whatever for direct connection to the operator. Note that the home direct service does not operate to and from all countries, and that the call could be charged at operator rates, which makes it

expensive for the person paying. Placing a call on your phone credit card is more expensive than paying the local tariff.

## Dialling Tones

In some countries, after you have dialled the international access code, you have to wait for a second dial tone before dialling the code for your target country and the number. Often the same applies when you ring from one city to another within these countries: wait for a dialling tone after you've dialled the area code for your target city. If you're not sure what to do, simply wait three or four seconds after dialling a code – if nothing happens, you can probably keep dialling.

## Phonecards

In major locations phones may accept credit cards: simply swipe your card through the slot and the call is charged to the card, though rates can be very high. Phone-company credit cards can be used to charge calls via your home country operator.

Stored-value phonecards are now almost standard all over Europe. You usually buy a card from a post office, telephone centre, newsstand or retail outlet and simply insert the card into the phone each time you make a call. The card solves the problem of finding the correct coins for calls (or lots of correct coins for international calls) and generally gives you a small discount.

## Call Costs

The cost of international calls varies widely from one country to another: a US$1.20 call from Britain could cost you US$6 from Turkey. The countries shown in the 'Telephone Codes & Costs' table that follows are rated from * (cheap) to *** (expensive), but rates can vary depending on which country you are calling to (for example, from Italy it's relatively cheap to call North America, but more expensive to call Australia). Reduced rates are available at certain times, usually from mid-evening to early morning, though it varies from country to country – check the local phone book or ask the operator for more details. Calling from hotel rooms can be very expensive.

## Telephone Codes & Costs

| | CC | cost (see text) | IAC | IO |
|---|---|---|---|---|
| Albania | 355 | *** | 00 | 12 |
| Andorra | 376 | ** | 00 | 821111 |
| Austria | 43 | * | 00 | 09 |
| Belarus | 375 | *** | 8(w)10 | (017) 233 2971 |
| Belgium | 32 | ** | 00 | 1224 (private phone) |
| | | | | 1223 (public phone) |
| Bosnia-Hercegovina | 387 | ** | 00 | 900/901/902 |
| Bulgaria | 359 | ** | 00 | 0123 (calls) |
| | | | | 0124 (inquiries) |
| Croatia | 385 | ** | 00 | 901 |
| Cyprus | 357 | *** | 00 | |
| Cyprus (Turkish) | 90+392 | | 00 | |
| Czech Republic | 420 | * | 00 | 1181/0149 |
| Denmark | 45 | ** | 00 | 141 |
| Estonia | 372 | *** | 000 | 165 |
| Finland | 358 | ** | 00, 990, 994, 999 | 020222 |
| France | 33 | * | 00(w) | 12 |
| Germany | 49 | * | 00 | 11834 |
| Gibraltar | 350 | *** | 00 | 100 |
| Greece | 30 | * | 00 | 161 |
| Hungary | 36 | * | 00(w) | 199 |
| Iceland | 354 | *** | 00 | 5335010 |
| Ireland | 353 | * | 00 | 114 |
| Northern Ireland | 44+28 | * | 00 | 155 |
| Italy | 39 | ** | 00 | 15 |
| Latvia | 371 | *** | 00 | 115 |
| Liechtenstein | 423 | *** | 00 | 114 |
| Lithuania | 370 | *** | 00 | 194/195 |
| Luxembourg | 352 | ** | 00 | 0010 |
| Macedonia | 389 | *** | 99 | 901 |
| Malta | 356 | ** | 00 | 194 |
| Moldova | 373 | *** | 8(w)10 | 973 |
| Morocco | 212 | *** | 00(w) | 12 |
| Netherlands | 31 | ** | 00 | 0800-0410 |
| Norway | 47 | ** | 00 | 181 |
| Poland | 48 | ** | 00 | 901 |
| Portugal | 351 | * | 00 | 099 |
| Romania | 40 | *** | 00 | 971 |
| Russia | 7 | ** | 8(w)10 | |
| Slovakia | 421 | ** | 00 | 0149 |
| Slovenia | 386 | ** | 00 | 115 |
| Spain | 34 | ** | 00(w) | 025 |
| Sweden | 46 | ** | 00 | 0018 |
| Switzerland | 41 | ** | 00 | 114 |
| Tunisia | 216 | ** | 00 | |
| Turkey | 90 | *** | 00 | 115 |
| UK | 44 | * | 00 | 155 |
| Ukraine | 380 | ** | 810 | 079/073 |
| Yugoslavia | 381 | *** | 99 | 901 |

CC – Country Code (to call into that country)
IAC – International Access Code (to call abroad from that country)
IO – International Operator (to make inquiries)
(w) – wait for dialling tone

Other country codes include: Australia ☎ 61, Canada ☎ 1, Hong Kong ☎ 852, India ☎ 91, Indonesia ☎ 62, Israel ☎ 972, Japan ☎ 81, Macau ☎ 853, Malaysia ☎ 60, New Zealand ☎ 64, Singapore ☎ 65, South Africa ☎ 27, Thailand ☎ 66, USA ☎ 1

# Language

This language guide contains pronunciation tips and basic vocabulary to help you get around Mediterranean Europe. For background information about each language see the individual country chapters. For more extensive coverage of the languages included here, see Lonely Planet's *Europe* and *Eastern Europe* phrasebooks.

## Albanian

### Pronunciation
Written Albanian is phonetically consistent and pronunciation shouldn't pose too many problems for English speakers. The Albanian **rr** is trilled and each vowel in a diphthong is pronounced. Some Albanian letters are present in English but are pronounced differently.

| | |
|---|---|
| ë | often silent; at the beginning of a word it's as the 'a' in 'ago' |
| c | as the 'ts' in 'bits' |
| ç | as the 'ch' in 'church' |
| dh | as the 'th' in 'this' |
| gj | as the 'gy' in 'hogyard' |
| j | as the 'y' in 'yellow' |
| q | between 'ch' and 'ky', similar to the 'cu' in 'cure' |
| th | as in 'thistle' |
| x | as the 'dz' in 'adze' |
| xh | as the 'j' in 'jewel' |
| zh | as the 's' in 'pleasure' |

### Basics
| | |
|---|---|
| Hello. | *Tungjatjeta/Allo.* |
| Goodbye. | *Lamtumirë.* |
| | *Mirupafshim.* (informal) |
| Yes. | *Po.* |
| No. | *Jo.* |
| Please. | *Ju lutem.* |
| Thank you. | *Ju falem nderit.* |
| That's fine. | *Eshtë e mirë.* |
| You're welcome. | *S'ka përse.* |
| Excuse me. | *Me falni.* |
| Sorry. (excuse me, forgive me) | *Më vjen keq.* or *Më falni, ju lutem.* |
| Do you speak English? | *A flisni anglisht?* |
| How much is it? | *Sa kushton?* |
| What's your name? | *Si quheni ju lutem?* |
| My name is ... | *Unë quhem ...* or *Mua më quajnë ...* |

### Getting Around
| | |
|---|---|
| What time does the ... leave/arrive? | *Në ç'orë niset/ arrin ...?* |
| boat | *barka/lundra* |
| bus | *autobusi* |
| tram | *tramvaji* |
| train | *treni* |
| | |
| I'd like ... | *Dëshiroj ...* |
| a one-way ticket | *një biletë vajtje* |
| a return ticket | *një biletë kthimi* |
| | |
| 1st class | *klas i parë* |
| 2nd class | *klas i dytë* |
| timetable | *orar* |
| bus stop | *stacion autobusi* |
| | |
| Where is ...? | *Ku është ...?* |
| Go straight ahead. | *Shko drejt.* |
| Turn left. | *Kthehu majtas.* |
| Turn right. | *Kthehu djathtas.* |
| near | *afër* |
| far | *larg* |

### Around Town
| | |
|---|---|
| a bank | *një bankë* |
| a chemist/pharmacy | *një farmaci* |
| the ... embassy | *... ambasadën* |
| my hotel | *hotelin tim* |
| the market | *pazarin* |
| newsagency | *agjensia e lajmeve* |
| the post office | *postën* |
| the stationers | *kartoleri* |
| the telephone centre | *centralin telefonik* |
| the tourist office | *zyrën e informimeve turistike* |
| | |
| What time does it open/close? | *Në ç'ore hapet/ mbyllet?* |

| Signs – Albanian | |
|---|---|
| *Hyrje* | **Entrance** |
| *Dalje* | **Exit** |
| *Informim* | **Information** |
| *Hapur* | **Open** |
| *Mbyllur* | **Closed** |
| *Policia* | **Police** |
| *Stacioni i Policisë* | **Police Station** |
| *E Ndaluar* | **Prohibited** |
| *Nevojtorja* | **Toilets** |
| *Burra* | **Men** |
| *Gra* | **Women** |

## Catalan

### Pronunciation
Catalan sounds are not hard for an English-speaker to pronounce. You should, however, note that vowels will vary according to whether they occur in stressed or unstressed syllables.

### Vowels
| | |
|---|---|
| a | when stressed, as the 'a' in 'father'; when unstressed, as in 'about' |
| e | when stressed, as in 'pet'; when unstressed, as in 'open' |
| i | as in 'machine' |
| o | when stressed, as in 'pot'; when unstressed, as the 'oo' in 'zoo' |
| u | as in 'humid' |

### Consonants
| | |
|---|---|
| b | pronounced 'p' at the end of a word |
| c | hard before a, o and u and at the end of a word; soft before e and i |
| ç | like 'ss' |
| d | pronounced 't' at the end of a word |
| g | hard before a, o and u; as the 's' in 'measure' before e and i |
| h | silent |
| j | as the 's' in 'pleasure' |
| r | as in English in the middle of a word; silent at the end of a word |
| rr | rolled with the tongue 'r', at the beginning of a word, or a doubled 'rr' in the middle of a word |
| s | as in 'so' at the beginning of a word; as 'z' in the middle of a word |
| v | as a 'b' in Barcelona; pronounced 'v' in some other areas |
| x | mostly as in English; sometimes 'sh' |

Other letters are approximately as in English. There are a few odd combinations:

| | |
|---|---|
| l.l | as 'll' in 'tell' |
| tx | as the 'ch' in 'cheese' |
| qu | as the 'k' in 'kite' |

### Greetings & Civilities
| | |
|---|---|
| Hello. | Hola. |
| Goodbye. | Adéu. |
| Yes. | Sí. |
| No. | No. |
| Please. | Sisplau/Si us plau. |
| Thank you (very much). | (Moltes) Gràcies. |
| You're welcome. | De res. |
| Excuse me. | Perdoni. |

| | |
|---|---|
| Help! | Ndihmë! |
| Call a doctor! | Thirrni doktorin! |
| Call the police! | Thirrni policinë! |
| Go away! | Zhduku!/Largohuni! |
| I'm lost. | Kam humbur rrugë. |

## Accommodation
| | |
|---|---|
| hotel | hotel |
| camping ground | kamp pushimi |
| Do you have any rooms available? | A keni ndonjë dhomë të lirë? |
| a single room | një dhomë më një krevat |
| a double room | një dhomë më dy krevat |
| one night | një natë |
| two nights | dy natë |
| How much is it per night/per person? | Sa kushton për një natë/për një njeri! |
| Does it include breakfast? | A e përfshin edhe mëngjesin? |

## Time, Days & Numbers
| | |
|---|---|
| What time is it? | Sa është ora? |
| today | sot |
| tomorrow | nesër |
| yesterday | dje |
| in the morning | në mëngjes |
| in the afternoon | pas dreke |
| Monday | e hënë |
| Tuesday | e martë |
| Wednesday | e mërkurë |
| Thursday | e enjte |
| Friday | e premte |
| Saturday | e shtunë |
| Sunday | e diel |

| | |
|---|---|
| 1 | një |
| 2 | dy |
| 3 | tre |
| 4 | katër |
| 5 | pesë |
| 6 | gjashtë |
| 7 | shtatë |
| 8 | tetë |
| 9 | nëntë |
| 10 | dhjetë |
| 100 | njëqind |
| 1000 | njëmijë |
| one million | një milion |

**LANGUAGE**

| | |
|---|---|
| Sorry. (forgive me) | *Ho sento/Perdoni.* |
| Do you speak English? | *Parla anglès?* |
| How much is it? | *Quant val?* |
| What's your name? | *Com es diu?* (polite) |
| | *Com et dius?* (informal) |
| My name is ... | *Em dic ...* |

## Getting Around

| | |
|---|---|
| What time does the ... leave? | *A quina hora surt ... ?* |
| bus | *l'autobús* |
| flight | *le vol* |
| train | *le tren* |
| | |
| I'd like a ... ticket. | *Voldria un bitllet ...* |
| one-way | *d'anada* |
| return | *d'anar i tornar* |
| | |
| bus station | *l'estació d'autobusos* |
| train station | *l'estació de tren* |
| baggage claim | *recollida d'equipatges* |
| | |
| Where is ...? | *On és ...?* |
| Turn left. | *Giri a mà esquerra.* |
| Turn right. | *Giri a mà dreta.* |
| near | *a prop* |
| far | *lluny de* |

## Around Town

| | |
|---|---|
| I'm looking for ... | *Estic buscant ...* |
| a bank | *un banc* |
| the market | *el mercat* |
| newsagency | *el quiosc* |
| pharmacy | *la farmàcia* |
| the police | *la policia* |
| the post office | *el correus* |
| a public toilet | *els lavabos públics* |
| the telephone centre | *la central telefònica* |
| the tourist office | *l'oficina de turisme* |
| | |
| What time does it open/close? | *A quina hora obren/tanquen?* |

## Accommodation

| | |
|---|---|
| hotel | *hotel* |
| guesthouse | *pensió* |
| youth hostel | *alberg juvenil* |
| camping ground | *càmping* |
| | |
| Do you have any rooms available? | *Hi ha habitacions lliures?* |
| | |
| a single room | *una habitació individual* |
| a double room | *una habitació doble* |
| for one night | *un nit* |
| for two nights | *dos nits* |

### Signs – Catalan

| | |
|---|---|
| **Entrada** | **Entrance** |
| **Sortida** | **Exit** |
| **Obert** | **Open** |
| **Tancat** | **Closed** |
| **Informació** | **Information** |
| **Prohibit** | **Prohibited** |
| **Comissaria** | **Police Station** |
| **Lavabos** | **Toilets** |

| | |
|---|---|
| How much is it per night/person? | *Quant val per nit/persona?* |
| Is breakfast included? | *Inclou l'esmorzar?* |

## Time, Days & Numbers

| | |
|---|---|
| What time is it? | *Quina hora és?* |
| today | *avui* |
| tomorrow | *demà* |
| yesterday | *ahir* |
| in the morning | *del matí* |
| in the afternoon | *de tarda* |
| | |
| Monday | *dilluns* |
| Tuesday | *dimarts* |
| Wednesday | *dimecres* |
| Thursday | *dijous* |
| Friday | *divendres* |
| Saturday | *dissabte* |
| Sunday | *diumenge* |

| | |
|---|---|
| 0 | *zero* |
| 1 | *un/una* |
| 2 | *dos/dues* |
| 3 | *tres* |
| 4 | *quatre* |
| 5 | *cinc* |
| 6 | *sis* |
| 7 | *set* |
| 8 | *vuit* |
| 9 | *nou* |
| 10 | *deu* |
| 100 | *cent* |
| 1000 | *mil* |
| | |
| one million | *un milió* |

# Croatian & Serbian

## Pronunciation

The writing systems of Croatian and Serbian are phonetically consistent: every letter is pronounced and its sound will not vary from word to word. With regard to the position of

## Serbian & Croatian Alphabets

| Cyrillic | Roman | English Pronunciation |
|---|---|---|
| А а | A a | as in 'rather' |
| Б б | B b | as in 'be' |
| В в | V v | as in 'vodka' |
| Г г | G g | as in 'go' |
| Д д | D d | as in 'do' |
| Ђ ђ | Đ đ | as the 'du' in British 'duty' |
| Е е | E e | as in 'there' |
| Ж ж | Ž ž | as the 's' in 'pleasure' |
| З з | Z z | as in 'zero' |
| И и | I i | as in 'machine' |
| Ј ј | J j | as the 'y' in 'young' |
| К к | K k | as in 'keg' |
| Л л | L l | as in 'let' |
| Љ љ | Lj lj | as the 'lli' in 'million' |
| М м | M m | as in 'map' |
| Н н | N n | as in 'no' |
| Њ њ | Nj nj | as the 'ny' in 'canyon' |
| О о | O o | as the 'aw' in 'shawl' |
| П п | P p | as in 'pop' |
| Р р | R r | as in 'rock' |
| С с | S s | as in 'safe' |
| Т т | T t | as in 'to' |
| Ћ ћ | Ć ć | as the 'tu' in 'future' |
| У у | U u | as in 'plume' |
| Ф ф | F f | as in 'fat' |
| Х х | h | as in 'hot' |
| Ц ц | C c | as the 'ts' in 'cats' |
| Ч ч | Č č | as the 'ch' in 'chop' |
| Џ џ | Dž dž | as the 'j' in 'judge' |
| Ш ш | Š š | as the 'sh' in 'shoe' |

stress, only one rule can be given: the last syllable of a word is never stressed. In most cases the accent falls on the first vowel in the word.

Serbian uses the Cyrillic alphabet, so it's worth familiarising yourself with it. Croatian uses a Roman alphabet and many letters are pronounced as in English.

The principal difference between Serbian and Croatian is in the pronunciation of the vowel 'e' in certain words. A long 'e' in Serbian becomes 'ije' in Croatian (eg, *reka, rijeka,* 'river'), and a short 'e' in Serbian becomes 'je' in Croatian (eg, *pesma, pjesma,* 'song'). Sometimes, however, the vowel 'e' is the same in both languages, as in *selo,* 'village'. There are also a number of variations in vocabulary between the two languages. In the following phraselist these are indicated with 'C' for Croatian and 'S' for Serbian.

## Basics

Hello.
   *Zdravo.*     Здраво.
Goodbye.
   *Doviđenja.*     Довиђења.
Yes.
   *Da.*     Да.
No.
   *Ne.*     Не.
Please.
   *Molim.*     Молим.
Thank you.
   *Hvala.*     Хвала.
That's fine/
You're welcome.
   *U redu je/*     У реду је/
   *Nema na čemu.*     Нема на чему.
Excuse me.
   *Oprostite.*     Опростите.
Sorry. (excuse me, forgive me)
   *Pardon.*     Пардон.
Do you speak English?
   *Govorite li*     Говорите ли
   *engleski?*     енглески?
How much is it ...?
   *Koliko košta ...?*     Колико кошта ...?
What's your name?
   *Kako se zovete?*     Како се зовете?
My name is ...
   *Zovem se ...*     Зовем се ...

## Getting Around

What time does the ... leave/arrive?
   *Kada ...*     Када ...
   *polazi/dolazi?*     полази/долази?
boat
   *brod*     брод
bus (city)
   *autobus*     аутобус
   *(gradski)*     (градски)
bus (intercity)
   *autobus*     аутобус
   *(međugradski)*     (међуградски)
train
   *voz* (S)/*vlak* (C)     воз
tram
   *tramvaj*     трамвај

one-way ticket
   *kartu u jednom*     карту у једном
   *pravcu*     правцу
return ticket
   *povratnu kartu*     повратну карту

1st class
*prvu klasu*     прву класу
2nd class
*drugu klasu*     другу класу

Where is the bus/tram stop?
*Gde je autobuska/tramvajska stanica?* (S)
*Gdje je autobuska/tramvajska postaja?* (C)
Где је аутобуска/трамвајска станица?
Can you show me (on the map)?
*Možete li mi pokazati (na karti)?*
Можете ли ми показати (на карти)?
Go straight ahead.
*Idite pravo napred* (S)/*naprijed.* (C)
Идите право напред.
Turn left.
*Skrenite lijevo* (C)/*levo.* (S)
Скрените лево.
Turn right.
*Skrenite desno.*
Скрените десно.
near
*blizu*
близу
far
*daleko*
далеку

## Around Town
I'm looking for ...
*Tražim ...*     Тражим ...
a bank
*banku*     банку
the ... embassy
*... ambasadu*     ... амбасаду
my hotel
*moj hotel*     мој хотел
the market
*pijacu*     пијацу
the post office
*poštu*     пошту
the telephone centre
*telefonsku*     телефонску централу
*centralu*
the tourist office
*turistički biro*     туристички биро

## Accommodation
hotel
*hotel*     хотел
guesthouse
*privatno*     приватно
*prenoćište*     преноћиште
youth hostel
*omladinsko*     омладинско
*prenoćište*     преноћиште
camping ground
*kamping*     кампинг

Do you have any rooms available?
*Imate li slobodne sobe?*
Имате ли слободне собе?
How much is it per night/per person?
*Koliko košta za jednu noć/po osobi?*
Колико кошта за једну ноћ/по особи?
Does it include breakfast?
*Dali je u cenu* (S)/*cijenu* (C) *uključen i doručak?*
Дали је у цену укључен и доручак?

I'd like ...
*Želim ...*
Желим ...
a single room
*sobu sa jednim krevetom*
собу са једним креветом
a double room
*sobu sa duplim krevetom*
собу са дуплим креветом

## Time, Days & Numbers
What time is it?
*Koliko je sati?*     Колико је сати?
today
*danas*     данас

| 8 | *osam* | осам |
| 9 | *devet* | девет |
| 10 | *deset* | десет |
| 100 | *sto* | сто |
| 1000 | *hiljada* (S) | иљада |
| | *tisuću* (C) | |

one million
*jedan milion* (S)   један милион
*jedan milijun* (C)

## Emergencies

Help!
*Upomoć!*
Упомоћ!
Call a doctor!
*Pozovite lekara!* (S)
*Pozovite liječnika!* (C)
Позовите лекара!
Call the police!
*Pozovite miliciju!* (S)
*Pozovite policiju!* (C)
Позовите милицију!
Go away!
*Idite!*
Идите!
I'm lost.
*Izgubio/Izgubila sam se.* (m/f) (S)
*Izgubljen/Izgubljena sam.* (m/f) (C)
Изгубио сам се/Изгубила сам се. (m/f)

tomorrow
*sutra*   сутра
yesterday
*juče* (S)   јуче
*jučer* (C)
in the morning
*ujutro*   ујутро
in the afternoon
*popodne*   поподне

Monday
*ponedeljak*   понедељак
Tuesday
*utorak*   уторак
Wednesday
*sreda* (S)   среда
*srijeda* (C)
Thursday
*četvrtak*   четвртак
Friday
*petak*   петак
Saturday
*subota*   субота
Sunday
*nedelja* (S)   недеља
*nedjelja* (C)

| 1 | *jedan* | један |
| 2 | *dva* | два |
| 3 | *tri* | три |
| 4 | *četiri* | четири |
| 5 | *pet* | пет |
| 6 | *šest* | шест |
| 7 | *sedam* | седам |

# French

## Pronunciation

French has a number of sounds which are difficult for Anglophones to produce. These include:

- The distinction between the 'u' sound (as in *tu*) and 'oo' sound (as in *tout*). For both sounds, the lips are rounded and projected forward, but for the 'u' the tongue is towards the front of the mouth, its tip against the lower front teeth, whereas for the 'oo' the tongue is towards the back of the mouth, its tip behind the gums of the lower front teeth.

- The nasal vowels. During the production of nasal vowels the breath escapes partly through the nose and partly through the mouth. There are no nasal vowels in English; in French there are three, as in *bon vin blanc* (good white wine). These sounds occur where a syllable ends in a single 'n' or 'm'; the 'n' or 'm' is silent but indicates the nasalisation of the preceding vowel.

- The 'r' sound. The standard 'r' of Parisian French is produced by moving the bulk of the tongue backwards to constrict the air flow in the pharynx while the tip of the tongue rests behind the lower front teeth. It's similar to the noise made by some people before spitting, but with much less friction.

## Basics

| Hello. | *Bonjour.* |
| Goodbye. | *Au revoir.* |
| Yes. | *Oui.* |
| No. | *Non.* |
| Please. | *S'il vous plaît.* |
| Thank you. | *Merci.* |
| That's fine, you're welcome. | *Je vous en prie.* |
| Excuse me. (attention) | *Excusez-moi.* |

| Sorry. (apology) | *Pardon.* |
| Do you speak English? | *Parlez-vous anglais?* |
| How much is it? | *C'est combien?* |
| What's your name? | *Comment vous appelez-vous?* |
| My name is ... | *Je m'appelle ...* |

## Getting Around

| When does the next ... leave/arrive? | *À quelle heure part/ arrive le prochain ...?* |
| boat | *bateau* |
| bus (city) | *bus* |
| bus (intercity) | *car* |
| tram | *tramway* |
| train | *train* |

| left luggage (office) | *consigne* |
| timetable | *horaire* |
| bus stop | *arrêt d'autobus* |
| tram stop | *arrêt de tramway* |
| train station | *gare* |
| ferry terminal | *gare maritime* |

| I'd like a ... ticket. | *Je voudrais un billet ...* |
| one-way | *aller simple* |
| return | *aller retour* |
| 1st-class | *de première classe* |
| 2nd-class | *de deuxième classe* |

| I'd like to hire a car/bicycle. | *Je voudrais louer une voiture/un vélo.* |

| Where is ...? | *Où est ...?* |
| Go straight ahead. | *Continuez tout droit.* |
| Turn left. | *Tournez à gauche.* |
| Turn right. | *Tournez à droite.* |
| near | *proche* |
| far | *loin* |

## Signs – French

| *Entrée* | **Entrance** |
| *Sortie* | **Exit** |
| *Renseignements* | **Information** |
| *Ouvert* | **Open** |
| *Fermée* | **Closed** |
| *Chambres Libres* | **Rooms Available** |
| *Complet* | **Full/No Vacancies** |
| *(Commissariat de) Police* | **Police Station** |
| *Interdit* | **Prohibited** |
| *Toilettes, WC* | **Toilets** |
| *Hommes* | **Men** |
| *Femmes* | **Women** |

## Emergencies – French

| Help! | *Au secours!* |
| Call a doctor! | *Appelez un médecin!* |
| Call the police! | *Appelez la police!* |
| Leave me alone! | *Fichez-moi la paix!* |
| I'm lost. | *Je me suis égaré/e.* |

## Around Town

| I'm looking for ... | *Je cherche ...* |
| a bank | *une banque* |
| a chemist/ pharmacy | *une pharmacie* |
| the ... embassy | *l'ambassade de ...* |
| my hotel | *mon hôtel* |
| the market | *le marché* |
| a newsagency | *un agence de presse* |
| the post office | *le bureau de poste* |
| a public telephone | *une cabine téléphonique* |
| a stationers | *une papeterie* |
| the tourist office | *l'office de tourisme/ le syndicat d'initiative* |

| What time does it open/close? | *Quelle est l'heure de ouverture/fermeture?* |

## Accommodation

| the hotel | *l'hôtel* |
| the guest house | *le pension (de famille)* |
| the youth hostel | *l'auberge de jeunesse* |

| Do you have any rooms available? | *Est-ce que vous avez des chambres libres?* |

| for one person | *pour une personne* |
| for two people | *pour deux personnes* |

| How much is it per night/per person? | *Quel est le prix par nuit/par personne?* |
| Is breakfast included? | *Est-ce que le petit déjeuner est compris?* |

## Time, Days & Numbers

| What time is it? | *Quelle heure est-il?* |
| today | *aujourd'hui* |
| tomorrow | *demain* |
| yesterday | *hier* |
| in the morning | *du matin* |
| in the afternoon | *de l'après-midi* |

| Monday | *lundi* |
| Tuesday | *mardi* |
| Wednesday | *mercredi* |
| Thursday | *jeudi* |
| Friday | *vendredi* |

| Saturday | *samedi* |
| Sunday | *dimanche* |

| 1 | *un* |
| 2 | *deux* |
| 3 | *trois* |
| 4 | *quatre* |
| 5 | *cinq* |
| 6 | *six* |
| 7 | *sept* |
| 8 | *huit* |
| 9 | *neuf* |
| 10 | *dix* |
| 100 | *cent* |
| 1000 | *mille* |

| one million | *un million* |

# Greek

## Pronunciation

Pronunciation of Greek letters is shown in the alphabet table below, using the closest-sounding English letter.

### Greek Alphabet

| Greek | English | Pronunciation |
| --- | --- | --- |
| A α | a | as in 'father' |
| B β | v | as in 'vine' |
| Γ γ | gh, y | like a rough 'g', or as the 'y' in 'yes' |
| Δ δ | dh | as the 'th' in 'then' |
| E ε | e | as in 'egg' |
| Z ζ | z | as in 'zoo' |
| H η | i | as in 'marine' |
| Θ θ | th | as in 'throw' |
| I ι | i | as in 'marine' |
| K κ | k | as in 'kite' |
| Λ λ | l | as in 'leg' |
| M μ | m | as in 'man' |
| N ν | n | as in 'net' |
| Ξ ξ | x | as the 'ks' in 'looks' |
| O o | o | as in 'hot' |
| Π π | p | as in 'pup' |
| P ρ | r | a slightly trilled 'r' |
| Σ σ | s | as in 'sand' ('ς' at the end of a word) |
| T τ | t | as in 'to' |
| Y υ | i | as in 'marine' |
| Φ φ | f | as in 'fit' |
| X χ | kh, h | as the 'ch' in Scottish *loch*, or as a rough 'h' |
| Ψ ψ | ps | as the 'ps' in 'lapse' |
| Ω ω | o | as in 'lot' |

## Letter Combinations

Some pairs of vowels are pronounced separately if the first has an acute accent (eg, ά), or the second has a dieresis (eg, ϊ). All Greek words of two or more syllables have an acute accent which indicates where the stress falls.

| εı, οı | i | as in 'marine' |
| αı | e | as in 'bet' |
| ου | u | as in 'plume' |
| μπ | b | as in 'be' |
| | mb | as in 'amber' (or as the 'mp' in 'ample') |
| ντ | d | as in 'do' |
| | nd | as in 'bend' (or as the 'nt' in 'sent') |
| γκ | g | as in 'go' |
| γγ | ng | as the 'ng' in 'angle' |
| γξ | ks | as in 'yaks' |
| τζ | dz | as the 'ds' in 'suds' |

The suffix of some Greek words depends on the gender of the speaker, eg, *asthmatikos* (m) and *asthmatikya* (f), or *epileptikos* (m) and *epileptikya* (f).

## Basics

| Hello. | *yasu* (informal) |
| | *yasas* (polite/plural) |
| Goodbye. | *andio* |
| Yes. | *ne* |
| No. | *okhi* |
| Please. | *sas parakalo* |
| Thank you. | *sas efharisto* |
| That's fine/ You're welcome. | *ine endaksi/parakalo* |
| Excuse me. (forgive me) | *signomi* |
| Do you speak English? | *milate anglika?* |
| How much is it? | *poso kani?* |
| What's your name? | *pos sas lene/ pos legeste?* |
| My name is ... | *me lene ...* |

## Getting Around

| What time does the ... leave/arrive? | *ti ora fevyi/ftani ...?* |
| boat | *to plio* |
| bus (city) | *to leoforio (ya tin poli)* |
| bus (intercity) | *to leoforio (ya ta proastia)* |
| tram | *to tram* |
| train | *to treno* |

| I'd like a ... ticket. | *tha ithela isitirio ...* |
| one-way | *horis epistrofi* |
| return | *me epistrofi* |
| 1st-class | *proti thesi* |
| 2nd-class | *dhefteri thesi* |

| left luggage | *horos aposkevon* |
| timetable | *dhromologhio* |
| bus stop | *i stasi tu leoforiu* |
| Go straight ahead. | *pighenete efthia* |
| Turn left. | *stripste aristera* |
| Turn right. | *stripste dheksya* |
| near | *konda* |
| far | *makria* |

## Around Town

| Where is a /the ...? | *pu ine ...?* |
| bank | *mia trapeza* |
| ... embassy | *i ... presvia* |
| hotel | *to ksenodhokhio* |
| market | *i aghora* |
| newsagency | *to efimeridhon* |
| pharmacy | *to farmakio* |
| post office | *to takhidhromio* |
| telephone centre | *to tilefoniko kentro* |
| tourist office | *to ghrafio turistikon pliroforion* |

| What time does it open/close? | *ti ora aniyi/klini?* |

## Accommodation

| a hotel | *ena xenothohio* |
| a youth hostel | *enas xenonas neoitos* |
| a camp site | *ena kamping* |

| I'd like a ... room. | *thelo ena dhomatio ...* |
| single | *ya ena atomo* |
| double | *ya dhio atoma* |

| How much is it ...? | *poso kostizi ...?* |
| per person | *ya ena atomo* |
| per night | *ya ena vradhi* |

| for one night | *ya mia nichta* |
| for two nights | *ya dhio nichtes* |

| Is breakfast included? | *simberilamvanete to proiono?* |

## Time, Days & Numbers

| What time is it? | *ti ora ine?* |
| today | *simera* |
| tomorrow | *avrio* |
| yesterday | *hthes* |
| in the morning | *to proi* |
| in the afternoon | *to apoyevma* |

| Monday | *dheftera* |
| Tuesday | *triti* |
| Wednesday | *tetarti* |
| Thursday | *pempti* |
| Friday | *paraskevi* |
| Saturday | *savato* |
| Sunday | *kiryaki* |

| 1 | *ena* |
| 2 | *dhio* |
| 3 | *tria* |
| 4 | *tesera* |
| 5 | *pende* |
| 6 | *eksi* |
| 7 | *epta* |
| 8 | *okhto* |
| 9 | *enea* |
| 10 | *dheka* |
| 100 | *ekato* |
| 1000 | *khilya* |

| one million | *ena ekatomirio* |

# Italian

## Pronunciation

Italian pronunciation isn't difficult once you learn a few basic rules. Although some of the more clipped vowels and stress on double letters require careful practice for English speakers, it's easy enough to make yourself understood.

## Vowels

| | |
|---|---|
| a | as in 'luther' |
| e | as the 'ay' in 'day', but without the 'y' sound |
| i | as in 'police' |
| o | as in 'dot' |
| u | as the 'oo' in 'tool' |

## Consonants

| | |
|---|---|
| c | as 'k' before a, o and u; as the 'ch' in 'choose' before e and i |
| ch | a hard 'k' sound |
| g | as in 'get' before a, o and u; as the 'j' in 'jet' before e and i |
| gh | as in 'get' |
| gli | as the 'lli' in 'million' |
| gn | as the 'ny' in 'canyon' |
| h | always silent |
| r | a rolled 'rrr' sound |
| sc | as the 'sh' in 'sheep' before e and i; as 'sk' before h, a, o and u |
| z | as the 'ts' in 'lights' or as the 'ds' in 'beds' |

Note that the i in ci, gi and sci isn't pronounced when followed by a, o or u, unless it's accented. Thus the name 'Giovanni' is pronounced 'joh-vahn-nee' – the 'i' sound after the 'G' is not pronounced.

## Stress

Double consonants are pronounced as a longer, more forceful sound than a single consonant.

Stress often falls on the next to last syllable, as in 'spaghetti'. When a word has an accent, the stress is on that syllable, as in città (city).

## Basics

| | |
|---|---|
| Hello. | Buongiorno. (polite) |
| | Ciao. (informal) |
| Goodbye. | Arrivederci. (polite) |
| | Ciao. (informal) |
| Yes. | Sì. |
| No. | No. |
| Please. | Per favore/Per piacere. |
| Thank you. | Grazie. |
| That's fine/ You're welcome. | Prego. |
| Excuse me. | Mi scusi. |
| Sorry. (excuse me/ forgive me) | Mi scusi/Mi perdoni. |
| Do you speak English? | Parla inglese? |
| How much is it? | Quanto costa? |
| What's your name? | Come si chiama? |
| My name is ... | Mi chiamo ... |

## Getting Around

| | |
|---|---|
| When does the ... leave/arrive? | A che ora parte/ arriva ...? |
| boat | la barca |
| bus | l'autobus |
| ferry | il traghetto |
| tram | il tram |
| train | il treno |
| bus stop | fermata d'autobus |
| train station | stazione |
| ferry terminal | stazione marittima |
| 1st class | prima classe |
| 2nd class | seconda classe |
| left luggage | deposito bagagli |
| timetable | orario |
| I'd like a one-way/ return ticket. | Vorrei un biglietto di solo andata/di andata e ritorno. |
| I'd like to hire a car/bicycle. | Vorrei noleggiare una macchina/bicicletta. |
| Where is ...? | Dov'è ...? |
| Go straight ahead. | Si va sempre diritto. |
| Turn left. | Giri a sinistra. |
| Turn right. | Giri a destra. |
| near | vicino |
| far | lontano |

## Around Town

| | |
|---|---|
| a bank | una banca |
| a chemist/pharmacy | una farmacia |
| the ... embassy | l'ambasciata di .. |
| my hotel | il mio albergo |
| the market | il mercato |
| a newsagency | un'edicola |
| post office | la posta |
| a stationers | un cartolaio |
| the telephone centre | il centro telefonico |
| the tourist office | l'ufficio di turismo |

## Signs – Italian

| | |
|---|---|
| Ingresso/Entrata | Entrance |
| Uscita | Exit |
| Informazione | Information |
| Aperto | Open |
| Chiuso | Closed |
| Camere Libere | Rooms Available |
| Completo | Full/No Vacancies |
| Polizia/Carabinieri | Police |
| Questura | Police Station |
| Proibito/Vietato | Prohibited |
| Gabinetti/Bagni | Toilets |
| Uomini | Men |
| Donne | Women |

| What time does it open/close? | A che ora (si) apre/chiude? |

## Accommodation

| hotel | albergo |
| guesthouse | pensione |
| youth hostel | ostello per la gioventù |
| camping ground | campeggio |

| Do you have any rooms available? | Ha delle camere libere/ C'è una camera libera? |
| How much is it per night/person? | Quanto costa per notte/ persona? |
| Is breakfast included? | È compresa la colazione? |

| a single room | una camera singola |
| a twin room | una camera doppia |
| a double room | una camera matrimoniale |
| for one night | per una notte |
| for two nights | per due notti |

## Time, Days & Numbers

| What time is it? | Che ora è? |
| | Che ore sono? |
| today | oggi |
| tomorrow | domani |
| yesterday | ieri |
| morning | mattina |
| afternoon | pomeriggio |

| Monday | lunedì |
| Tuesday | martedì |
| Wednesday | mercoledì |
| Thursday | giovedì |
| Friday | venerdì |
| Saturday | sabato |
| Sunday | domenica |

| 1 | uno |
| 2 | due |
| 3 | tre |
| 4 | quattro |
| 5 | cinque |
| 6 | sei |
| 7 | sette |
| 8 | otto |
| 9 | nove |
| 10 | dieci |
| 100 | cento |
| 1000 | mille |
| e million | un milione |

### Emergencies – Italian

| Help! | Aiuto! |
| Call a doctor! | Chiama un dottore/ un medico! |
| Call the police! | Chiama la polizia! |
| Go away! | Vai via! |
| I'm lost. | Mi sono perso. (m) |
| | Mi sono persa. (f) |

# Maltese

You'll have no problems getting around Malta using English, but knowing a few words in Maltese will always be welcome.

## Pronunciation

| ċ | as the 'ch' in child |
| g | as in good |
| ġ | 'soft' as the 'j' in job |
| għ | silent; lengthens the preceding or following vowel |
| h | silent, as in 'hour' |
| ħ | as the 'h' in 'hand' |
| j | as the 'y' in 'yellow' |
| ij | as the 'igh' in 'high' |
| ej | as the 'ay' in 'day' |
| q | a glottal stop; like the missing 't' in the Cockney pronunciation of 'bottle' |
| x | as the 'sh' in shop |
| z | as the 'ts' in 'bits' |
| ż | soft as in 'buzz' |

## Basics

| Hello. | Merħba. |
| Good morning/ Good day. | Bonġu. |
| Goodbye. | Saħħa. |
| Yes. | Iva. |
| No. | Le. |
| Please. | Jekk jogħġbok. |
| Thank you. | Grazzi. |
| Excuse me. | Skużani. |
| Do you speak English? | Titkellem bl-ingliż? |
| How much is it? | Kemm? |
| What's your name? | X'ismek? |
| My name is ... | Jisimni ... |

## Getting Around

| When does the boat leave/arrive? | Meta jitlaq/jasal il-vapur? |
| When does the bus leave/arrive? | Meta titlaq/jasal il-karozza? |

| | |
|---|---|
| I'd like a ... ticket. | *Nixtieq biljett ...* |
| one-way | *'one-way'* |
| return | *'return'* |
| 1st-class | *'1st-class'* |
| 2nd-class | *'2nd-class'* |
| | |
| left luggage | *hallejt il-bagalji* |
| bus/trolleybus stop | *xarabank/coach* |
| | |
| I'd like to hire a car/bicycle. | *Nixtieq nikri karozza/rota.* |
| Where is ...? | *Fejn hu ...?* |
| Go straight ahead. | *Mur dritt.* |
| Turn left. | *Dur fuq il-lemin.* |
| Turn right. | *Dur fuq il-ix-xellug.* |
| near | *il-vicin* |
| far | *il-boghod* |

## Around Town

| | |
|---|---|
| the bank | *il-bank* |
| chemist/pharmacy | *l-ispiżerija* |
| the ... embassy | *l'ambaxxata ...* |
| the hotel | *hotel/il-lakanda* |
| the market | *is-suq* |
| the post office | *il-posta* |
| a public telephone | *telefon pubbliku* |
| shop | *hanut* |
| stamp | *timbru* |
| | |
| What time does it open/close? | *Fix'hin jiftah/jaghlaq?* |

## Accommodation

| | |
|---|---|
| Do you have a room available? | *Ghandek kamra jekk joghogbok?* |
| | |
| Do you have a room for ...? | *Ghandek kamra ghal ...?* |
| one person | *wiehed* |
| two people | *tnejn* |
| one night | *lejl iljieli* |
| two nights | *zewgt iljieli* |
| | |
| Is breakfast included? | *Il-breakfast inkluż?* |

| Signs – Maltese | |
|---|---|
| *Dhul* | **Entrance** |
| *Hrug* | **Exit** |
| *Informazzjoni* | **Information** |
| *Miftuh* | **Open** |
| *Maghluq* | **Closed** |
| *Tidholx* | **No Entry** |
| *Pulizija* | **Police** |
| *Toilets* | **Toilets** |
| *Rgiel* | **Men** |
| *Nisa* | **Women** |

| Emergencries – Maltese | |
|---|---|
| Help! | *Ajjut!* |
| Call a doctor. | *Qibghad ghat-tabib.* |
| Police! | *Pulizija!* |
| I'm lost. | *Ninsab mitluf.* |
| hospital | *sptar* |
| ambulance | *ambulans* |

## Time, Days & Numbers

| | |
|---|---|
| What's the time? | *X'hin hu?* |
| today | *illum* |
| tomorrow | *ghada* |
| yesterday | *il-bierah* |
| morning | *fil-ghodu* |
| afternoon | *nofs in-nhar* |
| | |
| Monday | *it-tnejn* |
| Tuesday | *it-tlieta* |
| Wednesday | *l-erbgha* |
| Thursday | *il-hamis* |
| Friday | *il-gimgha* |
| Saturday | *is-sibt* |
| Sunday | *il-hadd* |

| | |
|---|---|
| 0 | *xejn* |
| 1 | *wiehed* |
| 2 | *tnejn* |
| 3 | *tlieta* |
| 4 | *erbgha* |
| 5 | *humsa* |
| 6 | *sitta* |
| 7 | *sebgha* |
| 8 | *tmienja* |
| 9 | *disgha* |
| 10 | *ghaxra* |
| 11 | *hdax* |
| 100 | *mija* |
| 1000 | *elf* |
| | |
| one million | *miljun* |

# Moroccan Arabic

## Pronunciation

Arabic is a difficult language to learn, but even knowing a few words can win you a friendly smile from the locals.

### Vowels

There are at least five basic vowel sounds that can be distinguished:

| | |
|---|---|
| a | as in 'had' (sometimes very short) |
| e | as in 'bet' (sometimes very short) |
| i | as in 'hit' |

o    as in 'hot'
u    as the 'oo' in 'book'

A stroke over a vowel (a macron) gives it a long sound. For example:

ā    as in 'far'
ē    as in 'there'
ī    as the 'e' in 'ear', only softer (often written as 'ee')
ō    as in 'for'
ū    as the 'oo' in 'food'

## Combinations
Certain combinations of vowels with vowels or consonants form other vowel sounds (diphthongs):

aw    as the 'ow' in 'how'
ai    as the 'i' in 'high'
ei, ay    as the 'a' in 'cake'

## Consonants
Many consonants are the same as in English, but there are some tricky ones:

j    as in 'John'
H    a strongly whispered 'h', almost like a sigh of relief
q    a strong guttural 'k' sound
kh    a slightly gurgling sound, like the 'ch' in Scottish *loch*
r    a rolled 'r' sound
s    as in 'sit', never as in 'wisdom'
sh    as in 'she'
z    as the 's' in pleasure
gh    called 'ghayn', similar to the French 'r', but more guttural

## Glottal Stop (')
The glottal stop is the sound you hear between the vowels in the expression 'oh oh!'. In Arabic it can occur anywhere in a word – at the beginning, middle or end. When the (') occurs before a vowel (eg, 'ayn), the vowel is 'growled' from the back of the throat. If it's before a consonant or at the end of a word, it sounds like a glottal stop.

## Basics
| | |
|---|---|
| Hello. | *as-salām 'alaykum* |
| Goodbye. | *ma' as-salāma* |
| Yes. | *īyeh* |
| No. | *la* |
| Please. | *'afak* |
| Thank you (very much). | *shukran (jazilan)* |

### Signs

| | |
|---|---|
| Entry | مدخل |
| Exit | خروج |
| Toilets (Men) | حمام للرجال |
| Toilets (Women) | حمام للنساء |
| Hospital | مستشفى |
| Police | الشرطة |
| Prohibited | ممنوع |

| | |
|---|---|
| You're welcome. | *la shukran, 'ala wajib* |
| Excuse me. | *smeH līya* |
| Do you speak English? | *wash kat'ref neglīzīya?* |
| I understand. | *fhemt* |
| I don't understand. | *mafhemtsh* |
| How much (is it)? | *bish-hal?* |
| What's your name? | *asmītak?* |
| My name is ... | *smītī ...* |

## Getting Around
| | |
|---|---|
| What time does the ... leave/arrive? | *emta qiyam/wusūl ...* |
| boat | *al-babūr* |
| bus (city) | *al-otobīs* |
| bus (intercity) | *al-kar* |
| train | *al-mashīna* |

| | |
|---|---|
| 1st class | *ddarazha llūla* |
| 2nd class | *ddarazha ttanīya* |
| train station | *maHattat al-mashīna/ al-qitar* |
| bus stop | *mawqif al-otobis* |

| | |
|---|---|
| Where can I hire a car/bicycle? | *fein yimkin ana akra tomobīl/beshklīta?* |
| Where is (the) ...? | *fein ...?* |
| Go straight ahead. | *sīr nīshan* |
| Turn right. | *dor 'al līmen* |
| Turn left. | *dor 'al līser* |

## Around Town
| | |
|---|---|
| the bank | *al-banka* |
| the embassy | *as-sifāra* |
| the market | *as-sūq* |
| the police station | *al-bolīs* |
| the post office | *al-bōsta, maktab al-barīd* |
| a toilet | *bayt al-ma, mirHad* |

## Emergencies – Arabic

| | |
|---|---|
| Help! | *'teqnī!* |
| Call a doctor! | *'eyyet at-tabīb!* |
| Call the police! | *'eyyet al-bolīs!* |
| Go away! | *sīr fHalek!* |

## Accommodation

| | |
|---|---|
| hotel | *al-otēl* |
| youth hostel | *dar shabbab* |
| camping ground | *mukhaym* |

| | |
|---|---|
| Is there a room available? | *wash kayn shī bīt xawīya?* |
| How much is this room per night? | *bshaHal al-bayt liyal?* |
| Is breakfast included? | *wash lftor mHsūb m'a lbīt?* |

## Time, Dates & Numbers

| | |
|---|---|
| What time is it? | *shHal fessa'a?* |
| today | *al-yūm* |
| tomorrow | *ghaddan* |
| yesterday | *al-bareh* |
| in the morning | *fis-sabaH* |
| in the evening | *fil-masa'* |

| | |
|---|---|
| Monday | *(nhar) al-itnēn* |
| Tuesday | *(nhar) at-talata* |
| Wednesday | *(nhar) al-arba'* |
| Thursday | *(nhar) al-khamīs* |
| Friday | *(nhar) al-juma'* |
| Saturday | *(nhar) as-sabt* |
| Sunday | *(nhar) al-ahad* |

Arabic numerals are simple enough to learn and, unlike the written language, run from left to right. In Morocco, European numerals are also often used.

| | |
|---|---|
| 1 | *wāHid* |
| 2 | *jūj* or *itnīn* |
| 3 | *talata* |
| 4 | *arba'a* |
| 5 | *khamsa* |
| 6 | *sitta* |
| 7 | *saba'a* |
| 8 | *tamanya* |
| 9 | *tissa'* |
| 10 | *'ashara* |
| 20 | *'asharin* |
| 100 | *miyya* |
| 1000 | *alf* |

| | |
|---|---|
| one million | *melyūn* |

# Portuguese

Portuguese pronunciation can be tricky for the uninitiated; like English, vowels and consonants have more than one possible sound depending on position and stress. Moreover, there are nasal vowels and diphthongs in Portuguese with no English equivalents.

## Vowels

| | |
|---|---|
| a | short, as the 'u' in 'cut' or long, as the 'ur' in 'hurt' |
| e | short, as in 'bet' or long, as in 'heir'; silent at the end of a word and in unstressed syllables |
| é | short, as in 'bet' |
| ê | long, as the 'a' in 'hay' |
| i | short, as in 'ring' or long, as in 'marine' |
| o | short, as in 'pot'; long as in 'note'; as the 'oo' in 'good' |
| ô | long, as in 'note' |
| u | as the 'oo' in 'good' |

## Nasal Vowels

Nasalisation is represented by an **n** or an **m** after the vowel, or by a tilde over it, eg, **ã**. The nasal 'i' exists in English as the 'ing' in 'sing'. For other vowels, practise by pronouncing a long 'a', 'ah', or 'e', 'eh', holding your nose, as if you have a cold.

## Diphthongs

Vowel combinations are relatively straightforward:

| | |
|---|---|
| au | as the 'ow' in 'now' |
| ai | as tin 'Thai' |
| ei | as the 'ay' in 'day' |
| eu | as 'e' followed by 'w' |
| oi | similar to the 'oy' in 'boy' |

## Nasal Diphthongs

Try the same technique as for nasal vowels. To say *não*, pronounce 'now' through your nose.

| | |
|---|---|
| ão | nasal 'ow' (owng) |
| ãe | nasal 'ay' (eing) |
| õe | nasal 'oy' (oing) |
| ui | similar to the 'uing' in 'ensuing' |

## Consonants

| | |
|---|---|
| c | as in 'cat' before **a**, **o** or **u**; as the 's' in 'sin' before **e** or **i** |
| ç | as the 'c' in 'celery' |
| g | as in 'go' before **a**, **o** or **u**; as the 's' 'treasure' before **e** or **i** |

| | |
|---|---|
| gu | as in 'guest' before e or i |
| h | never pronounced when word-initial |
| nh | as the 'ni' in 'onion' |
| lh | as the 'lli' in 'million' |
| j | as the 's' in 'treasure' |
| m | not pronounced when word-final – it simply nasalises the previous vowel, eg, *um* (oong), *bom* (bõ) |
| qu | as the 'k' in 'key' before e or i; elsewhere as in 'queen' |
| r | when word-initial, or when doubled (rr) within a word it's a harsh, guttural sound similar to the 'ch' in Scottish *loch*; in the middle or at the end of a word it's a rolled 'r' sound |
| s | as in 'so' when word-initial and when doubled (ss) within a word; as the 'z' in 'zeal' when between vowels; as 'sh' when it precedes a consonant, or at the end of a word |
| x | as the 'sh' in 'ship', as the 'z' in 'zeal', or as the 'x' in 'taxi' |
| z | as the 's' in 'treasure' before a consonant or at the end of a word |

## Word Stress

Word stress is important in Portuguese, as it can affect meaning. In words with a written accent, the stress always falls on the accented syllable.

Note that Portuguese uses masculine and feminine word endings, usually '-o' and '-a' respectively. Thus, to say 'thank you', a man will use *obrigado* and a woman, *obrigada*.

## Basics

| | |
|---|---|
| Hello/Goodbye. | *Bom dia/Adeus.* |
| Yes. | *Sim.* |
| No. | *Não.* |
| Please. | *Se faz favor.* |
| Thank you. | *Obrigado/a.* (m/f) |
| You're welcome. | *De nada.* |
| Excuse me. | *Com licença.* |
| Sorry. (forgive me) | *Desculpe.* |
| Do you speak English? | *Fala Inglês?* |
| How much is it? | *Quanto custa?* |
| What's your name? | *Como se chama?* |
| My name is ... | *Chamo-me ...* |

## Getting Around

| | |
|---|---|
| What time does the ... leave/arrive? | *A que horas parte/ chega ...?* |
| boat | *o barco* |
| bus (city) | *o autocarro* |
| bus (intercity) | *a camioneta* |
| tram | *o eléctrico* |
| train | *o comboio* |

### Signs – Portuguese

| | |
|---|---|
| *Entrada* | Entrance |
| *Saída* | Exit |
| *Informações* | Information |
| *Aberto* | Open |
| *Fechado* | Closed |
| *Quartos Livres* | Rooms Available |
| *Posto Da Polícia* | Police Station |
| *Proíbido* | Prohibited |
| *Empurre/Puxe* | Push/Pull |
| *Lavabos/WC* | Toilets |
| *Homens (h)* | Men |
| *Senhoras (s)* | Women |

| | |
|---|---|
| bus stop | *paragem de autocarro* |
| train station | *estação ferroviária* |
| timetable | *horário* |

| | |
|---|---|
| I'd like a ... ticket. | *Queria um bilhete ...* |
| one-way | *simples/de ida* |
| return | *de ida e volta* |
| 1st-class | *de primeira classe* |
| 2nd-class | *de segunda classe* |

| | |
|---|---|
| I'd like to hire ... | *Queria alugar ...* |
| a car | *um carro* |
| a bicycle | *uma bicicleta* |

| | |
|---|---|
| Where is ...? | *Onde é ...?* |
| Go straight ahead. | *Siga sempre (a direito/ em frente).* |
| Turn left. | *Vire à esquerda.* |
| Turn right. | *Vire à direita.* |
| near | *perto* |
| far | *longe* |

## Around Town

| | |
|---|---|
| a bank | *um banco* |
| the chemist/ pharmacy | *a farmácia* |
| the ... embassy | *a embaixada de ...* |
| my hotel | *o meu hotel* |
| the market | *o mercado* |
| the post office | *o correio* |
| the newsagency | *a papelaria* |
| the stationers | *a tabacaria* |
| the telephone centre | *a central de telefones* |
| the tourist office | *o (posto de) turismo* |

| | |
|---|---|
| What time does it open/close? | *A que horas abre/ fecha?* |

## Accommodation

| | |
|---|---|
| hotel | *hotel* |
| guesthouse | *pensão* |
| youth hostel | *pousada da juventude* |
| camping ground | *parque de campismo* |

## Emergencies – Portuguese

| | |
|---|---|
| Help! | *Socorro!* |
| Call a doctor! | *Chame um médico!* |
| Call the police! | *Chame a polícia!* |
| Go away! | *Deixe-me em paz!/* |
| | *Vai-te embora!* (inf) |
| I'm lost. | *Estou perdido/a.* (m/f) |

| | |
|---|---|
| Do you have any rooms available? | *Tem quartos livres?* |
| How much is it per night/per person? | *Quanto é por noite/ por pessoa?* |
| Is breakfast included? | *O pequeno almoço está incluído?* |

| | |
|---|---|
| a single room | *um quarto individual* |
| a twin room | *um quarto duplo* |
| a double bed room | *um quarto de casal* |
| for one night | *para uma noite* |
| for two nights | *para duas noites* |

### Time, Days & Numbers

| | |
|---|---|
| What time is it? | *Que horas são?* |
| today | *hoje* |
| tomorrow | *amanhã* |
| yesterday | *ontem* |
| morning | *manhã* |
| afternoon | *tarde* |

| | |
|---|---|
| Monday | *segunda-feira* |
| Tuesday | *terça-feira* |
| Wednesday | *quarta-feira* |
| Thursday | *quinta-feira* |
| Friday | *sexta-feira* |
| Saturday | *sábado* |
| Sunday | *domingo* |

| | |
|---|---|
| 1 | *um/uma* |
| 2 | *dois/duas* |
| 3 | *três* |
| 4 | *quatro* |
| 5 | *cinco* |
| 6 | *seis* |
| 7 | *sete* |
| 8 | *oito* |
| 9 | *nove* |
| 10 | *dez* |
| 11 | *onze* |
| 20 | *vinte* |
| 21 | *vinte e um/uma* |
| 30 | *trinta* |
| 40 | *quarenta* |
| 100 | *cem* |
| 1000 | *mil* |
| one million | *um milhão* |

# Slovene

## Pronunciation

Slovene pronunciation isn't difficult. The alphabet consists of 25 letters, most of which are very similar to English. It doesn't have the letters 'q', 'w', 'x' and 'y', but the following letters are added: ê, é, ó, ò, č, š and ž. Each letter represents only one sound, with very few exceptions, and the sounds are pure and not diphthongal. The letters l and v are both pronounced like the English 'w' when they occur at the end of syllables and before vowels.

Though words like *trn* (thorn) look unpronounceable, most Slovenes add a short vowel like an 'a' or the German 'ö' (depending on dialect) in front of the 'r' to give a Scot's pronunciation of 'tern' or 'tarn'.

| | |
|---|---|
| c | as the 'ts' in 'its' |
| č | as the 'ch' in 'church' |
| ê | as the 'a' in 'apple' |
| e | as the 'er' in 'opera' (when unstressed) |
| é | as the 'ay' in 'day' |
| j | as the 'y' in 'yellow' |
| ó | as the 'o' in 'more' |
| ò | as the 'o' in 'soft' |
| r | a rolled 'r' sound |
| š | as the 'sh' in 'ship' |
| u | as the 'oo' in 'good' |
| ž | as the 's' in 'treasure' |

## Basics

| | |
|---|---|
| Hello. | *Pozdravljeni.* (polite) |
| | *Zdravo/Živio.* (informal) |
| Good day. | *Dober dan!* |
| Goodbye. | *Nasvidenje!* |
| Yes. | *Da.* or *Ja.* (informal) |
| No. | *Ne.* |
| Please. | *Prosim.* |
| Thank you (very much). | *Hvala (lepa).* |
| You're welcome. | *Prosim/Ni za kaj!* |

## Signs – Slovene

| | |
|---|---|
| *Vhod* | **Entrance** |
| *Izhod* | **Exit** |
| *Informacije* | **Information** |
| *Odprto* | **Open** |
| *Zaprto* | **Closed** |
| *Prepovedano* | **Prohibited** |
| *Stranišče* | **Toilets** |

| | |
|---|---|
| Excuse me. | *Oprostite.* |
| What's your name? | *Kako vam je ime?* |
| My name is ... | *Jaz sem ...* |
| Where are you from? | *Od kod ste?* |
| I'm from ... | *Sem iz ...* |

## Getting Around

| | |
|---|---|
| What time does ... leave/arrive? | *Kdaj odpelje/ pripelje ...?* |
| boat/ferry | *ladja/trajekt* |
| bus | *avtobus* |
| train | *vlak* |
| | |
| one-way (ticket) | *enosmerna (vozovnica)* |
| return (ticket) | *povratna (vozovnica)* |
| bus stop | *avtobusno postajališče* |
| train station | *železniska postaja* |
| | |
| Where is ...? | *Kje je ...?* |
| Go straight ahead. | *Pojdite naravnost naprej.* |
| Turn left. | *Obrnite levo.* |
| Turn right. | *Obrnite desno.* |
| near | *blizu* |
| far | *daleč* |

## Around Town

| | |
|---|---|
| Where is the/a ...? | *Kje je ...?* |
| bank | *banka* |
| consulate | *konzulat* |
| embassy | *ambasada* |
| exchange | *menjalnica* |
| post office | *pošta* |
| telephone centre | *telefonska centrala* |
| tourist office | *turistični informa- cijski urad* |

## Accommodation

| | |
|---|---|
| hotel | *hotel* |
| guesthouse | *gostišče* |
| youth hostel | *počitniški dom* |
| camping ground | *kamping* |
| | |
| Do you have a ...? | *Ali imate prosto ...?* |
| bed | *posteljo* |
| cheap room | *poceni sobo* |
| single room | *enoposteljno sobo* |
| double room | *dvoposteljno sobo* |
| | |
| for one night | *za eno noč* |
| for two nights | *za dve noči* |
| | |
| How much is it per night? | *Koliko stane za eno noč?* |
| How much is it per person? | *Koliko stane za eno osebo?* |
| Is breakfast included? | *Ali je zajtrk vključen?* |

## Time, Days & Numbers

| | |
|---|---|
| today | *danes* |
| tonight | *nocoj* |
| tomorrow | *jutri* |
| in the morning | *zjutraj* |
| in the evening | *zvečer* |
| | |
| Monday | *ponedeljek* |
| Tuesday | *torek* |
| Wednesday | *sreda* |
| Thursday | *četrtek* |
| Friday | *petek* |
| Saturday | *sobota* |
| Sunday | *nedelja* |

| | |
|---|---|
| 1 | *ena* |
| 2 | *dve* |
| 3 | *tri* |
| 4 | *štiri* |
| 5 | *pet* |
| 6 | *šest* |
| 7 | *sedem* |
| 8 | *osem* |
| 9 | *devet* |
| 10 | *deset* |
| 100 | *sto* |
| 1000 | *tisoč* |
| | |
| one million | *milijon* |

# Spanish

## Pronunciation
### Vowels

Unlike English, each of the vowels in Spanish has a uniform pronunciation which doesn't vary. For example, the Spanish **a** has one pronunciation rather than the numerous pronunciations we find in English, such as in 'cat', 'cake', 'cart', 'care', 'call'. An acute accent (as in *días*) generally indicates a stressed syllable and doesn't change the sound of the vowel. Vowels are pronounced clearly even if they are in unstressed positions or at the end of a word.

a   as the 'u' in 'nut', or a shorter sound than the 'a' in 'art'

e   as in 'met'

i   somewhere between the 'i' in 'marine' and the 'i' in 'flip'

o   similar to the 'o' in 'hot'

u   as in 'put'

## Consonants

Some Spanish consonants are pronounced as per their English counterparts. The pronunciation of others is dependent on following vowels and also on which part of Spain you happen to be in. The Spanish alphabet also contains three consonants that aren't found in the English alphabet: **ch**, **ll** and **ñ**.

b   as in 'but' when word-initial or preceded by a nasal; elsewhere it's almost a cross between English 'b' and 'v'

c   a hard 'c' as in 'cat' when followed by **a**, **o**, **u** or a consonant; as the 'th' in 'thin' before **e** and **i**

ch   as in 'church'

d   as in 'do' when word-initial; elsewhere as the 'th' in 'then'

g   as in 'get' when word-initial and before **a**, **o** and **u**; elsewhere much softer. Before **e** or **i** it's a harsh, breathy sound, similar to a forceful 'h' in 'hit'

h   silent

j   a harsh, guttural sound similar to the 'ch' in Scottish *loch*

ll   as the 'lli' in 'million'; some pronounce it rather like the 'y' in 'yellow'

ñ   a nasal sound, as the 'ni' in 'onion'

q   as the 'k' in 'kick'; **q** is always followed by a silent **u** and is combined only with the vowels **e** (as in *que*) and **i** (as in *qui*)

r   a rolled 'r' sound; longer and stronger when initial or doubled

s   as in 'see'

v   the same sound as **b**

x   as the 'ks' sound in 'taxi' when between vowels; as the 's' in 'see' when it precedes a consonant

z   as the 'th' in 'thin'

## Semiconsonant

Spanish also has the semiconsonant **y**. When at the end of a word or when standing alone as a conjunction it's pronounced like the Spanish **i**. As a consonant, it's somewhere between the 'y' in 'yonder' and the 'g' in 'beige', depending on the region.

### Signs – Spanish

| | |
|---|---|
| *Entrada* | Entrance |
| *Salida* | Exit |
| *Información* | Information |
| *Abierto* | Open |
| *Cerrado* | Closed |
| *Habtaciones Libres* | Rooms Available |
| *Completo* | Full/No Vacancies |
| *Comisaría* | Police Station |
| *Prohibido* | Prohibited |
| *Servicios/Aseos* | Toilets |
|   *Hombres* | Men |
|   *Mujeres* | Women |

### Basics

| | |
|---|---|
| Hello. | *¡Hola!* |
| Goodbye. | *¡Adiós!* |
| Yes. | *Sí.* |
| No. | *No.* |
| Please. | *Por favor.* |
| Thank you. | *Gracias.* |
| You're welcome. | *De nada.* |
| I'm sorry. (forgive me) | *Lo siento/Discúlpeme.* |
| Excuse me. | *Perdón/Perdoneme.* |
| Do you speak English? | *¿Habla inglés?* |
| How much is it? | *¿Cuánto cuesta?* |
| What's your name? | *¿Cómo se llama?* |
| My name is ... | *Me llamo ...* |

### Getting Around

| | |
|---|---|
| What time does the next ... leave/arrive? | *¿A qué hora sale/ llega el próximo ...?* |
| boat | *barco* |
| bus (city) | *autobús, bus* |
| bus (intercity) | *autocar* |
| train | *tranvía* |
| | |
| I'd like a ... ticket. | *Quisiera un billete ...* |
| one-way | *sencillo/de sólo ida* |
| return | *de ida y vuelta* |
| 1st-class | *de primera clase* |
| 2nd-class | *de segunda clase* |
| | |
| left luggage | *consigna* |
| timetable | *horario* |
| bus stop | *parada de autobus* |
| train station | *estación de ferrocarril* |
| | |
| I'd like to hire ... | *Quisiera alquilar ...* |
| a car | *un coche* |
| a bicycle | *una bicicleta* |

| Where is ...? | ¿Dónde está ...? |
| Go straight ahead. | Siga/Vaya todo derecho. |
| Turn left. | Gire a la izquierda. |
| Turn right. | Gire a la derecha/recto. |
| near | cerca |
| far | lejos |

## Around Town

| a bank | un banco |
| chemist/pharmacy | la farmacia |
| the ... embassy | la embajada ... |
| my hotel | mi hotel |
| the market | el mercado |
| newsagency/ stationers | papelería |
| the post office | los correos |
| the telephone centre | el locutorio |
| the tourist office | la oficina de turismo |

| What time does it open/close? | ¿A qué hora abren/ cierran? |

## Accommodation

| hotel | hotel |
| guesthouse | pensión/casa de huéspedes |
| youth hostel | albergue juvenil |
| camping ground | camping |

| Do you have any rooms available? | ¿Tiene habitaciones libres? |

| a single room | una habitación individual |
| a double room | una habitación doble |
| a room with a double bed | una habitación con cama de matrimonio |
| for one night | para una noche |
| for two nights | para dos noches |

| How much is it per night/person? | ¿Cuánto cuesta por noche/persona? |
| Is breakfast included? | ¿Incluye el desayuno? |

## Time, Days & Numbers

| What time is it? | ¿Qué hora es? |
| today | hoy |
| tomorrow | mañana |
| yesterday | ayer |
| in the morning | de la mañana |
| in the afternoon | de la tarde |

| Monday | lunes |
| Tuesday | martes |
| Wednesday | miércoles |

### Emergencies – Spanish

| Help! | ¡Socorro!/¡Auxilio! |
| Call a doctor! | ¡Llame a un doctor! |
| Call the police! | ¡Llame a la policía! |
| Go away! | ¡Váyase! |
| I'm lost. | Estoy perdido/ perdida. (m/f) |

| Thursday | jueves |
| Friday | viernes |
| Saturday | sábado |
| Sunday | domingo |

| 1 | uno/una |
| 2 | dos |
| 3 | tres |
| 4 | cuatro |
| 5 | cinco |
| 6 | seis |
| 7 | siete |
| 8 | ocho |
| 9 | nueve |
| 10 | diez |
| 11 | once |
| 12 | doce |
| 13 | trece |
| 14 | catorce |
| 15 | quince |
| 16 | dieciéis |
| 100 | cien/ciento |
| 1000 | mil |

| one million | un millón |

# Turkish

## Pronunciation

The new Turkish alphabet is phonetic and thus reasonably easy to pronounce once you've learned a few basic rules. Each Turkish letter is pronounced, there are no diphthongs, and the only silent letter is ğ.

## Vowels

Turkish vowels are pronounced as follows:

| A a | as the 'a' in 'art' or 'bar' |
| E e | as in 'fell' |
| İ i | as 'ee' |
| I ı | as the 'a' in 'ago' |
| O o | as in 'hot' |
| U u | as the 'oo' in 'moo' |
| Ö ö | as the 'ur' in 'fur' |
| Ü ü | as the 'ew' in 'few' |

Note that both **ö** and **ü** are pronounced with pursed lips.

## Consonants
Most consonants are pronounced as in English, with a few exceptions:

| | |
|---|---|
| **Ç ç** | as the 'ch' in 'church' |
| **C c** | as English 'j' |
| **Ğ ğ** | not pronounced; draws out the preceding vowel a bit |
| **G g** | as in 'gun' |
| **H h** | as the 'h' in 'half' |
| **J j** | as the 's' in 'treasure' |
| **S s** | as in 'stress' |
| **Ş ş** | as the 'sh' in 'shoe' |
| **V v** | as the 'w' in 'weather' |

## Basics
| | |
|---|---|
| Hello. | *Merhaba.* |
| Goodbye. | *Allahaısmarladık/* *Güle güle.* |
| Yes. | *Evet.* |
| No. | *Hayır.* |
| Please. | *Lütfen.* |
| Thank you. | *Teşekkür ederim.* |
| That's fine/ You're welcome. | *Bir şey değil.* |
| Excuse me. | *Affedersiniz.* |
| Sorry/Pardon. | *Pardon.* |
| Do you speak English? | *İngilizce biliyor musunuz?* |
| How much is it? | *Ne kadar?* |
| What's your name? | *Adınız ne?* |
| My name is ... | *Adım ...* |

## Getting Around
| | |
|---|---|
| What time does the next ... leave/arrive? | *Gelecek ... ne zaman kalkar/gelir?* |
| ferry/boat | *feribot/vapur* |
| bus (city) | *şehir otobüsü* |
| bus (intercity) | *otobüs* |
| tram | *tramvay* |
| train | *tren* |

| | |
|---|---|
| I'd like ... | *... istiyorum* |
| a one-way ticket | *gidiş bileti* |
| a return ticket | *gidiş-dönüş bileti* |
| 1st-class | *birinci mevkii* |
| 2nd-class | *ikinci mevkii* |

| | |
|---|---|
| left luggage | *emanetçi* |
| timetable | *tarife* |
| bus stop | *otobüs durağı* |
| tram stop | *tramvay durağı* |
| train station | *gar/istasyon* |
| ferry/ship dock | *iskele* |

| | |
|---|---|
| I'd like to hire a car/bicycle. | *Araba/bisiklet kirala mak istiyorum.* |

| | |
|---|---|
| Where is a/the ...? | *... nerede?* |
| Go straight ahead. | *Doğru gidin.* |
| Turn left. | *Sola dönün.* |
| Turn right. | *Sağa dönün.* |
| near | *yakın* |
| far | *uzak* |

## Around Town
| | |
|---|---|
| a bank | *bir banka* |
| a chemist/pharmacy | *bir eczane* |
| the ... embassy | *... büyükelçiliği* |
| my hotel | *otelimi* |
| the market | *çarşı* |
| the newsagency | *haber agensı* |
| the post office | *postane* |
| the stationers | *kırtasiyeci* |
| the telephone centre | *telefon merkezi* |
| the tourist office | *turizm danışma bürosu* |

| | |
|---|---|
| What time does it open/close? | *Ne zamam açılır/kapanır?* |

## Accommodation
| | |
|---|---|
| hotel | *otel(i)* |
| guesthouse | *pansiyon* |
| student hostel | *öğrenci yurdu* |
| camping ground | *kampink* |

| | |
|---|---|
| Do you have any rooms available? | *Boş oda var mı?* |

| | |
|---|---|
| a single room | *tek kişilik oda* |
| a double room | *iki kişilik oda* |
| one night | *bir gece* |
| two nights | *iki gece* |

| | |
|---|---|
| How much is it per night/per person? | *Bir gecelik/Kişibaşına kaç para?* |
| Is breakfast included? | *Kahvaltı dahil mi?* |

### Signs – Turkish
| | |
|---|---|
| **Giriş** | **Entrance** |
| **Çikiş** | **Exit** |
| **Danişma** | **Information** |
| **Açik** | **Open** |
| **Kapali** | **Closed** |
| **Boş Oda Var** | **Rooms Available** |
| **Dolu** | **Full/No Vacancies** |
| **Polis/Emniyet** | **Police** |
| **Polis Karakolu/ Emniyet Müdürlüğü** | **Police Station** |
| **Yasak(tir)** | **Prohibited** |
| **Tuvalet** | **Toilets** |

## Emergencies – Turkish

| | |
|---|---|
| Help!/Emergency! | *İmdat!* |
| Call a doctor! | *Doktor çağırın!* |
| Call the police! | *Polis çağırın!* |
| Go away! | *Gidin/Git!/Defol!* |
| I'm lost. | *Kayboldum.* |

## Time, Days & Numbers

| | |
|---|---|
| What time is it? | *Saat kaç?* |
| today | *bugün* |
| tomorrow | *yarın* |
| yesterday | *dün* |
| morning | *sabah* |
| afternoon | *öğleden sonra* |

| | |
|---|---|
| Monday | *Pazartesi* |
| Tuesday | *Salı* |
| Wednesday | *Çarşamba* |
| Thursday | *Perşembe* |
| Friday | *Cuma* |
| Saturday | *Cumartesi* |
| Sunday | *Pazar* |

| | |
|---|---|
| January | *Ocak* |
| February | *Şubat* |
| March | *Mart* |
| April | *Nisan* |
| May | *Mayıs* |
| June | *Haziran* |
| July | *Temmuz* |
| August | *Ağustos* |
| September | *Eylül* |
| October | *Ekim* |
| November | *Kasım* |
| December | *Aralık* |

| | |
|---|---|
| 1 | *bir* |
| 2 | *iki* |
| 3 | *üç* |
| 4 | *dört* |
| 5 | *beş* |
| 6 | *altı* |
| 7 | *yedi* |
| 8 | *sekiz* |
| 9 | *dokuz* |
| 10 | *on* |
| 11 | *on bir* |
| 12 | *on iki* |
| 13 | *on üç* |
| 100 | *yüz* |
| 1000 | *bin* |
| one million | *bir milyon* |

# Thanks

Many thanks to the travellers who used the last edition and wrote to us with helpful hints, useful advice and interesting anecdotes:

Marlies Aanhaanen, Jodi Adams, Peter Adams, Nick Adlam, Sabine Agena, Amie Albrecht, Brooke Aldrich, Ruth Alexander, Rod Allan, Pedro Alvarez, Sheila Aly, Kelly Anderson, Sarah Andrews, Philip Anthony, Mike Appleyard, Christine Aquilina, Mary Ara, Daniel Arenas, Phoenix Arrien, Elena Arriero, N Arulraj, Karin Arver, Hiroyuki Asakuno, Ragnar Aschim, Catherine Ashford, Jerry Azevedo, Theo Baak, Brendon Bailey, Kate Baker, Ramon Baker, Rebecca Balsamo, Anne Bancroft, Christine Barbour, Ann Barker, Deon & Jacqueline Barnes, Dr R J Barnes, Craig Baron, Alan Bartlett, Amy Bartlett, Andrew Baynham, Wes Beard, John Bedford, CB Belcher, Jacqui Belgrave, Peggy Bendall, Jacob Bendtsen, Tony Benfield, George & Brenda Berry, Jeff Berry, Tara Bessette, Javier Betancourt, Gordon Bettenay, Michelle Beveridge, Tim Bewer, Andrzej Bielecki, Sylvain Biemont, Alexandre Billette, Peter Birch, Dane Birdseye, Massimo Bisiachi, Lars Björk, Jan & Ulrika Bjorkman, Louise & Brad Bland, Fernando Blasco, Cindy & Maggie Blick, Virginia Bloch-Jorgensen, Richard Bluett, Geert Boeije, Sarah Boniface, Andre Bosmans, Inge Bouwman, Joanna & Don Box, RS Boylen, Mahmut Boynudelik, Domi Branger, Ben Brehmer, Evan Brinder, Sjoukje Broer, David Browning, Gayle Brownlee, Jonathan Bryan, Ang Bryans, Helene Budinski, Martin Buekers, Jan Bullerdieck, Victoria Burford, HG Burnab, Cameron Bush, Michelle Bush, Rob Butler, Emanuel Buttigieg, Gerald Cadieux, Andrew Cameron, Tui Cameron, Drew Caputo, Sid Cara, Richard S Carnell, Maggie Carter, Scott Casban, Terry Casstevens, Luigi Ceccarini, Myriam Champagne, Dorothy Chatwin, Julian Chen, Yee Cheng, Alison Cheung, Terrie Chin, Kah Chong, Mark Christian, Joel Chusid, Niko Cimbur, Christopher Clarke, Daniele Clavenzani, Diana Clough, Bevan Cobb, Ian Coggin, Robyn Cohen, Helen Conway, Julie & Bruce Cook, Cliff Cordy, Andrew Cork, Michael Counsell, Paolo Criscione, David Critics, Sarok Csaba, Ricardo Cuan, Muireann Cullen, Carrie Cunningham, R Curran, Jennifer Currie, John Curry, P Cuypers, Zelko Cvitkovic, Madi Dale, Robert K Daly, Pat Daniel, Tania Daniels, Jane d'Arcy, Neil Datta, Shaun Davidson, Susan & Stewart Davison, Jeannie & Keith de Jong, John Deacon, Michael R Decker, Carine Delvaux, RJ Dempsey, Marius den Hartog, Carine Derch, David Deutscher, Robin Deweerdt, Kostis Diamantopoulos, Carlos Diaz, Katja Diezel, Rob Dighton, Marianna Dioxini, Jan Ditheridge, Rachel Dodds, Matjaz Dolenc, Nicola Doran, Kelly Douglas, Andreas Drechsler, Jason Dressler, Terry Drew, Pattie Dubaere, Liesbeth Dubois, Claire Duiker, Nick Duke, Rob Duncan, John Dunkelberger, Sarah Dunlop, Sonya Dykstra, John Dynan, Richard Eardley, Matt Eaton, Jack Egerton, Dave Eggelton, Bernie Eglinton, Veronica Egron, Robin Eley Jones, Sara Elison, Phillip Elrod, Caghan Elsiz, Kim Elton, Marleen Enschede, Gennevene Ensor, Nikita Eriksen-Hamel, Zeyda Erol, Diane Fahey, Trasy Fahle, Victor Falzon, Bernard Farjounel, Gillian Farley, Annie & Stephen Faustino, Andrea Fechter, Ryan Fennell, Armando Ferra, Wendy Finch-Turner, Philippa Fleetwood, Cait Fogarty, Richard Forsaith, Jordi Fortia-Huguet, Barbara Foster, Majorie Foster, Liz Foulis, Nicky Francis, Emmanuel Andre Vincent Frechette, Gemma French, Jan Frith, Louise Fryer, Reyes Moran Fuertes, Dave Fuller, Werner Furrer, Helene Gabriel, Andy Ganner, Reshma Ganpat, Jenny Garcia, Julio Garcia-Lopez, Alissa Garner, Gaelen Gates, Donatella Gatti, Josef Gaug, Anne Geange, Terry Geisecke, Johnny Ghanem, Louise & Dave Giles, Luke Gillian, Paul W Gioffi, Alberto Giorgiutti, Ewan Girvan, David Glasson, Ian Glennon, Arno Gloeckner, David Godfrey, Joel Goldsmith, Juan Gonzalez-Dominguez, Athina Gorezis, K Gorringe, Gorrit Goslinga, Jodie Goulden, Neale Gover, Paul Graalman, Rene Granacher, Gordon Grant, Nancy Grant, Deborah Gravrock, Beth Gray, Frank Greenhill, Nicole Grima, Kreso Gudelj, Pauline Gummer, Kumar Gupta, Shelly Habel, Stefan Haberl, Samantha Hack, Erja Haenninen, Kathy Hagen, Sally Hagen, Nardia Haigh, Alasdair Hamblin, Roswitha Hammer, Sharyn Hammond, John Hanks, Maria Hannon, Lars Folmer Hansen, Luc & Anja Hansenne-Geril, F Harmelin, Zach Rohaizad Roj Haron, Philip Harper, Jonathan Harris, Peter Harris, Stephen & Akkelin Harris, John Harrison, Steve Harrison, Susie Hartmann, Richard Harvey, Joseph Harwell, Chloe Harwood, Thomas Haunstein, Tony Hayman, Esther Hecht, Barry

Hennessy, Lisa Herb, Maria Heritage, NG Hetterley, Peter Hicks, Frank Higginson, Alyson & David Hilbourne, Kate Hill, Timothy Hill, Trev Hill, Nick Hind, Kym Hirst, Jan & Mirjam Hissink, Jonah Hister, Simon Ho, Matt Hodges, Jaap Hoftijzer, Belinda Hogan, Ville Holmberg, Gerald Holt, Clarie Hood, Melanie Hoods, Erik Hoogcarspel, Chong Hoong Yin, Fran Hopkins, Megan Hopkins, Barry Horowitz, Eileen Horowitz, Roger Horton, Jenny Horwood, Andrew Hoshkiw, Brent Hourd, Matt Howes, Stephen Howse, Paula Huber, Matt Huddleston, Kevin Hudson, John Hulme, Mary Hunt, Mary Hutchings, Joanne Hutchinson, Steuart Hutchinson, Christine Ingemorsen, Sabahattin Ismail, Chris James, Peter James, Anton Jansen, Tom Jansing, Jennifer Jansma, Rok Jarc, J Jarman, Massoud Javadi, Jason K Jew, Miles Johnston, Arthur Jones, Chris Jones, Hywel Jones, Scott L Jones, Beate Josephi, AJ Julicher, Alfie Kaech, Niki Kalogiratou, Lili Kalp, Aviva Kamm, Aziz Kara, Thecle Kentfield, Svensson Kerstin, Melita Khawly, Gail & Peter Kirby, Dean & John Klinkenberg, Paul Knudsen, Buket Kop, Igor Korsic, Minette Korterink, Robin Kortright, Juraj Kosticky, AH & J Koutsaplis, Carlo Krusich, Ralph Kuehn, Cintia Kurimoto, Peter Kurze, Wan Kwong Young, Stephen Lamb, Peter Lamont, Karen Lamorey, Jo Lane, Fabio Lanzavecchia, John Lea, Marc Lees, Dr PA Lekhi, Debbie Lelek, Dr Ing Christoph Lenssen, Desmond Leow, Birgitte Lerno, Franck Lesage, Sacha Lethborg, Len Levine, Joe Lewardowski, Rebecca Lewis, Paul Lewtas, George Liangas, Daniel Lieberfeld, Anja Lieder, Rich Lillywhite, Paul Lindsay-Addy, Jeroen Lintjens, Harriet Little, Lisa Long, Barbara Lopes-Cardozo, Berny Lottner, Serena Love, Matthew Low, Michael Low, Terry & Katherine Lustig, Peter Lyon, Oliver Lyttelton, Lachlan MacArthur, Mike Maglalang, Eric Markowitz, Betty Marriott, Alberto Martin, H Martin, Steve Martin, Eleni Martini, LD Mathews, Peta Mathias, Graeme Mawson, Jeff McCartney, Kathryn McDonnell, Brenda McDowell, Jamie McGraw, Delia McInerney, Brends McIntyre, Kevin McIntyre, Sarah McLellan, Paul McLoughlin, Andrew McMahon, Jodi McMillan, Janet Mead, George Meeker, Lori Mendel, Kathy Meredith, Muhamed Mesic, Pierre Messier, Bas Metolli, Patrice Meunier, Kevin Micallef, Stefano Micchia, Karen Mickle, George Miller, P A P Miller, Ming Ming Teh, Haleema Mini, Nicki Miquel, Richard Cousineau de la Mirande, Arkajyoti Misra, Claire Missing, Kenny Mitchell, Barbara Molin, Jesse Monsour, Robert Moon,

Rebekah Moore, Maura Moralic, Inge Mossige, Katie Mountford, Marcus Muhlethaler, K Mulzer, Dave Munn, Chris Munro, Simon Munt, Jasper & Vincent Murphy, Kate Murray, Maeve Murray, Helen Myers, Karen Myhill-Jones, Dan Nadel, MaryAnne Nelson, Ross Nelson, T Nelson, Heico Neumeyer, Steve Newcomer, Sara Newhall, Scott Newman, Christine Newtown, Vicky Nicholas, Judith Nielsen, Maria Mejer Nielsen, Ippolito Nievo, Borut Nikolas, Bjorn Norheim, Rudy Nuytten, Davor Obradovic, Debbie O'Bray, Judith O'Brien, Kevin O'Donovan, Carrie Oelberger, Ricardo Olaeta, Shannon O'Loughlin, Jacquie Olsen, Dana Olson, Stephen O'Neil, Rick Owen, Darja Pahic, Anne Palmer, Craig Palmer, Pasco Panconcelli, John Papageorgiou, Paula Park, Clinton Parkes, James Parkhurst, Thea Parkin, L Patrick-Ferry, Baz Pattison, Stuart Pattullo, Roger Peake, Antoine Pecoud, Carol Peddie, William Peden, Nicole Peel, Craig Peers, Jan M Pennington, Claus Penz, Rosa Maria Perales-Barrero, Alfredo Perez, Jane Perry, Dudas Peter, Rick Petkovsek, Renee Petry, Ooi Lin Pheh, Karen Pickering, Niki Pilidou, David Pitchford, Zoli Pitman, David John Pitts, Sean Plamondon, Paul Plaza, Dimitris Ploumides, Vanessa Pollett, Rita Portelli, Ezra Pound, Pirasri Povatong, Beth Powell, Carlo Pozzi, Cristina Pratas, Georgina Preston, Scott Prysi, Alan Quinn, Maria Ralph, Francesco Randisi, Bernt Rane, Andrea Rausch, Scott Reardon, Sergio Rebelo, Annette Reeves, Melinda Reidinger, Charlie Rich, Tony Richmond, Kornelia Ring, Jan Doeke Rinzema, Judith Ripoli, F Risi, F Roberts, Dr A Robertson, Dan Robinson, Melina Rodde, Andrea & Piper Roelen, H Roivas, Paul Roos, Brenda Roscoe, Nicolas Rosenbaum, Matthew Rothschild, Maureen Roult, Angela Rowe, JD Rowe, John Rowe, Alison Rowlands, Stephen Rowlands, TherTse Rozijan, Esa Ruotsalainen, Heather Ryan, Patti Ryan, Krysztof Rybak, Sandra Saccone, Karen Sackler Novick, John Sadler, Beth & Kevin Salt, Robert Saltzstein, Rachel Samsonowitz, Stefan Samuelsson, Aidan Santer, Markku Sarubin, V & M Sarubin, Suzanne Sataline, Gerard Sayers, Julien Scaife, Rachel Scanlon, Judith Schaniel, Etienne Scheeper, Carola Schellack, Peg Schlekat, Jacqueline Schliebs, Jeremias Schmidt, Inga Schonning, Bram Schout, Rebecca Schroeder, Suzy Scorer, Paul Sebastianelli, Shirley Seit, Oliver Selwyn, Brett Shackelford, Nadeem Shah, Eyal Shaham, U Shalit, Gwen & Norm Shannon, Robert & Ruth Shannon, Mark & Stephanie Shattuck, Barbara Sheerman-Chase, Norman Shepherd, Pushparcy

Shetty, Brian Shunamon, Bilal Sidani, Bogdan Siewierski, Dragan Simic, Vern & Cindy Simpson, Heidi Sinclair, Anneke Sips, Anica W Siric, Rebecca Skinner, Greg Slade, Kara Slaughter, Kerry Smallman, Brendan Smith, Kate Smith, Mackay Smith, K Smith-Jones, Andrew Sneddon, Kim Sowman, Eduardo Spaccasassi, Gary Spinks, Steven Stahl, Maarten Stam, Joesph T Stanik, Steven Stefanovic, Chris Stephenson, Sheila Stephenson, Hans Sterkendries, Kim Stewart, Bjarne Stig Hansen, Elena Stocco, Ivan Stockley, Derek Stone, Bill & Ann Stoughton, Phini Strati, Samo Stritof, Tom Stroka, Stuart Suckling, Paul Sullivan, Timothy Sullivan, Tarren Summers, Sonja Sun Johnsen, Johnny Sundberg, Flemming Svenningsen, Travis Swenson, Barry & Wanda Syner, Oscar Szanto, Lamija M Tabak-Didic, Zara Tai, Alan Tan, Andrew Tan, Kiri Tan, vo Tence, Mark Teramae, Ravindran Thanikaimoni, Peter Thayer, Anthony Thompson, Bruce Thompson, Sarah Thompson, Kristien Thys, Robert Tissing, Brian Tlongan, Paul Tod, J Toth, Abi Tovarloza, Janet Townsend, Michael Tracy, Liesl Trotter, Derek Trowell, Metaxia Tsoukatos, Kim Tuorila, Dean Turner, Helen Twitt, Sharda Ugra, Yusuf Usul, Dorothea Vafiadis, Con Vaitsas, Rimas Valaitis, Marco van de Sande, Hanny van den Bergh, Constant van der Heijden, Marlies van den Nieuwendijk, Wikke Van Dijk, Maarten van Galen, Nootje & Marcel van Gorp, Brigette van Haasteren, Frank van Rijn, S Vanderdonck, Nigel Varey, Brendan Vargas, Kim Vaughan, Thomas Vaughan, Florens Versteegh, Susan Viner, Colin Viney, Jens von Scheele, George S Vrontos, Dean Vuletic, Pauline Waddell, Stephen Wahl, Nick Walmsley, Karen Walsh, P Walsh, Beryl & Jim Walter, Jeremy Watts, John & Pat Webb, David Weightman, David Westland, Peter Wheelan, John White, Thelma White, Winston White, Ruben Wickenhauser, Veryan Wilkie-Jones, Aled Williams, Alwyn Williams, Jason Williams, Lance Williams, Bob Wing, Roxanne Winkler, Alexander Winter, Alex & Rhonda Wittmann, Justin Wong, Joanne Woo, Peta Woodland, Natalie Wray, Dion & Donna Wright, Sherryn Wyatt, Andrew Wyss, John Yates, Yoram Yom-Tov, Imran Yusuf, Karla Zimmerman, Felix Zimmermann, Zoran Zinzovski

# LONELY PLANET

## Guides by Region

Lonely Planet is known worldwide for publishing practical, reliable and no-nonsense travel information in our guides and on our Web site. The Lonely Planet list covers just about every accessible part of the world. Currently there are 16 series: Travel guides, Shoestring guides, Condensed guides, Phrasebooks, Read This First, Healthy Travel, Walking guides, Cycling guides, Watching Wildlife guides, Pisces Diving & Snorkeling guides, City Maps, Road Atlases, Out to Eat, World Food, Journeys travel literature and Pictorials.

**AFRICA** Africa on a shoestring • Botswana • Cairo • Cairo City Map • Cape Town • Cape Town City Map • East Africa • Egypt • Egyptian Arabic phrasebook • Ethiopia, Eritrea & Djibouti • Ethiopian Amharic phrasebook • The Gambia & Senegal • Healthy Travel Africa • Kenya • Malawi • Morocco • Moroccan Arabic phrasebook • Mozambique • Namibia • Read This First: Africa • South Africa, Lesotho & Swaziland • Southern Africa • Southern Africa Road Atlas • Swahili phrasebook • Tanzania, Zanzibar & Pemba • Trekking in East Africa • Tunisia • Watching Wildlife East Africa • Watching Wildlife Southern Africa • West Africa • World Food Morocco • Zambia • Zimbabwe, Botswana & Namibia
**Travel Literature:** Mali Blues: Traveling to an African Beat • The Rainbird: A Central African Journey • Songs to an African Sunset: A Zimbabwean Story

**AUSTRALIA & THE PACIFIC** Aboriginal Australia & the Torres Strait Islands •Auckland • Australia • Australian phrasebook • Australia Road Atlas • Cycling Australia • Cycling New Zealand • Fiji • Fijian phrasebook • Healthy Travel Australia, NZ & the Pacific • Islands of Australia's Great Barrier Reef • Melbourne • Melbourne City Map • Micronesia • New Caledonia • New South Wales • New Zealand • Northern Territory • Outback Australia • Out to Eat – Melbourne • Out to Eat – Sydney • Papua New Guinea • Pidgin phrasebook • Queensland • Rarotonga & the Cook Islands • Samoa • Solomon Islands • South Australia • South Pacific • South Pacific phrasebook • Sydney • Sydney City Map • Sydney Condensed • Tahiti & French Polynesia • Tasmania • Tonga • Tramping in New Zealand • Vanuatu • Victoria • Walking in Australia • Watching Wildlife Australia • Western Australia
**Travel Literature:** Islands in the Clouds: Travels in the Highlands of New Guinea • Kiwi Tracks: A New Zealand Journey • Sean & David's Long Drive

**CENTRAL AMERICA & THE CARIBBEAN** Bahamas, Turks & Caicos • Baja California • Belize, Guatemala & Yucatán • Bermuda • Central America on a shoestring • Costa Rica • Costa Rica Spanish phrasebook • Cuba • Cycling Cuba • Dominican Republic & Haiti • Eastern Caribbean • Guatemala • Havana • Healthy Travel Central & South America • Jamaica • Mexico • Mexico City • Panama • Puerto Rico • Read This First: Central & South America • Virgin Islands • World Food Caribbean • World Food Mexico • Yucatán
**Travel Literature:** Green Dreams: Travels in Central America

**EUROPE** Amsterdam • Amsterdam City Map • Amsterdam Condensed • Andalucía • Athens • Austria • Baltic States phrasebook • Barcelona • Barcelona City Map • Belgium & Luxembourg • Berlin • Berlin City Map • Britain • British phrasebook • Brussels, Bruges & Antwerp • Brussels City Map • Budapest • Budapest City Map • Canary Islands • Catalunya & the Costa Brava • Central Europe • Central Europe phrasebook • Copenhagen • Corfu & the Ionians • Corsica • Crete • Crete Condensed • Croatia • Cycling Britain • Cycling France • Cyprus • Czech & Slovak Republics • Czech phrasebook • Denmark • Dublin • Dublin City Map • Dublin Condensed • Eastern Europe • Eastern Europe phrasebook • Edinburgh • Edinburgh City Map • England • Estonia, Latvia & Lithuania • Europe on a shoestring • Europe phrasebook • Finland • Florence • Florence City Map • France • Frankfurt City Map • Frankfurt Condensed • French phrasebook • Georgia, Armenia & Azerbaijan • Germany • German phrasebook • Greece • Greek Islands • Greek phrasebook • Hungary • Iceland, Greenland & the Faroe Islands • Ireland • Italian phrasebook • Italy • Kraków • Lisbon • The Loire • London • London City Map • London Condensed • Madrid • Madrid City Map • Malta • Mediterranean Europe • Milan, Turin & Genoa • Moscow • Munich • Netherlands • Normandy • Norway • Out to Eat – London • Out to Eat – Paris • Paris • Paris City Map • Paris Condensed • Poland • Polish phrasebook • Portugal • Portuguese phrasebook • Prague • Prague City Map • Provence & the Côte d'Azur • Read This First: Europe • Rhodes & the Dodecanese • Romania & Moldova • Rome • Rome City Map • Rome Condensed • Russia, Ukraine & Belarus • Russian phrasebook • Scandinavian & Baltic Europe • Scandinavian phrasebook • Scotland • Sicily • Slovenia • South-West France • Spain • Spanish phrasebook • Stockholm • St Petersburg • St Petersburg City Map • Sweden • Switzerland • Tuscany • Ukrainian phrasebook • Venice • Vienna • Wales • Walking in Britain • Walking in France • Walking in Ireland • Walking in Italy • Walking in Scotland • Walking in Spain • Walking in Switzerland • Western Europe • World Food France • World Food Greece • World Food Ireland • World Food Italy • World Food Spain **Travel Literature:** After Yugoslavia • Love and War in the Apennines • The Olive Grove: Travels in Greece • On the Shores of the Mediterranean • Round Ireland in Low Gear • A Small Place in Italy

# LONELY PLANET

## Mail Order

L onely Planet products are distributed worldwide.They are also available by mail order from Lonely Planet, so if you have difficulty finding a title please write to us. North and South American residents should write to 150 Linden St, Oakland, CA 94607, USA; European and African residents should write to 10a Spring Place, London NW5 3BH, UK; and residents of other countries to Locked Bag 1, Footscray, Victoria 3011, Australia.

**INDIAN SUBCONTINENT & THE INDIAN OCEAN** Bangladesh • Bengali phrasebook • Bhutan • Delhi • Goa • Healthy Travel Asia & India • Hindi & Urdu phrasebook • India • India & Bangladesh City Map • Indian Himalaya • Karakoram Highway • Kathmandu City Map • Kerala • Madagascar • Maldives • Mauritius, Réunion & Seychelles • Mumbai (Bombay) • Nepal • Nepali phrasebook • North India • Pakistan • Rajasthan • Read This First: Asia & India • South India • Sri Lanka • Sri Lanka phrasebook • Tibet • Tibetan phrasebook • Trekking in the Indian Himalaya • Trekking in the Karakoram & Hindukush • Trekking in the Nepal Himalaya • World Food India **Travel Literature:** The Age of Kali: Indian Travels and Encounters • Hello Goodnight: A Life of Goa • In Rajasthan • Maverick in Madagascar • A Season in Heaven: True Tales from the Road to Kathmandu • Shopping for Buddhas • A Short Walk in the Hindu Kush • Slowly Down the Ganges

**MIDDLE EAST & CENTRAL ASIA** Bahrain, Kuwait & Qatar • Central Asia • Central Asia phrasebook • Dubai • Farsi (Persian) phrasebook • Hebrew phrasebook • Iran • Israel & the Palestinian Territories • Istanbul • Istanbul City Map • Istanbul to Cairo • Istanbul to Kathmandu • Jerusalem • Jerusalem City Map • Jordan • Lebanon • Middle East • Oman & the United Arab Emirates • Syria • Turkey • Turkish phrasebook • World Food Turkey • Yemen **Travel Literature:** Black on Black: Iran Revisited • Breaking Ranks: Turbulent Travels in the Promised Land • The Gates of Damascus • Kingdom of the Film Stars: Journey into Jordan

**NORTH AMERICA** Alaska • Boston • Boston City Map • Boston Condensed • British Columbia • California & Nevada • California Condensed • Canada • Chicago • Chicago City Map • Chicago Condensed • Florida • Georgia & the Carolinas • Great Lakes • Hawaii • Hiking in Alaska • Hiking in the USA • Honolulu & Oahu City Map • Las Vegas • Los Angeles • Los Angeles City Map • Louisiana & the Deep South • Miami • Miami City Map • Montreal • New England • New Orleans • New Orleans City Map • New York City • New York City City Map • New York City Condensed • New York, New Jersey & Pennsylvania • Oahu • Out to Eat – San Francisco • Pacific Northwest • Rocky Mountains • San Diego & Tijuana • San Francisco • San Francisco City Map • Seattle • Seattle City Map • Southwest • Texas • Toronto • USA • USA phrasebook • Vancouver • Vancouver City Map • Virginia & the Capital Region • Washington, DC • Washington, DC City Map • World Food New Orleans **Travel Literature:** Caught Inside: A Surfer's Year on the California Coast • Drive Thru America

**NORTH-EAST ASIA** Beijing • Beijing City Map • Cantonese phrasebook • China • Hiking in Japan • Hong Kong & Macau • Hong Kong City Map • Hong Kong Condensed • Japan • Japanese phrasebook • Korea • Korean phrasebook • Kyoto • Mandarin phrasebook • Mongolia • Mongolian phrasebook • Seoul • Shanghai • South-West China • Taiwan • Tokyo • Tokyo Condensed • World Food Hong Kong • World Food Japan **Travel Literature:** In Xanadu: A Quest • Lost Japan

**SOUTH AMERICA** Argentina, Uruguay & Paraguay • Bolivia • Brazil • Brazilian phrasebook • Buenos Aires • Buenos Aires City Map • Chile & Easter Island • Colombia • Ecuador & the Galapagos Islands • Healthy Travel Central & South America • Latin American Spanish phrasebook • Peru • Quechua phrasebook • Read This First: Central & South America • Rio de Janeiro • Rio de Janeiro City Map • Santiago de Chile • South America on a shoestring • Trekking in the Patagonian Andes • Venezuela **Travel Literature:** Full Circle: A South American Journey

**SOUTH-EAST ASIA** Bali & Lombok • Bangkok • Bangkok City Map • Burmese phrasebook • Cambodia • Cycling Vietnam, Laos & Cambodia • East Timor phrasebook • Hanoi • Healthy Travel Asia & India • Hill Tribes phrasebook • Ho Chi Minh City (Saigon) • Indonesia • Indonesian phrasebook • Indonesia's Eastern Islands • Java • Lao phrasebook • Laos • Malay phrasebook • Malaysia, Singapore & Brunei • Myanmar (Burma) • Philippines • Pilipino (Tagalog) phrasebook • Read This First: Asia & India • Singapore • Singapore City Map • South-East Asia on a shoestring • South-East Asia phrasebook • Thailand • Thailand's Islands & Beaches • Thailand, Vietnam, Laos & Cambodia Road Atlas • Thai phrasebook • Vietnam • Vietnamese phrasebook • World Food Indonesia • World Food Thailand • World Food Vietnam

**ALSO AVAILABLE:** Antarctica • The Arctic • The Blue Man: Tales of Travel, Love and Coffee • Brief Encounters: Stories of Love, Sex & Travel • Buddhist Stupas in Asia: The Shape of Perfection • Chasing Rickshaws • The Last Grain Race • Lonely Planet ... On the Edge: Adventurous Escapades from Around the World • Lonely Planet Unpacked • Lonely Planet Unpacked Again • Not the Only Planet: Science Fiction Travel Stories • Ports of Call: A Journey by Sea • Sacred India • Travel Photography: A Guide to Taking Better Pictures • Travel with Children • Tuvalu: Portrait of an Island Nation

# LONELY PLANET

You already know that Lonely Planet produces more than this one guidebook, but you might not be aware of the other products we have on this region. Here is a selection of titles that you may want to check out as well:

**Madrid City Map**
ISBN 1 74059 332 7
US$5.99 • UK£3.99

**Europe on a Shoestring**
ISBN 1 74059 314 6
US$24.99 • UK£14.99

**Europe phrasebook**
ISBN 1 86450 224 X
US$8.99 • UK£4.99

**Cycling France**
ISBN1 86450 036 0
US$19.99 • UK£12.99

**Barcelona Condensed**
ISBN 1 74059 335 9
US$11.99 • UK£5.99

**World Food Greece**
ISBN 1 86450 113 8
US$13• UK£8.99

**Read This First: Europe**
ISBN 1 86450 136 7
US$14.99 • UK£8.99

**Paris**
ISBN 1 74059 306 5
US$15.99 • UK£9.99

**Walking in Italy**
ISBN 1 74059 244 1
US$19.99 • UK£12.99

**Available wherever books are sold**

# Index

## Abbreviations

## Text

**Bold** indicates maps.

**Bold** indicates maps.

**Bold** indicates maps.

# MAP LEGEND

## CITY ROUTES

| | |
|---|---|
| Freeway | Freeway |
| Highway | Primary Road |
| Road | Secondary Road |
| Street | Street |
| Lane | Lane |
| | On/Off Ramp |

| | |
|---|---|
| | Unsealed Road |
| | One Way Street |
| | Pedestrian Street |
| | Stepped Street |
| | Tunnel |
| | Footbridge |

## REGIONAL ROUTES

| | |
|---|---|
| | Tollway, Freeway |
| | Primary Road |
| | Secondary Road |
| | Minor Road |

## BOUNDARIES

| | |
|---|---|
| | Internationa |
| | Stat |
| | Disputer |
| | Fortified Wa |

## HYDROGRAPHY

| | |
|---|---|
| | River, Creek |
| | Canal |
| | Lake |

| | |
|---|---|
| | Dry Lake; Salt Lake |
| | Spring; Rapids |
| | Waterfalls |

## TRANSPORT ROUTES & STATIONS

| | |
|---|---|
| | Train |
| | Underground Train |
| | Metro |
| | Tramway |
| | Funicular Railway |

| | |
|---|---|
| | Ferry |
| | Walking Trai |
| | Walking Tou |
| | Path |
| | Pier or Jetty |

## AREA FEATURES

| | |
|---|---|
| | Building |
| | Park, Gardens |

| | |
|---|---|
| | Market |
| | Sports Ground |

| | |
|---|---|
| | Beach |
| | Cemetery |

| | |
|---|---|
| | Forest |
| | Plaza |

## POPULATION SYMBOLS

| | | |
|---|---|---|
| ✪ **CAPITAL** National Capital | ● **CITY** City | ● Village Village |
| ◉ **CAPITAL** State Capital | ● Town Town | Urban Area |

## MAP SYMBOLS

| | | |
|---|---|---|
| ◼ Place to Stay | ▼ Place to Eat | ● Point of Interest |

| | | | | | | |
|---|---|---|---|---|---|---|
| ✈ Airport | | Cinema | | Museum | | Swimming Pool |
| ❸ Bank | | Embassy, Consulate | | Police Station | | Synagogue |
| ⊕ Border Crossing | ☕ Fountain | | Post Office | | Taxi Rank |
| Bus Station | ✚ Hospital | | Pub or Bar | | Telephone |
| Cable Car, Funicular | Internet Cafe | | Ruins | | Theatre |
| Castle, Chateau | Mosque | | Shopping Centre | ❶ Tourist Information |
| Cathedral, Church | ⚑ Monument | ⚲ Ski Field | | Zoo |

*Note: not all symbols displayed above appear in this book*

# LONELY PLANET OFFICES

## Australia
Locked Bag 1, Footscray, Victoria 3011
☎ 03 8379 8000  fax 03 8379 8111
email: talk2us@lonelyplanet.com.au

## USA
150 Linden St, Oakland, CA 94607
☎ 510 893 8555  TOLL FREE: 800 275 8555
fax 510 893 8572
email: info@lonelyplanet.com

## UK
10a Spring Place, London NW5 3BH
☎ 020 7428 4800  fax 020 7428 4828
email: go@lonelyplanet.co.uk

## France
1 rue du Dahomey, 75011 Paris
☎ 01 55 25 33 00  fax 01 55 25 33 01
email: bip@lonelyplanet.fr
www.lonelyplanet.fr

**World Wide Web: www.lonelyplanet.com *or* AOL keyword: lp**
**Lonely Planet Images: lpi@lonelyplanet.com.au**